TWELFTH EDITION

ACCOUNTANTS' HANDBOOK

VOLUME ONE:

FINANCIAL ACCOUNTING AND GENERAL TOPICS

DISCARD

Update Service

BECOME A SUBSCRIBER!

Did you purchase this product from a bookstore?

If you did, it's important for you to become a subscriber. John Wiley & Sons, Inc. may publish, on a periodic basis, supplements and new editions to reflect the latest changes in the subject matter that you *need to know* in order to stay competitive in this ever-changing industry. By contacting the Wiley office nearest you, you'll receive any current update at no additional charge. In addition, you'll receive future updates and revised or related volumes on a 30-day examination review.

If you purchased this product directly from John Wiley & Sons, Inc., we have already recorded your subscription for this update service.

To become a subscriber, please call **1-877-762-2974** or send your name, company name (if applicable), address, and the title of the product to:

mailing address: **Supplement Department**
                                 John Wiley & Sons, Inc.
                                 One Wiley Drive
                                 Somerset, NJ 08875
e-mail: **subscriber@wiley.com**
fax: **1-732-302-2300**

For customers outside the United States, please contact the Wiley office nearest you:

Professional & Reference Division
John Wiley & Sons Canada, Ltd.
22 Worcester Road
Etobicoke, Ontario M9W 1L1
CANADA
Phone: 416-236-4433
Phone: 1-800-567-4797
Fax: 416-236-4447
Email: canada@wiley.com

John Wiley & Sons Australia, Ltd.
33 Park Road
P.O. Box 1226
Milton, Queensland 4064
AUSTRALIA
Phone: 61-7-3859-9755
Fax: 61-7-3859-9715
Email: brisbane@johnwiley.com.au

John Wiley & Sons, Ltd.
The Atrium
Southern Gate, Chichester
West Sussex PO 19 8SQ
ENGLAND
Phone: 44-1243-779777
Fax: 44-1243-775878
Email: customer@wiley.co.uk

John Wiley & Sons (Asia) Pte., Ltd.
2 Clementi Loop #02-01
SINGAPORE 129809
Phone: 65-64632400
Fax: 65-64634604/5/6
Customer Service: 65-64604280
Email: enquiry@wiley.com.sg

TWELFTH EDITION
ACCOUNTANTS' HANDBOOK

VOLUME ONE:
FINANCIAL ACCOUNTING AND GENERAL TOPICS

LYNFORD GRAHAM
D.R. CARMICHAEL

WILEY

JOHN WILEY & SONS, INC.

For general information on our other products and services, or technical support, please contact our Customer Care Department within the United States at 800-762-2974, outside the United States at 317-572-3993 or fax 317-572-4002.

Wiley also publishes its books in a variety of electronic formats. Some content that appears in print may not be available in electronic books.

For more information about Wiley products, visit our Web site at *www.wiley.com*.

ISBN: 978-1-118-17182-0 (book); 978-1-118-25280-2 (ebk); 978-1-118-25286-4 (ebk); 978-1-118-25287-1 (ebk)

Printed in the United States of America

10 9 8 7 6 5 4 3 2 1

CONTENTS

PREFACE

The twelfth edition of *Accountants' Handbook* continues the tradition established in the first edition nearly 90 years ago of providing a comprehensive single reference source for understanding current financial statement and reporting issues. It is directed to accountants, auditors, executives, bankers, lawyers, and other preparers and users of accounting information. Its presentation and format facilitates the quick comprehension of complex accounting-related subjects updated for today's rapidly changing business environment.

This edition of the *Handbook* continues the presentation of two soft-cover volumes; this edition contains a total of 43 chapters. To provide a resource with the encyclopedic coverage that has been the hallmark of this *Handbook* series, this edition again focuses on financial accounting and related topics, including those auditing standards and audit reports that are the common ground of interest for accounting and business professionals.

A few years make quite a difference in the modern accounting and auditing world. Sarbanes-Oxley is part of the fabric of today's business environment, but we wrestle with a codification of generally accepted accounting principles that has reoriented our approach to citing the accounting literature and day-to-day updates on U.S. and Securities and Exchange Commission progress toward adopting International Financial Reporting Standards in the United States. Auditors of public companies continue to follow the growing Standards of the Public Company Accounting Oversight Board, and such Standards continue to diverge from those set by the Auditing Standards Board of the American Institute of Certified Public Accountants and adopted by the Government Account-ability Office in its Yellow Book Standards. In 2011, the AICPA implemented a new codification of its literature, more aligned with the presentation format of the International Federation of Accoun-tant's International Audit and Attest Standards Board format. The "clarity" standards are designed to better highlight the requirements of the standards and significantly align AICPA and IAASB Standards. Chapter 3 in this edition (by Tom Jones) reviews the recent revolution in accounting standards and the contemporary issues in merging U.S and international GAAP. There are also new chapters on fair value (Mark Zyla) and private company valuation issues (Neil Beaton). A new and comprehensive chapter on financial institutions by Zabihollah Rezaee addresses contemporary industry issues including those raised in the Dodd-Frank Financial Reform Act of 2010. We are in the middle of a significant revolution in the health care industry, and there remain a myriad of uncertainties surrounding the future in this industry at the date of publication.

In addition, most chapters have incorporated some international accounting perspectives when possible. Fraud continues to be an important element in our business environment, as we continue to focus on fraud and fraud-related issues. These topics have become more prominent in the business literature and in practice, and management and auditors have, by law and regulation, assumed greater responsibility for preventing and detecting fraud.

References to the professional accounting literature in this edition include references to the new Financial Accounting Standards Board Codification (Accounting Standards Codification, or ASC) in each chapter. Sometimes the original literature is also cited, where it can be helpful in understanding the development of thought and can help orient us to the prior literature. We have retained the chapter by Reed Storey on the development of the conceptual framework and plan to carry it forward because of its unique insight and historical content. In this edition we have also eliminated a number of redundant and overlapping chapters and those that were very specific to historical issues.

This edition of the *Handbook* is divided into two convenient volumes. *Volume One: Financial Accounting and General Topics* includes:

- A comprehensive review of the framework of accounting guidance today and the organizations involved in its development, including the development of international standards
- A compendium of specific guidance on general aspects of financial statement presentation, disclosure, and analysis, including SEC filing regulations
- Coverage of specific financial statement areas from cash through shareholders' equity, including coverage of financial instruments

Volume Two: Special Industries and Special Topics includes:

- Comprehensive coverage of the specialized environmental and accounting considerations for key industries, including a chapter on the film industry
- Coverage of accounting standards applying to pension plans, retirement plans, and employee stock compensation and other capital accumulation plans
- Diverse topics, including reporting by partnerships, estates and trusts, and valuation, bankruptcy, and forensic accounting

The specialized expertise of the individual authors remains a critical element in this edition, as it has been in all prior editions. Although the editor worked with the authors, in the final analysis, each chapter is the work and presents the viewpoint of the individual author or authors.

Content of the chapters in this edition has been prepared and/or reviewed by professionals practicing in accounting firms, financial executives, university professors, and financial analysts and executives. Every major international accounting firm is represented among the authors. These professionals bring to bear their own and their firms' experiences in dealing with accounting practice problems. All of the authors and technical reviewers are recognized authorities in their fields and have made significant contributions to the twelfth edition of the *Handbook*.

Our greatest debt is to the authors and reviewers of this edition. We deeply appreciate the value and importance of their time and efforts. We also acknowledge our debt to the editors of and contributors to 11 earlier editions of the *Handbook*. This edition draws heavily on the accumulated knowledge of those earlier editions.

Finally, we wish to thank John DeRemigis and Brandon Dust at John Wiley & Sons, Inc., for handling the many details of organizing and coordinating this effort.

For convenience, the pronoun "he" is used in this book to refer nonspecifically to the accountant and the businessperson. We intend this pronoun to include women.

L. Graham
D. R. Carmichael

ABOUT THE EDITOR

Lynford Graham, CPA, PhD, CFE, is a Certified Public Accountant with more than 30 years of public accounting experience in audit practice and national policy development groups. He is a visiting professor of accountancy and executive in residence at Bentley University in Waltham, Massachusetts. He was a partner and the director of audit policy for BDO Seidman, LLP, and was a national accounting and SEC consulting partner for Coopers & Lybrand, responsible for the technical issues research function and database, auditing research, audit automation and audit sampling techniques. Prior to joining BDO Seidman LLP, Dr. Graham was an associate professor of accounting and information systems and a graduate faculty fellow at Rutgers University in Newark, NJ, where he taught financial accounting courses. Dr. Graham is a member of the American Institute of Certified Public Accountants and a past member of the AICPA Auditing Standards Board. He is a Certified Fraud Examiner and a member of the Association of Certified Fraud Examiners. Throughout his career he has maintained an active profile in the academic as well as the business community. In 2002 he received the Distinguished Service Award of the Auditing Section of the AAA. His numerous academic and business publications span a variety of topical areas including information systems, internal controls, expert systems, audit risk, audit planning, fraud, sampling, analytical procedures, audit judgment, and international accounting and auditing. Dr. Graham holds an MBA in industrial management and PhD in business and applied economics from the University of Pennsylvania (Wharton School).

ABOUT THE CONTRIBUTORS

Michael A. Antonetti, CPA, CMA, is a partner with Crowe Horwath LLP. Mr. Antonetti has over 20 years of experience providing assurance and business advisory services to clients in many industries including manufacturing, distribution, banking, professional services, transportation and hospitality. Mr. Antonetti's experience also includes assisting clients with merger, acquisition, and divestiture transactions and application of related accounting standards. Mr. Antonetti also serves clients with international operations in Europe, Asia, and North and South America.

Yogesh Bahl, CPA, MBA, has more than 18 years of experience in leading global forensic investigations, delivering dispute consulting services, and helping companies manage enterprise risks. He leads the National Life Sciences Practice and the Northeast Antifraud practice. Yogesh specializes in assisting companies manage issues involving accounting, third parties, strategic alliances, and intellectual property. He has helped companies address and resolve multimillion-dollar issues involving accounting and finance, business partner reporting, unclear contract terms, and supply chain infiltration. In addition, Yogesh's experience includes strengthening the financial and audit-related provisions in various types of agreements including licensing, collaboration, distribution, and co-promotion agreements. By leveraging his advisory experience with corporations, Yogesh is effective when testifying on industry practice, breach of contract, accounting, and intellectual property matters.

Noah P. Barsky, PhD, CPA, CMA, is an associate professor at the Villanova School of Business. He earned his BS and MS in accounting from The Pennsylvania State University and his PhD from the University of Connecticut. His professional experience includes practice in the fields of accounting and finance as an analyst, auditor, and business consultant as well as instructional design and delivery for global professional services firms. He has been recognized with multiple national and international awards and grants for his scholarly writing and curriculum innovation.

Neil Beaton, CPA, ABV, CFAI, ASA, MBA is a managing director with Alvarez & Marsal Valuation Services in Seattle, Washington. He specializes in the valuation of public and privately held businesses and intangible assets for purposes of litigation support (marriage dissolutions, lost profits claims and others), acquisitions, sales, buy-sell agreements, ESOPs, incentive stock options, and estate planning and taxation. He also performs economic analysis for personal injury claims and for wrongful termination and wrongful death actions. His primary areas of concentration are valuations of early-stage, venture-backed company and litigation support across a broad spectrum of financial and economic matters. With more than 23 years of valuation and litigation support experience, Mr. Beaton has been involved in valuing companies in all major industries and has provided expert testimony in a number of domestic and international venues. Prior to joining A&M, Mr. Beaton spent nine years with Grant Thornton, where he most recently served as the Global Lead of Complex Valuation. He is a co-chair of the AICPA's Valuation of Private Equity Securities Task Force and a member of the AICPA's Mergers & Acquisitions Disputes Task Force. He is a member of the Business Valuation Update Editorial Advisory Board and on the Board of Experts, *Financial Valuation and Litigation Expert*.

Benedetto Bongiorno, CPA, CRE, has more than 40 years of public accounting experience providing auditing, accounting, and consulting services to both public and private real estate companies.

He has served as national director of real estate for Deloitte & Touche and BDO and has many years of experience in research and practical application of specially developed substantive analytical audit procedures and technologically based tools. He has made major contributions in public accounting, both in real estate and financial audits and in the field of continuous audit. As a cofounder and head of audit and accounting consulting services at Natural Decision Systems, Inc., he was awarded U.S. patents in both continuous assurance and internal control. Mr. Bongiorno continues to apply his extensive expertise in improving real evaluation techniques, transparency, and cost-effective auditing strategies through consulting for public accounting firms as well as both public and privately held companies.

Brad A. Davidson, CPA, is partner in charge of the Securities and Exchange Commission competency center of the national office of Crowe Horwath LLP. The Assurance Professional Practice group (or national office) has responsibility for technical consultations, quality control, and communications of current SEC and accounting developments. Brad specializes in the financial institutions industry. He serves as Crowe's representative to the Center for Audit Quality's SEC Regulations Committee, which meets quarterly with SEC staff to discuss emerging financial reporting issues. In December 2010, Brad served as steering committee chair of the American Institute of Certified Public Accountants annual national conference on current Securities and Exchange Commission and Public Company Accounting Oversight Board developments. Earlier in his career, he completed a two-year professional fellowship with the AICPA in Washington, DC.

Jason Flynn, FSA, MAAA, is a principal in the Human Capital Total Rewards practice at Deloitte Consulting LLP, where he provides broad technical guidance and advisory consulting with regard to pension and retiree medical benefit plans to a wide spectrum of clients including multinational clients. Jason serves as a national leader for Deloitte Consulting's retirement practice.

Sydney Garmong, CPA, is partner in the audit practice with Crowe Horwath LLP and located in Washington, DC. Her primary responsibility is to address accounting and regulatory issues affecting financial institutions. She is a member of the American Institute of Certified Public Accountants Depository Institutions Expert Panel, which maintains an ongoing liaison with various regulatory and standard-setting agencies that impact financial institutions, including the federal bank regulators, the Securities and Exchange Commission, and the Financial Accounting Standards Board. In addition to addressing technical issues, Sydney is a frequent speaker at industry and regulatory conferences. Prior to joining Crowe Horwath, she was a senior manager at the AICPA in Washington, DC. During her time with the AICPA, she addressed financial institution and financial instrument accounting, auditing, and regulatory matters.

Martha Garner, CPA, is a managing director in PricewaterhouseCoopers' national office specializing in health care, not-for-profit, and governmental accounting and financial reporting matters. She currently chairs the American Institute of Certified Public Accountants' Health Care Expert Panel and has served on numerous Financial Accounting Standards Board, Government Accounting Standards Board, and AICPA task forces and committees. She is a contributing author for *Montgomery's Auditing* (John Wiley & Sons, 1998) and the *Financial and Accounting Guide for Not-for-Profit Organizations* (John Wiley & Sons, 2012), and has authored articles and publications on a variety of accounting topics.

Timothy Geddes, FSA, MAAA, is a senior manager in the Human Capital Total Rewards practice at Deloitte Consulting LLP, where he provides broad technical guidance and advisory consulting with regard to pension and retiree medical benefit plans to a wide spectrum of domestic and multinational clients. Timothy serves on the American Academy of Actuaries Pension Committee and has spoken at numerous national actuarial meetings.

Frederick Gill, CPA, is senior technical manager on the Accounting Standards Team at the American Institute of Certified Public Accountants, where he provides broad technical support to the

Accounting Standards Executive Committee. During his over 20 years with the AICPA, he participated in the development of numerous AICPA Statements of Position, Audit and Accounting Guides, Practice Bulletins, issues papers, journal articles, and practice aids. He was a member of the U.S. delegation to the International Accounting Standards Committee, represented the U.S. accounting profession on the United Nations Intergovernmental Working Group of Experts on International Standards of Accounting and Reporting, and was a member of the National Accounting Curriculum Task Force. Previously he held several accounting faculty positions.

Alan S. Glazer, PhD, CPA (inactive), is the Henry P. and Mary B. Stager Professor of Business at Franklin & Marshall College, Lancaster, Pennsylvania. He was associate director of the Independence Standards Board's conceptual framework project and has been a consultant to several AICPA committees. His articles on auditor independence, not-for-profit organizations, and other issues have been published in the *Journal of Accountancy*, *CPA Journal*, *Issues in Accounting Education*, *Accounting Horizons*, and other academic and professional journals. He is also coauthor of a three-volume series of portfolios on financial statement analysis published by Bloomberg BNA.

Lynne M. Glennon, CPA, MST, is a full-time instructor for DePaul University's Master of Science in Taxation program. She currently teaches accounting for income taxes, transactions in property, and taxation of corporations and shareholders on campus as well as online for a national CPA firm. Prior to teaching full time, she worked in both industry and public accounting for 20 years as a tax director and tax consultant. As director of tax planning for Global Hyatt Corporation, she was primarily responsible for tax planning support on large-scale restructurings and mergers, acquisitions and dispositions, and management and control of the federal audit process, including communications with the Internal Revenue Service. As senior manager in Deloitte & Touche's lead tax services group, she focused on corporate and partnership taxation and served a number of multinational clients in the manufacturing, distribution, and service industries. Ms. Glennon is a Certified Public Accountant in the State of Illinois and a member of the American Institute of Certified Public Accountants. She is a graduate of the University of Notre Dame with a BA in economics; her MST degree is from DePaul University.

Bill Godshall, CPA. Since joining Coopers & Lybrand in 1990, Bill has had extensive experience in the energy and mining sector of assurance practices at two international accounting firms. He has worked on oil and gas audit and attestation engagements; utility audits, controls projects, and attestation engagements; and mining joint venture costs reviews. Bill also assisted his energy and mining clients with special accounting and auditing projects in the areas of derivatives, asset retirement obligations, leasing, and other complex topics. Bill spent two years at the Public Company Accounting Oversight Board, where he authored the inspection guidance for derivative accounting and auditing areas that is still in place today. In addition, Bill led the inspection of the audits of several energy and natural resource Securities and Exchange Commission issuers. Bill joined Frazier & Deeter's assurance practice in 2005 and serves as the lead partner for the assurance group's quality control function.

Richard A. Green, CPA, has over 25 years of auditing, accounting, and consulting experience, including all phases of external and internal auditing. Mr. Green leads the Sacramento public sector assurance practice of Macias Gini & O'Connell LLP. He served on the Governmental Accounting Standards Board Task Force on Pension Accounting Research and was recently appointed to the American Institute of Certified Public Accountants' State and Local Government Expert Panel Pension Comment Letter Task Force. Mr. Green is the engagement partner on the largest pension plan in the nation, the State of California Public Employees' Retirement System.

Frank J. Grippo, MBA, CPA, CFE, is an associate professor of accounting at William Paterson University in Wayne, NJ. He earned his BS in accounting from Seton Hall University and his MBA from Fairleigh Dickinson University. Prior to teaching, he was an auditor with Arthur Andersen & Co. His firm performs financial and accounting consulting for various nonprofit organizations, specializing in internal control structures, auditing, and fraud detection. Clients include well-known health and welfare, religious, and educational organizations.

Wendy Hambleton, CPA, is an audit partner working in the National SEC Department in BDO Seidman LLP's Chicago office. Prior to joining the SEC Department, Ms. Hambleton worked in the firm's Washington, DC, practice office. She works extensively with clients and engagement teams to prepare SEC filings and resolve related accounting and reporting issues. Ms. Hambleton coauthors a number of internal and external publications, including the AICPA's *Guide to SEC Reporting* and Warren Gorham & Lamont's *Controller's Handbook* chapter on public offering requirements.

Philip M. Herr, JD, CPA, PFS, is a senior case design analyst in the advance markets unit of AXA Equitable Life Insurance Company located in New York City. He is a former adjunct professor at Fairleigh Dickinson University, School of Continuing Education, and New Jersey City University. Phil specializes in the areas of: tax; estate and trusts; business succession and planning; personal financial planning; Employee Retirement Income Security Act issues and transactions; retirement, employee benefit, and executive compensation planning; and the use of life insurance, annuities, and insurance products. Phil is admitted to the New York and U.S. Tax Court Bars and is a member of the New York State Bar Association, American Institute of Certified Public Accountants, New York State Society of Certified Public Accountants, and Association for Advanced Life Underwriting. Phil holds life, health, and variable insurance licenses in New Jersey and New York and Financial Industry Regulatory Authority 7, 24, 55, 63 and 65 securities licenses.

Frank Hydoski, PhD, is a director in the New York Forensics & Dispute Services practice of Deloitte Financial Advisory Services LLP. He is responsible for developing new products and approaches in forensic accounting and investigations for clients in both the private and public sector. Mr. Hydoski is internationally recognized for his work in complex investigations, especially those requiring information technologies to facilitate forensic analysis. He was the chief investigator examining the United Nations Oil-for-Food Programme and led a crucial part of the massive forensic effort in the investigation of Holocaust-era accounts held by Swiss banks.

Henry R. Jaenicke, PhD, CPA, was the C. D. Clarkson Professor of Accounting at Drexel University. He is the author of *Survey of Present Practices in Recognizing Revenues, Expenses, Gains, and Losses* (FASB, 1981) and is the coauthor of the twelfth edition of *Montgomery's Auditing* (John Wiley & Sons, 1998). He has served as a consultant to several American Institute of Certified Public Accountants committees, the Independence Standards Board, and the Public Oversight Board.

Richard R. Jones, CPA, is a senior partner in the National Accounting Standards Professional Practice Group of Ernst & Young LLP, where he is responsible for assisting the firm's clients in understanding and implementing today's complex accounting requirements. Mr. Jones's fields of expertise are in the areas of impairments, equity accounting, real estate, leasing, and various financing arrangements.

Tom Jones was the vice chairman of the International Accounting Standards Board from its founding in 2001 until 2009. Prior to this he was a trustee and vice chairman of the Financial Accounting Foundation, which oversees the Financial Accounting Standards Board. He was a member of the ITF and was chairman of the American Bankers Association CFO Committee. He has been elected to the Financial Executives International Accounting Hall of Fame. Mr. Jones's corporate experience includes 20 years with Citibank/Citicorp as executive vice president and principal financial officer. He previously served for 15 years with IT&T in Italy, Belgium, and New York.

Ira G. Kawaller is the founder and principal of Kawaller & Co., a boutique consulting firm that specializes in assisting commercial enterprises with their use of derivative contracts. He is also the managing partner of the Kawaller Fund. He can be reached at Kawaller@kawaller.com; additional biographical information about Dr. Kawaller can be accessed at *www.kawaller.com/Ira_Kawaller_vita.pdf*.

Darin W. Kempke, CPA, is a partner at KPMG LLP in its Philadelphia office. He is the national audit sector leader for KPMG's power and utility practice. He has been working with power and utility clients (regulated and nonregulated) all over the world in his 21-plus years in the industry both with Arthur Andersen LLP and currently with KPMG LLP. He specializes in business and accounting services to regulated and nonregulated energy companies, provides energy thought leadership for publications and the KPMG Global Energy Institute, is a frequent speaker on the power and utility conference and webinar circuit. He spent time in the KPMG LLP Department of Professional Practice working on energy issues including derivatives, leases, emissions, and variable interest entities. He is a Certified Public Accountant licensed in Missouri, Kansas, New York, New Jersey, Pennsylvania, and the District of Columbia. He is a graduate of the University of Kansas with a BS in accounting and a BS in business administration.

Cynthia L. Krom, PhD, CPA, CFE, is assistant professor of accounting and organizations at Franklin & Marshall College, Lancaster, Pennsylvania. She is active in the New York State Society of Certified Public Accountants as well as the American Accounting Association. She has published articles on the Bank Secrecy Act and terrorism financing in professional journals, and her research interests include strategic bankruptcy and accounting history.

Richard F. Larkin, CPA, is technical director of not-for-profit accounting and auditing for BDO USA, LLP, in Bethesda, MD. Previously he was the technical director of the Not-for-Profit Industry Services Group in the national office of PricewaterhouseCoopers. He is a Certified Public Accountant with over 40 years of experience serving not-for-profit organizations as independent accountant, board member, treasurer, and consultant. He teaches, speaks, and writes extensively on not-for-profit industry matters and is active in many professional and industry organizations. He has been a member of the Financial Accounting Standards Board Not-for-Profit Advisory Task Force and the American Institute of Certified Public Accountants Not-for-Profit Organizations Committee and chaired the AICPA Not-for-Profit Audit Guide Task Force. He participated in writing both the third and fourth editions of *Standards of Accounting and Financial Reporting for Voluntary Health and Welfare Organizations*, and the AICPA Practice Aid *Financial Statement Presentation and Disclosure Practices for Not-for-Profit Organizations* (1999). He graduated from Harvard College and has an MBA from Harvard Business School. He is a coauthor of the fourth, fifth, and sixth editions of *Financial and Accounting Guide for Not-for-Profit Organizations* (John Wiley & Sons).

Elizabeth Lindsay-Ochoa, JD, LLM (Taxation), joined AXA Equitable in July 2002. Her primary focus is in estate and charitable planning. She has presented to Certified Public Accountants, attorneys, and financial professionals on charitable and estate-planning topics. Speaking engagements have included the Association of Fundraising Professionals International Conference on Fundraising; the American Bar Association Real Property, Trust and Estate; and the ABA Tax Section and the Association for Advanced Life Underwriting. Liz has written articles for the *Tax News Quarterly*, *Probate and Property*, and *National Underwriter*. She also has submitted comments to Congress, the Federal Deposit Insurance Company, and the Internal Revenue Service as part of her committee work for the ABA. Liz graduated from Michigan State University with a BA in telecommunications. In 2001, she received her JD from Thomas M. Cooley Law School and, in 2005, her LLM (taxation) from the University of Denver. Previously, Liz was a fellow with the Charitable Planning and Organizations Committee with the ABA's RPTE section (2005–2007). She is the chair of the Non-Tax Issues Affecting the Planning and Administration of Estates and Trust and an acquisitions editor for ABA RPTE publications. Liz is admitted to practice law in Michigan, Colorado (inactive), New York, and Connecticut. She is a member of the Colorado and Michigan Bar Associations and the National Committee on Planned Giving. She also holds Financial Industry Regulatory Authority Series 7, 66 and 24 securities registrations.

James Mraz, CPA, MBA, is a professor of accounting and business at the University of Maryland University College. Mr. Mraz has taught accounting and business for over 30 years in several colleges. Mr. Mraz has also conducted accounting accuracy reviews for John Wiley & Sons since 2005 and completed the instructor's manual for Prentice Hall's Accounting Information System's textbook. Mr. Mraz was a government auditor for 33 years while serving in the Marine Corps, Department of Health & Human Services, and the Department of Defense. Mr. Mraz served as chief financial officer for a resale and recreation government organization.

Grant W. Newton, PhD, CPA, CIRA, is a professor of accounting at Pepperdine University. He is the author of the two-volume set *Bankruptcy and Insolvency Accounting: Practice and Procedures: Forms and Exhibits, Sixth Edition* (John Wiley & Sons, 2006) and coauthor of *Bankruptcy and Insolvency Taxation, Second Edition* (John Wiley & Sons, 1994). He is a frequent contributor to professional journals and has lectured widely to professional organizations on bankruptcy-related topics.

Don M. Pallais, CPA, has his own practice in Richmond, VA. He is a former member of the American Institute of Certified Public Accountants Auditing Standards Board and the AICPA Accounting and Review Services Committee. He has written a host of books, articles, and continuing professional education courses on accounting topics.

Cynthia Pon, CPA, has over 20 years of professional experience providing auditing, accounting, and consulting services to the private and public sectors. Ms. Pon leads the San Francisco Bay Area public sector assurance practice of Macias Gini & O'Connell LLP, bringing extensive experience in federal, state, and local financial and compliance auditing. She is experienced in the application of generally accepted accounting principles and has been recognized by the Governmental Accounting Standards Board for her leadership in assisting California governments with early implementation of its standards. Ms. Pon also serves on the Government Finance Officers Association Special Review Committee for Comprehensive Annual Financial Report awards and has instructed numerous governmental clients on a variety of accounting and audit issues and challenges.

Zabihollah Rezaee, PhD, CPA, is the Thompson-Hill Chair of Excellence and Professor of Accountancy at the University of Memphis and has served a two-year term on the Standing Advisory Group of the Public Company Accounting Oversight Board. He received his BS degree from the Iranian Institute of Advanced Accounting, his MBA from Tarleton State University in Texas, and his PhD from the University of Mississippi. Professor Rezaee holds a number of certifications, including Certified Public Accountant, Certified Fraud Examiner, Certified Management Accountant, Certified Internal Auditor, Certified Government Financial Manager, Certified Sarbanes-Oxley Professional, Certified Corporate Governance Professional, and Certified Governance Risk Compliance Professional. He has also been a finalist for the SOX Institute's SOX MVP 2007, 2009, and 2010 Award. Professor Rezaee has published over 180 articles in a variety of accounting and business journals and made more than 200 presentations at national and international conferences. He has also published seven books: *Financial Institutions, Valuations, Mergers, and Acquisitions: The Fair Value Approach* (John Wiley & Sons, 2007); *Financial Statement Fraud: Prevention and Detection* (John Wiley & Sons, 2002); *U.S. Master Auditing Guide, Third Edition* (Commerce Clearing House, 2004); Audit Committee Oversight Effectiveness Post-Sarbanes-Oxley Act; *Corporate Governance Post-Sarbanes-Oxley: Regulations, Requirements, and Integrated Processes (John Wiley & Sons, 2007); Corporate Governance and Business Ethics* (John Wiley & Sons, 2008); and *Financial Services Firms: Governance, Regulations, Valuations, Mergers and Acquisitions* (John Wiley & Sons, 2011).

Francis E. Scheuerell, Jr., CPA, is a managing director at Navigant Consulting and is a Certified Public Accountant and certified management accountant. Frank has almost 30 years of diverse business experience in all areas of financial management and technical accounting, including accounting for business combinations, restatements, corporate restructurings, spin-offs, inventory, leases, revenue recognition, income taxes, equity method investments, segments, and consolidations, including variable interest entities. He has extensive experience addressing accounting and reporting issues for the real estate, construction, health care, hospitality, software, entertainment, retail, and manufacturing industries. Frank has served as an interim executive and/or consultant for numerous billion-dollar companies facing complex and extensive financial reporting issues. He has managed teams restating financial results and rebuilding financial reporting infrastructures while helping to restore regulator and investor confidence in those organizations. Frank has represented and testified on behalf of clients at Securities and Exchange Commission and NASDAQ hearings. Additionally, he has served as an expert witness in a securities litigation case. He has assisted numerous clients with their initial public offering or private place memorandums. He is an accomplished public speaker and author of numerous articles, publications, and continuing professional education seminars. Frank was a Project Manager—Research and Technical Activities for the Financial Accounting Standards Board and is a graduate of Illinois State University.

Jae K. Shim, PhD, is a professor of accounting and finance at California State University, Long Beach, and chief executive officer of Delta Consulting Company, a financial consulting and training firm. Dr. Shim received his MBA and PhD degrees from the University of California at Berkeley (Haas School of Business). He has been a consultant to commercial and nonprofit organizations for over 30 years. Dr. Shim has also published numerous articles in professional and academic journals and has over 50 college and professional books to his credit.

Reed K. Storey, PhD, CPA, had more than 30 years of experience on the framework of financial accounting concepts, standards, and principles, working with both the Accounting Principles Board, as director of Accounting Research of the American Institute of Certified Public Accountants, and the Financial Accounting Standards Board, as senior technical advisor. He was also a member of the accounting faculties of the University of California, Berkeley, the University of Washington, Seattle, and Bernard M. Baruch College, CUNY, and a consultant in the executive offices of Coopers & Lybrand (now PricewaterhouseCoopers LLP) and Haskins & Sells (now Deloitte & Touche, LLP).

B. Scott Teeter, MBA, CMA, is the vice president of land acquisition and development for the Austin/San Antonio, TX, division of Ryland Homes. He earned his BS in finance from The Pennsylvania State University and his MBA from the Wharton School of the University of Pennsylvania.

Daniel Thomas, EA, MAAA, is a specialist leader in the Human Capital Total Rewards practice at Deloitte Consulting LLP, where he serves as an actuarial specialist for the Deloitte audit teams and as a technical resource and reviewer within Deloitte's pension actuarial practice.

George I. Victor, CPA, is a partner in Giambalvo, Stalzer & Company, CPAs, P.C., and is the firm's director of quality control, where he is responsible for formulating the firm's accounting and auditing policy standards, including monitoring, consulting, technical research, staff training, and review of completed engagements. Mr. Victor has extensive experience in providing accounting and advisory services to both privately held and Securities and Exchange Commission–reporting companies. He also provides consulting services in areas of quality control, U.S. generally accepted accounting principles, and International Financial Reporting Standards matters to other certified public accounting firms in the United States and abroad. He is a member of the American Institute of Certified Public Accountants as well as the New York State Society of CPAs, where he serves as a member of its board of directors, chaired various committees, and serves as a member of the Editorial Board of the *CPA Journal*. He is an adjunct professor at the City University of New York. Mr. Victor has been published or quoted in various professional journals and books and frequently lectures on accounting and auditing related topics.

Jan R. Williams, PhD, CPA, is the Ernst & Young Professor and Dean, College of Business Administration, at the University of Tennessee. He is past president of the American Accounting Association and a frequent contributor to academic and professional literature on financial reporting and accounting education. Most recently he has been involved in the redesign of the CPA Examination and is a frequent speaker on this and other topics of professional significance.

Caroline H. Walsh, CPA, has over 33 years of specialized experience in auditing and consulting for local government agencies, nonprofit, and corporate enterprises. Ms. Walsh serves as the Quality Control Partner at Macias Gini & O'Connell LLP and leads the firm's Professional Standards Group. From October 2006 through 2009, Ms. Walsh served on the American Institute of Certified Public Accountants American Institute of Certified Public Accountants State and Local Government Expert Panel, where her role was to provide review and technical support services for the public accounting profession, including drafting and updating the AICPA guides for Audits of State and Local Governments and Government Auditing Standards and Circular A-133 Audits. Since 2009, Ms. Walsh has participated on the Expert Panel Task Force, which reviews and comments on the recent *Governmental Accounting Standards Board* due process documents related to accounting and reporting for pension benefits. In 2009, she was appointed for a three-year term to the GASB Advisory Committee, a standing committee whose members review the GASB staff's annual proposed changes and additions to the GASB's *Comprehensive Implementation Guide*.

David M. Zavada, CPA, MPA, is a partner with Kearney & Company in Alexandria, VA, where he specializes in providing accounting and audit services to the federal government. He is a former chief of the Financial Standards and Grants Branch within the Office of Federal Financial Management at the Office of Management and Budget and deputy to the Controller of the U.S. Government. He was director of the Office of Financial Management at the Department of Transportation, Federal Aviation Administration, and served as the Assistant Inspector General, Office of Audits at the Department of Homeland Security. In all of these positions David played a leadership role in developing and implementing government-wide financial management policies.

Mark L. Zyla, CPA/ABV, CFA, ASA, is managing director of Acuitas, Inc., an Atlanta, GA–based valuation and litigation consultancy firm. As a valuation specialist, Mark has provided consulting for numerous valuations in financial reporting and other types of engagements. He was the 2011 chair of the American Institute of Certified Public Accountants National Business Valuation Conference and presented AICPA's Fair Value Measurement Workshop. He is the author of *Fair Value Measurements, Second Edition: Practical Guidance and Implementation* (John Wiley & Sons).

CHAPTER 1

FINANCIAL ACCOUNTING AND AUDITING ORGANIZATIONS

Lynford Graham, CPA, PhD, CFE
Bentley University

Editor's Note: This chapter aggregates some key contributions of Chapters 1, 5, 9, and 28 from the 11th edition, for reader convenience and to reduce redundancy.

1.1 ROLE OF FINANCIAL ACCOUNTING AND AUDITING IN THE U.S. ECONOMY

This chapter provides background on the environment in which financial accountants carry on their activities, including the specific organizations that regulate or otherwise affect those activities. Auditing is the attestation of independent certified public accountants (CPAs) to third parties that the financial accounting presentation is "fairly presented" and free of material misstatement. Although the accounting and auditing profession were for many years largely self-regulated, major events such as the stock market crash of 1929 and the more recent implosion of a number of megacompanies such as Enron and WorldCom have led to regulatory oversight of the accounting and auditing professions. No financial accountant or manager can practice properly without understanding these organizations and how they not only constrain but also assist the performance of financial accounting and reporting services.

The globalization of accounting and auditing is a major trend that will impact the practice of accounting in profound ways. While a point of discussion for decades, the current movement of U.S. accounting practice toward an international set of accounting standards and auditing practice is a reality today. The questions seem to be how far and how fast this transition will go, and what the consequences to preparers and users of financial statements will be.

(a) OBJECTIVE OF FINANCIAL ACCOUNTING. An important beginning point for understanding the social role and importance of financial accounting is identifying the objective that it should meet. Although there are many opinions, the most authoritative and influential is this definition provided by the Financial Accounting Standards Board (FASB) in its Conceptual Framework project, which was intended to develop a unified theory of accounting (see Section 1.3(a)(v)):

> Financial reporting should provide information that is useful to present and potential investors and creditors and other users in making rational investment, credit, and similar decisions.

Thus, according to this definition, the goal is to provide information that allows users to reach better decisions than they would without it. For simplicity, the FASB uses the term *financial reporting* to encompass the activities of financial accounting and reporting, which includes presenting both financial statements and the additional financial information that accompanies them.

Usefulness may exist at the individual company level if management provides reports to investors and creditors when seeking financing or fulfilling various stewardship reporting responsibilities. Although this perspective undoubtedly explains why some aspects of accounting are regulated, it does not really provide an adequate basis for understanding the substantial governing structure. Instead, an economy-wide perspective is needed.

(b) A WIDER ECONOMIC PERSPECTIVE. Two key points help explain why financial accounting is important for the entire economy. The first point is the connection between the general benefit to society from the information that is presented in financial statements. The second point is that effective capital markets are central to an efficient and healthy economy and explains how effective capital markets are efficient processors of information.

(i) Linking the Economy to Fair Financial Statements. Exhibit 1.1 shows the links between economy and the benefit to society and the availability of useful financial statements. A sound economy is an important ingredient in providing for the benefit of society's members.

Although a variety of factors contribute to a sound economy, such as an abundance of natural resources, a stable political system, and an appropriate work ethic, one of the most critical is the availability of sufficient capital resources. Without adequate capital markets, manufactured goods and services cannot be produced or distributed to persons who want or need them at prices that are reasonable.

In turn, sufficient capital resources are made available through effective and efficient capital markets in which those who need capital can obtain it from those who are ready to provide it. If these market participants can conduct their activities in an environment based on fair financial reporting and correct data, they are able to establish fair prices for the capital in the form of expected returns. Consequently, fair reporting will encourage the flow of more capital into the markets.

In order for the markets to be effective, their participants must reach good decisions about where to invest or obtain capital under appropriate terms for the risks involved. If decisions are made haphazardly, capital will not be allocated in a reasonable fashion, and the economy will not perform as well because of the misallocation of resources.

Naturally, many different kinds of information are useful to decision makers. Some may relate to a particular company, an industry, or the national and world economies. Some types of information may be rooted in past events, whereas others are predictions of future events and conditions. Of particular importance to the capital markets is company financial information.

A significant source of financial information is the financial statements (and accompanying information) that are published for market participants. Although this information by itself is insufficient for making the capital markets work well, the absence of reliable financial information makes the allocation of resources and capital into guesswork.

The important economic role of financial statements causes society to be concerned about the activities of financial accountants and justifies setting up controls and other regulatory devices to

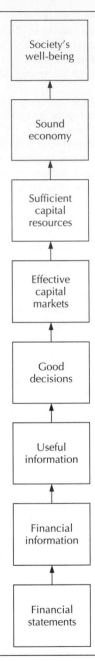

Exhibit 1.1   Role of Financial Accounting in Society

help ensure the availability and usefulness of the information. As should be expected, these controls are aimed at preventing irregularities in the financial reporting system. Every significant study of business and audit failures of the past half century has concluded that lapses in internal controls were a major contributor to the calamity. Chapter 7 in this *Handbook* is devoted to the reporting on internal controls that was made mandatory for public companies by the Sarbanes-Oxley Act of 2002.

(ii) Market Efficiency.   The word *efficiency* is used in two different ways to describe markets. In economic theory, an efficient market is capable of allocating resources quickly and without friction. These allocations are efficient because equilibrium prices (where supply and demand curves cross) are reached quickly and uniformly across the entire market. In order to be efficient in allocating resources, a market must have a number of characteristics, including competition among a large number of buyers and sellers. Perhaps most important, it must have large amounts of useful information about the resources that are being traded. As described, a role for financial accounting is to provide this information to the capital markets.

A second meaning of *efficiency* refers to a market's ability to gather and process this information. In this sense, an efficient market is able to respond quickly and appropriately to new relevant and reliable information, without regard to its source. This concept has been developed and advanced over the last 30 years in finance and accounting research into the functioning of U.S. capital markets, especially the New York Stock Exchange (NYSE).

On one level, this proposition that capital markets are efficient processors of information makes a great deal of sense because there are large incentives for market participants to gather and analyze useful information and then react to it quickly before others learn about it. These incentives also encourage participants to seek out information wherever it can be found, even (perhaps especially) if it is not in published financial statements. In fact, the most useful information is that which no one else knows.

This point does not mean that financial statements are not useful to the capital markets; however, it does suggest that financial statements play a different role from the one that has traditionally been attributed to them. While criticized as not being timely for making some investment decisions, financial statements still serve a role in confirming, with an independent auditor's opinion, the financial position and performance of the company. The knowledge that such confirmation is forthcoming is a deterrent to exaggerated press releases and unreasonably optimistic forecasts.

This point means that sophisticated market participants must clearly understand accounting principles and the impact of management's choices among the available alternative principles. Because of this understanding, the market is able to react appropriately to the signals that it receives. As a result of this sophistication, the market does not react naively to accounting choices that present differing results. For example, a decision by management of one company to use last-in, first out (LIFO) inventory costing and a similar-size company to use the first-in, first-out (FIFO) method in a period of rising prices will lead to higher reported earnings for the FIFO entity. An efficient market should be able to see through this difference, and because the tax bill for the higher-income entity would be higher, the market might even penalize the FIFO company for its choice of accounting principle. An efficient capital market should not be misled by accounting policy choices. In addition, an efficient market would be able to understand and act on the effects of unreported revenues and expenses. For example, a major controversy was created by a 1993 proposal (eventually leading to Statement of Financial Accounting Standards [SFAS] No. 123 *Accounting for Stock-Based Compensation*) that would cause companies to report compensation expense equal to the value of stock options granted to their employees. A naive view of the market would argue that recognizing this expense would produce lower stock prices because it would cause reported income to be lower. This view assumes that the market is either unaware of or oblivious to the effects of the compensation because such effects are not currently included in the earnings calculation. Some opponents of the proposal argued that this expense should not be reported because it is not a real cost. If they are right in the sense that the expense does not really exist, then the act of reporting it would not affect stock prices because the efficient capital market would simply ignore the reported amount and establish appropriate stock prices despite the noise in the financial statements.

In addition to the logical arguments in favor of the proposition that U.S. capital markets are efficient, a great deal of academic research has generated evidence that suggests that they are generally *quite* efficient. While markets are not perfectly efficient, there is abundant support for the broad notion that they are savvy in considering differences generated solely by choosing different accounting methods.

(c) PARTICIPANTS IN THE FINANCIAL REPORTING SYSTEM.   Financial accounting does not take place in a sterile arena; rather, the people who conduct it have very real but quite different interests in the process and its outcome.

The primary communication channel is between financial statement preparers and financial statement users. Generally, preparers are accountants who work for corporations or other entities that need capital resources or that have stewardship reporting responsibilities. Users are investors, creditors, or advisors to those who want to commit resources to an entity or who have already done so. The self-interests of preparers and users clearly are in potential conflict. Management also has an interest in reliable financial information in managing the business. Indeed, an important component in the Internal Controls Framework of the Committee of Sponsoring Organizations (COSO) is Information and Communication, and that includes managerial and financial information. A weakness in this component alone would require that a company assert its internal control is ineffective.

Preparers want the reporting system to provide information that will help them get low-cost capital or that will cause them to appear to have lived up to their responsibilities. However, the efficiency of the capital markets suggests that preparers (and the stockholders of their companies) are likely to be better off if more information is reported. The size of many 10-K (Securities and Exchange Commission [SEC] filings) Annual reports attests to the volumes of information our regulators and standard setters consider "important."

Users, in contrast, are looking for inexpensive, timely, and dependable information that will enable them to make new decisions or evaluate old ones. As described, they are not well served by information that misleads them through bias. If users receive unreliable information, the cost of capital will rise to compensate them for the added but unknown risks. If this mistrust is widespread, the economy will suffer because the capital markets will not be as efficient. Users also tend to want readily available, abundant information. This tendency is counterbalanced by the desire to have unique information or insight, which is important to earning higher returns (because no one else is privy to it).

To reduce the uncertainty about the dependability of the financial statements, the services of auditors provide independent assurance that the financial statements are fairly presented and a free of material misstatement of amounts or disclosures. In effect, auditors add credibility to the financial statements. However, like the other participants, auditors have self-interests. In particular, they prefer dealing with information that is objective and can be verified because they are concerned (and reasonably so) about the possibility of second guessing by users who suffer losses after using audited information that turns out to have been incorrect. The trend in financial accounting standards to make broader use of fair values in lieu of historical costs and to recognize gains and losses through income based on market valuations rather than objective transactions exacerbate their concerns. This work contains several chapters devoted to fair value and issues surrounding their use. Many chapters have expanded coverage of the use of fair values in specific accounts and industries. In summary, the three main participating groups have conflicting interests. In general, preparers want information that can be cheaply produced and will reflect their stewardship in the best light; users want timely, accurate, and (if possible) unique information or insight that no one else has; and auditors want information that can be audited and objectively supported. In contrast, society needs the capital market to have widely available and inexpensive decision-useful information. Because of these conflicts, financial accounting and auditing will continue to be subject to regulation and oversight.

1.2 ACCOUNTING STANDARDS IN THE UNITED STATES

Three primary bodies are involved in the development of U.S. accounting standards: the SEC, the FASB, and the Governmental Accounting Standards Board (GASB). Organizations such as the American Institute of Certified Public Accountants (AICPA) have influence over the standards but not standard-setting authority.

1.3 ROLE OF THE SECURITIES AND EXCHANGE COMMISSION

Although the SEC's jurisdiction is limited to publicly held corporations, its role as the primary regulator and protector of the country's capital markets has given it substantial influence over all financial accounting practice. A more thorough discussion of the role of the SEC can be found in Chapter 5 of this *Handbook* by Wendy Hambleton.

(a) BACKGROUND OF THE SECURITIES AND EXCHANGE COMMISSION.   The SEC was established by the Securities Exchange Act of 1934 and was charged with enforcing not only that statute but also the Securities Act of 1933. Previously, the 1933 Act had been administered by the Federal Trade Commission.

The SEC's prime mission is to achieve and maintain stable and effective capital markets for securities traded in interstate commerce. The nature of today's capital markets and communications networks makes it difficult to issue a security that is *not* traded across state borders. The SEC uses a variety of methods to accomplish its mission. The most basic is regulation of the activities of those corporations that have issued or would like to issue securities.

Under the 1933 Act, securities must be "registered" before they can be issued to the public. The purpose of registration is to establish a complete and widely available public record of information about the registrant and the securities. For example, registration creates a substantial amount of public information about the officers, directors, and other agents of the corporation, including promoters and underwriters. It also publicizes the company's plans for using the capital raised by issuing the securities. In the case of a company that has existed previously, registration also requires the presentation of financial statements and other financial data.

If the company meets the reporting requirements, the securities are allowed to "go public," regardless of their inherent riskiness. Thus, the registration process is designed to accomplish disclosure about the securities rather than to evaluate their merits. Although some states conduct merit reviews for securities traded within their borders, this approach would be very difficult to accomplish on a national level. Furthermore, many individuals believe that the capital markets should be as free as possible, as long as fraud and other forms of deceit are prohibited.

The 1934 Act went beyond the initial registration to require substantial ongoing disclosures about the corporation, its officers and directors, and its financial condition and results of operations and other activities. Thus, companies that have securities registered under the 1933 Act must provide quarterly and annual reports to the SEC as well as ad hoc reports when crucial events occur. Again, the goal is to allow the capital markets to work effectively by getting information to market participants. The SEC Staff may review the filed information for its compliance with the disclosure requirements, but there is no review of the merits of the management's behavior as described in the reports. For example, nothing in the SEC's processes prevents managers from paying large salaries to themselves, as long as the amount is disclosed. The idea is that disclosure will allow the market itself to discipline those managers who abuse their fiduciary duties. Of course, the disclosure requirement may very well have been designed to deter inappropriate behavior, because management would expect to have to suffer the consequences of publishing information about their activities. Nevertheless, the excesses of top corporate executive compensation is a contemporary topic of debate in the media and has raised the interest of regulators.

The 1934 Act also gave authority to the SEC to regulate securities exchanges (such as the NYSE and the American Stock Exchange) and those brokers and dealers who belong to them or otherwise conduct business for buyers and sellers of securities. This authority was expanded through the Investment Advisers Act of 1940 to encompass all who offer investment counseling. The fundamental goal of this arena of regulation is to increase market participants' confidence by reducing the likelihood of incompetence, fraud, or deceit. The line of reasoning is that if these problems can be reduced, more people are likely to invest, and if more people invest, the competition will bring about a more efficient allocation of capital.

Other legislation has given the SEC additional authorities and jurisdiction in the capital markets, but their contents are generally beyond the scope of this discussion, which focuses on the effect of the SEC on financial accounting. Specific categories of regulations and publications affect financial accountants and their clients.

It is especially important to note that the 1934 Act gave the SEC specific authority to establish accounting principles to be used by registrants in filed financial statements. This authority led to the issuance of Accounting Series Release (ASR) No. 4, *Administrative Policy on Financial Statements,* in 1938, which stated that the principles used in the filings would have to enjoy "substantial authoritative support." It also stated that disclosure of a departure from such supported principles would not be an acceptable substitute for applying them.

The role the SEC has historically played in resisting attempts to introduce fair value into the accounting process is interesting. First arising in rate-regulated entities as a means to ask for rate increases, the suggestion of fair values continued to be pressed until the door was opened to the practice in recent years. This is detailed in an excellent article by Steve Zeff.[1] The acceptance of fair values and recognition of income and expense based on fluctuations in market values continues to be controversial since it creates income effects based on temporal situations and often requires the use of imprecise measurement techniques to determine values. Chapter 24, "Fair Value Measurements," by Mark L. Zyla, and Chapter 25, "Valuation of Assets and Liabilities in Nonpublic Companies," by Neil J. Beaton, in this *Handbook* provide additional insight into the theory and application of fair value principles in the modern accounting environment.

Due to resource and expertise constraints, the SEC takes an oversight role in today's accounting standard-setting process, preferring on occasion to exercise its right to overrule the standards proposed by the FASB or its predecessor, the Accounting Principles Board (APB). The SEC is an active observer of the accounting standard–setting process.

(b) STRUCTURE OF THE SECURITIES AND EXCHANGE COMMISSION.   Because the SEC is an independent agency, it does not exist within any of the three traditional branches of government (executive, legislative, or judicial). All five commissioners are appointed by the president and are confirmed by the Senate. In order to help maintain balance and thereby boost public confidence in the capital markets, no more than three commissioners can be members of the same political party. The basic term for a commissioner is five years with the possibility of unlimited reappointments. However, history shows that it is unusual for a commissioner to complete an entire term. Most commissioners are attorneys by training, although some have had other backgrounds. One commissioner is designated by the president to serve as the chairperson and has special administrative responsibilities and acts as a spokesperson for the entire commission. However, the chairperson has only one vote and thus actually has no more authority than the other commissioners.

As is true with most major organizations, a large professional staff supports the work of the commissioners. The SEC has approximately 3,500 employees at its Washington, DC, headquarters and its 11 regional offices across the country. A number of divisions and offices deal with particular regulatory activities. The three that financial accountants are most likely to come into contact with are:

- Division of Corporation Finance (DCF)
- Office of the Chief Accountant (OCA)
- Division of Enforcement

In dealing with their responsibilities, all three report directly and independently to the SEC. However, they also work closely with one another to coordinate their activities and to avoid contradictions and confusion. Exhibit 1.2 is a diagram of their interrelationships and the points of usual interface with the public.

(c) DIVISION OF CORPORATION FINANCE.   The largest of these three sections of the SEC is the DCF, or Corp Fin. Its fundamental responsibility is to process filed documents received from registrants

---

[1] S. Zeff, "The SEC Rules Historical Cost Accounting: 1934 to the 1970s," *Accounting and Business Research,* International Accounting Policy Forum (2007).

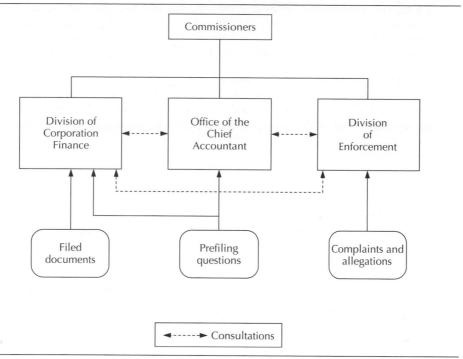

Exhibit 1.2   SEC Accounting Activities and Suborganizations

to determine whether they comply with the appropriate disclosure regulations. The DCF staff consists of attorneys, accountants, and financial analysts and is organized by industry specialties. The director is advised by a chief accountant for the division, who is not the same person as the SEC's chief accountant.

In the process of reviewing filings, the DCF Staff encounters questions about the suitability of the accounting principles applied to registrants' transactions or situations. Some registrants are careful to raise these kinds of questions before they file documents in order to determine the principles that the staff believes are applicable. In either situation, the DCF Staff often resolves these questions using published generally accepted accounting principles (GAAP) or precedents established in earlier cases. In more complicated or groundbreaking situations, the DCF chief accountant consults with the SEC's OCA.

(d) OFFICE OF THE CHIEF ACCOUNTANT.   The SEC's primary adviser on financial accounting issues and policy is the chief accountant, who is appointed by the chairperson and serves at his or her discretion. The OCA is supported by a professional staff, all of whom are experienced accountants, except for one attorney. As indicated in Exhibit 1.2, the OCA works with the DCF chief accountant to resolve issues raised in filings or by prefiling questions. The diagram also shows that some of these prefiling questions may come directly to the OCA.

In order to identify the accounting and auditing practices that have "substantial authoritative support," the OCA first tries to determine what the authoritative literature says about the issue, turning to its own pronouncements and interpretations only when that literature is silent or ambiguous. In conducting their research, the OCA Staff members frequently consult with the FASB Staff. It is also common for the registrant who raised the question to meet with the SEC Staff to explain the facts and circumstances surrounding the issue and to present its point of view. When the question cannot be resolved satisfactorily from the literature, the OCA develops an answer with the goal of providing "full and fair disclosure." To present a united position on the issue, the OCA and DCF establish together what ought to be done. If the registrant does not agree with the answer, SEC procedures allow it to appeal to the full SEC. However, as a practical matter, registrants seldom make this appeal because the commissioners virtually always support the Staff.

A significant source of information about the likely views of the Staff and the likely acceptable accounting treatments are precedence established by other published reports that have been filed with the SEC. Precedence is not the final determination, but it is a consideration when the issuer can identify similar situations where the proposed accounting practice was followed. The Electronic Data-Gathering, Analysis, and Retrieval (EDGAR) electronic database maintained by the SEC is a readily available source of SEC filings for research and the determination of precedence.

In addition to dealing with situation-specific issues, OCA also advises the SEC on major policy matters affecting financial reporting. This role involves preparing recommendations that new SEC rules be created for registrants. It also involves overseeing standard setters, such as the FASB and the Public Company Accounting Oversight Board (PCAOB).

(e) DIVISION OF ENFORCEMENT.   The third segment of the SEC staff that commonly interfaces with financial accountants is the Division of Enforcement, which is charged with investigating violations of the statutes and regulations and recommending disciplinary action. Information about possible violations comes from a wide variety of sources, including the OCA and DCF, as well as news reports and direct complaints from individuals. When violations appear to be other than merely inadvertent or technical, the Division of Enforcement is responsible for determining whether and how to pursue a case and for discovering the facts. In some situations, the division may recommend that the Commission reach a settlement with the alleged offenders without a judicial finding. Although the findings are made public, the subjects generally neither admit nor deny the allegations, even though some discipline may be accepted (such as suspension or permanent disbarment from practicing before the Commission). In far fewer situations, the Commission orders cases to be turned over to a U.S. Attorney's Office for prosecution in a federal court. Naturally, the Division of Enforcement Staff cooperates fully with the U.S. attorneys in pursuing these cases.

For violations of statutes or regulations involving accountants, Commission procedures require that the chief accountant of the Division of Enforcement consult with the OCA to ensure that the proper facts have been uncovered and that the authoritative literature has indeed been violated. These violations typically include failure to maintain proper books and records, preparing financial statements that do not comply with GAAP, issuing an unqualified audit opinion on statements that do not comply with GAAP, or conducting an audit without complying with generally accepted auditing standards (GAAS). Although the Division of Enforcement does not have to obtain concurrence from the OCA to go ahead with a case involving accounting or accountants, a lack of concurrence would make it difficult to persuade the SEC that a violation occurred.

(f) REGULATIONS AND PUBLICATIONS.   Because the SEC is a government agency, its accounting literature is structured differently from the pronouncements published by the FASB and other standard setters. This discussion provides an overall view of that structure in order to help the reader understand the SEC's regulations and publications. Those interested in more detailed descriptions of SEC financial reporting requirements will need to consult materials developed by one of several reporting services or large accounting firms. Like other agencies, the Commission publishes its pronouncements in the daily *Federal Register,* copies of which are then compiled and republished by proprietary organizations for sale to practicing accountants and attorneys, as well as libraries and others. Today, electronic services that maintain the current SEC literature are widely used by corporations and auditors to ensure that changes to the rules and regulations are properly considered.

The two main sources of the SEC's authority over accounting are the Securities Act of 1933 and the Securities Exchange Act of 1934. Five other statutes also affect accounting, but less directly. They include the Public Utility Holding Company Act of 1935, the Trust Indenture Act of 1939, the Investment Company Act of 1940, the Investment Advisor Act of 1940, and the Security Investor

Protection Act of 1970, and, most recently, the Sarbanes-Oxley Act of 2002. These statutes give the SEC the authority to create rules and regulations that interpret the requirements to be met by companies under its jurisdiction.

For accountants, the most familiar regulations under the 1933 and 1934 Securities Acts are Regulation S-X (17 Code of Federal Regulations [CFR] 210) and Regulation S-K (17 CFR 229). Regulation S-X describes the accounting and auditing requirements that registrants must meet, including not only the financial statements but also the qualifications of (including independence) and reports filed by accountants who practice before the SEC.

Some registrants are not required to comply with Regulation S-K; for example, small companies that fall under Regulation D of 17 CFR 230 are exempt, as are investment advisers.

At the next level below regulations and forms are SEC Releases, which are essentially official communications between the SEC and the public. They announce changes in the regulations and forms, interpret the regulations, describe various SEC enforcement activities, or declare general SEC policy. The SEC issues these publications only after a majority vote of the commissioners.

Several types of releases are related to the statutes and regulations. Releases concerning matters under the 1933 Act are called *Securities Releases.* When they are published in the *Federal Register,* they are given a number with a "33-" prefix. Releases concerning the 1934 Act are called *Exchange Act Releases* and have a "34-" prefix in the *Register.* Releases concerned with Regulations S-X and S-K fall into two categories. As might be expected, Financial Reporting Releases (FRR) announce changes and interpretations of these two Regulations. They are published with an "FR-" prefix, although they are commonly identified in the accounting literature as "FRR." It is possible for a single release to have more than one designation. In fact, it is not uncommon to find a release carrying all three.

Accounting and Auditing Enforcement Releases (AAER) announce enforcement or other disciplinary actions against individuals, firms, and registrants who have been alleged or proven to be in violation of the federal securities laws or who have otherwise fallen under the SEC's disciplinary powers. They are published under the prefix of "AAER."

Until 1982, the SEC issued ASRs, concerning both financial reporting matters and enforcement actions. In that year, the separate FR and AAER series were created to avoid the confusion of dealing with the two different kinds of actions in one series. The effective portions of the ASRs were codified in FR-1.

The fourth level of literature, Staff advice, is directed from the SEC Staff to registrants and other interested parties with regard to its interpretation of the regulations and forms. To help avoid arbitrary or otherwise inconsistent policies, these communications are generally subjected to substantial internal review involving two or more divisions or offices, including, for example, the OCA, DCF, and the Office of the General Counsel.

Although Staff advice lacks the official standing of SEC releases, a registrant faces substantial difficulty in successfully opposing it in a filing. As with every Staff decision, the registrant can appeal to the commissioners for an exception, but history has shown that few are willing to go to the expense and trouble, and fewer still succeed in overturning the Staff's position.

Three categories of Staff advice are of interest to accountants. Staff Accounting Bulletins (SABs) are probably the most familiar. They are issued by DCF and the OCA. An SAB is published to describe an interpretation that the Staff has made either for a series of filings with similar facts and situations or for one filing that dealt with an unusual situation or that took a novel approach to the authoritative literature. The SAB assists registrants through a troubled area or lets them know that a particular approach will not pass Staff review.

(g) SUMMARY. Even though the SEC has jurisdiction over public corporations only, without doubt it has exerted, and will continue to exert, a substantial influence on financial accounting by private corporations as well. The philosophy of fair and full disclosure permeates the practice of financial accounting for all companies, and the SEC's standards for independence and competence of auditors are fairly well established throughout the profession. The enforcement activities of the SEC are also important because they establish and defend norms of behavior expected of financial accountants.

A major issue in today's marketplace is how the SEC will weigh in on the issue of convergence of U.S. GAAP with International Accounting Standards (IAS). This work discusses this issue in more detail, as we look forward into the future of financial reporting in Chapter 3 in this Handbook.

Affiliating with a corporation registered with the SEC puts special demands on its internal and external accountants. No one should venture into this type of practice without substantial training and experience or without competent legal counsel. The requirements are extensive and complicated, and the penalties for not meeting the standards are considerable.

1.4 FINANCIAL ACCOUNTING STANDARDS BOARD

The Financial Accounting Standards Board (FASB) has a unique status as a private organization charged with protecting the public interest. (The GASB, a related organization, is discussed in Section 1.5) The SEC endorses it through its 1973 ASR No. 150 (now codified within FR-1) as the source of "substantial authoritative support" for determining the acceptability of accounting practices for filings with the SEC. It has also been endorsed at the state level to the extent that state boards of accountancy include a requirement for complying with FASB pronouncements in their ethics codes. The FASB does not receive funds directly from either the SEC or state boards.

Although other private sector bodies, such as the AICPA and Financial Executives International (FEI), endorse and finance the FASB, it is, by intent and design, independent of any of them. Of course, these endorsements are contingent on the FASB's maintaining an attitude of protecting the public interest.

(a) BRIEF HISTORY.   Beginning in 1938 with the issuance of ASR No. 4, the SEC has given the accounting profession the task to deliberate and propose GAAP.

Shortly after ASR No. 4's release, the American Institute of Accountants (the forerunner of the AICPA) upgraded the level of funding, staffing, and activity of its Committee on Accounting Procedures (CAP). Over the next 20 years, it produced 51 Accounting Research Bulletins (ARBs), including the all-encompassing ARB No. 43, *Restatement and Revision of Accounting Research Bulletins.* The CAP did not survive because it suffered from two political shortcomings.

1. It never was given authority by the institute's council to establish standards that would be binding on the membership.
2. It existed within the institute, a fact that created at least the appearance that auditors' interests (and their clients' interests) were likely to be preferred to the public interest.

In response to criticism, the AICPA formed the APB in 1958 and again increased the funding and staffing over the previous levels. During the next 15 years, the APB issued 31 opinions and 4 statements. In an effort to establish credibility, the APB's initial membership consisted of the top managing partners of major firms and other comparably influential accountants. Over time, the membership level slipped somewhat into lower levels of management, but highly competent technical experts continued to serve on the APB. In 1964, the AICPA council acted to correct one of the deficiencies carried forward from the CAP by requiring members of the institute to identify and justify their clients' departures from principles established by the APB. However, the second weakness still existed in that the APB was perceived as elevating auditors' and clients' interests above the interest of the general public in achieving full and fair disclosure for more effective capital markets.

In 1971, in response to growing sentiments and suggestions that the APB needed to be replaced by a government agency, the AICPA organized the Study Group on Establishing Financial Accounting Standards, under the chairmanship of Francis M. Wheat. The following year, the study group recommended creating an autonomous standard-setting body that would overcome the weaknesses of the CAP and the APB. That is, it would be granted authority to establish binding GAAP, but it would not be housed within the AICPA. Thus, it would be more likely to escape the appearance of dominance by the interests of auditors and their clients. The proposal was accepted by six sponsoring organizations that provided adequate funding and other support to get the FASB established and operating in 1973. The original six sponsors were the AICPA, the FEI, the Institute of Management Accountants (IMA), the American Accounting Association (AAA), the Securities Industry Association, and the Association for Investment Management and Research (AIMR). A critical event of the first year was the SEC's issuance of ASR No. 150.

Initially, the APB was still heavily dependent on the IMA and auditors for its funding and credibility. However, the previous concerns of dominance were raised in congressional hearings in 1975 and 1976, and the APB's bylaws were changed to make it less subject to the appearance of control by auditors and preparers.

The first chair was a respected practitioner, Marshall Armstrong, who had been a member of the APB from 1963 through 1969. He was succeeded in 1978 by Donald J. Kirk, who had been a charter member of the FASB. Kirk served as chair through the end of 1986, when he was replaced by Denny Beresford, who served until June 30, 1997. Edmund Jenkins, formerly of Arthur Andersen & Company, took over as the chair on July 1, 1997. Robert Herz, formerly of PricewaterhouseCoopers, became chair on July 1, 2002. The current chair as of December 23, 2010, is Leslie Seidman.

A more in-depth history of U.S. financial accounting standard setting from a technical perspective is provided in Chapter 2 in this work by Reed K. Storey, which is brought forward from previous editions of the *Accountant's Handbook*.

(b) STRUCTURE OF THE FINANCIAL ACCOUNTING STANDARDS BOARD. The FASB is actually only one part of a three-part organization, which also consists of the Financial Accounting Foundation (FAF) and the Financial Accounting Standards Advisory Council (FASAC). The relationships among these entities, the GASB, and the Governmental Accounting Standards Advisory Council (GASAC) are diagrammed in Exhibit 1.3.

The FAF is a nonprofit, tax-exempt Delaware corporation, managed by a 16-member board of trustees. The FAF is responsible primarily for raising operating funds and appointing members of the two boards and their Advisory Councils. A third unofficial function of the FAF is to shield board members from the kinds of pressures to compromise the public interest that shut down

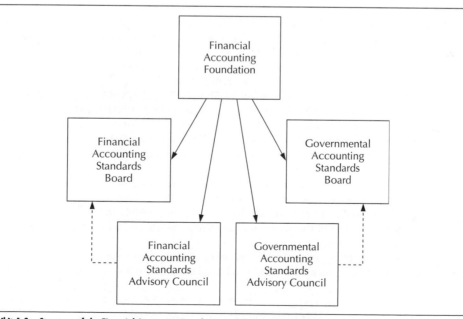

Exhibit 1.3   Structure of the Financial Accounting Foundation and the Standards Boards

the CAP and the APB. Eleven trustees are appointed by the governing boards of the sponsoring organizations, and the rest are selected by the other trustees. The creation of the GASB caused expansion of the FAF board to include three trustees selected by a consortium of organizations involved with local and state governments.

The FAF bylaws strictly forbid trustees from tampering with the boards' procedures in order to affect the standards that they issue. Of course, their control of appointments and reappointments gives the trustees substantial indirect influence.[2] A major controversy arose in 1996 concerning the composition of the FAF board after SEC chair Arthur Levitt grew dismayed by the lack of any kind of defense by the FAF against public claims by some leaders in the FEI that the FASB was "broken and in need of substantive repair."[3] He began to privately urge the FAF to voluntarily restructure itself to have a majority of its 16 members consist of individuals who unquestionably represent the public. (At the time, at least eight of the trustees, and possibly one other, were members of the preparer community.) When the negotiations broke down, Levitt took the issue public, first with a speech and then with a widely distributed letter that threatened to reconsider the standing of the SEC's ASR No. 150. This release delegates rule-making authority to the FASB.

As a result of the controversy, the FAF and SEC issued a joint press release in July 1996 that announced the appointment of four new trustees, all of whom met Levitt's criterion of being public representatives. Levitt accomplished his goal that preparers would no longer dominate the trustees or the FASB.

The FASAC was conceived as an experienced and informed microcosm of constituencies with the sole duty of providing feedback. It has operated that way with a membership ranging from 20 to 35 members who serve up to three one-year terms. Only the full-time chair receives compensation. The FASAC has no fundraising responsibilities and does not attempt to take a vote or reach a consensus on the issues. Rather, its job is to offer advice on projects that might be added to the agenda and on preliminary positions for existing projects.

The FASB itself is comprised of full-time members who must sever their relationships with their previous employers or partnerships. Each is appointed for a five-year term and can be reappointed for another. A member appointed to fill an unscheduled vacancy is eligible to serve up to two additional full terms. The FAF trustees designate the chair, who has significant administrative responsibilities, including the leadership of FASB Board meetings. In addition, the chair is the FASB's most visible spokesperson.

(c) BOARD PUBLICATIONS.   Although the FASB exists primarily to create financial accounting standards, it also provides interpretations. In addition, it was given the assignment of developing broad theoretical concepts of financial accounting. Its position in the regulatory process and the demand from many accountants for detailed rules combine to create the need for implementation guidance. As might be expected, the FASB's publications reflect these tasks.

The main category of publications consists of SFASs. They are numbered consecutively, and 175 SFASs were issued before the Codification was issued on July 1, 2009, and became effective for financial reports issued after September 15, 2009. The Codification brought together all the related authoritative literature at the time into a single document, arranged by topic and subtopic.

The FASB's implemented Codification of existing accounting pronouncements also exists as a searchable database of accounting standards at *http://asc.fasb.org/home*. Seventeen Accounting Standards Updates (ASUs) were issued in 2009 and 29 were issued in 2010. Going forward, the ASUs will be the mechanism to update the Codification. Practitioners continue to transition to this dramatic change in the professional literature, For purposes of this edition, most references in the various chapters will be to the historical releases (e.g., SFASs) with disclosure of the relevant Codification topical sections.

ASR No. 150 specifically recognizes the authority of these pronouncements, and they receive similar support in state accountancy statutes and regulations. In addition, they are recognized by

---

[2] See P. B. W. Miller, R. J. Redding, and P. R. Bahnson, *The FASB: The People, the Process and the Politics,* 4th ed. (Burr-Ridge, IL: Irwin-McGraw-Hill, 1998), pp. 183–186.
[3] Ibid., pp. 186–192.

the council of the AICPA as GAAP for the membership; any member not treating them as such will have violated Ethics Rule 203. Thus, financial statements must be prepared in accordance with these standards if they are to receive an unqualified audit opinion.

Another category of publication, Financial Interpretations (FINs), also establishes GAAP. However, relatively few have been issued since 1984, primarily because of the emphasis placed on other media for providing the kind of guidance that Interpretations were initially created to provide. Interpretations are numbered consecutively, and 48 have been issued.

A third category of FASB document is the Statement of Financial Accounting Concepts (SFAC). These statements describe broader underlying concepts that the FASB has determined to use in developing its Standards. The statements do not constitute GAAP; accordingly, they are not identified as such by regulatory bodies or ethics codes. Nonetheless, knowledge of these Statements is helpful for understanding the content of Standards and for anticipating the direction of future Standards. Concepts Statements are also numbered consecutively, and seven have been issued. SFAC No. 6, *Elements of Financial Statements,* replaced SFAC No. 3, *Elements of Financial Statements of Business Enterprises,* with the result that only six are in effect. These Concepts Statements have also been merged into the Codification.

A fourth FASB category of publication comprises Financial Technical Bulletins (FTBs), which are actually issued by the FASB Research Staff. They are narrow in scope and interpret the existing authoritative literature (i.e., ARBs, Accounting Principles Board Opinions [APBOs], SFASs, and FINs) to apply to situations not covered in it directly. Although FASB members have the ability to prevent issuance of proposed FTBs, they do not formally vote to authorize their publication. FTB are numbered in annual series, such as "85-3"; this number is the third one issued in 1985. The FASB initiated FTBs in order to systematize informal advice that its staff was disseminating by telephone and letters; the use of FTBs expanded in the mid-1980s to reduce the earlier practice of issuing many highly detailed standards and interpretations. This change also allowed FASB members to focus their efforts on more substantive issues.

To mitigate the need for narrow FASB pronouncements while still providing quick responses to new problems (called *timely guidance* in FASB jargon), the Emerging Issues Task Force (EITF) was created in 1984. The director of the FASB's Research Staff chairs this group, which consists of about 15 technical experts from major and regional accounting firms and large corporations. It meets periodically to tackle complex new problems by applying the existing literature. Transactions and events that have already transpired are the source of some issues, whereas others are based on proposed transactions. The SEC's chief accountant is an active participant in the discussions, despite being officially identified as only an observer. The chief accountant and the OCA Staff are the prime beneficiaries of the EITF's activity because it often addresses issues that were brought to the OCA by registrants and their accountants.

When the EITF faces an issue, it seeks a consensus, which is considered to exist if no more than two or three members object to a proposed solution. If more object, there is no consensus, with the consequence that the OCA is left to implement its own views. Alternatively, the task force may recommend that the full FASB consider dealing with the issue. Prior to 1988, EITF consensuses were not published, although minutes of the meetings were available from the FASB. In 1988, the FASB began to publish highly condensed summaries of the issues and their resolutions. These summaries are presented as a public service because the outcomes are not necessarily the opinion of either a majority of the FASB or the FASB's Staff. Nevertheless, they hold a position in the GAAP hierarchy. A consensus is acceptable for SEC filings as long as the OCA does not have a serious objection to its outcome. Like FTBs, EITF issues are numbered in annual series. While assigned status first by the auditing profession in Statement of Auditing Standards (SAS) No. 69, *The Meaning of Present Fairly in Conformity with Generally Accepted Accounting Principles,* to fill a void in the accounting literature, the implementation of a GAAP hierarchy by the FASB (SFAS No. 162, *The Hierarchy of Generally Accepted Accounting Principles*) recently obviated the need for this SAS in the auditing literature.

In addition to the documents just mentioned, the FASB also produces numerous other publications. Its Staff sometimes issues implementation guides, in the form of questions and answers, on more complex financial accounting standards. These implementation guides are yet another level in the GAAP hierarchy. Research Reports are developed in response to Staff or consultant efforts to identify a problem, review the literature related to a set of issues, or propose answers. Discussion Memorandums and Invitations to Comment solicit views from the FASB's constituents in early stages of deliberations. Three newsletters inform the public of the FASB's activities: *Action Alert, Status Report,* and *Highlights.* Another widely distributed item is Facts about FASB, which describes the organization's mission, procedures, and membership.

Like many other organizations, the FASB has a site on the World Wide Web (*www.fasb.org*) that it uses for a variety of purposes. The site provides the public with access to press releases, major FASB communications (including letters to the FASB from prominent commentators and responses from the FASB), and e-mail access to board and staff members. FASB exposure drafts can be downloaded from the FASB Web site.

(d) DUE PROCESS PROCEDURES. Like many other regulatory agencies, the FASB has established procedures to ensure that parties affected by new regulations have an opportunity to express their views on the issues and positions on the issues are identified. Another desirable effect is that the public's participation bolsters the credibility of the output. Although the term *due process* may imply a rigid set of procedures, there is actually enough flexibility to allow the FASB some freedom in determining how extensively to pursue various activities. These six steps, however, are followed:

1. Admission to the agenda
2. Preliminary deliberations
3. Tentative resolution
4. Further deliberations
5. Final resolution
6. Subsequent review

All six steps are public. Board meetings take place at the headquarters in Norwalk, Connecticut, and are open to all who want to attend, up to the room's capacity. Under the FASB's sunshine policy, FASB members are not allowed to discuss the issues privately in groups consisting of more than three persons. This arrangement was adopted in the mid-1970s after criticism that the previous policy of closed-door meetings caused some constituents to feel that their views were not being considered.

A project is admitted to the agenda only after substantial preliminary debate. The set of problems to be addressed in the project must meet three criteria.

1. There must be diverse practice.
2. The diversity must create significant differences in financial statements, such that there is a potential for users to be misled or to incur excessive analysis costs.
3. There must be a sufficiently high probability that the issues can be resolved in a manner that justifies using FASB resources.

Problems are identified by the FASB and Staff but more often come from constituents and the SEC. The EITF deliberations have also created some projects.

The next step is to engage in early deliberations. Early during this stage, the Research Staff attempts to frame the issues and sound out FASB members and constituents. For major projects, the Staff may create a task force of interested experts from various constituencies to assist its inquiries. Occasionally the FASB will publish a Discussion Memorandum or an Invitation to Comment at this phase. There may be public hearings for especially significant or controversial projects in order to allow constituents to express their views and to allow board members and Staff to question persons who testify. Board meetings will generally be devoted to questions from the members to the Staff and to each other. As the phase draws to a close, the Staff efforts turn to helping the members find the common ground on which to build a majority vote.

The third phase is the tentative resolution. At this point in the process, the FASB has voted to issue an Exposure Draft (ED), which is a proposed Standard, Concepts Statement, or Interpretation. More controversial projects may have another round of public hearings. Dissenting board members' views are included in the ED, as is a summary of the basis for the majority's conclusions.

During the further deliberations step of the due process, the Staff and FASB attempt to digest the comments received in response to the ED. During this phase, FASB members generally aim at fine-tuning the proposal to deal with unanticipated minor glitches. If significant changes are needed, a second ED may be necessary.

The final resolution phase is short and consists merely of taking votes from the FASB members either for or against the ballot draft of the Standard (or other pronouncement). The published document includes not only the majority's view but also the dissenters', if any. It describes the comments from the constituents and the FASB's reactions to them. Many Standards include an appendix illustrating the application of the requirements. Once this point is reached, the Staff's efforts turn to responding to implementation problems.

In summary, the due process is molded to fit the situation. The FASB specifically disavows any notion that the due process allows it to "count noses" to determine what a majority of the constituency wants. Its role is more judicial than legislative, and the FASB members must reach a conclusion about what is best, even if particular groups are strongly opposed to the new accounting Standard.

(e) CONCEPTUAL FRAMEWORK.   An important key to understanding the overall direction of the FASB's efforts to reform financial accounting is its project to identify a coherent theory of financial reporting, called the *conceptual framework.*

Because the CAP and APB were criticized for not developing a unified theoretical basis for resolving issues, the FASB's inaugural agenda included the task of identifying concepts that it could use in setting standards.

A critical initial decision in the project was to develop the framework from the top down by identifying the objectives of financial reporting and then working down to more specific concepts. This approach (also called *deductive*) had been tried before, most notably by Sprouse and Moonitz in the AICPA's Accounting Research Study (ARS) No. 3, *A Tentative Set of Broad Accounting Principles for Business Enterprises* (1962) and by the Trueblood Study Group in its report *Objectives of Financial Statements* (1973).[4] The opposite approach (called *bottom-up or inductive*) of looking at practice and identifying common threads had also been tried, most notably in APB Statement No. 4, *Basic Concepts and Accounting Principles Underlying Financial Statements of Business Enterprises* (1970). APB Statement No. 4 also used the top-down approach. Although there are several advantages and disadvantages to the two approaches, the main difference between them is that the bottom-up approach tends to encourage applying old solutions for new problems, whereas the top-down approach tends to lead to new solutions for old problems. Thus, the determination of the FASB to pursue a top-down framework created a substantially greater likelihood that significant changes in GAAP could be supported. Accordingly, the framework project was (and has continued to be) controversial.

SFAC No. 1, *Objectives of Financial Reporting by Business Enterprises,* was issued in 1978. It presented a hierarchy of objectives, the most important being the provision of "information that is useful to present and potential investors and creditors and other users in making rational investment, credit, and other decisions."

SFAC No. 1 is significant because it establishes that the interests of the public and financial statement users are to be ranked above the interests of auditors and preparers. User needs are also the compass auditors use in determining materiality, a critical auditing concept that shapes the nature and scope of auditing procedures applied.

SFAC No. 2, *Qualitative Characteristics of Accounting Information,* was issued in 1980. It identifies qualities of information that make it useful for meeting the objective described in SFAC

---

[4] AICPA Trueblood Study Group, *Objectives of Financial Statements* (New York: AICPA, 1973).

No. 1. The three primary qualities are relevance, reliability, and comparability. The important point to observe is that the FASB chose qualities that reflect user needs instead of the needs of auditors (who prefer defensible information) and preparers (who prefer controllable and inexpensive information).

The third phase of the framework culminated in 1980 with the issuance of SFAC No. 3 was superseded in 1985 by SFAC No. 6, which also encompasses the elements of financial statements issued by not-for-profit entities. The business elements identified by the FASB included the familiar assets, liabilities, owners' equity, revenues, expenses, gains, and losses; however, the FASB's decision to make the assets and liabilities the keystone elements was enormously significant. That is, it defined all the other elements, including "comprehensive income," that were defined in terms of assets and liabilities. With this decision, the FASB essentially turned away from the familiar matching concept of income that had dominated practice for decades with its emphasis on the income statement and its deemphasis of the balance sheet. Instead, under the conceptual framework, income is measured by changes in assets and liabilities because both the income statement and the balance sheet are considered useful and important.

SFAC No. 4, *Objectives of Financial Reporting by Nonbusiness Organizations,* was also issued in 1980. (Subsequent to issuing SFAC No. 4 but before issuing SFAC No. 6, the FASB determined that the term *not-for-profit* was preferable to *nonbusiness.* In particular, the managers of a number of these entities complained that they did not like the inference that they were not "businesslike" in the way they operated.) It was the outgrowth of the FASB's decision to deal with all entities, public or private. This Statement broke new ground because there had not been a significant effort to establish top-down concepts in this area. As might be expected, the main objective is similar to the one in SFAC No. 1; specifically, it says that the financial statements of not-for-profit organizations should provide "information that is useful to present and potential resource providers and other users in making rational decisions about the allocation of resources to those organizations."

By starting with this objective, the FASB again put into place the potential for substantial reform because it would be necessary to show how existing practices met this objective.

The FASB encountered major roadblocks when it entered into the project's next phase, "recognition and measurement," because it was here that decisions would be reached on whether, when, and at what amount assets, liabilities, and changes in them should be reflected in the financial statements. The fundamental issue was whether there should be a movement toward including more market value information in the statements. Naturally, this phase of the project attracted much attention and created substantial controversy. In 1985, after more than three years of debate, six FASB members agreed to issue SFAC No. 5, *Recognition and Measurement in Financial Statements of Business Enterprises,* which was clearly a compromise. It says that things recognized in the statements should be elements and that the amount reported for them should be relevant and reliable. In effect, all that was accomplished was to affirm the contents of the preceding concepts statements. SFAC No. 5 also identified the cash flow statement as a conceptual member of the set of financial statements, and the FASB eventually issued SFAS No. 95, *Statement of Cash Flows,* which requires its presentation. SFAC No. 5 also identified two possible income statements, one of which would focus on earnings, whereas the other would report comprehensive income, which might include changes in current value. In 1997, after two years of deliberations, the FASB issued SFAS No. 130, *Reporting Comprehensive Income,* which requires companies to report the amount of comprehensive income, either at the bottom of its regular income statement or in a separate statement. This amount equals the reported net income plus and minus the changes in various unrealized changes in equity that are reported on the balance sheet. The Standard addresses only the display of comprehensive income and does not introduce any new measurement requirements. However, the Standard does set into place a means for reporting other components of comprehensive income.

In 2000, the FASB issued SFAC No. 7, *Using Cash Flow Information and Present Value in Accounting Measurements.* Although accounting measurements are best determined using observable exchange transactions, sometimes measurements must be based on estimated cash flows. This Concepts Statement provides a framework for using cash-flow- based techniques for accounting measurements. SFAC No. 7 specifies that accounting measurements based on present value concepts should reflect the uncertainties associated with the underlying cash flows. SFAC No. 7 also introduces the expected cash flow approach to present value calculations. Present value calculations historically often are based on a single set of estimated cash flows and a single discount rate, where the discount rate reflects the uncertainties associated with the cash flows. Concept Statement No. 7 states that a range of estimated cash flows should be considered and that this range of cash flows should be assigned their respective probabilities and then discounted. Measurement of the fair value of an entity's liabilities is to reflect the credit standing of the entity.

What, then, is the significance of the conceptual framework?

1. It sets in place the possibility for significant changes in GAAP.
2. It puts users' needs (and thus the public interest) at the highest priority level.
3. It establishes that the statement of financial position should not be merely a resting place for debit and credit balances waiting to be "matched" in the future; rather, it should provide useful information about assets and liabilities.
4. It rejects matching in favor of reporting changes in assets and liabilities as income, thus raising the possibility that gains and losses from fair value changes could be recognized as income.
5. It defines a number of important terms that are used in the FASB's communications with its constituents and in its internal discussions. Far from being an empty academic theoretical exercise, the framework is perhaps the most significant set of pronouncements that the FASB has issued. The more that practitioners know about it, the more they will be capable of dealing with the FASB and the changes that its pronouncements will bring about.

(f) STANDARDS OVERLOAD.   One pervasive problem that just will not go away is *standards overload*. Originally this phrase described the issuance of numerous detailed standards, but more recently it has come to encompass the issuance of complex standards that are difficult to implement, especially by smaller nonpublic companies. Exhibit 1.4 symbolizes this situation, showing that the FASB has received rule-making authority from the SEC to establish GAAP for use by public companies while, at the same time, it has received rule-making authority from state boards and the AICPA to establish GAAP for use by private companies. It should be noted that these delegations of authority

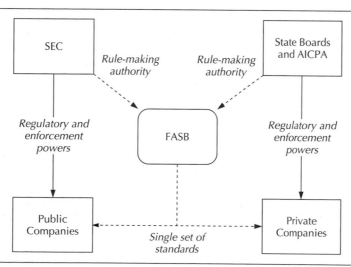

Exhibit 1.4   Conflicting Authorities and Standards Overload

do not grant the FASB any enforcement or broad policy-making powers. In fact, they have created the narrow but complex task of developing a single set of financial accounting standards that apply to both public and private companies.

The FASB's dilemma is that too much emphasis on the information needs of public companies ignores the practical constraints affecting private companies. Because the SEC exerts the greatest political influence, it seems likely that FASB will continue to focus on the needs of more sophisticated users and will issue Standards that may be difficult for private companies to implement. This choice leaves the state boards and the AICPA in a difficult relationship with some of their constituents and members, but there does not appear to be any way out of this dilemma.

Under active study and debate today is the application of different standards according to whether the company is private or public. Survey responses have consistently shown that a different set of GAAP for private companies would be perceived as inferior and that users probably would demand that public company principles be applied in private companies' statements. The IAS arena may provide some clues as to how standards for larger and smaller entities might coexist.

Apart from the issue of private and public company standards is the ever present debate over principles versus rules-based standards. Little can be added to that debate at this point. One can see from litigation and the analysis of failed audits that detailed accounting standards in themselves do not prevent bad things from happening. Some feel that detailed rules invite a gaming of structuring the transactions that seem to meet the letter of the standard. However, does that mean that less precise standards would be better? Would the SEC and auditors have more or less ammunition to urge a more "fair" presentation with less precise standards? If companies and their auditors cannot interpret the spirit of the rules when more detail is provided, are they likely to be more insightful and forceful with less? These questions plague concerned managements as well as auditors.

(g) SOME CRITICISMS OF THE STANDARDS.   The failure of Enron, largely due to the disclosure of financial reporting improprieties, resulted in some criticism of the FASB. Enron transferred nonperforming assets and liabilities into various special-purpose entities (SPEs). The objective of these maneuvers was to shield the company from recognizing losses on these nonperforming assets and to reduce its perceived risk by reducing its reported debt level. At the time, accounting rules for SPEs did not require consolidation of assets and liabilities transferred to the SPE with the financial statements of the sponsoring entity if an outside investor made an equity contribution of 3 percent or more of the SPE's total capitalization. Enron did not meet this requirement because some of the outside capital allegedly contributed to the SPE was not really at risk. Enron had guaranteed some of the capital investments made by outside investors using its own stock as the form of guarantee.

Although Enron did not comply with the existing accounting requirements, the FASB still was subject to stinging criticism because a number of parties alleged that the current accounting rules for SPEs were too lax, and the FASB's Standards are too detailed, and detailed Standards provide incentives for preparers to design transactions that meet their letter but not their spirit. The FASB has issued an Interpretation (*Consolidation of Variable Interest Entities,* Interpretation No. 46 to ARB No. 51, *Consolidated Financial Statements*) to tighten the rules related to nonconsolidation of SPEs. Moreover, the FASB historically has been criticized for failing to require companies to expense stock options. Changes in the Standards require more companies to record compensation as a result of granting stock options. The implementation of the 2004 revisions (FASB No. 123R) on stock compensation requires the use of the fair value method in measuring the expensing stock options.

While a goal has been to isolate the FASB from political and constituent pressure, the economic downturn in 2009 prompted the FASB to issue some additional guidance regarding the reaction to market conditions. Some of that guidance had the effect of softening the landing that otherwise the existing rules might require. Because accounting is linked to our economy and society, it is difficult to insulate it from the pressures that extraordinary times can place on it. It is a continuing challenge to maintain the integrity of the accounting standard-setting process.

1.5 GOVERNMENTAL ACCOUNTING STANDARDS BOARD

In response to needs expressed by various groups, a study was undertaken in the early 1980s to consider how to establish financial accounting standards for state and local governmental units. (The federal government's uniqueness has caused the application of governmental accounting standards to be limited to state and local entities.) Standards were being established through professional organizations composed of governmental accountants, but they had not been endorsed by the Council of the AICPA; consequently there was some concern over whether they constituted GAAP. The study group's report recommended the creation of the GASB that would be under the administration of the FAF. After several years of discussion and opposition, the trustees agreed to set up the GASB, and it began operations in 1984.

The constituencies of GASB overlap those of the FASB to a limited extent. The preparers consist of elected and appointed officials who are accountable to the voting public for the use and safekeeping of funds appropriated or otherwise entrusted to them, and thus they do not coincide with the preparers regulated by the FASB. The auditor constituency is essentially the same as for the FASB, although the actual individuals are different because of specialization issues. Users of the financial statements of governmental units are different from users of business statements. In effect, when governmental units go into the capital markets to obtain debt funding, they are competing with corporations for investors' attention. There is no regulatory agency comparable to the SEC with jurisdiction over governmental units; consequently the GASB has no constituent like the SEC. State boards are interested in the GASB's efforts because their licensees act as auditors for governmental units.

Without an endorsement by the SEC, the authority of GASB for setting standards is not quite as clear-cut as that of the FASB. It does have power, however, because a variety of professional societies, including the AICPA, endorse its efforts. It also has increased influence because of its affiliation with the FASB.

(a) STRUCTURE OF THE GOVERNMENTAL ACCOUNTING STANDARDS BOARD. The GASB has five members, with only the chair serving on a full-time basis. The other four members serve part time and meet as needed for formal meetings and consultations. In addition, the GASB has a full-time director of research and technical activities. The GASB's headquarters are located in the same building as the FASB and the FAF. Although the FASB and GASB operate independently, they do share some facilities, including the board meeting room and the library, as well as their accounting and human resource management staff.

The Governmental Accounting Standards Advisory Committee serves the same purpose as the FASAC, but it is not as large and does not have a full-time chair.

The GASB's due process procedures are essentially the same as the FASB's and include similar steps. Some of the deliberations are more difficult to accomplish because of the geographical dispersion of the part-time members.

(b) JURISDICTION ISSUE. A persistent problem in the relationship between the FASB and the GASB has been the overlapping of their jurisdictions in some segments of the economy. In fact, the issue of which board should provide standards for these segments was the major stumbling block to the GASB's establishment.

Some organizations subject to the overlapping jurisdiction are utilities and providers of educational and health services. For example, some universities are operated by governments, others are private, and still others are combinations. The same situation exists for utilities, hospitals, and nursing homes. The jurisdiction issue turned first on the question of whether all these entities should be required to use the same accounting principles in order to achieve comparability. If so, the next question was which board should establish those principles.

As long as there were no conflicts over the principles to be used, the jurisdiction dispute did not cause a practical problem. However, that situation did not exist for long because the two boards reached opposing conclusions concerning the recognition of depreciation. Thus, the unresolved issue continued to chafe both organizations and to confuse their constituents.

It was resolved in late 1989 when the FAF's trustees first voted to implement and then shortly thereafter rejected a recommendation offered by two special committees that reviewed the structures of the FASB and the GASB. The final resolution left the jurisdiction as it had originally been defined, with the GASB holding power over state and local government entities, whereas the FASB was given responsibility for all others. In addition, it was agreed that the GASB would give careful consideration to the need for comparability when setting standards for public sector entities in industries that also include private companies.

For those readers interested in state and local government issues, Chapter 33 of this *Handbook,* by Cynthia Pon, Richard A. Green, and Caroline H. Walsh, will be of interest.

1.6 FEDERAL ACCOUNTING STANDARDS ADVISORY BOARD

The needs of users of public, private, and state and local government financial reports can differ from the needs of the users of federal reports. Before the establishment of a separate body to consider GAAP in the context of federal financial accounting issues, the practice of federal accounting was a loose confederation of laws and federal directives and accounting principles drawn from the private sector and the state and local government sector.

However, since October 1999, the Federal Accounting Standards Advisory Board (FASAB) has been the body designated by the AICPA Council to establish GAAP and the GAAP hierarchy for federal reporting entities.

The federal GAAP hierarchy includes a priority sequence of documents and releases that guide accounting and reporting practice. That hierarchy includes FASAB Statements of Federal Financial Accounting Standards (SFFAS) and Interpretations, Technical Bulletins, Technical Releases of the Accounting and Auditing Policy Committee, and implementation guides. For further information see SFFAS No. 34, *The Hierarchy of Generally Accepted Accounting Principles, Including the Application of Standards Issued by the Financial Accounting Standards Board,* paragraph 5. Like the other standard setters, the FASAB operates in the sunshine with a structured due process from reaching decisions.

Volume Two of this work contains Chapter 32 by David M. Zavata, which provides a fuller summary of the development of federal accounting principles and how the myriad of constituencies and agencies interact within the federal environment. While the general financial statement reader does not confront reports prepared under federal accounting guidelines often, these principles govern an immense and growing portion of U.S. economic dollars. The Web site *www.fasab.gov/* may also be a helpful source of information about this important body and its activities.

1.7 AMERICAN INSTITUTE OF CERTIFIED PUBLIC ACCOUNTANTS

Prior to 1973, the role of accounting standard setter was held by the AICPA or its predecessor body. After the formation of the FASB, the AICPA continued to play a role in accounting standard setting through the occasional issuance of Statements of Position (SOPs) through the Accounting Standards Executive Committee (AcSEC) and the issuance of Accounting and Audit Guides for various industries.

Prior to 2002, AcSEC examined accounting issues, generally ones with more narrow industry implications, that had not reached the FASB's agenda or that the FASB had decided against adding to its agenda. Accordingly, AcSEC and the FASB were in frequent contact, and FASB Staff members attend AcSEC meetings. The primary form of output from AcSEC was an SOP, which must be followed by institute members. Under SAS No. 69, AcSEC SOPs were considered "level b" pronouncements in the GAAP hierarchy. SOPs constitute GAAP if no "level a" pronouncement existed.

In response to FASB concerns about the nature and development process surrounding various the standard-setting activities, and a recognition that the EITF was also a mechanism for addressing narrow issues that the Board did not place on its agenda, AcSEC discontinued issuing SOPs.

AcSEC and the AICPA will no longer issue general-purpose SOPs or ask the FASB to clear SOPs or practice bulletins.

The AICPA and AcSEC will continue to issue Accounting and Audit Guides. These Guides are a very valuable and unique service to members as they focus on interpreting auditing and accounting literature for company accountants and auditors with a topical (e.g., Audit Sampling) or industry (e.g., Airline Industry) focus. The practices described in the Guides should be followed or departures should be justified. No other accounting or auditing standard setter or professional organization issues authoritative guides such as these.

Today, the AICPA actively participates in commentary on various accounting issues before the FASB and professional issues that reach congressional attention. However, today the AICPA has a negligible role in directly setting accounting standards.

1.8 U.S. AUDITING STANDARDS

The field of U.S. auditing standards dramatically changed with the implementation of the Sarbanes-Oxley Act of 2002. Before that the AICPA, through the ASB and a variety of committees, had been primarily responsible for setting auditing standards for both public and private companies. The Sarbanes-Oxley Act established that the newly created PCAOB would have the authority to establish auditing standards (after SEC clearance) and conduct CPA firm inspections for public company auditors. Those companies not required to follow PCAOB jurisdiction (e.g., private companies, nonprofit entities, and governmental entities) could continue to follow AICPA auditing standards.

Since the PCAOB is a newer organization and its charge is over a vast amount of capital in the U.S. economy, it will receive considerable discussion in this chapter.

The influence of International Audit and Attest Standards Board (IAASB) is also a strong force in current standard-setting activity and will be discussed with the AICPA role.

1.9 PUBLIC COMPANY ACCOUNTING OVERSIGHT BOARD

(a) BACKGROUND. Congress created the PCAOB as a response to various accounting-related scandals including Enron, WorldCom and others. The state of outrage in the country to these allegations of financial reporting fraud is reflected by the overwhelming votes in favor of Sarbanes-Oxley in both houses of Congress. The Act passed the Senate 99 to 0, and only 3 votes were cast against it in the House of Representatives.

The Sarbanes-Oxley Act has 11 sections. These sections address:

1. The PCAOB
2. Auditor independence
3. Corporate responsibility
4. Enhanced financial disclosures
5. Analyst conflicts of interest
6. Commission resources and authority
7. Studies and reports
8. Corporate and criminal fraud accountability
9. White-collar crime penalty enhancements
10. Corporate tax returns
11. Corporate fraud and accountability

The first four and the last four sections are likely to be of greatest interest to practicing CPAs.

The Sarbanes-Oxley Act created new requirements for publicly held companies and others and revamped the regulatory system for auditors of public companies. For decades, various studies of accounting and auditing failures had concluded that deficiencies in internal controls were at the root of these failures. In addition, recently there was a noted increase in the frequency of restatements of the financial reports of public companies, leading to concerns that faith in the securities markets could be undermined by frequent errors in reported earnings, financial position, or disclosures.

The AICPA has retained the authority for standard setting for audits of financial statements of privately held companies and governments and for quality control for firms that perform those audits, where it has been since the 1930s. While there was no prohibition on the PCAOB working in some way with the existing U.S. auditing standard setter, the AICPA Auditing Standards Board (ASB), the PCAOB decided to maintain a very independent position in fulfilling its mission directed to public companies. This has led to increasing divergence in the auditing standards and independent quality inspections for public and nonpublic companies and is an important practice issue for auditors with public and nonpublic clients.

The AICPA has issued an auditing interpretation (AU 9508.89) explaining that if an auditor applies PCAOB Standards in the audit of a nonpublic company, the auditor must also comply with generally accepted auditing standards and the audit report should refer to both sets of standards.

Despite the use of the word *accounting* in its name, the focus of the PCAOB is on the auditing of public companies.

The PCAOB opened its doors in January 2003 and held its first meeting that month. The SEC reported, on April 25, 2003, that the PCAOB was organized and had the capacity to carry out its legislated duties, the final critical step in its establishment.

(b) AUTHORITY.   Sarbanes-Oxley defines the PCAOB's authority and revises the Securities Act of 1934 to recognize it. PCAOB was established to

> oversee the audit of public companies that are subject to the securities laws, and related matters, in order to protect the interests of investors and further the public interest in the preparation of informative, accurate, and independent audit reports for companies the securities of which are sold to, and held by and for, public investors. (Section 101(a))

The PCAOB's authority is subordinate to that of the SEC. Sarbanes-Oxley did not affect the SEC's authority to enforce the nation's securities laws, including regulating auditors, taking action against them, or setting accounting, auditing, or independence standards. The SEC maintains budgetary authority over the PCAOB and must approve proposed substantive rules before they take effect.

The PCAOB regulates auditors of issuers, which are described under Sarbanes-Oxley in this way:

> The term "issuer" means an issuer (as defined in section 3 of the Securities Exchange Act of 1934 (15 USC 78(c)), the securities of which are registered under section 12 of that Act (15 USC 78l), or that is required to file reports under section 15(d) (15 USC 78o(d)), or that files or has filed a registration statement that has not yet become effective under the Securities Act of 1933 (15 USC 77a et seq.), and that it has not withdrawn. (Section 2(a)(7))

It has authority over both domestic and foreign auditing firms that prepares or issue audit reports on U.S. public companies or that play a substantial role in the preparation or issuance of such reports.

The PCAOB's primary public-interest functions include:

- Registering accounting firms that audit public companies
- Establishing and maintaining standards for auditing, quality control, ethics, and independence related to the preparation of audit reports for public companies
- Conducting inspections of registered firms
- Conducting investigations and disciplinary proceedings against registered firms and associated individuals, including imposing sanctions when justified

Although state boards of accountancy can choose to adopt PCAOB Standards instead of those of the AICPA, Sarbanes-Oxley Section 209 explicitly notes that "the standards approved by the [PCAOB] should not be presumed to be applicable . . . for small and medium sized nonregistered public accounting firms."

The PCAOB's Practice Standards apply to all auditors, including staff and independent contractors (called *associated persons*), who participate in an audit of a public company. Registered firms also must comply with the board's Quality Control Standards.

(c) STRUCTURE.   The PCAOB is not an agency of the U.S. government, and its Staff members are not government employees. It is a nonprofit corporation that can be dissolved only by an act of Congress.

The PCAOB's Washington office is home to the board, the executive staff, and the standard-setting function. Its Web site is *www.pcaobus.org*. It has several satellite offices around the country, primarily focused on inspections.

The PCAOB's budget is subject to SEC approval. The bulk of its funding comes from an allocation of accounting support fees assessed on public companies and from registration and annual fees from the registered auditing firms.

The PCAOB has the authority to assess monetary penalties against auditors, but any amounts collected are donated to a merit scholarship program for undergraduate and graduate students in accredited accounting degree programs.

(i) Board Members, Staff, and Advisory Groups.   There are five members of the board. The board members serve full time and cannot engage in any other professional or business activity. They are appointed by the SEC, in consultation with the chair of the Federal Reserve and the secretary of the Treasury. To ensure the oversight group includes representation of various user groups and not just accountants, only two of the members can be current or former CPAs; however, a CPA cannot be appointed chairperson if he or she practiced as a CPA within five years of appointment to the board. Board members serve five-year terms, and no member can serve more than two terms.

The board is supported by a staff of several hundred accountants, attorneys, and others. Many of the accountants were partners or staff in auditing firms before joining the PCAOB Staff.

The board has established organizational functions in this way:

- The Division of Registration and Inspections creates the registry of accounting firms and performs inspections of the firms.
- The Office of the Chief Auditor and Professional Standards advises the board on standard setting.
- The Division of Enforcement and Investigations performs investigations of possible violations of law or professional standards and recommends disciplinary actions to the board.
- The Office of General Counsel provides legal advice and assists the board's rulemaking functions.
- The Office of Operations is responsible for information technology, human resources, and finance.
- The Office of Research and Analysis provides the PCAOB with assessment of risk and related insights.
- The Offices of Public Affairs and Government Relations assist the PCAOB in communications with the public, Congress, and the news media.
- The international affairs staff advises the PCAOB on international issues.

The PCAOB has the authority to create advisory groups to make recommendations regarding standards. It has officially convened a Standing Advisory Group (SAG) to assist the board in reviewing existing standards, in formulating new ones, and in evaluating proposed standards projects. Periodically, the PCAOB convenes ad hoc groups to advise Staff on specific practice issues.

(d) FIRM REGISTRATION. Under Sarbanes-Oxley, only firms registered with PCAOB may "prepare or issue, or . . . participate in the preparation or issuance of, any audit report with respect to any issuer" (section 102(a)). Thus, any firm—domestic or foreign—that plays a substantial role in an audit of a public company must be registered. However, a firm can voluntarily register with the PCAOB even if it does no audits of public clients.

It is illegal for a nonregistered firm to audit or participate in the audit of a public company. Accordingly, a firm must maintain its registration and needs to consider whether other firms that it relies on for the audits of subsidiaries or other elements of the company are registered.

Registered firms must:

- Follow the PCAOB Standards in auditing, quality control, and independence.
- Pay the required registration fees.
- Undergo periodic inspections.
- Cooperate with PCAOB-initiated investigations.

The application form for registration, called *Form 1,* asks for a substantial amount of information. While Sarbanes-Oxley calls for some of this information to be publicly available, firms can request that certain proprietary or confidential information be protected from public disclosure.

The registration fee and annual fee are assessed based on the number of public clients the firm audits.

A firm may withdraw from PCAOB registration, but the PCAOB may delay the withdrawal for up to 18 months while it carries out inspection, investigation, or disciplinary proceedings.

(e) STANDARDS. Sarbanes-Oxley gave the PCAOB the authority to approve, modify, or establish its own standards for auditing, quality control, and independence. The PCAOB determined that it would establish its own standards. The PCAOB Standards are not characterized as generally accepted because their authority does not derive from general acceptance but rather from regulatory authority.

To provide initial, transitional standards for the PCAOB, it adopted the existing AICPA SASs (through SAS No. 101, *Auditing Fair Value Estimates and Disclosures*), Attest Standards, Quality Control Standards, and Rules 101 and 102 of the Code of Professional Conduct as of April 16, 2003. The PCAOB also adopted the existing Independence Standards Board pronouncements and interpretations. Since that date, the PCAOB has been editing and replacing elements of those transitional Standards and issuing its own Standards for public company audit practice.

(i) Sarbanes-Oxley Mandated Provisions. Although the PCAOB will issue new Standards and amend or replace the interim ones, Sarbanes-Oxley explicitly calls for the PCAOB to require:

- Audit firms to prepare work papers and other information related to the audit report, in sufficient detail to support the auditor's conclusions, and to maintain them for at least seven years.
- A concurring or second-partner review and approval of audit reports.
- An audit report that includes a description of tests and findings related to the entity's internal control, including an evaluation of the effectiveness of internal control, an evaluation of the assessment of internal control made by management, and a description of material weaknesses in control or material noncompliance with controls the auditor discovered. This provision only applies today to the accelerated SEC filers. Nonaccelerated filers were exempted from separate auditor attestation by the Financial Reform Act of 2010. Chapter 7 in this *Handbook* on internal controls reporting provides additional detail regarding company responsibilities under the Sarbanes-Oxley Act of 2002.
- Quality control standards that deal with:
  ○ Monitoring of professional ethics and independence
  ○ Consultation on accounting and auditing questions
  ○ Supervision of audit work
  ○ Hiring, professional development, and advancement of personnel

○ Acceptance and continuation of engagements
○ Internal inspection

Sarbanes-Oxley requires auditors to report directly to the audit committee or, when there is none, the board of directors. It also requires the auditor to report on a timely basis to the audit committee all critical accounting policies and procedures used; alternative accounting treatments discussed with management, along with their ramifications and the treatment the auditor preferred; and other written communications between the firm and management, such as management letters or schedules of unadjusted differences.

The auditor of a public company, under the law, may also provide to that company nonaudit services, such as tax services, only with the advance approval of the company's audit committee. However, the law specifically prohibits auditors of public companies from also providing these services to those companies:

- Bookkeeping or other accounting services
- Financial information systems design and implementation
- Appraisal or valuation services, fairness opinions, or contribution-in-kind reports
- Actuarial services
- Internal audit outsourcing services
- Management or human resource functions
- Broker or dealer, investment advisor, or investment banking services
- Legal services and expert services unrelated to the audit

Sarbanes-Oxley requires that partners on an audit rotate off after performing audit services for that company for five consecutive years. It also prohibits auditors from taking certain senior financial positions with the companies they audit if they worked on the audit less than a year before the initiation of the current audit.

(ii) Standard-Setting Process.   Standards are approved on a majority vote of PCAOB members. The members are assisted by the chief auditor's staff and, as necessary, ad hoc participation from outsiders.

The PCAOB is assisted by its SAG. Chaired by the chief auditor, the SAG reviews existing Standards, evaluates proposals to amend them, and recommends new ones to the PCAOB. Its contribution is advisory only, but it provides the views of a diverse spectrum of backgrounds and viewpoints.

The PCAOB's standard-setting process involves these six steps:

1. The proposed Standard is discussed by the board at an open meeting. The briefing papers that provide background and recommendations are available on the PCAOB Web site, and the meetings are Webcast and archived on the Web site.
2. The proposed Standard is issued for comment. An ED is made available on the PCAOB Web site for at least 21 days. Hard copies of the ED are generally not produced or mailed out for comment.
3. The draft, revised as appropriate following exposure, is discussed and approved for issuance by the PCAOB at a public meeting. The approved rule is made available on the PCAOB Web site.
4. The final rule is filed with the SEC for its review. The SEC has the final approval power over PCAOB Standards.
5. The SEC publishes a notice of filing for the PCAOB's rule in the *Federal Register,* and comments are received for at least 35 days.
6. The SEC decides whether to approve the PCAOB Standard. The SEC can only accept or reject the rule; it cannot make revisions. If the rule is approved, it is printed in the *Federal Register* and becomes a PCAOB Standard.

PCAOB Standards contain three parts: a release, the standard, and the background and basis for conclusions. The PCAOB Staff has indicated that all three sections, having been approved by the PCAOB, are authoritative, and auditors are required to follow the guidance in any of these sections.

The PCAOB Staff also issues interpretive guidance in the form of Staff Questions and Answers or other Staff releases on specific topics. Although this guidance does not constitute PCAOB rules and is not approved by the PCAOB, the Staff considers it in interpreting the rules when questions arise in inspections or investigations.

(f) REQUIRED INSPECTIONS.   The PCAOB is charged by Congress with conducting:

> a continuing program of inspections to assess the degree of compliance of each registered public accounting firm and associated persons of that firm with [Sarbanes-Oxley], the rules of the [PCAOB], the rules of the [SEC], or professional standards, in connection with its performance of audits, issuance of audit reports, and related matters involving issuers. (Sarbanes-Oxley Section 104(a)).

The Division of Registration and Inspection is responsible for the inspection program.

All firms that audit public companies are required to undergo PCAOB inspection. A registered firm with no public clients is not subject to inspection.

Foreign registered firms may request that the board rely on a non-U.S. inspection. In that case, PCAOB will determine the degree, if any, to which it will rely on the non-U.S. inspection. The PCAOB considers the level of the non-U.S. inspection program's independence, rigor, and inspection work program.

Sarbanes-Oxley calls for annual inspections of firms with more than 100 public clients and inspections at least every three years for firms with 100 or fewer public clients, although it allows the PCAOB to adjust this schedule. In addition, the PCAOB may also conduct special inspections at its own discretion or SEC request. Since inception, the PCAOB has not been able to meet the targeted audit schedule for firms with 100 or fewer public clients, as there are far more firms with only one or a few public clients[5] than were expected.

(i) Inspection Scope.   The PCAOB inspection is similar in concept to the peer reviews of public company auditors that had been administered by the AICPA, but there are some significant differences. The inspection is not done by another public accounting firm but by the PCAOB Staff. Whereas peer reviews were intended primarily as a way to improve the firm's practice, inspections can be more punitive: Negative results may be communicated to the SEC or state boards of accountancy and disclosed to the public. In addition, an identified deficiency might lead to a PCAOB investigation.

Inspections focus on two general aspects of a firm's practice: practice management and individual audits. The focus for smaller firms is different from that for larger ones, taking into account the structural differences resulting from smaller size.

In assessing the firm's practice management, the inspectors review policies and procedures and interview personnel. They focus on seven significant areas:

1. The tone at the top—that is, management's commitment to quality auditing practices—and whether the expectation for quality practices is communicated unambiguously to the partners and staff

2. Whether compensation and promotion within the firm are driven by technical proficiency, not just the ability to generate new business

3. How the firm monitors compliance with applicable independence rules, including those related to nonaudit services both for the firm and those in its alliances and joint ventures

---

[5] In 2006, it was anecdotally reported that there were nearly 1,000 such CPA firms.

4. What factors the firm considers in client acceptance and continuance, including whether the engagements accepted are within the firm's competence and how the audit work addresses identified risks

5. The effectiveness of the firm's internal inspection process, including consideration of actions the firm takes to address identified problems

6. The effectiveness of the firm's audit policies and procedures, including how policies are identified, developed, and communicated

7. How the firm coordinates the use of foreign affiliates for audits of foreign subsidiaries of U.S. clients, including how the firm satisfies itself about the foreign affiliates' knowledge of U.S. technical requirements

The inspection involves detailed review of the work papers and interviews with those who did the work, including staff at all levels and nonaudit personnel, such as tax or information technology specialists. PCAOB inspectors also selectively interview members of the engagement clients' audit committees to gain their perspectives on the audit and auditor communications.

The tone-at-the-top and compensation review aspects of inspections are beyond what practitioners experienced in the past peer review program of the AICPA. This important expansion in the inspection program addresses issues faced by some CPA firms when business considerations impinge on professionalism. While these topics are difficult to inspect, the fact that they are part of the inspection program provides a strong deterrent to adopting policies and practices that may negatively impact the profession as a whole.

(ii) Inspection Results. At the conclusion of the inspection, the PCAOB prepares a draft report, which is made available to the firm. A firm that disagrees with the findings can file a response within 30 days. The PCAOB then reviews the draft report and the firm's response, if any, and after due consideration, issues a final report. A firm that continues to disagree with the findings can appeal to the SEC to review the PCAOB report.

The final inspection report is sent to the SEC. The report is made available to the public except that criticisms or defects identified in the firm's quality control system are not made public unless they are not corrected to the PCAOB's satisfaction within a year of the inspection report. The public disclosure excludes certain confidential or proprietary information and information privileged under the rules of evidence.

The PCAOB may refer information emanating from the review, along with the firm's response to the report, to relevant state licensing authorities.

(g) INVESTIGATIONS. The PCAOB's Office of Investigations and Enforcement can investigate possible violations of accounting and auditing standards by registered firms. Allegations of potential violations might come from PCAOB inspections, information forwarded to the PCAOB (its Web site has a facility for such reporting), or public information that comes to the PCAOB's attention.

Informal inquiries and formal investigations, along with related documents provided to PCAOB, are confidential until presented in connection with a public proceeding. Thus, until made public, they are protected from discovery by plaintiffs' counsel. The PCAOB may, however, make such documents available to the SEC, U.S. or state attorneys general, or other applicable federal or state regulatory authorities.

In conducting an investigation, the PCAOB can call for testimony, audit work papers, or other documents from a firm or other person involved in the audit. Registered firms are required to cooperate with the investigation; failure to do so can be the basis for disciplinary action.

The PCAOB has the authority to sanction any registered firm or associated individual who it determines violated Sarbanes-Oxley, PCAOB rules, securities laws relating to the preparation and issuance of audit reports, or professional standards. Sanctions may include:

- Suspension or revocation of registration
- Temporary or permanent suspension or bar of a person from further association with any registered public accounting firm.

- Temporary or permanent limitation on the activities, functions, or operations of the firm or person (e.g., prohibiting a firm from accepting new audit clients for a period of time; requiring a firm to assign a reviewer or supervisor to an associated person, to terminate one or more audit engagements, and to make functional changes in the firm or the engagement team)
- A civil money penalty for each such violation to a maximum of $100,000 for an individual and $2 million for a firm or, if the violation is intentional, reckless, or knowing or involves repeated instances of negligence, $750,000 for an individual and $15 million for a firm
- Censure
- Additional professional education or training
- Requiring the firm to engage an independent monitor, subject to PCAOB approval, to observe and report on the firm's future compliance with relevant laws or standards
- Requiring the firm to engage counsel or another consultant to design policies to comply with relevant laws or standards
- Requiring the firm or associated person to adopt or implement policies, or to undertake other actions, to improve audit quality or to comply with relevant laws or standards
- Requiring a firm to obtain an independent review and report on one or more engagements

Any sanctions imposed can be appealed to the SEC.

In an early poster-boy case, a small firm was suspended from public practice as a result of the PCAOB program. That decision was subsequently upheld when challenged.

For investigations of foreign firms, the PCAOB may rely on the investigation or sanction of the firm by a non-U.S. authority.

The PCAOB reports the name of the individual or firm sanctioned, a description of the sanction and the basis for its imposition, and other information it deems appropriate to the SEC, the appropriate state or foreign licensing authority, and the public.

Since inception, the PCAOB has withstood a challenge to the constitutionality of the Sarbanes-Oxley Act of 2002 and thus its authority. The Dodd-Frank Financial Reform Act of 2010 suspended the Sarbanes-Oxley requirement that auditors of nonaccelerated filers file a separate report on internal controls along with the required 10-K reports. (Note that this provision had never been implemented and had been the source of SEC deferrals since inception.) The 2010 Act retained the requirement that managements of all public companies report on the effectiveness of their internal controls annually. For additional information on these current requirements, see Chapter 7 in this *Handbook*.

(h) WHITE-COLLAR CRIME PENALTY ENHANCEMENTS.   The Sarbanes-Oxley Act amends the U.S. Code by increasing both the criminal penalties for mail and wire fraud from 5 years to 20 years. In addition, the Act imposes criminal penalties on chief executive officers (CEOs) and chief financial officers when they certify financial reports that do not comport with the requirements of the Sarbanes-Oxley Act. The penalties are a fine up to $1 million and imprisonment for up to 10 years for improper certifications and a fine up to $5 million and imprisonment up to 20 years for *willfully* improper certifications. For example, making misrepresentations or lying to an auditor can be a serious offense and has led to the imprisonment of a CEO.

1.10 AMERICAN INSTITUTE OF CERTIFIED PUBLIC ACCOUNTANTS

The largest and still most influential of the professional accounting trade organizations is the AICPA. The AICPA has approximately 330,000 members, a size that permits a large professional staff to provide member services and assist volunteers that serve on professional committees. Each member must be licensed as a CPA by some jurisdiction but need not practice as a public accountant. Less than half of the AICPA's membership is in public practice; the majority of members are in industry, government, or education. Membership in the AICPA is voluntary.

In response to assertions from congressional staff, the AICPA undertook a major restructuring in 1977 to establish a more rigorous self-regulatory system. Even though concern over alleged shortcomings was not backed up by enacted legislation, the AICPA created the Division for CPA Firms, whereas previously it had only individual memberships. Members of this division commit themselves to standards of quality and quality control, including triennial peer reviews of their quality control systems. Subsequent to the Sarbanes-Oxley Act, the AICPA created a structure of "centers" to improve member service. The former SEC Practice Section became the Center for Public Company Accounting Firms. These centers continue to evolve in terms of member composition and organization.

As a result of a major change in policy approved by AICPA membership in 1988, all members in public practice will be subject to quality control reviews, even if they do not belong to the Division for CPA Firms. However, these reviews will not be as extensive as full peer reviews, and the AICPA will not release the results to the public.

Despite efforts to raise the perceived quality of AICPA self-monitoring and peer review, the failures of Enron, WorldCom, and other entities in the late 1990s and early 2000s led to a serious erosion of AICPA authority and influence over setting standards and self-monitoring through peer reviews. The Sarbanes-Oxley Act has replaced the AICPA's system of self-regulation and peer reviews for public companies with Standards and inspections by the PCAOB. The PCAOB inspection process is an examination by independent professionals in the employ of the PCAOB, not an examination by "peers." The peer system was criticized when obvious firm deficiencies were revealed after a firm had "passed" a peer review.

The AICPA continues with its programs to nonissuers (private, not-for-profit, and government groups) of setting auditing standards through the ASB, an expanded 19-member panel with representation from the major CPA firms, and specific representation from user groups, government, and academia.

(a) TECHNICAL AUDITING STANDARDS. The auditing standards of the AICPA are set today by the ASB. Estimates are that over 300,000 nonpublic company audit reports are issued annually. In contrast, there are fewer than 15,000 public companies, but the capitalization of the largest 20 percent of these public companies dwarfs the value of the smaller public and private entities that are audited.

The ASB uses a thorough due process, including the issuance of EDs of proposed Standards and its ASB meetings are open to the public. Beginning in the late 1990s, the ASB actively participated in the standard-setting activities of the International Auditing and Attest Standards Board (IAASB), and has initiated the process of converging U.S. and international auditing standards.

(i) Risk Assessment Standards. In 2005–2006, the ASB issued a series of new pervasive Standards designed to enhance the risk assessment process and to clarify numerous auditor responsibilities. The Risk Assessment Standards[6] were mostly a refinement of existing literature, but by defining and distinguishing more carefully between suggestions and requirements in the Standards, they sought more uniform application of the Standards in practice.[7]

A simple example of the seeking of uniform implementation is the restated need for the auditor to assess the adequacy of the design of internal controls over financial reporting in all audits as a basis for the required risk assessment. Under prior Standards, it had become a practice to assess

---

[6] Technically, the Risk Assessment Standards were defined by the AICPA as SASs Nos. 104 through 111. However, SAS Nos. 102 and 103 contained important definitions of the words *must* and *should* in the new Standards and important documentation guidance regarding these Standards. In addition, SAS No. 112, later reissued as SAS No. 115, *Communicating Internal Control Related Matters Identified in an Audit,* provided important guidance regarding auditor communication of internal control deficiencies to management and governance. In a practical sense, SAS Nos. 102 through 112 were part of the same project and are often viewed in practice as part of the Risk Assessment suite of Standards.

[7] See J. Fogarty, L. Graham, and D. Schubert, "Assessing and Responding to Risks in a Financial Statement Audit" (and Part 2), *Journal of Accountancy* (July 2006, January 2007).

internal controls only when the audit strategy called for placing reliance on them. A pivotal point in the change introduced by SAS No. 109, *Understanding the Entity and Its Environment and Assessing the Risks of Material Misstatement,* in this respect was what the definition of *should* means in the Standards: Is it a wise suggestion or a requirement? That issue was resolved in SAS No. 102, *Defining Professional Requirements in Statements on Auditing Standards,* which established the term *should* as a presumptive requirement.

Another important point was the clarification in SAS No. 112, *Communicating Internal Control Related Matters Identified in an Audit,* that required communications regarding weakness and significant deficiencies in internal control should be communicated annually and in writing to management and those in the governance function. This change was mandated to reduce the risk of misunderstanding and any confusion between voluntary "management comments" with ancillary efficiency suggestions, and important, required auditor communications. SAS No. 112 also reminded auditors that it was the company's responsibility to design, document, and maintain the system of internal control, not the auditor's responsibility

Some of the other noteworthy conclusions and matters of emphasis in the risk assessment suite include:

- A reminder that the term *reasonable assurance* indicates a "high" level of assurance in the context of the Standards (e.g., 90% or greater assurance)
- A reminder that materiality, a cornerstone of audit planning, is based on user needs and should be related to a logical base (e.g., revenues, expenses, net income, etc.) respective to the user(s) of the financial statements
- A reminder that macro- and microeconomic and industry and business risks be considered (including internal control) as part of the audit and that such assessments can be considered when determining the nature and extent of other procedures to be performed
- An explicit statement that controls tests can be carried forward for two additional periods when there are no changes in the control
- A clarification that inquiry alone is not sufficient as evidence
- A reminder that sample results need to be projected to the population from which they were drawn and aggregated for purposes of determining whether adjustments to the financial statements are required to fairly present the financial statements and as a benchmark to assess the sufficiency of audit procedures and results in achieving a low-risk opinion that the financial statements are not materially misstated

The genesis of the Risk Assessment Standards was a joint project undertaken with the IAASB to bring the core auditing Standards of the two bodies into greater alignment. Included in that suite of joint Standards was SAS No. 99, *Consideration of Fraud in a Financial Statement Audit.* In the United States, the existing SAS No. 82 (also *Consideration of Fraud in a Financial Statement Audit*) and the proposed revisions to that document were further enhanced based on the early findings from Enron and other period frauds and audit failures and released as a separate SAS (SAS No. 99) in advance of the other Standards. The Sarbanes-Oxley Act caused the AICPA to delay the finalization of the Risk Assessment Standards in the United States pending possible PCAOB collaboration with that effort. However the PCAOB decided not to collaborate with the AICPA but to create a separate body of audit literature. A risk standards suite for audits of public companies was released in 2010 by the PCAOB.

The Sarbanes-Oxley Act charges the PCAOB with establishing or adopting auditing standards applicable to audits of SEC registrants. The Act clearly permits the PCAOB to adopt or modify auditing standards issued by the ASB. In the period subsequent to the PCAOB's formation in 2002-2003, it was not clear whether it would work with or independently of the ASB going forward. Pending resolution of that issue, the proposed suite of AICPA risk assessment standards from 2002 was placed on hold.

After formation, the chief auditor of the PCAOB, Dr. Douglas Carmichael, made it clear that the PCAOB intended to rewrite all the existing auditing standards for public companies. As a starting point for the auditing literature going forward, the PCAOB adopted the AICPA authoritative literature as it stood in April 2003 and then began to write its own Standards, modifying that literature going forward.

Since the PCAOB has so far not adopted any of the ASB Standards subsequent to SAS No. 101, the auditing Standards literature is diverging at a rapid rate. Representatives of the ASB, PCAOB and Government Accountability Office (GAO) meet periodically to discuss issues of mutual interest. In addition, the PCAOB regularly monitors the activities of the IAASB. Many auditors of private and public companies are concerned today about the complexity and confusion of working in an environment where there are two main bodies of auditing literature.

In 2011, the PCAOB implemented its own suite of the risk assessment standards

CPAs with practices spanning public and nonpublic clients need to adapt their audit practices to cope with multiple literatures and requirements that are similar but not the same. Inspections carried out by the PCAOB only relate to public clients and the PCAOB Standards literature.

(ii) Clarity and Convergence.   The joint projects between the IAASB and the ASB continued during the transitional implementation period for public company auditing. Beginning in 2004, the ASB initiated the Clarity Project, based on a proposal to the membership and a comment letter process. In 2007, it issued a Discussion Paper for public comment.[8] One purpose for this project was to provide a consistent format for all Auditing Standards going forward, clarifying the requirements in a standard from the suggestions and context guidance material that SASs often contain. Another purpose was to align U.S. GAAS with the format adopted by the IAASB for its Standards.

In order to continue to participate in deliberations with the IAASB, convergence of U.S. GAAS with the International Standards of Auditing (ISAs) was expected by the International Federation of Accountants (IFAC). There are and there may remain some differences between the Standards of the two bodies, such as U.S. requirements for performing group audits, but the Clarity Project has further narrowed any perceived differences in the two bodies of literature.

While no material differences were intended to be introduced with the recently issued Risk Assessment suite of Standards, some aspects of the literature have been modified. For example, some elements such as the illustration of the SAS No. 39 (*Audit Sampling*) and SAS No. 47 (*Audit Risk and Materiality in Conducting an Audit*) audit risk model, as modified by SAS No. 111, (*Audit Sampling*) were removed from the clarified Standard and will be resident only in related audit guides.

The format of the newly clarified Standards will be:

- Introduction and objective of the Standard
- Definitions
- Requirements
- Application material ("A" paragraphs)
- Special considerations—government and smaller entities
- Differences from IAASB Standards

Once implemented, the 10 "general standards," long a cornerstone of U.S. auditing practice, will disappear. The individual SASs will describe the specific objectives of the respective Standards. Users of the newly formatted Standards should not confuse "A" paragraphs with appendix or material of lesser importance. Users are required to read both the requirements and "A" paragraphs when comprehending and following GAAS. Of further note, the Standards will identify differences not from past U.S. Standards but from the ISAs of the IAASB.[9]

---

[8] AICPA, "Improving the Clarity of ASB Standards: Discussion Paper," March 20, 2007.
[9] See AICPA, "The AICPA's Guide to Clarified and Converged Standards for Auditing and Quality Control" AICPA, 2011.

(iii) Technical Assistance.   In addition to these activities, the AICPA Staff also provides technical assistance to members who have encountered questions in conducting their accounting, auditing, and tax practices. Specifically, members can call or write the AICPA Staff with their questions and receive guidance on how to resolve them. In many cases, all that is needed is to steer the member to the right portion of the authoritative literature. In other cases, the members are seeking concurrence with a position they have reached on their own. Both services are especially valuable to sole practitioners because they do not have the resources to provide a double check on their research and conclusions.

(b) SERVICES OFFERED BY CERTIFIED PUBLIC ACCOUNTANTS.   The term *independent accountant* is used interchangeably with "independent auditor" and "independent public accountant." Generally, the term is limited to either CPAs or public accountants licensed to perform audits and express opinions on financial statements under applicable state accountancy laws.

Only licensed CPAs who are independent of the client can issue audit opinions on public companies (SEC registrants). That is the one unique privilege held by CPAs. In other areas such as tax, consulting, and valuation, the service space is shared with other professionals.

Because they are knowledgeable about accounting principles and accounting systems, tax matters, and the like, independent accountants provide a wide range of services in addition to audits. These include accounting and review services, tax services, consulting services, personal financial planning, and others. Recently the range of their services has become contentious because of potential conflicts of interests with auditing and other professional services.

(i) Auditing.   An audit involves the application of a variety of procedures and techniques to obtain evidential matter sufficient for the independent accountant to express an informed opinion about whether the financial statements conform to GAAP. When serving as an auditor, the independent accountant is guided by the AICPA's Code of Professional Conduct and a variety of Standards promulgated by professional bodies established for that purpose.

Rule of Conduct 202 of the AICPA's Code of Professional Conduct provides: "A member who performs auditing, review, compilation, management consulting, tax or other professional services shall comply with standards promulgated by bodies designated by [the AICPA]."

SASs are pronouncements issued by the ASB of the AICPA to guide auditing practice. As Rule 202 indicates, SASs are enforceable under the Code; but perhaps of equal importance, courts generally view adherence to SASs as the standard for assessing an auditor's liability.

For audits of nonpublic companies, the SASs specify required auditing procedures, provide guidance on important areas of judgment often encountered in audits, and establish the form and content of the auditor's report. They are issued individually in a numbered series and are codified periodically. Today, electronic versions of the Standards often provide the most convenient form for use in practice. The Standards are published annually in hard copy.

The Auditor's Standard Report on Comparative Financial Statements Independent Auditor's Report

We have audited the accompanying balance sheets of ABC Company as of December 31, 2012, and 2011, and the related statements of income, retained earnings, and cash flows for the years then ended. These financial statements are the responsibility of the Company's management. Our responsibility is to express an opinion on these financial statements based on our audits.

We conducted our audits in accordance with auditing standards generally accepted in the United States of America. Those standards require that we plan and perform the audit to obtain reasonable assurance about whether the financial statements are free of material misstatement. An audit includes examining, on a test basis, evidence supporting the amounts and disclosures in the financial statements. An audit also includes assessing the accounting principles used and significant estimates made by management, as well as evaluating the overall financial statement presentation. We believe that our audits provide a reasonable basis for our opinion.

In our opinion, the financial statements referred to above, present fairly, in all material respects, the financial position of ABC Company as of [at] December 31, 2012, and 2011, and the results of its operations and its cash flows for the years then ended in conformity with accounting principles generally accepted in the United States of America.

[Signed]

[Date]

A number of points in the auditor's report deserve special attention.

- First and perhaps foremost is the requirement that auditors be independent of the client on which an opinion is rendered. The AICPA has extensive literature defining personal and familial relationships that can impair independence. The SEC has also developed an extensive literature that applies to public companies. An auditor's need to be independent limits his or her involvement in accounting for transactions, preparing financial statements, and performing certain services such as the design and implementation of accounting information systems. Regulatory agencies, such as the Department of Labor, may impose additional constraints on the auditor beyond the AICPA literature when auditing entities under their jurisdiction.

- The term *reasonable assurance* has been clarified to mean a high level of assurance in both the AICPA and PCAOB literature. The term *reasonable* is used in the context of delivering a professional service.

- Misstatements can occur because of inadvertent error or fraud. SASs Nos. 82 and 99 clarified that the auditor plans the audit to detect material misstatement whether due to error or fraud.

- The profession continues to struggle to convince the public that the financial statements are the responsibility of management, despite an explicit statement of that today in the auditor's opinion. Previously, the heavy involvement of the auditor in creating the financial statements when companies were incapable of doing so lent some legitimacy to this general misunderstanding. Today such a situation would be noted as a material weakness in internal controls. Auditors are cautious not to cross the line regarding auditing their own work.

- "Presenting fairly, in all material respects" does not mean the financial statements are accurate to the penny. Such precision would rarely be achievable. The concept of materiality is used to set the scope of the audit procedures to detect material misstatement whether they are individual or aggregate misstatements.

- The opinion also extends to the footnote disclosures in the financial statements.

Modifications to and Departures from the Standard Report. The auditor's Standard Report is called a "clean opinion" since it does not raise any specific issues regarding the fairness of the presented financial statements. Users have to be alert if the auditor includes an "emphasis" paragraph into the opinion that directs readers to some matter, often already disclosed in the financial statements, such as a contingent liability arising from related party transactions, litigation, or regulation that may be important to the user. This matter of emphasis does not change the meaning of the opinion to users.

When management is faced with liquidity or regulatory challenges such that the entity's continuance as a going concern is threatened, the auditor may insert a specific paragraph into the report noting this. In general, if management has a plausible plan for addressing the issue, such a warning might not be issued. While neither management nor the auditor can use a crystal ball to predict future events, the timeline in the Standards for making judgments regarding the need for such disclosures is within one year. In such situations, users should be particularly alert to the reasons that might be disclosed in the auditor's report as well as relationships and disclosures in the financial statement that are relevant to the issue of going concern. Forced liquidations in bankruptcy can depress the marketability and market prices of assets, resulting in more exposure to shareholders than that indicated by the financial statement amounts, many of which may be stated on a basis that the entity is a going concern. Management resistance to such disclosures on the basis that they might create a self-fulfilling prophecy unfortunately results in fewer of these disclosures than might serve users better. This is all the more reason for users to pay special attention to these disclosures when they do occur.

Occasionally, an auditor judges an item in the financials as not accounted for according to GAAP, so he or she may issue an "except for" opinion ("In our opinion except for the [e.g., insert departure from GAAP]...".). Nevertheless, the issue may not distort the overall fairness of the financial statements, and thus the auditor can still provide assurance on the overall financial statements. Since such situations often create an environment where the auditor and management reach a common conclusion that avoids the disclosure, users need to be especially mindful of these types of disclosures. Careful reading of the footnotes may also reveal areas where management and the auditor might not agree. Litigation experience has shown that the unintelligible footnote is often an indicator of an important issue.

While less common, adverse or disclaimer opinions can be issued. When an entity is required to be audited by creditor or contractual provisions, the auditor may have to say something, even if a clean opinion cannot be obtained. In an *adverse* opinion, the auditor states that the accompanying statements "do not present fairly..." and goes on to identify the reasons. Thus, sufficient evidence is obtained to make such a statement. Occasionally, a *disclaimer* opinion is necessary when the auditor cannot obtain sufficient information on which to base an opinion. Significant uncertainties caused by weather (e.g., earthquakes or floods) or political unrest or war may preclude gathering sufficient evidence on which to base an opinion on the overall financial statements.

(ii) Accounting Services.   Accounting services include all forms of involvement with financial statements or financial information other than an audit, such as bookkeeping, compilation of financial statements from a trial balance, and review of financial statements. The accountant's responsibilities for the unaudited financial statements of a nonpublic company are set forth in the Statements on Standards for Accounting and Review Services (SSARS) services, a numbered series of pronouncements issued by the Accounting and Review Services Committee of the AICPA.

The accountant should not submit unaudited financial statements of a nonpublic entity to the client or others unless, as a minimum, he or she complies with the provisions of the Statement applicable to a compilation engagement. Thus, the only types of report an accountant may issue in connection with the unaudited financial statements of a nonpublic company are for the accounting services of a compilation or review.

In general, the public needs to be informed of the differences between these services and an audit and the specific assurance the report is providing.

(iii) Tax Services.   The accountant may be called on to deal with a variety of tax problems, including those involving federal and state income taxes, estate and inheritance taxes, sales and use taxes, payroll taxes, and property taxes. The field of *income taxes* is especially important. The services rendered by the accountant in this area include determination of taxable income, preparation of tax returns and claims for refunds, representation of clients before taxing authorities, and cooperation with lawyers in the settlement of tax suits by litigation. The AICPA publishes Statements on Standards for Tax Services (SSTSs) that are enforceable tax practice standards for members of the AICPA. These Standards apply to all members regardless of the jurisdictions in which they practice and the types of taxes with respect to which they are providing services.

(iv) Consulting and Other Services.   The AICPA's Management Consulting Services Executive Committee issues pronouncements related to the conduct of a variety of consulting services. Statement on Standards for Consulting Services, *Consulting Services: Definitions and Standards,* describes the consulting process as "activities relating to the determination of client objectives, fact-finding, definition of the problems or opportunities, evaluation of alternatives, formulation of proposed action, communication of results, implementation, and follow-up." The process includes:

- Counseling management in its analysis, planning, organizing, operating, and controlling functions
- Conducting special studies, preparing recommendations, proposing plans and programs, and providing advice and technical assistance in their implementation

- Reviewing and suggesting improvement of policies, procedures, systems, methods, and organizational relationships
- Introducing new ideas, concepts, and methods to management

The independent public accountant may be called on to make special investigations or to report in connection with the special requirements of a government agency. Those services may require aspects of tax, consulting, and accounting and auditing skills. Newer services that are supported by the AICPA via credentials and guidance include elder care services and personal financial planning.

Special services often involve those other than an audit of one or more financial statements. These services also include application of agreed-on procedures to specified elements, accounts, or items of a financial statement or to nonfinancial information or preparing a valuation report.

Valuation services performed by CPAs are guided by Statements of Standards of Valuation Services (SSVSs) authored by the AICPA Consulting Services Executive Committee. SSVS No. 1, *Valuation of a Business, Business Ownership Interest, Security, or Intangible Asset* (2007), and provides guidance in performing procedures and reporting on valuation services.

Objectivity is required in all professional services; the valuation analyst must comply with AICPA Code of Professional Conduct Rule 102, *Integrity and Objectivity,* and be impartial, intellectually honest, disinterested, and free from conflicts of interest.

(c) CPA EXAMINATIONS. The AICPA produces, administers, and grades the Uniform CPA Examination under contract to individual state boards of accountancy. This service includes writing the exam to specifications established through the National Association of State Boards of Accountancy (NASBA), maintaining security over the questions, delivering the exams to the sites, and reading and grading the exam. The AICPA then sends the results to the state board, which, in turn, notifies the candidates.

Today the CPA Examination is administered as a 14-hour computerized exam. It is offered periodically throughout the year, rather than only in May and November as was the case previously. The exam covers auditing and attestation, financial accounting and reporting, regulation, and business environment and concepts.

The AICPA does not license CPAs to practice; states do. States also determine the number of CPAs that will be licensed in that state and determine the number and composition of hours of education required before candidates can be licensed in their state. Some years ago, a move was started to require 150 hours of college education before a candidate could become a CPA. This extra year of college was a hardship for many, and a number of states do not have the 150-hour requirement. States also determine the required hours and composition of hours of continuing professional education (CPE) that qualify a CPA to maintain a current license. For example, states may set a specific minimum number of hours of tax, ethics, or accounting and auditing within the licensing period. States may also terminate a CPA's license to practice in that state. The AICPA may censure or expel a member from the association but cannot remove a CPA's license.

A majority of states have adopted official cross-state recognition of licensing to facilitate commerce in their states. Certain "retirement" states have long been reluctant to recognize out-of-state licenses to avoid a glut of part-time practitioners within the state depressing the local demand for professional services. Overall, the states' licensing system has worked well but is cumbersome when a CPA practice spans various states.

1.11 STATE BOARDS AND OTHER ORGANIZATIONS

(a) ROLE OF THE STATE BOARDS OF ACCOUNTANCY.   The other main category of governmental agencies affecting the practice of financial accounting comprises the 54 state boards of accountancy in the United States. (One board exists in each of the 50 states, the District of Columbia, Puerto Rico, the Virgin Islands, and Guam.) They have three primary regulatory missions: granting the initial license to practice public accounting, ensuring the maintenance of competency through continuing education, and disciplining licensees who fail to maintain their competency or who act in an unethical manner. States can also designate an authority to be followed for auditing (e.g., AICPA, PCAOB) or promulgate their own requirements. For example, New York and California adopted audit documentation regulations in advance of the new requirements in SAS No. 103, *Audit Documentation.*

Because of the variety of forms (and names) for the boards, it is difficult to draw generalities. Some boards are separate freestanding agencies, whereas others are part of larger state regulatory bodies that license other professions and service providers. Funding for boards comes from general budget appropriations, dedicated credits from licensing fees, or some combination. Some boards are permanent, and others are subject to periodic sunset reviews designed to avoid overregulation.

An accountancy board's first responsibility is to award the license to practice, which may do no more than allow the licensees to identify themselves as CPAs. In many states, the license is a legal requirement for performing the attest function (audit or review) for financial statements. The Internal Revenue Service accepts the CPA's license as sufficient qualification to practice before it by representing clients in the audit and appeals procedures. The SEC requires a CPA to sign the audit opinion on public company financial statements.

All states require candidates to successfully complete the Uniform CPA Examination prepared, administered, and graded by the AICPA. In a few states, it is possible to pass the CPA exam and be certified without being licensed. The license is granted in some states only after the candidate has completed an experience requirement. Other states do not differentiate between certification and licensing. Most states have an experience requirement (e.g., two years or one year with a master's degree), but some do not. Over 40 states have passed laws that do or will require the completion of an additional year's course work beyond the bachelor's degree before certification (the 150-hour requirement). The additional credits do not have to result in an additional degree, but most programs are set up to issue some sort of degree.

Most state boards require their licensees to participate in formal CPE. Typically, CPAs need 40 hours of class time (or its equivalent) per year to continue practicing. Some boards regulate CPE by specifying minimum hours in certain topics or by recognizing only courses offered by authorized providers, whereas others require only a report of hours completed.

Most states now require peer reviews on a periodic basis for firms and practitioners performing assurance services. These requirements differ by state, and the Web site of the licensing authority of each state is the best source of information regarding the program. California, despite its size and proportion of economic activity, recently has enacted a mandatory peer review program.

A majority of state boards promulgate ethical standards of conduct through regulations interpreting the authorizing statutes; others have incorporated the AICPA ethics rules directly into their statutes. By and large, the ethics codes of state boards are the same as the AICPA's Code of Conduct, although local political factors often create differences. Because most states do not grant their boards sufficient funds to support a full-time staff for investigating allegations of unethical behavior, they must compete with other agencies for investigators' time and effort. In extreme cases, a finding of a violation will lead to revoking the individual's CPA license; however, boards do not mete out this punishment very often. Rather, they impose some rehabilitative discipline, such as a temporary suspension or the completion of additional CPE. In virtually all states, individuals automatically lose their licenses if they are convicted of a felony.

State boards typically are composed of unpaid volunteer practitioners who serve for three to five years. Often at least one of the board members is not an accountant but represents the general public. This arrangement lends more credibility to the board, which may suffer from a fox-in-the-henhouse image caused by having only accountants regulate accountants. A difficulty in using volunteers is that the boards tend to get only part-time effort. Larger states achieve more continuity and sustained effort by having a full-time executive director and staff.

Substantial ethics enforcement activity occurs at the state level and is controlled through a cooperative agreement with the AICPA, referred to as JEEP (Joint Ethics Enforcement Program). Recent years have seen state organizations playing a more active part in representing the profession's interests in state legislatures. Through the JEEP, the Ethics Division of the AICPA Staff works with state societies and members of AICPA ethics subcommittees to conduct investigations of alleged violations or to concur with findings conducted at the state level. These investigations attempt to establish only prima facie evidence that a section of the Code of Conduct was violated without trying to determine whether the member intended to violate it. JEEP leverages the expertise of the AICPA Staff to improve the overall quality and efficiency of the work that would otherwise have to be separately performed at the state level. This quality control helps ensure that the investigations protect the rights of the respondents while appropriate evidence is gathered. Information about possible violations comes from other CPAs, clients, enforcement agencies, and public information, such as the *Wall Street Journal,* the *Public Accounting Report,* and SEC Accounting and Auditing Enforcement Releases. Despite the large investment in ethics enforcement, the most extreme disciplinary action that the AICPA can take is to revoke membership, in which case the CPA is no longer subject to the AICPA's authority. However, the public embarrassment and negative press may be substantial. States can and do revoke licenses to practice.

Although the dispersion of certification authority across all states creates inefficiencies and inconsistencies, this arrangement is compatible with the policy of protecting states' rights against federal domination. Some professionals believe that this arrangement has outlived its usefulness, particularly for disciplining unethical accountants. Until such time as a federal agency is given a national licensing authority, however, financial accountants wanting to practice as auditors will need to be certified by one or more state boards.

(b) ROLE OF PROFESSIONAL SOCIETIES.   Although similar to the AICPA, state societies of CPAs are separately funded and operated entities. They are also a curious blend of regulatory authority and service providers. Individuals who want to influence the profession in their state consider membership to be essential. All states also have their own professional organizations, which are called societies, associations, or institutes, according to local preference. In many cases, they duplicate and complement the activities of the AICPA by offering CPE, publishing newsletters and journals, and providing opportunities for service and leadership through committee membership.

In order to gain by shared effort and to provide services efficiently, state boards have formed their own trade organization, the NASBA. This group (which includes all 54 U.S. licensing authorities) provides a forum for developing unified positions on issues that can be used in individual states more effectively. For example, the NASBA directors agreed in 1989 to change the specifications for the Uniform CPA Examination. They also have developed a model code of ethics and a model accountancy law to apply in each state. These documents could be (and were) used to persuade state lawmakers to bring their statutes and regulations up to a national norm. NASBA also assists state boards faced by legislative threats of closure under sunset reviews. NASBA has taken on a broader role in certifying CPE, which is important when CPAs take education courses in different jurisdictions or where states have not developed their own detailed standards for CPE.

Other national societies exist, including several that are fairly large. Two of these are the IMA and the FEI, both of which generally consist of individuals who are not in public practice. Indeed, they can be characterized as organizations representing the interests of statement preparers. The IMA was originally called the National Association of Cost Accountants and still draws most of its membership from management accountants. Nonetheless, it has played a leadership role in financial accounting standard setting through its position as one of the sponsoring organizations of the FASB. The primary units of the IMA are its local chapters, which operate autonomously in order to best meet the interests of their own members. The association also has developed a set of Standards of Ethical Conduct for Management Accountants, which requires the accountant to tell the truth to all who receive financial reports, including management and external users. The IMA administers the CMA (Certified Management Accountant) examination and awards the CMA certificate to persons meeting all the requirements. (See *www.imanet.org*.)

The FEI is smaller than the IMA because it draws its membership from those accountants who have substantial responsibilities in the financial area of their companies (e.g., chief financial officers, controllers), including reporting. In addition, the FEI limits the number of members from any given company. However, because FEI members occupy higher-level positions in large entities, the FEI often has more influence, particularly in dealing with the FASB as another of the sponsoring organizations.

Another national organization is the AAA, which was originally created as a professional society for accounting educators. Through the middle of the twentieth century, the membership was more eclectic and included not only instructors but many practitioners. However, during the 1970s and 1980s, the AAA lost a large number of its members who were practicing accountants and became more and more oriented toward academic issues and services. Apart from the influence of individual members and the AAA's participation as a "sponsoring organization" of the FASB (and COSO), it does not affect financial accounting practice to any great degree. Some issues that relate to market reactions to accounting treatments may be of interest to standard setters when forming opinions on accounting treatments. Additionally, the AAA through its committee structure may issue comment letters on pending matters in accounting and auditing.

As the major organization of accounting educators, the AAA hopes to influence the long-term theoretical development of financial and other kinds of accounting. To this end, its greatest emphasis has been on promoting and disseminating research in accounting and finance. The AAA publishes three main journals, *The Accounting Review, Accounting Horizons,* and *Issues in Accounting Education. The Accounting Review* tends to include the most rigorous research articles published by the AAA. *Accounting Horizons* tends to publish more applied research articles. There are various sections with specialized focus in research and education, such as the Auditing Section, Information Systems Section and the Taxation Section. The AAA is a sponsoring organization of the FASB, and one FASB member seat has always been occupied by an academic accountant. Additionally, the ASB generally has at least one academic member. The SEC has a fellowship program where one or two academic fellows may serve for a year to assist the SEC and help academics who may not be steeped in recent public practice experience to understand the workings of the SEC and its mission. However, the AAA does not have substantial influence on accounting standards.

1.12 GOVERNMENT ACCOUNTABILITY OFFICE

Two chapters in this work are devoted to accounting in the state and local environment (Chapter 33, Pon, et.al.) and in the federal government environments (see Chapter 32 in this *Handbook*). These chapters provide additional insight into the GAO and other audit agencies that are relevant to audits of these entities. This chapter provides a general description of the role of the GAO.

After World War I, the Budget and Accounting Act of 1921 transferred auditing responsibilities and accounting functions from the Treasury Department to a new agency, the General Accounting Office. Independent of the executive branch, the GAO was given broad responsibilities to investigate the efficiency and effectiveness of federal spending. The agency is considered a part of the legislative branch and is an audit and investigative arm of the U.S. Congress. It has been characterized as a congressional watchdog because of its mission to evaluate the effectiveness of financial reporting in the public sector as well as evaluate and measure performance audits that evaluate the effectiveness of various government programs. On July 7, 2004, the agency took the new name of the Government Accountability Office as a result of the GAO Human Capital Reform Act of 2004, Public Law 108–271, 118 Stat. 811 (2004). David Walker, then comptroller general, noted that the name change better reflected the role of the agency.

The agency is headed by the comptroller general of the United States, a nonpartisan and professional position, who is appointed by the president for a single 15-year term. This helps insulate the agency from temporal political pressures. The GAO states in its mission statement on its Web site: "We provide Congress with timely information that is objective, fact-based, nonpartisan, non-ideological, fair, and balanced." As of December 22, 2010, the comptroller general is Gene L. Dodaro, an internal appointment from within the GAO. The GAO's updated Strategic Plan (e.g., 2010–2015) for serving the Congress is made publicly available by the Web site posting (e.g., *www.gao.gov/new.items/d10559sp.pdf*).

Annually, the GAO issues an audit report on the U.S. government. The 2010 Financial Report of the United States Government, like prior reports, resulted in a disclaimer of opinion because of various limitations, including significant uncertainties and a lack of a cost basis for many assets included in the asset base.

The GAO operates in what might be classified as three major areas:

1. Financial statement audits
2. Compliance audits
3. Operational audits

(a) FINANCIAL STATEMENT AUDITS.   The GAO establishes Standards for audits of government organizations, programs and activities, and federal assistance received by various organizations. Generally accepted government auditing standards (GAGAS) are to be followed by auditors when auditing relevant entities. Generally, these Standards track with the SASs issued by the AICPA for nonpublic audits with some extensions of requirements, often due to the dual compliance objectives of the audits. The extensions beyond GAAS are more noticeable in the documentation and reporting areas, but SAS No. 103 considerably narrowed the differences in documentation.[10] The GAGAS Standards are often referred to as the "Yellow Book" due to the color of the cover of the published Standards. These Standards extend GAAS by adding additional guidance, such as requiring:

- That the reader be informed of the relevant accounting standards used and GAGAS is the relevant audit standard used
- Follow-up on prior audit findings and issues
- Reporting on noncompliance that was encountered
- That material weaknesses and reportable conditions be communicated to relevant users (e.g., granting agencies) outside of management and governance.

The GAO Yellow Book is a public document and can be obtained on the Web at (*www.gao .gov/yellowbook*). Additional information regarding the GAO and its Standards are also available at this and the general GAO Web site (*www.gao.gov*).

(b) COMPLIANCE AUDITS.   AICPA Standards guide CPAs in the performance of audits that have a compliance component as well as a financial statement audit component or when engaged to report on compliance. AU 801, *Compliance Audits,* was recently clarified by SAS No. 117 (also *Compliance Audits*) to be more explicit about which provisions in GAAS also applied when an auditor is engaged to perform a compliance audit. This clarification was prompted by a 2007 GAO review of a sample of Office of Management and Budget (OMB) A-133Single Audit Act compliance audits where confusion was noted regarding the applicability of some general GAAS Standards in the performance of compliance audits by CPAs.

When the audit falls under the Single Audit Act of 1984 (amended in 1996), additional guidance on auditing federal programs is set forth in an annual release from the OMB.[11] A Single Audit engagement includes three elements:

1. A financial statement audit under GAGAS for fair presentation
2. A report on the Schedule of Federal Awards
3. Reporting on compliance with relevant laws and regulations and grant terms

---

[10] See R. Whittington, L. Graham, G. Fischbach, and J. Ahern, "Advancing the Audit Documentation Standard," *Journal of Accountancy* (June 2006).

[11] Broadly, the provisions apply when an entity receives $500,000 or more in federal funding. Monies expended under the American Recovery and Reinvestment Act of 2009 are also included. Depending on the risks associated with the program, between 25 and 50 percent of the aggregate award amounts should be included in the tested populations. Thus, some awards may not be subject to auditor testing.

This annual OMB A-133 circular, "Audits of States, Local Governments, and Non-Profit Organizations," adds further to the Yellow Book standards. The purpose of the Single Audit Act was to reduce the number of audits of entities by government and auditor organizations for various purposes, therefore achieving more synergism and efficiency in the process.

In practice, financial and compliance audits have different objectives. The financial audit, like the GAAS audit, seeks high assurance that the financial statements are free of material misstatement. The auditor strategy for achieving that objective is a matter of judgment. A controls-based or substantive-based audit can be designed, subject to the minimum requirements that govern controls assessment and the performance of some substantive tests. The compliance audit seeks assurance that the entity has complied with the various laws and regulations surrounding the expenditure of federal funds. Consequently, regulations may require certain tests and extents of testing of controls over compliance as well as setting certain minimum sample sizes for the performance of substantive compliance tests. While clearly there is a relationship between compliance and fair financial reporting, these are separate concepts, and various criteria, such as materiality, may be defined differently for the various audit reports. Often the auditor performs separate tests to meet many of these separate objectives. For example, if a compliance criteria is the use of prevailing wage rates as specified by the Department of Labor (e.g., Davis-Bacon Act) when expending federal funds for payroll, that is a different objective from the financial statement objective verifying that the wages paid were complete, accurate, and properly recorded in the correct period. The multiplicity of Standards and agency regulations applicable to government entities greatly increases the education and expertise demands on today's CPAs who perform these services.

As an example of the specificity of compliance requirements, the 14 controls identified by the Single Audit Act that require auditor assessment and testing are listed next.

1. Allowed activities
2. Allowable costs
3. Cash management
4. Davis-Bacon Act
5. Eligibility
6. Equipment and real property management
7. Matching or required level of effort of the grantee (where required by the terms of the grant)
8. Period expended
9. Procurement
10. Program income
11. Real property acquisition
12. Reporting
13. Subrecipient monitoring (when relevant)
14. Special tests and provisions

Under some circumstances the attestation (AT series), and not the auditing, standards might be applicable to engagements that are undertaken to examine certain compliance issues such as reporting on the effectiveness of internal controls. This might occur more often when management is required to assert, with auditor review, to certain aspects of regulatory compliance required by regulations that do not relate specifically to the financial statements of the entity as a whole.

Generally, a compliance audit expands the reporting requirements to include the grantor or the report user. Issues of significant deficiencies in internal control, fraud, or abuse might not be reported publicly as a result of the financial statement audit reporting requirements, but they may generate required communications with users or grantors in a compliance audit. Specific reporting requirements might be created for compliance audits. For example, an actual (not extrapolated from a sample) error of $10,000 or more in compliance triggers a finding that needs to be reported in the Schedule of Findings and Questioned Costs. However, the extrapolated amount of a finding might give rise to a contingency of significance for financial audit purposes.

Special audit and disclosure requirements were set up in 2009 for American Recovery Act funds. Because of the sheer size and potential sensitivity of these funds, a public Web site has been set up to disclose and report on the quarterly expenditures and results. All American Recovery Act awards are designated by OMB as "high inherent risk," triggering higher levels of auditor testing than otherwise (see *www.recovery.gov*).

(c) OPERATIONAL AUDITS.   The watchdog function of the GAO is evident in the performance of various program effectiveness (performance) audits. These reports have uncovered significant instances of waste and inefficiency in government. Issuing nearly 1.000 reports annually on various programs and on issues raised by the Congress for investigation, the agency has a multitude of specialists from various fields to assist in the evaluation of program performance, which often goes well beyond the analysis of financial data. For example, the analysis may be as diverse as looking at an advanced weapons system to reported fraud in a food stamp program.

The reports issued are often termed "blue books" based on the color of the covers used over the years. The GAO prides itself in verifying and reviewing all the numerical and information presented as factual contained in these reports so that Congress and the public can place reliance on what is reported therein.

Generally all of the GAO reports are available at the GAO Web site unless they might compromise national security interests.

1.13 ROLE OF INTERNATIONAL FINANCIAL ACCOUNTING AND AUDITING INSTITUTIONS

The increasing globalization of commerce is contributing to the trends in accounting and auditing to converge Standards. It is hard to ignore the obvious desire to converge and conform accounting and auditing Standards across borders. Whether this will result in better practice in all countries or just some countries is a subject of continuing debate.

1.14 INTERNATIONAL ACCOUNTING STANDARDS BOARD

The IASB promulgates the current international accounting standards. The current hierarchy of IASB literature is:

- International Financial Reporting Standards (IASs issued by IASB)
- International Accounting Standards (issued by the predecessor International Accounting Standards Committee)
- Interpretations from the International Financial Reporting Interpretations Committee (IFRIC) or the Standing Interpretations Committee (SIC)

The IASC issued 40 ISAs prior to the formation of the IASB in 2001. Many of these ISAs have been replaced or modified by subsequent International Financial Reporting Standards (IFRSs). Relatively few Interpretations have been issued to date, in keeping with the desire to establish principles-based Standards in lieu of detailed rules. Nevertheless, some issues can develop quickly and the flexibility of the international interpretive bodies to address these issues serves a similar role as the EITF in the United States.

Still relevant in IASB standard setting is the *Framework for the Preparation of Financial Statements,* a document developed by the predecessor IASC. Like the Conceptual Framework in the United States, the IASC Framework document is not authoritative but guides the application of accounting thought to assist in solving existing and emerging issues in a consistent manner (see *www.iasplus.com/standard/framewk.htm*). The FASB and IASB seek to produce a joint Framework going forward.

While a timetable for adoption of the IASB Standards in the United States was set forth by the SEC in 2008, there is a current reconsideration of that commitment and schedule. Additional insight to the development and contemporary issues regarding IASs is provided in Chapter 3 in this *Handbook* by Tom Jones.

(a) HISTORY OF THE IASB.   The IASB began in 1966 with the formation of the AISG. The members of the AISG were representatives of the accounting profession from Canada, the United Kingdom, and the United States. The AISG was formed to perform comparative studies of the major accounting issues among the three originating countries.

In 1973, the AISG formed a committee consisting of representatives from professional accounting organizations from Australia, Canada, France, Germany, Japan, Mexico, the Netherlands, the United Kingdom and Ireland, and the United States. In June 1973, those nine professional organizations founded the IASC. The founding countries constituted the initial board of the IASC.

In 1977, with the formation of the IFAC, the international professional activities of the IASC were organized under IFAC, which later agreed that the IASC would have complete autonomy in setting IASs and in the issuance of discussion documents on international accounting issues.

The work of the IASC was developed and published by its board after due process procedures involving consultation on a worldwide basis. The due process procedures, which involved the issuance of EDs of proposed Standards, provided financial information users, preparers, and auditors with the opportunity to express their views. In setting its technical agenda and in developing IASs, the IASC board consulted with various advisory bodies, including an International Consultative Group, member bodies, and other standard-setting organizations.

In 1997, the IASC board formed the Strategy Working Party (SWP) to consider the structure of the IASC after it completed a "Core Standards" development process.[12] SWP issued its discussion paper, *Shaping IASC for the Future,* enumerating the working party's recommendations on the necessary structural changes to the IASC in meeting its long-term objectives. The SWP's recommendations, although extensive, retained many elements of the existing IASC structure.

In its final report, the SWP noted:

> The comment letters and consultations with interested parties also reflected various views on the attributes that are considered desirable to establish the legitimacy of a standard setting organization. The primary attributes identified were the representativeness of the decision making body, the independence of its members, and technical expertise. As applied to the IASC structure, the legitimacy of IASC's Standards is considered by some to be established through direct participation of key constituents in the decision making process. The other view is that legitimacy is established if the development of Standards is undertaken by an autonomous body of relatively few, full-time and highly skilled experts who are independent of perceived economic incentives which might interfere with their role on the decision making body.[13]

Based on the SWP's final recommendations, the IASC was renamed the IASB and restructured around the basic objectives of the development of a high-quality set of global accounting standards, formation of an independent standard-setting board, and broad geographic representation among its members.

---

[12] In 1995, the IASC board entered into an agreement with IOSCO to complete a core set of international accounting Standards by 1999. Upon successful completion of the agreed-on core set of Standards, IOSCO agreed to review them and consider endorsement of IASs for cross-border securities offerings among its member countries. In 1998, IOSCO reviewed those Standards and, in 2000, recommended 30 for cross-border offerings and listings.

[13] Strategic Working Party of the International Accounting Standards Committee, *Recommendations on Shaping the IASC for the Future: A Report of the International Accounting Standards Committee* (London: International Accounting Standards Committee, 1999, p. 6).

(b) STRUCTURE OF THE INTERNATIONAL ACCOUNTING STANDARDS BOARD.   The IASB is the standard-setting body of the larger IASC Foundation (the Foundation). The Foundation's objectives are to:

- Develop a single set of high-quality, understandable, and enforceable global accounting Standards, transparent, and comparable information in financial statements and other financial reporting to enable users to make economic decisions.
- Promote the use and rigorous application of those Standards.
- Consider the special needs of small and medium-size entities and emerging economies.
- Bring about convergence of national and IASs to high-quality solutions.

The operating structure of the Foundation consists of the trustees, the IASB (also called the board), the Standards Advisory Council (SAC), and the IFRIC (IFR Interpretations Committee).

(c) INTERNATIONAL ACCOUNTING STANDARDS BOARD TRUSTEES.   The trustees are appointed for a three-year, renewable term. The trustees consist of 22 individuals appointed by the current trustees.

Further, to ensure broad global representation, the convened group must consist of six representatives each appointed from North America, from Europe, and from the Asia/Pacific region. The remaining four representatives can be from any region, so long as overall geographic balance is maintained.

The composition of the trustees should provide a balance of professional backgrounds, including auditors, preparers, users, academics, and other officials serving the public interest. Two trustees normally are senior partners of prominent international accounting firms.

Trustees must meet at least twice each year. They have these responsibilities:

- Handle fundraising activities for the IASB.
- Appoint the members of the IASB, including those with liaison responsibilities with national standard-setting organizations, monitor its effectiveness, and annually review the IASB's strategy.
- Appoint the members of the SAC and the IFRIC.
- Approve the annual budget.
- Promote the IASB and the objective of rigorous application of its Standards.
- Establish and amend the operating procedures for the IASB, the Standard Interpretations Committee, and the Standards Advisory Committee.

(d) INTERNATIONAL ACCOUNTING STANDARDS BOARD.   The trustees' group has broad geographic representation. In contrast, representation on the IASB is based on the individual's technical accounting proficiency and practical experience. The criteria for selection include:

- Demonstrated technical competency and knowledge of financial accounting and reporting
- The ability to analyze accounting issues and to consider the implications of the analysis for the decision process
- Effective oral and written communication skills
- Capability to consider varied viewpoints and impartial and well-reasoned decision making
- Understanding of the global financial, business, and economic environment in which the IASB operates
- Ability to work in a collegial environment
- Integrity, objectivity, and discipline
- Commitment to the Foundation's mission and to serving the public interest

IASB board members are appointed by the trustees. The board consists of 14 members, 12 full time and 2 part time.

The IASB has full responsibility for all technical accounting matters, including the preparation and issuance of the IASs and the associated EDs of financial reporting Standards. Other IASB responsibilities include:

- Publish EDs on all projects and regularly publish draft statements of principles or other discussion documents for public comment on major projects.
- Retain full discretion over the technical agenda of the IASB and over the assignment of technical projects, in organizing the conduct of the technical work, including the outsourcing of technical accounting research or other work to national standard setters or other organizations.
- Establish procedures for reviewing comments received from the IASB constituency on documents issued for public comment.
- Form steering committees or other types of specialist advisory groups to provide advice on major projects.
- Consult the SAC on major projects, agenda decisions, and work priorities.

Each IASB member has one vote on any issue presented for vote by the board. Nine of the 14 members must approve a financial reporting Standard, ED, final Standard, or Interpretation for publication and issuance. Other IASB decisions, including publication of a discussion paper, require a simple majority of the IASB members present at a meeting attended by at least 60 percent of the board.

Except for certain administrative matters, the IASB opens its meeting to the public. When deemed necessary, the IASB may use a public hearing meeting format to discuss specified agenda topics or approve the use of field tests to ensure that proposed accounting approaches are practical and workable.

Except in limited circumstances, IASB EDs of proposed financial reporting Standards, discussion documents, and other similar public documents receive a comment period of 90 days. Under exceptional circumstances, the IASB may issue an ED for 60 days.

(e) STANDARDS ADVISORY COUNCIL.   The SAC, which consists of at least 30 members with diverse geographic and professional backgrounds, provides a forum for organizations and individuals with an interest in international financial reporting to participate in the standard-setting process. Members of the SAC are appointed for renewable three-year terms.

As constituted, the SAC's objectives are:

- Advising the IASB on agenda decisions and board priorities
- Informing the IASB of the diverse views of representative organizations and individuals on major standard-setting projects
- Advising the IASB and the trustees on other issues, as requested

In addition, the IASB must consult the SAC in advance of any proposed changes to the IASB constitution.

The SAC meets with the IASB at least three times each year. Meetings between the SAC and the IASB are open to the public.

(f) INTERNATIONAL FINANCIAL REPORTING INTERPRETATIONS COMMITTEE.   The IFRIC consists of 12 members appointed by the trustees. The director of technical activities, a staff position, or other senior member of the IASB Staff is the chair of the IFRIC and a nonvoting member. In addition, the trustees may appoint representatives of regulatory organizations to observe the meetings of the IFRIC. Although not granted voting status, the regulatory observers are permitted to speak at the meetings. Currently, representatives from the International Organizations of Securities Commissions (IOSCO) and the European Commission are observers of IFRIC meetings.

Members of the IFRIC include accountants in public practice and industry and financial statement users.

In the absence of specific authoritative guidance, the IFRIC reviews emerging accounting issues that might be subject to divergent or unacceptable accounting treatment, with the goal of reaching consensus on the appropriate accounting approach. The framework of the IASB and existing IFRSs guide IFRIC interpretations. As constituted, the IFRIC's responsibilities include:

- Interpreting the application of IFRSs and providing timely guidance on financial reporting issues not specifically addressed in existing international accounting guidance
- Working with national standard-setting organizations to bring about convergence of national accounting standards and IFRSs to high-quality solutions
- Publishing draft interpretations for public comment and, when developing a final Interpretation, considering comments received and issuing a final Interpretation within a reasonable time period

Before issuance, IFRIC's drafts and final Interpretations must be approved by the IASB.

The IFRIC meets as often as necessary, currently about every two months. Each IFRIC member has one vote and is expected to represent his or her own independent views rather than the views of any firm, organization, or other constituency with which the member may be associated. Although an IFRIC member may send an alternate, as approved by the IFRIC chair, such alternates may speak at meetings but are not granted voting privileges.

Except for meetings during which certain administrative matters are discussed, the IFRIC's meetings are open to the public.

(g) INTERNATIONAL FINANCIAL REPORTING STANDARDS.   IFRSs are international authoritative guidance on how particular economic events and transactions should be reported in a company's financial statements and reports.

IFRSs are established within the context of the IASC conceptual accounting framework that was approved in 1989. The framework assists the IASB in the development of future Standards; in its periodic review of existing Standards; and in promoting the convergence of regulations, accounting Standards, and procedures relating to the presentation of financial statements. However, the framework is not an authoritative IAS and does not define Standards for any particular measurement or disclosure issue. The framework addresses general-purpose financial statements that a company prepares and presents to meet the common information needs of a wide range of financial information users. It:

- Defines the objectives of financial statements and underlying assumptions
- Identifies the qualitative characteristics of financial statements
- Defines the basic elements of financial statements and the concepts for recognition and measurement of the financial statement elements
- Defines the concepts of capital and capital maintenance

At present, the IASB has no authority to require or enforce compliance with IFRSs. However, for cross-border securities issuances, many countries allow foreign companies to apply IFRSs when those companies prepare financial reports for issuance to the public. Such countries may require certain reconciliations or additional footnote explanations of differences between reported information and local accounting and financial reporting Standards. To identify the changing status of IFRSs in specific countries, consult *www.IASB.org*.

The IOSCO reviewed 30 ISAs for consideration for cross-border reporting by its member countries. Based on that review and subject to the appropriate reconciliation, disclosures, and interpretations, in May 2000, the President's Committee of IOSCO recommended that IOSCO members permit multinational issuers to use the 30 approved Standards to prepare their financial reporting information for cross-border offerings and listings. Further, as of January 1, 2005, the European Union (EU) requires all publicly listed companies to prepare their financial statements in conformity with IFRSs.

(i) Procedures for the Development of International Financial Reporting Standards.   Potential IASB financial accounting and reporting topics may be suggested to the IASB by its board members, members of the SAC, national accounting standard-setting organizations, regulatory organizations, the IASB Staff, and other interested individuals and IASB constituents. Once an item is added to its technical agenda, the IASB is given responsibility for determining the scope of that project. Development of an IFRS may involve these steps:

- Establishment of an advisory committee to consult with the IASB on issues involved in the project
- Preparation and issuance of a discussion document to obtain comments on the topic and proposed guidance from interested parties
- Preparation and issuance of an ED for public comment, after deliberation and consideration of the public comments received
- Issuance of a final IFRS, after deliberation and consideration of public comments received on the ED

A current list of outstanding IFRSs can be found at the official Web site, *www.ifrs.org*.

(ii) Acceptance of IFRS for SEC Purposes by Foreign Private Issuers.   In March 2008, the SEC indicated that it would accept financial statements prepared in accordance with IFRS for purposes of the filing requirements by foreign private issuers without reconciliation to U.S.GAAP (SEC Release 33–8879). Prior to this change, Regulation S-X and Form 20-F required reconciliation to U.S. GAAP to be acceptable for filing purposes

1.15 INTERNATIONAL ORGANIZATION OF SECURITIES COMMISSIONS

IOSCO was created in 1983. Its members represent national securities regulators and representatives from national securities exchanges that have responsibility for securities regulation and the administration of securities laws. IOSCO's objectives (*www.iosco.org*) are to:

- to cooperate in developing, implementing and promoting adherence to internationally recognized and consistent standards of regulation, oversight and enforcement in order to protect investors, maintain fair, efficient and transparent markets, and seek to address systemic risks;
- to enhance investor protection and promote investor confidence in the integrity of securities markets, through strengthened information exchange and cooperation in enforcement against misconduct and in supervision of markets and market intermediaries; and
- to exchange information at both global and regional levels on their respective experiences in order to assist the development of markets, strengthen market infrastructure and implement appropriate regulation.

IOSCO has three membership categories: ordinary (115), associate (11), and affiliate (67) members. Its activities to promote convergence began in 1989, when it released a report stating that cross-border offerings would be facilitated by the development of a global set of accounting standards. At that time, IOSCO decided to focus its activities on the efforts of the IASC (now the IASB).

In 1998, IOSCO adopted a comprehensive set of Objectives and Principles of Securities Regulation (IOSCO Principles), targeted as a benchmark for securities markets.

Today IOSCO is comprised of and regulates over 100 jurisdictions and its membership represents more than 95% of the world's securities markets.

In 2003, the organization endorsed a comprehensive methodology (IOSCO Principles Assessment Methodology) to provide a way to objectively assess the effective implementation of the IOSCO Principles in the jurisdictions of its members and the development of practical action plans to correct identified deficiencies.

In 2005, IOSCO agreed the IOSCO multilateral Memorandum of Understanding as a benchmark for international cooperation among securities regulators, "facilitating cross-border cooperation, reducing global systemic risk, protecting investors and ensuring fair and efficient securities markets."

In its report on the IASB core Standards, IOSCO discusses the supplemental treatments that IOSCO members may want to consider when deciding on the implementation. IOSCO is also working with the IAASB to develop a similar work plan to consider recommending IAS to its members for cross-border auditing and assurance engagements.

Since its inception, the U.S. SEC has had considerable influence on the leadership and direction of IOSCO. The decline of the relative dominance of the United States in worldwide securities trading has weakened U.S. influence on this international body.

1.16 EUROPEAN UNION

In 1957, the Treaty of Rome created the EC (European Community). In 1967, three existing communities—the European Economic Community, the European Coal and Steel Community, and the European Atomic Energy Community—were merged. In 1993, the European Community became the EU (European Union). Currently, a single Commission, a Council of Ministers (the Council), and a European Parliament exercise the powers and responsibilities incorporated in the separate treaties comprising the EU.

The Council represents the governments of its member states and is the EU's decision-making body. It deliberates proposals developed by the representatives in the Commission. A qualified majority vote by Council is generally required for approval of all proposals. Council votes are weighted based on the population of the individual member countries.

(a) COUNCIL DIRECTIVES. EU Directives are one approach used to harmonize company law throughout member states. Directives are developed through a complex and lengthy process, including ratification by its member states. Once Directives are ratified, each member state adopts and implements it, although national authorities are given some latitude on matters of implementation.

Directives address all aspects of company law, including accounting and auditing. Of the relevant company Directives that have been issued, two have significantly influenced European efforts to converge accounting and financial reporting: the Fourth and Seventh Directives, which are discussed next. The Eighth Directive addresses the qualification of accounting professionals authorized to conduct statutory audits.

The Fourth Directive, issued in 1978, is applicable to public and private companies with the exception of banks and insurance companies. According to this Directive, in preparing financial reports, companies must provide a "true and fair" view of their assets, liabilities, financial position, and results of operations. The guidance of the Fourth Directive includes:

- The format for a company's balance sheet and profit and loss statement
- The minimum footnote disclosure requirements and the contents of the annual report
- A section addressing the valuation rules and concepts considered in preparing financial statements and reported information

The Seventh Directive, issued in 1983, applies to groups of companies that include at least one public or private limited liability company. The Directive requires member states to mandate, under certain specified criteria, consolidation accounting between parent companies and their controlled subsidiaries.

(b) EUROPEAN UNION—RECENT DEVELOPMENTS. The EU has stressed support of convergence of accounting and financial reporting standards around those issued by the IASC (now IASB). For example:

- In 1999, the EC issued its action plan to improve the Single Market for Financial Services over a five-year period. In that action plan, the Commission noted that the IASC Standards represent the benchmark for companies that intend to participate in cross-border securities transactions.

- In 2000, the EC issued a report, *EU Financial Reporting Strategy: The Way Forward,* which contains its recommendations on an approach to European convergence. In that report, the EC recommends making it mandatory for all EU-listed companies to prepare consolidated financial statements in accordance with IASs. Further, the report proposed amending existing Directives and developing an IAS endorsement mechanism with the goal of achieving European application of IASs by January 1, 2005. In June 2002, the EC adopted a regulation requiring listed companies to prepare consolidated financial reports in accordance with IAS (now IFRSs).

- The EU, through its various committees on accounting issues, has been a vocal supporter and sometimes critic of IASB proposals. For example, in 2004, the EU objected to certain provisions of the revised IAS on accounting and reporting for derivative transactions. Rather than reject the revised Standard in total, the EU accepted a modified version of the final Standard, IAS No. 39, *Financial Instruments: Recognition and Measurement,* and requested that the IASB reconsider certain provisions. In response, the IASB reconsidered those provisions and issued amendments. In 2005, the EU accepted the amended Standard for use by listed companies in EU member states. It is clear that the EU intends to continue to be an active participant in IASB activities.

- In 2005, the EU approved amendments to the Eighth Directive. Consistent with some of the provisions of the Sarbanes-Oxley Act in the United States, the amendments establish public oversight of the auditing profession and increase audit committee oversight over the acceptance and conduct of the corporate audit. In addition, similar to the acceptance of IFRSs issued by the IASB, the amendments make the application of IAASB auditing Standards mandatory for all statutory audits.

The EU's recent activities make it clear that, subject to its review and evaluation of IFRSs, its objective is promote convergence of accounting Standards with the guidance of the IASB.

1.17 INTERNATIONAL AUDITING—INTERNATIONAL FEDERATION OF ACCOUNTANTS

IFAC is a nongovernmental global professional organization of national accounting groups that represent accountants employed in public practice, business and industry, the public sector, and education that interact regularly with the accounting profession. IFAC was established in 1977 as a result of the growth in international trade and multinational business enterprises coupled with a significant increase in investors' attraction to investments outside of their national borders and the associated increase in cross-border capital flows.

IFAC's stated mission is

to strengthen the worldwide accountancy profession and [to] contribute to the development of strong international economies by establishing and promoting adherence to high-quality professional standards, furthering the international convergence of such standards and speaking out on public interest issues,

where applicable. IFAC accomplishes its mission through its communications with national professional accounting organizations that are its official members and through its interactions with the many other professional organizations that rely on or have an interest in the activities of the international accounting profession.

In 2001, IFAC issued a paper, *Enhancing Financial Reporting and Auditing,* containing initiatives proposed to strengthen IFAC and improve the global professional accounting self-regulatory structure. The main elements of the initiatives include:

- Strengthening the processes and broadening the membership of the IAASB (formerly the International Auditing Practices Committee)

- Establishing a self-regulatory regime for firms performing transnational audits, comprising the Forum of Firms and its executive arm, the Transnational Audit Committee (an IFAC standing committee)
- Establishing a global Public Oversight Board
- Introducing a program for monitoring the compliance by IFAC member bodies with IFAC Standards and other pronouncements

IFAC's current structure reflects implementation of many of the recommendations proposed in the paper.

(a) MEMBERSHIP.   Membership in IFAC is open to accountancy organizations recognized by law or general consensus within their countries as substantial national organizations of good standing within the accounting profession. In 2011, IFAC has 164 member organizations in 125 countries representing more than 2.5 million accountants.

Members of IFAC are expected to:

- Make to fulfill IFAC's mission and objectives.
- Provide financial support of IFAC.
- Demonstrate compliance with the obligations set out in the Statements of Membership Obligations (SMOs), which are issued or revised periodically. (SMOs are issued by the IFAC board and provide clear benchmarks to current member organizations to assist them in meeting their membership requirements.)

(b) GOVERNANCE OF THE INTERNATIONAL FEDERATION OF ACCOUNTANTS.   IFAC is governed by an organization consisting of IFAC Council, the board, and standing technical committees. See Section (c)(ii) for more information on these standing committees.

(c) COUNCIL.   The Council consists of one representative from each member body of IFAC. The Council meets one time each year and is responsible for deciding constitutional questions and electing the IFAC board. Council members retain one vote on any issue addressed to the Council during its meeting. Other Council responsibilities include:

- Appointing a nominating committee
- Electing board members, based on the recommendations of the nominating committee
- Electing from its members, based on the recommendations of the nominating committee, the deputy president, who replaces the president for a term of two years
- Monitoring the progress and achievement of IFAC
- Admitting and expelling members, as appropriate
- Determining the basis for financial contributions from members
- Determining IFAC's strategic initiatives, budgetary priorities, and other major policy matters

(i) International Federation of Accountants Board.   The Council, based on the recommendations of the nominating committee, elects the board, which is comprised of the president and 21 individuals from 18 countries. These members are elected for up to three-year terms and are responsible for setting policy and overseeing IFAC operations, implementing programs, and the work of IFAC boards and committees. The board has broad regional representation as no more than two members may be from any single country.[14] The board is elected for up to three-year terms and meets three times each year.

---

[14] Except that the country of the president may have an additional representative on the board. See Part 5 of the IFAC Constitution dated November 2004.

(ii) Standing Committees. The standing committees work toward achieving the broad objectives of IFAC by issuing guidance that member organizations are committed to implement in their own countries. The standing committees include:

- *Transnational Auditors Committee (TAC).* TAC is the executive committee of the Forum of Firms. Membership in the Forum of Firms is open to all accounting firms that perform or wish to perform audits of transnational audits. Member firms are expected to conform to certain quality control standards and are subject to an evolving global peer review process to assess the firm's compliance with the quality control standards. TAC is responsible for coordinating the global peer review process and supervising the development of additional guidance regarding transnational audit work.
- *Compliance Advisory Panel.* The CAP oversees the implementation and operation of the IFAC compliance program. The CAP also makes recommendations to the IFAC board about the membership application process, including recommending new applicants for membership.
- *IAASB International Auditing and Assurance Standards Board.* This board works to improve the uniformity of auditing practices and related services by issuing pronouncements on a variety of audit and assurance functions and by promoting global acceptance of their Standards.
- *Ethics Committee.* The Ethics Committee consults and advises the board on all aspects of ethical issues, develops appropriate guidance on these issues for the board's ultimate approval, and promotes an understanding of ethical issues among its member bodies. In addition, the Ethics Committee continually monitors and stimulates debate on a wide range of ethical issues to ensure that its guidance is responsive to the expectations of its constituency.
- *International Public Sector Accounting Standards Board.* This board issues accounting and auditing pronouncements and conducts educational and research programs aimed at improving the financial management and accountability of national governments, regional and local governments, related governmental agencies, and the constituencies they serve.
- *Education Committee.* This committee develops standards and guidelines, conducts research, and facilitates the exchange of information to ensure that accountants are adequately trained. An important Education Committee focus is assisting developing nations in the advancement of accounting education.
- *Professional Accountants in Business Committee (PAIB).* PAIB publishes guidance, sponsors research programs, and facilitates the international exchange of ideas to develop and support financial and management accounting professionals. The Financial and Management Accounting Committee also works to increase public awareness, understanding, and demand for the services of these professionals worldwide.
- *Nominating Committee.* This committee makes recommendations regarding the composition of IFAC boards, committees, and task forces.

Occasionally, IFAC's Council appoints small working groups, ad hoc committees, or special task forces to address significant issues that warrant focused attention.

(d) INTERNATIONAL STANDARDS ON AUDITING. The IAASB issues ISAs and guidance on the application of the ISAs. The IAASB consists of 18 members. The chair is a full-time position; the remaining 17 members are volunteer, part-time positions. Members are appointed by the IFAC board based on recommendations from the IFAC Nominating Committee. The IAASB has broad geographical representation.

The IAASB meets about four times each year. Meetings, which are open to the public, are held in New York and several locations around the world. Information about meeting locations, the agenda, and minutes are available on the IFAC Web site (*www.ifac.org*).

In developing its auditing and assurance guidance, the IAASB establishes subcommittees to prepare and present draft auditing Standards and Statements. Subcommittees are composed of IAASB committee members, technical auditors from member organizations, and International Federation of

Accountants (IFAC) Staff. The IAASB deliberates on draft Standards and Statements at its regular meetings. After extensive discussion and debate, the subcommittee prepares an ED of a Statement or Standard for public issuance. Comments received on the ED are summarized and discussed at subsequent subcommittee meetings, and a revised document is prepared for discussion at an IAASB meeting. The IAASB deliberates on the revised draft and associated public comments and makes recommendations to the subcommittee, which are used to prepare a final document.

Each IAASB member has one vote on any document received. A final Standard requires approval of at least 75 percent of attending members.

The IAASB issues three types of formal guidance:

1. *ISAs,* which are applied in the audit of financial statements and adapted to the audit of other information and related services.
2. *International Standards on Assurance Engagements (ISAEs),* which are applied to assurance engagements performed by professional accountants in public practice when such engagements are not covered by an ISA or an International Auditing Practices Statement.
3. *International Auditing Practices Statements (IAPSs),* which provide practical assistance to auditors in implementing ISAs and promoting good practice. IAPSs do not have the authority of ISAs.

Neither ISAs nor ISAEs override local or national auditing or assurance services regulations, respectively.

The IAASB also issues various Discussion Papers with the intention of promoting discussion or debate on auditing and assurance issues affecting the accounting profession, presenting findings, or describing situations of interest relating to auditing and assurance issues. A Discussion Paper does not carry the authority of either an ISA or an IAPS.

Recently the format of the ISAs has been modified to facilitate incorporation of auditing requirements into local country law, as required in some international locations. The length of some auditing Standards would have made it awkward to bring the existing Standards into the law, so in practice only the requirements section of the ISA is brought into the country law. A major difference in the reformatted ("clarified") Standards is that the requirements of the Standard are set apart from the explanatory and other contextual material in it. Requirements are always expressed by the phrase "the auditor shall."[15] The format followed in the ISAs is the current direction taken in the clarified U.S. Standards. In addition, the reconciliation at the end of the U.S. reformatted Standards identifies any differences between U.S. and IAASB Standards.

ISAs now follow the format: Introduction, Objective, Definitions, Requirements, and Application and Other Explanatory Material. As of 2011, the final set of clarified Standards consists of 36 remaining ISAs and one International Standard on Quality Control (ISQC 1), including 16 Standards that contain new and revised requirements.

1.18 SUMMARY AND COMMENTARY

This chapter has shown how financial accounting is important to society because of its contribution to the economy by helping the capital markets operate more effectively. Because of the importance of this social goal, and because history has shown that abusive accounting tends to occur as preparers attempt to gain unfair advantages, financial accounting is significantly regulated

---

[15] To date, the U.S. clarified Standards continue to use the terms *must* and *should* to denote requirements. Internationally, one country protested the use of the term *must* in International Standards because when it was translated into its native language, the term was one used to describe the type of commands that are directed at young children. *Shall* was a more acceptable term. This is another example of how cultural and language differences can introduce complexities when writing technical accounting and auditing pronouncements.

by governmental agencies, by private standard-setting bodies that are endorsed and supported by governmental agencies, and by professional organizations. This regulation deals with reporting standards, competency standards, and ethical standards.

The regulation of accounting involves politics because of the conflicting interests among financial statement preparers, auditors, users, and regulators. The tension among these interests helps bring about change and improvement, but only at the risk of not fully serving the public interest. The current structure has evolved with what appears to be the central goal of protecting the public, but that mission will be attained only through careful vigilance and oversight.

While the trend toward globalization is unmistakable, the surrender of local decision making regarding accounting and auditing regulation is a step that many developed countries continue to approach with caution. The international bodies have been patient in permitting nonconforming countries to make contributions to the standard-setting process. However, the longer-range intent of these bodies is unmistakable: Adopt the international Standards you are helping to create or face declining influence or expulsion from the international process. This has been made clear by the IASB and IAASB.[16]

While not contributing to the harmony and good relations among members that mutual committee service engenders, drawing such lines in the sand does force decisions about where you are going. To date, many accounting and auditing bodies have had the opportunity to observe existing practices and policies developed in the more mature markets countries and have compared and contrasted the approaches and results obtained. With such existing models to consider, simplification and harmonization may have been enhanced. Some questions need to be addressed on the front end, since reparations may be difficult on the back end once the decision is made. These include:

- Will this process work the same way when topics are being debated that might be first experienced or recognized in only one or two of the participating countries?

- Will intimidation of countries to commit and join the process help or hurt the implementation process for international accounting and auditing Standards?

- Will the combined body be respectful of the fact that the issue may have originated in one environment or the other and may reflect issues likely to impact only a few environments? Comments and writings have criticized U.S. Standards for being detail oriented. Will ideology and nationalist issues be an impediment to addressing issues on a timely basis?

- Do detailed Standards grow out of a desire to issue detailed Standards, or do they grow from more complex and detailed issues that are recognized in practice and where harmonization on principles alone is unlikely? If the latter is the case, we may wind up in the same place in the long run anyway. If principles are cross-industry, why did the IASC develop an ISA on the agricultural industry?

- What role will the FASB and the ASB serve once their standard-setting roles have been assimilated into the international bodies? Will a void develop between the practicing profession and the standard-setting process?

- What past or existing international body will serve as a role model for how the international standards process will create greater harmony and commerce? The effectiveness of the United Nations in meeting its lofty goals is not a great endorsement for the likely effectiveness of international bodies.

- How will the SEC exercise its congressional mandate to oversee the profession in the United States in the context of the international standard-setting process?

- How will the PCAOB participate in the new standard-setting process, or will continue to "do its own thing" as it relates to setting U.S. public company audits?

---

[16] M. Lamoreaux, "New IASB Leader Embraces Challenges: An Interview with Chairman Hans Hoogervorst," *Journal of Accountancy* (September 2011); and A. Hickley and N. York, "IFRS Tiff Heats Up as US Banks Weigh In," *Global Financial Strategy News,* August 11, 2011, at *www.gfsnews.com*.

- Will the environment in which auditors operate (e.g., regulatory, professional, and economic) be conducive to their making tough judgments on principles-based issues? There is considerable evidence that the SEC has been a major resolution resource for issues that U.S. auditors and clients disagree on. Will the dynamics change when the system changes, and how?

Only time will tell.

1.19 ADDITIONAL READING

Afterman, A. *SEC Regulation of Public Companies.* Englewood Cliffs, NJ: Prentice-Hall, 1995.

American Institute of Certified Public Accountants. Report of the Study Group on the Objectives of Financial Statements, *Objectives of Financial Statements.* New York: Author, 1973.

———."Where Will the SEC Take the IFRS Roadmap?: An AICPA Analysis of Comment Letters on the SEC's Proposal." April 27, 2009. *www.ifrs.com/updates/aicpa/IFRS_SEC.html*

———."The AICPA's Guide to Clarified and Converged Standards for Auditing and Quality Control." *www.aicpa.org/research/standards/auditattest/asb/downloadabledocuments/clarity/aicpa_guide_to_clarity.pdf.*

BDO Seidman, LLP. *SEC Guidelines: Rules and Regulations.* Warren, Gorham and Lamont. 2005.

Blanchet, Jeannot. "Global Standards Offer Opportunity," *Financial Executiv e* (March/April 2002): 2–3.

Bragg, S. *Wiley Practitioner's Guide to GAAS 2012.* Hoboken, NJ: John Wiley & Sons, 2011.

Choi, F., and G. Meek. *International Accounting,* 7th ed. Englewood Cliffs, NJ: Prentice-Hall, 2010.

Epstein, B., and E. Jermakowicz. *2010 Interpretations and Applications of International Financial Reporting Standards.* Hoboken, NJ: John Wiley & Sons, 2010.

Financial Accounting Standards Board. Statement of Financial Accounting Concepts No. 1, *Objectives of Financial Reporting by Business Enterprises.* Stamford, CT: Author, 1978.

———. Statement of Financial Accounting Concepts No. 2, *Qualitative Characteristics of Accounting Information.* Stamford, CT: Author, 1980.

———. Statement of Financial Accounting Concepts No. 3, *Elements of Financial Statements of Business Enterprises.* Stamford, CT: Author, 1980.

———. Statement of Financial Accounting Concepts No. 4, *Objectives of Financial Reporting by Nonbusiness Organizations.* Stamford, CT: Author, 1980.

———. Statement of Financial Accounting Concepts No. 5, *Recognition and Measurement in Financial Statements of Business Enterprises.* Stamford, CT: Author, 1980.

———. Statement of Financial Accounting Concepts No. 6, *Elements of Financial Statements.* Stamford, CT: Author, 1985.

———. Statement of Financial Accounting Concepts No. 7, *Using Cash Flow Information and Present Value in Accounting Measurements.* Norwalk, CT: Author, 2000.

Hooks, K. *Auditing and Assurance Services: Understanding the Integrated Audit.* Hoboken, NJ: John Wiley & Sons, 2011.

Miller, Paul B. W., Rodney J. Redding, and Paul R. Bahnson. *The FASB: The People, the Process, and the Politics,* 4th ed. Burr Ridge, IL: Irwin-McGraw-Hill, 1998.

Oliverio, Mary Ellen. "The New Structure for International Accounting Standards," *CPA Journal* (May 2000): 20–26.

Public Oversight Board and Staff. *The Panel on Audit Effectiveness Report and Recommendations.* Stamford, CT: Author, 2000.

Ravlic, Tom. "The IOSCO Role: Making International Rules," *Australian CPA* (August 1999): 54–56.

Sarbanes-Oxley Act of 2002, 107th Congress, 2d Session.

Securities and Exchange Commission. Progress Report of the SEC Advisory Committee on Improvements to Financial Reporting SEC Release 33–8896, issued February 14, 2008.

Strategy Working Party of the International Accounting Standards Committee. *Recommendations on Shaping the IASC for the Future: A Report of the International Accounting Standards Committee.* London: IASC, 1999.

Tidrick, D. "A Conversation with James J. Leisenring, IASB Member," *CPA Journal* (March 2002): 48–51.

1.20 SELECTED WEB SITES

American Institute of Certified Public Accountants: *www.aicpa.org*

Federal Accounting Standards Advisory Board: *www.fasab.gov*

Financial Accounting Standards Board: *www.fasb.org/home*

Government Accountability Office: *www.gao.gov*

International Federation of Accountants / International Auditing and Attest Standards Board: *http://ifac.org*

International Financial Reporting Standards/International Accounting Standards Board: *www.ifrs.org/Home.htm*

International Organizations of Securities Commissions: *www.iosco.org*

FRAMEWORK OF FINANCIAL ACCOUNTING CONCEPTS AND STANDARDS: A HISTORICAL PERSPECTIVE

Reed K. Storey, PhD, CPA
Financial Accounting Standards Board

2.1 FINANCIAL ACCOUNTING AND REPORTING

The principal role of financial accounting and reporting is to serve the public interest by providing information that is useful in making business and economic decisions. That information facilitates the efficient functioning of capital and other markets, thereby promoting the efficient and equitable allocation of scarce resources in the economy. To undertake and fulfill that role, financial accounting in the twentieth century has evolved from a profession relying almost exclusively on the experience of a handful of illustrious practitioners into one replete with a set of financial accounting standards and an underlying conceptual foundation.

An underlying structure of accounting concepts was deemed necessary to provide to the institutions entrusted with setting accounting principles or standards the requisite tools for resolving accounting problems. Financial accounting now has a foundation of fundamental concepts and objectives in the Financial Accounting Standards Board's (FASB) *Conceptual Framework for Financial Accounting and Reporting,* which is intended to provide a basis for developing the financial accounting standards that are promulgated to guide accounting practice.

The FASB's conceptual framework and its antecedents constitute the major subject matter of this chapter. Some significant terms, organizations, and authoritative pronouncements need to be identified or briefly introduced. They already may be familiar to most readers or will become so in due course.

(a) FINANCIAL ACCOUNTING STANDARDS BOARD AND GENERAL PURPOSE EXTERNAL FINANCIAL ACCOUNTING AND REPORTING. *Financial accounting and reporting* is the familiar name of the branch of accounting whose precise but somewhat imposing full proper name is *general-purpose external financial accounting and reporting.* It is the branch of accounting concerned with general-purpose financial statements of business enterprises and not-for-profit organizations. General-purpose financial statements are possible because several groups, such as investors, creditors, and other resource providers, have common interests and common information needs. General-purpose financial reporting provides information to users who are outside a business enterprise or not-for-profit organization and lack the power to require the entity to supply the accounting information they need for decision making; therefore, they must rely on information provided to them by the entity's management. Other groups, such as taxing authorities and rate regulators, have specialized information needs but also the authority to require entities to provide the information they specify.

General-purpose external financial reporting is the sphere of authority of the FASB, the private-sector organization that since 1973 has established generally accepted accounting principles in the United States. General-purpose external financial accounting and reporting provides information that is based on generally accepted accounting principles and is audited by independent certified public accountants (CPAs). Generally accepted accounting principles result and have resulted primarily from the authoritative pronouncements of the FASB and its predecessors.

The FASB's standards pronouncements—Statements of Financial Accounting Standards (often abbreviated FASB Statement, SFAS, or FAS) and FASB Interpretations (often abbreviated FIN)—are recognized as authoritative by both the Securities and Exchange Commission (SEC) and the American Institute of Certified Public Accountants (AICPA).

The FASB succeeded the Accounting Principles Board (APB), whose authoritative pronouncements were the APB Opinions. In 1959 the APB had succeeded the Committee on Accounting Procedure, whose authoritative pronouncements were the Accounting Research Bulletins (often abbreviated ARB), some of which were designated as Accounting Terminology Bulletins (often abbreviated ATB).

With respect to the long name *general-purpose external financial reporting,* this chapter does what the standards-setting bodies also have done: For convenience, it uses the shortcut term *financial reporting.*

(b) MANAGEMENT ACCOUNTING AND TAX ACCOUNTING.   Financial accounting and reporting is only part of the broad field of accounting. Other significant kinds of accounting include management accounting and tax accounting.

Management accounting is internal accounting designed to meet the information needs of managers. Although the same accounting system usually accumulates, processes, and disseminates both management and financial accounting information, managers' responsibilities for making decisions and planning and controlling operations at various administrative levels of a business enterprise or not-for-profit organization require more detailed information than is considered necessary or appropriate for external financial reporting. Management accounting includes information that is normally not provided outside an organization and is usually tailored to meet specific management information needs.

Tax accounting is concerned with providing appropriate information needed by individuals, corporations, and others for preparing the various returns and reports required to comply with tax laws and regulations, especially the Internal Revenue Code. It is significant in the administration of domestic tax laws, which are to a large extent self-assessing. Tax accounting is based generally on the same procedures that apply to financial reporting. There are some significant differences, however, and taxing authorities have the statutory power to prescribe the specific information they want taxpayers to submit as a basis for assessing the amount of income tax owed and do not need to rely on information provided to other groups.

2.2 WHY WE HAVE A CONCEPTUAL FRAMEWORK

"Accounting principles" has proven to be an extraordinarily elusive term. To the nonaccountant (as well as to many accountants) it connotes things basic and fundamental, of a sort which can be expressed in few words, relatively timeless in nature, and in no way dependent upon changing fashions in business or the evolving needs of the investment community.

The Wheat Report

Principle. A general law or rule adopted or professed as a guide to action; a settled ground or basis of conduct or practice.

Accounting Research Bulletin No. 7

A recurring theme in financial accounting in the United States in the twentieth century has been the call for a comprehensive, authoritative statement of basic accounting *principles.* It has reflected a widespread perception that something more fundamental than rules or descriptions of methods or procedures was needed to form a basis for, explain, or govern financial accounting and reporting practice. A number of organizations, committees, and individuals in the profession have developed or attempted to develop their own variations of what they have diversely called *principles, standards, conventions, rules, postulates,* or *concepts.* Those efforts met with varying degrees of success, but by the 1970s none of the codifications or statements had come to be accepted or relied on in practice as the definitive statement of accounting's basic principles.

The pursuit of a statement of accounting principles has reflected two distinct schools of thought: that accounting principles are generalized or drawn from practice without reference to a systematic theoretical foundation or that accounting principles are based on a few fundamental premises that together with the principles provide a framework for solving specific problems encountered in practice. Early efforts to codify or develop accounting principles were dominated by the belief that principles are essentially a "distillation of experience," a description generally attributed to George O. May, one of the most influential accountants of his time, who used it in the title of a book, *Financial Accounting: A Distillation of Experience.*[1] However, as accounting has matured and its role in society has increased, momentum in developing accounting principles has shifted to those accountants who have come to understand what has been learned in many other fields: that reliance on experience alone leads only so far because environments and problems change; that until knowledge gained through experience is given purpose, direction, and internal consistency by a conceptual foundation, fundamentals will be endlessly reargued and practice blown in various directions by the winds of changing perceptions and proliferating accounting methods; and that only by studying and understanding the foundations of practices can the path of progress be discovered and the hope of improving practice be realized.

The conceptual framework project of the FASB represents the most comprehensive effort thus far to establish a structure of objectives and fundamentals to underlie financial accounting and reporting practice. To understand what it is, how it came about, and why it took the form and included the concepts that it did requires some knowledge of its antecedents, which extend back more than 60 years.

(a) SPECIAL COMMITTEE ON COOPERATION WITH STOCK EXCHANGES.   The origin of the use of *principle* in financial accounting and reporting can be traced to a special committee of the American Institute of Accountants (American Institute of Certified Public Accountants since 1957). The Special Committee on Cooperation with Stock Exchanges, chaired by George O. May, gave the word special significance in the attest function of accountants. That significance is still evident in audit reports signed by members of the Institute and most other CPAs attesting that the financial statements of their clients present fairly, or do not present fairly, the client's financial position, results of operations, and cash flows "in conformity with generally accepted accounting principles." The committee laid the foundation that has been the basis of both subsequent progress in identifying or developing and enunciating accounting principles and many of the problems that have accompanied the resulting principles.

In 1930 the Institute undertook a cooperative effort with the New York Stock Exchange aimed at improving financial disclosure by publicly held enterprises. It was widely believed that inferior accounting and reporting practices had contributed to the stock market decline and depression that began in 1929. The Exchange was concerned that its listed companies were using too many different accounting and reporting methods to reflect similar transactions and that some of those methods were questionable. The Institute wanted to make financial statements more informative and authoritative, to clarify the authority and responsibility of auditors, and to educate the public about the conventional nature of accounting and the limitations of accounting reports.

The Exchange's Committee on Stock List and the Institute's Special Committee on Cooperation with Stock Exchanges exchanged correspondence between 1932 and 1934. The special committee's report, comprising a series of letters that passed between the two committees, was issued to Institute members in 1934 under the title *Audits of Corporate Accounts* (reprinted in 1963). The key part was a letter dated September 22, 1932, from the Institute committee.

(i) "Accepted Principles of Accounting."   The special committee recommended that an authoritative statement of the broad accounting principles on which "there is a fairly general agreement" be formulated in consultation with a small group of qualified persons, including accountants, lawyers, and corporate officials. Within that framework of "accepted principles of accounting," each company would be free to choose the methods and procedures most appropriate for its financial statements, subject to requirements to disclose the methods it was using and to apply them consistently. Audit certificates (reports) for listed companies would state that their financial statements were prepared in accordance with "accepted principles of accounting." The special committee anticipated that its

---

[1] George O. May, *Financial Accounting: A Distillation of Experience* (New York: Macmillan, 1943).

program would improve financial reporting because disclosure would create pressure from public opinion to eliminate less-desirable practices.

The special committee did not define "principles of accounting," but it illustrated what it had in mind. It gave two explicit examples of accepted broad principles of accounting:

> It is a generally accepted principle that plant value should be charged against gross profits over the useful life of the plant....

> Again, the most commonly accepted method of stating inventories is at cost or market, whichever is lower.[2]

It also listed five principles that it presumed would be included in the contemplated statement of "broad principles of accounting which have won fairly general acceptance":

1. Unrealized profit should not be credited to income account of the corporation either directly or indirectly, through the medium of charging against such unrealized profits amounts, which would ordinarily fall to be charged against income account. Profit is deemed to be realized when a sale in the ordinary course of business is affected, unless the circumstances are such that the collection of the sale price is not reasonably assured. An exception to the general rule may be made [for industries in which trade custom is to take inventories at net selling prices, which may exceed cost].

2. Capital surplus [other paid-in capital], however created, should not be used to relieve the income account of the current or future years of charges, which would otherwise fall to be made there against. This rule might be subject to the exception that [permits use of quasi-reorganization].

3. Earned surplus [retained earnings] of a subsidiary company created prior to acquisition does not form a part of the consolidated earned surplus of the parent company and subsidiaries; nor can any dividend declared out of such surplus properly be credited to the income account of the parent company.

4. While it is perhaps in some circumstances permissible to show stock of a corporation held in its own treasury as an asset, if adequately disclosed, the dividends on stock so held should not be treated as a credit to the income account of the company.

5. Notes or accounts receivable due from officers, employees, or affiliated companies must be shown separately and not included under a general heading such as Notes Receivable or Accounts Receivable.[3]

The Institute submitted the committee's five principles for acceptance by its members in 1934, and they are now in ARB No. 43, *Restatement and Revision of Accounting Research Bulletins* (issued 1953), Chapter 1A, "Rules Adopted by Membership" [paragraphs 1–5].

The special committee's use of the word *principle* set the stage not only for the Institute's efforts to identify "accepted principles of accounting" but also for future confusion and controversy over what accountants mean when they use the word *principle*.

But Were They "Principles"?   The special committee's examples of broad principles of accounting were much less fundamental, timeless, and comprehensive than what most people perceive to be principles. They had little or nothing in them that made them more basic or less concrete than conventions or rules. Moreover, the special committee itself referred to them as rules in describing exceptions to them, the Institute characterized them as rules in submitting them for approval by its

---

[2] Audits of Corporate Accounts: Correspondence between the Special Committee on Cooperation with Stock Exchanges of the American Institute of Accountants and the Committee on Stock List of the New York Stock Exchange, 1932–1934 (New York: American Institute of Accountants, 1934), p. 7. Reprinted New York: American Institute of Certified Public Accountants, 1963, and in Stephen A. Zeff, Forging Accounting Principles in Five Countries: A History and an Analysis of Trends (Champaign, IL: Stipes Publishing, 1972), pp. 237–247.

[3] Ibid., p. 14. Lengthy exceptions in items 1 and 2 are summarized rather than quoted in full.

members, and the chairman of the special committee later conceded that they were nothing more than rules:

> When the committee . . . undertook to lay down some of the basic principles of modern accounting, it found itself unable to suggest more than half a dozen which could be regarded as generally acceptable, and even those were rules rather than principles, and were, moreover, admittedly subject to exception.[4]

Not surprisingly, the special committee's use of the word *principles* was soon challenged. In a contest sponsored by the Institute for its fiftieth anniversary celebration in 1937, Gilbert R. Byrne's essay entitled "To What Extent Can the Practice of Accounting Be Reduced to Rules and Standards?" won first prize for the best answer to the question posed in the title. He complained about accountants' propensity to downgrade principle by equating it with terms such as *rule, convention,* and *procedure.*

> [R]ecent discussions have used the term "accounting principles" to cover a conglomeration of accounting practices, procedures, conventions, etc.; many, if not most, so-called principles may merely have to do with methods of presenting items on financial statements or technique of auditing, rather than matters of fundamental accounting principle.[5]

Stephen Gilman made the same point in his careful analysis of terms in five chapters of his book, *Accounting Concepts of Profit.*

> With sublime disregard of lexicography, accountants speak of "principles," "tenets," "doctrines," "rules," and "conventions" as if they were synonymous.[6]

Gilman also quoted an excerpt from the *Century Dictionary* that he thought pertinent "because of the confusion noted in some accounting writings [about] the distinction between 'principle' and 'rule' ":

> There are no two words in the English language used so confusedly one for the other as the words *rule* and *principle.* You can make a *rule;* you cannot make a *principle;* you can lay down a *rule;* you cannot, properly speaking, lay down a *principle.* It is laid down for you. You can establish a *rule;* you cannot, properly speaking, establish a *principle.* You can only declare it. *Rules* are within your power, *principles* are not. A *principle* lies back of both *rules* and precepts; it is a general truth, needing interpretation and application to particular cases.[7]

Byrne, Gilman, and others pointed out that the form of accountant's report recommended by the special committee made accountants look foolish by requiring them to express opinions based on the existence of principles they actually could not specify. In that form of report, an accountant expressed the opinion that a client's financial statement is "fairly present, *in accordance with accepted principles of accounting consistently maintained by the company during the year under review,* its position . . . and the results of its operations." According to Byrne, that opinion presumed that accepted principles of accounting actually existed and accountants in general knew and agreed on what they were. In fact, "While there have been several attempts to enumerate [those principles], to date there has been no statement upon which there has been general agreement."[8]

That diagnosis was confirmed by Gilman as well as by Howard C. Greer:

> . . . the entire body of precedent [the "accepted principles of accounting"] has been taken for granted.

---

[4] George O. May, "Improvement in Financial Accounts," *Journal of Accountancy* (May 1937): 335.

[5] Gilbert R. Byrne, "To What Extent Can the Practice of Accounting Be Reduced to Rules and Standards?" *Journal of Accountancy* (November 1937): 366. Reprinted in Maurice Moonitz and A. C. Littleton, eds., *Significant Accounting Essays* (Englewood Cliffs, NJ: Prentice-Hall, 1965), pp. 103–115.

[6] Stephen Gilman, *Accounting Concepts of Profit* (New York: Ronald Press, 1939)–p. 169.

[7] Ibid., p. 188.

[8] Byrne, "To What Extent Can the Practice of Accounting Be Reduced to Rules and Standards?" p. 368.

It is as though each accountant felt that while he himself had never taken the time or the trouble to make an actual list of accounting principles, he was comfortably certain that someone else had done so....

[T]he accountants are in the unenviable position of having committed themselves in their certificates [reports] as to the existence of generally accepted accounting principles while between themselves they are quarreling as to whether there are any accounting principles and if there are how many of them should be recognized and accepted.[9]

There is something incongruous about the outpouring of thousands of accountants' certificates [reports] which refer to accepted accounting principles, and a situation in which no one can discover or state what those accepted accounting principles are. The layman cannot understand.[10]

Byrne argued that lack of agreement on what constituted accepted accounting principles resulted "in large part because there is no clear distinction, in the minds of many, between that body of fundamental truths underlying the philosophy of accounts which are properly thought of as *principles,* and the larger body of accounting rules, practices, and conventions which derive from principles, but which of themselves are not principles."[11] His prescription for accountants was to use *principle* in its most commonly understood sense of being more fundamental and enduring than rules and conventions.

If accounting, as an organized body of knowledge, has validity, it must rest upon a body of principles, in the sense defined in *Webster's New International Dictionary:*

"A fundamental truth; a comprehensive law or doctrine, from which others are derived, or on which others are founded; a general truth; an elementary proposition or fundamental assumption; a maxim; an axiom; a postulate." ...

Accounting principles, then, are the fundamental concepts on which accounting, as an organized body of knowledge, rests.... [T]hey are the foundation upon which the superstructure of accounting rules, practices and conventions is built.[12]

Gilman, in contrast, could find no principles that fit Byrne's definition. He concluded that most, if not all, of the propositions that had been put forth as principles of accounting should be relabeled "as doctrines, conventions, rules, or mere statements of opinion."[13] He called on accountants to admit that there were no accounting principles in the fundamental sense and to waste no more time and effort on attempts to identify and state them.

May's Attempts to Rectify "Considerable Misunderstanding."   In several articles and a book, George O. May responded to those and other criticisms of "accounting principles" and explained what the special committee, as well as several other Institute committees of which he was chairman, had done and why. He detected, in the criticisms and elsewhere, what he described as "considerable misunderstanding" of both the nature of financial accounting and the committees' work on accounting principles and thought it necessary to get the matter back on the right track.

Although he acknowledged that "in the correspondence the [special] Committee had used the words 'rules,' 'methods,' 'conventions,' and 'principles' interchangeably,"[14] May considered questions such as whether the propositions should be called rules or principles not to be matters "of any real importance." As Byrne had pointed out, if there were any principles that fit his definition, "they must be few in number and extremely general in character (such as 'consistency' and

---

[9] Gilman, *Accounting Concepts of Profit,* pp. 169 and 171.

[10] Howard C. Greer, "What Are Accepted Principles of Accounting?" *Accounting Review* (March 1938): 25.

[11] Byrne, "To What Extent Can the Practice of Accounting Be Reduced to Rules and Standards?" p. 368.

[12] Ibid., pp. 368 and 372.

[13] Gilman, *Accounting Concepts of Profit,* p. 257.

[14] May, *Financial Accounting,* p. 42.

'conservatism')."[15] Thus, they would afford less precise guidance than the more concrete principles illustrated by the special committee. Those who scolded the special committee for misusing "principles" had apparently forgotten that "accounting rules and principles are founded not on abstract theories or logic, but on utility."[16]

May urged the profession and others to focus efforts to improve financial accounting, as had the special committee, on the questions "of real importance"—the consequences of the necessarily conventional nature of accounting and the limitations of accounting reports. He explained the philosophy underlying the recommendation of the special committee and summarized that philosophy in the introductory pages of his book:

> In 1926, ... I decided to relinquish my administrative duties and devote a large part of my time to consideration of the broader aspects of accounting. As a result of that study I became convinced that a sound accounting structure could not be built until misconceptions had been cleared away, and the nature of the accounting process and the limitations on the significance of the financial statements which it produced were more frankly recognized.
>
> It became clear to me that general acceptance of the fact that accounting was utilitarian and based on conventions (some of which were necessarily of doubtful correspondence with fact) was an indispensable preliminary to real progress....
>
> Many accountants were reluctant to admit that accounting was based on nothing of a higher order of sanctity than conventions. However, it is apparent that this is necessarily true of accounting as it is, for instance, of business law. In these fields there are no principles, in the fundamental sense of that word, on which we can build; and the distinctions between laws, rules, standards, and conventions lie not in their nature but in the kind of sanctions by which they are enforced. Accounting procedures have in the main been the result of common agreement between accountants.[17]

He also reiterated and amplified a number of points the special committee had emphasized in *Audits of Corporate Accounts* concerning what the investing public already knew or should understand about financial accounting and reporting, such as, that because the value of a business depended mainly on its earning capacity, the income statement was more important than the balance sheet and should indicate to the fullest extent possible the earning capacity of the business during the period on which it reported; that because the balance sheet of a large modern corporation was to a large extent historical and conventional, largely comprising the residual amounts of expenditures or receipts after first determining a proper charge or credit to the income account for the year, it did not, and should not be expected to, represent an attempt to show the present values of the assets and liabilities of the corporation; and that because financial accounting and reporting was necessarily conventional, some variety in accounting methods was inevitable.

Special Committee's Definition of Principle.   May not only identified the definition of *principle* the special committee had used but also explained why it had chosen that particular meaning. In his comment on Byrne's essay, he recalled the committee's discussion and searching of dictionaries before choosing the "perhaps rather magniloquent word 'principle' ... in preference to the humbler 'rule.'" The definition of "principle" in the *Oxford English Dictionary* that came closest to defining the sense in which the special committee used the word was the seventh definition:

> A general law or rule adopted or professed as a guide to action; a settled ground or basis of conduct or practice.

---

[15] George O. May, "Principles of Accounting," *Journal of Accountancy* (December 1937): 424. (The article was a comment on Byrne's essay.)

[16] George O. May, "Terminology of the Balance Sheet," *Journal of Accountancy* (January 1942): 35.

[17] May, *Financial Accounting,* pp. 2 and 3.

The time and effort spent in searching dictionaries was fruitful—the committee found exactly the definition for which it was looking:

> [The]...sense of the word "principle" above quoted seemed...to fit the case perfectly. Examination of the report as a whole will make clear what the committee contemplated; namely, that each corporation should have a code of "laws or rules, adopted or professed, as a guide to action," and that the accountants should report, first, whether this code conformed to accepted usages, and secondly, whether it had been consistently maintained and applied.[18]

Thus, the special committee opted for the lofty *principle* rather than the more precise *rule* or *convention* because the definition that best fit the committee's needs was a definition of *principle,* albeit an obscure one, not a definition of *rule* or *convention.* Moreover, *rule* and *convention* carried unfortunate baggage:

> [The] word "rules" implied the existence of a ruling body which did not exist; the word "convention" was regarded as not appropriate for popular use and in the opinion of some would not convey an adequate impression of the authority of the precepts by which the accounts were judged.[19]

Principle, however, conveyed desirable implications:

> It used to be not uncommon for the accountant who had been unable to persuade his client to adopt the accounting treatment that he favored, to urge as a last resort that it was called for by "accounting principles." Often he would have had difficulty in defining the "principle" and saying how, why, and when it became one. But the method was effective, especially in dealing with those (of whom there were many) who regarded accounting as an esoteric but well established body of learning and chose to bow to its authority rather than display their ignorance of its rules. Obviously, the word "principle" was an essential part of the technique; "convention" would have been quite ineffective.[20]

Rules were elevated into principles because the committee thought it necessary to use a word with the force or power of *principle* to prevent the auditor's authority from being lost on the client.

(ii) The Best-Laid Schemes.　The special committee's program focused on what individual listed companies and their auditors would do. Each corporation would choose from "accepted principles of accounting" its own code of "laws or rules, adopted or professed, as a guide to action" and within that framework would be free to choose the methods and procedures most appropriate for its financial statements but would disclose the methods it was using and would apply them consistently. An auditor's report would include an opinion on whether or not each corporation's code consisted of accepted principles of accounting and was applied consistently. The Stock Exchange would enforce the program by requiring each listed corporation to comply in order to keep its listing.

The Institute was to sponsor or lead an effort in which accountants, lawyers, corporate officials, and other "qualified persons" would formulate a statement of "accepted principles of accounting" to guide listed companies and auditors, but it was not to get into the business of specifying those principles. The special committee had explicitly considered and rejected "the selection by competent authority out of the body of acceptable methods in vogue today [the] detailed sets of rules which would become binding on all corporations of a given class." The special committee also had avoided using *rule* because the word implied a rule-setting body that did not exist, and it had no intention of imposing on anyone what it considered to be an unnecessary and impossible burden. "Within quite

---

[18] May, "Principles of Accounting," pp. 423 and 424, emphasis added.
[19] May, *Financial Accounting,* p. 42.
[20] Ibid., p. 37.

wide limits, it is relatively unimportant to the investor what precise rules or conventions are adopted by a corporation in reporting its earnings if he knows what method is being followed and is assured that it is followed consistently from year to year."[21] Moreover, the committee felt that no single body could adequately assess and allow for the varying characteristics of individual corporations, and the choice of which detailed methods best fit a corporation's circumstances thus was best left to each corporation and its auditors. Because financial accounting was essentially conventional and required estimates and allocations of costs and revenues to periods, the utility of the resulting financial statements inevitably depended significantly on the competence, judgment, and integrity of corporate management and independent auditors. Although there had been a few instances of breach of trust or abuse of investors, the committee had confidence in the trustworthiness of the great majority of those responsible for financial accounting and reporting.

In the end, the special committee's recommendations were never fully implemented. Nonaccountants were not invited to participate in developing a statement of accepted accounting principles. In fact, although the Institute submitted the special committee's five principles for acceptance by its members, it attempted no formulation of a statement of broad principles, even by accountants. Nor did the Exchange require its listed companies to disclose their accounting methods.

Special Committee's Heritage.   The only recommendation to survive was that each company should be permitted to choose its own accounting methods within a framework of "accepted principles of accounting." The committee's definition of *principle* also survived, and "accepted principles of accounting" became "generally accepted."

The special committee's definition of *principle* — "A general law or rule adopted or professed as a guide to action; a settled ground or basis of conduct or practice" — was incorporated verbatim in Accounting Research Bulletin No. 7, *Report of the Committee on Terminology* (George O. May, chairman), in 1940, but it was attributed to the *New English Dictionary* rather than to the *Oxford English Dictionary*. When ARB 1–42 were restated and revised in 1953, the same definition of "principle," by then attributed only to "Dictionaries," was carried over to Accounting Terminology Bulletin No. 1, *Review and Résumé.*

"Generally" was added to the special committee's "accepted principles of accounting" in *Examination of Financial Statements by Independent Public Accountants,* published by the Institute in 1936 as a revision of an auditing publication, *Verification of Financial Statements* (1929). According to its chairman, Samuel J. Broad, the revision committee inserted "generally" to answer questions such as ". . . accepted by whom? business? professional accountants? the SEC? I heard of one accountant who claimed that if a principle was accepted by him and a few others it was 'accepted.' "[22]

In retrospect, the legacy of institutionalizing that definition of principle has been that the terms *principle, rule, convention, procedure,* and *method* have been used interchangeably, and imprecise and inconsistent usage has hampered the development and acceptance of subsequent efforts to establish accounting principles. Moreover, within the context of so broad a definition of *principle,* the combination of the latitude given management in choosing accounting methods, the failure to incorporate into financial accounting and reporting the discipline that would have been imposed by the profession's adopting a few, broad, accepted accounting principles, and the failure to enforce the requirement that companies disclose their accounting methods gave refuge to the continuing use of many different methods and procedures, all justified as "generally accepted principles of accounting," and encouraged the proliferation of even more "generally accepted" accounting methods.

Finally, despite the reluctance of the Institute to become involved in setting principles or rules, it eventually assumed that responsibility after the U.S. SEC was created.

---

[21] *Audits of Corporate Accounts,* pp. 8 and 9.
[22] Zeff, *Forging Accounting Principles in Five Countries,* p. 129.

(iii) Securities Acts and the Securities and Exchange Commission—"Substantial Authoritative Support."
The Securities Exchange Act of 1934 established the SEC and gave it authority to prescribe accounting and auditing practices to be used by companies in the financial reports required of them under that Act and the Securities Act of 1933. The SEC, like the Stock Exchange before it, became increasingly concerned about the variety of accounting practices approved by auditors. Carman G. Blough, first Chief Accountant of the SEC, told a round-table session at the Institute's fiftieth anniversary celebration in 1937 that unless the profession took steps to develop a set of accounting principles and reduce the areas of difference in accounting practice, "the determination of accounting principles and methods used in reports to the Commission would devolve on the Commission itself. The message to the profession was clear and unambiguous."[23]

In April 1938, the Chief Accountant issued Accounting Series Release (ASR) No. 4, *Administrative Policy on Financial Statements,* requiring registrants to use only accounting principles having "substantial authoritative support." That made official and reinforced Blough's earlier message: If the profession wanted to retain the ability to determine accounting principles and methods, the Institute would have to issue statements of principles that could be deemed to have "substantial authoritative support." Through ASR 4, the Commission reserved the right to say what had "substantial authoritative support" but also opened the way to give that recognition to recommendations on principles issued by the Institute.

(b) COMMITTEE ON ACCOUNTING PROCEDURE, 1938–1959. The Institute expanded significantly its Committee on Accounting Procedure (not principles) and gave it responsibility for accounting principles and authority to speak on them for the Institute—to issue pronouncements on accounting principles without the need for approval of the Institute's membership or governing Council. The committee was intended to be the principal source of the "substantial authoritative support" for accounting principles sought by the SEC.

The president of the Institute was the nominal chairman of the Committee on Accounting Procedure. Its vice chairman and guiding spirit was George O. May.

(i) No Comprehensive Statement of Principles by the Institute. The course the committee would follow for the next 20 years was set at its initial meeting in January 1939. Carman G. Blough, who had left the Commission and become a partner of Arthur Andersen & Co. and who was a member of the committee, recounted in a paper at a symposium at the University of California at Berkeley in 1967 how the committee chose its course:

> At first it was thought that a comprehensive statement of accounting principles should be developed which would serve as a guide to the solution of the practical problems of day to day practice....
>
> After extended discussion it was agreed that the preparation of such a statement might take as long as five years. In view of the need to begin to reduce the areas of differences in accounting procedures before the SEC lost patience and began to make its own rules on such matters, it was concluded that the committee could not possibly wait for the development of such a broad statement of principles.[24]

The committee thus decided that the need to deal with particular problems was too pressing to permit it to spend time and effort on a comprehensive statement of principles.

Statements of Accounting Principles by Others. Although the Institute attempted no formulation of a statement of broad accounting principles, two other organizations did. Both statements were written by

---

[23] Ibid., p. 134.

[24] Carman G. Blough, "Development of Accounting Principles in the United States," *Berkeley Symposium on the Foundations of Financial Accounting* (Berkeley: Schools of Business Administration, University of California, 1967), pp. 7 and 8.

professors, and each was an early representative of one of the two schools of thought about the nature and derivation of accounting principles.

American Accounting Association's Theoretical Basis for Accounting Rules And Procedures. "A Tentative Statement of Accounting Principles Underlying Corporate Financial Statements," by the Executive Committee of the American Accounting Association (AAA) in 1936, was based on the assumption "that a corporation's periodic financial statements should be continuously in accord with a single coordinated body of accounting theory."[25] The phrase *Accounting Principles Underlying Corporate Financial Statements* emphasized that improvement in accounting practice could best be achieved by strengthening the theoretical framework that supported practice. The "Tentative Statement" was almost completely ignored by the Institute, and its effect on accounting practice at the time was minimal. However, two of its principles (one a corollary of the other) and a monograph by W. A. Paton and A. C. Littleton based on it proved to have long-lasting influence and are described shortly.

Sanders, Hatfield, and Moore's Codification of Accounting Practices. In contrast to the AAA's attempt to derive a coordinated body of accounting theory, *A Statement of Accounting Principles,* by Thomas Henry Sanders, Henry Rand Hatfield, and Underhill Moore, two professors of accounting and a professor of law, respectively, was a compilation through interviews, discussions, and surveys of "the current practices of accountants" and reflected no systematic theoretical foundation. It was prepared under sponsorship of the Haskins & Sells Foundation and was published in 1938 by the Institute, which distributed it to all Institute members as "a highly valuable contribution to the discussion of accounting principles."

The report was excoriated for its virtually exclusive reliance on experience and current practice as the basis for principles, its reluctance to criticize even the most dubious practices, and its implication that accountants had no greater duty than to ratify whatever management wanted to do with its accounting as long as what it did was legal and properly disclosed. Many, perhaps most, of the characteristics criticized were inherent in what the authors were asked to do—formulate a code of accounting principles based on practice and the weight of opinion and authority. Even so, the report tended to strike a dubious balance between auditors' independence and duty to exercise professional judgment on the one hand and their deference to management on the other.

It was, nevertheless, "the first relatively complete statement of accounting principles and the only complete statement reflecting the school of thought that accounting principles are found in what accountants do." It was a successful attempt to codify the methods and procedures that accountants used in everyday practice and "was in fact a 'distillation of practice.' "[26] Moreover, since the Committee on Accounting Procedure adopted and pursued the same view of principles and incorporated existing practice and the weight of opinion and authority in its pronouncements, *A Statement of Accounting Principles* probably was a good approximation of what the committee would have produced had it attempted to codify existing "accepted principles of accounting."

Sets of Principles by Individuals. Three less ambitious efforts in 1937 and 1938—eight principles in Gilbert R. Byrne's prize-winning essay,[27] nine accounting principles and conventions in D. L. Trouant's book *Financial Audits,*[28] and six accounting principles in A. C. Littleton's "Tests for Principles"[29]—provided examples, rather than complete statements, of principles. Each described what *principles* meant and gave some propositions to illustrate the nature of principles or to show how propositions could be judged to be accepted principles. The resulting principles were

---

[25] Page 188 of the "Tentative Statement," which was published in *Accounting Review* (June 1936): 187–191. Reprinted in *Accounting and Reporting Standards for Corporate Financial Statements and Preceding Statements and Supplements* (Iowa City, IA: American Accounting Association, 1957, pp. 60–64.

[26] Reed K. Storey, *The Search for Accounting Principles* (New York: American Institute of Certified Public Accountants, 1964), p. 31. Reprinted (Houston, TX: Scholars Book Company, 1977).

[27] Byrne, "To What Extent Can the Practice of Accounting Be Reduced to Rules and Standards?" p. 372.

[28] D. L. Trouant, *Financial Audits* (New York: American Institute Publishing Co., 1937), pp. 5–7.

[29] A. C. Littleton, "Tests for Principles," *Accounting Review* (March 1938): 16–24.

substantially similar to those of the special committee. For example, all three authors included the conventions that revenue usually should be realized (recognized) at the time of sale and that cost of plant should be depreciated over its useful life. An interesting exception was Trouant's first principle—"Everything having a value has a claimant"—and the accompanying explanation: "In this axiom lies the basis of double-entry bookkeeping and from it arises the equivalence of the balance-sheet totals for assets and liabilities."[30] That proposition not only was more fundamental than most principles of the time but also was distinctive in referring to the world in which accounting takes place rather than to the accounting process.

Principles from Resolving Specific Problems.   None of those five efforts to state principles of accounting seems to have had much effect on practice, although Sanders, Hatfield, and Moore's *A Statement of Accounting Principles* may indirectly have affected the decision of the Committee on Accounting Procedure to tackle specific accounting problems first: "[A]nyone who read it could not fail to be impressed with the wide variety of procedures that were being followed in accounting for similar transactions and in that way undoubtedly it helped to point up the need for doing something to standardize practices."[31]

In any event, the Committee on Accounting Procedure decided that to formulate a statement of broad accounting principles would take too long and elected instead to use a problem-by-problem approach in which the committee would recommend one or more alternative procedures as preferable to other alternatives for resolving a particular financial accounting or reporting problem. The decision to resolve pressing and controversial matters that way was described by members of the committee as "a decision to put out the brush fires before they created a conflagration."[32]

(ii) Accounting Research Bulletins.   The committee's means of extinguishing the threatening fires were the ARB. From September 1939 through August 1959 it issued 51 ARBs on a variety of subjects. Among the most important or most controversial (or both) were No. 2, *Unamortized Discount and Redemption Premium on Bonds Refunded* (1939); No. 23, *Accounting for Income Taxes* (1944); No. 24, *Accounting for Intangible Assets* (1944); No. 29, *Inventory Pricing* (1947); No. 32, *Income and Earned Surplus* [*Retained Earnings*] (1947); No. 33, *Depreciation and High Costs* (1947); No. 37, *Accounting for Compensation in the Form of Stock Options* (1948); No. 40 and No. 48, *Business Combinations* (1950 and 1957); No. 47, *Accounting for Costs of Pension Plans* (1956); and No. 51, *Consolidated Financial Statements* (1959).

Each ARB described one or more accounting or reporting problems that had been brought to the committee's attention and identified accepted principles (conventions, rules, methods, or procedures) to account for the item(s) or otherwise to solve the problem(s) involved, sometimes describing one or more principles as preferable. Because each Bulletin dealt with a specific practice problem or a set of related problems, the committee developed or approved accounting principles (to use the most common descriptions) case by case, ad hoc, or piecemeal.

Piecemeal Principles Based on Practice, Experience, and General Acceptance.   As a result of the way the committee operated and the bases on which it decided issues before it, the ARB became classic examples of George O. May's dictum that "the rules of accounting, even more than those of law, are the product of experience rather than of logic."[33] Despite having "research" in the name, the ARBs, rather than being the product of research or theory, were much more the product of existing practice, the collective experience of the members of the Committee on Accounting Procedure, and the need to be generally accepted.

Since the committee had not attempted to codify a comprehensive statement of accounting principles, it had no body of theory against which to evaluate the conventions, rules, and procedures that it considered. Although individual ARBs sometimes reflected one or more theories apparently

---

[30] Trouant, *Financial Audits,* p. 5.

[31] Blough, "Development of Accounting Principles in the United States," p. 7.

[32] Ibid., p. 8.

[33] May, *Financial Accounting,* p. vii.

suggested or applied by individual members or agreed on by the committee, as a group they reflected no broad, internally consistent, underlying theory. On the contrary, they often were criticized for being inconsistent with each other. The committee used the word "consistency" to mean that a convention, rule, or procedure, once chosen, should continue to be used in subsequent financial statements, not to mean that a conclusion in one Bulletin did not contradict or conflict with conclusions in others.

The most influential unifying factor in the ARBs as a group was the philosophy that underlay *Audits of Corporate Accounts,* a group of propositions that May and the Special Committee on Cooperation with Stock Exchanges had described as pragmatic and realistic—not theoretical and logical. For example, the Bulletins clearly were based on the propositions that the income statement was far more important than the balance sheet; that financial accounting was primarily a process of allocating historical costs and revenues to periods rather than of valuing assets and liabilities; that the particular rules or conventions used were less significant than consistent use of whichever ones were chosen; and that some variety in accounting conventions and rules, especially in the methods and procedures for applying them to particular situations, was inevitable and desirable.

Most of the work of the Committee on Accounting Procedure, like that of most Institute committees, was done by its members and their partners or associates, and the ARBs reflected their experience. The experience of Carman G. Blough also left its mark on the Bulletins after he became the Institute's first full-time director of research in 1944. The Institute had established a small research department with a part-time director in 1939, which did some research for the committee but primarily performed the tasks of a technical staff, such as providing background and technical memoranda as bases for the Bulletins and drafting parts of proposed Bulletins. Committee members and their associates did even more of the committee's work as the research department also began to provide staff assistance to the Committee on Auditing Procedure in 1942 and then increasingly became occupied with providing staff assistance to a growing number (44 at one time) of other technical committees of the Institute.

The accounting conventions, rules, and procedures considered by the Committee on Accounting Procedure and given its stamp of approval as principles in an ARB were already used in practice, not only because the committee had decided to look for principles in what accountants did but also because only principles that were already used were likely to qualify as "generally accepted." General acceptance was conferred by use, not by vote of the committee. Each Bulletin, beginning with ARB 4 in December 1939, carried this note about its authority: "Except in cases in which formal adoption by the Institute membership has been asked and secured, the authority of the bulletins rests upon the general acceptability of opinions . . . reached."

The committee was authorized by the Institute to issue statements on accounting principles, which the Institute expected the SEC to recognize as providing "substantial authoritative support," but the committee had no authority to require compliance with the Bulletins. It could only add a warning to each Bulletin "that the burden of justifying departure from accepted procedures must be assumed by those who adopt other treatment."

The committee's reliance on general acceptability of principles developed or approved case by case, ad hoc, or piecemeal invited challenges to its authority whenever it tried either to introduce new accounting practices or to proscribe existing practices. Moreover, although the SEC also dealt with accounting principles case by case, ad hoc, or piecemeal, its power to say which accounting principles had substantial authoritative support—its own version of general acceptability—limited what the committee could do without the Commission's concurrence.

Challenges to the Committee's Authority.   The Committee on Accounting Procedure introduced interperiod income tax allocation in ARB No. 23, *Accounting for Income Taxes* (December 1944). The reason it gave for changing practice was that "income taxes are an expense that should be allocated, when necessary and practicable, to income and other accounts, as other expenses are allocated. What the income statement should reflect . . . is the [income tax] expense properly allocable to the income included in the income statement for the year" (page 186 [fourth page of ARB 23], carried over with some changes to ARB No. 43, *Restatement and Revision of Accounting Research Bulletins* (June 1953), Chapter 10B, "Income Taxes," paragraph 4).

A committee of the New Jersey Society of Certified Public Accountants reviewed ARB 23 soon after its issue and questioned whether the new procedures it recommended were "accepted procedures" at the date of its issue. General acceptability, the committee contended, depended on the extent to which procedures were applied in practice, which only time would tell. The committee proposed that the Institute submit a new Bulletin to a formal vote a year after issue because approval of a Bulletin by more than 90 percent of its members would demonstrate its general acceptability and authority.[34]

The Institute ignored the proposal, but the New Jersey committee had in effect challenged the authority of the Committee on Accounting Procedure to change accounting practice, raising an issue that would not go away. The Institute's Executive Committee or its governing council found it necessary to reaffirm the committee's authority a number of times in the following years,[35] and in the committee's final year its authority to change practice was challenged in court, again on a matter involving income tax allocation. Three public utilities, subsidiaries of American Electric Power, Inc., sought to enjoin the Committee on Accounting Procedure from issuing a letter dated April 15, 1959, interpreting a term in ARB No. 44 (revised), *Declining-Balance Depreciation* (July 1958).

> The object of the letter was to express the Committee's view that the "deferred credit" used in tax-allocation entries was a liability and not part of stockholders' equity. The three plaintiff corporations alleged that classification of the account as a liability would cause them "irreparable injury, loss and damage." They also claimed that the letter was being issued without the Committee's customary exposure, thus not allowing interested parties to comment. The Federal District Court ruled against the plaintiffs. An appeal to the Second Circuit Court of Appeals was lost, the Court saying inter alia, "We think the courts may not dictate or control the procedures by which a private organization expresses its honestly held views." Certiorari was denied by the U.S. Supreme Court, and the committee's letter was issued shortly thereafter [July 9, 1959].[36]

Neither the Institute's repeated reconfirmations of the committee's status nor its success in court corrected the weaknesses inherent in accounting principles whose authority rested on their general acceptability. The Institute did not finally face up to the problem until almost two decades later when the authority of the APB was challenged on another income tax matter—accounting for the investment credit.

Influence of the Securities and Exchange Commission. Because accounting principles in the ARBs would be acceptable in SEC filings only if the Commission deemed them to have "substantial authoritative support," two committees of the Institute carefully cultivated a working relationship with the Commission to try to ensure that the Bulletins met that condition. The Committee on Cooperation with the SEC met regularly with the SEC's accounting staff and occasionally with the Commissioners. The Committee on Accounting Procedure and the director of research met with representatives of the SEC as needed and took great pains to keep the Chief Accountant informed about the committee's work, not only sending him copies of drafts of proposed Bulletins but also seeking his comments and criticisms and, if possible, his concurrence. Efforts to secure his agreement usually were successful.[37]

---

[34] "Comments on 'Accounting for Income Taxes,'" A Statement by the Committee on Accounting Principles and Practice of the New Jersey Society of Certified Public Accountants, *Journal of Accountancy* (March 1945): pp. 235–240.

[35] Zeff, *Forging Accounting Principles in Five Countries,* pp. 160–167.

[36] Ibid., p. 166.

[37] Ibid., pp. 150 and 151; Blough, "Development of Accounting Principles in the United States," pp. 8 and 9. Carman G. Blough, first Chief Accountant of the SEC (1935–1938), became a charter member of the Committee on Accounting Procedure and later became the first full-time director of research of the Institute. Chief Accountants during the life (1938–1959) of the Committee on Accounting Procedure were William W. Wentz (1938–1947), Earle C. King (1947–1956), and Andrew Barr (1956–1972), whose term also included most of the life (1959–1973) of the committee's successor, the Accounting Principles Board.

Some differences of opinion between the Committee on Accounting Procedure and the Commission were inevitable, of course, but they were the exception rather than the rule. Most disagreements were settled amicably, as was the long-running disagreement over the current operating performance and all-inclusive or clean surplus theories of income. The committee and the Commission sometimes were able to work out a compromise solution. The committee often adopted the Commission's view, at least once withdrawing a proposed Accounting Research Bulletin because of the Commission's opposition and at other times apparently being discouraged from issuing Bulletins by the Commission. The Commission occasionally adopted the committee's view or at least delayed issue of its own accounting releases pending issue of a Bulletin by the Institute.

The Commission affected accounting practice indirectly through its influence on the ARB. It also directly exercised its power to say whether or not a set of financial statements filed with it met the statutory requirements by means of rulings and orders, some published but most private.

The Commission published some formal rules, mostly on matters of disclosure rather than accounting principles. For example, the first regulations promulgated by the newly formed SEC required income statements to disclose sales and cost of goods sold, information that many managements had long considered to be confidential. Over 600 companies, about a quarter of those required to file registration statements in mid-1935, risked delisting of their securities by refusing to disclose publicly the required information. The Commission granted hearings to a significant number of them and also heard arguments of security analysts, investment bankers, and other users of financial statements that the information was necessary. The Commission then "notified all of the companies affected that the information was necessary for a fair presentation and that this need overcame any arguments that had been advanced against it."[38]

The companies had little choice but to comply, and the effect of the rule was to put reporting of sales and cost of sales in the United States decades ahead of most of the rest of the world. The controversy surrounding initial application of the rule subsided, and reporting sales and cost of goods sold has been common practice for so long that few people now know of its once controversial nature or of the Commission's part in promulgating it.

The Commission largely exercised its power behind the scenes through informal rulings and orders in "deficiency letters" on registrants' financial statements. The recipient of a deficiency letter could decide either to amend the financial statements to comply with the SEC's ruling or go to Washington to try to convince the staff, and anyone else at the Commission who would listen, of the merits of the accounting that the staff had challenged. If that informal conference process failed to produce agreement, a registrant could do little except comply or withdraw the registration and forgo issuing the securities. The only appeal to the Commission of a staff ruling on an accounting issue was in the form of a hearing to determine whether a stop order should be issued to prevent the registration from becoming effective because it contained misrepresentations—in effect "a hearing to determine whether or not [the registrant was] about to commit a fraud . . . . [Since b]usinessmen who have any reputation do not put themselves in the position of putative swindlers merely to determine matters of accounting,"[39] those private administrative rulings effectively settled most accounting questions.

The SEC's far-reaching rule that assets must never be accounted for at more than their cost was promulgated in that way. "[N]either the Securities and Exchange Commission nor the accounting profession issued rules or guidelines directly proscribing write-ups [of assets] or supplemental disclosures of current values. The change was brought about by the intervention of the SEC's staff, who 'discouraged' both practices through informal administrative procedures."[40] "[T]he SEC took a stand from the very beginning . . . . establish[ing] its position so early [that] we often overlook

---

[38] Blough, "Development of Accounting Principles in the United States," p. 10.

[39] A. A. Berle Jr., "Accounting and the Law," *Accounting Review* (March 1938): 12. Reprinted in *Journal of Accountancy* (May 1938): 372.

[40] R. G. Walker, "The SEC's Ban on Upward Asset Revaluations and the Disclosure of Current Values," *Abacus* (March 1992): 3 and 4.

the fact that in [the basis for accounting for assets] the Commission never gave the profession a chance to even consider the matter insofar as registrants are concerned."[41]

In the sense that the commission's role has long been forgotten or unknown, experience with the cost rule was similar to that of the rule requiring disclosure of sales and cost of sales. But the similarity ended there. The cost rule involved accounting principle rather than disclosure. And, instead of subsiding as did resistance to the disclosure rule, controversy surrounding the cost rule intensified and in the years following the Second World War led to a major and long-lasting division within the Institute.

Because of widespread concern about the effects on financial statements of the high rate of inflation during the war and the greatly increased prices of replacing assets after the war, the Institute had created the Study Group on Business Income, financed jointly with the Rockefeller Foundation. Its report concluded that financial statements could be meaningful only if expressed in units of equal purchasing power. It advocated accounting that reflected the effects of changes in the general level of prices on the cost of assets already owned and the resulting costs and expenses from their use,[42] a change in accounting considered necessary by many Institute leaders and members.

While the Study Group was still at work, the Committee on Accounting Procedure, supported by many other Institute leaders and members and by the SEC, issued ARB No. 33, *Depreciation and High Costs* (December 1947), which rejected "price-level depreciation" and suggested instead that management annually appropriate net income or retained earnings in contemplation of replacing productive facilities at higher price levels. The Bulletin effectively blocked use of depreciation in excess of that based on cost in measuring net income that had been contemplated or adopted by a few large companies but also provoked an active opposition to the committee's action.

Prominent among those who criticized the committee for in effect applying the SEC's cost rule instead of facing up to the accounting problems caused by the effects of changes in the general price level was George O. May,[43] who had been instrumental in creating the Study Group on Business Income. He served as consultant to and then as a member of the group and later would be a joint author of its report. He criticized the committee's action for prejudging and undermining the Study Group's efforts, thereby foreclosing any real discussion of "the relation between changes in the price level and the concept of business income."[44] He considered ARB 33 to be, however, only one of a number of missteps over the following decade that showed that the committee had lost its way. He also criticized the committee, among other things, for failing to cast aside outmoded conventions in favor of others more consonant with the changed conditions in the economy and for adopting public utility accounting procedures such as the Federal Power Commission's "original (or predecessor) cost"—cost to the corporate or natural person first devoting the property to the public service rather than cost to the present owner—that the committee itself earlier had held to be contrary to generally accepted accounting principles.[45]

Despite the criticisms, the committee held its course, though not without some wavering. It twice considered issuing a Bulletin approving upward revaluations of assets but each time dropped the attempt in the face of the unequivocal opposition of the SEC. Although the number of dissents to the cost rule increased each time the committee revisited the question of changing price levels,

---

[41] Blough, "Development of Accounting Principles in the United States," p. 10.

[42] *Changing Concepts of Business Income,* Report of the Study Group on Business Income (New York: Macmillan, 1952), pp. 1–4, 103–109.

[43] George O. May, "Should the LIFO Principle Be Considered in Depreciation Accounting When Prices Vary Widely?" *Journal of Accountancy* (December 1947): 453–456.

[44] George O. May, "Income Accounting and Social Revolution," *Journal of Accountancy* (June 1957): 38.

[45] John Lawler, "A Talk with George O. May," *Journal of Accountancy* (June 1955): 41–45; George O. May, "Business Combinations: An Alternative View," *Journal of Accountancy* (April 1957): 33–36; and an unpublished memorandum dictated by May in 1958 and quoted in Paul Grady, ed., *Memoirs and Accounting Thought of George O. May* (New York: Ronald Press, 1962), pp. 277–279.

the committee "was unable to marshal a two-thirds majority in favor of a new policy"[46] and in 1958 dropped the subject from its agenda.

Whether it was influencing accounting practice directly through publishing rules or establishing them in informal rulings and private conferences with registrant companies or indirectly through the Committee on Accounting Procedure, the SEC generally seems to have had its way.

Decision to Issue Principles Piecemeal Reaffirmed.   The Committee on Accounting Procedure had to deal ad hoc with the SEC's comments on and objections to its Bulletins, issued or proposed, because it had no comprehensive statement of principles on which to base responses to the Commission's own ad hoc comments and rulings. Although the committee had decided early not to take the time required to develop a statement of broad principles on which to base solutions to practice problems (p. 2–12), the need for a comprehensive statement or codification of accounting principles continued to be raised occasionally, and the committee periodically revisited the question. Each time it decided against a project of that kind.

One of those occasions was in 1949, when the committee reconsidered its earlier decision and began work on a comprehensive statement of accounting principles. Ultimately, however, it again abandoned the project as not feasible and instead in 1953 issued ARB 43, *Restatement and Revision of Accounting Research Bulletins.* ARB 43 superseded the first 42 ARBs, except for three that were withdrawn as no longer applicable and eight that were reports of the Committee on Terminology and were reviewed and published separately in Accounting Terminology Bulletin No. 1, *Review and Résumé.* Although ARB 43 brought together the earlier Bulletins and grouped them by subject matter, "this collection retained the original flavor of the bulletins, i.e., a group of separate opinions on different subjects."[47]

Thus, the decision of the Committee on Accounting Procedure at its first meeting to put out brush fires as they flared up rather than to codify accepted accounting principles to provide a basis for solving financial accounting and reporting problems set the course that the committee pursued for its entire 21-year history. All 51 ARBs reflected that decision.

Influence of the American Accounting Association.   During the 21 years that the Committee on Accounting Procedure was issuing the ARBs, the AAA revised its 1936 "Tentative Statement of Accounting Principles Underlying Corporate Financial Statements" in 1941, 1948, and 1957, including eight Supplementary Statements to the 1948 Revision. In the "Tentative Statement," as already noted, the executive committee of the AAA emphasized that improvement in accounting practice could best be achieved by strengthening the theoretical framework that supported practice and attempted to formulate a comprehensive set of concepts and standards from which to derive and by which to evaluate rules and procedures. Principles were not merely descriptions of procedures but standards against which procedures might be judged.

The executive committee of the Association, like the committees of the Institute concerned with accounting principles, regarded the principles as being derived from accounting practice, although the means of derivation differed—distillation or compilation according to the Institute and theoretical analysis according to the Association. Thus, the "Tentative Statement" set forth 20 principles, each a proposition embodying "a corollary of this fundamental axiom":

> Accounting is . . . not essentially a process of valuation, but the allocation of historical costs and revenues to the current and succeeding fiscal periods. [p. 188]

Although the AAA's intent was to emphasize accounting's conceptual underpinnings, the "Tentative Statement" was substantially less conceptual and more practice oriented than might appear, not only because its principles were derived from practice but also because its "fundamental axiom" was essentially a description of existing practice. The same description of accounting was inherent in the report of the Special Committee on Cooperation with Stock Exchanges, was voiced by

---

[46] Zeff, *Forging Accounting Principles in Five Countries,* pp. 155–157 and 165–166.
[47] Storey, *The Search for Accounting Principles,* p. 43.

George O. May at the annual meeting of the Institute in October 1935[48] and was evident in most of the ARBs.

That the principles in the Statements of the AAA were significantly like those in the ARBs should come as no surprise. "Inasmuch as both the Institute and the Association subscribed to the same basic philosophy regarding the nature of income determination, it was more or less inevitable that they should reach similar conclusions, even though they followed different paths."[49]

The AAA's 1941 and 1948 revisions generally continued in the direction set by the 1936 "Tentative Statement." Some changes began to appear in some of the Supplementary Statements to the 1948 Revision and in the 1957 Revision. They probably were too late, however, to have had much effect on the ARBs, even if the Committee on Accounting Procedure had paid much attention.

Long-lasting influence on accounting practice of the "Tentative Statement," as noted earlier, came some time after it was issued and mostly indirectly through two of its principles on "all-inclusive income" (one a corollary of the other) and a monograph by W. A. Paton and A. C. Littleton.

"All-Inclusive Income" versus "Avoiding Distortion of Periodic Income." "A Tentative Statement of Accounting Principles Underlying Corporate Financial Statements" strongly supported what was later called the *all-inclusive income* or *clean surplus theory*. The principle (No. 8, p. 189), which gave the theory one of its names, was that an income statement for a period should include all revenues, expenses, gains, and losses properly recognized during the period "regardless of whether or not they are the results of operations in that period." The corollary (No. 18, p. 191), which gave the theory its other name, was that no revenues, expenses, gains, or losses should be recognized directly in earned surplus (retained earnings or undistributed profits).

The SEC later strongly supported that accounting, and it became a bone of contention between the SEC and the Committee on Accounting Procedure. The committee generally favored the "current operating performance" theory of income, which excluded from net income extraordinary and nonrecurring gains and losses "to avoid distorting the net income for the period." The disagreement broke into the open with the issue of ARB No. 32, *Income and Earned Surplus* [Retained Earnings] (December 1947), whose publication in the January 1948 issue of *The Journal of Accountancy* was accompanied by a letter from SEC Chief Accountant Earle C. King saying that the "Commission has authorized the staff to take exception to financial statements which appear to be misleading, even though they reflect the application of Accounting Research Bulletin No. 32 (p. 25)." Two more Bulletins, ARB No. 35, *Presentation of Income and Earned Surplus* (October 1948), and ARB No. 41, *Presentation of Income and Earned Surplus (Supplement to Bulletin No. 35)* (July 1951), followed as the committee and the SEC tried to work out a number of compromises. Each effort proved unsatisfactory to one or both parties.

Years later the APB would adopt an all-inclusive income statement in APB Opinion No. 9, *Reporting the Results of Operations* (December 1966). That accounting and reporting has since been modified by admitting some significant exceptions, primarily by FASB Statement No. 12, *Accounting for Certain Marketable Securities* (December 1975),[50] and FASB Statement No. 52, *Foreign Currency Translation* (December 1981). Thus, net income reported under current generally accepted accounting principles cannot accurately be described as all-inclusive income, but the idea of all-inclusive income is still generally highly regarded, and many still see it as a desirable goal to which to return.

---

[48] George O. May, "The Influence of Accounting on the Development of an Economy," *Journal of Accountancy* (January 1936): 15.

[49] Storey, *The Search for Accounting Principles,* p. 45.

[50] FASB Statement No. 12 was superseded by FASB Statement No. 115, *Accounting for Certain Investments in Debt and Equity Securities* (May 1993), which retained the provision requiring that unrealized holding gains and losses on certain securities be excluded from net income and directly added to or deducted from equity.

"Matching of Costs and Revenues" and "Assets Are Costs."   Two members of the AAA executive committee that issued "A Tentative Statement of Accounting Principles Underlying Corporate Financial Statements" in 1936 undertook to write a monograph to explain its concepts. The result, *An Introduction to Corporate Accounting Standards,* by W. A. Paton and A. C. Littleton (1940), easily qualifies as the academic writing that has been most influential in accounting practice. Although the monograph rejected certain existing practices—such as last in, first out (LIFO) and cost or market, whichever is lower—it generally rationalized existing practice, providing it with what many saw as a theoretical basis that previously had been lacking.

The monograph accepted two of the premises that underlay the ARBs: (1) that periodic income determination was the central function of financial accounting—"the business enterprise is viewed as an organization designed to produce income"[51]—and (2) that (in the words of the "fundamental axiom" of the AAA's 1936 "Tentative Statement") accounting was "not essentially a process of valuation, but the allocation of historical costs and revenues to the current and succeeding fiscal periods."

> The fundamental problem of accounting, therefore, is the division of the stream of costs incurred between the present and the future in the process of measuring periodic income. The technical instruments used in reporting this division are the income statement and the balance sheet....
> The income statement reports the assignment [of costs] to the current period; the balance sheet exhibits the costs incurred which are reasonably applicable to the years to come.[52]

The monograph described the periodic income determination process as the "matching of costs and revenues," giving it not only a catchy name but also strong intuitive appeal—a process of relating the enterprise's efforts and accomplishments. The corollary was that most assets were "deferred charges to revenue," costs waiting to be "matched" against future revenues:

> The factors acquired for production which have not yet reached the point in the business process where they may be appropriately treated as "cost of sales" or "expense" are called "assets," and are presented as such in the balance sheet. It should not be overlooked, however, that these "assets" are in fact "revenue charges in suspense" awaiting some future matching with revenue as costs or expenses.

> The common tendency to draw a distinction between cost and expense is not a happy one, since expenses are also costs in a very important sense, just as assets are costs. "Costs" are the fundamental data of accounting....

> The balance sheet thus serves as a means of carrying forward unamortized acquisition prices, the not-yet-deducted costs; it stands as a connecting link joining successive income statements into a composite picture of the income stream.[53]

Not surprisingly, those who had supported the accounting principles developed in the ARBs but were uncomfortable with those principles' apparent lack of theoretical support found highly attractive the theory that "matching costs and revenues" not only determined periodic net income but also justified the practice of accounting for most assets at their historical costs or an unamortized portion thereof.

However, just as the institutionalizing of a broad definition of accounting principles had caused problems for the Committee on Accounting Procedure itself and later for the APB, the institutionalizing of "matching costs with revenues," "costs are assets," and "avoiding distortion of periodic income" also caused problems for the FASB in developing a conceptual framework for financial accounting and reporting. The FASB found those expressions not only to be ingrained in accountants' vocabularies and widely used as reasons for or against particular accounting or reporting

---

[51] W. A. Paton and A. C. Littleton, *An Introduction to Corporate Accounting Standards* (Ann Arbor, MI: American Accounting Association, 1940), p. 23.

[52] Ibid., p. 67.

[53] Ibid., pp. 25 and 67.

procedures but also to be generally vague, highly subjective, and emotion laden. They have proven to be of minimal help in actually resolving difficult accounting issues.

(iii) Failure to Reduce the Number of Alternative Accounting Methods. The Institute's effort aimed at improving accounting by reducing the number of acceptable alternatives probably did improve accounting by culling out some "bad" practices.

> There are those who seem to believe that very little progress has been made towards the development of accounting principles and the narrowing of areas of differences in the principles followed in practice.
>
> It is difficult for me to see how anyone who has knowledge of accounting as it was practiced during the first quarter of this century and how it is practiced today can fail to recognize the tremendous advances that have taken place in the art.[54]

A number of the practices for whose acceptance Sanders, Hatfield, and Moore's *Statement of Accounting Principles* had been lambasted[55] had disappeared by about 1950. It is uncertain, however, how much of that improvement was due to the ARBs and how much to other factors, such as the good professional judgment of corporate officials or auditors or the SEC's rejection of some egregious procedures.

Ironically, the end result was an overabundance of "good" practices that had survived the process. That plethora of sanctioned alternatives for accounting for similar transactions continued to thrive despite the committee's charge to reduce the number of alternative procedures because, just as Will Rogers never met a man he didn't like, the committee rarely met an accounting principle it didn't find acceptable.

> Two factors contributed to the increase in the number of accepted alternatives: (1) the committee on accounting procedure failed to make firm choices among alternative procedures, and (2) the committee was clearly reluctant to condemn widely used methods even though they were in conflict with its recommendations. For example, in its very first pronouncement on a specific problem—unamortized discount and redemption premium on refunded bonds [ARB 2] the committee considered three possible procedures, of which it rejected one and accepted two.
>
> The committee had a clear preference—it praised the method of amortization of cost over the remaining life of the old bonds as consistent with good accounting thinking regarding the relative importance of the income statement and the balance sheet. It condemned immediate writeoff as a holdover of balance-sheet conservatism which was of "dubious value if attained at the expense of a lack of conservatism in the income account, which is far more significant" [ARB 2, p. 13]. Nevertheless, the latter method had "too much support in accounting theory and practice and in the decisions of courts and commissions for the committee to recommend that it should be regarded as unacceptable or inferior." [ARB 2, p. 20]
>
> ... The solution turned out to be a "live-and-let-live" policy. The major thing accomplished by the bulletin was the elimination of a method [amortization over the life of the new issue] which was not widely used anyway. And this type of solution was characteristic of the bulletins, rather than exceptional.
>
> The extreme to which this attitude was sometimes carried is exemplified in the Institute's inventory bulletin [ARB 29], a classic example of trying to please everyone. The committee accepted almost every conceivable inventory [pricing] procedure, except the discredited base-stock method. The committee therefore passed up the opportunity to narrow the range of acceptable alternative procedures in the area of inventory [pricing].... Instead, the individual practitioner was left with

---

[54] Blough, "Development of Accounting Principles in the United States," p. 12.
[55] The report contained statements to the effect that (1) impairments of net worth in the form of catastrophic losses might be listed on the asset side, (2) deficits of new companies might be shown as assets, (3) capital losses might be carried as deferred charges if charging them against the income of a single period would distort profit, etc. Storey, *The Search for Accounting Principles,* p. 30.

the high-sounding but useless admonition that the method chosen should be the one which most clearly reflected periodic income.[56]

The proliferation of accepted alternative principles was probably inherent in an approach that championed disclosure and consistency in use of procedures over specific principles and consistency between principles.

Most of the controversial subjects covered by the ARB came back to haunt the Committee on Accounting Procedure's successor, the APB. The case-by-case, ad hoc, or piecemeal approach produced few lasting solutions to financial accounting and reporting problems.

(c) ACCOUNTING PRINCIPLES BOARD—1959–1973. The American Institute of Accountants changed its name to the American Institute of Certified Public Accountants in June 1957, and in October of that year the new president of the AICPA, Alvin R. Jennings, proposed that the Institute reorganize its efforts in the area of accounting principles.[57] His recommendation came at a time when the Committee on Accounting Procedure was under fire for, among other things, failing to reduce the number of alternative accounting procedures. A growing number of Institute members sensed that the committee's firefighting approach to accounting principles had gone about as far as it could and expressed an urgent need for the committee to abandon that effort and to do what it had theretofore been reluctant to do—formulate or codify a comprehensive statement of accounting principles.

Jennings called for an increased research effort to reexamine the basic assumptions of accounting and to develop authoritative statements to guide accountants. He appointed a Special Committee on Research Program, and its report, *Organization and Operations of the Accounting Research Program and Related Activities,* in December 1958, provided the basis for the organization of an APB and an Accounting Research Division. The committee set a lofty goal:

> The general purpose of the Institute in the field of financial accounting should be to advance the written expression of what constitutes generally accepted accounting principles, for the guidance of its members and others. This means something more than a survey of existing practice. It means continuing effort to determine appropriate practice and to narrow the areas of difference and inconsistency in practice. In accomplishing this, reliance should be placed on persuasion rather than on compulsion. The Institute, however, can, and it should, take definite steps to lead in the thinking on unsettled and controversial issues.[58]

The APB in September 1959 replaced the Committee on Accounting Procedure as the senior technical committee of the Institute with responsibility for accounting principles and authority to issue pronouncements on accounting principles without the need for approval of the Institute's membership or governing Council. The Board's 18 members were members of the Institute, and thus CPAs, who, like members of the Committee on Accounting Procedure, continued their affiliations with their firms, companies, and universities while serving without compensation on the Board.

The APB was originally envisioned as the instrument through which a definitive statement of accounting principles would finally be achieved—what the Wheat Report later would call a

---

[56] Storey, *The Search for Accounting Principles,* pp. 49 and 50.

[57] Alvin R. Jennings, "Present-Day Challenges in Financial Reporting," *Journal of Accountancy* (January 1958): 28–34. Reprinted in Stephen A. Zeff, *The Accounting Postulates and Principles Controversy of the 1960s* (New York: Garland Publishing, 1982).

[58] "Report to Council on the Special Committee on Research Program," *Journal of Accountancy* (December 1958): 62 and 63. Reprinted in *Organization and Operations of the Accounting Research Program and Related Activities* (New York: American Institute of Certified Public Accountants, 1959); in Zeff, *Forging Accounting Principles in Five Countries,* pp. 248–265; and in Zeff, *The Accounting Postulates and Principles Controversy of the 1960s.*

"'grand design' of accounting theory upon which all else would rest."[59] The report of the Special Committee on Research Program in 1958 outlined a hierarchy of postulates, principles, and rules to guide the APB's work:

> The broad problem of financial accounting should be visualized as requiring attention at four levels: first, postulates; second, principles; third, rules or other guides for the application of principles in specific situations; and fourth, research.
>
> Postulates are few in number and are the basic assumptions on which principles rest. They necessarily are derived from the economic and political environment and from the modes of thought and customs of all segments of the business community. The profession . . . should make clear its understanding and interpretation of what they are, to provide a meaningful foundation for the formulation of principles and the development of rules or other guides for the application of principles in specific situations . . . .
>
> A fairly broad set of co-ordinated accounting principles should be formulated on the basis of the postulates. The statement of this probably should be similar in scope to the statements on accounting and reporting standards issued by the American Accounting Association. The principles, together with the postulates, should serve as a framework of reference for the solution of detailed problems.
>
> Rules or other guides for the application of accounting principles in specific situations, then, should be developed in relation to the postulates and principles previously expressed. Statements of these probably should be comparable as to subject matter with the present accounting research bulletins. They should have reasonable flexibility.
>
> Adequate accounting research is necessary in all of the foregoing.[60]

The report of the Special Committee on Research Program contemplated that the APB would quickly concern itself with providing the conceptual context from which would flow the rules or procedures to be applied in specific situations. The APB would then use the postulates and principles in choosing between alternate rules and procedures to narrow the areas of difference and inconsistency in practice.

(i) Postulates and Principles.   Following that prescription, the new Accounting Research Division published Accounting Research Study No. 1, *The Basic Postulates of Accounting,* by Maurice Moonitz in 1961, and Accounting Research Study No. 3, *A Tentative Set of Broad Accounting Principles for Business Enterprises,* by Robert T. Sprouse and Maurice Moonitz in 1962. Accounting Research Studies (ARSs) were not publications of the APB and thus did not constitute official Institute pronouncements on accounting principles. On the authority of the Director of Accounting Research, Maurice Moonitz, they were issued for wide exposure and comment.

In an article entitled "Why Do We Need 'Postulates' and 'Principles'?" Moonitz explained that postulates and principles were necessary to give accounting "the integrating structure it needs to give more than passing meaning to its specific procedures. It will provide 'experience' with the aid it needs from 'logic' to explain why it is that some procedures are appropriate and others are not."[61] An integrating structure would provide accounting with a mechanism by which to rid itself of procedures that clearly were not in harmony with the authoritatively stated principles.

---

[59] *Establishing Financial Accounting Standards,* Report of the Study on Establishment of Accounting Principles (New York: American Institute of Certified Public Accountants, March 29, 1972), p. 15. Often called the Wheat Report, after the group's chairman, Francis M. Wheat, a former SEC commissioner.

[60] "Report to Council of the Special Committee on Research Program," p. 63.

[61] Maurice Moonitz, "Why Do We Need 'Postulates' and 'Principles'?" *Journal of Accountancy* (December 1963): 46. Reprinted in Zeff, *The Accounting Postulates and Principles Controversy of the 1960s.*

Among the most significant contributions of those ARSs was their development of the terms postulates and principles, especially postulates, which Moonitz explained in his article:

> "[P]ostulates" is used . . . to denote those basic propositions of accounting which describe the accountant's understanding of the world in which he lives and acts. The propositions are therefore generalizations about the environment of accounting, generalizations based upon a more or less comprehensive view and understanding of that environment. The term "principles" is used to denote those basic propositions which stem from the postulates and refer expressly to accounting issues.[62]

To qualify as a postulate, a proposition had to meet two conditions: It must be "self-evident," an assertion about the environment in which accounting functions that is universally accepted as valid; and it must be "fruitful for accounting," that is, it must "relate to (be inferred from) a world that does exist and not to one that is a fiction." Moonitz also noted that self-evident is not, as some who commented on ARS 1 seemed to have believed, the same as trivial.[63] An example from ARS 1 to which he referred made his point: "Most of the goods and services that are produced are distributed through exchange, and are not directly consumed by the producers" (Postulate A-2. Exchange). In that straightforward observation lie the reasons that accounting is concerned with production and distribution of goods and services and with exchange prices; if it is further observed that most exchanges are for cash, the reasons that accounting is concerned with cash prices and cash flows become apparent. As Moonitz observed, the "proposition is an extraordinarily fruitful one for accounting."[64]

Emphasis on a basis for accounting principles comprising self-evident propositions about the real-world environment in which accounting functions, and on which it reports, constituted a significant shift in thinking. Accountants' earlier emphasis, largely in a conceptual vacuum, had been on the conventional nature of accounting and the resulting necessity for conventional procedures, allocations, opinion, and judgment to produce the numbers in income statements and balance sheets. That emphasis provided an unstable and uncertain basis for accounting principles.

> Accounting is often described as "conventional" in nature, and its principles as "conventions." The two terms, conventions and conventional, are ambiguous; the statement that accounting is conventional may be true or false depending on which meaning is intended. It is true if it refers to such things as the use of Arabic numerals, the use of the dollar sign, or the sequence in which assets, liabilities, revenues, and expenses are listed in financial statements because other symbols and forms could be used to convey precisely the same message. It is not true if the statement means that any proposition which accountants accept is a valid one. As a farfetched example, assume that all uninsured losses, without exception, were to be converted into "assets" by the expedient of calling them "deferred charges against future operations." This convention would not make assets out of losses; it would merely give the approval of accountants to a false assertion concerning the enterprise that suffered the losses, and would place accountants and accounting in an unfavorable light in the eyes of those who knew what had happened.
>
> Suppose, however, that the assertion about accounting principles as "conventions" is intended to convey the idea that they are generalizations, inferences drawn from a large body of data, and that they are not intended to be literal descriptions of reality. "Conventions" and "conventional" are clearly valid descriptions, then, but not because accounting is unique. Instead, accounting is like every other field of human endeavor in this one respect: Its basic propositions are generalizations or abstractions and not minute descriptions of every aspect of "reality."[65]

---

[62] Ibid., p. 43.

[63] Ibid., pp. 44 and 45.

[64] Maurice Moonitz, *The Basic Postulates of Accounting, Accounting Research Study No. 1* (New York: American Institute of Certified Public Accountants, 1961), p. 22. Reprinted in Zeff, *The Accounting Postulates and Principles Controversy of the 1960s.*

[65] Moonitz, "Why Do We Need 'Postulates' and 'Principles'?" pp. 45 and 46.

Postulates that were self-evident propositions about the real world and also fruitful for account-ing were needed to provide a solid basis for accounting principles and rules—"a platform from which to start," "a place to stand"—and "a place to stand" was prerequisite to real improvement in accounting practice. "Failure by accountants to agree on a 'place to stand' will mean continued operation in mid-air, as unstable and uncertain in the future as in the past."[66]

In the more than 30 years since the two studies were published, their valuable contributions to accounting thought increasingly have been recognized. Some of the conclusions and recommen-dations of ARS 3, *A Tentative Set of Broad Accounting Principles for Business Enterprises,* such as use of replacement costs of inventories and plant and equipment and accounting for the effects of changes in the general price level, have remained controversial and still are largely unaccept-able to many accountants. In contrast, most of the conclusions of ARS 1, *The Basic Postulates of Accounting,* long ago became commonplace in accounting literature. For example, the basic idea that the foundation for accounting principles lies in self-evident propositions about the environment in which accounting functions was incorporated into APB Statement No. 4, *Basic Concepts and Accounting Principles Underlying Financial Statements of Business Enterprises,* in 1970. By 1975 that basic idea had become an essential part of the FASB's conceptual framework.

When ARS 3 was published in April 1962, however, each copy contained a Statement of the Accounting Principles Board (later designated APB Statement No. 1) passing judgment on both studies: "The Board believes . . . that while these studies are a valuable contribution to accounting thinking, they are too radically different from present generally accepted accounting principles for acceptance at this time."

It was not the APB's finest hour. Even though general dissatisfaction with the state of existing practice had been the reason for the APB's creation and the new emphasis on research, the Board and many others reacted as if they had been caught by surprise that the studies recommended some significant changes in existing practice. Moreover, instead of letting consideration of the studies follow the anticipated course of wide circulation and exposure and receipt of comments from interested readers before the Board considered the studies, the Board reacted first, spoiling any opportunity of receiving unbiased comments on the studies. The experience seems to have adversely affected for years the Board's approach to postulates and principles.

The experience may have made the APB "disillusioned with, or at least skeptical toward, the potential that fundamental or 'theoretical' research might have for solving accounting problems. . . . [T]he Board seemed to abandon the hope of the Special Committee on Research Program that such research could serve as a foundation for pronouncements on accounting principles."[67] In any event, the Board did little or nothing more on accounting postulates and principles until 1965, except to authorize the project that in March 1965 became ARS No. 7, *Inventory of Generally Accepted Accounting Principles,* by Paul Grady, the second Director of Accounting Research. In 1965, the Board renewed efforts on fundamental matters—which it then called basic concepts and principles rather than postulates and principles—to comply with recommendations to the Institute's governing Council by the Special Committee on Opinions of the Accounting Principles Board (the Seidman Committee), but most Board members seemed to lack enthusiasm for the effort.

By the summer of 1962, when the Board hoped that it had put behind it the fuss over the postulates and principles studies, three years had passed since an Institute committee had issued a pronouncement on accounting principles. The Board turned its attention from postulates and prin-ciples and toward solving specific problems, just as had the Committee on Accounting Procedure.

(ii) The Accounting Principles Board, the Investment Credit, and the Seidman Committee.   When the Board decided to tackle the thorny issue of accounting for the investment credit, which was enacted in federal income tax law for the first time in October 1962, it inadvertently created an ideal scenario for fueling doubts about its effectiveness and authority. The law provided that a company acquiring a depreciable asset other than a building could deduct up to 7 percent of the cost of the asset from its

---

[66] Ibid., p. 45.

[67] Zeff, *Forging Accounting Principles in Five Countries,* pp. 177 and 178.

income tax otherwise payable in the year the asset was placed in service. Two accounting methods sprang up—the "flow-through" method, by which the entire reduction in tax was included in income of the year the asset was placed in service, and the "deferral" method, by which the tax reduction was included in net income over the productive life of the acquired property.

APB Opinion No. 2, *Accounting for the "Investment Credit,"* was issued in December 1962, setting forth the Board's choice of the deferral over the flow-through method. Some of the large accounting firms then popularly called the Big Eight almost immediately made it known that they would not expect their clients to abide by the Opinion. The SEC ruled that both methods had substantial authoritative support, making either acceptable and thereby effectively undercutting the Board's position. Fifteen months later, the Board issued APB Opinion No. 4 (Amending No. 2), *Accounting for the "Investment Credit,"* reaffirming its opinion that the investment credit should be accounted for by the deferral method. It recognized, however, the inevitable effect of the SEC's action on the authority of APB Opinion No. 2:

> [T]he authority of Opinions of this Board rests upon their general acceptability. The Board, in the light of events and developments occurring since the issuance of Opinion No. 2, has determined that its conclusions as there expressed have not attained the degree of acceptability which it believes is necessary to make the Opinion effective.
>
> In the circumstances the Board believes that . . . the alternative method of treating the credit as a reduction of Federal income taxes of the year in which the credit arises is also acceptable. [paragraphs 9 and 10]

The APB's authority had been severely undermined. Did APB Opinions still have to pass the test of general acceptance, as did the ARB before them, or did they constitute generally accepted accounting principles solely because the APB had issued them? The Board voted to bring the matter to the Executive Committee and the governing Council of the AICPA.

In May 1964, after an extended and heated debate, Council adopted a resolution "that it is the sense of this Council that [audit] reports of members should disclose material departures from Opinions of the Accounting Principles Board." Pursuant to a directive in the resolution, the Institute formed a Special Committee on Opinions of the Accounting Principles Board to suggest ways of implementing the resolution and to review the entire matter of the status of APB Opinions and the development of accounting principles and practices for financial reporting.

The special committee reported to Council on its first charge in October 1964, and Council adopted a resolution and transmitted it to Institute members in a Special Bulletin, *Disclosure of Departures from Opinions of the Accounting Principles Board.* It declared that members of the Institute should see to it that a material departure from APB Opinions (or from ARBs still in effect)—even if the auditor concluded that the departure rested on substantial authoritative support—was disclosed in notes to the financial statements or in the auditor's report. Since Council adopted recommendations that "1. 'Generally accepted accounting principles' are those principles which have substantial authoritative support [and] 2. Opinions of the APB constitute 'substantial authoritative support,'" the authority of APB Opinions no longer depended on their passing a separate test of general acceptability.

The special committee, commonly referred to as the Seidman Committee after its second chairman, J. S. Seidman,[68] reported to Council on its second charge in May 1965, reiterating that an authoritative identification of generally accepted accounting principles was essential if an independent CPA was to fulfill his or her primary function of attesting to the conformity of financial statements with generally accepted accounting principles. Its Recommendation No. 1 was that:

> At the earliest possible time, the [Accounting Principles] Board should:
>
> **a.** Set forth its views as to the purposes and limitations of published financial statements . . . .
> **b.** Enumerate and describe the basic concepts to which accounting principles should be oriented.

---

[68] The first chairman, William W. Werntz, died shortly after the special committee reported to Council on its first charge.

c. State the accounting principles to which practices and procedures should conform.

d. Define such phrases in the auditor's report as "present fairly" and "generally accepted accounting principles." ...

e. Define the words of art employed by the profession, such as "substantial authoritative support," "concepts," "principles," "practices," "procedures," "assets," "liabilities," "income," and "materiality."[69]

The committee made that recommendation acknowledging that the Special Committee on Research Program had contemplated that the APB would have accomplished the task described by that time in its life, but it exculpated the Board: "This planned course ran into difficulty because current problems commanded attention and could not be neglected."[70]

However, the need for a solid conceptual foundation for accounting no longer could be neglected either:

[I]t remains true that until the basic concepts and principles are formulated and promulgated, there is no official bench mark for the premises on which the audit attestation stands. Nor is an enduring base provided by which to judge the reasonableness and consistency of treatment of a particular subject. Instead, footing is given to controversy and confusion.[71]

... Accounting, like other professions, makes use of words of art. Since accounting talks to the public, the profession's meaning, as distinguished from the literal dictionary meaning, must be explained to the public.

For example, ...

What is meant by the expression "generally accepted accounting principles"? How is "generally" measured? What are "accounting principles"? Where are they inscribed, and by whom? ...

By "accepted," is the profession aiming at what is popular or what is right? There may be a difference. The ... Special Committee on Research Program said that "what constitutes generally accepted accounting principles ... means more than a survey of existing practice."

Then again, "accepted" by whom—the preparer of the financial statement, the profession, or the user?[72]

The profession has said that generally accepted accounting principles are those with "substantial authoritative support." What does that expression mean? What yardstick is to be applied to the words "substantial" and "authoritative"? What are the guidelines to prevent mere declaration, or use by someone, somewhere, from becoming the standard?

Many other expressions in accounting need explanation and clarification for the public. They include such words as "concepts," "principles," "practices," "procedures," "assets," "liabilities," "income," and "materiality."

Until the profession deals with all these matters satisfactorily, first for itself and then for understanding by the consumer of its product, there will continue to be an awkward failure of communication in a field where clear communication is vital.[73]

Accounting Principles Board Statement No. 4. Issued in October 1970, APB Statement No. 4, *Basic Concepts and Accounting Principles Underlying Financial Statements of Business Enterprises,* was the Board's response to the Seidman Committee's recommendations. For those who had hoped for definitive answers to the Seidman Committee's questions or a statement of accounting's fundamental concepts and principles, APB Statement No. 4 was a disappointment. The Board gave

---

[69] *Report of Special Committee on Opinions of the Accounting Principles Board* (New York: American Institute of Certified Public Accountants, Spring 1965), p. 12.

[70] Ibid., p. 13.

[71] Ibid.

[72] Ibid., pp. 13 and 14.

[73] Ibid., p. 15.

every indication of having issued it primarily to comply, somewhat grudgingly, with the Seidman Committee's recommendations.

The definition of generally accepted accounting principles in APB Statement No. 4 and its description of their nature and how they become accepted, although couched in the careful language that characterized the Statement, merely reiterated what the Institute had been saying about them for over 30 years.

> Generally accepted accounting principles incorporate the consensus* at a particular time as to...[the items that should be recognized in financial statements, when they should be recognized, how they should be measured, how they should be displayed, and what financial statements should be provided].
>
> ...Generally accepted accounting principles encompass the conventions, rules, and procedures necessary to define accepted accounting practice at a particular time.... includ[ing] not only broad guidelines of general application, but also detailed practices and procedures.
>
> Generally accepted accounting principles are conventional—that is, they become generally accepted by agreement (often tacit agreement) rather than by formal derivation from a set of postulates or basic concepts. The principles have developed on the basis of experience, reason, custom, usage, and, to a significant extent, practical necessity.[74]

---

*Inasmuch as generally accepted accounting principles embody a consensus, they depend on notions such as *general acceptance* and *substantial authoritative support,* which are not precisely defined....

Generally accepted accounting principles were a mixture of conventions, rules, procedures, and detailed practices that were distilled from experience and identified as principles primarily by observing existing accounting practice.

The basic concepts in Chapters 3 to 5 of APB Statement No. 4 were a mixed bag. On one hand, the definitions of assets, liabilities, and other "basic elements of financial accounting" were what George J. Staubus, who gave the Statement a generally positive review, called the Definitions Mess. All of the definitions were defective because the only essential distinguishing characteristic of assets (or liabilities) was that they were "recognized and measured as assets [or liabilities] in conformity with generally accepted accounting principles," and the other definitions depended on the definitions of assets and liabilities.[75]

On the other hand, the basic concepts also included new ideas (at least for Institute pronouncements) and normative propositions, and at least some of the concepts looked to what financial accounting ought to be in the future, not just to what it already was. These are examples:

- The basic purpose of financial accounting is to provide information that is useful to owners, creditors, and others in making economic decisions (paragraphs 40 and 73).
- Financial accounting is shaped to a significant extent by the nature of economic activity in individual business enterprises (paragraph 42).
- The transactions and other events that change an enterprise's resources, obligations, and residual interest include exchange transactions, nonreciprocal transfers, and other external events as well as production and other internal events (paragraph 62).
- Certain qualities or characteristics such as relevance, understandability, verifiability, neutrality, timeliness, comparability, and completeness make financial information useful (paragraphs 23 and 87–105).

---

[74] *Basic Concepts and Accounting Principles Underlying Financial Statements of Business Enterprises,* Statement of the Accounting Principles Board No. 4 (New York: American Institute of Certified Public Accountants, 1970), paragraphs 137–139.
[75] George J. Staubus, "An Analysis of APB Statement No. 4," *Journal of Accountancy* (February 1972): 39.

- To make comparisons between enterprises as meaningful as possible, "differences between enterprises' financial statements should arise from basic differences in the enterprises themselves or from the nature of their transactions and not merely from differences in financial accounting practices and procedures" (paragraph 101).

Anyone familiar with the report of the Trueblood Study Group on objectives of financial statements and the FASB's conceptual framework will recognize that those and similar ideas later appeared in one or both of those sources.

Nevertheless, in describing itself, APB Statement No. 4 virtually ignored that it contained anything that was new, normative, or forward-looking, emphasizing instead that it looked only at the present and the past, even in describing its basic concepts. The Board was adamant that it had not passed judgment on the existing structure and apparently was almost equally reluctant to admit that it had broken new ground:

> The Statement is primarily descriptive, not prescriptive. It identifies and organizes ideas that for the most part are already accepted . . . . [T]he Statement contains two main sections that are essentially distinct—(a) Chapters 3–5 on the environment, objectives, and basic features of financial accounting and (b) Chapters 6–8 on present generally accepted accounting principles. The description of present generally accepted accounting principles is based primarily on observation of accounting practice. Present generally accepted accounting principles have not been formally derived from the environment, objectives, and basic features of financial accounting [that is, from the basic concepts.]*

> The aspects of the environment selected for discussion are those that appear to influence the financial accounting process directly. The objectives of financial accounting and financial statements discussed are goals toward which efforts *are presently directed.* [Emphasis added.] The accounting principles described are those that the Board believes are generally accepted *today.* *The Board has not evaluated or approved present generally accepted accounting principles except to the extent that principles have been adopted in Board Opinions. Publication of this Statement does not constitute approval by the Board of accounting principles that are not covered in its Opinions.* [Emphasis in the original.] [paragraphs 3 and 4]

---

*For some unexplained reason, the Statement does not use the term *basic concepts* after defining it in paragraph 1: "The term basic concepts is used to refer to the observations concerning the environment, the objectives of financial accounting and financial statements, and the basic features and basic elements of financial accounting discussed in Chapters 3–5 of the Statement" (paragraph 1, footnote 2). The rest of the Statement uses instead the full definition in footnote 2 or, as in this sentence, some shorter variation of it.

The expected contribution of the basic concepts in the Statement was generally vague, and still in the future.

> The Statement is a step toward development of a more consistent and comprehensive structure of financial accounting and of more useful financial information. It is intended to provide a framework within which the problems of financial accounting may be solved, although it does not propose solutions to those problems and does not attempt to indicate what generally accepted accounting principles should be. Evaluation of present accounting principles and determination of changes that may be desirable are left to future pronouncements of the Board. [paragraph 6]

Those paragraphs seemed to deflate unduly the most laudable parts of the Statement, almost as if the Board had gone out of its way to disparage the effort or otherwise to lower expectations about it. Instead of emphasizing that APB Statement No. 4 had begun to lay a basis for delineating what accounting ought to be and suggesting positive steps needed to build on it, the Board chose to characterize the Statement as primarily descriptive, thereby casting it into the category of uncritical description of what accounting already was. Once again, accounting principles had been defined as being essentially the product of experience.

However, there were by then too many people within and outside the profession who could no longer be satisfied with that view of accounting principles. Principles distilled from experience could lead only so far, and that point had long since been reached. For 15 to 20 years, principles distilled from experience had created more problems than they had solved, and a growing number of people interested in accounting principles had become convinced that principles had to be defined to mean a higher order of things than conventions or procedures. Dissatisfaction with the APB's performance in this area was mounting, and there was increasing pressure for the Board to state "the objectives of financial statements" as a basis for moving forward.

(iii) End of the Accounting Principles Board. At the same time, the APB was constantly under pressure from the SEC and others to confront current, specific problems encountered in practice and to issue Opinions on subjects seemingly far removed from the domain of principles, such as the presumed overstating of sales prices in some real estate sales with long-term financing, accounting for nonmonetary transactions, and reporting the effects of disposing of a segment of a business.

The SEC's urgency to deal with specific practice problems and widespread criticism of the use of the pooling of interests method influenced the APB and its staff to expend extra effort to produce an opinion on a highly controversial subject—accounting for business combinations—on which the Accounting Research Division had completed two related ARS: No. 5, *A Critical Study of Accounting for Business Combinations,* by Arthur R. Wyatt, and No. 10, *Accounting for Goodwill,* by George R. Catlett and Norman O. Olson.

Although the Board worked diligently and analyzed the problems about as well as could be expected in the absence of postulates and principles or other conceptual foundation, it became hopelessly deadlocked. It could find no solutions acceptable to a two-thirds majority to the problems of choosing between the purchase and pooling of interests methods for accounting for a business combination and of whether and how to capitalize goodwill and, if capitalized, whether to amortize it. Yet, it felt compelled to issue an Opinion because the SEC was almost certain to issue its own rule if the APB failed to do so.

The experience produced two Opinions in 1970, APB Opinion No. 16, *Business Combinations,* and No. 17, *Intangible Assets,* as well as more intense criticism of, and threats of legal action against, the Board. In a section entitled "Opinions 16 and 17—Vesuvius Erupts," Stephen A. Zeff reported that neither the Board's "hard-won compromise" nor the "'pressure-cooker' manner in which it was achieved" pleased anyone. "These two Opinions, perhaps more than any other factor, seem to have been responsible for a movement to undertake a comprehensive review of the procedure for establishing accounting principles."[76]

In January 1971, AICPA president Marshall S. Armstrong convened a conference to consider how the Institute might improve the process of establishing accounting principles, and two study groups were appointed to explore ways of improving financial reporting. The group chaired by Francis M. Wheat was formed to "examine the organization and operation of the APB and [to] determine what changes are necessary to attain better results faster."[77] The Wheat Group was primarily concerned with the processes and means by which accounting principles should be established. The Accounting Objectives Study Group, under the chairmanship of Robert M. Trueblood, was organized to review the objectives of financial statements and the technical problems in achieving those objectives.

The APB's days were numbered, although that was not yet clear, and perhaps not even suspected, in 1971, and the Board went on with its work. It issued almost half of its total of 31 Opinions after wheels were put in motion to develop an alternative structure that would eventually replace it.

Despite the criticisms the APB received for Opinions Nos. 16 and 17 and others and although some of its Opinions provided only partial solutions that would need to be revisited in the future, on balance its Opinions were successful. In several problem areas, the APB succeeded in remedying, sometimes almost completely and often to a significant degree, the greatest ill of the time by

---

[76] Zeff, *Forging Accounting Principles in Five Countries,* p. 216.

[77] *Establishing Financial Accounting Standards,* p. 87.

carrying out the charge it received at its creation: "to determine appropriate practice and to narrow the areas of difference and inconsistency in practice."[78] APB Opinions such as No. 9, *Reporting the Results of Operations;* No. 18, *The Equity Method of Accounting for Investments in Common Stock;* and No. 20, *Accounting Changes,* laid to rest long-standing controversies. APB Opinion No. 22, *Disclosure of Accounting Policies,* required implementation in 1972 of one of the key recommendations made in *Audits of Corporate Accounts* in 1932: Each company would disclose which methods it was using. Some of the most controversial APB Opinions—such as No. 5, *Reporting of Leases in Financial Statements of Lessee;* No. 8, *Accounting for the Cost of Pension Plans;* No. 11, *Accounting for Income Taxes;* No. 16, *Business Combinations;* No. 17, *Intangible Assets;* No. 21, *Interest on Receivables and Payables;* and No. 26, *Early Extinguishment of Debt*—caused some consternation and often fierce opposition, but both industry and public accountants learned to live with them, and later the FASB encountered opposition when it proposed changing some of them.

The report of the Wheat Group in March 1972, *Establishing Financial Accounting Standards,* concluded that many of the APB's problems were fatal flaws. The APB was weakened by nagging doubts about its independence, the inability of its part-time members to devote themselves entirely to the important problems confronting it, and the lack of coherence and logic of many of its pronouncements, which resulted from having to compromise too many opposing points of view. The group's solution was directed toward remedying those flaws, which, in its opinion, required a new arrangement.

The Wheat Report proposed establishment of a Financial Accounting Foundation, with trustees whose principal duties would be to appoint the members of a FASB and to raise funds for its operation. The Board would comprise seven members, all of whom would be salaried, full time, and unencumbered by other business affiliations during their tenure on the Board, and some of whom would not have to be CPAs. The group recommended "Standards" Board rather than "Principles" Board because

> the APB (despite the prominence in its name of the term "principles") has deemed it necessary throughout its history to issue opinions on subjects which have almost nothing to do with "principles" in the usual sense [which "connotes things basic and fundamental, of a sort which can be expressed in few words, relatively timeless in nature, and in no way dependent upon changing fashions in business or the evolving needs of the investment community"].[79]

"Standard"—which connotes something established by authority or common consent as a pattern or model for guidance or a basis of comparison for judging quality, quantity, grade, level, and so on, and may need to be spelled out in some detail—was more descriptive than "principles" for most of what the APB did and what the FASB was expected to do.

The Wheat Group's diagnosis of the APB's terminal condition became the popular explanation, but it was not the only one. Oscar S. Gellein, a member of the APB during its final years and a member of the FASB during its early years, offered a perceptive analysis:

> The conditions most often identified with the problems of the APB were perceived conflicts of interests causing a waffling of positions and part-time effort where full-time effort was needed. In retrospect, those probably were not as significant as the absence of a structure of fundamental notions that would elevate the level at which debate begins and provide assurance of considerable consistency to the standards pronounced. The APB repetitively argued fundamentals. The same fundamentals were argued in taking up projects near the end of its tenure as were argued in connection with early projects. Even the most fundamental of fundamentals—assets, liabilities, revenue, expense—were never defined nor could the definitions be inferred from APB pronouncements.[80]

---

[78] "Report to Council of the Special Committee on Research Program," pp. 62 and 63.
[79] Ibid., p. 13.
[80] Oscar S. Gellein, "Financial Reporting: The State of Standard Setting," *Advances in Accounting, Vol. 3,* Bill N. Schwartz, ed. (Greenwich, CT: JAI Press, 1986), p. 13.

Thus, it may have been the Board's continual rejection of the ineluctable need to develop an underlying philosophy as a basis for accounting principles in favor of the Committee on Accounting Procedure's "brush fire" approach that most directly contributed to the way it was perceived and ultimately to its demise. The APB had never been able to achieve a consensus on the conceptual aspects of its work, which had effectively been pushed aside by the Board's efforts to narrow the areas of difference in accounting practice by a problem-by-problem treatment of pressing issues. Although the ARS on basic postulates and broad principles of accounting and APB Statement No. 4 had made conceptual contributions that would prove fruitful in the hands of the Study Group on the Objectives of Financial Statements and the FASB, the APB steadfastly refused to take credit for, or even acknowledge, those contributions. Thus, accounting was still without a statement of fundamental principles at the end of the APB's tenure, and its absence would continue to plague the profession until the FASB, mostly on its own initiative, did something about it.

(d) FINANCIAL ACCOUNTING STANDARDS BOARD FACES DEFINING ASSETS AND LIABILITIES.   The FASB, which was not part of the AICPA, began operations in Stamford, Connecticut, on January 2, 1973, with Marshall S. Armstrong, the first chairman, and a small staff. The other six Board members and additional staff joined the group during the first half of the year, and the FASB was fully operational by the time it succeeded the APB at midyear.

Meanwhile, the Institute had approved a restated code of professional ethics that in a new Rule 203 covered for the first time infractions of the recommendations adopted by Council in 1964 regarding disclosure of departures from APB Opinions:

> A member shall not express an opinion that financial statements are presented in conformity with generally accepted accounting principles if such statements contain any departure from an accounting principle promulgated by the body designated by Council to establish such principles.

Council at its May 1973 meeting designated the FASB as the body to establish principles covered by Rule 203. The APB issued its final two Opinions—No. 30 and No. 31—and went out of business on June 30, 1973.

Later that year, the SEC's ASR No. 150, *Statement of Policy on Establishment and Improvement of Accounting Principles and Standards,* reaffirmed the policy set forth 35 years earlier in ASR 4 and declared that the Commission would recognize FASB Statements and Interpretations as having, and contrary statements as lacking, substantial authoritative support.

The FASB set its first technical agenda of seven projects in early April 1973, including a project called Broad Qualitative Standards for Financial Reporting. The Board undertook the project in expectation of receiving the report of the Trueblood Study Group, noting:

> [A]s [the Board] develops specific standards, and others apply them, there will be a need in certain cases for guidelines in the selection of the most appropriate reporting.... [and] the report of the special AICPA committee on objectives of financial statements chaired by Robert Trueblood will be of substantial help in this project.[81]

The FASB received the report of the Trueblood Study Group, *Objectives of Financial Statements,* in October 1973.[82] The Study Group had concluded:

> Accounting is not an end in itself.... [T]he justification for accounting can be found only in how well accounting information serves those who use it. Thus, the Study Group agrees with the conclusion drawn by many others that "The basic objective of financial statements is to provide information useful for making economic decisions." [p. 61]

---

[81] FASB, Status Report, June 18, 1973, pp. 1 and 4.
[82] *Objectives of Financial Statements,* Report of the Study Group on the Objectives of Financial Statements (New York: American Institute of Certified Public Accountants, October 1973). Often called the Trueblood Report, after the group's chairman, Robert M. Trueblood.

The report's other 11 objectives were more specific; for example, the next two identified the purposes of financial statements with meeting the information needs of those with "limited authority, ability, or resources to obtain information and who rely on financial statements as their principal source of information about an enterprise's economic activities" and with providing information useful to actual and potential owners and creditors in making decisions about placing resources available for investment or loan (p. 62). The report also included a group of seven "qualitative characteristics of reporting" that information "should possess . . . to satisfy users' needs" (p. 57).

Soon afterward, the FASB announced that the scope of "Broad Qualitative Standards for Financial Reporting" had been broadened because

> [m]embers of the Standards Board believe that the . . . project should encompass the entire conceptual framework of financial accounting and reporting, including objectives, qualitative characteristics and the information needs of users of accounting information.[83]

The Board also for the first time used the title "Conceptual Framework for Accounting and Reporting."

(i) Were They Assets? Liabilities?   In the meantime, two other original projects confronted the new Board with the key questions of what constituted and what did not constitute an asset or a liability. The FASB's first technical agenda included some unfinished projects inherited from the APB. One was on accounting for research and development and similar costs, which eventually resulted in FASB Statement No. 2, *Accounting for Research and Development Costs* (October 1974), and FASB Statement No. 7, *Accounting and Reporting by Development Stage Enterprises* (June 1975); the other was on accruing for future losses, which eventually resulted in FASB Statement No. 5, *Accounting for Contingencies* (March 1975). Principal questions raised by those projects were: Do expenditures for research and development, start-up, relocation, and the like result in assets? Do "reserves for self-insurance," "provisions for expropriation of overseas operations," and the like constitute liabilities? decreases in assets?

The Board quite naturally turned to the definitions of assets and liabilities in APB Statement No. 4, which were the pertinent definitions in the authoritative accounting pronouncements. The definitions proved to be of no use to the FASB in deciding the major questions raised by the projects or to anyone else in trying to anticipate how the Board would decide the issues in the two projects.

The Board had to turn elsewhere for useful definitions of assets and liabilities to resolve the issues in those projects, and Board members learned that an early priority of the Board's conceptual framework project would have to be providing definitions of assets and liabilities and other elements of financial statements to fill a yawning gap in the authoritative pronouncements.

The reasons that the FASB found the definitions of assets and liabilities in APB Statement No. 4 to be useless underlay the Board's subsequent actions on the conceptual framework project. The related topics, the proliferation of questionable deferred charges and credits, the pervasive influence of the belief in "proper matching to avoid distorting periodic net income," and the common use of the expressions "assets are costs" and "costs are assets" help explain not only why Board members took the initiative in establishing a conceptual framework for financial accounting and reporting but also why the Board adopted the basic concepts that it did. Robert T. Sprouse used the term *what-you-may-call-its* to describe certain deferred charges and deferred credits routinely included in balance sheets as assets and liabilities without much consideration of whether they actually were assets or liabilities,[84] and the name has become widely used; expressions such as "proper matching," "nondistortion of periodic net income," and "assets are costs" originated in the 1930s and 1940s, as noted in describing the influence of the AAA on U.S. accounting practice, and became widely used in the 1950s, 1960s, and 1970s.

---

[83] FASB, News Release, December 20, 1973.

[84] Robert T. Sprouse, "Accounting for What-You-May-Call-Its," *Journal of Accountancy* (October 1966): 45–53.

Assets, Liabilities, and What-You-May-Call-Its.   The introduction to the definitions of assets and liabilities in APB Statement No. 4 said: "The basic elements of financial accounting—assets, liabilities . . . —are related to . . . economic resources, economic obligations . . . " (paragraph 130), suggesting that the Statement's discussion of economic resources and obligations provided a basis for the definitions of assets and liabilities. The Statement did define economic resources and economic obligations in a way that both accountants and nonaccountants would understand them to be, or to be synonymous with, what they also generally understood to be assets and liabilities:

> Economic resources are the scarce means (limited in supply relative to desired uses) available for carrying on economic activities. The economic resources of a business enterprise include: 1. *Productive resources* . . . the means used by the enterprise to produce its product . . . 2. *Products* . . . . 3. *Money* 4. *Claims to receive money* 5. *Ownership interests in other enterprises.*

> The economic obligations of an enterprise at any time are its present responsibilities to transfer economic resources or provide services to other entities in the future . . . . Economic obligations include: 1. *Obligations to pay money* 2. *Obligations to provide goods or services.* (paragraphs 57 and 58)

Moreover, the first sentence of the parallel definitions of assets and liabilities in paragraph 132 did identify assets with economic resources and liabilities with economic obligations:

$$\left\{ \begin{matrix} \text{Assets} \\ \text{Liabilities} \end{matrix} \right\} \text{economic} \left\{ \begin{matrix} \text{resources} \\ \text{obligations} \end{matrix} \right\} \text{of an enterprise that are recognized and measured}$$

in conformity with generally accepted accounting principles.

The second sentence of the definitions broke the relationships between assets and economic resources and between liabilities and economic obligations, however, by including what-you-may-call-its in both assets and liabilities:

$$\left\{ \begin{matrix} \text{Assets} \\ \text{Liabilities} \end{matrix} \right\} \text{also include certain deferred} \left\{ \begin{matrix} \text{charges} \\ \text{credits} \end{matrix} \right\} \text{that are not} \left\{ \begin{matrix} \text{resources} \\ \text{obligations} \end{matrix} \right\}$$

but that are recognized and measured in conformity with generally accepted accounting principles.

The definitions actually defined nothing: Assets were whatever (economic resources and what-you-may-call-its) generally accepted accounting principles recognized and measured as assets, and liabilities were whatever (economic obligations and what-you-may-call-its) generally accepted accounting principles recognized and measured as liabilities. The definitions also were circular: Since the FASB was the body responsible for determining generally accepted accounting principles, research and development costs would be assets, and self-insurance reserves would be liabilities, if the Board said they were.

Nevertheless, APB Statement No. 4's definitions of assets and liabilities actually were descriptions of items recognized as assets and liabilities in practice. But why should balance sheets include as assets and liabilities items that lacked essential characteristics of what most people would understand to be assets and liabilities—items that involved no scarce means of carrying out economic activities, such as consumption, production, or saving, or items that involved no obligations to pay cash or provide goods or services to other entities?

Proper Matching to Avoid Distorting Periodic Net Income.   The Board issued a Discussion Memorandum—a neutral document that describes issues and sets forth arguments for and against particular solutions or procedures but gives no Board conclusions—for each of the two projects and scheduled public hearings. At the hearings, respondents to the Discussion Memorandums were able to explain or clarify their analyses of the issues, and Board members could ask questions to pursue certain points made in comment letters and otherwise make sure they understood respondents' proposed solutions to the issues raised by the Discussion Memorandums and their underlying reasoning.

The Board discovered in the comment letters and the hearings that many respondents were less interested in what constituted assets and liabilities than in whether capitalizing and amortizing research and development costs and accruing self-insurance reserves "properly matched" costs with revenues and thus did not "distort periodic net income." Many of the respondents argued that "proper matching" required research and development and similar costs to be capitalized and amortized over their useful lives. Similarly, many argued that "proper matching" required self-insurance and similar costs to be accrued or otherwise "provided for" each period, whether or not the enterprise suffered damage from fire, earthquake, heavy wind, or other cause during the period. Unless the Board required proper matching of costs and revenues, many respondents counseled, periodic income of the affected enterprises would be distorted.

Board members were largely frustrated in their attempts to pin down what respondents meant by "proper matching" and "periodic income distortion," but the reasons for the proliferation of what-you-may-call-its emerged clearly. The following four snippets paraphrase what Board members heard at the hearings on research and development and similar costs and accounting for contingencies. Two of them are clear standing alone; two are understandable only if the questions being answered also are included.

1. **Q.** In other words, you would focus on the measurement of income? You would not be concerned about the balance sheet?

   A. Yes. I think that is the major focus.

2. Much of the controversy over accrual of future loss has focused on whether a company had a liability for future losses or not. However, the impact on income should be overriding. The credit that arises from a provision for self-insurance is not a liability in the true sense, but that in and of itself should not keep it out of the balance sheet. APB Opinion No. 11 recognized deferred tax credits in balance sheets even though all agreed that the credit balances were not liabilities. Income statement considerations were considered paramount in that case, and similar thinking should prevail in accounting for self-insurance.

3. Defining assets does not really solve the problem of accounting for research and development expenditures and similar expenses. If some items that do not meet the definition of an asset are included in expenses of the current period, they may well distort the net income of that period because they do not relate to the revenues of that period. That accounting also may distort the net income of other periods in which the items more properly belong. The Board should focus on deferrability that gets away from the notion of whether or not those costs are assets and concentrates on the impact of deferral on the determination of net income.

4. **Q.** One of your criteria for capitalization is that net income not be materially distorted. Do you have any operational guidelines to suggest regarding material distortion?

   A. The profession has been trying to solve that one for a great many years and has been unsuccessful. I really do not have an answer.

   Q. Then, is material distortion a useful criterion that we can work with?

   A. Yes, I believe it is. Despite the difficulty, I think it is necessary to work with that criterion. It is a matter of applying professional judgment.[85]

Board members were not satisfied with the kinds of answers just illustrated.

Members of the FASB concluded early that references to vague notions such as "avoiding distortion" and "better matching" were neither an adequate basis for analyzing and resolving controversial financial accounting issues nor an effective way to communicate with one another and with the FASB's constituency.[86]

---

[85] Public Record—Financial Accounting Standards Board, 1974, Vol. 1, *Discussion Memorandum on Accounting for Research and Development and Similar Costs Dated December 28, 1973 (1007), Part 2*, pp. 171 and 172, 189 and 190; 1974, Vol. 3, *Discussion Memorandum on Accounting for Future Losses* Dated March 13, 1974 (1006), Part 2, pp. 18 and 19, 65.

[86] Robert T. Sprouse, "Commentary on Financial Reporting—Developing a Conceptual Framework for Financial Reporting," *Accounting Horizons* (December 1988): 127.

Many of the responses indeed were vague, and it soon became clear that proper matching and distortion of periodic net income were largely in the eye of the beholder. Respondents said essentially that although they had difficulty in describing proper matching and distorted income, they knew them when they saw them and could use professional judgment to assure themselves that periodic net income was determined without distortion in individual cases. The thinking and practice described in the comment letters and at the hearings seemed to make income measurement primarily a matter of individual judgment and provided no basis for comparability between financial statements. To Board members, the arguments for including in balance sheets items that could not possibly qualify as assets or liabilities—what-you-may-call-its—sounded a lot like excuses to justify smoothing reported income, thereby decreasing its volatility.

The experience generally strengthened Board members' commitment to a broad conceptual framework—one beginning with objectives of financial statements and qualitative characteristics (the Trueblood Report) and also defining the elements of financial statements and including concepts of recognition, measurement, and display—and affected the kind of concepts it would comprise.

(ii) Nondistortion, Matching, and What-You-May-Call-Its.   The proliferation of what-you-may-call-its and durability of apparently widely held and accepted notions of accounting such as the overriding importance of "avoidance of distortion of periodic income" and "proper matching of costs with revenues" were the legacy of 40 years of accountants' emphasis on the accounting process and accounting procedures instead of on the economic things and events on which financial accounting is supposed to report. As a result, an accounting convention or procedure with narrow application but a catchy name was elevated to the focal point of accounting: Matching of costs and revenues to determine periodic net income for a period became the major function of financial accounting, and whatever was left over from the matching procedure (mostly "unexpired" costs and "unearned" receipts) was carried over to future periods as assets or liabilities, depending on whether the leftover items were debits or credits.

Although Paton and Littleton's AAA monograph, *An Introduction to Corporate Accounting Standards* (1940), popularized the term *matching of costs and revenues* and provided existing practice with what many saw as a theoretical basis that previously had been lacking, the roots of the emphasis on proper matching and nondistortion of periodic net income were older. For example, the basic rationale—that the single most important function of financial accounting was determination of periodic net income and that the function of a balance sheet was not to reflect the values of assets and liabilities but to carry forward to future periods the costs and credits already incurred and received but needed to determine net income of future periods—appeared in the report of the Institute's Special Committee on Cooperation with Stock Exchanges:

> It is probably fairly well recognized by intelligent investors today that the earning capacity is the fact of crucial importance in the valuation of an industrial enterprise, and that therefore the income account is usually far more important than the balance-sheet. In point of fact, the changes in the balance-sheets from year to year are usually more significant than the balance-sheets themselves.
>
> The development of accounting conventions has, consciously or unconsciously, been in the main based on an acceptance of this proposition. As a rule, the first objective has been to secure a proper charge or credit to the income account for the year, and in general the presumption has been that once this is achieved the residual amount of the expenditure or the receipt could properly find its place in the balance-sheet at the close of the period, the principal exception being the rule calling for reduction of inventories to market value if that is below cost.[87]

That thinking led in two related directions that came together only later as the argument that proper matching was needed to avoid distorting periodic net income, which was so popular in the comment letters and hearings on whether to defer research and development expenditures or accrue future losses. The nondistortion and matching arguments seem to have developed separately in the 1940s and 1950s and made common cause only later.

---

[87] *Audits of Corporate Accounts,* p. 10.

Nondistortion and the Balance Sheet as Footnote.   Since the purpose of income measurement was to indicate the earning power of an enterprise as well as to help appraise the performance of the enterprise and the effectiveness of management, periodic income was expected to be an indicator of the long-run or normal trend of income. The usefulness of the net income of a period as a long-run or normal measure was distorted therefore by including in it the effects of unusual or random events—gains or losses with no bearing on normal performance because they were extraordinary, caused by chance, or tended to average out over time—that could cause significant extraneous fluctuations in reported net income.

Emphasis on nondistortion of periodic net income surfaced in discussions of the effects of extraordinary and nonrecurring gains and losses in comparing the current operating performance and all-inclusive or clean-surplus theories of income, briefly described earlier, but also was later applied to accounting for recurring transactions and other events. The emphasis on stability and nondistortion of reported net income seems to have increased in the late 1940s and 1950s. Herman W. Bevis, who described the need to avoid distorting periodic net income in more detail and with more careful terminology than many accountants, set forth the underlying philosophy.

> If the corporation watches the general economy, the latter also watches the corporation. For example, one of the important national economic indicators is the amount of corporate profits (and the dividends therefrom). Fluctuations in this particular index have important implications both for the private sector and with respect to the government's revenues from taxation; they also have a psychological effect on the economic mood of the nation. There is no doubt that, given a free choice between steadiness and fluctuation in the trend of aggregate corporate profits, the economic well-being of the nation would be better served by the former. Thus . . . society will welcome any contribution that the accounting discipline can make to the avoidance of artificial fluctuations in reported yearly net incomes of corporations. Conversely, the creation by accounting of artificial fluctuations will be open to criticism.[88]

The primary accounting tool for avoiding artificial fluctuations was accrual accounting, which "reflects the fact that the corporation's activities progress much more evenly over the years than its cash outflow and inflow" and "attempts to transfer the income and expense effect of cash receipts and disbursements, other transactions, and other events from the year in which they arise to the year or years to which they more rationally relate."[89] However, accrual accounting was sometimes too general, and further guidance was needed. Bevis described four guidelines for repetitive transactions and events, which had been developed out of long experience, beginning with the transaction guideline and the matching guideline:

1. Record the effect on net income of transactions and events in the period in which they arise unless there is justification for recording them in some other period or periods.
2. Where a direct relationship between the two exists, match costs with revenues.[90]

To Bevis, in contrast to most accountants of the time, who tended to describe matching of costs and revenues very broadly, the matching guideline was of restricted application because "matching attempts to make a direct association of costs with *revenues.*" Its application to a merchandising operation was obvious: "Carrying forward of the inventory of unsold merchandise so as to offset its cost against the revenue from its sale is clearly useful in determining the net income of each of the two years," although its use with some costing methods, such as LIFO, was at least questionable. Another clear application was to "the effecting of a sale [which] can be matched with a liability to pay a sales commission." Otherwise, however, "the ordinary business operation is so complex that revenues are the end product of a variety of corporate activities, often over long periods of time; objective evidence is lacking to connect the cost of most of the activities

---

[88] Herman W. Bevis, *Corporate Financial Reporting in a Competitive Environment* (New York: Macmillan, 1965), p. 30.
[89] Ibid., pp. 94 and 96.
[90] Ibid., pp. 97 and 100.

with any particular revenues." To emphasize that the matching guideline applied "to relatively few types of items," Bevis illustrated the kind of situations to which it clearly did not apply: "The matching guideline can become potentially dangerous when it attempts to match *today's real costs* with *hopes of tomorrow's revenues,* as in deferring research and development costs to be matched against hoped-for, but speculative, future revenues."[91]

In viewing matching narrowly, Bevis essentially agreed with George O. May, to whose memory the book was dedicated. May (in a report written with Oswald W. Knauth for the Study Group on Business Income) noted that it had become common, especially in academic circles, "to speak of income determination as being essentially a process of 'matching costs and revenues'" but warned: "Only in part are costs 'matched' against revenues, and 'matching' gives an inadequate indication of what is actually done.... [I]t would be more accurate to describe income determination as a process of (1) matching product costs against revenues, and (2) allocating other costs to periods."[92]

Bevis also noted that the matching guideline was "sometimes confused with the allocation of costs to periods. Taxes, insurance, or rent, for example, may be paid in advance and properly allocated to the years covered. However, this allocation is to a *period,* and one would be hard pressed to establish any direct connection between—i.e., to match—these costs and specific sales of the period to which they are allocated." Those kinds of allocations came not under the matching guideline but rather under the much broader systematic and rational guideline:

> **3.** Where there is justification for allocating amounts affecting net income to two or more years, but there is no direct basis for measuring how much should be associated with each year, use an allocation method that is systematic and rational.[93]

An essential companion of the systematic and rational guideline was the nondistortion guideline:

> **4.** From among systematic and rational methods, use that which tends to minimize distortions of periodic net income.[94]

Illustrations of "specific allocation practices that are designed to avoid or minimize distortions of net income among years" included self-insurance provisions, provisions for costs of dry-docking ships for major overhauls, and provisions for costs of relining of blast furnaces. For all of them, "a rational practice is to spread the costs over a reasonable period of time."

All three of the nondistortion practices described were potential what-you-may-call-its—deferred credits that did not qualify as liabilities. They were recognized not because they were liabilities incurred by the enterprise but because they would lessen the volatility of reported net income.

As already noted in describing the hearing on accruing future losses, not even those who advocated accruing self-insurance provisions and reserves argued that the reserves were liabilities. They argued for accruing the reserves to ensure proper matching and to avoid distorting periodic net income despite the fact that the resulting reserves were not liabilities. Similarly, the effect on net income, "to spread the costs over a reasonable period of time," was the principal consideration in accruing provisions for dry-docking ships and relining blast furnaces.

An enterprise does not incur a liability for costs that later will be expended in dry-docking a ship or relining a blast furnace by operating the ship or using the furnace. Rather, it begins to incur the pertinent liabilities only when it dry-docks the ship and begins to scrape off the barnacles or otherwise overhaul her or when it shuts down the furnace and starts the relining, but certainly not before making a contract with one or more other entities to do the work.

---

[91] Ibid., pp. 100 and 101.

[92] *Changing Concepts of Business Income,* Report of the Study Group on Business Income (New York: Macmillan, 1952), pp. 28 and 29.

[93] Bevis, *Corporate Financial Reporting,* p. 101.

[94] Ibid., p. 104.

Costs of dry-docking a ship or relining a furnace might legitimately be recognized between dry-dockings or relinings by recognizing them as decreases in the carrying amount of the asset because accumulations of barnacles reduce the ship's efficiency or use of the furnace wears out the lining, but proponents of accruing costs to avoid distortion of periodic net income usually have not argued that way. Since their attention has focused almost entirely on the effect on reported net income, they have not been much concerned with "niceties" of whether periodically recognizing the cost increased liabilities or decreased assets. They have been likely to dismiss questions of that kind on the grounds that they are "merely geography" in the financial statements—an insignificant detail. Lack of concern about assets and liabilities was a distinguishing characteristic of true believers in the matching or nondistortion "gospel."

Bevis reflected that kind of focus on nondistortion of periodic net income and lack of concern about the resulting balance sheet:

> [T]he amounts at which many assets and liabilities are stated in the balance sheet are a by-product of methods designed to produce a fair periodic net income figure. The objective is *not* to produce a liquidating value or a current fair market value of assets. This approach is consistent with the primary interest of the stockholder in periodic income, as opposed to liquidating or "pounce" values in a not-to-be-liquidated enterprise.[95]

Indeed, he came up with the most imaginative—and pertinent—description in the entire nondistortion and proper-matching literature of the way proponents see a balance sheet—as a footnote to an income statement:

> [T]wo-thirds of the items on the asset side of the balance sheet [a "Composite Statement of Financial Position" of "100 Large Industrial Corporations" in the Appendix] . . . are not assets in the sense of either being or expected to be directly converted to cash. They represent a huge amount of "deferred costs," mostly past cash expenditures, which are to be included as costs in future income statements. . . . Among all the footnotes explaining and elaborating on the income statement, this makes the balance sheet the biggest footnote of all.[96]

The same idea had been expressed less flatteringly by Professor William Baxter of the University of London (London School of Economics):

> [A group] of accountants bent on belittling the balance-sheet and elevating the revenue account . . . tend to dismiss the balance-sheet as a mere appendage of the revenue account—a mausoleum for the unwanted costs that the double-entry system throws up as regrettable by-products.[97]

Although Bevis defined matching narrowly and gave it only a limited place in periodic income determination, relying more on the rational and systematic guideline and the nondistortion guideline, his was probably a minority view. Most accountants who have emphasized the need for nondistorting income determination procedures have considered careful timing of recognition of revenues and expenses by proper matching to be critical in avoiding distortion of periodic income.

Proper Matching and "Assets Are Costs."   In contrast to Bevis's and May's narrow definitions of matching, most accountants have described matching of costs and revenues broadly, making matching either (1) one of two central functions of financial accounting or (2) *the* central function of financial

---

[95] Ibid., p. 107.

[96] Ibid., p. 94.

[97] W. T. Baxter, ed., *Studies in Accounting* (London: Sweet & Maxwell Ltd., 1950), "Introduction." Reprinted as "Introduction to the First Edition" in second and third editions: W. T. Baxter and Sidney Davidson, eds., *Studies in Accounting Theory* (London: Sweet & Maxwell Ltd., 1962) and Baxter and Davidson, eds., *Studies in Accounting* (London: Institute of Chartered Accountants in England and Wales, 1977), p. x.]

accounting. Either way, matching encompasses allocations of costs using systematic and rational procedures, such as depreciation and amortization, which Bevis explicitly excluded from matching.

Accountants of the first group, whose use of matching has been the narrower of the two, have described periodic income determination as a two-step process: revenue recognition or "realization" and matching of costs with revenues (expense recognition). To them, matching not only recognized perceived direct relationships between costs and revenues, such as between cost of goods sold (product costs) and sales, but also recognized perceived indirect relationships between costs and revenues through mutual association with the same period. The latter would include relationships such as those between, on one hand, costs recognized as expenses in the period incurred and depreciation and other costs allocated to the same period by a rational and systematic procedure and, on other hand, revenues allocated to the same period by "realization." That is, matching encompassed both matching product costs with specific revenues (Bevis's and May's definitions) and what usually has been called allocation—matching other costs with periods. For example, this definition clearly encompassed both kinds of matching:

> Matching is one of the basic processes of income determination; essentially it is a process of determining relationships between costs...and (1) specific revenues or (2) specific accounting periods.[98]

Accountants of the second group have used matching of costs and revenues in the broadest possible sense—as a synonym for periodic income determination—making matching *the* central function of financial accounting. To them, matching encompassed both revenue recognition or "realization" and expense recognition. Matching dictated what has been included in income statements, as it did in both of these definitions:

> **matching** 1. The principle of identifying related revenues and expense with the same accounting period.[99]
>
> By means of accounting we seek to provide these test readings [of progress made] by a periodic matching of the costs and revenues that have flowed past "the meter" in an interval of time.[100]

The degree to which matching of costs and revenues had become the central function of financial accounting in the minds of many accountants by the time of the FASB's projects on research and development expenditures and similar costs and accruing future losses was indicated by Delmer Hylton's description in 1965, which was by no means an overstatement:

> Concurrent with the ascendency of the income statement in recent years, we have also witnessed increasing emphasis on the accounting convention known as "matching revenue with expense." In fact, it seems that most innovations in accounting in recent years have been justified essentially as better performing this matching process. In the minds of many accountants, this single convention outweighs all others; in other words, if a given procedure can be asserted to conform to the matching concept, nothing else need be said: the matter is settled and the procedure is justified.[101]

That is basically what Board members read and heard in the comment letters and public hearings on accounting for research and development expenditures and similar costs and accruing future losses. The need for proper matching of costs and revenues to avoid distorting periodic net income was the overriding consideration in many letters and in the prepared statements and answers of a significant number of those who appeared at the hearings and responded to Board members' questions. They showed little or no interest in whether research and development expenditures resulted in assets and whether reserves for self-insurance were liabilities.

---

[98] APB Opinion No. 11, *Accounting for Income Taxes* (1967), paragraph 14(d).

[99] Eric L. Kohler, *A Dictionary for Accountants,* 5th ed. (Englewood Cliffs, NJ: Prentice-Hall, 1975), p. 307.

[100] Paton and Littleton, *An Introduction to Corporate Accounting Standards* (1940), p. 15.

[101] Delmer Hylton, "On Matching Revenue with Expense," *Accounting Review* (October 1965): 824.

Rather, those deferred charges and deferred credits belonged in the balance sheet because they were needed for proper matching to avoid distorting periodic net income. And what were most assets, anyway, except deferred or "unexpired" costs, as Paton and Littleton's monograph had said:

> [A]ssets are costs. "Costs" are the fundamental data of accounting, and . . . . it is possible to apply the term "cost" equally well to an asset acquired, a service received, and a liability incurred. Under this usage assets, or costs incurred, would clearly mean charges awaiting future revenue, whereas expenses, or costs applied, would mean charges against present revenue.[102]

That usage followed from the monograph's view that periodic income measurement was not only a process of matching costs and revenues but also the focal point of accounting.

> The factors acquired for production which have not yet reached the point in the business process where they may be appropriately treated as "cost of sales" or "expense" are called "assets," and are presented as such in the balance sheet . . . . [T]hese "assets" are in fact "revenue charges in suspense" awaiting some future matching with revenue as costs or expenses . . . .

> The fundamental problem of accounting . . . is the division of the stream of costs incurred between the present and the future in the process of measuring periodic income . . . . The balance sheet . . . serves as a means of carrying forward unamortized acquisition prices, the not-yet-deducted costs; it stands as a connecting link joining successive income statements into a composite picture of the income stream.[103]

Long before the time of the FASB projects on research and development costs and self-insurance reserves, however, Paton had recognized that matching had become an obsession of many accountants. It had been carried much too far and had been the cause of downgrading the meaning and significance of assets.

> For a long time I've wished that the Paton and Littleton monograph had never been written, or had gone out of print twenty-five years or so ago. Listening to Bob Sprouse take issue with the "matching" gospel, which the P & L monograph helped to foster, confirmed my dissatisfaction with this publication . . . . The basic difficulty with the idea that cost dollars, as incurred, attach like barnacles to the physical flow of materials and stream of operating activity is that it is at odds with the actual process of valuation in a free competitive market. The customer does not buy a handful of classified and traced cost dollars; he buys a product, at prevailing market price. And the market price may be either above or below any calculated cost . . . .

> For a long time I've been touting the idea that the central element in business operation is the *resources* (in hand or in prospect) and that the main objective of operation is the efficient utilization of the available assets.[104]

His intermediate accounting textbook, published a mere dozen years after the monograph, was entitled *Asset Accounting.*[105]

(iii) An Overdose of Matching, Nondistortion, and What-You-May-Call-Its.   Board members had, as former chairman Donald J. Kirk once put it, cut their accounting teeth on matching, nondistortion, assets are costs, and similar notions. Some of them may have entertained some doubts about some of the ideas before serving on the Board, but it was the paramount importance that was attributed to those ideas in early comment letters and at the early hearings that made the Board increasingly

---

[102] Paton and Littleton, *An Introduction to Corporate Accounting Standards,* pp. 25 and 26.

[103] Ibid., pp. 25 and 67.

[104] William A. Paton, "Introduction," in Williard E. Stone, ed., *Foundations of Accounting Theory: Papers Given at the Accounting Theory Symposium, University of Florida, March 1970* (Gainesville: University of Florida Press, 1971), pp. x and xi.

[105] William A. Paton, with the assistance of William A. Paton, Jr., *Asset Accounting* (New York: Macmillan, 1952).

uncomfortable with them. Those notions seemed to be open-ended; no one could explain the limits, if any, on matching or nondistortion procedures or how to verify that proper matching or nondistortion had been achieved. The experience made most, if not all, Board members highly skeptical about arguments that the need for proper matching to avoid distortion of periodic net income was the "be-all and end-all of financial accounting"[106] with little or no concern expressed about whether the residuals left over after matching actually were assets or liabilities.

Among other things, those early experiences had graphically demonstrated to Board members that once accountants had come to perceive assets primarily as costs, they often failed to distinguish assets in the real world from the entries in the accounts and financial statements. What-you-may-call-its were a consequence of the habit of using "costs" and "assets" interchangeably—"assets were costs; costs were assets"—without worrying about whether the costs actually represented anything in the real world.

The "Pygmalion Syndrome" (after the legendary sculptor who fell in love with his statue of a woman) was at work. That name was given by the noted physicist J. L. Synge to "the tendency of many people to confuse conceptual models of real-world things and events with the things and events themselves."[107] Perhaps the most common example has been the habit of lawyers, accountants, corporate directors and officers, stockholders, and others to describe a dividend as paid "out of surplus (retained earnings)." That habit led a prominent lawyer to chide:

> Distributions are never paid "out of surplus," they are paid out of assets; surplus cannot be distributed—assets are distributed. No one ever received a package of surplus for Christmas.[108]

The fact that the matching literature was so full of references to "unexpired" costs that "expired" when matched against revenues also caused a prominent professor of finance to admonish that accountants had confused matters by defining

> depreciation as "expired capital outlay"—in other words, as "expired cost"—thereby transferring the word from a value to a cost category. But this definition was a dodge rather than a solution, and the fact that it still enjoys some currency among accounting writers who must be aware of its spurious character illustrates the tenacity of convenient though specious phrases. For cost does not "expire." What may be said gradually to expire is the economic significance of the asset as it grows older, in short, its utility or its value. "Expired cost" is therefore mumbo jumbo, and a reversion to the old association of depreciation with loss in value would be a far more sensible alternative.[109]

As Board members began to look at problems likely to come onto the Board's agenda, they began to see more what-you-may-call-its in their future. In addition to self-insurance reserves and provisions for removing barnacles from ships or relining blast furnaces, which have already been described, a significant number of what-you-may-call-its were part of existing practice in the early 1970s, had been or were being proposed to become part of practice, or had recently been proscribed:

- Unamortized debt discount
- Deferred tax credits and deferred tax charges
- Deferred gains and losses on securities in pension funds
- Deferred gains on translating foreign exchange balances (the APB issued in late 1971 an exposure draft of a proposal to permit deferral of losses on foreign exchange balances but dropped the subject without issuing an Opinion.)

---

[106] Sprouse, "Commentary on Financial Reporting—Developing a Conceptual Framework for Financial Reporting," p. 127.

[107] Loyd C. Heath, "Accounting, Communication, and the Pygmalion Syndrome," *Accounting Horizons* (March 1987): 1.

[108] Bayless Manning, *A Concise Textbook on Legal Capital,* 2nd ed. (Mineola, NY: Foundation Press, 1981), pp. 33 and 34.

[109] James C. Bonbright, *Principles of Public Utility Rates* (New York: Columbia University Press, 1961), pp. 195 and 196.

- Deferred gains or losses on sales of long-term investments
- Deferred gains or losses on sale-and-leaseback transactions
- Negative goodwill remaining after reducing to zero the noncurrent assets acquired in a business combination

Since several of those what-you-may-call-its were part of topics that might well come before the Board within a few years, Board members thought it essential to ensure that the Board would not have to face those kinds of matters without the necessary tools. They were not anxious to repeat their experiences with research and development expenditures and similar costs and accruing future losses. They not only wanted to get in place a broad conceptual framework to provide a basis for sound financial accounting standards but also had some firm ideas of the kinds of concepts that were needed.

Kirk later described his own thinking at the time, and other Board members probably would concur with most of what he said:

Among the projects on the Board's initial agenda were accounting for research and development costs and accounting for contingencies. The need for workable definitions of assets and liabilities became apparent in those projects and served as a catalyst for the part of the framework projects that became FASB Concepts Statement No. 3, *Elements of Financial Statements of Business Enterprises* (1980)....

To me, the definitions were the missing boundaries that were needed to bring the accrual accounting system back under control. The definitions have, I hope, driven a stake part way through the "nondistortion" guideline. But I am realistic enough to know, having dealt with the subjects of foreign currency translation and pension cost measurement, that the aversion to volatility in earnings is so strong that the notion of "nondistortion" will not die easily.[110]

Kirk's reference to volatility of reported net income was not accidental—that has been and will continue to be a major bone of contention between the FASB and its constituents. Managements have been and continue to be concerned that volatility of periodic net income will affect adversely the market prices of their enterprises' securities and hence their cost of capital. The Board's general response to that concern has been that accounting must be neutral, and if financial statements are to represent faithfully an entity's net income, the presence of volatility must be reported to investors and creditors. For example, former Board member Robert T. Sprouse probably expressed the thinking of many Board members:

I submit...that minimizing the volatile results of actual economic events should be primarily a matter for management policy and strategy, not a matter for accounting standards. To the extent volatile economic events actually occur, the results should be reflected in the financial statements. If it is true that volatility affects market prices of securities and the related costs of capital, it is especially important that, where it actually exists, volatility be revealed rather than concealed by accounting practices. Otherwise, financial statements do not faithfully represent the results of risks to which the enterprise is actually exposed.

To me, the least effective argument one can make in opposing a proposed standard is that its implementation might cause managers or investors to make different decisions.... The very reason for the existence of reliable financial information for lenders and investors...is to help them in their comparisons of alternative investments. If stability or volatility of financial results is an important consideration to some lenders and investors, all the more reason that the degree of stability or volatility should be faithfully reflected in the financial statements.[111]

---

[110] Donald J. Kirk, "Looking Back on Fourteen Years at the FASB: The Education of a Standard Setter," *Accounting Horizons* (March 1988): 15.

[111] Robert T. Sprouse, "Commentary on Financial Reporting—Economic Consequences: The Volatility Bugaboo," *Accounting Horizons* (March 1987): 88.

That kind of problem is nothing new. For example, almost 50 years earlier, Paton made essentially the same point as Sprouse in writing about the effects on income of the choice of inventory methods:

> [Sanders, Hatfield, and Moore] quote, with apparent approval, the following statement from Arthur Andersen: "The practice of equalizing earnings is directly contrary to recognized accounting principles." But . . . they go out of their way to support a European practice, the base-stock inventory method, which . . . has been vigorously revived and sponsored in recent years [in the United States] under the "last in, first out" label, which represents nothing more nor less than a major device for equalizing earnings, to avoid showing in the periodic reports the severe fluctuations which are inherent in certain business fields. . . . Actually, we do have good years and bad years in business, fat years and lean years. There is nothing imaginary about this condition—particularly in the extractive and converting fields, where this agitation centers. . . . It may be that in some situations the year is too short a period through which to attempt to determine net income (as surely the month and quarter often are), but if this is the case, the solution lies not in doctoring the annual report, but in lengthening the period. Certainly it is not good accounting to issue reports for a copper company, for example, which make it appear that the concern has the comparative stability of earning power of the American Telephone and Telegraph Co.[112]

The earlier description of the experiences of Board members that led them to support a broad conceptual framework project and to develop firm ideas about the kinds of concepts needed has focused on the projects on accounting for research and development expenditures and similar costs and accounting for contingencies, including accruing future losses. Those projects were highly significant experiences for Board members, as the preceding indicates, but later projects have provided additional or similar experiences. As the comments on volatility of income suggest, the education of Board members and members of the constituency is a continuing process in which the conceptual framework has been both a source of disagreement and controversy and a significant help in setting sound financial accounting standards.

(iv) Initiation of the Conceptual Framework.   Confronted with the fruits of decades of the profession's lethargy and inability to fashion a statement defining accounting's most basic concepts, the FASB, on its own initiative and motivated by the experiences of its members, decided to undertake the development of a statement of basic concepts that went beyond the objectives of financial statements to definition, recognition, measurement, and display of the elements of financial statements. In 1973 it initiated a conceptual framework project that was intended to be at once both the reasoning underlying procedures and a standard by which procedures would be judged.

A deliberative, authoritative body with responsibility for accounting standards finally had decided to do what the Committee on Accounting Procedure and the APB had been implored to do but had never felt strongly was a part of their mission. The FASB concluded that accounting did possess a core of fundamental concepts that were neither subject to nor dependent on the moment's particular, transitory consensus. Accounting had achieved the stage in its development that made it imperative and proper to place before its constituents a definitive statement of its fundamental principles.

2.3 FINANCIAL ACCOUNTING STANDARDS BOARD'S CONCEPTUAL FRAMEWORK

In an open letter to the business and financial community, which prefaced the booklet, *Scope and Implications of the Conceptual Framework Project* (December 2, 1976), Marshall S. Armstrong, the first chairman of the FASB, expressed some of the Board's aspirations for the conceptual framework project:

---

[112] William A. Paton, "Comments on 'A Statement of Accounting Principles,'" *Journal of Accountancy* (March 1938): 199 and 200.

The conceptual framework project will lead to definitive pronouncements on which the Board intends to rely in establishing financial accounting and reporting standards. Though the framework cannot and should not be made so detailed as to provide automatically an accounting answer to a set of financial facts, it will determine bounds for judgment in preparing financial statements. The framework should lead to increased public confidence in financial statements and aid in preventing proliferation of accounting methods.

The excerpt highlighted a significant characteristic of the conceptual framework project. Although Board members were aware of the widespread criticism directed at the Committee on Accounting Procedure and the Accounting Principles Board for their collective inability to provide the profession with an enduring framework for analyzing accounting issues, the FASB's stimulus was entirely different from that of its predecessors. It was not reacting to instructions or recommendations to establish basic concepts by groups such as the AICPA's Special Committees on Research Program or Opinions of the APB, the Wheat Group, or the SEC. Rather, the Board undertook the self-imposed task of providing accounting with an underlying philosophy because Board members had concluded that to discharge their standards-setting responsibilities properly, they needed a set of fundamental accounting concepts for their own guidance in resolving issues brought before the Board.

The idea that the conceptual framework was intended to benefit the FASB by guiding its ongoing work in establishing accounting standards was embodied in the Preface, entitled "Statements of Financial Accounting Concepts," to each Concepts Statement:

The Board itself is likely to be the most direct beneficiary of the guidance provided by the Statements in this series. They will guide the Board in developing accounting and reporting standards by providing the Board with a common foundation and basic reasoning on which to consider merits of alternatives.

Armed with the conviction that a coordinated set of pervasive concepts was prerequisite to establishing sound and consistent accounting standards, the FASB in late 1973 formally expanded the scope of its original concepts project, "Broad Qualitative Standards for Financial Reporting," and changed its name. The new title—"Conceptual Framework for Accounting and Reporting: Objectives, Qualitative Characteristics and Information"—for the first time used the words "conceptual framework" by which the project would become identified.

The Board concluded at the outset that it was unrealistic to attempt to devise a complete conceptual framework and adopt it by a single Board action. It already had experienced an urgent need for a definitive statement about some of the most fundamental components of the envisioned conceptual framework—the objectives of financial reporting and definitions of the elements of financial statements. The absence of meaningful definitions of assets and liabilities in the accounting literature had already hindered the FASB's work on the other projects on its agenda.

The project was conceived as comprising six major parts, as illustrated by Exhibit 2.1. (A seventh part was added in 2000. See Subsection 2.3(b)(v).) The parts were expected to be undertaken in the order shown by moving down the pyramid and from left to right at each level.

The numbers in parentheses in Exhibit 2.1 reflect that although six Concepts Statements were issued, their numbers did not correspond to the order just described for the six boxes in the exhibit because (a) the Statement on qualities of useful information was finished before the Statement on elements of financial statements; (b) not-for-profit organizations were included within the scope of the framework, resulting in Concepts Statement No. 4, which pertained only to not-for-profit organizations, and in Concepts Statement No. 6, which amended Concepts Statement No. 2 and replaced Concepts Statement No. 3, making them applicable to not-for-profit organizations; and (c) little conceptual work was actually completed on the topics in the two lower levels of Exhibit 2.1, and what was done on all three topics was included in a single Concepts Statement, No. 5.

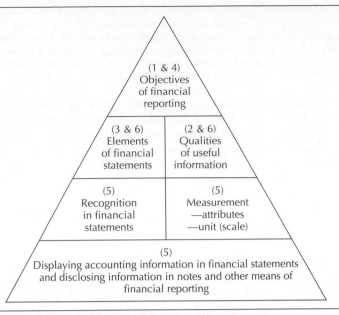

Exhibit 2.1   FASB's Conceptual Framework for Financial Accounting and Reporting

Exhibit 2.2 shows the six Concepts Statements by topic and date of issue and explains how they fit together in relation to Exhibit 2.1.

The conceptual framework constitutes the subject matter of the remainder of this chapter, which considers, among other things, the underlying philosophy of and emphasis in the framework, the effects on it of matters discussed earlier in the chapter, the ways that it has been and might be used by the FASB and others in improving financial accounting and reporting practice, and a more detailed look at some of the concepts. The discussion is divided into two sections: It looks at the conceptual framework first as a body of concepts that underlies financial accounting and reporting in the United States and then as five interrelated Concepts Statements, each focused on one of four parts of the framework: objectives of financial reporting, qualitative characteristics of accounting information, elements of financial statements, and recognition and measurement and display in financial statements.

No. 1 "Objectives of Financial Reporting by Business Enterprises" (November 1978)

No. 2 "Qualitative Characteristics of Accounting Information" (May 1980)

No. 3 "Elements of Financial Statements of Business Enterprises" (December 1980)

No. 4 "Objectives of Financial Reporting by Nonbusiness Organizations" (December 1980)

No. 5 "Recognition and Measurement in Financial Statements of Business Enterprises" (December 1984)

No. 6 "Elements of Financial Statements" (December 1985)

No. 2 amended by No. 6 to apply to not-for-profit organizations as well as to business enterprises]

No. 3 superseded by No. 6, which applies to both business enterprises and not-for-profit organizations

No. 5 also briefly covers display in financial statements and disclosure in notes and other means of financial reporting

Exhibit 2.2   Six Concepts Statements

(a) FRAMEWORK AS A BODY OF CONCEPTS.   The Concepts Statements as a group reflect a number of sources and other influences, most of which have already been introduced or otherwise noted, including:

- The Trueblood Study Group's report, *Objectives of Financial Statements* (October 1973), whose 12 objectives and seven "qualitative characteristics of reporting" and supporting discussion and analysis directly affected the two Concepts Statements on objectives and the one on qualitative characteristics and indirectly affected the others
- Board members' experiences in trying to set standards in the absence of an accepted conceptual basis, which was a significant factor both in the FASB's having a conceptual framework and in the kinds of concepts it comprises
- Conceptual work of the APB and Accounting Research Division, primarily ARS 1 and 3 on basic postulates and broad principles of accounting and the basic concepts part of APB Statement No. 4
- Conceptual work of others reported in the literature, including the work of individuals, the AAA's concepts and standards statements, and developments in Canada, the United Kingdom, Australia, New Zealand, and other countries
- Conceptual work of the FASB itself, including preparatory work on its original concepts project and development of Discussion Memorandums and Exposure Drafts that led to the Concepts Statements and related projects, such as that on materiality; and the fruits of "due process," such as some excellent comment letters and exchanges of views at a number of hearings

Some of the most fundamental concepts in the framework had their roots in those sources and influences. The three examples of fundamental concepts under the next three headings combine ideas from one or more Concepts Statements and illustrate those connections.

(i) Information Useful in Making Investment, Credit, and Similar Decisions

Financial accounting and reporting is not an end in itself but is intended to provide information that is useful to present and potential investors, creditors, other resource providers, and other users outside an entity in making rational investment, credit, and similar decisions about it.

The FASB generally followed the report of the Trueblood Study Group on objectives of financial statements in focusing the objectives of financial reporting on information useful in investment, credit, and similar decisions, instead of on information about management's stewardship to owners or information based on the operating needs of managers. The description of Concepts Statement No. 1 later in this chapter shows the influence of the Trueblood Study Group's objectives on the FASB's objectives.

That focus on information for decision making represented a fundamental change in attitude toward the purposes of financial statements. Before the Trueblood Study Group's report, APB Statement No. 4 was the only AICPA pronouncement identifying financial reporting with the needs of investors and creditors for decision making rather than with the traditional accounting purpose of reporting on management's stewardship. A vocal minority, which still is heard from occasionally, has insisted that the primary function of accounting by an enterprise is to serve management's needs and that the objectives should reflect that purpose. It has never been obvious why proponents of that view think that a body such as the APB or FASB should be establishing objectives and setting standards for information that is primarily for internal and private use and that management can require in whatever form it finds most useful. The message intended apparently is that management, not the APB, FASB, or similar body, should decide what information financial statements are to provide to investors, creditors, and others.

The Study Group, which may have been influenced to some extent by APB Statement No. 4, emphasized the role of financial statements in investors' and creditors' decisions and identified the purposes of financial statements with the decisions of investors and creditors, existing or prospective, about placing resources available for investment or loan. The Study Group's recommendations became the starting point for the FASB to build a conceptual framework.

(ii) Representations of Things and Events in the Real-World Environment

The items in financial statements represent things and events in the real world, placing a premium on representational faithfulness and verifiability of accounting information and neutrality of both standards setting and accounting information.

The FASB's decision to ground its concepts in the environment in which financial accounting takes place and the economic things, events, and activities that exist or happen there, instead of on accounting processes and procedures, was influenced significantly by Accounting Research Study 1 on basic postulates of accounting and the section of APB Statement No. 4 on basic concepts. The postulates in ARS 1 were, as already described, self-evident propositions about the environment in which accounting functions—a world that does exist and not one that is a fiction—that were fruitful for accounting.

For example, the observation that most of the goods and services produced in the United States are not directly consumed by their producers but are sold for cash or claims to cash suggests both why financial accounting is concerned with production and distribution of goods and services and with exchange prices and why investors, creditors, and other users of financial statements are concerned with cash prices and cash flows.

That focus of financial accounting on the environment and the things and events in it that are represented in financial statements constituted a fundamental change from the earlier emphasis on the conventional nature of accounting and the conventional procedures and allocations used to produce the numbers in financial statements. Thus, the Concepts Statements devote considerable space to describing activities such as producing, distributing, exchanging, saving, and investing in what they variously call the "real world," "economic, legal, social, political, and physical environment in the United States," or "U.S. economy," and what is involved in representing those economic things and events in financial statements. Concepts Statement No. 1 notes a significant consequence of that focus on things and events in the environment that is pertinent to the definitions of the elements of financial statements.

The information provided by financial reporting pertains to individual business enterprises.... Since business enterprises are producers and distributors of scarce resources, financial reporting bears on the allocation of economic resources to producing and distributing activities and focuses on the creation of, use of, and rights to wealth and the sharing of risks associated with wealth. [paragraph 19]

Thus, the elements of financial statements are assets and liabilities and the effects of transactions and other events that change assets and liabilities—that change and transfer wealth.

(iii) Assets (and Liabilities)—Fundamental Element(s) of Financial Statements

The fundamental elements of financial statements are assets and liabilities because all other elements depend on them:

Equity is assets minus liabilities;

Investments by owners,
Distributions to owners, and
Comprehensive income and its
    components—revenues, expenses,
    gains, and losses— } are { inflows, outflows, or other increases decreases in assets and liabilities

Because liabilities depend on assets—liabilities are obligations to pay or deliver assets—assets is the most fundamental element of financial statements.

Soon after its inception, the FASB needed definitions of assets and liabilities and found many examples of two types of definition in the accounting literature.

Definitions of one type identified assets with economic resources and wealth, emphasizing the service potential, or benefits, and economic values that an asset confers on the holding or owning entity. Similarly, they identified liabilities with amounts or duties owed to other entities, emphasizing the payment or expenditure of assets required of the debtor or owing entity to satisfy the claim. They were definitions that described things that most people could recognize as assets and liabilities because they had experience in their everyday lives as well as in their business activities with rights to use economic resources and with obligations to pay debts.

Three sets of definitions of assets and liabilities by the AAA, Robert K. Mautz, and Eric L. Kohler, respectively,[113] are examples of the numerous definitions the FASB considered that had those characteristics:

Assets are economic resources devoted to business purposes within a specific accounting entity; they are aggregates of service-potentials available for or beneficial to expected operations.

An asset may be defined as anything of use to future operations of the enterprise, the beneficial interest in which runs to the enterprise. Assets may be monetary or nonmonetary, tangible or intangible, owned or not owned.

asset Any owned physical object (tangible) or right (intangible) having economic value to its owner; an item or source of wealth . . .

The interests or equities of creditors (liabilities) are claims against the entity arising from past activities or events which, in the usual case, require for their satisfaction the expenditure of corporate resources.

Liabilities are claims against a company, payable in cash, in other assets, or in service, on a fixed or determinable future date.

liability 1. An amount owing by one person (a debtor) to another (a creditor), payable in money, or in goods or services: the consequence of an asset or service received or a loss incurred or accrued . . .

The FASB also found a second type of definition of assets and liabilities that included economic resources and obligations but also let in some ultimately undefinable what-you-may-call-its—such as deferred tax charges and credits, deferred losses and gains, and self-insurance reserves—items that are not economic resources or obligations of an entity but were included in its balance sheet as assets or liabilities "to achieve 'proper' matching of costs and revenues" or "to avoid distorting periodic net income" (pp. 2–33–2–47 of this chapter).

Prime examples of the second type of definition were those in APB Statement No. 4, paragraph 132, which explicitly included what-you-may-call-its in its definitions of assets and liabilities:

Assets—economic resources of an enterprise that are recognized and measured in conformity with generally accepted accounting principles. Assets also include certain deferred charges that are not resources but that are recognized and measured in conformity with generally accepted accounting principles.

Liabilities—economic obligations of an enterprise that are recognized and measured in conformity with generally accepted accounting principles. Liabilities also include certain deferred credits that are not obligations but that are recognized and measured in conformity with generally accepted accounting principles.

---

[113] American Accounting Association, Committee on Concepts and Standards Underlying Corporate Financial Statements, *Accounting and Reporting Standards for Corporate Financial Statements and Preceding Statements and Supplements* (Iowa City, IA: Author, 1957), pp. 3 and 7. Robert K. Mautz, "Basic Concepts of Accounting," *Handbook of Modern Accounting,* Sidney Davidson, ed. (New York: McGraw-Hill, 1970), pp. 1–5 and 1–8 (chapter 1, pp. 5 and 8). Kohler, *A Dictionary for Accountants,* pp. 39 and 291.

Those definitions were circular and open-ended, however, being both determinants of and determined by generally accepted accounting principles and saying in effect that assets and liabilities were whatever the Board said they were.

In trying to use the definitions in APB Statement No. 4 to set financial accounting standards for research and development expenditures and accruing future losses, Board members found that assets and liabilities defined as fallout from periodic recognition of revenues and expenses were too vague and subjective to be workable. That experience strongly reinforced the conceptual and practical superiority of definitions of assets and liabilities based on resources and obligations that exist in the real world rather than on deferred charges and credits that result only from bookkeeping entries.

APB Statement No. 4's definitions proved to be of little help to the Board in deciding whether results of research and development expenditures qualified as assets or whether reserves for self-insurance qualified as liabilities because they permit almost any debit balance to be an asset and almost any credit balance to be a liability. They were hardly better than the definitions that they had replaced, which also included what-you-may-call-its and were circular and open-ended in the same ways:

> [T]he word "asset" is not synonymous with or limited to property but includes also that part of any cost or expense incurred which [according to generally accepted accounting principles] is properly carried forward upon a closing of books at a given date.
>
> ...Thus, plant, accounts receivable, inventory, and a deferred charge are all assets in a balance-sheet classification.
>
> The last named is not an asset in the popular sense, but if it may be carried forward as a proper charge against future income, then in an accounting sense, and particularly in a balance-sheet classification, it is an asset....
>
> ...Thus, the word ["liability"] is used broadly to comprise not only items which constitute liabilities in the popular sense of debts or obligations...but also credit balances to be accounted for which do not involve the debtor and creditor relation. For example, capital stock, deferred credits to income, and surplus are balance-sheet liabilities in that they represent balances to be accounted for by the company; though these are not liabilities in the ordinary sense of debts owed to legal creditors.[114]

Definitions of that kind provide no effective limits or restraints on the matching of costs and revenues and the resulting reported net income. If balance sheets at the beginning and end of a period include debits and credits that are labeled assets and liabilities but that result from book-keeping entries and are assets only "in an accounting sense" or "in a balance-sheet classification" or are only "balance-sheet liabilities," the income statement for the period will include components of income that are equally suspect—namely, debits and credits that are labeled revenues, expenses, gains, or losses but that result from the same bookkeeping entries as the what-you-may-call-its in the balance sheet. They have resulted not from transactions or other events that occurred during the period but from shifting revenues, expenses, gains, or losses from earlier or later periods to match costs and revenues properly or to avoid distorting reported periodic income.

---

[114] Accounting Research Bulletin No. 9 (Special), *Report of the Committee on Terminology* (May 1941), pp. 70 and 71. The definitions in ARB 9 were carried over to Accounting Terminology Bulletin No. 1, *Review and Résumé* (August 1953), paragraphs 26 and 27, but, for some unexplained reason, "deferred credits to income," the only part of the liability definition comparable to "deferred charges" in the asset definition, was deleted. Assets are probable future economic benefits obtained or controlled by a particular entity as a result of past transactions or events (Concepts Statement 6, paragraph 25). Liabilities are probable future sacrifices of economic benefits arising from present obligations of a particular entity to transfer assets or provide services to other entities in the future as a result of past transactions or events (Concepts Statement 6, paragraph 35).

Thus, when the Board defined the elements of financial statements in Concepts Statement No. 3 (and used the same definitions in Concepts Statement No. 6), it defined assets and liabilities in essentially the same way as the three sets of definitions by the AAA, Mautz, and Kohler, emphasizing the benefits that assets confer on their holders and the obligations to others that bind those with liabilities to pay or expend assets to settle them.

Assets are probable future economic benefits obtained or controlled by a particular entity as a result of past transactions or events. [Concepts Statement No. 6, paragraph 25]	Liabilities are probable future sacrifices of economic benefits arising from present obligations of a particular entity to transfer assets or provide services to other entities in the future as a result of past transactions or events. [Concepts Statement No. 6, paragraph 35]

The definitions that were adopted exclude all what-you-may-call-its. Deferred charges and credits that "need to be carried forward for matching in future periods" can no longer be included in assets and liabilities merely by meeting definitions no more restrictive than "assets are costs" and "liabilities are proceeds."

Although definitions identifying assets with economic resources and wealth and liabilities with amounts or duties owed to other entities had been common in the accounting literature from the turn of the century to the 1970s, the definitions in APB Statement No. 4 actually reflected accounting practice at the time the FASB was developing its definitions. Thus, its definitions represented a fundamental change from the emphasis on financial accounting as primarily a process of matching costs and revenues.

Misunderstanding and Controversy about the Financial Accounting Standards Board's Defining Assets and Liabilities as the Fundamental Elements.   Both of the other fundamental concepts described earlier—that the objective of financial reporting is to provide information useful in making investment, credit, and similar decisions and that items in financial statements represent things and events in the real-world environment—also constituted significant changes in perceptions of the purpose and nature of financial accounting and reporting. Both caused concern among many members of the FASB's constituency at the beginning and drew some criticism and opposition. With time, however, both concepts seem to have been understood reasonably well, their level of acceptance has increased, and active opposition has subsided.

In contrast, this third concept—that assets and liabilities are the fundamental elements of financial statements—still is undoubtedly the most controversial, and the most misunderstood and misrepresented, concept in the entire conceptual framework.

Two Views of Income.   The FASB's emphasis on assets and liabilities in the definitions of the elements of financial statements became a focus of controversy in the development of the conceptual framework because it highlighted the tension in accounting thought and practice between two widely held and essentially incompatible views about income:

- Income is an enhancement of wealth or command over economic resources.
- Income is an indicator of performance of an enterprise and its management.

That difference of opinion about income usually has involved the question of whether certain items should be reported in the net income for a period or should be excluded from net income and reported directly in equity. It most often has been described as the issue of how to display the effects of unusual, extraordinary, or nonrecurring happenings and prior period adjustments, which underlay the disagreement between the SEC and the Institute's Committee on Accounting Procedure over the all-inclusive and current-operating-performance types of income statement, and has troubled accounting standards-setting bodies for more than half a century.

> Standard setters, including the Committee on Accounting Procedure, the Accounting Principles Board, and the Financial Accounting Standards Board, have issued more pronouncements dealing with display of the effects of unusual and nonrecurring events than any other subject.[115]

It also underlies differences between comprehensive income and earnings, recently manifesting itself most prominently in the issue of whether to extend the traditional display of unusual, non-recurring, or extraordinary events—to exclude them from net income and report them directly in equity—to recurring but often volatile holding gains and losses that largely are beyond the control of an entity and its management.

Difference of opinion about whether income is wealth enhancement or performance indicator likewise underlay the controversy that followed issue of the FASB Discussion Memorandum on definitions of elements of financial statements and their measurement (December 2, 1976), but the matter went deeper than financial statement display. In the FASB's conceptual framework, definitions of elements of financial statements are more fundamental than recognition, measurement, or display in financial statements (see Exhibit 2.1), and the Discussion Memorandum emphasized definition rather than display.

The Board referred to the two views of income or earnings as the *asset and liability view* and the *revenue and expense view* and described the difference between them for purposes of defining elements of financial statements as whether definitions of assets and liabilities should be the controlling definitions or should depend on definitions of revenues and expenses.

> The conceptual issue in choosing between the asset and liability view and the revenue and expense view concerns selecting the most fundamental elements whose precise definitions control the definitions of the other elements. [p. 35]

Former Board member Oscar Gellein (writing in 1984) described the issue as one of identifying the elements that have what he called conceptual primacy and said that the question of which concepts had primacy was "[a] central issue [that] pervades the FASB's effort to construct a conceptual framework."[116] That question was the first issue in the Discussion Memorandum.

> Should the asset and liability view ... [or] the revenue and expense view ... be adopted as the basis underlying a conceptual framework for financial accounting and reporting? [p. 36][117]

According to the Discussion Memorandum, proponents of the asset and liability view hold that assets should be defined as the economic resources of an enterprise (its scarce means of carrying out economic activities such as exchange, production, saving, and investment), that liabilities should be defined as its obligations to transfer assets to other entities in the future, and that definitions of income and its components should depend on the definitions of assets and liabilities. Thus, no revenues or gains can occur unless an asset increases or a liability decreases, and no expenses or losses can occur unless an asset decreases or a liability increases. As a result, income reflects an increase in wealth of the enterprise, and a loss reflects a decrease in its wealth.

---

[115] Oscar S. Gellein, "Periodic Earnings: Income? or Indicator?" *Accounting Horizons* (June 1987): 61.
[116] Oscar S. Gellein, "Financial Reporting: The State of Standard Setting," *Advances in Accounting*, Vol. 3, Bill N. Schwartz, ed. (Greenwich, CT: JAI Press, 1986), pp. 14 and 15.
[117] A third view described in the Discussion Memorandum, the nonarticulation view, is omitted.

Accounting Research Bulletins

No. 8, *Combined Statement of Income and Earned Surplus (Retained Earnings)* (February 1941)

No. 32, *Income and Earned Surplus* (December 1947)

No. 35, *Presentation of Income and Earned Surplus* (October 1948)

No. 41, *Presentation of Income and Earned Surplus* (Supplement to Bulletin No. 35) (July 1951)

No. 43, *Restatement and Revision of Accounting Research Bulletins* (June 1953) Chapter 2(b), "Combined Statement of Income and Earned Surplus" Chapter 8, "Income and Earned Surplus"

APB Opinions

No. 9, *Reporting the Results of Operations [Income]* (December 1966)

No. 20, *Accounting Changes* (July 1971)

No. 30, *Reporting the Results of Operations—Reporting the Effects of Disposal of a Segment of a Business, and Extraordinary, Unusual and Infrequently Occurring Events and Transactions* (June 1973)

FASB Statements

No. 4, *Reporting Gains and Losses from Extinguishment of Debt* (an amendment of APB Opinion No. 30) (March 1975)

No. 16, *Prior Period Adjustments* (June 1977)

Proponents of the revenue and expense view, in contrast, hold that income is a measure of performance of an enterprise and its management, that income results from proper matching of costs and revenues, and that most nonmonetary assets and liabilities are by-products of the matching process. Proper matching of costs and revenues involves timing their recognition to relate effort (expenses) and accomplishment (revenues) for a period. Thus, the effects of past expenditures or receipts that are deemed to be expenses or revenues of future periods are recognized as assets or liabilities (deferred charges or deferred credits) whether or not they relate to economic resources or obligations to transfer resources to other entities in the future.

Asset and Liability View and Conceptual Primacy of Assets and Liabilities.   Although Concepts Statements Nos. 3 and 6 neither mentioned the asset and liability view and the revenue and expense view nor explained how or why the Board had settled on one of them, the definitions themselves left no doubt about which view the Board had endorsed. Following the steps it had set down in the Discussion Memorandum, it first identified assets and liabilities as "the most fundamental elements whose precise definitions control the definitions of the other elements" (p. 35 of the Discussion Memorandum). The Board then used the most fundamental definitions—assets and liabilities—in defining all of the other elements. For example, equity is assets minus liabilities. Investments by and distributions to owners and comprehensive income and its components—revenues, expenses, gains, and losses—are inflows, outflows, or other increases and decreases in assets and liabilities. (Assets actually is the most fundamental element of financial statements because the definition of liabilities depends on the definition of assets—liabilities are obligations to pay or deliver assets.) The emphasis on assets and liabilities in the definitions of the elements of financial statements in Concepts Statement No. 3 showed that the Board had adopted the asset and liability view and rejected the revenue and expense view.

Assets and (to a lesser extent) liabilities have conceptual primacy, while income and its components—revenues, expenses, gains, and losses—do not.

Every conceptual structure builds on a concept that has primacy. That is simply another way of saying some element must be given meaning before meaning can be attached to others. I contend that assets have that primacy. I have not been able to define income without using a term like asset, resources, source of benefits, and so on. In short, meaning can be given to assets without first defining income, but the reverse is not true. That is what I mean by conceptual primacy of assets. No one has ever been successful in giving meaning to income without first giving meaning to assets.[118]

The Board's early experiences had convinced it that definitions of assets and liabilities that depended on definitions of income and its components did not work. As already noted, those kinds of definitions proved to be of little help to the Board in deciding whether results of research and development expenditures qualified as assets or whether reserves for self-insurance qualified as liabilities because they permit almost any debit balance to be an asset and almost any credit balance to be a liability.

In addition, the Board had attempted to test whether revenues and expenses could be defined without first defining assets and liabilities. It asked respondents to the Discussion Memorandum to submit for its consideration precise definitions of revenues and expenses that were wholly or partially independent of economic resources and obligations (assets and liabilities) and capable of general application in a conceptual framework. That no one was able to do that without having to resort to subjective guides, such as proper matching and nondistortion of income, was a significant factor in the Board's ultimate rejection of the revenue and expense view.

> Attempts to identify a good match based on the primacy of revenue and expense have been unsuccessful so far. There is a serious question as to whether revenue and expense can be defined independent of assets and liabilities.[119]

Thus, revenues and expenses could not fulfill the function of concepts having primacy, which

> are the concepts used to define other concepts. They prevent the systems from being open-ended and potentially circular. They are the concepts that are used to test for unity and maintenance of a consistent direction—they are the anchor.[120]

Instead, the Board found that definitions that made assets and liabilities essentially fallout of the process of matching revenues and expenses provided no anchor. They excluded almost nothing from income because they excluded almost nothing from assets and liabilities. The definitions were primarily conventional, not conceptual, and had made periodic income measurement largely a matter of individual judgment and personal opinion. The resulting accounting lacked the conceptual underpinning that provides, among other things, "the means for judging whether one solution is better than another... [and] the restraints necessary to prevent proliferation of perceptions and resulting diversity of accounting methods for substantially similar circumstances."[121] That is, the Board found the revenue and expense view to be part of the problem rather than part of the solution.

In contrast, the Board's definitions of assets and liabilities limited what can be included in all of the other elements. The Board's choice of the asset and liability view limited the population of assets and liabilities to the underlying economic resources and obligations of an enterprise. The resulting definitions impose limits or restraints not only on what can be included in assets and liabilities but also on what can be included in income. The only items that can meet the definitions of income and its components—revenues, expenses, gains, and losses—are those that increase or decrease the wealth of an enterprise.

The Board based its definitions of elements of financial statements on the conceptual primacy of assets and liabilities for both conceptual and practical reasons. However, that decision was to put

---

[118] Oscar S. Gellein, "Primacy: Assets or Income?" *Research in Accounting Regulation,* Vol. 6, Gary John Previts, ed. (Greenwich, CT: JAI Press, 1992), p. 198.

[119] Gellein, "Financial Reporting: The State of Standard Setting," p. 17.

[120] Ibid., p. 15.

[121] Ibid., p. 13.

the Board at odds with many of its constituents because, among other reasons, "both [conceptual primacy], and the implications of the FASB position on it are still rather widely misunderstood."[122]

Revenue and Expense View and Its Hold on Practice.   The revenue and expense view had been the basis for accounting practice and for most authoritative accounting pronouncements for over 40 years when the Board looked closely at it in the 1970s. The FASB saw clear evidence of its pervasiveness in practice and in accountants' minds in its early projects on research and development expenditures and accruing future losses. An emphasis on the "proper matching of costs and revenues," a concern for avoiding "distortion of periodic net income," and a willingness to allow what-you-may-call-its to appear in balance sheets are all characteristics of the revenue and expense view of income, which has been described extensively earlier in this chapter without referring to it by that name.[123] When the Board issued the Discussion Memorandum, the revenue and expense view was the only view of accounting that most of its constituents knew.

Many of them apparently could not, or would not, believe that the Board's primary concern was the need for a set of definitions that worked. That reaction probably was to have been expected. Definitions of assets and liabilities have not been significant in the thinking underlying the revenue and expense view, which has focused on the need to measure performance by relating efforts expended with the resulting accomplishments and has emphasized proper matching and nondistortion of periodic net income as the means of achieving that association of effort and accomplishment. Its proponents might find it difficult to believe that definitions of assets and liabilities could be considered to be fundamental concepts.

Unfortunately, the issue became highly emotional, and many of those who did not accept the Board's explanations looked for other explanations for its decision. Although the Board had defined assets and liabilities in a way that could accurately be described as venerable, many members of the Board's constituency found something unusual, perhaps even sinister, in the Board's definitions of elements of financial statements.

For example, a popular criticism of the asset and liability view charged the FASB with having the intent

- To downgrade the importance of net income and the income statement by making the balance sheet more important than the income statement
- To supplant accounting based on completed transactions and matching of costs and revenues with a "new" accounting based on the valuation of assets and liabilities at current values or costs

That many of the comment letters the Board received on the Discussion Memorandum echoed those charges mostly reflected the success of an illustrated-lecture tour by Robert K. Mautz, partner of Ernst & Ernst (now Ernst & Young LLP), in which he urged members of 65 to 70 chapters of the Financial Executives Institute to reject the asset and liability view.[124]

Board and staff members became concerned that discussion of the FASB's decision to base its definitions of elements of financial statements on the conceptual primacy of assets and liabilities had gone astray. The focus had been shifted from the definitions to some oversimplified and essentially irrelevant distinctions between the asset and liability and revenue and expense views concerning which financial statement is more useful and which measurement basis goes with which view.

> Conceptual primacy has nothing to do with the question of what information is most useful or of how it is measured. It refers only to the matter of definitional dependency.[125]

---

[122] Ibid., p. 14.

[123] Most accountants had never heard the terms *revenue and expense view* and *asset and liability view* until the FASB used them in its 1976 Discussion Memorandum on elements of financial statements.

[124] Pelham Gore, *The FASB Conceptual Framework Project, 1973–1985, An Analysis* (Manchester, UK: Manchester University Press, 1992), pp. 94 and 95.

[125] Gellein, "Financial Reporting: The State of Standard Setting," p. 15.

The Discussion Memorandum had tried to keep the emphasis on the definitions, explaining why the relative usefulness of income statements and balance sheets was never a real issue between the two views:

> [A]dvocates of the asset and liability view agree with advocates of the revenue and expense view that the information in a statement of earnings is likely to be more useful to investors and creditors than the information in a statement of financial position. That is, both groups agree that earnings measurement is the focus of financial accounting and financial statements. [paragraph 45]

Concepts Statement No. 1 was unequivocal in identifying information about income as most useful to investors, creditors, and other users:

> The primary focus of financial reporting is information about an enterprise's performance provided by measures of earnings and its components. Investors, creditors, and others who are concerned with assessing the prospects for enterprise net cash inflows are especially interested in that information. [paragraph 43][126]

Thus, to say that the asset and liability view downgrades the significance of net income and the income statement by making the balance sheet more significant than the income statement at best reflects misunderstanding of the conceptual primacy of assets and liabilities and of the asset and liability view used by the Board. At worst, it misrepresents the Board's reasons for accepting the asset and liability view and rejecting the revenue and expense view of income.

The idea that the Board chose the asset and liability view to impose some kind of current value accounting on an unwilling world reflects the same misunderstanding and misrepresentation. None of the Concepts Statements except No. 5, *Recognition and Measurement in Financial Statements of Business Enterprises,* says anything about how assets or liabilities should be measured, and Concepts Statement No. 5 does not embrace a "new" accounting based on the valuation of assets and liabilities at current values or costs. If anything, it favors "historical-cost accounting" and erects barriers to current values or costs, for example, placing a higher hurdle for recognizing current values or costs than for recognizing historical costs: "Information based on current prices should be recognized if it is sufficiently relevant and reliable to justify the costs involved and more relevant than alternative information" (paragraph 90). Moreover, Concepts Statement No. 5 and numerous speeches made and articles written by Board members while the Concepts Statements were in progress furnish abundant evidence that Board members never were sufficiently of the same mind on the relative merits and weaknesses of current cost or value and so-called historical cost for measuring assets and liabilities for the Board accurately to be characterized as "having the intent" to adopt any particular measurement model for assets and liabilities.

Since Board members' continual public denials of that kind of intent and their explanations of what the Board actually was trying to accomplish were publicly brushed aside by many members of the Board's constituency, the unfortunate result was a generally unenlightening digression that served no purpose except to cast aspersions on Board members' veracity and integrity and to polarize opinion. It made little or no contribution to the conceptual framework, but it did reveal a deep-seated distrust of a conceptual framework, or perhaps of concepts generally, on the part of many accountants and a fear, easily triggered by, for example, labeling the asset and liability view a "valuation approach," that the FASB might be in the process of turning the world of accounting upside down.

---

[126] That paragraph echoed paragraph 171 of *Tentative Conclusions on Objectives of Financial Statements of Business Enterprises,* which was issued in a package with the Discussion Memorandum: *Earnings* for an enterprise for a period measured by accrual accounting [is] generally considered to be the most relevant indicator of relative success or failure of the earning process of an enterprise in bringing in needed cash. Measures of periodic earnings are widely used by investors, creditors, security analysts, and others.

The revenue and expense view is still deeply ingrained in many accountants' minds, and their first reaction to an accounting problem is to think about "proper matching of costs and revenues." Time will be needed for them to become accustomed to thinking first about effects of transactions or other events on assets and liabilities (or both) and then about how the effect on assets and liabilities has affected revenues, expenses, gains, or losses. Many will be able to make that adjustment only with difficulty, and a significant number simply will make no attempt to do so, clinging instead to the revenue and expense view. The FASB's experience suggests that a long tradition of ad hoc accounting principles has fostered a propensity to resist restraints on flexibility, especially those that limit an enterprise's ability to decide what can be included in income for a period.

Yet the hold of the revenue and expense view on practice is destined to decline. Definitions reflecting the revenue and expense view have been weighed in the balance and found wanting, not only by the FASB but also by other standards-setting bodies.

> The conceptual frameworks of the standard-setting bodies [in Australia, Canada, the United Kingdom and the United States and the International Accounting Standards Committee] do rest on the bedrock of the balance sheet. This may be inevitable, given that advocates of a p[rofit] & l[oss] account-driven approach have so far failed to produce rigorous, coherent and consistent definitions of its elements that refer to underlying events rather than the recognition process itself.[127]

Countries besides the United States that have adopted or are in the process of adopting conceptual frameworks or statements also generally have developed definitions of elements of financial statements that reflect the conceptual primacy of assets and liabilities. Thus, standards setters in Australia, Canada, and the United Kingdom, as well as the International Accounting Standards Committee, all have definitions that are generally similar to those of the FASB.

To those familiar with the FASB's experience with the Discussion Memorandum on elements of financial statements, the related Exposure Drafts, and Concepts Statement No. 3, what has happened recently in some of those countries is (in the words of Yogi Berra) "*déjà vu* all over again." At the annual Financial Times financial reporting conference in the United Kingdom in September 1993, for example,

> David Lindsell, senior technical partner at Ernst & Young, reiterated his firm's criticism of the A[ccounting] S[tandards] B[oard]'s conceptual approach (*Accountancy,* October 1993, page 11). Whereas the ASB's Statement of Principles makes the balance sheet the "focal point of the accounts" and "treats financial reporting primarily as a process of valuation," E&Y believes that the primary focus should be on "the measurement of earnings, and that the balance sheet should be seen as a residual statement, derived after measuring the company's profits and not the other way round."[128]
>
> Essentially E&Y accuses the ASB of focusing on the balance sheet at the expense of the p[rofit] & l[oss] account and argues for a return to pure historical cost accounting.... [S]ince E&Y went public with its criticism, it has heard from a lot of people, particularly finance directors, who have expressed sympathy with its arguments.[129]

International harmonization of accounting practice is likely to continue to be in the direction of phasing out the revenue and expense view.

However, change is likely to be rather deliberate, and at least in the United States, features of the revenue and expense view are likely to be part, though a shrinking part, of financial statements for some time to come. The Board has said that it "intends future change to occur in the gradual,

---

[127] Brian Rutherford, "Accountancy Issues—They Manipulate, You Smooth. I Self-Hedge: Perhaps the World's Finest Know a Thing or Two After All," *Accountancy* (June 1995): 95.

[128] "News—ASB under Fire," *Accountancy* (November 1993): 16.

[129] Brian Singleton-Green, "The ASB: Critics That Won't Be Pacified," *Accountancy* (November 1993): 26.

evolutionary way that has characterized past change" (Concepts Statement No. 5, paragraph 2). And, although it precluded self-insurance reserves and similar what-you-may-call-its in balance sheets, the Board has permitted other what-you-may-call-its to avoid unduly disrupting practice. For example, it explicitly responded to concerns about volatility of reported net income expressed by respondents to the Exposure Draft that preceded FASB Statement No. 87, *Employers' Accounting for Pensions* (December 1985), concluding that to require accounting that was conceptually appropriate under the definitions in Concepts Statement No. 3 would be too great a change from past practice to be adopted in a single step. Thus, Statement No. 87 "retains three fundamental aspects of past pension accounting" despite their conflict with the Concepts Statements and accounting principles applied elsewhere (paragraph 84). One of the three—delaying recognition of actuarial gains and losses to spread over future periods the recognition of gains or losses that have already occurred to a liability for pensions or pension plan assets—requires recognizing in the accounts a number of what-you-may-call-its even though they do not qualify as assets or liabilities under the Board's definitions. The Board's perception of a need for expedients of that kind means that at least some "what-you-may-call-its" in balance sheets and the related arguments about "proper matching of costs and revenues" and "avoiding distortion of periodic net income" are likely to disappear only gradually.

(iv) Functions of the Conceptual Framework.   The Preface of each FASB Concepts Statement has carried the following, or a similar, description (this excerpt is from Concepts Statement No. 6):

> The conceptual framework is a coherent system of interrelated objectives and fundamentals that is expected to lead to consistent standards and that prescribes the nature, function, and limits of financial accounting and reporting. It is expected to serve the public interest by providing structure and direction to financial accounting and reporting to facilitate the provision of evenhanded financial and related information that helps promote the efficient allocation of scarce resources in the economy and society, including assisting capital and other markets to function efficiently.

> Establishment of objectives and identification of fundamental concepts will not directly solve financial accounting and reporting problems. Rather, objectives give direction, and concepts are tools for solving problems.

The FASB's conceptual framework is intended to be primarily a set of tools to help the Board in setting sound financial accounting standards and to help members of the Board's constituency not only understand and apply those standards but also contribute significantly to their development. It is not expected automatically to provide ready-made, unique, and obviously logical answers to complex financial accounting or reporting problems, but it should help to solve them by:

- Providing a set of common premises as a basis for discussion
- Providing precise terminology
- Helping to ask the right questions
- Limiting areas of judgment and discretion and excluding from consideration potential solutions that are in conflict with it
- Imposing intellectual discipline on what traditionally has been a subjective and ad hoc reasoning process

Those contributions of the conceptual framework have all been introduced at least indirectly earlier in this chapter, and the last two were cited as factors in the FASB's conclusions in the preceding discussion of assets as the fundamental element of financial statements. The following paragraphs add a few points on the first three.

A critical function of the conceptual framework is to provide a set of common premises from which to begin discussing specific accounting problems and developing solutions for them. The accounting profession's earlier efforts to establish accounting principles have shown that if experience is the frame of reference, no one can be sure of the starting point, if one exists at all, because everyone's experience is different. The FASB's predecessors tried to use experience as a common point of departure, but when confronted with the same problems, people with different experiences too often offered widely different solutions, and financial accounting was inundated with multiple solutions to the same problems. The problems of communication and understanding between those supporting the revenue and expense view and those supporting the asset and liability view offer a striking illustration.

A framework of coordinated concepts as the frame of reference, in contrast, can change that picture. The FASB and its constituency start from common ground, vastly increasing the likelihood that they can communicate with and understand each other on the complex and difficult problems that often arise in financial accounting and reporting. A set of common premises does not guarantee agreement, but it does avoid the problems and wasted time that result if those discussing a matter talk past each other because they actually are not talking about the same thing. It also promotes consensus once a problem is solved. For example, Donald J. Kirk, former chairman of the FASB, noted that the conceptual framework was undertaken "with the expectation that it would articulate definitions and concepts that would diminish the need for and details in standards; it was to be the 'relief' from the so-called 'firefighting' [approach] for which the FASB's predecessors had been criticized."[130]

A related purpose of the conceptual framework is to provide a precise terminology. Good terminology serves much the same function as a set of common premises: "Loose terminology encourages loose thinking. Precision in the use of words does not solve human controversies, but at least it paves the way for clear thinking." [131] The FASB's conceptual framework has contributed significantly to precise terminology through its careful definitions of the elements of financial statements in Concepts Statement No. 6 and the qualitative characteristics of accounting information in Concepts Statement No. 2.

The conceptual framework helps to ask the right questions. Indeed, the FASB has emphasized that contribution as much as any. For example, the definitions of elements of financial statements not only make clear which are the right questions but also the order in which to ask them:

What is the asset?

What is the liability?

Did an asset or liability or its value change?

Increase or decrease?

By how much?

Did the change result from:

An investment by owners?

A distribution to owners?

Comprehensive income?

Was the source of comprehensive income what we call:

Revenue?

Expense?

Gain?

Loss?

To start at the bottom and work up the list will not work. That is what ad hoc accounting has tried to do over many years, resulting in assets and liabilities in balance sheets that cannot meet the definitions.

---

[130] Donald J. Kirk, "Looking Back on Fourteen Years at the FASB: The Education of a Standard Setter," *Accounting Horizons* (March 1988): 11.

[131] Austin Wakeman Scott, *Abridgement of the Law of Trusts* (Boston: Little, Brown, 1960), p. 28.

The conceptual framework does not guarantee logical solutions to accounting problems. The results depend significantly on those who use the concepts to establish financial accounting standards. But it does provide valuable tools to standards setters.

> Standard setters' instincts alone are not adequate to maintain direction—to discriminate between a solution that better lends usefulness to a standard than another solution, and at the same time maintain consistency. Their instincts need conceptual guidance.

> . . . The objectives build on the role of financial reporting and underlie the definitions of financial statement elements. Acceptance of the definitions provides the necessary discipline for order. Instead of arguing about the definitions, the FASB, as well as its constituents, now focuses attention on whether a matter in a given situation meets the conditions of a definition. That contributes to efficiency and furthers the chances of consistency.[132]

(b) FINANCIAL ACCOUNTING STANDARDS BOARD CONCEPTS STATEMENTS. The Concepts Statements set forth the objectives and conceptual foundation of financial accounting that are the basis for the development of financial accounting and reporting standards. This section of the chapter discusses the individual Concepts Statements in a logical order according to their subject matter. The objectives of financial reporting constitute the subject matter of Concepts Statement No. 1, *Objectives of Financial Reporting by Business Enterprises,* and Concepts Statement No. 4, *Objectives of Financial Reporting by Nonbusiness Organizations.* The qualities that make accounting information useful for investment, credit, and other resource allocation decisions are described in Concepts Statement No. 2, *Qualitative Characteristics of Accounting Information.* Concepts Statements No. 3 and No. 6 define the *Elements of Financial Statements.* Finally, Concepts Statement No. 5, *Recognition and Measurement in Financial Statements of Business Enterprises,* describes a complete set of financial statements and what is meant by recognition and measurement.

(i) Objectives of Financial Reporting. After the FASB received the report of the Trueblood Study Group, *Objectives of Financial Statements,* in October 1973, it issued a Discussion Memorandum, *Conceptual Framework for Accounting and Reporting: Consideration of the Report of the Study Group on the Objectives of Financial Statements,* in June 1974. The Discussion Memorandum was based primarily on the Trueblood Report's 12 objectives of financial statements and seven qualitative characteristics of reporting. The Board held a public hearing in September and began to develop its own conclusions on the objectives.

Concepts Statement No. 1. In December 1976, the Board published for comment a draft entitled *Tentative Conclusions on Objectives of Financial Statements of Business Enterprises* and a Discussion Memorandum, *Conceptual Framework for Financial Accounting and Reporting: Elements of Financial Statements and Their Measurement.* Although the Trueblood Report included an objective of financial statements for governmental and not-for-profit organizations, the FASB had decided to concentrate its initial efforts on formulating objectives of financial statements of business enterprises. Following a public hearing on those publications the following August, the Board issued an Exposure Draft, *Objectives of Financial Reporting and Elements of Financial Statements of Business Enterprises,* in December 1977. Concepts Statement No. 1, *Objectives of Financial Reporting by Business Enterprises,* was issued in November 1978.

The change in title between the Tentative Conclusions and the Exposure Draft indicated a change in the Board's perspective from a focus on financial statements to financial reporting. To a significant extent, it reflected comments received on the Tentative Conclusions document. The change also emphasized that financial statements were the primary, but not the only, means of conveying financial information to users. During the Board's consideration of objectives, it had decided that for general purpose external financial reporting, the objectives of financial statements and the objectives of financial reporting are essentially the same, although, as the Statement said,

---

[132] Gellein, "Financial Reporting: The State of Standard Setting," p. 13.

some information is better provided by financial statements and other information is better provided by other means of financial reporting (paragraph 5).

That brief sketch of the background of the Statement has touched only certain points. Concepts Statement No. 1, like all of the Concepts Statements, contains an appendix on its background (paragraphs 57–63).

Concepts Statement No. 1 and the Trueblood Group's Objectives.   The FASB accepted the starting point and basic objective in the report of the Trueblood Study Group and, although some differences in direction had begun to appear in the supporting discussion, accepted in a general way the group's second and third objectives. These excerpts are from the Study Group's report:

> Accounting is not an end in itself....

> The basic objective of financial statements is to provide information useful for making economic decisions.

> An objective of financial statements is to serve primarily those users who have limited authority, ability, or resources to obtain information and who rely on financial statements as their principal source of information about an enterprise's economic activities.

> An objective of financial statements is to provide information useful to investors and creditors for predicting, comparing, and evaluating potential cash flows to them in terms of amount, timing, and related uncertainty. [pp. 61–62]

These excerpts are from Concepts Statement No. 1:

> Financial reporting is not an end in itself but is intended to provide information that is useful in making business and economic decisions—for making reasoned choices among alternative uses of scarce resources in the conduct of business and economic activities. [paragraph 9]

> The objectives in this Statement...stem primarily from the informational needs of external users who lack the authority to prescribe the financial information they want from an enterprise and therefore must use the information that management communicates to them. [paragraph 28]

> Potential users of financial information most directly concerned with a particular business enterprise are generally interested in its ability to generate favorable cash flows because their decisions relate to amounts, timing, and uncertainties of expected cash flows. To investors, lenders, suppliers, and employees, a business enterprise is a source of cash in the form of dividends or interest and perhaps appreciated market prices, repayment of borrowing, payment for goods or services, or salaries or wages. They invest cash, goods, or services in an enterprise and expect to obtain sufficient cash in return to make the investment worthwhile. They are directly concerned with the ability of the enterprise to generate favorable cash flows and may also be concerned with how the market's perception of that ability affects the relative prices of its securities. (paragraph 25)

> Financial reporting should provide information that is useful to present and potential investors and creditors and other users in making rational investment, credit, and similar decisions. [paragraph 34]

None of the other nine objectives of the Study Group was adopted in recognizable form in Concepts Statement No. 1. Many of them were about matters that the Board had decided to include in the recognition, measurement, and display parts of the conceptual framework.

Concepts Statement No. 4.   By 1977 the fiscal problems of a number of large cities, including New York and Cleveland, had prompted public officials and private citizens increasingly to question the relevance and reliability of financial reporting by governmental and not-for-profit organizations. That concern was reflected in many legislative initiatives and widely publicized allegations of serious deficiencies in the financial reporting of various kinds of not-for-profit organizations.

The Board began to consider concepts underlying general purpose external financial reporting by not-for-profit organizations by commissioning a research report to identify the objectives of financial reporting by organizations other than business enterprises. That report, *Financial Accounting in Nonbusiness Organizations,* by Robert N. Anthony, was published in May 1978. Rather than delay progress on the objectives of financial reporting by business enterprises by attempting to include not-for-profit organizations within its scope, the Board decided to proceed with two separate objectives projects. It issued a Discussion Memorandum based on the research report, followed by an Exposure Draft. Then, *Objectives of Financial Reporting by Nonbusiness Organizations* was issued as Concepts Statement No. 4 in December 1980. After Concepts Statement No. 4 was issued, the FASB changed the key term from *nonbusiness* to *not-for-profit organizations.*

Effects of Environment and Information Needs of Resource Providers.   Concepts Statement No. 1 and Concepts Statement No. 4 have the same structure. Both sets of objectives are based on the fundamental notion that financial reporting concepts and standards should be based on the information needs of users of financial statements who make decisions about committing resources to either business enterprises or not-for-profit organizations with the expectation of pecuniary reward or to not-for-profit organizations for reasons other than expectations of monetary return of or return on resources committed. From that broad focus, the Statements narrow the focus, on one hand, to the primary interest of investors, creditors, and other users in the prospects of receiving cash from their investments in or loans to business enterprises and the relationship of their prospects to those of the enterprise, and, on the other hand, to the needs of resource providers for information about a not-for-profit organization's services, its ability to continue to provide them, and the relationship of management's stewardship to the organization's performance. Finally, both Statements focus on the kinds of information that financial reporting can provide to meet the respective needs of both groups.

The objectives of financial reporting cannot be properly understood apart from the environmental context in which they have been developed—the real world in which financial accounting and reporting takes place. They are affected by the economic, legal, political, and social environment of the United States. The objectives "stem largely from the needs of those for whom the information is intended, which in turn depend significantly on the nature of the economic activities and decisions with which the users are involved" (Concepts Statement No. 1, paragraph 9). Thus, Concepts Statement No. 1 describes the highly developed exchange economy of the United States, in which:

- Most goods and services are exchanged for money or claims to money instead of being consumed by their producers.

- Most productive activity is carried on through investor-owned business enterprises whose operations are controlled by directors and professional managers acting in the interests of investor-owners.

- Well-developed securities markets tend to allocate scarce resources to enterprises that use them efficiently.

- Productive resources are generally privately rather than government owned, although government intervenes in the resource allocation process through taxation, borrowing and spending for government operations and programs, regulation, subsidies, or monetary and fiscal policy.

Cash is important in the economy "because of what it can buy. Members of the society carry out their consumption, saving, and investment decisions by allocating their present and expected cash resources" (Concepts Statement No. 1, paragraph 10). Entities' efficient allocation of cash and other economic resources is a means to the desired end of a well-functioning, healthy economy. The following excerpt from Concepts Statement No. 1 describes how financial reporting can contribute to achieving that social good. It refers to reporting about business enterprises, but its premise relates as well to the objectives of financial reporting of not-for-profit organizations.

The effectiveness of individuals, enterprises, markets, and government in allocating scarce resources among competing uses is enhanced if those who make economic decisions have information that reflects the relative standing and performance of business enterprises to assist them in evaluating alternative courses of action and the expected returns, costs, and risks of each. The function of financial reporting is to provide information that is useful to those who make economic decisions about business enterprises and about investments in or loans to business enterprises. [paragraph 16]

Business enterprises and not-for-profit organizations have both similarities and differences in their operating environments that affect the information needs of those who make decisions about them and thus affect the objectives of financial reporting. Both kinds of entities have transactions with suppliers of goods and services who expect to be paid for what they provide, with employees who expect to be paid for their work, and with lenders who expect to be repaid with interest. Both entities may sell the goods or services they produce, although to survive, business enterprises charge prices sufficient to cover their costs, usually plus a profit, whereas not-for-profit organizations often may sell below cost or at nominal prices or may even give their outputs to beneficiaries without charge.

Not-for-profit organizations commonly need certain kinds of control arrangements more than do business enterprises. Although not-for-profit organizations must often compete not only with each other but also with business enterprises for goods and services, employees, and lendable funds, the operating performance of business enterprises generally is subject to the discipline of market controls to a greater extent than is the performance of not-for-profit organizations because business enterprises must compete in equity markets for funds to finance their operations while not-for-profit organizations do not. Spending mandates and budgets to control uses of resources are significant factors in obtaining and allocating resources for not-for-profit organizations to compensate for the lesser influence of direct market competition.

Business enterprises and not-for-profit organizations also differ in their relationships to some significant resource providers. Business enterprises have stockholders or other owners who invest with the expectation of receiving profits commensurate with the risks incurred. In contrast, not-for-profit organizations have no owners in the same sense as business enterprises and often receive significant amounts of resources by gift or donation from those who do not expect pecuniary returns. Those contributors are interested in the services the organizations provide and receive compensation for their contributions by nonfinancial means, such as by seeing the purposes and goals of the organizations advanced.

Objectives of Financial Reporting by Business Enterprises.   The objectives of financial reporting by business enterprises are derived from the information needs of investors, creditors, and others outside an enterprise who generally lack the authority to prescribe the information they want and thus must rely on information that management communicates to them. They are the primary users of the information provided by general purpose external financial reporting, whose primary objective is to

> provide information that is useful to present and potential investors and creditors and other users in making rational investment, credit, and similar decisions. [Concepts Statement No. 1, paragraph 34]

The objectives of general purpose external financial reporting are not derived from and do not comprehend satisfying the information needs of all potential users. Regulatory and taxing authorities, for example, have needs for special kinds of financial information that is not normally provided by financial reporting but also have the statutory authority to obtain the specific information they need. Thus they do not have to rely on information provided to other groups. Management is interested in the information provided by external financial reporting but also has ready access not only to that information but also to a great deal of internal information that is normally unavailable to those outside the enterprise. Management's primary role in external financial reporting is that of a provider or communicator of information for use by investors, creditors, and others outside the enterprise who must rely on management for information.

In emphasizing the information needs of investors, creditors, and similar users, the FASB recognized that external financial reporting cannot satisfy the particular and perhaps diverse needs of various individual users who look to the information provided by financial reporting for assistance in making resource allocation decisions. However, those who make investment, credit, and similar decisions do have common, overlapping interests in the ability of a business enterprise to generate favorable cash flows. It is the common interest in an enterprise's cash flow potential that the objectives of external financial reporting seek to satisfy.

The objectives in Concepts Statement No. 1 focus financial reporting on a particular kind of economic decision—the decision to commit or to continue to commit cash or other resources to a business enterprise with the expectation of payment or of future return of and return on the investment, usually in cash but sometimes in other goods and services. That kind of decision is made by investors, creditors, suppliers, employees, and other potential users of financial information, and they are interested in net cash inflows to the enterprise because their own prospects for receiving cash flows from investments in, loans to, or other participation in an enterprise depend significantly on its ability to generate favorable cash flows.

> Financial reporting should provide information to help present and potential investors and creditors and other users in assessing the amounts, timing, and uncertainty of prospective cash receipts from dividends or interest and the proceeds from the sale, redemption, or maturity of securities or loans. The prospects for those cash receipts are affected by an enterprise's ability to generate enough cash to meet its obligations when due and its other cash operating needs, to reinvest in operations, and to pay cash dividends and may also be affected by perceptions of investors and creditors generally about that ability, which affect market prices of the enterprise's securities. Thus, financial reporting should provide information to help investors, creditors, and others assess the amounts, timing, and uncertainty of prospective net cash inflows to the related enterprise. [Concepts Statement No. 1, paragraph 37]

Concepts Statement No. 1 explicitly recognizes that financial reporting does not and cannot provide all of the information needed by those who make economic decisions about business enterprises. It is but one source. Information provided by financial reporting needs to be combined with information about, among other things, the general economy, political climate, and prospects for an enterprise's particular industry or industries.

The objectives ultimately focus on the kind of information that fulfills the users' needs described and that the accounting system can provide better than other sources: information about assets, liabilities, and changes in them. Thus financial reporting should

> provide information about the economic resources of an enterprise, the claims to those resources (obligations of the enterprise to transfer resources to other entities and owners' equity), and the effects of transactions, events, and circumstances that change resources and claims to those resources. [Concepts Statement No. 1, paragraph 40]

That includes information about an enterprise's assets, liabilities, and owners' equity; information about enterprise performance provided by measures of comprehensive income (called *earnings* in Concepts Statement No. 1) and its components; information about liquidity, solvency, and funds flows; information about management stewardship and performance; and management's explanations and interpretations [paragraphs 41–54].

Objectives of Financial Reporting by Not-for-Profit Organizations.   The objectives of financial reporting by not-for-profit organizations are derived from the information needs of external resource providers who, like investors and creditors of business enterprises, generally cannot prescribe the information they want and thus must rely on information that management communicates to them. They are the primary users of the information provided by general purpose external financial reporting, whose primary objective is to

> provide information that is useful to present and potential resource providers and other users in making rational decisions about the allocation of resources to those organizations. [Concepts Statement No. 4, paragraph 35]

Resource providers encompass those who receive direct compensation for providing resources, including lenders, suppliers, and employees, as well as members, contributors, taxpayers, and others who are concerned with a not-for-profit organization's activities but who are not directly and proportionately compensated financially for their involvement.

The objectives flow from the common interests of those who provide resources to not-for-profit organizations in the services those organizations provide and in their continuing ability to provide services. Because the goals of not-for-profit organizations are to provide services rather than to generate profits,

> [f]inancial reporting should provide information to help present and potential resource providers and other users in assessing the services* that a [not-for-profit] organization provides and its ability to continue to provide those services. They are interested in that information because the services are the end for which the resources are provided. The relation of the services provided to the resources used to provide them helps resource providers and others assess the extent to which the organization is successful in carrying out its service objectives. [Concepts Statement No. 4, paragraph 38]

*The term "services" in this context encompasses the goods as well as the services a [not-for-profit] organization may provide.

The kinds of controls imposed on the operations of not-for-profit organizations to compensate for the reduced influence of markets significantly affect the objectives of their financial reporting. Alternative controls, such as specific budgetary appropriations that may limit the amount an organization is allowed to spend for a particular program or donor-imposed restrictions on the use of resources, usually place a special stewardship responsibility on managers to ensure that resources are used for their intended purposes. Those kinds of spending mandates tend to have a pervasive effect on the conduct and control of the activities of not-for-profit organizations. Because of the nature of the resources entrusted to managers of not-for-profit organizations, Concepts Statement No. 4 identifies the evaluation of management stewardship and performance information as an objective of the financial reporting of not-for-profit organizations:

> Financial reporting should provide information that is useful to present and potential resource providers and other users in assessing how managers of a [not-for-profit] organization have discharged their stewardship responsibilities and about other aspects of their performance. [Concepts Statement No. 4, paragraph 40]

Management stewardship is of concern to investors and creditors of business enterprises and resource providers of not-for-profit organizations. Both kinds of resource providers hold management accountable not only for the custody and safekeeping of an organization's resources but also for their efficient and effective use. Concepts Statement No. 1 identifies comprehensive income as the common focus for assessing management's stewardship or accountability (paragraph 51). Since profit figures are not available for not-for-profit organizations, Concepts Statement No. 4 instead delineates information about an organization's performance as the focus for assessing management stewardship. It says that financial reporting can provide information about the extent to which managers have acted in accordance with provisions specifically designated by donors. Information about departures from budget mandates or donor-imposed stipulations that may adversely affect an organization's financial performance or its ability to provide a satisfactory level of services is important in assessing how well managers have discharged their stewardship responsibilities.

The objectives of not-for-profit organizations, like those of business enterprises, ultimately focus on the kind of information that the accounting system can provide better than other sources:

> Financial reporting should provide information about the economic resources, obligations, and net resources of an organization and the effects of transactions, events, and circumstances that change resources and interests in those resources. [Concepts Statement No. 4, paragraph 43]

Resources are the lifeblood of an organization in the sense that it must have resources to render services. Since resource providers tend to direct their interest to information about how an organization acquires and uses its resources, financial reporting should provide information about an organization's assets, liabilities, and net assets; information about its performance, such as about the nature of and relation between resource inflows and outflows and about service efforts and accomplishments; information about liquidity; and managers' explanations and interpretations (paragraphs 44–55).

Keeping the Objectives in Perspective.   Financial accounting information is not intended to measure directly the value of a business enterprise. Nor is it intended to determine or influence the decisions that are made with information it provides about business enterprises and not-for-profit organizations. Its function is to provide the neutral or unbiased information that investors, creditors, various resource providers, and others who are interested in the activities of business enterprises and not-for-profit organizations can use in making those decisions. If financial information were directed toward a particular goal, such as encouraging the reallocation of resources toward particular business enterprises or industries or in favor of certain programs or activities of not-for-profit organizations, it would not be serving its broader objective of providing information useful for resource allocation decisions.

Moreover, as Concepts Statement No. 1 says, financial reporting is not financial analysis:

> Investors, creditors, and others often use reported [income] and information about the components of [income] in various ways and for various purposes in assessing their prospects for cash flows from investments in or loans to an enterprise. For example, they may use [income] information to help them (a) evaluate management's performance, (b) estimate "earning power" or other amounts they perceive as "representative" of long-term earning ability of an enterprise, (c) predict future [income], or (d) assess the risk of investing in or lending to an enterprise. They may use the information to confirm, reassure themselves about, or reject or change their own or others' earlier predictions or assessments. Measures of [income] and information about [income] disclosed by financial reporting should, to the extent possible, be useful for those and similar uses and purposes.

> However, accrual accounting provides measures of [income] rather than evaluations of management's performance, estimates of "earning power," predictions of [income], assessments of risk, or confirmations or rejections of predictions or assessments. Investors, creditors, and other users of the information do their own evaluating, estimating, predicting, assessing, confirming, or rejecting. For example, procedures such as averaging or normalizing reported [income] for several periods and ignoring or averaging out the financial effects of "nonrepresentative" transactions and events are commonly used in estimating "earning power." However, both the concept of "earning power" and the techniques for estimating it are part of financial analysis and are beyond the scope of financial reporting. [paragraphs 47 and 48; *income* has been substituted for *earnings,* which the Board replaced with *comprehensive income* after Concepts Statement No. 1]

(ii) Qualitative Characteristics of Accounting Information.   "The objectives of financial reporting underlie judgments about the qualities of financial information, for only when those objectives have been established can a start be made on defining the characteristics of the information needed to attain them" (Concepts Statement No. 2, paragraph 21). Having concluded in Concepts Statement No. 1 that to provide information useful for making investment, credit, and similar decisions is the primary objective of financial reporting, the FASB elaborated on the corollary to that objective in Concepts Statement No. 2: that the usefulness of financial information for decision making should be the primary quality to be sought in determining what to encompass in financial reporting. The qualities that make accounting information useful have been designated its "qualitative characteristics." The term was originally used by the Trueblood Study Group, but the idea of articulating the qualities of information that contribute to its usefulness in decision making has its genesis in the authoritative literature in APB Statement No. 4. That Statement described them as "qualitative objectives," which "aid in determining which resources and obligations and changes should be measured and reported and how they should be measured and reported to make the information most useful" (paragraph 84).

Both APB Statement No. 4 and the Trueblood Report are direct antecedents of the FASB Concepts Statements because emphasis on decision making by investors and creditors represented a departure from the AICPA's traditional view that financial statements primarily reported to present stockholders on management's stewardship of the corporation. Unless stewardship means mere custodianship, however, stockholders need essentially the same information for that purpose as they do for making investment decisions (Concepts Statement No. 1, paragraphs 50–53).

Concepts Statement No. 2.   Concepts Statement No. 2, *Qualitative Characteristics of Accounting Information,* is described as a bridge between Concepts Statement No. 1 and the other Statements on elements of financial statements, recognition and measurement, and display. It connects the Statements on objectives, which concern the purposes of financial reporting, with the later Concepts Statements and Standards Statements, which deal with how to attain those purposes, by sharing "with its constituents [the Board's] thinking about the characteristics that the information called for in its standards should have. It is those characteristics that distinguish more useful accounting information from less useful information" (paragraph 1).

When Concepts Statement No. 2 was issued, the Board noted that its discussion of the qualitative characteristics referred primarily to business enterprises but that it had tentatively concluded that the qualities also applied to the financial reporting of not-for-profit organizations. In Concepts Statement No. 6, in 1985, the Board formally amended Concepts Statement No. 2 to apply to both business enterprises and not-for-profit organizations by giving it a new paragraph 4:

> The qualities of information discussed in this Statement apply to financial information reported by business enterprises and by not-for-profit organizations. Although the discussion and the examples in this Statement are expressed in terms commonly related to business enterprises, they generally apply to not-for-profit organizations as well. "Objectives of financial reporting by business enterprises," "investors and creditors," "investment and credit decisions," and similar terms are intended to encompass their counterparts for not-for-profit organizations, "objectives of financial reporting by not-for-profit organizations," "resource providers," "resource allocation decisions," and similar terms.

Accountants are required to make a large number of choices—about the criteria by which assets and liabilities and revenues and expenses are to be recognized and the attribute(s) of assets and liabilities to be measured; about whether to allocate; about methods of allocation; about the level of aggregation or disaggregation of the information to be disclosed in financial reports. Accounting standards issued by the designated standards-setting body narrow the scope for individual choice, but accounting choices will always have to be made, whether between choices for which no standard has been promulgated or between alternative ways of implementing a standard.

> To maximize the usefulness of accounting information, subject to considerations of the cost of providing it, entails choices between alternative accounting methods. Those choices will be made more wisely if the ingredients that contribute to "usefulness" are better understood. [Concepts Statement No. 2, paragraph 5]

By defining the qualities that make accounting information useful, Concepts Statement No. 2 is intended to enable the Board and its staff to provide direction for developing accounting standards consistent with the objectives of financial reporting, which are oriented toward providing useful information for making investment, credit, and similar decisions:

> The central role assigned here to decision making leads straight to the overriding criterion by which all accounting choices must be judged. The better choice is the one that, subject to considerations of cost, produces from among the available alternatives information that is most useful for decision making. [Concepts Statement No. 2, paragraph 30]

Hierarchy of Accounting Qualities.   Concepts Statement No. 2 examines the characteristics that make accounting information useful, and the FASB has gone to considerable effort to lay out what usefulness means. Usefulness for making investment, credit, and similar decisions is the most

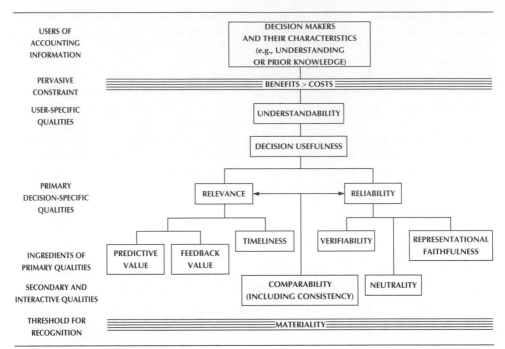

Exhibit 2.3   Hierarchy of Accounting Qualities
Source: Financial Accounting Standards Board, Statement of Financial Accounting Concepts No. 2, par. 32.

important quality in its "Hierarchy of Accounting Qualities": "The characteristics of information that make it a desirable commodity guide the selection of preferred accounting policies from among available alternatives.... Without usefulness, there would be no benefits from information to set against its costs. The hierarchy is represented in [Exhibit 2.3]" (Concepts Statement No. 2, paragraph 32).

Usefulness is a high-level abstraction. To serve as a meaningful criterion or standard against which to judge the results of financial accounting, usefulness needs to be made more concrete and specific by analyzing it into its components at lower levels of abstraction. The two primary components of usefulness are relevance and reliability. While those concepts are more concrete than usefulness, they are still quite abstract. That is why Concepts Statement No. 2 focuses at a still more concrete level, where the concepts of predictive value and feedback value, timeliness, representational faithfulness, verifiability, neutrality, and comparability together serve as criteria for determining information's usefulness.

For accounting standards setting, usefulness cannot be interpreted to mean whatever a particular individual interprets it to mean. A judgment that a piece of information is useful must be the result of a careful analysis that confirms first that the information possesses the qualities at the most concrete level of the hierarchy. Is it timely and does it have predictive or feedback value or both? Is it representationally faithful, verifiable, and neutral? If it has those characteristics, it is relevant and reliable. Only then, if information has survived that kind of examination, can it be deemed useful.

The exhibit also shows two constraints, primarily quantitative rather than qualitative in nature. The pervasive constraint is that the benefits of information should exceed its cost. Information that would be useful for a decision may be just too expensive to justify providing it. The second constraint is a *materiality threshold,* meaning that "the requirement that information be reliable can still be met even though it may contain immaterial errors, for errors that are not material will not perceptibly diminish its usefulness" (paragraph 33).

The hierarchy distinguishes between user-specific and decision-specific qualities because whether a piece of information is useful to a particular decision by a particular decision maker depends in part on the decision maker. Usefulness depends on a decision maker's degree of prior knowledge of the information as well as on his or her ability to understand it.

> The better informed decision makers are, the less likely it is that any new information can add materially to what they already know. That may make the new information less useful, but it does not make it less relevant to the situation. If an item of information reaches a user and then, a little later, the user receives the same item from another source, it is not less relevant the second time, though it will have less value. For that reason, relevance has been defined in this Statement (paragraphs 46 and 47) in terms of the capacity of information to make a difference (to someone who does not already have it) rather than in terms of the difference it actually does make. The difference it actually does make may be more a function of how much is already known (a condition specific to a particular user) than of the content of the new messages themselves (decision-specific qualities of information). [Concepts Statement No. 2, paragraph 37]

Similarly, the ability to understand a pertinent piece of information relates more to the characteristics of users for whom the information is intended than to the information itself. Even though information may be relevant to a decision, it will not be useful to a person who cannot understand it.

In Concepts Statement No. 1, the Board said that information provided by financial reporting "should be comprehensible to those who have a reasonable understanding of business and economic activities and are willing to study the information with reasonable diligence" (paragraph 34). But information's relevance may transcend the ability of a user to recognize its import:

> Financial information is a tool and, like most tools, cannot be of much direct help to those who are unable or unwilling to use it or who misuse it. Its use can be learned, however, and financial reporting should provide information that can be used by all—nonprofessionals as well as professionals—who are willing to learn to use it properly. Efforts may be needed to increase the understandability of financial information. Cost-benefit considerations may indicate that information understood or used by only a few should not be provided. Conversely, financial reporting should not exclude relevant information merely because it is difficult for some to understand or because some investors or creditors choose not to use it. [Concepts Statement No. 1, paragraph 36]

> Understandability of information is governed by a combination of user characteristics and characteristics inherent in the information, which is why understandability and other user-specific characteristics occupy a position in the hierarchy of qualities as a link between the characteristics of users (decision makers) and decision-specific qualities of information. [Concepts Statement No. 2, paragraph 40]

The two primary decision-specific qualities that make accounting information useful for decision making are relevance and reliability. If either is missing completely from a piece of information, the information will not be useful. In choosing between accounting alternatives, one should strive to produce information that is both as relevant and as reliable as possible, but at times it may be necessary to sacrifice some degree of one quality for a gain in the other.

Relevance

> To be relevant to investors, creditors, and others for investment, credit, and similar decisions, accounting information must be capable of making a difference in a decision by helping users to form predictions about the outcomes of past, present, and future events or to confirm or correct expectations. [Concepts Statement No. 2, paragraph 47]

That definition of relevance is more explicit than the dictionary meaning of relevance as bearing on or relating to the matter in hand. As alluded to earlier, prior knowledge of information may diminish its value but not its relevance and, hence, its usefulness, for it is information's ability to "make a difference" that makes it relevant to a decision.

Statements about relevance of financial statement information must answer the question "relevant to whom for what purpose?" For information to be judged relevant, an object to which it is relevant must always be understood.

Predictive Value and Feedback Value. To be relevant, information must have predictive value or feedback value or both.

> Information can make a difference to decisions by improving decision makers' capacities to predict or by confirming or correcting their earlier expectations. Usually, information does both at once, because knowledge about the outcome of actions already taken will generally improve decision makers' abilities to predict the results of similar future actions. Without a knowledge of the past, the basis for a prediction will usually be lacking. Without an interest in the future, knowledge of the past is sterile. [Concepts Statement No. 2, paragraph 51]

David Solomons, consultant on and major contributor to Concepts Statement No. 2, said in his book, *Making Accounting Policy,* that "whereas predictive value is forward-looking and is derived directly from its power to guide decisions, feedback value is derived from what information tells about the past." He gives as an example of a balance sheet item with predictive value the allowance for uncollectible receivables, which is the amount of accounts receivable that is not expected to produce future cash flows. The most important figure in financial statements with feedback value is the earnings figure, which "conveys information about the success of the ventures that have been invested in and also about the performance of the managers who have been responsible for running the business."[133]

To say that accounting information has predictive value is not to say that in itself it constitutes a prediction (Concepts Statement No. 2, paragraph 53). Predictive value means value as an input into a predictive process, not value directly as a prediction. It is "the quality of information that helps users to increase the likelihood of correctly forecasting the outcome of past or present events" (Concepts Statement No. 2, glossary). Information about the present state of economic resources or obligations or about an enterprise's past performance is commonly a basis for expectations. Information is relevant if it can reduce the uncertainty surrounding a decision. It is relevant "if the degree of uncertainty about the result of a decision that has already been made is confirmed or altered by the new information; it need not alter the decision" (Concepts Statement No. 2, paragraph 49).

Timeliness. To be relevant, information also must be timely. Timeliness means "[h]aving information available to a decision maker before it loses its capacity to influence decisions" (Concepts Statement No. 2, glossary). Information that is not available when it is needed or becomes available only long after it has value for future action is useless. "Timeliness alone cannot make information relevant, but a lack of timeliness can rob information of relevance it might otherwise have had" (Concepts Statement No. 2, paragraph 56).

Reliability. Reliability is the quality of information that allows those who use it to depend on it with confidence. "The reliability of a measure rests on the faithfulness with which it represents what it purports to represent, coupled with an assurance for the user, which comes through verification, that it has that representational quality" (Concepts Statement No. 2, paragraph 59). The hierarchy of qualities decomposes reliability into two components, representational faithfulness and verifiability, with neutrality shown to interact with them.

Representational Faithfulness. Representational faithfulness is "correspondence or agreement between a measure or description and the phenomenon it purports to represent. In accounting, the phenomena to be represented are economic resources and obligations and the transactions and events that change those resources and obligations" (Concepts Statement No. 2, paragraph 63). The FASB's conceptual framework emphasizes that accounting is a representational discipline. It represents things in the financial statements that exist in the real world. Therefore, the correspondence between the accounting representation and the thing being represented is critical.

---

[133] David Solomons, *Making Accounting Policy: The Quest for Credibility in Financial Reporting* (New York: Oxford University Press, 1986), pp. 89 and 90.

Concepts Statement No. 2 uses an analogy with mapmaking to illustrate what it means by representational faithfulness:

> A map represents the geographical features of the mapped area by using symbols bearing no resemblance to the actual countryside, yet they communicate a great deal of information about it. The captions and numbers in financial statements present a "picture" of a business enterprise and many of its external and internal relationships more rigorously—more informatively, in fact—than a simple description of it. [paragraph 24]

Just as the lines and shapes on a road map represent roads, rivers, and geographical boundaries, so also descriptions and amounts in financial statements represent cash, property, sales, and a host of things owned or owed by an entity as well as transactions and other events and circumstances that affect them or their values. The items in financial statements have a higher degree of reliability as quantitative representations of economic things and events in the real world—and therefore more usefulness to investors and other parties interested in an entity's activities—if they faithfully represent what they purport to represent. Since the benefit of the information is representational and not aesthetic, to take "artistic license" with the data decreases rather than increases its benefit. Just as a cartographer cannot add roads, bridges, and lakes where none exist, an accountant cannot add imaginary items to financial statements without spoiling the representational faithfulness, and ultimately the usefulness, of the information.

Striving for representational faithfulness does not comprehend creating an exact replica of the activities of an enterprise. Perfect information is as beyond the reach of accountants as it is of nonaccountants.

> The financial statements of a business enterprise can be thought of as a representation of the resources and obligations of an enterprise and the financial flows into, out of, and within the enterprise—as a model of the enterprise. Like all models, it must abstract from much that goes on in a real enterprise. No model, however sophisticated, can be expected to reflect all the functions and relationships that are found within a complex organization. To do so, the model would have to be virtually a reproduction of the original. In real life, it is necessary to accept a much smaller degree of correspondence between the model and the original than that. One can be satisfied if none of the important functions and relationships are lost.... The mere fact that a model works—that when it receives inputs it produces outputs—gives no assurance that it faithfully represents the original. Just as a distorting mirror reflects a warped image of the person standing in front of it..., so a bad model gives a distorted representation of the system that it models. The question that accountants must face continually is how much distortion is acceptable. [Concepts Statement No. 2, paragraph 76]

Completeness. Completeness of information is an important aspect of representational faithfulness, and thus of reliability, because if financial statements are to faithfully represent an enterprise's financial position and changes in financial position, none of the significant financial functions of the enterprise or its relationships can be lost or distorted. Completeness is defined as "the inclusion in reported information of everything material that is necessary for faithful representation of the relevant phenomena" (Concepts Statement No. 2, glossary). Financial statements are incomplete, and therefore not representationally faithful, if, for example, an enterprise owns an office structure but reports no "building" or similar asset on its balance sheet.

Completeness also is necessary to relevance, the other primary quality that makes accounting information useful:

> Relevance of information is adversely affected if a relevant piece of information is omitted, even if the omission does not falsify what is shown. For example, in a diversified enterprise a failure to disclose that one segment was consistently unprofitable would not, before the issuance of FASB Statement No. 14, *Accounting for Segments of a Business Enterprise,* have caused the financial reporting to be judged unreliable, but that financial reporting would have been (as it would now be) deficient in relevance. [Concepts Statement No. 2, paragraph 80]

Although completeness implies showing what is material and feasible, it must always be relative. Financial statements cannot show everything or they would be prohibitively expensive to provide.

Verifiability is "the ability through consensus among measurers to ensure that information represents what it purports to represent or that the chosen method of measurement has been used without error or bias" (Concepts Statement No. 2, glossary). Verifiability is an essential component of reliability—to be reliable, accounting information must be both representationally faithful and verifiable: "The reliability of a measure rests on the faithfulness with which it represents what it purports to represent, coupled with an assurance for the user, which comes through verification, that it has that representational quality" (Concepts Statement No. 2, paragraph 59). Verifiability fulfills a significant but relatively narrow function.

> In summary, verifiability means no more than that several measurers are likely to obtain the same measure. It is primarily a means of attempting to cope with measurement problems stemming from the uncertainty that surrounds accounting measures and is more successful in coping with some measurement problems than others.... [A] measure with a high degree of verifiability is not necessarily relevant to the decision for which it is intended to be useful. [Concepts Statement No. 2, paragraph 89]

Three ideas are the focus of the discussion in Concepts Statement No. 2 of verifiability and its relation to reliability:

1. Accounting information is verifiable if accounting measures obtained by one measurer can be confirmed or substantiated by having other measurers measure the same phenomenon with essentially the same results.

   > Verification implies consensus. Verifiability can be measured by looking at the dispersion of a number of independent measurements of some particular phenomenon. The more closely the measurements are likely to be clustered together, the greater the verifiability of the number used as a measure of the phenomenon.
   >
   > Some accounting measurements are more easily verified than others. Alternative measures of cash will be closely clustered together, with a consequently high level of verifiability. There will be less unanimity about receivables (especially their net value), still less about inventories, and least about depreciable assets.... [Concepts Statement No. 2, paragraphs 84 and 85]

2. The purpose of verification is to confirm the representational faithfulness of accounting information—to provide a significant degree of assurance to a user that accounting measures essentially agree with or correspond to the economic things and events that they represent (Concepts Statement No. 2, paragraphs 59, 81, and 86). Accounting information may not be representationally faithful because measurer bias or measurement bias (or both) gives a measure the tendency to be consistently too high or too low instead of being equally likely to fall above and below what it represents. Measurer bias is introduced if a measurer, unintentionally through lack of skill or intentionally through lack of integrity, or both, wrongly applies the chosen measurement method. Measurement bias results from using a biased measurement method (Concepts Statement No. 2, paragraphs 77, 78, and 82). Representational faithfulness is adversely affected if information is intentionally biased to attain a predetermined result or induce a particular mode of behavior, a possibility that is discussed in the next section on neutrality.

3. The extent to which verifiability adds reliability to accounting information depends on whether

   > an accounting measure itself has been verified or only ... the procedures used to obtain the measure have been verified. For example, the price paid to acquire a block of marketable securities or a piece of land is normally directly verifiable, while the amount of depreciation for a period is normally only indirectly verifiable by verifying the depreciation method, calculations used, and consistency of application. [Concepts Statement No. 2, paragraph 87]

In present practice, for example, the result of measuring the quantity of an inventory is directly verifiable, while the result of measuring the carrying amount or book value of the inventory is only indirectly verifiable—the auditing process checks on the accuracy or verity of the inputs and recalculates the outputs but does not verify them.

> For quantities there is a well-defined formal system (perpetual inventory system) which specifies the relevant empirical inputs (receipts and issues) and the output provides an expectation or prediction of the quantity on hand. The physical count is a separate [or direct] verification of that output.
>
> For book values there is disagreement about the formal system (LIFO or FIFO) and disagreement about the relevant inputs (which costs are to be attached [to inventory] and which are to be expensed). The output [book value of the inventory on hand] . . . is not separately verifiable.[134]

Measures of the quantity of the inventory resulting from the perpetual inventory system and the physical count verify each other if they essentially agree. Independent measures of a phenomenon need not use the same measurement process. In the absence of a perpetual inventory system, however, verifying the quantity of the inventory requires at least two independent physical counts or a third way to measure the quantity of the inventory.

It makes a difference to the reliability of accounting information whether an accounting measure itself is verified or only the procedures used to obtain the measure are verified because even if disagreements about choice of method and relevant inputs are ignored or resolved, merely rechecking the mechanics does not verify the representational faithfulness of the measure, leaving its reliability in doubt.

> Direct verification of accounting measures tends to minimize both personal bias introduced by a measurer (measurer bias) and bias inherent in measurement methods (measurement bias). Verification of only measurement methods tends to minimize measurer bias but usually preserves any bias there may be in the selection of measurement or allocation methods. [Concepts Statement No. 2, paragraph 87]
>
> The elimination of measurer bias alone from information does not insure that the information will be reliable. Even though several independent measurers may agree on a single measurement method and apply it honestly and skillfully, the result will not be reliable if the method used is such that the measure does not represent what it purports to represent. [Concepts Statement No. 2, paragraph 86]

The distinguishing characteristic of accounting measures that normally are directly or separately verifiable as representing what they purport to represent is that they measure market prices in transactions between independent entities (Concepts Statement No. 2, paragraphs 65 and 67). Two or more independent measurers are likely to obtain essentially the same measures in each instance, and the separate measures will tend to cluster. Some will show more dispersion than others, and relatively few, if any, will be as tightly clustered as separate measures of cash, but whether or not they reasonably represent what they purport to represent is verifiable.

The distinguishing characteristic of accounting measures whose representational faithfulness normally cannot be verified because only the procedures used to obtain the measure are verifiable is that they result from allocations, which interpose between the resulting measures and the market prices on which they are based a calculation or other means of allotting the cost or other past price to time periods or individual assets. As a result, the inputs and procedures of the allocation process often are readily verifiable, but the outputs—the resulting measures—are not (Concepts Statement No. 2, paragraphs 65–67). Two or more independent measurers are unlikely to obtain essentially the same measures in each instance, and the separate measures will tend to be dispersed or scattered rather than clustered. The reliability of the accounting measures themselves cannot be

---

[134] Robert R. Sterling, "On Theory Construction and Verification," *Accounting Review* (July 1970): 450, footnote 16.

verified because verifying only the procedures that produced them does not confirm or substantiate their representational faithfulness.

Since the point is likely to be misunderstood, it should explicitly be noted that the inability to verify the representational faithfulness of an accounting measure does not necessarily mean that the measure does not represent what it purports to represent. It generally means only that no one can know the extent to which the measure has or does not have that representational quality. Since the extent to which it represents faithfully the economic phenomenon it purports to represent is unknown, however, the measure cannot accurately be described as reliable.

Concepts Statement No. 2 also uses the difference between verifying a measure and verifying the method used to obtain it to show that reliability requires both representational faithfulness and verifiability. It illustrates how an accounting measure may be unreliable despite the verifiability of the allocation process that produced it using as an example the once-widespread practice, proscribed by FASB Statement No. 5, *Accounting for Contingencies,* for reasons described earlier in this chapter, of accruing "self-insurance reserves" by recognizing an annual expense or loss equal to a portion of expected future losses from fire, flood, or other casualties. Expectations of future losses could be actuarially computed for an enterprise with a large number of "self-insured" assets, and the methods of allocating expected losses to periods could be readily verified. Nevertheless, the representational faithfulness of the resulting measures would be extremely low, if not missing entirely. The "reserve for self insurance" in a balance sheet was a "what-you-may-call-it"—a deferred credit that did not qualify as a liability because the "self-insured" enterprise owed no one the amount of the reserve, or anything like it—and the allocated expense or loss in an income statement reported hypothetical effects of nonexistent transactions or events in years in which the enterprise suffered no casualties and, except by coincidence, grossly underreported losses incurred in years in which the enterprise's uninsured assets actually were damaged or destroyed by fire, flood, earthquake, hurricane, or the like.

Since the representational faithfulness of measures resulting from allocation procedures cannot be verified by rechecking the mechanics of how the measures were obtained, so-called historical cost accounting and other systems or models that depend heavily on allocations of prices in past transactions generally are considerably less reliable than is usually supposed. Concepts Statement No. 2 puts in perspective the oft-heard generalization that historical costs are "hard" information while current market prices are "soft" information—that historical cost information is reliable while current price information is not:

> More than one empirical investigation has concluded that accountants may agree more about estimates of the market values of certain depreciable assets than about their carrying values. Hence, to the extent that verification depends on consensus, it may not always be those measurement methods widely regarded as "objective" that are most verifiable. [paragraph 85]

Considerable confusion about reliability of accounting information results from the propensity of accountants and others to use reliable, objective, and verifiable interchangeably even though the three terms are not synonyms if used precisely. Reliable is a broader term than verifiable, comprising not only verifiability but also representational faithfulness. Objective is a narrower term than verifiable. It means being independent of the observer, implying that objective accounting information is free of measurer bias—not affected by the hopes, fears, and other thoughts and feelings of the measurer—but saying little or nothing about measurement bias. "Objectivity" and "objective" should assume the narrower meaning in accountants' vocabularies and be replaced by "verifiability" and "verifiable" to describe measures whose representational faithfulness can be confirmed through consensus of independent measurers and thus are reliable.

Neutrality. Neutrality is concerned with bias and thus is a factor in reliability of accounting information. It is the "absence in reported information of bias intended to attain a predetermined result or to induce a particular mode of behavior" (Concepts Statement No. 2, glossary). Accounting information is neutral if it "report[s] economic activity as faithfully as possible, without coloring the image it communicates for the purpose of influencing behavior in *some particular direction*" (paragraph 100).

A common perception and misconception is that displaying neutrality means treating everyone alike in all respects. It would not necessarily show a lack of neutrality to require less disclosure of a small company than of a large one if it were shown that an equal disclosure requirement placed an undue economic burden on the small company. Solomons says that neutrality "does not imply that no one gets hurt." His response to the argument that accounting policy can never be neutral because in any policy choice someone gets his or her preference and someone else does not clarifies the meaning of neutrality:

> The same thing could be said of the draft, when draft numbers were drawn by lot. Some people were chosen to serve while others escaped. It was still, by and large, neutral in the sense that all males of draft age were equally likely to be selected. It is not a necessary property of neutrality that everyone likes the results; the absence of intentional bias is at the heart of the concept.[135]

Neutrality requires that information should be free from bias toward a predetermined result, but that is not to say that standards setters or those who provide information according to promulgated standards should not have a purpose in mind for financial reporting. Accounting should not be without influence on human behavior, but it should not slant information to influence behavior in a particular way to achieve a desired end.

> Neutrality in accounting is an important criterion by which to judge accounting policies, for information that is not neutral loses credibility. If information can be verified and can be relied on faithfully to represent what it purports to represent—*and if there is no bias in the selection of what is reported*—it cannot be slanted to favor one set of interests over another. [Concepts Statement No. 2, paragraph 107]

Former Board member Arthur R. Wyatt emphasized the crucial nature of the quality of neutrality in Concepts Statement No. 2 to the FASB's process and to the widespread acceptability of its resulting standards:

> Early on ... the FASB undertook work to develop a conceptual framework, in part so that it could develop standards that had a logical cohesion, and in part so that the results of its deliberations could be evaluated to assess whether the resulting standards flowed from logical premises or may have been the result of lobbying activities or pressure politics.[136]

The Board unequivocally rejected the view that financial accounting standards should be slanted to foster a particular government policy or to favor one economic interest over another:

> The notion of neutrality within the Board's conceptual framework is that in resolving issues the Board will attempt to reach conclusions that result in reliable and relevant information and not conclusions that favor one segment of society to the detriment of one or more other segments.... [T]he notion of neutrality emphasizes that in developing the standard the Board ... is not overtly striving to reallocate resources for the benefit of one group to the detriment of others.[137]

On several occasions, Donald J. Kirk, former Board chairman, also made the point that neutrality is essential to fulfilling the objective of providing relevant and reliable information to investors,

---

[135] Solomons, *Making Accounting Policy,* p. 234.

[136] Arthur R. Wyatt, "Accounting Standards and the Professional Auditor," *Accounting Horizons* (June 1989): 97.

[137] Ibid.

creditors, and other users, and to prevent standards setting from becoming an exercise in directing resources to a preferred group. For example:

> [N]eutrality of information keeps financial reporting standards as a part of a measurement process, rather than a purposeful resource allocation process.... It is the emphasis on neutrality of information, as well as the independence of the standard setters from undue influence, that ensures the continued success of private sector standard setting.[138]

To protect the public interest in useful accounting information, what is needed is *not* "good business sense," *nor* even "good public policy," but rather "neutrality" (i.e., "absence in reported information of bias intended to attain a predetermined result or to induce a particular mode of behavior"). The chairman of the SEC made the point about the importance of neutrality in his statement on oil and gas accounting:

> If it becomes accepted or expected that accounting principles are determined or modified in order to secure purposes other than economic measurement—even such virtuous purposes as energy production—we assume a grave risk that confidence in the credibility of our financial information system will be undermined.[139]

Neutrality in standards setting is so significant that it has been incorporated into the FASB's Mission Statement, and Concepts Statement No. 2 itself explains why neutrality is so critical to the Board and to the standards-setting process. The first and last words in the section entitled "Neutrality" are:

> Neutrality in accounting has a greater significance for those who set accounting standards than for those who have to apply those standards in preparing financial reports, but the concept has substantially the same meaning for the two groups, and both will maintain neutrality in the same way. Neutrality means that either in formulating or implementing standards, the primary concern should be the relevance and reliability of the information that results, not the effect that the new rule may have on a particular interest.

> The Board's responsibility is to the integrity of the financial reporting system, which it regards as its paramount concern. [Concepts Statement No. 2, paragraphs 98 and 110]

Comparability.   Comparing alternative investment or lending opportunities is an essential part of most, if not all, investment or lending decisions. Investors and creditors need financial reporting information that is comparable, both for single enterprises over time and between enterprises at the same time. Comparability is a quality of the relationship between two or more pieces of information—"the quality of information that enables users to identify similarities in and differences between two sets of economic phenomena" (Concepts Statement No. 2, glossary). Comparability is achieved if similar transactions and other events and circumstances are accounted for similarly and different transactions and other events and circumstances are accounted for differently.

Comparability has been the subject of much disagreement among accountants. Some have argued that enterprises and their circumstances are so different from one another that comparability between enterprises is an illusory goal, and to include it as an aim of financial reporting is to promise to investors and creditors something that ultimately cannot be delivered. In that view, the best that can be hoped for is that individual enterprises will use their chosen accounting procedures consistently over time to permit comparisons with other enterprises and that honorable auditors will be able to attest to the consistent application of "generally accepted accounting principles."

---

[138] Kirk, "Looking Back on Fourteen Years at the FASB: The Education of a Standard Setter," p. 13.
[139] Donald J. Kirk, "Reflections on a 'Reconceptualization of Accounting': A Commentary on Parts I–IV of Homer Kripke's Paper, 'Reflections on the FASB's Conceptual Framework for Accounting and on Auditing,'" *Journal of Accounting, Auditing & Finance* (Winter 1989): 95. The excerpt quoted is from Harold M. Williams, chairman, Securities and Exchange Commission, "Accounting Practices for Oil and Gas Producers" (Washington, D.C., 1978), p. 12.

The problem with that view of comparability is that it allows an excessive degree of latitude in reporting practice. It was the dominant view during the 1930s and 1940s and did permit, or even encouraged, the proliferation of alternative accounting procedures that characterized the period, many in situations in which few significant differences in enterprises or circumstances were ever reasonably substantiated. The result was an intolerable lack of comparability, which was responsible for much of the criticism directed toward financial accounting and eventually led to the replacement of the Committee on Accounting Procedure by the APB.

Today, with the objectives of financial reporting focused on decision making, comparability is one of the most essential and desirable qualities of accounting information. Investors and creditors can no longer be expected to tolerate blanket claims of differences in circumstances to justify undue use of alternative accounting procedures. Only actual differences in transactions and other events and circumstances warrant different accounting.

Concepts Statement No. 2 notes that the need for comparable information is a fundamental rationale for standards setting:

> The difficulty in making financial comparisons among enterprises because of the use of different accounting methods has been accepted for many years as the principal reason for the development of accounting standards. [paragraph 112]

Some critics have focused on the standards setter's pursuit of comparability, calling it "uniformity," and mistakenly implying that standards are issued to require all enterprises to use the same accounting methods despite underlying differences. Comparability is, however, the antithesis of uniformity:

> Comparability should not be confused with identity, and sometimes more can be learned from differences than from similarities if the differences can be explained. The ability to explain phenomena often depends on the diagnosis of the underlying causes of differences or the discovery that apparent differences are without significance . . . . Greater comparability of accounting information, which most people agree is a worthwhile aim, is not to be attained by making unlike things look alike any more than by making like things look different. [Concepts Statement No. 2, paragraph 119]

In fact, uniformity of practice may be a greater threat to comparability than is too much flexibility in choice of accounting method. Investors and creditors can often discern and compensate for lack of comparability caused by alternative procedures, but they usually have no way of detecting a lack of comparability caused by forced uniformity of practice.

Consistency, meaning "conformity from period to period with unchanging policies and procedures" (Concepts Statement No. 2, glossary), has long been regarded as an important quality of information provided by financial statements. For example, it was an explicit part of the recommendation of the Special Committee on Cooperation with Stock Exchanges in 1932. Auditors are required to point out changes in accounting principles or in the method of their application that have a material effect on the comparability of a client's financial statements.

Consistent use of accounting methods, whether from one period to another within a single firm or within a single period across firms, is a necessary but not a sufficient condition of comparability. Consistency in applying accounting methods over time contributes to comparability, provided that the methods consistently applied were reasonably comparable to begin with. Lack of comparability will never be transformed into comparability by consistent application. If what is measured and reported has representational faithfulness, an accurate analysis of similarities and differences will be possible, and comparability is enhanced. However, in the same way that lack of timeliness can deprive information of relevance it might otherwise have had, inconsistent use of comparable information can ruin whatever comparability the information might otherwise have had.

Concern for consistency does not mean that accountants should not be open to new and better methods and standards. A change need not inhibit comparability if its effects are properly disclosed.

Conservatism.   A word needs to be said about conservatism, an important doctrine in most accountants' minds, but not a separate qualitative characteristic in the FASB's hierarchy of qualities that make accounting information useful. The FASB has described conservatism as "a prudent reaction to uncertainty to try to ensure that uncertainties and risks inherent in business situations are adequately considered" (Concepts Statement No. 2, paragraph 95). That is quite different from the traditional meaning of conservatism in financial reporting, which usually connoted deliberate, consistent understatement of net assets and profits, summed up by the admonition to "anticipate no profits but anticipate all losses." That view developed during a time when balance sheets were considered the primary (and often only) financial statement, and bankers or other lenders were their principal external users. Since understating assets was thought to provide a greater margin of safety as security for loans and other debts, deliberate understatement was considered a virtue.

The traditional application of conservatism introduced into reporting a preference "that possible errors in measurement be in the direction of understatement rather than overstatement of net income and net assets" (APB Statement No. 4, paragraph 171). In practice that often meant depressing reported net income by excessive depreciation or undervaluation of inventory or deferring recognition of income until long after sufficient evidence of its existence became available.

That kind of conservatism has now become discredited because it conflicts with the information's comparability, with its representational faithfulness and neutrality, and thus with its reliability. Any kind of bias, whether overly conservative or overly optimistic, influences the timing of recognition of net income or losses and may mislead investors as they attempt to evaluate alternative investment opportunities. Information that adds to uncertainty is inimical to informed and rational decision making and betrays the fulfillment of the objectives of financial reporting.

> The appropriate way to treat uncertainty is to disclose its nature and extent honestly, so that those who receive the information may form their own opinions of the probable outcome of the events reported. That is the only kind of conservatism that can, in the long run, serve all of the divergent interests that are represented in a business enterprise. It is not the accountant's job to protect investors, creditors, and others from uncertainty, but only to inform them about it. Any attempt to understate earnings or financial position consistently is likely to engender skepticism about the reliability and the integrity of what is reported. Moreover, it will probably be ultimately self-defeating.[140]

Materiality.   The final item on the hierarchy, characterized as a constraint or *threshold for recognition,* is materiality, which is a *quantitative,* not a qualitative, characteristic of information. Materiality judgments pose the question: "Is this item large enough for users of the information to be influenced by it?" [Concepts Statement No. 2, paragraph 123]. Materiality means:

> the magnitude of an omission or misstatement of accounting information that, in the light of surrounding circumstances, makes it probable that the judgment of a reasonable person relying on the information would have been changed or influenced by the omission or misstatement. [Concepts Statement No. 2, glossary]

Popular usage of *material* often makes it a synonym for *relevant,* but the two are not synonymous in Concepts Statement No. 2. Information may be relevant in the sense that it is capable of making a difference and yet the amounts involved are immaterial—too small to matter in a decision. To illustrate the difference between materiality and relevance, Concepts Statement No. 2 (paragraph 126) provides an example of an applicant for employment who is negotiating with an employment agency. On one hand, information about the nature of the duties, salary, hours, and benefits is relevant, as well as material, to most prospective employees. On the other hand, whether the office floor is carpeted and whether the cafeteria food is of good quality are relevant, but probably not material, to a decision to accept the job. The values placed on them by the applicant are too small to influence the decision.

---

[140] Solomons, *Making Accounting Policy,* p. 101.

However, materiality judgments go beyond magnitude itself to the nature of the item and the circumstances in which the judgment has to be made. Items too small to be thought material if they result from routine transactions may be considered material if they arise in abnormal circumstances. Therefore, one must always think in terms of a threshold over which an item must pass, considering its nature and the attendant circumstances as well as its relative amount, that separates material from immaterial items.

Where the threshold for recognition occurs with regard to a materiality decision is a matter of judgment. Many accountants would like to have more quantitative guidelines or criteria for materiality laid down by the SEC, the FASB, or other regulatory agency. The FASB's view has been that materiality judgments can best be made by those who possess all the facts. In recognition of the fact that materiality guidance is sometimes needed, the appendices to Concepts Statement No. 2 include a list of quantitative guidelines that have been applied both in the law and in the practice of accounting. However, if and when those guidelines specify some minimum size stipulated for recognition of a material item, they do not preclude recognition of a smaller segment. There is still room for individual judgment in at least one direction.

Costs and Benefits. Information is subject to the same pervasive cost-benefit constraint that affects the usefulness of other commodities: Unless the benefits to be derived from information equal or exceed the cost of acquiring it, it will not be pursued. Financial information is unlike other commodities, however, in being a partly private and partly public good since "the benefits of information cannot always be confined to those who pay for it" (Concepts Statement No. 2, paragraph 135), and the balancing of costs and benefits cannot be left to the market.

Cost-benefit decisions about accounting standards generally have to be made by the standards-setting body—now the FASB. Both costs and benefits of accounting standards cut across the whole spectrum of the Board's constituency, with the benefits only partly accruing to those who bear the costs and the balance between costs and benefits reacting very imperfectly to supply and demand considerations. Moreover, individuals, be they providers, users, or auditors of accounting information, are not in a position to make cost-benefit assessments due to lack of sufficient information as well as probable biases on the matter.

Cost-benefit decisions are extremely difficult because both costs and benefits often are subjective and difficult or impossible to measure reliably. Cost-benefit analysis is at best a fallible tool. Although the Board is committed to doing the best it can in making cost-benefit assessments and Board members indeed have taken the matter seriously in facing the question in several standards in which it has arisen, cost-benefit measures and comparisons are too unreliable to be the deciding factor in crucial standards-setting decisions.

Impact of the Qualitative Characteristics. In the 25 years since the Trueblood Study Group, and later the FASB, authoritatively clarified the objectives of financial reporting and the consequent primacy of usefulness of financial information for decision making, an evolution in accounting thought has slowly taken place:

> Once decision making is seen as the primary objective of financial reporting, it is inevitable that the usefulness of financial information for making decisions should be the primary quality to be sought in deciding what is to be reported and how that reporting is to be done. This is not quite the truism that it seems to be, for . . . only a minority of the respondents to an FASB inquiry in 1974 favored the adoption of that objective. Since 1974 there has been a striking change in attitude among persons interested in financial reporting, and decision usefulness has become widely accepted as the most important quality that financial information should have.[141]

The qualitative characteristics have also had an impact on practice. Former FASB vice chairman Robert T. Sprouse, in an appearance at a Harvard Business School conference entitled "Conceptual

---

[141] Ibid., p. 86.

Frameworks for Financial Accounting" in October 1982, described their contribution to accounting debate:

> I must confess that initially, although it was clear that certain identified qualitative characteristics of accounting information constituted an essential component of a conceptual framework for general purpose, external financial reporting, I was skeptical about their contribution to the standard setting process. It seemed to go without saying that accounting information should be relevant and reliable; I doubted that explicit acknowledgment of such qualities would be very useful to preparers, auditors, users, and standard setters in making decisions about financial reporting issues. I was wrong.
>
> The qualitative characteristics project has proven to be extremely valuable, particularly in improving communications among the many and varied organizations and individuals who are involved in resolving financial reporting issues. Statement No. 2 has established a language that has significantly enhanced the degree of precision and level of understanding in discussions of those matters. Increasingly, position papers and comment letters submitted to the FASB refer to specific qualitative characteristics to support positions that are advocated, recommendations that are proffered, and criticisms that are aimed at Board proposals. Similarly, in Board discussions and deliberations it is no longer sufficient to argue that something is relevant or irrelevant and reliable or unreliable. One must specify whether it is predictive value that is enhanced or lacking or whether representational faithfulness would be achieved or be absent, or whether it is some other aspect of relevance or reliability that is affected. The result has been greater precision in thinking about issues and greater understanding in communicating about them.[142]

(iii) Elements of Financial Statements.   Concepts Statement No. 1 said that "financial reporting should provide information about the economic resources of an enterprise, the claims to those resources (obligations of the enterprise to transfer resources to other entities and owners' equity), and the effects of transactions, events, and circumstances that change resources and claims to those resources" (paragraph 40). Concepts Statement No. 6 (and previously Concepts Statement No. 3) provides the means for carrying out that objective. It defines the elements of financial statements—the economic resources of an entity, the claims to those resources, and changes in them—about which information is relevant to investors, creditors, and other users of financial statements for investment, credit, and similar decisions.

> The elements defined in this Statement are a related group with a particular focus—on assets, liabilities, equity, and other elements directly related to measuring performance and status of an entity. Information about an entity's performance and status provided by accrual accounting is the primary focus of financial reporting. [Concepts Statement No. 6, paragraph 3]

Concepts Statement No. 3.   Concepts Statement No. 3, *Elements of Financial Statements of Business Enterprises,* issued in December 1980, defined 10 elements: assets, liabilities, equity, investments by owners, distributions to owners, and comprehensive income and its components: revenues, expenses, gains, and losses. The Statement introduced the term *comprehensive income,* the name adopted by the Board for the concept that was called "earnings" in Concepts Statement No. 1 and the other conceptual framework documents previously issued, including the *Tentative Conclusions on Objectives of Financial Statements of Business Enterprises* (December 1976); the Discussion Memorandum, *Conceptual Framework for Financial Accounting and Reporting: Elements of Financial Statements and Their Measurement* (December, 1976); and the Exposure Draft, *Objectives of Financial Reporting and Elements of Financial Statements of Business Enterprises* (December 1977). As its title shows, the first Exposure Draft in the conceptual framework project dealt with both objectives and elements.

---

[142] *Conceptual Frameworks for Financial Accounting,* Proceedings of a conference at the Harvard Business School, October 1–2, 1982, H. David Sherman, ed. (Cambridge, MA: President and Fellows of Harvard College, circa 1984), p. 33.

During 1978, the Board divided the subject matter of the Exposure Draft. One part developed into Concepts Statement No. 1 on objectives, and another part became the basis for a revised Exposure Draft, *Elements of Financial Statements of Business Enterprises,* which was issued in December 1979. The substance of that Exposure Draft became Concepts Statement No. 3.

The Board's work on not-for-profit reporting was advancing concurrently, and Concepts Statement No. 4, *Objectives of Financial Reporting by Nonbusiness Organizations,* was issued with Concepts Statement No. 3 in December 1980. The four Concepts Statements constituted a single conceptual framework for financial accounting and reporting by all entities. The Board voiced its expectation in Concepts Statements Nos. 2 and 3 that the qualitative characteristics and definitions of elements of financial statements should apply to both business enterprises and not-for-profit organizations.

> Although the discussion of the qualities of information and the related examples in this Statement refer primarily to business enterprises, the Board has tentatively concluded that similar qualities also apply to financial information reported by nonbusiness organizations. [Concepts Statement No. 2, paragraph 4]

> Assets and liabilities are common to all organizations, and the Board sees no reason to define them differently for business and nonbusiness organizations. The Board also expects the definitions of equity, revenues, expenses, gains, and losses to fit both business and nonbusiness organizations. [Concepts Statement No. 3, paragraph 2]

The Board saw no need for two separate statements on elements as it had for the objectives.

To solicit views on applying the qualitative characteristics and definitions of elements to both business enterprises and not-for-profit organizations, the Board issued an Exposure Draft, *Proposed Amendments to FASB Concepts Statements 2 and 3 to Apply Them to Nonbusiness Organizations,* in July 1983. The Board reaffirmed the conclusion that the qualitative characteristics applied to not-for-profit organizations and issued a revised Exposure Draft, *Elements of Financial Statements,* in September 1985. Concepts Statement No. 6, *Elements of Financial Statements,* was issued in December 1985, superseding Concepts Statement No. 3 and extending that Statement's definitions to not-for-profit organizations. Most of Concepts Statement No. 3 was carried over into the parts of Concepts Statement No. 6 concerned with business enterprises or with both kinds of entities. Paragraph numbers were changed, however, because Concepts Statement No. 6 has numerous paragraphs that relate only to not-for-profit organizations or that explain how the definitions in Concepts Statement No. 3 apply to not-for-profit organizations.

Concepts Statement No. 6.   Concepts Statement No. 6 defines the same 10 elements of financial statements that Concepts Statement No. 3 had defined: Seven are elements of the financial statements of both business enterprises and not-for-profit organizations—assets, liabilities, equity (business enterprises) or net assets (not-for-profit organizations), revenues, expenses, gains, and losses; and three are elements of financial statements of business enterprises only—investments by owners, distributions to owners, and comprehensive income. The Statement also defines three classes of net assets of not-for-profit organizations, characterized by the presence or absence of donor-imposed restrictions, and the changes in those classes during a period—changes in permanently restricted, temporarily restricted, and unrestricted net assets. For business enterprises, equity is defined only in total.

To try to avoid later confusion, Concepts Statement No. 6 is precise about what is an element and what is not. For example, cash, inventories, land, and buildings are items that fit the definition of assets, but they are not elements. Assets is the element:

> Elements of financial statements are the building blocks with which financial statements are constructed—the classes of items that financial statements comprise. *Elements* refers to broad classes, such as assets, liabilities, revenues, and expenses. Particular economic things and events, such as cash on hand or selling merchandise, that may meet the definitions of elements are not

elements as the term is used in this Statement. Rather, they are called *items* or other descriptive names. This Statement focuses on the broad classes and their characteristics instead of defining particular assets, liabilities, or other items. [paragraph 5]

The Statement then emphasizes that the elements in financial statements stand for things and events in the real world:

> The items that are formally incorporated in financial statements are financial representations (depictions in words and numbers) of certain resources of an entity, claims to those resources, and the effects of transactions and other events and circumstances that result in changes in those resources and claims. That is, symbols (words and numbers) in financial statements stand for cash in a bank, buildings, wages due, sales, use of labor, earthquake damage to property, and a host of other economic things and events pertaining to an entity existing and operating in what is sometimes called the "real world." [paragraph 6]

The definitions are of the real-world things and events, not of what is recognized in financial statements. That is, the definition of assets, for example, refers to assets such as the inventory in the warehouse, not to the word "inventory" and the related amount in the balance sheet.

A thing or event and its representation in financial statements commonly are called by the same name. For example, both the amount deposited in a checking account and its representation in the balance sheet are called cash in bank.

Elements of financial statements are of two types: those that constitute financial position or status at a moment in time and those that are changes in financial position over a period of time. Assets, liabilities, and equity or net assets describe levels or amounts of resources or claims to or interests in resources at a moment in time. All other elements—revenues, expenses, gains, and losses (and for business enterprises, comprehensive income, and investments by and distributions to owners)—describe the effects of transactions and other events and circumstances that affect an entity over a period of time. The interrelation between the two types of elements is called articulation:

> The two types of elements are related in such a way that (a) assets, liabilities, and equity (net assets) are changed by elements of the other type and at any time are their cumulative result and (b) an increase (decrease) in an asset cannot occur without a corresponding decrease (increase) in another asset or a corresponding increase (decrease) in a liability or equity (net assets). Those relations are sometimes collectively referred to as *articulation*. They result in financial statements that are fundamentally interrelated so that statements that show elements of the second type depend on statements that show elements of the first type and vice versa. [Concepts Statement No. 6, paragraph 21]

The elements of financial statements are defined in relation to particular entities, which may be business enterprises, not-for-profit organizations, other economic units, or people. For example, items that qualify as assets under the definition are assets of particular entities.

Definition of Assets.   There is no more fundamental concept in accounting than assets. Assets, or economic resources, are the lifeblood of both business enterprises and not-for-profit organizations. Without assets—to exchange for, combine with, or transform into other assets—those entities would have no reason to exist.

> Economic resources or assets and changes in them are central to the existence and operations of an individual entity. Both business enterprises and not-for-profit organizations are in essence resource or asset processors, and a resource's capacity to be exchanged for cash or other resources or to be combined with other resources to produce needed or desired scarce goods or services gives it utility and value (future economic benefit) to an entity.

> Since resources or assets confer their benefits on an enterprise by being exchanged, used, or otherwise invested, changes in resources or assets are the purpose, the means, and the result of

an enterprise's operations, and a business enterprise exists primarily to acquire, use, produce, and distribute resources. [Concepts Statement No. 6, paragraphs 11 and 15]

Because the concept of assets is so fundamental, one would think that the issue of what is or is not an asset would have been settled long ago. All accountants claim to know an asset when they see one, yet differences of opinion arise about whether some items called assets are assets at all and should be included in balance sheets. Those differences of opinion surfaced at the FASB's first hearings, as already described, and those experiences convinced early Board members that workable definitions of assets and liabilities were imperative.

The FASB decided on the conceptual primacy of assets and liabilities, meaning that the definitions of all the other elements of financial statements are derived from the definitions of assets and liabilities. Since the definition of assets is critical, Concepts Statement No. 6 provides a carefully worded definition with three essential facets, adds nine paragraphs explaining the characteristics of assets, and devotes a significant part of Appendix B to the Statement to elaborating the concept of assets. All of those sections are part of the definition of assets.

The definition of assets is in paragraph 25:

Assets are probable future economic benefits obtained or controlled by a particular entity as a result of past transactions or events.

Paragraph 26 then describes the trio of characteristics that qualify an item as an asset:

An asset has three essential characteristics: (a) it embodies a probable future benefit that involves a capacity, singly or in combination with other assets, to contribute directly or indirectly to future net cash inflows, (b) a particular entity can obtain the benefit and control others' access to it, and (c) the transaction or other event giving rise to the entity's right to or control of the benefit has already occurred.

The definition indicates the appropriate questions to ask in trying to decide whether or not a particular item is an asset: Is there a future economic benefit? If so, to which entity does it belong? What made it an asset of that entity?

Future Economic Benefits.   Assets commonly are items that also can be characterized as economic resources—the scarce means through which people and other economic units carry out economic activities such as consumption, production, and exchange. All economic resources or assets have "service potential" or "future economic benefit," the scarce capacity to provide services or benefits to the people or other entities that use or hold them.

Future economic benefit is the essence of an asset (paragraphs 27–31). An asset has the capacity to serve the entity by being exchanged for something else of value to the entity, by being used to produce something of value to the entity, or by being used to settle its liabilities.

The most obvious evidence of future economic benefit is a market price. Anything that is commonly bought and sold has future economic benefit.... Similarly, anything that creditors or others commonly accept in settlement of liabilities has future economic benefit, and anything that is commonly used to produce goods or services, whether tangible or intangible and whether or not it has a market price or is otherwise exchangeable, also has future economic benefit. Incurrence of costs may be significant evidence of acquisition or enhancement of future economic benefits. [Concepts Statement No. 6, paragraphs 172 and 173]

All value of economic (scarce) goods and services derives ultimately from the utility of consumers' goods and services, which are used primarily by individuals and families. Their capacity to satisfy human needs or wants creates demand not only for them but also for the producers' goods and services, used primarily by business enterprises and other producers, that provide economic benefit by being used, directly or indirectly, to produce consumers' goods and services or other producers' goods and services. Cash is the asset par excellence because of what it can buy. "It can be exchanged for virtually any good or service that is available or it can be saved and exchanged for them in the future" (Concepts Statement No. 3, paragraph 23) and is the medium for settling most liabilities.[143]

At least two questions need to be asked about the presence or absence of future economic benefit to determine whether or not an entity has an asset: Did the item obtained by an entity truly represent a future economic benefit in the first place, and does all or any of the future economic benefit to the entity remain at the time the issue of its being an asset is considered?

Concepts Statement No. 6 says that most assets presently included in financial statements qualify as assets under its definition because they have future economic benefits (paragraph 177). They include cash, accounts and notes receivable, interest and dividends receivable, and investments in the securities of other entities. Inventories of raw materials, work-in-process, and finished goods and productive resources such as property, plant, and equipment also qualify as assets, but some "assets" that have often been described in accounting literature as "deferred costs" or "deferred charges to revenues" either fail to qualify as assets or may perhaps represent assets but cannot reliably be recognized as assets.

Deferred costs that fail to qualify as assets are what-you-may-call-its—deferred costs that do not represent economic resources but are said to be assets "because they must be deferred and matched with future revenues to avoid distorting net income." For reasons described earlier, the Board firmly rejected the argument that "costs are assets," and Concepts Statement No. 6 is explicit:

> Although an entity normally incurs costs to acquire or use assets, costs incurred are not themselves assets. The essence of an asset is its future economic benefit rather than whether or not it was acquired at a cost . . . .
>
> . . . [I]ncurrence of a cost may be evidence that an entity has acquired one or more assets, but it is not conclusive evidence. Costs may be incurred without receiving services or enhanced future economic benefits. Or, entities may obtain assets without incurring costs—for example, from investment in kind by owners or contributions of securities or buildings by donors. The ultimate evidence of the existence of assets is the future economic benefit, not the costs incurred. [paragraphs 179 and 180]

Deferred costs that may or may not represent assets are victims of the pervasive uncertainty in business and economic affairs that often obscures whether or not some items have the capacity to provide future economic benefits to an entity and thus should be recognized as assets. A question arises whether an item received should be recognized as an asset or as an expense or loss if the value of future benefit obtained is uncertain or even doubtful or if the future benefit may be short-lived or of highly uncertain duration. Expenditures for research and development, advertising, training, development of new markets, relocation, and goodwill are examples of items for which management's intent clearly is to obtain or augment future economic benefits but for which there is uncertainty about the extent, if any, to which the expenditures succeeded in creating or increasing future economic benefits. That uncertainty led to FASB Statement No. 2, *Accounting for Research and Development Costs,* in which the Board for primarily practical reasons required entities to recognize the expenditures as expenses or losses rather than as assets. If research and development or advertising costs actually result in new or greater future economic benefit, that benefit qualifies as an asset. The practical problems are in determining whether future economic benefit is actually present and in quantifying it, especially if realization of benefits is far down the road, or perhaps never.[144]

---

[143] L. Todd Johnson and Reed K. Storey, *Recognition in Financial Statements: Underlying Concepts and Practical Conventions,* FASB Research Report (Stamford, CT: Financial Accounting Standards Board, 1982), pp. 91–94.

[144] This paragraph paraphrases paragraphs 44, 45, and 173 of Concepts Statement No. 6 and briefly summarizes the conclusions of FASB Statement No. 2, *Accounting for Research and Development Costs,* whose development raised questions that helped Board members decide that a definition of assets was essential.

Services provided by other entities can be assets of an entity only momentarily as they are received and used, and they commonly are recognized as expenses when received, but the right to receive services for specified or determinable future periods qualifies as an asset.

Control by a Particular Entity.   The definition defines assets in relation to specific entities. An asset is an asset of some entity. No asset can simultaneously be an asset of more than one entity, although some physical assets may provide future economic benefits to two or more entities at the same time. That is, some assets comprise separable bundles of benefits that may be unbundled and held simultaneously by two or more entities so that each has an asset. For example, a building may provide future economic benefits to its owner, to an entity that leases space in it, and to an entity that holds a mortgage on it. Each has an interest in a different aspect of the same building, and each expects to receive cash flows from having one or more of the bundles of benefits.

An entity must control an item's future economic benefit to be able to consider the item as its asset. To enjoy an asset's benefits, an entity generally must be in a position to deny or regulate access to that benefit by others, for example, by permitting access only at a price.

> Thus, an asset of an entity is the future economic benefit that the entity can control and thus can, within limits set by the nature of the benefit or the entity's right to it, use as it pleases. The entity having an asset is the one that can exchange it, use it to produce goods or services, exact a price for others' use of it, use it to settle liabilities, hold it, or perhaps distribute it to owners. [Concepts Statement No. 6, paragraph 184]

An entity usually gains the ability to control an asset's future economic benefits through a legal right. However, an entity still may have an asset without having an enforceable legal right to it if it can obtain and control the benefit some other way, for example, by maintaining exclusive access to the asset's benefits by keeping secret a formula or process.

Occurrence of a Past Transaction or Event.   Items become assets of an entity as the result of transactions or other events or circumstances that have already occurred. An entity has an asset only if it has the present ability to obtain that asset's future economic benefits. If an entity anticipates that it may in the future control an item's future economic benefits but as yet does not have that control, it cannot claim that item as its asset because the transaction, other event, or circumstance conferring that control has not yet occurred.

> Since the transaction or event giving rise to the entity's right to the future economic benefit must already have occurred, the definition excludes from assets items that may in the future become an entity's assets but have not yet become its assets. An entity has no asset for a particular future economic benefit if the transactions or events that give it access to and control of the benefit are yet in the future. [Concepts Statement No. 6, paragraph 191]

Similarly, once acquired, an asset continues as an asset of an entity as long as the transactions, other events, or circumstances that use up or destroy its future economic benefit or deprive the entity of its control are in the future.

Definition of Liabilities.   The definition of *liabilities* in paragraph 35 of Concepts Statement No. 6 has the same structure as the definition of assets in paragraph 25. The parallelism of the two definitions was deliberate.

> Liabilities are probable future sacrifices of economic benefits arising from present obligations of a particular entity to transfer assets or provide services to other entities in the future as a result of past transactions or events.

> Paragraph 36 describes the three characteristics that an item must possess to be a liability:

> A liability has three essential characteristics: (a) it embodies a present duty or responsibility to one or more other entities that entails settlement by probable future transfer or use of assets at a specified or determinable date, on occurrence of a specified event, or on demand, (b) the duty

or responsibility obligates a particular entity, leaving it little or no discretion to avoid the future sacrifice, and (c) the transaction or other event obligating the entity has already happened.

The definition prompts the following questions when trying to decide if a particular item constitutes a liability: Is there an obligation requiring a future sacrifice of assets? If so, which entity is obligated? What past transaction or event made it a liability of that entity?

Required Future Sacrifice of Assets. Liabilities commonly arise as the consequence of financial instruments, contracts, and laws invented to facilitate the functioning of a highly developed economy by permitting delays in payment and delivery in return for interest or other compensation as the price for enduring delay. Entities routinely incur liabilities to acquire the funds, goods, and services they need to operate and just as routinely settle the liabilities they incur, usually by paying cash. For example, borrowing cash results in an obligation to repay the amount borrowed, usually with interest; using employees' knowledge, skills, time, and effort results in an obligation to pay compensation for their use; or selling products with warranties results in an obligation to pay cash or to repair or replace the products that prove defective. Liabilities come in a vast array of forms, but they all entail a present obligation requiring a nondiscretionary future sacrifice of some economic benefit:

> The essence of a liability is a duty or requirement to sacrifice assets in the future. A liability requires an entity to transfer assets, provide services, or otherwise expend assets to satisfy a responsibility to one or more other entities that it has incurred or that has been imposed on it. [Concepts Statement No. 6, paragraph 193]

Although most liabilities arise from exchanges between entities, most of which are contractual in nature, some obligations are imposed by laws or governmental regulations that require sacrificing assets to comply.

Receipt of proceeds—cash, other assets, or services—without an accompanying cash payment is often evidence that a liability has been incurred, but it is not conclusive evidence. Other transactions and events generate proceeds—cash sales of goods or services or other sales of assets, cash from donors' contributions, or cash investments by owners—without incurring liabilities. Liabilities can be incurred without any accompanying receipt of proceeds, for example, by imposition of taxes. It is the obligation to sacrifice economic benefits in the future that signifies a liability, not whether proceeds were received by incurring it.

Most liabilities presently included in financial statements qualify as liabilities under the definition because they require a future sacrifice of assets. They include accounts and notes payable, wages and salaries payable, long-term debt, interest and dividends payable, and obligations to honor warranties and to pay pensions, deferred compensation, and taxes. Subscriptions or rents collected in advance or other "unearned revenues" from deposits and prepayments received for goods or services to be provided are also liabilities because they obligate an entity to provide goods or services to other entities in the future. Those kinds of items sometimes have been referred to as deferred credits or reserves in the accounting literature.

Obligation of a Particular Entity

> To have a liability, an entity must be obligated to sacrifice its assets in the future—that is, it must be bound by a legal, equitable, or constructive duty or responsibility to transfer assets or provide services to one or more other entities. [Concepts Statement No. 6, paragraph 200]

A liability entails an obligation—legal, moral, or ethical—to one or more other entities to convey assets to them or provide them with services in the future. Not all probable future sacrifices of assets are liabilities of an entity. An intent or expectation to enter into a contract or transaction to transfer assets does not constitute a liability until an obligation to another entity is taken on.

The obligation aspect of liabilities is not emphasized as strongly in the definition in the Concepts Statement as it perhaps might have been. The Board became enamored with making the one-sentence definitions of assets and liabilities parallel to accentuate the symmetry between future benefits of assets and future sacrifices of liabilities.

The definition of an asset emphasizes its "service potential" or "future economic benefit," "the scarce capacity to provide services or benefits to the entities that use them" (paragraph 28), the common characteristic possessed by all assets. The definition of a liability puts first "future sacrifices of assets" to make it parallel with the asset definition, but it would have been more precise to focus on an entity's *obligation* to another entity to transfer assets or to provide services to it in the future. Future sacrifices of assets, after all, are the consequence—not the cause—of an obligation to another entity. Liabilities are present obligations of a particular entity to transfer assets or provide services to other entities in the future requiring probable future sacrifices of economic benefits as a result of past transactions or events.

Some kinds of assets and liabilities are mirror images of one another. Receivables and payables are the most obvious example. Entity X has an asset (a receivable) because Entity Y has a liability (a payable) to transfer an asset (most commonly cash) to Entity X. Unless Entity Y has the liability, Entity X has no asset. Those relationships hold for rights to receive and obligations to pay or deliver cash, goods, or services. In fact, they hold for most contractual relationships involving a right to receive and an obligation to deliver. Receivables and payables cancel each other in national income accounting, for example, leaving land, buildings, equipment, and similar assets as the stock of productive resources of the economy.

Most kinds of assets are not receivables, and a host of assets have no liabilities as mirror images. For example, the benefit from owning a building does not stem from an obligation of another entity to provide the benefit. The building itself confers significant benefits on its owner. The owner may, of course, enhance the benefits from the building by obtaining the right to services provided by others, who incur corresponding obligations, but that is a separate contractual arrangement involving both rights and obligations for the contracting parties.

Consequently, the Board's concern with the symmetry between the future benefits of assets and the future sacrifices of liabilities tended to overshadow the obligation to another entity that is the principal distinguishing characteristic of a liability. The definition of liabilities in Concepts Statements 3 and 6 and the accompanying explanations might well have profited from a brief description such as that in FASB Statement No. 5, *Accounting for Contingencies,* paragraph 70.

> The economic obligations of an enterprise are defined in paragraph 58 of *APB Statement No. 4* as "its present responsibilities to transfer economic resources or provide services to other entities in the future." Two aspects of that definition are especially relevant to accounting for contingencies: first, that liabilities are *present* responsibilities and, second, that they are obligations to *other entities.* Those notions are supported by other definitions of liabilities in published accounting literature, for example:
>
> Liabilities are claims of creditors against the enterprise, arising out of past activities, that are to be satisfied by the disbursement or utilization of corporate resources.*
>
> A liability is the result of a transaction of the past, not of the future.‡

---

*American Accounting Association, *Accounting and Reporting Standards for Corporate Financial Statements and Preceding Statements and Supplements* (Sarasota, FL: AAA, 1957), p. 16.

‡Maurice Moonitz, "The Changing Concept of Liabilities," *Journal of Accountancy,* May 1960, p. 44.

Occurrence of a Past Transaction or Event.   Items become liabilities of an entity as the result of transactions or other events or circumstances that have already occurred. An entity has a liability only if it has a present obligation to transfer assets to another entity. Budgeting the payments required to enact a purchase results neither in acquiring an asset nor in incurring a liability because no transaction or event has yet occurred that gives the entity access to or control of future economic benefits or binds it to transfer assets.

Once incurred, a liability remains a liability of an entity until it is satisfied, usually by payment of cash, in another transaction or is otherwise discharged or nullified by another event or circumstance affecting the entity.

Nonessential Characteristics of Assets and Liabilities.   The word *probable* is included in the asset and liability definitions with its general, not accounting or technical, meaning and refers to that which can reasonably be expected or believed on the basis of available evidence or logic but is neither certain nor proved.[145] Its use was intended to indicate that something does not have to be certain or proved to qualify as an asset or liability. The first Exposure Draft did not contain the word *probable*. It identified assets with "economic resources—cash and future economic benefits—" saying that a "resource other than cash... must, singly or in combination with other resources, contribute directly or indirectly to future cash inflows ..." and identified liabilities with "obligations... to other entities," saying that "the obligation must involve future sacrifice of resources." [146] The Board received many comment letters that said, in essence, "almost nothing can ever be an asset or liability because you have said that it has to be certain, and everything except cash is uncertain."

The Board thus inserted *probable* into the definition, but perhaps *expected* would have been a better word. As long as someone thinks that an item has value and is willing to pay for it, the item has value and meets the definition of assets, even if the expectation turns out to have been mistaken. It is easy to read more into the use of *probable* than was intended. *Probable* is not an essential part of the definitions; its function is to acknowledge the presence of uncertainty and to say that the future economic benefits or sacrifices do not have to be certain to qualify the items in question as assets and liabilities, not to specify a characteristic that must be present.

Although the application of the definitions of assets and liabilities commonly requires some assessment of probabilities, degrees of probability are not part of the definitions. The degree of probability of a future economic benefit (or of a future cash outlay or other sacrifice of future economic benefits) and the degree to which its amount can be estimated with reasonable reliability, both of which are required to recognize an item as an asset (or a liability), are recognition and measurement matters.

The asset and liability definitions screen out items that lack one or more of the three essential characteristics that assets and liabilities, respectively, must possess. Assets and liabilities have other features that help identify them. Assets may be acquired at a cost, tangible, exchangeable, or legally enforceable. Liabilities usually require the obligated entity to pay cash to one or more entities and are also legally enforceable. However, the difference between those features and the three characteristics identified by Concepts Statement No. 6 as essential to assets and liabilities is that the absence of a nonessential feature, by itself, is not sufficient to disqualify an item from being an asset or liability. For example, absence of a market price or exchangeability of an asset does not negate future economic benefit that can be obtained by use of the asset instead of by its exchange, although it may cause recognition and measurement problems. In contrast, absence of even one of the three essential characteristics does preclude an item from being an asset or liability:

> [A]n item does not qualify as an asset of an entity under the definition in paragraph 25 if (a) the item involves no future economic benefit, (b) the item involves future economic benefit, but the entity cannot obtain it, or (c) the item involves future economic benefit that the entity may in the future obtain, but the events or circumstances that give the entity access to and control of the benefit have not yet occurred (or the entity in the past had the ability to obtain or control the future benefit, but events or circumstances have occurred to remove that ability). Similarly, an item does not qualify as a liability of an entity under the definition in paragraph 35 if (a) the item entails no future sacrifice of assets, (b) the item entails future sacrifice of assets, but the entity is not obligated to make the sacrifice, or (c) the item involves a future sacrifice of assets that the entity will be obligated to make, but the events or circumstances that obligate the entity have not yet occurred (or the entity in the past was obligated to make the future sacrifice, but events or circumstances have occurred to remove that obligation). [Concepts Statement No. 6, paragraph 168]

---

[145] *Webster's New World Dictionary of the American Language,* Second College Edition (New York: Simon and Schuster, 1982), p. 1132.
[146] FASB Exposure Draft, *Objectives of Financial Reporting and Elements of Financial Statements of Business Enterprises* (December 29, 1977), paragraphs 47 and 49.

Equity or Net Assets. *Equity of business enterprises* and *net assets of not-for-profit organizations* have the same definition.

> Equity or net assets is the residual interest in the assets of an entity that remains after deducting its liabilities.
>
> The equity or net assets of both a business enterprise and a not-for-profit organization is the difference between the entity's assets and its liabilities. [Concepts Statement No. 6, paragraphs 49 and 50]

Nevertheless, both terms should be used with care to assure that the referent is clear. Differences between business enterprises and not-for-profit organizations and the ways they carry out their respective missions, particularly the relative importance of transactions with owners to business enterprises and of gifts or donations to not-for-profit organizations, result in significant differences between the equity or net assets of the two kinds of entities.

> A major distinguishing characteristic of the equity of a business enterprise is that it may be increased through investments of assets by owners who also may, from time to time, receive distributions of assets from the entity. Owners invest in a business enterprise with the expectation of obtaining a return on their investment as a result of the enterprise's providing goods or services to customers at a profit....
>
> In contrast, a not-for-profit organization has no ownership interest or profit purpose in the same sense as a business enterprise and thus receives no investments of assets by owners and distributes no assets to owners. Rather, its net assets often are increased by receipts of assets from resource providers (contributors, donors, grantors, and the like) who do not expect to receive either repayment or economic benefits proportionate to the assets provided but who are nonetheless interested in how the organization makes use of those assets and often impose temporary or permanent restrictions on their use. [Concepts Statement No. 6, paragraphs 51 and 52]

Thus, whether a particular use of either equity or net assets refers to a business enterprise or a not-for-profit organization often is significant to investors, creditors, and other resource providers.

A footnote referenced to paragraph 50 notes that although the terms are interchangeable, "[t]his Statement generally applies the term *equity* to business enterprises, which is common usage, and the term *net assets* to not-for-profit organizations, for which the term *equity* is less commonly used." That terminology has the advantage of being both common and consistent, but what assures consistent clarity of meaning is Concepts Statement No. 6's careful use of the terms. It usually gives the complete names—equity of a business enterprise and net assets of a not-for-profit organization—using the shortcuts "equity" and "net assets" only if the referent is clear from the context. As a result, even if it interchanged the terms—net assets of a business enterprise or equity of a not-for-profit organization—the meaning would still be unmistakable.

Equity or Net Assets as a Measure of Wealth. Although the term *wealth* is not part of most accountants' technical vocabularies, as explained earlier the definitions of the elements of financial statements in Concepts Statement No. 6 (carried over from Concepts Statement No. 3) make an enterprise's wealth and changes therein the major subject matter of financial accounting and reporting. The definitions of assets, liabilities, and equity in Concepts Statement No. 6 are all in terms of wealth. The Statement identifies assets with "economic resources.... the scarce means that are useful for carrying out economic activities, such as consumption, production, and exchange," whose "common characteristic ... is 'service potential' or 'future economic benefit,' the scarce capacity to provide services or benefits to the entities that use them" (Concepts Statement No. 6, paragraphs 27 and 28). That is, the definition of assets refers to economic resources, rights to economic resources, and other things in the real-world environment in which financial accounting and reporting takes place that constitute wealth, and the definition of liabilities refers to obligations to transfer wealth to other entities. As a result, the definition of equity or net assets refers to net wealth of a business enterprise or a not-for-profit organization, and the remaining definitions refer to increases and decreases in wealth over time.

Equity of Business Enterprises.   Equity of business enterprises represents the ownership interests of those who invest funds in a business enterprise with the expectation of obtaining a return on their investment as a result of the enterprise's operating at a profit. Since equity ranks after liabilities as a claim to or interest in the assets of the enterprise, it is a *residual* interest. Changes in it result from profits and losses as well as from investments by and distributions to owners. Equity is often referred to as "risk capital," for in an uncertain world owners not only benefit if an enterprise is profitable but also are the first to bear the risk that an enterprise may be unprofitable.

> Equity in a business enterprise is the ownership interest, and its amount is the cumulative result of investments by owners, comprehensive income, and distributions to owners. That characteristic, coupled with the characteristic that liabilities have priority over ownership interest as claims against enterprise assets, makes equity not determinable independently of assets and liabilities. Although equity can be described in various ways, and different recognition criteria and measurement procedures can affect its amount, equity always equals net assets (assets minus liabilities). That is why it is a residual interest. [Concepts Statement No. 6, paragraph 213]

Liabilities and equity are mutually exclusive claims to or interests in an enterprise's assets by other entities, and liabilities take precedence over ownership interests. Although the line between equity and liabilities is clear in concept, it increasingly has been obscured in practice by introduction of financial instruments having characteristics of both liabilities and equity. Convertible debt instruments and redeemable preferred stock are common examples of securities with both debt and equity characteristics, which may cause problems in accounting for them.

Investments by and Distributions to Owners.   Equity of a business enterprise is increased and decreased by investments by owners and distributions to owners—unique transactions "between an enterprise and its owners *as owners* rather than as employees, suppliers, customers, lenders, or in some other nonowner role" (Concepts Statement No. 6, paragraphs 60 and 68).

> Investments by owners are increases in equity of a particular business enterprise resulting from transfers to it from other entities of something valuable to obtain or increase ownership interests (or equity) in it. Assets are most commonly received as investments by owners, but that which is received may also include services or satisfaction or conversion of liabilities of the enterprise.

> Distributions to owners are decreases in equity of a particular business enterprise resulting from transferring assets, rendering services, or incurring liabilities by the enterprise to owners. Distributions to owners decrease ownership interest (or equity) in an enterprise. [Concepts Statement No. 6, paragraphs 66 and 67; footnote reference omitted]

Not-for-profit organizations have no comparable transactions.

A business enterprise may make discretionary distributions to owners, usually by the formal act of declaring a dividend, but it is not obligated to do so. Many enterprises have several classes of equity, each with different priority claims on enterprise assets in discretionary distributions or in the event of liquidation, depending on the degree to which they bear relatively more of the risk of unprofitability. All classes of equity depend to some extent on enterprise profitability for distributions of assets, and no class has an unconditional right or absolute claim to the assets of an enterprise except in the event of liquidation of the enterprise, and even then, owners must stand behind creditors, who have a priority right to enterprise assets (Concepts Statement No. 6, paragraph 62).

Comprehensive Income of Business Enterprises.   Investors, creditors, and others focus on comprehensive income to help them assess an enterprise's prospects for generating net cash inflows because, in the long run, it is through comprehensive income that they obtain a return on their investments, loans, or other association with an enterprise. Thus, the Concepts Statements recognize the significance of income and information about income of an enterprise to investors, creditors, and others.

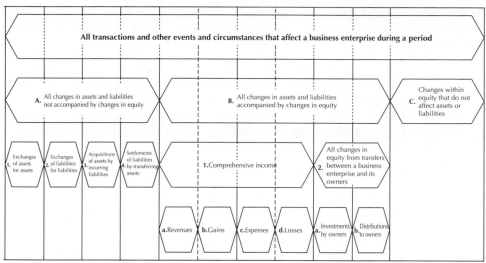

Exhibit 2.4   **Transactions and Other Events that Change Assets, Liabilities, and Equity of Business Enterprises**
Source: Financial Accounting Standards Board, Statement of Financial Accounting Concepts No. 6, par. 64.

Equity is originally created by owners' investments in an enterprise and may from time to time be augmented by additional investments by owners. Equity is reduced by distributions by the enterprise to owners. However, the distinguishing characteristic of equity is that it inevitably is affected by the enterprise's operations and other events and circumstances affecting the enterprise (which together constitute comprehensive income . . .). [Concepts Statement No. 6, paragraph 63]

The primary focus of financial reporting is information about an enterprise's performance provided by measures of [comprehensive income][147] and its components. [Concepts Statement No. 1, paragraph 43]

Concepts Statement No. 6 defines *comprehensive income* as

the change in equity of a business enterprise during a period from transactions and other events and circumstances from nonowner sources. It includes all changes in equity during a period except those resulting from investments by owners and distributions to owners. [paragraph 70]

Comprehensive income and investments by and distributions to owners—class B in Exhibit 2.4—account for all changes in equity of a business enterprise during a period. The exhibit not only distinguishes the sources of changes in equity in class B from each other but also distinguishes them from other transactions and events affecting the enterprise during a period. Class A comprises exchange transactions that change assets or liabilities, or both, but do not change equity. They are common in most business enterprises. Events in class C are less familiar—changes within equity that do not affect assets or liabilities or change the amount of equity, such as stock dividends, conversions of preferred stock into common stock, and some stock recapitalizations.

---

[147] Concepts Statement No. 1 said *earnings,* but in Concepts Statement No. 3 (paragraph 1, footnote 1) the Board changed the name of the concept to *comprehensive income* and reserved the term *earnings* for possible use to designate a component part of comprehensive income. The Board used *earnings* in that way in Concepts Statement No. 5.

Revenues, Expenses, Gains, and Losses.   Concepts Statements Nos. 3 and 6 define the components of comprehensive income—revenues, expenses, gains, and losses—as well as comprehensive income (paragraph references are from Concepts Statement No. 6):

> *Revenues* are inflows or other enhancements of assets of an entity or settlements of its liabilities (or a combination of both) from delivering or producing goods, rendering services, or other activities that constitute the entity's ongoing major or central operations. [paragraph 78]

> *Expenses* are outflows or other using up of assets or incurrences of liabilities (or a combination of both) from delivering or producing goods, rendering services, or carrying out other activities that constitute the entity's ongoing major or central operations. [paragraph 80]

> *Gains* are increases in equity (net assets) from peripheral or incidental transactions of an entity and from all other transactions and other events and circumstances affecting the entity except those that result from revenues or investments by owners. [paragraph 82]

> *Losses* are decreases in equity (net assets) from peripheral or incidental transactions of an entity and from all other transactions and other events and circumstances affecting the entity except those that result from expenses or distributions to owners. [paragraph 83]

Revenues and expenses represent actual or expected cash inflows and outflows usually associated with the ongoing major operations and earning and financing activities of an enterprise, leaving other more peripheral and incidental changes in equity to be described as various kinds of gains and losses.

> Revenues and gains are similar, and expenses and losses are similar, but some differences are significant in conveying information about an enterprise's performance. Revenues and expenses result from an entity's ongoing major or central operations and activities—that is, from activities such as producing or delivering goods, rendering services, lending, insuring, investing, and financing. In contrast, gains and losses result from incidental or peripheral transactions of an enterprise with other entities and from other events and circumstances affecting it. Some gains and losses may be considered "operating" gains and losses and may be closely related to revenues and expenses. Revenues and expenses are commonly displayed as gross inflows or outflows of net assets, while gains and losses are usually displayed as net inflows or outflows.

> ...Distinctions between revenues and gains and between expenses and losses in a particular entity depend to a significant extent on the nature of the entity, its operations, and its other activities. Items that are revenues for one kind of entity may be gains for another, and items that are expenses for one kind of entity may be losses for another. For example, investments in securities that may be sources of revenues and expenses for insurance or investment companies may be sources of gains and losses in manufacturing or merchandising companies. Technological changes may be sources of gains or losses for most kinds of enterprises but may be characteristic of the operations of high-technology or research-oriented enterprises. [Concepts Statement No. 6, paragraphs 87 and 88]

The definitions of revenues, expenses, gains, and losses are less precise and serve a different purpose than the definitions of the six elements described in the preceding pages: assets, liabilities, equity, investments by owners, distributions to owners, and comprehensive income. Those six constitute the complete set of definitions of fundamental elements of financial statements of business enterprises. They are mutually exclusive and collectively are both necessary and sufficient to account for the wealth and net wealth of an enterprise at any time and for all changes in its net wealth during a period, including the changes comprising profit or loss (or income) for the period.[148]

---

[148] As noted earlier, the definitions in Concepts Statements Nos. 3 and 6 are of things and events in the real world and not of their representations in financial statements. Limitations on financial statements' reporting of an enterprise's wealth and changes in wealth stem from accounting's inability to recognize

In contrast, distinctions between revenues and gains and between expenses and losses are not needed to determine comprehensive income. Since comprehensive income is determined by changes in assets and liabilities, it can be derived without separating it into its various components.

Revenues, expenses, gains, and losses are useful not to define comprehensive income but to show how it is obtained.

> In the diagram [Exhibit 2.4], dashed lines rather than solid boundary lines separate revenues and gains and separate expenses and losses because of display considerations.... [T]his Statement ... do[es] not precisely distinguish between revenues and gains on the one hand or between expenses and losses on the other. Fine distinctions between revenues and gains and between expenses and losses, as well as other distinctions *within* comprehensive income, are more appropriately considered as part of display or reporting. [Concepts Statement No. 6, paragraph 64]

Definitions of the components of comprehensive income are significant because to satisfy the objectives of financial reporting, that is, to provide information intended to be useful to investors and creditors in assessing an enterprise's performance or profitability, requires more information about comprehensive income than just its amount. Investors and creditors want and need to know how and why equity has changed, not just the amount that it has changed. The sources of comprehensive income are significant to those attempting to use financial statements to help them with investment, credit, and similar decisions.

> Information about various components of comprehensive income is usually more useful than merely its aggregate amount to investors, creditors, managers, and others who are interested in knowing not only that an entity's net assets have increased (or decreased) but also *how* and *why*. The amount of comprehensive income for a period can, after all, be measured merely by comparing the ending and beginning equity and eliminating the effects of investments by owners and distributions to owners, but that procedure has never provided adequate information about an entity's performance. Investors, creditors, managers, and others need information about the causes of changes in assets and liabilities. [Concepts Statement No. 6, paragraph 219]

Comprehensive income is an all-inclusive income concept and results from many and varied sources. The primary source of comprehensive income is an enterprise's major or central operations, but income also can often be generated by peripheral or incidental activities in which an enterprise engages. Moreover, the economic, legal, social, political, and physical environment in which an enterprise operates creates events and circumstances—such as, price changes, interest rate changes, technological changes, impositions of taxes and regulations, discovery, growth or accretion, shrinkage, vandalism, thefts, expropriations, wars, fires, and natural disasters—that can affect comprehensive income but that may be partly or wholly beyond the control of individual enterprises and their managements (Concepts Statement No. 6, paragraphs 74 and 75; the examples are from paragraph 32).

Those many and varied transactions and other events that constitute sources of comprehensive income—central and peripheral, planned and unplanned, controllable and noncontrollable—result in receipts that may differ in stability, risk, and predictability. Thus the desire for information about the various sources of comprehensive income underlies the distinctions between revenues, expenses, gains, and losses.

Different components of income are useful to distinguish revenue generated from the production and sale of products from return on investments in marketable securities in an income statement. The primary purpose of separating comprehensive income into revenues and expenses and gains and losses is to make the display of information about an enterprise's sources of comprehensive income as useful as possible.

---

all wealth and changes in wealth in financial statements and accountants' historic reluctance to recognize even what can be recognized and measured with reasonable reliability.

Net Assets of Not-for-Profit Organizations.   A not-for-profit organization has no ownership interests that can be sold or transferred or that convey entitlement to a share of a residual distribution of resources in the event of liquidation of the organization. It thus does not receive investments of assets by owners and is generally prohibited from distributing assets as dividends to its members or officers. Increases in its net assets result from receipt of assets from resource providers who expect to receive neither repayment nor return on the assets. However, some resource providers may impose permanent or temporary restrictions on the uses of the assets they contribute to be able to influence an organization's use of those assets. Thus, Concepts Statement No. 6 (paragraphs 92–94) divides net assets of not-for-profit organizations into three mutually exclusive classes—permanently restricted net assets, temporarily restricted net assets, and unrestricted net assets. Restrictions restrain the organization from using part of its resources for purposes other than those specified, for example, to settle liabilities or to provide services outside the purview of the restrictions.

Briefly, permanently restricted net assets is the part of net assets resulting from inflows of assets whose use by the organization is limited by donor-imposed stipulations that neither expire nor can be satisfied or otherwise removed by any action of the organization. Stipulations that require resources to be permanently maintained but that permit the organization to use the income derived from the donated assets are often called *endowments.*

Temporarily restricted net assets is the part of net assets governed by donor-imposed stipulations that can expire or be fulfilled or removed by actions of the organization in accordance with those stipulations. Once the stipulation is satisfied, the restriction is gone.

Unrestricted net assets is the part of net assets resulting from all revenues, expenses, gains, and losses that are not changes in permanently or temporarily restricted net assets. The only limits on unrestricted net assets are the broad limits encompassing the nature of the organization, which are specified in its articles of incorporation or bylaws, and perhaps limits resulting from contractual agreements (e.g., loan covenants) entered into by the organization in the course of its operations.

Although a not-for-profit organization does not have ownership interests or comprehensive income in the same sense as a business enterprise, to be able to continue to achieve its service and operating objectives, it needs to maintain net assets such that resources made available to it at least equal the resources needed to provide services at levels satisfactory to resource providers and other constituents. To assess an organization's success at maintaining net assets, resource providers need information about the components of changes in net assets—revenues, expenses, gains, and losses. The definitions of revenues, expenses, gains, and losses of business enterprises also apply to not-for-profit organizations and

> include all transactions and other events and circumstances that change the amount of net assets of a not-for-profit organization. All resource inflows and other enhancements of assets of a not-for-profit organization or settlements of its liabilities that increase net assets are either revenues or gains and have characteristics similar to the revenues or gains of a business enterprise. Likewise, all resource outflows or other using up of assets or incurrences of liabilities that decrease net assets are either expenses or losses and have characteristics similar to expenses or losses of business enterprises. [Concepts Statement No. 6, paragraph 111]

A not-for-profit organization's central operations—its service-providing efforts, fund-raising activities, and most exchange transactions—by which it attempts to fulfill its service objectives are the sources of its revenues and expenses. Gains and losses result from activities that are peripheral or incidental to its central operations and from interactions with its environment, which give rise to price changes, casualties, and other effects that may be largely beyond the control of an individual organization and its management.

Accrual Accounting and Related Concepts.   Concepts Statement No. 6 also defines several "terms of art" or significant financial accounting and reporting concepts that are used extensively in the conceptual framework.

Transactions, Events, and Circumstances.   *Transactions and other events and circumstances* affecting an entity is a phrase used throughout the conceptual framework to describe the sources or causes of changes in assets, liabilities, and equity. Real-world occurrences that are reflected in financial statements divide into two categories: events and circumstances. They can be further divided into this hierarchy:

Events
Transactions
    Exchanges
    Nonreciprocal transfers
Other external events
Internal events
Circumstances

Events are by far the most important, encompassing external happenings, including transactions, and internal happenings. The breakdown of events into those various components highlights differences that are important to financial accounting.

> An event is a happening of consequence to an entity. It may be an internal event that occurs within an entity, such as using raw materials or equipment in production, or it may be an external event that involves interaction between an entity and its environment, such as a transaction with another entity, a change in price of a good or service that an entity buys or sells, a flood or earthquake, or an improvement in technology by a competitor. [paragraph 135]

Transactions are external events that include reciprocal transfers of assets and liabilities between an entity and other entities called *exchanges and nonreciprocal transfers* between an entity and its owners or between an entity and entities other that its owners in which one of the participants is often a passive beneficiary or victim of the other's actions:

> A transaction is a particular kind of external event, namely, an external event involving transfer of something of value (future economic benefit) between two (or more) entities. The transaction may be an exchange in which each participant both receives and sacrifices value, such as purchases or sales of goods or services; or the transaction may be a nonreciprocal transfer in which an entity incurs a liability or transfers an asset to another entity (or receives an asset or cancellation of a liability) without directly receiving (or giving) value in exchange. Nonreciprocal transfers contrast with exchanges (which are reciprocal transfers) and include, for example, investments by owners, distributions to owners, impositions of taxes, gifts, charitable or educational contributions given or received, and thefts. [paragraph 137]

Investments by and distributions to owners are nonreciprocal transfers because they are events in which an enterprise receives assets from owners and acknowledges an increased ownership interest or disperses assets to owners whose interests decrease. They are not exchanges from the point of view of the enterprise because it neither incurs any obligations nor sacrifices any of its assets in exchange for owners' investments, and it receives nothing of value to itself in exchange for the assets it distributes with the payment of a dividend.

Circumstances, in contrast, are not events but the results of events. They provide evidence of often imperceptible events that may already have happened but that are discernible only in retrospect by the resulting state of affairs. They are important in financial reporting because they often have accounting consequences.

> Circumstances are a condition or set of conditions that develop from an event or a series of events, which may occur almost imperceptibly and may converge in random or unexpected ways to create situations that might otherwise not have occurred and might not have been anticipated. To see the circumstance may be fairly easy, but to discern specifically when the event or events that caused it occurred may be difficult or impossible. For example, a debtor's going bankrupt or a thief's stealing gasoline may be an event, but a creditor's facing the situation that its debtor is bankrupt or a warehouse's facing the fact that its tank is empty may be a circumstance. [paragraph 136]

Accrual Accounting.   The objectives of financial reporting are served by accrual accounting, which generally provides a better indication of an entity's assets, liabilities, and performance than does information about cash receipts and payments. Accrual accounting is defined in paragraph 139 of Concepts Statement No. 6:

> Accrual accounting attempts to record the financial effects on an entity of transactions and other events and circumstances that have cash consequences for the entity in the periods in which those transactions, events, and circumstances occur rather than only in the periods in which cash is received or paid by the entity. Accrual accounting is concerned with an entity's acquiring of goods and services and using them to produce and distribute other goods or services. It is concerned with the process by which cash expended on resources and activities is returned as more (or perhaps less) cash to the entity, not just with the beginning and end of that process. It recognizes that the buying, producing, selling, distributing, and other operations of an entity during a period, as well as other events that affect entity performance, often do not coincide with the cash receipts and payments of the period.

Accrual accounting is based not only on cash transactions but also on all the transactions, events, and circumstances that have cash consequences for an entity but involve no concurrent cash movement. By accounting for noncash assets, liabilities, and comprehensive income, accrual accounting links an entity's operations and other transactions, events, and circumstances that affect it with its cash receipts and outlays, thereby providing information about its assets, liabilities, and changes in them that cannot be obtained by accounting only for its cash transactions.

Concepts Statement No. 6 also provides technical definitions of the following procedures used to apply accrual accounting (emphasis added):

> *Accrual* is concerned with expected future cash receipts and payments: It is the accounting process of recognizing assets or liabilities and the related liabilities, assets, revenues, expenses, gains, or losses for amounts expected to be received or paid, usually in cash, in the future. *Deferral* is concerned with past cash receipts and payments—with prepayments received (often described as collected in advance) or paid: It is the accounting process of recognizing a liability resulting from a current cash receipt (or the equivalent) or an asset resulting from a current cash payment (or the equivalent) with deferred recognition of revenues, expenses, gains, or losses. Their recognition is deferred until the obligation underlying the liability is partly or wholly satisfied or until the future economic benefit underlying the asset is partly or wholly used or lost. [paragraph 141]

> *Allocation* is the accounting process of assigning or distributing an amount according to a plan or a formula. It is broader than and includes *amortization,* which is the accounting process of reducing an amount by periodic payments or write-downs. Specifically, amortization is the process of reducing a liability recorded as a result of a cash receipt by recognizing revenues or reducing an asset recorded as a result of a cash payment by recognizing expenses or costs of production. [paragraph 142]

> *Realization* in the most precise sense means the process of converting noncash resources and rights into money and is most precisely used in accounting and financial reporting to refer to sales of assets for cash or claims to cash.... *Recognition* is the process of formally recording or incorporating an item in the financial statements of an entity. [paragraph 143]

> *Matching* of costs and revenues is simultaneous or combined recognition of the revenues and expenses that result directly and jointly from the same transactions or other events. In most entities, some transactions or events result simultaneously in both a revenue and one or more expenses. The revenue and expense(s) are directly related to each other and require recognition at the same time. In present practice, for example, a sale of product or merchandise involves both revenue (sales revenue) for receipt of cash or a receivable and expense (cost of goods sold) for sacrifice of the product or merchandise sold to customers. [paragraph 146]

That is a narrow definition of matching, similar to the definitions of Herman W. Bevis and George O. May described earlier in the chapter. The definition excludes from matching the systematic and rational allocation of revenues or costs to periods by a formula and makes matching a single process in measuring comprehensive income, not a synonym for the entire periodic income determination process, as it commonly has been.

Concepts Statement No. 6 also includes an example on debt discount, premium, and issue cost (paragraphs 235–239) to illustrate precise technical differences between some of those terms.

(iv) Recognition and Measurement. Recognition and measurement originally had been viewed as separate components of the conceptual framework. Two research studies on recognition matters were commissioned by the FASB: *Recognition of Contractual Rights and Obligations: An Exploratory Study of Conceptual Issues* (1980), by Yuji Ijiri, and *Survey of Present Practices in Recognizing Revenues, Expenses, Gains, and Losses* (1981), by Henry R. Jaenicke. Those studies focused, respectively, on the timing of the initial recognition of assets and liabilities and on the related subsequent timing of recognition of revenues and expenses. A third study, *Recognition in Financial Statements: Underlying Concepts and Practical Conventions,* by L. Todd Johnson and Reed K. Storey, was published in 1982.

Meanwhile, a project on financial reporting and changing prices was to consider measurement. The direction of the original measurement project was changed, however, because of the urgency caused by the increasing prices of the late 1960s and 1970s and the SEC's issuance of ASR No. 190, *Notice of Adoption of Amendments to Regulation S-X Requiring Disclosure of Certain Replacement Cost Data,* which required certain publicly held companies to disclose replacement cost information about inventories, cost of sales, productive capacity, and depreciation. Instead of remaining part of the conceptual framework, the measurement project resulted in FASB Statement No. 33, *Financial Reporting and Changing Prices* (1979).

Concepts Statement No. 5. Recognition decisions often cannot be separated from measurement decisions, particularly if the decision relates to when to recognize changes in assets and liabilities. Recognition and measurement were eventually combined in the conceptual framework because most Board members became convinced that certain recognition questions, which were among the most important to be dealt with, were so closely related to measurement issues that it was unproductive to try to handle them separately. The product of that union was Concepts Statement No. 5, *Recognition and Measurement in Financial Statements of Business Enterprises,* issued in December 1984.

Financial Statements. Concepts Statement No. 5 includes concepts that relate recognition and measurement to the earlier Concepts Statements. For example, it is the part of the conceptual framework in which the FASB describes the financial statements that should be provided and how those financial statements contribute to the objectives of financial reporting.

> Financial statements are a central feature of financial reporting—a principal means of communicating financial information to those outside an entity. In external general purpose financial reporting, a financial statement is a formal tabulation of names and amounts of money derived from accounting records that displays either financial position of an entity at a moment in time or one or more kinds of changes in financial position of the entity during a period of time. Items that are recognized in financial statements are financial representations of certain resources (assets) of an entity, claims to those resources (liabilities and owners' equity), and the effects of transactions and other events and circumstances that result in changes in those resources and claims. The financial statements of an entity are a fundamentally related set that articulate with each other and derive from the same underlying data. [paragraph 5]

To satisfy the objectives of financial reporting—to provide information that is useful to investors and creditors and other users in making rational investment, credit, and similar decisions; to provide information to help them assess the amounts, timing, and uncertainty of prospective net cash inflows to an enterprise; and to provide information about the economic resources, claims to those resources (obligations to transfer resources to other entities and owners' equity), and changes in and claims to those resources—requires a full set of articulated financial statements that report:

Financial position at the end of the period

Earnings (net income) for the period

Comprehensive income (total nonowner changes in equity) for the period

Cash flows during the period

Investments by and distributions to owners during the period (Concepts Statement No. 5, paragraph 13)

A full set of financial statements provides information about an entity's financial position and changes in its financial position. Financial position, as depicted in a balance sheet, is determined by the relationship between an entity's economic resources (assets) and obligations (liabilities), leaving a residual (net assets or owners' equity). In addition, information about earnings, comprehensive income, cash flows, and transactions with owners are different kinds of information about the effects of transactions and other events and circumstances that change assets and liabilities during a period—that is, they are information about different kinds of changes in financial position.

Not all information useful for investment, credit, and similar decisions that financial accounting is able to provide can be reported in financial statements. Concepts Statement No. 5 includes a diagram (Exhibit 2.5) illustrating the many kinds of information that investors and creditors may contemplate consulting when deciding whether to invest in or loan funds to an enterprise. Financial statements provide only part of the information useful for investment, credit, and similar decisions. Financial reporting also encompasses notes to financial statements and parenthetical disclosures, which provide information about accounting policies or explain information recognized in the financial statements. Supplementary information about the effects of changing prices or management discussion and analysis provides information that may also be relevant for making decisions but is deemed not to meet the criteria necessary for recognition in financial statements. Financial statements are unique because the information they provide is distinguished by its capacity and need to withstand the scrutiny of accounting recognition.

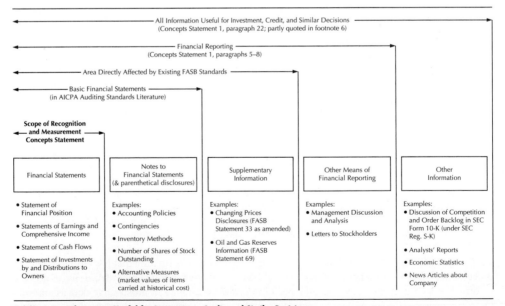

Exhibit 2.5   Information Useful for Investment, Credit, and Similar Decisions
Source: Financial Accounting Standards Board, Statement of Financial Accounting Concepts No. 5, par. 5.

Concepts Statement No. 5, expanding the one-sentence definition in Concepts Statement No. 3, defines *recognition* as

> the process of formally recording or incorporating an item into the financial statements of an entity as an asset, liability, revenue, expense, or the like. Recognition includes depiction of an item in both words and numbers, with the amount included in the totals of the financial statements. For an asset or liability, recognition involves recording not only acquisition or incurrence of the item but also later changes in it, including changes that result in removal from the financial statements. [paragraph 6]

A slight shift in emphasis discloses another characteristic of recognition: "Recognition attempts to represent or depict in financial statements the effects on an entity of real-world economic things and events.[149] That description is congruent with the idea expressed throughout the conceptual framework that financial reporting is concerned with providing information about things and events that occur in the real world in which accounting takes place.

Concepts Statement No. 5 affirms the value of information disclosed in notes or other supplementary information as essential to understanding the information recognized in financial statements, but it also makes it clear that

> disclosure by other means is *not* recognition. Disclosure of information about the items in financial statements and their measures that may be provided by notes or parenthetically on the face of financial statements, by supplementary information, or by other means of financial reporting is not a substitute for recognition in financial statements for items that meet recognition criteria. Generally, the most useful information about assets, liabilities, revenues, expenses, and other items of financial statements and their measures (that with the best combination of relevance and reliability) should be recognized in the financial statements. [paragraph 9]

Although information provided by notes to financial statements or by other means is valuable and ought to be made available to investors, creditors, and other users, it is not a substitute for recognition in the body of financial statements with the amounts included in the financial statement totals.

Comprehensive Income and Earnings.   Concepts Statement No. 5 says that a full set of financial statements should report both comprehensive income and earnings. Since the distinction between comprehensive income and earnings in the Statement is another manifestation of the difference of opinion about whether income is an enhancement of wealth (command over economic resources) or an indicator of performance of an enterprise and its management, the Statement implies that financial statements should report both kinds of information. Present practice reports neither earnings nor comprehensive income, although a statement of net income based on present generally accepted accounting principles may report either or both if there are no changes in accounting principles or no holding gains or losses reported as direct increases or decreases in equity instead of in net income.

Comprehensive income was defined in Concepts Statement No. 3 as an all-inclusive income concept:

> Comprehensive income is the change in equity (net assets) of an entity during a period from transactions and other events and circumstances from nonowner sources. It includes all changes in equity during a period except those resulting from investments by owners and distributions to owners. [paragraph 56]

The same definition was carried over into Concepts Statement No. 6, paragraph 70.

Comprehensive income is the only concept of income defined in the FASB's conceptual framework.[150] Although Concepts Statement No. 5 referred a half dozen times to "the concept of

---

[149] Johnson and Storey, *Recognition in Financial Statements,* p. 2.

[150] Comprehensive income is one of six mutually exclusive elements of financial statements of business enterprises whose definitions are necessary and sufficient to form a complete or closed set. The other five are assets, liabilities, equity, investments by owners, and distributions to owners.

earnings" and gave earnings much more attention than comprehensive income, neither Concepts Statement No. 5 nor any other Concepts Statement defined earnings or its close relative net income. Instead, Concepts Statement No. 3, paragraph 1, footnote 1 (carried over into Concepts Statement No. 6), explained that the Board had changed to *comprehensive income* the name of the concept that was called *earnings* in Concepts Statement No. 1 and other conceptual framework documents previously issued and had reserved the term earnings for possible use to designate a component part of comprehensive income.

Later, Concepts Statement No. 5 did use the term *earnings* to describe a component part of comprehensive income that corresponds to net income in current practice, except that it excludes the so-called catch-up adjustment required by paragraph 19(b) of APB Opinion No. 20, *Accounting Changes,* to be included in net income.[151]

> Earnings and comprehensive income have the same broad components—revenues, expenses, gains, and losses—but are not the same because certain classes of gains and losses are included in comprehensive income but are excluded from earnings. [paragraph 42]

The Statement described a two-step relationship between earnings and comprehensive income:

Revenues − expenses + most gains − most losses = Earnings

$\pm$ Cumulative effect on prior years of a change in accounting principle = Net income

$\pm$ Gains and losses included in comprehensive income but excluded from net income[152]

− Comprehensive income.

The Concepts Statements describe but do not define earnings and net income because they cannot be defined. Both result from applying generally accepted accounting principles and are

---

[151] Both earnings and net income as Concepts Statement No. 5 uses the terms are what Concepts Statements Nos. 3 and 6 described as intermediate components of comprehensive income: "Comprehensive income consists of not only its basic components—revenues, expenses, gains, and losses—but also various intermediate components or measures that result from combining the basic components . . . in various ways to obtain several measures of enterprise performance with varying degrees of inclusiveness. . . . Those intermediate" components or measures are, in effect, subtotals of comprehensive income and often of one another (Concepts Statement No. 3, paragraph 62; Concepts Statement No. 6, paragraph 77 is almost the same). Each Statement explains that: "Although cash resulting from various sources of comprehensive income is the same, receipts from various sources may vary in stability, risk, and predictability . . . indicating a need for information about various components of comprehensive income" (paragraphs 61 and 76, respectively).

[152] This term, which is more descriptive and accurate than Concept Statement No. 5's *other nonowner changes in equity,* was used in FASB Statement No. 109, *Accounting for Income Taxes* (February 1992), and implied in a number of other FASB Statements. This entry is from Statement No. 109's glossary:

Gains and losses included in comprehensive income but excluded from net income
  Under present practice, gains and losses included in comprehensive income but excluded from net income include certain changes in market values of investments in marketable equity securities classified as noncurrent assets, certain changes in market values of investments in industries having specialized accounting practices for marketable securities, adjustments from recognizing certain additional pension liabilities, and foreign currency translation adjustments. Future changes to generally accepted accounting principles may change what is included in this category. [paragraph 289]
  Concepts Statement No. 5, FASB Statement No. 109, and other FASB Statements refer only to *gains and losses* that are included in comprehensive income but excluded from earnings. In some kinds of enterprises, however, increases and decreases in equity from holding assets or owing liabilities while their prices change involve activities that constitute ongoing major or central operations and thus qualify as revenues and expenses instead of gains and losses.

determined by what is done in practice at a particular time—the meaning of each changes with changes in generally accepted accounting principles. Thus, paragraph 35 of Concepts Statement No. 5 says:

> The Board expects the concept of earnings to be subject to the process of gradual change or evolution that has characterized the development of net income. Present practice has developed over a long time, and that evolution has resulted in significant changes in what net income reflects, such as a shift toward what is commonly called an *all-inclusive income statement.* Those changes have resulted primarily from standard-setting bodies' responses to several factors, such as changes in the business and economic environment and perceptions about the nature and limitations of financial statements, about the needs of users of financial statements, and about the need to prevent or cure perceived abuse(s) in financial reporting. Those factors sometimes may conflict or appear to conflict. For example, an all-inclusive income statement is intended, among other things, to avoid discretionary omissions of losses (or gains) from an income statement, thereby avoiding presentation of a more (or less) favorable report of performance or stewardship than is justified. However, because income statements also are used as a basis for estimating future performance and assessing future cash flow prospects, arguments have been advanced urging exclusion of unusual or nonrecurring gains and losses that might reduce the usefulness of an income statement for any one year for predictive purposes.

Those kinds of arguments also have been advanced urging exclusion of recurring gains and losses that increase the volatility of reported net income, and the FASB has to some extent responded. For example, FASB Statement No. 12, *Accounting for Certain Marketable Securities* (1975), and FASB Statement No. 52, *Foreign Currency Translation* (1981), excluded from net income certain holding gains and losses (gains and losses from holding assets or owing liabilities while their prices change). Briefly, Statement No. 12 required the carrying amount of a marketable equity securities portfolio to be the lower of its aggregate cost and market value but required that changes in the carrying amount of a noncurrent marketable equity securities portfolio "be included in the equity section of the balance sheet [that is, not included in net income] and shown separately" (paragraph 11). Similarly, Statement No. 52 provided that "translation adjustments [as defined in the Statement] shall not be included in determining net income but shall be reported separately and accumulated in a separate component of equity" (paragraph 13). The Board had taken a step away from the APB's decision to make reported net income all-inclusive—"net income should reflect all items of profit and loss recognized during the period with the sole exception of the prior period adjustments" (APB Opinion No. 9, *Reporting the Results of Operations* [December 1966], paragraph 17)—and had set the stage for the distinction between earnings and comprehensive income that it made in Concepts Statement No. 5.

As might have been expected, comprehensive income generally has been criticized for being too inclusive, among other things including volatile holding gains and losses that are excluded from net income or earnings. For example, John W. March's dissent to Concepts Statement No. 5 reflected the common view that periodic income determination should focus on performance rather than report gains and losses from all sources that increase or decrease wealth. These are the first and penultimate paragraphs of his dissent:

> Mr. March dissents from this Statement because (a) it does not adopt measurement concepts oriented toward what he believes is the most useful single attribute for recognition purposes, the cash equivalent of recognized transactions reduced by subsequent impairments or loss of service value—instead it suggests selecting from several different attributes without providing sufficient guidance for the selection process; (b) it identifies all nonowner changes in assets and liabilities as comprehensive income and return on equity, thereby including in income, incorrectly in his view, capital inputs from nonowners, unrealized gains from price changes, amounts that should be deducted to maintain capital in real terms, and foreign currency translation adjustments; (c) it uses a concept of income that is fundamentally based on measurements of assets, liabilities, and changes in them, rather than adopting the Statement's concept of earnings as the definition of

income; and (d) it fails to provide sufficient guidance for initial recognition and derecognition of assets and liabilities.

The description of earnings (paragraphs 33–38) and the guidance for applying recognition criteria to components of earnings (paragraphs 78–87) is consistent with Mr. March's view that income should measure performance and that performance flows primarily from an entity's fulfillment of the terms of its transactions with outside entities that result in revenues, other proceeds on resource dispositions (gains), costs (expenses) associated with those revenues and proceeds, and losses sustained. However, Mr. March believes that those concepts are fundamental and should be embodied in definitions of the elements of financial statements and in basic income recognition criteria rather than basing income on measurements of assets, liabilities, and changes in them.[153]

As March suggested, Concepts Statement No. 5 contains good, brief descriptions of the goal of periodic income determination in the minds of those who think it should focus on performance.

> ...Earnings is a measure of performance for a period and to the extent feasible excludes items that are extraneous to that period—items that belong primarily to other periods.... [paragraph 34]

> Earnings focuses on what the entity has received or reasonably expects to receive for its output (revenues) and what it sacrifices to produce and distribute that output (expenses). Earnings also includes results of the entity's incidental or peripheral transactions and some effects of other events and circumstances stemming from the environment (gains and losses). [paragraph 38]

Concepts Statement No 5, as noted earlier, devoted much more attention to earnings than to comprehensive income, and for more than 10 years the Board did nothing more about its conclusion that a full set of financial statements reports comprehensive income (paragraph 13). Most people had, to their knowledge, never seen a statement that reports comprehensive income and may have had difficulty picturing it and its relation to an income statement in present practice.

As a result of Statements Nos. 12 and 52 and other FASB Statements of which they were forerunners, net income is less all-inclusive than it was, say, after issuance of APB Opinion No. 30, *Reporting the Results of Operations—Reporting the Effects of Disposal of a Segment of a Business, and Extraordinary, Unusual and Infrequently Occurring Events and Transactions* (June 1973). Since the FASB has not required a statement of comprehensive income, pronouncements such as Statements Nos. 12 and 52 that exclude volatile holding gains and losses from net income and bury them directly in equity have made it possible for many U.S. enterprises to report periodic income that reflects their domestic and foreign operations as less risky than they actually are.

That may be about to change. The Board recently has been talking about how to report both earnings, or its close relative net income, and comprehensive income and has issued an Exposure Draft, *Reporting Comprehensive Income* (June 20, 1996).[154] The Board's effort seems to have been encouraged by *Financial Reporting in the 1990s and Beyond* (1993), a report by the Financial Accounting Policy Committee of the Association for Investment Management and Research (AIMR) intended to express the views of AIMR members on financial reporting.

> Throughout the report, there are repeated recommendations that the FASB needs to develop its concept of "comprehensive income." [page 5]

> We refer to comprehensive income several times above and have urged the FASB to construct the bridge from concept to standard. It is needed for better and more useful financial reporting in several areas.

---

[153] March's dissent to Concepts Statement No. 5 constituted a retroactive dissent to Concepts Statement No. 3, to which he had assented. The dissent explicitly repudiated Concepts Statement No. 3's definition of comprehensive income and would replace it in the definitions of the elements of financial statements with Concepts Statement No. 5's "concept of earnings."

[154] Author's note: FASB Statement No. 130, *Reporting Comprehensive Income,* was issued in June 1997.

... The F[inancial] A[ccounting] P[olicy] C[ommittee] has consistently supported the all-inclusive income statement format.... We consider income to include all of an enterprise's wealth changes except those engendered from transactions with its owners. We have profound misgivings about the increasing number of wealth changes that elude disclosure on the income statement. Yet individual items may be interpreted differently. That calls for a display of comprehensive income that allows components of different character to be seen and evaluated separately. [page 63]

Capital Maintenance.   Maintenance of capital is a financial concept or abstraction needed to measure comprehensive income. Since comprehensive income is a residual concept, not all revenues of a business enterprise for a period are comprehensive income because the sacrifices necessary to produce the revenues must be considered. Capital used up during the period must be recovered from revenues or other increases in net assets before any of the return may be considered comprehensive income. A concept of capital maintenance is critical for distinguishing an enterprise's return *on* investment from return *of* investment because an enterprise receives a profit or income—a return on investment—only after its capital has been maintained or recovered.

Two major concepts of capital maintenance exist, the financial capital concept and the physical capital concept (which is often described as maintaining operating capability, that is, maintaining the capacity of an enterprise to provide a constant supply of goods or services).

In Concepts Statement No. 5, the Board decided that the concept of financial capital maintenance is the basis for a full set of articulated financial statements.

A return on financial capital results only if the financial (money) amount of an enterprise's net assets at the end of a period exceeds the financial amount of net assets at the beginning of the period after excluding the effects of transactions with owners. The financial capital concept is the traditional view and is the capital maintenance concept in present financial statements. [paragraph 47]

Financial capital maintenance can be measured either in units of money (for example, nominal dollars) or in units of constant purchasing power (e.g., 1982–1984 dollars or 2007 dollars).

The Board rejected the physical capital concept, which holds that

a return on physical capital results only if the physical productive capacity of the enterprise at the end of the period (or the resources needed to achieve that capacity) exceeds the physical productive capacity at the beginning of the period, also after excluding the effects of transactions with owners. [paragraph 47]

The general procedure for maintaining physical capital is to value assets, such as inventories, property, plant, and equipment at their current replacement costs and to deduct expenses, such as cost of goods sold and depreciation, at replacement costs from revenues to measure periodic return on capital. The increases and decreases in replacement costs of those assets while they are held by the enterprise are included in owners' equity as a "capital maintenance adjustment" rather than in return on capital as "holding gains and losses." The idea underlying the measurement of return on capital in the physical capital concept is that increases in wealth that are merely increases in prices of things that an enterprise must continue to hold to engage in operations do not constitute return on capital but part of the capital to be maintained.

The principal difference between the two concepts is in the treatment of holding gains and losses resulting from the effects of price changes during a period on assets while held and on liabilities while owed.

Under the financial capital concept, if the effects of those price changes are recognized, they are conceptually holding gains and losses ... and are included in the return on capital. Under the physical capital concept, those changes would be recognized but conceptually would be capital maintenance adjustments that would be included directly in equity and not included in return on capital. Both earnings and comprehensive income as set forth in this Statement, like present net income, include holding gains and losses that would be excluded from income under a physical capital maintenance concept. [paragraph 48]

Measurement and Attributes.   By definition, recognition includes the depiction of an item in both words and numbers. The need to quantify the information about an item to be recognized introduces the issue of its *measurement.*

> Measurement involves choice of an attribute by which to quantify a recognized item and choice of a scale of measurement (often called "unit of measure"). [Concepts Statement No. 5, paragraph 3]

Attribute is defined and explained in footnote 2 to paragraph 2 of Concepts Statement No. 1:

> "Attributes to be measured" refers to the traits or aspects of an element to be quantified or measured, such as historical cost/historical proceeds, current cost/current proceeds, etc. Attribute is a narrower concept than measurement, which includes not only identifying the attribute to be measured but also selecting a scale of measurement (for example, units of money or units of constant purchasing power). "Property" is commonly used in the sciences to describe the trait or aspect of an object being measured, such as the length of a table or the weight of a stone. But "property" may be confused with land and buildings in financial reporting contexts, and "attribute" has become common in accounting literature and is used in this Statement.

Since recognition often involves recording changes in assets and liabilities, it often raises the question of whether the amount of an attribute should be changed or whether a different attribute should be used in its place. In any event, since the changes in an asset or liability and in the attribute occur at the same time, it is often difficult to separate recognition from measurement problems.

Five different attributes of assets and liabilities are used in present accounting practice. The following is based on paragraph 67 of Concepts Statement No. 5, which describes the attributes and gives examples of the kinds of assets for which each attribute is commonly reported:

1. *Historical cost.* The amount of cash or its equivalent paid to acquire an asset, usually adjusted after acquisition for amortization or other allocations (e.g., property, plant, equipment, and most inventories).

2. *Current cost.* The amount that would have to be paid if the same or an equivalent asset were acquired currently (e.g., some inventories).

3. *Current market value.* The amount that could be obtained by selling an asset in orderly liquidation (e.g., marketable securities).

4. *Net realizable value.* The nondiscounted amount into which an asset is expected to be converted in due course of business less direct costs necessary to make that conversion (e.g., short-term receivables).

5. *Present (or discounted) value of future cash flows.* The present value of future cash inflows into which an asset is expected to be converted in due course of business less present values of cash outflows necessary to obtain those inflows (e.g., long-term receivables).

Recognition and Measurement—Description Rather than Concepts.   The preceding pages have described several areas in which Concepts Statement No. 5 has furthered the conceptual framework, at least to some extent—in identifying what a full set of financial statements comprises, in expanding and clarifying what constitutes recognition, in explaining the relationship between comprehensive income and its component part, earnings, and in endorsing financial capital maintenance.

Although the Statement's name implies that it gives conceptual guidance on recognition and measurement, its conceptual contributions to financial reporting are not really in those two areas. As a result of compromises necessary to issue it, much of Concepts Statement No. 5 merely describes present practice and some of the reasons that have been used to support or explain it but provides little or no conceptual basis for analyzing and attempting to resolve the controversial issues of recognition and measurement about which accountants have disagreed for years.

The FASB knew all along that recognition and measurement concepts would be controversial. Each component of the conceptual framework—the objectives, the qualitative characteristics, the elements of financial statements, recognition and measurement—is successively less abstract and more concrete than the one before. Recognition and measurement are the most concrete and least abstract of the components because they are necessarily at the point at which concepts and practice converge. They are the components in which practicing accountants have been most interested because they determine what actually gets into the numbers and totals in the financial statements. While few practitioners may be interested in what they may see as abstractions—such as objectives, qualitative characteristics, and definitions—most are interested in a change in revenue recognition or the measured attribute of an asset, or perhaps in reporting the effects of inflation, and they usually feel that they have a vested interest in the Board's decisions regarding recognition and measurement and in resisting changes that may adversely affect their future reporting.

Accountants have strongly held, and ultimately polarizing, views about which is the most relevant and reliable attribute to be measured and about the circumstances needed for recognizing changes in attributes and changes in the amounts of an attribute. Proponents of the present model—which often is mislabeled historical cost accounting because it is actually a mixture of historical costs, current costs, current exit values, net realizable values, and present values—fiercely defend it and broach no discussion of alternatives for fear that any change would portend its abandonment in favor of current value accounting, a term that is used generically to refer to the continuous use of any attribute other than historical cost. Similarly, proponents of various current cost or current value models are equally unyielding, often almost as critical of other current value or current cost models that compete with their own favorite model as they are of the historical-cost model for its failure to recognize the realities of changing values and changing prices.

The Board was as badly split on recognition and measurement as the constituency. Although most Board members could see the deficiencies in the current model, a majority of the Board could not accept a current value or current cost measurement system, even at a conceptual level. Therefore, instead of indicating a preferred accounting model or otherwise offering conceptual guidance about measurement, Concepts Statement No. 5 merely acknowledged that present practice consists of a mix of five attributes for measuring items in financial statements and said that the Board "expects the use of different attributes to continue" (paragraph 66). Beyond that, it said that "information based on current prices should be recognized if it is sufficiently relevant and reliable to justify the costs involved and more relevant than alternative information" (paragraph 90), which was extremely weak guidance. Whereas a neutral exposition of alternatives was appropriate for a Discussion Memorandum, a litany of present measurement practices with neither conceptual analysis or evaluation nor guidance for making choices was not proper for a Concepts Statement.

In merely describing current practice, Concepts Statement No. 5 is a throwback to statements of accounting principles produced by the "distillation of experience" school of thought—an essentially practical, not a conceptual, effort. Its prescriptions for improving practice are reminiscent of those of the Committee on Accounting Procedure or the APB: Measurement problems will be resolved on a case-by-case basis. Unfortunately, that approach worked only marginally well for those now-defunct bodies.

Oscar Gellein called the discussion of recognition in the Exposure Draft that ultimately became part of Concepts Statement No. 5 "a helpful distillation of current recognition practices." However, he also saw that the Statement would not advance financial reporting in the area of recognition and measurement:

> The umbrella is broad enough to cover virtually all current practices, but not conceptually directed toward either narrowing those practices or preventing their proliferation.... Recognition is the watershed issue in the conceptual framework in the sense that hierarchically it is the ultimate stage of conceptual concreteness. Without that kind of conceptual guidance, there is the risk of reversion to ad hoc rules in determining accounting methods.[155]

---

[155] Gellein, "Financial Reporting: The State of Standard Setting," p. 14.

David Solomons criticized Concepts Statement No. 5 for distorting the process of formulating future accounting standards.[156] He noted that in several places it asserts that concepts are to be developed as the standards-setting process evolves, citing these examples:

> The Board expects the concept of earnings to be subject to the process of gradual change or evolution that has characterized the development of net income. [paragraph 35]

> Future standards may change what is recognized as components of earnings.... Moreover, because of the differences between earnings and comprehensive income, future standards also may recognize certain changes in net assets as components of comprehensive income but not as components of earnings. [paragraph 51]

> The Board believes that further development of recognition, measurement, and display matters will occur as the concepts are applied at the standards level. [paragraph 108]

Solomons was not at all persuaded by the Board's apparent argument, represented by those excerpts, that concepts could be a by-product of the standards-setting process:

> These appeals to evolution should be seen as what they are—a cop-out. If all that is needed to improve our accounting model is reliance on evolution and the natural selection that results from the development of standards, why was an expensive and protracted conceptual framework project necessary in the first place? It goes without saying that concepts and practices should evolve as conditions change. But if the conceptual framework can do no more than point that out, who needs it? And, for that matter, if progress is simply a matter of waiting for evolution, who needs the FASB?[157]

Concepts Statement No. 5 almost seems to have anticipated the challenges to its legitimacy as a Statement of recognition and measurement concepts and capitulated in its second and third paragraphs, which could serve as its epitaph:

> The recognition criteria and guidance in this Statement are generally consistent with current practice and do not imply radical change. Nor do they foreclose the possibility of future changes in practice. The Board intends future change to occur in the gradual, evolutionary way that has characterized past change.

> This Statement also...notes that...the Board expects the use of different attributes.... [and] nominal units of money (that is, unadjusted for changes in purchasing power over time)...to continue.

Concepts Statement No. 5 does make some noteworthy conceptual contributions—they are just not on recognition and measurement.

(v) Using Cash Flow Information and Present Value in Accounting Determinations. Cash flow information and present value are used in some accounting determinations now, but their application is not consistent. Further, those devices are not used in other accounting determinations in which they might be used. The reason for both of those conditions has been the lack of an authoritative framework within which to consider the issues involved.

To rectify that lack, the FASB initiated a project in October 1988 that culminated in publication of its Concepts Statement No. 7, *Using Cash Flow Information and Present Value in Accounting Measurements,* in February 2000. The Statement considers issues in determining amounts but not issues in recognition. It is confined to determinations at initial recognition, fresh-start determinations, and amortization based on future cash flows, in situations other than those in which transactions involving cash or other assets paid or received are involved or in which observations of fair values in the marketplace are available.

---

[156] David Solomons, "The FASB's Conceptual Framework: An Evaluation," *Journal of Accountancy* (June 1986): 122.

[157] Ibid.

The Board defines *fair value* of an asset (or liability) in its Concepts Statement No. 7 much the same as it always has:

> The amount at which an asset (or liability) could be bought (or incurred) or sold (or settled) in a current transaction between willing parties, that is, other than in a forced or liquidation sale.

That definition is ambiguous. It does not say who the "willing parties" are. One of the willing parties must be the owner of the asset. If the owner is not willing to sell, there would be no "current transaction." The other must be a prospective buyer who is willing to pay at least as much as the minimum amount for which the owner is willing to sell. For many if not most assets, no such buyer exists.

The FASB avoids the ambiguity in its definition of *fair value* in its Preliminary Views, *Reporting Financial Instruments and Certain Related Assets and Liabilities at Fair Value,* issued on December 14, 1999:

> Fair value is an estimate of the price an entity would have realized if it had sold an asset or paid if it had been relieved of a liability on the reporting date in an arm's-length exchange motivated by normal business considerations. That is, it is an estimate of an exit price determined by market interactions. [paragraph 47]

Why the FASB issued two different definitions of *fair value* at about the same time is not clear. Subsequently in this supplement, the assumption is made that *fair value* refers to the maximum amount any buyer is willing to pay for the asset, that is, the asset's current selling price, which generally agrees with the definition in the Preliminary Views.

Cash flow information and present value are linked. Present value is considered for use only in connection with the use of future cash flow information in accounting determinations. The Statement provides a framework for using future cash flows at the basis for accounting determinations. The framework describes the objective of using present value in such determinations and provides general principles for its use, especially when the amount of future cash flows, their timing, or both are uncertain.

Fundamental Questions Relevant to Determinations that Use Present Value Techniques.   The Statement addresses the following fundamental questions relevant to determinations that use future cash flows and present value techniques:

- What is the objective, or objectives, of present value when it is used in determinations at initial recognition of assets or liabilities?
- Does the objective differ in subsequent fresh-start determinations of assets and liabilities?
- Do determinations of liabilities require objectives, or present problems, different from those of determinations of assets?
- How should estimates of cash flows and interest rates be developed?
- What is the objective, or objectives, of present value when it is used in the amortization of existing assets and liabilities?
- If present value is used in the amortization of assets and liabilities, how should the technique be applied when estimates of cash flows change?

Time Value of Money.   Present value techniques (discounting using the compound interest formula) are used for the purpose of incorporating in accounting determinations the time value of money. The time value of money refers to the fact that the earlier money is to be obtained, the more valuable the prospective receipt is; and the later money needs to be paid, the less burdensome the obligation to pay it is. Those facts are reflected in accounting determinations involving future cash receipts or future cash payments that incorporate present value techniques. The Board justifies its consideration of present value techniques based on the facts that present value is one of the foundations of economics and corporate finance, that the computation of present value is part of most modern asset-pricing models, and that the present value of future cash flows is implicit in all market prices.

The Board does not say what the implicit relationship is. It is the following: (1) The seller believes that the present value of the future cash receipts the seller could obtain in the future from using the object being sold is *less than* the amount of money represented by the price involved in the sale or *less than* the present value the seller could receive from an alternative investment the seller could make with the proceeds of sale—that is why the seller is willing to sell at the price of the sale—and (2) the buyer believes that the present value of the future cash receipts the buyer will receive in the future from using the object being sold is *more than* the amount of money represented by the price involved in the sale—that is why the buyer is willing to buy at the price of the sale. Thus, the price of the sale does not equal the present value as seen by either the buyer or the seller.

The Statement illustrates the time value of money with (1) an asset with a contractual cash receipt of $10,000 due in one day, certain of receipt (though nothing about the future is certain); (2) an asset with a contractual cash receipt of $10,000 due in 10 years, certain of receipt; (3) an asset with a contractual cash receipt of $10,000 dues in one day, with the receipt to be equal to or less than $10,000; (4) an asset with a contractual cash receipt of $10,000 due in 10 years, with the receipt to be equal to or less than $10,000; and (5) an asset with an expected cash receipt of $10,000 due in 10 years, with the receipt to be at least $8,000 but not more than $12,000. By reporting the assets all at the amounts contracted or expected to be received, they would all be reported at the gross amounts of $10,000. That would be misleading, because they are not economically the same—they differ on timing and certainty of receipt—and a buyer who wants to maximize his or her resources would not agree to pay the same amount for all of the assets.

Elements of Present Value Determinations.   Discounting the gross amounts $10,000 using present value techniques and discount rates and periods that reflect the diverse timing and diverse certainty of receipt of the assets would reflect the time value of money and work to counteract the misleading effect. The following are the elements of such a present value calculation:

- An estimate of the amounts and timing of anticipated future cash receipts and payments related to the asset
- Anticipated possible variations in those amounts or timing
- The interest rate that would reflect the pure time value of money (i.e., not involving uncertainty), which is the risk-free interest rate (U.S. government securities or U.S. government–backed securities are considered to be risk free. But are they? Confederate debt and the bonds of Tsar Nicholas II, for example, were not.)
- The interest-rate premium for bearing the uncertainty
- Other, sometimes unidentifiable, factors, such as illiquidity and market imperfections

Using Present Value to Approximate Fair Value at Initial Recognition and for Fresh-Start Determinations.   Fair value incorporates all of those elements. When used in accounting determinations at initial recognition and fresh-start determinations, present values are used only to approximate fair values that cannot be determined directly from the market.

The Board states that the fair value, if determinable, would encompass the consensus view of those interested in buying the asset, of the asset's utility, future cash flow, uncertainties surrounding the cash flows, and discount in the price demanded for the uncertainties. (There is, however, no such consensus view. There is only one view for each prospective buyer, which differs among prospective buyers. The term *consensus* implies that the prospective buyers agree. The fair value is the maximum price any prospective buyer would be willing to pay for the asset, not a consensus price.)

The usual determination of the amount of an asset at initial recognition is its cash price in the exchange in which it is acquired if it is acquired in an exchange in which there is a cash price (the Board notes an exception related to unstated rights or privileges described in APB Opinion No. 21).

If an asset is acquired other than in such an exchange, the Board states that its amount should be determined when acquired at fair value. If the asset is acquired in a nonmonetary exchange, its amount should be determined to be the fair value of the asset surrendered to obtain it, in conformity with APB Opinion No. 29.

Fair value can be determined most satisfactorily by reference to the price in a recent exchange for cash involving an asset similar to the asset whose amount is being determined. If there is no such exchange, the Board contends that amounts may have to be determined by estimating the future cash flows involved with the asset and applying present value techniques. The objective in determining the discount rate in the present value calculation is that contained in APB Opinion No. 21:

> The objective is to approximate the rate which would have resulted if an independent borrower and an independent lender had negotiated a similar transaction under comparable terms and conditions with the option to pay the cash price upon purchase or to give a note for the amount of the purchase which bears the prevailing rate of interest to maturity.

The principles that apply to determinations at initial recognition apply equally for fresh-start determinations. Because an asset subject to a fresh-start determination is not then acquired in an exchange involving a cash price, its amount cannot be determined directly at such a price. Determining its amount is necessarily confined to concepts involving fair value, as discussed above for assets acquired other than in exchanges involving a cash price.

The Board lists the following existing accounting conventions alternative to fair value that incorporate the elements of a present value calculation listed above to diverse extents: value-in-use (entity-specific determinations), effective-settlement determinations for liabilities, and cost-accumulation or cost-accrual determinations. Each of those conventions contains factors that are specific to the reporting entity: It adds factors not contemplated in the price of an exchange involving the kind of asset involved and assumptions of the entity's management not made by buyers and sellers in the market, or it excludes factors contemplated by buyers and sellers in the market, or both. The alternative conventions are related to the fact that the best estimate by the entity's management of the present value of uncertain future cash flows may differ from the fair value of those cash flows. The reasons the management's expectations might differ from those expected by buyers and sellers in the market include:

- The management might intend to use the asset or settle the liability in a manner different from that contemplated by the buyers and sellers.
- The management might prefer to retain the risk involved in a liability rather than transfer the risk to another party.
- The entity might benefit, for example, from tax or zoning variances, private information, trade secrets, or processes not otherwise available.
- The entity might be able to take advantage of internal resources not available at the entity's cost to realize or pay amounts involved in the asset or liability.

Those items represent contemplated future comparative advantages enjoyed by the reporting entity relative to the asset or liability over those enjoyed by other buyers or sellers in the market. If the amount of an asset or liability is determined at initial recognition or at a fresh start using one of those alternative conventions and the offset to the amount is to revenue or expense, the contemplated future comparative advantage is reported in income at initial recognition or fresh-start determination. If the amount of an asset or liability is determined at those times using fair value, the contemplated future comparative advantage is reported in the periods in which it realizes assets or settles liabilities at amounts that differ from fair value.

Some suggest that the amounts of assets and liabilities be determined at initial recognition or at a fresh start at amounts that incorporate the contemplated future comparative advantages, because they contend that that would better help users of financial statements assess the amounts and timing of prospective cash receipts to them. The FASB points out, however, that such reporting ignores the uncertainties involved in the prospective cash flows. It further points out that though knowledge of management's expectations is often useful and informative, the market is the final arbiter of asset and liability values, and that fair value, which incorporates those values, results in neutral, complete, and representational faithful determinations of the economic characteristics of the asset or liability. Further, the alternative conventions imply various discount rates, such as an asset-earning rate, an incremental-borrowing rate, or an embedded interest rate, with no conceptual basis for choosing among them. For all of those reasons, the FASB has decided that, as stated above, the amount of an asset or liability should be determined at initial recognition or at a fresh start at fair value. It points out, however, that a lack of other data might sometimes require incorporating the expectations of the reporting entity's management in implementing the fair value principle.

Implementing the Determination of Fair Value Using Present Value Techniques.   To implement the determination of fair value using present value techniques, the risk-free interest rate must be determined, future cash flows must be estimated, the uncertainty involved in those cash flows must be estimated, and other factors affecting the estimated cash flow, such as possible variations in their amounts or timing, illiquidity, or market imperfections, must be considered. There are two ways to incorporate those factors in the calculation. First, the uncertainty and the other factors may be used to determine risk-adjusted estimates of the future cash flows and the pure risk-free interest rate applied to them. Second, the risk-free interest rate may be adjusted for the uncertainty and the other factors to determine a risk-adjusted interest rate and applied to the unadjusted estimated future cash flows.

Before getting into the details of determining the factors required for the calculation of present value, the Board lists general principles to follow to avoid biasing the calculation:

- To the extent possible, estimated cash flows and interest rates should reflect assumptions that would be considered in contemplating an arm's-length transaction for cash.
- Interest rates used should reflect assumptions consistent with those inherent in the estimated cash flows. For example, an interest rate of 12 percent should be applied to contractual cash flows of a loan with characteristics that reflect that rate.
- Estimated cash flows and interest rates should not be deliberately overstated or understated to obtain a desired reporting result.
- The estimated cash flows and interest rates should reflect the range of possible outcomes.

If the asset or liability consists of contractual cash flows (a promised series of future cash receipts or payments), they should be used as the future cash flows in the calculation. A single interest rate, often described as "the rate commensurate with the risk," is consistent for assets and liabilities with contractual cash flows with the manner in which marketplace participants describe assets and liabilities, such as a "12 percent bond." Such an approach is useful for determinations in which comparable assets and liabilities can be observed in the marketplace.

However, that approach is unsuited for complex problems of amount determination, including determination of the amounts of nonfinancial assets and liabilities for which there is no market for the asset or liability or for a comparable asset or liability. If no contractual cash flows are involved, the cash flows must be estimated. To determine the present value of such an asset or liability, the observable rate of interest of a comparable asset or liability must be used. The comparable asset or liability must have cash flows whose characteristics are similar to those of the asset or liability whose amount is being determined. The following must be done to do so:

- Identify the set of cash flows that will be discounted.
- Identify another asset or liability in the marketplace that appears to have similar cash flow characteristics.
- Compare the cash flow sets from the two items to make sure that they are similar (e.g., are both sets contractual cash flows, or is one contractual and the other an estimated cash flow?).

- Evaluate whether there is an element in one item that is not present in the other (e.g., is one less liquid than the other?).
- Evaluate whether both sets of cash flows are likely to behave (vary) in a similar fashion under changing economic conditions (FASB Concepts Statement No. 7, par. 44).

In complex situations, the future cash flows should be determined by the expected cash flow approach. That approach uses the sum of probability-weighted amounts in a range of possible estimated amounts. The Board illustrates that as follows for uncertain amounts. The probabilities of cash flows are $100 with a probability of 10 percent, $200 with a probability of 60 percent, and $300 with a probability of 30 percent. The expected cash flow is ($100 × 10%) + ($200 × 60%) + ($300 × 30%) = $220. It illustrates that for uncertain timing of receipts or payments as follows. An estimated cash flow of $1,000 may be received or paid in one year with a probability of 10 percent, in two years with a probability of 60 percent, or in three years with a probability of 30 percent. The comparable interest rates are 5 percent for one year, 5.25 percent for two years, and 5.5 percent for three years. The expected present value is ([$1,000 discounted at 5% for one year = $952.38[158]] × 10%) + ([$1,000 discounted at 5.25% for two years = $902.73[159]] × 60%) + ([$1,000 discounted at 5.5% for three years = $851.61[160]] × 30%) = $95.24 + $541.64 + $255.48 = $892.36.

Those illustrations go beyond the use of present value techniques for "contractual rights to receive money or contractual obligations to pay money on fixed or determinable dates" (APB Opinion No. 21, par. 2). Such techniques cannot reflect uncertainties in timing. Calculations such as those illustrated are not routinely used by accountants. They are required, however, in determinations of pensions, other postretirement benefits, and some insurance liabilities. They are allowed for determination of impairment of long-lived assets and estimating the fair value of financial instruments. The Board answers those who may object to applying probabilities to highly subjective estimates of future cash flows by stating that the approach without applying probabilities uses the same subjective estimates without the "computational transparency" of the illustrated approach.

The Board discusses these situations as examples in which the information needed to implement the calculations is limited:

- The estimated amount is between $50 and $250, with no amount more likely than another. The estimated expected cash flow is ($50 + $250) ÷ 2 = $150.
- The estimated amount is between $50 and $250, and $100 is most likely. The probabilities are not known. The estimated expected cash flow is ($50 + $100 + $250) ÷ 3 = $133.33.
- It is estimated that there is a 10 percent probability that the amount will be $50, a 30 percent probability that the amount will be $250, and a 60 percent probability that the amount will be $100. The estimated expected cash flow is ($50 × 10%) + ($250 × 30%) + ($100 × 60%) = $140.

Obtaining the data to make such complex calculations can be expensive. The Board states that, as usual, the cost of implementing this technique should be commensurate with the benefits to be obtained from it by the users of financial statements.

The Board notes objections to the expected cash flow technique in selected circumstances. For example, an asset or liability has an expected cash flow of $10 with a 90 percent probability and an expected cash flow of $1,000 with a 10 percent probability. The technique arrives at a fair value of ($10 × .9) + ($1,000 × .1) = $109. They say that represents neither the $10 nor the $1,000. The Board says the $109 represents the fair value, which neither the $10 nor the $1,000 represents.

---

[158] $952.38 × 1.05 = $1,000.
[159] $902.73 × 1.0525 × 1.0525 = $1,000.
[160] $851.61 × 1.055 × 1.055 × 1.055 = $1,000.

Relationship to Accounting for Contingencies.   Statement of Concepts No. 7 focuses on determination of amounts, not on recognition. In contrast, FASB Statement of Standards No. 5 and FASB Interpretation No. 14 focus on recognition of loss "contingencies." (That is a misnomer. Statement No. 5 calls for recognition of a loss if it is probable that an asset *has been* impaired or a liability or an increase in a liability *has been* incurred and that future events will confirm the loss. There is nothing contingent about such events.) Nevertheless, the Statements interact.

For example, determining the fair value of a loan involves expectations about potential default, but recognizing a loss under Statement No. 5 requires that it be probable that a loss has been incurred. The Board presents an illustration that it states raises issues that are "intractable" and beyond the scope of Statement No. 7. If the preceding illustration is changed to make the 90 percent probability a cash flow of $0, the expected cash flow is $100 but Statement No. 5 would seem to call for recognition of the liability at $0. Or, if a reporting entity had 10 potential liabilities with the characteristics of this illustration with the outcomes of the 10 independent of one another, some would conclude that a probable loss is $1,000, because one in 10 will probably materialize. Statement No. 5 would on that basis report a loss of $1,000, but Statement No. 7 would report no loss.

Some losses are reported by adjustment to the existing amortization or reporting convention not involving a current interest rate, not through a fresh-start determination. Such adjustments are beyond the scope of Statement No. 7. A fresh-start determination such as required by FASB Statement of Standards No. 121 is consistent with Statement No. 7.

FASB Interpretation No. 14 prescribes a determination of an amount equal to the minimum value in the range involved. That is inconsistent with Statement No. 7.

Risk and Uncertainty.   The fair value estimate should include the amount sellers are able to receive for bearing the risk inherent in the cash flows from the asset, if it is identifiable, determinable, and significant. Including an arbitrary adjustment for risk or arbitrarily excluding an adjustment for risk in unacceptable. Matrix pricing, option-adjusted spread models, and fundamental analysis are ways to estimate the risk adjustment. However, if no reliable estimate of the risk premium can be obtained or if it is small compared with the potential error in estimating the future cash flows, the risk-free interest rate may be preferable to use.

The uncertainty involved in the risk of owning the asset should be described clearly. For example, a lender on 1,000 loans may set the interest rate based on the view that some loans will default, whereas another lender on 1,000 loans may set the interest rate based on the view that 150 loans will default. Determination of the present value in those situations should make the distinction.

A purchaser of an asset with a given certain expected future cash flow would pay more for the asset than for an asset with the same expected future cash flow but that involves uncertainty. That is because people prefer to avoid uncertainty (are "risk-averse"). For that reason, the Board concludes that uncertainty should be factored into determination of present value to approximate fair value. The risk premium, the premium for uncertainty, is often difficult to determine. The Statement describes approaches to the problem, including portfolio theory, behavioral finance theory, and the Capital Asset Pricing Model, including problems with and disputes over each.

Relevance and Reliability.   Calculations to determine fair values in the absence of readily observable market values, whether to determine future cash flows or present values, use estimates and therefore are inherently imprecise. Nevertheless, though different conclusions may be reached about the amount and timing of future cash flows and adjustments for uncertainty and risk, the use of expected future cash flows and simplifying assumptions permits the determination of present values that are sufficiently reliable and much more relevant than undiscounted amounts.

Present Value in the Determination of Liability Amounts.   The Statement discusses techniques to estimate the fair value of a liability at initial recognition or at a fresh start. The objective is to estimate the value of the assets to either settle the liability with the holder or transfer the liability to an entity of comparable credit standing. One way is to estimate the price at which the liability can be sold as an asset to another entity. The other way is to estimate the price the reporting entity would have to pay another entity to assume the liability. Both of those involve the credit standing of the reporting entity. The price at which the liability can be sold or that the reporting entity would have to pay another entity to assume the liability is affected by the perceived risk of holding the liability as an asset. The greater the perceived risk, the less another entity would agree to pay to obtain the liability as an asset (the greater the required effective interest rate), and vice versa.

In complex liabilities, such as a liability with a range of possible outflows, the effect of risk may be more effectively included by computing expected cash flows.

Including the reporting entity's credit standing in the determination of the amount at which to report a liability at initial recognition and at a fresh start has been controversial, with some contending that such reporting involves a paradox—income is reported when the reporting entity's credit standing declines. The FASB is adamant, however: "there is no rationale for why, in initial or fresh-start measurement, the recorded amount of a liability should reflect something other than the price that would exist in the marketplace."[161] In fact, Lorensen has presented such a rationale, an argument in favor of reporting a liability at its risk-free funding rate.[162]

The FASB goes on to disagree that there is a paradox:

A change in credit standing represents a change in the relative positions of the two classes of claimants (shareholders and creditors) to an entity's assets. If the credit standing diminishes, the fair value of creditors' claims diminishes. The amount of shareholders' residual claim to the entity's assets may appear to increase, but that increase probably is offset by losses that may have occasioned the decline in credit standing. Because shareholders usually cannot be called on to pay a corporation's liabilities, the amount of their residual claims approaches, and is limited by, zero. Thus, a change in the position of borrowers necessarily alters the position of shareholders, and vice versa.

The failure to include changes in credit standing in the measurement of a liability ignores economic differences between liabilities. Consider the case of an entity that has two classes of borrowing. Class One was transacted when the entity had a strong credit standing and a correspondingly low interest rate. Class Two is new and was transacted under the entity's current lower credit standing. Both classes trade in the marketplace based on the entity's current credit standing. If the two liabilities are subject to fresh-start measurement, failing to include changes in the entity's credit standing makes the classes of borrowings seem different—even though the marketplace evaluates the quality of their respective cash flows as similar to one another. (Statement of Concepts No. 7, paragraphs 86–88)

The main objection to the FASB's defense is that it relies on the effects on parties separate from the reporting entity: the creditors and the shareholders. The financial report on a reporting entity should be solely about effects of events on the reporting entity, not on any other entity. Regardless of changes in the values of claims to the creditors or rights of shareholders, the reporting entity has the same obligation to make the same payments, unchanged by changes affecting the creditors or shareholders.

The FASB states that the reporting entity's reported shareholders' equity "may appear" to increase using the kind of reporting it prefers in the face of a decline in the credit standing of the reporting entity. In fact, it does increase. The FASB says that the increase probably is offset by losses that may have occasioned the decline in credit standing. The message is that it is correct to, in effect, reverse reporting such losses. No justification for such a reversal is offered or apparent.

Though, as the FASB states, the marketplace evaluates the quality of the respective cash flows of the Class One and Class Two liabilities it illustrates as similar to one another, their promised cash flows are different, because their interest payments are different, reflecting the difference in the credit standing between the times they were incurred. Under the reporting recommended by Lorensen, they would appear different. Were their required cash flows the same, they would appear the same under the reporting recommended by Lorensen.

---

[161] Statement of Concepts No. 7, paragraph 85.
[162] Leonard Lorensen, "Accounting Research Monograph No. 4," *Accounting for Liabilities* (New York: AICPA, 1992).

Interest Methods of Allocation.   All methods of so-called systematic and rational allocation use formulas selected at the beginning of the periods of allocation. They are said to report changes in value, utility, or substance of assets and liabilities over time, though the FASB states that "they are not measurements." Interest methods of allocation use the compound interest formula, for example, for amortization of discount or premium as prescribed by APB Opinion No. 21. They are considered most relevant to circumstances in which a borrowing and a lending is involved, similar assets or liabilities are allocated using the interest method, a set of estimated future cash flows is closely associated, and the calculation at initial recognition was based on present value.

Applying an interest method of allocation requires description of the kind of cash flow (promised, expected, etc.), the kind of interest rate to be used (effective or other), application of the rate (constant effective or a series of annual), and how to report changes in the amount or timing of the estimated cash flows. Changes in market interest rates are ignored. Changes in estimates of cash flows are included in a fresh-start calculation or affect the interest amortization plan. The plan may be affected by a prospective approach, computing a new effective interest rate, a catch-up approach, adjusting the carrying amount of the asset or liability to the amount it would have been had the new estimate been made originally, or a retrospective approach based on actual cash flows to date and newly estimated remaining cash flows. The FASB expresses a preference for the catch-up approach. Though some consider the retrospective approach best, the cost of applying it may be prohibitive.

2.4 INVITATION TO LEARN MORE

This chapter is more a generous introduction to the FASB's conceptual framework. About half of the chapter is concerned with the antecedents of the conceptual framework, why the FASB undertook it, and why it contains the particular set of concepts that it does. The framework cannot really be understood without that background. The descriptions of the various Concepts Statements emphasized their major conclusions and some of the explanation they provide but did not go into them deeply enough to provide a substitute for reading them. Readers are urged to read the Concepts Statements themselves.

The FASB has used the completed parts of the framework with considerable success. The Board's constituents also have learned to use the framework, partly at least because they have discovered that they are more likely to influence the Board if they do. Both the Board and the constituents have also found that at times the concepts appear to work better than at other times, and undoubtedly they sometimes could have been more soundly applied. As much of the chapter suggests, some parts of the conceptual framework are still controversial, partly at least because long-held views die hard. The framework remains unfinished, although the Board gives no sign of completing it. Despite the fact that the Board has left it incomplete, the FASB's conceptual framework

- Is the first reasonably successful effort by a standards-setting body to formulate and use an integrated set of financial accounting concepts
- Has fundamentally changed the way financial accounting standards are set in the United States
- Has provided a basis for discussion for the International Accounting Standards Committee and several national standards-setting bodies in other English-speaking countries, which have been influenced by the FASB's Concepts Statements, sometimes to the point of adopting the same or virtually the same set of concepts

The Concepts Statements can continue to contribute significantly to better financial accounting and reporting standards. However, the conceptual framework is primarily a set of tools in the hands of standards setters. To live up to their promise, sound concepts require "the right blend of characteristics in standard setters—independence of mind, intellectual integrity, judicial temperament, and a generous portion of wisdom."[163]

---

[163] Kirk, "Looking Back on Fourteen Years at the FASB: The Education of a Standard Setter," p. 17.

Looking forward, challenges will be presented by the current business environment—where joint ventures, licensing arrangements and multiple subsidiaries blur the lines of the traditional entity, and the extension of fair value accounting into more areas of the financial accounting model gives rise to greater subjectivity in financial reporting when seeking greater relevance in the information content.[164]

2.5 SOURCES AND SUGGESTED REFERENCES

American Accounting Association, Committee on Concepts and Standards Underlying Corporate Financial Statements. *Accounting and Reporting Standards for Corporate Financial Statements and Preceding Statements and Supplements*. Iowa City, Iowa: Author, 1957.

———. "A Tentative Statement of Accounting Principles Underlying Corporate Financial Statements," *Accounting Review*, June 19, 1936, 187–191; Reprinted in *Accounting and Reporting Standards for Corporate Financial Statements and Preceding Statements and Supplements,* pp. 60–64.

American Institute of Accountants. Accounting Research Bulletin No. 43, *Restatement and Revision of Accounting Research Bulletins*. New York: Author, 1953.

———. *Audits of Corporate Accounts: Correspondence between the Special Committee on Cooperation with Stock Exchanges of the American Institute of Accountants and the Committee on Stock List of the New York Stock Exchange, 1932–1934*. New York: Author, 1934. Reprinted: New York: American Institute of Certified Public Accountants, 1963; and in Zeff, *Forging Accounting Principles in Five Countries* (full reference below), pp. 237–247.

American Institute of Certified Public Accountants. APB Statement No. 4, *Basic Concepts and Accounting Principles Underlying Financial Statements of Business Enterprises*. New York: Author, 1970.

———. *Establishing Financial Accounting Standards*. (Often called the Wheat Report, after the chairman, Francis M. Wheat, a former SEC commissioner.) New York: Author, March 29, 1972.

———. *Report of Special Committee on Opinions of the Accounting Principles Board*. (Often called the Seidman Report, after the chairman, J. S. Seidman.) New York: Author, 1965.

Anton, H. R. "Objectives of Financial Accounting: Review and Analysis," *Journal of Accountancy* (January 1976). 40–51.

Baxter, W. T., ed. "Introduction." *Studies in Accounting*. London: Macmillan, 1950. [Reprinted as "Introduction to the First Edition" in second and third editions: W. T. Baxter and Sidney Davidson, eds., *Studies in Accounting Theory* (London: Sweet & Maxwell Ltd., 1962); and Baxter and Davidson, eds. *Studies in Accounting* (London: Institute of Chartered Accountants in England and Wales, 1977.)]

Berle, A. A. Jr. "Accounting and the Law," *Accounting Review* (March 1938): 9–15. Reprinted in *Journal of Accountancy* (May 1938): 368–378.

Bevis, H. W. *Corporate Financial Reporting in a Competitive Environment*. New York: Macmillan, 1965.

Blough, C. G. "Development of Accounting Principles in the United States," *Berkeley Symposium on the Foundations of Financial Accounting*. Berkeley: Schools of Business Administration, University of California, 1967, pp. 1–14; discussions by Carl Devine, pp. 15–19, and Stephen A. Zeff, pp. 20–25.

Bonbright, J. C. *Principles of Public Utility Rates*. New York: Columbia University Press, 1961.

Byrne, G. R. "To What Extent Can the Practice of Accounting Be Reduced to Rules and Standards?" *Journal of Accountancy* (November 1937): 364–379. Reprinted in M. Moonitz and A. C. Littleton, eds., *Significant Accounting Essays*. Englewood Cliffs, NJ: Prentice-Hall, 1965, pp. 103–115.

Carey, J. L. *The Rise of the Accounting Profession to Responsibility and Authority, 1937–1969*. New York: American Institute of Certified Public Accountants, 1970.

CFA Institute. *A Comprehensive Business Reporting Model: Financial Reporting for Investors*. Charlottesville, VA: Author, 2005.

---

[164] Steven H. Wallman, "The Future of Accounting and Disclosure in an Evolving World: The Need for Dramatic Change," *Accounting Horizons* (September 1995). For a further discussion of issues facing contemporary and future financial reporting see also: *Financial Reporting in the 1990s and Beyond,* a report of the Association for Investment Management and Research (AIMR), Peter H. Knutson, principal author (Charlottesville, VA: AIMR, 1993), and *A Comprehensive Business Reporting Model: Financial Reporting for Investors* (Charlottesville, VA: CFA Institute, 2005). In addition, Chapter 3 of this *Handbook* addresses the challenges faced in the near term related to establishing accounting standards.

Chambers, R. J. "Why Bother with Postulates?" *Journal of Accounting Research* (Spring 1963): 3–15. Reprinted in Zeff, *The Accounting Postulates and Principles Controversy of the 1960s* (full reference below).

Chatfield, Michael. "Postulates and Principles." In *A History of Accounting Thought*, rev. ed. Huntington, NY: Robert E. Krieger, 1977.

Committee on Accounting Principles and Practice of the New Jersey Society of Certified Public Accountants. "Comments on 'Accounting for Income Taxes.'" *Journal of Accountancy* (March 1945): 235–240.

FASB. Discussion Memorandum, *Conceptual Framework for Financial Accounting and Reporting: Elements of Financial Statements and Their Measurement*. Stamford, CT: Author, December 2, 1976.

_____. Special Bulletin, *Disclosure of Departures from Opinions of the Accounting Principles Board*. New York: Author, 1964. Reprinted in Zeff, *Forging Accounting Principles in Five Countries* (full reference below), pp. 266–268.

Financial Accounting Standards Board. *Scope and Implications of the Conceptual Framework Project*. Stamford, CT: Author, 1976.

Gellein, O. S. "Financial Reporting: The State of Standard Setting." In *Advances in Accounting*, Vol. 3, ed. Bill N. Schwartz. Greenwich, CT: JAI Press., 1986, pp. 3–23.

_____. "Periodic Earnings: Income? or Indicator?" *Accounting Horizons* (June 1987): 59–64.

_____. "Primacy: Assets or Income?" In *Research in Accounting Regulation*, Vol. 6, ed. Gary John Previts. Greenwich, CT: JAI Press, 1992, pp. 198–199.

Gilman, S. *Accounting Concepts of Profit*. New York: Ronald Press, 1939, pp. 167–257.

Gore, P. *The FASB Conceptual Framework Project, 1973–1985, An Analysis*. Manchester, UK: Manchester University Press, 1992.

Grady, P., ed. *Memoirs and Accounting Thought of George O. May*. New York: Ronald Press, 1962.

Greer, H. C. "What Are Accepted Principles of Accounting?" *Accounting Review* (March 1938): 25–30.

Heath, Loyd C. "Accounting, Communication, and the Pygmalion Syndrome," *Accounting Horizons* (March 1987): 1–8.

Hylton, D. "On Matching Revenue with Expense," *Accounting Review* (October 1965): 824–828.

Ijiri, Y. "Recognition of Contractual Rights and Obligations: An Exploratory Study of Conceptual Issues." Financial Accounting Standards Board Research Project. Stamford, CT, FASB 1980.

Jaenicke, H. R. "Survey of Present Practices in Recognizing Revenues, Expenses, Gains and Losses" Financial Accounting Standards Board Research Project. Stamford, CT., FASB, 1981.

Jennings, A. R. "Present-Day Challenges in Financial Reporting." *Journal of Accountancy* (January 1958): 28–34. Reprinted in Zeff, *The Accounting Postulates and Principles Controversy of the 1960s* (full reference below).

Johnson, L. T., and R. K. Storey. *Recognition in Financial Statements: Underlying Concepts and Practical Conventions*. FASB Research Report. Stamford, CT: Financial Accounting Standards Board, 1982.

Kirk, D. J. "Commentary on the Limitations of Accounting—A Response [to Eugene H. Flegm]." *Accounting Horizons* (September 1989): 98–104.

_____. "Looking Back on Fourteen Years at the FASB: The Education of a Standard Setter," *Accounting Horizons* (March 1988): 8–17.

_____. "Reflections on a 'Reconceptualization of Accounting': A Commentary on Parts I–IV of Homer Kripke's Paper, 'Reflections on the FASB's Conceptual Framework for Accounting and on Auditing,"' *Journal of Accounting, Auditing & Finance* (Winter 1989): 83–105.

Knutson, P. H. *Financial Reporting in the 1990s and Beyond*. Charlottesville, VA: Association for Investment Management and Research, 1993.

Knutson, P. H. *A Report of the AIMR Financial Accounting Policy Committee, Financial Reporting in the 1990s and Beyond*. Charlottesville, VA: AIMR, 1993. (The AIMR is now known as the CFA Institute.)

Kohler, E. L. *A Dictionary for Accountants*, 5th ed. Englewood Cliffs, NJ: Prentice-Hall, 1975.

Lawler, J. "A Talk with George O. May," *Journal of Accountancy* (June 1955): 40–45.

Littleton, A. C. "Tests for Principles," *Accounting Review* (March 1938): 16–24.

Luper, O. L., and Paul Rosenfield. "The APB Statement on Basic Concepts and Principles," *Journal of Accountancy* (January 1971): 46–51.

Manning, B. *A Concise Textbook on Legal Capital*, 2nd ed. Mineola, NY: Foundation Press, 1981.

Mautz, R. K. "Basic Concepts of Accounting." In *Handbook of Modern Accounting*, ed. Sidney Davidson, pp. 1-1–1-15. New York: McGraw-Hill, 1970.

May, G. O. "The Influence of Accounting on the Development of an Economy," *Journal of Accountancy* (January 1936): 11–22.

———. "Improvement in Financial Accounts," *Journal of Accountancy* (May 1937): 333–369.

———. "Principles of Accounting," *Journal of Accountancy* (December 1937): 423–425.

———. "Terminology of the Balance Sheet," *Journal of Accountancy* (January 1942): 35–36.

———. *Financial Accounting: A Distillation of Experience*. New York: Macmillan, 1943.

———. "The Nature of the Financial Accounting Process," *Accounting Review* (July 1943): 189–193.

———. "Should the LIFO Principle Be Considered in Depreciation Accounting When Prices Vary Widely?" *Journal of Accountancy* (December 1947): 453–456.

———. "Business Combinations: An Alternative View," *Journal of Accountancy* (April 1957): 33–36.

———. "Income Accounting and Social Revolution," *Journal of Accountancy* (June 1957): 36–41.

———. "Generally Accepted Principles of Accounting," *Journal of Accountancy* (January 1958): 23–27.

Moonitz, M. *The Basic Postulates of Accounting*. Accounting Research Study No. 1. New York: American Institute of Certified Public Accountants, 1961. Reprinted in Zeff, *The Accounting Postulates and Principles Controversy of the 1960s* (full reference below).

———. "The Changing Concept of Liabilities," *Journal of Accountancy* (May 1960): 41–46.

———. "Why Do We Need 'Postulates' and 'Principles'?" *Journal of Accountancy* (December 1963): 42–46. Reprinted in Zeff, *The Accounting Postulates and Principles Controversy of the 1960s* (full reference below).

———. *Obtaining Agreement on Standards in the Accounting Profession*. Studies in Accounting Research No. 8. Sarasota, FL: American Accounting Association, 1974.

"News—ASB under Fire," *Accountancy* (November 1993): 16.

Paton, W. A., with the assistance of William A. Paton Jr. *Asset Accounting*. New York: Macmillan Company, 1952.

Paton, W. A. "Comments on 'A Statement of Accounting Principles,'" *Journal of Accountancy* (March 1938): 196–207.

———. Introduction. In *Foundations of Accounting Theory: Papers Given at the Accounting Theory Symposium, University of Florida, March 1970*, ed. Williard E. Stone. Gainesville: University of Florida Press, 1971.

Paton, W. A., and A. C. Littleton. *An Introduction to Corporate Accounting Standards*. Ann Arbor, MI: American Accounting Association, 1940.

"Report to Council of the Special Committee on Research Program." *Journal of Accountancy* (December 1958): 62–68. [Reprinted in Zeff, *Forging Accounting Principles in Five Countries* (full reference below), pp. 248–265; and in Zeff, *The Accounting Postulates and Principles Controversy of the 1960s* (full reference below).

Rutherford, B. "Accountancy Issues—They Manipulate. You Smooth. I Self-Hedge: Perhaps the World's Finest Know a Thing or Two After All," *Accountancy* (June 1995): 95.

Sanders, T. H., H. R. Hatfield, and U. Moore, *A Statement of Accounting Principles*. New York: American Institute of Accountants, 1938. Reprinted, Columbus, OH: American Accounting Association, 1959.

Scott, A. W. *Abridgement of the Law of Trusts*. Boston: Little, Brown, 1960.

Shattke, R. W. "An Analysis of Accounting Principles Board Statement No. 4," *Accounting Review* (April 1972): 233–244.

Sherman, H. D., ed. *Conceptual Frameworks for Financial Accounting*, Proceedings of a conference at the Harvard Business School, October 1–2, 1982. Cambridge, MA: President and Fellows of Harvard College, circa 1984.

Singleton-Green, B. "The ASB: Critics That Won't Be Pacified," *Accountancy* (November 1993): 26.

Solomons, D. "The FASB's Conceptual Framework: An Evaluation," *Journal of Accountancy* (June 1986): 114–124.

———. *Making Accounting Policy: The Quest for Credibility in Financial Reporting*. New York: Oxford University Press, 1986.

Sprouse, R. T. "Accounting for What-You-May-Call-Its," *Journal of Accountancy* (October 1966): 45–53.

———. "Commentary on Financial Reporting—Developing a Conceptual Framework for Financial Reporting," *Accounting Horizons* (December 1988): 121–127.

———. "Commentary on Financial Reporting—Economic Consequences: The Volatility Bugaboo," *Accounting Horizons* (March 1987): 88.

Sprouse, R. T., and M. Moonitz, *A Tentative Set of Broad Accounting Principles for Business Enterprises*. Accounting Research Study No. 3. New York: American Institute of Certified Public Accountants, 1962.

Staubus, G. J. "An Analysis of APB Statement No. 4," *Journal of Accountancy* (February 1972): 36–43.

Sterling, R. R. "On Theory Construction and Verification," *Accounting Review* (July 1970): 444–457.

Storey, R. K. "Conditions Necessary for Developing a Conceptual Framework." FASB *Viewpoints*, March 3, 1981. Excerpted in *Journal of Accountancy* (June 1981): 84–96, and (with unauthorized revisions by the editor, some of which changed the meaning) in *Financial Analysts Journal* (May-June 1981): 51–58.

———. *The Search for Accounting Principles*. New York: American Institute of Certified Public Accountants, 1964. Reprinted, Houston, TX: Scholars Book Company, 1977.

Storey, R. K., and S. Storey, "The Framework of Financial Accounting and Concepts." Special Report. Norwalk, CT: FASB, 1998.

Study Group on Business Income. *Changing Concepts of Business Income*. New York: Macmillan Company, 1952.

Study Group on the Objectives of Financial Statements. *Objectives of Financial Statements*. (Often called the Trueblood Report, after the chairman, Robert M. Trueblood.) New York: American Institute of Certified Public Accountants, October 1973.

Trouant, D. L. *Financial Audits*. New York: American Institute Publishing, 1937.

Walker, R. G. "The SEC's Ban on Upward Asset Revaluations and the Disclosure of Current Values," *Abacus* (March 1992): 3–35.

Wallman, S. H. "The Future of Accounting and Disclosure in an Evolving World: The Need for Dramatic Change," *Accounting Horizons* (September 1995).

Wyatt, A. R. "Accounting Standards and the Professional Auditor," *Accounting Horizons* (June 1989): 96–102.

———. "Commentary on Interface Between Teaching/Research and Teaching/Practice," *Accounting Horizons* (March 1989): 125–128.

Zeff, Stephen A. *The Accounting Postulates and Principles Controversy of the 1960s*. New York: Garland Publishing, 1982.

———. *Forging Accounting Principles in Five Countries: A History and an Analysis of Trends*. Champaign, IL: Stipes Publishing, 1972.

CHAPTER 3

FUTURE DIRECTIONS IN FINANCIAL ACCOUNTING STANDARDS: THE POTENTIAL ROLE OF INTERNATIONAL ACCOUNTING STANDARDS

Tom Jones

3.1 INTRODUCTION

The objective of the International Accounting Standards Board (IASB) is a single set of high-quality financial reporting standards used globally. Why is this a desirable objective?

First, there are cost benefits. The international standards dramatically reduce costs to preparers and also to auditors and to some extent to analysts. This applies primarily to multinational companies that in the past have had to deal with many different accounting conventions and disclosure requirements in their foreign operations. They have had to meet local accounting standards in their subsidiaries overseas and then convert those results into U.S. generally accepted accounting principles (GAAP) for Securities and Exchange Commission (SEC) and shareholder reporting.

At least they now deal mainly with only two sets of accounting conventions—U.S. GAAP and international GAAP—but even this involves two sets of books for every affected operating unit, and this remains expensive. IBM is a prime example of a company with more operations outside the United States complying with international standards than in the United States complying with U.S. GAAP. One global enterprise, Ford Motor Company, has moved to international standards worldwide—for every unit, including its management reporting for domestic U.S. operations. The broader goal of this particular company is to build on a unified global accounting system as a key part and driver of globalizing its entire operations.

It is also the case that U.S.-based multinationals are the only companies in the world that are required to keep two sets of books; since foreign registrants are now permitted to file in the United States without reconciliation to U.S. GAAP, this implies some acceptance by the SEC that international GAAP has significant legitimacy.

Cost benefits are not limited to large multinationals. Many of the smaller listed companies believe that the move to international standards will be very expensive and will yield few benefits. Nothing could be further from the truth, and this erroneous view is fostered by scaremongering by opponents of U.S. adoption of international standards and by a lack of teaching and information on the subject.

3.2 NECESSARY TRANSITION PERIOD

The transition to international GAAP in the United States will likely not take place without a lengthy preparation time, probably about five years. Most companies renew operating systems fairly frequently, and obviously changes in the next few years should take into account potential international accounting information requirements. This will dramatically reduce the cost of the transition if considered at the time of systems updates.

In addition, the Financial Accounting Standards Board (FASB) and the IASB are working very hard right now to convert to identical standards in each area where they are currently active. A prime example is revenue recognition, which was an area of significant difference between FASB and IASB, mostly attributable to the multitude of detail rules in current U.S. GAAP. A new standard currently being contemplated would make principles-based revenue recognition identical in both jurisdictions. Obviously, the larger and more important the area of full convergence, the lower will be the cost of adoption.

Also, the cost of conversion, as modest as many believe it will be, is a one-time item.

3.3 CASE FOR ADOPTING ONE SET OF PRINCIPLES-BASED STANDARDS

A logical way for the United States to adopt international standards would be to eliminate the unnecessary length and large body of rules-based requirements, written in accountant "techno-speak" language that is incomprehensible to all but a few. If the United States adopts this approach, there will be quite dramatic savings in the future in terms of the lower amount of investment and effort complying with the current complex requirements. While cost savings are important, the savings in the human resource area are probably equally important. In the past, preparers had to ensure that accounting staff were educated in many different accounting theories; often the first language of these staff members was not English. Imagine the cost and waste of resources this caused, often in countries with limited resources that would be better used for purposes other than competing accounting theories.

No less significant are the improvements in comparability. Opponents of international standards argue that comparability will suffer, but a few moments reflection will convince you that with emerging economies growing rapidly and markets globalizing—and with U.S. markets now occupying only about 30 percent[1] of the total global equity markets, comparability globally will obviously be improved.

---

[1] The Committee on Capital Markets Regulation (CCMR) also reported that the U.S. share of global market capitalization was 31.6 percent compared to an average of 45.7 percent from 1996 to 2006. It is, however, true that the U.S. share of global equity trading was 45.8 percent compared to a historical average of 50.6 percent. (See press release of August 18, 2011, from CCMR at *www.capmktsreg.org*.) The world federation of exchanges (*www.world-exchanges.org/*) reports that the United States share of domestic market capitalization declined from 52 percent in 2001 to 31 percent in 2009.

In summary, the combination of these factors should make for more efficient capital markets—and a reduced cost of capital. Academic research[2] has shown that in a number of countries that have adopted international standards, the cost of capital has indeed been reduced.

It is important to remember that accounting is not rocket science. It does not need to be highly complicated or to be written in incomprehensible language. In fact, I believe that complexity in accounting standards is usually a sign of too many rules and too few principles and is therefore a sign of weakness in the standards. The more complex the standard, the easier it is for inventive accountants to "lawyer the words" and find ways around it. Prime examples of this can be found in consolidation standards, where the IASB has a simple principle: "If you have control, you must consolidate." The standard illustrates that control is a fact. It may be ownership of more than 50 percent, but it may equally be the exercise of control over the board or over company policies or benefits. These and other factors may be evidence of the requirement for consolidation even without majority ownership or even without any ownership. It is clear that you cannot easily find ways around the standard by tweaking ownership percentages and that judgment of the facts is required to make a decision as to whether consolidation is required or not. I posit that there would have been far fewer subsidiaries omitted from the books of the banks in the 2008 crisis had that been the rule in the United States. In fact, when Deutsche Bank moved from U.S. standards to international standards in 2007, it was required to consolidate approximately 200 vehicles that had not been consolidated under U.S. GAAP, and of course the lessons of Enron's adventures in accounting do not need repeating. I should hasten to add that U.S. standards on consolidation have been significantly strengthened in recent years, and the United States and international standards on this and many other subjects should be identical after completion of the current round of joint deliberations on these standards.

Another example of the evils of complexity is in the area of lease accounting. Many standards, including both international and U.S. standards, have had rather complex rules regarding how lease obligations should be treated. This, of course, means whether they should appear on the balance sheet or not. Needless to say, these rules have resulted in less than an appropriate number of leases ever appearing on balance sheets as liabilities. This is a gross distortion of liabilities and of any ratios based on assets or liabilities. It is the simple result of giving adventurous preparers a challenge to work around and defeat complex rules. A proposed replacement by both the IASB and the FASB will include a simple principle stating that if a lease has been entered into, the discounted cost of lease payments through the entire contract must be reported as a liability. It will be very hard to find imaginative ways to avoid that standard, and accounting credibility and comparability will benefit as a result.

One other change introduced by the IASB based on the experience of a number of national standard setters is to discourage the issuance of industry-specific standards. The IASB prefers to use product-specific standards so that preparers do not shop around for the most advantageous accounting methodologies. An example of this lies in the banking and insurance industries, where it is possible for an identical product to be accounted for differently depending on whether the preparer is classified as an insurer or as a bank. Many commentators in the United States see the

---

[2] See: C. Dargenidou, S. McLeay, and I. Raonic, "Expected Earnings Growth and the Cost of Capital: An Analysis of Accounting Regime Change in the European Financial Market," Cass Business School Research Paper, 2006. C.D. Lee, S.M. Walker, I.R. Christensen, Research Report 105, "Mandating IFRS: Its Impact on the Cost of Equity Capital in Europe," Certified Accountants Education Trust, London, 2008. G. Lee and Y. Chen, "Asset Liquidity, Cost of Capital and IFRS Adoption," presented at the 2010 Accounting and Finance Association of Australia and New Zealand Conference, January, 10 2010; *http://ssrn.com/abstract=1534316*. N. S. Soderstrom and K. J. Sun, "IFRS Adoption and Accounting Quality: A Review," *European Accounting Review* 16, no. 4 (2007): 675–702. S. Shi and J.-B. Kim, "Enhanced Disclosures Via IFRS and Stock Price Synchronicity Around the World: Do Analyst Following and Institutional Infrastructure Matter?", October 2007. Available at *SSRN: http://ssrn.com/abstract=1026190*

absence of industry-specific standards as a weakness. It takes a real effort to change that mind-set and recognize that while product-specific accounting may be required, industry-specific accounting is a trap. Much of the complexity in U.S. rules has been caused by industry specialization, and global experience tells us that not only it is not necessary but that it carries heavy cost burdens, leads to real differences in accounting, can lend itself to opinion shopping, and usually is a way for an industry to look for exceptions from basic rules. A number of years ago special accounting for railroads was abolished, and life continued as usual.

In my view, accounting standards need not be highly complex, and I believe that the last 10 years have given some proof of that. However, the objective of a single set of high-quality accounting standards used in every jurisdiction is a breathtaking thought. It certainly would not have seemed very likely 10 years ago when the IASB was first formed, but when you consider that the result of multiple sets of differing standards is that a transaction may be accounted for differently because it takes place in Birmingham, Alabama, rather than Birmingham, England, the result is absurdity.

It is also a fact that many of the differences between the various competing standard setters in the past were insignificant. In some cases, countries developed their own versions of existing U.S., U.K., or French standards with no meaningful differences between their end product and their "model" except the pride of authorship. Obviously there are issues of principle, which must be addressed head on. For example, the charging of stock option compensation to earnings was a prime example of an issue of principle that had to be addressed in accounting, but many of the differences that accounting technicians and academics argue over and that accumulate to make the differences between competing accounting rules are truly insignificant and create confusion while yielding no benefit whatsoever. This topic of stock compensation was hotly debated in and outside the United States and heavily lobbied by businesses exerting pressure on politicians to influence the process. In both cases, the end accounting result was similar, but a war was fought on two fronts to accomplish that end result. How unnecessary.

3.4 HISTORICAL PERSPECTIVE

Accounting systems have been with us for a very long time. History tells us that double-entry bookkeeping was invented in northern Italy or more likely somewhere east of there about 500 years ago and that long before that time, records of crops and the changing seasons were maintained. However, the emphasis on high-quality financial reporting started with the invention of joint stock companies whose investors who did not necessarily have access to the books of account. While this trend started in Europe, the past 50 or 60 years have seen the United States invest more effort, more money, more time, and more thinking into the subject of comprehensive high-quality financial reporting than any other country.

Accounting history in the United States is complicated. There have been many players, including the part-time Accounting Principles Board and its successor, the Financial Accounting Standards Board. The American Institute of Certified Public Accountants (AICPA) has also had a continuing hand in accounting standard setting through its Accounting Standards Executive Committee (AcSEC) and other groups issued industry-specific guidance. In addition, the SEC has at times been active in steering the direction of accounting through its rulings, Staff Accounting Bulletins, and through speeches or staff announcements. Of course, Congress retains the ultimate right to override all these other bodies, although it has only occasionally done so in the past and today is an active participant in FASB standard-setting projects. This early confusion over standards setting was somewhat alleviated with the formation of the FASB in 1973. A good deal of the duplication and confusion has been cleaned up, particularly with the recently completed "codification" project, which pulled together all the relevant and related rules standards and guidance into one place by topical area. This is a major improvement in a somewhat messy situation. If all the accounting literature (standards, interpretations and clarifications issued by the FASB the SEC and predecessor parallel bodies such as the Accounting Principals Board, Railroad Accounting Board, AcSec, etc.) were printed, it would probably reduce the total number of pages from about 25,000 to an estimated 15,000 pages or so.

In the period from 1973 to the late 1980s, the FASB clearly was the world gold standard in accounting, and it could have become the de facto global standard setter. This is especially true because at that time U.S. capital markets made up significantly more than half of the world's capital markets. However, there was little enthusiasm at the board level or amongst the trustees for this extension of the board's mission. I was a member of the Board of Trustees at the time, and I remember the debate and the consideration of the amount of change in staffing, consultation, politics, and workload to expand the mission to a global focus and include other country's views. This was enough to blunt any enthusiasm that existed, and it probably was a wise decision not to take on the task of global standard setting at that time.

Unfortunately, in the late 1980s and the early 1990s, there were many changes, including the acceleration of growth in capital markets outside the United States and a major and sustained increase in the volume and complexity of the FASB's standards, rules, and guidance.

There was also rapid growth in innovative financial products and techniques as a result of the information technology revolution, enabling inventive minds to find work-arounds to almost any standards containing detailed rules. At one time, a source of pride for a large certified public accounting firm was a dedicated group available on almost a 24/7 basis to help structure financial transactions to meet business objectives.

In addition, there was increasing interest around the world in finding accounting that would add credibility and therefore improve a nation's ability to raise capital. There also was increasing concern, even alarm, over the quality of financial reporting and auditing around the world, particularly in the emerging economies.

Finally, there was a huge and commendable effort by FASB chairman Ed Jenkins, and his successor, Bob Herz, to turn back the clock toward a more principles-based set of standards and a less contorted form of language in the standards issued.

In European accounting, there was a somewhat different picture with a wide variation in traditions. The Dutch, for example, were very early practitioners in accounting aimed at joint stock companies (i.e., shareholder-focused companies). In fact, the Dutch accounting body was created before its equivalents in the United States or the United Kingdom.

Scandinavia also tended toward the equity-focused basis of accounting, as did the United Kingdom. In other parts of continental Europe, however, accounting tended to be focused on creditors or bondholders, or toward distributable income as a key ingredient.

By the 1990s, Europe's commercial union, the European Union (EU), had become highly successful. However, fundraising and equity markets had not kept pace, and of course political unity was and remains elusive. This is part of the reason for the euro problems—a common currency but a large number of different economic strategies.

Setting aside the currency issues, it was apparent that given its commercial success, the creation of a common equity market for Europe was a high priority. While the currency experiment could continue, it was essential to have uniform accounting standards. This was the Lamfalussy plan,[3] named for the chairman of the committee of "wise men" who created it. Europe's dilemma arose because of the different accounting approaches adopted by various countries within the union and the fact that it would be difficult to persuade 27 countries to adopt the accounting standards of any one country. For this reason, the existing International Accounting Standards Committee (IASC; predecessor of the IASB) seemed to offer a better alternative. [4]

---

[3] The Lamfalussy report, "The Application of the Lamfalussy Process to EU Securities Markets Legislation," was initially published February 15, 2001. See next footnote for final version and source.

[4] European Commission Staff, "The Application of the Lamfalussy Process to EU Securities Markets Legislation," (Final Version) November 15, 2004. See: *http://ec.europa.eu/internal_market/securities/docs/lamfalussy/sec-2004-1459_en.pdf*

While these discussions were going on in Europe, other countries and other institutions were active. The Japanese had a complex but advanced set of accounting standards, and many countries (e.g., Australia and Canada), were also at the forefront of developments. Other groups were thinking about the issue of accounting standards, prominent among them the United Nations and the Organization for Economic Cooperation and Development.

Another interesting contender in the movement toward rationalizing/standardizing accounting standards was known as the G4 +1. This organization was a completely informal discussion group dealing with accounting issues of the day. It included heavyweight accounting standard setters, such as the United States, the United Kingdom, Canada, Australia, New Zealand, and the IASC. The group produced some very high quality research, but why it was known as the G4 +1 when in fact it was 5+1 is lost in the mysteries of time. One thing is obvious, however: This was a very Anglo-Saxon–oriented group, with the IASC the only representative of other jurisdictions. Nevertheless, it remained purely a discussion group and did not really have aspirations to become a standard-setting body. To his credit, Ed Jenkins proposed that the group abolish itself upon the formation of the new IASB, and this was a welcome endorsement of the newly forming body.

The IASC is also relevant since it was the predecessor body to the IASB. It was initiated in London in 1973—coincidentally the same year as the formation of the FASB in the United States—as a result of the very active role of its chief supporter, Sir Henry Benson. Benson was a British auditor who, with amazing perspicacity, forecast that while the IASC may be new to the scene, it would come to have great significance by the turn of the century. Indeed, exactly 27 years later, in 2001, it became the basis for the formation of the International Accounting Standards Board.

During its 27 years of existence, the IASC gradually advanced its professionalism and credibility but really did not become anything other than a collator of accounting methodologies in use around the world, with many of its standards containing accounting options—sometimes multiple options to appease various constituencies. It also had no ability to require countries to use its standards or to enforce them in any way. No country required use of the IASC standards, although a number of companies voluntarily complied and they did serve as default standards in a number of countries, including Italy. Despite these handicaps, the IASC was a large group of people—70 to 80 people around the table—from a wide geographic spectrum sharing the common goal of improving accounting. Most of the participants were very part time volunteers. Nevertheless, the credibility of the IASC improved over its lifetime. It certainly could not have undertaken the role subsequently played by the IASB, but it did provide a neutral and credible base for the formation of a new board with more teeth.

Turning now from the various aspiring standard setters, there was obviously a considerable amount of political maneuvering happening behind the scenes. There was an urgent need for a single set of standards in Europe, in order for its capital markets to consolidate and grow. There was equally an interest in the United States because of its worldwide purview of investments. The developing countries also needed to improve credibility, particularly those that wished to make inward investment more attractive. Even Japan, despite its wealth and advanced development, was still looking for more inward investment and therefore needed credible accounting to attract that capital.

It was clear that for most countries, the transition to international standards would be difficult. There was a somewhat grudging acceptance that a beefed-up IASC was the most likely organization to make progress. The IASC also recognized that it would need to relinquish its position in favor of a stronger full-time board, which would have the required impact. There was strong support for the concept of an enhanced IASC from Bob Denham, a visionary chairman of the Financial Accounting Foundation (FAF) and from David Ruder, a former SEC chairman and a member of the FASB's board of trustees. Ed Jenkins, chairman of the FASB, was also a strong supporter.

In September 1996, a strategy working party was created to determine how best to move forward. There was broad involvement, as demonstrated by this list of the members of the working party.

Edward Waitzer, chairman	Partner, Stikeman, Elliott
	Former chairman, Ontario Securities Commission
	Former chairman, International Organization of Securities Commissions (IOSCO) Technical Committee
Georges Barthes de Ruyter	Chairman, Conseil National de la Comptabilite
	Former chairman, IASC
Sir Brian Carsberg	Secretary-General, IASC
Anthony Cope	Board member, FASB
Stig Enevoldsen	Chairman, IASC
Frank Harding	President, International Federation of Accountants (IFA)
Kazuo Hiramatsu	Professor of accounting, Kwanei Gakuin University
	Member, Business Accounting Deliberation Council
Brigitta Kantola	Vice President, Finance and Planning,
	International Finance Corporation
Jacques Manardo	Chairman—Europe, Deloitte Touche Tohmatsu International
David Ruder	Professor of law, Northwestern University
	Trustee, Financial Accounting Foundation
	Former chairman, U.S. Securities and Exchange Commission
Werner Seifert	Chief executive officer, Deutsch Borse
Michael Sharpe	Past chairman, IASC
Peter Sjostrand	Partner, BZ Group (Switzerland)
	Board member, Pharma Vision
Sir David Tweedie	Chairman, Accounting Standards Board (UK)

As progress toward a transition was mapped out by the working party, a key meeting of the IASC took place in Venice in November 1999, when after lengthy negotiations between the IASC and the SEC conducted through Mike Crooch, a committee member, and Lynn Turner, chief accountant at the SEC (on behalf of then chairman of the SEC Arthur Levitt), the board unanimously voted itself out of existence in favor of a proposed strengthened IASB.

While the strategy working party was deliberating, the International Organization of Securities Regulators (IOSCO) was a highly involved and interested observer. IOSCO's members worked together to produce an extensive list of issues and subjects that it desired to see resolved before it gave its full support to a new board. This list contained hundreds of recommendations, many of them in potential conflict with each other, but it did get to the heart of many of the issues facing the IASC standards and gave guidance for the IASB's first five years of work programs.

Behind these scenes of major change lay the fact that Arthur Levitt, an influential and very active chairman of the SEC, had concluded that the world would not in fact accept an American-dominated FASB as its standard setter. Yet he had become alarmed as significant companies (particularly in the late 1990s in some Asian emerging markets) suddenly faced financial problems and in some cases bankruptcy shortly after receiving clean audit reports from one or other of the major multinational audit firms.

Investigating this phenomenon, Levitt understood that accounting based on local conventions was being audited by major audit firms using local auditing requirements, leading to very unsatisfactory reporting. This caused him to put his full weight behind the effort to create the IASB, presumably based on the experience of his chief accountant who attended IASC meetings as an observer.

3.5 FORMATION AND STRUCTURE OF THE IASB

It is unknown whether Levitt really believed that the IASB would come to dominate standard-setting globally or whether he simply believed that it would be healthy for the IASB and the FASB to compete in a friendly way to achieve better standards. In any event, it was Levitt's support that led the way. At his urging, the agreement of the structure for the new IASB was completed. Also at his urging, the IASC as one of its last acts appointed a nominating committee of very senior statesman, as the next list demonstrates.

Arthur Levitt, Jr.	Chairman, U.S. Securities and Exchange Commission
Karl H. Baumann	Chairman, Supervisory Board, Siemens AG
	Deputy chairman, DRSC (German national accounting standard setters)
James E. Copeland, Jr.	Chief executive officer, Deloitte Touche Tohmatsu
Howard Davies	Chairman, U.K. Financial Services Authority
Michel Prada	Chairman, French Commission des Operations de Bourse
Andrew Sheng	Chairman, Hong Kong Securities and Futures Commission
James D. Wolfensohn	President, World Bank

The sole objective of this group was the appointment of the first group of trustees who would oversee the IASB. The nominating committee very quickly persuaded Paul Volcker to become the first chairman of the trustees, and together they arranged the appointment of the initial slate of trustees. Volcker completed two terms as chairman, bringing welcome stature to the new organization and defending the independence of the group with force and style. He was clearly a major asset to the IASB. The quality and prestige of the first group of trustees is well illustrated by the next list.

Paul A. Volcker, Chairman	Former chairman, U.S. Federal Reserve Board
Roy Andersen	Deputy chairman and chief executive officer (CEO),
	Liberty Life Group
John H. Biggs	Chairman, TIAA-CREF
Andrew Crockett	General manager, Bank for International Settlements
Roberto Teixeira Da Costa	Former chairman, Brazilian Comissao de Valores Mobiliarios
Guido A. Ferrarini	Professor of law, University of Genoa
	Chairman, Ogilvy Renault, Barristers and Solicitors
L. Yves Fortier	Former Ambassador of Canada to the United Nations
Toshikatsu Fukuma	Chief Financial Officer (CFO), Mitsui & Co., Ltd
Cornelius Herkstroter	Former president, Royal Dutch Petroleum
Hilmar Kopper	Chairman, Supervisory Board, Deutche Bank
Philip A. Laskaway	Chairman, Ernst & Young International
Charles Yeh Kwong Lee	Chairman, Hong Kong Exchange and Clearing Ltd.
Sir Sidney Lipworth	Chairman, U.K. Financial Reporting Council
Didier Pineau-Valencienne	Chairman, Association Francaise des Enterprises Privees
Jens Roder	Senior partner, PricewaterhouseCoopers
David S. Ruder	Former chairman, U.S. Securities and Exchange Commission
	Director, several publicly listed companies
Kenneth H. Spencer	Chairman, Australian Accounting Standards Board
William C. Steere, Jr.	Chairman and CEO, Pfizer Inc.
Koji Tajika	Co-chairman, Deloitte Touche Tohmatsu

As part of its negotiations, the strategy working party concluded that the board should consist of 14 members at least 12 of whom were to be full time. This number later increased to 16 with up to 3 part-time members. This was a significantly larger group than the United States had wanted but significantly smaller than the alternative two chambered proposals or a much larger part-time body desired by Europe.

The characteristics desired in the new standards were:

- Prepared by a predominantly technical board
- Producing standards based on principles rather than rules

- With few interpretations because if the standards were indeed principles based there should be very little need for interpretation (this turned out to be true)
- Written in an understandable and translatable way (implementation guidance and examples of application are of course useful but are considered to be quite separate from the standards themselves)

The board was technically qualified but also was geographically widespread as indicated by this list of the initial board members in 2001.

Sir David Tweedie, chairman	United Kingdom	Academic, standard setter
Tom Jones, vice chairman	United States	Preparer
Mary E. Barth	United States	Auditor, academic
Hans-Georg Bruns	Germany	Preparer
Anthony T. Cope	United States	Analyst
Robert P. Garnet	South Africa	Preparer, analyst
Gilbert Gelard	France	Auditor, preparer
Robert H. Hertz	United States	Auditor
James Leisenring	United States	Standard setter
Warren McGregor	Australia	Standard setter
Patricia O'Malley	Canada	Standard setter
Harry K. Schmidt	Switzerland	Preparer
Geoffrey Whittington	United Kingdom	Academic, standard setter
Tatsumi Yamada	Japan	Auditor

The choice of David Tweedie as chairman was unanimous and was almost a foregone conclusion. He was clearly the most visible and the most reputable candidate. It is mainly due to his independence, tenacity, technical ability, and political skills that the board achieved such success in its first 10 years.

3.6 STRUCTURE AND PROCESS OF THE IASB

The structure and governance of the new organization was heavily influenced by and is in fact based on the structure of the FAF and the FASB in the United States. Trustees set the due process rules, hire and fire the board members, and fulfill the fundraising role. The board members are completely independent in terms of technical accounting decisions, which must, of course, comply with the due process as outlined by the trustees and must be totally independent of any other body or any previous employer. (The part-time board members are exempt from this requirement.)

The board operates through regular board meetings, normally one week each month. The trustees appoint working groups of outside experts for every major project and also appoint a standards advisory committee (SAC), which meets quarterly. Roundtables are organized in the case of particularly difficult technical standards and an interpretations committee (the International Financial Reporting Interpretations Committee (IFRIC)) meets approximately six times a year.

Sunshine rules apply. Every meeting, whether board, trustees, working groups, or roundtables, must be publicly advertised and must be open to public observation. No more than five board members may discuss a technical issue in private.

One significant difference between this initial structure and the US accounting standard setting structure, is that there is no oversight body monitoring actions of the trustee's. In the United States, this is a role assumed by the SEC. This shortcoming was eliminated during a change in the constitution after about five years when a monitoring board was appointed consisting of five securities regulators (including the chairman of the SEC) together with an observer from the Basel banking committee. This oversight is quite similar to the equivalent SEC oversight within the United States.

The appointment of the board in April 2001 resulted in about four years of very hard work, responding to criticisms and suggestions by IOSCO and also by the European Commission, and in general to make the standards suitable for European and other countries to adopt in 2005. The European commission did in fact adopt the standards in 2005 giving the IASB a credible start. It was notable that a number of other countries also adopted in 2005, including Australia, which had a very well-established and reputable position as a leader in accounting standards setting. This broad project to prepare the standards for use in 2005 was collectively known as the improvements project, and although it did not answer every issue—it is silent on insurance accounting, for example—it nevertheless resulted in a set of standards that have stood the test of time well in situations that had greater impact in the United States. There were the expected bouts of criticism, particularly in Europe, about the effort required to achieve the transition, but a couple of years later there was general agreement, at least by preparers, that IASB had improved accounting in Europe.

Each country or jurisdiction that uses international standards must of course have its own process for implementing those standards. Some have chosen to adopt all standards and interpretations automatically as issued unless they make an exception; Australia is one example. Others including Europe have chosen an active endorsement process of one kind or another. In Europe, the entire collection of existing standards in 2005 was adopted together with all subsequent standards and interpretations with one minor exception—a "carve-out" of about 11 paragraphs of one standard in the initial package of standards adopted in 2005. This carve-out is very unfortunate; it has given rise to a view that the standards are not being implemented in a disciplined way in every country. In fact, there are differences in the rigor with which countries enforce the standards but, in general, over the first 10 years, the movement has been very much toward full adoption with no exceptions and no argument. The carve-outs in Europe, which could not be eliminated because of the objections of a very small number of European companies—29 out of 8000—will likely disappear with the implementation of the new standards on financial instruments being developed jointly between the FASB and the IASB.

It is important to note that adoption can be achieved in a number of ways, some more expensive and wasteful than others. With about 120 countries having adopted the standards or being in the process of doing so, there is much experience to draw from. The examples of Denmark and Germany are good ones to illustrate good and bad ways to implement. Denmark has made very efficient use of international standards by abolishing its local GAAP for listed companies and abolishing separate accounting rules for tax or statistical purposes wherever possible. Germany took the opposite path and has imposed international standards on top of all existing local requirements and has applied them only to holding companies as opposed to subsidiaries. This is about as inefficient a way to achieve adoption as it is possible to imagine right now.

In other cases, adoption has been too enthusiastic, and international standards have been applied even to small, unlisted businesses. This is clearly a mistake and has been remedied by the introduction of a small and medium enterprise standard within the past few years. The SME standard has achieved enormous success with approximately 60 countries already using it. It covers the entire spectrum of accounting in only 250 pages. It also gives added impetus to further simplify the full standards used by listed companies. The United States is currently considering separate standards for small enterprises. One might hope that the United States takes advantage of the international experience in this area.

The international convergence efforts are supported by the G20 (the largest economies in the world) who at their September 2009 meeting called on international accounting bodies to redouble their efforts to achieve convergence. The current status for some those countries are:

Argentina	Required for fiscal years beginning on or after January 1, 2011
Australia	Required for all private sector reporting entities and as the basis for public sector reporting since 2005

Brazil	Required for consolidated financial statements of banks and listed companies from December 31, 2010
Canada	Required from January 1, 2011, for all listed entities and permitted for private sector entities including not-for-profit organizations
China	Substantially converged national standards
European Union	All member states of the EU are required to use International Financial Reporting Standards (IFRS) as adopted by the EU for listed companies since 2005
France	Required via EU adoption and implementation process since 2005
Germany	Required via EU adoption and implementation process since 2005
India	Substantially converged national standards
Indonesia	Convergence process ongoing; a decision about a target date for full compliance with IFRSs is expected to be made in 2012

Approximately 100 additional countries either have adopted or have a date certain for future adoption. this listing is kept up to date and can also be accessed through *www.IASplus.com*.

3.7 STANDARDS IN FORCE

Some idea of the coverage of international standards can be seen in this list of standards and interpretations in force in 2010. Interpretations number less than three per year on average, giving credence to the belief that principles-based standards require much less interpretation. Resisting the demands for excessive interpretation requires courage, and the interpretations committee (IFRIC), consisting of 12 volunteer external experts, has done a great job in this respect.

International Financial Reporting Standards International Accounting Standards

IAS No. 1	Presentation of Financial Statements
IAS No. 2	Inventories
IAS No. 7	Statement of Cash Flows
IAS No. 8	Accounting Policies, Changes in Accounting Estimates and Errors
IAS No. 10	Events after the Reporting Period
IAS No. 11	Construction Contracts
IAS No. 12	Income Taxes
IAS No. 16	Property, Plant and Equipment
IAS No. 17	Leases
IAS No. 18	Revenue
IAS No. 19	Employee Benefits
IAS No. 20	Accounting for Government Grants and Disclosure of Government Assistance
IAS No. 21	The effects of Changes in Foreign Exchange Rates
IAS No. 23	Borrowing Costs
IAS No. 24	Related Party Disclosures
IAS No. 26	Accounting and Reporting by Retirement Benefit Plans
IAS No. 27	Consolidated and Separate Financial Statements
IAS No. 28	Investments in Associates
IAS No. 29	Financial Reporting in Hyperinflationary Economies
IAS No. 31	Interests in Joint Ventures
IAS No. 32	Financial Instruments: Presentation
IAS No. 33	Earnings per Share
IAS No. 34	Interim Financial Reporting
IAS No. 36	Impairment of Assets

IAS No. 37	Provisions, Contingent Liabilities and Contingent Assets
IAS No. 38	Intangible Assets
IAS No. 39	Financial Instruments: Recognition and Measurement
IAS No. 40	Investment Property
IAS No. 41	Agriculture

Interpretations

IFRIC No. 1	Changes in Existing Decommissioning, Restoration and Similar Liabilities
IFRIC No. 2	Members' Shares in Co-operative Entities and Similar Instruments
IFRIC No. 4	Determining Whether an Arrangement contains a Lease
IFRIC No. 5	Rights to Interests arising from Decommissioning, Restoration and Environmental Rehabilitation Funds
IFRIC No. 6	Liabilities arising from Participating in a Specific Market-Waste Electrical and Electronic Equipment
IFRIC No. 7	Applying the Restatement Approach under IAS 29 Financial Reporting in Hyperinflationary Economies
IFRIC No. 9	Reassessment of Embedded Derivatives
IFRIC No. 10	Interim Financial Reporting and Impairment
IFRIC No, 11	Interpretation on Group and Treasury Share Transactions
IFRIC No. 12	Service Concession Arrangements
IFRIC No. 13	Customer Loyalty Programmes
IFRIC No. 14	IAS 19: The Limit on a Defined Benefit Asset, Minimum Funding Requirements and Their Interaction
IFRIC No. 15	Agreements for the Construction of Real Estate
IFRIC No. 16	Hedges of a Net Investment in a Foreign Operation
IFRIC No. 17	Distributions of Non-Cash Assets to Owners
IFRIC No. 18	Transfers of Assets from Customers
IFRIC No. 19	Extinguishing Financial Liabilities with Equity Instruments
SIC[5] 7	Introduction of the Euro
SIC 10	Government Assistance: No Specific Relation to Operating Activities
SIC 12	Consolidation: Special Purpose Entities
SIC 13	Jointly Controlled Entities—Non-Monetary Contributions by Venturers
SIC 15	Operating Leases: Incentives
SIC 21	Income Taxes: Recovery of Revalued Non-Depreciable Assets
SIC 25	Income Taxes: Changes in the Tax Status of an Entity or Its Shareholders
SIC 27	Evaluating the Substance of Transactions Involving the Legal Form of a Lease
SIC 29	Service Concession Arrangements: Disclosures
SIC 31	Revenue: Barter Transactions Involving Advertising Services
SIC 32	Intangible Assets: Web Site Costs

These lists are expanding, and the cooperative agreement between the FASB and the IASB will lead to new and revised standards that are common to both in a number of areas. Some examples are a new comprehensive standard for financial instruments, a common standard for revenue recognition, a common standard for lease accounting, and possibly a new insurance standard that will remedy one of the true defects in accounting today. That defect is the fact that insurance accounting (specifically life insurance) is different in many countries, that it is written in a rather arcane language understood only by insurance experts, and that technology is bringing banking and insurance closer so that current differences in accounting treatments are a particular problem. Think,

---

[5]Standards Interpretation Committee.

for example, of a small subsidiary regulated by the weakest banking regulator, and therefore using bank accounting, trading heavily in derivatives. This subsidiary is hidden inside a global insurance company, and practically bankrupted its parent.

Other standards already part of the IASB suite are very similar, even though they were written before the formal partnership between the FASB and the IASB. Examples of these are the acquisition and merger accounting standard and the stock compensation standard.

3.8 IMPEDIMENTS TO IMPLEMENTATION

One objection raised in the move to international standards was the belief that cultural differences would create problems for a number of countries in adopting the standards. Experience with about 120 countries shows that most of the so-called cultural differences are in fact legal differences. The IASB position on legal differences is very simple: If a country wishes to adopt international standards, it must make whatever changes in the law are required. If it does not wish to change the law, it should not attempt to use international standards. As far as I know, the only area that is continuing to debate the issue of cultural differences is the Middle East, where some countries believe that Arabic banking requires separate and different standards. Personally I doubt this; many foreign corporations operate banks in the Middle East and seem to manage quite well.

Following the wave of adoptions in 2005 to 2007, a number of large countries are now implementing or on track to implement international standards. For this reason, there is some pressure to issue new standards and then after 2011 to have a stable platform for these countries to implement. This is somewhat in conflict with the U.S. trend to take a longer period to produce more complicated common standards.

This leads to a discussion of the U.S. position. Much of the enthusiasm by countries around the world, particularly Japan and China, was based on the assumption that the United States, which had been responsible for setting in motion the IASB, would be on board 10 years later. This has not yet happened, although the United States appears still to be supportive. There is excellent cooperation at the level of the two technical boards, FASB and IASB, but countries around the world are beginning to ask why they should fully adopt international standards if the United States does not. They are also asking themselves why the United States should have four board members and five trustees—more than any other country—when it is one of the very few countries that has not yet committed to a date for adoption.

If the United States does not commit to adoption, other major players may also opt out and we will have lost our best chance of stabilizing the accounting world. If the United States commits to adoption but retains all the detailed rules, interpretations, and guidance that exist today, it will have the worst of all worlds and will have given up the chance to move to a more principles-based approach.

One must also sympathize with the complexity of the U.S. adoption decision. The SEC is given legal authority over accounting standards in the United States and has actively participated in the discussions and deliberations of the FASB. Indeed, many of the accounting issues raised to the Emerging Issues Task Force are issues prompted from the SEC's review of filings and questions from U.S. corporations. In the past, the SEC has had a large voice in international accounting and securities laws. Today, U.S. equity markets are no longer as dominant as in the past. Some important questions:

- How can the SEC meet its legal responsibilities to regulate accounting principles in the United States in this new environment?
- What influence will the United States have in the international deliberations going forward?
- Will it be necessary for the SEC to insert interpretive guidance for U.S. companies if the international mechanism for issuing interpretations is reluctant or slow to respond to issues and U.S. perceived needs for guidance? Does that put the United States at risk of being in a situation similar to the one it is currently facing regarding detailed rules and guidance?

- If the past advice of the IASB was to decouple from international standards when there is a conflict with local law, does that imply that the United States needs to change the authority given the SEC in order to adopt international standards as GAAP for financial reporting?

These questions have no easy-to-implement solutions. Answers need to be forthcoming before, not after, a decision to change is made.

The accounting world has come a long way. In the 1980s, the IASC was looking for harmonization. In the 1990s, the IASC was looking for convergence. In the 2000s, the IASB was looking for adoption. It would appear that the SEC has invented a new term, *condorsement*. I hope this is not an indication of the worst-of-all-worlds solution described earlier.

3.9 MYTHS AND MISCONCEPTIONS ABOUT INTERNATIONAL STANDARDS

A variety of myths and misperceptions about international standards should be openly debated. Here the author presents his views on the myths and suitable responses.

Myth 1. Detailed rules are superior to principles-based standards even though they are longer and much more complex because they guard against inappropriate accounting.

Response. The opposite seems to be true. Detailed rules provide a bright line from which creative minds can game how to get around those rules. As soon as you hedge the principle with rules, you open the door to accounting games.

Myth 2. U.S. rules and interpretations result in lower numbers of accounting and financial frauds in the United States than in other countries.

Response. Although no compelling academic research has been done, a simple listing of well-known accounting frauds would indicate that fraud is still present in the United States. A skeptic might say that the United States discovers the frauds but others do not or that they do not get the press coverage of U.S. companies. The Parmalat accounting fraud in Italy that grew over a decade shows that fraud is not culturally selective, but big cheese attracts big rats. Of course, with the amount of capitalization at stake in the United States, it is not clear what would have been the case had more principles-based standards been adopted, although my belief is that principles-based standards would have improved many situations, for example the issue of off balance sheet subsidiaries in the banking industry.

Myth 3. International standards are not consistently applied by all companies under IASB standards.

Response. Consistent application and enforcement of all the standards is in the hands of the securities regulators in each jurisdiction. Obviously some regulators will be more effective than others, but enforcement is not the role of IASB, any more than it is the role of the FASB.

Myth 4. International standards are untried and untested.

Response. This was a common criticism in the early days, but with the standards having been implemented for more than five years in countries with environments just as complicated as the United States, the standards by now are in fact well and truly tried and tested.

Myth 5. International standards are shorter, simpler, and carry fewer interpretations, only because they are younger and have not had the time to become complex and to require interpretations.

Response. The new board in 2001 made an absolute commitment to maintain the shorter, simpler, more principles-based approach and to permit very few interpretations. That record has been maintained for 10 years, and the new management team in London has repeated the commitment. There is no evidence to suggest that this criticism is justified

Myth 6. International standards cannot deal with all the cultural differences that will occur around the world.

Response. I would repeat my comment that we have seen very little evidence of any cultural differences that would impact the accounting result of a transaction. I have raised this issue hundreds of times during meetings over the past 10 years, and in almost every instance a circumstance that was described as a cultural difference turned out to be purely a legal difference.

Myth 7. International standards are more subject to political interference and manipulation than U.S. standards.

Response. Both sets of standards are subject to political pressure. Obviously an elected governing body has the final say, whether it is the U.S. Congress or any other country's government. In general, interference has taken place only during grave crises, and it applies at least equally to both standards setters. An example was the stock option accounting debate, hotly lobbied inside and outside the United States. The final standards reached by both bodies were similar and resisted similar political pressures. With proper organizational mechanisms in place, this need not be an issue.

Myth 8. Funding is a major weakness for the IASB and could threaten its independence.

Response. Given the enthusiasm around the world for the rationalization of international standards and given the very modest cost structure of the IASB, it is highly unlikely that the world would permit the organization to disappear because of a lack of funding. In the last few years the efforts of the Board of Trustees to secure long-term commitments to funding has been successful in many countries. Indeed, using resources to achieve similar ends in separate environments will be more costly.

Myth 9. International standards that are principles based are more difficult to defend in court than a system that has more specific rules and guidance.

Response. I have had many discussions with the legal professions in a number of countries including the United States. There is no evidence whatsoever that judges cannot understand the difference between a principle and a rule. In fact, if a case is based in a rules-based environment, the court will look at the rules and may indeed ignore substance over form. In a principles-based environment, judges will more closely examine the judgment behind the decision. The court will also look for contemporaneous recording of that judgment, and it will decide accordingly.

Myth 10. The adoption of international standards by the United States would be very expensive.

Response. As I indicated earlier, the cost would in fact be quite modest if adoption provides a suitable introduction transition period, say five years. It would be even less if the FASB and IASB are successful in introducing common standards in a number of key areas currently under review. In any case, this is a one-time cost that could yield benefits forever if it results in the elimination of the extraordinary cost of complying with the huge body of complex rules contained in the FASB's standards today.

3.10 SOURCES AND SUGGESTED REFERENCES

Ball, R. "Mandatory International Financial Reporting Standards (IFRS): Pros and Cons for Investors," *Accounting and Business Research*, International Accounting Policy Forum, 2006, pp. 5–27.

Barth, M. E. "Global Financial Reporting: Implications for U.S. Academics." *Accounting Review* 83, no. 5 (2008): 1159–1179.

Delotte Global Services Limited.. "IAS Plus," 2008; *www.iasplus.com/restruct/whatis.htm*

PricewaterhouseCoopers. "U.S. GAAP and IFRS Convergence," 2011; *www.pwc.com/us/en/issues/ifrs-reporting/ifrs-gaap-convergence.jhtml*

Important Web Sites

IFAC: *http://ifac.org/*

IFRS and IASB: *www.ifrs.org/Home.htm*

CHAPTER 4

FINANCIAL STATEMENTS: FORM AND CONTENT

Jan R. Williams, PhD, CPA
College of Business Administration University of Tennessee

This chapter has been updated for this edition by the editors.

4.1 INTRODUCTION

Financial statements are one of management's primary means of communicating with external parties about the financial activities of the enterprise. Through financial statements, interested parties outside a company are able to learn a great deal about the financial effects of business transactions and the accumulated resources and obligations of the reporting enterprise.

This chapter presents a broad overview of the form and content of financial statements as a means of introducing these important communication tools. The purpose is to introduce financial statements, to illustrate how they interrelate or articulate with each other, and to suggest the types of information that can be gleaned from them. Later chapters develop in more depth the content and underlying accounting principles of specific elements of financial statements.

The chapter reviews the objectives of financial reporting, including financial statements, and identifies the principles supporting the preparation of financial statements. Then the chapter provides individual reviews and illustrations of the primary financial statements: the balance sheet, the income statement, the statement of stockholders' equity, and the statement of cash flows. Articulation of financial statements is then covered, followed by a discussion of the role of supplemental and note disclosure. The chapter ends with a discussion of some of the limitations of general-purpose financial statements as communication tools.

The convergence of U.S. and international accounting principles introduces some fundamental reconciliation problems and may lead to financial statements that look different from the statements prepared today in the United States. Some of the presentation and formatting issues are identified later in this chapter. More detailed differences are described in individual chapters in this *Handbook*.

4.2 PRINCIPLES UNDERLYING FINANCIAL STATEMENTS

(a) OBJECTIVES OF FINANCIAL REPORTING.   The Financial Accounting Standards Board (FASB) is the authoritative body responsible for establishing financial reporting standards in the United States. The FASB has established several objectives of financial reporting. *Financial reporting* is a broad term used to identify all means by which investors, creditors, and other interested parties learn about the financial activities of an enterprise. One of the most important parts of the financial reporting environment is the preparation and distribution of financial statements, particularly public company financial statements that are audited by an independent certified public accountant (CPA).

Three primary objectives of financial reporting, which are carried out in part through the preparation of financial statements, are:

1. To provide information that is useful to present and potential investors and creditors and other users in making rational investment, credit, and similar decisions (Statement of Financial Accounting Concepts (SFAC) No. 1, par. 34)
2. To provide information to help current and potential investors and creditors and other users assess the amounts, timing, and uncertainty of prospective cash receipts from dividends and

interest and the proceeds from the sale, redemption, or maturity of securities or loans (SFAC No. 1, par. 37)

3. To provide information about the economic resources of the enterprise, claims to those resources, and the effects of transactions, events, and circumstances that change resources and claims to resources (SFAC No. 1, par. 40)

4. In explaining these objectives, the FASB points out that information provided should be comprehensible to those who have a reasonable understanding of business and economic activities and are willing to study the information with reasonable diligence. Thus, the orientation of financial statements is toward the reasonably informed user of financial information—neither the extreme highest in terms of knowledge (e.g., professional financial analysts) nor the extreme lowest (e.g., the naive investor with little knowledge of business activities).

(b) SELECTED UNDERLYING PRINCIPLES. Many broad principles underlie the preparation of financial statements. The next paragraphs briefly set forth several principles that are important for an introductory understanding of the financial statements.

(i) Multiple Sources of Information. Financial statements are only one of many sources of financial information about a reporting enterprise. Management may communicate financial and other information to interested parties in a variety of ways, some of which are through governmental organizations such as the Securities and Exchange Commission (SEC). News releases and direct contact with owners and others are other means of communication within the financial reporting framework. Many times these communications include financial statements or refer to information taken from financial statements.

(ii) Approximate Measures. The content of financial statements results, in part, from approximate rather than exact measures of business activities. Many estimates and assumptions are required to partition ongoing business activities into relatively short periods of time, such as one year. Although the financial statements have an appearance of precision because items are measured in terms of a monetary unit, determining many of the amounts requires judgments that impose uncertainty and on into the resulting financial statement items.

(iii) Historical Orientation. The orientation of financial statements is primarily historical inasmuch as they report activities and events that have already occurred. Reporting on historical events, however, sometimes requires estimates of the present and the future. The recent expansion of the permitted use of fair value for monetary assets, investments, and liabilities reflects a desire to present more relevant and current data, sometimes at the expense of accuracy.

(iv) General-Purpose Financial Statements. The primary financial statements are general purpose in nature in that they are designed to meet the information needs of a wide variety of financial statement users and are not specifically tailored to the unique needs of any particular user group. These general-purpose statements are intended primarily for external users who lack the authority to dictate the specific information they receive. Users who do have the authority to dictate the nature of such information are not the primary audience of general-purpose financial statements.

For examples, lenders may wish to receive specific information regarding cash flows and liquidity at intervals more frequent than the published financial statements (e.g, monthly). They can require this information as a condition of making loans.

(v) Accrual Accounting. Financial statements are based on accrual accounting principles. Accrual accounting attempts to measure the financial impact of events and transactions when they occur and not simply when the cash consequences of those events and transactions take place. The cash effects of certain transactions may occur earlier or later than the transaction itself, and accountants attempt to report at the time of the substantive financial effects rather than only the cash effects.

(vi) Explanatory Notes and Disclosures. The usefulness of financial statements is believed to be enhanced by explanations and details outside the body of the statements themselves. For this reason, financial statements frequently are accompanied by notes and other supplemental disclosures providing a variety of information that would otherwise not be available. A discussion of supplemental and note disclosure is presented later in this chapter.

A complete set of financial statements generally includes a balance sheet, an income statement, a statement of stockholders' equity, and a statement of cash flows. In the following sections, each of these statements is illustrated and described. Because of the overview nature of this chapter, all of the disclosures that would normally accompany the statements are not presented. Rather, the focus is on the basic structure of each statement, the definitions of the primary elements of the statements, and the interrelationship of the statements.

4.3   BALANCE SHEET

A balance sheet, also called a *statement of financial position,* is a listing of the quantifiable resources that an enterprise has to operate with as well as a listing of claims against those resources represented by both creditors and owners. In the report form of the statement, the quantifiable resources, called *assets,* are listed first, followed by the claims of creditors and owners. In the account form of the statement, the assets typically are presented on the left and the claims to the assets on the right side of the statement. An important relationship in the balance sheet is that the claims to the assets equal, or balance exactly, the amount of the assets presented. The balance sheet is discussed in FASB Accounting Standards Codification (ASC) 210.

Another way to view the balance sheet is that it represents the quantifiable resources of the enterprise and a description of the three primary sources from which those resources have been garnered. The first source is creditors—those who have loaned or otherwise provided resources to the company for its use, expecting a return on those loaned amounts as well as eventual repayment of them. The second source is the owners, called *stockholders* in a corporation, who have committed resources to the company, expecting some combination of return and enhanced value of the investment through the effective employment of resources by the enterprise. The third source also is considered an owner source but results from the assets earned by the enterprise having been retained for its future use rather than having been distributed back to the owners on a periodic basis.

Exhibit 4.1 illustrates a balance sheet for the hypothetical Morristown Products, Inc. It is prepared in the report form, first listing assets, followed by liabilities and stockholders' equity. This is a *classified balance sheet,* with the various major categories further categorized as described next.

(a) ASSETS.   *Assets* are defined as probable future economic benefits obtained or controlled by the enterprise as a result of past transactions or events (Statement of Financial Concepts [SFAC] No. 6, par. 25). Assets have three essential characteristics:

1. They embody a probable future economic benefit in the form of a direct or indirect future net cash inflow.
2. A particular enterprise (e.g., the owner) can obtain the benefit and control others' access to it.
3. The transaction or other event giving rise to the enterprise's right to control the benefit has already occurred (SFAC No. 6, par. 26).

Assets typically are presented in the balance sheet in terms of current and noncurrent classifications.

(i) Current Assets.   *Current assets* are assets that are expected to become cash, sold, or consumed in the near future (Accounting Research Bulletin [ARB] No. 43, chap. 3, par. 4). These assets are considered liquid in that they represent cash or near-cash resources from which the company can satisfy obligations as they become due. The primary purpose of listing current assets is to communicate information about the various stages of a company's short-term cash-to-cash cycle, including the

MORRISTOWN PRODUCTS, INC.
Balance Sheet
December 31, 20X0, 20X1, and 20X2
(in thousands of dollars)

	20X2	20X1	20X0
Assets			
Current assets			
Cash	$ 8	$ 13	$ 10
Marketable securities	6	5	5
Accounts receivable	50	40	45
Merchandise inventory	100	90	75
Prepaid expenses	7	4	5
	$171	$152	$140
Property, plant, and equipment			
Equipment	$100	$100	$100
Building	250	200	200
Land	60	60	50
	$410	$360	$350
Less: accumulated depreciation	(105)	(90)	(75)
	305	270	275
Investments	67	67	50
Total assets	$543	$489	$465
Liabilities			
Current liabilities			
Accounts payable	$ 52	$ 45	$ 40
Accrued expenses	40	32	35
	$ 92	$ 77	$ 75
Noncurrent liabilities			
Bonds payable	200	200	200
Total liabilities	$292	$277	$275
Stockholders' equity			
Preferred stock	$ 20	$ 20	$ 20
(500 shares @ $40 par value)			
Common stock	110	110	100
(10,000 shares @ $10 par value in 2000;			
shares @ $10 par value in 2001 and 2002)			
Additional paid-in capital	35	35	30
Retained earnings	86	47	40
Total stockholders' equity	$251	$212	$190
Total liabilities and stockholders' equity	$543	$489	$465

Exhibit 4.1   Sample Balance Sheet

amount invested in each stage of that cycle. Exhibit 4.2 depicts a typical short-term cash cycle for a company that invests cash in merchandise inventory. That inventory is held until sold to customers on credit, thus creating accounts receivable that subsequently are converted into cash. Assuming the purchase of inventory takes place at a dollar amount below the price of the sale of that same inventory, the eventual addition to cash when the receivable is collected is greater than the original reduction in cash when the item was purchased. This short-term or operating cycle is intended to be a primary source of increased cash, which is then available for future use in continued operations.

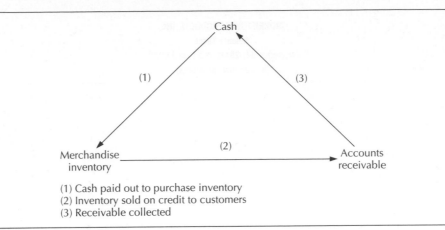

(1) Cash paid out to purchase inventory
(2) Inventory sold on credit to customers
(3) Receivable collected

Exhibit 4.2   Sample Income Statement

Current assets typically are listed in their order of liquidity in the balance sheet, beginning with cash itself. Some companies hold certain highly liquid investments as cash equivalents and combine them with cash as a current asset in the balance sheet. In Exhibit 4.1, cash is followed by marketable securities, accounts receivable, merchandise inventory, and prepaid expenses, in that order. Marketable securities are considered current assets if management invests in them when excess cash is available and disinvests when that cash is needed again for operating purposes. If the intent of management is to retain the investment for a longer period of time, the securities would not be classified as current. Marketable securities presented in the current asset section of a balance sheet may be thought of as secondary sources of cash that are readily available to the company when needed. Accounts receivable represent the result of credit sales transactions that have not yet been collected in cash. Merchandise inventory represents the company's investment in assets held for resale and expected to be sold in the near future. Prepaid expenses represent advance payments of items that will be used by the company in the coming accounting period. Prepaid expenses are different from other current assets in that they will not become cash in the near future, but they conserve the use of cash in the near future.

The time period for distinguishing current assets from other assets is usually one year. Some companies, however, have a short-term cash-to-cash cycle, or operating cycle, of more than one year. For example, if inventory is required to be held through an aging process, the time between the initial investment of cash in inventory and the eventual return of that cash through the sale of the inventory may be quite long. If a company's operating cycle is longer than one year, the longer period of the cycle is used to identify current assets. If the company has several cycles within a year, a year is used.

(ii) Noncurrent Assets.   Noncurrent assets are assets that do not meet the definition of current assets. These may represent a variety of resources available to the enterprise and may vary considerably among enterprises, depending on the nature of the business activity in which the enterprise is involved. Many companies require property, plant, and equipment, sometimes referred to as *fixed* or *plant assets,* in order to operate. In Exhibit 4.1, Morristown Products, Inc., presents equipment, buildings, and land under a property, plant, and equipment caption. The amounts so presented generally represent the cost of those assets to the enterprise. Over time, that cost is recognized as an expense in the income statement of the enterprise, a subject covered in Section 4.7 of this chapter. The accumulation of those expense amounts is identified in the balance sheet as accumulated depreciation and is subtracted from the cost of the assets. Over time, the accumulated depreciation would ordinarily increase in amount as illustrated in Exhibit 4.1.

A variety of other noncurrent assets may be held by a company at any particular point in time. The balance sheet of Morristown Products, Inc., illustrates one such asset, investments. These are most likely securities of other enterprises that the company is holding with the intent of not converting to cash in the near future. Thus, they are properly identified as other than current assets.

(b) LIABILITIES. *Liabilities* are probable future sacrifices of economic benefits arising from present obligations of the reporting enterprise to transfer assets or provide services to other entities in the future as a result of past transactions or events (SFAC No. 6, par. 35). Liabilities have three essential characteristics:

1. They embody a present duty or responsibility that is expected to be settled by probable future transfer of assets.
2. The duty or responsibility obligates a particular enterprise.
3. The transaction or event obligating the enterprise has already occurred (SFAC No. 6, par. 36).

Liabilities typically are presented in the balance sheet in terms of current and noncurrent classifications.

(i) Current Liabilities. *Current liabilities* are liabilities that are expected to be satisfied with the use of current assets (ARB No. 43, Ch. 3, par. 7). Ordinarily, current liabilities are those that will be due within one year or operating cycle, if longer. There are instances where such short-term obligations are not presented as current liabilities, however, because they are not expected to be satisfied using current assets. For example, if a company has a long-term debt obligation outstanding and throughout the period of the debt provides for repayment by investing in a fund to be used only for that purpose, the debt obligation is not a current liability in its last year, because the asset source used for repayment is not a current asset.

Exhibit 4.1 illustrates two examples of current liabilities: accounts payable and accrued expenses. The former most likely results from the purchase of merchandise inventory from suppliers and represents debts that will be paid within a very short time. Accrued expenses may arise from a variety of sources related to the application of accrual accounting procedures and may represent the enterprise's obligation to pay wages to employees, interest to creditors, taxes to government, and other similar items.

(ii) Noncurrent Liabilities. *Noncurrent liabilities* are liabilities that do not meet the definition of current liabilities. They are part of the long-term financing of the enterprise and are expected to be repaid at some distant date. Bonds payable is used as an example of such an arrangement in Exhibit 4.1.

(iii) Working Capital and the Current Ratio. Current assets and current liabilities are listed and their totals reported in the balance sheet as previously explained. The excess of total current assets over total current liabilities is referred to as *working capital*. The total of current assets compared to the total of current liabilities is commonly referred to as the *current ratio*. Working capital and the current ratio are thought to be helpful in evaluating the entity's ability to meet its obligations as they come due (i.e., the entity's liquidity).

(c) STOCKHOLDERS' EQUITY. *Equity* is the residual interest in the enterprise after deducting liabilities from assets (SFAC No. 6, par. 49). A corporate organization titles that equity as stockholders' equity. Other forms of business organization, such as sole proprietorships and partnerships, commonly refer to it simply as *owner's equity* or *owners' equity*.

(i) Contributed Equity. Corporations sell stock as evidence of ownership in the company. This stock may be labeled preferred or common stock. Although a detailed discussion of these types of stock is beyond the scope of this chapter, preferred stock will receive distributions of assets to owners, called *dividends,* before common stock. Also, should the company liquidate, preferred stockholders have a preference in receiving assets over common stockholders. The stocks typically have an identified par or stated value at which they are carried in the corporate balance sheet, as illustrated in Exhibit 4.1 ($40 par for preferred and $10 par for common).

Because preferred and common stock will not necessarily sell to stockholders at precisely their par values, additional accounts may be found in the stockholders' equity section of the balance sheet representing additional sources of assets. In Exhibit 4.1, the account additional paid-in capital is an example of such an account. The preferred stock, common stock, and additional paid-in capital accounts combined represent the contributed or paid-in equity of the enterprise—those amounts that have been committed to the enterprise by owners for the enterprise's use.

(ii) Retained Earnings.   The final element of stockholders' equity is retained earnings. This amount represents a source of enterprise assets from profitable past operations beyond the amount of such assets that have been distributed to owners in the form of dividends. Typically companies do not distribute assets to stockholders that are equal to the amount of their earnings. Rather, they withhold a portion of earned assets for future operations, including expansion of business activities and other uses.

The balancing feature can be seen in Exhibit 4.1 inasmuch as the assets equal the total of the liabilities and stockholders' equity (e.g., $543,000 in 2002). The balance sheet is based on this primary underlying principle, and it represents a basic tenet of financial reporting. The balance sheet has been described as a still photograph of a business at a point in time, in terms of its assets, liabilities, and owners' equity—a simple but appropriate analogy that identifies what this important financial statement attempts to communicate.

When comprehensive income arises, it is accumulated as a component of retained earnings. See the discussion of comprehensive income in Subsection 4.4(d)(iv).

(iii) Subclassifying Stockholders' Equity.   In explaining the term *equity,* the FASB has observed that distinctions within equity, such as those between common and preferred stock, between contributed and earned capital, and between stated or legal capital and other equity, are primarily matters of presentation, implying that this information may be of limited value to financial statement users (SFAC No. 6, footnote 29).

4.4 INCOME STATEMENT

Continuing the analogy of the balance sheet as a still photograph of an enterprise at a point in time, the income statement can then be described as a motion picture that identifies certain dimensions of the enterprise over a period of time. The income statement is discussed in ASC 225. Exhibit 4.3 shows the relationship of the balance sheet and the other financial statements, including the income statement, in terms of time. Exhibit 4.4 provides an income statement for Morristown Products, Inc., for the years 20X1 and 20X2. This income statement relates to, or articulates with, the balance sheet presented in Exhibit 4.1. It describes the profit-directed activities of the company in terms of its revenues and expenses, leading to a final figure of net income or net loss.

(a) REVENUES.   *Revenues* are inflows or other enhancements of assets of an enterprise or settlement of its liabilities from delivering or producing goods, rendering services, or carrying out other activities that constitute the entity's ongoing major or central operations (SFAC No. 6, par. 78).

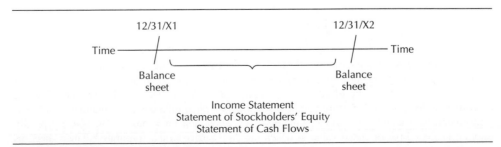

Exhibit 4.3   Relationship of Financial Statements

MORRISTOWN PRODUCTS, INC.
Income Statement
For years ended December 31, 20X1 and 20X2
(in thousands of dollars)

	20X2	20X1
Sales	$ 500	$ 400
Cost of sales	240	180
Gross margin	$ 260	$ 220
Expenses:		
Selling and administrative	$ 135	$ 155
Depreciation	15	15
	150	170
Income from operations	$ 110	$ 50
Interest expense	20	20
Income before income taxes	$ 90	$ 30
Provision for income taxes	27	9
Net income	$ 63	$ 21
Earnings per share	$5.60	$1.87

Exhibit 4.4   Sample Income Statement

The nature of an enterprise's revenues depends on the type of business activity. For a manufacturing enterprise, revenues consist of sales of its manufactured product to retailers or other enterprises that will sell to the ultimate consumer. For a service enterprise, revenues represent the value of the services provided to its customers or clients for a period of time. Revenues typically are the first items listed in an income statement, as is the case in Exhibit 4.4 with the sales figure for Morristown Products, Inc. See Chapter 12 for additional detail regarding this critical account.

(b) EXPENSES. *Expenses* are outflows or other using up of assets or incurrences of liabilities from delivering or producing goods, rendering services, or carrying out other activities that constitute the entity's ongoing major or central operations (SFAC No. 6, par. 80). Sacrifices of resources are necessary in order for an enterprise to create revenues. These sacrifices are in the form of asset outflows or creation of liabilities that, in turn, will result in asset outflows when those liabilities are eventually paid. Expenses attempt to measure these asset outflows or reductions. Many expense categories are presented in the typical income statement of a business enterprise, as is the case in Exhibit 4.4—cost of sales, selling and administrative, depreciation, interest, provision for income taxes. All of these represent various types of expenses that are required to create the asset enhancements or revenues related to these expenses.

The income statement is based on an accounting principle called *matching*. Revenues ordinarily can be readily associated with specific business activity that relates to specific periods of time. Once the revenues for a period of time have been identified, the accountant attempts to associate with those revenues all expenses that relate to (1) that same period of time and/or (2) the generation of those specific revenues. These amounts are then matched, meaning that the expenses are subtracted from the revenues, to determine the results of operations for the period. The result is called *net income* if revenues exceed expenses; it is called *net loss* if expenses exceed revenues.

(c) PRESENTATION ISSUES. In a multiple-step income statement, illustrated in Exhibit 4.4, several subtotals appear within the statement. Examples are gross margin, income from operations, and income before income tax. These descriptions are intended to help the reader of the statement understand the important relationships that underlie the statement. *Gross margin* measures the difference between sales and cost of sales. *Cost of sales* is the direct cost of acquiring (or manufacturing) the items sold. Gross margin is a broad concept of profit in that it deducts from sales only the direct cost of those items sold and does not include other costs of business operations that are necessary, but less direct. *Income from operations* attempts to measure the excess of sales over those expenses that are most closely tied to ongoing business operations. In the case of Morristown Products, Inc., in Exhibit 4.4, interest payments on borrowings and income taxes have been omitted from the determination of income from operations on the basis that they are less closely related to ongoing business activities than are the other expenses identified earlier in the statement—cost of sales, selling and administrative, and depreciation. Income before income taxes indicates the profitability of the company after recognizing all related expenses except income tax. Net income is the final indication of profitability for the period of time covered. The subtotals preceding net income in Exhibit 4.4 are not found in all income statements but are placed there at the discretion of the preparer for the convenience and understanding of the financial statement reader. An income statement that omits these subtotals is called a *single-step income statement.*

Earnings per share (EPS) is an indication of the net income recalculated on a per-share-of-common-stock basis. Referring again to Exhibit 4.4, in 20X1, net income per share of common stock was $1.87, and for 20X2, the amount was $5.60. This figure is calculated by taking the amount of net income, reducing it by any dividend requirements for preferred stock, and dividing the result by the weighted average number of shares of common stock outstanding for the year.

Income statements may include gains and losses other than those illustrated in Exhibit 4.4. Gains and losses may result from a variety of peripheral business activities; that is, they do not relate to the primary, ongoing central activities of the enterprise. These types of gains and losses occur less frequently than revenues and expenses that are defined as the enterprise's primary revenue-producing activities.

(d) SPECIAL ISSUES: EXTRAORDINARY ITEMS DISCONTINUED OPERATIONS, AND OTHER COMPREHENSIVE INCOME

(i) Extraordinary Items.   Extraordinary items are separated out from the recurring operating items in a special line item (net of tax) after net income from operations. This alerts the reader to their special nature. To be extraordinary, these charges must be (1) unusual in nature and (2) infrequent in occurrence. Determination of this categorization can sometimes be difficult and can create an incentive for management to classify unpleasant results as extraordinary items to discount their effect on share values. Examples of such items may include seizure of assets by a foreign government and natural disasters (e.g., earthquakes, volcanoes). However, flood damage in a floodplain area would not be extraordinary. (See ASC 225-20-45.)

(ii) Unusual Gains and Losses.   Sometimes material events will be unusual or infrequent (but not both), and they may be accorded a special treatment to alert readers to their nature. Generally accepted accounting principles (GAAP) prohibits these items be shown net of tax to emphasize that they are not extraordinary and should not receive a separate EPS calculation as extraordinary items do. In a single-step income statement presentation, these items might be merged with costs and expenses before the income tax expense line. Examples of such items includes sales of assets, write-downs of inventory, and gains and losses from foreign currency exchange rates. A concern with these items is that their determination may be highly judgmental and might be used divert reader attention from other operating costs and expenses, when such a distinction might not be warranted.

(iii) Discontinued Operations.   When the entity has committed to a plan to dispose of an identified segment or product line in its business, separate recognition is made in the income statement for the income or losses from continuing to operate the segment before disposal and ultimately the loss or gain on the disposal of the segment. The segment is considered disposed of when there remains no significant involvement of the entity in these operations. These amounts are separately reported net of tax after income from continuing operations (ASC 205-20-45).

(iv) Other Comprehensive Income.   The recognition or unrealized gains and losses due to changes in the fair value of assets like investments give rise to items that are accumulated in shareholder's equity in a separate category termed comprehensive income (ASC 220). To segregate these potential gains and losses from those that are actually realized from transactions, special treatment is accorded these items.

Comprehensive income (cumulative) is part of the stockholders' equity section of the balance sheet. However, period changes in the balance may be presented in three ways;

1. As a separate (income) statement (e.g., comprehensive income statement) that begins with net income; recognizes the unrealized gain or loss, net of tax; and ends with comprehensive income.

2. As an extension of the income statement (e.g., combined statement of comprehensive income) that is preceded by net income and ends in total comprehensive income.

3. As an expanded presentation of the period changes in the account in the statement of stockholders' equity. This presentation bypasses the income statement.

(v) Corrections of an Error. When later-discovered errors (e.g., mathematical mistakes, improper applications of GAAP) in prior reported financial statements are material, correction is made by adjusting the retained earnings in the period of identification and correction and restating any income statements currently presented that are affected by the error for the proper amounts that should have appeared in those statements. These error adjustments are also termed prior-period adjustments (see ASC 250). Note that corrections of estimates from prior periods are handled as adjustments in the current and affected future income accounts, not as corrections of errors, unless an error was associated with the incorrect estimate. The subtlety in some situations between these two distinctions often creates discussions between entities and their auditors and can be a source of contention in legal cases that involve financial reporting.

4.5 STATEMENT OF STOCKHOLDERS' EQUITY

A required disclosure in a complete set of financial statements of a corporation is an identification of the changes in stockholders' equity in terms of dollars by major category and numbers of shares of stock (Accounting Principles Board [APB] Opinion No. 12, par. 10). This disclosure can be made in several different forms, such as a note or supplemental schedule to the other financial statements, or a separate financial statement. The statement of stockholders' equity is discussed in ASC 215. Because many companies today make this presentation in the form of a separate financial statement, Exhibit 4.5 takes that approach in Morristown Products, Inc.'s statement of stockholders' equity.

MORRISTOWN PRODUCTS, INC.
Statement of Stockholders' Equity
for Years Ended December 31, 20X1 AND 20X2
(in Thousands of Dollars)

	Contributed Equity			
	Preferred Stock	Common Stock	Additional Paid-in Capital	Retained Earnings
Dec. 31, 20X0	$20	$100	$30	$40
Sale of 1,000 shares of common stock		10	5	
Net income				21
Dividends				(14)
Dec. 31, 20X1	$20	$110	$35	$47
Net income				63
Dividends				(24)
Dec. 31, 20X2	$20	$110	$35	$86

Exhibit 4.5   Sample Statement of Stockholders' Equity

Like the income statement, the statement of stockholders' equity covers activity during a period of time rather than at a specific point in time. The columns represent the major categories of stockholders' equity: contributed equity—preferred stock, common stock, and additional paid-in capital—and retained earnings. The statement begins with the balance at the end of the period prior to that covered in the statement. In Exhibit 4.5, the statement covers 20X1 and 20X2, so the statement begins with the balances in the stockholders' equity accounts at the end of 20X0.

The rows in the statement indicate activities that resulted in changes in the major categories of stockholders' equity—sale of common stock, net income, and dividends. Notice that the sale of common stock in 20X1 affects only the contributed equity accounts inasmuch as they are intended to include those amounts contributed to the enterprise by stockholders. In this case, common stock increased by the par value of the shares sold, $10,000, and additional paid-in capital increased by $5,000. This means that the stock sold for 1.5 times its par value, or $15 per share. The increase in the number of shares is disclosed in the caption to the left describing the sale of common stock.

Net income and dividends affect only retained earnings, as illustrated in Exhibit 4.5. Net income increases the retained earnings balance, and dividends decrease that balance.

The exhibit shows the relationship of the financial statements covered earlier to the statement of stockholders' equity. For example, the net income amount included in the retained earnings column of Exhibit 4.5 is taken directly from the income statement for each year as indicated in Exhibit 4.4. Also, the various stockholders' equity accounts at December 31 of each year correspond to the amounts presented in the company's balance sheet at the end of each year in Exhibit 4.1. For example, the December 31, 20X2, balances of preferred stock ($20,000), common stock ($110,000), additional paid-in capital ($35,000), and retained earnings ($86,000) in the balance sheet correspond to the amounts in the final row of the statement of stockholders' equity in Exhibit 4.5.

4.6 STATEMENT OF CASH FLOWS

One of the central objectives of financial reporting is to provide information that is useful to external parties in assessing the amount, timing, and uncertainty of prospective cash flows to them. One factor of particular importance in this assessment is the cash position and changes in position of the enterprise itself. As a result, the fourth key financial statement is the statement of cash flows.

The statement of cash flows presents information about an enterprise's cash receipts and payments during a period of time (Statement of Financial Accounting Standards(SFAS) No. 95, par. 4). This statement is similar in concept to the income statement and statement of stockholders' equity in that it covers activity during a period of time rather than just at a point in time. In its simplest form, the statement of cash flows indicates the enterprise's primary sources of cash and the primary ways the enterprise used that cash. These changes are presented in a manner that reconciles the change in cash from the beginning to the end of the accounting period. The statement of cash flows is discussed in ASC 230; however, individual accounting transactions may have specific requirements regarding their presentation in the statement of cash flows. Readers need to be alert for the specific points of guidance.

The statement of cash flows for Morristown Products, Inc., is included in Exhibit 4.6. This statement is presented in three categories: cash flows from operating activities, cash flows from investing activities, and cash flows from financing activities. At the bottom of the statement, the net change in cash is presented as a reconciling figure to show how the cash balance either increased or decreased between the beginning and ending of the accounting period covered by the statement.

(a) OPERATING ACTIVITIES.   Cash flows from operating activities generally describe the cash flow effects of those transactions presented in the enterprise's income statement. Because the income statement is prepared on an accrual basis, revenues and expenses reported in that statement may not represent the cash effects of those transactions during the same accounting period. For example, revenues generally are recognized at the point of sale, but cash may not be received from the sale until the company collects the related receivable at a later date. Expenses, however, may have been paid before or after the period in which the expense is recognized in the income statement. Depreciation, for example, represents an expense that attempts to measure the cost of services rendered during a period of time by the enterprise's plant assets. The cash to purchase those assets may have been paid in an earlier accounting period.

MORRISTOWN PRODUCTS, INC.
Statement of Cash Flows
for the Years Ended December 31, 20X1 and 20X2
(in Thousands of Dollars)

	20X2	20X1
Cash Flows from Operating Activities		
Cash received from customers	$490	$405
Cash paid to suppliers	(243)	(190)
Cash paid for selling and administrative expenses	(130)	(157)
Cash paid for interest	(20)	(20)
Cash paid for income taxes	(27)	(9)
Net cash provided by operating activities	$ 70	$ 29
Cash Flows from Investing Activities		
Payment to purchase land		$(10)
Payment to purchase investments		(17)
Payment to purchase marketable securities	$ (1)	
Payment to purchase building	(50)	
Net cash used in investing activities	(51)	(27)
Cash Flows from Financing Activities		
Sale of common stock		$ 15
Payment of dividends	(24)	(14)
Net cash provided by (used in) financing activities	(24)	1
Net increase (decrease) in cash	$ (5)	$ 3
Cash at beginning of year	13	10
Cash at end of year	$ 8	$ 13
Reconciliation of Net Income to Net Cash Provided by Operating Activities		
Net income	$ 63	$ 21
Adjustments to reconcile net income to net cash provided by operating activities:		
Depreciation	$ 15	$ 15
Change in current assets and liabilities:		
Accounts receivable	(10)	5
Inventory	(10)	(15)
Prepaid expenses	(3)	1
Accounts payable	7	5
Accrued expenses	8	(3)
	7	8
Net cash provided by operating activities	$ 70	$ 29

Exhibit 4.6   Sample Statement of Cash Flows

These three types of cash inflows from operating activities are presented in the statement of cash flows, as appropriate:[1]

1. Cash receipts from sales of goods or services
2. Cash receipts from returns on loans to and investments in other enterprises
3. Other cash receipts that do not stem from transactions classified as investing and financing activities

[1] FASB SFAS No. 95 provided significant guidance in the preparation of the cash flow statement. The updated guidance from SFAS No. 95 can be located in ASC 230 (primarily), 310, 815, 830, and 942.

The five cash outflows from operating activities typically presented in the statement of cash flows are:

1. Cash payments to acquire goods for manufacture or sale
2. Cash payments to suppliers and employers for goods or services
3. Cash payments to governments for taxes, duties, fines, and other fees or penalties
4. Cash payments to lenders and other creditors for interest
5. Other cash payments that are not classified as investing and financing cash outflows

The types of cash flows from operating activities of a particular enterprise depend on the nature of that enterprise's activities. Exhibit 4.6 presents the cash flows from operating activities first in the statement of cash flows in five categories that are deemed appropriate for this enterprise's particular business activities. The result is a figure of net cash flows from operating activities (e.g., $70,000 for 20X2), implying a netting of positive and negative cash flows within that category.

The relationship of net cash flows from operating activities to the company's net income is shown in a disclosure presented as part of the statement of cash flows. In that disclosure, net income is adjusted for noncash items to show the reader of the statement why net income and net cash flows from operating activities are different amounts. For example, for 20X2 net income was $63,000 and net cash flows from operating activities was $70,000. The difference is due to several noncash items that affected net income but did not provide or use cash during the year. (This disclosure is found at the bottom of the statement of cash flows in Exhibit 4.6.)

(b) INVESTING ACTIVITIES.   Cash flows from investing activities present the enterprise's cash flow activities in terms of investments in assets. Specifically, cash inflows ordinarily are presented in one of these three categories:

1. Receipts from collections or sales of loans made by the enterprise to other enterprises
2. Receipts from sales of equity instruments of other enterprises
3. Receipts from the sales of property, plant and equipment, and other productive assets

Cash outflows from investing activities typically are presented in one of these three categories:

1. Payments for loans made to other enterprises and investments in other enterprise's debt instruments
2. Payments to acquire equity instruments of other enterprises
3. Payments to purchase property, plant, and equipment, and other productive assets

In Exhibit 4.6, the cash flow from investing activities is presented for Morristown Products, Inc., resulting in negative cash flow of $51,000 for 20X2. During the year the company had only two types of transactions in investing category—purchase of marketable securities and purchase of building—both of which represent negative cash flows.

(c) FINANCING ACTIVITIES.   Financing activities represent positive and negative cash flows of the enterprise from debt and equity financing transactions. Typical cash inflows from financing activities are:

- Proceeds from selling stock
- Proceeds from issuing bonds, mortgages, notes, and other debt instruments

Negative cash flows from financing activities include:

- Payments of dividends or other distributions to owners
- Repayments of amounts borrowed

Referring again to Exhibit 4.6, the third major section of the statement of cash flows of Morristown Products, Inc., is the cash flows from financing activities. For 20X2, the net amount is a reduction of $24,000, resulting from a single transaction—payment of dividends. For 20X1, however, the net amount from financing activities is a positive $1,000 amount when the amount received from the sale of common stock ($15,000) is offset by the amount of dividends paid ($14,000).

4.7 ARTICULATION OF FINANCIAL STATEMENTS

Reference has been made several times to the relationship of the four financial statements. Selected specific examples have shown where the items in one of the statements relate directly to the items in another financial statement.

The four financial statements are derived from the same underlying transactions and the same financial measurements of those transactions. The statements present different types of information about the enterprise's activities during a period of time and thus are not alternatives to each other. All are necessary for the reader to get as complete an understanding as is possible through the medium of financial statements.

Attempting to demonstrate the articulation of financial statements in a single illustration is an impossible undertaking. Exhibit 4.7 illustrates several of the most important relationships that

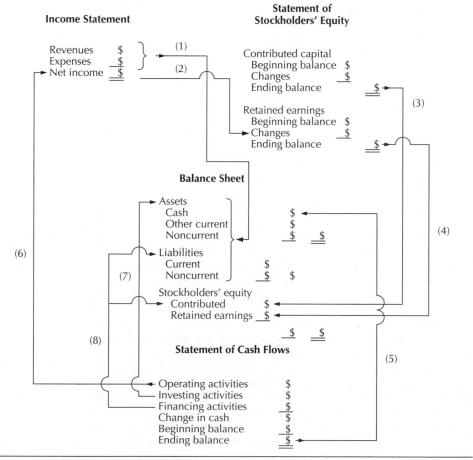

Exhibit 4.7   Relationships of Financial Statements

underlie the four financial statements presented earlier: the balance sheet, the income statement, the statement of stockholders' equity, and the statement of cash flows. The next list summarizes the eight relationships identified by numbers in parentheses in Exhibit 4.7.

1. Revenues and expenses, presented in the income statement, result in changes in assets and liabilities in the balance sheet.

2. Net income flows into the statement of stockholders' equity and is an important determinant of the end-of-period balance in retained earnings.

3. The ending balances of contributed equity accounts in the statement of stockholders' equity correspond to the same amounts in the stockholders' equity section of the balance sheet.

4. The ending balance of retained earnings in the statement of stockholders' equity corresponds to the balance in retained earnings in the stockholders' equity section of the balance sheet.

5. The ending cash balance in the statement of cash flows corresponds to the amount of cash presented on the balance sheet.

6. Cash flows from operating activities in the statement of cash flows reflect the cash effects of those transactions included in the determination of net income. A reconciliation of net income and net cash flows from operating activities is presented as part of the statement of cash flows.

7. Investing activities in the statement of cash flows reflect positive and negative cash flows from changes in assets whose ending balances are included in the balance sheet.

8. Financing activities in the statement of cash flows reflect positive and negative cash flows from debt and equity financing transactions. The end-of-period balances in debt and equity are presented in the balance sheet.

4.8 FINANCIAL STATEMENT DISCLOSURE

One of the underlying principles of financial statement preparation is adequate or fair disclosure. This means that financial statements and the notes and other supplemental information accompanying them must include all available relevant information to keep them from being misleading. In determining whether a specific item of information should be disclosed, the accountant must judge whether that information would make a difference in the decision of a reasonably prudent reader of the financial statements. If the information would be important to such a person, it should be disclosed.

Many disclosure requirements are specified in the authoritative accounting literature, such as the Statements of Financial Accounting Standards and more recently the recodification of these Standards by the FASB. Because of the extensive nature of these requirements, accountants frequently use checklists to ensure that they have not overlooked important information. The American Institute of Certified Public Accountants as well as various private vendors compile such checklists. Some securities law firms also compile such checklists for the use of their clients. Companies are responsible for ensuring that all required disclosures related to GAAP and SEC (public companies only) requirements are made. Auditors also use checklists to independently examine the completeness and fairness of the disclosures.

Exhibit 4.8 presents a sample checklist for the balance sheet category of related party transactions. The three columns to the right indicate the alternative responses for the financial statement preparer: Yes (disclosure has been made), No (disclosure has not been made but is required), and N/A (disclosure is not applicable in this case).

Disclosure takes several forms. The strongest form of disclosure is to include the information in the body of the financial statements. In fact, the statements themselves are a form of disclosure. Including certain words, phrases, and dollar amounts in the statement is one means of disclosing the information. Classification within the financial statements is also an important form of disclosure.

	Yes	No	N/A
Related Party Transactions Generally, (ASC 850)			
For related party transactions, do disclosures include:			
1. The nature of the relationships involved?	—	—	—
2. For each period for which an income statement is presented.			
3. A description of the transaction, including transactions to which no amounts or nominal amounts were ascribed? This includes guarantees or other terms.	—	—	—
4. Other information deemed necessary to an understanding of the effects of the transaction on the financial statements?	—	—	—
5. The dollar amount of transactions?	—	—	—
6. The effect of any changes in the method of establishing the terms from that used in the preceding period?	—	—	—
7. Amounts due from or to related parties as of the date of each balance sheet presented and, if not otherwise apparent, the terms and manner of settlement?	—	—	—
8. If representations about transactions with related parties are made, do they note that the related party transactions were consummated at arm's length, and if such assertions are made, can they be substantiated?	—	—	—
9. If (a) the reporting entity and one or more other enterprises are under common ownership or management control and (b) the existence of the control could result in operating results or financial position of the reporting entity being significantly different from that if the enterprise were autonomous, is the nature of the controlled relationships disclosed (even if there are no transactions between the enterprises)?	—	—	—
10. Are the nature and extent of leasing transactions with related parties appropriately disclosed?	—	—	—
11. Are combined financial statements considered for entities under common control?	—	—	—
12. Are economic dependencies such as with customers, suppliers, borrowers or lenders fully disclosed?	—	—	—

Exhibit 4.8   Sample Financial Statement Disclosure Checklist

A great deal of information is presented in conjunction with financial statements but outside the body of the statements. This information typically is labeled as notes to the financial statements. These notes include both text and numerical information that intend to further inform the reader about matters that have been included in summary fashion in the statements or have been excluded entirely from the financial statements. The reader should not interpret such notes as secondary or unimportant. In fact, notes often occupy more page space than the statements themselves and include very important information that would not be available if the reader were limited to the information that can be contained in the financial statements themselves.

The auditor's report might also direct the reader to specific information in the notes. If management has no viable plan to mitigate a near-term significant risk of bankruptcy, the auditor's report should indicate a going-concern qualification and generally will direct the reader to specific information in the notes to the financial statements. Even in the absence of a going-concern situation, the notes might reveal a risk of business disruption due to limited entity liquidity.

(a) BROAD DISCLOSURE REQUIREMENTS.   The next paragraphs discuss several areas of broad disclosure requirements that do not relate to any one financial statement element. Rather, they are more pervasive in nature and apply to the financial statements as a whole.

(i) Accounting Policies.   The basic elements of the financial statements are identified and measured by applying accounting policies, many of which have been established by the FASB and other policy-setting bodies within the accounting profession. In some areas, alternative policies are available, and companies are required to disclose to readers of financial statements those policies that have been adopted in the preparation of the financial statements (ASC 235).

The inventory accounting policy statement is particularly important because of the disclosure about the accounting method used in determining the amount of inventories. Companies may account for inventories by a variety of techniques, such as first in, first out (FIFO), last in, first out (LIFO), and several averaging methods. The method used in determining the amount of inventory may have an important impact on the amounts in the income statement, balance sheet, and other financial statements and is considered important information in interpreting financial statements.

(ii) Related Party Transactions.   *Related parties* are individuals or companies with the ability to influence the financial transactions of each other. Disclosure of related party transactions may be important for a complete understanding of the financial statements of companies engaged in such transactions.

Notes to financial statements should include a description of transactions between related parties, such as transactions between a principal stockholder and the company, between a corporate officer and the company, and between a subsidiary company and its parent company (ASC 850).

(iii) Subsequent Events.   Financial statements cover a specific time period or point in time. These statements are not immediately available at the end of the accounting period but are usually published several weeks later. The period of time between the end of the accounting period and the issuance of the financial statements is called the *subsequent period.*

During the subsequent period, events may occur or information may become available that should be communicated in the financial statements. If the information reflects conditions that existed at the end of the previous accounting period, the items and amounts in the financial statements may require adjustment in order to appropriately reflect the company's financial position and results of operations for the previous period. If the information reflects conditions that arose after the end of the previous accounting period, it may be necessary to disclose that information in the form of notes to the statements so that they reflect all relevant information.

(iv) Doubt Concerning Continued Existence.   Financial statements typically are prepared on the assumption that the enterprise is a going concern. This means that, in the absence of information to the contrary, it is reasonable to expect the company to continue in existence for the foreseeable future. Failing to meet this assumption could considerably impact the valuation of assets and liabilities. In bankruptcy, financial balances might require valuation on a liquidation rather than on a going-concern basis.

Should accountants preparing the financial statements determine that this assumption is not reasonable and that a significant question about continued existence exists, that information must be disclosed in notes to the financial statements.

In 2011, the AICPA issued Statement of Auditing Standards (SAS) 122, which introduced a recodification of the existing AICPA Auditing Standards. Former SAS No. 59 is now recodified as AU-C 570, *The Auditor's Consideration of and Entity's Ability to Continue as a Going Concern.* In late 2011, the Auditing Standards Board approved a revision of this section as a new SAS. Public company audit requirements are set by the Public Company Accounting Oversight Board, which has retained the former codified version of SAS No. 59 in Section 341.

(v) Contingent Liabilities.   *Contingent liabilities* are liabilities that involve a great deal of uncertainty as to their existence and amount. Often they exist as a result of lawsuits against an enterprise or other situations that may, in the future, require the enterprise to transfer assets in settlement of a claim.

If certain conditions are met, contingent liabilities should be formally entered into the accounting records and become a part of the financial statements. Many contingent liabilities, however, are less certain and typically are disclosed in notes to the financial statements. This is frequently the case with pending lawsuits, where the certainty of loss, including the amount of loss, is unknown when the financial statements are issued. Disclosure in this manner puts the reader on notice as to the possible negative consequences of events that have already taken place but do not meet the objectivity standards necessary for inclusion in the body of the financial statements (ASC 450-20).

(vi) Significant Risks and Uncertainties.   The volatility of the business and economic environment dictates a need for disclosure about significant risks and uncertainties that confront business enterprises. Four areas for which information is required in conjunction with financial statements are described next.

1. Nature of operations (i.e., description of major products or services and principal markets)
2. Use of estimates in the preparation of financial statements (i.e., explanation that the preparation of financial statements in conformity with GAAP requires the use of management's estimates)
3. Certain significant estimates (i.e., disclosure of specific estimates that have material impact on the financial statements)
4. Current vulnerability due to certain concentrations (i.e., disclosure of (a) concentrations in the volume of business with a particular customer, supplier, lender, grantor, or contributor; (b) concentrations in revenue from particular products, services, or fund-raising events; (c) concentrations in the available sources of materials, labor, or services; and (d) concentrations in the market or geographic area in which an entity conducts its operations (ASC 450).

(vii) Disclosure Recommendations of the AICPA Special Committee on Financial Reporting.   A special committee of the AICPA, charged with making broad recommendations to improve financial reporting through improved disclosure, has recommended enhanced supplementary disclosures that are intended to help users of financial statements evaluate the reporting entity's prospects. Among other recommendations, this group states that standard setters should:

- Develop a comprehensive model of business reporting, indicating the types and timing of information that users need to value and assess the risk of their investments
- Improve understanding of costs and benefits of business reporting, recognizing that definitive quantification of costs and benefits is not possible
- Improve financial statement disclosures in these areas:
  ○ Business segment information
  ○ Innovative financial instruments
  ○ Identity, opportunities, and risks of off-balance-sheet financing arrangements
  ○ Effects of core and noncore activities and events and measure at fair value noncore assets and liabilities
  ○ Uncertainty of measurements of certain assets and liabilities
  ○ Reporting on fourth quarter separately and including business segment information in interim reports

In addition to these specific recommendations, the Special Committee made general recommendations that standard setters search for and eliminate less relevant disclosures, improve the display in financial statements, expand interim reporting requirements, improve comparability and consistencies of information, and provide key statistics and ratios to assist users of financial statements.[2]

(b) DISCLOSURES RELATED TO SPECIFIC FINANCIAL STATEMENT ELEMENTS.   Whereas the examples of disclosure just discussed are broad in nature and do not relate to specific financial statement elements, other disclosures focus attention on individual items in the balance sheet, income statement, or other financial statements. Examples of several of these disclosures are briefly identified and discussed in the next subsections.

(i) Debt and Equity Investments.   Companies may have invested cash in debt and equity instruments of other companies and, as a result, may have investments among the assets in their balance

---

[2] AICPA, Comprehensive Report of the Special Committee on Financial Reporting, *Improving Business Reporting—A Customer Focus* (New York: Author, 1994), pp. 123–125.

sheets. Accepted accounting procedures call for separating these investments into three portfolios—trading, available for sale, and held to maturity—based primarily on the intent of management for holding the investment. Trading securities may include both debt and equity investments and are presented as current assets in the balance sheet. Available-for-sale securities include both debt and equity investments for which the enterprise has no immediate plans to sell but does not plan to hold indefinitely (equity securities) or until maturity (debt securities). Held-to-maturity investments include only those debt investments for which the intent is to hold until maturity. Available-for-sale and held-to-maturity investments usually are presented as noncurrent assets.

Information disclosed in notes to the balance sheet about these investments includes their fair value, gross unrealized holding gains and losses, and amortized cost by category as well as information about realized gains and losses included in the income statements (ASC 470).

(ii) Inventories.   In addition to disclosing information about the accounting policy employed in accounting for inventories, detailed information about the dollar amounts of inventories must be disclosed. For example, a manufacturing company may have several types of inventories—raw materials, work in process, and finished goods. The financial statements or related notes should include an indication of the dollar amounts of each of these types of inventories (ASC 330).

(iii) Plant Assets and Depreciation.   Plant assets include land, buildings, equipment, furniture, fixtures, and other long-lived assets that are required to accomplish the business purposes of an enterprise. Plant assets are subject to depreciation whereby a portion of the cost of the asset is written off as an expense during those years in which the asset is used. The remaining unamortized cost is presented in the balance sheet as an asset.

Information about the amount of plant assets in individual categories, such as equipment and fixtures, is believed to be important to readers of financial statements. In addition, information about the cost of those assets and the portion of the cost that has been written off as depreciation to date is also important. This information may be presented in the body of the financial statements but often is found in notes to the financial statements (ASC 360).

(iv) Long-Term Debt.   The amount of long-term debt is presented in the enterprise's balance sheet. That amount may be made up of many different debt issues having different interest rates, maturity dates, and other characteristics. Information about the details of individual debt issues that make up the total of long-term debt frequently is found in the notes to financial statements in order to avoid unnecessary details in the statements themselves (ASC 470).

(v) Capital Structure.   A corporation may have one or more types of preferred and common stock in its capital structure. Information about the characteristics of individual issues of capital stock, such as the number of shares the corporation is authorized to issue, the par or stated value, and the dividend rate, is disclosed in the financial statement or related notes. If an entity has issued redeemable stock (i.e., stock that must be repurchased by the issuing company at a future date), the amount of the redemption requirement must be disclosed for each of the next five years, usually in notes to the financial statements. Also, the preference of preferred stock in liquidation must be presented in the aggregate on the face of the balance sheet (ASC 505).

Just a few examples of the types of information usually disclosed in conjunction with financial statements have been described. Disclosures in a variety of other areas, such as leases, pensions, and income taxes, can be quite long and complex. They include a great deal of information that would otherwise be unknown to the user of the financial statements.

(c) SPECIAL DISCLOSURES OF PUBLICLY HELD COMPANIES.   Publicly held companies must adhere to a higher disclosure standard in certain areas than companies that are not publicly held. Due to the unique reporting responsibilities of publicly held companies, the FASB has limited certain disclosure requirements to publicly held companies. In addition, the SEC requires public companies to make additional disclosure. Several of these are briefly discussed next.

(i) Segment Disclosures. Publicly held companies are required to report detailed information about their reportable operating segments. This information generally is reported as supplemental to the financial statements and is prepared on the same basis as is used internally for evaluating segment performance. Operating segments are components of an enterprise about which separate financial information is available that is evaluated regularly by the chief operating decision maker in deciding how resources should be allocated within the enterprise. Segment reporting requirements also include information about operations in different geographic areas and reliance on major customers (ASC 280).

(ii) Earnings per Share. The EPS figures are required only in the income statements of publicly held companies. These are presented as part of the income statement and indicate the amount of net income attributable to each share of outstanding common stock, after providing for dividends that would be required on preferred stock. Nonpublic companies are not required to make these disclosures in their income statements. Public companies whose capital structure includes financial instruments and other contractual arrangements that would reduce EPS (called *potential common stock*) are required to make a dual presentation of EPS—basic EPS and diluted EPS. Basic EPS reflects the historical amount of EPS of common stock, and diluted EPS is a pro forma amount that anticipates the dilutive effect of potential common stock (ASC 260).

(iii) Interim Reporting. Companies may provide information to their stockholders and others on a more frequent basis than annually. Many companies provide information regularly on a quarterly basis.

Publicly held companies that report regularly on an interim basis must meet certain specific disclosure standards. These standards specify the information that must be presented, as a minimum, in these reports (ASC 270).

(d) DISCLOSURE OVERLOAD. The accounting profession and the investing community have expressed concern that too much disclosure may be required by the authoritative accounting literature, causing users to get lost in the details and miss the primary message being communicated. Standards overload, if in fact such exists, is believed by many to be caused by the fact that reporting needs of users of the financial statements of large, public companies drive the establishment of standards, most of which are then applicable to all companies, including smaller, private companies. The AICPA Special Committee searched, without much success, for current disclosure requirements that could be eliminated. While it was unable to find current requirements that do not provide useful information for the complex business environment and types of transactions companies engage in, it did recommend that standard setters and regulators continue the search in hopes of simplifying financial statement disclosures.

4.9 LIMITATIONS OF FINANCIAL STATEMENTS

Financial statements are important means of communications between management and external parties, primarily investors and creditors. These statements are subject to certain limitations, several of which are introduced in this final section.

(a) STABLE MONETARY UNIT ASSUMPTION. Financial statements are prepared with an underlying assumption of a stable monetary unit. Accountants recognize that the monetary unit does, in fact, change in value over time. In the United States, the monetary unit is the dollar, and in recent years, the changes in value have been declines as the general level of prices has risen consistently. Experiments have been undertaken to measure the impact of changing prices on the financial statements. To date, however, no single approach has been accepted, nor is any adjustment for changing prices required in financial statements prepared in accordance with accepted accounting principles.

Perhaps the best way to describe the underlying assumption is not as a stable monetary unit but rather as a monetary unit with changes in value from period to period that are not large enough to have a material impact on the financial statements. Astute readers of financial statements should be generally aware that some distortion may exist because of the impact of changing prices and that the failure to adjust for such changes represents a limitation of financial statements.

During a brief period of high inflation in the United States, an FASB Standard (SFAS No. 33) was issued on changing prices. At the point at which inflation subsided, interest in price-level adjusted financial statements evaporated.

(b) HISTORICAL ORIENTATION.   Financial statements are essentially historical representations of business activity. Frequently they are used to anticipate the future, and their historical orientation imposes a limitation on their value in this regard. Despite the historical orientation of the statements, accountants must consider the future to make many of the judgments that are required in reporting about past activities. For example, in determining an appropriate amount of depreciation on a plant asset for an accounting period, the accountant must make an assumption concerning how long the reporting entity will use that asset.

The greater use of fair values in financial reporting marks a turning away from the traditional historical cost basis of the financial statements. Debate continues regarding how far the fair value concept can be reliably and objectively applied in financial statements.

(c) JUDGMENT AND ESTIMATION.   While financial statements have an appearance of great precision, they are tentative in nature and require judgment and estimation. Any attempt to partition ongoing business activity into relatively short periods of time, such as a year or quarter, requires judgment and estimation about future events and about the outcome of incomplete past events. Although accountants attempt to apply an objectivity standard to the extent possible, in many instances they must resort to judgment and estimation to determine important amounts that affect the elements of the financial statements. The extensive use of fair values in reporting and in measuring asset impairment adds additional judgment and estimation to the process of accounting.

(d) MANAGEMENT ABILITY TO INFLUENCE CONTENT.   Within limits, management has the ability to influence the content of financial statements. Certain end-of-period activities can have an important effect on the relationships that investors and creditors consider particularly important in assessing the financial activities of the enterprise.

Sometimes these actions can have a manipulative effect on earnings and liquidity.

(e) UNRECORDED ITEMS.   The accounting system does not attempt to capture all aspects of business activity that may be important factors in the success of the enterprise. One example of an item that may be very important to the future well-being of the enterprise is its human resources. For many companies, its management personnel and labor force may be its most valuable asset, but nowhere in the balance sheet does a value for this item appear. Other assets, such as goodwill or certain intellectual property, may be measured when a business is combined with another entity. In the absence of some reliable measure of their value, such as in a business combination, such values are not recorded.

Financial statements are limited to those elements that can be measured with reasonable objectivity and that are required by GAAP. They should be viewed as only partial, not complete, representations of the business enterprise.

(f) FLEXIBILITY VERSUS UNIFORMITY.   An ongoing debate in the accounting profession is flexibility versus uniformity. This controversy asks the question: Should enterprises have latitude in the manner in which they identify and measure the elements of the financial statements (i.e., flexibility), or should all enterprises follow precisely the same rules and procedures in preparing statements (i.e., uniformity)?

At present, elements of both flexibility and uniformity exist in GAAP. In some areas, enterprises have great latitude in accounting for and presenting certain items in their financial statements. In other areas, enterprises are essentially limited to a single process or procedure. The FASB seeks to identify areas of financial reporting where unjustified differences exist in practice. One objective of the FASB is to narrow these areas of difference in practice so that all enterprises account for similar transactions in essentially the same manner. This is a long process, however, and undoubtedly both flexibility and uniformity in different areas of accounting can be expected to exist for years to come.

4.10 INTERNATIONAL PERSPECTIVE

The convergence of U.S. GAAP and international standards could have a significant impact on the appearance of the basic financial statements. IFRS differences are identified as they relate to individual financial statement elements in other chapters of this *Handbook*. Some general presentation differences that are currently identified between U.S. GAAP and IFRS financial statements that will need to be addressed should the two approaches be converged are discussed next.

International Accounting Standard (IAS) 1, *Presentation of Financial Statements,* and IAS 7, *Cash Flow Statements,* as amended, provide the basic international accounting standards related to presentation.

(a) GENERAL ISSUES. On the initial adoption of IFRS, the presentation of the first statements will require the full retroactive application of the to all prior financial statements for comparability purposes. Information not readily accessible may be needed to convert the financial statements to IFRS Standards. While many large companies may already have such statements and have wrestled with obtaining the required data, smaller companies may not have thought through all of the data requirements necessary to make the conversion. The conversion process the entity to identify a date (generally the earliest financial statement date presented) for the conversion, prepare an opening balance sheet under IFRS, select acceptable accounting principles under IFRS, and apply those principles retrospectively to adjust other disclosures from previously reported-on financial statements that appear in the current financial statements for comparative purposes. Extensive disclosures will be necessary to explain the transition changes.

Additionally, to date, IFRS has not established a formal hierarchy of accounting standards and guidance (beyond IFRS).

(b) BALANCE SHEET AND CASH FLOW ISSUES. IFRS generally requires a classified balance sheet presentation (grouping of similar items together under a caption). However, under IFRS, assets and liabilities are usually listed in reverse liquidity order (e.g., cash is the last item listed current assets category). Noncurrent assets (e.g., long-term investments; property, plant, and equipment; and intangibles) are shown *first* in the balance sheet, followed by current assets. Shareholder equities similarly are listed *before* noncurrent liabilities, which are followed by current liabilities in the equities section of the IFRS balance sheet. IFRS, unlike GAAP, does not discourage the use of the term *reserves.* There may also be numerous other potential terminology differences with GAAP (e.g., *share premium* rather than *paid in capital in excess of par value*). IFRS additionally permits more offsetting of certain items in the balance sheet than GAAP.

In the cash flow statement under IFRS, cash and cash equivalents can include liquid investments and be netted with short-term borrowings, such as bank overdrafts. Certain noncash investing and financing activities (e.g., exchanges of nonmonetary assets) are required to be disclosed only in the notes under IFRS while these items may be shown under GAAP in the statement of cash flows. IFRS also permits alternatives for disclosing certain items, such as interest, dividends, and taxes, in the statement of cash flows. GAAP requires that interest and dividends be reported as operating activities.

(c) INCOME STATEMENT ISSUES. IFRS does not permit the separate treatment of extraordinary items as a separate caption in the income statement. SEC rules for public companies require more income statement captions and key summary points (e.g., income from operations) and presentation requirements than current IFRS requirements. Under IFRS, the revaluation of property, plant, and equipment as well as intangibles is permitted as a component of other comprehensive income.

4.11 REFERENCES TO THE HISTORICAL ACCOUNTING LITERATURE

Accounting Principles Board. APB Opinion No. 12, *Omnibus Opinion—1967*. New York: AICPA, 1967.

————. APB Opinion No. 22, *Disclosure of Accounting Policies*. New York: AICPA, 1972.

————. APB Opinion No. 28, *Interim Financial Reporting*. New York: AICPA, 1973.

American Institute of Certified Public Accountants. Accounting Research Bulletin No. 43, Chapter 3, *Working Capital*. New York: Author, 1953.

————. Accounting Research Bulletin No. 43, Chapter 4, "Inventory Pricing". New York: Author, 1953.

————. *Checklists and Illustrative Financial Statements for Corporations*. New York: Author, 2001.

————. Comprehensive Report of the Special Committee on Financial Reporting, *Improving Business Reporting—A Customer Focus*. New York: Author, 1994.

————. Statement on Auditing Standards No. 12, *Subsequent Events*. New York: Author, 1972.

————. Statement on Auditing Standards No. 59, *The Auditor's Consideration of an Entity's Ability to Continue as a Going Concern*. New York: Author, 1988.

————. Statement of Position No. 94-6, *Disclosure of Certain Significant Risks and Uncertainties*. New York: Author, 1994.

Financial Accounting Standards Board. Statement of Financial Accounting Concepts No. 1, *Objectives of Financial Reporting by Business Enterprises*. Stamford, CT: Author, 1978.

————. Statement of Financial Accounting Concepts No. 6, *Elements of Financial Statements*. Stamford, CT: Author, 1985.

————. Statement of Financial Accounting Standards No. 5, *Accounting for Contingencies*. Stamford, CT: Author, 1975.

————. Statement of Financial Accounting Standards No. 21, *Suspension of the Reporting of Earnings Per Share and Segment Information by Nonpublic Enterprises*. Stamford, CT: Author, 1978.

————. Statement of Financial Accounting Standards No. 57, *Related Party Disclosures*. Stamford, CT: Author, 1982.

————. Statement of Financial Accounting Standards No. 95, *Statement of Cash Flows*. Stamford, CT: Author, 1987.

————. Statement of Financial Accounting Standards No. 115, *Accounting for Certain Investments in Debt and Equity Securities*. Norwalk, CT: Author, 1993.

————. Statement of Financial Accounting Standards No. 128, *Earnings per Share*. Stamford, CT: Author, 1997.

————. Statement of Financial Accounting Standards No. 129, *Disclosure of Information about Capital Structure*. Stamford, CT: Author, 1997.

————. Statement of Financial Accounting Standards No. 131, *Disclosures about Segments of an Enterprise and Related Information*. Stamford, CT: Author, 1997.

CHAPTER 5

SECURITIES AND EXCHANGE COMMISSION REPORTING REQUIREMENTS

Wendy Hambleton, CPA
BDO USA, LLP

5.1   SECURITIES AND EXCHANGE COMMISSION

(a) CREATION OF THE SECURITIES AND EXCHANGE COMMISSION.   Congress created the Securities and Exchange Commission (SEC, or the Commission) through the Securities Exchange Act of 1934 (the 1934 Act). The Securities Act of 1933 (the 1933 Act) was administered by the Federal Trade Commission before the SEC was established.

The 1933 Act and 1934 Act (the Securities Acts) are the main securities statutes of importance to accountants. The Commission also administers the Public Utility Holding Company Act of 1935, the Trust Indenture Act of 1939, the Investment Company Act of 1940, and the Investment Advisers Act of 1940. In addition, the Commission administers the Securities Investor Act of 1970 and also serves as adviser to the U.S. District Court in connection with Federal Bankruptcy Act reorganization proceedings involving registrants. More recently, the Sarbanes-Oxley Act of 2002 has provided additional rules and regulations for publicly traded companies, their management, board members and advisers. The SEC's Web site is *www.sec.gov*.

(b) ORGANIZATION OF THE SECURITIES AND EXCHANGE COMMISSION.   The Commission is an independent agency of five commissioners. No more than three may be of the same political party. They are appointed by the President of the United States (with advice and consent of the Senate) to five-year terms, one term expiring in June of each year.

One commissioner is designated by the President as chair of the Commission. The Commission has a professional staff, consisting of lawyers, accountants, engineers, financial analysts, economists, and administrative and clerical employees, which is organized into 23 divisions and offices including administrative offices. Descriptions of the 11 key nonadministrative divisions and offices and their responsibilities are presented next:

1. *Office of International Affairs.* Primarily responsible for negotiating understandings between the SEC and foreign securities regulators and for coordinating enforcement programs pursuant to those agreements. It also consults with other divisions and offices concerning the effect of the internationalization of the securities markets on their responsibilities and programs and works as a liaison to emerging markets around the world

2. *Division of Trading and Markets.* Regulates and oversees securities exchanges, national securities associations, and brokers-dealers, and administers the statistical functions.

3. *Division of Enforcement.* Supervises enforcement activities under the statutes administered by the Commission and institutes civil and administrative actions. The division works with law enforcement agencies in the United States and around the world to initiate criminal cases as appropriate.

4. *Division of Investment Management.* Administers the Investment Company Act of 1940, the Investment Advisers Act of 1940, and the Public Utility Holding Company Act of 1935 by reviewing investment company and investment adviser filings, assisting with enforcement matters involving investment companies and advisers, and interpreting laws and regulations.

5. *Division of Corporation Finance.* Accountants deal primarily with this division on SEC matters. This division is described in greater detail in Section 5.1(c).

6. *Office of Administrative Law Judges.* Conducts hearings and brings rules on allegations of securities law violations initiated by the Commission.

7. *Office of the General Counsel.* The General Counsel is the chief law officer of the Commission. This office coordinates the SEC's involvement in judicial proceedings and provides legal advice and assistance.

8. *Office of the Chief Accountant.* The Chief Accountant is the Commission's principal adviser on accounting and auditing matters. The Office of the Chief Accountant:

    a. Develops policy with respect to accounting and auditing matters and financial statement requirements

    b. Supervises implementation of policies on accounting and auditing matters

    c. Reviews complex, new, or controversial accounting and auditing problems of registrants

    d. Considers registrants' appeals of decisions by the Division of Corporation Finance on accounting matters

    e. Serves as liaison with and oversees the private sector standards-setting process working closely with the Financial Accounting Standards Board (FASB) and the International Accounting Standards Board (IASB) as well as the American Institute of Certified Public Accountants (AICPA)

    f. Considers accountants' independence

    g. Prepares Financial Reporting Releases (FRRs) and (in conjunction with the Division of Corporation Finance), Staff Accounting Bulletins (SABs)/Staff Legal Bulletins (SLBs)

    h. Assists counsel in administrative proceedings relating to accounting and auditing matters

9. *Office of Compliance Inspections and Examinations.* Conducts examination and inspection programs for self-regulatory organizations, broker-dealers, transfer agents, investment companies, and investment advisers.

10. *Office of Investor Education and Advocacy.* Created by the SEC specifically to serve individual investors. The office makes sure the concerns and problems encountered by individual investors are known throughout the SEC and considered when the Agency takes action. It also carries out the SEC's investor education program.

11. *Division of Risk, Strategy and Financial Innovation.* Created by the SEC in 2009 to identify risks and trends in the financial markets. The division performs strategic analysis and identifies new trends in financial markets and systemic risks.

The main offices of the Commission are located at 100 F Street NE, Washington, DC 20549. There are also 11 regional offices. The regional offices are the field representatives of the Commission. It is their responsibility to provide enforcement and inspection capabilities throughout the country.

(c) DIVISION OF CORPORATION FINANCE. Because accountants generally deal more with the Division of Corporation Finance than with the other SEC divisions, its duties and operations are considered here in greater detail.

(i) Responsibilities.   The division's principal responsibility is to ensure that financial information included in SEC filings is in compliance with the rules and regulations of the SEC. Its duties include:

1. Reviewing and commenting on
   a. Registration statements for initial public offerings (IPOs)
   b. Annual and quarterly filings
   c. Proxy materials
2. Consulting with registrants and their advisers on accounting and filing issues
3. Issuing interpretive guidance in the form of the *Financial Reporting Manual,* Compliance and Disclosure Interpretations, PowerPoint presentations, and other informal guidance
4. Monitoring the use of IFRS by foreign private issuers
5. Working in conjunction with other divisions to issue concept releases, new rules, SABs and SLBs

The SEC does not pass on the merits of any proposed security issue. Although the SEC sets accounting and disclosure requirements that, in some cases, may be over and above those required by generally accepted accounting principles (GAAP), it does not generally prescribe the use of specific auditing procedures other than those related to certain regulated industries. It is the responsibility of the independent registered public accounting firm to determine whether the financial statements included in the filing have been audited in accordance with auditing standards adopted by the Public Company Accounting Oversight Board (PCAOB).

(ii) Organization.   The division is supervised by a director who is aided by 3 deputy directors, 8 associate directors, and 12 assistant directors.

The division also has a chief counsel who interprets the securities laws and a chief accountant who supervises compliance in accounting and auditing matters. The chief accountant does not set policy; in novel or complex accounting situations, he or she may confer with the Commission's chief accountant.

Each assistant director office is staffed primarily by attorneys and accountants. Each office is responsible for certain specific industries, so that each reviewer is familiar with a registrant's type of business and can treat accounting and reporting matters consistently. A registrant is assigned to an industry group and then to a particular office based on the company's primary Standard Industrial Classification (SIC) Code.

Once a company's initial filing is assigned to an assistant director office for review, all subsequent matters relating to that company are generally handled by that office. The company's assignment to its specific office is shown in the Electronic Data Gathering, Analysis, and Retrieval system (EDGAR) after the basic company information. The assistant director offices have access to the Office of Engineering for assistance in technical areas such as mining. The Office of the Chief Accountant has valuation expertise as well.

(iii) Review Procedures.   Filings with the division are customarily reviewed by an accountant and an attorney or financial analyst. The accountant's review will be directed toward determining adequate disclosure and compliance with GAAP and the applicable rules of the SEC. This review will also determine the appropriateness of the accounting and disclosures based on information in the textual section of the filing. As required by the Sarbanes-Oxley Act, every registrant is reviewed in some manner at least once every three years.

Comments from the review may result in issuing the registrant a "comment letter." The assistant director approves comments made by the attorney or financial analyst, and a senior assistant chief accountant clears comments made by the accountant. If there are troublesome accounting problems, the division's chief accountant may confer with the Office of the Chief Accountant. In unusual situations, the Office of the Chief Accountant may bring the matter to the Commission's attention.

To minimize SEC comments regarding potential problem areas in the filing, the registrant may request a prefiling conference with the Commission's staff. Such conferences may also be held after the filing to resolve matters in the comment letter. The SEC has developed protocol for contacting the Office of the Chief Accountant or the Division of Corporation Finance for accounting issues. This protocol can also be found on the SEC's Web site in the section "Information for Accountants." After a registrant has provided the written information, it can also request a face-to-face meeting to resolve the issue if necessary.

The registrant also may refer matters to the Office of the Chief Accountant and, in rare instances, to the Commission. This can occur either before filing or after receipt of the letter of comments.

Because of the significant volume of filings it receives on an annual basis, the division has adopted a selective review program. Registration and transactional proxy statements are given priority over the 1934 Act reports because of the tight time schedules associated with such filings. The selective review criteria are directed at reviewing all key filings, and registrants should expect all registration statements for initial public offerings to be thoroughly reviewed. If a registration or proxy statement is selected for review, the registrant will be notified.

Normally the division attempts to review a registration statement and provide initial comments within 30 days after the filing date. Comments are generally provided in writing and may be sent via e-mail.

Periodic reports under the 1934 Act may be reviewed on a selective basis after the filing date. Depending on the number and severity of the deficiencies, the SEC Staff will either require the registrant to amend the periodic report or may require only that the changes be implemented in future filings.

The 1934 Act permits the SEC to suspend trading in any security "for a period not exceeding 10 days" if it is in the public interest and is necessary to protect investors. Based on a Supreme Court decision, the SEC does not have the authority to issue suspensions beyond the initial 10 days.

(iv) EDGAR—Electronic Data Gathering Analysis and Retrieval System. The SEC utilizes its EDGAR system as its primary means of accepting filings from registrants. With a very few exceptions, most forms filed with the SEC are required to be filed electronically, including responses to comment letters and other information. Responses to comment letters and other correspondence do not become immediately available publicly; rather they only become publicly available after the completion of the filing review. Anyone with access to the Internet can review public filings made via EDGAR. The SEC's Web site contains a section related to EDGAR and how to use the system.

(v) Extension of Time to File. If a filing is not expected to be made on a timely basis, the SEC rules require that companies submit a notification on Form 12b-25, indicating the reason for extension, no later than one business day after the due date of the report. In addition, the rules provide relief where reports are not timely filed if a timely filing would involve unreasonable effort or expense. Under this provision, a report will be considered to be filed on a timely basis if these three provisions are met:

1. The required notification on Form 12b-25 (a) discloses that the reasons causing the inability to file on time could not be eliminated without unreasonable effort or expense, and (b) undertakes that the document will be filed no later than the 15th day following the due date (by the fifth day with respect to Form 10-Q).

2. There is a statement, attached as an exhibit to Form 12b-25, from any person other than the registrant (e.g., the independent accountant) whose inability to furnish a required opinion, report, or certification was the reason the report could not be timely filed without unreasonable effort or expense.

3. The report is filed within the represented time period.

This procedure does not require a response by the SEC.

Periodic reports that are filed late with the SEC may (1) prevent the registrant from using short-form registration statements on Form S-3, (2) cause injunctive action to compel filing, (3) make Rule 144 unavailable for the sale of shares by company officers, directors, or insiders (thus requiring registration of those shares before they can be sold), or (4) result in suspension of trading in the registrant's securities. The exchange often acts quickly to suspend trading of a security if the company has not filed information on a timely basis.

(d) RELATIONSHIP BETWEEN THE ACCOUNTING PROFESSION AND THE SECURITIES AND EXCHANGE COMMISSION. The SEC and the accounting profession have cooperated with each other in developing GAAP. Through its FRRs, SABs, and SLBs, the SEC has informed the accounting profession of its opinions on accounting and reporting. In addition, the chief accountant and certain members of his or her staff attend meetings of the FASB, including the Emerging Issues Task Force (EITF), and technical committees of the AICPA.

In turn, as stated in FRR 1 (Section 101):

> [T]he Commission intends to continue its policy of looking to the private sector for leadership in establishing and improving accounting principles and standards through the FASB with the expectation that the body's conclusions will promote the interests of investors. For the purpose of this policy, principles, standards, and practices promulgated by the FASB in its Statements and Interpretations will be considered by the Commission as having substantial authoritative support, and those contrary to such FASB promulgations will be considered to have no such support.

Although there has been an attempt to eliminate the differences between GAAP requirements and SEC accounting and reporting requirements, there are still certain key differences. Some of the additional requirements for SEC registrants are listed next.

- *Assets subject to lien (S-X Rule 4-08(b)).* The rule requires the disclosure of the nature and approximate amount of assets mortgaged, pledged, or subject to liens.
- *Financial information of unconsolidated subsidiaries and 50-percent-or-less-owned equity method investees (S-X Rule 4-08(g) and 3-09).* Depending on the significance of the investment, the SEC may require separate audited financial statements of the investee.
- *Income tax expense (S-X Rule 4-08(h)).* Additional disclosure regarding the components of income tax expense (domestic foreign, other, etc.) and a numerical reconciliation between the reported income tax expense and the pretax income multiplied by the statutory rate is generally required.
- *Related party transactions (S-X Rule 4-08(k)).* Related party balances are disclosed on the face of the financial statements.
- *Disclosure of the composition of "other" current assets, current liabilities, assets, and liabilities if the total exceeds certain thresholds (S-X Rule 5-02.8, 5-02.17, 5-02.20, 5-20.24).*
- *Guarantor financial statements (S-X Rule 3-10).* Depending on the significance and other criteria regarding the guarantors, the SEC may require separate financial information regarding guarantor and nonguarantor entities included in the consolidated financial statements.

For more detailed information related to these and other differences, see Section 5.4.

(e) SARBANES-OXLEY ACT OF 2002. In response to several significant restatements by public companies in late 2001 and early 2002, both the House of Representatives and the U.S. Senate proposed bills that could affect almost everyone associated with public companies. The two bills were quickly reconciled into the Sarbanes-Oxley Bill, which the President signed in late July 2002 and thus became the Sarbanes-Oxley Act (the Act).

The Act is very broad in scope and, numerous questions of interpretation have arisen and will continue to arise. A broad overview of certain provisions of the Act is presented next.

(i) Implications for Public Company Officers and Directors

Certifications. Chief executive officer (CEO) and chief financial officer (CFO) certifications regarding annual and quarterly reports are required in accordance with two separate provisions of the Act. In certifications provided in response to Section 302 of the Act, the officers must each state:

- They have reviewed the report.
- Based on their knowledge:
  - The report contains no untrue material fact and does not omit a material fact that would make the statements misleading, and
  - The financial statements and other financial information in the report present fairly, in all material respects, the operations and financial condition of the company.
- They are responsible for establishing and maintaining internal controls.
- They have designed internal controls to ensure that material information relating to the issuer and its consolidated subsidiaries is made known to such officers by others within the company and its consolidated subsidiaries during the period in which the periodic reports are being prepared.
- They have evaluated the effectiveness of internal controls as of the end of the period covered by the report and have presented their conclusions about such effectiveness based on their evaluation.
- They have disclosed to the issuer's auditors and the audit committee all significant deficiencies and/or material weaknesses in the controls and any fraud involving management or other employees who have a significant role in the issuer's internal controls.
- They have indicated in the report whether there were any significant changes in internal controls or other factors that might significantly affect internal controls subsequent to the date of their evaluation, including any corrective actions taken in response to deficiencies and/or material weaknesses.

Pursuant to Section 906 of the Act, such officers must also provide a certification for each periodic report containing financial statements filed with the SEC that:

- The periodic report complies fully with the requirements of Section 13(a) or 15(d) of the Securities Exchange Act of 1934.
- The information provided presents fairly, in all material respects, the financial condition and results of operations of the company.

Maximum penalties for knowing violations of this section of the Act are fines of up to $1 million and/or imprisonment for up to 10 years; willful violations carry fines of up to $5 million and/or imprisonment of up to 20 years.

Internal Control Reports. Companies must also file a report on internal control with their annual reports. This report must acknowledge management's responsibility for establishing and maintaining an adequate internal control structure and procedures for financial reporting and include an assessment as to the effectiveness of such structure as of its fiscal year-end.

Loans to Officers and Directors. The Act, subject to certain limited exceptions, makes it unlawful for a company to extend credit to its directors and executive officers. However, existing loans were grandfathered, provided they are not materially modified or renewed.

Penalties for Violations of Securities Laws. Under the Act, corporate officers are subject to new penalties. If a company restates its financial statements due to material noncompliance with financial reporting requirements, as a result of misconduct, any bonuses and other incentive-based or equity-based compensation received by the CEO and CFO during the 12 months following the filing of the noncompliant document, as well as any profits realized from the sale of securities during that period, must be returned to the company.

There are other provisions in the Act addressing corporate code of ethics, insider trading, and other issues.

(ii) Implications for Audit Committees

General Audit Committee Requirement and Responsibilities.   All public companies must have an audit committee. If one is not appointed, the entire board will be deemed to be functioning as the audit committee. The committee will be responsible for:

- Appointment, compensation, and oversight of auditors, including resolution of any disagreements between management and the auditors
- Establishing procedures for receiving and addressing complaints, including anonymous submissions, concerning accounting, internal control, or auditing matters
- Engaging independent counsel or other advisers, as necessary, with funding to be provided by the company

Each audit committee member must be independent. Under the independence definition in the Act, the member may not receive fees from the company for any consulting, advisory, or other services (other than for services on the board) and may not be affiliated with either the company or its subsidiaries in any capacity other than as a director.

Financial Expertise Requirement and Disclosure.   Companies must disclose whether at least one member of the audit committee qualifies as a "financial expert." When making such a determination, a company should consider an individual's:

- Educational and professional background
- Knowledge of GAAP and financial statements
- Experience in preparing or auditing financial statements for comparable companies
- Experience with internal accounting controls
- Understanding of audit committee functions

(iii) Implications for Independent Auditors

Public Company Accounting Oversight Board.   The Act required the creation of the PCAOB. The PCAOB is comprised of five financially literate members (two current or former certified public accountants [CPAs] and three non-CPAs). Members, appointed by the SEC after consultation with the chairman of the Federal Reserve Board and the Secretary of the Treasury, may not be connected with any public accounting firm other than as retired members receiving fixed continuing payments and in general may not be employed or engaged in any other professional or business activity. The PCAOB is funded through fees collected from public companies, which are assessed based on its level of market capitalization.

The PCAOB's duties include adopting standards (e.g., auditing, quality control, ethics, and independence) related to the preparation of audit reports for public companies, conduct inspections of registered accounting firms, and conduct investigations and disciplinary proceedings, as necessary. When conducting investigations, the PCAOB is able to request and compel testimony, through subpoena requests, of public accounting firms and issuers. The PCAOB has the authority, subject to SEC review, to impose sanctions on accounting firms that are not in compliance with the Act.

Public Accounting Firms.   All accounting firms that audit public companies are required to register with the PCAOB. This requirement also extends to foreign accounting firms that audit a public company (a foreign private issuer as well as a U.S. company). Registered firms serving more than 100 public companies are subject to annual quality reviews conducted by the PCAOB. All other firms will be reviewed, at a minimum, on a triennial basis.

Auditor Independence Standards.   The Act imposed new restrictions on the types of services a public accounting firm could perform for a public company when it is serving as that company's auditor. Prohibited services include:

- Bookkeeping services
- Financial information systems design and implementation
- Appraisal or valuation services, fairness opinions, or contribution-in-kind reports
- Actuarial services
- Internal audit outsourcing services
- Management functions or human resources
- Broker or dealer, investment adviser, or investment banking services
- Legal services and expert services unrelated to the audit

Other nonaudit services, including tax services, may be provided but only if approved in advance by the company's audit committee. Approval of all nonaudit services must be disclosed in periodic reports.

The Act provides for mandatory rotation of the audit partner and engagement quality review partner such that neither can act in that capacity for more than five years. Accounting firms are also prohibited from auditing a public company if an individual from the accounting firm who participated in the company's audit during the one year preceding the initiation of the audit holds a financial oversight role at the company.

If a company meets the criteria of an accelerated filer (generally a public float of greater than $75 million), then its registered public accounting firm must also attest to and report on its internal controls over financial reporting as part of an integrated audit engagement. If a company has a material weakness in internal controls, the auditors must issue an adverse opinion on its internal control over financial reporting (ICFR).

Financial Disclosures.   The SEC added rules to require disclosure in quarterly and annual reports of material off-balance-sheet transactions, arrangements, obligations, and other relationships with related parties that may have a material current or future effect on financial condition and results of operations.

Additionally, the SEC issued rules covering non-GAAP financial information included in any periodic report, annual report, or press release. Key disclosures include:

- A numerical reconciliation to the most comparable GAAP metric
- Disclosure about the uses of the non-GAAP metric
- Discussion of changes in the non-GAAP metric

Such non-GAAP metrics are generally prohibited from inclusion in the financial statements

(f) QUALIFICATIONS AND INDEPENDENCE OF PUBLIC ACCOUNTANTS PRACTICING BEFORE THE SEC.   To qualify for practice before the SEC, the public accountant auditing the financial statements must be independent, in good standing in the profession, and entitled to practice under the laws of his or her place of residence or principal office (Rule 2-01 of Regulation S-X). The firm must be registered with the PCAOB.

Both the SEC and the PCAOB have independence rules that cover public accountants who audit or play a substantial role in the audit of a public company. The rules focus on relationships or other services that would be deemed to impair the independence of the registered public accounting firm. The rules prohibit certain nonaudit services and require permitted nonaudit services (including tax services) to be preapproved by the company's audit committee. The rules also require annual disclosure of the amount and types of fees paid to the public accounting firm and the audit committee's preapproval policies of those fees.

(g) SEC'S FOCUS ON ACCOUNTING FRAUD.   The SEC's mission is to protect investors. Accounting fraud is one of the areas of significant concern. SEC officials have noted two types of accounting fraud: cooked books and cute accounting. Cooking the books involves falsifying books and records either by creating or accelerating revenues or by deferring or concealing expenses. Cute accounting involves misapplying or stretching accounting principles and interpretations to obtain the desired, albeit distorted, financial picture. Both the accounting profession and corporate officials have been reminded by the SEC of their responsibilities to the public investor. More specifically:

- The SEC will carefully review Form 8-K reports to monitor changes in accountants. CPA firms should use caution when taking on new clients. A firm should review the work of the predecessor accountants to determine whether the change in accountants was the result of a company's refusing to comply with GAAP or violating federal securities laws. The SEC will take action against companies that shop for the most favorable accounting interpretations. The enforcement division will pursue not only these companies but also accounting firms that attempt to gain clients by disregarding GAAP.

- Accountants should treat with healthy skepticism any changes in accounting policies or individual transactions that increase revenues or reduce expenses.

- Accountants should avoid the tendency to rationalize otherwise questionable accounting positions. Firms should not take the view that "if it is not proscribed, it's permitted" but instead should use accounting procedures that follow both the letter and the spirit of SEC and FASB pronouncements.

- Companies have a duty to disclose adverse nonpublic information (e.g., loss of a major customer) in the management's discussion and analysis section of Form 10-K. Furthermore, independent accountants are obligated not to sign off on filings if significant information is missing.

The SEC is concerned with opinion shopping and requires companies and their former auditors to make certain disclosures upon a change in outside auditor. FRR 31 provides additional guidance as to these disclosures.

FRR 31 explains that

the term *disagreements* should be interpreted broadly, to include any difference of opinion on any matter of accounting principles or practices, financial statement disclosure, or auditing scope or procedures, which if not resolved to the former accountant's satisfaction would have caused it to refer to the subject matter of the disagreement in connection with its report.

It further explains that preliminary differences of opinion that are "based on incomplete facts" are not disagreements if the differences are resolved by obtaining more complete factual information.

When an independent accountant who was the principal accountant for the company or who audited a significant subsidiary and was expressly relied on by the principal accountant resigns declines to stand for reelection or is dismissed, the registrant must also disclose:

- Whether the former accountant resigned, declined to stand for reelection, or was dismissed, and the date of this action

- Whether there was an adverse opinion, disclaimer of opinion, or qualification or modification of opinion as to uncertainty, audit scope, or accounting principles issued by such accountant for either of the two most recent years, including a description of the nature of the opinion

- Whether the decision to change accountants was recommended by or approved by the audit committee or a similar committee, or by the board of directors in the absence of such special committee

Finally, the rules also require disclosure of certain "reportable events" during the two most recent fiscal years or any subsequent interim period preceding the resignation or dismissal of the accountant. "Reportable events" include the auditors having advised the registrant:

- That the internal controls necessary to develop reliable financial statements do not exist
- That information has come to the auditor's attention that led him or her to no longer be able to rely on management's representations, or that has made him or her unwilling to be associated with the financial statements
- Of his or her need to significantly expand the audit scope or of information having come to the auditor's attention during the last two fiscal years and any subsequent interim period that, if further investigated, may (a) materially impact the fairness or reliability of either a previously issued audit report or the underlying financial statements or the financial statements issued or to be issued for a subsequent period or (b) cause him or her to be unwilling to rely on management's representations or to be associated with the financial statements and because of the change in auditors, the auditor did not expand his or her scope or conduct a further investigation
- That information has come to the auditor's attention that what he or she has concluded materially impacts the fairness or reliability of either (a) a previously issued audit report or the underlying financial statements or (b) the financial statements relating to a subsequent period, and unless the matters are resolved to the auditor's satisfaction, the auditor would be prevented from rendering an unqualified report and, because of the change in auditors, the matter has not been resolved

Disagreements and reportable events are intended to include both oral and written communications to the registrant. Because these communications deal with sensitive areas that may impugn the integrity of management, they will have to be handled with extreme care on the part of all involved.

The time frame for reporting these changes is listed next.

- The Form 8-K reporting the change should be filed by the end of the fourth business day following the day the former auditor is dismissed or notifies its client of its resignation or decision not to stand for reelection.
- The letter from the former auditor should be filed by the registrant within two business days after it is received by the registrant.
- The registrant should request the former auditor to furnish its letter "as promptly as possible." To facilitate prompt responses, the rule requires the registrant to provide the former auditor with a copy of its report no later than the day the initial Form 8-K is filed with the SEC.
- The auditor who is aware that a required filing related to a change of accountants has not been made by the registrant should consider advising the registrant in writing of that reporting responsibility with a copy to the Commission.

In addition, the PCAOB has a rule requiring auditors to communicate auditor changes directly to the SEC. Under that rule, when a firm has resigned, declined to stand for reelection, or been dismissed, it should notify the former client within five business days that the auditor-client relationship has ceased and should simultaneously send a copy to the SEC.

(h) FOREIGN CORRUPT PRACTICES ACT.   The Foreign Corrupt Practices Act of 1977 (FCPA) deals with (1) payments to foreign officials and (2) internal accounting control.

(i) Payments to Foreign Officials.   The FCPA makes it illegal to offer anything of value to any foreign official, foreign political party, and so on (other than employees of foreign governments, etc., whose duties are ministerial or clerical), for the purpose of exerting influence in obtaining or retaining business. The prohibition against payments to foreign officials, as stated in this law, applies to all U.S. domestic concerns regardless of whether they are publicly or privately held. The FCPA may also apply to foreign subsidiaries of U.S. companies.

(ii) Internal Accounting Control.   The FCPA makes it illegal for companies subject to SEC jurisdiction to fail to:

- Keep books and records, in reasonable detail, that accurately and fairly reflect the transactions and disposition of the company's assets
- Devise and maintain a system of internal accounting controls that will provide reasonable assurance that:
  - Transactions are properly recorded in accordance with management's authorization.
  - Financial statements are prepared in conformity with GAAP and accountability for assets is maintained.
  - Access to company assets is permitted only with management's authorization.
  - The recorded assets are checked and differences reconciled at reasonable intervals.

Shortly after the FCPA became effective, the SEC issued Accounting Series Releases (ASRs) No. 242, which states:

> It is important that issuers subject to the new requirements review their accounting procedures, systems of internal accounting controls and business practices in order that they may take any actions necessary to comply with requirements contained in the Act.

To aid management in evaluating internal accounting control (which could be beneficial in judging whether a company complies with the accounting requirements of the FCPA), the AICPA formed a Special Advisory Committee on Internal Accounting Control. This committee issued a report that defines internal accounting control, develops related objectives (categorized by the committee as authorization, accounting, and asset safeguarding), and discusses what management should be doing with respect to an evaluation of these controls.

According to the committee's report, the internal accounting control environment should be a significant factor in management's assessment of the company's system. Along those lines, the report of the Special Advisory Committee on Internal Control (1979) states: "It is unlikely that management can have reasonable assurance that the broad objectives of internal accounting control are being met unless the company has an environment that establishes an appropriate level of control consciousness."

The role of top management and the board of directors in establishing an appropriate internal accounting control environment is significant. The report considers the factors that shape such an environment to include "creating an appropriate organizational structure, using sound management practices, establishing accountability for performance, and requiring adherence to appropriate standards for ethical behavior, including compliance with applicable laws and regulations."

A strong control environment may include, for example, clearly defined accounting policies and procedures, clearly established levels of responsibility and authority, periodic evaluations of employees to determine that their performance is consistent with their responsibilities, budgetary controls, and an effective internal audit function. A strong control environment will provide more assurance that the company's internal accounting control procedures are followed. A poor internal accounting control environment, however, could negate the effect of specific controls (e.g., employees may hesitate to challenge management override of control procedures).

After assessing the control environment, management should evaluate the internal accounting control system. There are several approaches to such an evaluation, depending, for example, on the organizational structure of the company and its type of business. The report uses a "cycle" approach in illustrating an evaluation of internal accounting control, although other approaches may be acceptable (e.g., by function or operating unit). Under the cycle approach, transactions are grouped into convenient cycles (e.g., revenues, expenditures, production or conversion, financing, and external financial reporting), and appropriate internal accounting control criteria are identified for each cycle. In addition, the existing control procedures and techniques used by the company to meet the related criteria should be evaluated.

Meeting internal accounting control criteria generally reduces the risk of material undetected errors and irregularities. Of course, there are inherent limitations to any system of internal accounting control. Even though internal accounting control procedures are performed and the related criteria are met, collusion or override can circumvent existing procedures. Even a strong system of internal accounting control can provide only reasonable assurance for the timely detection of errors or irregularities. However, nonachievement of criteria increases the likelihood that (1) transactions not authorized by management will occur, (2) transactions will not be properly recorded, and (3) assets will be subject to unauthorized access.

The FCPA's legislative history recognizes that the aggregate cost of specific internal controls should not exceed the expected benefits to be derived. Therefore, the report concludes that if it is determined that an internal accounting control criterion is not met, management should evaluate the "cost/benefit" considerations of modifying existing procedures or adding new ones. In determining the aggregate cost, consideration should be given to the direct and indirect dollar cost (e.g., additional personnel, new forms) and whether the new or modified procedure slows the decision-making process or has other deleterious effects on the company. To measure the expected benefit, management should evaluate the likelihood that an error or irregularity could result in a loss to the company or in a misstatement in its financial statements, and evaluate the extent of such loss or misstatement.

Because the system of internal accounting control depends on employees' performing their assigned duties, the report indicates that management should establish a program to obtain reasonable assurance that the controls continue to function properly. The nature of the monitoring program will vary from company to company and will depend on the company's size and organizational structure, the degree of managerial involvement in its day-to-day operations, and the complexity of its accounting system. Ordinarily, monitoring occurs through supervision, representations, audits, or other compliance tests, and so on.

(i) AUDIT COMMITTEES. The SEC, the New York Stock Exchange (NYSE) and the Nasdaq all have certain independence requirements for audit committee members of registrants or companies that list on the respective exchange. The SEC's rules require that audit committee members be members of the board of directors and generally not accept compensation from the registrant except for services as a board member and that they may not otherwise be an affiliated person of the registrant or a subsidiary. Directors who are members of current management or who serve the company in an advisory capacity, such as consultants or legal counsel, and relatives of executives are not considered independent directors. Former company executives who serve as directors can serve on the audit committee if, in the opinion of the board, that person will exercise independent judgment and will materially aid and assist the function of the committee. The SEC also requires registrants to disclose if the audit committee has a financial expert and if not, why it does not.

The NYSE and Nasdaq both require listed companies to have audit committees composed of at least three members meeting the independence criteria just noted. In addition, NYSE audit committee members must be financially literate (as defined in the NYSE rules), and Nasdaq audit committee members must be able to read and understand financial statements.

(j) CONTACT WITH SEC STAFF. Contact with the SEC Staff can be both formal and informal and can occur in various situations including:

- *Registration.* The SEC review of 1933 Act registration statements is described later. The company issuing the securities and its lawyers, underwriters, and accountants work closely with SEC Staff to produce a document that the SEC will not contend lacks full disclosure.
- *Filing Reviews.* A filing review is an SEC Staff review of a 1934 Act filing including annual reports, current reports and proxy statements and issuance of a comment letter.
- *Investigation.* The SEC Staff, typically from the enforcement division, can make an informal investigation when it believes securities laws have been violated. Such investigations may be prompted by market activity in a stock that is not justified by publicly available

information or by news accounts of possible wrongdoing, complaints from the investing public, references from stock exchanges and the National Association of Securities Dealers, or references from other law enforcement agencies. People do not have to assist the SEC Staff in its investigation and instead can force the Staff to proceed immediately to a formal investigation, authorized by the Commission when justified. The formal order of investigation will name the SEC Staff members who are authorized to issue subpoenas for the production of witnesses and documents.

- *Interpretation.* As a general rule, the U.S. legal system does not allow people to obtain interpretations of the law before an act is committed. Only through litigation can a person know whether a violation has occurred. However, administrative agencies often provide some exceptions to the rule.

A formal interpretation from the SEC is obtained by receiving a no-action letter. This communication is a SEC Staff promise not to recommend to the Commission that it take action if the facts submitted by the applicant and described in the letter are found to be accurate. The Commission has always honored its Staff's no-action letters. Typical no-action letters involve exemption from 1933 Act registration and refusals by corporations to include a stockholder proposal in the company's proxy material.

The SEC will respond to informal questions related to interpretations of rules and the like. In certain circumstances, the Staff will respond to questions without requiring disclosures of the name of the registrant. Generally, these "no-name" inquiries are on more general questions. In fact-specific questions, the Staff will often request a written submission regarding the facts and circumstances and will request that the name of the registrant be disclosed in the submission. The Staff has a specific protocol it suggests that registrants use if they wish to submit an issue to the SEC Staff members to obtain their views. These issues typically cover interpretations of which financial statements need to be filed by a registrant and for what periods as well as unique or unclear accounting interpretations.

(k) CURRENT REFERENCE SOURCES.   To keep abreast of SEC developments, accountants and others mainly consult these publications:

- *The Federal Securities Law Reporter,* published by Commerce Clearing House (New York), is a loose-leaf service containing all federal securities laws, SEC rules, forms, interpretations and decisions, and court decisions on securities matters.
- The *SEC News Digest* is a daily summary of important SEC developments it is available on the SEC's Web site.
- The SEC's Web site, *www.sec.gov*, provides the full extent of all SEC releases and of speeches made by members of the Commission and its Staff.

5.2 SECURITIES ACT OF 1933

(a) TRANSACTIONS COVERED.   The preamble to the 1933 Act states that the Act is intended "to provide full and fair disclosure of the character of securities sold in interstate and foreign commerce and through the mails, and to prevent frauds in the sale thereof, and for other purposes."

The 1933 Act does not cover the most common sale of securities: sales of issued and outstanding securities. Those transactions, on a stock exchange, in the over-the-counter (OTC) market or otherwise, are regulated by the 1934 Act. The 1933 Act covers only the original sale of the security by the issuer, along with sales by persons in control of an issuer.

There are two primary aspects to the 1933 Act regulation of securities offerings:

1. The sale must be registered with the SEC, and purchasers must be furnished with much of the information contained in the registration statement in the form of a prospectus (1933 Act, Sections 5, 6).

2. Purchasers of the securities who suffer losses within a specified time period may recover their losses if the registration statement contained a materially misleading statement (1933 Act, Section 11). Recovery can be obtained from the issuer. However, the proceeds from the sale may have been squandered; therefore, recovery is permitted from directors, underwriters, and any expert, such as an accountant, if the material misrepresentation was in the audited financial statements. All defendants, other than the issuer, may avoid liability by proving their due diligence in reviewing the registration statement.

(b) AUDITORS' RESPONSIBILITIES.   As to the audited financial statements, auditors must prove that they had,

> after reasonable investigation, reasonable ground to believe, and did believe, at the time . . . the registration statement became effective, that the statements [in the audited financial statements] were true and that there was no omission to state a material fact required to be stated therein or necessary to make the statements therein not misleading. [1933 Act, § 11(b)(3)]

Section 11(c) of the Act states: "The standard of reasonableness shall be that required of a prudent man in the management of his own property."

The *BarChris* case—*Escott v. BarChris Construction Corp.*, 283 F. Supp. 643, U.S. District Court, Southern District of New York, 1968—was the first, and remains the most important, case regarding liability for a misleading 1933 Act registration statement. A major accounting firm was among the defendants found not to have fulfilled due diligence requirements. The court stated: "Accountants should not be held to a standard higher than that recognized in their profession." However, the court relied heavily on the failure of the firm to follow its own guidelines for reviewing events since the date of the statements for the purpose of ascertaining whether the audited financial statements were misleading at the time the registration statement became effective. The complete text of the *BarChris* case appears in *Regulating Transactions in Securities*.[1]

(c) MATERIALITY.   When the Securities Acts require plaintiffs to prove that information was false, untrue, or misleading, the plaintiffs must also show that the information was material to investors. In general, neither the statutes nor the SEC's rules and regulations offer quantitative tests or useful verbal descriptions of the meaning of *materiality*. For example, as to the information required to be filed in a 1933 Act registration statement, information is material if "an average prudent investor ought reasonably to be informed [of it]" (1933 Act, Rule 405).

Many cases involve attempts to further define materiality. In the *BarChris* case, the judge used the test of "a fact which if it had been correctly stated or disclosed would have deterred or tended to deter the average prudent investor from purchasing the securities in question." Starting in the mid-1970s, some courts admitted that they would have to apply materiality standards in a flexible manner, reflecting the context in which the misleading statement was made (e.g., a 1933 Act registration statement, a 1934 Act registration statement or periodic report, a proxy statement, a case involving insider trading or tipping, etc.).

In SAB No. 99, *Materiality* (August 12, 1999), the SEC Staff states that accountants and independent auditors should not rely exclusively on quantitative benchmarks to determine materiality in preparing or auditing financial statements. Misstatements are not immaterial simply because they fall beneath a numerical threshold.

(i) Assessing Materiality.   A company or its independent auditor becomes aware that combined misstatements or omissions overstate net income 4 percent and earnings per share $0.02 (4 percent). No item in the consolidated financial statements is misstated by more than 5 percent, nor are there any particularly egregious circumstances, such as self-dealing or misappropriation. Management and the independent auditor conclude that the accounting is permissible.

---

[1] J.L.Wiesen. *Regulating Transactions in Securities* (St. Paul, MN: West Publishing Co.: 1975).

The Staff concludes that the materiality of items may not be determined based simply on whether they fall beneath any percentage threshold set by management or the independent auditor. The Staff does not object to the use of a percentage threshold as an initial step in determining materiality. But that is only the beginning. A full analysis of relevant conditions is required. Materiality concerns the significance of an item to users of financial statements. A matter is material if it is substantially likely that a reasonable person would consider it important. The context of the surrounding circumstances or the total mix of information requires assessment. Both quantitative and qualitative factors are involved. The FASB, the AICPA auditing literature, and the U.S. Supreme Court have emphasized these matters concerning materiality.

The SEC Staff thus believes that there are numerous circumstances in which misstatements below 5 percent could be material and that qualitative factors could cause quantitatively small misstatements to be material. Examples of such factors are presented next.

- Whether the misstatement is based on a precise measurement or on an estimate and the degree of imprecision inherent in the estimate. A misstatement of a given amount in the former case is more likely to be material than in the latter case.
- Whether the misstatement masks a change in earnings trends or other trends.
- Whether the misstatement hides a failure to meet analysts' consensus expectations for the company.
- Whether the misstatement changes a loss into income or vice versa.
- Whether the misstatement affects the company's compliance with regulatory requirements.
- Whether the misstatement affects the company's compliance with contractual requirements.
- Whether the misstatement increases management's compensation, for example, by satisfying requirements for the award of incentive compensation.

The potential market reaction to a misstatement is too blunt an instrument to be used by itself in determining its materiality. However, the demonstrated volatility of the price of a company's securities in response to certain kinds of disclosures may provide guidance as to whether investors consider quantitatively small misstatements material. Expectations based, for example, on a past pattern of market performance that a known misstatement may cause a significant positive or negative market reaction should be considered in determining the materiality of the item.

The intent of management may provide significant evidence of materiality, particularly if management has intentionally misstated items to manage reported earnings, presumably believing that the amounts and trends that result would be significant to users of the financial statements. The SEC Staff believes that investors generally would consider significant a management practice to overstate or understate earnings just short of a percentage threshold to manage earnings and an accounting practice that, in essence, made all earnings amounts subject to a management-directed margin of misstatement.

The location of an item may affect its materiality. For example, a misstatement of the revenue and operating profit of a relatively small segment represented by management to be important to future profitability is more likely to be material to investors than a misstatement of the same percentage of a routine segment.

(ii) Aggregating and Netting Misstatements.   In determining the effects on the financial statements taken as a whole, each misstatement should be considered separately, and the aggregate effect should also be considered. The effects on individual line item amounts, subtotals, and totals should be considered. Misstatements of material amounts, such as of revenue, are not cured by misstatements of other amounts, such as of expenses. In considering the effect of misstatements on subtotals or totals, care should be taken in offsetting a misstatement of an amount based on an estimate and an amount capable of precise measurement.

SAB No. 108, *Considering the Effects of Prior Year Misstatements when Quantifying Misstatements in Current Year Financial Statements,* clarifies that management and auditors also need to consider the impact of potential misstatements on both a rollover and an iron curtain basis.

In other words, consideration needs to be given to the impact of correcting the cumulative error in the balance sheet as well as the current-year income statement impact. If the misstatement to the current-year income statement due to correcting the cumulative error in the balance sheet is material, then prior-year financial statements may need to be amended.

(iii) Intentional Immaterial Misstatements. Management may try to manage earnings by intentionally adjusting various financial statement items in a manner not in conformity with GAAP. The adjustments are not material separately or in the aggregate.

The SEC Staff concludes that in certain circumstances, intentional immaterial misstatements are unlawful. The Staff believes that the FASB's statement in each of its Statements of Standards that it need not be applied to immaterial items does not cover intentional misstatements. Sections 13(b)(2)–(7) of the Exchange Act require registrants to make and keep books, records, and accounts that, in reasonable detail, accurately and fairly reflect the transactions and dispositions of the assets of the registrant and must maintain internal accounting controls sufficient to provide reasonable assurances that, among other things, transactions are recorded as necessary to permit the preparation of financial statements in conformity with GAAP. In this context, the terms *reasonable assurance* and *reasonable detail* are not based on materiality but on the level of detail and degree of assurance that would satisfy prudent officials in the conduct of their own affairs. Reasonableness in this context is not solely based on the significance of the item to investors. It reflects instead a judgment as to whether an issuer's failure to correct a known misstatement implicates the purposes underlying the accounting provisions of Sections 13(b)(2)–(7) of the Exchange Act. Also, U.S. Code Sections 78 m(4) and (5) provide that criminal liability may be imposed if a person knowingly fails to implement a system of internal accounting controls or knowingly falsifies books, records, or accounts. These factors should be considered in assessing whether a misstatement results in a violation of a registrant's duty to keep books and records that are accurate in reasonable detail:

- It is reasonable to treat misstatements that are clearly inconsequential differently from more significant ones.
- It is likely never reasonable to record or not to correct known misstatements in an ongoing senior management effort to manage earnings.
- Small misstatements need not be corrected if it would involve major expenditures. But not correcting any misstatement at little cost is not reasonable.
- Not correcting an item that agrees with one of two or more reasonable interpretations of authoritative accounting guidance may be reasonable. However, if there is little ground for reasonable disagreement, the case for not correcting a misstatement is correspondingly weaker.

An independent auditor who discovers an illegal act as defined by Section 10A(b) of the Exchange Act, regardless of whether it is perceived to materially affect the financial statements being audited irrespective of netting, must, unless it is clearly inconsequential, among other things, inform the appropriate level of management and be sure that the audit committee is adequately informed. The independent auditor may also have to reevaluate the degree of audit risk in the engagement; determine whether to revise the nature, timing, and extent of audit procedures; and consider whether to resign. The intentional misstatement may also suggest to the independent auditor the existence of reportable conditions or material weaknesses in internal accounting control designed to detect and deter improper financial reporting or a lax tone set by top management. The independent auditor must report such conditions to the audit committee.

If the independent auditor determines that the company or the board of directors has failed to take remedial action, then the auditor may need to report directly to the SEC.

(d) SMALLER REPORTING COMPANIES. During 2007, the SEC acted on the 2006 recommendations of its Advisory Committee on Smaller Public Companies by finalizing rules that extended reporting relief to a category of registrants defined as "smaller reporting companies." Smaller reporting companies are defined as companies with less than $75 million of public float. These rules eliminated the

Topic	Difference
Annual periods to be presented	Article 8 requires only two years of financial statements
Financial statements of acquired businesses	Under Article 8, no more than two years of financial statements are required
Financial statement disclosures	Most of the disclosures required by Reg. S-X that exceed the requirements of GAAP are not required.
Separate financial statement of significant equity investees	Not required
Financial statements schedules	Not required

Exhibit 5.1   Differences Between General Regulation S-X and Article 8 of Regulation S-X Requirements

Topic	Difference
Description of business	Registration statements need to discuss the business historical development for only three years, instead of five
Selected financial data	Not required
Selected quarterly financial information	Not required
Risk factors	Not required
Performance graph	Not required
Table of contractual obligations	Not required
Market risk disclosures	Not required
Executive compensation	Specific disclosures and the number or individuals covered by certain disclosures is less comprehensive than for regular filers

Exhibit 5.2   Principal Differences Between General Regulation S-K Requirements and Those for Smaller Reporting Companies

former category of filers defined as "small business issuers" and the related small business forms, and moved the financial and nonfinancial reporting requirements for smaller reporting companies from Regulation S-B into Regulation S-X and Regulation S-K, respectively

Existing registrants measure their market capitalization as of the end of their most recent fiscal second quarter. For a company filing an IPO or an initial registration statement, the public float is calculated as of a date within 30 days of the filing date and is determined based on the number of shares held by nonaffiliates before the offering and the estimated IPO price. Registrants with no public float (e.g., only publicly issued debt) can be considered as smaller reporting companies if its annual revenue is less than $50 million.

Registrants qualifying as a smaller reporting company may elect on an item-by-item basis whether to comply with the regular filer rules or the smaller reporting company rules. Exhibits 5.1 and 5.2 identify some important differences in the rules for smaller public companies.

(e) EXEMPTIONS FROM REGISTRATION.   This section discusses the exemptions from the registration process and the simplified filings available to a company contemplating an offering under the 1933 Act.

The 1933 Act gives to the SEC the authority to establish rules for exempting securities from registration, if offered in small issues or if offered to a limited number of investors. Rules 501 through 509 of the 1933 Act, referred to as *Regulation D,* cover limited offerings and sales of securities, whereas Rules 251 through 263, called *Regulation A,* cover the small offering exemptions.

(i) Regulation D.   Regulation D was adopted in 1982 to allow small businesses to raise capital without the burdens imposed by the registration process.

The regulation comprises Rules 501 to 508. Rules 501 to 503 contain definitions, terms, and conditions that generally apply throughout the regulation. Rules 504 to 506 provide the three exemptions from registration under Regulation D:

- Rule 504 relates to offerings where the aggregate sales price does not exceed $1 million in a 12-month period. This exemption is not available to companies subject to the 1934 Act reporting requirements or to an investment company registered under the Investment Company Act of 1940 or certain development-stage companies.
- Rule 505 relates to offerings up to $5 million in a 12-month period to an unlimited number of "accredited" investors (defined later) and to a limit of 35 other purchasers not meeting the accredited investor definition. This exemption is not available to registered investment companies.
- Rule 506 permits offerings, without regard to the dollar amount, to no more than 35 purchasers meeting certain sophistication standards and an unlimited number of accredited investors. This exemption requires, among other things, that the issuer reasonably believe that the nonaccredited purchaser, or representative, has adequate knowledge and experience in finance and business to evaluate the merits and risks of the securities offered. This rule has no qualifications as to the issuer.
- Rule 507 addresses the disqualifying provision relating to exceptions under Rules 504, 505, and 506.
- Rule 508 relates to the insignificant deviations from a term, condition, or requirement of Regulation D.

Accredited Investor.   An accredited investor includes institutions or individuals who come within, or whom the issuer reasonably believes come within, any of these nine categories:

1. An institutional investor, such as a bank, insurance company, or an investment company registered under the Investment Company Act of 1940
2. A private business development company, as defined in the Investment Advisers Act of 1940
3. An employee benefit plan qualifying under the Employee Retirement Income Security Act (ERISA) with total assets over $5 million, if the plan's investment decisions are made by a bank, insurance company, or registered investment adviser
4. A tax-exempt organization under the Internal Revenue Code with total assets in excess of $5 million
5. Any director, executive officer, or general partner of the issuer
6. Any trust, with total assets in excess of $5 million, not formed for the specific purpose of acquiring the securities offered whose purchase is directed by a sophisticated person
7. A person whose individual net worth or joint net worth with spouse at the time of the purchase exceeds $1 million
8. A person whose individual income for each of the two most recent years is in excess of $200,000 or income jointly with that person's spouse in excess of $300,000 and reasonably expects income in excess of $200,000 (or jointly $300,000) in the current year
9. Any entity in which all the equity owners are accredited investors

Disclosure Requirements.   The disclosure requirements of Regulation D are based on the nature of the issuer and the size of the offering depending on these three items:

1. An issuer offering securities under Rule 504 and 504a or to only accredited investors is not required to furnish disclosures.
2. Companies not subject to the 1934 Act reporting requirement must furnish:
   - For offerings up to $2 million, the same kind of information as would be required in Part II of Form 1-A and Article 8 of Regulation S-X, except that the issuer's balance sheet, which must be dated within 120 days of the start of the offering, must be audited.
   - For offerings up to $7.5 million, the same information required for smaller reporting companies filing an S-1. Generally, financial statements for the two latest years are required.

If audited financial statements cannot be obtained without reasonable effort and expense, then only the balance sheet need be audited, which must be dated within 120 days.

○ For offerings over $7.5 million, the same information specified in the form a registrant would qualify to use that would be required in a full registration statement. If audited financial statements cannot be obtained without reasonable effort and expense, then only the balance sheet need be audited, which must be dated within 120 days.

Limited partnerships may furnish income tax basis financial statements if their preparation in conformity with GAAP would be unduly burdensome or costly.

3. Companies subject to the 1934 Act reporting requirements are required to furnish:

○ Either: The latest annual stockholders' report, related proxy statement and, if requested, Form 10-K, *or* the information (but not the Form itself) contained in the most recent Form 10-K or registration statement on Form S-1 or Form 10.

○ Most recent interim filings.

Conditions to Be Met.   In addition to the qualifications to be met by issuers under Rules 504 and 505, Regulation D includes these limitations and conditions:

• Except as provided in Rule 504, no form of general solicitation or general advertising can be used by the issuer or any person acting on its behalf to offer the securities. The issuer or the person acting on its behalf (e.g., an underwriter) must have a preexisting relationship with the offeree.

• Except as provided in Rule 504, securities sold under Regulation D will be "restricted" securities with limited transferability. Each stock certificate issued should include a legend stating the security is restricted as to transferability.

(ii) Regulation A.   Regulation A allows a company to publicly offer its securities without registration under the 1933 Act. Instead, an offering statement (Form 1-A) is filed and qualified with the SEC. Two principal attractions of Regulation A are that only two years of financial statements are necessary, and the financial statements may be unaudited if audited information is not already available. Further, the completion of a Regulation A offering does not automatically subject the issuer to 1934 Act reporting. The limit for securities offerings under Regulation A is $5 million in any 12-month period (of which $1.5 million can be sales by selling security holders). Issuers are allowed to test the waters before filing the offering statement with the SEC. Also, Form 1-A allows the optional use of a user-friendly question-and-answer form (the Small Company Offering Registration (SCOR) form) used by several states for the registration of Regulation D offerings. Under the rules for prefiling communications, issuers can solicit indications of interest through the distribution or publication of preliminary materials. In general, the content of these materials is unregulated, except that it is limited to factual information. However, the preliminary materials must include a brief general description of the company's business and products, the business experience of the chief executive officer, and a statement that no money is being solicited or accepted until the qualification and delivery of the offering circular. Any solicitation of interest material must be filed with the SEC on the date it is first used, and oral communications to gauge investor interest are permitted once the solicitation of interest document is filed. However, the rules also require that the use of the solicitation statement must be discontinued once the preliminary offering statement has been filed, and they call for a 20-day lapse between the last use of the solicitation statement and the first sale of any securities.

(iii) Other Exemptions.   Other exemptions from the registration requirement are:

• Offerings restricted to residents of the state in which the issuer is organized and does business, provided the issuer has at least 80 percent of its revenue and assets within the state and at least 80 percent of the net proceeds of the offering are used within the state (Rule 147)

- Securities of some governmental agencies
- Offerings of small business investment companies (Regulation E)

(f) "GOING PRIVATE" TRANSACTIONS.   Companies may repurchase their shares from the public and, in turn, become privately held. When shares are held by fewer than 300 shareholders or fewer than 500 shareholders if there are minimal assets and the company no longer lists on a national exchange, a company can choose to cease filing and go private. If the registrant is engaging in a transaction to go private, SEC Rule 13e-3, which prohibits going private transactions that are fraudulent, deceptive, or manipulative may apply. Under the rule, companies are required to state whether the transaction is fair to stockholders unaffiliated with management and to provide a detailed discussion of the material factors on which that belief is based. Among the factors that should be addressed are: (1) the purpose of the transaction and what other alternatives were considered; and (2) whether the consideration offered to unaffiliated stockholders constitutes fair value in relation to current and historical market prices, net book value, going concern value, liquidation value, purchase price in previous purchases, and any report, opinion, or appraisal obtained on the fairness of the consideration.

Rule 13e-4, relating to an issuer's tender offer for its own securities, also imposes stringent disclosure requirements and other responsibilities on registrants. The rule requires that:

1. An issuer's tender offer remain open for at least 20 business days.
2. A shareholder tendering stock have the right to withdraw within the first 15 business days or after 40 business days following the announcement if the company has not acted on its offer.
3. Officers, directors, and major shareholders disclose all their stock transactions during the 40 business days preceding the purchase offer.
4. An issuer accept tendered securities on a pro rata basis if a greater number of securities is tendered than the issuer is obliged to accept within 20 days of an offer.

(g) INITIAL FILINGS.   The information requirements for initial and other registration statements and annual filings are very similar and are based on an integrated disclosure system. The rules applicable to Form 10-K require much of the same financial statement information required in a registration statement. However, there are some unique aspects of initial filings. Initial filings are most commonly filed on Form S-1, but other forms may be used in specific circumstances. Form S-3, however, is available only to an existing registrant and is considered an abbreviated form.

The most commonly used forms for registration under the 1933 Act are listed next.

S-1	General form to be used when no other form is specifically prescribed. Disclosures are similar to those required for Form 10-K.
S-3	For companies that have been reporting to the SEC for 12 or more months and meet a "float" test ($75 million or more of voting and nonvoting stock held by nonaffiliates). Form S-3 allows maximum incorporation by reference and requires the least disclosure in the prospectus. Form S-3 may also be used for certain other types of transactions without meeting the float test.
S-4	For securities to be issued in certain business combinations and that are to be redistributed to the public.
S-6	For unit investment trusts registered under the Investment Company Act of 1940 on Form N-8B-2.
S-8	For securities to be offered to employees under certain stock option, stock purchase, or similar plans.
S-11	For registration of securities issued by certain real estate investment trusts and by companies whose primary business is acquiring and holding real estate.
F-1, F-3, and F-4	Registration of the securities of certain foreign private issuers including certain forms specifically for Canadian issuers.

The SEC requires issuers to write the cover page, summary, and risk factors section of prospectuses in plain English. The SEC also gives guidance to issuers of prospectuses on how to make the entire prospectus clear, concise, and understandable. Further, it issued *A Plain English Handbook: How to Create Clear SEC Disclosure Documents,* (available at *www.sec.gov/pdf/handbook.pdf* which provides techniques and tips on how to create plain-English disclosure documents.

The organization, language, and design of the covered sections of the prospectus should conform to plain-English principles and be easy to read. Qualities of writing involved in plain English include short sentences; definite, concrete, everyday language; the active voice; tabular presentation or bullet lists for complex information whenever possible; no legal jargon or highly technical business terms; and no multiple negatives. The sections should be designed to make them inviting to the readers. The text should be formatted and the document designed to highlight information important to investors.

The SEC requires registrants to use these techniques in writing prospectuses:

- Sections, paragraphs, and sentences must be clear and concise.
- Short explanatory sentences and bullet lists should be used whenever possible.
- Terms used should ordinarily be made understandable in context. Terms should be defined in glossaries only if they cannot be made understandable in context and if defining the terms that way facilitates understanding of the disclosure.
- Legal and highly technical business terminology should be avoided.

The SEC requires registrants to avoid these conventions:

- Legalistic or overly complex presentations that cloud the substance of the disclosure
- Vague boilerplate explanations readily subject to differing interpretations
- Complex information taken from legal documents without clear and concise explanation
- Repetition that adds to the length of the prospectus without adding to the quality of the information

The goal of the guidance on how to make the entire prospectus clear, concise, and understandable is to rid the entire prospectus of legalese and repetition so that information important to investors is not blurred.

The SEC Staff assists registrants in complying with the rule.

5.3 SECURITIES EXCHANGE ACT OF 1934

(a) SCOPE OF THE ACT.   The 1934 Act has six principal parts:

1. Creation and operation of the SEC
2. Regulation of stock exchanges and the OTC market
3. Regulation of brokers and dealers
4. Corporate disclosure requirements
5. Regulation of corporate managers, large stockholders, and preparers of filed statements
6. Prohibition against fraud in securities transactions

(b) CORPORATE DISCLOSURE REQUIREMENTS

(i) Registration of Securities.   Unlike the registration of securities transactions under the 1933 Act, under the 1934 Act registration is a one-time event for an issue of securities.

Issuers of securities registered on a national securities exchange (listed securities), and companies that have assets exceeding $1 million and 500 or more shareholders of record, must register by filing Form 10. The information required in Form 10 is very similar to the information required in an annual report, which is discussed later. This form requires 16 items of information:

   1. Business

  1A. Risk Factors

   2. Financial information

   3. Properties

   4. Security ownership of certain beneficial owners and management

   5. Directors and executive officers

   6. Executive compensation

   7. Certain relationships any related transactions

   8. Legal proceedings

   9. Market price of and dividends on the registrants' common equity and related stockholder matters

  10. Recent sales of unregistered securities

  11. Description of registrants' securities to be registered

  12. Indemnification of directors and officers

  13. Financial statements and supplementary data

  14. Changes in and disagreements with accountants on accounting and financial disclosure

  15. Financial statements and exhibits

(ii) Periodic Reports.   Registrants under the 1934 Act (as defined earlier), or any issuer that ever sold securities pursuant to an effective 1933 Act registration statement and has 300 or more shareholders of record, must file periodic reports with the Commission. Principally, these reports are Form 10-K (an annual report), Form 10-Q (a quarterly report), and Form 8-K (current report).

These reporting requirements may be eliminated for companies with equity securities registered under Section 12(b) or 12(g) of the 1934 Act if:

- The number of holders of record of a class of security decreases at any time to less than 300 (and the company has filed at least one Form 10-K)
- The company certifies that it had fewer than 500 holders of record *and* on the last day of each of the last three fiscal years the total assets have not exceeded $10 million (and the company has filed at least three Form 10-Ks since its most recent registered securities offering)

For companies with a class of security registered under the 1933 Act—that is, not Section 12(b) or 12(g) companies—these reporting requirements, as required solely by Section 15(d) of the 1934 Act, may be suspended if:

- Ownership falls below 300 persons at the *beginning* of a fiscal year and a 1933 Act filing does not become effective during that year (a company whose securities were registered with the SEC on or before August 20, 1964, may discontinue filing if the value of the outstanding securities of the registered class falls below $1 million, even though there are at least 300 holders of record); or
- The company certifies that it had fewer than 500 holders of record and, on the last day of each of its last three fiscal years, its total assets have not exceeded $10 million *and* a 1933 Act filing does not become effective during that year.

A company that desires an exemption from periodic reporting should file Form 15 with the SEC.

Exchange Act Rule 12b-15 covers the procedures for amending previous Exchange Act filings:

1. Registrants are required to make amendments under cover of the form being amended. The fact that the filing is an amendment will be designated by adding the letter "A" after the form title (e.g., Form 10-K/A).

2. Amendments are required to set forth the complete text of each item amended rather than only revised words or lines.

5.4 FORM 10-K AND REGULATIONS S-X AND S-K

Form 10-K is the annual report required to be filed by companies whose securities are registered with the SEC. The due date of the filing varies based on the classification of the registrant as a smaller reporting company, nonaccelerated filer, accelerated filer, and large accelerated filer. Annual reports of smaller reporting companies and nonaccelerated filers are due 90 days after the end of the registrant's fiscal year; accelerated filers' annual reports are due 75 days after the end of the registrant's fiscal year; and large accelerated filers' annual reports are due 60 days after their fiscal year-end.

The filings are reviewed by the Division of Corporation Finance. As indicated in Subsection 5.1(c)(iii), the SEC Staff may review Form 10-K on a selective basis after the filing date. However, the filings that are reviewed are subjected to close scrutiny.

The SEC issues a set of instructions concerning the preparation of Form 10-K. Form 10-K is prepared using Regulation S-X, which prescribes requirements for the form, content, and periods of financial statements and for the accountant's reports, and Regulation S-K, which prescribes the other disclosure requirements.

The Form 10-K text (as distinguished from financial statements and related notes) generally is prepared by the company with assistance, if necessary, from the attorneys.

The accountant should read the entire Form 10-K text for the omission of pertinent information in the financial statements and to avoid inconsistencies between the financial statements and the text. Also, the accountant may become aware of information in the text that he or she believes to be misleading (see Statement of Accounting Standards No. 8, *Other Information in Documents Containing Audited Financial Statements*).

Form 10-K and related documents must be submitted electronically via the EDGAR system.

(a) REGULATION S-X.   The form and content of and requirements for financial statements included in filings with the SEC are set forth in Regulation S-X. Regulation S-X rules, in general, are consistent with GAAP but contain certain additional disclosure items not provided for by GAAP, as discussed later.

Regulation S-X is organized into 13 articles:

- *Article 1—Application of Regulation S-X.* Contains certain definitions that are used throughout Regulation S-X.
- *Article 2—Qualifications and Reports of Accountants.* Contains the SEC rules on the qualification and independence of accountants and the requirements for accountants' reports.
- *Article 3—General Instructions as to Financial Statements.* Contains the instructions as to the various types of financial statements (e.g., registrant, businesses acquired or to be acquired, significant unconsolidated subsidiaries) required to be filed, and the periods to be covered.
- *Article 3A—Consolidated and Combined Financial Statements.* Governs the preparation of consolidated or combined financial statements by a registrant.

- *Article 4—Rules of General Application.* Contains certain disclosure requirements not provided for by GAAP and also contains accounting rules for registrants engaged in oil- and gas-producing activities.
- *Article 5—Commercial and Industrial Companies.* Contains the instructions regarding the contents of and disclosures for the balance sheet and income statement line items for commercial and industrial companies as well as the requirements for financial statement schedules.
- *Articles 6 to 9.* Contain financial statement and schedule instructions, in a manner similar to Article 5, for certain special types of entities as listed:

Article 6	Registered Investment Companies
Article 6A	Employee Stock Purchase, Savings, and Similar Plans
Article 7	Insurance Companies
Article 9	Bank Holding Companies

Note that Article 8 on committees issuing certificates of deposit was removed in 1985.

- *Article 10—Interim Financial Statements.* Contains instructions as to the form and content of the interim financial statements required by Article 3 and by the quarterly report on Form 10-Q.
- *Article 11—Pro Forma Financial Information.* Contains presentation and preparation requirements for pro forma financial statements and a financial forecast filed in lieu of a pro forma statement of income.
- *Article 12—Form and Content of Schedules.* Sets out the detailed requirements for the various financial statement schedules required by Articles 5, 6, 6A, 7, and 9.

(b) ACCOUNTANTS' REPORTS.   The form and content of accountants' reports are prescribed by Rule 2-02 of Regulation S-X.

In those situations where other independent accountants have audited the financial statements of any branch or consolidated subsidiary of the registrant, Rule 2-05 of Regulation S-X sets forth the reporting requirements in addition to the requirements set forth in the PCAOB's audit standards. (This section is covered by the interim standards adopted by the PCAOB.) Where part of an audit is made by an independent accountant other than the principal accountant and his or her report is referred to by the principal accountant, or when the prior period's financial statements are audited by a predecessor accountant, the separate report of the other accountant must be included in the filing. However, such separate reports are not required to be included in annual reports to stockholders.

The SEC generally will not accept opinions that are qualified for scope or fairness of presentation. The SEC will reject opinions that contain an explanatory paragraph that addresses the uncertainty of the registrant's ability to recover its investment in specific assets, for example, a significant receivable, an investment security or interest, or certain deferred costs. Since GAAP require such assets to be stated not in excess of their net recoverable amount, the SEC Staff views such modifications as indicative of a scope of limitation (i.e., the auditor was unable to determine that the asset was stated at or below net recoverable value).

However, the SEC will accept an audit report that contains a going-concern paragraph if the filing contains full and fair disclosure as to the registrant's financial difficulties and the plans to overcome them. Also, an audit report with a fourth explanatory paragraph describing an accounting change is acceptable.

Any filings made via EDGAR include a typed signature of the accountant. The registrant is required to keep a manually signed copy of the accountant's report in its files for five years after the filing of the related document.

(c) GENERAL FINANCIAL STATEMENT REQUIREMENTS. Article 3 of Regulation S-X establishes uniform instructions governing the periods to be covered for financial statements included in most registration statements and reporting forms filed with the SEC. These are:

- Audited balance sheets as of the end of the last two fiscal years
- Audited statements of income, comprehensive income, stockholders' equity, and cash flows for each of the last three fiscal years (the same financial statements are required in annual reports to stockholders furnished pursuant to Section 14a-3 of the proxy rules [Regulation 14A])

Additionally, for 1933 Act filings, Article 3, in general, requires in specified circumstances unaudited interim financial statements for a current period along with financial statements for the comparable period of the prior year. It also allows audited statements of income, comprehensive income, stockholders' equity, and cash flows for a nine-month period to substitute for one of the required fiscal year periods in certain specified circumstances or when permitted by the SEC Staff.

Article 3 codifies the Staff position that 1933 Act filings by companies that have not yet completed their first fiscal year must include audited financial statements as of a date within 135 days of the date of the filing.

(d) CONSOLIDATED FINANCIAL STATEMENTS. Rule 3A-02 requires a registrant to file consolidated financial statements that clearly exhibit the financial position and results of operations of the registrant and its subsidiaries. A brief description of the principles followed in consolidating the financial statements and in determining the entities included in consolidation is required to be disclosed in the notes to the financial statements. If there has been a change in the entities included in the consolidation or in their fiscal year-ends, such changes should also be disclosed.

The latest year of consolidated subsidiaries must be within 93 days of the registrant's fiscal year-end. If there are differences in year-end, the registrant must disclose the closing date of the subsidiary and the effect of intervening events that materially affect the financial position or results of operation.

(e) REGULATION S-X MATERIALITY TESTS. Some of the additional disclosures required by Rules 5-02 and 5-03 of Regulation S-X, based on stated levels of materiality, are summarized next. These disclosures may be made either on the face of the financial statements or in a note.

- *Notes receivable.* Show separately if amount represents more than 10 percent of aggregate receivables.
- *Other current assets and other assets.* State separately any amount in excess of 5 percent of total current assets and total assets, respectively.
- *Other current liabilities and other liabilities.* State separately any amount in excess of 5 percent of total current liabilities and total liabilities, respectively.
- *Net sales and gross revenues.* State separately each component representing 10 percent of total sales and revenues.

(f) CHRONOLOGICAL ORDER AND FOOTNOTE REFERENCING. The SEC has no preference as to the chronological order (i.e., left to right or right to left) used in presenting the financial statements. However, the same order must be used consistently throughout the filing, including numerical data in narrative sections.

The financial statements are not required to be referenced to applicable notes unless it is appropriate for an effective presentation.

(g) ADDITIONAL DISCLOSURES REQUIRED BY REGULATION S-X. Regulation S-X requires certain significant disclosures to the financial statements not required by GAAP. A summary of the most common additional requirements (exclusive of those relating to specialized industries) is presented next. However, if amounts involved are immaterial, disclosures may be omitted.

- *Assets subject to lien (Rule 4-08(b)).* The nature and approximate amount of assets mortgaged, pledged, or subject to liens and an identification of the related obligation.

- *Restrictions on the payment of dividends (Rule 4-08(e)).* A description of the most restrictive limit on the payment of dividends by the registrant and the amount of retained earnings or net income restricted or free of restrictions. Additionally, the amount of consolidated retained earnings representing the undistributed earnings of 50-percent-or-less-owned equity method investees must be disclosed. As discussed in more detail later in this section, disclosure may also be required of restrictions on the ability of subsidiaries to transfer funds to the parent, and in some cases separate parent-company-only financial information may be required. The disclosure requirements are based on specified materiality tests.

- *Financial information of unconsolidated subsidiaries and 50-percent-or-less-owned equity method investees (Rules 3-09 and 4-08(g)).* This requirement is discussed in detail later in this section.

- *Related party transactions (Rules 1-02(t) and 4-08(k)).* Regulation S-X requires disclosure of material related party balances on the face of the balance sheet, income statements, and statement of cash flows (in addition to the footnote disclosures required by GAAP).

- *Income taxes (Rule 4-08(h)).* The additional SEC disclosures relating to income taxes are discussed in Sections 5.1(d) and 5.2(k).

- *Redeemable preferred stock (Rule 5-02(28)).* The presentation and disclosure requirements for preferred stocks or other equity securities having certain mandatory redemption features are discussed in Section 5.4(m).

- *Defaults (Rule 4-08(c)).* Disclose the facts and amounts concerning any default in principal, interest, sinking fund, or redemption requirement, or any breach of a covenant that has not been cured. If a waiver has been obtained, the registrant must state the amount involved and the period of the waiver.

- *Warrants or rights outstanding (Rule 4-08(i)).* Disclose the title and aggregate amount of securities underlying warrants or rights outstanding; and the date and price at which the warrants or rights are exercisable.

- *Accounting policies for certain derivative instruments (Rule 4-08(n)).* Disclose the accounting policies used for derivative financial instruments and derivative commodity instruments and the methods of applying these policies that materially affect the determination of financial position, cash flows, or results of operations. The disclosure should include:

  a. A discussion of the methods used to account for derivatives

  b. The types of derivatives accounted for under each method

  c. The criteria required to be met for use of each accounting method

  d. The accounting method used if the specific criteria are not met

  e. The accounting for the termination of derivatives designed as hedges

  f. The accounting for derivatives if the designated item matures or is otherwise terminated

  g. Where and when derivatives and their related gains and losses are reported in the financial statements

(h) OTHER SOURCES OF DISCLOSURE REQUIREMENTS. The SEC publishes the opinions of the Commission on major accounting questions and on the form and content of financial statements and financial disclosures in FRRs. These opinions (originally called Accounting Series Releases), which supplement Regulations S-X and S-K, have been codified by the SEC to present their contents in an organized manner. The SEC's "Codification of Financial Reporting Policies" contains all current releases relating to financial statement information.

SABs are interpretations and practices followed by the Division of Corporation Finance and the Office of the Chief Accountant. SABs are not SEC rules; instead, they are a means of documenting the SEC Staff's views on matters relating to accounting and disclosure practices. An SAB usually deals with a specific question posed to the SEC relating to a specific situation. However, the Staff has indicated that the guidance included in the SABs should be applied in similar cases. Although the SABs are not formal rules of the SEC, they do reflect the Staff's current thinking and represent the position that will be taken on various accounting and disclosures matters. As a result, SABs should be followed when preparing information to be included in a filing with the SEC.

The SLBs reflect the views of the SEC Staff but are not rules or regulations (similar to SABs).

(i) RESTRICTIONS ON TRANSFER BY SUBSIDIARIES AND PARENT-COMPANY-ONLY FINANCIAL INFORMATION. Regulation S-X emphasizes the disclosure of restrictions on subsidiaries' ability to transfer funds to the parent by requiring these disclosures in certain instances:

- Footnote disclosure describing and quantifying the restrictions on the subsidiaries (Rule 4-08(e)).
- Condensed parent-company-only financial information as a financial statement schedule (Rules 5-04 and 12-04).

The next footnote disclosures are required when the sum of (1) the proportionate share of subsidiaries' consolidated and unconsolidated net assets (after intercompany eliminations) that are restricted from being loaned or advanced, or paid as a dividend to the parent without third party consent *and* (2) the parent's equity in undistributed earnings of 50-percent-or-less-owned equity method investees exceed 25 percent of consolidated net assets as of the latest fiscal year-end:

- Any restrictions on all subsidiaries' ability to transfer funds to the parent in the form of cash dividends, loans, or advances
- The separate total amounts of consolidated and unconsolidated subsidiaries' restricted net assets at the end of the latest year

In addition, the rules require presentation of condensed parent company financial position, results of operations, and cash flows in a financial statement schedule (Schedule I) when the restricted net assets of consolidated subsidiaries exceed 25 percent of consolidated net assets at the end of the latest year (Rules 5-04 and 12-04). The condensed data may be in Form 10-Q format and should disclose, at a minimum, material contingencies, the registrant's long-term obligations and guarantees, cash dividends paid to the parent by its subsidiaries and investees during each of the last three years, and a five-year schedule of maturities of the parent's debt.

In determining the amount of restricted net assets, where the limitations on funds that may be loaned or advanced differ from any dividend restriction, the least restrictive amount should be used in the computation. For example, if a subsidiary is prohibited from paying dividends but can lend funds to the parent without limitation, the subsidiary's net assets will be considered unrestricted. Illustrations of situations involving restrictions may include loan agreements that require a subsidiary to maintain certain working capital or net assets levels. The amount of the subsidiary's restricted net assets should not exceed the amount of its net assets included in consolidated net assets. (Acquisition of a subsidiary in a "purchase" transaction can result in a significant difference in this regard.) Furthermore, consolidation adjustments should be pushed down to the subsidiary for the purpose of this test.

In computing net assets, redeemable preferred stock and noncontrolling interests should be excluded from equity.

(j) FINANCIAL INFORMATION REGARDING UNCONSOLIDATED SUBSIDIARIES AND 50-PERCENT-OR-LESS-OWNED EQUITY METHOD INVESTEES. Depending on their significance, Regulation S-X can require the presentation of both:

- Footnote disclosure of summarized financial statement information for unconsolidated subsidiaries and 50-percent-or-less-owned equity method investees
- Separate financial statements for one or more unconsolidated subsidiaries or 50-percent-or-less-owned equity method investees

It should be noted that under GAAP, unconsolidated subsidiaries that are not consolidated generally consist of a relatively narrow group of subsidiaries for which control is temporary or ineffectual.

Summarized financial statement footnote information as to assets, liabilities, and results of operations of unconsolidated subsidiaries and 50-percent-or-less-owned equity method investees is required when any one of the next tests—significant subsidiary tests of Rule 1-02(w)—are met on an individual or aggregate basis (Rule 4-08(g)).

- *Investment test.* The amount of the registrant's and its other subsidiaries' investments in and advances to such subsidiaries and other companies exceeds 10 percent of the total assets of the parent and its consolidated subsidiaries as shown in the most recent consolidated balance sheet. For a proposed business combination to be accounted for as a pooling of interests, this condition is also met when the number of common shares exchanged or to be exchanged exceeds 10 percent of the registrant's total common shares outstanding at the date the combination is initiated.

- *Asset test.* The amount of the registrant's and its other subsidiaries' proportionate share of the total assets (after intercompany eliminations) of such subsidiaries and other companies exceeds 10 percent of the total assets of the parent and its consolidated subsidiaries as shown in the most recent consolidated balance sheet.

- *Income test.* The registrant's and its other subsidiaries' equity in the income from continuing operations before income taxes and extraordinary items and cumulative effect of an accounting change of such subsidiaries or other companies exceeds 10 percent of the income of the registrant and its consolidated subsidiaries for the most recent fiscal year. However, if such consolidated income is at least 10 percent lower than the average of such income for the last 5 fiscal years, then the average income may be substituted in the determination. Any loss year should be excluded when computing average income. Additionally, when preparing the income statement test on an aggregate basis, unconsolidated subsidiaries, and 50-percent-or-less-owned equity method investees that report losses should not be aggregated with those reporting income.

According to Rule 1-02(bb), the summarized information should include:

- *For financial position.* Current and noncurrent assets and liabilities, redeemable preferred stock, and minority interests. In the case of specialized industries where classified balance sheets ordinarily are not presented, the major components of assets and liabilities should be shown.

- *For results of operations.* Gross revenues or net sales, gross profit, income (loss) from continuing operations before extraordinary items and cumulative effect of accounting changes, and net income (loss).

The summarized data is required for the same periods as the audited consolidated financial statements (insofar as it is practicable). In presenting the data, unconsolidated subsidiaries should not be combined with 50-percent-or-less-owned investees. Furthermore, if the significant subsidiary test is met, the summarized information should be provided for *all* such companies.

In addition to the requirement for footnote disclosure of summarized financial information, separate financial statements are required for any unconsolidated subsidiary or 50-percent-or-less-owned equity method investee that individually meets the Rule 1-02(w) test using 20 percent instead of 10 percent. These separate statements should cover, insofar as is practicable, the same periods as the audited consolidated financial statements and should be audited for those periods in which the 20 percent test is met.

The SEC has eliminated the asset test when determining whether separate audited financial statements of all (both domestic and foreign) equity investees must be provided under Reg. S-X rule 3-09. However, it should be noted that the SEC did not change the Reg. S-X Rule 4-08(g) requirement to provide summary financial information in the notes to the financial statements if equity investees are significant based on any of the three (i.e., assets, investment, and income) significance tests.

Combined or unconsolidated financial statements may be presented when two or more unconsolidated subsidiaries, or two or more 50-percent-or-less-owned investees, meet the 20 percent test.

The inclusion of those separate financial statements required by Rule 3-09 does not eliminate the need to present summarized footnote information pursuant to Rule 4-08(g), and the existence of one 20 percent entity will also automatically trigger the footnote disclosure of summarized information for all entities on an aggregate basis.

Next are listed two informal interpretations by the SEC Staff of the significant subsidiary test under Rule 1-02(w)(2):

1. Rule 1-02(w)(2) of Regulation S-X states that a subsidiary is significant if the parent's (registrant's) and its other subsidiaries' proportionate share of the total assets (after intercompany eliminations) of the subsidiary exceeds 10 percent of consolidated assets.

   The next interpretations are directed to the phrase *after intercompany eliminations.* The term *tested subsidiary* (used later) refers to the subsidiary being tested to determine whether it is a significant subsidiary. Receivables of the tested subsidiary from members of the consolidated group should be eliminated before determining the consolidated group's proportionate share of total assets of the tested subsidiary. Receivables from unconsolidated subsidiaries and 50-percent-or-less-owned persons of the tested subsidiary should not be eliminated before determining the consolidated group's proportionate share of total assets of the tested subsidiary.

   No adjustments would be made to consolidated assets included in the denominator of the fraction, because all appropriate intercompany eliminations are already made in consolidation. Although the phrase *after intercompany eliminations* is not used in Rule 1-02(w)(3), adjustments to income from continuing operations before income taxes for intercompany profits should be made to the entity being tested similar to those made in recording earnings of the entity in consolidation.

2. Rule 1-02(w)(3) states that a subsidiary is significant if the parent's and its other subsidiaries' equity in the income from continuing operations before income taxes, extraordinary items, and cumulative effect of an accounting change of the subsidiary exceeds 10 percent of such income of the parent and its consolidated subsidiaries, provided that if such income of the parent and its consolidated subsidiaries is at least 10 percent lower than the average of such income for the last five fiscal years such average may be substituted in the determination.

   The alternative five-year average income substitution is applicable only to the parent and its consolidated subsidiaries and is not applicable to the subsidiary being tested. In computing the five-year average income, loss years should be assigned a zero, and the denominator should be 5.

   In situations where there is a loss figure for one but not both sides of the equation in the computation of the income test, the income test should be made by determining the percentage effect of the parent's and its other subsidiaries' equity in the income or loss from continuing operations before income taxes, extraordinary items, and the cumulative effect of an accounting change of the tested subsidiary on the income or loss of the parent and its subsidiaries (excluding the income or loss of the tested subsidiary).

(k) DISCLOSURE OF INCOME TAX EXPENSE.   Rule 4-08(h) of Regulation S-X requires detailed disclosures relating to income tax expense. These rules originally required significant additional disclosures as compared to GAAP; however, since the issuance of the SEC's rules, GAAP has changed and includes almost all of the same requirements so there are minimal incremental requirements. Registrants should disclose:

- The components of income before income tax expense as either domestic or foreign if the foreign amount equals or exceeds 5 percent of total income before income tax expense
- The components of the income tax expense (i.e., current and deferred) stating separately the amounts applicable to U.S. federal, foreign, and other income taxes, if foreign or other income taxes equal or exceed 5 percent of the tax expense component
- The components of deferred tax liabilities (i.e., depreciation, warranty costs)
- A reconciliation (in dollars or percentages) between the reported income tax expense and the amount computed by multiplying income by the statutory federal rate, showing separately any item that exceeds 5 percent of the amount computed by multiplying income before tax by the applicable statutory federal tax rate

In those cases where the registrant is a foreign entity, the statutory rate prevailing in the foreign country should be used in making the reconciliation from the statutory rate to the effective rate.

(I) DISCLOSURE OF COMPENSATING BALANCES AND SHORT-TERM BORROWING ARRANGEMENTS. Regulation S-X calls for disclosure of compensating balances (Rule 5-02(1)) and short-term borrowing arrangements (Rule 5-02(19)). The purpose of the rules is to provide information on liquidity of the registrant (i.e., short-term borrowings and maintenance of compensating balances) and cost of short-term borrowing.

(i) Disclosure Requirements for Compensating Balances. A *compensating balance* is that portion of any demand deposit (i.e., certificate of deposit [CD], checking account balance) maintained by a company as support for existing or future borrowing arrangements.

Compensating balances that are legally restricted under an agreement should be segregated on the balance sheet. An example is a situation where a CD must be held for the duration of a loan. If the compensating balance is maintained against a short-term borrowing arrangement, it should be included as a current asset; if held against a long-term borrowing arrangement, it should be treated as a noncurrent asset.

The existence of a compensating balance arrangement, regardless of whether the balance is legally restricted and even if the arrangement is not reduced to writing, requires these six disclosures in the notes to financial statements for the latest fiscal year:

1. A description of the arrangement.
2. The amount of the compensating balance, if determinable (e.g., a percentage of short-term borrowings, a percentage of unused lines of credit, an agreed-upon average balance).
3. The required balance, under certain arrangements, may be expressed as an average over a period of time. The average required amount may differ materially from that held at year-end.
4. Material changes in amounts of compensating balance arrangements during the year.
5. Noncompliance with a compensating balance requirement and possible bank sanctions whenever such sanctions may be immediate and material.
6. Compensating balances maintained for the benefit of affiliates, officers, directors, principal stockholders, or similar parties.

There is a materiality guideline for determining whether disclosure or segregation is required. Usually compensating balances that exceed 15 percent of liquid assets (current cash balances and marketable securities) are considered material.

Some considerations in computing compensating balances include these:

- A compensating balance may include funds that would be held in any case as a minimum operating balance. Such operating balances should not be subtracted from the compensating balance. It may be desirable, however, to disclose the dual purpose of such amounts in the footnotes.

- Amounts disclosed or segregated in the financial statements should be on the same basis as the cash amounts shown in those statements. However, the book amounts and bank amounts for cash may differ because of outstanding checks, deposits in transit, and funds subject to collection. To reconcile the book and bank accounts, the compensating balance amount agreed to by the bank should be adjusted by the estimated float (i.e., outstanding checks less deposits in transit).

(ii) Disclosure Requirements for Short-Term Borrowings. The notes to financial statements should disclose the weighted average interest rate on short-term borrowings outstanding as of the date of each balance sheet presented if significant; and the amount and terms of unused lines of credit (Rule 5-02(19)). There must be separate disclosure for lines that support a commercial paper borrowing or similar arrangement. If a line of credit may be withdrawn under certain circumstances, this situation also must be disclosed.

A company may maintain lines of credit with a number of banks. If the aggregate amount of credit lines exceeds the debt limit under any one agreement, only the usable credit should be disclosed.

(m) REDEEMABLE PREFERRED STOCK. Rules 5-02(28), (29), and (30) require that amounts relating to equity securities should be separately classified as (1) preferred stock with mandatory redemption requirements, (2) preferred stock without mandatory redemption requirements, and (3) common stock. Redeemable preferred stock, or another type of stock with the same characteristics, may not be concluded under the general heading of "stockholders' equity" or combined with other stockholders' equity captions, such as additional paid-in capital and retained earnings.

The rule defines *redeemable preferred stock* as any class of stock (not just preferred) that (1) the issuer undertakes to redeem at a fixed or determinable price on a fixed or determinable date or dates, (2) is redeemable at the option of the holder, or (3) has conditions for redemption that are not solely within the control of the issuer, such as provisions for redemption out of future earnings.

The rule also requires registrants to provide a general description of each issue of redeemable preferred stock, including its redemption terms, the combined aggregate amounts of expected redemption requirements each year for the next five years, and other significant features similar to those for long-term debt.

The rules do not require any change in the calculation of debt/equity ratios for the purpose of making materiality computations to determine if an item requires disclosure or for determining compliance with existing loan agreements. However, where ratios or other data involving amounts attributable to stockholders' equity are presented, such ratios or other data should be accompanied by an explanation of the calculation. If the amounts of redeemable preferred stock are material and the ratios presented are calculated treating the redeemable preferred stock as equity, the ratios should also be presented as if the redeemable preferred stock were classified as debt.

According to SAB Topic 3-C *Redeemable Preferred Stock,* when preferred stock is issued for less than its mandatory redemption value, the stated value should be increased periodically by accreting the difference, using the interest method, between stated value and the redemption value. The periodic accretions should be included with cash dividend requirements of preferred stock in computing income applicable to common stock unless the preferred stock is a common stock equivalent.

Although Rules 5-02(27)and the related FRR Section 211 speak to preferred stocks that require redemption, the SEC Staff applies those provisions to any equity security that has conditions requiring redemption that are outside the control of the issuer. Several EITF consensus positions (now included in the codification) have applied FRR Section 211, by analogy, to stock purchase warrants and stock issued under certain employee stock plans.

With the general decline in interest rates, it is not uncommon for companies to find that the dividend rates on their outstanding preferred stocks exceed what they believe to be a current rate. The response of many companies in this position has been to either (1) redeem these preferred stocks (typically at a premium to their carrying values), or (2) induce their conversion. As long as redemption of the preferred stock is not outside the control of the issuer (i.e., the security is not a "mandatorily redeemable" preferred stock), accounting practice for such transactions has been to record the excess of (1) the fair value of the consideration transferred to the preferred stockholders over (2) the carrying amount of the preferred stock as a charge to additional paid-in capital. However, the SEC Staff has stated that it believes that such amounts should be treated as reductions of income applicable to common shareholders (in a manner similar to the treatment of dividends on preferred stock) for earnings per share calculation purposes.

(n) REGULATION S-X SCHEDULES.   The schedules required by Regulation S-X support information presented in the financial statements and can be filed 30 days after the due date of the report as an amendment on Form 10-K/A. Each schedule has detailed instructions as to what information is required. It is essential to understand these instructions and tie the schedules in to the related items in the financial statements. The information required by any schedule may be included in the financial statements and related notes, in which case the schedule may be omitted.

The following schedules are required to be audited if the related financial statements are audited.

Schedule No.	Description
I	Condensed financial information of registrant
II	Valuation and qualifying accounts
III	Real estate and accumulated depreciation
IV	Mortgage loans on real estate
V	Supplemental information concerning property-casualty insurance operations

As noted, certain schedules are required for other specific industries as described in Regulation S-X 6–9.

(o) REGULATION S-K.   Regulation S-K contains the disclosure requirements for the "textual" (non-financial statement) information in filings with the SEC. Regulation S-K is divided into 10 major classifications:

1. *General.* Including the Commission's policy on projections, rules on incorporation by reference, use of non-GAAP financial measures and smaller reporting companies (Item 10)
2. *Business.* Including a description of property and legal proceedings (Items 101, 102, and 103)
3. *Securities of the registrant.* Including market price and dividends (Items 201 and 202)
4. *Financial information.* Including selected financial data, supplementary financial information, management's discussion and analysis (MD&A) of financial condition and results of operations and disagreements with accountants and market risk disclosures, disclosure controls and procedures and ICFR (Items 301–308)
5. *Management and certain security holders.* Including directors, executive officers, promoters, and control persons; executive compensation; security ownership of certain beneficial owners and management; and certain relationships and related transactions, code of ethics and corporate governance (Items 401–407)
6. *Registration statement and prospectus provisions* (Items 501–512)
7. *Exhibits* (Item 601)
8. *Miscellaneous* (Items 701–703)
9. *List of industry guides* (Items 801 and 802)
10. *Roll-up transactions* (Items 901–915)

(p) STRUCTURE OF FORM 10-K. Form 10-K comprises four parts that are structured to facilitate incorporation by reference from the annual stockholders' report and the proxy statement for the election of directors. This format reflects the SEC's ongoing program of promoting the integration of reporting requirements under the 1933 and 1934 Acts. The parts of the Form 10-K are as follows:

Part I

Item 1	Business
Item 1A	Risk Factors
Item 1B	Unresolved Staff Comments
Item 2	Properties
Item 3	Legal Proceedings
Item 4	Reserved

Part II

Item 5	Market for Registrant's Common Equity and Related Stockholder Matters
Item 6	Selected Financial Data
Item 7	Management's Discussion and Analysis of Financial Condition and Results of Operations
Item 7A	Quantitative and Qualitative Disclosures about Market Risk
Item 8	Financial Statements and Supplementary Data
Item 9	Changes in and Disagreements with Accountants on Accounting and Financial Disclosures
Item 9A	Controls and Procedures

Part III

Item 10	Directors and Executive Officers of the Registrant
Item 11	Executive Compensation
Item 12	Security Ownership of Certain Beneficial Owners and Management
Item 13	Certain Relationships and Related Transactions
Item 14	Principal Accounting Fees and Services

Part IV

Item 15	Exhibits and Financial Statement Schedules

(i) Part I of Form 10-K. The information called for by Parts I and II *may* be incorporated by reference from the annual stockholders' report if that report contains the required disclosures. Where information is incorporated by reference, Form 10-K should include a cross-reference schedule indicating the item numbers incorporated and the related pages in the referenced material. The cross-referencing would be included on the cover page and in Item 14 of Form 10-K.

Item 1—Business (Item 101 of Regulation S-K). This caption requires the disclosures specified by Regulation S-K relating to the description of business, which are segregated into the next major categories:

- *General development of the business during the latest fiscal year.* The registrant should discuss the year organized and its form of organization; any bankruptcy proceedings, business combinations, acquisitions or dispositions of material assets not in the ordinary course of business; and any changes in the method of conducting its business.

- *Financial information about industry segments for the last three fiscal years (or for each year the registrant has been engaged in business, whichever period is shorter).* If significant trends relating to segments are identified in the five-year Selected Financial Data required under Item 6, it may be advisable to include the segment data for the additional years in Item 1.

- *Narrative description of business.* This caption requires a description of the registrant's current and planned business for each reportable segment and should include information on principal products and services, markets, distribution methods, new products, sources and availability of raw materials, patents, seasonality of business, practices relating to working capital items, dependence on major customers, backlog, government contracts, and competition. In addition, research and development activities, number of employees, and compliance with environment-related laws (including disclosure of material estimated capital expenditures for environmental control facilities for the succeeding fiscal year) should be discussed. The number of employees disclosed should be as of the latest practicable data.

- *Financial information about geographic areas as discussed in Accounting Standard Codification 280 for the last three fiscal years (or shorter period, if applicable).* Information should include information about the foreign countries from which the registrant derives revenues and information about any individual material foreign jurisdiction.

Item 1A—Risk Factors (Item 503(c) of Regulation S-K).   A registrant should describe the specific risk factors that an investor should be aware of in evaluating the company and its future prospects.

Item 1B—Unresolved Staff Comments.   This section requires all accelerated filers to disclose in Form 10-K unresolved comments from the SEC Staff that the issuer believes are material and that are more than 180 days old.

Item 2—Properties (Item 102 of Regulation S-K).   A description of the principal properties owned or leased should be identified. The registrant should briefly discuss the location and general character of the property and indicate any outstanding encumbrances. The industry segments in which the properties are used should be included.

The suitability, adequacy, capacity, and utilization of the facilities should be considered. The SEC has indicated this item will be read in conjunction with the Staff's review of the discussion of "capital resources" in the MD&A (Item 7 of Form 10-K).

Additional information is required for registrants engaged in oil- and gas-producing activities.

Item 3[2]—Legal Proceedings (Item 103 of Regulation S-K).   This caption primarily requires disclosure of legal proceedings that are pending or that were terminated during the registrant's fourth quarter and involve claims for damages in excess of 10 percent of consolidated current assets. Such disclosure generally includes the name of the court or agency, the date instituted, the principal parties, a description of the factual basis alleged to underlie the proceeding, and the relief sought (if pending). For terminated proceedings, disclosure would include termination date and description of disposition. Disclosure is not required for litigation that is ordinary, routine, and incidental to the company's business.

Environmental actions brought by a governmental authority are required to be disclosed unless the registrant believes that any monetary sanctions will be less than $100,000. Any material bankruptcy, receivership, or similar proceeding of the registrant should also be described.

In determining whether disclosure under Item 3 is required, FRR 36 indicates that amounts a company may be required to pay toward remedial costs do not represent sanctions under Items 103.

Any legal proceedings to which a director, officer, affiliate, or owner of record (actually or beneficially) of more than 5 percent of the voting stock is a party adverse to the registrant should also be disclosed.

Annual Report Disclosure of Certain Tax Penalties.   The American Jobs Creation Act of 2004 added Section 6707A to the Internal Revenue Code to (1) provide a monetary penalty for the failure to include on any tax return any information required to be disclosed with respect to certain "reportable" transactions, as described in Section 1.6011-4(b) of the Income Tax Regulations, and (2) require SEC registrants to disclose any such penalties they are required to pay. The Internal Revenue Service issued Revenue Procedure 2005-51 to provide more detailed guidance with respect to the required disclosures. (The requirements are not reflected in any of the SEC's rules or forms.)

---

[2] Note that Item 4 is currently reserved for future use.

(ii) Part II of Form 10-K

Item 5—Market for Registrant's Common Equity and Related Stockholder Matters (Items 201, 701, and 703 of Regulation S-K). The next information is required under this caption:

- The registrant should provide information relating to principal trading markets and common stock prices for the last two years. If the principal market is an exchange (i.e., New York, American, or other stock exchange), the quarterly high and low sales prices should be disclosed. Where there is no established public trading market, a statement should be furnished to that effect. If the principal market is not an exchange (i.e., the securities are traded on the NASDAQ or in the OTC market), the high- and low-bid information should be disclosed.
- The approximate number of shareholders for each class of common stock as of the latest practicable date is required to be disclosed.
- The frequency and amount of any cash dividends declared on common stock during the past two years and any restrictions on the registrant's present ability to pay dividends are required. If no dividends have been paid, the registrant should so state. When dividends have not been paid in the past although earnings indicated an ability to do so, and the registrant does not intend to pay dividends in the foreseeable future, a statement to that effect should be included under this item. Registrants with a dividend-paying history are encouraged, but not required, to indicate whether dividends will continue in the future. Such forward-looking information is covered by the SEC's safe-harbor rules on projections.
- When there are restrictions (including restrictions on the ability of subsidiaries to transfer funds to the registrant) that materially limit the registrant's dividend-paying ability, a discussion of these matters should be included in this caption or should be cross-referenced to the applicable portion of MD&A or to the required disclosures in the notes to the financial statements.
- For any sales of unregistered securities sold by the registrant:
  - **a.** Securities sold including the title, amount, and date
  - **b.** Name of persons or class of persons to whom the securities were sold
  - **c.** Consideration received
  - **d.** Exemption from registration claimed
  - **e.** Terms of conversion if applicable
- Registrants that have repurchased shares must provide disclosures covering repurchases made on a monthly basis. Information includes:
  - **a.** Total number of shares repurchased
  - **b.** Average price paid per share
  - **c.** Total number of shares purchased during the month as part of a publicly announced share repurchase plan
  - **d.** Maximum number of shares or approximate dollar amount that may yet be purchased under share repurchase plans

Item 6—Selected Financial Data (Item 301 of Regulation S-K). This item is intended to highlight significant trends in the registrant's financial condition as well as its results of operations. The next summary should be provided, in columnar form, for the last five fiscal years (or shorter period, if applicable) and any additional years necessary to keep the information from being misleading:

- Net sales (or operating revenues)
- Income (loss) from continuing operations and related earnings per common share data
- Total assets

- Long-term obligations (including long-term debt, capital leases, and preferred stock subject to mandatory redemption features)
- Cash dividends declared per common share (if a dividend was not declared, the registrant should state so)

A registrant may provide additional information to enhance the understanding of, or highlight trends in, its financial position or results of operations. The selected financial data should also include a description of matters that materially affect the comparability of the data (e.g., accounting changes, business combinations, or dispositions) as well as a discussion of material uncertainties that might cause the data not to be indicative of the registrant's future financial condition or operating results.

When a registrant chooses to use a non-GAAP metric, it must include certain additional disclosures including a reconciliation from the non-GAAP metric to the most comparable GAAP metric. Non-GAAP metrics may not be more prominent than that GAAP metric and must describe why the metric is important to users.

Item 7—Management's Discussion and Analysis of Financial Condition and Results of Operations (Item 303 of Regulation S-K).   The SEC expects each registrant to tailor the MD&A to its own specific circumstances. As a result there are no prescribed methods of disclosing the required information. The primary focus is centered on the company's earnings, liquidity, and capital resources for the three-year period covered by the financial statements. MD&A may also include other relevant information that promotes an understanding of a registrant's financial condition, changes in financial condition, or results of operations.

The use of boilerplate analysis is discouraged. MD&A should not merely repeat numerical data, such as dollar or percentage changes, contained in or easily derived from the financial statements. Instead, the registrant should provide meaningful commentary as to *why* changes in liquidity, capital resources, and operations have occurred. The reasons an expected change did not occur should also be included. The emphasis should be on trends, regardless of whether they are favorable or not.

The discussion on each topic should not be solely from a historical perspective. A registrant must also discuss any known trends, demands, commitments, events, or uncertainties that are reasonably likely to have a material effect on future financial condition, liquidity, or results of operations (such as unusually large promotional expenses, large price increases, and strikes).

The SEC's continuing focus on the importance of MD&A attained a new level in 1992 with the first-ever enforcement action taken solely due to the inadequacy of MD&A disclosures. While the SEC has tacked on MD&A deficiency allegations in previous cases of improper financial reporting, *In the Matter of Caterpillar, Inc.* (Accounting and Auditing Enforcement Release No. 363), there was no financial reporting question.

Seriously deficient MD&As may result in an enforcement action, even if the financial statements and other narrative disclosures are in compliance. Companies would be wise to review their procedures for complying with the MD&A requirements. Particular issues that should be evaluated include:

- The adequacy of "systems" in place to gather the information necessary to prepare MD&A (this would include both information about past results and information about known trends, demands, commitments, events, or uncertainties)
- The extent to which matters that are significant enough to require discussion at the board of directors level are considered for disclosure in MD&A
- The extent to which the company's MD&A does more than update boilerplate and provides the investor with an opportunity to see the company "through the eyes of management"

In 1989, the SEC completed an MD&A project that was intended to study MD&As in actual filings to determine what could be done to improve the information therein. An interpretive release

(FRR 36) providing guidance for the improvement of MD&A was issued on May 18, 1989. FRR 36 and Accounting Series Release (ASR) No. 299 contain examples illustrating particular points that the Staff believes require emphasis. This study is still relevant and, along with additional interpretive releases, provides the basis for many of the Staff's comments related to MD&A. The next discussion of the financial areas that are to be addressed in MD&A incorporates this guidance.

- *Liquidity and capital resources.* Liquidity and capital resources may be discussed together because of their interrelationship. Disclosure is required of internal and external sources of liquidity.

  In this context, *liquidity* relates to a company's ability to generate sufficient cash flow on both a long-term and short-term basis. The liquidity discussion should go beyond a review of working capital at specific dates or a mechanical analysis of changes in cash flows. It should cover sources of liquidity, trends, or unusual demands indicating material changes in liquidity and remedial action required to meet any projected deficiencies. The discussion of liquidity should not be limited to cash flow. The registrant should consider changes in other working capital items and future sources of liquidity, such as financing capabilities and securities transactions.

  The Staff will expect companies to discuss liquidity trends that may not be obvious from the balance sheet. For example, if a company pays off its line of credit at year-end due to the business cycle but is dependent on it during the year, it needs to provide information so that an investor understands the significance of the line of credit or short-term borrowings to the registrant.

  For entities with going-concern opinions, the registrant should disclose its financial difficulties and plans to overcome the difficulties and provide a detailed discussion of its ability or inability to generate sufficient cash to support its operations during the 12-month period following the date of the financial statements.

  Indicators of liquidity should be disclosed in the context of the registrant's particular business. For example, working capital may be an appropriate measure of liquidity for a manufacturing company but might not be so for a bank. Even if working capital is considered to be a measure of a company's liquidity, indicators ordinarily should go beyond working capital. Depending on the nature of the company, liquidity indicators may also include unused credit lines, debt–equity ratios, bond ratings, and debt covenant restrictions.

  If the financial statements, as required by Regulation S-X, disclose restrictions on the ability of subsidiaries to transfer funds to the parent, the liquidity discussion should indicate the impact of these restrictions on the parent.

  Capital resources are not specifically defined by the Commission, but equity, debt, and off-balance-sheet financing arrangements are used as examples. MD&A should describe any material commitments for capital expenditures, their purpose, and the planned source of funds to pay for those capital items. Trends in capital resources, including anticipated changes among the mix of equity, debt, and any off-balance-sheet financing arrangements, should be discussed. Forward-looking information, such as the total anticipated cost of a new plant or the company's overall capital budget, is encouraged by the SEC but not required. Although this information would be useful and is expressly covered by the SEC's safe-harbor rule for projections, the advisability of including such information ordinarily should be reviewed with legal counsel. Known data that will have an impact on future operations (e.g., known increases in labor or material costs, commitments for capital expenditures) is not considered forward-looking data and is required to be disclosed.

  Income taxes can have a material impact on the cash flows of the company, so therefore generally they are an item that should be discussed. The income tax footnote provides a reconciliation from the statutory rate to the effective rate, but it does not provide any context for the reconciling items and whether that effective rate will continue in the future. Registrants with material taxes should include some of these discussions in the MD&A. Also for net deferred tax assets, if material, the registrant should discuss uncertainties surrounding realization of the assets and management assumptions.

- *Results of operations.* A description is required of any unusual or infrequent events or trans-actions and any trends or uncertainties that are expected to affect future sales or earnings. The extent to which sales changes are attributable to volume and prices also should be described. In addition, events that management expects to cause a material change in the relationship between costs and revenues should be discussed, along with the expected change. Regis-trants should also disclose if they expect inflation to have a material impact on the financial statements.

  The SEC believes that, in some cases, a discussion of interrelationships may be the most helpful way of describing the reasons for changes in several individual items. For example, certain costs may be directly related to sales, so a discussion of the reasons for a change in sales may also serve to explain the changes in a related item. A repetition of the same explanation is neither required nor useful.

  The SEC has been very focused on disclosures related to segments. It believes that MD&A should adequately explain variances on a segment-by-segment basis. MD&A should also highlight any instances where a segment contributes a disproportionate amount of income or loss as compared to its revenue levels.

  The Commission has stated that its focus on MD&A disclosures will continue, and principal targets of enforcement will include the failure of companies to address continued operating trends and financial institutions not candidly addressing loan loss problems. The SEC has also warned that the antifraud provisions applicable to filings under the Securities Acts also apply to all public statements made by persons speaking on behalf of the registrant. Therefore, company spokespersons should exercise care when making statements that can reasonably be expected to be made known to the financial community and ultimately relied on by the public investor.

  For Accounting Standards Updates that have been issued but not yet adopted, a brief description of the standard and its anticipated adoption date, the method of adoption and impact on the financial statements to the extent reasonably estimable is required.

- *Contractual obligations.* In a separately captioned section of the MD&A, tabular disclosure must be provided about these types of contractual obligations:

  ○ Long-term debt

  ○ Capital leases obligations

  ○ Operating leases

  ○ Purchase obligations

  ○ Other long-term obligations reflected on the balance sheet.

  Amounts due in less than one year, one to three years, three to five years, and more than five years must be provided for each category. In addition, the table should be accompanied by footnotes necessary to describe material contractual provisions or other material information to the extent necessary for an understanding of the timing and amount of the contractual obligations.

- *Additional interpretive guidance.* The SEC issued FRR 72 to provide guidance regarding MD&A. The release does not create new legal requirements or modify existing legal require-ments but provides guidance to help companies prepare MD&A disclosure that is easier for an investor to understand and that better satisfies the SEC's stated objectives.

  The guidance reminds companies of existing disclosure requirements and provides addi-tional guidance regarding the overall presentation and focus of MD&A. Suggestions for improved presentation include:

  ○ Use of an executive-level overview

  ○ Tabular presentation of relevant financial or other information

  ○ Deletion of information carried forward from past-years' MD&A that is no longer relevant

  ○ Reformatting the MD&A to discuss the most significant items first

○ Emphasis on analysis of financial information as opposed to simply discussion (i.e., the underlying reasons for and implications of material trends, events, demands and commitments, and uncertainties)

○ Discussion of known material trends and uncertainties, including quantification of their material effects to the extent the information is reasonably available

○ Use of key performance indicators, including both financial and nonfinancial measures.

○ Liquidity and capital resources. Specifically, suggesting registrants focus on the cash requirements (using the table of contractual obligations as a starting point) and the sources of cash to satisfy the requirements

- *Critical accounting policies.* The SEC provided guidance regarding the need to disclose critical accounting policies in FRR 60 (Release No. 33-8040), *Cautionary Advice Regarding Disclosure about Critical Accounting Policies.* To elicit improved disclosure in this area, in April 2002, the SEC proposed rules that are contained in Release No. 33-8098, Proposed Rule: *Disclosure in Management's Discussion and Analysis about the Application of Critical Accounting Policies.* That proposal would mandate presenting this information in a separate section of MD&A.

Both FRR 60 (Release No. 33-8040) and the proposed rule discuss that companies should provide disclosure in MD&A that allows investors to understand the manner and degree to which the reported operating results, financial condition, and changes in financial condition depend on estimates involved in applying accounting policies that entail uncertainties and subjectivity. To do this, a company should provide disclosures about (1) the critical accounting estimates it made in applying its critical accounting policies and (2) the initial adoption of an accounting policy that has a material impact on its financial presentation. The disclosures should focus on the most recent fiscal year and any subsequent interim period presented. Currently, many companies present this information in a separate section of the MD&A immediately preceding or following the discussion of the results of operations.

Since final rules have not been issued on critical accounting policies and estimates, FRR 60 is the official applicable guidance. However, the Staff believes that the postponed rules in Release No. 33-8098 also call for disclosures that investors will find useful. Therefore, registrants should also consider the items called for in that proposal when preparing their disclosures.

Critical accounting policy disclosures should communicate uncertainties and how they might affect the financial statements. The Staff commented that repeating disclosure from the accounting policies footnote does not satisfy the MD&A requirements to disclose known uncertainties that are reasonably likely to materially affect future operating results. Critical accounting estimates disclosure should focus on numbers in the financial statements that are sensitive to material change from external factors. The disclosure should provide insight into:

○ The assumptions used in deriving estimates, particularly those that factor into fair value estimations

○ How the estimate was arrived at, including all assumptions that factored into the initial estimate and how susceptible the estimate is to variability

○ If any of the assumptions have changed from the prior period, the reason for the change and resulting impact on the estimate

○ Factors that could cause the estimate to change in the future and the potential magnitude of future changes

Item 7A—Quantitative and Qualitative Disclosures About Market Risk (Item 305 of Regulation S-K).   The disclosures must be made in all filings containing annual financial statements. Summarized quantitative disclosures must also be provided for the preceding fiscal year, although comparative information is not required for the first fiscal year in which the information is presented.

The quantitative and qualitative disclosures are intended to help investors better understand specific market risk exposures of registrants, thereby allowing them to better manage market risks in their investment portfolios.

Item 305 requires separate disclosures for instruments entered into for trading purposes and for purposes other than trading

In addition, within each of these portfolios, market risk must be described separately for each category of risk (e.g., interest rate risk, foreign currency exchange rate risk, and commodity price risk). Materiality is to be evaluated based on both:

- The materiality of the fair values of the market risk-sensitive instruments outstanding at the end of the latest fiscal year
- The materiality of potential near-term (generally up to one year) losses in future earnings, fair values, and cash flows from reasonably possible near-term changes in market rates or prices

If market risk is determined to be material under *either* definition (present or future), market risk disclosures are required.

Based on this definition of materiality, entities with no derivatives (e.g., banks with significant fixed rate loans outstanding, entities with material amounts of marketable securities, or entities with receivables or payables denominated in foreign currencies) will be required to make Item 305 disclosures.

- *Quantitative disclosures.* The quantitative information requirements are very detailed and specific. In summary, the information can be disclosed in three different ways. The alternatives are:

  a. A tabular presentation that shows fair values, contract terms, and expected future cash flow amounts for market risk-sensitive instruments

  b. A sensitivity analysis showing the potential loss in future earnings, fair values, or cash flows of market risk-sensitive instruments resulting from one or more selected hypothetical changes in interest rates, foreign currency exchange rates, commodity prices, or other relevant market rate or price changes over a selected period of time

  c. Value at risk disclosures that express the potential loss in earnings, fair values, or cash flows of market risk-sensitive instruments over a selected period of time, with a selected likelihood of occurrence, from changes in interest rates, foreign currency exchange rates, commodity prices, or other relevant market rates or prices

  The rules provide great flexibility in selecting the method to be used for each portfolio (trading and nontrading) and category of risk. Furthermore, the methods, once selected, can be changed if the registrant discloses the reason for the change and provides comparable disclosures for the current and previous years. Additionally, registrants who believe providing quantitative year-end information may hurt their competitive position may provide the sensitivity analysis or value-at-risk disclosures for the average, high, and low amounts for the fiscal year.

  In addition, disclosures regarding the methods and assumptions used are required. Registrants must also discuss (after the initial year) the reasons for material quantitative changes in market risk exposures as compared to the preceding fiscal year.

  Registrants are also encouraged, but not required, to provide market risk disclosures regarding market risk-sensitive instruments and transactions other than those specifically required by Item 305 (e.g., commodity positions, anticipated transactions). Disclosures for these items may be combined with the disclosures for the required instruments. Disclosure for these items is suggested, but not required. Because their cash flows may be difficult to estimate. For example, a U.S. company that imports a significant portion of the products it sells from Japan may find it difficult to estimate the impact on anticipated transactions of changes in the yen/dollar exchange rate.

  Registrants are therefore also required to discuss limitations that cause the quantitative information to not fully reflect the market risk exposures of the entity. Such limitations include (1) failing to provide the voluntary disclosures discussed in the preceding paragraph and (2) the fact that market risks related to leverage, options, or prepayment features may not be fully communicated through the required disclosures.

The SEC believes that much of the information to prepare the tabular presentation is currently available and that the additional recordkeeping costs to implement this approach should not be great, particularly since (1) financial institutions already disclose a significant amount of the information required in a tabular presentation pursuant to Industry Guide 3 and (2) the tabular presentation alternative is similar to the gap analysis commonly provided by financial institutions. However, the SEC believes that the sensitivity analysis or value at risk disclosure alternatives may require significant additional costs if a registrant does not already use one of these methodologies to manage market risk.

- *Qualitative disclosures.* The qualitative disclosures are intended to make the quantitative information more meaningful by placing it in the context of the registrant's business. Registrants are required to describe (1) the primary market risk exposures at the end of the latest fiscal year, (2) how those exposures are managed (i.e., description of objectives, strategies, and instruments, if any, used), and (3) known or expected changes in exposures or risk management practices as compared to those in effect during the most recently completed fiscal year.

The Private Securities Litigation Reform Act of 1995 established a safe harbor from liability in private lawsuits for certain forward-looking statements. This safe harbor was extended to the Item 305 disclosures. The safe harbor does not apply to financial statements, so the Item 305 disclosures must be made outside the financial statements.

Item 8—Financial Statements and Supplementary Data

- *Financial statements.* Article 3 of Regulation S-X contains uniform instructions governing the periods to be covered by financial statements included in annual stockholders' reports and in most 1933 Act and 1934 Act filings. The basic financial statement requirements for Form 10-K are:
  - Audited balance sheets as of the end of the most recent two fiscal years
  - Audited statements of income, comprehensive income, changes in stockholders' equity, and cash flows for the most recent three fiscal years

  These financial statements may be incorporated into the 10-K by reference from the annual stockholders' report.

  The financial statement schedules required by Regulation S-X, as well as any separate financial statement required by Rule 3-09, are not included in Item 8 but instead are presented in Item 14.

- *Supplementary financial information (Item 302 of Regulation S-K).*
  - Selected quarterly financial data

    The next data are required to be disclosed for each full quarter within the latest two fiscal years and any subsequent interim periods for which income statements are presented:
    - Net sales, gross profit, income (loss) before extraordinary items and cumulative effect of a change in accounting, per share data based on such income (loss) (basic and diluted) and net income (loss). The registrant may also be required to disclose per share data for discontinued operations, extraordinary items, and net income (losses). SAB Topic 6-G-1 states that companies in specialized industries should, in lieu of "gross profit," present quarterly data in the manner most meaningful to their industry.
    - A description of the effect of any disposals of segments of a business and extraordinary, unusual, or infrequently occurring items.
    - The aggregate effect and nature of year-end or other adjustments that are material to the results of the quarter.
    - An explanation, in the form of a reconciliation, of differences between amounts presented in this item and data previously reported on Form 10-Q filed for any quarter (e.g., where a pooling of interests occurs or where an error is corrected).

The interim data disclosures are not required for parent-company-only financial statements that are presented in a schedule in Item 14 of Form 10-K. The data also need not be included for supplemental financial statements for unconsolidated subsidiaries or 50-percent-or-less-owned companies accounted for by the equity method unless the subsidiary or affiliate is a registrant that does not meet the conditions for exemption from the disclosure rule. The SEC requires timely quarterly reviews of a company's interim financial statements by its independent auditors prior to the filing of its Form 10-Q with the Commission. The independent auditor is required to follow "professional standards and procedures for conducting such reviews, as adopted or established by the PCAOB, as may be modified or supplemented by the Commission." These auditing procedures are set forth in Auditing Standards Codification (AU) Section 722, *Interim Financial Information,* as are the steps an auditor must take when, as the result of performing a review of the interim financial information of a public entity or certain other procedures, the auditor becomes aware that interim financial information filed or to be filed with the SEC is materially misstated.

AU Section 722 requires auditors to perform certain review procedures with respect to the quarterly data. It also provides guidance for an auditor's reporting responsibilities regarding the review of quarterly financial data. Specifically, the auditor's report should be expanded if the quarterly financial data required by Item 302 are (1) omitted or (2) have not been reviewed.

Item 9—Changes in and Disagreements with Accountants on Accounting and Financial Disclosures (Item 304 of Regulation S-K).

The SEC has long been concerned about the relationships between the registrant and its independent accountants. During the 1980s, the growing number of allegations about opinion shopping encouraged the SEC to adopt new disclosure requirements to provide increased public disclosure of possible opinion-shopping situations. In FRR 31, dated April 7, 1988, the Commission stated:

> The auditor must, at all times, maintain a "healthy skepticism" to ensure that a review of a client's accounting treatment is fair and impartial. The willingness of an auditor to support a proposed accounting treatment that is intended to accomplish the registrant's reporting objectives, even though that treatment might frustrate reliable reporting, indicates that there may be a lack of such skepticism and independence on the part of the auditor. The search for such an auditor by management may indicate an effort by management to avoid the requirements for an independent examination of the registrant's financial statements. Engaging an accountant under such circumstances is generally referred to as "opinion shopping." Should this practice result in false or misleading financial disclosure, the registrant and the accountant would be subject to enforcement and/or disciplinary action by the Commission.

In 1986 and 1988, the SEC made significant amendments to Item 304 to require additional disclosures about changes in and disagreements with accountants. Disagreements and "other reportable events" are required to be disclosed in Form 8-K and in proxy statements sent to shareholders. The same disclosures are generally required in Form 10-K. However, if a Form 8-K has been filed reporting a change in accountants and there were no reported disagreements or reportable events, the Form 10-K does not require a repetition of the disclosures.

Item 9A—Controls and Procedures (Items 307 and 308 of Regulation S-K)

Evaluation and Reporting Requirements—Disclosure Controls and Procedures (Item 307). Rules 13a-15(b) and 15d-15(b) require each issuer's management to evaluate, with the participation of the issuer's principal executive and principal financial officers, or persons performing similar functions, the effectiveness of the issuer's disclosure controls and procedures, as of the end of each fiscal quarter (including the fourth quarter). Regulation S-K Item 307 requires disclosure of management's conclusions regarding the effectiveness of the registrant's disclosure controls and procedures.

Evaluation and Reporting Requirements—Internal Control over Financial Reporting (Item 308). The Commission adopted through Release 33-8238 rules to implement Section 404 of Sarbanes-Oxley and require management to evaluate and report on the effectiveness of a registrant's internal controls in each annual report. Among other actions, the rules require

- Management (other than that of a registered investment company) to *evaluate* the effectiveness of the issuer's ICFR as of the end of each fiscal year.

  The issuer's principal executive and financial officers must participate. The evaluations must be based on a framework that is a suitable, recognized control framework that has been established by a body or group that has followed due process procedures, including a broad distribution of the framework for public comment. The Committee of Sponsoring Organizations (COSO) framework will satisfy the SEC's criteria. However, the rules do not mandate the use of a particular framework.

  The rules do not specify the methods for or procedures to be performed in evaluating ICFR. However, the rules state that in conducting the evaluation and developing an assessment of the effectiveness of internal controls, a company must maintain evidential matter, including documentation, to provide reasonable support for management's conclusions. In addition, inquiry alone will not provide an adequate basis for management's assessment. The assessment must be based on procedures sufficient to both

  ○ Evaluate the internal control over financial reporting's design effectiveness and

  ○ Test its operating effectiveness.

  While nonmanagement personnel may perform this work, management must actively supervise the entire process.

- Management to *report* on a company's internal controls in each annual report. Companies must include in their annual reports a report of management on the company's ICFR (Regulation S-K Item 308(a)). Management reporting on ICFR has been required for all public companies for fiscal years ending on or after December 15, 2007.

- The report must include

  ○ A statement of management's responsibility for establishing and maintaining adequate ICFR.

  ○ A statement identifying the framework used by management to evaluate the effectiveness of the company's ICFR.

  ○ Management's assessment of the effectiveness of the company's ICFR as of the end of the company's most recent fiscal year, including a statement as to whether the company's ICFR is effective or not.

  ○ A statement that the registered public accounting firm that audited the company's financial statements has issued an attestation report on the registrant's ICFR.

    With regard to management's assessment of the effectiveness of the company's internal controls,

  ○ A negative assurance statement indicating that nothing has come to management's attention to suggest that the company's ICFR is not effective is not acceptable.

  ○ The report must include disclosure of any material weaknesses in the company's ICFR.

  ○ Management is not permitted to conclude that the company's ICFR is effective if there are one or more material weaknesses.

  ○ It is the Commission's judgment that an aggregation of significant deficiencies could constitute a material weakness.

    The rules do not specify where the internal control report must appear in the company's annual report. Companies typically place the report either in Section 9A, near MD&A disclosure, or in a portion of the document immediately preceding the financial statements.

- A company's *auditors to issue an attestation report* on the registrant's ICFR. The auditor's attestation report must be filed as part of the annual report and should be placed in the same location as management's internal control report (Regulation S-K Item 308(b)). The SEC had temporarily exempted nonaccelerated filers from the ICFR auditor attestation requirement. However, the Dodd-Frank Act, which was signed into law on July 21, 2010, permanently exempted nonaccelerated filers from the requirement to have their auditors attest to their ICFR. In September 2010, the Commission conformed its rules to the Dodd-Frank Act. The

SEC now deems the management reports on ICFR of nonaccelerated issuers to be filed, not furnished, and these filers no longer need to provide a statement that an auditors' report on ICFR was not provided.

- Management to disclose each quarter (including the fourth quarter) material changes during the quarter in internal controls.
- Regulation S-K Item 308(c).
  - Registrants must disclose material changes in ICFR that have occurred during a quarter (including the fourth quarter). However, the rules do not require a quarterly report on the effectiveness of a company's internal controls.

Item 9B—Other Information.   The registrant must disclose under this item any information required to be disclosed in a report on Form 8-K during the fourth quarter of the year covered by this Form 10-K, but not reported, whether otherwise required by this Form 10-K or not. If disclosure of such information is made under this item, it need not be repeated in a report on Form 8-K that would otherwise be required to be filed with respect to such information or in a subsequent report on Form 10-K.

(iii) Part III of Form 10-K.   The information required in this part may be incorporated by reference from the proxy statement relating to election of directors if such statement is to be filed within 120 days after year-end. If the information is omitted from the Form 10-K and the proxy statement ultimately is not filed within the 120-day period, it will be necessary to amend the Form 10-K by filing a Form 10-K/A to include the omitted information. The reportable information and captions are described in the next subsections.

Item 10—Directors and Executive Officers of the Registrant (Items 401 and 405, 406, and Portions of 407 of Regulation S-K).
The information reportable under this caption includes a listing of directors and executive officers and information about each individual. *Directors* includes all persons nominated or chosen to become directors. The information includes name, age, positions held with the registrant, business experience for the last five years, other directorships held, and other information that an investor might want to know about an individual serving as an executive officer or director. In addition, as discussed previously, additional disclosures are made related to the audit committee.

The SEC defines *executive officers* as the president, secretary, treasurer, vice president in charge of a principal function or business, or any person with policy-making functions affecting the entire entity even if he has no title.

Disclosure of family relationships among directors and executive officers and a brief account of their previous business experience for the past five years is also required. Any involvement in certain legal or bankruptcy proceedings during the past five years should be disclosed.

For directors, the registrant must also disclose the particular experience, qualifications, attributes, or skills that led the board to conclude the person should serve as director.

Registrants that were organized within the last five years or that have recently become subject to the reporting requirements of the Exchange Act are also required to disclose certain legal and bankruptcy proceedings that have occurred during the past five years and involve a promoter or control person.

Also, pursuant to Item 405 of Regulation S-K, the registrant must disclose certain information on the identity of officers, directors, or owners of more than 10 percent of any class of stock who during the latest year were late in the filing of any of the "insider trades" reports (Forms 3, 4, and 5) required under Section 16 of the 1934 Act. Pursuant to Item 406, there are additional disclosures related to corporate governance.

Item 11—Executive Compensation (Item 402 and Portions of Item 407 of Regulation S-K).   The SEC executive compensation rules require registrants to disclose information regarding all components of executive and director compensation—not to require any particular practice or regulate the amounts of such compensation. The rules require registrants to report the entire grant date fair value of option and stock awards to executives and directors in the summary compensation table (SCT) and director compensation table (DCT) in the year of grant, regardless of the extent to which the award had vested. Full grant date fair value disclosures are also required in the grants of plan-based awards table. The SEC believes that aggregate grant date fair value disclosure is meaningful to shareholders and better reflects the compensation committee's decision with regard to stock and option awards.

Five named executive officers are included in the SCT. However, the principal executive officer (PEO, formerly the CEO) *and* the principal financial officer (PFO) are named executive officers regardless of compensation level. The other three named executives are the most highly compensated executive officers identified on the basis of *total* compensation, not simply salary and bonus. *Total compensation* for this purpose includes all compensation listed in the SCT except for nonqualified deferred compensation earnings and the accumulated net change in pension value.

Briefly, the principal disclosure requirements include:

- SCT provides a three-year summary of compensation paid. It includes annual compensation (salary, bonuses, etc.), earned long-term compensation (including restricted stock awards, the number of options and stock appreciation rights [SARs] granted, long-term incentive plan payouts, and restricted stock holdings), nonequity incentive plan compensation, certain information about pension values, and all other compensation. By requiring information covering three years, this table is designed to provide investors with information to evaluate trends in executive compensation.
- The grants of plan-based awards table summarizes the number and terms of options/SARs granted during the last fiscal year. It also requires information about the potential value of the grants as discussed. Outstanding equity awards at fiscal year-end table summarizes information on all equity awards that remain outstanding, unexercised or unearned at year-end.
- The option exercises and stock vested table summarizes options exercised and stock awards that vested during the last fiscal year and the aggregate value received.
- The postemployment benefits table requires disclosures of the present value of accumulated benefit, the number of years of credited service, and other relevant information.
- The nonqualified deferred compensation table includes information about the full amount of nonqualified deferred compensation obligations.
- Compensation discussion and analysis (CD&A) requires registrants to analyze and discuss the material factors underlying compensation policies and decisions reflected in the data presented in the tables in the same manner that they discuss operations and financial condition in MD&A.

The Commission provided these key questions that registrants are required to address in their CD&As:

- What are the objectives of the company's compensation programs?
- What is the compensation program designed to reward?
- What is each element of compensation?
- Why does the company choose to pay each element?
- How does the company determine the amount (and, where applicable, the formula) for each element?
- How does each element and the company's decisions regarding that element fit into the company's overall compensation objectives and affect decisions regarding other elements?

The rules also require disclosure of information about compensation of directors, employment contracts and termination agreements, and compensation committee interlocks and insider participation.

Equity Compencation Plans. The information on equity compensation plans should be provided on an aggregate basis and categorized between those plans that were approved by shareholders and those that were not. For each plan that has not been approved by shareholders, the registrant should include a brief description of the material features of the plan. Copies of such plans should also be filed as exhibits unless they are immaterial in amount or significance.

These disclosures are required in annual reports on Forms 10-K and 10-KSB for fiscal years ending on or after March 15, 2002. They are also required in proxy statements for meetings of shareholders occurring on or after June 15, 2002, where the registrant is submitting a compensation plan for shareholder approval.

Item 12—Security Ownership of Certain Beneficial Owners and Management (Items 201(d) and 403 of Regulation S-K). The next disclosures are required for all equity compensation plans (including individual compensation arrangements) in effect as of the end of the most recent fiscal year:

- The number of securities to be issued upon exercise of outstanding options, warrants, and rights
- The weighted average exercise price of outstanding options, warrants, and rights
- The number of securities remaining available for future issuance under equity compensation plans

The information reportable related to security ownership and certain beneficial owners is required for owners of more than 5 percent of any class of voting securities and for all officers and directors. The name and address of the owner, the amount and nature of beneficial ownership, and the class and percentage ownership of stock should be presented in the prescribed tabular form.

Item 13—Certain Relationships and Related Transactions (Item 404 and 407(a) of Regulation S-K). Certain transactions in excess of $120,000 must be disclosed that have taken place during the last fiscal year or are proposed to take place, directly or indirectly, between the registrant and any of its directors (including nominees), executive officers, more-than-5 percent stockholders, or any member of their immediate family. In addition, special rules apply to disclosure of payments between the registrant and entities in which directors have an interest (including significant customers, creditors, and suppliers, and law firms or investment banking firms where fees exceeded 5 percent of the firm's gross revenues).

If the registrant is indebted, directly or indirectly, to any individual just mentioned, and such indebtedness has exceeded $120,000 at any time during the last fiscal year, Item 13 requires that the individual, nature of the liability, the transaction in which the liability was incurred, the outstanding balance at the latest practicable date, and other pertinent information be disclosed.

This section of the filing also requires disclosures regarding director independence.

Item 14—Principal Accounting Fees and Services (Item 9(e) of Schedule 14A). The instructions for this section are found in Item 9(e) of Schedule 14A and call for disclosures related to fees paid to the principal auditor for specific categories: audit fees, audit related fees, tax fees, and all other fees. The disclosures cover the two most recent fiscal years.

(iv) Part IV of Form 10-K

Item 15—Exhibits and Financial Statement Schedules. This item relates to Regulation S-X schedules, the financial statements required in Form 10-K but not in the annual stockholders' report (i.e., financial statements of unconsolidated subsidiaries or 50-percent-or-less-owned equity method investees, or financial statements of affiliates whose securities are pledged as collateral), and exhibits required by Item 601 of Regulation S-K (including a list of the registrant's significant subsidiaries) and, for electronic filers only, a financial data schedule.

All financial statements, schedules, and exhibits filed should be listed under this item. Where any financial statement, financial statement schedule, or exhibit is incorporated by reference, the incorporation by reference should be set forth in a schedule included in this item.

The financial statement schedules at Item 14 must be covered by an accountant's report. If the financial statements in Item 8 have been incorporated by reference from the annual stockholders' report, Item 14 should include a separate accountant's report covering the schedules. Such a report usually makes reference to the report incorporated by reference in Item 8, indicates that the audit referred to in that report also included the financial statement schedules, and expresses an opinion on whether the schedules present fairly the information required to be presented therein. When the financial statements are *not* incorporated by reference from the annual report, the 10-K must include an opinion on both the financial statements required by Item 8 and the financial statement schedules required by Item 14. This is accomplished by either of two methods:

1. The report appearing in Item 8 may cover only the financial statements with a separate report included in Item 14 on the financial statement schedules.

2. The report appearing in Item 8 may cover both the financial statements and financial statement schedules by including the schedules in the scope paragraph and by adding a third paragraph that contains an opinion on the schedules.

XBRL Exhibit. In 2008, the SEC adopted amendments that require issuers to provide to the Commission financial statements in interactive data format using Extensible Business Reporting Language (XBRL). The rules apply to public companies and foreign private issuers that prepare their financial statements in accordance with U.S. GAAP and foreign private issuers that prepare their financial statements using IFRS as issued by the IASB. An issuer will be required provide the XBRL data as an exhibit to its annual and quarterly reports, transition reports, Form 8-K and 6-K reports containing updated or revised versions of financial statements that appeared in a periodic report, and registration statements, and on its corporate Web site if it maintains one.

(v) Signatures.   The required signatories include the PEO, PFO, controller or principal accounting officer, and at least a majority of the board of directors. The name of each person who signs the report must be typed or printed beneath his or her signature. Signatures for any electronic submission are in typed form rather than manual format. However, manually signed pages (or other documents acknowledging the typed signature) must be obtained *prior* to the electronic filing. The registrant must retain the original signed version of the document for a period of five years after the filing and provide it to the SEC or the Staff upon request.

(vi) Certifications.   The rules require companies to provide Section 302 and 906 certifications as exhibits to the periodic reports to which they relate. The Section 302 certification is exhibit number 31 in the Regulation S-K Item 601 exhibit table; the Section 906 certification is exhibit number 32.

(q) ANNUAL REPORT TO STOCKHOLDERS.   Rules 14a-3 and 14c-3 of the 1934 Act give the SEC the right to regulate the financial statements included in the stockholders' annual report. Although an annual stockholders' report must be sent to the SEC, technically it is not a "filed" document. Therefore, the annual stockholders' report is not subject to the civil liability provisions of Section 18 of the 1934 Act unless it is an integral part of a required filing, such as when incorporated by reference in Form 10-K. Yet an annual stockholders' report is subject to the antifraud provisions set forth in Section 10b and Rule 10b-5 of the 1934 Act. The proxy solicitation (or information statement if proxies are not being solicited) for an annual stockholders' meeting at which directors will be elected must be accompanied or preceded by an annual report that contains:

• Audited consolidated balance sheets as of the end of the two most recent fiscal years
• Statements of income, comprehensive income (if applicable), shareholders equity, and cash flows for each of the three most recent fiscal years

The requirements of Regulation S-X must be met except for the next rules, which are excluded:

- Certain provisions of Article 3 (e.g., financial information for businesses acquired and to be acquired, separate financial statements of subsidiaries not consolidated and 50-percent-or-less owned persons, separate financial statements of guarantors, separate financial statements of affiliates whose securities serve as collateral for the registrant's securities)
- Article 11 (pro forma financial information)
- Article 12 (financial statement schedules)

The similar disclosure requirements allow registrants to use extensive incorporation by reference to the annual stockholders' report in SEC filings. As such, the annual stockholders' report is often expanded to meet the disclosure requirements of Items 1 through 4 of Form 10-K to allow incorporation by reference. In some cases, the Form 10-K and the annual report are combined into one document.

The annual stockholders' report also must contain a statement, in boldface, that the company will provide the annual report on Form 10-K, without charge, in response to written requests. The report must indicate the name and address of the person to whom such a written request is to be directed. The statement may alternatively be included in the proxy statement.

(i) Content of Annual Report to Stockholders. The SEC has long recognized that the annual stockholders' report is the most effective method of communicating financial information to stockholders. It believes these reports should be readable and informative and prefers that they be written without boilerplate. The SEC allows registrants to use their discretion in determining the format of the annual stockholders' report, as long as the information required is included and can easily be located. To improve the presentation of data, the SEC encourages the use of charts and other graphic illustrations, as long as they are consistent with the information in the financial statements.

5.5 FORM 10-Q

In addition to the comprehensive annual report on Form 10-K, the Commission requires a registrant to file a Form 10-Q for each of the first three quarters of its fiscal year. Form 10-Q is due either 40 or 45 days after the end of the quarter depending on accelerated filer status; one is not required for the fourth quarter. If the registrant is a listed company, it also must file Form 10-Q with the appropriate stock exchange. The basic requirements of Form 10-Q are listed next.

- The form is required to be filed by any company (1) whose securities are registered with the SEC, and (2) which is required to file annual reports on Form 10-K.
- Information must be submitted on a consolidated basis and must be reviewed in accordance with PCAOB auditing standards by the company's independent auditor prior to the filing.

A uniform set of instructions for interim financial statements is included in Article 10 of Regulation S-X, as an extension of the SEC's integrated disclosure program. In addition, certain requirements for the current Form 10-Q are contained in FRR Sections 301, 303, 304, and 305. Interpretations of the rules are provided in SAB Topic 6-G. Accounting Series Releases 177 and 286—Relating to Amendments to Form 10-Q, Regulation S-K, and Regulations S-X Regarding Interim Financial Reporting.

A registrant may elect to incorporate by reference all of the information required by Part I to a quarterly stockholder report or other published document containing the information. Other information also may be incorporated by reference in answer or partial answer to an item in Part II, provided the incorporation by reference is clearly identified. The SEC permits a combined quarterly stockholder report and Form 10-Q *if* the report contains all information required by Part I and all other information (cover page, signature, Part II) is in the combined report or included on Form 10-Q with appropriate cross-referencing.

(a) STRUCTURE OF FORM 10-Q.   Form 10-Q consists of two parts. Part I contains financial informa-tion, and Part II contains other information such as legal proceedings and changes in securities.

(i) Part I—Financial Information

Item 1—Financial Statements.   The financial statements should be prepared in accordance with Rule 10-01 of Regulation S-X and ASC 270. An understanding of these requirements is essential in preparing Form 10-Q.

The financial statements may be condensed and should include a condensed balance sheet, income statement, and statement of cash flows for the required periods. The statements are not required to be audited or reviewed by independent accountants.

Balance sheets as of the end of the latest quarter and the end of the preceding fiscal year are required. A comparative balance sheet as of the end of the previous year's corresponding interim date need be included only when, in the registrant's opinion, it is necessary for an understanding of seasonal fluctuations.

Only the major captions set forth in Article 5 of Regulation S-X are required to be disclosed, except that the components of inventory (raw materials, work in process, finished goods) must also be presented on the balance sheet or in the notes. Thus, even if a company uses the gross profit method or similar method to determine cost of sales for interim periods, management will have to estimate the inventory components.

There is also a materiality rule for disclosure of major balance sheet captions. Those that are less than 10 percent of total assets *and* that have not changed by more than 25 percent from the preceding fiscal year's balance sheet may be combined with other captions.

Income statements for the latest quarter and the year to date and for the corresponding periods of the prior year are to be provided. Statements may also be presented for the 12-month period ending with the latest quarter and the corresponding period of the preceding year.

For example, if a company reports on a November 30, 20XB, fiscal year-end, its Form 10-Q for the quarter ended August 31, 20XB, would include comparative income statements for the nine months ended August 31, 20XB and 20XA, and for the three months ended August 31, 20XB and 20XA.

Only major captions set forth in Article 5 of Regulation S-X are required to be disclosed. However, a major caption may be combined with others if it is less than 15 percent of average net income for the latest three fiscal years *and* has not changed by more than 20 percent as compared to the related caption in the income statement for the corresponding interim period of the preceding year (except that bank holding companies must present securities gains or losses as a separate item, regardless of the amount or percentage change). In computing average net income, only the amount classified as net income should be used. Loss years should be excluded unless losses were incurred in all three years, in which case the average loss should be used. As with the balance sheet, retroactive reclassification of the prior year is required to conform with the current year's classification in the income statement.

Statements of cash flows for the year to date and for the corresponding period of the prior year are to be presented. In addition, the statement may be presented for the 12-month periods ending with the latest quarter and the corresponding period of the prior year. The statement of cash flows may be condensed, starting with a single amount for net cash flows from operating activities. Additionally, individual items of financing and investing cash flows, and disclosures about noncash investing or financing transactions, need be presented only if they exceed 10 percent of the average net cash flows from operating activities for the last three years. In computing the average, any years that reflect a net cash outflow from operations should be excluded, unless all three years reflect a net cash outflow, in which case the average outflow should be used for the test.

Seven other important provisions of the rules relating to financial information are listed next.

1. Detailed footnote disclosures and Regulation S-X schedules are not required. However, dis-closures must be adequate so as not to make the presented information misleading. It would appear that the two preceding sentences are contradictory. There is, however, a presumption

that financial statement users have read or have access to the audited financial statements containing detailed disclosures for the latest fiscal year, in which case most continuing footnote disclosures could be omitted.

Regulation S-X specifically requires disclosure of events occurring since the end of the latest fiscal year having a material impact on the financial statements, such as changes in:

a. Accounting principles and practices.

b. Estimates used in the statements.

c. Status of long-term contracts.

d. Capitalization, including significant new borrowings, or modification of existing financing arrangements.

e. If material contingencies exist, disclosure is required even if significant changes have not occurred since year-end.

f. In addition, based on existing pronouncements and informal statements by the SEC, the next matters, if applicable, should be considered for disclosure:

  i. Significant events during the period (i.e., unusual or infrequently occurring items, such as material write-downs of inventory or goodwill)

  ii. Significant changes in the nature of transactions with related parties

  iii. The basis for allocating amounts of significant costs and expenses to interim periods if different from those used for the annual statements

  iv. The nature, amount, and tax effects of extraordinary items

  v. Significant variations in the customary relationship between income tax expense and income before taxes

  vi. The amount of any last-in, first-out (LIFO) liquidation expected to be replaced by year-end or the effect of a material liquidation during the quarter

  vii. Significant new commitments or changes in the status of those previously disclosed

Although it is not mentioned in the rules, registrants may consider it desirable to indicate with a legend on Form 10-Q that the financial statements are condensed and do not contain all GAAP-required disclosures that are included in a full set of financial statements.

2. The interim financial statements should contain a statement representing that they reflect all normally recurring adjustments that are, in management's opinion, necessary for a fair presentation in conformity with GAAP. Such adjustments would include estimated provisions for bonuses and for profit-sharing contributions normally determined at year-end.

3. The registrant may furnish additional information of significance to investors, such as seasonality of business, major uncertainties, significant proposed accounting changes, and backlog. In that connection, ordinarily it would be appropriate to include a statement that the interim results are not necessarily indicative of results to be obtained for the full year.

4. For disposals of a significant portion of the business or for combinations accounted for as purchases, the effect on revenues and net income (including earnings per share) must be disclosed. In addition, in the case of purchases, pro forma disclosures in accordance with ASC 805 are required.

5. If the prior-period information has been retroactively restated after the initial reporting of that period, disclosure is required of the effect of the change.

6. If an accounting change was made, the date of the change and the reasons for making it must be disclosed. In addition, in the first Form 10-Q filed after the date of an accounting change, a letter from the accountants (referred to as a *preferability letter*) must be filed as an exhibit in Part II, indicating whether they believe the change to be a preferable alternative accounting principle under the circumstances. If the change was made in response to an FASB requirement, no such letter need be filed.

The SEC Staff acknowledges that where objective criteria for determining preferability have not been established by authoritative bodies, the determination of the preferable accounting treatment should be based on the registrant's business judgment and business planning (e.g., expectations regarding the impact of inflation, consumer demand for the company's products, or a change in marketing methods). The Staff believes that the registrant's judgment and business planning, unless they appear to be unreasonable, may be accepted and relied on by the accountant as the basis of the preferability letter.

If circumstances used to justify a change in accounting method become different in subsequent years, the registrant may not change back to the principle originally used without again justifying that the original principle is preferable under current conditions.

Item 2—Management's Discussion and Analysis of Financial Condition and Results of Operations (Item 303(b) of Regulation S-K). The MD&A must be provided pursuant to Item 303(b) of Regulation S-K and should discuss substantially the same issues covered in the MD&A for the latest Form 10-K, specifically focusing on:

- Material changes in financial condition for the period from the latest fiscal year-end to the date of the most recent interim balance sheet and, if applicable, the corresponding interim period of the preceding fiscal year
- Material changes in results of operations for the most recent year-to-date period, the current quarter, and the corresponding periods of the preceding fiscal year

In preparing the discussion, companies may presume that users of the interim financial information have access to the MD&A covering the most recent fiscal year. The MD&A should address any seasonal aspects of its business affecting its financial condition or results of operations and identify any significant elements of income from continuing operations that are not representative of the ongoing business. The impact of inflation does not have to be discussed.

The MD&A should be as informative as possible. As discussed, the registrant should avoid the use of boilerplate analysis and not merely repeat numerical data easily derived from the financial statements. Information about material changes to contractual obligations should be disclosed.

Item 3—Quantitative and Qualitative Disclosures about Market Risk (Item 305 of Regulation S-K).   Market risk information is required to be presented if there have been material changes in the market risks faced by a registrant or in how those risks are managed since the end of the most recent fiscal year. Interim information is not required until after the first fiscal year-end in which the disclosures are made.

Item 4—Controls and Procedures (Item 307 and 308(c) of Regulation S-K).   Item 4 requires the PEO and PFOs to evaluate the effectiveness of disclosure controls and procedures as of the end of each quarter. Regulation S-K Item 307 requires disclosure of the conclusions of such evaluations.

(ii) Part II—Other Information.   The registrant should provide the information below in Part II under the applicable captions. Any item that is not applicable may be omitted *without* disclosing that fact.

Item 1—Legal Proceedings (Item 103 of Regulation S-K).   A legal proceeding has to be reported in the quarter in which it first becomes a reportable event or in subsequent quarters in which there are material developments. For terminated proceedings, information as to the date of termination and a description of the disposition should be provided in the Form 10-Q covering that quarter.

Item 1A—Risk Factors.   Item 1A requires disclosure of any material changes to the factors reported in response to Item 1A of the issuer's annual report on Form 10-K.

Item 2—Unregistrered Sales of Equity Securities and Use of Proceeds (Item 701 and 703 of Regulation S-K).   Any sales of equity securities not registered under the Securities Act not previously reported, including a description of the securities sold, the purchasers, the consideration received, the exemption from registration claimed, and the terms of conversions (if any), should be disclosed.

For first registration statements filed under the Securities Act, the issuer must report on the use of proceeds in the first periodic report filed after the registration statement's effective date and in each subsequent periodic report (i.e., Form 10-K or 10-Q) until the offering is terminated or all proceeds applied, whichever is later. The registrant must quantify the use of proceeds to date (i.e., to invest in property and plant, to acquire businesses, to repay debt) and identify any direct or indirect payments to directors, officers, or 10 percent or more stockholders.

Registrants are also required to disclose the same information related to repurchases of stock as required in the form 10-K.

Item 3[3]—Defaults on Senior Securities.   Disclosure is required of a default (with respect to principal or interest) not cured within 30 days of the due date, including any grace period, if the related indebtedness exceeds five percent of consolidated assets. A default relating to dividend arrearages on preferred stock should also be disclosed.

Item 5—Other Information.   Events not previously reported on Form 8-K may be reported under this caption. Such information would not be required to be repeated in a report on Form 8-K.

Item 6—Exhibits and Reports on Form 8-K.   This caption should include a listing of exhibits filed with Form 10-Q (Item 601 of Regulation S-K) and a listing of Form 8-K reports filed during the quarter, showing the dates of any such reports, items reported, and financial statements filed.

Inapplicable exhibits may be omitted without referring to them in the index. Where exhibits are incorporated by reference, that fact should be noted.

XBRL Exhibit. All domestic registrants (foreign private issuers using IFRS will be required to file XBRL schedules as soon as the XBRL taxonomy is approved) are required to include XBRL schedules with the quarterly report.

(iii) Signatures.   The form must be signed by the PFO or chief accounting officer of the registrant as well as another duly authorized officer. If the PFO or chief accounting officer is also a duly authorized signatory, one signature is sufficient provided the officer's dual responsibility is indicated.

Signatures for any electronic submission are in typed form rather than manual format. However, manually signed pages (or other documents acknowledging the typed signatures) must be obtained *prior* to the electronic filing. The registrant must retain the original signed document for a period of five years after the filing of the related document and provide it to the SEC or the staff upon request.

5.6 FORM 8-K

(a) OVERVIEW OF FORM 8-K REQUIREMENTS.   A company that is required to file annual reports on Form 10-K is required to file current reports on Form 8-K if any specified reportable events take place. Form 8-K reports are due within four business days after occurrence of the event.

The Form 8-K items are organized in this way:

- Section 1—Registrant's Business and Operations
  - Item 1.01   Entry into a Material Definitive Agreement
  - Item 1.02   Termination of a Material Definitive Agreement
  - Item 1.03   Bankruptcy or Receivership
- Section 2—Financial Information
  - Item 2.01   Completion of Acquisition or Disposition of Assets
  - Item 2.02   Results of Operations and Financial Condition

---

[3] Item 4 is reserved for future use.

- ○ Item 2.03   Creation of a Direct Financial Obligation or an Obligation under an Off-Balance Sheet Arrangement of a Registrant
- ○ Item 2.04   Triggering Events That Accelerate or Increase a Direct Financial Obligation or an Obligation under an Off-Balance Sheet Arrangement
- ○ Item 2.05   Costs Associated with Exit or Disposal Activities
- ○ Item 2.06   Material Impairments
- Section 3—Securities and Trading Markets
- ○ Item 3.01   Notice of Delisting or Failure to Satisfy a Continued Listing Rule or Standard; Transfer of Listing
- ○ Item 3.02   Unregistered Sales of Equity Securities
- ○ Item 3.03   Material Modifications to Rights of Security Holders
- Section 4—Matters Related to Accountants and Financial Statements
- ○ Item 4.01   Changes in Registrant's Certifying Accountant
- ○ Item 4.02   Non-Reliance on Previously Issued Financial Statements or a Related Audit Report or Completed Interim Review
- Section 5—Corporate Governance and Management
- ○ Item 5.01   Changes in Control of Registrant
- ○ Item 5.02   Departure of Directors or Certain Officers; Election of Directors; Appointment of Certain Officers; Compensatory Arrangements of Certain Officers
- ○ Item 5.03   Amendments to Articles of Incorporation or Bylaws; Change in Fiscal Year
- ○ Item 5.04   Temporary Suspension of Trading under Registrant's Employee Benefit Plans
- ○ Item 5.05   Amendments to the Registrant's Code of Ethics, or Waiver of a Provision of the Code of Ethics
- ○ Item 5.06   Changes in Shell Company Status
- ○ Item 5.07   Submission of Matters to a Vote of Security Holders
- Section 6—Asset-Backed Securities
- ○ Item 6.01   ABS Informational and Computational Method
- ○ Item 6.02   Change of Servicer or Trustee
- ○ Item 6.03   Change in Credit Enhancement or Other External Support
- ○ Item 6.04   Failure to Make a Required Distribution
- ○ Item 6.05   Securities Act Updating Disclosure
- Section 7—Regulation FD
- ○ Item 7.01   Regulation FD Disclosure
- Section 8—Other Events
- ○ Item 8.01   Other Events
- Section 9—Financial Statements and Exhibits
- ○ Item 9.01   Financial Statements and Exhibits

If substantially the same information required for Form 8-K has been previously reported by the registrant in a filing with the SEC (such as in Part II of Form 10-Q or in a proxy statement), there is no need to include it on a Form 8-K.

If, within the four business days, a registrant issues a press release or other document that includes information meeting some or all of the requirements of Form 8-K, the information may be incorporated by reference to the document. The document incorporated by reference should be included as an exhibit to Form 8-K.

A few of the events and the required disclosures are discussed in more detail next.

(i) Item 2.01—Completion of Acquisition or Disposition of Assets.   Disclosure is required of any acquisitions or dispositions of a significant amount of assets, other than in the ordinary course of business. Disclosures would include the transaction date, description of the assets, the purchase or sales price, the parties involved and any relationships between them, sources of funds used, and the use of assets acquired.

An acquisition or disposition is "significant" if:

- For an acquisition or disposition of assets (versus a business), the net book value of the assets or the purchase price or sales price exceeds 10 percent of the registrant's consolidated assets before the transaction, *or*
- The interest in the business bought or sold meets the test of a significant subsidiary at the 20 percent level.

Financial statements may be required to be filed for the acquired business, depending on its relative significance. The determination of significance is made by applying the significant subsidiary tests in comparing the latest annual financial statements of the acquired business to the registrant's latest annual consolidated financial statements filed at or before the acquisition (Rule 3-05 of Regulation S-X). The income and asset test should be as of the latest fiscal year; *provided, however,* that if the registrant has, since the end of the most recent fiscal year, consummated an acquisition for which historical and pro forma financial information has been filed on Form 8-K, then the pro forma amount in that Form 8-K for the latest fiscal year may be used. (*Note:* Registrants who believe their specific circumstances warrant the use of later financial information in other situations should consult with the Division of Corporation Finance, which will evaluate such requests on a case-by-case basis.)

- If, based on such tests, none of the conditions exceeds 20 percent, financial statements are not required.
- If any condition exceeds 20 percent, but none exceeds 40 percent, financial statements are required for the latest year prior to acquisition (audited) and for any interim periods required by Rules 3-01 and 3-02 of Regulation S-X (unaudited).
- If any condition exceeds 40 percent but does not exceed 50 percent, financial statements are required for the two most recent years (audited), and for any interim periods (unaudited).
- If any condition exceeds 50 percent, financial statements are required for the three latest years (audited), as required in Form 10-K, and for any interim periods (unaudited). However, only two years of financial statements are required if the acquired business revenues, in its most recent year, are less than $50 million or the registrant is a smaller reporting company.

If the acquired business or equity investee is a foreign entity, the entity's financial statements can be (1) presented in U.S. GAAP or (2) presented in IFRS as issued by the IASB or (3) presented in local GAAP if a reconciliation from local GAAP to U.S. GAAP is provided when the significance exceeds 30 percent.

Even if the reconciliation of U.S. GAAP does not need to be presented, reconciliation work will still be required with respect to the financial statements of foreign equity investees. This is because (1) the local GAAP financial statements of the foreign equity investees must still be converted to U.S. GAAP in order to properly apply the equity method of accounting and (2) Reg. S-X Rule 4-08(g) requires summary financial information regarding equity investees in accordance with U.S. GAAP in the notes to the primary financial statements.

Domestic issuers may now update the financial statements of acquired foreign businesses or foreign equity investees included in their filings on the same time schedule as foreign issuers. Regulation S-X governs the form and content of these financial statements. S-X schedules are not required.

If a portion of a business is being acquired, such as a division or a single product line, the registrant should provide audited financial statements only on the portion of the business acquired. Therefore, the registrant may, depending on the circumstances and with the permission of the SEC, present a "statement of assets acquired and liabilities assumed" (excluding amounts not included in the acquisition, such as intercompany advances) instead of a balance sheet and a "statement of revenues and direct expenses" for the business acquired instead of an income statement. A registrant, when acquiring a division or product line whose operations are included in the consolidated financial statements of a larger entity, should determine as soon as possible if the accountant reporting on the consolidated financial statements of the seller is able to report on the portion being acquired.

A significant acquisition or disposition under Item 2.01 will also require presentation of pro forma financial information giving effect to the event. The purpose of pro forma data is to provide investors with information about the continuing impact of a transaction and assist them in analyzing future prospects of the registrant. The main provisions of the rule (Regulation S-X, Article 11) are listed next.

- The pro forma financial statements should consist of a condensed balance sheet as of the end of the most recent period and condensed income statements for the latest fiscal year and the interim period from the latest fiscal year-end to the date of the pro forma balance sheet. (Interim data for the corresponding period of the prior year is optional.)

- Only the major captions of Article 5 of Regulation S-X need be presented. For the balance sheet, captions that amount to less than 10 percent of total assets may be combined; income statement captions less than 15 percent of average net income for the latest three years may likewise be combined.

- The pro forma statements should be preceded by an introductory paragraph describing the transaction and should be accompanied by explanatory notes.

- Ordinarily, the statements should be in columnar form, presenting historical statements, pro forma adjustments, and the pro forma totals. Care should be taken in combining pro forma adjustments to the same line item. Sufficient detail must be provided to allow for a clear understanding of the amount and nature of required adjustments. For a purchase business combination, the footnotes should tabularly indicate the components and allocation of the purchase price.

- If the acquired business's fiscal year differs from that of the registrant by more than 93 days, the income statement of the acquired business for the latest year should be updated. This can be done by adding and deducting comparable interim periods. In that case, there should be disclosure of the periods combined and the revenues and income for periods excluded or for periods included more than once (e.g., an interim period included both as part of the fiscal year and subsequent interim period).

- The pro forma income statement should end with income (loss) from continuing operations Material nonrecurring items and related tax effects that will affect net income within the next 12 months should be disclosed separately. Nonrecurring items included in the historical financial statements that are not directly attributable to the transaction should *not* be excluded from the pro forma financial statements.

  If the assets acquired include assets relating to operations that the acquirer intends to dispose of, the Staff will not object to the presentation of those assets as a single line item in the pro forma balance sheet, provided the operations are not expected to be continued for more than a short period (i.e., 12 months) prior to disposal.

- Adjustments to the pro forma income statement should assume that the transaction was consummated at the beginning of the earliest fiscal year and should include factually supportable adjustments that are directly attributable to the transaction and expected to have a continuing effect. Adjustments to the balance sheet should assume that the transaction had occurred at the balance sheet date and should include factually supportable adjustments that are directly attributable to the transaction (regardless of whether they have a continuing impact or are nonrecurring).

If an acquired entity was previously part of another entity, adjustments might be necessary when corporate overhead, interest, or income taxes had not been allocated by management on a reasonable basis. Similarly, if the acquired business was an S corporation or a partnership, adjustments should be made to reflect estimated officer salaries and income taxes. For dispositions, the adjustments should include deletion of the divested business and adjustments of expenses incurred on behalf of that business (e.g., advertising costs). For transactions accounted for as a purchase, the adjustments should reflect any the income statement of the purchase transaction (e.g., the impact of additional depreciation and amortization on the fair value of the acquired assets and interest on debt incurred to make the acquisition).

- Tax effects of pro forma adjustments should be shown separately and ordinarily should be calculated at the statutory rate in effect during the periods presented.

- In certain unusual instances, there may only be a limited number of clearly understandable adjustments, in which case a narrative description of the transaction may be substituted for the pro forma statements.

- Historical and pro forma per share data, including the number of shares used in the computation, should be disclosed on the face of the pro forma income statement. If common shares are to be issued in the transaction, the per share data should be adjusted to reflect assumed issuance at the beginning of the period presented.

- A financial forecast may be presented in lieu of the pro forma income statement. The forecast should be in the same detail as the pro forma income statements and should cover at least 12 months from the date of the most recent balance sheet included in the filing or the estimated consummation date of the transaction, whichever is later. Historical information for a recent 12-month period should be presented in a parallel column. The forecast should be presented in accordance with AICPA guidelines, with clear disclosure of underlying assumptions. Registrants rarely present a forecast in lieu of pro forma financial statements.

The determination of what constitutes a "business" for the purpose of determining whether financial statements are required to be included in the filing is a facts-and-circumstances test. This test would require an evaluation of whether there is sufficient continuity of the acquired entity's operations before and after the transaction so that presentation of prior financial data is meaningful for an understanding of future operations. There is a presumption that a subsidiary or division is a business, although a smaller component or an entity also could qualify. Among the matters to be considered are:

- Whether the type of revenue-producing activity will remain generally the same
- Whether physical facilities, employee base, marketing system, sales force, customer base, operating rights, production methods, or trade names will remain

Form 8-K provides for an automatic extension of up to a total of 75 days from the consummation of a business combination to file the historical audited financial statements and the pro forma financial information (a 71-day extension from the initial 4-day due date).

A registrant should provide all available information required under Items 2.01 and 9.01 for the business acquisition. The registrant may, at its option, include unaudited financial statements in the initial report on Form 8-K. No further extensions beyond the 71 days will be considered. The SEC has emphasized that the availability of the extension should not be an invitation for nontimely filing of the required information. Pro forma financial statements depicting a disposition are required to be included in the Item 2.01 Form 8-K filed within four business days of the disposition. The 71-day grace period does not apply to business dispositions.

(ii) Item 4.01—Changes in Registrant's Certifying Accountant.   Certain disclosures are required in Form 8-K as a result of the resignation by (or declination to stand for reelection after completion of the current audit) or dismissal of a registrant's independent accountant or the engagement of a new accountant. Such changes in the accountant for a significant subsidiary on whom the principal accountant expressed reliance in his or her report would also be reportable events.

The Commission is concerned about changes in accountants and the potential for opinion shopping. Generally all 8-Ks reporting a change in accountant are reviewed by the Staff. When an independent accountant who was the principal accountant for the company or who audited a significant subsidiary and was expressly relied on by the principal accountant resigns (or declines to stand for reelection) or is dismissed, the registrant must make these four disclosures:

1. Whether the former accountant resigned, declined to stand for reelection, or was dismissed, including the date thereof and whether:
   a. There was an adverse opinion, disclaimer of opinion, or qualification or modification of opinion as to uncertainty, audit scope, or accounting principles issued by such accountant for either of the two most recent years, including a description of the nature of the opinion.
   b. The decision to change accountants was recommended by or approved by the audit committee or a similar committee or by the board of directors in the absence of such special committee.
2. Whether during the two most recent fiscal years and any subsequent interim period preceding the resignation, declination, or dismissal there were any disagreements with the former accountant on any matter of accounting principles or practices, financial statement disclosure, or auditing scope or procedure, which disagreement(s), if not resolved to the satisfaction of the former accountant, would have caused the accountant to make reference to the subject matter of the disagreement(s) in connection with his or her report. If such disagreement occurred, the registrant must disclose:
   a. The nature of the disagreement
   b. Whether any audit committees (or similar body) or board of directors discussed the subject matter of the disagreement with the former accountant
   c. Whether the registrant has authorized the former accountant to respond fully to the successor accountant concerning the matter

   The term *disagreements* should be interpreted broadly but should not include preliminary differences of opinion that are "based on incomplete facts" if the differences are resolved by obtaining more complete factual information.
3. Whether there were any "reportable events" during the two most recent fiscal years or any subsequent interim period preceding the resignation, declination, or dismissal, including:
   a. The auditor having advised the registrant that the internal controls necessary to develop reliable financial statements do not exist
   b. The auditor having advised the registrant that information has come to the auditor's attention that led him or her to no longer be able to rely on management's representations or that has made him or her unwilling to be associated with the financial statements
   c. The auditor having advised the registrant that there is a need to significantly expand the audit scope or that information has come to the auditor's attention during the last two fiscal years and any subsequent interim period that, if further investigated, may (1) materially impact the fairness or reliability of either a previously issued audit report or the underlying financial statements or the financial statements issued or to be issued for a subsequent period or (2) cause the auditor to be unwilling to rely on management's representations or to be associated with the financial statements and due to the change in auditors, the auditor did not expand his scope or conduct a further investigation
   d. The auditor having advised the registrant that information has come to the auditor's attention that he or she has concluded materially impacts the fairness or reliability of either (1) a previously issued audit report or the underlying financial statements or (2) the financial statements relating to a subsequent period and, unless the matter is resolved to the auditor's satisfaction, the auditor would be prevented from rendering an unqualified report and, due to the change in auditors, the matter has not been resolved

4. When a new independent accountant has been engaged, the registrant must identify the newly engaged accountant and the date of the engagement. In addition, if, during the two most recent fiscal years or subsequent interim period, the registrant or someone on its behalf consulted the newly engaged accountant regarding the application of accounting principles as to any specific transaction, either completed or proposed, the type of audit opinion that would be rendered on the registrant's financial statements, or any matter of disagreement or a reportable event with the former accountant. If such a consultation took place, the Form 8-K must:

    a. Describe the accounting issue and the newly engaged accountant's view. Any written opinion issued by the new accountant must be filed as an exhibit, and the new accountant must be provided the opportunity to review the disclosure and furnish a letter to the SEC that clarifies or expresses disagreement with the registrant's disclosure of its views.

    b. State whether the former accountant was consulted regarding such issues and, if so, describe the former accountant's views.

Disagreements and reportable events are intended to be communicated to the registrant orally and in writing. Because these are sensitive areas that may impugn the integrity of management, communication will have to be handled with extreme care on the part of all involved.

The auditor who is aware that a required filing related to a change of accountants has not been made by the registrant should consider advising the registrant in writing of that reporting responsibility with a copy to the Commission.

The PCAOB adopted as part of its interim standards a rule of the Center for Public Company Audit Firms of the AICPA (successor to the Securities and Exchange Commission Practice Section (SECPS)), which also requires the auditor to provide written notification, within five business days, that the auditor has resigned, has decided not to stand for reelection, or has been dismissed. The purpose of this "five-day" letter is to provide early notification to the SEC in advance of the Form 8-K filing due date. This letter is addressed to the client, with a copy to the SEC (generally faxed), and states simply that the relationship has been terminated.

Additionally, Item 304 of Regulation S-K requires the registrant to disclose similar information about auditor changes during the two years preceding the filing of registration statements for initial public offerings.

(iii) Item 4.02—Non-Reliance on Previously Issued Financial Statements or a Related Audit Report or Completed Interim Review. Item 4.02 requires a company to provide certain disclosures when a company's previously issued financial statements should no longer be relied on because of an error (as addressed in ASC 250 (SFAS No. 154, *Accounting Changes and Error Corrections*)). The disclosures must be made whether the company (Item 4.02a) or its independent auditors (Item 4.02b) make this determination. In either case, the company must disclose:

1. The date of the determination and identification of the financial statements and years or periods covered that should no longer be relied on

2. A statement that the audit report should no longer be relied on

3. A brief description of the facts underlying the determination to the extent known to the company at the time of filing

4. A statement as to whether the audit committee, the full board if there is no audit committee, or an authorized officer has discussed the matter giving rise to the determination with the company's independent accountant

If the company's independent accountant makes the determination, the company must provide the accountant with a copy of the disclosures it is making under this item no later than the day it files the Form 8-K. The company must also ask the accountant to furnish as promptly as possible a letter addressed to the SEC, stating whether the accountant agrees with the company's disclosure and if not, why not. The company must then amend the Form 8-K to file the accountant's letter as an exhibit within two business days of receipt of the letter.

If the registrant determines that its previously issued financial statements can no longer be relied on because of errors or its auditor advises that the previously issued audit report or completed interim review should no longer be relied on, the company must file a Form 8-K within four business days. If the registrant determines that an error and an associated restatement are not material (and that a Form 8-K filing is therefore not necessary), the Staff advises that the company should be prepared to support its conclusion. Also, the Staff may question the timing of the Form 8-K if it is filed shortly before an amended Form 10-K or 10-Q filing. Given the time it usually takes to prepare restated financial statements, this suggests that the Form 8-K may not have been filed within four business days of the date the registrant concluded the financial statement should not be relied on. The Staff observe that registrants are always required to file Item 4.02 Form 8-Ks when prior financial statement should not be relied on and that it is not appropriate to disclose this information in quarterly or annual reports.

5.7 PROXY STATEMENTS

(a) OVERVIEW.   Because of the geographic dispersion of the owners of a public company, it is unlikely that a quorum could be obtained at any meeting that required a vote of the shareholders. As a result, the use of proxies and proxy statements developed to facilitate such votes. A *proxy* is broadly defined as any authorization given to someone by security holders to act on their behalf at a stockholders' meeting. The term *proxy* also refers to the document used to evidence such authorization. Persons soliciting proxies must comply with Regulation 14A and the 1934 Act, which prescribes the content of documents to be distributed to stockholders before, or at the same time as, such solicitation occurs.

The informational content of the proxy statement provided to the stockholders depends on the action to be taken by the stockholders. Schedule 14A prescribes the informational content required based on the specific circumstances.

When the vote is solicited for (1) an exchange of one security for another, (2) mergers or consolidations, or (3) transfers of assets, the transaction constitutes an "offer to sell securities." As such, a registration statement is required under the 1933 Act and can be filed on Form S-4 (Form F-4 for foreign private issuers in similar transactions).

(b) REGULATION 14A.   The SEC derives its authority to regulate the solicitation of proxies from the Exchange Act and from the Investment Company Act of 1940. Section 14(a) of the Exchange Act states:

> It shall be unlawful for any person, by the use of the mails or by any means or instrumentality of interstate commerce or of any facility of a national securities exchange or otherwise, in contravention of such rules and regulations as the Commission may prescribe as necessary or appropriate in the public interest or for the protection of investors, to solicit or to permit the use of his name to solicit any proxy or consent or authorization in respect of any security (other than an exempted security) registered pursuant to Section 12 of this title.

Based on this statutory authority, the SEC established Regulation 14A to regulate proxy solicitations. Regulation 14A consists of these rules:

14a-1	Definitions
14a-2	Solicitations to Which Rules 14a-3–14a-15 Apply
14a-3	Information to Be Furnished to Security Holders
14a-4	Requirements as to Proxy
14a-5	Presentation of Information in Proxy Statements
14a-6	Filing Requirements

14a-7	Obligation of Registrants to Provide a List of, or Mail Solicitation Materials to, Security Holders
14a-8	Shareholder Proposals
14a-9	False or Misleading Statements
14a-10	Prohibition of Certain Solicitations
14a-11	Shareholder Nominations
14a-12	Solicitation Before Furnishing a Proxy Statement
14a-13	Obligation of Registrants in Communicating with Beneficial Owners
14a-14	Modified or Superseded Documents
14a-15	Differential and Contingent Compensation in Connection with Roll-up Transactions
14a-16	Internet Availability of Proxy Materials
14a-17	Electronic Shareholder Forums
14a-18	Disclosure Regarding Nominating Shareholders and
	Nominees Submitted Pursuant to Applicable State of Foreign Law, or a Registrant's Governing Documents
14a-20	Shareholder Approval of Executive Compensation of TARP Recipients

Because of the complexity of these rules, most are not discussed in detail here. However, it is important to remember that proxies and proxy statements are different from other SEC filings because they are required to be sent directly to the security holders. Registration statements are filed directly with the SEC. Annual reports on Form 10-K are filed with the SEC and are furnished to the shareholder only on request. Typically, the proxy materials must be given to the shareholders at least 20 days prior to the meeting date. Companies listed on the NYSE provide shareholders 30 days to review the materials.

The proxy rules require companies to provide shareholders with proxy cards to give them more opportunity to participate in corporate elections. Shareholder proxy cards must (1) indicate whether the proxy is solicited on behalf of the board of directors, (2) enable shareholders to abstain from voting on directors and other proxy matters as well as to approve or disapprove each matter, and (3) allow shareholders to vote for or withhold authority to vote for each nominee for the board of directors. Registrants may provide their proxy materials on the Internet and provide shareholders with a notice of Internet availability of proxy materials instead of mailing a hard copy of the materials to each shareholder. Shareholders can request and the registrant must provide paper copies of the materials.

(c) SEC REVIEW REQUIREMENTS.   Except as noted in this section, Rule 14a-6 requires that preliminary copies of the proxy statements and related materials be filed with the SEC at least 10 calendar days prior to the date definitive copies of such material are first sent or given to security holders. Such materials should be appropriately marked as "Preliminary Copies," and the date definitive materials are to be mailed to the shareholders must be stated in the filing. Earlier submission (usually more than 20 days) is advisable to allow time for any changes that may be required as a result of the SEC's selective review process.

Preliminary proxy materials need not be filed with the Commission if the solicitation relates to any meeting of security holders at which the only matters to be acted on include these six:

1. The election of directors
2. The election, approval, or ratification of accountant(s)
3. A shareholder proposal
4. With respect to a registered investment company or business development company, a proposal to continue, without change, any advisory or other contract or agreement that has been the subject of a proxy solicitation for which proxy material has previously been filed

5. With respect to an open-end registered investment company, a proposal to increase the number of shares authorized to be issued

6. The approval or ratification of certain compensation plans (i.e., restricted stock, SARs, or stock options) or amendments to such plans. This exemption does not, however, extend to the approval of awards made pursuant to such plans.

Information in preliminary proxy material will be made available to people requesting it after the definitive proxy is filed, unless an application for confidential treatment for such information is made at the time of filing the preliminary proxy material and approved by the SEC. Such preliminary material will also be made available to people requesting it if no definitive filing is anticipated.

Before the registrant files the preliminary material, the accountant should read the entire text and compare it with the financial statements. This procedure is intended to avoid inconsistencies and misleading comments of which the accountant may have knowledge and to ascertain that the financial statements include disclosures mentioned in the text that are appropriate for a fair presentation of the financial statements in conformity with GAAP.

If the audit has not been completed, the SEC requires that a letter from the independent accountant accompany the preliminary material. The letter should state that the accountant has considered the preliminary material and will allow the use of his or her report on the financial statements. This letter is addressed to the registrant, who, in turn, submits it to the SEC. When preparing the letter, the accountant should avoid using general terms such as "considered" or "reviewed" in describing the work and should avoid expressing approval, either directly or indirectly, of the sufficiency of disclosures in the text. The accountant should state that he or she has read the preliminary proxy statements and will upon completion of the audit allow use of the report on the financial statements. The financial statements covered by the report, and the date of the report, should be specified in the letter. When a proxy statement is prepared for a proposed merger, the letter should relate only to the company with which the accountant is familiar.

Copies of the definitive material that are mailed to stockholders should be filed with the SEC no later than the date such material is mailed to the stockholders.

If changed circumstances or new events arising between the time the proxy solicitation is mailed and the stockholders' meeting date cause the proxy material to be materially false and misleading, the corrected material should be disseminated promptly to the stockholders and to the SEC (with markings clearly indicating the changes).

CHAPTER 6

MANAGEMENT DISCUSSION AND ANALYSIS

Sydney K. Garmong, CPA
Crowe Horwath LLP

Brad A. Davidson, CPA
Crowe Horwath LLP

6.1 OVERVIEW

(a) INTRODUCTION. Management must include, as part of Form 10-K filings, a section entitled "Management Discussion and Analysis of Financial Condition and the Results of Operations" (commonly referred to as Management Discussion & Analysis [MD&A]). The governing regulation is Section 229.303 of Regulation S-K and is referred to as Item 303. As stated in Item 303, the objective of the MD&A is "to provide to investors and other users information relevant to an assessment of the financial condition and results of operations of the registrant as determined by evaluating the amounts and certainty of cash flows from operations and from outside sources." The MD&A should permit shareholders and users to see and understand the specific decisions made through the eyes of management. The Securities and Exchange Commission (SEC) has stated:

> The Commission has long recognized the need for a narrative explanation of the financial statements, because a numerical presentation and brief accompanying footnotes alone may be insufficient for an investor to judge the quality of earnings and the likelihood that past performance is indicative of future performance. MD&A is intended to give the investor an opportunity to look at the company through the eyes of management by providing both a short- and long-term analysis

of the business of the company. The Item asks management to discuss the dynamics of the business and to analyze the financials. [Securities Act Release No. 6711, April 24, 1987, 52 Federal Register (FR) 13715]

The SEC has especially emphasized the need for prospective disclosures:

The MD&A requirements are intended to provide, in one section of a filing, material historical and prospective textual disclosure enabling investors and other users to assess the financial condition and results of operations of the registrant, with particular emphasis on the registrant's prospects for the future. [Release Nos. 33-6835; 34-26831, May 18, 1989]

This is notably similar to the statement given by the Financial Accounting Standards Board (FASB) on the purpose of financial reporting in general:

Financial reporting should include explanations and interpretations to help users understand financial information provided. For example, the usefulness of financial information as an aid to investors, creditors, and others in forming expectations about a business enterprise may be enhanced by management's explanations of the information. Management knows more about the enterprise and its affairs than investors, creditors, or other "outsiders" and can often increase the usefulness of financial information by identifying certain transactions, other events, and circumstances that affect the enterprise and explaining their financial impact on it. [par. 54, FASB Concepts Statement, *Objectives of Financial Reporting by Business Enterprises*]

Additionally, the Financial Analysts Federation has endorsed the MD&A:

We have supported the efforts of the SEC to make these disclosures meaningful. The MD&A, when properly prepared, can be extremely valuable in helping users understand the results of operations and, by extension, the factors which will affect future operating results. [Letter dated September 30, 1986, from Anthony Cope, Chairman, SEC Liaison Committee of the Financial Analysts Federation, to Jonathan Katz, Secretary, SEC]

In sum, both the SEC and the investment community strongly support the MD&A requirement. Furthermore, in light of SEC enforcement actions, particular care should be exercised in drafting the MD&A.

(b) BRIEF HISTORY.   The requirement for a management discussion section originated in 1968 when the SEC adopted the *Guides for Preparation and Filing of Registration Statements* (Securities Act Release No. 33-4936). These guides required a summary of earnings, which was to address unusual conditions affecting net income. In 1974, this summary was mandated for filings under the Securities Exchange Act and was broadened to include a discussion of underlying trends in profitability. Although specific topics to be discussed were not specified, recommendations were made. The SEC wanted to keep the requirements flexible, allowing management to discuss those items peculiar to its business, in order to prevent a "boilerplate" presentation. However, corporations generally fulfilled the requirement by providing percentage changes of financial statement line items (which investors could calculate themselves) without providing substantive reasons for the changes.

In 1977, the SEC's Advisory Committee on Corporate Disclosure reiterated that corporate management, in fact, be given broad latitude in their discussions but that better direction be provided. To elicit more meaningful prospective analyses, the SEC granted protection under safe harbor rules in 1979.[1] Then in 1980, the MD&A requirement was substantially expanded and rewritten. Although "soft" information was to be provided, the overriding belief was that the potential

---

[1] The safe harbor rule protects issuers from liability for forward-looking information, if such information has a reasonable basis and is disclosed in good faith. Otherwise, fraud actions under Rule 10b-5 may be brought against the firm.

relevance surpassed problems of verifiability. The 1980 requirements changed the MD&A from a summary of earnings only to an analysis of liquidity, capital resources, and results of operations.

In May 1989, the SEC issued an Interpretive Release, *Management's Discussion and Analysis of Financial Condition and Results of Operations; Certain Investment Company Disclosures,* which provided guidance, particularly on prospective or "forward-looking" disclosures.[2] This is significant in that the examples included in the release can serve as standards against which the SEC can measure the adequacy of registrant disclosures. The entire 1989 release is known as FR 36. (See *www.sec.gov/rules/interp/33-6835.htm.*)

With respect to currently known trends, the 1989 release points out that management must assess whether the trend, demand, commitment, event, or uncertainty is likely to happen. If a matter is not likely, no disclosure is required. However, management must be able to make a determination that a matter is not likely. If management cannot make such a determination, it must evaluate the consequences based on the assumption that the event will happen and then disclose the effects if the consequences are material. The release distinguishes currently known trends from anticipated trends.

Examples of known trends affecting future operations include reductions in the registrant's product prices, erosion in market share, changes in insurance coverage, likely nonrenewal of a material contract, discontinuation of a growth trend, and implementation of recently enacted legislation. With respect to future liquidity, the release indicates that the SEC expects registrants to discuss both short- and long-term liquidity, and to use the framework of the statement of cash flows as a basis of discussion (i.e., future operating, investing, and financing cash flows).[3]

To underscore the SEC's insistence on enhanced prospective disclosures, the SEC issued this warning in footnote 28 in its May 1989 Interpretative Release:

> Where a material change in a registrant's financial condition (such as a material increase or decrease in cash flows) or results of operations appears in a reporting period and the likelihood of such change was not discussed in prior reports, the Commission staff as part of its review of the current filing will inquire as to the circumstances existing at the time of the earlier filings to determine whether the registrant failed to discuss a known trend, demand, commitment, event or uncertainty as required by Item 303. [Release Nos. 33-6835; 34-26831, May 18, 1989]

Prior to the passage of the Sarbanes-Oxley Act of 2002 (SOX), the SEC issued additional guidance for MD&A. After the passage of SOX, two of the three releases were formally codified and incorporated into Regulation S-K through SEC rule making.

In 2001, the SEC issued *Cautionary Advice Regarding the Use of "Pro Forma" Financial Information in Earnings Releases* (also referred to as FR 59). In response to Section 401(b) of

---

[2] Although the 1989 release emphasizes prospective analysis, the historical analysis of the 1980 release is also required. The 1989 release interprets, but does not supersede, the 1980 release. Therefore, by continuing to require a discussion of historical changes as well as prospective events, the SEC underscores its belief that a better understanding of the causes of past performance is necessary for investors to assess the likelihood that the past is indicative of the future.

[3] As a matter of interest, the 1989 release mentions one known, future, material event that need not be disclosed. Merger negotiations do not have to be discussed in the MD&A unless the registrant has otherwise disclosed them. The SEC acknowledges that the risk of disclosure may jeopardize the transaction. There are other disclosure items that are required under different SEC releases and that may be disclosed in the MD&A. For instance, the SEC's Financial Reporting Release No. 6 (1982) mentions the MD&A as an appropriate place to discuss the degree of exposure to exchange rate risks, the functional currencies used to measure significant foreign operations, and the nature of the translation component of equity. Also, in its Staff Accounting Bulletin (SAB) No. 74 (1987), the SEC states that the MD&A may be used to discuss the impact (if known or reasonably estimable) of a future adoption of a recently issued accounting standard.

SOX and to codify guidance in FR 59, the SEC amended Regulation S-K with the issuance of the final rule, *Conditions for Use of Non-GAAP Financial Measures,* on January 22, 2003 (also referred to as FR 65).

The SEC also issued, in 2001, *Cautionary Advice Regarding Disclosure About Critical Accounting Policies* (referred to as FR 60). On May 10, 2002, the SEC proposed a rule entitled *Disclosure in Management's Discussion and Analysis about the Application of Critical Accounting Policies.* This proposal remains outstanding.

During 2001, the SEC also issued a statement entitled *Commission Statement About Management's Discussion and Analysis of Financial Condition and Results of Operations* (referred to as FR 61). This release primarily addressed liquidity and capital resources disclosures. In response to section 401(a) of SOX and to codify FR 61, the SEC amended Regulation S-K with the issuance of a final rule entitled *Disclosure in Management's Discussion and Analysis About Off-Balance-Sheet Arrangements and Aggregate Contractual Obligations* (also referred to as FR 67).

After the passage of SOX , the SEC continued issue MD&A guidance. During 2003, the SEC issued interpretative guidance entitled *Commission Guidance Regarding Management's Discussion and Analysis of Financial Condition and Results of Operations* (referred to as FR 72).

The SEC has continued to focus on MD&A disclosures on liquidity and capital resources. During 2010, the SEC issued an interpretative guidance entitled *Commission Guidance on Presentation of Liquidity and Capital Resources Disclosures in Management's Discussion and Analysis* (referred to as FR 83).

Exhibit 6.1 provides the full text of Section 229.303 (Item 303), "Management's Discussion and Analysis of Financial Condition and Results of Operations," of Regulation S-K. Exhibit 6.2 lists, in chronological order, the major SEC releases related to the MD&A.

TITLE 17 — COMMODITY AND SECURITIES EXCHANGES
CHAPTER II — SECURITIES AND EXCHANGE COMMISSION
PART 229 STANDARD INSTRUCTIONS FOR FILING FORMS UNDER SECURITIES ACT
Subpart 229.300 Financial Information
Section 229.303 (Item 303) Management's discussion and analysis of financial condition and results of operations.

a. *Full fiscal years.* Discuss registrant's financial condition, changes in financial condition and results of operations. The discussion shall provide information as specified in paragraphs (a)(1) through (5) of this Item and also shall provide such other information that the registrant believes to be necessary to an understanding of its financial condition, changes in financial condition, and results of operations. Discussions of liquidity and capital resources may be combined whenever the two topics are interrelated. Where in the registrant's judgment a discussion of segment information or of other subdivisions of the registrant's business would be appropriate to an understanding of such business, the discussion shall focus on each relevant, reportable segment or other subdivision of the business, and on the registrant as a whole.

   1. *Liquidity.* Identify any known trends or any known demands, commitments, events, or uncertainties that will result in or that are reasonably likely to result in the registrant's liquidity increasing or decreasing in any material way. If a material deficiency is identified, indicate the course of action that the registrant has taken or proposes to take to remedy the deficiency. Also identify and separately describe internal and external sources of liquidity, and briefly discuss any material unused sources of liquid assets.

   2. *Capital resources.*

      i. Describe the registrant's material commitments for capital expenditures as of the end of the latest fiscal period, and indicate the general purpose of such commitments and the anticipated source of funds needed to fulfill such commitments.

      ii. Describe any known material trends, favorable or unfavorable, in the registrant's capital resources. Indicate any expected material changes in the mix and relative cost of such resources. The discussion shall consider changes between equity, debt, and any off-balance-sheet financing arrangements.

   3. *Results of operations.*

      i. Describe any unusual or infrequent events or transactions or any significant economic changes that materially affected the amount of reported income from continuing operations and, in each case, indicate the extent to which income was so affected. In addition, describe any other significant components of revenues or expenses that, in the registrant's judgment, should be described in order to understand the registrant's results of operations.

Exhibit 6.1   Item 303 of Regulation S-K

    ii. Describe any known trends or uncertainties that have had or that the registrant reasonably expects will have a material favorable or unfavorable impact on net sales or revenues or income from continuing operations. If the registrant knows of events that will cause a material change in the relationship between costs and revenues (such as known future increases in costs of labor or materials or price increases or inventory adjustments), the change in the relationship shall be disclosed.

    iii. To the extent that the financial statements disclose material increases in net sales or revenues, provide a narrative discussion of the extent to which such increases are attributable to increases in prices or to increases in the volume or amount of goods or services being sold or to the introduction of new products or services.

    iv. For the three most recent fiscal years of the registrant, or for those fiscal years in which the registrant has been engaged in business, whichever period is shortest, discuss the impact of inflation and changing prices on the registrant's net sales and revenues and on income from continuing operations.

4. *Off-balance-sheet arrangements.*

    i. In a separately-captioned section, discuss the registrant's off-balance-sheet arrangements that have or are reasonably likely to have a current or future effect on the registrant's financial condition, changes in financial condition, revenues or expenses, results of operations, liquidity, capital expenditures, or capital resources that are material to investors. The disclosure shall include the items specified in paragraphs (a)(4)(i)(A), (B), (C), and (D) of this Item to the extent necessary to an understanding of such arrangements and effect and shall also include such other information that the registrant believes is necessary for such an understanding.

        A. The nature and business purpose to the registrant of such off-balance-sheet arrangements;

        B. The importance to the registrant of such off-balance-sheet arrangements in respect of its liquidity, capital resources, market risk support, credit risk support, or other benefits;

        C. The amounts of revenues, expenses, and cash flows of the registrant arising from such arrangements; the nature and amounts of any interests retained, securities issued, and other indebtedness incurred by the registrant in connection with such arrangements; and the nature and amounts of any other obligations or liabilities (including contingent obligations or liabilities) of the registrant arising from such arrangements that are or are reasonably likely to become material and the triggering events or circumstances that could cause them to arise; and

        D. Any known event, demand, commitment, trend, or uncertainty that will result in or is reasonably likely to result in the termination, or material reduction in availability to the registrant, of its off-balance-sheet arrangements that provide material benefits to it, and the course of action that the registrant has taken or proposes to take in response to any such circumstances.

    ii. As used in this paragraph (a)(4), the term *off-balance-sheet arrangement* means any transaction, agreement, or other contractual arrangement to which an entity unconsolidated with the registrant is a party, under which the registrant has:

        A. Any obligation under a guarantee contract that has any of the characteristics identified in paragraph 3 of FASB Interpretation No. 45, *Guarantor's Accounting and Disclosure Requirements for Guarantees, Including Indirect Guarantees of Indebtedness of Others* (November 2002) ("FIN 45"), as may be modified or supplemented, and that is not excluded from the initial recognition and measurement provisions of FIN 45 pursuant to paragraphs 6 or 7 of that Interpretation;

        B. A retained or contingent interest in assets transferred to an unconsolidated entity or similar arrangement that serves as credit, liquidity, or market risk support to such entity for such assets;

        C. Any obligation, including a contingent obligation, under a contract that would be accounted for as a derivative instrument, except that it is both indexed to the registrant's own stock and classified in stockholders' equity in the registrant's statement of financial position, and therefore excluded from the scope of FASB Statement of Financial Accounting Standards (SFAS) No. 133, *Accounting for Derivative Instruments and Hedging Activities* (June 1998), pursuant to paragraph 11(a) of that Statement, as may be modified or supplemented; or

        D. Any obligation, including a contingent obligation, arising out of a variable interest (as referenced in FASB Interpretation No. 46, *Consolidation of Variable Interest Entities* [January 2003], as may be modified or supplemented) in an unconsolidated entity that is held by, and material to, the registrant, where such entity provides financing, liquidity, market risk, or credit risk support to, or engages in leasing, hedging, or research and development services with, the registrant.

5. *Tabular disclosure of contractual obligations.*

    i. In a tabular format, provide the information specified in this paragraph (a)(5) as of the latest fiscal year end balance sheet date with respect to the registrant's known contractual obligations specified in the table that follows this paragraph (a)(5)(i). The registrant shall provide amounts, aggregated by type of contractual obligation. The registrant may disaggregate the specified categories of contractual obligations using other categories suitable to its business, but the presentation must include all of the obligations of the registrant that fall within the specified categories. A presentation covering at least the periods specified shall be included. The tabular presentation may be accompanied by footnotes to describe provisions that create, increase, or accelerate obligations, or other pertinent data to the extent necessary for an understanding of the timing and amount of the registrant's specified contractual obligations.

Exhibit 6.1   *Continued*

Contractual obligations	Total	Payments due by period			
		Less than 1 year	1–3 years	3–5 years	More than 5 years
[Long-Term Debt Obligations]					
[Capital Lease Obligations]					
[Operating Lease Obligations]					
[Purchase Obligations]					
[Other Long-Term Liabilities Reflected on the Registrant's Balance Sheet under GAAP]					
Total					

ii. *Definitions*:. The following definitions apply to this paragraph (a)(5):

   A. *Long-Term Debt Obligation* means a payment obligation under long-term borrowings referenced in FASB SFAS No. 47 *Disclosure of Long-Term Obligations* (March 1981), as may be modified or supplemented.

   B. *Capital Lease Obligation* means a payment obligation under a lease classified as a capital lease pursuant to FASB SFAS No. 13 *Accounting for Leases* (November 1976), as may be modified or supplemented.

   C. *Operating Lease Obligation* means a payment obligation under a lease classified as an operating lease and disclosed pursuant to FASB SFAS No. 13 *Accounting for Leases* (November 1976), as may be modified or supplemented.

   D. *Purchase Obligation* means an agreement to purchase goods or services that is enforceable and legally binding on the registrant that specifies all significant terms, including: fixed or minimum quantities to be purchased; fixed, minimum, or variable price provisions; and the approximate timing of the transaction.

Instructions to Paragraph 303(a):

   1. The registrant's discussion and analysis shall be of the financial statements and other statistical data that the registrant believes will enhance a reader's understanding of its financial condition, changes in financial condition and results of operations. Generally, the discussion shall cover the three-year period covered by the financial statements and shall use year-to-year comparisons or any other formats that in the registrant's judgment enhance a reader's understanding. However, where trend information is relevant, reference to the five year selected financial data appearing pursuant to Item 301 of Regulation S-K may be necessary. A smaller reporting company's discussion shall cover the two-year period required in Article 8 of Regulation S-X and shall use year-to-year comparisons or any other formats that in the registrant's judgment enhance a reader's understanding.

   2. The purpose of the discussion and analysis shall be to provide to investors and other users information relevant to an assessment of the financial condition and results of operations of the registrant as determined by evaluating the amounts and certainty of cash flows from operations and from outside sources.

   3. The discussion and analysis shall focus specifically on material events and uncertainties known to management that would cause reported financial information not to be necessarily indicative of future operating results or of future financial condition. This would include descriptions and amounts of (A) matters that would have an impact on future operations and have not had an impact in the past, and (B) matters that have had an impact on reported operations and are not expected to have an impact upon future operations.

   4. Where the consolidated financial statements reveal material changes from year to year in one or more line items, the causes for the changes shall be described to the extent necessary to an understanding of the registrant's businesses as a whole; provided, however, that if the causes for a change in one line item also relate to other line items, no repetition is required and a line-by-line analysis of the financial statements as a whole is not required or generally appropriate. Registrants need not recite the amounts of changes from year to year which are readily computable from the financial statements. The discussion shall not merely repeat numerical data contained in the consolidated financial statements.

   5. The term *liquidity* as used in this Item refers to the ability of an enterprise to generate adequate amounts of cash to meet the enterprise's needs for cash. Except where it is otherwise clear from the discussion, the registrant shall indicate those balance sheet conditions or income or cash flow items which the registrant believes may be indicators of its liquidity condition. Liquidity generally shall be discussed on both a long-term and short-term basis. The issue of liquidity shall be discussed in the context of the registrant's own business or businesses. For example a discussion of working capital may be appropriate for certain manufacturing, industrial, or related operations but might be inappropriate for a bank or public utility.

Exhibit 6.1   *Continued*

6. Where financial statements presented or incorporated by reference in the registration statement are required by Rule 4-08(e)(3) of Regulation S-X to include disclosure of restrictions on the ability of both consolidated and unconsolidated subsidiaries to transfer funds to the registrant in the form of cash dividends, loans, or advances, the discussion of liquidity shall include a discussion of the nature and extent of such restrictions and the impact such restrictions have had and are expected to have on the ability of the parent company to meet its cash obligations.

7. Any forward-looking information supplied is expressly covered by the safe harbor rule for projections. See Rule 175 under the Securities Act, Rule 3b-6 under the Exchange Act and Securities Act Release No. 6084 (June 25, 1979).

8. Registrants are only required to discuss the effects of inflation and other changes in prices when considered material. This discussion may be made in whatever manner appears appropriate under the circumstances. All that is required is a brief textual presentation of management's views. No specific numerical financial data need be presented except as Rule 3-20(c) of Regulation S-X otherwise requires. However, registrants may elect to voluntarily disclose supplemental information on the effects of changing prices as provided for in SFAS No. 89, *Financial Reporting and Changing Prices*, or through other supplemental disclosures. The Commission encourages experimentation with these disclosures in order to provide the most meaningful presentation of the impact of price changes on the registrant's financial statements.

9. Registrants that elect to disclose supplementary information on the effects of changing prices as specified by SFAS No. 89, *Financial Reporting and Changing Prices*, may combine such explanations with the discussion and analysis required pursuant to this Item or may supply such information separately with appropriate cross reference.

10. All references to the registrant in the discussion and in this Item shall mean the registrant and its subsidiaries consolidated.

11. Foreign private registrants also shall discuss briefly any pertinent governmental economic, fiscal, monetary, or political policies or factors that have materially affected or could materially affect, directly or indirectly, their operations or investments by U.S. nationals.

12. If the registrant is a foreign private issuer, the discussion shall focus on the primary financial statements presented in the registration statement or report. There shall be a reference to the reconciliation to United States generally accepted accounting principles, and a discussion of any aspects of the difference between foreign and United States generally accepted accounting principles, not discussed in the reconciliation, that the registrant believes is necessary for an understanding of the financial statements as a whole.

13. The attention of bank holding companies is directed to the information called for in Guide 3 (Sec. 229.801(c) and Sec. 229.802(c)).

14. The attention of property-casualty insurance companies is directed to the information called for in Guide 6 (Sec. 229.801(f)).

Instructions to Paragraph 303(a)(4):

1. No obligation to make disclosure under paragraph (a)(4) of this Item shall arise in respect of an off-balance-sheet arrangement until a definitive agreement that is unconditionally binding or subject only to customary closing conditions exists or, if there is no such agreement, when settlement of the transaction occurs.

2. Registrants should aggregate off-balance-sheet arrangements in groups or categories that provide material information in an efficient and understandable manner and should avoid repetition and disclosure of immaterial information. Effects that are common or similar with respect to a number of off-balance-sheet arrangements must be analyzed in the aggregate to the extent the aggregation increases understanding. Distinctions in arrangements and their effects must be discussed to the extent the information is material, but the discussion should avoid repetition and disclosure of immaterial information.

3. For purposes of paragraph (a)(4) of this Item only, contingent liabilities arising out of litigation, arbitration, or regulatory actions are not considered to be off-balance-sheet arrangements.

4. Generally, the disclosure required by paragraph (a)(4) shall cover the most recent fiscal year. However, the discussion should address changes from the previous year where such discussion is necessary to an understanding of the disclosure.

5. In satisfying the requirements of paragraph (a)(4) of this Item, the discussion of off-balance-sheet arrangements need not repeat information provided in the footnotes to the financial statements, provided that such discussion clearly cross-references to specific information in the relevant footnotes and integrates the substance of the footnotes into such discussion in a manner designed to inform readers of the significance of the information that is not included within the body of such discussion.

b. *Interim periods.* If interim period financial statements are included or are required to be included by Article 3 of Regulation S-X, a management's discussion and analysis of the financial condition and results of operations shall be provided so as to enable the reader to assess material changes in financial condition and results of operations between the periods specified in paragraphs (b) (1) and (2) of this Item. The discussion and analysis shall include a discussion of material changes in those items specifically listed in paragraph (a) of this Item, except that the impact of inflation and changing prices on operations for interim periods need not be addressed.

1. *Material changes in financial condition.* Discuss any material changes in financial condition from the end of the preceding fiscal year to the date of the most recent interim balance sheet provided. If the interim financial statements include an interim balance sheet as of the corresponding interim date of the preceding fiscal year, any material changes in financial condition from that date to the date of the most recent interim balance sheet provided also shall be discussed. If discussions of changes from both the end and the corresponding interim date of the preceding fiscal year are required, the discussions may be combined at the discretion of the registrant.

Exhibit 6.1   *Continued*

2. *Material changes in results of operations.* Discuss any material changes in the registrant's results of operations with respect to the most recent fiscal year-to-date period for which an income statement is provided and the corresponding year-to-date period of the preceding fiscal year. If the registrant is required to or has elected to provide an income statement for the most recent fiscal quarter, such discussion also shall cover material changes with respect to that fiscal quarter and the corresponding fiscal quarter in the preceding fiscal year. In addition, if the registrant has elected to provide an income statement for the twelve-month period ended as of the date of the most recent interim balance sheet provided, the discussion also shall cover material changes with respect to that twelve-month period and the twelve-month period ended as of the corresponding interim balance sheet date of the preceding fiscal year. Notwithstanding the above, if for purposes of a registration statement a registrant subject to paragraph (b) of Rule 3-03 of Regulation S-X provides a statement of income for the twelve-month period ended as of the date of the most recent interim balance sheet provided in lieu of the interim income statements otherwise required, the discussion of material changes in that twelve-month period will be in respect to the preceding fiscal year rather than the corresponding preceding period.

Instructions to Paragraph (b) of Item 303:

1. If interim financial statements are presented together with financial statements for full fiscal years, the discussion of the interim financial information shall be prepared pursuant to this paragraph (b) and the discussion of the full fiscal year's information shall be prepared pursuant to paragraph (a) of this Item. Such discussions may be combined.

2. In preparing the discussion and analysis required by this paragraph (b), the registrant may presume that users of the interim financial information have read or have access to the discussion and analysis required by paragraph (a) for the preceding fiscal year.

3. The discussion and analysis required by this paragraph (b) is required to focus only on material changes. Where the interim financial statements reveal material changes from period to period in one or more significant line items, the causes for the changes shall be described if they have not already been disclosed: *Provided, however,* that if the causes for a change in one line item also relate to other line items, no repetition is required. Registrants need not recite the amounts of changes from period to period which are readily computable from the financial statements. The discussion shall not merely repeat numerical data contained in the financial statements. The information provided shall include that which is available to the registrant without undue effort or expense and which does not clearly appear in the registrant's condensed interim financial statements.

4. The registrant's discussion of material changes in results of operations shall identify any significant elements of the registrant's income or loss from continuing operations which do not arise from or are not necessarily representative of the registrant's ongoing business.

5. The registrant shall discuss any seasonal aspects of its business which have had a material effect upon its financial condition or results of operation.

6. Any forward-looking information supplied is expressly covered by the safe harbor rule for projections. See Rule 175 under the Securities Act, Rule 3b-6 under the Exchange Act and Securities Act Release No. 6084 (June 25, 1979).

7. The registrant is not required to include the table required by paragraph (a)(5) of this Item for interim periods. Instead, the registrant should disclose material changes outside the ordinary course of the registrant's business in the specified contractual obligations during the interim period.

c. *Safe harbor.*

1. The safe harbor provided in section 27A of the Securities Act of 1933 and section 21E of the Securities Exchange Act of 1934 ("statutory safe harbors") shall apply to forward-looking information provided pursuant to paragraphs (a)(4) and (5) of this Item, provided that the disclosure is made by: an issuer; a person acting on behalf of the issuer; an outside reviewer retained by the issuer making a statement on behalf of the issuer; or an underwriter, with respect to information provided by the issuer or information derived from information provided by the issuer.

2. For purposes of paragraph (c) of this Item only:

   i. All information required by paragraphs (a)(4) and (5) of this Item is deemed to be a *forward looking statement* as that term is defined in the statutory safe harbors, except for historical facts.

   ii. With respect to paragraph (a)(4) of this Item, the meaningful cautionary statements element of the statutory safe harbors will be satisfied if a registrant satisfies all requirements of that same paragraph (a)(4) of this Item.

d. *Smaller reporting companies.* A smaller reporting company, as defined by Sec. 229.10(f)(1), may provide the information required in paragraph (a)(3)(iv) of this Item for the last two most recent fiscal years of the registrant if it provides financial information on net sales and revenues and on income from continuing operations for only two years. A smaller reporting company is not required to provide the information required by paragraph (a)(5) of this Item.

47 FR 11401, Mar. 16, 1982, as amended at 47 FR 29839, July 9, 1982; 47 FR 54768, Dec. 6, 1982; 52 FR 30919, Aug. 18, 1987; 68 FR 5982, 5999, Feb. 5, 2003; 73 FR 958, Jan. 4, 2008.

Exhibit 6.1   *Continued*

The following are SEC releases pertinent to MD&A regulation in chronological order.

- Securities Act Release No. 4936 (December 9, 1968) (33 FR 18617), *Guides for Preparation and Filing of Registration Statements under the Securities Act of 1933*. This was the first requirement for a narrative discussion of the results of operations, which was incorporated in registration statements.

- Securities Act Release No. 5520 (September 3, 1974) (39 FR 31894), *Commission's Guidelines for Registration and Reporting*. This required a narrative discussion about the results of operations to accompany all periodic financial statements.

- Securities Act Release No. 5992 (November 7, 1978) (43 FR 53251), *Guide for Reports or Memoranda Concerning Registrants*. This release set forth a "safe harbor" for forward-looking information. As a result, the government or private plaintiffs are prevented from alleging fraud in suits where forward-looking projections fail to materialize, as long as they have a reasonable basis and are disclosed in good faith.

- Securities Act Release No. 6231 (September 2, 1980) (45 FR 63630), *Amendments to Annual Report Form, Related Forms, Rules, Regulations, and Guides; Integration of Securities' Acts Disclosure System*. This release expanded the required discussion to include liquidity, capital resources, as well as the results of operations. It also required discussion of certain prospective information. It remains in force.

- Securities Act Release No. 6349 (September 28, 1981), 23 SEC Docket 962 [not published in the *Federal Register*]. This release reported deficiencies in complying with the 1980 requirement and gave examples of disclosures to assist companies in drafting the MD&A.

- Securities Act Release No. 6711 (April 24, 1987) (52 FR 13715), (April 17, 1987), *Concept Release on Management's Discussion and Analysis of Financial Condition and Results of Operations*. This release was referred to as the Concept Release. Its main purpose was to seek comment from various parties to proposed changes in the MD&A requirements made by the accounting profession.

- Securities Act Release Nos. 33-6835; 34-26831; IC-16961; FR-36; (May 18, 1989) (54 FR 22427), *Management's Discussion and Analysis of Financial Condition and Results of Operations; Certain Investment Company Disclosures; Certain Investment Company Disclosures*. This release gave more examples of MD&A disclosures, particularly those pertaining to prospective information.

- Securities Act Release Nos. 33-8039, 34-45124, FR-59 (December 4, 2001) (*Federal Register:* December 10, 2001, Volume 66, Number 237), *Cautionary Advice Regarding the Use of "Pro Forma" Financial Information in Earnings Releases*. This release provides cautionary advice regarding the use of "pro forma" financial information in earnings releases.

- Securities Act Releases Nos. 33-8040, 34-45149, FR-60 (December 12, 2001) (*Federal Register,* December 17, 2001, Volume 66, Number 242), *Cautionary Advice Regarding Disclosure About Critical Accounting Policies*. This release provides cautionary advice regarding disclosure about critical accounting policies.

- Securities Act Release Nos. 33-8056; 34-45321; FR-61 (January 22, 2002) (*Federal Register,* January 25, 2002, Volume 67, Number 17), *Commission Statement About Management's Discussion and Analysis of Financial Condition and Results of Operations*. This release sets forth certain views of the Securities and Exchange Commission regarding disclosure in MD&A concerning liquidity and capital resources including off-balance-sheet arrangements; certain trading activities that include non-exchange-traded contracts accounted for at fair value; and effects of transactions with related and certain other parties.

- Securities Act Release Nos. 33-8098; 34-45907 (*Federal Register,* May 20, 2002, Volume 67, Number 97). Proposed rule, *Disclosure in Management's Discussion and Analysis About the Application of Critical Accounting Policies*. The SEC proposed disclosure requirements that would enhance investors' understanding of the application of companies' critical accounting policies. The proposals would encompass disclosure in two areas: accounting estimates a company makes in applying its accounting policies and the initial adoption by a company of an accounting policy that has a material impact on its financial presentation. This proposal remains outstanding at date of this publication.

- Release No. 33-8176; 34-47226; FR-65 (*Federal Register,* January 30, 2003, Volume 68, Number 20), *Conditions for Use of Non-GAAP Financial Measures*. This final rule addresses public companies' disclosure or release of certain financial information that is calculated and presented on the basis of methodologies other than in accordance with generally accepted accounting principles (GAAP). The SEC also adopted a new disclosure regulation, Regulation G, which requires public companies that disclose or release such non-GAAP financial measures to include, in that disclosure or release, a presentation of the most directly comparable GAAP financial measure and a reconciliation of the disclosed non-GAAP financial measure to the most directly comparable GAAP financial measure. The SEC also adopted amendments to Item 10 of Regulation S-K to provide additional guidance to those registrants that include non-GAAP financial measures in SEC filings.

- Securities Act Release Nos. 33-8182, 34-47264, FR-67 (*Federal Register,* February 5, 2003, Volume 68, Number 24), *Disclosure in Management's Discussion and Analysis about Off-Balance-Sheet Arrangements and Aggregate Contractual Obligations*. This final rule requires a registrant to provide an explanation of its off-balance-sheet arrangements in a separately captioned subsection of the MD&A section of a registrant's disclosure documents. The amendments also require registrants (other than small business issuers) to provide an overview of certain known contractual obligations in a tabular format. Securities Act *Relea*se Nos. 33-8350, 34-48960, FR-72 (*Federal Register,* December 29, 2003, Volume 68, Number 248), *Commission Guidance Regarding Management's Discussion and Analysis of Financial Condition and Results of Operations*. This interpretation is intended to elicit more meaningful disclosure in MD&A in a number of areas, including the overall presentation and focus of MD&A, with general emphasis on the discussion and analysis of known trends, demands, commitments, events, and uncertainties, and specific guidance on disclosures about liquidity, capital resources, and critical accounting estimates.

Exhibit 6.2   MD&A-Related SEC Releases

- Securities Act Release Nos. 33-8876, 34-56994, 39-2451 (*Federal Register:* January 4, 2008, Volume 73, Number 3), *Smaller Reporting Company Regulatory Relief and Simplification.* This final rule amends the disclosure and reporting requirements under the Securities Act of 1933 and the Securities Exchange Act of 1934 to expand the number of companies that qualify for its scaled disclosure requirements for smaller reporting companies. Companies that have less than $75 million in public equity float will qualify for the scaled disclosure requirements under the amendments. Companies without a calculable public equity float will qualify if their revenues were below $50 million in the previous year. To streamline and simplify regulation, the amendments move the scaled disclosure requirements from Regulation S-B into Regulation S-K.

- Securities Act Release Nos. 33-9144, 34-62934, FR-83 (*Federal Register,* September 28, 2010, Volume 75, Number 187), *Commission Guidance on Presentation of Liquidity and Capital Resources Disclosures in Management's Discussion and Analysis.* This guidance that is intended to improve discussion of liquidity and capital resources in MD&A of financial condition and results of operations in order to facilitate understanding by investors of the liquidity and funding risks facing the registrant.

Exhibit 6.2   *Continued*

(c) GENERAL GUIDANCE ON MD&A.   Companies are required, in the MD&A, to provide investors and other users with material information that is necessary to understand the company's financial condition and operating performance as well as its prospects for the future. On December 19, 2003, the SEC issued interpretative guidance entitled *Commission Guidance Regarding Management's Discussion and Analysis of Financial Condition and Results of Operations* (referred to as FR 72). This guidance is intended to elicit more meaningful disclosure in MD&A in a number of areas, including the overall presentation and focus of MD&A, with general emphasis on the discussion and analysis of known trends, demands, commitments, and events and uncertainties, and with specific guidance on disclosures about liquidity, capital resources, and critical accounting estimates. It provides guidance to assist companies in preparing MD&A disclosure that is easier to follow and understand and contains information that more completely satisfies the SEC's previously enunciated principal objectives of MD&A. The release captures the objective of the MD&A in this way:

> The purpose of MD&A is not complicated. It is to provide readers information necessary to an understanding of [a company's] financial condition, changes in financial condition and results of operations. The MD&A requirements are intended to satisfy three principal objectives:
>
> - To provide a narrative explanation of a company's financial statements that enables investors to see the company through the eyes of management;
> - To enhance the overall financial disclosure and provide the context within which financial information should be analyzed; and
> - To provide information about the quality of, and potential variability of, a company's earnings and cash flow, so that investors can ascertain the likelihood that past performance is indicative of future performance
>
> MD&A should be a discussion and analysis of a company's business as seen through the eyes of those who manage that business. Management has a unique perspective on its business that only it can present. As such, MD&A should not be a recitation of financial statements in narrative form or an otherwise uninformative series of technical responses to MD&A requirements, neither of which provides this important management perspective. Through this release we encourage each company and its management to take a fresh look at MD&A with a view to enhancing its quality. We also encourage early top-level involvement by a company's management in identifying the key disclosure themes and items that should be included in a company's MD&A.
>
> Based on our experience with many companies' current disclosures in MD&A, we believe there are a number of general ways for companies to enhance their MD&A consistent with its purpose. The recent review experiences of the staff of the Division of Corporation Finance, including its Fortune 500 review, have led us to conclude that additional guidance would be especially useful in the following areas:
>
> - The overall presentation of MD&A;
> - The focus and content of MD&A (including materiality, analysis, key performance measures and known material trends and uncertainties);

- Disclosure regarding liquidity and capital resources; and
- Disclosure regarding critical accounting estimates.

Therefore, in this release, we emphasize the following points regarding overall presentation:

- Within the universe of material information, companies should present their disclosure so that the most important information is most prominent;
- Companies should avoid unnecessary duplicative disclosure that can tend to overwhelm readers and act as an obstacle to identifying and understanding material matters; and
- Many companies would benefit from starting their MD&A with a section that provides an executive-level overview that provides context for the remainder of the discussion.

We also emphasize the following points regarding focus and content:

- In deciding on the content of MD&A, companies should focus on material information and eliminate immaterial information that does not promote understanding of companies' financial condition, liquidity and capital resources, changes in financial condition, and results of operations (both in the context of profit and loss and cash flows);
- Companies should identify and discuss key performance indicators, including non-financial performance indicators, that their management uses to manage the business and that would be material to investors;
- Companies must identify and disclose known trends, events, demands, commitments, and uncertainties that are reasonably likely to have a material effect on financial condition or operating performance; and
- Companies should provide not only disclosure of information responsive to MD&A's requirements, but also an analysis that is responsive to those requirements that explains management's view of the implications and significance of that information and that satisfies the objectives of MD&A.

For the full text of FR 72, see *www.sec.gov/rules/interp/33-8350.htm*.

As discussed in FR 72, the SEC provides several recommendations to assist registrants in improving their MD&A disclosures. The SEC believes that the presentation of the MD&A of too many companies may have become unnecessarily lengthy, difficult to understand, and confusing. It asserts that many companies can improve their MD&A by focusing on the most important information disclosed to investors. Disclosure should emphasize material information that is required or promotes understanding and deemphasize immaterial information that is not required and does not promote understanding. Companies should prepare MD&A with a strong focus on the most important information, provided in a manner intended to address the objectives of MD&A. The SEC recommends, in FR 72, consideration of these points:

- Companies should consider whether a tabular presentation of relevant financial or other information may help a reader's understanding of MD&A.
- Companies should consider whether the headings they use assist readers in following the flow of, or otherwise assist in understanding, MD&A, and whether additional headings would be helpful in this regard.
- Many companies' MD&A could benefit from adding an introductory section or overview that would facilitate a reader's understanding.
- While all required information must of course be disclosed, companies should consider using a "layered" approach. Such an approach would present information in a manner that emphasizes, within the universe of material information that is disclosed, the information and analysis that is most important.

(d) RECENT DEVELOPMENTS

(i) Smaller Reporting Companies. The SEC has adopted amendments to its disclosure and reporting requirements under the Securities Act of 1933 and the Securities Exchange Act of 1934 to expand the number of companies that qualify for its scaled disclosure requirements for smaller reporting companies. On December 19, 2007, the SEC issued a final rule, *Smaller Reporting Company Regulatory Relief and Simplification* (Releases Nos. 33-8876; 34-56994; 39-2451; File No. S7-15-07).

Companies that have less than $75 million in public equity float qualify for the scaled disclosure requirements under the amendments. Companies without a calculable public equity float will qualify if their revenues were below $50 million in the previous year. To streamline and simplify regulation, the amendments move the scaled disclosure requirements from Regulation S-B into Regulation S-K.

Specific to the MD&A requirements, the final rule allows smaller reporting companies to provide only two years of analysis if the company is presenting only two years of financial statements, instead of the three years of analysis required of larger companies that are required to provide three years of financial statements; also, smaller reporting companies are exempt from providing tabular disclosure of contractual obligations.

The final rule is available at: *www.sec.gov/rules/final/2007/33-8876.pdf*.

The SEC also issued additional guidance for smaller public companies:

- *Smaller Reporting Company Compliance and Disclosure Interpretations,* available at: *www.sec.gov/info/smallbus/src-cdinterps.htm*
- *Small Entity Compliance Guide,* available at: *www.sec.gov/info/smallbus/secg/s3f3-secg.htm*

(ii) MD&A Disclosures on Fair Value and Liquidity and Capital Resources. In December 2008, the staff of the SEC participated in the American Institute of Certified Public Accountants' (AICPA) National Conference on Current SEC and Public Company Accounting Oversight Board (PCAOB) Developments. During this conference, the SEC staff made several presentations including two that identified best practices for fair value MD&A disclosures and considerations for preparing the liquidity and capital resources section of the MD&A. The slides are available at: *http://sec.gov/news/speech/2008/spch120908wc-slides.pdf/* .

Fair Value Disclosures. The SEC's top ten best practices for fair value MD&A disclosures, as noted on slides 34 to 60, include these areas:

1. When to provide a sensitivity analysis
2. Alternative valuation technique disclosures
3. Details of other-than-temporary impairment charges on available-for-sale securities
4. Broker/pricing services
5. Collateral underlying mortgage-backed securities, collateralized debt obligations, collateralized loan obligations, and so on.
6. Quantitative disclosure of effects of the company's own credit risk and counterparty credit risk
7. Consideration of illiquidity in valuations
8. Key drivers of value for each significant Level 3 asset/liability grouping
9. Inputs that became unobservable when transfers to Level 3 occur
10. Transfers in or out of Level 3

These best practices were developed from two "Dear CFO" letters sent to 30 public companies in March 2008 and September 2008 by the SEC and posted to its Web site, given the much broader applicability of the guidance. The goal of these "Dear CFO" letters was to provide suggestions to improve transparency surrounding fair value measurements.

Subsequent to the issuance of the "Dear CFO" letters and the SEC staff speech, the FASB amended U.S. generally accepted accounting principles (GAAP) to improve financial statement disclosures about fair value. The primary changes for fair value disclosures were issued in 2010 and

2011 with the issuances of two Accounting Standards Updates (ASUs): ASU 2010-06, *Fair Value Measurements and Disclosures* (Topic 820): *Improving Disclosures About Fair Value Measurements;* and ASU 2011-04, *Fair Value Measurement* (Topic 820): *Amendments to Achieve Common Fair Value Measurement and Disclosure Requirements in U.S. GAAP and IFRSs.*

Liquidity and Capital Resources Disclosures.   The SEC's top ten considerations for companies when preparing the liquidity and capital resources section of the MD&A were developed by the SEC staff not only to provide investors with a clear picture of the company's current financial condition but also to provide investors with the opportunity to evaluate the company's future prospects.

The SEC's top ten best practices for liquidity and capital resources MD&A disclosures, as noted on slides 76 to 87, include:

1. Introductory Discussion: Provide greater analysis of the sources and uses of cash.
2. Operating Activities: Discuss changes in cash received from customers and other sources, and cash paid to suppliers and employees, and so on.
3. Operating Activities: Discuss any known trends and uncertainties that are reasonably expected to have material effects on the separate sources and uses of cash.
4. Investing Activities: Evaluate capital expenditures on a discretionary and nondiscretionary basis and discuss any anticipated funding sources.
5. Financing Activities: Discuss the sufficiency of the unused availability (or the estimated utilization), the anticipated circumstances requiring its use, any uncertainty surrounding the ability to access funds when needed, and any implications from not being able to access the funds.
6. Credit Ratings: Discuss the factors that may materially influence credit ratings, the potential implications of known or reasonably likely changes in credit ratings or credit rating outlook, and management's expectations.
7. Financial Covenants: Discuss any uncertainty or trends surrounding future compliance with financial covenants, and the material implications of a breach. Consider also providing company specific calculations when the actual ratios under the agreement are provided in a filing. Refer to FR 72 for disclosure suggestions when breach of covenant is reasonably likely.
8. Financial Covenants: Discuss the capacity for additional borrowing under the most restrictive covenant, whether there is otherwise an ability to raise these funds, and whether this amount is sufficient or insufficient for current and long-term needs.
9. Current Market Conditions: Discuss any uncertainties and reasonably likely implications related to:
   a. Committed and uncommitted loan facilities from banks and other lending institutions
   b. The commercial paper market
   c. Cash and securities held at banks and other financial institutions
   d. Illiquid investments
   e. Future pension funding
   f. Share repurchase programs and dividend payments
10. General: Prepare a user-friendly "Liquidity and Capital Resource" section that:
   a. Can be read as a stand-alone document
   b. Prominently displays the most critical information
   c. Can be meaningful without supplemental investor calculations
   d. Excludes superfluous information
   e. Avoids boilerplate language
   f. Includes management insight

The SEC also issued, on September 17, 2010, an interpretative release entitled *Commission Guidance on Presentation of Liquidity and Capital Resources Disclosures in Management's Discussion and Analysis* (referred to as FR 83). The release was effective September 28, 2010, and was issued to improve discussion of liquidity and capital resources in MD&A in order to facilitate understanding by investors of the liquidity and funding risks facing the registrant. The three primary areas addressed in the release are liquidity disclosure, leverage ratio disclosures, and contractual obligation table disclosures.

The release is available at: *www.sec.gov/rules/interp/2010/33-9144.pdf* .

6.2 CURRENT GUIDANCE

(a) OVERALL REQUIREMENTS.   For large-accelerated and accelerated filers, the MD&A must cover the three most recent fiscal years and the two interyear comparisons. For smaller reporting companies,[4] the MD&A must cover the two most recent fiscal years.

Registrants need not discuss the earliest year in comparison to the preceding year unless the discussion is necessary for an understanding of a trend of the registrant's financial position or results of operations. The general requirements, as summarized from Item 303, are summarized next.

- Discuss the registrant's financial condition, changes in financial condition and results of operations.
- With respect to all of the categories just listed, registrants are required to identify any currently known trends, demands, commitments, events, or uncertainties that are reasonably expected to have material affects on the registrant's liquidity, capital resources, and results of operations, or that would cause reported financial information not to be necessarily indicative of future operating results or financial condition.
- Provide such other information that the registrant believes to be necessary to an understanding of its financial condition, changes in financial condition and results of operations.
- These issues must also be discussed by business segments to the extent necessary, in the registrant's judgment, for an understanding of the business as a whole.
- Address both positive and negative aspects of a company's financial condition and results of operations.
- Where the consolidated financial statements reveal material changes from year to year in one or more line items, describe the causes for the changes to the extent necessary to an understanding of the registrant's businesses as a whole.

The required disclosures are ultimately conditional on passing both a "materiality" and a "cost" threshold. Immaterial effects or events need not be (but may be) disclosed.[5] As stated in Item 303:

---

[4] The SEC defines a "smaller reporting company" as one with public float of less than $75 million. Public float is computed at the end of the second quarter, using one year's information. If there is no public float, then a revenue test is used. The revenue test for a "smaller reporting company" is whether the company has revenue of under $50 million.

[5] The SEC discussed materiality in SAB No. 99, *Materiality,* August 12, 1999. Further, the SEC relies on the decisions rendered by the Supreme Court in two separate cases. In *TSC Industries Inc. v. Northway* (1980), the Court stated that "an omitted fact is material if there is a substantial likelihood that reasonable shareholders would consider it important." The Court further explained: "To fulfill the materiality requirement, there must be a substantial likelihood that the disclosure of the omitted fact would have been viewed by the reasonable investor as having significantly altered the 'total mix' of information made available." In *Basic, Inc. v. Levinson* (1988), the Court addressed materiality as it relates to possible future events: "Materiality will depend at any given time upon a balancing of both the indicated probability that the event will occur and the anticipated magnitude of the event in light of the totality of the company activity." Finally, and most important, for both past events and possible future events, the Court stated: "Materiality depends on the facts and is to be determined on a case by case basis." Therefore, materiality is a relative concept.

"The information provided pursuant to this Item need only include that which is available to the registrant without undue effort or expense and which does not clearly appear in the registrant's financial statements."

The full requirements are contained in Exhibit 6.1. Regulation S-K requires disclosure in these areas:

a. Liquidity

b. Capital resources

c. Results of operations

d. Off-balance-sheet arrangements

e. Tabular disclosure of contractual obligations[6]

(b) CRITICAL ACCOUNTING ESTIMATES. On December 12, 2001, the SEC issued an interpretative release entitled *Cautionary Advice Regarding Disclosure About Critical Accounting Policies* (referred to as FR 60). The SEC's rules governing MD&A have long required disclosure about trends, events, or uncertainties known to management that would materially affect reported financial information; the SEC observed, in FR 60, that disclosure responsive to these requirements could be enhanced. For example, environmental and operational trends, events, and uncertainties typically are identified in MD&A, but the implications of those uncertainties for the methods, assumptions, and estimates used for recurring and pervasive accounting measurements are not always addressed. Communication between investors and public companies could be improved if management explained in MD&A the interplay of specific uncertainties with accounting measurements in the financial statements.

The SEC encourages public companies to include in their MD&A full explanations, in plain English, of their critical accounting policies, the judgments and uncertainties affecting the application of those policies, and the likelihood that materially different amounts would be reported under different conditions or using different assumptions. The objective of this disclosure is consistent with the objective of MD&A.

The SEC pointed out that investors may lose confidence in a company's management and financial statements if sudden changes in its financial condition and results occur but were not preceded by disclosures about the susceptibility of reported amounts to change, including rapid change. In FR 60,[7] the SEC alerted public companies to the importance of employing a disclosure regimen in these ways:

1. Each company's management and auditor should bring particular focus to the evaluation of the critical accounting policies used in the financial statements. As part of the normal audit process, auditors must obtain an understanding of management's judgments in selecting and applying accounting principles and methods. Special attention to the most critical accounting policies will enhance the effectiveness of this process. Management should be able to defend the quality and reasonableness of the most critical policies, and auditors should satisfy themselves thoroughly regarding their selection, application, and disclosure.

2. Management should ensure that disclosure in MD&A is balanced and fully responsive. To enhance investor understanding of the financial statements, companies are encouraged to explain in MD&A the effects of the critical accounting policies applied, the judgments made in their application, and the likelihood of materially different reported results if different assumptions or conditions were to prevail.

3. Prior to finalizing and filing annual reports, audit committees should review the selection, application, and disclosure of critical accounting policies. Consistent with auditing standards, audit committees should be apprised of the evaluative criteria used by management in their selection of the accounting principles and methods. Proactive discussions between the audit

---

[6] Smaller public companies (as defined) are not required to provide tabular disclosure of contractual obligations.

[7] www.sec.gov/rules/other/33-8040.htm

committee and the company's senior management and auditor about critical accounting policies are appropriate.

4. If companies, management, audit committees, or auditors are uncertain about the application of specific GAAP principles, they should consult with our accounting staff. We encourage all those whose responsibility it is to report fairly and accurately on a company's financial condition and results to seek out our staff's assistance. We are committed to providing that assistance in a timely fashion; our goal is to address problems before they happen.

On May 10, 2002, the SEC proposed a rule entitled *Disclosure in Management's Discussion and Analysis About the Application of Critical Accounting Policies.* The proposal encompassed disclosure in two areas:

1. *Accounting estimates a company makes in applying its accounting policies.* Under the first part of the proposals, a company would have to identify the accounting estimates reflected in its financial statements that required it to make assumptions about matters that were highly uncertain at the time of estimation. Disclosure about those estimates would then be required if different estimates that the company reasonably could have used in the current period, or changes in the accounting estimate that are reasonably likely to occur from period to period, would have a material impact on the presentation of the company's financial condition, changes in financial condition, or results of operations. A company's disclosure about these critical accounting estimates would include a discussion of:

   ○ The methodology and assumptions underlying them

   ○ The effect the accounting estimates have on the company's financial presentation

   ○ The effect of changes in the estimates

2. *The initial adoption by a company of an accounting policy that has a material impact on its financial presentation.* Under the second part of the proposals, a company that has initially adopted an accounting policy with a material impact would have to disclose information that includes:

   ○ What gave rise to the initial adoption

   ○ The impact of the adoption

   ○ The accounting principle adopted and method of applying it

   ○ The choices it had among accounting principles

   Companies would place all of the new disclosure in the MD&A section of their annual reports, registration statements, and proxy and information statements. In addition, in the MD&A section of their quarterly reports, U.S. companies would have to update the information regarding their critical accounting estimates to disclose material changes.

This proposal remains outstanding.

Many estimates and assumptions involved in the application of GAAP have a material impact on reported financial condition and operating performance and on the comparability of such reported information over different reporting periods. As previously discussed, the SEC's December 2001 Release, FR 60, reminded companies that, under the existing MD&A disclosure requirements, a company should address material implications of uncertainties associated with the methods, assumptions, and estimates underlying the company's critical accounting measurements. In its follow-up statement, FR 72, the SEC states that:

- When preparing disclosure under the current requirements, companies should consider whether they have made accounting estimates or assumptions where: The nature of the estimates or assumptions is material due to the levels of subjectivity and judgment necessary to account for highly uncertain matters or the susceptibility of such matters to change; and

- The impact of the estimates and assumptions on financial condition or operating performance is material.

If so, companies should provide disclosure about those critical accounting estimates or assumptions in their MD&A.

(c) NON-GAAP MEASURES. On December 4, 2001, the SEC issued a release entitled *Cautionary Advice Regarding the Use of "Pro Forma" Financial Information in Earnings Releases* (referred to as FR 59). The SEC issued this release to registrants that present their earnings and results of operations on the basis of methodologies other than GAAP. This is often referred to as *pro forma* financial information. The SEC states that pro forma financial information can serve useful purposes for public companies that wish to focus investors' attention on critical components of financial results to provide a meaningful comparison to results for the same period of prior years or to emphasize the results of core operations. However, the SEC observed that to a large extent, this has been the intended function of disclosures in a company's MD&A section of its reports.

In response to Section 401(b) of SOX and to codify guidance in FR 59, the SEC amended Regulation S-K. The SEC subsequently adopted new rules and amendments to address public companies' disclosure or release of certain financial information that is calculated and presented on the basis of methodologies other than in accordance with GAAP. The final rule, *Conditions for Use of Non-GAAP Financial Measures,* was issued on January 22, 2003. The disclosure regulation, Regulation G, requires public companies that disclose or release such non-GAAP financial measures to include, in that disclosure or release, a presentation of the most directly comparable GAAP financial measure and a reconciliation of the disclosed non-GAAP financial measure to the most directly comparable GAAP financial measure. The final rule also adopted amendments to provide additional guidance to those registrants that include non-GAAP financial measures in SEC filings.

Here is a recap of the requirements:

REGULATION G

- *Application.* This regulation applies whenever a registrant required to file reports under Section 13(a) or 15(d) of the Exchange Act (other than a registered investment company), or a person acting on the registrant's behalf, discloses or releases publicly any material information that includes a non-GAAP financial measure. Typically, this information is furnished under Item 2.02 of Form 8-K.

- *Requirements.* The registrant must present the most directly comparable GAAP measure and a reconciliation of the differences between the non-GAAP measure disclosed or released with the most directly comparable GAAP measure. With regard to forward-looking information, a quantitative reconciliation is required only to the extent available without unreasonable efforts. If all of the information necessary is not available without unreasonable efforts, the registrant must identify the information that is unavailable and disclose probable significance.

ITEM 10(E) OF REGULATION S-K

- *Application.* This regulation applies to a registrant's filings with the SEC (e.g., 10-K, 10-Q, 20-F, S-1, F-1).
- *Requirements.* The registrant must present:
  - With equal or greater prominence, the most directly comparable GAAP measure
  - A reconciliation of the differences between the non-GAAP measure and the most directly comparable GAAP measures
  - A statement disclosing why management believes the presentation of the non-GAAP measure provides useful information to investors regarding the registrant's financial condition and results of operations
  - To the extent material, a statement disclosing the additional purposes, if any, for which management uses the non-GAAP measure

Subsequent to the enactment of these rules and regulations and the release of the SEC staff interpretative guidance, the SEC staff noted questions and inconsistencies in a recent study of registrant filings. As a result, in January 2010, the SEC's Division of Corporate Finance issued new Compliance and Disclosure Interpretations (C&DIs) on the use of non-GAAP financial measures. The C&DIs replace the interpretative guidance in the SEC staff's "Frequently Asked Questions

Regarding the Use of Non-GAAP Measures" (FAQs), which was issued in June 2003, but the rules on non-GAAP financial measures (Regulation G and Item 10(e) of Regulation S-K) were not amended.

The issuance of the C&DIs was a result of the SEC staff's review of its June 2003 interpretations in an effort to eliminate any actual or perceived restrictions in the FAQs on the disclosure of non-GAAP information that were not consistent with the actual rules. In addition, they were issued to ensure that non-GAAP guidance is being read in a manner that provides clarity and flexibility to companies with respect to reporting information in their filings that they believe provides the most meaningful indicators of how they are doing and is consistent with other communications (e.g., through communications such as earnings calls and press releases).

(d) EFFECT OF NEWLY ISSUED BUT NOT YET EFFECTIVE ACCOUNTING STANDARDS.   Public companies must discuss the effect of newly issued, but not yet effective, accounting standards. SEC Staff Accounting Bulletin (SAB) *Disclosure of the Impact That Recently Issued Accounting Standards Will Have on the Financial Statements of the Registrant When Adopted in a Future Period* (SAB No. 74) requires disclosure of the expected impacts on financial information to be reported in the future and is required in the financial statements if the change to the new accounting standard will be accounted for in future periods by restatement of the current financials. Additionally, disclosure in the financials is to be considered when the change will be accounted for prospectively or as a change in accounting principle.

6.3 RELATED ACCOUNTING LITERATURE

(a) RISKS AND UNCERTAINTIES.   The financial statements disclosures under GAAP have similar objectives as the MD&A disclosures. In 1994, the AICPA's Accounting Standards Executive Committee (AcSEC) issued Statement of Position (SOP) 94-6, *Disclosure of Certain Significant Risks and Uncertainties.* This SOP, subsequently codified in FASB's Accounting Standards Codification (ASC) 275, *Risks and Uncertainties,* requires an entity to disclose, in the notes to the financial statements, forward-looking information about certain significant estimates and concentrations. This is a GAAP requirement rather than a MD&A requirement and is applicable to both public and private entities. As discussed in ASC 275-10-05-2:

> The central feature of this Subtopic's disclosure requirements is selectivity: specified criteria serve to screen the host of risks and uncertainties that affect every entity so that required disclosures are limited to matters significant to a particular entity.

> The disclosures focus primarily on risks and uncertainties that could significantly affect the amounts reported in the financial statements in the near term or the near-term functioning of the reporting entity. The risks and uncertainties this Subtopic addresses can stem from any of the following:

> **a.** The nature of the entity's operations
> **b.** The use of estimates in the preparation of the entity's financial statements
> **c.** Significant concentrations in certain aspects of the entity's operations.

> Namely, an entity must disclose:

> **1.** Nature of operations
> **2.** Use of estimates in the preparation of financial statements
> **3.** Certain significant estimates
> **4.** Current vulnerability due to certain concentrations

The first two disclosures are always required. Disclosures about risks (related to concentrations) and uncertainties (concerning estimates) are required if specified criteria are met. The statement became effective for fiscal years ending after December 15, 1995. A summary of the required disclosures is presented next. For a complete understanding, readers should refer to the full text of ASC 275. (see: *https://asc.fasb.org/subtopic&trid=2134480*—a subscription service)

(b) NATURE OF OPERATIONS. The financial statements should include a description of the major products or services the entity sells or provides and its principal markets, including the locations of those markets. If the entity operates in more than one business, the disclosure should also indicate the relative importance of its operations in each business and the basis for the determination—for example, assets, revenues, or earnings. Disclosures about the nature of operations do not need to be quantified. The relative importance could be conveyed by use of terms such as "predominately," "about equally," or "major."

(c) USE OF ESTIMATES IN THE PREPARATION OF FINANCIAL STATEMENTS. Financial statements should include an explanation that the preparation of financial statements in conformity with GAAP requires the use of management's estimates.

(d) CERTAIN SIGNIFICANT ESTIMATES. Uncertainties concerning estimates that affect financial statement amounts (such as a valuation allowance for deferred tax assets or the carrying amount of inventory or a long-term contract) if it is at least reasonably possible the estimates will change in the near term and the effect of the change could be material to the financial statements must be disclosed.

As stated in ASC 275-10-50-8:

Disclosure regarding an estimate shall be made when known information available before the financial statements are issued or are available to be issued indicates that both of the following criteria are met:

a. It is at least reasonably possible that the estimate of the effect on the financial statements of a condition, situation, or set of circumstances that existed at the date of the financial statements will change in the near term due to one or more future confirming events. (The term reasonably possible as used in this Subtopic is consistent with its use in Subtopic 450-20 to mean that the chance of a future transaction or event occurring is more than remote but less than likely.)

b. The effect of the change would be material to the financial statements.

(e) CURRENT VULNERABILITY DUE TO CERTAIN CONCENTRATIONS. Financial statements should include risks related to concentrations in volume of business, sources of supply, revenue, or market or geographic area if it is at least reasonably possible that the concentrations could have a severe impact on operations within the near term. As stated in ASC 275-10-50-16:

Vulnerability from concentrations arises because an entity is exposed to risk of loss greater than it would have had it mitigated its risk through diversification. Such risks of loss manifest themselves differently, depending on the nature of the concentration, and vary in significance. Financial statements shall disclose the concentrations described in paragraph 275-10-50-18 if, based on information known to management before the financial statements are issued or are available to be issued (as discussed in Section 855-10-25), all of the following criteria are met:

a. The concentration exists at the date of the financial statements.

b. The concentration makes the entity vulnerable to the risk of a near-term severe impact.

c. It is at least reasonably possible that the events that could cause the severe impact will occur in the near term.

Concentrations, including known group concentrations, are required to be disclosed if they meet the criteria of paragraph 275-10-50-16. Group concentrations exist if a number of counterparties or items that have similar economic characteristics collectively expose the reporting entity to a particular kind of risk. Some concentrations may fall into more than one of these categories:

- Volume of business with a particular customer, supplier, lender, grantor, or contributor
- Revenue from particular products, services, or fundraising events
- Source of supply of materials, labor, services, or licenses or other rights
- Market or geographic area in which operations are conducted

6.4 EXTERNAL AUDITOR INVOLVEMENT

The external auditor is required follow Statement of Auditing Standards (SAS) No. 8, *Other Information in Documents Containing Audited Financial Statements,* when other information, such as the MD&A, is presented with the audited financial statements and the independent auditor's report. SAS 8[8] was issued by the AICPA in December 1975 and in the codification, the reference is AU Section 550, *Other Information in Documents Containing Audited Financial Statements.* As excerpted from par. 4 of SAS 8, the auditor has the responsibility to read the other information, such as the MD&A:

> Other information in a document may be relevant to an audit performed by an independent auditor or to the continuing propriety of his report. The auditor's responsibility with respect to information in a document does not extend beyond the financial information identified in his report, and the auditor has no obligation to perform any procedures to corroborate other information contained in a document. However, he should read the other information and consider whether such information, or the manner of its presentation, is materially inconsistent with information, or the manner of its presentation, appearing in the financial statements.

For a complete understanding, readers should refer to the full text of the standard. The full text of SAS 8 is available on the PCAOB Web site at: *http://pcaobus.org/Standards/Auditing/Pages/AU550 .aspx*

Management may wish to engage the external auditor to perform additional procedures related to the MD&A. To accommodate such an engagement, the AICPA issued, in 2001, Statement on Standards for Attestation Engagements No. 10, *Attestation Standards: Revision and Recodification,* which is relevant to the external auditor's association with MD&A. In the codification, the reference is attestation standards (AT) Section 701, *Management's Discussion and Analysis.* This statement provides performance and reporting guidance and applies to engagements where management has opted to engage the external auditor to examine and to review the MD&A included in audited financial statements or in other documents. The full text of AT Section 701 can be accessed on the PCAOB's Web site at: *http://pcaobus.org/Standards/Attestation/Pages/AT701.aspx*.

---

[8] In April 2003, the PCAOB adopted certain preexisting standards as its interim standards. Pursuant to Rule 3200T, Interim Auditing Standards consist of generally accepted auditing standards, as described in the AICPA's Auditing Standards Board's Statement of Auditing Standards No. 95, in existence on April 16, 2003, to the extent not superseded or amended by the Board.

CHAPTER 7

INTRODUCTION TO INTERNAL CONTROL ASSESSMENT AND REPORTING

Lynford Graham, CPA, PhD, CFE

Bentley University

7.1 INTRODUCTION

The Sarbanes-Oxley Act of 2002[1] made significant changes to many aspects of the financial reporting process. One of those changes is a requirement that management evaluate the effectiveness of its internal control over financial reporting and provides a report on this evaluation. Additionally, the company's independent auditors are required to report on the effectiveness of internal control in conjunction with their traditional audit of the company's financial statements.

The motivation for this requirement arose out of the business and audit failures in the early 2000s. Corporate names such as Enron, WorldCom, and Global Crossing dominated the news with

---

[1] United States Congress, The Public Company Accounting Reform and Investor Protection Act of 2002 (Sarbanes-Oxley Act), Pub. L. No. 107-204, 116 Stat. 745, July 30, 2002.

tales of financial reporting shenanigans and corporate executive misdirections. The root foundation for requiring this controls reporting remedy is a long trail of academic and professional research that concluded time and time again that weaknesses in internal controls were an underlying cause of these types of problems. In addition, a rising proportion of restatements of previously issued financial reports was also observed. These factors contributed to a conclusion that investor confidence in the U.S. securities market was at risk. In light of recent emerging strengths in international securities markets, the trend had to be reversed.

While a much-discussed aspect of the Sarbanes-Oxley Act has been the requirement for corporations to report publicly on internal controls, other provisions of the act have had significance for the business community and the auditing profession. Those provisions include:

- Establishment of the Public Company Accounting Oversight Board (PCAOB) as the auditing standards setting and inspection body over public company audits
- Strengthened independence rules for independent auditors and limitations on providing certain nonaudit services for audit clients
- Strengthened penalties for corporate executive misconduct
- More accountability for corporate financial executives for establishing, maintaining, and monitoring internal controls and quarterly certifications regarding significant changes in internal controls
- Additional penalties for corporate executives not complying with the rules

In years subsequent to 2004, the Securities and Exchange Commission (SEC) and the PCAOB (Auditing Standard No. 5) issued revised guidance to companies and auditors, designed to ease the burdens of compliance as a result of cost concerns. Nonaccelerated filer entities (capitalization under $75 million) finally began reporting on the effectiveness of their controls in 2008. In July 2010, the Dodd-Frank Wall Street Reform and Consumer Protection Act (Pub. L. 111-203, July 21; Dodd-Frank) suspended the requirement that auditors separately assess, test, and report on the internal controls reports of nonaccelerated filer public companies. All public companies will, however, continue to report on the effectiveness of their internal controls following SEC guidelines. Auditors of nonaccelerated filers will read and assess the disclosures made by companies regarding their internal controls under other auditing standards (Auditing Standards codification (AU) Section 550).

(a) EFFECTIVENESS OF SARBANES-OXLEY REQUIREMENTS TO DATE.   It is difficult to quantitatively assess the success of the Sarbanes-Oxley Act at this time. We are aware that restatements, fraud, and financial statement misstatement have not ended, but the extent to which they would be higher in the absence of the requirements is not easily measured. Anecdotal evidence and information gathered for an academic research study[2] indicate the identification of many deficiencies in internal control in even the largest and most well controlled entities. In a study of 44 accelerated filer audit engagements over two years (2004 and 2005) that yielded 76 data observations, nearly 4,000 deficiencies of various magnitudes were identified and documented by entities and auditors. It was found that management's classifications of the severity of deficiencies that were also assessed by the auditor were often understated, adding credence to the value of independent auditor involvement. More than 65 percent of the time, companies underrated the severity of deficiencies they found, relative to the way the auditor assessed these deficiencies. Also, the auditor seems to have been the primary source of deficiency identification (over 70 percent of the total deficiencies), and control tests were the predominant discovery vehicle for uncovering the control deficiencies (again over 70 percent). The remediation of material weaknesses identified during the year resulted in a more modest reported number of ineffective control opinions than would have been the case if all weaknesses (and not just those remaining at year-end) were determinant of controls effectiveness.

---

[2] Jean C. Bedard and Lynford Graham, "Detection and Severity Classification of Sarbanes-Oxley Section 404 Internal Control Deficiencies, and Archival Evidence on Remediation of Sarbanes-Oxley Section 404 Internal Control Deficiencies." *Accounting Review* 86, no 3 (2011): 825–855.

By that measure, the requirements seem to be identifying issues that should result in fewer financial statement misstatements and restatements. In light of the importance of auditor procedures in identifying and classifying control deficiencies, it is surprising that Dodd-Frank suspended the auditor attestation provision. Instead, Dodd-Frank places considerable reliance on company performance of control assessment and evaluation procedures, which have not been shown to be sufficient and effective based on research on the early years of implementation . . .

Evidence also shows that after an initial rise in restatements after the introduction of the internal controls requirements (i.e., a number of past misstatements were uncovered by the procedures), subsequent years show a decline and leveling off of the upward trends of pre-Sarbanes years. Also, some research studies show that a lower cost of capital is associated with companies with effective internal controls. A 2008 report of the Association of Certified Fraud Examiners noted that companies that implemented such antifraud controls as a fraud hotline experienced over 60 percent less loss due to fraud. The implementation of other controls and audit-related procedures also revealed significant reductions in the losses due to fraud. Clearly gains are being made. But the cost-benefit remains in debate. While the lessened requirements of the SEC's guidance[3] and the new PCAOB Auditing Standard No. 5, *An Audit of Internal Control over Financial Reporting That Is Integrated with an Audit of Financial Statements,*[4] are designed to enhance efficiency, the intent is to not lessen the effectiveness of the intended legislation for companies and auditors.

There have been some studies of factors that influence the costs of Sarbanes-Oxley compliance. In one study of 2,451 accelerated filers that reported on their internal controls in both 2004 and 2005,[5] some findings are worthy of note:

- The smaller of the filers in this group reported a greater proportion of the material weaknesses. This may have implications for the nonaccelerated filers that may become subject to auditor assessment and testing in 2010.
- Audit fees were relatively higher for companies reporting a material weakness.
- Audit fees generally declined in the second year of implementation. Greater reductions were found in companies with effective internal controls.
- Audit fees for companies reporting a material weakness in the second year increased.

Because many of the documentation costs and project organizational costs are first-year costs, a general reduction in audit and compliance costs in the second year of implementation can be expected. However, the message here is that establishing effective company internal controls is one controllable factor in reducing compliance costs, even before considering the possible effects of the revised SEC or auditing guidance.

7.2 DEFINITION OF *INTERNAL CONTROL*

For the purposes of complying with the internal control reporting requirements of the Sarbanes-Oxley Act, the SEC rules provide the working definition of the term *internal control over financial reporting.* Rule 13a-15(f) states:

> The term internal control over financial reporting is defined as a process designed by, or under the supervision of, the issuer's principal executive and principal financial officers, or persons

---

[3] Securities and Exchange Commission, *Commission Guidance Regarding Management's Report on Internal Control over Financial Reporting under Section 13(a) or 15(d) of the Securities Exchange Act of 1934,* Release Nos. 33-8810; 34-55929; FR 77; File No. S7-24-06.

[4] Public Company Accounting Oversight Board, Auditing Standard No. 5, *An Audit of Internal Control over Financial Reporting That Is Integrated with an Audit of Financial Statements,* PCAOB Release No. 2007-005, May 24, 2007.

[5] Jean C. Bedard, Lynford Graham, Rani Hoitashi, and Udi Hoitashi, "Sarbanes-Oxley Section 404 and Internal Controls," *CPA Journal* (October 2007).

performing similar functions, and effected by the issuer's board of directors, management and other personnel, to provide reasonable assurance regarding the reliability of financial reporting and the preparation of financial statements for external purposes in accordance with generally accepted accounting principles and includes those policies and procedures that:

1. Pertain to the maintenance of records that in reasonable detail accurately and fairly reflect the transactions and dispositions of the assets of the issuer;

2. Provide reasonable assurance that transactions are recorded as necessary to permit preparation of financial statements in accordance with generally accepted accounting principles, and that receipts and expenditures of the issuer are being made only in accordance with authorizations of management and directors of the issuer; and

3. Provide reasonable assurance regarding prevention or timely detection of unauthorized acquisition, use or disposition of the issuer's assets that could have a material effect on the financial statements.

When considering the SEC's definition, you should note these issues:

- The term *internal control* is a broad concept that extends to all areas of the management of an enterprise. The SEC definition narrows the scope of an entity's consideration of internal control to the preparation of the financial statements—hence the use of the term *internal control over financial reporting.*

- The SEC intends its definition to be consistent with the definition of internal controls that pertains to financial reporting objectives that was provided in the Committee of Sponsoring Organizations (COSO) of the Treadway Commission 1992 COSO Report:[6] The rule makes explicit reference to the use or disposition of the entity's assets—that is, the safeguarding of assets.

7.3 MANAGEMENT'S REQUIRED REPORTS ON INTERNAL CONTROL

(a) ANNUAL REPORTING REQUIREMENTS.   Section 404 of the Sarbanes-Oxley Act (SOX 404) requires chief executive officers (CEOs) and chief financial officers (CFOs) to annually evaluate and report on the effectiveness of the entity's internal control over financial reporting. This report is contained in the company's Form 10-K, which is filed annually with the SEC. The SEC has adopted rules for its registrants that effectively implement the requirements of SOX 404.

Under the SEC rules (final rule adopted in 2003),[7] the company's 10-K must include:[8]

A. *Management's Annual Report on Internal Control over Financial Reporting.* Provide a report on the company's internal control over financial reporting that contains:

1. A statement of management's responsibilities for establishing and maintaining adequate internal control over financial reporting

2. A statement identifying the framework used by management to evaluate the effectiveness of the company's internal control over financial reporting

3. Management's assessment of the effectiveness of the company's internal control over financial reporting as of the end of the most recent fiscal year, including a statement as to whether or not internal control over financial reporting is effective. This discussion must include disclosure of any material weakness in the company's internal control over

---

[6] Committee of Sponsoring Organizations (COSO), *Internal Control—Integrated Framework* (New York: American Institute of Certified Public Accountants, 1992).

[7] Securities and Exchange Commission, *Final Rule: Management's Report on Internal Control over Financial Reporting and Certification of Disclosure in Exchange Act Periodic Reports,* Release Nos. 33-8238; 34-47986; IC-26068; File Nos. S7-40-02; S7-06-03.

[8] See Regulation S-K, Item 308 (17 CFR §229.308).

financial reporting identified by management. Management is not permitted to conclude that the registrant's internal control over financial reporting is effective if there are one or more material weaknesses in the company's internal control over financial reporting.

B. *Changes in Internal Control over Financial Reporting.* Disclose any change in the company's internal control over financial reporting that has materially affected, or is reasonably likely to materially affect, the company's internal control over financial reporting. The company's annual report filed with the SEC also should include management's fourth-quarter report on the effectiveness of the entity's disclosure controls and procedures, as described in this chapter. The SEC final rules also require a company to file, as part of the company's annual report, the attestation report of the registered public accounting firm that audited the company's financial statements.

(i) Effective Dates. The requirement to disclose material changes in the entity's internal control became effective on August 14, 2003. The effective date for the other provisions of the rules described—that is, management's report on the effectiveness of internal control and the related auditor attestation—become effective at different times, depending on the filing status of the company.

- *Accelerated filer.* A company that is an accelerated filer as of the end of its first fiscal year ending on or after November 15, 2004, must begin to comply with the internal control reporting and attestation requirements in its annual report for that fiscal year.[9]
- *Nonaccelerated filer.* Smaller companies are required to comply with the new rules for their first fiscal year ending on or after December 15, 2008, with independent auditor reports on the effectiveness of internal control scheduled to begin the following year.[10]

(b) QUARTERLY REPORTING REQUIREMENTS. Section 302 of the Sarbanes-Oxley Act requires quarterly reporting on the effectiveness of an entity's "disclosure controls and procedures." Item 307 of SEC Regulation S-K implements this requirement for the company's quarterly Form 10-Q filings by requiring management to:

> [d]isclose the conclusions of the company's principal executive and principal financial officers, or persons performing similar functions, regarding the effectiveness of the company's disclosure controls and procedures as of the end of the period covered by the report, based on the evaluation of these controls and procedures.

In addition to reporting on disclosure controls, the company's quarterly reports also must disclose material changes in the entity's internal control over financial reporting.

Note that for these quarterly filings, management is *not* required to evaluate or report on internal control over financial reporting. That evaluation is required on an *annual basis only.*

(i) Disclosure Controls and Procedures. With these rules, the SEC introduces a new term, *disclosure controls and procedures,* which is different from *internal controls over financial reporting* defined earlier. SEC Rule 13a-15(e) defines disclosure controls and procedures as those that are:

> [d]esigned to ensure that information required to be disclosed by the issuer in the reports that it files or submits under the Act is recorded, processed, summarized, and reported within the time periods specified in the Commission's rules and forms. Disclosure controls and procedures

---

[9] *Accelerated filer* is defined in Exchange Act Rule 12b-2. Generally, companies with a market capitalization of $75 million or more are considered accelerated filers.

[10] In October 2009, the SEC granted another extension on the requirement for companies to include an auditor report regarding the effectiveness of internal controls. In 2010, the auditor report requirement was suspended by the 2010 Financial Reform Act.

include, without limitation, controls and procedures designed to ensure that information required to be disclosed by an issuer in the reports that it files or submits under the Act is accumulated and communicated to the issuer's management, including its principal executive and principal financial officers, or persons performing similar functions, as appropriate to allow timely decisions regarding required disclosure.

Thus, "disclosure controls and procedures" would encompass the controls over all material financial and nonfinancial information in Exchange Act reports. Information that would fall under this definition that would not be part of an entity's internal control over financial reporting might include the signing of a significant contract, changes in a strategic relationship, management compensation, or legal proceedings.

In relation to its rule requiring an assessment of disclosure controls and procedures, the SEC also advised all public companies to create a disclosure committee to oversee the process by which disclosures are created and reviewed, including:

- Review of 10-Q, 10-K, and other SEC filings; earnings releases; and other public information for the appropriateness of disclosure
- Determination of what constitutes a significant transaction or event that requires disclosure
- Determination and identification of significant deficiencies and material weaknesses in the design or operating effectiveness of disclosure controls and procedures
- Assessment of CEO and CFO awareness of material information that could affect disclosure

The existence and effective operation of an entity's disclosure committee can have a significant effect on the nature and scope of management's work to evaluate the effectiveness of the entity's internal control. For example:

- The effective functioning of a disclosure committee may be viewed as an element that strengthens the entity's control environment.
- The work of the disclosure committee may create documentation that engagement teams can use to reduce the scope of their work.

7.4 MANAGEMENT CERTIFICATIONS

In addition to providing a report on the effectiveness of its disclosure controls and internal control over financial reporting, the company's principal executive officer and principal financial officer are required to sign two certifications, which are included as exhibits to the entity's 10-Q and 10-K. These two certifications are required by the Sarbanes-Oxley Act:

1. Section 302, which requires a certification to accompany each quarterly and annual report filed with the SEC.
2. Section 906, which added a new Section 1350 to Title 18 of the U.S. Code, and which contains a certification requirement subject to specific federal criminal provisions. This certification is separate and distinct from the Section 302 certification requirement.

Exhibit 7.1 provides the text of the Section 302 certification. This text is provided in SEC Rule 13a-14(a) and should be used exactly as set forth in the rule.

Exhibit 7.2 provides an example of the Section 906 certification. Note that some certifying officers may choose to include a "knowledge qualification," as indicated by the optional language within the parentheses. Officers who choose to include this language should do so only after consulting with their SEC counsel. Unlike the Section 302 certification, which requires a separate certification for both the CEO and CFO, the company can provide only one 906 certification, which is then signed by both individuals.

I, [identify the certifying individual], certify that:

1. I have reviewed this [specify report] of [identify registrant];

2. Based on my knowledge, this report does not contain any untrue statement of a material fact or omit to state a material fact necessary to make the statements made, in light of the circumstances under which such statements were made, not misleading with respect to the period covered by this report;

3. Based on my knowledge, the financial statements, and other financial information included in this report, fairly present in all material respects the financial condition, results of operations and cash flows of the registrant as of, and for, the periods presented in this report;

4. The registrant's other certifying officer(s) and I are responsible for establishing and maintaining disclosure controls and procedures (as defined in Exchange Act Rules 13a-15(e) and 15 d-15(e)) and internal control over financial reporting (as defined in Exchange Act Rules 13a-15(f) and 15 d-15(f)) for the registrant and have:

   a. Designed such disclosure controls and procedures, or caused such disclosure controls and procedures to be designed under our supervision, to ensure that material information relating to the registrant, including its consolidated subsidiaries, is made known to us by others within those entities, particularly during the period in which this report is being prepared;

   b. Designed such internal control over financial reporting, or caused such internal control over financial reporting to be designed under our supervision, to provide reasonable assurance regarding the reliability of financial reporting and the preparation of financial statements for external purposes in accordance with generally accepted accounting principles;

   c. Evaluated the effectiveness of the registrant's disclosure controls and procedures and presented in this report our conclusions about the effectiveness of the disclosure controls and procedures, as of the end of the period covered by this report based on such evaluation; and

   d. Disclosed in this report any change in the registrant's internal control over financial reporting that occurred during the registrant's most recent fiscal quarter (the registrant's fourth fiscal quarter in the case of an annual report) that has materially affected, or is reasonably likely to materially affect, the registrant's internal control over financial reporting; and

5. The registrant's other certifying officer(s) and I have disclosed, based on our most recent evaluation of internal control over financial reporting, to the registrant's auditors and the audit committee of the registrant's board of directors (or persons performing the equivalent functions):

   a. All significant deficiencies and material weaknesses in the design or operation of internal control over financial reporting which are reasonably likely to adversely affect the registrant's ability to record, process, summarize, and report financial information; and

   b. Any fraud, whether or not material, that involves management or other employees who have a significant role in the registrant's internal control over financial reporting.

Exhibit 7.1   Section 302 Certification, SEC Rule 13a-14(a)/15d-14(a)

An initial concern was that the required certification process would result in a mass exodus of company executives, reluctant to make the explicit disclosures and certifications required. While there is evidence that some executives did feel strongly enough about the new risks to change positions, there has been no observed mass exodus. In the early years of SOX implementation, the increased focus on the responsibilities and liabilities of the boards of directors and audit committees has made it more difficult to recruit directors, but again, there is no evidence of a crisis in oversight.

In the view of many, the increased focus on governance and competence at the board level seems to have strengthened corporate governance.

A great deal of the information included in financial statements and other reports filed with the SEC originates in areas of the company that are outside the day-to-day or direct control of the CEO and CFO. Because of the significance of information prepared by others, it is becoming common for the CEO and CFO to request those individuals who are directly responsible for supplying this

In connection with the [annual/quarterly] report of [name of registrant] (the "Company") on Form (10-K/10-Q] for the period ended (the "Report"), the undersigned in the capacities listed below, hereby certify, pursuant to 18 U.S.C. ss. 1350, as adopted pursuant to Section 906 of the Sarbanes-Oxley Act of 2002, that

   i. The Report fully complies with the requirements of Section 12(a) or 15(d) of the Securities Exchange Act of 1934; and

   ii. The information contained in the Report fairly presents, in all material respects, the financial condition and results of operations of the company.

Exhibit 7.2   Section 906 Certification, 18 U.S.C. Section 1350

information to certify it. This process is known as *subcertification,* and it usually involves providing a written affidavit to the CEO and CFO that will in turn allow them to sign their certifications in good faith.

Items that may be the subject of subcertification affidavits include:

- Adequacy of specific disclosures in the financial statements or other reports filed with the SEC, such as management's disclosure and analysis included in the entity's 10-Q or 10-K
- Accuracy of specific account balances
- Compliance with company policies and procedures, including the company's code of conduct
- Adequacy of the design and/or operating effectiveness of departmental internal controls and disclosure controls
- Accuracy of reported financial results of the department, subsidiary, or business segment

7.5 INDEPENDENT AUDITOR'S RESPONSIBILITIES

Exhibit 7.3 describes the relationship among the various rule-making bodies, companies, and their auditors regarding the reporting on internal control. As described previously, management of a public company is required to report on the effectiveness of the entity's internal control on an annual basis, and the company's independent auditors are required to review this report. The SEC is responsible for setting rules to implement the Sarbanes-Oxley Act requirements. Those rules include guidance for reporting by the CEO and CFO on the entity's internal control over financial reporting and disclosure controls, but they do not provide any guidance or set standards for the independent auditors. The PCAOB sets the auditing standards, which have a direct effect on auditors and how they plan and perform their engagements.

In addition, the auditing standards will have an indirect effect on the company as it prepares for the audit of the internal control report. Just as in a financial statement audit, the company should be able to support its conclusions about internal control and provide documentation that is sufficient for the auditor to perform an audit. Thus, in preparing for the audit of its internal control report, it is vital for management, and those who assist managers, to have a good understanding of what the independent auditors will require.

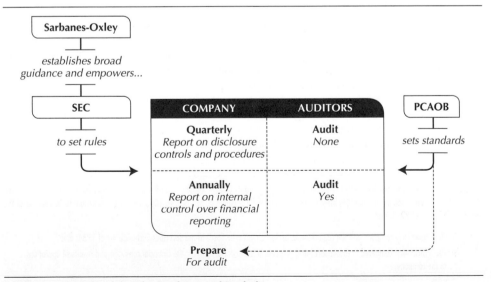

Exhibit 7.3   Relationship of the Rules, Regulations, and Standards

7.6 AUDIT STANDARDS

In June 2004, the SEC approved PCAOB Auditing Standard No. 2, *An Audit of Internal Control over Financial Reporting Performed in Conjunction with an Audit of Financial Statements.* That standard required auditors for the first time to conduct two audits of their publicly traded clients: the traditional audit of financial statements and a new audit of internal control. The standard was revised and reissued as Auditing Standard No. 5 in response to concerns that the original standard required unnecessary procedures without corresponding benefits and to take advantage of the experience gained in the first several years of implementation. There was no intent to lessen the effectiveness of the standard.

The Auditing Standard can have a significant effect on the way in which company management conducts its own required assessment in internal control effectiveness. For example, the standard:

- Requires auditors to makes their own assessment of the effectiveness of the company's internal control. Since management and the auditor are seeking to arrive at the same conclusion, careful consideration should be made of both the SEC and the PCAOB guidance by both companies and auditors. Auditors will read management's disclosures regarding internal control. If management makes a misstatement in its disclosures or fails to have an adequate basis for its statements and conclusions about internal controls, the auditors will need to note this in their opinion, if the issue cannot be resolved.

- Allows the auditor to rely on the work performed by the company in its self-assessment process to support his or her conclusion on internal control effectiveness. However, to rely on this work to the maximum extent, certain conditions regarding the objectivity and competence of the work performed and the people who performed it must be met.

- Establishes the definition of a *material weakness* in internal control. To conclude that internal control is effective, management should have reasonable assurance that there were no material weaknesses in internal control in any of the five COSO components as of the reporting date.

Subsequent to the original auditing standard, both the PCAOB and the SEC released interpretive question-and-answer guidance that today has for the most part been folded into the most recent guidance issued. An important step in planning a SOX 404 compliance engagement is for management to have read the most current guidance and any outstanding staff positions issued by the PCAOB and the SEC.

(a) RELATIONSHIP WITH MANAGEMENT'S ASSESSMENT. The SEC rules relating to the scope of management's assessment of internal control effectiveness remain rather conceptual. In practice, companies frequently encounter situations for which the SEC has not provided guidance. In those situations, companies may look to the Auditing Standard to help determine which business units or controls should be included in their assessment.

Auditing Standard No. 5 provides conceptual guidance on the required scope of the auditor's assessment of the company's internal control. This guidance is written in the context of the independent auditor's responsibilities, but of course the nature and extent of procedures performed by management may shape the nature and extent of procedures the auditor performs to achieve his or her required high level of assurance that the controls are operating effectively.

If the company's self-assessment process does *not* include the required elements or it does not gather sufficient evidence to support its conclusions, the auditor should discuss the situation with management. If the independent auditor concludes that the company process was inadequate to support the assertion, the auditor would need to point that out in a modification of his or her audit report. A general audit requirement is that whenever the independent auditor believes a disclosure in the financial statements or in accompanying materials is misleading or unsupported, the auditor needs to point this out, even if it is not directly a part of the financial statements and disclosures. As a practical matter, most companies take steps to ensure that their assessment process provides support for their assertion on internal controls.

(b) DOCUMENTATION.   Independent auditors will evaluate the adequacy of management's support for their assertion regarding internal control. That support includes documentation of the design of management's process to assess the effectiveness of its controls as well as documentation of the existing controls and procedures performed to confirm the effective operation of its controls. Without adequate documentation by the company of its assessment process, the auditor is hampered in his or her assessment or may be unable to conclude that management has support for its disclosed assertion. Lack of or deficient controls documentation in itself is considered a control deficiency.

The SEC guidance on management's responsibilities includes general conceptual documentation guidance. Companies are well advised to discuss with the independent auditors the nature and extent of their planned documentation to anticipate any differing views or expectations regarding company documentation.

More robust documentation and testing of the company process can lead to efficiencies in the required audit work. Since under Auditing Standard No. 5 more reliance can be placed on company procedures when they are objectively and competently performed, better company documentation and attention to the assessment process can enhance the ability of auditors to rely on procedures already performed by management.

(c) SCOPE OF TEST WORK.   The Auditing Standard provides limited guidance on the nature, timing, and extent of the auditor's procedures for a number of situations, including:

- Extent of testing of manual and automated controls
- Required procedures when the entity uses a service organization to process transactions
- Required procedures when the entity engages others, including internal auditors, to perform procedures as part of the company assessment process
- Updated test work that may be required when the original testing was performed at an interim date, well in advance of the reporting date

(d) USE OF WORK OF INTERNAL AUDITORS AND OTHERS.   Both the Sarbanes-Oxley Act and the PCAOB Auditing Standard describe a two-pronged approach for providing financial statement users with useful information about the reliability of a company's internal control:

1. Management assesses and reports on the effectiveness of the entity's internal control.
2. The company's independent auditors issue a separate, independent opinion on the effectiveness of the company's internal control (accelerated filers).

In this scheme, it is vital that the two participants perform their duties independently of each other. While auditors may sometimes rely on the company's procedures, companies *cannot* use any auditor-performed procedures as a basis for their required attestation. The company attestation should stand on its own. COSO makes it clear that the independent auditor is not an element of the internal control system of a company, and it is that control system that is the focus of the controls attestation.

Keep in mind that the company is required to perform a thorough assessment of the company's internal control. That assessment is prioritized by a risk assessment of the more vulnerable financial statement reporting areas. As much as possible, management will want to provide the results of its work to the independent auditors, so the auditors will have a clear understanding of management's assessment and will not have to duplicate the company's efforts. In fact, cross communication of findings between the auditor and management is expected by the PCAOB and SEC.

(i) Independent Auditor's Use of the Company's Internal Control Work.   An important efficiency concession in recent guidance on the performance of the audit of internal controls is the relaxation on the limitations on the reliance the independent auditor can place on the work of others, providing that the work of others is shown to be objective and competently performed. The work of others includes the relevant work performed by:

- Internal auditors
- Other company personnel

- Third parties, such as consultants working under the direction of management or the audit committee

The independent auditor's ability to rely on the work of others has some limits. For example, in identified high-risk areas or in areas requiring significant subjective judgment, the independent auditor will often perform more of the procedures supporting the auditor opinion.

(ii) Using the Work of Others.   To determine the extent to which the independent auditor may use the company's work, the independent auditor:

- Considers the nature of the controls subjected to the work of others. In general, auditors will probably want to perform some of their own tests on the controls related to accounts that have a high risk of material misstatement.
- Evaluates the objectivity of the individuals who performed the work. The more objective the company's project team, the more likely the independent auditors will be to rely on their work.
- Tests some of the work performed by others to evaluate the quality and competence of their work.

Auditors cannot rely on procedures performed by individuals who are not objective (e.g., employees self-assessing their own work) or on work not competently performed. Both characteristics (objectivity and competence) are necessary.

To encourage the company's independent auditors to make as much use as possible of the company's own assessment of internal control, company management should have a clear understanding of the conditions that must be met for the independent auditors to use the work. To help the independent auditors determine that those criteria have been met, companies may wish to ensure their documentation includes information relevant to compliance with the key requirements of the Auditing Standard and make this documentation available to the independent auditors early on in their audit planning process. For example, such information might include:

- Obtaining the resumes of project team members showing their education level, experience, professional certifications, and continuing education
- Documenting the company's policies regarding the assignment of individuals to work areas
- Documenting the organizational status of the project team and how they have been provided access to the board of directors and audit committee
- Determining that the internal auditors follow the relevant internal auditing standards
- Establishing policies that ensure that the *documentation* of the work performed includes:
  - A description of the scope of the work
  - Work programs that document when and by whom the work is to be completed
  - Evidence of supervision and review
  - Conclusions about the work performed

(e) DETERMINATION OF MATERIAL WEAKNESSES.   The SEC reporting rules require entity management to disclose any material weaknesses in internal control. A company cannot assess its controls as effective if one or more material weaknesses remain as of the reporting date of the assertion regarding the effectiveness of internal control. Weaknesses and deficiencies identified in the course of the assessment and satisfactorily remediated before the reporting date are not considered in the final assessment of the effectiveness of the internal controls. For example, numerous material weaknesses might be identified in the course of the assessment of controls; if successfully remediated, the company and auditor can state that internal controls are effective as of the reporting date. However, weaknesses discovered in a financial statement quarter during the year are likely to trigger disclosures as part of the Section 302 quarterly reporting requirements. Engagements to assess the effectiveness of internal controls should be planned and performed in a way that will detect material weaknesses. Thus, it is critical that you have a working definition of the term. The Auditing Standard provides these definitions:

- A control deficiency exists when the design or operation of a control does not allow management or employees, in the normal course of performing their assigned functions, to prevent or detect misstatements on a timely basis.
- A material weakness is a deficiency, or a combination of deficiencies, in internal control over financial reporting, such that there is a reasonable possibility that a material misstatement of the company's annual or interim financial statements will not be prevented or detected on a timely basis. The term *reasonable possibility* is related to the use of that term in Financial Accounting Standards Board Statement No. 5, *Accounting for Contingencies,* and refers to a likelihood assessment that is more than remote.
- A significant deficiency is a deficiency, or a combination of deficiencies, in internal control over financial reporting that is less severe than a material weakness yet important enough to merit attention by those responsible for oversight of a registrant's financial reporting.

An issue relevant to the material weakness determination is that it remains a subjective judgment, and reasonable persons might disagree on the severity assessment in some situations. In assessing the severity of a deficiency, related compensating, redundant, or monitoring controls should be considered to see if they would be sufficiently effective to limit the severity of any controls deficiency to less than a material weakness or significant deficiency. The SEC and PCAOB agree that there are at least four situations that are indicators of a material weakness; however, there is no "automatic" classification.

1. Identification of fraud, whether material or not, on the part of senior management
2. Restatement of previously issued financial statements to reflect the correction of a material misstatement
3. Identification of a material misstatement of the financial statements in the current period in circumstances that indicate the misstatement would not have been detected by the company's internal control over financial reporting (ICFR)
4. Ineffective oversight of the company's external financial reporting and internal control over financial reporting by the company's audit committee

As a final check on the reasonableness of a weakness classification, the PCAOB; states:

If the auditor determines that a deficiency, or combination of deficiencies, might prevent prudent officials in the conduct of their own affairs from concluding that they have reasonable assurance that transactions are recorded as necessary to permit the preparation of financial statements in conformity with generally accepted accounting principles, then the auditor should treat the deficiency, or combination of deficiencies, as an indicator of a material weakness. (PCAOB AS No. 5, Para 70)

This final check is a sort of plausibility test that asks if it would make sense to a businessperson that the classification is less than a material weakness (or significant deficiency). All material weaknesses are not created equal. Investors and financial experts usually consider both the existence of a weakness as well as the nature of a material weakness when assessing the implications of the disclosure. A material weakness in the control environment due to an ineffective governance function or a poor tone at the top is likely to generate a more significant user response than a weakness in a transaction-related control or as a result of an infrequently encountered transaction, such as a merger. This is why management must identify the nature of any material weaknesses in their report on the effectiveness of internal control.

(f) WORKING WITH THE INDEPENDENT AUDITORS.   To render an opinion on either the financial statements or the effectiveness of internal control, the company's independent auditors are required to maintain their independence, in accordance with applicable SEC rules. These rules are guided by certain underlying principles, which include:

- The audit firm must not be in a position where it audits its own work.
- The auditor must not act as management or as an employee of the client.

Although maintaining independence is primarily the responsibility of the auditors, several of the PCAOB independence requirements impose certain responsibilities on management and the audit committee. These requirements include:

- *Preapproval by the audit committee.* Each internal control–related service to be provided by the auditor must be preapproved by the audit committee. The audit committee should not pre-approve internal control-related services as a broad service category, but should approve *each* service. (See PCAOB Staff Questions and Answers, June 23, 2004 and revised July 27, 2004, Questions 3 and 4).
- *Independence in fact and appearance.* The company's audit committee and independent auditors must be diligent to ensure that independence is maintained both in fact and in appearance.

No matter how detailed the independence rules may become, they cannot possibly address every possible interaction between the company and its auditors. During the initial implementation of SOX 404, many situations arose that called into question whether the auditor could interact with the company in a particular way and still maintain its independence.

For example, if the company was unsure whether its documentation of internal control would be acceptable, could it approach its auditors for advice? If the auditors made recommendations on how to improve the documentation and the company then incorporated those recommendations, would that put the audit firm in the position of auditing its own work when it reviewed that documentation? The form and content of the company's documentation of its internal control is the responsibility of management. If the auditor becomes significantly involved in that decision, does that imply that it is acting in the capacity of management?

In the initial implementation of SOX 404, it became common for auditors to provide little advice to their clients on internal control matters. Concerned about possibly violating the independence rules, they chose to largely remove themselves from their clients' efforts.

As a practical matter, both the SEC and the PCAOB understood that the public interest is not well served if the independent auditors are completely uninvolved with the company's efforts to understand and assess its internal control. There must be some sharing of information between the company and its auditors, and the auditors must be able to provide help and advice on some matters without dictating company practices and approaches.

Under the independence provisions of SOX, auditors were permitted to only provide certain limited levels of assistance to management in documenting their internal controls and making recommendations for changes to internal controls. In the early days of SOX (e.g., 2002–2005) this was broadly interpreted by many as limiting the independent auditor's role to that of a scribe in the company documentation process.

The PCAOB later provided more extensive guidance on how company management may solicit advice from and share advice with its auditors on internal control matters. The guidance from the staff was in answer to a question directed specifically to an auditor's review of the company's draft financial statements or its providing advice on the adoption of a new accounting principle or emerging issue—services that historically have been considered a routine part of a quality audit.

When management seeks the assistance of the company's auditors to help with its internal control assessment, it should make it clear that management retains the ultimate responsibility for internal control. The PCAOB places the burden on management to clearly communicate with the auditor the nature of the advice it is seeking and the purpose for which the auditor is being involved.

7.7 TOP-DOWN, RISK-BASED APPROACH FOR EVALUATING INTERNAL CONTROL

As indicated previously, both the SEC and the PCAOB periodically issue staff position papers to clarify how to address specific circumstances. On May 16, 2005, in response to information that was gathered about the first year of implementation, both the SEC and the PCAOB issued guidance that addressed the most significant problems encountered with the implementation of Auditing Standard No. 2. Of the five main areas addressed in the guidance, these are the most relevant to company management:

- *Use a risk-based, top-down approach.* The PCAOB emphasized that auditors should use a top-down approach, and company management would be wise to use this same approach. In a top-down approach, you begin with an evaluation of entity-level controls, such as the control environment and shared software and information technology controls, and from there move to the testing of detailed activity-level controls.

- One of the key principles of the top-down approach is that the decision of which controls to document and test is based an assessment of risk as well as materiality. Controls that mitigate significant risks should be documented and assessed. Those that mitigate less significant risks would be subject to considerably less, if any, testing and evaluation.

- *Auditors and company management should engage in direct and timely communication with each other.* As described earlier in this chapter, during the first year of compliance, there was often a lack of communication between the two. Ultimately the PCAOB made it clear that the auditor should be responsive to client requests for advice, provided that company management would take final responsibility for internal control.

- *Auditors should make as much use as possible of quality work on internal control performed by the company.* This guidance should help companies keep down the cost of compliance, but it also means that companies have to perform their assessment with objective and qualified individuals in a way that is consistent with the requirements of Auditing Standard No. 5.

(a) PRINCIPLES OF A TOP-DOWN, RISK-BASED APPROACH. Controls in the COSO *Internal Control Integrated Framework* are comprised of five components. Some of those components often involve the entity as a whole, such as the control environment and risk assessment. Other components, such as activity controls, operate more at the transaction level. Entity-level controls are generally pervasive and can affect many different financial statement accounts. For example, the tone at the top of an organization can establish an environment of honesty and ethics, which can set the tone for employee-expected behavior and adherence to policies. Since management override has been so often identified as an underlying fraud characteristic, the risk of management override is an important "top-side" consideration. As another example, a company's hiring and training policies will affect the way in which individual control procedures are performed. Companies that hire qualified people, train them properly, and evaluate them fairly will have much greater success when it comes time for those people to perform their jobs. The converse also is true. In that sense, hiring and training policies can have an effect on many different financial statement accounts. A less than fully competent controller or financial officer can unwittingly make errors that auditors will need to catch to prevent misstatements. That lack of competence is a control environment issue and may require the auditor to assign staff with stronger accounting backgrounds and test more period transactions. Failures in the control environment or certain other far-reaching or overarching controls can render tests of the underlying transaction controls less meaningful.

Activity-level controls, however, often may be restricted to transactions. Controls over cash disbursements generally will affect cash disbursements only and will have no impact on other specific noncash accounts, such as goodwill or the depreciation of fixed assets.

In the first year of implementation, many companies and their auditors adopted a bottom-up approach in which they started by identifying all of the companies' activity-level controls and then documenting and testing each of these to determine whether internal control as a whole was effective. This was because companies and auditors were more familiar with transaction controls than, say, the information and communication and monitoring components of COSO. As you can imagine, when fundamental, pervasive, or entity-level controls were identified as deficient late in the audit, the prior tests of any underlying controls that had already been tested became suspect and in some cases needed to be repeated after redesigns and remediations of the deficient controls. As such, this strategy was highly inefficient. As later clarified, *top-down* also means testing the highest-level control that meets the required precision of the control effectiveness, so if there are detailed controls over each stage of processing an invoice for payment as well as a final detailed supervisory review of the payment support before payment, then testing the supervisory review may be sufficient to meet the objectives of the control, and the underlying controls may not need to be individually evaluated or tested. This assumes that the identified supervisory review covers all the relevant assertions that are covered by the other controls.

In a top-down approach, you begin at the risk assessment and then go to the top, at the entity level. You then identify the most significant accounts and transaction types and risks of the organization and the control objectives for those accounts and transactions. Once you determine the control objectives, you identify those controls, starting with the entity and top-side controls that are in place to meet those objectives. Then you test and evaluate those controls.

By using a top-down approach, the company:

- Tests only those controls related to significant risks of misstatement in the accounts and transactions. This eliminates the need to focus attention on other controls in those areas that do not pose a risk that the company's financial statements could be materially misstated.
- Tests the minimum number of controls necessary to meet the control objective. Redundant controls or controls operating at a level lower than other effective controls (and there are many of these) need not be tested.

Implementing a top-down approach requires company management to exercise its judgment. How do you decide which accounts and transactions are significant and which are insignificant? If you are not going to test all the control activities for significant accounts and transactions, how do you determine which ones to test?

To make these and other decisions, you should consider the related risk of material misstatement of the financial statements. Control activities are designed to meet identified risks of misstatement. For example, one of the risks of misstatement is that the company may fail to record all of its accounts payable as of year-end. To mitigate this risk, management will design and implement procedures at the company to make sure that that all payables get recorded in the proper period.

Do these controls need to be documented and tested? It depends on the relative significance of the risk of failing to record all accounts payable. What is the likelihood that the failure to record all accounts payable would result in a material misstatement of the company's financial statements? If material amounts are or could be outstanding at year-end, then the risk is probably not negligible. In a business where cash is used for most transactions, then the misstatement risk posed by accounts payable might be negligible. The question needs to be resolved on a company-by-company and account-by-account basis. While the guidance seems to imply to some that only a few significant controls will be identified and need to be tested, in practice a good risk assessment will identify many significant areas where controls are needed. More controls will be identified when estimates and judgments are involved, when few entity-level controls are present, and when the company is comprised of more locations and business segments. Few material accounts are without risk of misstatement when the effectiveness of internal controls is not considered in making the risk assessment. There have been major frauds and misstatements of financial statements associated with just about every account in the balance sheet and income statement, including even the supposedly safe ones (e.g., cash, fixed assets, deferred costs).

Performing an assessment of internal control is not a paint-by-numbers exercise. It is a process that requires a great deal of objective and subjective judgment. The primary benchmark for making these judgments is the risk that the financial statements would be materially misstated if a material misstatement is introduced through an account and an effective control is not in place to identify and correct the misstatement.

Recently the more relaxed guidance for companies and auditors (including the PCAOB Staff Guidance of January 23, 2009) has raised the question as to whether the pendulum has swung too far in the other direction.

- Have companies attached the required annual importance to the controls identification and assessment process now that this task has been performed for several years?

- Are company assessments alone (SOX 404a) effective when the auditor is not reporting separately on internal control?
- Have companies obtained evidence or other bases supporting their risk assessments, particularly when the assessment eliminates or drastically reduces further assessment and testing in a financial reporting area?
- Are control environment factors or other compensating controls being credited too heavily when assessing the impact of missing or deficient detail controls?

Research and empirical data may help the profession assess the validity of these issues.

7.8 COORDINATING WITH THE INDEPENDENT AUDITORS

The SEC makes clear in its guidance that the company is not obligated to follow any specific course in meeting its requirements, and the auditor cannot dictate the way the company goes about its assessment. Nevertheless, it is recommended that companies consider the needs and expectations of the entity's independent auditors when planning their project to assess internal controls. Proper understanding between the company and the independent auditors will facilitate an effective and efficient audit. A lack of coordination with the auditors could result in a variety of negative unforeseen consequences, including:

- A lack of sufficient support for management's assertion, which will prompt a comment by the auditor in its report (and probably a comment to the company by the SEC)
- Duplication of effort
- Reperformance of certain tests
- Performance of additional tests or expansion of the scope of the engagement
- Misunderstandings relating to the definition or reporting of material weaknesses

Some of the key areas where consideration on SEC and PCAOB requirements will be useful include:

- The overall engagement process and approach
- The scope of the project, including locations or business units to be included, based on a risk assessment
- Preliminary identification of significant controls in meeting the risks
- The nature of any internal control deficiencies noted by the auditors during past audits of the entity's financial statements
- An understanding about what will constitute a significant deficiency or material weakness
- The nature and extent of the documentation of controls
- The nature and extent of the documentation of tests of controls
- The degree to which the auditors might be able to rely on the results of your test work to reach their conclusion
- The identification and evaluation of the monitoring component of the COSO framework

7.9 A NEW ERA

The passage of the Sarbanes-Oxley Act signaled the start of a new era in financial reporting, on par with the requirement of 70 years ago that the company's financial statements be audited by an independent certified public accountant (CPA). At that time, the capital markets looked to the CPA profession for help in implementing this new requirement. Now members of the profession—whether in public practice or employed in industry—seem equally well positioned to make a significant contribution as our country's financial reporting process embarks on another new direction.

CHAPTER 8

ACCOUNTING FOR BUSINESS COMBINATIONS

James Mraz, CPA, MBA

Professor of Accounting
University of Maryland: University College

8.1 BACKGROUND

For the 30 years prior to June 30, 2001, accounting for business combinations in the United States was governed by Accounting Principles Board (APB) Opinion No. 16, *Business Combinations,* APB Opinion No. 17, *Intangible Assets,* and their various amendments and interpretations. Those standards provided for two methods of accounting for business combinations—the pooling of interests method and the purchase method—and for amortization of goodwill and other intangible assets recognized under the purchase method over a period not longer than 40 years.

Effective July 1, 2001, those pronouncements were replaced by Statement of Financial Accounting Standards (SFAS) No. 141, *Business Combinations* and SFAS No. 142, *Goodwill and Other Intangible Assets.* In December 2007, SFAS No. 141 was revised and replaced by Statement of Financial Standards Revised [SFAS(R); Accounting Standards Codification ASC 805] *Business Combinations.* The new standards fundamentally change the method of accounting for business combinations and goodwill and other intangible assets. SFAS No. 141(R) requires that all business combinations be accounted for by a single method—the acquisition method. And whereas Opinion No. 17 had presumed that goodwill and all other intangible assets were wasting assets (i.e., finite lived) that should be amortized in determining net income, SFAS No. 142 makes no such presumption. Instead, under SFAS No. 142 goodwill and intangible assets that have indefinite useful lives are not amortized but rather are tested at least annually for impairment. Any intangible assets that have finite useful lives continue to be amortized over their useful lives, but without the constraint of an arbitrary 40-year ceiling.

SFAS No. 141(R) does not change many of the provisions of Opinion No. 16 related to the application of the acquisition method. For example, it does not significantly change the guidance for determining the cost of an acquired entity and allocating that cost to the assets acquired and liabilities assumed, the accounting for contingent consideration, and the accounting for preacquisition contingencies.

8.2 SCOPE

Statement No. 141(R) applies to a transaction or other event that meets the definition of a business combination. A *business combination* is a transaction or other event in which an acquirer obtains control of one or more businesses.

Control is generally indicated by ownership by one company (Accounting Research Bulletin [ARB] No. 51, *Consolidated Financial Statements,* paragraph 2, as amended by SFAS No. 94, *Consolidation of All Majority-Owned Subsidiaries*).

(a) IDENTIFYING A BUSINESS COMBINATION.   An entity shall determine whether a transaction or other event is a *business combination* by applying the definition, which requires that the assets acquired and liabilities assumed constitute a *business.* If the assets acquired are not a business, the reporting entity shall account for the transaction or other event as an asset acquisition.

A business combination may be structured in a variety of ways for legal, taxation, or other reasons, which include but are not limited to:

1. One or more businesses become subsidiaries of an acquirer or the net assets of one or more businesses are legally merged into the acquirer.
2. One combining entity transfers its net assets or its owners transfer their equity interests to another combining entity or its owners.
3. All of the combining entities transfer their net assets or the owners of those entities transfer their equity interests to a newly formed entity (sometimes referred to as a roll-up or put-together transaction).
4. A group of former owners of one of the combining entities obtains control of the combined entity.

Each of the listed entities represents a business combination regardless of whether the form of consideration given is cash, other assets, a business or a subsidiary of the entity, debt, common or preferred stock, or a combination of those forms. An exchange of a business for a business also constitutes a business combination.

The acquisition of some or all of the equity interests held by minority stockholders of a subsidiary is not a business combination. However, the acquisition of some or all of the stock held by minority stockholders of a subsidiary—regardless of whether acquired by the parent, the subsidiary itself, or another affiliate—is accounted for by the acquisition method under SFAS No. 141(R). The term *business combination* as used in this Statement also excludes both (a) transfers by an entity of some or all of its net assets to a newly formed substitute entity chartered by the transferor entity; and (b) transfers of net assets or exchanges of shares between entities under common control, such as between a parent corporation and its subsidiary or between two subsidiary corporations of the same parent. The assets and liabilities transferred in such transactions are recorded in the accounts of the entity that received the net assets or shares at the amounts recorded in the accounts of the entity that made the transfer as the date of the transfer or exchange.

8.3 ACQUISITION METHOD OF ACCOUNTING

Application of the acquisition method of accounting requires:

1. Identifying the acquirer
2. Determining the acquisition date
3. Recognizing and measuring the identifiable assets acquired, the liabilities assumed, and any noncontrolling interest in the acquiree
4. Recognizing and measuring goodwill or a gain from a bargain purchase.

(a) IDENTIFYING THE ACQUIRING COMPANY.   The *acquiring entity* is the entity that obtains control over the other entity or entities involved in the business combination. An entity that transfers cash or other assets or incurs liabilities to acquire the assets or equity interests of another entity and obtain control over the other entity is generally the acquiring entity. The identities of the acquiring entity and the acquired entity are usually evident in a business combination effected by the issuance of stock. The acquiring entity normally issues the stock and commonly is the larger entity. However, the facts and circumstances surrounding a business combination sometimes indicate that a smaller entity acquires a larger one. Also, in some business combinations, the combined entity assumes the name of the acquired entity, or it is the acquired entity that issues the stock, which is commonly referred to as a *reverse acquisition.*

In identifying which entity is the acquiring entity in a business combination involving two or more entities, all pertinent facts are considered, particularly the relative voting rights in the combined entity after the combination and the composition of the board of directors and the senior management of the combined entity. In identifying which of the shareholder groups retained or received the larger portion of the voting rights in the combined entity, the existence of any major voting block, unusual or special voting arrangements, and options, warrants, or convertible securities is considered.

If a new entity is formed to issue stock to effect a business combination, one of the existing combining entities is considered the acquiring entity on the basis of the evidence available. The guidance in the two preceding paragraphs applies to that determination.

- The Securities and Exchange Commission (SEC) Staff Accounting Bulletin (SAB) No. 97, Topic 2, provides some additional guidance in identifying the acquiring company and indicates that other factors must also be considered in identifying which company is the acquirer.

Paragraph A12 of SFAS No. 141(R) provides other pertinent facts and circumstances that are to be considered in identifying the acquirer in a business combination:

- *The relative voting rights in the combined entity after the business combination.* The acquirer usually is the combining entity whose owners as a group retain or receive the largest portion of the voting rights in the combined entity. In determining which group of owners retains or receives the largest portion of the voting rights, an entity shall consider the existence of any unusual or special voting arrangements and options, warrants, or convertible securities.
- *The existence of a large minority voting interest in the combined entity if no other owner or organized group of owners has a significant voting interest.* The acquirer usually is the combining entity whose single owner or organized group of owners holds the largest minority voting interest in the combined entity.
- *The composition of the governing body of the combined entity.* The acquirer usually is the combining entity whose owners have the ability to elect or appoint or to remove a majority of the members of the governing body of the combined entity.
- *The composition of the senior management of the combined entity.* The acquirer usually is the combining entity whose former management dominates the management of the combined entity.

- *The terms of the exchange of equity interests.* The acquirer usually is the combining entity that pays a premium over the precombination fair value of the equity interests of the other combining entity or entities.

The application of the guidance in paragraphs A10-A15 of SFAS No. 141(R) and SAB No. 97, Topic 2, may result in treating the legal acquirer as the acquiree for purchase accounting purposes. Such is the case in a reverse acquisition as described next.

(i) Reverse Acquisitions. The term *reverse acquisition* refers to a business combination accounted for by the purchase method in which the company that issues its shares or gives other consideration to effect a business combination is determined to be the acquiree. Reverse acquisition is typically based on the fact that the shareholders of the issuer will have less than a majority of voting control of the combined entity. Reverse acquisitions often involve a shell company or a blind pool created for the purpose of raising capital and using such assets to acquire an interest in an operating company by issuing its shares to acquire all of the stock of an operating company. A reverse acquisition often is characterized by the continued operations of the operating company under its precombination management, with little or no management involvement by officers and directors of the shell or blind pool.

A reverse acquisition occurs when the entity that issues securities (the legal acquirer) is identified as the acquiree for accounting purposes based on the guidance in paragraphs A10–A15 of SFAS No. 141(R). The entity whose equity interests are acquired (the legal acquiree) must be the acquirer for accounting purposes for the transaction to be considered a reverse acquisition.

In a reverse acquisition, the legal acquirer continues in existence as the legal entity whose shares represent the outstanding common stock of the combined company. In some instances, the legal acquirer is a public company whose shares are listed on an exchange. By effecting a reverse acquisition, the accounting acquirer can thereby gain access to the public market without going through an initial public offering.

(ii) Measuring the Consideration Transferred in a Reverse Acquisition. In a reverse acquisition, the accounting acquirer usually issues no consideration for the acquiree. Instead, the accounting acquiree usually issues its equity shares to the owners of the accounting acquirer. Accordingly, the acquisition date fair value of the consideration transferred by the accounting acquirer for its interest in the accounting acquiree is based on the number of equity interests the legal subsidiary would have had to issue to give the owners of the legal parent the same percentage equity interest in the combined entity that results from the reverse acquisition. The fair value of the number of equity interests calculated in that way can be used as the fair value of consideration transferred in exchange for the acquiree.

(b) DETERMINING THE COST OF THE ACQUIRED EQUITY. The cost of an acquired company must be measured by the fair value of the consideration given or the fair value of the acquired company, whichever is the more clearly evident. If stock is actively traded, its quoted market price, after making allowance for market fluctuations, additional quantities issued, issue costs, and so on, is normally better evidence of the fair value than are appraisal values of the net assets of an acquired company. Although the fair value of the individual assets acquired and liabilities assumed must be determined in connection with the accounting for a business combination by the acquisition method, often it is difficult to value goodwill or other intangible assets separately or to determine the existence of negative goodwill.

If the quoted market price is not the fair value of stock, either preferred or common, the consideration received is estimated even though measuring directly the fair values of assets received is difficult. Both the consideration received, including goodwill, and the extent of the adjustment of the quoted market price of the stock issued are weighed to determine the amount to be recorded. All aspects of the acquisition, including the negotiations, are studied, and independent appraisals may be used as an aid in determining the fair value of securities issued. Consideration other than stock distributed to effect an acquisition may provide evidence of the total fair value received.

The cost of an acquired entity and the values assigned to assets acquired and liabilities assumed are determined as of the date of acquisition (see Section 8.3(1) of this chapter). The statement of income of an acquiring entity for the period in which a business combination occurs includes income of the acquired entity after the date of acquisition by including the revenue and expenses of the acquired operations based on the cost to the acquiring entity.

(i) Fair Value of Consideration Given.   Many business combinations are effected through the issuance of cash or other assets or securities, the incurrence or assumption of liabilities, or a combination thereof. Frequently, information required to measure the value of the consideration given is readily available. Cash is measured at its face amount, and assets, such as marketable securities, at fair value. Paragraph 22 of SFAS No. 141 required that consideration also be given to the market price of securities for a reasonable period before and after the date the terms of the combination are agreed to and announced. Liabilities are measured at the present value of future cash payments.

Often valuation issues arise when the consideration given includes securities that are closely held, restricted or thinly traded, preferred stock, debentures, or treasury stock. The valuation of securities that are not readily traded is typically performed by someone with an appropriate level of expertise to make such judgments, such as a reputable investment banker. The next four paragraphs discuss various considerations in these situations.

Preferred stock issued to effect a business combination may have characteristics of debt securities or equity securities, or it may have significant characteristics of both types of securities. Consideration should be given to the fair value of the acquiree and the debt versus equity characteristics of the preferred stock, including:

- The stated dividend rate of the preferred stock compared with market rates for similar securities
- The tax implications to the holders of the securities and the effect of such implications on the value of similar securities
- Redemption, liquidation, or conversion rights that will affect the valuation of the stock
- Any other factors that may have a unique bearing on the fair value of such securities

Debentures or other debt instruments issued to effect an acquisition should be recorded at their fair value (i.e., present value based on market rates of interest determined in accordance with APB Opinion No. 21) and a premium or discount recorded if the stated interest rate differs materially from the current yield for a comparable security.

When the consideration given in a business combination includes treasury stock, the principles of fair value still apply. That is, the purchase price is measured by the fair value of the securities given as consideration following the requirements of paragraph 22 of SFAS No. 141, as discussed. In all likelihood, this fair value will differ from the carrying value or cost of the treasury shares. Thus, a charge or credit to additional paid-in capital will be necessary for the difference between the value and the recorded cost of the treasury shares.

The cost of a purchase business combination is generally determined at the initiation date of the combination with recognition that security prices may need a short period of time to reflect market valuations associated with the proposed combination.

(ii) Calculating the Fair Value of the Consideration Transferred.   As a result of the issuance of 150 common shares by Entity A (legal parent, accounting acquiree), Entity B's shareholders own 60 percent of the issued shares of the combined entity (i.e., 150 of 250 issued shares). The remaining 40 percent are owned by Entity A's shareholders. If the business combination had taken the form of Entity B issuing additional common shares to Entity A's shareholders in exchange for their common shares in Entity A, Entity B would have had to issue 40 shares for the ratio of ownership interest in the combined entity to be the same. Entity B's shareholders would then own 60 of the 100 issued shares of Entity B—60 percent of the combined entity. As a result, the fair value of the consideration effectively transferred by Entity B and the group's interest in Entity A is $1,600 (40 shares with a per share fair value of $40). The fair value of the consideration effectively transferred should be based on the most reliable measure. In this example, the quoted market price of Entity

A's shares provides a more reliable basis for measuring the consideration effectively transferred than the estimated fair value of the shares in Entity B, and the consideration is measured using the market price of Entity A's shares—100 shares with a per share fair value of $16.

(iii) Stock Options of the Acquiree. The acquiree in a business combination may have options outstanding at the initiation date. In such instances, the acquirer may assume the obligation of the acquiree to issue shares upon exercise of the options, it may require the acquiree to redeem all of the outstanding options, or it may permit the options to remain outstanding without change. If the options are permitted to remain outstanding without change, their existence ordinarily has no impact on the purchase price because it is assumed that the purchase price reflects any dilution expected to result from their exercise. The exercise of the options will result in creation of, or addition to, minority interest in the acquired company. Accordingly, consideration would need to be given to the outstanding options in the allocation of the purchase price. If the acquirer assumes the acquiree's obligation to issue shares upon exercise of the options, an adjustment of the purchase price is required.

If the options are assumed by the acquirer an amount equal to the difference between the exercise price and the fair value of the securities at the acquisition date, issuable by the acquiree upon exercise, should be recorded as a part of the purchase price. However, the exercise of such options should not be assumed in recording the shares issuable in connection with the business combination. Such shares may be common stock equivalents or other potentially dilutive securities, and consideration should be given to them in the computation of earnings per share of the combined company in accordance with SFAS No. 128, *Earnings per Share.* However, only the difference between the exercise price and the fair value of the securities issuable should be recorded on the acquisition date. For example, if the fair value of the acquirer's stock is determined to be $100 per share and the exercise price of outstanding options is $45 per share, the difference, $55 per share, should be included in the computation of the purchase price with a corresponding credit to additional paid-in capital. The $45 option exercise price should not be recorded until the option is exercised.

Accordingly, if the acquirer settles outstanding options for cash or stock, or by assuming the obligation for these options, the consideration given results in an adjustment to the purchase price of the acquisition. If, however, the acquiree settles the options for cash or other consideration before, after, or as part of the acquisition, compensation expense would be recorded by the acquiree.

(iv) Stock Options of the Acquirer. An acquirer may exchange its share-based payment awards (replacement awards) for awards held by employees of the acquiree. Exchanges of share options or other share-based payment awards in conjunction with a business combination are modifications of share-based payment awards in accordance with Statement No. 123 (revised 2004), *Share-Based Payment.* In some situations, acquiree awards may expire as a consequence of a business combination. If the acquirer replaces those awards even though it is not obligated to do so, all of the fair value–based measure of the replacement awards shall be recognized as compensation cost in the postcombination financial statements.

(v) Fair Value of the Acquired Company. As noted earlier, there may be instances where the fair value of the company acquired is more clearly evident than the fair value of the consideration given. For example, this might be the case where the acquiree is a shell company or a blind pool where assets are essentially monetary assets subject to reasonable independent valuations. In other situations where the purchase price must be determined based on the value of the assets acquired, reference should be made to industry price/earnings ratios, opinions of investment bankers, independent appraisals of the acquiree's net assets (including intangibles and goodwill), the value indicated by the negotiations, recent security transactions for both companies to the combination, and any other indicators of value that are available.

(vi) Determining the Acquisition Date. Paragraph 11 of SFAS No. 141(R) states that the acquirer shall identify the acquisition date, which is the date on which it obtains control of the acquire. The date on which the acquirer obtains control of the acquiree generally is the date on which the acquirer legally transfers the consideration, acquires the assets, and assumes the liabilities of the acquiree—the closing date.

(c) DIRECT COSTS OF THE BUSINESS COMBINATION.   Under SFAS No. 141(R) (ASC 805–10–25–23) acquisition-related costs are excluded from the measurement of the consideration paid, because such costs are not part of the fair value of the acquiree and are not assets.

Direct costs incurred in the business combination include finder's fees as well as advisory, legal, accounting, valuation, and other professional or consulting fees.

Indirect, ongoing costs include the cost to maintain a mergers and acquisition department as well as other general administrative costs, such as managerial or secretarial time and overhead that are allocated to the merger but would have existed in its absence.

The acquirer shall account for acquisition-related costs as expenses in the periods in which the costs are incurred and the services are received.

If a business combination is effected through the issuance of equity securities, the cost of the acquired company should be measured by the fair value of those equity securities. The resulting credit to shareholders' equity should be reduced by the cost of registration and issuance of those securities.

Interpretation No. 35, *Criteria for Applying the Equity Method of Accounting for Investments in Common Stock,* an interpretation of APB Opinion No. 18 requires that, if registration costs will not be incurred or paid until after the acquisition date, such costs should be accrued as a liability with a corresponding reduction in the amount credited to additional paid-in capital. The result of this adjustment generally will be recognized as a charge to goodwill.

Typical direct costs of acquisition include:

- Debt placement and other bank-related fees in connection with debt incurred to finance the acquisition
- Refinancing fees associated with the acquiree's debt that require refinancing upon a change in ownership
- Prepayment penalties associated with the acquiree's debt that is prepaid in order to restructure the financing of the combined company and provide the acquisition lender with the first mortgage on all assets of the combined company
- Fees paid to investment bankers (see also discussion of SAB No. 77 in the next paragraph)
- Fees paid for outside accounting, legal, engineering, or appraisal services

In March 1988, the SEC issued SAB No. 77, which addressed the treatment of certain debt issue costs incurred in connection with financing used in a business combination accounted for by the purchase method. The SAB uses the example of a company that retained an investment banker to provide the following services:

- Advisory services in structuring the acquisition
- Arrangement of bridge financing on an interim basis
- Structuring of permanent financing at a subsequent date

The SAB requires that the investment banker's fees (whether separately billed or not) be allocated to the services provided and that the fees for the bridge financing and permanent financing be accounted for as debt issue costs rather than direct costs of the acquisition.

(i) Acquisition Costs Incurred by the Acquiree.   An acquiree may incur accounting, legal, engineering, and other consulting fees in connection with a business combination. These costs normally would be expensed by the acquiree unless it can be demonstrated that the costs are nonduplicative direct costs of the acquisition and are clearly incurred by the acquiree for the benefit of the acquirer. *Nonduplicative acquisition costs* are those that are more clearly associated with the distinct activities of the acquirer rather than with the costs that benefit the combined companies or the acquiree's stockholders; such costs normally would have been incurred by the acquirer absent an arrangement between the parties for the acquiree to pay such costs.

In the absence of a reimbursement arrangement between the acquirer and the acquiree, costs incurred by the acquiree incidental to the acquisition should be expensed. These acquisition costs must be evaluated based on the facts and circumstances of the specific acquisition.

(ii) Plant Closing Costs and Employee Severance Costs. Subparagraph 37k of SFAS No. 141 indicated that, in allocating the purchase price to the assets acquired and liabilities assumed, a liability should be recorded for plant closing expenses incidental to the acquisition. SFAS No. 141(R) requires that assets acquired be recorded at their fair value. Financial Technical Bulletin (FTB) No. 85–5, *Issues Relating to Accounting for Business Combinations,* addresses the costs of closing duplicate facilities resulting from an acquisition. It distinguishes between costs of closing plants owned by the acquiree and costs of closing the acquirer's plants. Only the direct costs of an acquisition should be included in the cost of the acquired company. The cost of closing the acquirer's facilities, which become duplicative as a result of the acquisition, should not be considered part of the cost of acquisition. Such plant closing costs would include employee severance costs, relocation costs, and other costs incidental to the closing of duplicate facilities. The Technical Bulletin also indicates that plant closing expenses, in general, are not part of the direct costs of the acquisition that are added to the value of securities or assets given to effect the acquisition in arriving at the total purchase price. Rather, a plant-closing liability is one factor to be considered in allocating the cost of the acquired company to the individual assets acquired and liabilities assumed. Ordinarily it is assumed that the costs of plant closing, employee relocation, and severance plans were considered in the negotiations and are an integral part of the bargained purchase price in a business combination. The costs of such plant closing, employee relocation, and severance plans should, therefore, be allocations of the purchase price and not additional costs of the acquisition.

(iii) Payments to Employees: Acquisition Cost versus Employee Compensation Arrangements. An acquisition agreement may include provisions for consideration to be paid to employees of the acquiree. The intent of such arrangements may be to compensate employees of the acquiree for past services, to act as a golden handcuff in retaining key executives of the acquiree during a specified period subsequent to the acquisition, or to serve as additional consideration in the purchase acquisition.

Payments made, or to be made, to employees of an acquiree should be evaluated carefully to determine if the substance of the transaction is compensation for services performed subsequent to the acquisition or a cost of the acquisition. Many of the considerations discussed earlier in this chapter with regard to employee/shareholder arrangements in a pooling should be considered in determining the purchase price in a business combination accounted for by the purchase method.

A provision that requires employees to remain in the service of the combined company for a specified extended period of time before payments are received, or where such payments seem to approximate normal compensation levels for the employees, generally indicates that the substance of such payments is compensation for services to be rendered in the period subsequent to the acquisition rather than additional cost of the acquisition.

Conversely, if only a short service period is required for the employees to vest, it could indicate that little or no benefit will be received in a period subsequent to the acquisition. Payments significantly in excess of employees' normal compensation may also indicate that the substance of the payments may represent compensation for services rendered prior to the acquisition or an additional cost of acquiring the target company.

Employee payments determined to be part of the acquisition cost represent a liability assumed in the acquisition rather than a direct cost of the acquisition that increases the total purchase price.

(iv) Discretionary Costs in Purchase Business Combinations. In many purchase business combinations, the management of the acquiring company expects to incur certain costs shortly after the merger to integrate the operations of the two companies or to exit certain activities or terminate or relocate certain employees of either the acquired or acquiring company. In May 1995, the Emerging Issues Task Force (EITF) addressed those matters and reached a consensus in Issue No. 95–3, *Recognition of Liabilities in Connection with a Purchase Business Combination.*

To the extent that an expected future cost is accrued as a liability at the time of a business combination, the cost of the acquisition increases. Since the identifiable assets are not affected, the amount of the accrued liability normally results in an increase to goodwill.

Issue No. 95–3 addresses three broad groups of costs expected to be incurred as a result of a purchase business combination:

1. Costs to exit an activity or to involuntarily terminate or relocate employees of the *acquired* company
2. Costs to exit an activity or to involuntarily terminate or relocate employees of the *acquiring* company
3. Costs to integrate the activities of the acquired company with those of the acquiring company

Examples would include salaries of management personnel during the integration phase and costs of training acquired personnel, upgrading the acquired company's physical facilities or computer systems, relocating acquired equipment, and consolidating or restructuring certain functions.

In resolving Issue No. 95–3, the EITF concluded that only the first group of costs (costs to exit an activity or to involuntarily terminate or relocate employees of the *acquired* company) are potentially recognizable as liabilities at the time of a purchase business combination, and then only under the conditions described in the next paragraph The second group of costs (costs related to activities or employees of the *acquiring* company) may not be accrued as liabilities and thereby added to the purchase cost, because the cost of a purchase acquisition is never allocated to the assets of the acquiring company (see FTB No. 85–5). The third group of costs—expenditures to integrate the activities of the acquired company with those of the acquiring company and any other exit, termination, or relocation costs relating to the acquired company that do not qualify for liability accrual—should be either expensed or capitalized when incurred based on the nature of the expenditure and the capitalization policy of the combined company.

Expected costs to exit an activity of the acquired company should be recognized as a liability as of the date of purchase of a business combination if:

- The cost was incurred pursuant to a formal plan. (Issue No. 95–3 identifies criteria for such a plan, including requirements that the plan be based on conditions existing as of the date of the merger and that it be finalized not longer than one year after the merger.)
- Action to implement the plan begins as soon as the plan is finalized.
- The cost is not incurred to generate revenues of the combined entity after the merger.
- The cost has no future economic benefit to the combined company.
- Either (a) the cost is incremental to other costs incurred by either the acquired or the acquiring company prior to the merger and will be incurred as a direct consequence of the plan to exit an activity of the acquired company or (b) the cost is the result of a premerger contractual obligation of the acquired company.

Expected costs to involuntarily terminate or relocate employees of the acquired company should be recognized as a liability as of the date of the purchase business combination if:

- The cost was incurred pursuant to a formal plan that clearly identifies the number of employees to be terminated or relocated, their job classifications or functions, and their locations.
- The details of the termination or relocation plan and related benefits are finalized and communicated to employees not longer than one year after the merger date.
- Action to implement the plan begins as soon as the plan is finalized.

If an estimated liability is accrued at the time of the combination and the actual amount ultimately turns out to be less, the excess should reduce the cost of the acquired company (i.e., reduce goodwill). If the cost ultimately turns out to be more than the original accrual, the portion of that excess arising in the first year after the combination is added to the cost of the acquired company; any excess cost incurred beyond a year after the merger is charged to expense when incurred.

Issue No. 95–3 specifies certain disclosures that must be made in the notes to the financial statements of the combined company both in the period in which the merger occurs and thereafter until the plan to exit activities or terminate or relocate employees is completed.

(d) CONTINGENT CONSIDERATION.   *Contingent consideration* usually is an obligation of the acquirer to transfer additional assets or equity interests to the former owners of an acquiree as part of the exchange for control of the acquiree if specified future events occur or conditions are met. However, contingent consideration also may give the acquirer the right to the return of previously transferred consideration if specified conditions are met.

The acquirer must classify an obligation to pay contingent consideration as a liability or as equity in accordance with FASB Statement No. 150, *Accounting for Certain Financial Instruments with Characteristics of both Liabilities and Equity,* EITF Issue No. 00–19, *Accounting for Derivative Financial Instruments Indexed to, and Potentially Settled in, a Company's Own Stock,* or other applicable generally accepted accounting principles (GAAP). For example, Statement No. 150 provides guidance on whether to classify as a liability a contingent consideration arrangement that is, in substance, a put option written by the acquirer on the market price of the acquirer's shares issued in the business combination. The acquirer must classify as an asset a right to the return of previously transferred consideration if specified conditions are met.

Some changes in the fair value of contingent consideration that the acquirer recognizes after the acquisition date may be the result of additional information about facts and circumstances that existed at the acquisition date that the acquirer obtained after that date. Such changes are measurement period adjustments in accordance with paragraphs 51–55 of SFAS No. 141(R). However, changes resulting from events after the acquisition date, such as meeting an earnings target, reaching a specified share price, or reaching a milestone on a research and development project, are not measurement period adjustments. The acquirer must account for changes in the fair value of contingent consideration that are not measurement period adjustments in this way:

a. Contingent consideration classified as equity shall not be remeasured and its subsequent settlement shall be accounted for within equity.

b. Contingent consideration classified as an asset or a liability is remeasured to fair value at each reporting date until the contingency is resolved. The changes in fair value are recognized in earnings unless the arrangement is a hedging instrument for which Statement 133, as amended by this Statement, requires the changes to be initially recognized in other comprehensive income.

A Bargain Purchase.   SFAS No. 141(R) defines a *bargain purchase* as a business combination in which the total acquisition-date fair value of the identifiable net assets acquired exceeds the fair value of the consideration transferred plus any noncontrolling interest in the acquiree, and it requires the acquirer to recognize that excess in earnings as a gain attributable to the acquirer. In contrast, SFAS No. 141 required the negative goodwill amount to be allocated as a pro rata reduction of the amounts that otherwise would have been assigned to particular assets acquired. SFAS No. 141(R) therefore improves the representational faithfulness and completeness of the information provided about both the acquirer's earnings during the period in which it makes a bargain purchase and the measures of the assets acquired in the bargain purchase.

(i) Contingencies Based on Earnings.   SFAS No. 141 required that additional consideration that is contingent on maintaining or achieving specified levels of earnings be recorded when resolved. These types of contingencies result in an adjustment to the purchase price of the acquiree based on the fair value of the consideration issued or issuable, with the fair value measured as of the date the contingency is resolved. The fair value of the consideration issued should be allocated to the assets acquired, generally as an adjustment to goodwill or negative goodwill.

As with all aspects of a business combination, evaluation should be made of the substance of contingency arrangements as well as their form.

The EITF addressed the question of whether contingent consideration that is embedded in a financial instrument or that is itself a separate financial instrument should be recorded by the issuer at fair value at acquisition date or recognized only when the contingency is resolved. In Issue No. 97–8, the EITF concluded that the contingent consideration should be recorded at fair value at acquisition date.

Some agreements provide that a portion of the consideration be placed in escrow to be distributed or to be returned to the transferor when specified events occur. Either debt or equity securities may be placed in escrow, and amounts equal to interest or dividends on the securities during the contingency period may be paid to the escrow agent or to the potential security holder. Such amounts are accounted for according to the accounting for the securities. That is, until the disposition of the securities in escrow is resolved, payments to the escrow agent are not recorded as interest expense or dividend distributions. An amount equal to interest and dividends later distributed by the escrow agent to the former stockholders is added to the cost of the acquired assets at the date distributed and amortized over the remaining life of the assets.

Contingent consideration usually is recorded when the contingency is resolved and consideration is issued or becomes issuable. In general, the issuance of additional securities or distribution of other consideration at resolution of contingencies based on earnings results in an additional element of cost of an acquired entity. In contrast, the issuance of additional securities or distribution of other consideration at resolution of contingencies based on security prices does not change the recorded cost of an acquired entity.

(ii) Contingencies Based on Security Prices.   Another type of contingency arrangement addressed by SFAS No. 141 is one in which the acquirer guarantees attainment of a specified price for its stock or maintenance of a specified security price during the contingency period. If the contingency price is not met, additional consideration in the form of cash, equity, or debt securities is given upon resolution of the contingency to make the current value of the total consideration equal the specified amount. The statement's use of the term *specified amount* refers to the total guaranteed value of the acquisition, including the value of the contingency. For example, if Company A proposes to acquire Company B for stock value at $10 million and cash of $50 million, but guarantees that the stock will have a value of $15 million after three years or Company A will pay cash or issue additional shares of stock sufficient to meet the $15 million guaranteed value, then the purchase price of Company B would be $65 million, represented by the $50 million cash exchanged, plus the $15 million of guaranteed stock value.

The authoritative literature does not provide guidance on discounting the guaranteed portion to be paid at the end of the contingency period. In practice, discounting has been used in some situations and not used in others. The SEC has taken the position in certain cases, primarily where the guarantee is issuable in stock rather than cash or other consideration, that acquisition cost associated with a guaranteed price contingency for stock should be determined without regard to discounting.

The issuance of additional securities or distribution of other consideration does not affect the cost of the acquired entity, regardless of whether the amount specified is a security price to be maintained or a higher security price to be achieved. On a later date when the contingency is resolved and additional consideration is distributable, the acquiring entity records the current fair value of the additional consideration issued or issuable. However, the amount previously recorded for securities issued at the date of acquisition is simultaneously reduced to the lower current value of the securities. Reducing the value of debt securities previously issued to their later fair value results in recording a discount on debt securities. The discount is amortized from the date the additional securities are issued.

A tax reduction resulting from imputed interest on contingently issuable stock reduces the fair value recorded for contingent consideration based on earnings and increases additional capital recorded for contingent consideration based on security prices.

The substance of some agreements for contingent consideration is to provide compensation for services or use of property or profit sharing, and the additional consideration given is accounted for as expenses of the appropriate periods.

Accounting for contingent consideration based on conditions other than those described are inferred from the procedures discussed. For example, if the consideration contingently issuable depends on both future earnings and future security prices, additional cost of the acquired entity is recorded for the additional consideration contingent on earnings, and previously recorded consideration is reduced to the current value of the consideration contingent on security prices. Similarly, if the consideration contingently issuable depends on later settlement of a contingency, an increase in the cost of acquired assets, if any, is amortized over the remaining life of the assets.

(iii) Earnings per Share Consequences of Contingent Share Arrangements. Paragraphs 30 through 35 of SFAS No. 128 provide guidance on the appropriate accounting for earnings per share under contingent share arrangements. In general terms, that statement requires that both primary and diluted earnings per share be adjusted to reflect contingently issuable shares when the conditions that give rise to the issuance of such contingent shares are currently being met. Additionally, if the conditions are not currently being met or must be met over a period of years, the number of contingently issuable shares included in diluted earnings per share is based on the number of shares, if any, that would be issuable if the end of the current reporting period were the end of the contingency period. Previously reported earnings per share data should not be restated to give retroactive effect to shares subsequently issued as a result of attainment of a specified increased earning level.

Paragraph 32 of SFAS No. 128, which provides guidance on accounting for shares contingently issuable based on market price of the stock at a future date, states:

> The number of shares contingently issuable may depend on the market price of the stock at a future date. In that case, computations of diluted EPS shall reflect the number of shares that would be issued based on the current market price at the end of the period being reported on if the effect is dilutive.

Paragraph 25 of SFAS No. 150 stipulates that entities that have issued mandatorily redeemable shares of common stock or entered into forward contracts that require physical settlement by repurchase of a fixed number of the issuer's equity shares of common stock in exchange for cash shall exclude the common shares that are to be redeemed or repurchased in calculating basic and diluted earnings per share. Any amounts, including contractual (accumulated) dividends and participation rights in undistributed earnings, attributable to shares that are to be redeemed or repurchased that have not been recognized as interest costs in accordance with paragraph 22 of SFAS No. 150 are to be deducted in computing income available to common shareholders (the numerator of the earnings per share calculation), consistently with the two-class method set forth in paragraph 61 of SFAS No. 128.

SFAS No. 160 Amended SFAS No. 128. The FASB considered how the classification of the noncontrolling interest as part of the equity of the consolidated group should affect the computation of earnings-per-share data. The FASB concluded that the presentation of earnings-per-share information is for the benefit of the parent's owners. Thus, although amounts for both the parent and the noncontrolling interest are reported in consolidated net income, the FASB decided the calculation of earnings-per-share data in consolidated financial statements that include subsidiaries that are less than wholly owned should be based on amounts attributable to the parent's owners. Thus, this statement amends Statement No. 128 so that earnings-per-share data will continue to be calculated the same way they were calculated before this statement was issued, based on amounts attributable to the parent's owners.

(iv) Adjustment of Acquisition Cost or Compensation Expense? SFAS No. 141 does not provide clear guidance as to when contingent consideration is an adjustment of the original acquisition cost and when it is compensation expense. An adjustment of the acquisition cost normally increases goodwill and is amortized over the remaining amortization period of the goodwill previously recognized in the acquisition. Recognizing contingent consideration as compensation expense is a current charge against earnings. Paragraph 27 of SFAS No. 141 states that, in general, the issuance of additional securities or distribution of other consideration at resolution of contingencies based on earnings shall result in an additional element of the cost of an acquired entity. Yet paragraph 34 says that if the substance of the agreement for contingent consideration is to provide compensation for services or use of property or profit sharing, the additional consideration given shall be accounted for as an expense of the appropriate periods. While paragraph 34 does not identify the kinds of contingencies that *may* make the additional consideration compensation expense, in practice they tend to be contingencies based on maintaining or achieving a level of earnings. In several recent cases, the SEC staff has taken the position that if the contingent consideration is based on earnings or other measure of financial performance and is paid to key employees (individuals who are in a position to directly affect financial performance, such as directors, officers, or senior managers), the contingent consideration is compensation expense.

The EITF addressed the matter in EITF Issue No. 95–8, *Accounting for Contingent Considera- tion Paid to the Shareholders of an Acquired Enterprise in a Purchase Business Combination.* The EITF reached a consensus that judgment is required to determine whether the consideration trans- ferred to settle an earnings- or performance-based contingency is compensation or is an additional purchase price for the acquired company. The published consensus identifies a number of factors and circumstances to consider in exercising that judgment. Examples that indicate compensation rather than additional purchase price include a requirement of continued employment for payment of the contingent amount, extra payments to those selling shareholders who remain as key employ- ees of the combined company, and contingent payments structured on terms similar to those of former profit-sharing arrangements of the acquired company.

(e) ACQUISITION OF MINORITY INTERESTS.   The discussion to this point has been concerned with various types of business combinations. An acquisition of stock held by minority stockholders of a subsidiary is not a business combination; paragraph 14 of SFAS No. 141, however, requires such acquisitions to be accounted for by the purchase method. Use of the purchase method of accounting is required whether the stock is acquired by the parent, the subsidiary itself, or other subsidiaries of the same parent. Additionally, the purchase method should be used if the effect of a transaction, irrespective of its form, is to reduce or eliminate the minority interest in a subsidiary. The adjustments necessary to give effect to the application of the purchase method are not ordinarily recognized in the separate financial statements of the subsidiary, and, accordingly, shares purchased directly by the subsidiary, or by the parent or other companies controlled by the parent and contributed to the subsidiary, should be accounted for as a capital transaction by the subsidiary. A more comprehensive discussion of the effects of purchase accounting on the separate financial statements of an acquired company (pushdown accounting) is included in Subsection 8.3(h)(i).

The purchase of fractional shares or shares held by dissenting stockholders as part of a plan of combination is not an acquisition of minority interest. In this circumstance, the general provisions of the statement would apply.

Interpretation No. 26, *Accounting for Purchase of a Leased Asset by the Lessee during the Term of the Lease,* an interpretation of FASB Statement No. 13, provides additional guidance on the acquisition of minority interest and indicates that purchase accounting is applicable when:

- A parent exchanges its common stock, assets, or debt for common stock held by minority shareholders of its subsidiary.
- The subsidiary buys as treasury stock the common stock held by minority shareholders.
- Another subsidiary of the parent exchanges its common stock or assets or debt for common stock held by the minority shareholders of an affiliated subsidiary.

These examples of acquisitions of minority interests raise questions regarding the appropriate accounting in certain circumstances when considered in relation to Interpretation No. 39, *Offset- ting of Amounts Related to Certain Contracts,* an interpretation of APB Opinion No. 10 and FASB Statement No. 105, which discusses combinations and exchanges between entities under common control. FTB No. 85–5 addresses the issues of downstream mergers and stock transactions between companies under common control. It emphasizes the point made in Interpretation No. 26 that acqui- sition of minority interest through a downstream merger should be accounted for by the purchase method, even though some would argue that such transactions may represent a combination of entities under common control.

FTB No. 85–5 also discusses in detail the accounting for stock transactions between companies under common control in relation to the acquisition of the minority interest of one subsidiary by issuing stock of another subsidiary. The accounting for such transactions between subsidiaries under common control depends on whether the minority shareholders are party to the exchange of shares.

Paragraph 6 of the Technical Bulletin indicates that, if shares owned by minority shareholders are exchanged by the minority shareholders for shares of ownership in another subsidiary of the parent, the transaction is recognized by the parent company as the acquisition of a minority interest and should be accounted for by the purchase method. If, however, minority shareholders are not party to an exchange of shares between the two subsidiaries (assuming one partially owned subsidiary issues its shares in exchange for the parent's shares of another subsidiary), the minority interest in the issuing subsidiary remains outstanding. This transaction should be accounted for in a manner similar to that for a pooling of interests under the guidance of Interpretation No. 39, because the substance of the transaction is simply a rearrangement of the parent's investment in its subsidiaries without change in the composition of any of the existing minority interests.

As can be seen from the preceding example, although the minority stockholders' interest in net assets of the subsidiaries has changed in each case, the accounting will depend on whether the minority shareholders participated in the transaction or if the exchange of shares occurred only between the parent and/or its subsidiaries.

(i) Exchange of Ownership Interests Between Entities under Common Control. EITF Issue No. 90–5, *Exchange of Ownership Interests Between Entities under Common Control,* deals with two situations that may arise when a parent company transfers its ownership in one subsidiary (Sub A) to another subsidiary (Sub B) in exchange for additional shares of Sub B. The parent's investment in Sub A differs from the value of the net assets in Sub A's financial statements because pushdown accounting appropriately was not applied.

The Task Force concluded that the consolidated financials of Sub B should reflect the assets and liabilities of Sub A at the historical cost in the consolidated financials of Sub B's parent and not at the historical cost in Sub A's financials. The parent's carrying amount is historical cost under Interpretation No. 39. The Task Force also noted that Sub B must be a substantive operating company.

The Task Force stated further that the acquisition be treated as a purchase acquisition in the consolidated statements of Sub B, conforming to the guidance contained in FTB No. 85–5, regardless of whether cash or stock is used to effect the transaction. However, if the exchange lacks substance, it should be accounted for based on carrying amounts. If stock is used, there must be an objective and reliable basis for measuring the value of the stock issued in order to record the transaction at fair value.

(ii) Accounting for Simultaneous Common Control Mergers. A recent set of issues that came before the Task Force (EITF Issue No. 90–13, *Accounting for Simultaneous Common Control Mergers*) involved transactions in which a parent company (Parent) obtains control of another company (Target) and almost simultaneously, as part of the planned transaction, Target issues additional shares to Parent in exchange for Parent's interest in a subsidiary (Subsidiary).

The Task Force concluded that the two-step transaction cannot be separated, but should be viewed as one transaction. Interpretation No. 39 does not apply, and Parent should account for the transfer of Subsidiary to Target as a purchase of Target under the Opinion. Furthermore, Parent should account for the transaction as a partial sale of Subsidiary to Target's minority shareholders and as a partial acquisition of Target. Gain or loss would be recognized by Parent on the portion of Subsidiary sold.

In preparing Parent's consolidated statements, Parent should step up Target's assets and liabilities to the extent acquired by Parent and step up Subsidiary's assets and liabilities to the extent Subsidiary was sold.

Subsidiary:	
70% of the $100 historical cost	$ 70
30% of the $250 fair value	75
Target:	
70% of the $500 fair value	350
30% of the $200 historical cost	60
Basis of combined entity	$ 555
Parent's basis in Target	$ 420
Minority interest	$ 135
	$ 555

Target's and Subsidiary's assets and liabilities would be valued in Target's separate financial statements at amounts totaling $510, based on the following calculation:

Subsidiary historical cost	$ 100
Target:	
70% of the $500 fair value	350
30% of the $200 historical cost	60
Basis of combined entity	$ 510

Exhibit 8.1   Example of the Application of the EITF Consensus on Issue No. 90–13, *Accounting for Simultaneous Common Control Mergers* **(Exhibit 90–13A)**

In the separate financial statements of Target, the transaction should be accounted for as a reverse acquisition of Target by Subsidiary. In Target's separate financials, its assets and liabilities would be reflected at fair value to the extent acquired. Subsidiary's assets and liabilities should not be revalued. The Task Force noted that this treatment is consistent with reverse acquisition accounting (Subsidiary has acquired an interest in Target) and gain or loss is not recognized at the Target–Subsidiary level.

The illustration in Exhibit 8.1 is reproduced from EITF Issue No. 90–13, with permission.

(f) IDENTIFYING ASSETS ACQUIRED AND LIABILITIES ASSUMED.   Before doing the allocation procedures described in Sections 8.3(f) and (g), the acquiring entity:

- Reviews the purchase consideration if other than cash to make sure that it has been valued in conformity with the guidance in Section 8.3(b)
- Identifies all of the assets acquired and liabilities assumed, including intangible assets

SFAS No. 141(R) provides a listing of examples of identifiable intangible assets acquired in a business combination.

Intangible assets designated with the symbol # are those that arise from contractual or other legal rights. Those designated with the symbol * do not arise from contractual or other legal rights but are separable. Intangible assets designated with the symbol # might also be separable, but separability is not a necessary condition for an asset to meet the contractual-legal criterion.

(i) Marketing-Related Intangible Assets.   Marketing-related intangible assets are primarily used in the marketing or promotion of products or services. Examples of marketing-related intangible assets are:

- Trademarks, trade names, service marks, collective marks, certification marks
- Trade dress (unique color, shape, package design)
- Newspaper mastheads
- Internet domain names
- Noncompetition agreements

(ii) Customer-Related Intangible Assets.   Examples of customer-related intangible assets are:

- Customer lists
- Order or production backlog
- Customer contracts and related customer relationships
- Noncontractual customer relationships

(iii) Artistic-Related Intangible Assets.   Artistic-related assets acquired in a business combination are identifiable if they arise from contractual or legal rights such as those provided by copyright Examples of contract-based intangible assets are:

- Licensing, royalty, standstill agreements
- Advertising, construction, management, service or supply contracts
- Lease agreements (whether the acquiree is the lessee or the lessor)
- Construction permits
- Franchise agreements
- Operating and broadcast rights
- Servicing contracts such as mortgage servicing contracts
- Employment contracts
- Use rights, such as drilling, water, air, timber cutting, and route authorities

(iv) Contract-Based Intangible Assets.   Contract-based intangible assets represent the value of rights that arise from contractual arrangements. Customer contracts are one type of contract-based intangible asset. If the terms of a contract give rise to a liability (e.g., if the terms of an operating lease or customer contract are unfavorable relative to market terms), the acquirer recognizes it as a liability assumed in the business combination. Examples of contract-based intangible assets are:

- Licensing, royalty, standstill agreements
- Advertising, construction, management, service or supply contracts
- Lease agreements (whether the acquiree is the lessee or the lessor)
- Construction permits
- Franchise agreements
- Operating and broadcast rights
- Servicing contracts such as mortgage servicing contracts
- Employment contracts
- Use rights such as drilling, water, air, timber cutting, and route authorities

(v) Technology-Based Intangible Assets.   Examples of technology-based intangible assets are:

- Patented technology
- Computer software and mask works
- Unpatented technology
- Databases, including title plants
- Trade secrets, such as secret formulas, processes, recipes

All identifiable assets acquired and liabilities assumed in a business combination, regardless of whether recorded separately in the financial statements of the acquired entity, are assigned a portion of the total cost of the acquired entity based on their fair values at the date of acquisition. Among other sources of relevant information, independent appraisals and actuarial or other valuations may be used as an aid in determining the fair values. The tax basis of an asset or liability is not a factor in determining its fair value.

(g) RECOGNIZING AND MEASURING THE IDENTIFIABLE ASSETS ACQUIRED, THE LIABILITIES ASSUMED AND ANY NONCONTROLLING INTEREST IN THE ACQUIREE

(i) Recognition and Measurement Principle.   Paragraph 12 of SFAS No. 141(R) stipulates that as of the acquisition date, the acquirer shall recognize, separately from goodwill, the identifiable assets acquired, the liabilities assumed, and any noncontrolling interest in the acquiree.

Recognition Conditions. To qualify for recognition as part of applying the acquisition method, the identifiable assets acquired and liabilities assumed must meet the definitions of assets and liabilities in FASB Concepts Statement No. 6, *Elements of Financial Statements,* at the acquisition date.

In addition, to qualify for recognition as part of applying the acquisition method, the identifiable assets acquired and liabilities assumed must be part of what the acquirer and the acquiree (or its former owners) exchanged in the business combination transaction rather than the result of separate transactions. The acquirer shall apply the guidance in paragraphs 57–59 of SFAS No. 141(R) to determine which assets acquired or liabilities assumed are part of the exchange for the acquiree and which, if any, are the result of separate transactions to be accounted for in accordance with their nature and the applicable GAAP.

Measurement Principle. The acquirer shall measure the identifiable assets acquired, the liabilities assumed, and any noncontrolling interest in the acquiree at their acquisition-date fair values.

Paragraphs A57–A61 of SFAS 141(R) provide guidance on measuring the fair values of particular identifiable assets and a noncontrolling interest in an acquiree.

Exceptions to the Recognition or Measurement Principles. This statement provides limited exceptions to its recognition and measurement principles. Paragraphs 23–33 of SFAS No. 141(R) specify the types of identifiable assets and liabilities that include items for which this statement provides limited exceptions.

(ii) Excess of the Fair Value of Acquired Net Assets over Cost.   In some cases, the sum of the fair values of identifiable assets acquired less liabilities assumed may exceed the cost of the acquired entity (excess). In those cases, the amounts that otherwise would be assigned to acquired intangible assets that are of a type that do not have an observable market are limited to the amount that would not create or increase an excess. If the excess is less than the fair values of those acquired intangible assets, it is allocated as a pro rata reduction of the fair values that otherwise would be assigned. If the excess is greater than the fair values of those intangible assets, the remaining excess is then allocated as a pro rata reduction of the fair values that otherwise would be assigned to all of the acquired depreciable nonfinancial assets and all of the acquired intangible assets that are of a type that have an observable market.

If any excess remains after those assets are reduced to zero, that excess is recognized as an extraordinary gain, as described in paragraph 11 of APB Opinion No. 30, *Reporting the Results of Operations—Reporting the Effects of Disposal of a Segment of a Business, and Extraordinary, Unusual and Infrequently Occurring Events and Transactions.* The extraordinary gain is recognized in the period in which the business combination is completed unless the combination involves contingent consideration that, if paid or issued, would be recognized as an additional element of cost of the acquired entity. If an extraordinary gain is recognized before the end of the allocation period, any subsequent adjustments to that extraordinary gain that result from changes to the purchase price allocation are recognized as an extraordinary item.

For contingent consideration based on earnings, an amount equal to the lesser of the maximum amount of the contingent consideration or excess is recognized as if it were a liability. When the contingency is resolved, the contingent consideration issued or issuable over the amount that was recognized as if it were a liability is recognized as an additional cost of the acquired entity. If the amount initially recognized as if it were a liability exceeds the fair value of the consideration issued or issuable, that excess is allocated as a pro rata reduction of the amount assigned to assets acquired. Any amount that remains after reducing those assets to zero is recognized as an extraordinary gain.

(iii) Last-In, First-Out Inventories.   Inventories accounted for under the last-in, first-out (LIFO) method by the acquired company should be valued at fair value in accordance with the provisions of SFAS No. 141(R) at the acquisition date. This fair value of the acquired inventories thereby becomes the LIFO base layer valuation for postacquisition purposes. Carryover of the acquiree's LIFO basis inventories for book purposes is not appropriate because that is not fair value at acquisition date.

(iv) Determining Costs to Complete, Selling Costs, and Normal Profit Margin.   The valuation of finished goods and work-in-process inventories requires consideration of costs to complete, selling costs, and normal profit margin for the completion and selling effort. The calculation of a normal profit margin should be based on an allocation of a normal gross profit among the preacquisition and postacquisition activities associated with the inventories. One guideline for determining the reasonable profit allowance (mentioned in SFAS No. 141, paragraph 37c) is to identify a reasonable dollar value profit margin for the particular item of inventory for the industry. This amount should then be reduced by the estimated selling costs associated with the product. The resulting amount should then be allocated between the preacquisition and postacquisition activities based on the ratio of selling expenses and completion costs to total manufacturing costs plus selling expenses.

(v) Identifiable Noncurrent Tangible and Intangible Assets.   The appraised value of noncurrent tangible and identifiable intangible assets is generally the best measure of fair value for allocating the purchase price of the acquisition. SFAS No. 141, consistent with SFAS No. 144, *Accounting for the Impairment or Disposal of Long-Lived Assets,* specifically suggests these two methods for allocating purchase price to plant and equipment, depending on the type of expected future use for those assets:

1. If the equipment is to be used for an extended period, the valuation should be based on current replacement costs for similar capacity, unless the expected future use of the assets indicates a lower value to the acquirer. The use of appraisal information or relevant published indices would be appropriate to establish replacement cost.
2. Equipment to be sold or held for later sale rather than used in postacquisition operations should be valued at current net realizable value.

Paragraph A19 of SFAS No. 141(R) requires that intangible assets that can be identified and named should be valued separately from goodwill and other identifiable assets acquired in the acquisition. Intangible assets typically found in an acquisition include those listed in Section 8.3(f) of this chapter (see also paragraphs A29–A31 of SFAS No. 141(R)). The critical factor in assessing whether a particular intangible asset should be valued separately in an acquisition is whether the intangible asset arises from contractual or legal rights or is capable of being separated from the entity and sold.

Identifiable intangible assets with fair values that are reliably measurable should not be included in goodwill. An intangible asset is recognized as an asset apart from goodwill if it arises from contractual or other legal rights (regardless of whether those rights are transferable or separable from the acquired entity or from other rights and obligations). If an intangible asset does not arise from contractual or other legal rights, it is recognized as an asset apart from goodwill only if it is separable, that is, it is capable of being separated or divided from the acquired entity and sold, transferred, licensed, rented, or exchanged (regardless of whether there is an intent to do so). However, for purposes of Statement No. 141, an intangible asset that cannot be sold, transferred, licensed, rented, or exchanged individually is considered separable if it can be sold, transferred, licensed, rented, or exchanged in combination with a related contract, asset, or liability. For purposes of Statement No. 141, an assembled workforce is not recognized as an intangible asset apart from goodwill.

(vi) Assignment of Purchase Price to Leases.   FASB Interpretation No. 21, *Accounting for Leases in a Business Combination,* provides guidance on valuing capital leases acquired. The interpretation indicates that the acquirer shall retain the previous classification of leases acquired in a business combination unless the provisions of the leases are modified as indicated in paragraph 9 of SFAS No. 13, *Accounting for Leases.* The amounts assigned to individual assets acquired and liabilities assumed at the date of the combination must be determined in accordance with the general guides for that type of asset or liability in paragraphs 36–39 of FASB Statement No. 141. The liability should be equal to the present value of the remaining lease payments, discounted at an appropriate current interest rate as of the acquisition date. The capital lease asset should be valued based on the underlying value of the asset itself. One method of estimating such a value in a situation in which the remaining useful life of the asset exceeds the lease terms would be to calculate the present value of the current fair rental value for similar used equipment using an appropriate current interest rate as of the acquisition date. The interpretation also indicates that subsequent to the initial recording, the leases should be accounted for in accordance with SFAS No. 13.

(vii) Research and Development Acquired.   FASB Interpretation No. 4, *Applicability of FASB Statement No. 2 to Business Combinations Accounted for by the Purchase Method,* an interpretation of FASB Statement No. 2, indicates that identifiable assets resulting from research and development (R&D) activities of an acquired company should be recorded in the business combination and that the purchase price should be allocated to the R&D asset. Some R&D assets acquired might include patents received or applied for, blueprints, formulas and specifications, designs for new products or processes, materials and supplies, equipment and facilities, and projects in process.

After allocation of the purchase price, an evaluation should be made to determine whether the identifiable R&D assets are to be used in the general R&D activities of the combined enterprise or will be used in a particular R&D project and have no alternative future use. Under SFAS No. 141(R) (ASC 805–20), in-process R&D is measured and recorded at fair value as an asset on the acquisition date. This requirement does not extend to R&D in contexts other than business combinations.

(viii) Long-Lived Assets Classified as Held for Sale.   Prior to the issuance of SFAS No. 121, EITF Issue No. 87–11, *Allocation of Purchase Price to Assets to Be Sold,* provided guidance on the accounting for a disposal group to be sold that was newly acquired in a purchase business combination, including, but not limited to, a segment of a business covered by Opinion No. 30, *Reporting the Results of Operations—Reporting the Effects of Disposal of a Segment of a Business, and Extraordinary, Unusual and Infrequently Occurring Events and Transaction*s. The guidance in Issue No. 87–11 extended the measurement provisions of Opinion No. 30 in determining the purchase price allocation under Opinion No. 16, *Business Combinations.* Accordingly, the disposal group was measured at the lower of its carrying amount or net realizable value, adjusted for future operating losses.

SFAS No. 121 subsequently required that a long-lived asset (disposal group) to be sold other than a segment of a business covered by Opinion No. 30 be measured at the lower of its carrying amount or fair value less cost to sell. However, it did not nullify Issue No. 87–11 to reflect that change for a long-lived asset (disposal group) to be sold that was newly acquired in a purchase business combination. Consequently, in implementing Statement No. 121, questions emerged about the impact of that statement on Issue No. 87–11. The primary issue was whether, and if so how, the measurement guidance provided by Issue No. 87–11 should be applied to a long-lived asset (disposal group) that was newly acquired in a purchase business combination. A related issue was how to account for the results of operations of the asset (disposal group) while it was classified as held for sale and whether future operating losses could be considered in measuring the fair value less cost to sell of the asset (disposal group). The EITF discussed that topic in Issue No. 95–21, *Accounting for Assets to Be Disposed of Acquired in a Purchase Business Combination* but did not reach a consensus.

SFAS No. 144 resolves Issue No. 95–21 by requiring that a long-lived asset (disposal group) classified as held for sale be measured at the lower of its carrying amount or fair value less cost to sell, whether previously held and used or newly acquired. This statement also requires that the results of operations of a long-lived asset (disposal group) classified as held for sale be recognized in the period in which those operations occur, whether reported in continuing operations or in discontinued operations. Therefore, this statement nullifies Issue No. 87–11.

Prior to this consensus, the SEC had required that the acquirer have a firm contract to sell the assets at the acquisition date before it would permit discounting of the net realizable value. The SEC staff accepted the EITF consensus and will require the accounting described by the EITF for those instances where the operations to be sold were identified as of the purchase date and, as of that date, there was a reasonable expectation that the operations would be sold within one year. At the December 1987 EITF meeting, the SEC representative indicated that the SEC staff would also require these disclosures in the financial statements and pro forma information that cover the reporting periods in which the consensus is applied:

- A description of the operations held for sale, a description of the method used to assign amounts to those assets, the expected disposal date, and the method used to account for those assets.
- Disclosures of the operation's profit or loss during the period that has been excluded from the consolidated income statement, together with a schedule reconciling that amount to the earnings received or losses funded by the parent that have been accounted for as an adjustment to the carrying amount of the assets. Allocated interest cost should be separately identified.
- Disclosure of any gain or loss on the ultimate disposition that has been treated as an adjustment of the original purchase price allocation.

In addition, the SEC expects registrants to review differences between actual and estimated cash flow and the estimated sales proceeds in order to determine if a loss should be reported for events that occur during the holding period.

In EITF Issue No. 90–6, the Task Force considered two events not addressed in Issue No. 87–11: (1) The acquiring company does not complete the sale of an operating unit (a line of business or a portion of a line of business) of an acquired company within one year of the purchase date, but the acquiring company still intends to sell the operating unit; and (2) the acquiring company decides not to sell the operating unit.

The Task Force concluded that Issue No. 87–11 be applied only to identified net assets held for sale that constitute a segment or a portion of a segment of a business. As to the holding period, a company may continue to apply the accounting of Issue No. 87–11 for up to one year from the purchase date if it is actively attempting to find a buyer and remains committed to a formal plan of sale. In addition, Issue No. 87–11 accounting may be continued for a short period beyond one year only in the event a firm contract exists for a sale to be completed soon after the end of the one-year period. At the end of the holding period, the acquiring company should discontinue accounting for the operating unit to be sold in accordance with Issue No. 87–11. Thereafter, the results of operations and incremental interest expense incurred in financing the purchase of the operating unit should be reported in the consolidated operations of the acquiring company generally as a single line item. The amounts pertaining to the operating unit (operating results, gain or loss on disposal, and interest expense) should be reported as part of income or loss from continuing operations, unless the operating unit qualifies as a segment of a business, in which case Opinion No. 30 applies.

Task Force members also considered other matters, such as the need to allocate the carrying value of the acquired unit at the end of the holding period, at least on a memo basis, to determine the operating results of the operations of the unit. Because the unit is still held for sale, no cumulative adjustment is made to reflect a reallocation of the unit's purchase price or reversal of the effects of applying Issue No. 87–11 accounting. There is also a need to continually reevaluate the net realizable value of the unit. A decrease in net realizable value should be reflected as losses to the acquiring company if attributable to specific identifiable economic events occurring subsequent to the purchase date. Other changes in net realizable value identified within the (Opinion No. 30) allocation period not so attributable should be accounted for as an adjustment to the allocation of the purchase price.

If a decision is made not to sell the operating unit of the acquired company within the holding period, the Task Force concluded that the purchase price of the acquired company should be reallocated. This reallocation should be based on amounts as of the purchase date as if the operating unit had never been held for sale, including reversal of the effects of having applied Issue No. 87–11 accounting to the transaction.

When a decision not to sell is reached after the end of the holding period, the purchase price of Company B should not be reallocated based on amounts as of the purchase date. Rather, the carrying amount of Subsidiary S as of the date the decision is made to keep Subsidiary S should be allocated to the current fair values of its identifiable assets and liabilities on that date and the remainder, if any, to goodwill. The current carrying amount of Subsidiary S at that date should be net of any impairment in the value of Subsidiary S since the date of purchase. Any such impairment is recognized as a current loss from operations. Any change in goodwill resulting from the allocation is amortized over its remaining life in accordance with Opinion No. 17.

The SEC observer indicated that it is expected that the registrant be able to demonstrate that the operation to be sold had been identified at the purchase date and there was at least a reasonable expectation of sale within one year. A mere intent to sell is insufficient. Moreover, the consensus for Issue Nos. 87–11 and 90–6 require, rather than merely permit, that kind of accounting in those circumstances.

The SEC staff would expect the financial statements and pro forma information covering all reporting periods to include:

- A description of the operations held for sale, the method used to assign amounts to those assets, the method used to account for those assets, and the expected disposal date.
- Disclosure of the operation's profit or loss that has been excluded from the consolidated income statement during the period together with a schedule reconciling that amount to the earnings received or losses funded by the parent that have been accounted for as an adjustment to the carrying amount of the assets. The amount of allocated interest cost should be separately identified.
- Disclosure of any gain or loss on the ultimate disposition that has been treated as an adjustment of the original purchase price allocation.
- Discussion in Management's Discussion and Analysis of Financial Condition and Results of Operations (MD&A) of any material effect on results of operations, liquidity, capital resources and known trends, commitments, or contingencies.

A decision not to sell after the holding period should be disclosed, including the reasons and an explanation of the adjustments including (1) the carrying amount of the subsidiary that will be allocated to the current fair values of its identifiable assets and liabilities (including the amount of operating profit or losses and interest capitalized pursuant to the consensus for Issue No. 87–11), and (2) the effect on comparability of the reporting periods.

Continual monitoring of cash flows, actual versus estimated, is required to determine whether an impairment loss should be reported in the income statement for events that have occurred subsequent to the purchase date.

(ix) Purchase Price of Pensions. SFAS No. 87, *Employers' Accounting for Pensions,* requires that business combinations accounted for by the purchase method include recognition of a liability to the extent the projected benefit obligation exceeds plan assets or, alternatively, recognition of an asset to the extent the plan assets exceed the projected benefit obligation. In applying the guidance of SFAS No. 87, any previously existing unrecognized net gain or loss, unrecognized prior-service cost, and unrecognized net obligation or net asset existing at the date of initial application of SFAS No. 87 are eliminated. Postacquisition pension expense for the acquired plan is based only on service cost, interest cost, and the actual return on assets until such time as unrecognized gains or losses and unrecognized prior service costs arise through the postacquisition operations of the plan. The liability or asset recorded for acquired pension costs is amortized or accreted based on the difference between pension funding and pension expense. If it is anticipated that the plan will be terminated or curtailed, the effects of such actions should be taken into consideration in measuring the projected benefit obligation used to determine the appropriate amount of the asset or liability to be recorded.

(x) Postretirement Benefits of the Acquiree. Paragraphs 86 through 88 of FASB Statement No. 106, *Employers' Accounting for Postretirement Benefits Other than Pensions,* provide guidance on accounting for postretirement plans acquired in a business combination that is accounted for by the purchase method. That guidance indicates that when an employer is acquired in a business combination that is accounted for by the purchase method under the opinion and that employer sponsors a single-employer defined benefit postretirement plan, the allocation of the purchase price to individual assets acquired and liabilities assumed must include a liability for the accumulated postretirement benefit obligation (APBO) in excess of the fair value of the plan assets or an asset for the fair value of the plan assets in excess of the APBO. The APBO assumed must be measured based on the benefits attributed by the acquired entity to employee service prior to the date the business combination is consummated, adjusted to reflect (1) any changes in assumptions based on the purchaser's assessment of relevant future events and (2) the terms of the substantive plan to be provided by the purchaser to the extent they differ from the terms of the acquired entity's substantive plan.

Further, if the postretirement benefit plan of the acquired entity is amended as a condition of the business combination (e.g., if the change is required by the seller as part of the consummation of the acquisition), the effects of any improvements attributed to services rendered by the participants of the acquired entity's plan prior to the date of the business combination must be accounted for as part of the APBO of the acquired entity. Otherwise, if improvements to the postretirement benefit plan of the acquired entity are not a condition of the business combination, credit granted for prior service must be recognized as a plan amendment. If it is expected that the plan will be terminated or curtailed, SFAS No. 106 requires that the effects of those actions must be considered in measuring the APBO. Otherwise, no future changes to the plan should be anticipated.

In addition, any previously existing unrecognized net gain or loss, unrecognized prior service cost, or unrecognized transition obligation or transition asset is eliminated for the acquired employer's plan. Subsequently, to the extent that the net obligation assumed or net assets acquired are considered in determining the amounts of contributions to the plan, differences between the purchaser's net periodic postretirement benefit cost and amounts it contributes will reduce the liability or asset recognized at the date of the combination.

(xi) Postemployment Benefits of the Acquiree. FASB Statement No. 112, *Employers' Accounting for Postemployment Benefits,* sets standards of accounting for an employer's cost of providing benefits to former or inactive employees after employment but before retirement. Examples of such benefits would be salary continuation, severance pay, and disability, medical, and life insurance coverage. In a sense, SFAS No. 112 is a companion to SFAS No. 106, which covers the costs of providing benefits to former employees after retirement date. SFAS No. 112 is less detailed than SFAS No. 106. For instance, it does not contain guidance on how to account for postemployment benefits acquired in a purchase business combination that would parallel the guidance in paragraphs 86–88 of SFAS No. 106. In the absence of explicit guidance in SFAS No. 112, the guidance in SFAS No. 106 should, logically, be analogized to postemployment benefit obligations of the acquired company that are assumed by the acquiring company; see Subsection 8.3(g)(x).

(xii) Fair Value of Liabilities Existing at the Acquisition Date. SFAS No. 141(R) requires that liabilities assumed in the acquisition be recorded at their fair value. Such liabilities include warranty accruals, vacation pay, deferred compensation, unfavorable leases, contracts, and commitments, as well as accounts and notes payable and other forms of long-term debt. Liabilities should be recorded at the present value of amounts to be paid and discounted at current interest rates. The objective of allocating fair value to liabilities assumed in the acquisition is to arrive at amounts assigned as though the acquirer had incurred the liabilities as of the acquisition date.

Certain components of equity should also be evaluated to determine if the substance of the security is more closely related to debt than to equity. For example, mandatory redeemable preferred stock, which typically is classified outside of the equity section due to the redemption characteristics, generally should be recorded at fair value at the date of acquisition. The amount of cash the preferred shareholders will receive is fixed, as in a debt arrangement, and generally the other redemption and dividend terms are fixed as well. There is little difference in substance between assuming long-term debt of a target company and assuming mandatorily redeemable preferred stock. Both types of securities represent potential claims against the company for cash.

The EITF discussed Issue No. 84–35a, *Liabilities Accrued in a Purchase Business Combination,* at its February 1985 meeting. Several types of liabilities were discussed, and no consensus was reached as to individual types of liabilities that should be accrued. However, the FASB staff expressed its belief that the literature is clear: Liabilities that exist at the acquisition date should be accrued at their fair values.

(xiii) Income Tax Effects on the Purchase Price Allocation.   This discussion of accounting for income taxes in connection with business combinations accounted for by the purchase method is based on the guidance provided in SFAS No. 109, *Accounting for Income Taxes.*

SFAS No. 109 requires recognition of a deferred tax liability or asset at the acquisition date for the income tax consequences of differences between the assigned values and the tax bases of the assets acquired and the liabilities assumed (except the portion of goodwill for which amortization is not deductible for tax purposes, unallocated negative goodwill, leveraged leases, and acquired (APB Opinion No. 23, *Accounting for Income Taxes—Special Areas Differences*). This change may seem to imply little more than a requirement to gross up the tax effects that would have been previously recognized on a net-of-tax basis under this opinion and APB Opinion No. 11, *Accounting for Income Taxes.* However, the change is much more significant:

- A net deferred tax asset is recognized in a purchase transaction if realization of the tax benefits for deductible temporary differences and carryforwards is more likely than not.

- If separate tax returns are expected to be filed in future years, only the available evidence of the acquired entity should be considered in determining if realization of acquired tax benefits is more likely than not.

- Tax benefits for temporary differences and carryforwards of the acquirer that were not recognized prior to the business combination may be recognized in the purchase price allocation by reducing the valuation allowance if realization is more likely than not.

- Discounting of the income tax consequences of temporary differences and carryforward benefits to their present values is prohibited.

Consistent with prior practice, no deferred income taxes are recorded for the amount assigned to goodwill that is not deductible for tax purposes. Also, deferred income taxes are not recorded for the difference between the financial reporting amount assigned to a leveraged lease acquired in a purchase business combination and the tax basis of that lease. EITF Issue No. 96–7, *Accounting for Deferred Taxes on In-Process Research and Development Activities Acquired in a Purchase Business Combination,* concludes that deferred taxes are not provided on the difference between book and tax bases of in-process research and development costs at acquisition date, and therefore in-process R&D is written off on a gross basis.

This accounting applies to both taxable and nontaxable purchase business combinations. A taxable business combination is distinguished from a nontaxable one in that, in a taxable transaction, the purchase price is assigned to the assets acquired and liabilities assumed both for income tax and financial reporting purposes, whereas in a nontaxable business combination, the predecessor's tax bases are carried forward. In both taxable and nontaxable business combinations, the amounts assigned to the individual assets acquired and liabilities assumed for financial statement purposes are often different from the amounts assigned or carried forward for tax purposes. A deferred tax liability or asset is recognized for each of these differences using the recognition and measurement criteria of SFAS No. 109.

The next example from paragraph 260 of SFAS No. 109 illustrates the recognition and measurement of a deferred tax liability and asset in a nontaxable business combination. The assumptions are:

- The enacted tax rate is 40 percent for all future years, and amortization of goodwill is not deductible for tax purposes.
- An enterprise is acquired for $20,000, and the enterprise has no leveraged leases.
- The tax basis of the net assets acquired is $5,000, and the assigned value (other than goodwill) is $12,000. Future recovery of the assets and settlement of the liabilities at their assigned values will result in $20,000 of taxable amounts and $13,000 of deductible amounts that can be offset against each other. Therefore, no valuation allowance is necessary.

The amounts recorded to account for the purchase transaction are:

Assigned value of the net assets (other than goodwill) acquired	$12,000
Deferred tax liability for $20,000 of taxable temporary differences	(8,000)
Deferred tax asset for $13,000 of deductible temporary differences	5,200
Goodwill—nondeductible	10,800
Purchase price of the acquired enterprise	$20,000

If a valuation allowance is recognized for the deferred tax asset for an acquired entity's deductible temporary differences or operating loss or tax credit carry forwards at the acquisition date, SFAS No. 109 indicates that the tax benefits for those items that are first recognized (i.e., by elimination of that valuation allowance) in financial statements after the acquisition date should be applied in this order:

1. To reduce to zero any goodwill related to the acquisition
2. Then to reduce to zero other noncurrent intangible assets related to the acquisition
3. Finally to reduce income tax expense

(xiv) Deferred Taxes Associated with Acquired Identifiable Intangible Assets with No Tax Basis. Differences in the tax and book bases of purchased intangible assets result in temporary differences under SFAS No. 109 even if the asset has no tax basis or if the amortization of the asset is not currently deductible for tax purposes. This is often the case in a nontaxable business combination where, for accounting purposes, a significant portion of the purchase price is allocated to identifiable intangible assets, such as franchise rights, patents, mortgage servicing rights, or other intangible assets with no tax basis.

The FASB staff concluded in Question 16 of its special report, *A Guide to Implementation of Statement 109 on Accounting for Income Taxes* (hereafter the Special Report), that these intangible assets should not be treated in a manner similar to goodwill. Question 16 states, in part:

A deferred tax liability or asset should be recognized for temporary differences related to intangible assets other than goodwill in accordance with the recognition and measurement requirements of Statement 109. Goodwill recognized in a business combination accounted for as a purchase is a residual—it is the excess of purchase price over the assigned values of the identifiable net assets acquired. Other intangible assets such as customer lists and trademarks are not residuals and are not included among the exceptions (which include goodwill) to comprehensive recognition of deferred taxes identified in paragraph 9 [of the statement].

SFAS No. 109 indicates that unallocated negative goodwill does not represent a temporary difference. However, negative goodwill that is allocated to (as a reduction of) the fair value of noncurrent assets will affect the deferred tax liability associated with the difference between book and tax bases for those assets. Accordingly, in determining the deferred tax liability for a business combination in which negative goodwill is allocated to noncurrent assets, the negative goodwill must be computed simultaneously with the deferred tax liability.

(xv) Tax Deductibility of Goodwill Amortization. The Omnibus Budget Reconciliation Act of 1993 was enacted on August 10, 1993, and provides that the tax basis of goodwill can be amortized over 15 years. For business combinations consummated after the enactment date, the guidance contained in paragraph 262 and 263 of SFAS No. 109 should be followed. Thus, if the combination results in goodwill for financial reporting purposes that exceeds goodwill for tax purposes, the excess will not result in a reported tax benefit. If, however, tax goodwill exceeds goodwill for financial reporting purposes, a tax benefit will be reported when those tax benefits are realized in tax returns in future years.

(xvi) Fair Value When Less than 100 Percent Acquired. Paragraph 35 of SFAS No. 141 states that, in a purchase business combination, the acquiring company should record at fair value the assets acquired and liabilities assumed. However, if the acquiring company in a purchase business combination acquires less than 100 percent of the outstanding common shares of the acquired company, the statement does not specify whether the identifiable assets and liabilities of the acquired company should be recorded at (1) 100 percent of their fair value on the date of the acquisition or (2) the acquiring company's proportionate share of their value on the date of the acquisition plus the minority interest's proportion of the preacquisition carrying amounts. In the first case, minority interest is recorded at minority's share of the fair value of the identifiable assets and liabilities. In the second case, minority interest is recorded at minority's share of the subsidiary's carrying amount. While the differences could be substantial, they do not affect the measurement of consolidated net income or earnings per share. They do affect the balance sheet and various amortizations and the amount of minority interest in consolidated income reported in the income statement.

Both approaches are followed in practice today, although the second approach (measure minority's share based on the acquired company's carrying amount) is far more common. Prior to the issuance of SFAS No. 141(R), the FASB was addressing the issue in a project on acquisition method procedures for business combinations.

(xvii) Concerns of Securities and Exchange Commission Staff. In the past several years, the SEC staff has required a number of registrants to restate their financial statements by reallocating portions of the cost of purchase business combination out of goodwill and into specifically identifiable assets—assets whose amortization periods are likely to be shorter than that for goodwill. Previously, under SFAS No. 141, the acquisition cost had to be allocated first to all identifiable assets acquired and liabilities assumed regardless of whether they had been recorded in the financial statements of the acquired entity (paragraph 35). Paragraph 37 contains some general guides for assigning amounts to individual assets acquired and liabilities assumed other than goodwill. SFAS 141(R) requires an acquirer to recognize the assets acquired, the liabilities assumed, and any non-controlling interest in the acquiree at the acquisition date, measured at their fair values as of that date, with limited exceptions. These days, with an increasing number of acquisitions of service and technology companies, significant portions of the acquisition cost may be attributable to other kinds of self-created identifiable intangible assets that were not recorded on the acquiree's books but that must be recognized under SFAS No. 141(R). The SEC staff has also taken the position that a portion of the acquisition cost that is assigned to purchased R&D should be capitalized and amortized as an intangible asset, not written off in its entirety immediately after the acquisition, if it meets the alternative future use test in paragraph 11c, Intangibles Purchased from Others, of SFAS No. 2, *Accounting for Research and Development Costs.* Normally, R&D would have an alternative future use if technological feasibility or marketability can be established.

(h) ASSETS AND LIABILITIES ARISING FROM CONTINGENCIES. FASB Statement No. 5, *Accounting for Contingencies,* defines a contingency as an existing condition, situation, or set of circumstances involving uncertainty as to possible gain or loss to an entity that will ultimately be resolved when one or more future events occur or fail to occur.

The guidance in Statement No. 5 *does not apply* in determining which assets or liabilities arising from contingencies to recognize as of the acquisition date. Instead

1. The acquirer shall recognize as of the acquisition date all of the assets acquired and liabilities assumed that arise from contingencies related to contracts (referred to as *contractual contingencies*), measured at their acquisition-date fair values.

2. For all other contingencies (referred to as *noncontractual contingencies*), the acquirer shall assess whether it is *more likely than not* as of the acquisition date that the contingency gives rise to an asset or a liability as defined in Statement of Financial Accounting Concepts Statement No. 6, *Elements of Financial Statements.* If that criterion is met as of the acquisition date, the asset or liability arising from a noncontractual contingency shall be recognized at that date, measured at its acquisition-date fair value. If that criterion is not met as of the acquisition date, the acquirer shall not recognize an asset or a liability at that date. The acquirer shall instead account for a noncontractual contingency that does not meet the more-likely-than-not criterion as of the acquisition date in accordance with other GAAP, including Statement No. 5, as appropriate. Paragraphs A62–A65 of SFAS No. 141(R) illustrate the application of the more-likely-than-not criterion.

The guidance of SFAS No. 5 should be used in determining whether a condition, situation, or set of circumstances constitutes a contingency of the acquiree at the date of acquisition. Contingencies arising from the acquisition itself are not preacquisition contingencies (e.g., litigation over the acquisition or the tax effects of the acquisition). These contingencies are the acquiring company's contingencies rather than preacquisition contingencies.

Paragraph 62 of SFAS 141(R) provides the subsequent accounting for an asset or a liability arising from a contingency recognized as of the acquisition date in accordance with paragraph 24 that would be in the scope of Statement 5 if not acquired or assumed in a business combination depends on when new information about the possible outcome of the contingency is obtained Absent new information about the possible outcome, the acquirer shall continue to report such an asset or a liability at its acquisition-date fair value. When new information is obtained about the possible outcome of the contingency, the acquirer shall evaluate that information and measure the asset or liability as follows:

a. A liability shall be measured at the higher of:
1. Its acquisition-date fair value; or
2. The amount that would be recognized if applying Statement 5.
b. An asset shall be measured at the lower of:
1. Its acquisition-date fair value; or
2. The best estimate of its future settlement amount.

Paragraph 26 of SFAS No. 141(R) stipulates that the acquirer shall recognize and measure a deferred tax asset or liability arising from the assets acquired and liabilities assumed in a business combination in accordance with FASB Statement No. 109, *Accounting for Income Taxes,* as amended by this Statement.

The acquirer shall account for the potential tax effects of temporary differences, carryforwards, and any income tax uncertainties of an aquiree that exist at the acquisition date or that arise as a result of the acquisition in accordance with SFAS Statement No. 109, as amended, and related interpretative guidance, including FASB Interpretation No. 48, *Accounting for Uncertainty in Income Taxes.*

The EITF concluded that all income tax uncertainties that exist at the time of or arise in connection with a purchase business combination should be accounted for pursuant to SFAS No. 109. Further, the Task Force reached a consensus that the guidance contained in Question 17 of the

Special Report on SFAS No. 109 should be applied to changes in estimates and final settlements of all income tax uncertainties that predate or result from a purchase business combination with the exception of uncertainties related to the valuation allowance of a deferred tax asset. The consensus does not, however, apply to changes in judgment about the realization of deferred tax assets because SFAS No. 109 provides guidance for changes in a valuation allowance related to an acquired deductible difference or carryforward. Further, the Task Force noted that the requirement for reduction of a valuation allowance established at the acquisition date applies only to initial recognition of an acquired benefit; all other changes in the valuation allowance due to a change in judgment about the realizability of the deferred tax asset should be included in income from continuing operations.

As indicated in Question 17 of the Special Report, deferred tax assets and liabilities at the date of a purchase business combination should be based on management's best estimate of the ultimate tax basis that will be accepted by the tax authority, and liabilities for prior tax returns of the acquired entity should be based on management's best estimate of the ultimate settlement. At the date of a change in management's best estimate of the ultimate tax basis of acquired assets, liabilities, and carryforwards, and at the date that the tax basis is settled with the tax authority, deferred tax assets and liabilities should be adjusted to reflect the revised tax basis and the amount of any settlement with the tax authority for prior-year income taxes. Similarly, at the date of a change in management's best estimate of items relating to the acquired entity's prior tax returns, and at the date that the items are settled with the tax authority, any liability previously recognized should be adjusted. The effect of those adjustments should be applied to increase or decrease the remaining balance of goodwill attributable to that acquisition. If goodwill is reduced to zero, the remaining amount of those adjustments should be applied initially to reduce to zero other noncurrent intangible assets related to that acquisition, and any remaining amount should be recognized in income.

The Task Force observed that interest on the final settlement with the tax authority that accrues subsequent to the acquisition date should not be included in the goodwill adjustment.

The Task Force also reached a consensus that the guidance in Question 17 of the Special Report is applicable to all purchase business combinations, regardless of whether the combination occurred prior to the adoption of SFAS No. 109 and regardless of the transition method used to adopt SFAS No. 109. SFAS No. 141(R) applies to all other preacquisition contingencies, and the application of the EITF consensus should be limited solely to income tax uncertainties relating to purchase business combinations.

(i) PUSHDOWN ACCOUNTING.   In October 1979, the American Institute of Certified Public Accountants (AICPA) Accounting Standards Executive Committee (AcSEC) prepared an Issues Paper entitled *Pushdown Accounting*. The Issues Paper's advisory committee dealt with determining the percentage change in ownership that would justify a new basis of accounting.

Members of AcSEC supported 90 percent as a minimum change of ownership that would justify pushdown accounting. At the time AcSEC decided to support pushdown accounting, it was not supported by practice or by other authoritative accounting or regulatory bodies. In January 1983, the Federal Home Loan Bank Board issued guidance in R-Memorandum No. 55 (which was superseded by R-55a in 1986) consistent with the Issues Paper, which permits but does not require pushdown accounting. The SEC also agreed in SAB No. 54 that the Staff believes that purchase transactions that result in an entity becoming substantially wholly-owned (as defined in Rule 1–02(z) of Regulation S-X) establish a new basis of accounting for the purchased assets and liabilities.

When initially applied in practice, a new basis of accounting in the separate financial statements of an acquired entity was generally applied when the change in ownership was at least 90 percent. However, since the AICPA Issues Paper was published in 1979, practice has developed to permit pushdown accounting when the change in ownership is 80 percent or greater. In the case of a step acquisition, pushdown accounting may be applied when an individual, company, or control group obtains 80 percent ownership or more of the acquired entity.

As noted, the SEC's position on pushdown accounting has been based on an entity becoming substantially wholly-owned rather than the substantial change in ownership concept discussed in the

1979 AcSEC Issues Paper. The SEC staff has indicated that SAB No. 54 was intended to require pushdown accounting when an entity became substantially wholly-owned even if accomplished through a step acquisition that takes a number of years to complete. In addition, the SEC will address each situation on an individual facts and circumstances basis.

In June 1985, the EITF discussed Issue No. 85–21, *Changes of Ownership Resulting in a New Basis of Accounting.* Several accounting issues regarding the application of pushdown accounting were discussed. No consensus views were reached by the EITF, and the EITF chairman indicated that pushdown issues would be dealt with in the standards phase of the FASB's consolidations project to the extent that it was addressed in the AcSEC Issues Paper on pushdown accounting. As a general rule, the SEC requires push down accounting when the ownership change is greater than 95% and objects to push-down accounting when the ownership change is less than 80%.[1]

In December 1991, the FASB issued a Discussion Memorandum entitled "An Analysis of Issues Related to New Basis Accounting." The discussion memorandum was published to solicit views on which, if any, transactions or events should result in changing the carrying amount of an entity's individual assets, including goodwill, and liabilities to amounts representing their current fair values.

As with all aspects of business combinations, an evaluation should be made of the change in ownership that results in the application of pushdown accounting to assure that the substance of the acquisition and the change in ownership, not just the legal form, determine the appropriate accounting. For example, 80 percent of a company (X) is owned by the public (Group A) and 20 percent is owned by two individuals, the president and a board member (Group B). Two unrelated individuals propose to form a holding company (HC) and capitalize it with $1 million. Then through a series of transactions with Group A and Group B shareholders, HC will acquire 90 percent of X's stock. HC will be 78 percent owned by the two unrelated individuals that formed HC and 22 percent by Group B. Even though X is 90 percent owned by HC, the application of pushdown accounting would be questionable. In evaluating the acquisition, one should look at the total change in ownership of X held by the two unrelated individuals after the transaction. After the acquisition, the unrelated individuals that formed HC own 78 percent of HC's 90 percent ownership interest in X, or approximately 70 percent. Between the Group A shareholders and Group B shareholders, there is a continuing ownership interest in X of 30 percent. It is unlikely that one could argue that a 70 percent change in ownership justifies the use of pushdown accounting.

(i) Pushdown of Parent Company Debt.   In applying the concepts of pushdown accounting, questions often arise regarding the pushdown of the acquirer's debt to its subsidiary. For example, a company (A) forms a subsidiary to acquire the net assets of another company. A has borrowed 100 percent of the purchase price, which exceeds the recorded basis of the net assets acquired. A intends to service this debt from the earnings of the subsidiary, whose cash flows are expected to be sufficient to cover the debt service on the loan. Should A's debt be pushed down to the subsidiary?

The subject of pushdown of parent company debt to a subsidiary was discussed by the EITF without reaching a consensus. In December 1987, the SEC released SAB No. 73, *Pushdown Basis of Accounting for Parent Company Debt Related to Subsidiary Acquisition.* The SAB requires that debt incurred or mandatory redeemable preferred stock issued by a parent to acquire substantially all of the common stock of a subsidiary should be pushed down along with the related purchase price adjustment if:

- The subsidiary is to assume the debt of the parent in a current or planned transaction.
- The proceeds of a debt or equity offering of the subsidiary will be used to retire all or part of the parent company's debt.
- The subsidiary pledges its assets as collateral or otherwise guarantees the parent company's debt.

---

[1] D. Jeter and P. Chaney, *Wiley Advanced Accounting* (Hoboken, NJ: John Wiley & Sons, 2007), p. 272.

(ii) Exceptions to Pushdown of Parent Company Debt.   SAB No. 73 does not require debt to be pushed down to the subsidiary if only the subsidiary's stock is pledged as collateral for the debt since, in the case of default, such a pledge would not give the parent's debt holders priority over the subsidiary's debt holders but rather would simply transfer the parent's common stock investment to the parent's debt holders. In addition, the SAB provides guidance on the required disclosures in the notes to financial statements and the registrant's Management's Discussion and Analysis of Financial Condition and Results of Operations.

The SEC has also indicated, in regard to the pushdown of parent-company debt to the separate financial statements of a subsidiary when pushdown accounting itself is not required because of the specific exclusions outlined in SAB No. 54, that pushdown of parent-company debt generally becomes an issue only when pushdown accounting is applied. However, the SEC may require pushdown accounting (and pushdown of the related parent-company debt) in situations where there is public debt, preferred stock, or significant minority interest, depending on the individual facts and circumstances.

(j) ALLOCATION PERIOD.   SFAS No. 141 does not specifically address the period of time subsequent to the acquisition date over which the research and fact gathering must be accomplished and the purchase price allocated. The reasonableness of the allocation period should be determined through an analysis of the specific facts and circumstances surrounding the business combination, including:

- The size and complexity of the entity acquired
- Information available to the acquirer prior to the consummation date
- The acquirer's management's knowledge of and expertise in the acquiree's business
- Demonstration by management of its ongoing efforts to avail itself of relevant information

In connection with the accounting for preacquisition contingencies, Appendix F of SFAS No. 141 defines the allocation period for preacquisition contingencies in this way:

> The period required to identify and measure the fair value of the assets acquired and the liabilities assumed in a business combination. The allocation period ends when the acquiring entity is no longer waiting for information that it has arranged to obtain and that is known to be available or obtainable. Thus, the existence of a pre-acquisition contingency for which an asset, a liability, or an impairment of an asset cannot be estimated does not, of itself, extend the allocation period. Although the required period will vary with circumstances, the allocation period should usually not exceed one year from the consummation of a business combination.

It is not unusual for a company to acquire another company in a business combination to be accounted for by the purchase method at or near the end of a reporting period or its fiscal year. The allocation of the purchase price may not be completed by the date the acquirer's financial statements are issued. In such cases, a preliminary allocation should be made, and disclosure should be made in the financial statements that further adjustments may arise as a result of finalization of the ongoing study. Changes subsequent to the issuance of financial statements in the allocation of purchase price should then be evaluated by determining (1) if the original allocation, as reported, was the result of preliminary evaluation of an ongoing data-gathering and evaluation process, which in management's opinion was not expected to differ significantly upon finalizing the study; and (2) whether the study was finalized in a reasonable period of time subsequent to the acquisition. Adjustments to preliminary amounts generally result in corresponding adjustments to goodwill.

The nature of an asset and not the manner of its acquisition determines an acquirer's subsequent accounting for the cost of that asset. The basis for measuring the cost of an asset—regardless of whether it is the amount of cash paid, the fair value of an asset received or given up, the amount of a liability incurred, or the fair value of stock issued—has no effect on the subsequent accounting for the cost, which is retained as the carrying amount of the asset, depreciated, amortized, or otherwise matched with revenue.

After initial recognition, goodwill and other intangible assets acquired in a business combination are accounted for in accordance with the provisions of SFAS No. 142.

SFAS No. 141(R) requires an acquirer to recognize the assets acquired, the liabilities assumed, and any noncontrolling interest in the acquiree at the acquisition date, measured at their fair values as of that date, with limited exceptions specified in the statement. SFAS No. 141(R) replaces SFAS No. 141's cost-allocation process, which required the cost of an acquisition to be allocated to the individual assets acquired and liabilities assumed based on their estimated fair values. SFAS No. 141's guidance resulted in not recognizing some assets and liabilities at the acquisition date, and it also resulted in measuring some assets and liabilities at amounts other than their fair values at the acquisition date.

(k) SAB STAFF ACCOUNTING BULLETIN NO. 61. In May 1986, the SEC issued SAB No. 61, *Adjustments to Allowances for Business Combination Loan Losses—Purchase Method Accounting.* The SAB indicates that, with rare exceptions, the SEC does not believe changes in allowances for loan losses are necessary as part of the allocation process in applying purchase accounting adjustments. The SEC believes that, assuming the appropriate methodology is followed by each party to the business combination, each company's estimate of the uncollectible portion of a loan portfolio would fall within a range of acceptability.

However, the SEC concedes that a purchase accounting adjustment may be required to reflect a difference in valuation of a portfolio of loans or receivables if the acquirer's intent with regard to ultimate recovery of the loans or receivables is demonstrably different from the plans or assumptions used by the acquiree in estimating its loan loss reserve. For example, the acquiree may have intended to hold the loans to maturity or to assist a troubled borrower through a long-term workout on the loan, whereas the acquirer plans to sell such loans or foreclose on the underlying collateral. The net carrying value of the loans recorded in purchase allocation should therefore be based on the acquirer's plan of recovery.

Loan losses and allowances for uncollectible accounts and similar reserves are typically not considered preacquisition contingencies. Reasonable methods of estimating such losses or allowances should be used by the acquiree and evaluated by the acquirer at the date of acquisition. Subsequent adjustments to the allowances to reflect the ultimate outcome or resolution of the receivables is presumed to be based on changes in the economic factors surrounding the particular receivable, the nature of the receivable, and the evaluation of the collectibility of the receivables in light of events occurring subsequent to the business combination. Accordingly, such changes in the related valuation accounts should not be accounted for as adjustments to the cost of the business combination.

The provisions and guidance of SAB No. 103.5, *Adjustments Allowances for Loan Losses in Connection with Business Combinations,* have also been applied to other assets acquired in a purchase business combination. The SEC staff has indicated the guidance should be interpreted broadly with its provisions applied to items such as warranty reserves, inventory obsolescence reserves, and bad debt reserves of nonfinancial institutions, among others.

(l) DATE USED TO RECORD THE ACQUISITION. Paragraph 10 of SFAS No. 141(R) indicates that the acquirer shall identify the acquisition date, which is the date on which it obtains control of the acquiree.

Paragraph 11 of SFAS No. 141(R) also indicates that the acquisition date is the date on which the acquirer obtains control of the acquiree generally is the date on which the acquirer legally transfers the consideration, acquires the assets, and assumes the liabilities of the acquiree—the closing date. However, the acquirer might obtain control on a date that is either earlier or later than the closing date. For example, the acquisition date precedes the closing date if a written agreement provides that the acquirer obtains control of the acquiree on a date before the closing date. An acquirer shall consider all pertinent facts and circumstances in identifying the acquisition date.

SFAS No. 141 also provides for the use of a convenience date, whereby the parties to the combination may designate as the effective date the end of an accounting period that falls between the initiation date and the consummation date. One condition for using a convenience date is that the written agreement for the acquisition provides that effective control of the acquired company is transferred to the acquirer by the effective date without restriction, except for those restrictions required to protect the stockholders of the acquiree. The restrictions permitted are those that prohibit significant changes in operations or disposal of assets, require normal payment of dividends, and the like.

In the event a convenience date is used, SFAS No. 141 requires that adjustments be made to the cost of the acquired company and net income for imputed interest at an appropriate current rate on the assets given, liabilities incurred, or stock issued as of the transfer date to acquire the company.

Factors that should be evaluated in determining if control has passed to the acquirer include:

- The combination has been approved by both companies' boards of directors.
- The acquiree does not do anything between the effective date and consummation date outside the ordinary course of business.
- Management of the combined entity takes over the day-to-day operations of the acquiree.
- Only one set of postacquisition accounting records is maintained from the effective date forward.
- Combined operational meetings involving employees of both companies are held.

Use of a convenience date subsequent to the consummation date is not permitted by SFAS No. 141.

(m) ADDITIONAL GUIDANCE FOR APPLYING THE ACQUISITION METHOD TO PARTICULAR TYPES OF BUSINESS COMBINATIONS

(i) Business Combination Achieved in Stages.   An acquirer sometimes obtains control of an acquiree in which it held an equity interest immediately before the acquisition date. For example, on December 31, 20X1, Entity A holds a 35 percent noncontrolling equity interest in Entity B. On that date, Entity A purchases an additional 40 percent interest in Entity B, which gives it control of Entity B. SFAS No. 141(R) refers to such a transaction as a *business combination achieved in stages,* sometimes also referred to as a step acquisition.

In a business combination achieved in stages, the acquirer shall remeasure its previously held equity interest in the acquiree at its acquisition-date fair value and recognize the resulting gain or loss, if any, in earnings. In prior reporting periods, the acquirer may have recognized changes in the value of its equity interest in the acquiree in other comprehensive income (e.g., because the investment was classified as available for sale). If so, the amount that was recognized in other comprehensive income must be reclassified and included in the calculation of gain or loss as of the acquisition date.

(ii) Business Combination Achieved without the Transfer of Consideration.   An acquirer sometimes obtains control of an acquiree without transferring consideration. The acquisition method of accounting for a business combination applies to those combinations. Such circumstances include:

1. The acquiree repurchases a sufficient number of its own shares for an existing investor (the acquirer) to obtain control.
2. Minority veto rights lapse that previously kept the acquirer from controlling an acquiree in which the acquirer held the majority voting interest.
3. The acquirer and acquiree agree to combine their businesses by contract alone. The acquirer transfers no consideration in exchange for control of an acquiree and holds no equity interests in the acquiree, either on the acquisition date or previously. Examples of business combinations achieved by contract alone include bringing two businesses together in a stapling arrangement or forming a dual listed corporation.

(n) DISCLOSURE IN FINANCIAL STATEMENTS.   The notes to the financial statements of a combined entity disclose this information in the period in which a material business combination is completed:

1. The name and a brief description of the acquired entity and the percentage of voting equity interests acquired
2. The primary reasons for the acquisition, including a description of the factors that contributed to a purchase price that results in recognition of goodwill
3. The period for which the results of operations of the acquired entity are included in the income statement of the acquiring entity
4. The cost of the acquired entity and, if applicable, the number of shares of equity interests (such as common shares, preferred shares, or partnership interests) issued or issuable, the value assigned to those interests, and the basis for determining that value
5. A condensed balance sheet disclosing the amount assigned to each major asset and liability caption of the acquired entity at the acquisition date
6. Contingent payments, options, or commitments specified in the acquisition agreement and the accounting treatment that will be followed should any such contingency occur
7. The amount of purchased research and development assets acquired and written off in the period and the line item in the income statement in which the amounts written off are aggregated
8. For any purchase price allocation that has not been finalized, that fact and the reasons for it; in subsequent periods, the nature and amount of any material adjustments made to the initial allocation of the purchase price
9. This information if the amount assigned to goodwill or to other intangible assets acquired is significant in relation to the total cost of the acquired entity:
   a. For intangible assets subject to amortization:
      i. The total amount assigned and the amount assigned to any major intangible asset class
      ii. The amount of any significant residual value, in total and by major intangible asset class
      iii. The weighted-average amortization period, in total and by major intangible asset class
   b. For intangible assets not subject to amortization, the total amount assigned and the amount assigned to any major intangible asset class
   c. For goodwill:
      i. The total amount of goodwill and the amount that is expected to be deductible for tax purposes
      ii. The amount of goodwill by reportable segment (if the combined entity is required to disclose segment information in conformity with SFAS No. 131, *Disclosures about Segments of an Enterprise and Related Information*) unless not practicable

The notes to the financial statements of an acquiring entity disclose the next information in the period in which individually immaterial business combinations have been completed if those combinations are material in the aggregate:

1. The number of entities acquired and a brief description of those entities
2. The aggregate cost of the acquired entities, the number of shares of stock issued or issuable, and the value assigned to those shares
3. The aggregate amount of any contingent payments, options, or commitments and the accounting treatment that will be followed should any such contingency occur (if potentially significant in relation to the aggregate cost of the acquired entities)

4. The information described in item 9 in the list on the previous page if the aggregate amount assigned to goodwill or to other intangible assets acquired is significant in relation to the aggregate cost of the acquired entities

In the period in which an extraordinary gain is recognized related to a business combination, the notes to the financial statements disclose the information required by paragraph 11 of APB Opinion No. 30. The notes to the financial statements also disclose, for any material business combination completed after the balance sheet date but before the financial statements are issued, the information required in items 1 to 9 in the list on the previous page (unless not practicable).

(i) Pro Forma Disclosures.   Paragraph 54 of SFAS No. 141 requires that pro forma results of operations be presented as supplemental information for the period in which the companies are combined and for the immediately preceding period.

(ii) Classification of Acquired Securities.   The FASB Statement No. 115, *Accounting for Certain Investments in Debt and Equity Securities,* requires an investor to classify its investments in debt and equity securities into three categories (held-to-maturity securities, trading securities, and available-for-sale securities) and prescribes different accounting for each. When such securities are obtained in a business combination accounted for by the purchase method, they should be classified based on the intent and ability of the acquiring company. This may mean reclassification from how those securities were classified in the financial statements of the acquired company. It may also mean a different classification in the separate statements of the acquired subsidiary versus consolidation.

(iii) Disclosures in Interim Financial Information.   The summarized interim financial information of a public business entity discloses the next information if a material business combination is completed during the current year up to the date of the most recent interim statement of financial position presented:

1. The information described in items 1 to 9 in the list on the previous page.
2. Supplemental pro forma information that discloses the results of operations for the current interim period and the current year up to the date of the most recent interim statement of financial position presented and for the corresponding periods in the preceding year as if the business combination had been completed as of the beginning of the period being reported on. That pro forma information displays, at a minimum, revenue, income before extraordinary items and the cumulative effect of accounting changes (including those on an interim basis), net income, and earnings per share.
3. The nature and amount of any material, nonrecurring items included in the reported pro forma results of operations.

(o) DISCLOSURES IN SECURITIES AND EXCHANGE COMMISSION FILINGS.   In Financial Reporting Release (FRR) No. 47, the SEC revised its rules with respect to disclosures relating to significant business acquisitions in filings under the 1933 and 1934 Securities Acts. These amendments reduce the number of years for which the acquired company's financial statements must be provided and, in some cases, eliminate the requirement to provide those financial statements in registration statements altogether.

(p) COMPARISON OF THE PURCHASE AND ACQUISITION METHODS OF ACCOUNTING.   Assume that ParentCo acquires 70 percent of the outstanding shares of SubCo for $1,000. Additional facts are:

- ParentCo estimates that the fair value of 100 percent of SubCo is $1,405.
  - Note that the fair value of SubCo may not ordinarily be calculated by extrapolating the purchase price paid to the remaining shares outstanding (i.e., $1,000/70% = $1,429 is not ordinarily the fair value). The reason is that a portion of the purchase price contains a payment for the ability to exercise control.

- In this case, the control premium would be $55, calculated as: $(\$1000-.7(\$1405))/(1-.7)$ = $55.
- It may be difficult to estimate the control premium, because it may have to be derived from an estimate of the full fair value of the acquired company, as above.
- The book value of SubCo's assets and liabilities approximate their fair value, except for one asset with a remaining useful life of 10 years. For that asset, the fair value exceeds the book value by $100.

The next table displays (1) the respective balance sheets of ParentCo and SubCo at the date of acquisition, (2) the consolidated results under the purchase and acquisition methods, and (3) the goodwill calculations under each method.[2]

	Parent	SubCo	Consolidated Purchase Method	Consolidated Acquisition Method
Investment in SubCo	$ 1,000			
Other assets	2,000	800	2,870	2,900
Goodwill			580	805
Total assets	$ 3,000	$ 800	$ 3,450	$ 3,705
Liabilities	$ 500	$ 300	$ 800	$ 800
Minority interest in SubCo			150	
Shareholders' Equity				
Non-controlling interest in SubCo				405
Owners' equity	2,500	500	2,500	2,500
Total liab. & owners' equity	$ 3,000	$ 800	$ 3,450	$ 3,705

Goodwill Calculations

Acquisition price	$ 1,000	$ 1,000
Non-controlling interest		405
Portion of SubCo's book value attributed to ParentCo	(350)	
Increment to book value of SubCo's net assets	(70)	
Fair value of assets acquired		(900)
Fair value of liabilities assumed		300
	$ 580	$ 805

The purchase method had a lot of warts, but it took the FASB decades to replace it. In essence, it was nothing more than a slavish application of the historic cost principle to mute the future effect of an acquisition on operating expenses. The idea was that if you purchased 70 percent of the outstanding shares of another company, revaluation of assets would take place only to the extent of the shares purchased. Among other things, this meant that the basis of the assets of a subsidiary acquired in a business combination transaction would be the sum of the fair value of the portion acquired and the historic cost of the portion not acquired. This is illustrated by the calculation of consolidated assets: $\$2,000 + \$800 + .7(\$900-800) = \$2,870$.

The acquisition method represents a full commitment to fair value, yet ironically, the FASB still does not require fair value for all assets and liabilities assumed. In other words, if the transaction results in the acquisition of control of an entity, assets acquired and liabilities assumed will be initially measured at 100 percent of their fair value—even if less than 100 percent of the outstanding shares are purchased. That is why consolidated assets are $30 higher in the illustration under the acquisition method.

---

[2] Example from *http://accountingonion.typepad.com/theaccountingonion/2008/01/fas-141r-and-fa.html.*

(q) EFFECTIVE DATE AND TRANSITION.   SFAS No. 141(R) should be applied prospectively to business combinations for which the acquisition date is on or after the beginning of the first annual reporting period beginning on or after December 15, 2008. Earlier application is prohibited.

Assets and liabilities that arose from business combinations whose acquisition dates preceded the application of this statement should not be adjusted upon application of this statement.

An entity, such as a mutual entity, which has not yet applied Statement No. 141 and FASB Statement No. 147, *Acquisitions of Certain Financial Institutions,* and that had one or more business combinations that were accounted for using the purchase method must apply the transition provisions in paragraphs A130 to A134. An entity that has not yet applied Statement No. 142 in its entirety should apply that statement in its entirety at the same time that it applies this statement.

8.4 LEVERAGED BUYOUT

(a) DEFINITION.   Authoritative accounting literature does not provide a definition of a leveraged buyout (LBO) transaction. However, an LBO can best be described as a financing technique for acquiring a company wherein a large portion of the purchase price is derived from borrowings, often some or all of which are secured by the underlying assets of the entity being acquired. In most LBO transactions, management of an existing company (OLDCO) and one or more new investors form a holding company (NEWCO) to acquire all of OLDCO's outstanding common stock.

A leverage buyout (LBO) occurs when a group of employees (generally a management group) and third-party investors create a new company to acquire all the outstanding common shares of their employer company.

(b) STRUCTURE.   There is no predetermined manner in which to structure an LBO; a structure is designed to meet the requirements of each transaction, giving appropriate consideration to existing and forecasted cash flows, capital expenditure and working capital needs, income tax considerations, potential dispositions, and lender requirements. There are, however, common elements in the structure of each LBO transaction.

(i) Legal Form.   NEWCOs are generally formed to acquire OLDCOs. Typically, there is no real economic incentive or disincentive to form NEWCO, although for practical purposes many companies acquired in an LBO transaction are publicly owned and are acquired through a tender offer and a NEWCO generally is formed to hold the tendered OLDCO shares prior to the closing of the tender offer. NEWCO may also be used to effect a squeeze-out merger, which is a mechanism used to acquire untendered shares. Depending on OLDCO's state of incorporation, a squeeze-out generally can be accomplished after two-thirds of OLDCO's stockholders have tendered their OLDCO stock to NEWCO. At that point, NEWCO may have the legal right to effect a merging of NEWCO into OLDCO, without shareholder approval, and force an exchange of cash or NEWCO securities for the untendered OLDCO stock.

Nonpublic companies acquired in an LBO generally have a limited number of stockholders; therefore, establishing NEWCO simply to acquire shares may be regarded as an unnecessary expense. However, for accounting purposes, the need to form NEWCO to acquire OLDCO is very important. That is, without forming NEWCO, the transaction can be accounted for only as a restructuring/recapitalization for which no change in accounting basis is appropriate.

(ii) Management Participation.   In most if not all LBOs, management has the critical role of managing OLDCO's assets to ensure repayment of borrowings and maximize value to NEWCO's stockholders. Accordingly, management's involvement in structuring the LBO transaction and, more important, its continued involvement in managing OLDCO after the acquisition often is crucial to the success of the LBO transaction. Accordingly, key members of OLDCO management generally are given a substantive incentive to ensure the continued successful operation of OLDCO. This is typically accomplished through management's investment in NEWCO.

Management may be granted options to acquire additional NEWCO stock, generally at a price based on the fair market value of the stock at the date of the LBO transaction. A vesting period of several years often is required before management is entitled to receive unrestricted ownership of the stock. The options and warrants provide the stockholders of NEWCO with a mechanism by which to ensure continued employment of key management. The granting of options and warrants also provides management the ability to acquire NEWCO equity at bargain rates (assuming that the fair market value of the stock rises) at a future date, thus obviating the need for them to make up-front cash investments.

(iii) Financing Arrangements. The borrowing required to fund an LBO may come from a variety of sources: commercial banks, insurance companies, other financial institutions, public investment, and so on. As mentioned, financing arrangements are dependent on cash flow needs for operations, debt service, and dividend distributions. Frequently, however, the financing consists of bank and institutional term loans, private investor debt and equity investments placed by investment bankers, and a bridge loan. The bridge loan is made available by the lenders until less expensive permanent financing is obtained.

Another factor that may affect the legal form of the transaction is the nature of the security required by lenders. That is, NEWCO as the acquirer generally incurs the indebtedness to acquire OLDCO. One or more lending institutions, however, may desire more security on their loans than a pledge of OLDCO stock owned by NEWCO. More specifically, some lending institutions require their loans to be placed in the legal entity that contains the operating assets, that is, OLDCO.

A number of LBO transactions have also included financing through the issuance of debt and/or equity securities to the former owners of OLDCO. Certain securities in an LBO may take the form of what is known as *paid-in-kind* (PIK) securities. These securities, for a specified period of years, pay interest or dividends by issuing additional securities. Such securities provide NEWCO relief from its cash flow needs in the early years following the LBO.

Numerous LBOs have also issued NEWCO common stock to OLDCO shareholders. This provides such shareholders with the potential for large profits frequently generated from postacquisition sales of assets or public offerings of NEWCO stock at prices in excess of the LBO acquisition price.

(iv) Tax Considerations. A multitude of factors affect the taxability of the transaction to OLDCO and its stockholders. There are, however, some common strategies to minimize income taxes to both parties. For example, OLDCO's management may wish to exchange part or all of its equity interest in OLDCO for an equity interest in NEWCO without paying tax on the appreciation in the OLDCO stock. This can be accomplished through the use of an acquisition holding company to which management transfers its OLDCO stock in exchange for NEWCO stock.

As another example, if a corporate seller of OLDCO has been filing a consolidated return, the buyer and seller may jointly make a §338(h)(10)election, the effect of which is to treat a stock acquisition as an asset purchase for tax purposes. This will allow higher depreciation deductions to offset postacquisition taxable income. The election may be beneficial to both the seller and the buyer for nontax reasons since the transaction is actually a stock rather than an asset transfer.

Other tax strategies will depend on the specific facts and circumstances of the entities and individuals involved in the transaction.

(c) HISTORICAL PERSPECTIVE. The determination of whether an LBO transaction was a purchase business combination, a step acquisition, or a treasury stock transaction was a difficult accounting problem that accountants had to solve as the pace of LBO transactions increased. In an LBO transaction in which OLDCO shareholders become NEWCO shareholders, the price paid by NEWCO to acquire their OLDCO stock could be considered as purchase price, a capital transaction, or a mixture of both.

Because GAAP was not clear regarding the accounting for LBO transactions, accountants were required to make some difficult decisions regarding the proper manner in which to account for the transactions. Not surprisingly, the decisions produced a variety of accounting results that often meant the difference between the write-up of assets to fair value, or a reduction of equity. In many cases, a reduction of equity resulted in NEWCO reporting a negative net worth. Although the underlying economics of LBO transactions are not changed based on whether the accounting results produce a write-up of assets or a reduction of equity, it is almost undeniable that a company attempting to raise capital will have an easier time doing so if it has positive, rather than negative, equity.

The SEC staff, along with the accounting profession, naturally became concerned regarding the diversity in accounting results and in the proper accounting for LBO transactions. Therefore, while the SEC staff internally adopted guidelines for determining the circumstances in which an LBO transaction should be accounted for as a purchase business combination, it raised the issue of accounting for LBO transactions at the EITF's May 1986 meeting so that the accounting profession would be more directly involved in establishing accounting guidance. The SEC staff and the profession were especially interested in resolving this issue because of its significance to investors, particularly when OLDCO shareholders become NEWCO shareholders.

The EITF reached a consensus on Issue No. 86–16, *Carryover of Predecessor Cost in Leveraged Buyout Transactions,* in July 1987. This consensus, however, did not address the accounting for transactions in which an OLDCO shareholder decreased ownership interest in NEWCO relative to what he or she owned in OLDCO. (These situations are sometimes referred to as *leveraged sell-offs.*) At about the same time, the SEC staff communicated to the EITF that LBO transactions seemed to be evolving and that they may not resemble the LBO transaction described in Issue No. 86–16.

In June 1988, the FASB staff raised Issue No. 88–16, *Basis in Leveraged Buyout Transactions When the Previous Owner's Interest Declines.* In dealing with Issue No. 88–16, the EITF formed a working group to formulate a proposal to deal with the varied matters covered by this issue. In the course of the various EITF and working group meetings, it was decided that one comprehensive consensus should be prepared that would encompass the matters addressed in Issue Nos. 86–16 and 88–16. In doing so, the EITF's conclusions were largely influenced by a desire on the part of the SEC staff to limit diversity in practice, prevent potential accounting abuses, and limit the number of circumstances requiring consultation with the SEC staff. The result of the EITF's efforts, reached by consensus at its May 1989 meeting, is predominantly an objective set of rules that define the accounting for all LBO transactions.

(d) ACCOUNTING FOR THE LEVERAGED BUYOUT TRANSACTION.   EITF Issue No. 88–16 indicates that the substance of the LBO transaction must be evaluated to determine whether it constitutes:

- A financial restructuring/recapitalization for which no change in accounting basis would be appropriate
- A step acquisition for which a partial change in accounting basis would be appropriate
- A purchase by new controlling investors for which a partial or complete change in basis, based on the fair value of the transaction, would be appropriate

The EITF's consensus guidance consists of an elaborate set of criteria that define when a new accounting basis is appropriate (situations in second and third bulleted items) and how to determine that new accounting basis.

In the context of basis adjustments to assets and liabilities acquired, LBOs are considered to be analogous to purchase business combinations discussed previously in this chapter.

The EITF consensus is divided into three sections. The first section addresses the circumstances in which a change in control has occurred; the second section addresses the calculation of NEWCO's recorded investment in OLDCO; and the third section addresses limitations on recording the basis otherwise calculated in the second section.

The basic accounting question relates to the net asset values (fair or book) to be used by the new corporation. Accounting procedures generally followed the rules advocated by the EITF in Consensus Position No. 88–16, which did not view LBOs as business combinations. FASB

Statement No. 141(R) did not comprehensively address this LBO issue but did indicate that this position was no longer applicable. The essence of the change suggests that the economic entity concept should be applied here as well; thus, LBO transactions are now to be viewed as business combinations.

(e) CHANGE IN CONTROL.   The EITF consensus specifies this general provision:

> A partial or complete change in accounting basis is appropriate only when there has been a change in control of voting interest; that is, a new controlling shareholder or group of shareholders must be established.

This provision stems from the underlying assumption that the establishment of a new controlling shareholder or control group results in a transaction similar to a purchase business combination, as opposed to a recapitalization restructuring for which a change in basis is not appropriate.

The consensus guidance establishes specific objective and subjective criteria to be evaluated in determining whether a new controlling shareholder or control group (defined in Subsections 8.4(e)(i) and (ii) has been established. Included in this determination is a definition of which shareholders are part of the control group. The consensus guidance also describes the accounting result if a change in control has not occurred.

(i) Objective Criteria.   Except for the most straightforward circumstance under which a change in control has occurred—that is, a single new shareholder gains the ability to unilaterally exercise control over NEWCO—the guidance in this section is based on two underlying assumptions:

1. New shareholders that meet the definition for inclusion in the NEWCO control group will act in concert to exercise control over NEWCO. This assumption concludes that by virtue of (a) the significance of the shareholders' economic interests in NEWCO and (b) the contemporaneous acquisition of NEWCO interests, such shareholders have similar goals and will consistently act together to control NEWCO.
2. Members of management have a commonality of interest among themselves that distinguishes them from being typical shareholders. This commonality of interest is derived from management's shared responsibility to achieve the objectives of the enterprise and their authority to establish policies and make decisions by which those objectives will be pursued.

These assumptions address circumstances wherein there has been a step acquisition by one or more parties. However, the EITF also recognized that there were some circumstances in which certain shareholders in the NEWCO control group had a step acquisition while other shareholders in the NEWCO control group decreased their ownership interest in NEWCO in relation to their percentage ownership interest in OLDCO. In this latter situation, it was not always clear whether there had been a change in control. Accordingly, the EITF provided explicit guidance to address this issue. This particular portion of the EITF consensus guidance was heavily debated because, in some circumstances, following the guidance could produce a potentially contentious result. For example, as Exhibit 8.2 demonstrates, Investor 2 has been excluded from the NEWCO3 control group for the reason indicated, yet Investors 1 and 2 clearly have a majority ownership in OLDCO and in NEWCO. The question follows then: If Investors 1 and 2 could have controlled OLDCO *and* NEWCO, has there actually been a change in control?

In applying the objective tests for determining whether there has been a change in control, the NEWCO shareholders were divided into three groups: management, shareholders with a greater percentage of residual interest in NEWCO than they held in OLDCO, and shareholders with the same or lower percentage of residual interest in NEWCO than they held in OLDCO. Each group of shareholders was believed to have characteristics distinct from the other groups.

Management shareholders are presumed to be part of the control group because they are presumed to have the ability to significantly influence the terms of the LBO transaction and the

The following examples illustrate the change in control criterion as described in Section 1(a) of the consensus (all ownership interests are fully diluted).

	OLDCO	NEWCO1	NEWCO2	NEWCO3	NEWCO4
Management	20%	60%	30%	0	40%
Investor 1	40	40	10	45%	20
Investor 2	40	0	0	15	0
Investor 3	0	0	30	20	20
Investor 4	0	0	30	20	20
Total	100%	100%	100%	100%	100%

NEWCO1 would qualify as a change in control under the criterion in Section 1(a)(i) of the consensus guidance (management obtains unilateral control of NEWCO1).

NEWCO2 would qualify as a change in control under the criterion in Section 1(a)(ii) of the consensus guidance because Investors 3 and 4, who are members of the NEWCO2 control group, obtain unilateral control of NEWCO2.

Assuming Investor 2 is not a member of the NEWCO3 control group, for example, because Investor 2 has no capital at risk in NEWCO other than a common stock interest, NEWCO3 would qualify as a change in control under the criterion in Section 1(a)(iii) of the consensus guidance.

NEWCO4 would not qualify as a change in control because management and Investor 1 are in NEWCO4's control group. A subset of the NEWCO4 control group (management and Investor 1) owned a majority voting interest in OLDCO. See Section 1(c) of the consensus guidance for the criteria for inclusion in the control group.

Exhibit 8.2   Examples of the Change in Control Criterion Used in the EITF Consensus on Issue No. 88–16
Source: Reprinted from Exhibit 88–16B of the EITF Consensus.

operations of OLDCO after the LBO transaction. Further, their participation in the LBO transaction indicates a commonality of interest between them and other members of the control group. However, in some instances, management has clearly not participated with the other members of the control group in promoting the LBO transaction, such as when management has pursued its own bid to acquire OLDCO and loses its quest to a rival bidder.

Therefore, in those unusual circumstances, the EITF believed that the commonality of interest linking management with the other members of the control group was absent, and management should not be presumed part of the NEWCO control group.

When the presumption that management is part of the NEWCO control group has been overcome, management is nevertheless considered a single shareholder in applying other tests required by the EITF consensus because management is still considered to have a commonality of interest among its members. This logic would seem to be borne out in situations such as the competing management bid described earlier.

When management is included in the NEWCO control group, it is included without regard to management's ownership interest in NEWCO. That is, there is no de minimis exception provided because of the significant influence that management is deemed to have in controlling NEWCO.

The NEWCO shareholders that have increased their ownership interest in relation to the percentage ownership interest that they had in OLDCO are divided into two groups based on their percentage ownership in NEWCO. This division was made so that shareholders representing the passive investing public could be excluded from the control group.

The NEWCO shareholders that have *decreased* their relative ownership interest were generally perceived as trying to pass control of OLDCO on to new shareholders. For example, the president of OLDCO owns 100 percent of OLDCO's outstanding stock and wants to retire, but either has an interest in retaining an equity kicker or the new owners are unable to borrow sufficient funds to buy out all of the president's equity in OLDCO. However, there were other examples in which it appeared that control was not being passed on to new owners. Accordingly, the EITF devised two tests designed to determine whether a shareholder was aligned with other members of the control group and, therefore, should be included in or excluded from the control group.

The first test, a voting-interest test, is applied to each individual shareholder. It determines whether a shareholder is aligned with other control group members based on the significance of that shareholder's voting ownership interest in NEWCO. This test employs a complicated set of criteria for determining what constitutes a voting interest.

For the individual shareholder being tested, all dilutive securities owned by that shareholder must be considered exercised when calculating the percentage voting interest. This fully diluted amount represents the maximum ownership interest that can be obtained by the shareholder. Dilutive securities held by other shareholders are treated as having been exercised when their terms are no less favorable than the terms of the dilutive securities held by the shareholder being tested. However, the effect of dilution cannot reduce the continuing shareholder's voting interest percentage below that which he can currently exercise.

Rights held by a continuing shareholder to purchase NEWCO stock at fair value at the time of exercise need not be considered in the voting-interest test if such rights are not exercisable for a substantive period of time (currently at least one year).

The second test, a capital-at-risk test, is also applied to individual shareholders. It determines whether a shareholder is aligned with other control group members based on the significance of the shareholder's economic interest in NEWCO. Although authoritative accounting literature defines control and significant influence based on the percentage of voting interest, many believe that a person holding a significant economic interest does have significant influence or may effectively control an entity.

(ii) Subjective Criteria. A basic tenet of accounting theory is that the substance of the transaction, rather than merely its legal form, should prevail in recording the event. For example, the EITF believed it would be inappropriate for a new shareholder to form NEWCO, have NEWCO acquire 100 percent of the outstanding common stock of OLDCO, sell 100 percent of NEWCO's common stock back to the original OLDCO stockholders, and conclude that a change in control had occurred. Accordingly, the EITF identified a number of factors that should be considered in assessing whether the change in control, determined as a result of applying the objective guidance, is truly a substantive change in control.

(iii) No Change in Control. When a change in control has not occurred, the consensus guidance states:

> If a change in control is deemed not to have occurred as a result of applying the above guidance, the transaction should be considered a recapitalization–restructuring for which a change in accounting basis is not appropriate. Refer to Section 1.d of EITF Issue No. 86–16, "Basis in Leveraged Buyout Transactions."

In other words, the transaction is accounted for as what is alternatively referred to as a *redemption, distribution,* or *effective dividend.*

SFAS No. 141(R) nullified EITF Issue No. 86–16.

(f) DETERMINING THE CARRYING AMOUNT OF NEWCO'S INVESTMENT IN OLDCO. The EITF consensus sets forth this general provision:

> The form of a transaction by which the investor obtains its interest in NEWCO does not change the accounting to be applied. In general, if an investor in NEWCO owned a residual interest in OLDCO, then the lesser of that investor's residual interest in OLDCO or NEWCO is carried over at the investor's predecessor basis. [Refer to Section 2 of EITF Issue No. 86–16.]

Again, although the acquisition of OLDCO by NEWCO could take many different forms as a result of legal, tax, or other implications, the EITF concluded that the substance of the transaction should provide the basis for recording the transaction.

The next paragraphs describe the calculation of the carrying amount of NEWCO's investment in OLDCO. They address OLDCO interests acquired from all continuing shareholders (i.e., those OLDCO shareholders who have acquired a NEWCO interest), differentiating between those who are and those who are not part of the NEWCO control group.

Continuing shareholders who are part of the NEWCO control group are viewed as having acquired OLDCO in step fashion. Accordingly, the historical cost accounting principles applicable to a step acquisition are applied. To the extent that a shareholder owns the same percentage of residual interest in NEWCO as in OLDCO, no recordable event has occurred with respect to that residual interest; that is, no exchange has taken place, and the historical cost basis in the OLDCO investment should not be changed. If there is a net increase in ownership, then the carrying amount of NEWCO's investment in OLDCO is generally determined in a manner that is similar to a step acquisition, and the increase in ownership is recorded at fair value.

Some continuing shareholders who are members of the NEWCO control group, however, actually decrease their relative ownership interests. These continuing shareholders are viewed as having retained a portion of their original interest in OLDCO. The portion of the OLDCO investment that has not been disposed of is one in which no exchange has taken place. Accordingly, the proportional historical cost basis for that portion of the investment that is retained is not changed.

Continuing shareholders who are not part of the NEWCO control group are further subdivided between those who own less than 5 percent of NEWCO and those who own 5 percent or more of NEWCO, but who own no more of NEWCO (as a percentage) than they held in OLDCO. (This latter group of shareholders was previously excluded from the control group because they had less than a 20 percent voting interest or less than 20 percent of the cumulative capital at risk in NEWCO.)

The first group, the passive investing public, is not considered party to the step acquisition of OLDCO. Therefore, its OLDCO interests acquired by NEWCO may be valued at fair value. The latter group of shareholders cannot, by prior definition, be considered the passive investing public since it owns 5 percent or more of NEWCO. Although individuals in this group were excluded from the NEWCO control group under the "Change in Control" section (Section 8.4(e)) discussed earlier, they, if viewed as a group, could have significant influence as NEWCO investors. Accordingly, their OLDCO interests will be valued by NEWCO at their predecessor basis if they collectively have significant influence (i.e., they own 20 percent or more) of NEWCO. If they do not collectively have significant influence over NEWCO, then their OLDCO interests may be valued at fair value.

The OLDCO interests acquired by NEWCO from noncontinuing shareholders may be valued at fair value as an exchange has clearly taken place.

In EITF Issue No. 90–12, the Task Force reached a consensus on the question of how NEWCO's investment in OLDCO should be allocated to individual assets and liabilities of OLDCO in an LBO within the scope of Issue No. 88–16, in which a portion of NEWCO's investment in OLDCO is valued at predecessor basis. The Task Force concluded that the allocation should be similar to a step acquisition (partial purchase method). The consensus does not require or change the practice in Issue No. 88–16 applications, retained earnings, and accumulated depreciation are reduced to zero after the allocation.

The SEC observer noted that a partial purchase application would split a net operating loss (NOL) carryforward, whereas in this case the entire NOL carryforward must be viewed as an acquired carryforward.

(g) LIMITATION OF THE CARRYING AMOUNT OF NEWCO'S INVESTMENT IN OLDCO.   The next paragraphs address the valuation of OLDCO based on the ability to validate the value of NEWCO securities issued to acquire OLDCO. Notwithstanding any conclusion reached under the previous section, this section may limit NEWCO's ability to record all or a portion of its investment in OLDCO at fair value. The EITF's general provision is:

> The fair value of any securities issued by NEWCO to acquire OLDCO should be objectively determinable. Fair value should not be used, whether or not the NEWCO securities are publicly traded, unless at least 80% of the fair value of consideration paid to acquire OLDCO equity interests comprises monetary consideration (the monetary test). Refer to Section 3 of EITF Issue No. 86–16.

The EITF consensus defines the element of the numerator and denominator in determining what percentage of the consideration paid by NEWCO constitutes monetary consideration.

If less than 80 percent of the total consideration paid by NEWCO to acquire OLDCO constitutes monetary consideration, then the OLDCO value as reported by NEWCO is limited to the percentage of monetary consideration paid. Accordingly, NEWCO may be required to record a larger portion of its investment in OLDCO at predecessor basis (i.e., larger than that which otherwise results from the application of step-acquisition accounting principles) as a result of an inability to objectively and reliably measure the value of the transaction.

The EITF consensus also addresses circumstances in which NEWCO equity interests have been acquired from OLDCO assets and, therefore, cannot result in NEWCO equity. For example, the controlling NEWCO shareholder may obtain his or her NEWCO equity interest from OLDCO assets by way of a loan or unusual bonus or other payment. In these circumstances, the cash paid results in a debit to NEWCO equity and a credit to the value of the OLDCO investment.

(h) LEVERAGED BUYOUT ACCOUNTING ILLUSTRATED.   Exhibit 8.3 illustrates the application of the EITF consensus guidance. This example is reprinted from Example 5 of Exhibit 88–16F of the EITF consensus. The consensus contains several additional examples of accounting for LBOs.

(i) INTERNATIONAL ACCOUNTING STANDARDS BOARD INTERNATIONAL FINANCIAL REPORTING STANDARD NO. 3, *BUSINESS COMBINATIONS.*   International Financial Reporting Standard (IFRS) No. 3, *Business Combinations,* was issued in March 2004 and superseded International Accounting Standard 22 Business Combinations. IFRS 3 defines a business combination as the bringing together of separate entities or business into one reporting entity. To be accounted for as a combination under IFRS 3, the entity being acquired generally must meet this definition of a business:

an integrated set of activities and assets conducted and managed for the purpose of providing:

a. a return to investors, or
b. lower costs or other economic benefits directly and proportionately to policyholders or participants. [Paragraph 2]

However, certain acquisitions of assets are treated as a combination even if they do not meet this definition. If an entity acquires a group of assets that do not meet the definition of a business, it should allocate the cost of the group of assets among the individual assets based on their relative fair values. If goodwill arises from the transaction, the transaction is accounted for as a business combination.

These types of transactions generally meet IFRS 3's definition of a business combination:

• The purchase of all assets, liabilities and rights to the activities of an entity
• The purchase of some of the assets, liabilities, and rights to activities of an entity that together meet the definition of a business
• The establishment of a new legal entity in which the assets, liabilities, and activities of combined businesses will be held

Like SFAS No. 141(R), IFAS 3 requires the acquisition method to be used for all business combinations.

Differences that exists between the requirements of IFRS 3 and SFAS No. 141(R) in the following areas are provided in Appendix G of SFAS No. 141(R):

• Scope exception for not-for-profit organizations
• Definition of acquirer and identifying the acquirer
• Definition of control
• Definition of fair value
• Operating leases

- Noncontrolling interest in an acquiree
- Assets and liabilities arising from contingencies
- Contingent consideration
- Subsequent measurement and accounting for assets, liabilities, or equity instruments
- Goodwill by reportable segment disclosures

| | OLDCO | | | NEWCO | |
	Shares	Book Value	Fair Value	Shares	Fair Value
Management	24	$ 2,400	$ 2,880	60	$ 2,880
Public	76	7,600	9,120	40	1,920
Total	100	$ 10,000	$ 12,000	100	$ 4,800

Method of Acquisition of OLDCO Interest

Source of cash:	
Debt	$ 7,200
Cash paid to public	$ 7,200
NEWCO common stock issued to public in exchange for OLDCO common stock (40 shares × $48)	1,920
NEWCO common stock issued to management in exchange for OLDCO common stock (60 shares × $48)	2,880
OLDCO fair value	$ 12,000

Application of the 80% Monetary Test

Monetary consideration	$ 7,200
Total consideration	$ 12,000
Portion monetary	60%

Accounting

The transaction meets the criteria of Section 1(a) of the consensus (management obtains unilateral control); therefore, a change in basis is appropriate.

Management's 24% interest should be recorded at predecessor basis in accordance with Section 2 of the consensus. The monetary test in Section 3 of the consensus is not met; therefore, only 60% of the OLDCO interests acquired should be recorded at fair value. The remaining interest acquired from OLDCO public shareholders should be recorded based on OLDCO's book value as a surrogate for public's predecessor basis.

	Percent	Amount
Summary of Accounting		
Valuation:		
Predecessor basis (24 shares × $ 110)	24	$ 2,640
OLDCO book value [(76% − 60%) × $ 10,000]	16	1,600
Fair value (60% × $12,000)	60	(7,200)
Total investment in OLDCO		11,440
Less NEWCO debt		(7,200)
NEWCO equity		$ 4,240
Analysis of NEWCO Equity Account		
Stock issued to management valued at predecessor basis		$ 2,640
Stock issued to public valued at OLDCO book value		1,600
NEWCO equity		$ 4,240

Exhibit 8.3   Example of the Application of the EITF Consensus on Issue No. 88–16
Source: Reprinted from Exhibit 88–16F of the EITF consensus.

Most of the differences identified in this appendix arise because of the board's decision to provide guidance for accounting for business combinations that is consistent with other existing FASB standards or IASB IFRSs. Many of those differences are being considered in current projects or are candidates for future convergence projects, which is why the Boards allowed those differences to continue at this time.

8.5 SOURCES AND SUGGESTED REFERENCES

Accounting Principles Board. APB Opinion No. 15, *Earnings per Share*. New York: AICPA, 1969.

———. APB Opinion No. 16, *Business Combinations*. New York: AICPA, 1970.

———. APB Opinion No. 17, *Intangible Assets*. New York: AICPA, 1970.

———. APB Opinion No. 21, *Interest on Receivables and Payables*. New York: AICPA, 1971.

———. APB Opinion No. 25, *Accounting for Stock Issued to Employees*. New York: AICPA, 1972.

———. Interpretations Nos. 1–39, *Business Combinations: Accounting Interpretations of APB Opinion No. 16*. New York: AICPA, 1970–1973.

American Institute of Certified Public Accountants. Issues Paper, *Pushdown Accounting*. New York: AICPA, 1979.

Baluch, C., et al. "Consolidation Theories and Push-Down Accounting: Achieving Global Convergence," *Journal of Finance and Accountancy*, www.aabri.com/manuscripts/10442.pdf

Devine, M. "Forecasting Post-Combination Earnings: FASB 141(R) Can Have a Dramatic Effect on Future Income Statements," *Journal of Accountancy* (December 2008).

Federal Home Loan Bank Board. R-Memorandum No. 55, *Pushdown Accounting*. Washington, DC: Author, 1983.

Financial Accounting Standards Board. EITF Issue No. 84–35, *Business Combinations: Sale of Duplicate Facilities and Accrual*. Stamford, CT: Author, 1984.

———. EITF Issue No. 84–35a, *Liabilities Accrued in a Purchase Business Combination*. Stamford, CT: Author, 1984.

———. EITF Issue No. 85–21, *Changes of Ownership Resulting in a New Basis of Accounting*. Stamford, CT: Author, 1985.

———. EITF Issue No. 85–45, *Business Combinations: Settlement of Stock Options and Awards*. Stamford, CT: Author, 1986.

———. EITF Issue No. 86–14, *Purchased Research and Development Projects in a Business Combination*. Stamford, CT: Author, 1986.

———. EITF Issue No. 86–16, *Carryover of Predecessor Cost in Leveraged Buyout Transactions*. Stamford, CT: Author, 1986.

———. EITF Issue No. 87–11, *Allocation of Purchase Price to Assets to Be Sold*. Stamford, CT: Author, 1987.

———. EITF Issue No. 88–16, *Basis in Leveraged Buyout Transactions When the Previous Owner's Interest Declines*. Norwalk, CT: Author, 1988.

———. EITF Issue No. 90–5, *Exchange of Ownership Interests Between Entities under Common Control*. Norwalk, CT: Author, April 19, 1990.

———. EITF Issue No. 90–6, *Accounting for Certain Events Not Addressed in Issue No. 87–11, Relating to an Acquired Operating Unit to Be Sold*. Norwalk, CT: Author, September 7, 1990.

———. EITF Issue No. 90–10, *Accounting for a Business Combination Involving a Majority-Owned Investee of a Venture Capital Company*. Norwalk, CT: Author, May 9, 1991.

———. EITF Issue No. 90–12, *Allocating Basis to Individual Assets and Liabilities for Transactions Within the Scope of Issue No. 88–16*. Norwalk, CT: Author, July 12, 1990.

———. EITF Issue No. 90–13, *Accounting for Simultaneous Common Control Mergers*. Norwalk, CT: FASB, September 7, 1990.

———. EITF Issue No. 93–2, *Effect of Acquisition of Employer Shares for/by an Employee Benefit Trust on Accounting for Business Combinations*. Norwalk, CT: Author, 1993.

_____. EITF Issue No. 93–7, *Uncertainties Related to Income Taxes in a Purchase Business Combination*. Norwalk, CT: Author, May 1993.

_____. EITF Issue No. 95–3, *Recognition of Liabilities in Connection with a Purchase Business Combination*. Norwalk, CT: Author, 1995.

_____. EITF Issue No. 95–8, *Accounting for Contingent Consideration Paid to the Shareholders of an Acquired Enterprise in a Purchase Business Combination*. Norwalk, CT:1995.

_____. EITF Issue No. 95–14, *Recognition of Liabilities in Anticipation of a Business Combination*. Norwalk, CT: Author, 1995.

_____. EITF Issue No. 96–7, *Accounting for Deferred Taxes on In-Process Research and Development Activities Acquired in a Purchase Business Combination*. Norwalk, CT: Author, May 23, 1996.

_____. EITF Issue No. 96–8, *Accounting for a Business Combination When the Issuing Company Has Targeted Stock*. Norwalk, CT: Author, May 23, 1996.

_____. EITF Issue No. 97–8, *Accounting for Contingent Consideration Issued in a Purchase Business Combination*. Norwalk, CT: Author, July 23–24, 1997.

_____. Determination of the Useful Life of Renewable Intangible Assets under FASB Statement No. 142, *Goodwill and Other Intangible Assets*, EITF Issue 03–9. Norwalk, CT: FASB, July 31, 2003.

_____. *FASB Special Report—A Guide to Implementation of Statement 109 on Accounting for Income Taxes—Questions and Answers*. Norwalk, CT: Author, March 1992.

_____. FASB Interpretation No. 4, *Applicability of FASB Statement No. 2 to Business Combinations Accounted for by the Purchase Method*. Stamford CT: FASB, 1975

_____. FASB Interpretation No. 9, *Applying APB Opinions No. 16 and 17 When a Savings and Loan Association or a Similar Institution Is Acquired in a Business Combination Accounted for by the Purchase Method*. Stamford, CT: Author, 1976.

_____. FASB Interpretation No. 21, *Accounting for Leases in a Business Combination*. Stamford, CT: Author, 1978.

_____. FASB Technical Bulletin No. 85–5, *Issues Relating to Accounting for Business Combinations*. Stamford, CT: Author, 1985.

_____. Statement of Financial Accounting Standard No. 13, *Accounting for Leases*. Stamford, CT: Author, 1976.

_____. Statement of Financial Accounting Standards No. 2, *Accounting for Research and Development Costs*. Stamford, CT: Author, 1974.

_____. Statement of Financial Accounting Standards No. 5, *Accounting for Contingencies*. Stamford, CT: Author, 1975.

_____. Statement of Financial Accounting Standards No. 38, *Accounting for Preacquisition Contingencies of Purchased Enterprises*. Stamford, CT: Author, 1980.

_____. Statement of Financial Accounting Standards No. 81, *Disclosure of Postretirement Health Care and Life Insurance Benefits*. Stamford, CT: Author, 1984.

_____. Statement of Financial Accounting Standards No. 87, *Employers' Accounting for Pensions*. Stamford, CT: Author, 1985.

_____. Statement of Financial Accounting Standards No. 109, *Accounting for Income Taxes.* Stamford, CT: Author, 1992.

_____. Statement of Financial Accounting Standards No. 112, *Employers' Accounting for Postemployment Benefits*. Norwalk, CT: Author, 1992.

_____. Statement of Financial Accounting Standards No. 115, *Accounting for Certain Investments in Debt and Equity Securities*. Norwalk, CT: Author, 1993.

_____. Statement of Financial Accounting Standards No. 121, *Accounting for the Impairment of Long-Lived Assets and for Long-Lived Assets to Be Disposed Of*. Norwalk, CT: Author, 1995.

_____. Statement of Financial Accounting Standards No. 141, *Business Combinations*. Norwalk, CT: Author, 2001.

_____. Statement of Financial Accounting Standards No. 142, *Goodwill and Other Intangible Assets*. Norwalk, CT: Author, 2001.

_____. Statement of Financial Accounting Standards No. 144, *Accounting for the Impairment or Disposal of Long-Lived Assets*. Norwalk, CT: Author, 2001.

International Accounting Standards Board. International Financial Reporting Standard No. 3, *Business Combinations*. London: Author, 2004.

Jacobs, J. "Accounting for Acquired In-Process R&D under SFAS 141(R)," *CPA Journal* (July 2010).

————. "Business Combinations in a New World," *CPA Journal* (Summer 2008), *www.picpa.org/Content/cpajournal/2008/summer/2.aspx.*

Miller, P. A. "New Day for Business Combinations: Recognizing the Whole Enterprise," *Journal of Accountancy* (June 2008).

Rashty, J., and J. O'Shaughnessy. "Accounting for Deferred Revenue Liabilities in Post-Business Combination Statements," *CPA Journal* (April 2011).

Securities and Exchange Commission. Accounting Series Release No. 146, *Effect of Treasury Stock Transactions on Accounting for Business Combinations*. Washington, DC: Author, 1973.

————. Financial Reporting Release No. 47, *Streamlining Disclosure Requirements Relating to Significant Business Acquisitions*. Washington, DC: Author, 1996.

————. Staff Accounting Bulletin Topic 2, Item A-2 (SAB No. 40), *Determination of the Acquiring Corporation*. Washington, DC: Author, 1981.

————. Staff Accounting Bulletin No. 54, *Application of Pushdown Basis of Accounting in Financial Statements of Subsidiaries Acquired by Purchase*. Washington, DC: Author, 1983.

————. Staff Accounting Bulletin No. 73, *Pushdown Basis of Accounting for Parent Company Debt Related to Subsidiary Acquisition*. Washington, DC: Author, 1987.

————. Staff Accounting Bulletin No. 76, *Effect of Certain De Minimis Sales by Affiliates in Compliance with the Requirements of ASR Nos. 130 and 135*. Washington, DC: Author, 1988.

————. Staff Accounting Bulletin No. 77, *Views Regarding Allocation of Debt Issue Costs in a Business Combination Accounted for as a Purchase*. Washington, DC: Author, 1988.

————. Staff Accounting Bulletin No. 96, *Business Combinations*. Washington, DC: Author, 1996.

————. "Statement of Policy and Interpretations in Regard to Accounting Series Release No. 146," Accounting Series Release No. 146-A. Washington, DC: Author, 1974.

————. "Technical Amendments to Rules, Forms, Schedules, and Codification of Financial Reporting Policies; Final Rule 17 CFR Parts 210, 211, 229 et al.," *Federal Register,* April 23, 2009.

CHAPTER 9

CONSOLIDATION, TRANSLATION, AND THE EQUITY METHOD

James Mraz, CPA, MBA
University of Maryland University College

9.1 OVERVIEW

Consolidation, translation, and the equity method are related sets of accounting practices used mainly in the preparation of consolidated financial statements. While circumstances and guidelines dictate when each of these methods are appropriate when preparing financial statements, there may remain circumstances where selection between the equity versus consolidation accounting methods are not as clear cut.

When nearly identical economic circumstances and relationships exist between entities, one would expect that the methods of accounting for related entities might reflect nearly identical results, but that is not the case all the time. The equity versus consolidation methods can produce different ratios and relationships in the aggregate accounts and can alter user perceptions of key financial benchmarks. Historically, bright-line tests based on ownership have provided guidelines for distinguishing between the accounting alternatives. More recently, qualitative concepts have entered the discussions, making when one method or the other might be appropriate, more fluid and subject to judgment. The fair value option for investments will replace the historical cost basis accounting methods when the consolidation option is exercised for a particular securities investment. When attempting to compare companies, users of financial statements should be mindful of the different presentations these accounting principles can take.

(a) CONSOLIDATION.   Consolidated financial statements present the financial position, results of operations, and cash flows of a consolidated group of companies essentially as if the group were a single enterprise with one or more branches or divisions. With limited exceptions, a consolidated group of companies includes a parent company and all subsidiaries in which the parent company has a direct or indirect controlling financial interest. Because the reporting entity for consolidated financial statements transcends the legal boundaries of single companies, consolidated financial statements have special features that must be considered in preparing and interpreting the statements.

The purpose of consolidated financial statements is to present, primarily for the benefit of the owners and creditors of the parent, the results of operations and the financial position of a parent and all its subsidiaries as if the consolidated group were a single economic entity. There is presumption that consolidated financial statements are more meaningful than separate financial statements and that they are usually necessary for a fair presentation when one of the entities in the consolidated group directly or indirectly has a controlling financial interest in the other entities.

(i) Consolidation Policy.   The usual condition for a controlling financial interest is ownership of a majority voting interest. Therefore, as a general rule, ownership by one entity, directly or indirectly, of more than 50 percent of the outstanding voting shares of another entity is a condition pointing toward consolidation. However, there are exceptions to this general rule. A majority-owned entity should not be consolidated if control does not rest with the majority owner (e.g., if the entity is in legal reorganization or in bankruptcy or operates under foreign exchange restrictions, controls, or other governmentally imposed uncertainties so severe that they cast significant doubt on the parent's ability to control the entity).

All subsidiaries—that is, all entities in which a parent has a controlling financial interest—should generally be consolidated. Today this includes subsidiaries in different lines of business from other entities. For example, a finance subsidiary of a manufacturing company used to be excludable based on its being in a different line of business. But today the general thinking is to consolidate this entity.

Control of an entity can be obtained either by obtaining (1) ownership of a majority of its outstanding voting interests (the controlled entity is referred to as a voting interest entity), or (2) contractual rights to receive the majority of the financial benefits and/or assuming contractual obligations to bear the majority of the financial consequences that occur in the future from the entity outperforming or underperforming its expectations (the controlled entity is referred to as a variable interest entity [VIE]).

Investments in unconsolidated subsidiaries, like other investments that give an investor the ability to exercise significant influence over the investee's operating and financial activities, are accounted for by the equity method, which is discussed in Section 9.1(d).

The fact that a particular subsidiary is located in a foreign country, has a large minority interest, or engages in principal activities substantially different from those of its parent is irrelevant to the consolidation requirement. That was not always the case, however. Until 1988, those factors were quite relevant and, indeed, were considered to be legitimate reasons for excluding a particular subsidiary from consolidation. The rules were changed by the issuance of Statement of Financial Accounting (SFAS) No. 94, *Consolidation of All Majority-Owned Subsidiaries,* and that no longer is the case. SFAS No. 94 (broadly, Financial Accounting Standards Board [FASB] Accounting Standards Codification [ASC] 810) requires consolidation of all majority-owned subsidiaries unless control is temporary or does not rest with the majority owners.

A difference in fiscal periods of a parent and a majority-owned subsidiary does not in itself justify the subsidiary's exclusion from consolidation. In that case, the subsidiary has to prepare, for consolidation purposes, financial statements for a period that corresponds with or closely approaches the parent's fiscal period.

If, however, where the difference between the parent's and the subsidiary's fiscal periods is not more than about three months, is usually is acceptable to use, for consolidation purposes, the subsidiary's financial statements for its fiscal period; when this is done, recognition should be given by disclosure or otherwise regarding the effect of any intervening events that materially affect consolidated financial position or results of operations.

(ii) Intercompany Amounts.   Only legal entities can own assets, owe liabilities, issue capital stock, earn revenues, enjoy gains, and incur expenses and losses. A group of companies as such cannot do those things. So the elements of consolidated financial statements are the elements of the financial statements of the members of the consolidated group of companies—the parent company and its consolidated subsidiaries. They are the assets owned by the member companies; the liabilities owed by the member companies; the equity of the member companies; and the revenues, expenses, gains, and losses of the member companies.

Some elements of the financial statements of member companies are not elements of the consolidated financial statements, however. The elements of the financial statements of a reporting entity are relationships and changes in relationships between the reporting entity and outside entities. But some elements of the financial statements of members of a consolidated group are relationships and changes in relationships between member companies, called *intercompany amounts.* (They would more accurately be described as intragroup amounts.) Intercompany amounts are excluded from consolidated financial statements.

It is convenient to prepare consolidated financial statements by starting with the financial statements of the member companies, which include intercompany amounts. The intercompany amounts are removed by adjustments and eliminations in consolidation. The items are:

- *Investment elimination.* This area includes the parent's investment in subsidiary and subsidiary's equity accounts. The retained earnings or deficit of a subsidiary at the date of acquisition by the parent is not included in consolidated retained earnings.
- *Intercompany receivables and payables.* This area includes debts of member companies to other member companies.
- *Intercompany advances.* These include advances to and from subsidiaries and advances to and from the parent company.

- *Intercompany sales purchases of inventories, fees, rents, interest, and the like.* This area includes sales of goods or provision of services from member companies to other member companies.
- *Intercompany profits.* These are the profits recorded by member companies in transactions with other member companies reflected in recorded amounts of assets of member companies at the reporting date.
- *Intercompany dividends.* These are dividends from members of the consolidated group to other members of the consolidated group.

After the intercompany amounts are eliminated, the consolidated financial statements present solely relationships and changes in relationships with entities outside the consolidated reporting entity. They present:

- Amounts receivable from and amounts payable to outside entities
- Investments in outside entities
- Other assets helpful in carrying out activities with outside entities
- Consolidated equity equal to the excess of those assets over those liabilities
- Changes in those assets, liabilities, and equity, including profits realized or losses incurred by dealings with outside entities

Consolidated financial statements present the financial affairs of a consolidated group of companies united for economic activity by common control.

(iii) Variable Interest Entities.   In 2003, the FASB issued FASB Interpretation (FIN) No. 46 (Revised December 2003), *Consolidation of Variable Interest Entities (VIEs)—An Interpretation of Accounting Research Bulletin (ARB) No. 51* (FASB ASC 810-10-05), to clarify the circumstances where and how VIEs should be consolidated. As defined in paragraph 2c of FIN-46R, interests in a VIE are contractual, ownership, or other interests in an entity that change with changes in the fair value of the entity's net assets, thus the term *variable interest entity*. VIEs are often are created for a specific purpose (e.g., to facilitate the securitization of receivables). In FIN-46R, VIEs are defined by the nature and amount of their equity investment and the rights and obligations of their equity investors. In June 2009, SFAS No. 167, *Amendments to FASB Interpretation No. 46(R)* (ASC 810), made several changes to FIN 46-R.

Paragraph 3b of SFAS No. 167 stipulates that the enterprise with a variable interest or interests that provide the enterprise with a controlling financial interest in a variable interest entity will have both of these characteristics:

a. The power to direct the activities of a variable interest entity that most significantly impact the entity's economic performance

b. The obligation to absorb losses of the entity that could potentially be significant to the variable interest entity or the right to receive benefits from the entity that could potentially be significant to the variable interest entity.

Entities deemed VIEs must follow the provisions of FIN-46R as amended by SFAS No. 167. Entities are deemed VIEs if they meet three requirements.

1. They should not be self-supportive, as in these instances:
  - The entity is thinly capitalized (i.e., the equity is insufficient to fund the entity's activities without additional subordinated financial support); or
  - The equity holders as a group possess at least one of the these five characteristics:
    a. Have insufficient equity investment at risk
    b. Have inadequate rights to make significant decisions about the entity's activities

    c. Possess no substantive voting rights

    d. Fail to absorb the prorated share of the entity's expected losses

    e. Fail to receive the prorated share of the entity's expected residual returns

2. The entities must have variable interests in the VIE (e.g., provide it with financial support).

3. The entity must be the VIE's primary beneficiary (e.g., one absorbing more than half of expected losses or receiving more than half of expected residual returns). If neither entity assumes more than half of the expected losses or expected gains, then there is no primary beneficiary and, therefore, no consolidation exists.

The issue of accounting for such entities received considerable public attention and accounting focus after revelations about the role of certain unconsolidated entities in possibly obscuring the underlying economic effect of certain transactions relating to Enron's financial statements. FIN-46R will make it harder to exclude debt from the balance sheet via specialized finance affiliates and likely will require more entities to be consolidated.

Entities holding a majority of voting stock will still follow the ownership-based guidelines for consolidation in ARB No. 51, *Consolidated Financial Statements.*

Variable interests may include:

- Investments in common or preferred stock
- Loans or notes
- Guarantees
- Certain insurance contracts and derivative contracts
- Leases, and service or management contracts

Not all entities that qualify as VIEs are consolidated. For example, when a VIE has sufficient equity at risk such that the VIE can operate on a stand-alone basis, there may be no need for another entity to consolidate the VIE.

This topic continues to be a complex area of practice. Familiarity with the interpretation's concepts and requirements is evolving, but FIN-46R provides much-needed guidance to shore up perceived weaknesses in the consolidation requirements when VIEs exist.

FIN-46R also identifies certain required disclosures for primary beneficiaries as well as for unconsolidated VIEs.

(iv) Disclosures. Paragraph 38 of SFAS No. 160, *Noncontrolling Interests in Consolidated Financial Statements,* stipulates that a parent with one or more less-than-wholly-owned subsidiaries should disclose for each reporting period:

    a. Separately, on the face of the consolidated financial statements, the amounts of consolidated net income and consolidated comprehensive income and the related amounts of each attributable to the parent and the noncontrolling interest (paragraphs A4 and A5).

    b. Either in the notes or on the face of the consolidated income statement, amounts attributable to the parent for the following, if reported in the consolidated financial statements (paragraph A4):

      (1) Income from continuing operations

      (2) Discontinued operations

      (3) Extraordinary items

    c. Either in the consolidated statement of changes in equity, if presented, or in the notes to consolidated financial statements, a reconciliation at the beginning and the end of the period of the carrying amount of total equity (net assets), equity (net assets) attributable to the parent, and equity (net assets) attributable to the noncontrolling interest. That reconciliation shall separately disclose (paragraph A6):

      (1) Net income

      (2) Transactions with owners acting in their capacity as owners, showing separately contributions from and distributions to owners

(3) Each component of other comprehensive income.

d. In notes to the consolidated financial statements, a separate schedule that shows the effects of any changes in a parent's ownership interest in a subsidiary on the equity attributable to the parent (paragraph A7).

Also, a member of a consolidated group that files a consolidated tax return discloses the next information related to income taxes in its own separately issued financial statements:

- The amount of current and deferred tax expense for each statement of earnings presented and any tax-related balances due to or from other group members as of each balance sheet date
- The principal provisions of the method by which the consolidated amount of current and deferred tax expense is allocated to members of the consolidated group and the nature and effect of any changes in that method

Paragraph 22E of SFAS No. 167 stipulates that in addition to disclosures required by other standards, an enterprise that is a primary beneficiary of a variable interest entity16c or an enterprise that holds a variable interest in a variable interest entity but is not the entity's primary beneficiary shall disclose:

a. Its methodology for determining whether the enterprise is the primary beneficiary of a variable interest entity, including, but not limited to, significant judgments and assumptions made. For example, one way to meet this disclosure requirement would be to provide information about the types of involvements an enterprise considers significant, supplemented with information about how the significant involvements were considered in determining whether the enterprise is the primary beneficiary.

b. If facts and circumstances change such that the conclusion to consolidate a variable interest entity has changed in the most recent financial statements (for example, the variable interest entity was previously consolidated and is not currently consolidated), the primary factors that caused the change and the effect on the enterprise's financial statements.

c. Whether the enterprise has provided financial or other support (explicitly or implicitly) during the periods presented to the variable interest entity that it was not previously contractually required to provide or whether the enterprise intends to provide that support, including:

1. The type and amount of support, including situations in which the enterprise assisted the variable interest entity in obtaining another type of support

2. The primary reasons for providing the support.

d. Qualitative and quantitative information about the enterprise's involvement (giving consideration to both explicit arrangements and implicit variable interests) with the variable interest entity, including, but not limited to, the nature, purpose, size, and activities of the variable interest entity, and how the entity is financed.

(b) BUSINESS COMBINATIONS.   A company can start a subsidiary by having it incorporated and investing resources in it. Including such a subsidiary in consolidated financial statements presents no special problem. The amount of the investment recorded by the parent company equals the initial equity of the subsidiary, each of which is eliminated in consolidation. Business combinations are the subject of Chapter 8 in this *Handbook.*

(c) TRANSLATION.   According to Paragraph 4 of SFAS No. 52, *Foreign Currency Translation,* the translation of the financial statements of each component entity of an enterprise should accomplish two objectives. It should:

1. Provide information that is generally compatible with the expected economic effects of a rate change on an enterprise's cash flows and equity

2. Reflect in consolidated statements the financial results and relationships of the individual consolidated entities as measured in their functional currencies in conformity with U.S. generally accepted accounting principles (GAAP)

Current accounting standards require that the translation adjustment (gain or loss) be reported currently in income or deferred as a component of stockholders' equity, depending on the method used to translate the accounts. The appropriate method is not a free choice but rather is dictated by the circumstances as described in SFAS No. 52 (ASC 830-30-45-12).

Financial statements of a parent company are stated in the domestic unit of currency, such as the U.S. dollar for U.S. parent companies. Financial statements of a foreign subsidiary are stated in a foreign unit of currency, a unit of currency other than the domestic unit of currency, such as the U.K. pound for U.K. subsidiaries. Such foreign currency financial statements cannot be consolidated with domestic currency financial statements; the result would be a set of financial statements stated in more than one unit of currency, which would make them unintelligible.

Before the financial statements of a foreign subsidiary can be consolidated with those of its parent company, therefore, the amounts in its foreign currency financial statements are changed to amounts stated in the domestic unit of currency. Changing the amounts from those stated in the foreign unit of currency to those stated in the domestic unit of currency is called *translation,* analogous to translation from one language to another. Translation is discussed and illustrated in Section 9.2.

Translation uses foreign exchange rates. Such rates are ratios of exchange, prices of units of one kind of currency in terms of units of another kind of currency, such as $(U.S.) 1.50 for £(U.K.) 1. Foreign exchange rates change, as all other prices do. That causes two problems in translation: (1) how to select the foreign exchange rates to use for translation; and (2) how to treat translation differences, which are defined as items unique to translated financial statements caused by translating amounts in a single set of financial statements at two or more foreign exchange rates.

(d) EQUITY METHOD. The equity method is used to account for investments that give an investor the ability to exercise significant influence over the investee's operating and financial activities, including investments in majority-owned subsidiaries that do not qualify for consolidation. The investee may be a corporation, a partnership, or a joint venture. An investment accounted for by the equity method is initially recorded at cost. After that, the investment's carrying amount is increased or decreased for the investor's share of changes in the underlying net assets of the investee and for certain other transactions and other events. Principles relating to the equity method are discussed in Section 9.3.

(e) COMBINED FINANCIAL STATEMENTS. Circumstances exist in which combined financial statements of commonly controlled corporations are likely to be more meaningful than their separate financial statements. Such circumstances include, for example, ownership by one person of a controlling interest in several corporations related in their operations.

If combined financial statements are prepared, they present only relationships and changes in relationships with entities outside the combined group. That means that intercompany sales and purchases, profit, and receivables and payables are eliminated. Intercompany stockholdings, if any, are eliminated.

The separate components of equity of each corporation are aggregated with the corresponding separate components of the other corporations. Presentation of a table showing each corporation's portion of each component of combined equity in either the balance sheet or the notes, though not required by the authoritative accounting literature, would likely enhance the usefulness of the combined statements.

(f) CONSOLIDATING STATEMENTS. If all else fails to present information on a group of related companies in a helpful way, consolidating statements are often used as an effective means of presenting the pertinent information. Such statements are essentially presentations as in worksheets used to derive consolidated financial statements together with notes and other kinds of necessary disclosures.

(g) SECURITIES AND EXCHANGE COMMISSION RULES AND REGULATIONS ON CONSOLIDATED FINANCIAL STATEMENTS.   Beyond the concepts and procedures involving all consolidated financial statements, the Security and Exchange Commission (SEC), in its Regulation S-X § 210.3A-02, has published regulations for registrants that file their consolidated financial statements with the commission.

(i) Selection of Reporting Entity.   The rules require that the application of principles for inclusion of subsidiaries in consolidated financial statements "clearly exhibit the financial position and results of operations of the registrant and its subsidiaries." A company not majority owned may not be consolidated. A subsidiary whose financial statements are as of a date or for periods different from those of the registrant may not be consolidated unless all the next conditions apply:

- The difference is not more than 93 days.
- The closing date of the subsidiary's financial information is expressly indicated.
- The necessity for using different closing dates is briefly explained.

Due consideration must be given to consolidating foreign subsidiaries operating under political, economic, or currency restrictions. If such foreign subsidiaries are consolidated, the effects, if determinable, of foreign exchange restrictions on the consolidated financial position and results of operations must be disclosed.

(ii) Intercompany Items and Transactions.   Intercompany items and transactions between members of a consolidated group generally are eliminated in consolidated financial statements, and unrealized intercompany profits and losses on transactions with investees accounted for by the equity method are also eliminated. If such items are not eliminated, the registrant is required to state its reason for not doing so.

(iii) Other Disclosures.   The SEC rules require brief descriptions in the notes to consolidated financial statements of the principles of consolidation followed and any changes in principles or in the composition of the companies constituting the consolidated group since the last set of consolidated financial statements was filed with the commission.

The rules require that consolidated financial statements also present:

- An explanation and reconciliation of differences between (1) the amount at which investments in consolidated subsidiaries are carried on the registrant's books and (2) the equity of the registrant in the assets and liabilities of the subsidiaries
- An explanation and reconciliation between (1) dividends received from unconsolidated subsidiaries and (2) earnings of unconsolidated subsidiaries
- An analysis of minority interest in capital stock, in retained earnings, and in net income of consolidated subsidiaries

9.2 FOREIGN CURRENCY TRANSLATION

A subsidiary or another unit within a consolidated group of companies (or within a company or an affiliated group of companies), such as a joint venture, a division, or a branch, may be a foreign operation, an operating unit that prepares foreign currency financial statements. Before such statements can be included in domestic currency consolidated financial statements, they ordinarily have to be translated into the domestic currency used in the consolidated financial statements, the currency of the parent company's country. SFAS No. 52 sets forth current GAAP for translation. (See FASBs ASC 830 and 830-30-40.)

(a) OBJECTIVES OF TRANSLATION. SFAS No. 52 states objectives to be achieved in translation in the face of changes in foreign exchange rates and ratios of exchange between two currencies. The principles in SFAS No. 52 were adopted with the intention: that the translation of the financial statements of each component entity of an enterprise should accomplish three objectives:

1. Provide information that is generally compatible with the expected economic effects of a rate change on an enterprise's cash flows and equity.
2. Reflect in consolidated statements the financial results and relationships of the individual consolidated entities as measured in their *functional currencies in conformity with U.S. GAAP.*
3. Present the consolidated financial statements of an enterprise in conformity with U.S. generally accepted accounting principles.

In SFAS No. 52, the FASB also considered whether to adopt another objective:

To use a "single unit of measure" for financial statements that include translated foreign amounts. (par. 70d)

The FASB did not adopt that objective (par. 75). It forces accountants to put into financial statements the equivalent of the four objectives. The FASB not only acknowledged that the principles in SFAS No. 52 require accountants to violate the single-unit-of-measure rule of arithmetic but defended it strenuously:

[The FASB] believes that, for an enterprise operating in multiple currency environments, a true "single unit of measure" does not, as a factual matter, exist.... The Board concluded that for many foreign entities, adhering to a "single unit of measure" was artificial and illusory. (pars. 85, 88)

But no unit of measure exists until it is defined for the purpose at hand. Moreover, if no single unit of measure could be soundly defined for multiple-currency environments, sound consolidation or combinations involving foreign operations would be impossible.

The single unit of measure should be the unit used in the parent company's financial statements.

(b) ASSUMPTIONS CONCERNING TRANSLATION. SFAS No. 52 states these assumptions concerning translation on which its principles are based:

- *Two types of foreign operations.* Foreign operations are of two types, which differ from each other so much that translation procedures for the two types have to differ. The two types are (1) self-contained and integrated foreign operations and (2) components or extensions of the parent company's domestic operations.
- *Self-contained and integrated foreign operations.* A foreign operation may be relatively self-contained and integrated in a foreign country. Such an operation should be treated in consolidated financial statements as a net investment of the parent company. The entire net investment, not merely certain assets and liabilities of the foreign operation, is exposed to the risk of changes in the exchange rate between the currency of the foreign country and the domestic currency. Though such changes affect the parent company's net investment, they do not affect its cash flows. The effects of such changes on a foreign operation should therefore be excluded from reported consolidated net income unless the parent company sells part or all of its investment in the foreign operation or completely or substantially liquidates its investment in the foreign operation.
- *Components or extensions of parent company domestic operations.* A foreign operation may be a direct and integral component or an extension of the parent company's domestic operations, such as an import or export business. It should be treated as an integral part of the parent

company's operations. Changes in the exchange rate between the currency of the country in which the foreign operation is conducted and the domestic currency directly affect certain individual assets and liabilities of the foreign operation (e.g., its foreign currency receivables and payables) and thereby affect the parent company's cash flows. The effects should be recognized currently in reported consolidated net income.

- *Functional currencies.* The most meaningful measuring unit for the assets, liabilities, and operations of a foreign operation is the currency of the primary economic environment in which the operation is conducted, its functional currency. Consolidated financial statements should therefore use one measuring unit for each functional currency of the operating units in the consolidated group of companies, including the domestic currency, which is the functional currency of the parent company. If only one measuring unit were used, the resulting information generally would be incompatible with the expected effects of changes in foreign exchange rates on the parent company's cash flows and equity. It would therefore be contrary to the basic objective of translation.

- *Highly inflationary economies.* Currencies of countries with highly inflationary economies are unsatisfactory as measuring units for financial reporting. A highly inflationary economy is one that has cumulative inflation of approximately 100 percent or more over three years. An operation in the environment of such a currency should be treated as if the domestic currency were its functional currency.

- *Effective hedges.* Some contracts, transactions, and balances are, in effect, hedges of foreign exchange risks. They should be treated that way regardless of their form.

(c) TASKS REQUIRED FOR TRANSLATION.   SFAS No. 52 (par. 69) states that to achieve the objectives of translation and to conform with its functional currency approach assumptions, four major tasks are required for each foreign operation:

1. Identifying the functional currency of the economic environment
2. Measuring all elements of the financial statements in the functional currency
3. Using the current exchange rate for translating from the functional currency to the reporting currency, if they are different
4. Distinguishing the economic impact of changes in exchange rates on a net investment from the impact of such changes on individual assets and liabilities that are receivable or payable in currencies other than the functional currency

(i) Identifying the Functional Currency.   SFAS No. 52 indicates that identifying the functional currency of a foreign operation by determining the primary economic environment in which the entity operates; normally, that is the currency of the environment in which an entity primarily generates and expends cash. Management is in the best position to obtain the pertinent facts and weigh their relative importance in determining the function currency for each operation. Economic factors are considered both individually and collectively to determine the functional currency, so that the financial results and relationships are measured with the greatest degree of relevance and reliability.

Exercise of management's judgment is simplified if a foreign operation is either clearly self-contained and integrated in a particular foreign country, so that the currency of that country obviously is its functional currency, or clearly a direct and integral component or extension of the parent company's operations, so that the domestic currency obviously is its functional currency.

On the other hand, a single subsidiary of a financial institution might have relatively self-contained and integrated operations in each of several different countries. In these circumstances each operation may be considered to be an entity as that term is used in SFAS No. 52; and, based on the facts and circumstances, each operation might have a different functional currency.

The functional currency of a foreign operation normally is the currency of the environment in which it primarily generates and expends cash. But sometimes observable facts are ambiguous in pointing to the functional currency. For example, if a foreign operation conducts significant amounts of business in two or more currencies, its functional currency might not be easily identifiable. For those operations, individual economic facts and circumstances need to be assessed.

SFAS No. 52, Appendix A, paragraph 42 provides guidance for making those assessments in particular circumstances. The guidance is grouped in sets of indicators: cash flow indicators, sales price indicators, sales market indicators, expense indicators, financing indicators, and intercompany transactions and arrangements indicators.

(ii) Remeasurement into the Functional Currency. Paragraph 12 of SFAS No. 52 requires that all of a foreign entity's assets and liabilities shall be translated from the entity's functional currency into the reporting currency using the current exchange rate. This paragraph also requires that revenues, expenses, gains, and losses be translated using the rates on the dates on which those elements are recognized during the period.

Most foreign operations prepare their financial statements in their functional currencies. Some, however, prepare their financial statements in other foreign currencies. Before the financial statements of a foreign operation are translated from its functional currency to the domestic currency, its foreign currency financial statements obviously have to be stated in its functional currency. If its financial statements are stated in another currency because its records are maintained in the other currency, they have to be remeasured into the functional currency before translation.

- *Remeasurement* is the process of translating the amounts of a foreign entity into its functional currency when they are stated in another currency.
- *Translation* is when accounts measured in the functional currency are translated converted into the reporting currency using the current rate method.

SFAS No. 52 (par. 10) states that the goal of remeasurement is "to produce the same results as if the entity's books of record had been maintained in the functional currency."

Remeasurement requires, as does translation, use of foreign exchange rates. For remeasurement, they are the rates between the foreign currency in which the financial statements of a foreign operation are stated and its foreign functional currency. Unlike translation, however, remeasurement requires the use of historical foreign exchange rates in addition to the current foreign exchange rate. Historical rates are rates at dates before the reporting date as of which certain financial statement items are recorded, such as items recorded at acquisition cost.

Three steps are involved in remeasurement.

1. Amounts to be remeasured at historical rates are distinguished from amounts to be remeasured at current rates.
2. The amounts are remeasured using the historical and current rates, as appropriate.
3. To recognize currently in income all exchange gains and losses from remeasurement of monetary assets and liabilities that are not denominated in the functional currency.

Amounts remeasured at historical rates generally are those stated in historical terms, such as acquisition cost, and related revenue and expenses, such as depreciation.

SFAS No. 52 specifies that amounts resulting from interperiod income tax allocation and amounts related to unamortized policy acquisition costs of stock life insurance companies are to be remeasured using the current rate.

To remeasure an amount recorded in a currency other than the functional currency at the lower of cost and market, its cost in the foreign currency is first remeasured using the historical exchange rate. That amount is compared with market in the functional currency, and the remeasured amount is written down if market value is lower than the remeasured cost. If the item had been written down in the records because the market was less than the cost in the currency in which it was recorded, the write-down is reversed if the market in the functional currency is more than the remeasured cost.

If an item is written down to market in the functional currency, the resulting amount is treated as cost in subsequent periods in which it is held in applying the lower of the cost and market rule.

The financial statements of a foreign operation in a highly inflationary economy are remeasured to the domestic currency in the same way they would be remeasured were the domestic currency its functional currency.

(iii) Translation Using the Current Rate.   Amounts remeasured into the domestic currency need not be translated, because the domestic currency is used as the reporting currency in the consolidated financial statements. Amounts measured in a foreign currency or remeasured into a foreign currency are all translated using the current foreign exchange rate between the foreign currency and the domestic currency.

For assets and liabilities, that is the rate at the reporting date. For income statement items, that is the rates as of the dates during the reporting period at which the items are recorded. An appropriately weighted average rate may be used to translate such items if they are numerous.

(iv) Translation Adjustments.   Translation adjustments arise from either consolidation or equity method accounting for a net investment in another entity having a different functional currency from that of the investor.[1] Translation adjustments result from the process of translating all amounts in foreign currency financial statements from the functional currency to U.S. dollars. Remeasurement of a foreign operation's foreign currency financial statements involves recognition in current income of exchange gains and losses. In contrast, translation adjustments are not recognized in current income but are accumulated in a separate component of equity.

The translation adjustments pertaining to a foreign operation are transferred from equity to gain or loss on disposition of the foreign operation when it is partly or completely sold or completely or substantially liquidated.

(d) TREATMENT OF FOREIGN COMPONENTS OR EXTENSIONS OF PARENT COMPANY OPERATIONS.   The functional currency of a foreign operation that is a component or extension of the parent company's operations is the domestic currency. If the foreign component prepares its financial statements in a foreign currency, those financial statements are remeasured into the domestic currency by procedures discussed earlier in Section 9.2(c)(ii). No translation is required for such a foreign operation.

(e) TREATMENT OF FOREIGN CURRENCY TRANSACTIONS.   Some transactions of a unit in a consolidated group of companies may take place in a currency other than the functional currency of the unit. For example, a unit whose functional currency is the Mexican peso may buy a machine on credit for U.K. pounds or may sell securities on credit for euros. Except in a forward exchange contract (discussed in Section 9.2(f)), the amounts in such a foreign currency transaction are measured at the transaction date at the foreign exchange rate at that date—in the example, between the peso and the pound or between the peso and the euro.

At the next reporting date or at an intervening date at which the receivable or payable is settled, the receivable or payable is remeasured at the rate current at that date. Changes in its amount as measured in the functional currency since the previous reporting date or an intervening date at which it was acquired are transaction gains or losses, to be included in current reported consolidated net income, except as discussed later in Section 9.2(f)(ii) .

To illustrate: Corporation P, whose functional currency is U.S. dollars, borrowed £(U.K.)1,000,000 on January 1, 20X1, and agreed to repay £100,000 on December 31, 20X1, and £1,100,000 on December 31, 20X2. Exchange rates were \$1.60/£1 at January 1, 20X1, and \$1.50/£1 at December 31, 20X1.

The payment of £100,000 on December 31, 20X1, is remeasured as interest expense of \$150,000. The liability in dollars at December 31, 20X1, is remeasured for the change in exchange rate and a transaction gain of \$100,000 is determined, for presentation in P's income statement for the year 20X1, as shown in Exhibit 9.1.

---

[1] See SFAS No. 52, Appendix C, paragraph 110.

		U.S. Dollars
Liability		
January 1, 20X1	£1,000,000 × $1.60/£1 =	$1,600,000
December 31, 20X1	£1,000,000 × $1.50/£1 =	1,500,000
Transaction gain		$ 100,000

Exhibit 9.1   Corporation P, Transaction Gain on Forward Exchange Contracts for the Year 20X1

(f) FORWARD EXCHANGE CONTRACTS.   Forward exchange contracts are contracts that require currencies of two countries to be traded in specified amounts at specified future dates and specified rates, called *forward rates*. Such contracts are foreign currency transactions that require special treatment.

Agreements that are, in substance, essentially the same as forward contracts (e.g., currency swaps) are accounted for in a manner similar to the accounting for forward contracts.

(i) Discounts or Premiums on Forward Exchange Contracts.   A forward exchange contract may involve a discount or premium. The discount or premium on a forward contract is the foreign currency amount of the contract multiplied by the difference between the contracted forward rate and the spot rate at the date of inception of the contract. Ordinarily, a discount or premium is allocated to income over the duration of the forward exchange contract. However, a discount or premium may be treated differently in two circumstances:

1. *If the contract is designated as and is effective as a hedge of a net investment in a foreign operation* (discussed later in Section 9.2(g)). If so, the discount or premium may be included with translation adjustments and thus not be reported in income.

2. *If the contract meets the tests of a hedge of an identifiable foreign currency commitment* (also discussed later in Section 9.2(g)(ii)). If so, the discount or premium may be included in the amount at which the foreign currency transaction related to the commitment is stated.

Paragraph 18 of SFAS No. 52 had provided the reporting entity the option to amortize the discount or premium of a derivative that is used as the hedging instrument.

However, SFAS No. 133 does not permit the premium or discount (also referred to as the forward points) on a foreign currency forward contract that is used to hedge the foreign exchange exposure of the entity's net investment in foreign operations to be accounted for separately. It supersedes paragraph 18 in SFAS No. 52 and requires all derivatives to be reported at fair value.

(ii) Gains or Losses on Forward Exchange Contracts.   A gain or loss on a forward exchange contract to be reported in the current reporting period is computed, except for a speculative forward contract, by multiplying the foreign currency amount of the forward contract by the difference between the spot rate at the balance sheet date and the spot rate at the date of inception of the forward contract (or the spot rate last used to measure a gain or loss on that contract for an earlier period). A gain or loss on a forward exchange contract is recognized in income as a transaction gain or loss in the period of the gain or loss, unless it is in one of the categories of transaction gains and losses excluded from net income, discussed later in Section 9.2(g).

To illustrate a forward exchange contract: On January 1, 20X1, P and Q enter into a contract in which Q agrees to buy £(U.K.)1,000,000 from P for $(U.S.)1,550,000, incorporating a forward rate of $1.55/£1, on December 31, 20X2. The exchange rate at January 1, 20X1, is $1.60/£1. The contract therefore involves a premium to P and a discount to Q of £1,000,000 × ($1.60/£1 − $1.55/£1) = $50,000.

Q makes this entry:

Foreign currency receivable	$1,600,000	
Payable to P		$1,550,000
Discount on foreign exchange contract		50,000

P makes this entry:

Receivable from Q	$1,550,000	
Premium on foreign exchange contract	50,000	
Foreign currency payable		$1,600,000

P and Q allocate the $50,000 to forward exchange gain or loss over the years 20X1 and 20X2. P makes this entry in each of the two years:

Amortization of premium on forward exchange contract	$25,000	
Premium on forward exchange contract		$25,000

Q makes this opposite entry in each of the two years:

Discount on forward exchange contract	$25,000	
Amortization of discount on forward exchange contract		$25,000

The exchange rate changes to $1.50/£1 at December 31, 20X1, and $1.45/£1 at December 31, 20X2. P records these entries based on the changes in the exchange rate:

December 31, 20X1		
Foreign currency payable	$100,000	
Forward exchange gain		$100,000
£1,000,000 × ($1.60/£1 − $1.50/£1) = $100,000		
December 31, 20X2		
Foreign currency payable	$ 50,000	
Forward exchange gain		$ 50,000
£1,000,000 × ($1.50/£1 − $1.45/£1) = $50,000		

Q records these opposite entries based on the changes in the exchange rate:

December 31, 20X1		
Forward exchange loss	$100,000	
Foreign currency receivable		$100,000
December 31, 20X2		
Forward exchange loss	$ 50,000	
Foreign currency receivable		$ 50,000

On settlement of the contract on December 31, 20X2, P makes this entry:

Foreign currency payable	$1,450,000	
Cash	$ 100,000	
Receivable from Q		$1,550,000

to record payment of $1,450,000 to buy £1,000,000 to give to Q, receipt of $1,550,000 from Q, and cancellation of the forward exchange receivable from Q.

Q makes this opposite entry:

Payable to P	$1,550,000	
Foreign currency receivable		$1,450,000
Cash		100,000

	Gain by P, Loss by Q, U.S. Dollars
Foreign exchange gain or loss on contract:	
Year 20X1—£1,000,000 × ($1.60/£1 − $1.50/£1) =	$100,000
Year 20X1—£1,000,000 × ($1.50/£1 − $1.45/£1) =	50,000
	150,000
Premium or discount on contract	(50,000)
Net gain or loss over the life of the contract	$100,000

Exhibit 9.2   Corporation P or Corporation Q, Gain or Loss on Forward Exchange Contracts Beginning in the Year 20X1

to record receipt of $1,450,000 on sale of £1,000,000 received from P, payment of $1,550,000 to P, and cancellation of the forward exchange payable to P.

The contract may be summarized as shown in Exhibit 9.2.

The net gain of P and loss of Q of $100,000 equal the difference between the forward rate and the rate on the settlement date times the amount of currency transferred:

$$(\$1.55/£1 − \$1.45/£1) \times £1,000,000 = 100,000$$

(g) EXCLUSION OF TRANSACTION GAINS AND LOSSES FROM INCOME.   Gains and losses on some foreign currency transactions are not recognized in income when they occur.

Gains and losses on these foreign currency transactions are not included in determining net income:

a. Foreign currency transactions that are designated as, and are effective as, economic hedges of a net investment in a foreign entity, commencing as of the designation date

b. Intercompany foreign currency transactions that are of a long-term investment nature (i.e., settlement is not planned or anticipated in the foreseeable future), when the entities to the transaction are consolidated, combined, or accounted for by the equity method in the reporting enterprise's financial statements

(i) Treatment as Translation Adjustments.   SFAS No. 52 (par. 20) requires gains and losses on the following foreign currency transactions not to be included in determining net income, but shall be reported in the same manner as translation adjustments:

(a) Foreign currency transactions that are designated as, and are effective as, economic hedges of a net investment in a foreign entity, commencing as of the designation date

(b) Intercompany foreign currency transactions that are of a long-term-investment nature (that is, settlement is not planned or anticipated in the foreseeable future), when the entities to the transaction are consolidated, combined, or accounted for by the equity method in the reporting enterprise's financial statements

(ii) Deferral of Transaction Gains and Losses.   Recognition of transaction gains and losses in consolidated income is deferred for such gains and losses resulting from transactions intended to hedge identifiable foreign currency commitments; they are included in accounting for the transaction resulting from the commitment. However, recognition of losses is not deferred if deferral would lead to recognition of losses in subsequent periods.

SFAS No. 52 (par. 21) states two conditions that have to be met for a foreign currency transaction to be considered a hedge of an identifiable foreign currency commitment:

1. The foreign currency transaction is designated as, and is effective as, a hedge of a foreign currency commitment.

2. The foreign currency commitment is firm.

(h) OTHER TOPICS IN FOREIGN CURRENCY TRANSLATION.   Other topics concerning translation by the current rate method include income tax considerations, intercompany profit eliminations, selection of exchange rates, approximations, and required disclosures.

(i) Income Tax Considerations.   Treatment of foreign operations involves some special income tax accounting treatments (FASB ASC 740):

- *Unremitted earnings.* Deferred taxes are not recognized on translation adjustments that meet the tests in Accounting Principles Board (APB) Opinion No. 23, *Accounting for Income Taxes—Special Areas,* concerning unremitted earnings.
- *Intraperiod allocation.* Income taxes related to transaction gains and losses or translation adjustments reported in separate components of the income statement or the statement of changes in equity are allocated to the separate components.

(ii) Intercompany Profit Eliminations.   An exception in the current rate method to the use of the current exchange rate for translation is the method to eliminate intercompany profits that are attributable to sales or other transfers between entities that are consolidated, combined, or accounted for by the equity method in the enterprise's financial statements. They are eliminated at the exchange rates at the dates of the sales or transfers, because those are the rates at which the profits are embedded in the recorded amounts. Such eliminations precede applying the current exchange rates to the foreign currency amounts.

To illustrate: Corporation P, a domestic parent company, sold a parcel of land last year to Corporation S, its foreign subsidiary, at a profit of $24,000, when the exchange rate was $1/zł8 (Polish zlotys). S recorded the land in zlotys. The current exchange rate is zł6 = $1. The profit is eliminated at zł8/$1. The remaining amount at which S has the land recorded is translated at zł6/$1. However, exchange restrictions between dollars and zlotys may be severe enough to call into question the soundness of including S in the consolidated reporting entity.

(iii) Selection of Exchange Rates.   The current foreign exchange rate is used for most translation required by SFAS No. 52 (FASB ASC 830). Circumstances in which the rates at the dates of transactions are used instead are discussed previously in paragraph 9.2(c)(ii). These are other special considerations in selecting exchange rates:

- If the two currencies involved could not be exchanged on the date of the transaction or the reporting date, the rate at which they could be exchanged at the first succeeding date is used.
- If the inability to exchange the two currencies is not merely temporary, including the foreign operation in a consolidated group or accounting for it by the equity method is questionable.
- Foreign currency transactions are translated at the rates at which they could have been settled at the dates of the transactions. Resulting receivables and payables are translated subsequently at the rates at which they could be settled at the reporting dates.
- If there is more than one rate at a particular date, the rate at which foreign currency could be exchanged for domestic currency to remit dividends is used.
- If the reporting date of the foreign currency financial statements being translated differs from the reporting date of the reporting entity in which the foreign operation is included, the current rate is the rate in effect on the reporting date of the foreign currency financial statements.

(iv) Approximations.   Approximations of the results of applying the required translation principles are acceptable if the cost of applying them to every detail exceeds the benefits of such precision and the results do not materially differ from what they would be by applying them to every detail. Judgment is required to determine whether to use approximation, because determining the extent of the differences precisely would require the very calculations to be avoided by approximations.

(i) DISCLOSURES CONCERNING FOREIGN OPERATIONS. These disclosures are required concerning foreign operations:

- The total transaction gains or losses, including, for this purpose, gains and losses on forward contracts other than those excluded from income
- An analysis of the changes in the separate component of equity for translation adjustments, including at least:
  - The beginning and ending accumulated balances
  - The net change from translation adjustments and gains and losses from hedges and intercompany balances treated the way translation adjustments are treated
  - Income taxes allocated to translation adjustments
  - Transfers from the equity component into income because of the partial or complete sale of an investment in a foreign operation or the complete or substantial liquidation of a foreign operation

9.3 EQUITY METHOD

Generally speaking, if a firm owns between 20 percent and 50 percent of another company, then the firm is considered to possess significant control over the company and should use the equity method to account for the subsidiary.

Cases in which an investment of 20 percent or more might not enable an investor to exercise significant influence include:

- The investee opposes the investor's acquisition of its stock.
- The investor and investee sign an agreement under which the investor surrenders significant shareholder rights.
- The investor's ownership share does not result in "significant influence" because majority ownership of the investee is concentrated among a small group of shareholders who operate the investee without regard to the views of the investor.
- The investor tries and fails to obtain representation on the investee's board of directors.

The equity method, which is the focus of APB Opinion No. 18, *The Equity Method of Accounting for Investments in Common Stock,* is used to account for investments in unconsolidated subsidiaries, corporate joint ventures, and common stock that provide the investor with the ability to exercise significant influence over the operating and financial policies of the investee. Paragraph 15 of SFAS No. 94 amended APB Opinion No. 18, which eliminated the requirement to use the equity method to account in consolidated financial statements for unconsolidated majority-owned subsidiaries.

Under the equity method, an investor initially records an investment at cost. It adjusts the carrying amount of the investment at the end of the period in which it is acquired and in succeeding periods by the investor's proportionate share of changes in the investee's assets and liabilities and for the effects of intercompany profits. The principles for determining the cost of an investment accounted for by the equity method are essentially the same as those for determining the cost of an investment leading to a business combination accounted for by the acquisition method, discussed in Chapter 8 of this *Handbook.*

(a) DIFFERENCES BETWEEN CONSOLIDATION AND THE EQUITY METHOD. Consolidating the financial statements involves combining the firms' income statements and balance sheets together to form one statement. The equity method does not combine the accounts in the statement, but it accounts for the investment as an asset and accounts for income received from the subsidiary.

An investor's net income for a period and its equity at a point in time with its investment accounted for by the equity method are generally the same as they are with the investee consolidated. Application of SFAS No. 34, *Capitalization of Interest Cost,* and SFAS No. 58, *Capitalization of Interest Cost in Financial Statements That Include Investments Accounted for by the Equity Method,* cause differences, however.

Under SFAS No. 34, the total amount of interest cost capitalized in a set of consolidated financial statements cannot exceed the total amount of interest cost incurred by all the members of the consolidated group after intercompany amounts are eliminated. Under SFAS No. 58, however, for investments accounted for by the equity method, the total amount of interest cost capitalized in the investor's financial statements cannot exceed the total amount of interest cost incurred solely by the investor. That is, interest costs incurred by an investee accounted for by the equity method are excluded in accounting for amounts in the investor's financial statements on which interest is capitalized. Interest cost incurred by the investee can be capitalized only on amounts in the investee's financial statements.

Paragraph 9 of SFAS No. 34, as amended by SFAS No. 58, lists the type of interest that must be capitaized:

    a. Assets that are constructed or otherwise produced for an enterprise's own use (including assets constructed or produced for the enterprise by others for which deposits or progress payments have been made)

    b. Assets intended for sale or lease that are constructed or otherwise produced as discrete projects (e.g., ships or real estate developments)

    c. Investments (equity, loans, and advances) accounted for by the equity method while the investee has activities in progress necessary to commence its planned principal operations provided that the investee's activities include the use of funds to acquire qualifying assets for its operations

However, interest cost must not be capitalized for inventories that are routinely manufactured or otherwise produced in large quantities on a repetitive basis because, in the FASB's judgment, the informational benefit does not justify the cost of so doing. In addition, interest must not be capitalized for these types of assets:

    a. Assets that are in use or ready for their intended use in the earning activities of the enterprise

    b. Assets that are not being used in the earning activities of the enterprise and that are not undergoing the activities necessary to get them ready for use

    c. Assets that are not included in the consolidated balance sheet of the parent company and consolidated subsidiaries

    d. Investments accounted for by the equity method after the planned principal operations of the investee begin

    e. Investments in regulated investees that are capitalizing both the cost of debt and equity capital

(b) USING THE EQUITY METHOD.   An investor generally uses the equity method to account for each of the following types of investments.

(i) Unconsolidated Subsidiaries.   If a subsidiary does not qualify for consolidation, its financial statement elements are not combined with corresponding elements of the parent company line by line but instead are reported in the parent company's balance sheet and income statement on one line on each statement, one called *investment in unconsolidated subsidiary* or the like and the other called *investment revenue* or the like.

(ii) Joint Ventures.   An enterprise may be formed and operated by a number of other enterprises as a joint venture—a separate business or means to carry out a specific project for the benefit of its investors, also called *venturers*. The venturers pool their resources, knowledge, and talents and share risks for the purpose of ultimately sharing rewards. In many joint ventures, each venturer has more than just a passive interest or investment; each participates—either directly or indirectly—in managing the venture. Investments in joint ventures are generally accounted for by the equity method.

(iii) Investments in Common Stock Involving Significant Influence.   In the absence of evidence to the contrary, an investor with an investment of from 20 to 50 percent of the voting common stock of an investee is presumed to have the ability to exercise significant influence over the financial and operating policies of the investee and, because of that, uses the equity method to account for such an investment. Conversely, in the absence of evidence to the contrary, an investor with an investment of less than 20 percent of the common stock of an investee is presumed not to have the ability to exercise significant influence over the financial and operating policies of the investee and, therefore, does not use the equity method to account for such an investment but uses the method discussed in Section 9.4(a).

The ability to exercise significant influence may be inferred from, for example:

- Representation on the investee's board of directors
- Participation in policy-making processes
- Material intercompany transactions
- Interchange of managerial personnel
- Technological dependency

The inability to exercise significant influence may be inferred from, for example:

- Opposition by the investee that challenges the investor's ability to exercise significant influence, such as litigation or complaints to government authorities
- An agreement by the investor surrendering significant rights as a stockholder
- Concentration of the majority ownership of the investee among a few stockholders, who operate the investee without regard to the views of the investor
- Inability of the investor to obtain representation on the investee's board of directors after attempting to do so
- Inability of the investor to obtain financial information necessary to apply the equity method after attempting to do so

No one item in either of those lists is the sole determining factor as to whether an investor has the ability to exercise significant influence over the investee. Instead, all items are considered collectively.

If an investor owns two investments of, say, 20 percent each in unrelated corporations, one investment might qualify for the equity method and the other might not, because their circumstances differ. Judgment is always necessary in determining whether an investment gives an investor the ability to exercise significant influence over the investee.

(c) APPLYING THE EQUITY METHOD.   This section discusses and illustrates application of the equity method.

Under the equity method, the investor's initial investment, in essence, comprises three bundles:

Bundle A. A proportionate share of the book values of the investee's assets and liabilities on the date of the purchase, PLUS

Bundle B. A proportionate share of the differences between the book values and the fair values of the investee's assets and liabilities on the date of the initial investment (commonly referred to as *net unrealized appreciation* or *unrealized depreciation*). The principles for determining the fair values of the investee's assets and liabilities parallel the principles in applying the purchase method of accounting for business combinations (discussed in Chapter 8 of this *Handbook*) PLUS.

Bundle C. Goodwill, which is the excess at the date of purchase of (1) the cost of the investment over (2) the investor's proportionate share of the fair values of the investee's assets and liabilities (the sum of A + B) at the date of the purchase. If (2) exceeds (1), this bundle is negative goodwill. The principles of accounting for goodwill and negative goodwill under the equity method parallel the principles to account for them in consolidation.

The investor adjusts the carrying amount of the investment in succeeding periods by its proportionate share of changes in each bundle and for the effects of intercompany profits.

(i) Bundle A. Changes in the investee's equity are caused by earnings or losses from operations, extraordinary items, prior-period adjustments, the payment of cash or property dividends, and other transactions by the investor or the investee in stock of the investee.

The investor charges the investment account for its proportionate share of the investee's earnings from operations and credits investment revenue. If the investee reports a loss, the investor credits the investment account for its proportionate share of the investee's loss from operations and charges investment revenue. A negative balance in the investment revenue account for a reporting period is disclosed as a loss from investment. The investor adjusts its investment account for its proportionate share of the investee's prior-period adjustments and extraordinary items and correspondingly charges or credits prior-period adjustments and extraordinary items in its own financial statements.

An investor recognizes receipt of a cash dividend by crediting its investment account.

(ii) Bundle B. The portion of the investment that represents the investor's proportionate share of the differences between the fair values and the book values of each of the investee's assets and liabilities at the date of the investment (unrealized appreciation or depreciation) is amortized to investment revenue over the remaining estimated useful lives of the underlying assets and liabilities.

(iii) Bundle C. The portion of the difference between the cost of an investment and the amount of underlying equity in assets and liabilities of an investee accounted for by the equity method that represents goodwill, known as *equity method goodwill,* is not amortized. Equity method goodwill is not tested for impairment in conformity with FASB Statement No. 142, *Goodwill and Other Intangible Assets.* Equity method investments continue to be tested for impairment in conformity with paragraph 19(h) of APB Opinion No. 18.

(iv) Intercompany Profit or Loss. Intercompany profit or loss on assets bought from or sold to an investee is eliminated in the period of sale by adjusting the investment and the investment revenue accounts. That entry is reversed in the period in which the asset is sold to unrelated parties. The amount of unrealized profit or loss to be eliminated depends on whether the underlying transactions are considered to be at arm's length. If the transactions are not considered to be at arm's length, all the intercompany profit or loss is eliminated. If, however, the underlying transactions are considered to be at arm's length, only the investor's proportional share of the unrealized profit or loss is eliminated.

(v) Special Considerations. Applying the equity method sometimes involves the next special considerations.

Preferred Dividends. An investor computes its proportionate share of the investee's net income or loss after deducting cumulative preferred dividends, regardless of whether they are declared.

Investee's Capital Transactions. An investor accounts for transactions between the investee and its stockholders (e.g., issuances and reacquisitions of its stock) that directly affect the investor's proportionate share of the investee's equity in the same way that such transactions of a consolidated subsidiary are accounted for.

Time Lag.   An investor's reporting period may differ from that of the investee or the financial statements of the investee may not be available in time for an investor to record in its financial statements the information necessary to apply the equity method currently. In either case, the investor applies the equity method using the investee's most recent available financial statements. The same lag in reporting is used each period for consistency.

Permanent Decline in Value.   The recorded amount of an investment accounted for by the equity method is normally not reduced for declines in market value. But if the decline brings that market value below the carrying amount of the investment and is judged to be permanent, the investment is written down to its recoverable amount, usually market value, and a loss is charged to current income. The distinction between a decline that is permanent and one that is not is often not clear. However, evidence of a permanent decline might be demonstrated by, for example, the investor's inability to recover the carrying amount of the investment, the investee's inability to sustain an earnings capacity that would justify the carrying amount of the investment, or a history of losses or market values substantially below cost.

To illustrate: On January 1, 20X4, Corporation P accounts for its investment in Corporation S by the equity method. The carrying amount is $24,000 and the market value of the investment is $13,000. If the decline is judged to be permanent, P discontinues applying the equity method and records this entry to reduce the investment to its recoverable amount, in this case market value:

Investment loss	$11,000	
Investment in Corporation S		$11,000

If the market subsequently recovers, $13,000, not $24,000, is the basis at which to resume applying the equity method.

Excessive Losses.   A company that accounts for an investment by the equity method ordinarily discontinues applying that method when the carrying amount of the investment in and net advances to the investee is reduced to zero, unless the investor has guaranteed obligations or is otherwise committed to providing further financial support for the investee. An investor resumes applying the equity method after the investee returns to profitable operations and the investor's proportionate share of the investee's subsequent net income equals the proportionate share of net losses the investor did not recognize during the period that application of the equity method was suspended.

Changed Conditions.   If an investment no longer qualifies for the equity method because the investor no longer has the ability to exercise significant influence over the investee, the investor stops applying the equity method and starts applying the cost method from that point on. The investor does not retroactively adjust the carrying amount of the investment to reflect what the carrying amount of the investment would have been had that method been applied since the investment was acquired.

To illustrate: On January 1, 20X4, Corporation P's investment in Corporation S ceases to give P the ability to exercise significant influence over S. On that date, the investment in Corporation S is reported in P's financial statements at $28,000. That becomes the investment's cost for purposes of applying the cost method from that point on.

If an investment accounted for by the cost method subsequently qualifies for the equity method because the investor subsequently gains the ability to exercise significant influence over the investee, the investor stops applying the method and starts applying the equity method from that point on. In that case, in contrast, the investor does retroactively adjust the carrying amount of the investment to what it would have been had it been accounted for by the equity method starting with its first acquisition by the investor, in a manner consistent with the accounting for a step-by-step acquisition of a subsidiary.

To illustrate: P acquired stock of S on January 1, 20X3, for $24,000. The investment did not give P the ability to exercise significant influence over S. The investment is reported in P's balance sheet on December 31, 20X3, at $24,000, in accordance with the cost method. Had the investment previously qualified for the equity method, the investment in S would have been reported in P's balance sheet at $32,000.

On January 1, 20X4, P gains the ability to exercise significant influence over S without a change in its holding of S's stock. P therefore increases its investment account to $32,000, as shown:

Investment in Corporation S	$8,000	
Retained earnings		$8,000

From then on, P applies the equity method the way it would have been applied had P first obtained the ability to exercise significant influence when it first acquired the investment.

(vi) Proportional Consolidation.   Proportional consolidation for representing the aggregate financial position of the parent and non–fully owned related entities, although not currently part of U.S. GAAP, is in use in some countries (e.g., Canada). Its origin was in the accounting for joint ventures. In the United States, some industries (e.g., construction) have used proportional consolidation.

Under this approach, the ownership percentage of the owner corporation of the other entity is used to determine an amount of each asset and liability of the other entity to aggregate into the consolidated totals. This may be an area of interest as differences between International Financial Reporting Standards (IFRS) and U.S. GAAP continue to be explored. IFRS permits both the equity and proportional consolidation methods (International Accounting Standard No. 31, *Interests in Joint Ventures*). In some circumstances, the method will result in different financial metrics when compared to the equity method treatment currently established as GAAP. It is anticipated that the equity method will be required when international standards are reconsidered.

(d) DISCLOSURES CONCERNING THE EQUITY METHOD.   The information in this section about investments accounted for by the equity method, as applicable, is disclosed on the face of the financial statements, in the notes to the financial statements, or in supporting schedules or statements:

- The names of the investees and the percentages of ownership.
- Reasons investments of 20 percent or more of the voting stock of an investee are not accounted for by the equity method.
- Reasons investments of less than 20 percent of the voting stock of an investee are accounted for by the equity method.
- The amounts of net unrealized appreciation or depreciation and how the amounts are amortized.
- The amounts of goodwill and how they are amortized.
- The quoted market prices of the investments, if available.
- Summarized information about the assets, liabilities, and results of operations of investments in unconsolidated subsidiaries or in corporate joint ventures, if they are material individually or collectively in relation to the financial position or results of operations of the investor. The information can be either about each investment accounted for by the equity method or combined information of all investments accounted for by the equity method.
- Descriptions of possible conversions, exercises of warrants or options, or other contingent issuances of stock of investees that may significantly affect the investor's shares of reported earnings.

9.4 HISTORICAL SUMMARY OF MAJOR PRONOUNCEMENTS

The next sections summarize some of the major pronouncements that deal with the topics covered in this chapter.

(a) CONSOLIDATION

- ARB No. 43, Chapter 12, "Foreign Operations and Foreign Exchange," provides criteria for the treatment of foreign subsidiaries in consolidated financial statements.

- ARB No. 51, *Consolidated Financial Statements,* describes the purpose of consolidated financial statements and selection of a consolidation policy, and discusses concepts underlying consolidation and procedures to prepare consolidated financial statements.

- SFAS No. 94, *Consolidation of All Majority-Owned Subsidiaries,* amends ARB No. 51 to require consolidation of all majority-owned subsidiaries unless control is temporary or does not rest with the majority owners.

- SFAS No. 160, *Noncontrolling Interests in Consolidated Financial Statements,* amends ARB No. 51 to improve the relevance, comparability, and transparency of the financial information that a reporting entity provides in its consolidated financial statements by establishing accounting and reporting standards for the noncontrolling interest in a subsidiary.

- SFAS No. 167, *Amendments to FASB Interpretation No. 46(R).* The objective of this Statement is to amend certain requirements of FASB Interpretation No. 46 (revised December 2003), to improve financial reporting by enterprises involved with variable interest entities and to provide more relevant information to users of financial statements.

- FIN No. 46(R), *Consolidation of Variable Interest Entities—An Interpretation of ARB No. 51,* was revised December 2003. This interpretation of ARB No. 51 replaces FASB Interpretation No. 46, Consolidation of Variable Interest Entities, addresses consolidation by business enterprises of variable interest entities.

- Emerging Issues Task Force (EITF) Issue No. 87-15, *Effect of a Standstill Agreement on Pooling-of-Interests Accounting,* holds that the existence of a standstill agreement does not by itself preclude an otherwise qualifying business combination from being accounted for by the pooling-of-interests method. (A standstill agreement is an agreement that prohibits a more than 10 percent shareholder from acquiring additional shares of the enterprise or its successors for a specified period.)

- EITF Issue No. 87-27, *Poolings of Companies That Do Not Have a Controlling Class of Common Stock,* concludes that a business combination may still qualify for the pooling-of-interests method even if the issuing company has to convert voting preferred stock into voting common stock so as to create a controlling class of common stock.

- EITF Issue No. 88-27, *Effect of Unallocated Shares in an ESOP on Accounting for Business Combinations,* specifies the circumstances in which unallocated shares held by an employee stock option plan should and should not be considered "tainted" for purposes of determining whether a business combination should be accounted for by the pooling of interests method.

- Financial Technical Bulletin (FTB) No. 85-5, *Issues Relating to Accounting for Business Combinations, Including Costs of Closing Duplicate Facilities of an Acquirer; Stock Transactions between Companies under Company Control; Downstream Mergers; Identical Common Shares for a Pooling of Interests; Pooling of Interests by Mutual and Cooperative Enterprises,* clarifies these matters:

  - That costs incurred to close duplicate facilities as a result of a business combination should not be considered part of the cost of the business combination

  - How a parent company should account for minority interest in an exchange of stock between two of its subsidiaries

  - That an exchange by a partially owned subsidiary of its common stock for the outstanding common stock of its parent should be accounted for under the purchase method

  - That the pooling-of-interests method may not be used to account for a business combination in which one company issues common stock identical to other outstanding common shares except that the issuer retains a right of first refusal to reacquire the shares issued in certain specified circumstances

○ That the conversion of a mutual or cooperative enterprise to a stock company within two years of a business combination does not by itself bar the combination from being accounted for by the pooling-of-interests method

- EITF Issue No. 94-2, *Treatment of Minority Interests in Certain Real Estate Investment Trusts,* and the related EITF Issue 95-7, *Implementation Issues Related to the Treatment of Minority Interests in Certain Real Estate Investment Trusts,* specify how, and at what amount, the sponsor's interest and partnership income or loss should be reported in the financial statements of a real estate investment trust (REIT).

- EITF Issue No. 96-16, *Investor's Accounting for an Investee When the Investor Has a Majority of the Voting Interest but the Minority Shareholder or Shareholders Have Certain Approval or Veto Rights,* describes circumstances in which certain rights held by the minority interest may preclude consolidation by the controlling shareholder.

- EITF Issue No. 97-2, *Application of FASB Statement No. 94 and APB Opinion No. 16 to Physician Practice Management Entities,* discusses circumstances in which interests in practice management entities should and should not lead to the consolidation of the entity's financial statements.

- EITF Issue No. 97-6, *Application of Issue No. 96-20 to Qualifying Special-Purpose Entities Receiving Transferred Financial Assets Prior to the Effective Date of FASB Statement No. 125,* reached a consensus that was nullified by the issuance of FASB Statement No. 140, *Accounting for Transfers and Servicing of Financial Assets and Extinguishments of Liabilities.*

- EITF Issue No. 99-16, *Accounting for Transactions with Elements of Research and Development Arrangements,* discusses reporting by an enterprise that is a party to a research and development arrangement through which it obtains the results of research and development funded partially or entirely by others.

- EITF Issue No. 00-4, *Majority Owner's Accounting for a Transaction in the Shares of a Consolidated Subsidiary and a Derivative Indexed to the Majority Interest in That Subsidiary,* discusses reporting by a parent company that owns a majority of a subsidiary's outstanding common stock and consolidates the subsidiary at the inception of a derivative contract of a type described in the Issue.

- EITF Issue No. 02-5, *Definition of "Common Control,"* in relation to FASB Statement No. 141, *Business Combinations,* discusses how to determine whether separate entities are under common control, in the context of Statement No. 141, when common majority ownership exists by an individual, a family, or a group affiliated in some other manner.

(b) FOREIGN CURRENCY TRANSLATION

- ARB No. 43, Chapter 12, "Foreign Operations and Foreign Exchange," provides criteria for the treatment of foreign subsidiaries in consolidated financial statements.

- SFAS No. 52, *Foreign Currency Translation,* specifies the accounting for foreign operations reported in the financial statements of a domestic company. It supersedes SFAS No. 8, *Accounting for the Translation of Foreign Currency Transactions and Foreign Currency Financial Statements.*

- FIN No. 37, *Accounting for Translation Adjustments upon Sale of Part of an Investment in a Foreign Entity,* prescribes that the accounting in SFAS No. 52 that applies to a sale or complete or substantially complete liquidation of an investment in a foreign entity also applies to a partial disposal by an enterprise of its ownership interest.

- EITF Issue No. 90-17, *Hedging Foreign Currency Risks with Purchased Options,* provides guidance on the accounting for purchased foreign currency options that are not specifically addressed in SFAS No. 52.

- EITF Issue No. 91-1, *Hedging Intercompany Foreign Risks,* concludes that (1) transactions between members of a consolidated group with different functional currencies can result in foreign currency risk that may be hedged for accounting purposes and (2) the appropriate accounting for the risk depends on the type of hedging instrument used.

- EITF Issue No. 91-4, *Hedging Foreign Currency Risks with Complex Options and Similar Transactions,* led to (1) a consensus on the type of information that should be disclosed by an entity that hedges foreign currency risks with complex or similar transactions and (2) an SEC staff position regarding the deferral of gains or losses on complex options and similar transactions.

- EITF Issue No. 92-4, *Accounting for a Change in Functional Currency When an Economy Ceases to Be Considered Highly Inflationary,* states that an entity with a foreign subsidiary operating in an economy that ceases to be considered highly inflationary should restate the functional currency accounting bases of nonmonetary assets and liabilities as of the date of cessation.

- EITF Issue No. 92-8, *Accounting for the Income Tax Effects under FASB Statement No. 109 of a Change in Functional Currency When an Economy Ceases to Be Considered Highly Inflationary,* states that deferred income taxes associated with temporary differences arising from a change in functional currency when an economy ceases to be considered highly inflationary should be reflected as an adjustment to the cumulative translation adjustment component of stockholders' equity.

- EITF Issue No. 93-10, *Accounting for Dual Currency Bonds,* discusses whether the effect of foreign currency exchange rates on dual currency bonds (bonds whose principal is repayable in U.S. dollars but whose periodic interest is payable in a foreign currency) should be recognized (1) as an adjustment of future interest expense or (2) currently as an adjustment of the liability's carrying amount.

- EITF Issue No. 97-7, *Accounting for Hedges of the Foreign Currency Risk Inherent in an Available-for-Sale Marketable Equity Security,* concludes that foreign currency transaction gains or losses on a foreign currency forward exchange contract or foreign currency–denominated liability should be reported in the Statement No. 115 separate component of stockholders' equity.

- EITF Issue No. 01-5, *Application of FASB Statement No. 52 to an Investment Being Evaluated for Impairment That Will Be Disposed Of,* discusses whether a reporting enterprise should include the accumulated foreign currency translation adjustment in the carrying amount of the investment in assessing impairment of an investment in a foreign entity that is held for disposal if the planned disposal will cause some or all of the accumulated foreign currency translation adjustments to be reclassified to net income.

(c) EQUITY METHOD

- APB Opinion No. 18, *The Equity Method of Accounting for Investments in Common Stock,* specifies the circumstances in which an investment in common stock should be accounted for by the equity method of accounting and the principles that apply to the method.

- SFAS No. 58, *Capitalization of Interest Cost in Financial Statements That Include Investments Accounted for by the Equity Method,* specifies the circumstances in which investments accounted for by the equity method should be considered qualifying assets for purposes of interest capitalization.

- FIN No. 35, *Criteria for Applying the Equity Method of Accounting for Investments in Common Stock,* clarifies that the presumptions concerning the applicability of the equity method may be overcome by predominant evidence to the contrary, based on an evaluation of all facts and circumstances relating to the investment.

- FTB FASB Technical Bulletin No. 79-19, *Investor's Accounting for Unrealized Losses on Marketable Securities Owned by an Equity Method Investee,* emphasizes that an investor should not combine the portfolios of its marketable securities with the portfolios of the marketable securities of its investees that are accounted for by the equity method, for purposes of determining the investor's unrealized losses on marketable securities.

- FASB Statement No. 142, *Goodwill and Other Intangible Assets,* indicates the treatment of equity method goodwill after it is first recognized.
- EITF Issue No. 98-13, *Accounting by an Equity Method Investor for Investee Losses When the Investor Has Loans to and Investments in Other Securities of the Investee,* provides guidance on how the equity method loss pickup from the application of APB Opinion No. 18, when the carrying amount of the common stock has been reduced to zero, interacts with the applicable literature relating to investments in the other securities of the investee, FASB Statement No. 114, *Accounting by Creditors for Impairment of a Loan* or FASB Statement No. 115, *Accounting for Certain Investments in Debt and Equity Securities.*
- EITF Issue No. 00-1, *Investor Balance Sheet and Income Statement Display under the Equity Method for Investments in Certain Partnerships and Other Ventures,* discusses whether there are circumstances in which proportionate gross presentation is appropriate under the equity method of accounting for an investment in a legal entity.
- EITF Issue No. 00-8, *Accounting by a Grantee for an Equity Instrument to Be Received in Conjunction with Providing Goods or Services,* discusses issues involved contemporaneous exchange of equity instruments for goods or services with contingent conditions.
- EITF Issue No. 00-12, *Accounting by an Investor for Stock-Based Compensation Granted to Employees of an Equity Method Investee,* discusses accounting for stock-based compensation based on the investor's stock granted to employees of an investee accounted for under the equity method when no proportionate funding by the other investors occurs and the investor does not receive any increase in the investor's relative ownership percentage of the investee.
- EITF Issue No. 01-2, *Interpretations of APB Opinion No. 29,* discusses how to account for the exchange of an equity method investment for a similar equity method investment.

9.5 SOURCES AND SUGGESTED REFERENCES

Brenner, V. C., V. C. Brenner Jr., and M. Jeancola "New Reporting Standards for Noncontrolling Interests: Benefits Include Greater Comparability and Conceptual Consistency," *CPA Journal* (July 2008).

Reinstein, A., G. H. Lander, and S. Danese, "Consolidation of Variable-Interest Entities: Applying the Provisions of FIN 46(R)," *CPA Journal* (August 2006).

Rosenfield, P. "Accounting for Foreign Operations," *Journal of Accountancy* (August 1987).

Simon, M. "The Who and How of the Equity Accounting Method," *Journal of Accountancy* (February 2001).

Soroosh, J., and J. T. Ciesielski, "Accounting for Special Purpose Entities Revised: FASB Interpretation 46(R)," *CPA Journal* (July 2004).

University of Cincinnati College of Law. *Security Lawyer's Deskbook*, "Security & Exchange Commission Regulation S-X: Rule 34-02—Consolidated Financial Statements of the Registrant and Its Subsidiaries." *http://taft.law.uc.edu/CCL/regS-X/SX3A-02.html*

CHAPTER 10

ANALYZING FINANCIAL STATEMENTS

Noah P. Barsky, PhD, CPA, CMA
Villanova University

Frank J. Grippo, MBA, CPA, CFE
William Paterson University

B. Scott Teeter, MBA, CMA
The Ryland Group, Inc.

10.1 SCOPE OF FINANCIAL STATEMENT ANALYSIS

(a) EXTERNAL USERS OF PUBLISHED FINANCIAL STATEMENTS. This section is concerned with the techniques of financial analysis employed by external users of financial statements. The techniques described are generally limited to analysis of publicly available financial statements or similar reports circulated privately. Principal emphasis is on the financial statements of companies whose shares are publicly traded. Chapter 25 of this *Handbook* is concerned with the valuation of companies whose shares are not publicly traded.

Management has available far more extensive internal financial data for control of the business and deployment of resources. In many respects, it may employ similar analysis as an external user, but in greater detail.

The common characteristic of external users is their general lack of authority to prescribe the information they want from an enterprise. They depend on general-purpose external financial reports provided by management. The objectives of these external users are aptly described by the Financial Accounting Standards Board (FASB) in Statement of Financial Accounting Concept No. 1 (CON 1), *Objectives of Financial Reporting by Business Enterprises:*

INFORMATION USEFUL IN INVESTMENT AND CREDIT DECISIONS

Financial reporting should provide information that is useful to present and potential investors and creditors and other users in making rational investment, credit, and similar decisions. The information should be comprehensible to those who have a reasonable understanding of business and economic activities and are willing to study the information with reasonable diligence. [par. 34]

(b) USER GROUPS AND THEIR ANALYTICAL OBJECTIVES. External users of financial information encompass a wide range of interests but can be classified into four general groups:

1. Equity investors (i.e. company owners)
2. Government—regulatory bodies, tax authorities, the executive and legislative branches
3. Creditors, such as bankers and suppliers
4. Other groups, including the general public, labor unions, employees, consumer groups, and research institutions

Each group has a particular objective in financial statement analysis but, according to the FASB, the primary users are equity investors and creditors. The information supplied to investors and creditors, however, is likely to be generally useful to other user groups as well. Hence financial accounting standards are geared to the purposes and perceptions of investors. For that reason, the analytical techniques in this chapter are geared to those primary audiences.

The underlying objective of financial analysis is the comparative measurement of risk and return in order to make investment or credit decisions. These decisions are based on some estimates of the future performance. General-purpose financial statements, which describe the past, provide one basis for projecting future cash flows. Many of the techniques used in this analytical process are broadly applicable to all types of decisions, but there are also specialized techniques concerned with specific investment interests or, put another way, specific risks and returns.

(i) Equity Investors.   Equity investors are primarily interested in the long-term earning power of the company and its ability to pay dividends. Since equity investors bear the residual risk in an enterprise, their analysis is often the most comprehensive. When the residual ownership risk might be more volatile, equity investors focus increasing attention on measuring comparative risks and diversifying these risks in investment portfolios.

(ii) Creditors.   This subgroup of investors emphasizes several specialized analytical approaches. Short-term creditors, such as banks and trade creditors, place more emphasis on the immediate *liquidity* of the business because they seek an early payback of their investment. Long-term investors in bonds, such as insurance companies and pension funds, are primarily concerned with the long-term asset position and earning power of the company. They seek assurance of the payment of interest and the capability of retiring or refunding the obligation at maturity. Credit exposure is often considered less risky than equity holdings and is more easily determinable.

(c) SOURCES OF FINANCIAL INFORMATION.   The term *financial statements* normally encompasses four statements:

1. Income statement
2. Balance sheet
3. Statement of changes in stockholders' equity (or changes in retained earnings)
4. Statement of cash flows

The notes to the financial statements are an integral part of disclosure and provide substantial amounts of supplementary information, such as the operations of major segments of the business, events subsequent to financial statement reporting dates, financial position of pension plans, and existing and potential off-balance sheet (OBS) obligations.

These statements are presented in both the annual and the quarterly reports to shareholders and in filings with the Securities and Exchange Commission (SEC). The SEC filings (registration statements for new security offerings, the 10-K annual report, and/or 10-Q quarterly report) often contain additional valuable information not presented in reports to shareholders. Shareholder reports often contain useful supplementary financial and statistical data and a narrative report by management. Therefore, any comprehensive analysis of a company should review both of these basic sources.

Industry data and other information about a company also may be obtained from sources outside the company. This discussion is confined to company-originated financial data.

(d) FRAMEWORK FOR ANALYSIS.   Investment analysis should begin with an evaluation of macroeconomic conditions including trends in the gross national product (GNP), personal consumption, and capital expenditures along with other relevant macro-variables. This analysis should be developed on a domestic and international level for insights into the relative investment potential across countries and industrial sectors. The competitive, economic, and technological factors affecting selected industries should be analyzed next; finally, there should be a comprehensive analysis of various firms in these industries. The analysis framework to achieve forecasts of earning power and market value can be outlined in this way:

1. Broad economic factors
   Gross domestic product (GDP)
   Personal consumption expenditures
   Inflations rates
   Capital expenditures
   Interest rates
   Currency rates
   Other relevant macrovariables, such as unemployment rates
2. Industrywide factors
   Product life cycle—sales and earnings
   Unit cost and unit sales price
      Trends over time
      Relative to other firms
   Economic and technological forces affecting industry competition
      Threat of new entrants
      Bargaining power of buyers
      Rivalry among existing competitors
      Threat of substitute products
      Bargaining power of suppliers
3. Firm-specific analyses
   Firm strategies in given economic and industrywide environment
   Earning power
   Leverage analysis

10.2 INCOME STATEMENT ANALYSIS

This section discusses the evaluation of earning power and risk through analysis of the revenue and expense components of the income statements. Various analytical techniques used to study trends and variability in revenues and the impact of costs incurred on risk are described. Such techniques help to determine if earnings are sustainable.

(a) EARNINGS POWER AND RISK.   In the long run, earnings power is the basis for credit and the source of cash return (interest or dividends) to the investor. The analyst seeks to project earning power over some future period associated with the length of the risk period. Therefore, it is the focus of income statement analysis.

Earnings power is an analytical concept and cannot be separately identified in the income statement. It is defined as the ability of a company to generate continuing earnings from the operating assets of the business over a period of years. Its characteristics include normality, stability (or variability), and growth. *Normality* is the normal level of earnings, absent strikes, floods, and other unusual nonrecurring events. It should exclude extraordinary items such as accounting adjustments and nonrecurring gains or charges. *Stability* is the absence of data variation around an estimated trend line. *Growth* is the rate of change (slope) in the trend line of earnings over a defined period. Generally, earning power is better represented by operating earnings than by total net income, which often includes unusual or nonrecurring elements. The analyst often normalizes and averages operating earnings data to determine earning power, which can then be forecasted and monetized to expected cash flow over time.

The risk element in earning power is the variability between actual and expected earnings, or the predictability of earnings. The earnings of some companies may fluctuate with some regularity in a cyclical pattern, whereas for others the fluctuations can be irregular and unpredictable. Fluctuation is tantamount to uncertainty when increasingly irregular and unpredictable. Thus, stocks of natural resource companies are often considered more risky than those of consumer product companies, because commodity prices are far less predictable.

(b) SALES AND REVENUE ANALYSIS. Sales and other operating revenues are the lifeblood of a business. Analysts compare a company's revenue factors with the industry and with competing companies to associate economic changes with internal company trends. Such comparisons of trends and variability determine the relative importance of price and volume.

(i) Trend Analysis. The most appropriate measure of a trend is determined by the revenue pattern. A stable trend is easily measured by a compound annual growth rate calculated on the endpoint values, but a highly variable pattern is better measured by a least squares calculation. Three patterns of sales trends are illustrated in Exhibit 10.1

Company A shows fairly steady growth, and a compound growth rate calculated between years 1 and 10 is a reasonable measure of trend. It can be presumed to have some predictive power, subject to an analysis of all factors affecting sales.

Company B shows a cyclical pattern with a compound growth rate calculated from year 1 to year 10 of 9.2 percent, although total sales for 10 years are the same as Company A. Obviously, a growth rate calculated from the bottom of one cycle to the peak of another one does not provide a sound basis for prediction. Two better methods can be used. One is to measure from one peak to the next peak (or from trough to trough). Thus year 1 (trough) to year 7 (trough) shows a compound growth rate of 6.0 percent; or year 4 (peak) to year 10 (peak), a rate of 1.9 percent. A second method is to fit a least squares trend line to the data. The slope of this line shows a growth rate of 4.8 percent, which is probably a more realistic long-term measure for this company.

Year	Company A Steady Growth		Company B Cyclical Pattern		Company C Unusual Development	
	Amount	% Change	Amount	% Change	Amount	% Change
1	$ 21.5		$ 8.1	20.5		
2	23.0	7.0	23.6	30.4	$ 21.5	4.9
3	24.0	4.3	28.1	19.1	23.0	7.0
4	25.7	7.1	35.7	17.0	24.5	6.5
5	28.1	9.3	29.0	(18.8)	26.0	6.1
6	29.6	5.3	27.5	(5.2)	26.5	1.9
7	31.3	5.7	26.0	(5.4)	28.0	5.7
8	34.5	10.2	29.0	11.5	29.0	3.6
9	35.0	1.4	32.0	10.3	40.0	10.3
10	36.3	3.7	40.0	25.0	50.0	25.0
10-year Total	$289.0		$289.0		$289.0	
% Change years 1–10		68.8		121.0		143.9
Compound growth rate years 1–10 (%)		6.0		9.2		10.4
Least squares growth rate (%)		6.0		4.8		9.1
Standard deviation		5.3		6.1		9.2

Exhibit 10.1   Measures of Sales Trends

Company C experiences an explosive sales growth at the end of the decade, enabling it to attain the same 10-year total as Companies A and B. The compound growth rate over the whole period is 10.4 percent, and the least squares growth rate is 9.1 percent. When it is recognized that the growth rate in the first eight years is only 5.1 percent compared with 31.3 percent in the last two years, the 10-year compound growth fails to describe the sales trend. In fact, there is no satisfactory measure to project the sales trends of Company C in comparison with the other companies. The company's recent sales experience must be analyzed before any projection can be made.

(ii) Variability.   These three companies illustrate widely differing sales patterns, leading to different levels of confidence in their persistence in future years. One indication of variability is the simple year-to-year percentage change in sales. Company A's year-to-year increases are close to the 10-year compound growth rate, whereas Company B swings widely above and below its 10-year trend line growth of 4.8 percent annually. The standard deviation is the statistical tool that measures the variation from the trend line. For Company A, it can be expected that about two-thirds of the expected values will fall within ± 5.3, or 18 percent, of the mean, whereas for Company C, the range is ± 9.2, or 32 percent of the mean. A's variability is less, and the certainty of its sales trend is greater, although not absolute.

(iii) Components of Sales Trends.   A sales trend can be understood better if the components of price and volume can be separated. Not many companies provide such information, but often it can be derived indirectly. If Company A sells a single product, the price of which is known, volume can be easily computed. For Company A, for example, the price rose at a 4.0 percent annual rate during the 10-year period.

Volume growth can be calculated as shown:

$$\text{volume growth over 10 years} = \frac{\text{Sales (year 10)}}{\text{Sales (year 10)}} - \frac{\text{Sales (year 1)}}{\text{Sales (year 1)}}$$

By dividing year 10 sales by year 10 price, we obtain a volume figure for that year. A similar exercise for the base year (year 1) provides a comparable figure. Conversely, volume may be known (e.g., steel production), so price can be derived from this equation, substituting volume for price.

Occasionally the components of sales change are presented in a variance analysis in an annual report. This is illustrated next.

Total sales increase in year 2	$150,000
Increase due to price ((Price 2 – Price 1) × Volume 1)	86,000
Increase due to volume ((Volume 2 – Volume 1) × Price 2)	64,000

In large diversified companies, gross sales are an aggregate of many diverse activities, and many other components of sales should be analyzed. In recent years, companies have been required to report sales (and earnings and other data) of the principal segments and geographic sources of the business.

Within a single product line or segment, there are also differences in the characteristics of sales components. One example is sales versus service revenues, or sales versus leasing. Most companies provide this breakdown where it is important. Sales of an expensive machine (e.g., a computer) may be expected to fluctuate from year to year, but service revenues will tend to build up steadily as the number of installed machines increases. Alternatively, buyers may shift between buying and leasing, although product shipments remain unchanged. The volatility and the current profitability of these revenue streams are quite different, and both must be analyzed to fully understand the sales trend.

When examining sales trends, the analyst must be wary of the effects of acquisitions and divestitures as well as the effects of changes in exchange rates. These issues are discussed in Sections 10.3(h) and 10.3(j).

Year	Company D Sales % Industry	Company E Sales % GNP	Company F Volume Index[a] Company	Company F Volume Index[a] Industry
1	23.5	.00065	100	100
2	27.4	.00072	105	105
3	28.1	.00075	112	117
4	29.3	.00070	113	120
5	30.2	.00068	115	123
5-year average	27.7	.00070	109	113

[a]Year 1 = 100.

Exhibit 10.2   Comparative Sales Trend Analysis

(iv) Comparative Trend Analysis.   A company cannot be analyzed in a vacuum. The outside forces affecting it and its responses are an important aspect of financial analysis. Sales can be tested against competition in the company's markets and general economic trends. There are a number of ways to do this, none of which is very difficult. Exhibit 10.2 is illustrative. Company D is gaining a share of the market. Company E had an earlier cyclical recovery but merely maintained its position relative to the economy over the full business cycle. Its greater cyclical variability is an important aspect of the appraisal of the company. Company F's slow revenue growth is due to lagging volume compared to its industry.

Although the comparison of similar companies is a necessary part of analysis, it is fraught with peril. No two companies are identical. Differences in sales trends may result from any of these issues:

- End markets may have different growth or cyclical characteristics.
- Major customers may differ; differences in customer sales trends will be reflected in new orders.
- Companies that are considered secondary suppliers will show greater variability than "primary" suppliers.
- Some companies have greater vertical integration than others in the same industry.
- In industries with high transportation costs, regional conditions may vary greatly (e.g., cement).

(c) COST AND EXPENSE ANALYSIS.   Many of the same analytical techniques applied to revenue analysis can also be utilized in expense analysis, but the predominant technique is profit margin analysis. The great diversity of business operations precludes any general standard for such profitability ratios. Such ratios are often used in internal trend analysis and comparisons.

(i) Classification of Costs.   In a typical industrial company, the principal expense categories are cost-of-goods-sold and selling, general, and administrative expenses. Sometimes these categories are subdivided. Often depreciation is shown separately rather than included in other categories. Because of these and other classification problems, these categories are rarely comparable from company to company.

For purposes of analysis, one should focus on gross profit (sales less cost of goods sold) or on operating income (before other income and expense, interest income and expense, and income taxes). Using income before interest charges facilitates the comparison of companies with different financial structures.

(ii) Margin Analysis.   A company's ability to control costs in relation to revenues is an important factor in earning power. These five ratios or margins are generally used to measure cost control in industrial companies:

1. $\text{Gross margin} = 1 - \dfrac{\text{Cost of goods sold}}{\text{Sales}}$

2. $\text{Expense ratio} = \dfrac{\text{Selling, general, and administrative expenses}}{\text{Sales}}$

3. $\text{Operating margin} = \dfrac{\text{Operating income}}{\text{Sales}}$

4. $\text{Pretax margin} = \dfrac{(\text{Operating income } + \text{ other income } - \text{ interest}}{\text{Sales}}$

5. $\text{Profit margin} = \dfrac{\text{Net income before extraordinary items}}{\text{Sales}}$

These ratios must be interpreted in relation to those in other companies in the same industry and over time within the company. Any given ratio has little meaning out of context. Margins must also be related to other facets of the business, such as the capital required and the turnover ratio, which is explained later in this section.

For example, a retail food chain typically shows a low operating margin because it rapidly passes through a high volume of products at a very low unit cost. Although a low operating margin would normally suggest considerable uncertainty about the continuity of operating income, the rapid turnover provides more opportunity to keep selling prices in line with costs.

In contrast, a capital-intensive industrial company may have a much wider operating margin, but typically it will have a higher proportion of fixed costs and more volatile sales. An electric utility company will show both a wide operating margin and steady sales, but its capital costs (e.g., interest) are also large.

Some lines of business have a very low gross margin, that is, the cost of the product is a high percentage of sales, meaning that value added by the company is modest. In such cases, the dynamics of expenses can be related better to the gross margin than to sales.

(iii) Analytical Adjustments.   When possible, nonrecurring items should be removed from earnings prior to analysis. These items include:

- Gains or losses from refinancing
- Capital gains or losses on asset sales
- Write-offs, especially "restructuring provisions" [see Section 10.3(f)]
- Transitional impacts of new accounting standards
- Results of discontinued operations
- Foreign currency translation gain or loss
- Settlement in a major lawsuit
- Asset impairment losses

These items may or may not have great significance for cash flow, but usually they are nonrecurring or infrequent and therefore cannot be projected in an assessment of future earning power. A loss on a facility closedown is largely an accounting adjustment that in effect recognizes a prior loss of earning power. It will not affect future years except perhaps indirectly in sales and costs. Foreign currency translation gains and losses are accounting adjustments arising from fluctuations in foreign exchange, and their economic significance to the business is often hard to judge. A gain from debt retirement is really a capital transaction unrelated to the operations of the business.

	Company X			Company Y		
	Year 1	Year 2	Year 3	Year 1	Year 2	Year 3
Sales Expense	$1,000	$1,100	$900	$1,000	$1,100	$900
Variable[a]	$ 500	$ 550	$450	$ 200	$ 220	$180
% of sales	50.0	50.0	50.0	20.0	20.0	20.0
Semivariable[b]	200	205	195	300	315	280
% of sales	20.0	18.6	21.7	30.0	28.6	31.1
Fixed[c]	200	200	200	400	400	400
% of sales	20.0	18.2	22.2	40.0	36.4	44.4
Total expense	900	955	845	900	935	860
% of sales	90.0	86.8	93.9	90.0	85.0	95.5
Operating income	$ 100	$ 145	$ 55	$ 100	$ 165	$ 40
% of sales	10.0	13.2	6.1	10.0	15.0	4.5

[a]Variable costs: direct labor, materials, and supplies.
[b]Semivariable costs: administrative expense, fuel, maintenance.
[c]Fixed costs: depreciation, rents, and interest.

Exhibit 10.3   Operating Leverage

(iv) Operating Leverage. The analyst should attempt to separate variable, semivariable, and fixed costs. This will permit better analysis of cost control in a fluctuating business environment. Companies usually do not reveal this information, but an analysis of cost and expense movement over a business cycle may give a general indication. All costs are variable in the long run, but over a business cycle, high fixed costs have a leverage effect on operating income.

In Exhibit 10.3, Company X's variable costs are a steady 50 percent of sales, whereas its fixed costs average only 20 percent of sales. Company Y has only 20 percent in variable costs but 40 percent in fixed costs and 30 percent in semivariable costs. In year 1, sales and profit margins are the same. With 10 percent increase in sales in year 2, Company Y shows a 65 percent gain in operating income compared with 45 percent for X. In the third year sales drop 18 percent, and Y suffers a 76 percent drop in operating income compared with 62 percent for X. Company Y has a more highly leveraged operating structure, making its income more sensitive to a change in sales.

(v) Fixed Charges. *Fixed charges* consist of interest and related expense and an interest factor on capitalized leases, both of which are contractual commitments and are deductible for income taxes. Preferred stock dividends are a fixed charge ahead of the common stock, but they lack the firm contractual commitment of debt and they are not deductible for income taxes.

The key measure of the burden of fixed charges is the interest coverage ratio. This is calculated as:

$$\text{Interest coverage ratio} = \frac{\text{Income before interest and taxes}}{\text{Fixed charges}}$$

This is expressed as "times fixed charges covered." For example, a result of 2.75 is often communicated as 2.75times covered.

If there are senior and subordinated classes of debt, the coverage ratio for the senior debt is calculated separately by using only the interest cost of the senior debt as the divisor. Coverage for the subordinated debt is calculated on an overall basis, as shown.

Interest on borrowed funds used for large construction and development projects is often required to be capitalized, under Accounting Standards Codification (ASC) 835, *Interest*. Capitalized interest should be added to interest expense in computing coverage ratios. Alternatively, interest earned should not be deducted from interest payable, although it can be included with other income. The bondholder is interested in earnings protection for all interest, regardless of accounting reductions.

The quality perception of fixed income securities is heavily influenced by the coverage ratio. But here again the ratio must be related to the type of business. A ratio of 2.50 times for an electric utility is satisfactory because earnings are stable and it is a regulated monopoly providing a basic service. For an industrial company, a ratio of 5.00 times or 6.00 times would be more appropriate for a highly rated issue because of more variable earnings in competitive markets.

The margin of safety is another ratio used to measure the adequacy of protection for fixed charges.

It is simply the percentage of revenues remaining after fixed charges or, in other words, the pretax margin. In terms of a bond, it shows the percentage by which revenue can decline without endangering full coverage of interest expense. It is useful in conjunction with the coverage ratio. For example, a company may have a small debt and a correspondingly high interest coverage ratio, but a low margin of safety. In such a case, any adversity could quickly wipe out interest coverage despite the low debt.

(vi) Preferred Dividend Coverage.   The coverage of preferred dividends should be calculated on a comprehensive basis, using this formula:

$$\text{Preferred dividend coverage} = \frac{\text{Income before interest and taxes}}{\text{Fixed charges} + \text{pretax preferred dividends}}$$

Because preferred dividends are paid out of income after income taxes, they must be grossed up before being inserted in the formula. Preferred dividends must be divided by (1 minus the marginal income tax rate) to compute the pretax earnings needed to pay the preferred dividend.

The prior deductions method, which simply divides net income by preferred dividends, is not a permissible method unless there is no interest expense. Otherwise this method gives a misleading indication of coverage (see Exhibit 10.4 for fixed charge coverage ratios).

(d) INCOME TAX ANALYSIS.   ASC 740, *Income Taxes,* provides income tax reporting standards. The accounting methods themselves are described in Chapter 17 of this *Handbook.* The purpose of this

---

Debt
$50, senior: Annual interest charges @ 10% = $5
$25, junior (subordinated): Annual interest charges @ 12% = $3
1 million shares of preferred stock: Annual dividend @ $1/share = $1

Partial Income Statement

Income before interest and taxes	$16
Interest: Senior debt	(5)
Junior debt	(3)
Pretax income	$8
Taxes @ 37.5%	3
Net income	5
Preferred dividend	(1)
Net income available for common stock	$ 4

Coverage Ratios
Senior debt: 16 ÷ 5 = 3.2x
Total debt: 16 ÷ 8 = 2.0 (Not 11 ÷ 3 = 3.67)
Preferred: 16 ÷ (5 + 3 + (1 ÷ .625)) = 16 ÷ 9.6 = 1.67 (Not 5 ÷ 1 = 5.0)

Exhibit 10.4   Fixed Charge Coverage Ratios for Company P ($ in millions)

section is to discuss the information available from footnote disclosures required by ASC 740 and the inferences that can be drawn from such data.

Pervasive differences in the objectives and methods of financial reporting and accounting for income taxes generate temporary differences in periodic tax liability and tax expense. (*Note:* Some differences are permanent in that revenues and expenses in the financial statements are never recognized on the tax return and vice versa. These differences are not discussed here since they do not generate deferred taxes and their cash consequences are unambiguous.) These differences are reported as deferred tax liabilities or deferred tax assets, but their cash consequences are not always obvious. In the United States, these differences are usually significant because tax-book conformity is required only in the case of last-in, first-out (LIFO) inventory valuation.

ASC 740 uses a modified liability method; the balance sheet accrual is intended to represent the future cash flow consequences of past events. Thus, a change in tax rates results in the balance sheet asset or liability being marked to market to reflect that change.

Deferred tax assets are fully recorded under the new standard. However, it requires firms to record a valuation allowance when an evaluation of future taxable income suggests that it is more likely than not that some or all of the deferred tax assets may not be realized. As changes in the valuation allowance are included in periodic income tax expense, such changes affect reporting earnings and can be used to manage earnings. In addition, changes in the valuation allowance complicate the assessment of effective tax rates.

ASC 740 also changed some of the "indefinite reversal" provisions of Accounting Principles Board (APB) Opinion Nos. 23 and 24. In particular, companies are required to provide deferred taxes on the reinvested earnings (post-1992) of domestic affiliates accounted for under the equity method. However, the provision of deferred taxes on the undistributed earnings of foreign affiliates remains discretionary.

The major issue of deferred tax accounting remains largely unsolved. What the financial analyst would like to know is what income tax payments (or refunds) can be expected in future years. Unfortunately, no mechanical accounting method predicts tax results with complete certainty.

Fortunately, the disclosure requirements of ASC 740, which expanded those of prior standards, provide useful raw material for analysis of the impact of income taxes on the firm. A brief discussion of the usefulness of these disclosures follows.

- *Disclosure of all deferred tax assets and liabilities.* The required disclosure of all components of tax expense should make it to reconcile income tax expense with income taxes paid.

- *Reconciliation of effective tax rate with statutory rate.* This reconciliation permits the analyst to understand the permanent differences between taxable and reported income as well as sources of income with tax rates that differ significantly from the statutory rate. This information facilitates forecasts of future net income under varying assumptions regarding the sources of pretax income.

- *Sources of deferred tax assets and liabilities for the current year and on a cumulative basis.* Such disclosure permits the analyst to evaluate the financial reporting methods of the firm. Significant sources may include depreciation, impairment, and other "restructuring" charges, revenue and expense recognition methods, and postretirement benefits.

- *The amount of any valuation allowance and the change for the year.* As the valuation allowance is highly judgmental, this disclosure makes the decision transparent so that the analyst can evaluate both the decision (which may signal operating expectations) and its impact on reported income and equity.

- *Unrecognized tax loss carryforwards.* These carryforwards may be available, in some circumstances, to shelter future income.

- *Unrecognized deferred tax liabilities related to the reinvested earnings of foreign affiliates and (pre-1992) domestic affiliates.* This disclosure facilitates the comparison of firms making different choices in this area. In addition, the income tax effects of possible intercompany dividends and dispositions can be evaluated.

Ultimately, therefore, as in most areas of financial reporting, disclosure requirements are the most valuable provisions of the new accounting standard. While companies must report a precise number for income tax expense, disclosures permit analysts to better understand the range of possible outcomes.

Furthermore, generally accepted accounting principles (GAAP) require companies to analyze the technical merits of their tax positions and to determine if these tax positions will be held up if they were ever examined by respective taxing authorities. Thus, if companies determine that it is unlikely that the tax position taken would be sustained, they would be required to record a liability and the tax benefit of their position would be required to be reduced.

Tax positions include such areas as research and development credits taken, capitalization of inventory, excess compensation, decisions to classify certain transactions as tax exempt, and the decision not to file a tax return in a particular state, among many other specific items.

There is a two-step approach to evaluate the company's position, specifically, recognition and measurement. Recognition means approaching the problem from a more-likely-than-not threshold. Basically this means that there must be a 50% likelihood that a position would be sustained if challenged by the taxing authorities. In performing the second step, measurement, the tax benefit of a position is the largest amount of the tax benefit that is more than 50% likely to be received if a settlement is made with the taxing authority. The company assesses the probability of possible benefit outcomes based on the taxing authority having full knowledge of all relevant information and determines the tax benefit that would be recognized in the financial statements based on the largest cumulative amount of benefit that is more than 50% likely to reflect the ultimate outcome.

(e) EARNINGS POWER ANALYSIS.   Having analyzed reported net income, the analyst can proceed to the comparison of one company with another and to the projection of future earnings. The types of ratio and trend analysis already discussed are applicable here:

- Net income margin on sales
- Trend over last 5 and 10 years, measured by compound growth rate, least squares trend, or averages for periods
- Variability over the same period as measured by the standard deviation from trend, or between cyclical peaks and troughs

These measures can be used to compare the company with others in the same industry and with companies in other industries. These comparisons usually reveal which companies have the most favorable trends in earning power.

10.3 ACCOUNTING AND REPORTING ISSUES

The impacts of various accounting and reporting issues on reported earnings, analysis of risk, and earnings power are discussed in this section.

(a) QUALITY OF EARNINGS.   Financial statements prepared in accordance with GAAP may fall short of meeting the needs of investment analysts for various reasons. GAAP-based financial reporting provides a record of significant accounting events but does not report all relevant economic events. The selection and quantification of economic events qualifying for accounting recognition is highly variable across firms. Within GAAP, management has considerable latitude in its choice of methods (LIFO versus first-in, first-out, [FIFO]; accelerated versus straight-line depreciation) and estimates (service lives; residual values) resulting in inconsistencies and measurement biases across firms and over time, in accordance with ASC 330, *Inventory*. Thus, an evaluation of the quality of earnings is an essential component of a comprehensive analysis of financial statements.

Bernstein and Siegel define *quality of earnings* as a measure (qualitative) of the comparative integrity, reliability, and predictive ability of reported earnings.[1] Thus, the quality of earnings

---

[1] L. A. Bernstein and J. G. Siegel, "The Concept of Earnings Quality," *Financial Analysts Journal* 35, no. 4 (July–August 1979): 72–75.

is determined by the degree to which selected accounting policies reflect economic reality and represent future earning power. This determination must be made across firms and over time for the firm, allowing an assessment of comparability (similarity of accounting policies between companies) and consistency (continuity over time). Various accounting issues requiring particular attention are discussed in the next sections.

(b) INVENTORY.   The principal methods of valuing inventories are LIFO, FIFO, and average cost, which are explained in Chapter 13. LIFO accounting results in lower reported income, lower current taxes, and better forecasts of future earnings when price levels are increasing and inventory quantities are constant or increasing. Despite tax benefits, many major industrial companies have not adopted LIFO. Earnings comparisons across firms can be misleading if no adjustment is made for differences in inventory accounting. Average cost earnings will fall between those computed using LIFO or FIFO. The LIFO earnings of a FIFO firm may be approximated by computing the LIFO effect as shown next:

$$\text{LIFO effect} = \text{FIFO beginning inventory} \times \text{percent changes in}$$

$$\text{specific price level (for major segment(s) of the firm)}$$

The LIFO effect is the difference in cost of goods sold between the LIFO and FIFO methods. Given the effective tax rate for the firm, the impact on income taxes and reported income can be determined. It is easier to determine the FIFO earnings of a LIFO firm since such firms will disclose the LIFO reserve or the difference between LIFO and FIFO ending inventories. The difference between two consecutive LIFO reserves is the LIFO effect for that time period. The LIFO reserve should be added to the LIFO ending inventory balance to approximate the current cost of inventories on hand. Earnings reported using LIFO generally will not reflect the same trend/growth rate represented by the same earnings stream under FIFO. A liquidation of LIFO layers will increase reported income and current taxes. This impact on net income is generally disclosed in the footnotes. However, liquidations may signal changes in future earnings and/or investment in the affected segment. The analyst should not confuse liquidations with declines in the LIFO reserve that are a result of decreases in inventory prices.

LIFO inventory accounting comes in different forms. A firm may use a single LIFO "pool" or many pools; that choice has an impact on LIFO liquidations. Pools generally contain products that are substantially identical. A second variant is pricing, as firms can construct internal price indices rather than using government-produced indices. Users should watch for changes in accounting estimates in these areas. Note that the LIFO variant used for financial reporting purposes may differ from that used for tax reporting, despite the conformity requirement.

(c) DEPRECIATION.   Periodic depreciation expense allocates the cost of long-lived assets to operating periods during which the assets are used in production. The expense is a function of the chosen depreciation method, asset lives, and residual values. Although a substantial number of companies use accelerated depreciation methods for income tax reporting, few do so for financial reporting. Those that do so will report lower and more conservative net income. The cash impact of depreciation is due to the tax savings generated by the depreciation method used for income tax reporting. The use of different depreciation methods in tax and financial reporting results in a difference between the tax liability and reported tax expense—that is, a deferred tax expense, which is disclosed in the footnotes. This deferred tax amount divided by the federal statutory tax rate gives an approximation of the difference in depreciation expense and can be used to adjust reported net income. Since depreciation expense is based on historical cost, it tends to overstate income when price levels are increasing. Thus, accelerated depreciation methods may provide a reasonable approximation of replacement or current cost depreciation.

Asset lives also affect reported depreciation expense. Management has some latitude in the determination of asset lives since judgment and experience are used in this choice. Footnote disclosure of depreciation policies can be used to compare asset lives of similar companies in the same industry. A comparison of the ratio of depreciation expense to gross fixed assets frequently eliminates the effects of different depreciation curves and different useful lives.

The average age of fixed assets used in operations may be computed by dividing the accumulated depreciation by depreciation expense. The ratio of gross property, plant, and equipment to depreciation expense reflects the average life assumption used in reporting. Increasing investment due to expansion or declining investment due to deteriorating business conditions will distort these ratios, suggesting the need for caution in interpreting trends in these ratios over time and across firms.

The third component of the depreciation calculation is residual value. Changes in estimates of residual value reduce the depreciable base and, therefore, depreciation expense.

The depreciation policy adopted for idled/underutilized facilities should be analyzed for inferences regarding the quantification and timing of unamortized costs expected to be recovered through future operations. Changes in depreciation policy may mask a deteriorating financial condition or pervasive asset impairment.

(d) EXPENSE DEFERRALS.   Discretionary costs are subject to management control, and earnings can be managed when expenses (such as marketing or research) are accelerated or deferred. The decision whether to capitalize or expense can also significantly affect reported income. The capitalization decision also increases reported cash flow from operations as expenditures are included in cash flow for investment. For example, some firms capitalize software development costs while others do not. While GAAP allows the capitalization of construction-related interest, not all firms do so.

Other areas that warrant attention include estimates related to:

- Deferral of marketing expenditures and sales commissions
- Accrual or deferral of major maintenance expenditures
- Credit loss accruals
- Warranty accruals

(e) REVENUE RECOGNITION.   Revenue generally is recognized when goods are sold or as services are rendered. Since the activities of one period may generate cash flows in subsequent periods, both the quantification and timing of revenue recognition present problems. The timing of sales and services, uncertainties regarding the collection of expected inflows, and expected future costs of providing services should be evaluated in the context of the firm's operations and compared to prevailing industry practices. Various specialized industries including franchising, real estate, motion pictures, and television require particular attention. The increasing reliance on fee-based services by the financial services sector of the economy and the growth of leasing also present challenging revenue recognition issues.

Revenue recognition has been a particular problem in recent years. Specific areas of concern include:

- Sales incentives such as discounts, undocumented right of return, and the granting of stock options
- Barter arrangements that create difficult measurement issues
- Recording revenue when an agreement is signed or when goods are ordered rather than over the agreement's term or when the goods are shipped
- Recognizing revenues for which the firm is merely an agent
- Reporting shipping and handling costs as revenues
- Premature recognition of revenues although the earnings process is not yet complete

While ASC 605, *Revenue Recognition* and SEC Staff Accounting Bulletin (SAB) 101 and, as updated as SAB 104, *Revenue Recognition in Financial Statements,* provide current authoritative guidance, reporting rules continue to evolve to meet increasingly complex business transactions.

(f) DISCONTINUED OPERATIONS, EXTRAORDINARY GAINS (LOSSES), AND UNUSUAL ITEMS. The assessment of future earnings power is a function of the predictability of income statistics. Thus, analysts are concerned with revenues and expenses directly related to the normal and recurring operations since they reflect future earning power. The inclusion of unusual or nonrecurring events would distort the predictability of reported income. Inconsistently applied definitions or interpretations of recurring versus nonrecurring events would reduce comparability across firms and may provide a basis for manipulation or smoothing of income. However, unusual and extraordinary data may be relevant to the evaluation of managerial efficiency.

Existing reporting standards require separate reporting of material, unusual, *and* infrequent events in the income statement. These events are evaluated with reference to the specific and similar firms in the same industry in light of the firm's environment. Qualifying extraordinary items are reported separately, net of tax effects, after operating income. The related earnings-per-share (EPS) amounts also are disclosed separately. Examples include expropriation of assets by foreign governments and gains or losses due to debt extinguishment.

Events that are either unusual or infrequent but not both may be reported on a separate line in the income statement but cannot be reported net of taxes. Additional footnote disclosure often accompanies these events, and it may provide insights into their effect on future earning power and cash flows.

ASC 360, *Property, Plant and Equipment,* requires the recognition of impairments when one or more impairment indicators are present and the expected gross cash flows from the assets are less than their carrying amount. The loss is measured as the difference between the fair value of the asset(s) or the present value of the cash flows and the carrying value of the asset(s). This two-step approach to recognition and measurement will leave the timing of recognition and amount of the impairment loss substantially at the discretion of management.

Impairments of long-lived assets, write-downs or write-offs (henceforth inclusively referred to as *impairments*), and restructurings generally are reported on a separate line in the income statement. Impairments and write-downs are due to substantial changes in technological or market conditions and eliminate past cash flows related to assets the firm may idle or continue to operate at reduced levels. Their contribution to future earnings and cash flows is uncertain as to timing and amount.

Restructuring provisions often include impairments and may reflect significant reorganizations of business. The nonimpairment-related components of restructuring include termination or severance costs in addition to various other current and future cash outflows.

The operating results of and the gain (loss) due to disposal of qualifying discontinued segments also must be reported separately, net of taxes, after income from continuing operations. The related EPS effects also are presented separately. Discontinued segments are reported separately if their assets, results of operations, and other activities can be clearly segregated from the assets, results of operations, and other activities of the firm. This segregation must be accomplished physically, operationally, and for financial reporting purposes.

(g) CHANGING PRICES. As financial statements are based largely on historical costs, price changes tend to reduce the usefulness of such statements. Whereas periods of high inflation have ushered in attempts to provide inflation-adjusted data, most financial statements provide little assistance to the user in gauging the effects of changing prices on the enterprise.

When the LIFO method of inventory valuation is used, the analyst can use required disclosures to make the necessary adjustments. Adding back the LIFO reserve (which must be disclosed) provides a reasonable estimate of the current value of inventories. When FIFO or average cost is used, inventories are already stated at close to current value.

For public companies, the 10-K annual report filed with the SEC may contain a considerable amount of information about the location and extent of real estate holdings. For some categories (shopping centers, hotels, etc.), industry rules of thumb may enable one to translate physical data (e.g., square footage) into market value data.

Clues may be available in the financial statements. Real estate taxes paid may indicate assessed values. When borrowings are secured by specific holdings, some inference about value can be made. The income (or cash flow) generated by real estate investments may be an indication of value. Assets acquired via a purchase method acquisition can be assumed to have been written up at that time; if goodwill was created, one can assume that the write-up was the maximum possible.

When natural resources are included in fixed assets, additional information may be provided. Companies with reserves of oil and natural gas are required under industry-specific GAAP to provide information about the physical quantities and their discounted present value based on current costs and prices. Although such data are based on estimates and preparers strongly discourage their use, these data are widely used in the financial community to value such reserves. For other natural resource holdings (coal, precious metals, etc.), only physical data must be disclosed. The analyst must make assumptions in order to value these holdings, but the result is usually closer to fair value than the historical cost of such holdings.

Investments may also require adjustment. If investee financial statements are available, they can be used to value the holding, perhaps by comparison with public companies in the same industry. In making such comparisons, the user should take care to adjust for differences in accounting methods and financial leverage. When investments include holdings of public companies, current market value can be used in place of cost in certain circumstance.

The discussion thus far has focused on balance sheet valuation. However, the income statement should also be adjusted for changing prices. To the extent that income includes holding gains resulting from price increases, whether realized or unrealized, the financial markets may discount reported earnings.

In the area of inventories, the use of LIFO removes the effect of rising prices from reported earnings. For non-LIFO inventories, an approximation must be made. If the company is in one line of business, a government or private price index may be employed to estimate the inflation component. The percentage price change should be multiplied by the starting inventory, and the result (after tax) should be subtracted from operating net income. For multiple lines of business, this should be done on a segmented basis when possible.

(h) FOREIGN OPERATIONS.   Financial statements of companies with foreign operations are made more complex by the effects of changing currency rates. The functional currencies chosen by a company for its foreign operations have an important effect on how currency changes affect reported earnings. Under ASC 830, *Foreign Currency Matters,* the translation of functional currency balance sheets into the reporting currency (U.S. dollar for U.S. companies) generates gains or losses that are deferred to a separate component of stockholders equity. Such gains or losses accumulate indefinitely unless a foreign subsidiary is sold or impairment is recognized.

The U.S. dollar must be used as the functional currency in a hyperinflationary economy (defined as three-year cumulative inflation exceeding 100 percent). As a result, translation gains and losses are included in earnings. Even when the translation effects of foreign currency changes are excluded from the income statement, reported sales and earnings may be materially affected by such changes. Revenues and costs incurred in foreign currencies are translated into the reporting currency using average exchange rates for the period. When the reporting currency rises, for example, foreign currency earnings and sales will appear to be smaller. In periods of large fluctuations of the dollar against other major currencies, such rate changes can have a significant impact on the apparent sales and earnings trends of companies with large foreign operations.

The analysis of foreign operations cannot be confined to looking at the accounting consequences of exchange rate changes. Such changes may have real economic consequences that are quite different from the accounting impacts. For most foreign operations, changing exchange rates do have an impact on local operations. To the extent that local operations compete with imports from or exports to other countries, currency rate changes will affect real profitability analysis of a company with foreign operations, therefore, requires two levels of analysis. First, the user must understand how the reported results of foreign operations have been affected by the currency rate changes alone. Second, the user must examine the underlying economic relationships in order to understand the trend of real profitability of such operations.

(i) POSTEMPLOYMENT BENEFITS. Companies with defined benefit pension plans must account for such plans in accordance with ASC 715, *Compensation—Retirement Benefits.* Because GAAP permits considerable latitude in making actuarial assumptions and provides for deferred recognition of differences between assumptions and realized results, both income statement and balance sheet may contain considerable noise.

The balance sheet generally includes only the cumulative differences between accrued pension cost and contributions actually made. The best measure of pension fund status is normally the difference between the fair value of fund assets and the projected benefit obligation. The gap between the amounts reflected on the balance sheet and the funded status results from deferred recognition of actuarial gains and losses, plan amendments, and the initial impact of ASC 715.

Replacing the amounts actually recognized with the funded status will reflect the actual plan status, as if the plan had been consolidated with the corporate parent. In some cases, when plan termination can be assumed, the accumulated benefit obligation may be a better measure of the liability. Note that both liability measures are highly sensitive to the choice of discount rate. That rate can vary from company to company and, for the same company, from year to year.

Pension cost and operation expense consists of four components: (1) service cost; (2) interest on the projected benefit obligation; and (3) assumed return on assets (ROA) may be considered the "normal" portion of pension cost; while (4) amortization components vary from year to year. Note that even the "normal" costs are sensitive to the choice of discount rate and assumed rate of ROA. Comparability and consistency cannot be assumed.

GAAP also distinguishes reporting for employers providing postemployment benefits other than pensions (known as other postemployment benefits, or OPEB). The accounting for such benefits is discussed in Chapter 27 in this *Handbook.*

From the analysis point of view, the new standard was an enormous improvement. As in the case of pensions, disclosures permit analysts to see behind the accounting conventions to the economics of the plans.

(i) Analysis of OPEB Disclosures. An important area of focus should be plan amendments. Because of the sharply rising cost of health care (the major component of the OPEB liability), many firms have introduced cost sharing, caps, and other provisions intended to limit the employer obligation. Such plan amendments, in many cases, reduce the reported liability. Many companies with amendments also report gains ultimately reduce plan expense and increase reported income.

(ii) Impact of Actuarial Assumptions. Companies that have adopted ASC 715 will have made a number of assumptions required to estimate both the benefit obligation and the postretirement benefit cost. Some of these assumptions, which must be disclosed, include:

- Asset and liability discount rates
- Expected long-term rate of return on plan assets
- Rate of compensation growth

In the case of postretirement benefits, the last two of these items are rarely significant. Because plan assets are minimal, the return assumption has little impact on benefit cost. The rate of compensation growth is also unimportant for most nonpension benefit plans. The discount rate, however, remains highly significant.

Because the discount rate is used to compute the present value of the benefit obligation, the latter is highly sensitive to the choice of rate. If experience with pensions is a guide, there will be considerable variation among companies, and the chosen rate will vary over time. A higher discount rate will reduce the benefit obligation (and therefore the transition liability) and the service cost (present value of benefits earned in current year) component of benefit cost.

For postretirement healthcare benefits, which are the most important nonpension benefits in most cases, the benefit obligation is also extremely sensitive to assumptions regarding the future cost of medical care. The most important of these assumptions is the healthcare cost trend rate. GAAP requires disclosure of:

- The trend rate used for the next year
- The pattern of rates used thereafter

For example, Caterpillar disclosed in its 2010 annual report that:

The annual rate of increase in health care costs was assumed at 7.4% for 2008, 7.0% for 2009, and 7.9% for 2010.

Such disclosures should be compared with those of other companies as lower trend rates result in reduced measures of both the liability and expense of postretirement health care plans.

These disclosures are intended to improve the comparability of the benefit obligations and costs of different employers when they are based on different assumptions. They also reveal the sensitivity of the benefit obligation to the trend rate assumption.

Caterpillar disclosed that a 1-percentage-point increase in trend rates for each future year would increase the accumulated pension benefit obligation (APBO) by approximately $2.0 billion. The different degree of sensitivity to changes in the trend rate can be dramatic, depending on company size and plan funding.

Caterpillar also reported in its 2010 annual report that a 1 percent increase (decrease) in the assumed healthcare cost trend rate would increase (decrease) the APBO by approximately $500 million. This two-sided disclosure shows the effect on the firm of both higher and lower healthcare inflation.

(iii) Impact of Mergers and Acquisitions.   As in the case of pensions, postretirement benefits must be explicitly recognized when an acquisition is accounted for using the purchase method of accounting. The transition liability is therefore shown on the acquirer's balance sheet following the effective date of the acquisitions. Such recognition means that no adjustment to net worth is required for purposes of analysis except for gains and losses deferred subsequent to the date of the acquisition.

(j) MERGERS AND ACQUISITIONS.   Companies that make significant acquisitions transform their financial statements. Analysis of such companies must attempt to understand the effects of these transactions.

U.S. GAAP and the International Financial Reporting Standards (IFRS) now both prohibit the use of the pooling (uniting) methods of reporting mergers and acquisitions. Under the purchase method, the assets and liabilities of the acquired company are revalued to current market; any excess of the purchase price over the fair value of nets assets acquired become goodwill. ASC 805, *Business Combinations,* requires a periodic assessment of goodwill for impairment.

Under the purchase method, the acquired firm is included in financial statements effective with the acquisition date. This creates an illusion of growth, especially when many small acquisitions make it impossible to track the contribution of each acquisition to operating results. Some firms become dependent on frequent acquisitions. If their stock price declines or access to credit is restricted, the growth trend may disappear.

The inclusion of the assets and liabilities of the acquired firm creates a discontinuity, instantly changing the financial ratios of the enterprise. The mix of historical cost (the assets and liabilities of the acquirer are not restated) and fair values (acquired firm) also hampers analysis. When the acquired firm was public and/or the acquisition is significant, there may be adequate disclosure to permit analysis of the effect of the acquisition on ratios and other performance indicators. When the acquired firm is reported as a segment, segment data may permit the analyst to track the effect of the acquisition on future operating results.

(k) PUSH-DOWN ACCOUNTING. When an entity that has been acquired in an acquisition accounted for by the purchase method issues its own financial statements, those statements may reflect that transaction. In most cases, the purchase method adjustments will be pushed down into the financial statements of the acquiree.

This is often seen when an acquired company has publicly held debt or preferred stock and, therefore, continues to publish separate financial statements. Such statements may also be presented to bank lenders, creditors, and customers.

The footnotes of these financial statements normally will show the effect of the purchase method adjustments. Users of such statements should bear in mind that the purchase method adjustments will distort ratios derived from both balance sheet and income statement data.

When companies that have been taken private through leveraged buyouts are taken public again, their statements usually will reflect push-down accounting. Comparisons of such entities with others that have not gone through the revaluation process must take into account the effects of push down on the balance sheet and income statement.

(l) ANALYSIS OF SEGMENT DATA. ASC 280, *Segment Reporting,* requires firms to provide data on each reportable segment of their business, both annually and for interim periods. The standard uses the management approach under which segment disclosures depend on the firm's internal organization. These data, augmented by the management discussion and analysis, generally are helpful in assessing the firm's operating results. However, four problems limit the usefulness of these data:

1. *Reported segment data depend on the data reported to top management.* Thus, firms that have skimpy internal information systems may report less data.

2. *Segment data may be based on a different accounting system than the U.S. GAAP used for consolidated reporting.* For example, data for regulated subsidiaries can be reported using regulatory GAAP if such data are used for internal reporting purposes. Similarly, foreign subsidiaries may report using local GAAP if such data are reported to top management.

3. *Reported segment data depend on internal allocation policies.* Thus, comparisons of firms with different policies will be difficult. The main use of segment data will remain the analysis of trends within each company.

4. *Companies with large foreign operations may provide less data about such geographic segments.* The segments' results may fluctuate due to economic and foreign currency volatility.

(m) ANALYSIS OF INTERIM RESULTS. When analyzing a company's financial statements, normally the latest annual data are supplemented by subsequent interim reports. Although use of interim data is essential because of its timeliness, some caution must be exercised.

For public companies, the user should always obtain the 10-Q quarterly reports filed with the SEC. Shareholder reports are often highly abbreviated. The 10-Q will contain financial statements that may be the equivalent of those found in the annual report except for footnotes.

The lack of footnotes sometimes limits the usefulness of interim reports. Whereas major accounting changes should be disclosed in the 10-Q, changes in estimates may not be. Some of the financial data may be condensed as well.

However, the major reason for caution in the use of interim data is the possibility of drawing misleading conclusions. Companies with a high degree of seasonality will produce interim results that are not an indicator of annual performance. Retailers, for example, produce a disproportionate part of earnings in the quarter that includes the Christmas selling period. A secondary peak around Easter is also normal. Interim results of seasonal companies should, therefore, be compared with the interim results of the corresponding period for prior years.

Accounting for income taxes may create some difficulty in interpreting interim results. As income tax expense is determined on an annual basis, interim tax expense must be estimated based on assumptions about the full year. Income tax expense for the first quarter, for example, must be determined by using the estimated tax rate for the full year. This rate must be re-estimated each quarter. Changes in the estimated tax rate may distort quarterly results.

The LIFO inventory accounting is also determined on an annual basis and depends on prices and physical inventory levels at the end of the year. Here again, quarterly results depend on estimates of the year-end position, and a new estimate must be made each quarter.

More generally, there is more scope for companies to "manage" earnings on a quarterly basis. Expenses can be deferred (or accrued) in ways that would not be permitted at a fiscal year-end. In addition, transactions may be accounted for differently after auditor guidance.

ASC 280 requires abbreviated segment reporting on an interim basis. Such data should facilitate the analysis of interim data and the use of such data to forecast future operating results.

(n) INTERNATIONAL REPORTING DIFFERENCES. The continued growth of international capital markets and trade has resulted in increasingly multinational enterprises with complex financial statements consolidating operations in various countries and prepared using their different reporting standards. However, the absence of globally accepted accounting standards makes it difficult to analyze and compare investments across countries. A brief discussion of various efforts to harmonize standards and achieve comparability follows.

(i) International Accounting Standards Board. Reorganized in 2001, the International Accounting Standards Board (IASB) has established IFRS that provide a credible alternative to U.S. GAAP. Its multinational members produced 41 standards as of June 30, 2011, a Framework for the Preparation and Presentation of Financial Statements (similar to the FASB's conceptual framework), and a Standing Interpretations Committee (similar to the FASB's Emerging Issues Task Force [EITF]).

A number of non-U.S. companies have adopted IAS IFRS. Starting in 2009, the SEC allowed foreign registrants to report based on IAS without a U.S. GAAP reconciliation. At the time of this publication, the timing, nature, and extent of harmonization of international reporting rules with U.S. GAAP remains uncertain.

(ii) Reporting by Foreign Issuers in the United States. Foreign firms may directly sell securities in the United States or their securities may be traded as depositary shares American Depository Receipts (ADRs). These companies may follow the registration and reporting requirements applicable to domestic companies or elect to report as foreign registrants on Forms 20-F and 6-K, which are comparatively less comprehensive. Foreign firms filing Form 20-F must reconcile reported income and equity to U.S. GAAP. The reconciliations contain information useful in understanding accounting differences and comparing alternative investments.

(o) ANALYSIS OF INVESTMENTS. The recognition of market values in historical cost financial statements has been one of the major accounting controversies of recent years. Strong support for mark-to-market accounting from the SEC has resulted in actions by the FASB that increase both disclosures of market values and their use in financial statements.

There are two basic issues. One is whether market value should supplant historic cost for investments. The argument for market value is greater relevance; the argument for historic cost is based on reliability. This issue, in practice, comes down to where to draw the line. There is little argument against carrying marketable equity securities, for example, at market value but enormous opposition to marking to market bank loans and fixed income investments expected to be held to maturity. A related issue concerns the advisability of marking to market only the asset side of the balance sheet while leaving liabilities at historic cost.

The second issue is the disposition of unrealized gains and losses. The choice is between immediate recognition in reported income and deferral via stockholders' equity.

ASC 320, *Investments—Debt and Equity Securities,* requires firms to categorize investments in debt and equity securities in these ways:

- *Debt securities classified as held to maturity.* Such investments are measured at amortized cost. Any realized gains or losses are included in reported income. This classification requires that the firm have both the intent and the ability to hold the securities until maturity.

- *Trading securities (debt and equity).* These investments are measured at fair (market) value as current assets. Unrealized (as well as realized) gains and losses are included in reported income.
- *Securities available for sale (debt and equity).* These securities, carried either as current or noncurrent assets, are also measured at fair value. However, unrealized gains and losses are reported as a separate component of stockholders' equity and excluded from reported earnings until sold.

For analysis purposes, three objectives arise related to investments:

1. All investment income should be removed from operating income; market value changes in particular (whether realized or unrealized) obscure the reported results of operations.
2. The total return (including market value changes) should be compared with benchmark return data in order to evaluate the investment performance of the investments.
3. When analyzing the balance sheet, all portfolios should be marked to market, given the greater relevance of market values. For unrealized gains and losses, deferred taxes should be provided when sale would generate tax payments or refunds.

Based solely on management intent, ASC 320 made no real difference as it simply replaced one arbitrary set of classifications with another. Investment returns still will have to be disentangled from operating results, and investments carried at cost have to be marked to market for analysis.

Such disclosures, however limited, should be valuable in providing estimates of market value for asset classes other than highly marketable equity and debt (for which market values are already disclosed). These disclosed values should be used, for analytic purposes, in place of historic cost in order to mark to market investment portfolios.

For financial institutions, however, the analyst must recognize that the assets are only half the story. To the extent that such institutions match the characteristics (such as duration) of asset and liability portfolios, market value changes for assets should be accompanied by approximately equal market value changes for liabilities. While, under ASC 320, financial firms are not prohibited from disclosing market values for liabilities, few do so, given the difficult measurement problems. Thus, while the analyst may be able to evaluate the investment performance of the asset portfolios, an evaluation of the effect of market value changes on real (economic) net worth of financial institutions may be elusive.

Recent GAAP related to fair value measurements also requires expanded footnote disclosures about fair value measurement. A common hierarchy was established to help companies measure fair values for their annual reports. There are three levels to the hierarchy. The most reliable is Level 1, because it is based on observable inputs, such as market prices for identical assets and liabilities, such as publicly listed companies. Less reliable is Level 2, because it is based on market-based inputs other than those that were included in Level 1. That is, rather than basing the valuation on market prices for identical assets and liabilities, the valuation is based on market prices for similar assets and liabilities. Finally, Level 3 is the least reliable, because it is based on unobservable inputs, such as the company's own assumption or data that are developed, for instance, by using present value or expected cash flow techniques.

(p) STOCK COMPENSATION PLANS. ASC 718, *Compensation—Stock Compensation,* requires disclosure of extensive data regarding stock options and similar compensation plans. Firms are required to disclose the pro forma effect on net income and EPS of recording the cost of such plans as an expense.

Since the FASB made income statement recognition of stock compensation expense voluntary, virtually no firm included these costs in net income. However, a few firms have decided to report these costs in net income. For analysis and valuation, when only pro forma data are available, they should be used instead of reported net income and EPS. As stock compensation plans often represent a significant element of compensation, omitting their cost overstates income relative to firms that use other forms of compensation that must be expensed.

(q) EARNINGS PER SHARE.   ASC 260, *Earnings Per Share,* requires reporting of basic and diluted EPS. Basic EPS excludes the effect of all dilutive securities. For valuation, only diluted EPS should be used. For trend analysis, however, especially over short time periods, basic EPS may be more useful as it ignores the effect on EPS of stock prices.

10.4 BALANCE SHEET ANALYSIS

(a) ELEMENTS OF THE BALANCE SHEET.   The balance sheet reports the status of the company's financial position at a point in time, in contrast to the income statement, which reflects the flow of operating and earning activities during a period. Because earnings are essential for an enterprise's financial health, primary analytical emphasis has focused on earning power; balance sheet analysis is equally important, however, for a comprehensive understanding of a company's financial position and progress.

The main components of the balance sheet are the enterprise's assets or financial resources and the equities or claims against those resources. Assets represent probable future economic benefits obtained or controlled by the enterprise as a result of past transactions or events. Assets may be physical or tangible—for example, inventories, plant and equipment, and natural resources. Some assets are intangible in that they represent legal claims or rights to economic resources—for instance, patents and copyrights.

Equities are either external claims against the enterprise's resources (i.e., liabilities), or they represent the "residual" interests of the firm's owners, called *stockholders'* or *owners' equity.* Liabilities are probable future sacrifices of economic resources because of the enterprise's present obligations to transfer resources or provide services to external claimants in the future as a result of past transactions or events. Examples are accounts payable, taxes, and bonds payable.

Owners' equity is the residual interest of the owners of the enterprise and represents the excess of the assets over liabilities. It includes preferred and common stock, additional paid-in capital, and the earnings retained in the enterprise. Owners' equity represents the capital invested in the firm by its owners.

Statement of Financial Accounting Concept No. 6 (CON 6) reorganizes the stockholders' equity section by introducing the concept of comprehensive income, defined as:

> the change in equity of a business enterprise during a period from transactions and other events and circumstances from nonowner sources. It includes all changes in equity during a period except those resulting from investments by owners and distributions to owners. [par. 70]

Thus, comprehensive income includes both net income and direct-to-equity adjustments (other comprehensive income) such as:

- Cumulative translation adjustments
- Minimum pension liability
- Unrealized gains and losses on available-for-sale securities
- Deferred gains and losses on cash flow hedges

While such reporting does not change financial statement measurements, it does organize the elements of other comprehensive income to facilitate their analysis. These elements represent economic changes that have not yet been recognized in net income but often have implications for securities valuation; they can be ignored only at the analyst's peril.

Assets and liabilities are defined as economic resources and claims against these resources. However, the financial reporting system emphasizes the recording of accounting events rather than economic events. Many relevant economic events receive no recognition in financial statements; for example, the impact of price-level changes on reported quantifications of assets and liabilities is virtually ignored since financial statements are based on historical costs.

The selection of economic events that receive accounting recognition is discretionary and highly variable across firms. Leases, which in substance may be installment purchases of assets, may not receive accounting recognition if the lease contract is structured to avoid capitalization criteria in accounting standards. Management may also select from different methods and use different estimates in quantifying selected accounting events (e.g., inventory valuation, depreciation methods, service lives, and pension costs). These factors lead to significant inconsistencies and measurement biases in the financial statements of different firms and of the same firm over time.

The explosive growth in OBS financing transactions, such as sales or securitization of receivables, take-or-pay contracts, and leases has increased the divergence between reported accounting and economic assets and liabilities. These transactions generally are structured as executory contracts, thereby avoiding accounting recognition [see Subsection 10.4(c)(vii)].

Balance sheet classification of reported assets and liabilities is based on their respective time cycles for realization. Current assets and liabilities are expected to be realized or paid within a 12-month period or within the normal operating cycle of the firm, whichever is longer. Long-term assets are intended for use in the business, such as plant and equipment, or are not intended for sale, such as investments in affiliates. Long-term liabilities such as bonds payable are due after one year. Owners' equity represents the residual interest and as such is the permanent capital invested in the firm. Balance sheet analysis revolves around the interrelationships among a firm's various components.

(b) LIQUIDITY ANALYSIS. Short-term lenders, suppliers, and creditors focus on the liquidity of the firm in their assessment of its risk level. The evaluation concerns the firm's ability to meet its maturing obligations at a given point in time; equally important are changes in that ability over time. Cash or cash equivalents become available through liquidation of short-term debt and equity instruments, collection of receivables, and conversion of inventories into receivables through sales, thence into cash. In ongoing businesses, continuing operations require new investments in inventories and receivables to replace those converted to cash. Thus, receivables and inventories are to a considerable extent "permanent capital," not liquid assets, except for seasonal businesses that experience troughs and peaks. However, as financial markets evolve, securitization of receivables and more effective inventory financing and management techniques may erode the permanence of capital invested in these liquid assets.

(i) Analytical Ratios. Two ratios traditionally are used in the assessment of short-term liquidity and financial flexibility: the current ratio and the quick ratio. They apply primarily to industrial, merchandising, and service companies rather than to utilities or financial services companies. These two ratios are defined as shown next:

$$\text{Current ratio} = \frac{\text{Current assets (cash and equivalents, receivables, and investories)}}{\text{Current liabilities (payable, accruals, taxes, and debt due in 1 year)}}$$

$$\text{Quick ratio} = \frac{\text{Cash and equivalents plus receivables}}{\text{Current liabilities}}$$

The application of these ratios is illustrated in Exhibit 10.5.

Company N begins the year (column A) with a current ratio of 2.0, which reflects an ample margin of current assets over current liabilities; the quick ratio of 1.2 indicates that liquid assets alone exceed all current liabilities. The quick ratio is a more conservative measure of relative liquidity in that it assumes liquidity is provided only by cash, cash equivalents, and receivables that normally can be realized in the short run without loss. Inventories usually are further removed from realization and may be subject to loss. Inventories of actively traded commodities—for example, wheat—can be very liquid and should be included among liquid assets in the quick ratio for relevant industries.

Using the Ratios. The measures of liquidity provide an indication of the firm's short-term ability to meet its obligations, but they are superficial by themselves, are limited in that they provide a picture at a specific point in time, and may be distorted at year-end.

	A	B	C
Cash	$10,000	$ 10,000	$25,000
Receivables	20,000	35,000	20,000
Inventory	20,000	55,000	20,000
Current assets	$50,000	$100,000	$65,000
Bank loan	—	35,000	—
Payables	5,000	15,000	5,000
Accruals	10,000	15,000	10,000
Taxes	10,000	10,000	15,000
Current liabilities	25,000	75,000	30,000
Net working capital	$ 25,000	$ 25,000	$35, 000
Ratios			
1. Current ratio	2.00	1.33	2.17
2. Quick ratio	1.20	0.60	1.50

Exhibit 10.5   Liquidity Ratios for Company N

The year-to-year trends and business characteristics also must be analyzed along with continued evaluation of the trend of earnings. A good liquidity position and financial flexibility can erode rapidly with losses and vice versa. If Company N's liquidity position changes in one year from column A to column B, an obvious deterioration has occurred. All liquidity ratios are lower, and receivables and inventory are higher, increasing the current assets. Current liabilities have increased since short-term bank debt has been used to finance the increase in current assets.

The analyst and short-term creditor should review the trends in and impact on operating cash flow and earnings through an analysis of trends in sales (by segments, where possible), the collectibility of receivables, and the salability of inventories to evaluate sources of increase in risk and decrease in financial flexibility. The ratio of operating cash flow to average current liabilities may provide insights into causes of changes in the current ratio:

$$\text{Operating cash flow to current liabilities} = \frac{\text{Cash provided by operations}}{\text{Average current liabilities}}.$$

Empirical research by Casey and Bartczak suggests that healthy firms exhibit ratios of 40 percent or better.[2]

However, the changes in and trends of liquidity ratios should be interpreted with caution. When the current ratio exceeds 1.00, equal increases (decreases) in current assets and current liabilities will decrease (improve) the current ratio but need not reflect a decline (improvement) in financial flexibility. Temporary plant shutdowns or recessions may reduce current liabilities or allow the firm to use up inventories with a resulting improvement in current ratios. In contrast, the firm may build up inventories, financing the increase with short-term debt in anticipation of increased sales. These actions may be appropriate but would depress current ratios.

The firm's liquidity position is also susceptible to manipulation. At year-end, purchases may be delayed or receivables sold and proceeds used to retire short-term debt. The use of averages in the ratios and a comparison of ratios over time will mitigate this problem to some extent. Acquisitions and divestitures also significantly distort current ratios. However, some disclosures in the statement of cash flows allow analysts to adjust for these effects.

---

[2] C. J. Casey and N. J. Bartczak, "Using Operating Cash Flow Data to Predict Financial Distress: Some Extension," *Journal of Accounting Research* (Spring 1985): 384–401.

Lenders providing short-term bank debt and publicly traded long-term debt generally control the liquidity risk by imposing requirements for maintenance of minimum current ratios or working capital. These indenture restrictions or debt covenants are disclosed in footnotes to financial statements and often are included in filings with the SEC 10-K reports. The analyst should monitor the firm's maintenance of liquidity ratios specified in debt covenants and evaluate accounting changes—for example, switching to FIFO inventory valuation from LIFO, which may mask deteriorating financial conditions.

The analyst should use footnote disclosures of significant accounting policies to adjust published figures to a more realistic basis. If the LIFO method is used for inventory accounting, the reported book value of inventories may well be far below current value. Footnote disclosures of LIFO reserves should be used to gross up LIFO inventories to equivalent FIFO amounts, improving the current ratio and augmenting comparability with FIFO companies. The marketable securities also should be adjusted from book to market values, allowing for tax effects. These adjustments would make the current assets more representative of the firm's liquidity position.

Seasonal and Cyclical Factors.   Most seasonal businesses have fiscal years ending at the conclusion of the sales cycle when the financial position is most liquid. At interim periods, the current ratios may change considerably from the previous year-end without any change in net working capital and financial flexibility.

Assume that Company N in Exhibit 10.5 is in the holiday season trade and columns A and C represent its financial position at successive January 31 fiscal year-ends, whereas column B reflects its position on October 31. To build inventories for the seasonal peak, the company borrows from its bank and finances receivables by allowing payables and accruals to build up in the normal course of business. At year-end, inventories are liquidated, receivables collected, bank loans repaid, and net profit of $10,000 is added to the net working capital or liquidity position. During the year, Company N also increases long-term debt to expand the plant.

Although the ratios in column B are the same as in the trend analysis in the first case, the circumstances are different. The lower liquidity ratios reflect a temporary condition just before the inventories begin to move into sales. At the end of the season (column C), the liquidity position has returned to "normal" with some improvement due to profitable operations. The analyst should evaluate firm performance relative to the normal pattern of the Christmas trade and industry performance. If the merchandise does not move at the holiday season, the year-end position will be column B rather than column C.

Highly cyclical industries or building contractors may display this same pattern of change over a longer period as volume increases and then subsides.

Fast-Turnover Business.   A retail grocery chain, for example, is mostly a cash business and usually has few or no receivables. It can operate adequately on a current ratio of less than 2.0. Cash is being received as quickly as sales are made, and payables and accruals accumulate and turn over at longer intervals. High daily cash receipts and quick inventory turnover allow such firms to raise cash for unanticipated needs very quickly.

Slow-Turnover Business.   A steel company, in contrast, will have very large inventories and receivables and typically will have a current ratio of 3.0, 4.0, or higher. However, the receivables and inventory are necessary for operations and may not be immediately available to meet current obligations. Hence, a steel company may be no more liquid than the retail grocery chain despite its nominally higher current ratio.

Companies with diverse businesses may include fast- and slow-turnover segments, manufacturing, retail, and financial operations and divisions with different or conflicting restrictions on current ratios. To the extent possible, the analyst should adjust for these differences using information in footnotes and segment reports.

(ii) Activity Ratios.   Liquidity analysis can be augmented by an assessment of how effectively the firm uses its liquid assets. Various activity ratios are used to analyze the operating cycle (i.e., the flow of materials into finished merchandise into receivables into cash).

The inventory turnover ratio provides an indicator of the efficiency of the firm's operations. It is calculated as shown:

$$\frac{\text{Cost of goods sold}}{\text{Average inventory}}$$

The number of days that inventory is on hand can be calculated as:

$$\frac{365}{\text{Inventory turnover}}$$

The turnover ratio and the number of days that inventory is on hand should be analyzed for trends over time and compared to similar firms in the industry. The latter comparison requires an adjustment for any differences in inventory methods. Ideally, for industries experiencing rising prices, the cost of goods sold should be stated in LIFO terms and the inventory balances should reflect current costs (FIFO). Thus, both numerator and denominator would reflect current costs. Use of LIFO inventory cost to compute turnover will inflate that ratio, especially if the LIFO reserve is high relative to LIFO cost.

The receivables turnover and the average number of days that receivables are outstanding indicate the effectiveness of the firm's credit policies and the length of time it takes to convert the receivables to cash:

$$\text{Receivables turnover} = \frac{\text{Net credit sales}}{\text{Average receivables}}$$

$$\text{Number of days receivables are outstanding} = \frac{365}{\text{Receivables turnover}}$$

These ratios are meaningful only when compared to credit terms used by the firm and, if possible, similar firms in the industry. If the credit terms are net 30 days but receivables are outstanding for 50 days on average, collections are slow. When receivables have been sold, the analyst should use footnote data to adjust turnover calculations [see Subsection 10.4(c)(vii)].

The total number of days that inventories are on hand and the number of days that receivables are outstanding indicate the length of the operating cycle of the firm—the amount of time it takes the firm to convert materials into cash. A review of these ratios over time and with similar companies would allow a cash flow forecast and indicate whether short-term obligations can be met with cash flows from operations. Thus, activity ratios are particularly relevant to short-term creditors, such as banks. Creditors should also monitor the earnings power, which is essential to maintain solvency and meet maturing obligations. Without adequate margins, the operating cycle will not produce the cash required to repay debts.

(c) ANALYSIS OF LONG-TERM ASSETS AND LIABILITIES.   Generally, noncurrent assets are stated at their historical cost book values adjusted for depreciation and rarely reflect their economic worth. However, noncurrent assets represent the firm's investments in manufacturing technologies and are relevant to an analysis of its growth prospects.

Investments in nonaffiliated companies are reported at acquisition costs and may well be marketable securities, in which case their current market value can be added to liquid assets that are a part of current assets. Investments in affiliated enterprises and joint ventures are reported at cost plus the proportionate interest in the investee's undistributed earnings. They may represent investments in emerging technologies or acquisitions of operating capacity in partnership with other firms. These investments usually are not available for sale, but they should be analyzed for elements of value different from carrying value. Footnotes often provide separate financial data for such investees. Direct borrowing may support these investments, or the firm may provide indirect guarantees of underlying debt. Since the investor reports its proportionate interest in the net assets of these investees, the debt component of these investments requires analysis. (See discussion on

OBS financing techniques, in Section 10.4(c)(vi). Property, plant, and equipment normally represent permanent investment, and their value to the firm is best measured by their contribution to income. The net carrying value is based on historical cost, which provides some idea of relative magnitude but usually is not indicative of current value. Supplementary note disclosures provide some measure of current value. However, these disclosures are no longer mandatory, which makes analysis difficult if not impossible.

Some types of property have a degree of liquidity, and secondary markets may provide current market values. Substituting these values for net book values may provide insights into a company's economic worth. Reserves of natural resources and commercial real estate are examples.

Oil and gas companies disclose the present values of their reserves of oil and gas; the analyst can use these data to derive an indication of market value. The adjusted valuations have a more practical analytical use than historical book values. Coal reserves and the timber content of forest properties are other examples of natural resource properties to which a similar analysis can be applied. Real estate investment trusts and hotel companies report changes in the market value of their commercial properties and the change in those values as a measure of income, supplementing their standard historical cost accounts.

Deferred charges are accounting numbers that do not represent assets but are incurred expenditures not yet reflected in income. Normally these have minor significance, but they should be examined carefully when they are large or increasing. Reported income may be overstated in such instances.

(i) Fixed Asset Turnover Ratio. A measure of the efficiency of capital investment can be derived as:

$$\frac{\text{Net sales}}{\text{Average fixed assets}}$$

This ratio reflects the sales generated by investments in productive capacity. Some caveats should be noted. Growing companies would report increasing investments in fixed assets resulting in a relatively low turnover. Significant acquisitions accounted for under the purchase method may also lower the turnover. In contrast, cutbacks in investments, discontinued operations, and write-offs will improve the ratio but with possibly negative implications for earning power. Finally, increased reliance on leasing accounted for as operating leases would have a favorable but comparatively misleading impact on this turnover ratio.

(ii) Capitalization Analysis. The analysis of a company's capital structure—the amount of debt relative to equity—is essential for an evaluation of its use of financial leverage and the measurement of its ability to meet its long-term obligations. The use of debt in the capital structure adds fixed costs through contractual interest payments, exerting a leverage effect on the residual return to stockholders. The higher the rate of ROA relative to the fixed after-tax cost of debt capital, the higher the residual return accruing to stockholders. However, the fixed nature of interest payments has an adverse effect on this return during recessions or declines in demand as the rate of ROA falls. Given the priority of debt claims relative to equity, a highly leveraged capital structure will have a negative impact on equity holders when adversity strikes. Conservative debt ratios enhance access to capital markets and improve the investment quality of the common stock.

The firm's ability to meet fixed interest and principal repayment obligations is a function of its earnings and cash-generating ability. The proportion of debt to equity capital and the stability of earnings and operating cash flows determine the riskiness of the firm's capital structure.

Long-term creditors use bond covenants to limit debt levels. Covenants that restrict dividend payments based on measures of cumulative profitability or net worth serve to restrict the firm's ability to strengthen stockholders' position relative to that of bondholders. The analyst should monitor the firm's maintenance of various ratios and relationships specified by bond covenants. Highly leveraged mergers and recapitalizations and their impact on bondholders emphasizes the importance of a detailed analysis of the protection implied by debt covenants.

LION COMPANY
Capitalization Table
(in US$ millions)

	12/31/2010		12/31/2011	
	Amount	% of Total Capital (BV)	Amount	% of Total Capital (BV)
Short-term debt	10	0.19	7	0.14
Long-term debt	3,844	73.12	3,846	76.94
Total Debt (Book Value)	3,854	73.31	3,853	77.08
Common stockholders' equity (Book Value)[1]	$1,403	26.69	$1,146	22.92
Total capital (Book Value)	$5,257	100.00	$4,999	100.00
Common stockholders' equity (Market Value)[2]	$1,800		$1,685	
Total capital (Market Value)	$5,654		$5,538	
Debt		%		%
to equity (BV)		274.7		336.2
to capital (BV)		73.3		77.1
Debt		%		%
to equity (MV)		214.09		228.71
to capital (MV)		68.16		69.58

Notes (2011 Calculations):
[1] From Balance Sheet, includes common stock, paid-in-capital, and retained earnings less treasury stock.
[2] From supplementary information in the Balance Sheet, based on number of shares outstanding and the closing market price on 12/31/2011 (117.56 × $14.33).

Exhibit 10.6   Sample Capitalization Table

(iii) Capitalization Table.   The capital structure of a company is usually presented in a capitalization table derived from the balance sheet. It shows the position and proportion of capital issues in relation to each other and the total capital of the company. Exhibit 10.6 illustrates such a table, of Lion Company, adapted from a real company's filings.

(iv) Debt Ratios.   Three ratios—debt to total capital, debt to equity, and total debt at book value—are used to evaluate the relationship between debt and equity. A comprehensive definition of *debt* includes current debt, long-term debt, capitalized lease obligations, and contractual obligations not afforded accounting treatment as liabilities, for example, take-or-pay payments and certain operating leases. Subsections 10.4(c)(vi) and (vii) discuss the analysis of these OBS financing transactions. Preferred stock may have some characteristics of debt and should be evaluated for the most appropriate classification. A detailed discussion of preferred stock follows this section. All subsidiary debt should be included in total capitalization to determine the total debt supported by the company's capital.

Debt ratios that are based on the balance sheet may be calculated as:

$$\text{Debt to total capital ratio} = \frac{\text{Total current and long-term debt} + \text{capitalized leases}}{\text{Total capital (total debt} + \text{leases} + \text{stockholder's equity)}}$$

This figure expresses debt as a percentage of total capital. Exhibit 10.6 shows that this ratio is 77.1 percent (73.3 percent in 2010) for Lion Company.

The debt-to-equity ratio is defined as:

$$\frac{\text{Total current and long-term debt} + \text{capitalized leases}}{\text{Total stockholders' equity}}$$

This ratio often is used interchangeably with the debt-to-capital ratio, which is preferred. In 2011, this ratio was 336.2 percent (274.7 percent in 2010) for Lion Company.

Total debt at book value should also be compared to the market value of total capital instead of book value:

$$\frac{\text{Total debt at book value}}{\text{Total debt and preferred stock} + \text{common stock at market}}$$

This ratio was 70.96 percent (70.03 in 2010) for Lion Company.

When the market value of total capital is well above book value, the debt ratio will be lower than the book value–based ratio; it will be presumed that the company's earning power and/or market conditions are favorable for issuance of debt to raise needed capital or refund existing debt. However, a continued trend of market value of equity at less than book value may signal deteriorating credit and restricted financial flexibility. Although this ratio will vary because of market fluctuations, it is a useful analytical tool.

These derivations can be altered to focus on senior debt (e.g., mortgage bonds and bank debt) when the capital structure includes junior debt (e.g., debentures or subordinated debt). The junior debt is subtracted from the numerator and added to the denominator, thereby becoming a part of the capital base that supports the senior debt. The debt ratio for senior debt alone is thus more favorable than for the entire debt.

Debt ratios must be viewed in context. The type of business, the variability and trend of earnings, and other relevant factors must be evaluated. For example, a finance company, which has liquid financial assets, and an electric utility, which may be a regulated monopoly providing a basic service, normally carry higher debt ratios than a cyclical manufacturing company.

(v) Preferred Stock Ratios. Preferred stock also has a claim on assets prior to the common stock, and its position and leverage effect are easily shown in the capitalization table. The preferred stock ratio can be classified by seniority (i.e., senior preferred stock and junior preference stock).

Adjustments may be necessary for the correct balance sheet presentation of preferred stocks. For purposes of analysis, preferred stock should be shown at liquidating value rather than at stated value because this is the true measure of its claim on assets. Any excess of liquidating value over stated value should be charged against retained earnings in the common equity.

A second issue is the classification of preferred stock subject to mandatory redemption. The SEC now requires that such stock be shown apart from stockholders' equity. This is based on the notion that mandatory redemption through a sinking or purchase fund makes the preferred stock a "temporary" form of capital analogous to debt. Stockholders' equity is considered "permanent" capital.

Preferred stock may be considered permanent capital (i.e., stockholders' equity) on legal grounds because failure to make dividend or sinking fund payments normally will not cause default or bankruptcy, as with a bond. The principal effect of such failure probably would be to block dividends on the common stock. This common equity nature is stronger in the case of convertible preferred, especially when conversion can be forced by calling the preferred.

However, nonconvertible, mandatorily redeemable preferred stock has the economic characteristics of debt. Thus, it should be treated as subordinated debt for purposes of analysis.

(vi) Off-Balance-Sheet Obligations. Balance sheet–based analyses of capital structure and leverage may understate firm risk because OBS activities and executory contracts do not receive accounting recognition. The OBS transactions are designed to transfer or share the risk of the firm's operations, and they have real current or future cash flow consequences. For example, long-term lease contracts may be, in substance, installment purchases of long-term assets, but they have been structured to avoid capitalization requirements of accounting standards, thereby eliminating balance sheet recognition of the asset and the related liability. Nonrecognition in the financial statements limits the usefulness of capital structure and risk indicators unless proper adjustments are made.

Executory contracts involve commitments to purchase or pay for a commodity or service over a period of time. No liability is recognized since no accounting obligation arises until an exchange transaction is completed. This legalistic definition of liabilities has contributed to their nonrecognition in financial statements.

Firms may engage in these transactions to avoid reporting adverse debt-to-equity ratios and to reduce the probability of technical default under restrictive covenants in debt indentures. Historical cost basis financial statements, which suppress the current value of assets, increase the incentive to engage in OBS transactions to keep liabilities off the books. A detailed review of footnote disclosures of OBS transactions and executory contracts is essential for a comprehensive analysis of capital structure.

(vii) Examples of Off-Balance-Sheet Financing Techniques.   The most common examples of the use of OBS financing techniques are discussed next. When analyzing a company, the analyst must watch for such transactions and make the appropriate adjustments when computing financial ratios.

Accounts Receivable.   Legally separate, wholly owned finance subsidiaries often are created to purchase receivables from the parent, which uses the proceeds to retire debt. When such subsidiaries are unconsolidated, the parent firms report significantly lower debt–equity ratios. In the past, parent companies used the equity method to account for their finance subsidiaries; that is, the consolidated balance sheet reported the parent's net investment in these units, suppressing the debt used to finance receivables. The FASB eliminated this nonconsolidation option, and all post-1987 financial statements must consolidate the assets and liabilities of controlled finance subsidiaries (after relevant intercompany eliminations). The analyst should compute consolidated debt–equity ratios because the parent generally supports finance subsidiary borrowings through extensive income-maintenance agreements and direct or indirect guarantees of its debt.

Receivables also may be financed by sale (or securitization) to unrelated parties with proceeds used to reduce debt. These transactions are effectively collateralized borrowing when receivables are transferred with recourse to the "seller." Footnote disclosures should be analyzed to determine whether the risks and rewards of controlling these receivables have been transferred to the "buyer." Where the "seller" retains these risks and rewards, the analyst should reinstate the receivables and treat the proceeds as debt in computing the debt–equity ratio as well as the current ratio, receivables turnover, and the return on average total capital.

Inventories.   Firms may finance inventory and raw material purchases through take-or-pay commitments whereby they contract to purchase or pay for minimum quantities over a specified time period. The present value of these future obligations should be included in computing debt ratios. Companies typically use take-or-pay contracts to ensure supplies of raw materials or availability of manufacturing capacity. Natural resource companies may use throughput contracts to guarantee distribution needs by contracting with pipelines to purchase or transport minimum quantities. Firms organize joint ventures with related companies or third parties where the take-or-pay commitments effectively guarantee the joint venture's long-term debt service requirements. In some cases, direct guarantees of joint venture or related companies' debt are disclosed in footnotes. The obligations under take-or-pay and throughput arrangements and the direct guarantees should be included in the computation of debt–equity ratios.

Natural resource firms may finance inventories through commodity-indexed debt where interest and/or principal repayments are a function of the price of underlying commodities. Changing commodity prices should be monitored to determine their impact on these liabilities and the debt–equity ratios.

Fixed Assets.   Firms acquire rights to fixed assets through lease contracts structured to avoid capitalization criteria in accounting standards. Footnote disclosure of these operating leases details minimum payments for each of the next five years and the total payments thereafter. Where this payment schedule depicts relatively stable and long-term payments over a period roughly equivalent to the average economic/useful life of similarly owned long-term assets or those undercapitalized leases, the analyst should capitalize these operating leases to adjust reported debt levels. The reported fixed assets, depreciation expense, and interest expense also should be adjusted in order to correctly calculate various affected ratios.

Joint Ventures. Firms acquire, control, or obtain access to distribution and manufacturing capacity through joint ventures and/or investments in affiliated and nonaffiliated companies. In some cases, the joint venture offers economies of scale and needed capacity or provides for a negotiated sharing of technologies, raw materials, or financial risk. The owners of these ventures enter into take-or-pay or throughput arrangements where the minimum guaranteed payments are designed to cover required debt service obligations. These agreements constitute the collateral for the venture's borrowings in the absence of substantial equity investments by various parties to the joint venture. Direct or indirect guarantees of venture's debt may also be present.

Generally, firms account for an investment in the joint ventures using the equity method, since no single firm holds a controlling interest. Thus, the balance sheet reports only the nominal net investment in the venture. Footnotes may disclose the assets, liabilities, and results of operations of the venture in a summarized format. These disclosures should be used for proportionate consolidation of the joint venture with the firm. Any direct or indirect guarantees of venture debt should be evaluated for adjustment to reported debt levels.

Investments. Some firms have issued long-term debt convertible into the common stock of related firms, held as investments. Potential motives for these transactions include lower interest costs on debt, benefits of tax deductibility of interest payments, the 80 percent exclusion from taxable income of dividends received from eligible investments, and control of the amount and timing of capital gains on conversion.

Currency and Interest Rate Exposure. Long-term debt in foreign currency denominations may increase the firm's exchange risk exposure. The mix of fixed and variable rate debt exposes the firm to interest rate risk.

Some firms also engage in interest rate and/or currency swaps related to outstanding debt. For example, a bond may be issued payable in fixed-rate Australian dollars and the proceeds swapped for variable-rate Swiss francs. The foreign currency–denominated debt also may be convertible into commodities or natural resources. Footnote disclosures vary widely, ranging from an acknowledgment of swap transactions to detailed analyses of the effect of swaps on currency and interest rate exposure. The analyst should monitor these disclosures to evaluate risk exposure.

Exhibit 10.7 ties together this discussion of OBS techniques, using Lion Company as an example. Lion makes extensive use of joint ventures, operating leases, and other OBS techniques. Adjustments for these obligations increase debt in 2011 from $3,853 to $5,291 ($3,854 to $5,207 in 2010), or 37 percent (35 percent in 2010). Even after adjustment of stated equity in 2011 to significantly higher market value, the debt-to-capital ratio rises from 77.1 percent (as computed in Exhibit 10.6) to 97.5 percent (from 73.3 percent to 95.4 percent in 2010). However, this exhibit is incomplete; a comprehensive adjustment requires additional analysis of the operations and financial structure of Lion's affiliates and other guarantees it provides to those affiliates and its partners in various joint ventures. The analyst should also recognize Lion's proportionate share of the present value of operating leases and noncancelable purchase obligations of its affiliates.

(viii) Property Analysis. The long-term capital of the company often is compared with its permanent investment in property and equipment. This is analogous to the ratio of mortgage loan to value in the financing of residential and commercial buildings. Since plant and equipment are carried at historical cost and normally are not available for sale, this ratio has limited practical significance. A better measure is the ratio of debt to total net tangible assets including net current assets.

A debt-to-property analysis may be more useful in the case of natural resource companies or companies with large real estate holdings. Frequently, the market value of natural resources holdings exceeds historical cost book values. Theoretically this market value is an indicator of funds available to support debt in an emergency. For some companies, these excess market values can be significant and may augment the potential value of the entire company in an acquisition.

LION COMPANY
Capitalization Table
(in US$ millions)

	12/31/2010		12/31/2011	
	Amount	% of Adjusted Total Capital (BV)	Amount	% of Adjusted Total Capital (BV)
Total Debt (Book Value)[1]	$ 3,854	$ 70.61	$ 3,853	$ 71.03
Adjustments:				
41% of Equitee's long-term liabilities[2]	922	16.89	958	17.66
58.75% of Lion-Tiger's long-term liabilities[2]	276	5.06	294	5.42
Fair value of long-term debt[3]	(77)	−1.41	—	—
Guarantees and contingent liabilities[4]	—	—	—	—
Capitalization of Lion's operating leases[5]	232	4.25	223	4.12
Adjusted total debt	$5,207	95.40	$5,291	97.55
Common stockholders' equity (BV)	$1,403	25.71	$1,146	21.13
Adjustments:				
Goodwill[6]	−$1,152	−21.11	−$1,102	−20.32
LIFO reserves[6]	—		—	
Fair value of investments and long-term receivables[6]	—		$89	1.64
Excess (shortfall) of present value of discounted cash flow over capitalized costs over capitalized costs of oil and gas reserves[6]				
Adjusted Common Stockholders Equity (BV)	— $ 251	4.60	— $ 133	2.45
Total capital (BV)	$5,257		$ 4999	
Total capital (BV)	$5,458	100.00	$5,424	100.00
Common stockholders' equity (market value [MV])[7]	$1,800		$1,685	
Total capital (MV)	$5,654		$5,538	
Adjusted total capital (MV)	$7,057		$6,684	
Adjusted Debt		%		%
to adjusted equity (BV)		2,074.4		3,978.4
to adjusted capital (BV)		95.4		97.5
Adjusted Debt		%		%
to equity (MV)		289.28		314.00
to adjusted capital (MV)		92.09		95.55

Notes (2011 Calculations):
[1] From Exhibit 10.6.
[2] From supplementary information in the Annual Report.
[3] From Note X, difference between fair value and carrying amount of debt, interest rate swaps, and other derivatives.
[4] Guarantees of the debt of affiliated companies, subsidiaries, and other relevant contingent liabilities should be included in adjustments to total debt. See discussion in the text and Lion's footnotes detailing its relationship and obligations to affiliates.
[5] From Note Y, present value of future rental payments under operating leases (see text for an explanation of the discount rate used).
[6] From Balance Sheet and footnotes.
[7] From Exhibit 10.6.

Exhibit 10.7   Sample Adjusted Capitalization Table

10.5 CASH FLOW ANALYSIS

Effective in 1987, the FASB replaced the "funds statement" with a statement of cash flows. From an analytic viewpoint, the change is most beneficial. The funds statement generally added little information to that available from the balance sheet and income statement.

In contrast, the statement of cash flows provides significant additional data for analysis requiring that:

1. The effect of acquisitions be removed from the balance sheet changes used to compute cash flows

2. The effects of changes in exchange rates be removed from balance sheet changes used to compute cash flows

3. Cash flows be separated into operating, investing, and financing activities

The first two requirements result in cash flow data that are unclouded by the effects of acquisitions and exchange rate factors. The third requirement means that such accounts as accounts receivable, accounts payable, accrued liabilities, long-term liabilities, and accounts labeled "other" or "miscellaneous" must be segregated into operating, investing, and financing functions by the financial statement preparer. As a result of these requirements, the statement of cash flows is far more accurate than the do-it-yourself estimates that were necessary earlier.[3]

(a) DIRECT VERSUS INDIRECT METHODS. GAAP permits the statement of cash flows to be prepared using either direct or indirect methods. Although the indirect method is used by virtually all preparers, the direct method is more suitable for analysis. In most cases, therefore, the analyst must prepare direct method statements. This can be done by rearranging the data given in the indirect method format. For example, combining sales with the change in operating accounts receivable produces cash receipts.[4]

As there is some evidence that the components of cash flow from operating activities are better indicators than the total, the analyst should use whatever detail is available. The ratio of each component to cash receipts, for example, should be looked at over time.

Cash flow used for investments should be compared with cash flow from operations. The difference is often called *free cash flow* and may be a useful indicator of the cash-generating ability of the enterprise. However, the analyst must compare the results of this exercise with the a priori expectations based on the type of business. For example, a company experiencing rapid growth may have little or no operating cash flow and free cash flow may be negative. In this case, the analyst would be primarily concerned with how this cash deficit was being financed. A proper balance between debt and equity should be struck.

However, a *cash cow* should generate cash flow from operations well in excess of capital needed for investment purposes. In this case, the analyst would be concerned with the use of the excess cash flow. If the free cash flow generated did not conform to the prior expectation, this would also be a cause for concern.

(b) COMPARING CASH FLOWS. Cash flow analysis is best done using data for a number of years. Cash flow for one period may be distorted by random events (strikes, abnormal volume due to price changes, etc.). For cyclical companies, the business cycle also will affect cash flows. Cyclical expansions generally require additional working capital; contractions generate cash as working capital is reduced.

For periods of less than one year, additional caution is required because of seasonality. The statement of cash flows for less than one year should be compared only with the statement for

---

[3] A. C. Sondhi, G. H. Sorter, and G. I. White, "Cash Flow Redefined: FAS 95 and Security Analysis," *Financial Analysts Journal* (November–December 1988): 19–20.

[4] J. Ronen and A. C. Sondhi, "Debt Capacity and Financial Contracting: Finance Subsidiaries," *Journal of Accounting, Auditing and Finance* (Spring 1989): 237–265.

the corresponding period of prior years when the business is at all seasonal. Otherwise, normal seasonal working capital variations will dominate any real trends.

When comparing different companies, allowance must be made for differences in financial structure. Under the provisions of Statement of Financial Accounting Standards No. 95, *Statement of Cash Flows* (now ASC Section 230, *Statement of Cash Flows*), cash flow from operating activities includes income from investments and interest expense (but not dividends paid). In order to facilitate intercompany comparisons, interest expense (after-tax) should be removed from operating cash flow and included in financing cash flow. When income from investments is significant, it should be removed (after-tax) from operating cash flow and included in investing cash flow. With these adjustments, cash flow from operations can be evaluated, and companies can be compared with the effects of financing decisions removed.

10.6 INTEGRATED ANALYSIS OF FINANCIAL STATEMENTS

A company's ROA provides a comprehensive measure of its profitability during a given period of time and is calculated as

$$\text{Return on assets} = \frac{\text{Net income}}{\text{Average total assets}}$$

The trends in this ratio allow an evaluation of the company's performance over time. It also should be compared with the ratio for similar firms over time and with an industry average. This return measure is affected by accounting and tax policy choices and the degree of leverage used by a firm over time and across firms. A measure using earnings before interest and income taxes (EBIT) overcomes these limitations and provides a measure of operating profitability unaffected by differences in leverage and tax effects. It is calculated as:

$$\frac{\text{Earnings before interest and taxes}}{\text{Average total assets}}$$

Further insights into operating performance over time may be obtained by evaluating the components of these return measures. One component is the net income (or EBIT) margin, which is a measure of the profitability in relation to sales. The second component, the asset turnover ratio, evaluates the effectiveness of the firm's use of assets in generating sales. Each component can be analyzed in greater detail to determine the underlying relationships affecting current return and their potential impact on returns over time. As illustrated below, the net income (or EBIT) margin can be decomposed further to evaluate changes in different sources of revenues and proportions of various expense categories over time. Inventory, receivables, and fixed asset turnover ratios can be analyzed to evaluate trends in the fixed asset turnover.

Net income margin or EBIT margin	×	Asset turnover	=	Return on assets
$\frac{\text{Net income}}{\text{Net sales}}$ or $\frac{\text{EBIT}}{\text{Net sales}}$	×	$\frac{\text{Net income}}{\text{Average total assets}}$	=	$\frac{\text{Net income}}{\text{Average total assets}}$ or $\frac{\text{EBIT}}{\text{Average total assets}}$
↓		↓		
Analysis of relevant revenue and expense breakdowns		Analysis of inventory, receivables, and fixed assets turnover		

Exhibit 10.8, adapted from a real SEC filing, shows that Woodbridge Company's ROA has improved from 3.75 percent in 2007 to 5.80 percent in 2011. In 2008, Woodbridge reported a decline

WOODBRIDGE COMPANY AND CONSOLIDATED SUBSIDIARIES

Year	Profit Margin[1] $\dfrac{\text{Net Income}}{\text{Sales}}$	×	Asset Turnover[2] $\dfrac{\text{Sales}}{\text{Avg. Total Assets}}$	=	Return on Assets[3] $\dfrac{\text{Net Income}}{\text{Avg. Total Assets}}$	×	Leverage[4] $\dfrac{\text{Avg. Total Assets}}{\text{Avg. Common Equity}}$	=	Return on Equity[5] $\dfrac{\text{Net Income}}{\text{Avg. Common Equity}}$
	(%)				(%)				(%)
2007	2.11	×	1.78	=	3.75	×	3.72	=	13.96
2008	3.11	×	0.94	=	2.93	×	3.13	=	9.17
2009	4.26	×	1.09	=	4.63	×	2.88	=	13.36
2010	0.88	×	1.18	=	1.04	×	3.25	=	3.36
2011	5.40	×	1.07	=	5.80	×	3.43	=	19.89

Net Income — Growth Rates (2007–2011)

	%
% Change	18.46
Compound Growth rate	9.89

Notes (2011 Calculations) Some calculations may differ slightly due to rounding.
[1] Profit margin (%) = (Net income/Sales) × 100 = (417/7719) × 100 = 5.4%
[2] Asset Turnover = Sales/Average total assets (7719/((7284 + 7092)/2)) = 1.07
[3] ROA = Profit margin × Asset turnover = 5.4 × 1.07 = 5.80%
[4] Leverage = Average total assets × Average common equity = (((7284 + 7092)/2)/((2266 + 1965)/2)) = 3.43
[5] ROE = ROA × Leverage = 5.80 × 3.43 = 19.89

Exhibit 10.8   Analysis of Return on Equity

continues

WOODBRIDGE COMPANY AND CONSOLIDATED SUBSIDIARIES

Year	Preinterest and Tax Margin[1] EBIT Sales		Asset Turnover[2] Sales Avg. Total Assets		Preinterest Return on Assets[3] EBIT Avg. Total Assets		Interest on Assets[4] Interest Expense Avg. Total Assets		Postinterest Return on Assets[5] EBT Avg. Total Assets		Leverage[6] Avg. Total Assets Avg. Common Equity		Pretax Return on Equity[7] EBT Avg. Common Equity
	(%)				(%)		(%)		(%)				(%)
2007	3.82	×	1.78	=	6.79	−	2.29	=	4.50	×	3.72	=	16.75
2008	6.84	×	0.94	=	6.45	−	1.88	=	4.57	×	3.13	=	14.28
2009	9.15	×	1.09	=	9.95	−	2.24	=	7.71	×	2.88	=	22.24
2010	8.55	×	1.18	=	10.07	−	2.93	=	7.14	×	3.25	=	23.18
2011	11.05	×	1.07	=	11.87	−	2.39	=	9.48	×	3.43	=	32.51

EBIT — Growth Rates (2007–2011)

	%
% Change	68.91
Compound Growth rate	13.78

Notes (2011 Calculations)

[1] Pre-interest and tax margin (%) = (EBIT/Sales) × 100 = (853/7719) × 100 = 11.05%
[2] Asset Turnover = Sales/Average total assets (7719/((7284 + 7092)/2)) = 1.07
[3] Preinterest ROA = Preinterest and tax margin × Asset turnover = 11.05 × 1.07 = 11.87
[4] Interest on Assets = (Interest expense × Average total assets) × 100 = (172/((7719 + 7092)/2)) × 100 = 2.39
[5] Postinterest ROA = Preinterest ROA − Interest on assets = 11.87 − 2.39 = 9.48
[6] Leverage = Average total assets × Average common equity = (((7284 + 7092)/2)/((2266 + 1965)/2)) = 3.43
[7] Pretax ROE = Postinterest ROA × Leverage = 9.48 × 3.43 = 32.51

Exhibit 10.8 *Continued*

in ROA due to a significant drop in asset turnover (beginning in 2008, previously consolidated units were reported on the equity method, significantly reducing reported sales) despite an increase in the profit margin. In 2010, a decline in the profit margin was not overcome by an improvement in asset turnover. However, the decline in the net income reflected a loss on discontinued operations. Excluding this loss, the profit margin (based on continuing operations) would have been 6.41 percent and the ROA 7.56 percent. In 2011, asset turnover declined but was more than offset by a significant improvement in reported profit margin. When we compute profit margins using income from continuing operations, 2011 reflects a decline in performance as compared to 2010. EBIT return rose nearly 190 percent to 11.05 percent in 2001 from 3.82 percent in 2007. However, 2007 and 2008 are not comparable to the other years because of the change to the equity method in 2008. From 2009 to 2011, EBIT margins have improved by approximately 21 percent.

Investors should also calculate the firm's ROE as:

$$\frac{\text{Net income}}{\text{Average common equity}}$$

The ROE should be analyzed over time and across firms, and it should be compared to the average ROE for the industry in which the firm operates. Woodbridge's ROE was 13.96 percent in 2007; it fell to 9.17 percent in 2008 and to 3.36 percent in 2010. As noted previously, the ROE reported in 2010 is affected by loss from discontinued operations. ROE from continuing operations would have been 24.5 percent, which is significantly higher than the 19.89 percent reported for 2011.

The trends in ROE can be further analyzed in terms of its components:

$$\text{ROE} = \frac{\text{Net income}}{\text{Average total assets}} \times \frac{\text{Average total assets}}{\text{Average common equity}}$$

$$= \text{Profit margin} \times \text{Asset turnover} \times \text{Leverage ratio}$$

$$= \frac{\text{Net income}}{\text{Net sales}} \times \frac{\text{Net sales}}{\text{Average total assets}} \times \frac{\text{Average total assets}}{\text{Average common equity}}$$

An analysis of these components shows that the decline (from 2007 to 2010) in ROE stemmed from the year 2010 fall in profit margins, lower asset turnover in 2008 to 2010 relative to 2007, and a resulting lower ROA. Significantly higher profit margins in 2011 generated the highest reported ROE. Note that asset turnover (1.07 times) remains lower than that reported in 2007 (1.78 times) and the improvement is all due to the higher profit margin. However, an ROE measure based on income from continuing operations shows a lower ROE in 2011 compared to 2010.

The third component, assets/equity, is a leverage measure: The higher the ratio, the lower the proportion of assets financed by common equity. This ratio has increased steadily from 3.13 in 2008 to 3.43 in 2011, despite a slight decline to 2.88 in 2009. The firm has decreased debt in 2008 and 2009 (it reported decreasing interest expense as a percentage of average total assets) while improving operating performance and generating higher cash flows.

10.7 FIXED INCOME ANALYSIS

Investors in fixed income securities are concerned with the safety of the expected interest payments and redemption of debt at maturity. Redemption at maturity depends on internal cash flows, the relationship of debt to equity, and other industry-specific and broad economic factors. Thus, fixed-income investors need a comprehensive analysis of all financial statements to develop insights into the investment risk relative to expected return.

(a) EARNINGS PROTECTION. The safety of interest payments is a function of the margin of earnings in excess of interest so that an unexpected decline in earnings will not jeopardize payment. The adequacy of coverage depends on the volatility of earnings. The greater the volatility, the higher the ratio necessary to ensure protection under adverse circumstances. A low ratio of 2.5 times may be adequate for a finance company, whose earnings are stable. In fact, captive finance subsidiaries (i.e., those conducting at least 70 percent of their operations with the parent) have income-maintenance agreements with the parent whereby it guarantees coverage ratios from 1.05 to 1.50 times fixed charges. A much higher ratio, five to six times, is desirable for an industrial company whose earnings fluctuate because of the business cycle. Greater coverage offers creditors greater assurance in such circumstances.

Another test of earnings adequacy is earning power—the return before interest expense on the total invested capital. This is given by the next equation:

$$\text{Return on invested capital} = \frac{\text{Earnings before interest and taxes}}{\text{Average invested capital}}$$

This is a useful long-term measure of strength. The margin of safety provided by the return on investment depends on the cost of debt. A return of 14 percent on invested capital is adequate when rates are 5 to 7 percent, but not at substantially higher rates. Recapitalization using high-yield debt significantly increases vulnerability and reduces the protection available to the creditors if it is not accompanied by a sustained increase in return on total invested capital.

Redemption at maturity should be evaluated by the analysis of cash flows and the balance sheet in conjunction with the income statement to determine the assurance of payment at maturity. First, the analyst must review the maturity schedule of the outstanding debt, as given in footnotes to the financial statements. The company may have a continuing run of maturing obligations, including sinking funds, or it may have a few widely spaced larger maturities. The analyst then should evaluate the firm's ability to meet the specified repayment schedule and amounts through internally generated funds (i.e., operating cash flows). The measure is:

$$\text{Years to pay} = \frac{\text{Total fixed obligations}}{\text{Operating cash flows}}$$

This ratio states the number of years required to pay off all debt by application of all internally generated cash flows. The logic is that debt maturities will have the first priority on all available funds. Normally this ratio ought to be in a range of 3 to 5 years. At 8 to 10 years, the repayment burden could be onerous. Increased use of debt will increase the ratio relative to past experience. High levels of internally generated cash flows will signify low years-to-pay and high credit standing.

In summary, whereas actual appropriation of all internal cash flow to debt reduction for several years would hamper the future growth of the business and be tantamount to liquidation, a high ratio of cash flow to debt gives a company considerable flexibility in financing its business internally and/or externally and therefore is a good indicator of credit quality. A useful adjustment to this ratio would require a deduction from operating cash flows of capital expenditures required to maintain productive capacity, a crude measure of which may be provided by the current cost equivalent of depreciation. The resulting ratio is more conservative but would facilitate a more comprehensive analysis. The analyst should also compute this ratio after adjusting for all OBS obligations. These adjustments would enable the analyst to compare different reported and OBS-inclusive capital structures.

The analyst should review the company's overall credit standing on the expectation that a new issue can be sold to refund a large maturing issue or recapitalize the firm. Here again, investors and analysts should carefully evaluate long-term earning power, interest coverage, the ratio of debt to total capital, OBS financing activities, and bond covenants to determine whether a refunding issue or recapitalization would be accepted in the marketplace. Many industrial bonds have sinking funds that retire most of the issue by maturity, but that is not the case for most utilities. Utilities must maintain a balanced capital structure and adequate coverage in order to maintain continued access to the bond market.

Exhibit 10.9 details bond protection ratios for Woodbridge over the period from 2007 to 2011. Generally, all the measures of protection and safety for creditors have improved over this period.

WOODBDRIDGE COMPANY AND CONSOLIDATED SUBSIDIARIES

	2007	2008	2009	2010	2011
Pretax Interest Coverage (x)[1]	2.97	3.44	4.44	3.44	4.96
Pretax Fixed Charge Coverage (x)[2]	2.07	2.27	2.98	2.54	3.34
EBITDA Coverage (%)[3]	6.34	4.83	6.07	4.64	6.41
Free Cash Flow/Total Debt (%)[4]	(3.29)%	130.15%	(10.78)%	(23.91)%	(4.26)%
Margin of Safety (%)[5]	2.54%	4.85%	7.09%	6.07%	8.82%
Pretax Return on Permanent Capital (%)[6]	10.35%	10.20%	15.24%	14.72%	17.01%
Operating Income/Net Sales (%)[7]	2.81%	0.73%	2.53%	2.46%	0.30%
Long-Term Debt/Capitalization (%)[8]	45.55%	42.05%	42.23%	46.78%	44.56%
Total Debt/Capitalization (%)[9]	47.90%	45.20%	47.36%	54.14%	46.50%
Current Assets/Total Debt[10]	1.58	1.02	1.02	0.09	1.08
Net Tangible Assets/Total Debt[11]	2.53	3.27	3.07	2.73	3.31

Notes (2011 Calculations)

[1] EBIT/(Interest expense + Capitalized interest) = 853/172 = 4.96
[2] ((EBIT + Gross rents)/(Interest expense + Capitalized interest + Gross rents)) = (853 + 119)/(172 + 119) = 3.34
[3] EBTDA/(Interest expense + Capitalized interest) = 1103/172 = 6.41
[4] Free operating cash flow/Total debt = (−87/2044) × 100 = −4.26%
[5] EBT/Net sales = (681/7719) = 8.82%
[6] [EBIT/(Average (Total debt + Deferred taxes + Minority interest + Equity)] × 100 = 17.01%
[7] Operating income/Net sales = (23/7719) × 100 = 0.30%
[8] Long-term debt/(Debt + Equity) = (1959/4396) × 100 = 44.56%
[9] Total debt/(Debt + Equity) = (2044/4396) × 100 = 46.50%
[10] Current assets/Total debt = 2213/2044 = 1.08
[11] Total assets − Intangibles/Total debt = (7284 − 528)/2044 = 3.31

Exhibit 10.9   Bond Protection Ratios For an Industrial Company

10.8 FINANCE COMPANY DEBT ANALYSIS

Finance companies have a large body of outstanding debt, and its quality is measured by slightly different criteria adapted to the special circumstances of this business, which involves the financing of sales and receivables of their parents and that of other, unaffiliated companies. Finance company assets are composed largely of financial obligations of third parties that are self-liquidating through relatively frequent payments of both principal and interest, allowing significantly greater leverage than that observed for industrial companies. Earnings depend on the loss experience on loans, the interest rate spread between loans and borrowings, and expense control. Finance subsidiaries and their industrial parents also have extensive operating agreements that call for income maintenance and direct or indirect parent guarantees of subsidiary debt, augmented by extensive debt covenants.

The ratios used to measure these factors are fundamentally the same as for other businesses, but they usually are expressed in a different form, and the standards are different. The analyst should also evaluate the operating agreement and bond covenants to evaluate finance company debt risk.[5]

ASC 942, *Financial Services—Depository and Lending,* requires the consolidation of leasing and finance subsidiaries that were previously reported under the equity method because of their heterogeneous operations. The standard requires continued disclosure of disaggregated information on finance subsidiaries. To the extent possible, the analyst should evaluate separate finance company data to evaluate the riskiness of finance company debt. An analysis of the parent–subsidiary contractual relationship is necessary for an evaluation of recourse to the parent. Lenders to the

---

[5] J. Ronen and A. C. Sondhi, "Debt Capacity and Financial Contracting: Finance Subsidiaries," *Journal of Accounting, Auditing and Finance* (Spring 1989): 237–265.

parent are concerned with both the risk in parent debt and the degree of support the parent is contractually obligated to provide to its subsidiaries. The effect of consolidation on traditional ratios will not always be in the expected direction and of anticipated magnitude because of differences between parent and subsidiary size, profitability, and growth rates over time and across firms. Disaggregated disclosures are necessary for a separate evaluation of finance company and parent debt. To the extent that continued availability of disaggregated disclosure is affected by FASB actions with respect to consolidated financial reporting, analysts will need to monitor these developments.

(a) OPERATING AGREEMENT.   Operating agreements govern the transactions between the parent and its financing subsidiary. An income maintenance agreement is used to provide a parent guarantee that the subsidiary's net income will be a prespecified multiple of its fixed charges; direct payments to the subsidiary are required when this multiple is not reached, thereby protecting investments in subsidiary debt. Operating agreements require that receivables be sold to subsidiaries at discounts competitive with those prevailing in the financial markets. Uncollectibles are charged to the parent, and the subsidiary often has the right to withhold a predetermined portion of the purchase price (a holdback reserve), which is refunded when receivables have been collected. Some agreements contain provisions for repossession and payments in the event of default.

In summary, the operating agreement serves to reduce the volatility and risk in subsidiary earnings and cash flows, thereby enhancing the protection available to the finance company's debt holders.

(b) ASSET PROTECTION RATIOS.   Since receivables are the principal assets of finance companies, asset protection for the debt is measured by the proportion of receivables to debt, as shown next:

$$\frac{\text{Gross receivables} - \text{unearned finance charges}}{\text{Total debt}}$$

This ratio should range from 110 to 120 percent, and it indicates the margin of liquid or financial assets over total debt. A similar ratio should also be calculated on senior debt. Refunding and call provisions in debt covenants provide additional protection. Generally, significant declines in receivables trigger a requirement to redeem outstanding debt at specified premiums. This covenant also limits investment in nonfinancial assets, which may be constrained by other, direct covenants.

(c) RESERVE AND LOSS RATIOS.   The quality of financial assets is critical to the earning power and credit quality of a finance company. This quality is measured by the rate of losses on collection of receivables and the adequacy of balance sheet reserves to absorb losses. The level of holdback reserves also indicates the continued parent equity in the subsidiary. Loss as a percentage of average receivables is defined as:

$$\frac{\text{Net losses on charge-offs for the year}}{\text{Average receivables (gross receivables} - \text{unearned finance charges})}$$

This ratio will vary depending on the type of business (retail versus wholesale; mix of products financed). A rising trend is an important signal. Losses can also be measured against net interest income on a trend basis.

Reserves as a percentage of receivables are defined as:

$$\frac{\text{Reserve for losses}}{\text{Gross receivables} - \text{unearned finance charges}}$$

The reserve is used to absorb losses and is replenished by charges to operations. To provide a proper cushion, the reserve should be 1.25 to 2 times annual losses.

(d) LOAN SPREADS.   Earnings in the finance (and banking) industry are developed by lending funds at a higher rate than that paid on borrowed funds (i.e., the net interest earned). This spread should be evaluated against the net investment in receivables to derive a rate of return:

$$\frac{\text{Net interest earned (interest revenues} - \text{interest expense)}}{\text{Average receivables (gross receivables} - \text{unearned charges)}}$$

(e) LIQUIDITY.   Finance companies are constantly in the market, rolling over short-term paper, refunding longer issues, and selling new debt. Liquidity therefore becomes a function of an adequate balance of debt between all sectors of the money market without an undue concentration of maturities, coupled with adequate bank lines of credit. To maintain the confidence of the market to accept paper under various economic conditions, consistent earnings trends, controlled operations, and debt levels are designed to accomplish these objectives, and the analyst should monitor these ratios and covenants over time to manage risk and return trade-offs.

(f) CAPITALIZATION.   Subordinated debt is usually a significant segment of the finance company's capital structure and must be evaluated separately from senior debt. Subordinated debt and equity together represent the capital base supporting the high levels of debt observed in finance companies. Senior debt normally is restricted to a multiple of the capital base, the aggregate of total debt, the liquid net worth, or a multiple of net worth. Covenants also contain similar restrictions on allowed subordinated debt. The ratio of senior debt to the capital base is frequently 2.5:1 to 3.5:1 for independent finance companies. Captives may use higher ratios because of access to parent company capital and some guarantees of minimum earnings. Bank credit departments use a similar ratio—"borrowing ratio"—which eliminates illiquid assets from the capital base. The ratio of senior debt to capital is:

$$\frac{\text{Total senior debt}}{\text{Subordinated debt} + \text{net worth}}$$

Thus, the allowed debt (senior and subordinated) is restricted to some multiple of equity or, in the case of subsidiaries, to the parent's equity investment and may incorporate subordinated debt owed to parent in the capital base. Along with requirements to maintain receivables levels, these covenants preserve collateral available in the finance company. The ratios just described and the covenants should be monitored by the analyst to evaluate finance company debt.

10.9 KEY RATIOS

Liquidity Analysis

1. Current ratio $= \dfrac{\text{Current assets (cash and equivalents, receivables and inventories)}}{\text{Current liabilities (payables, accruals, taxes, and debt due in 1 year)}}$

2. Quick ratio $= \dfrac{\text{Cash and equivalents plus receivables}}{\text{Current liabilities}}$

3. Operating cash flow to current liabilities $= \dfrac{\text{Cash provided by operations}}{\text{Average current liabilities}}$

Activity Ratios

4. Inventory turnover $= \dfrac{\text{Cost of goods sold}}{\text{Average inventory}}$

The number of days inventory is on hand can be calculated as:

$$\frac{365}{\text{Inventory turnover}}$$

5. Receivables turnover $= \dfrac{\text{Net credit sales}}{\text{Average receivables}}$

6. Number of days receivables are outstanding $= \dfrac{365}{\text{Receivables turnover}}$

7. Fixed asset turnover ratio $= \dfrac{\text{Net sales}}{\text{Average fixed assets}}$

MARGIN ANALYSIS

8. Gross margin $= 1 - \dfrac{\text{Cost of goods sold}}{\text{Sales}}$

9. Expense ratio $= \dfrac{\text{Selling, general, and administrative expenses}}{\text{Sales}}$

10. Operating margin $= \dfrac{\text{Operating income}}{\text{Sales}}$

11. Pretax margin $= \dfrac{\begin{array}{c}\text{Income before income tax}\\ \text{(Operating income + other income − interest)}\end{array}}{\text{Sales}}$

12. Profit margin $= \dfrac{\text{Net income before extraordinaryitems}}{\text{Sales}}$

DEBT RATIOS

13. Interest coverage ratio $= \dfrac{\text{Income before interest and taxes}}{\text{Fixed charges}}$

14. Margin of safety $= \dfrac{\text{Income after fixed charges before income taxes}}{\text{Sales}}$

15. Preferred dividend coverage $= \dfrac{\text{Income before interest and taxes}}{\text{Fixed charges + pretax preferred dividends}}$

16. Debt to total capital ratio $= \dfrac{\text{Total current and long-term debt + capitalized leases}}{\text{Total capital (total debt + leases + stockholders'equity)}}$

17. Debt-to-equity ratio $= \dfrac{\text{Total current and long-term debt + capitalized leases}}{\text{Total stockholders' equity}}$

or

$$\dfrac{\text{Total debt at book value}}{\text{Total debt and preferred stock + common stock at market}}$$

INTEGRATED ANALYSIS OF FINANCIAL STATEMENTS

18. Return on assets $= \dfrac{\text{Net income}}{\text{Average total assets}}$

or

$$\dfrac{\text{Earnings before interest and taxes}}{\text{Average total assets}}$$

DECOMPOSITION OF MARGIN AND RETURN RATIOS

19.

Net income margin			
or	× Asset turnover	=	Return on assets
EBIT margin			

$$\frac{\text{Net income}}{\text{Net sales}} \qquad\qquad \frac{\text{Net income}}{\text{Average total assets}}$$

$$\text{or} \qquad \times \frac{\text{Net sales}}{\text{Average total assets}} \qquad = \qquad \text{or}$$

$$\frac{\text{EBIT}}{\text{Net sales}} \qquad\qquad \frac{\text{EBIT}}{\text{Average total assets}}$$

$$\downarrow \qquad\qquad \downarrow$$

Analysis of relevant   Analysis of inventory,
revenue and expense   receivables, and fixed
breakdowns   asset turnover

20. $\text{ROE} = \dfrac{\text{Net income}}{\text{Average common equity}}$

DECOMPOSITION OF RETURN ON EQUITY

21.

$$\text{ROE} = \frac{\text{Net income}}{\text{Average total assets}} \times \frac{\text{Average total assets}}{\text{Average common equity}}$$

or

$$= \text{Profit margin} \times \text{Asset turnover} \times \text{Leverage ratio}$$

$$= \frac{\text{Net income}}{\text{Net sales}} \times \frac{\text{Net sales}}{\text{Average total assets}} \times \frac{\text{Average total assets}}{\text{Average common equity}}$$

OTHER EARNINGS AND ASSET PROTECTION RATIOS

22. $\text{Return on invested capital} = \dfrac{\text{Earnings before interest and taxes}}{\text{Average invested capital}}$

23. Number of years to pay off debt by application of internally generated cash flows =

$$\frac{\text{Total fixed obligations}}{\text{Operating cash flows}}$$

24. $\text{Asset protection ratio} = \dfrac{\text{Gross receivables} - \text{unearned finance charges}}{\text{Total debt}}$

25. $\text{Reserve and loss ratio} = \dfrac{\text{Net losses on charge-offs for the year}}{\text{Average receivable (gross receivables} - \text{unearned finance charges})}$

26. $\text{Reserves as a percentage of receivables} = \dfrac{\text{Reserve for losses}}{\text{Gros receivables} - \text{unearned finance charges}}$

27. Loan spreads $= \dfrac{\text{Net interest earned (interest revenues} - \text{interest expense)}}{\text{Average receivables (gross receivables} - \text{unearned charges)}}$

28. Ratio of senior debt to capital $= \dfrac{\text{Total senior debt}}{\text{Subordinated debt} + \text{net worth}}$

10.10 SOURCES AND SUGGESTED REFERENCES

Barsky, N. P., A. H. Catanach Jr., and S. C. Rhoades-Catanach. "Analyst Tools for Detecting Financial Reporting Fraud," *Commercial Lending Review* (Fall 2003): 31–36.

Barsky, N. P., and J. C. Thibodeau. "Financial Viability in the Retail Industry," *Journal of Financial Education* 26, no. 1 (2000): 82–90.

Beneish, M., and M. Vargus. "Insider Trading, Earnings Quality, and Accrual Mispricing," *Accounting Review* (October 2002): 755–791.

Bernstein, L. A., and J. G. Siegel. "The Concept of Earnings Quality," *Financial Analysts Journal* 35, no. 4 (July–August 1979): 72–75.

Bradshaw, M., S. Richardson, and R. Sloan. "Do Analysts and Auditors Use Information in Accruals?" *Journal of Accounting Research* (June 2001): 45–74.

Bragg, S. M. *Wiley GAAP Guide*. Hoboken, NJ: John Wiley & Sons, 2011.

Casey, C. J., and N. J. Bartczak. "Using Operating Cash Flow Data to Predict Financial Distress: Some Extensions," *Journal of Accounting Research* (Spring 1985); 384–401.

Fisher, D. "Cash Doesn't Lie," *Forbes*, July 18, 2011, pp. 54–55.

Friedlob, G. T., L. L. Schliefer, and F. G. Plewa. *Essentials of Corporate Performance Measurement*. Hoboken, NJ: John Wiley & Sons, 2002.

Jablonsky, S. F., and N. P. Barsky. *The Manager's Guide to Financial Statement Analysis*, 2nd ed. Hoboken, NJ: John Wiley & Sons, 2001.

Hafzalla, N., R. Lundholm, and E. Van Winkle. "Percent Accruals," *Accounting Review* (January 2011): 209–236.

Ronen, J., and A. C. Sondhi. "Debt Capacity and Financial Contracting: Finance Subsidiaries," *Journal of Accounting, Auditing and Finance* (Spring 1989): 237–265.

Securities and Exchange Commission. "Notice of Adoption of Amendments to Regulation S-X Requiring Disclosure of Certain Replacement Cost Data," *Accounting Series Release No. 190*. Washington, DC: Author, 1976.

Sondhi, A. C., G. H. Sorter, and G. I. White. "Cash Flow Redefined: FAS 95 and Security Analysis," *Financial Analysts Journal* (November–December 1988); 19–20.

White, G. I., A. C. Sondhi, and D. Fried. *The Analysis and Use of Financial Statements*, 3rd ed. Hoboken, NJ: John Wiley & Sons, 2003.

CHAPTER **11**

CASH, LOANS, AND INVESTMENTS

Michael A. Antonetti, CPA, CMA
Crowe Horwath LLP

11.1 INTRODUCTION TO CASH

(a) NATURE AND IMPORTANCE OF CASH. Cash is both the beginning and the end of the operating cycle (cash-inventory-sales-receivables-cash) in the typical business enterprise, and almost all transactions affect cash either directly or indirectly. Cash transactions are probably the most frequently recurring type entered into by a business because, except for barter transactions, every

The information contained in this chapter does not necessarily represent the views of Crowe Horwath LLP.

sale leads to a cash receipt and every expense to a cash disbursement. Cash is recognized as the most liquid of the assets and thus has prominence for users who are focusing on issues of liquidity.

Cash derives its primary importance from its dual role as a medium of exchange and a unit of measure. As a medium of exchange, it has a part in the majority of transactions entered into by an enterprise. Assets are acquired and realized, and liabilities are incurred and liquidated, in terms of cash. Thus, cash generally is the most active asset possessed by a company. As a unit of measure, it sets the terms on which all properties and claims against the company are stated in its financial statements.

(b) CASH ACCOUNTING AND CONTROL. The major challenge in accounting for cash is maintaining adequate control over the great variety and quantity of cash transactions. Cash receipts may come from such diverse sources as cash sales, cash on delivery (COD) transactions, collections on accounts and notes receivable, loans, security issues, income from investments, and sales of such properties as retired assets, scrap, and investments. Disbursements may be made for a variety of expense items, for cash purchases and in payment of various liabilities, for dividends, and for taxes. Thus, the variety of cash transactions in itself presents inherent problems.

The quantity of cash transactions constitutes another source of difficulty. To handle expeditiously the volume of cash transactions calls for appropriate equipment, careful organization and segregation of duties, planning of procedures, and design of appropriate forms. Information as to available cash balances is of daily interest to the management of every company, and this information must be accurate and prompt if it is to be useful.

(c) MISREPRESENTED CASH BALANCES. Companies sometimes misrepresent their cash balance to improve the appearance of their financial liquidity. For example, cash receipts may be recorded for a few days after the close of a fiscal period and reported as receipts of the preceding period. An improved cash position is thus reported. If this balance is then used as a basis for reducing outstanding receivables, the ratio of current assets to current liabilities appears better than if it was recorded appropriately.

11.2 ACCOUNTING FOR AND REPORTING CASH

(a) DEFINITION OF *CASH*. Cash exists both in physical and book entry forms: physical in the form of coin and paper currency as well as other negotiable instruments of various kinds, and book entry in various forms, such as commercial bank deposits and savings deposits. In addition to coin and paper currency, other kinds of physical cash instruments that are commonly reported as cash for financial accounting purposes include certificates of deposit (CDs) with original maturities of three months or less, bank checks, demand bills of exchange (in some cases), travelers' checks, post office or other money orders, bank drafts, cashiers' checks, certain short-term Treasury bills with an original maturity of three months or less, and money market funds.

All these forms of cash involve credit and depend for their ready acceptance on the integrity and liquidity of some person or institution other than those offering or accepting them as cash. This is true even for coin and paper currency, which is ultimately dependent on the credit of the government issuing it. Given this integrity and liquidity, the book entry forms and other physical instruments are properly viewed as cash because of their immediate convertibility into cash in its currency form at the will of the holder. Convertibility in the case of savings accounts, CDs, and other time deposits may be something less than immediate depending on stipulated conditions imposed by the depository, but the assurance of such convertibility makes these items a generally accepted form of cash.

The definition of *cash* also includes the concept that the instrument is so near its maturity that there is insignificant risk of changes in value because of changes in interest rates. Generally, only investments with original maturities of three months or less qualify for presentation as cash equivalents.

Original maturity means original maturity to the entity holding the investment. For example, both a three-month U.S. Treasury bill and a three-year U.S. Treasury note purchased three months from maturity qualify as cash equivalents. However, a Treasury note purchased three years ago does not become a cash equivalent when its remaining maturity is three months. According to the Financial Accounting Standards Board (FASB) Codification Master Glossary, examples of items commonly considered to be cash equivalents are Treasury bills, commercial paper, money market funds, and federal funds sold (for an entity with banking operations).

Before and especially during the financial crisis experienced in 2008 and 2009, the classification of certain financial instruments was more closely scrutinized as markets for the instruments became inactive and called into question their timely conversion into cash. For example, some companies invested in auction rate securities. Such securities are long-term variable-rate bonds tied to short-term interest rates that are reset through a "Dutch auction" process that typically occurs every 7 to 35 days. The holder can participate in the auction and liquidate the auction rate securities to prospective buyers through a broker or dealer. The holder typically does not have the right to put the security back to the issuer. The Securities and Exchange Commission (SEC) staff has concluded in its Current Issues and Rulemaking Projects (CIRP), *Current Accounting and Disclosure Issues in the Division of Corporation Finance,* dated November 30, 2006 (section IIH3), that because the auction rate securities have long-term maturity dates and there is no guarantee the holder will be able to liquidate its holdings, these securities do not meet the definition of cash equivalents in the FASB Codification Master Glossary.

(b) CLASSIFICATION AND PRESENTATION.   The presentation of cash in the balance sheet is largely an issue of appropriate classification and description. Because of its importance in evaluating an entity's financial condition, cash must be stated as accurately as possible. This calls for careful analysis of each component of cash so that no items will improperly be included in, or excluded from, current assets. In this connection, the FASB Codification Master Glossary defines *current assets* as:

> Cash and other assets or resources commonly identified as those that are reasonably expected to be realized in cash or sold or consumed during the normal operating cycle of the business.

It defines *operating cycles* as:

> The average time intervening between the acquisition of materials or services and the final cash realization constitutes an operating cycle.

Paragraph 3 of the Accounting Standards Codification (ASC) 210-10-45, *Balance Sheet, Overall, Other Presentation Matters,* notes that a one-year time period is to be used as a basis for the segregation of current assets in cases where there are several operating cycles within a year. However, if the period of the operating cycle is more than 12 months, as in, for instance, the tobacco, distillery and lumber businesses, the longer cycle must be used. If an entity has no clearly defined operating cycle, then one year governs.

Thus, the definition of *current assets* includes cash and cash equivalents, although, as noted next, not all cash and cash equivalents are classified as current assets.

Paragraph 4 of ASC 210-10-45 includes the concept that the nature of current assets excludes from that classification such resources as cash and claims to cash that are restricted as to withdrawal or use for other than current operations, are designated for expenditure in the acquisition or construction of noncurrent assets, or are segregated for the liquidation of long-term debts. Even though not actually set aside in special accounts, funds that are clearly to be used in the near future for the liquidation of long-term debts, payments to sinking funds, or similar purposes must also, under this concept, be excluded from current assets. However, if such funds are considered to offset maturing debt that has properly been set up as a current liability, they may be included with the current asset classification.

As the one asset that is liquid—that is, expendable with no intermediary transactions or conversions—cash assumes the position of prime importance in the balance sheet and generally is presented as the first item among the assets of the enterprise. Four examples of presentation are:

1. Cash and cash equivalents
2. Cash
3. Cash and equivalents
4. Cash combined with marketable securities

Generally, the form shown in example 1 is widely used, but the important point is that cash subject to withdrawal restrictions should not be combined with cash of immediate availability. In this regard, O'Reilly et al. state: "The cash caption on the balance sheet should include cash on hand and balances with financial institutions that are immediately available for any purpose and cash equivalents."[1]

(c) RESTRICTED CASH.   Cash restricted as to use by agreement, such as amounts deposited in escrow or for a specified purpose subject to release only at the order of a person other than the depositor, should not be classified in the balance sheet as cash and, unless deposited to meet an existing current liability, presumably should be excluded from current assets. Cash is sometimes received from customers in advance payment for work being performed under contract or under similar circumstances. Such cash is properly designated as cash in the balance sheet but may be properly classified as a current asset only if the resulting customer's deposit is classified as a current liability. Cash restricted as to withdrawal because of inability of the depository to meet demands for withdrawal (such as deposits in banks in receivership) is not a current asset and should not be designated in the balance sheet as cash without an appropriate qualifying caption.

In regard to cash awaiting use for construction or other capital purposes or held for the payment of long-term debt, O'Reilly et al. state:

> Cash sometimes includes balances with trustees, such as sinking funds or other amounts not immediately available, for example, those restricted to uses other than current operations, designated for acquisition or construction of noncurrent assets, or segregated for the liquidation of long-term debt. Restrictions are considered effective if the company clearly intends to observe them, even though the funds are not actually set aside in special bank accounts. The facts pertaining to those balances should be adequately disclosed, and the amounts should be properly classified as current or noncurrent.[2]

(d) BANK OVERDRAFTS.   ASC 210-20, *Balance Sheet, Offsetting,* provides guidance regarding offsetting assets and liabilities in the balance sheet. Overdrafts can be of two kinds: (1) an actual bank overdraft, resulting from payment by the bank of checks in an amount exceeding the balance available to cover such checks; (2) a book overdraft, arising from issuance of checks in an amount in excess of the balance in the account on which drawn, although such checks have not cleared through the bank in an amount sufficient to exhaust the account.

Actual bank overdrafts represent the total of checks honored by the bank without sufficient funds in the account to cover them; such an overdraft is the bank's way of temporarily loaning funds to its customer. Accordingly, bank overdrafts (other than those that arise in connection with a zero-balance or similar arrangement with a bank) represent short-term loans and should be classified as liabilities if the right of offset does not exist.

Book overdrafts representing outstanding checks in excess of funds on deposit generally should be classified as liabilities and cash reinstated at the balance sheet date. Such credit book balances

[1] Vincent M. O'Reilly, Patrick J. McDonnell, Barry N. Winograd, James S. Gerson, and Henry R. Jaenicke, *Montgomery's Auditing,* 12th ed. (New York: John Wiley & Sons, 1998), chap. 17, p. 16.
[2] Ibid., chap. 17, p. 17.

should not be viewed as offsets to other cash accounts except where the legal right of setoff exists within the same bank due to the existence of other positive balances in that bank.

(e) FOREIGN BALANCES.   Cash in foreign countries may properly be included in the balance sheet as cash if stated at its equivalent in U.S. currency at the prevailing rate of exchange and if no exchange restrictions exist to prevent the transfer of such monies to the domicile of the owner. Depending on circumstances and the extent to which such cash balances may be subject to exchange control or other restrictions, the amount of cash so included should be considered for disclosure, by being stated separately, parenthetically, or otherwise. The question of exchange restrictions (or economic conditions) preventing transfer of cash across national boundaries is of prime importance, and cash in foreign countries should be classified as a current asset only if appropriate review establishes that no significant restrictions or conditions exist with respect to the amounts involved. If restrictions exist but ultimate transfer seems probable, the cash may be included in the balance sheet in a noncurrent classification.

Difficulty in stating foreign cash balances at their equivalent in U.S. currency occurs when more than one rate of exchange exists. In this situation, the use of an exchange rate related to earnings received from the foreign subsidiary for the purpose of translating foreign currency accounts is recommended. ASC 830-30-45, *Foreign Currency Matters, Translation of Financial Statements, Other Presentation Matters,* paragraphs 6 to 9, provide guidance on the selection of exchange rates.

(f) COMPENSATING CASH BALANCES.   It is not uncommon for banks to require that a current or prospective borrower maintain a compensating balance on deposit with the bank. Frequently, the required compensating balance is based on the average outstanding loan balance. A compensating deposit balance may also be required to assure future credit availability (including maintenance of an unused line of credit). The compensating balance requirement may be (1) written into a loan or line of credit agreement, (2) the subject of a supplementary written agreement, or (3) based on an oral understanding. In some instances, a fee is paid on an unused line of credit (or commitment) to ensure credit availability.

The SEC originally defined compensating balances in Accounting Series Release (ASR) No. 148, *Disclosure of Compensating Balances and Short-Term Borrowing Arrangements,* now codified in the *Codification of Financial Reporting Policies,* Section 203.02a, done in this way:

> A compensating balance is defined as that portion of any demand deposit (or any time deposit or certificate of deposit) maintained by a corporation (or by any other person on behalf of the corporation) which constitutes support for existing borrowing arrangements of the corporation (or any other person) with a lending institution. Such arrangements would include both outstanding borrowings and the assurance of future credit availability.

For SEC registrants, requirements for the disclosure of restrictions on the withdrawal or use of cash and cash items, such as compensating balance arrangements, are set forth in Rule 5-02.1 of Regulation S-X:

CASH AND CASH ITEMS.

> Separate disclosure shall be made of the cash and cash items which are restricted as to withdrawal or usage. The provisions of any restrictions shall be described in a note to the financial statements. Restrictions may include legally restricted deposits held as compensating balances against short-term borrowing arrangements, contracts entered into with others, or company statements of intention with regard to particular deposits; however, time deposits and short-term certificates of deposit are not generally included in legally restricted deposits. In cases where compensating balance arrangements exist but are not agreements which legally restrict the use of cash amounts shown on the balance sheet, describe in the notes to the financial statements these arrangements and the amount involved, if determinable, for the most recent audited balance sheet required and for any subsequent unaudited balance sheet required in the notes to the financial statements. Compensating balances that are maintained under an agreement to assure future credit availability

shall be disclosed in the notes to the financial statements along with the amount and terms of such agreement.

Guidelines and interpretations for disclosure of compensating balance arrangements are described within the codification of SEC Financial Reporting Release (FRR) No. 203, *Disclosure of Compensating Balances and Short-Term Borrowing Arrangements,* and SEC Staff Accounting Bulletin (SAB) Topic 6H, Accounting Series Release 148, *Disclosure of Compensating Balances and Short-Term Borrowing Arrangements (Adopted November 13, 1973 as Modified by ASR 172 Adopted on June 13, 1975 and ASR 280 Adopted on September 2, 1980).* These provide useful information in evaluating the need for segregation and disclosure of compensating balance arrangements, including determination of the amount to be disclosed. Cash float and other factors should be considered.

Although no other authoritative literature requires compensating balance disclosures in the financial statements of non-SEC registrants, disclosure of material compensating balances will usually be necessary for fair presentation of the financial statements in accordance with generally accepted accounting principles (GAAP). Consequently, the disclosure of material compensating balance arrangements in financial statements of non-SEC reporting companies, whether maintained under a written agreement or under an informal agreement confirmed by the bank, is usually considered necessary as an "informative disclosure" under the third standard of reporting. It should be noted that compensating balances may also relate to an agreement or an understanding relative to future credit availability (including unused lines of credit). Compensating balances related to future credit availability should be disclosed as well as those related to outstanding borrowings.

(i) Disclosure.   In circumstances where compensating balances relative to outstanding loans and future credit availability are not legally restricted as to withdrawal, note disclosure is appropriate.

(ii) Segregation in the Balance Sheet.   Cash that is not subject to withdrawal should be classified as a noncurrent asset to the extent that such cash relates to the noncurrent portion of the debt that causes its restriction. To the extent legally restricted cash relates to short-term borrowings, it may be included with unrestricted amounts on one line in financial statements of non-SEC reporting companies, provided the caption is appropriate and there is disclosure of the restricted amounts in the notes, for example, "Cash and restricted cash (Note 3)." Rule 5-02.1 of Regulation S-X requires SEC-reporting companies to disclose separately funds legally restricted as to withdrawal, but FRR No. 203.02.b is more specific in its requirement to segregate all legally restricted cash in the balance sheet.

No single example is appropriate for the disclosure of all compensating balance arrangements and future credit availability (including unused lines of credit) because the terms of loan agreements vary greatly. However, the next hypothetical examples illustrate methods of disclosing the details of compensating balance agreements and future credit availability.

Next is an example of disclosure where withdrawal of the compensating balance was legally restricted at the date of the balance sheet.

CASH ITEMS DISCLOSED ON BALANCE SHEET

SEC-Reporting Companies

Current assets

Cash	$3,500,000
Restricted cash compensating balances (Note X)	$6,000,000

Non-SEC Reporting Companies

Current assets $9,500,000

Cash and restricted cash (Note X)

Note X. Compensating Balances

A maximum of $100,000,000 is available to the company under a revolving credit agreement. Under the terms of the agreement, the company is required to maintain on deposit with the bank a compensating balance, restricted as to use, of 10 percent of the outstanding loan balance. At December 31, 20XX, $6,000,000 of the cash balance shown in the balance sheet was so restricted after adjusting for differences of "float" between the balance shown by the books of the company and the records of the bank.

For SEC-reporting companies, the following disclosure should be added to the above note:

This "float" amount consisted of $3,000,000 of unpresented checks less $500,000 of deposits of delayed availability at the agreed-upon schedule of 1.5 days' deposits.

Next is an example of disclosure for both SEC and non-SEC reporting companies where withdrawal of the compensating balance was not legally restricted at the date of the balance sheet.

Current assets

   Cash (Note X) $10,000,000

Note X. Compensating Balances

Under an informal agreement with a lending bank, the company maintains on deposit with the bank a compensating balance of 5 percent of an unused line of credit and 10 percent of the outstanding loan balance. At December 31, 20XX approximately $5,800,000 of the cash balance shown in the balance sheet represented a compensating balance.

(g) UNUSED LINES OF CREDIT.   Rules 5-02.19 and 22 of Regulation S-X require that the amount and terms (including commitment fees and the conditions under which commitments may be withdrawn) of unused lines of credit or unused commitments for financing arrangements be disclosed. The term *unused lines of credit* is used for short-term financing arrangements; the term *unused commitments* refers to long-term financing arrangements. The requirements of Regulation S-X are:

5.02.19 ACCOUNTS AND NOTES PAYABLE. (b) The amount and terms (including commitment fees and the conditions under which lines may be withdrawn) of unused lines of credit for short-term financing shall be disclosed, if significant, in the notes to the financial statements. The weighted average interest rate on short term borrowings outstanding as of the date of each balance sheet presented shall be furnished in a note. The amount of these lines of credit which support a commercial paper borrowing arrangement or similar arrangements shall be separately identified.

5.02. 22. BONDS, MORTGAGES, AND OTHER LONG TERM DEBT, INCLUDING CAPITALIZED LEASES. (b) The amount and terms (including commitment fees and the conditions under which commitments may be withdrawn) of unused commitments for long-term financing arrangements that would be disclosed under this rule if used shall be disclosed in the notes to the financial statements if significant.

Many future credit arrangements are informal. Even formal arrangements may be withdrawn by lending institutions on very short notice, usually resulting from an adverse change in the financial position of a company. Therefore, limitations relating to the subsequent use of such lines of credit make it particularly difficult to provide informative and adequate disclosure so that the reader does not get a more favorable picture than is warranted. Because of the uncertainty of the duration of some lines of credit, disclosure of these types of lines of credit in financial statements requires the exercise of individual judgment based on the facts of the particular situation, and disclosures should include the limitations and conditions of subsequent use. Unused lines of credit or commitments that may be withdrawn at the mere option of the lender need not be disclosed but, if disclosed, the nature of the arrangement should be disclosed as well.

(i) Fee Paid for Future Credit Availability. A commitment fee has an effect on the cost of borrowing that is similar to that of a compensating balance. If a fee is paid to a lending bank for an unused line of credit or commitment, such fee should be disclosed if significant (Rule 502.19b of Regulation S-X).

(ii) Disclosure. Next is an example of disclosure of binding bank credit arrangements. Information of this nature may be combined with note disclosure of indebtedness.

> Note X. Unused Lines of Credit
>
> Bank lines of credit under which notes payable of $105,000,000 were outstanding at December 31, 20XX, aggregated $152,500,000. The use of these lines generally is restricted to the extent that the Company is required periodically to liquidate its indebtedness to individual banks for 30 to 60 days each year. Borrowings under such agreements are at interest rates ranging from $1/4$ to $1/2$ of 1% above the prime rate, plus a commitment fee of $1/4$ to $1/2$ of 1% on the unused available credit. Commitments by the banks generally expire one year from the date of the agreement and are generally renewed.
>
> For SEC-reporting companies, this disclosure should be added to the above note:
>
> Total commitment fees paid on the unused lines of credit amounted to $175,000 for 20XX, $195,000 for 20XX, and $180,000 for 20XX.

(h) CONCENTRATION OF CREDIT RISK. Disclosures related to cash balances should include the existence of uninsured cash balances that represent a significant concentration of credit risk. American Institute of Certified Public Accountants (AICPA) Technical Questions and Answers Section 2000, Section 2110, Cash Paragraph 2110.06, *Disclosure of Cash Balances in Excess of Federally Insured Amounts,* provides this guidance:

> *Inquiry.* Should the existence of cash on deposit with banks in excess of Federal Deposit Insurance Corporation (FDIC)-insured limits be disclosed in the financial statements?
>
> *Reply.* The existence of uninsured cash balances should be disclosed if the uninsured balances represent a significant concentration of credit risk. Credit risk as defined in the FASB Codification Master Glossary includes risk associated with changes in the obligor's creditworthiness, default and changes in the spread over the benchmark interest rate with respect to a hedged item's credit sector at inception of the hedge. As a result, bank statement balances in excess of FDIC-insured amounts represent credit risk.
>
> An example of disclosure for this circumstance might be:
>
> The Company maintains its cash in bank deposit accounts which, at times, may exceed federally insured limits. The Company has not experienced any losses in such account. The Company believes it is not exposed to any significant credit risk on cash and cash equivalents.

On July 21, 2010, the president signed the Dodd-Frank Wall Street Reform and Consumer Protection Act (the Dodd-Frank Act) into law. There will be a permanent increase in deposit insurance for banks, thrifts, and credit unions to $250,000, which is retroactive to January 1, 2008. Cash limits on protection by the Securities Investor Protection Corporation is also increased from $100,000 to $250,000, subject to periodic adjustments for inflation.

(i) Fair Value Disclosures. ASC 825-10-50, *Financial Instruments, Overall Disclosure,* requires disclosure of fair values of financial instruments. The disclosure should include the method and significant assumptions used to estimate fair value. Due to the short-term maturity of cash and cash equivalents, this requirement is often met by the following sample disclosure:

> *Cash and Cash Equivalents.* The carrying amount approximates fair value because of the short-term maturity of those instruments.

11.3 LOANS

(a) INTRODUCTION. Although not the primary focus of their business, manufacturers, wholesalers, retailers, and service companies may nevertheless originate loans in connection with their revenue-generating activities. The FASB Codification Master Glossary defines a loan, as:

> A contractual right to receive money on demand or on fixed or determinable dates that is recognized as an asset in the creditor's statement of financial position. Examples include but are not limited to accounts receivable (with terms exceeding one year) and notes receivable. [par. 4]

However, there are certain requirements, as discussed, for any type of credit arrangement, including trade receivables. In contrast, one of the most significant activities for financial institutions is the origination and acquisition of loans in order to generate interest revenue. Chapter 30 discusses matters of interest to financial institutions and entities involved in lending and deposit taking activities.

(b) RECOGNITION AND MEASUREMENT. ASC 310-10-35, *Receivables, Overall, Subsequent Measurement,* states that:

> Loans and trade receivables that management has the intent and ability to hold for the foreseeable future or until maturity or payoff shall be reported in the balance sheet at outstanding principal adjusted for any chargeoffs, the allowance for loan losses (or the allowance for doubtful accounts), any deferred fees or costs on originated loans, and any unamortized premiums or discounts on purchased loans. [par. 47]

Generally, interest income on loans is accrued at the contractual rate, and premiums and discounts are amortized using the interest method in accordance with ASC 835-30-25, *Interest, Imputation of Interest, Recognition.* Additional guidance is also included in ASC 835-30-55, *Interest, Imputation of Interest, Implementation Guidance and Illustrations,* paragraphs 2 and 3. ASC 835-30-25 discusses the appropriate accounting when the face amount of a note does not reasonably represent the present value of the consideration given or received in the exchange. ASC 835-30-15, *Interest, Imputation of Interest, Scope and Scope Exceptions,* paragraph 3, excludes from its scope

- Receivables and payables arising from transactions with customers or suppliers in the normal course of business that are due in customary trade terms not exceeding approximately one year.
- Amounts that do not require repayment in the future but rather will be applied to the purchase price of the property, goods, or service involved; for example, deposits or progress payments on construction contracts, advance payments for acquisition of resources and raw materials.
- Amounts intended to provide security for one party to an agreement (e.g., security deposits, retainages on contracts).
- The customary cash lending activities and demand or savings deposit activities of financial institutions whose primary business is lending money.
- Transactions where interest rates are affected by the tax attributes or legal restrictions prescribed by a governmental agency (e.g., industrial revenue bonds, tax exempt obligations, government guaranteed obligations, income tax settlements).
- Transactions between parent and subsidiary entities and between subsidiaries of a common parent.
- The application of the present value measurement (valuation) technique to estimates of contractual or other obligations assumed in connection with sales of property, goods, or service (e.g., a warranty for product performance).

Non-interest-bearing loans, loans with unrealistic interest rates, and loans obtained in exchange for property, goods, or services with fair values materially different from the principal amount of

This example is an illustration of the guidance in paragraphs 835-30-45-1 through 45-3 related to the balance sheet presentation of notes that are discounted.

	December 31	
	1970	1969
Presentation 1—Discount presented in caption		
NOTE RECEIVABLE FROM SALE OF PROPERTY:		
$1,000,000 face amount, non-interest-bearing, due December 31, 1975 (less unamortized		
discount based on imputed interest rate of 8%—1970, $320,000; 1969, $370,000)	$ 680,000	$ 630,000
Presentation 2—Discount presented separately		
NOTE RECEIVABLE FROM SALE OF PROPERTY:		
Non-interest-bearing note due December 31, 1975	$ 1,000,000	$ 1,000,000
Less unamortized discount based on imputed interest rate of 8%	320,000	370,000
Note receivable less unamortized discount	$ 680,000	$ 630,000
Presentation 3—Several notes involved		
LONG-TERM DEBT (Note 1):		
Principal amount	$ 24,000,000	$ 24,000,000
Less unamortized discount	2,070,000	2,192,000
Long-term debt less unamortized discount	$ 21,930,000	$ 21,808,000

Note 1—Long-Term Debt
Long-term debt at December 31, 1970 consisted of the following:

	Principal	Unamortized Discount
6% subordinated debentures, due 1984 (discount is based on imputed interest rate of 7%)	$ 20,000,000	$ 1,750,000
6½% bank loan, due 1973	3,000,000	—
Non-interest-bearing note issued in connection with acquisition of property, due 1975		
(discount is based on imputed interest rate of 8%)	1,000,000	320,000
Total	$ 24,000,000	$ 2,070,000

Exhibit 11.1   Example 2: Balance Sheet Presentation of Discounted Notes

the loan lead to the recognition of premiums and discounts, unless the fair value options is elected. ASC 835-30-45, *Interest, Implementation of Interest, Other Presentation Matters,* paragraph 1A, states that the discount or premium resulting from the determination of present value in cash or noncash transactions is not an asset or liability separable from the note that gives rise to it. Therefore, the discount or premium must be reported in the balance sheet as a direct deduction from or addition to the face amount of the note. It must not be classified as a deferred charge or deferred credit. The description of the note must include the effective interest rate. The face amount must also be disclosed in the financial statements or in the notes to the statements. Example 2 in ASC 835-30-55, *Interest, Imputation of Interest, Implementation Guidance and Illustrations,* paragraph 8, provides an example of the balance sheet presentation (see Exhibit 11.1).

Nonrefundable fees and costs associated with an entity's lending activities are most prevalent for financial institutions and the accounting for these fees and costs is discussed in Chapter 30.

Some acquired loans may have experienced a decline in credit quality. ASC 310-30, *Receivables, Loans and Debt Securities Acquired with Deteriorated Credit,* addresses the accounting and reporting for those loans. Loans that have been acquired should be evaluated to determine whether the provisions of ASC 310-30 should be applied.

(c) LOAN IMPAIRMENT AND INCOME RECOGNITION.   ASC 450-20, *Contingencies, Loss Contingencies,* and ASC 310-10-35, *Receivables, Overall, Subsequent Measurement,* address the accounting by creditors for impairment of certain loans. According to ASC 310-10-35, a loan is impaired when, based on current information and events, it is probable that a creditor will be unable to collect all the contractual interest and principal as scheduled in the loan agreement. It applies to all creditors. While both topics address loan impairment, Topic 450, *Contingencies,* generally addresses smaller-balance homogenous loans while Topic 310, *Receivables,* addresses all loans except those specifically excluded as noted in ASC 310-10-35, paragraph 13:

- Large groups of smaller-balance homogeneous loans that are collectively evaluated for impairment. Those loans may include but are not limited to credit card, residential mortgage, and consumer installment loans.
- Loans that are measured at fair value or at the lower of cost or fair value, for example, in accordance with ASC Topic 948, *Financial Services—Mortgage Banking.*
- Leases as defined in ASC Topic 840, *Leases.*
- Debt securities as defined in ASC Topic 320, *Investments—Debt and Equity Securities.*

The guidance does not specify how a creditor should identify loans that are to be evaluated for impairment. However, in practice, a number of different mechanisms are employed to identify loans for impairment evaluation. These mechanisms include but are not limited to:

- Loans or receivables over a specified dollar amount
- Past-due reports
- Reports from regulatory examiners
- Reviews of incomplete loan files of financial institutions
- Identification of those borrowers facing financial difficulties or operating in industries facing such difficulties
- Loss statistics pertaining to certain categories of loans
- Loan files lacking current financial data related to borrowers and guarantors
- Loans secured by collateral that is not readily marketable or that is susceptible to deterioration in realizable value

(i) Impairment Measurement Guidelines. The measurement of impairment should take into account both contractual interest payments and contractual principal payments consistent with the original payment terms of the loan agreement. For loans within the scope of ASC 310-10, the creditor should measure impairment based on the present value of expected future cash flows discounted at the loan's effective interest rate. A loan's effective interest rate is defined in the FASB Codification Master Glossary as "the rate of return implicit in the loan, that is, the contractual interest rate adjusted for any net deferred loan fees or costs, premium, or discount existing at the origination or acquisition of the loan."

ASC 310-10-35 provides that as a practical expedient, creditors may measure impairment based on a loan's observable market price or the fair value of the collateral if the loan is a collateral dependent loan. If the latter approach is used, Topic 820, *Fair Value Measurement,* applies. Paragraph 23 of ASC 310-10-35 indicates that if a creditor uses the fair value of the collateral to measure impairment of a collateral-dependent loan and repayment or satisfaction of a loan is dependent on the sale of the collateral, the fair value of the collateral must be adjusted to consider estimated cost to sell. However, if repayment or satisfaction of the loan is dependent only on the operation, rather than the sale, of the collateral, the measure of impairment should not incorporate cost to sell the collateral. Furthermore, when a creditor determines that foreclosure is probable, impairment must be measured based on the fair value of the collateral.

When valuations are based on appraisals, particular attention should be given to the objectivity and competence of the specialist providing the appraisal and the methods and assumptions used to develop the appraised fair value. Additionally, the appraisal should be assessed as to its suitability for the purpose. For example, "appraisals" sometimes are obtained to assess the feasibility of a commercial development project (e.g., a golf course and condominium complex) and assume the existence of the completed project. Such an "appraisal" might not be useful in assessing the "as is" fair value of a property comprised mostly of raw land in foreclosure. While companies are not precluded from appraising collateral internally, the increased objectivity of third-party appraisals may provide more objective valuations to assist management in decision making and also permit auditors to also rely on the work of a specialist performing the appraisal. Valuations are the subject of Chapters 24 and 25 in this *Handbook*.

In any event, a valuation allowance should be established if the recorded investment in the loan (including accrued interest, net deferred loan fees or costs, and unamortized discount or premium) exceeds the impaired measure (e.g., present value of cash flows using the loan's original effective rate, fair value of collateral, or observable market price of loan). The recognition of such an allowance is accompanied by a corresponding charge to bad debt expense.

(ii) Income Recognition.   Once a loan has been impaired, some entities, particularly financial institutions, suspend the accrual of interest because, in those circumstances, such accruals do not reflect economic reality.

ASC 310-10-35 does not address how a creditor should recognize, measure, or display interest income on an impaired loan. Some accounting methods for recognizing income may result in a recorded investment in an impaired loan that is less than the present value of expected future cash flows (or, alternatively, the observable market price for the loan or the fair value of the collateral). In those cases, no additional impairment is recognized. An entity is required to disclose its accounting policy for recognizing interest on impaired loans. Some accounting methods may include recognition of interest income using a cost-recovery method, a cash-based method, or some combination of those methods. The recorded investment in an impaired loan may also be less than the present value of expected future cash flows (or, alternatively, the observable market price for the loan of the fair value of the collateral) because the creditor has charged off part of the loan.

ASC 310-10-35, paragraph 40, describes two accounting methods to account for changes in the net carrying amount of an impaired loan subsequent to the initial measure of impairment:

(a) Under the first income recognition method, a creditor shall accrue interest on the net carrying amount of the impaired loan and report other changes in the net carrying amount of the loan as an adjustment to bad-debt expense.

(b) Under the second income recognition method, a creditor shall recognize all changes in the net carrying amount of the loan as an adjustment to bad-debt expense.

Creditors must disclose the amount of interest income that represents the change in present value due to the passage of time.

Those income recognition methods are not required, and a creditor is not precluded from using either of those methods.

(d) TROUBLED DEBT RESTRUCTURINGS.   Occasionally, a loan may be restructured to meet a borrower's changing circumstances, and a new loan is recognized. The guidance for accounting for troubled debt restructurings by creditors is covered in ASC 310-40, *Receivables, Troubled Debt Restructuring by Creditors*. The guidance for accounting for troubled debt restructurings by debtors is included in ASC 470-60, *Debt, Troubled Debt Restructurings by Debtors*. The discussion here focuses on guidance provided in ASC 310-40.

The FASB Codification Master Glossary defines a troubled debt restructuring in this way:

A restructuring of debt constitutes a troubled debt restructuring if the creditor for economic or legal reasons related to the debtor's financial difficulties grants a concession to the debtor that it would not otherwise consider.

For example, the creditor may modify the debt terms including interest rates or amounts, payment terms and/or amounts and maturity date(s) or accepting the transfer of assets or equity interest in debtor to partially or fully settle the debt.

In addition, paragraph 16 of ASC 310-40-15, *Receivables, Troubled Debt Restructurings by Creditors, Scope and Scope Exceptions,* provides in part that the concession is granted by the creditor in an attempt to protect as much of its investment as possible. For example, a creditor may restructure the terms of a debt to alleviate the burden of the debtor's near-term cash requirements, or the creditor may accept cash or other assets or an equity interest in the debtor in satisfaction of the debt, even though the value received is less than the amount of the debt. Although troubled debt that is fully satisfied by foreclosure, repossession, or other transfer of assets or by grant of equity securities by the debtor, is, technically, not restructured, that kind of event is covered by ASC 340-40 and ASC 470-60. ASC 340-40-15 provides other examples of circumstances that do not qualify as troubled debt restructurings, including when the fair value of cash or other assets accepted by the creditor in full satisfaction of its receivable at least equals the recorded investment or when the creditor reduces the effective interest rate to reflect a decrease in market interest rates or a decrease in the risk. Also, certain transactions where the creditor is accounting for the receivable at market value in accordance with specialized industry practice are not accounted for as troubled debt restructurings, as described in ASC 310-40-35, *Receivables, Troubled Debt Restructurings by Creditors, Subsequent Measurement,* paragraph 2

Paragraphs 2 through 4 of ASC 310-40-40, *Receivables, Troubled Debt Restructurings by Creditors, Derecognition,* provide guidance on accounting for the full settlement of receivables in a troubled debt restructuring. Creditors that receive assets or an equity interest in the debtor in full satisfaction of the loan should account for the restructuring at the fair value of the assets or equity interest received or the fair value of the loan, whichever is more clearly determinable. If the fair value of the assets less cost to sell or equity interest received is less than the recorded investment in the receivable, losses, to the extent they are not offset against allowances for uncollectable amounts, should be included in net income. The fair value of the receivable may be used only if the fair value of the receivable is more clearly evident than the fair value of the assets received.

ASC 310-40-35 provides guidance on accounting for the partial settlement of receivables in a troubled debt restructuring. In the case of a partial satisfaction of the loan, the loan is reduced by the fair value less cost to sell of the assets received. Paragraph 12 requires that the effective interest rate to be used for a loan restructured in a troubled debt restructuring be the original contractual rate and not the rate specified in the restructuring agreement.

ASC 310-40-50, *Receivables, Troubled Debt Restructurings, Disclosure,* provides disclosure requirements related to troubled debt restructurings. A key item that creditors must disclose is the amount of commitments, if any, to lend additional funds to debtors owing receivables whose terms have been modified in troubled debt restructurings (ASC-310-40-50-1).

In April 2011, the FASB issued Accounting Standards Update 2011-02 (ASU 2011-02), *A Creditor's Determination of Whether a Restructuring Is a Troubled Debt Restructuring.* This ASU was issued to improve financial reporting by creating greater consistency in the way GAAP is applied for various types of debt restructurings. The ASU clarifies which loan modifications constitute troubled debt restructurings. It is intended to assist creditors in determining whether a modification of the terms of a receivable meets the criteria to be considered a troubled debt restructuring, for purposes of both recording an impairment loss and disclosure of troubled debt restructurings. Although the ASU does not amend the accounting for troubled debt restructurings, it is expected that application of the clarifications contained in it will result in more modifications being considered troubled debt restructurings.

In evaluating whether a restructuring constitutes a troubled debt restructuring, a creditor must separately conclude that both of these two issues exist: (1) the restructuring constitutes a concession, and (2) the debtor is experiencing financial difficulties. The provisions of this ASU clarify the guidance on a creditor's evaluation of whether it has granted a concession and whether a debtor is experiencing financial difficulties. With regard to determining whether a concession has been granted, the ASU clarifies that creditors are precluded from using the effective interest method to determine whether a concession has been granted. Instead, creditors must now focus on other considerations, such as the value of the underlying collateral, evaluation of other collateral or guarantees, the debtor's ability to access other funds at market rates, interest rate increases, and whether the restructuring results in a delay in payment that is insignificant. In addition, the ASU provides "a not all inclusive" list of six indicators for creditors to consider when determining if a debtor is experiencing financial difficulties, which can be found in ASC 310-40-15-20.

For public companies, the new guidance is effective for interim and annual periods beginning on or after June 15, 2011, and applies retrospectively to restructurings occurring on or after the beginning of the fiscal year of adoption. As a result of applying the amendments, an entity may identify receivables that are newly considered impaired. For purposes of measuring impairment of those receivables, an entity should apply the amendments prospectively. For example, a December 31 year-end public company will be required to adopt the provisions of the ASU on July 1, 2011. If the company entered into a loan modification between the dates of January 1 and June 30, it would be required to apply the provisions contained in the ASU to that loan modification to determine if the modification is a troubled debt restructuring. Any impairment resulting from a receivable now considered a troubled debt restructuring would be recognized in the period ending September 30, 2011.

A public entity should disclose the total amount of receivables and the allowance for credit losses as of the end of the period of adoptions related to those receivables that are newly considered impaired. An entity should also disclose information required by ASC 310-10-50, paragraphs 33 and 34, which was previously deferred by ASU 2011-01, *Receivables (Topic 310), Deferral of the Effective Date of Disclosure about Troubled Debt Restructuring in Update No. 2100-20,* for public entities.

The ASU is effective for nonpublic entities for annual periods ending on or after December 15, 2012, including interim periods within those annual periods. Early adoption is permitted for public and nonpublic entities.

(e) NOTES RECEIVED FOR CAPITAL STOCK.   An entity sometimes may receive a note from the sale of capital stock or as a contribution to paid-in capital. Paragraph 2 of ASC 505-10-45, *Equity, Overall, Other Presentation Matters,* provides that reporting the note as an asset is generally not appropriate, except in very limited circumstances when there is substantial evidence of ability and intent to pay within a reasonably short period of time. Consequently, the predominant practice is to offset the notes and stock in the equity section. However, such notes may be recorded as an asset if collected in cash before the financial statements are issued or are available to be issued.

(f) DISCLOSURES.   There are a number of disclosure requirements related to loans. ASC 310-10-50, *Receivable, Overall, Disclosure;* ASC 310-30-50, *Receivables, Loans and Debt Securities Acquired with Deteriorated Credit Quality, Disclosure;* ASC 450-20-50, *Contingencies, Loss Contingencies, Disclosure;* and ASC 460-10-50, *Guarantees, Overall, Disclosure,* provide guidance on these requirements. ASU 2010-20, *Receivable (Topic 310), Disclosures About Credit Quality of Financing Receivables and the Allowance for Loan Losses,* was issued in July 2010 to require additional disclosures regarding the allowance for loan losses and credit quality of its financing receivables. The provisions of ASU 2010-20 are effective for public entities for interim and annual periods beginning after December 15, 2010 and nonpublic entities for annual reporting periods beginning after December 15, 2011.

Disclosure requirements specific to financial institutions are included in ASC 942, *Financial Services Depository and Lending.*

11.4 DEBT SECURITIES

(a) INTRODUCTION.   According to the FASB Codification Master Glossary, a *security*

includes a share, participation, or other interest in property or in an entity of the issuer or an obligation of the issuer that is represented by an instrument issued in bearer or registered form or in books maintained to record transfers by or on behalf of the issuer, is commonly dealt in on securities exchanges or markets or is commonly recognized as a medium of investment and is either one of a class or series or by its terms is divisible into a class or series of shares, participations, interest, or obligations.

An entity may invest in debt securities (e.g., bonds) to generate interest revenue and/or to realize gains from their sale at increased market prices. ASC 320, *Investments, Debt and Equity Securities,* is the primary standard applicable to investments in debt securities. The FASB Codification Master Glossary defines *debt securities* in part as those securities that represent "a creditor relationship with an entity." These securities include:

- U.S. Treasury securities, U.S. government agency securities, municipal securities, corporate bonds, convertible debt, commercial paper, all securitized debt instruments, such as collateralized mortgage obligations (CMOs) and real estate mortgage investment conduits (REMICs), and interest-only and principal-only strips
- A CMO (or other instrument) that is issued in equity form but is required to be accounted for as a nonequity instrument regardless of how that instrument is classified (i.e., whether equity or debt) in the issuer's statement of financial position
- Preferred stock that by its terms either must be redeemed by the issuing enterprise or is redeemable at the option of the investor
- Excluded from the definition of debt securities are unsecuritized loans, options on debt securities, accounts receivable, option contracts, financial futures contracts, forward contracts, and lease contracts.

Generally, ASC 320 applies to all entities, including cooperatives and mutual entities (such as credit unions and mutual insurance entities) and trusts, that do not report substantially all of their securities at fair value. ASC 320 does not apply to enterprises whose specialized accounting practices include accounting for substantially all investments in debt and equity securities at market value or fair value, with changes in value recognized in earnings (income) or in the change in net assets. Not-for-profit organizations are also excluded from the scope of ASC 320 with the exception of accounting for the impairment of certain securities.

(In addition, since ASC 320 generally requires that investments in debt securities that are not properly classified as held to maturity be presented at fair value, enterprises that already use similar measurement guidelines in accounting for these investments—for example, brokers and dealers in securities, defined benefit pension plans, and investment companies—are excluded from the scope of ASC 320. Certain financial assets subject to prepayment are measured like investment in debt securities. Those assets include interest-only strips, retained interests in securitizations, loans, other receivables, or other financial assets that can contractually be prepaid or otherwise settled in such a way that the holder would not recover substantially all of its recorded investment, except for instruments that are within the scope of ASC 815, *Derivatives and Hedging.*

ASC 325-40, *Investments—Other, Beneficial Interest in Securitized Financial Assets,* provides interest income recognition and measurement guidance for interests retained in a securitization transaction accounted for as a sale. The scope of ASC 325-40 includes retained beneficial interests in securitization transactions that are accounted for as sales and certain purchased beneficial interests in securitized financial assets. The scope, as noted in ASC 325-40-15, includes beneficial interests that:

a. Are either debt securities under ASC 320-10, *Investments—Debt and Equity Securities,* or required to be accounted for like debt securities under ASC 860-20-35, *Transfers and Servicing, Sales of Financial Assets, Subsequent Measurement,* paragraph 2.

b. Involve securitized financial assets that have contractual cash flows (e.g., loans, receivables, debt securities, and guaranteed lease residuals, among other items). Thus, the guidance on ASC 325-40 does not apply to securitized financial assets that do not involve contractual cash flows (e.g., common stock equity securities, among other items). See ASC 320-10-35,

Subsequent Measurement, paragraph 38, for guidance on beneficial interest involving securitized financial assets that do not involve contractual cash flows.

c. Do not result in consolidation of the entity issuing the beneficial interest by the holder of the beneficial interests.

d. Are not within the scope of Subtopic 310-30.

e. Are not beneficial interests in securitized financial assets that have both of the next characteristics:

    1. Are of high credit quality (e.g., guaranteed by the U.S. government, its agencies, or other creditworthy guarantors, and loans or securities sufficiently collateralized to ensure that the possibility of credit loss is remote)

    2. Cannot contractually be prepaid or otherwise settled in such a way that the holder would not recover substantially all of its recorded investment

ASC 325-40-35 provides that if, upon evaluation, based on current information and events there is a favorable (or an adverse) change in cash flows expected to be collected from the cash flows previously projected, then the investor must recalculate the amount of accretable yield for the beneficial interest on the date of evaluation as the excess of cash flows expected to be collected over the beneficial interest's reference amount. The reference amount is equal to the initial investment minus cash received to date minus other-than-temporary impairments recognized in earnings to date plus the yield accreted to date. A favorable (or an adverse) change in cash flows expected to be collected is considered in the context of both timing and amount of the cash flows expected to be collected. Based on cash flows expected to be collected, interest income may be recognized on a beneficial interest even if the net investment in the beneficial interest is accreted to an amount greater than the amount at which the beneficial interest could be settled if prepaid immediately in its entirety. The adjustment should be accounted for prospectively as a change in estimate.

In addition, if the fair value of the beneficial interest has declined below its reference amount, the entity should determine whether the decline is other than temporary.

(b) INITIAL RECOGNITION AND MEASUREMENT. Upon acquisition, debt securities are classified into one of three categories: (1) held to maturity, (2) available for sale, or (3) trading. Generally, these securities are initially recorded at cost with appropriate identification of premium or discounts. Paragraph 8A of ASC 310-40, *Receivables, Troubled Debt Restructuring by Creditor, Derecognition,* states that "the initial cost basis of a debt security of the original debtor received as part of a debt restructuring should be the security's fair value at the date of the restructuring."

ASC 320-10-25, *Investments—Debt and Equity Securities, Overall, Recognition,* provides guidance on classification of debt securities upon acquisition as discussed in the next subsections.

(i) Held to Maturity. At acquisition, an entity should determine that has the positive intent and ability to hold a debt security to maturity. An entity that has the positive ability and intent to hold a security to maturity should classify such security as a held-to-maturity security. Otherwise, the security should be classified as trading or available for sale. The positive intent and ability to hold a debt security to maturity is more than the mere absence of intent to sell. If there is uncertainty regarding the intention to hold a debt security to maturity (e.g., if would be sold to meet liquidity needs, because of changes in market rates or yields on alternative investment or foreign exchange risk), it does not qualify for held-to-maturity classification. Specific scenarios in which debt securities should not be classified as held to maturity include

- A security that can contractually be prepaid or otherwise settled in such a way that the holder would not recover substantially all of its recorded investment
- A mortgage-backed interest-only certificate
- A debt security that is considered available to be sold as part of an entity's asset-liability management activities

- Securities maintained as part of a dynamic hedging program where changes in external factors require that certain securities be sold to maintain an effective hedge
- Securities that may need to be sold to implement tax-planning strategies
- Convertible debt securities
- An insurance entity or other regulated entity should not classify securities as held to maturity nor indicate to regulators that those securities could be sold to meet liquidity needs in a defined interest rate scenario whose likelihood of occurrence is reasonably possible but not probable

In addition, a documented policy to initially classify all debt securities as held to maturity but then automatically transfer every security to available for sale when it reaches a predetermined point before maturity so the entity has flexibility to sell the securities is not consistent with the held-to-maturity classification.

(ii) Trading.   Debt securities are classified as trading securities if they are acquired with the intent of selling them in the near term and holding them only for a short period of time. The "near term" contemplates a holding period generally measured in hours or days rather than months or years. However, the classification of a security as trading is not precluded because the entity does not intend to sell it in the near term.

(iii) Available for Sale.   Debt securities that have readily determinable fair values and are not classified as held-to-maturity or trading securities are classified as available-for-sale securities.

(c) ACCOUNTING AFTER ACQUISITION.   Gains and losses realized upon the sale of debt securities are included in earnings. Sale accounting is appropriate only for transfers of financial assets in which the transferor surrenders control over those financial assets. Otherwise, the transferor should account for the transfer as a secured borrowing with pledge of collateral. Generally, interest income is recognized at the contractual rate, and premiums and discounts are amortized using the interest method. The amount at which a debt security is presented in the statement of financial position depends on its classification, as discussed below. The accounting requires the determination of fair value for securities not classified as held to maturity. The FASB Codification Master Glossary defines *fair value* as "the price that would be received to sell an asset or paid to transfer a liability in an orderly transaction between market participants at the measurement date. If a quoted market price is available for an instrument, the fair value to be used is generally the product of the number of trading units of the instrument times its market price." If a quoted market price is not available for a debt security, pricing techniques such as discounted cash flow analysis, matrix pricing, option-adjusted spread models, and fundamental analysis can be used to obtain an estimate of fair value.

ASC 825-10-50 requires additional disclosures when the fair value option is used for financial assets and liabilities. The fair value disclosure requirements have been updated by ASU 2011-4, *Amendments to Achieve Common Fair Value Measurement and Disclosure Requirements in U. S. GAAP and IFRS,* which is effective on a prospective basis, for public entities for interim and annual reporting periods beginning after December 15, 2011. For nonpublic entities, the disclosures are effective for annual reporting periods beginning after December 15, 2011. Early adoption is permitted for nonpublic entities only for interim periods beginning after December 15, 2011.

The appropriateness of a security's classification must be reassessed at each reporting date. In making this assessment, prior sales and transfers should be considered. Transfers to another category are discussed in Subsection 11.4(c)(iv).

(i) Held to Maturity.   Debt securities classified as held to maturity are carried at amortized cost. Like loans, premiums and discounts pertaining to these securities generally are amortized using the interest method.

In assessing the appropriateness of the held-to-maturity designation at each reporting date, paragraphs 6 through 11 of ASC 320-10-25 provide that transfers or sales due to the next six changes in circumstances do not taint the held-to-maturity classification of other debt securities:

1. Evidence of a significant deterioration in the issuer's creditworthiness (e.g., a downgrading of an issuer's published credit rating)

2. A change in tax law that eliminates or reduces the tax-exempt status of interest on the debt security (but not a change in tax law that revises the marginal tax rates applicable to interest income)

3. A major business combination or major disposition (such as sale of a components of an entity) that necessitates the sale or transfer of held-to-maturity securities to maintain the enterprise's existing interest rate risk position or credit risk policy (See ASC 320-10-25, paragraphs 12 and 13, for a description of transactions that do and do not taint the held to maturity classification.)

4. A change in statutory or regulatory requirements significantly modifying either what constitutes a permissible investment or the maximum level of investments in certain kinds of securities, thereby causing an enterprise to dispose of a held-to-maturity security. (Also see the next full text paragraph.)

5. A significant increase by the regulator in the industry's capital requirements that causes the enterprise to downsize by selling held-to- maturity securities (Also see the next full text paragraph).

6. A significant increase in the risk weights of debt securities used for regulatory risk-based capital purposes. (Also see the next full text paragraph).

It is not appropriate to apply these exceptions to situations that are similar, but not the same as, those just listed.

If a regulator directs a particular institution (rather than all institutions supervised by that regulator) to sell or transfer held-to-maturity securities (e.g., to increase liquid assets), those sales or transfers are not consistent with item 4, which describes a change in regulations applicable to all entities affected by the legislation or regulator enacting the change. The same is true of items 5 and 6. However, it is possible that the circumstances causing a regulator to direct an institution to sell securities could be considered an event that is isolated, nonrecurring, and unusual that could not have been reasonably anticipated, as described in the next paragraph.

In addition to the changes in circumstances just listed, certain other events may cause the entity to sell or transfer a held-to-maturity security without necessarily calling into question (tainting) its intent to hold other debt securities to maturity. Such events must meet all of the next four conditions to avoid tainting the entity's intent to hold other debt securities to maturity in the future:

1. The event is isolated.
2. The event is nonrecurring.
3. The event is unusual for the reporting entity.
4. The event could not have been reasonably anticipated.

Other than extremely remote disaster scenarios (such as a run on a bank or an insurance entity), very few events would meet all four of those conditions. Extremely remote disaster scenarios should not be anticipated by an entity in deciding whether it has the positive intent and ability to hold a debt security to maturity.

(ii) Trading. Debt securities classified as trading securities are carried at fair value. The resulting unrealized gain or loss is reflected in earnings.

(iii) Available for Sale. Debt securities classified as available for sale are carried at fair value. With the exception of fair value hedges, unrealized holding gains and losses for available-for-sale securities (including those classified as current assets) are excluded from earnings and reported in other comprehensive income (OCI), net of related deferred income taxes. These unrealized gains and losses should include the entire change in the fair value of foreign currency–denominated available-for-sale debt securities, not just the portion attributable to changes in exchange rates. Changes in the value of fair value hedges should be recognized in earnings during the period of the hedge pursuant to ASC 815.

(iv) Transfers Between Categories. Changes in the classification of investments in debt securities are accounted for at fair value. The next table summarizes the proper accounting for transfers as outlined in ASC 320-10-35.

Transfer From	Transfer To	Accounting Principles
Trading	Available for Sale	The unrealized holding gain or loss at the date of the transfer will have already been recognized in earnings and shall not be reversed.
	Held to Maturity	The unrealized holding gain or loss at the date of the transfer will have already been recognized in earnings and shall not be reversed.
Available for Sale	Trading	The portion of the unrealized holding gain or loss at the date of the transfer that has not been previously recognized in earnings shall be recognized in earnings immediately.
	Held to Maturity	The unrealized holding gain or loss at the date of the transfer shall continue to be reported in a separate component of shareholders' equity, such as accumulated other comprehensive income, but shall be amortized over the remaining life of the security as an adjustment of yield in a manner consistent with the amortization of any premium or discount.
Held to Maturity	Trading	The portion of the unrealized holding gain or loss at the date of the transfer that has not been previously recognized in earnings shall be recognized in earnings immediately.
	Available for Sale	The unrealized holding gain or loss at the date of the transfer shall be reported in other comprehensive income.

(d) IMPAIRMENT. Impairment of debt and equity securities is discussed in ASC 320-10-35, *Investments—Debt and Equity Securities, Overall, Subsequent Measurement.* The scope of ASC 320-10-35 excludes the next items.

As noted in ASC320-10-35, ASC 944-325-35-1 applies to Insurance entities are required to report equity securities at fair value.

- Entities shall not look through the form of their investment to the nature of the securities held by an investee. For example, an investment in shares of a mutual fund that invests primarily in debt securities would be assessed for impairment as an equity security.
- A bifurcated host instrument under ASC 815-15, *Derivatives and Hedging, Embedded Derivatives,* should be evaluated under this impairment guidance.
- Debt and equity securities with the scope of ASC 958-320, *Not-for-Profit Entities, Investments—Debt and Equity Securities,* and that are held by an entity that reports a performance indicator as defined in ASC 954-225-45, *Health Care Entities, Income Statement, Other Presentation Matters,* should apply this impairment guidance.
- ASC 320-10-35, paragraphs 25 through 27, provide guidance on cost method investments.

Temporary declines in the fair value of securities below amortized cost are not recognized since it is generally held that such declines will ultimately reverse. However, the evaluation of whether impairment is considered other than temporary requires judgment in the application of intent and ability to hold held-to-maturity and available-for-sale securities as well as the potential for the investment to recover losses in fair value. The measurement of impairment can be described in a three-step model:

Step 1. *Determine whether an investment is impaired (i.e., fair value is less than cost).* Generally, cost equals amortized cost less any previous write-downs.

Step 2. *Evaluate whether the impairment is other than temporary.* Other than temporary does not mean permanent, and an investment does not have to be deemed permanently impaired in order to require a write-down.

Step 3. *If the impairment is deemed to be other than temporary, recognize an impairment loss equal to the difference between the carrying amount and its fair value, measured as of the balance sheet date.* Further, the fair value becomes the new cost basis of the investment and should not be adjusted for subsequent recoveries in fair value.

For Step 1, ASC 320-10-35, paragraphs 20 through 29, discusses impairment:

Impairment shall be assessed at the individual security level (referred to as an investment). Individual security level means the level and method of aggregation used by the reporting entity to measure realized and unrealized gains and losses on its debt and equity securities (For example, equity securities with the same CUSIP number purchased in separate lots may be aggregated on an average cost basis). [A CUSIP number is an identification number assigned to all stocks and registered bonds. The Committee on Uniform Securities Identification Procedures (CUSIP) oversees the entire CUSIP system.] An investment is impaired if the fair value of the investment is less than its cost. An investor shall assess whether an investment is impaired in each annual or interim reporting period. An investor shall not combine separate contracts (a debt security and a guarantee or other credit enhancement) for purposes of determining whether a debt security is impaired or can contractually be prepaid or otherwise settled in such a way that the investor would not recover substantially all of its cost.

For investments other than cost-method if the fair value of the investment is less than its cost, proceed to Step 2.

ASC 320-10-35, paragraphs 25 through 27, discusses the consideration of impairment for cost investments. Because the fair value of cost-method investments is not readily determinable, the evaluation of whether an investment is impaired is determined in this way:

(a) If an entity has estimated the fair value of a cost-method investment (for example, for disclosure under *ASC 825-10-50 Financial Instruments, Overall, Disclosure*), that estimate shall be used to determine if the investment is impaired for the reporting periods in which the investor entity estimates fair value. If the fair value of the investment is less than its cost, proceed to Step 2. An entity may not estimate the fair value of a cost-method investment because it is not practicable to estimate the fair value of the investment or because the fair value disclosure requirements of ASC 825-10-50 do not apply.

(b) For reporting periods in which an entity has not estimated the fair value of a cost-method investment, the entity shall evaluate whether an event or change in circumstances has occurred in that period that may have a significant adverse effect on the fair value of the investment (an impairment indicator). Impairment indicators include, but are not limited to:

1. A significant deterioration in the earnings performance, credit rating, asset quality, or business prospects of the investee

2. A significant adverse change in the regulatory, economic, or technological environment of the investee

3. A significant adverse change in the general market condition of either the geographic area or the industry in which the investee operates

4. A bona fide offer to purchase (whether solicited or unsolicited), an offer by the investee to sell, or a completed auction process for the same or similar security for an amount less than the cost of the investment

5. Factors that raise significant concerns about the investee's ability to continue as a going concern, such as negative cash flows from operations, working capital deficiencies, or noncompliance with statutory capital requirements or debt covenants.

In addition, if an investment was previously tested for impairment under Step 2 and the Entity concluded that the investment was not other-than-temporarily impaired, the Entity shall continue to evaluate whether the investment is impaired (that is, shall estimate the fair value of the investment) in each subsequent reporting period until either (a) the investment experiences a recovery of fair value up to (or beyond) its cost or (b) the Entity recognizes an other-than-temporary impairment loss.

If an impairment indicator is present, the investor shall estimate the fair value of the investment. If the fair value of the investment is less than its cost, proceed to Step 2.

For Step 2, ASC 320-10-35, paragraphs 30 through 33I, discusses whether an impairment is other than temporary. When the fair value of an investment is less than its amortized cost at the balance sheet date of the reporting period for which impairment is assessed, the impairment is either temporary or other than temporary. ASC 320-10-35, paragraphs 33A through 33I, provides this guidance relative to debt securities:

If an entity has decided to sell the debt security, other-than-temporary impairment shall be considered to have occurred.

When the impairment is other than temporary, the entity should, in Step 3, recognize an impairment loss equal to the difference between the investment's cost and its fair value.

The entity does not intend to sell the debt security, but available evidence indicates it is more likely than not it will be required to sell the security before the recovery of its amortized cost basis (for example, whether its cash or working capital requirements or contractual or regulatory obligations indicate that the security will be required to be sold before a forecasted recovery occurs).

If an entity does not expect to recover the entire amortized cost of the security (based on comparing the present value of the cash flows expected to be collected with the amortized cost basis), even if it does not intend to sell the security.

ASC 320-10-35, paragraphs 33d and 33e, provides additional guidance on applying the present value techniques to debt securities and debt securities that are beneficial interest.

There are numerous factors to consider in circumstances not covered by the specific criteria mentioned above when estimating whether a credit loss exist and the period of time over which the debt security is expected to recover. These factors include but are not limited to

a. The length of time and extent to which the fair value has been less than the amortized cost basis.
   Adverse conditions specifically related to the security, an industry or geographic area; for example, changes in the financial condition of the underlying obligors such as changes in technology, the discontinuance of a segment of the business that may impact the future earnings potential of the issuer

b. or underlying loan obligors and changes in the quality of the credit enhancement.

c. The historical and implied volatility of the fair value of the security.

d. The payment structure of the debt security.

e. Failure of the user of the security to make scheduled interest or principal payments.

f. Any changes to the rating of the security

g. By a rating agency.

h. Recoveries or additional declines in fair value after the balance sheet date.

In making its other than temporary impairment assessment, an entity shall consider all available information relevant to the collectibility of the security, including information about last events, current conditions, and reasonable and supportable forecast, when developing the estimate of cash flows expected to be collected. That information should include all of the following:

a. The remaining payment terms of the security

b. Prepayment speeds

c. The financial condition of the issuer(s)

d. Expected defaults

e. The value of any underlying collateral.

An entity shall also consider how other credit enhancements affect the expected performance of the security, including consideration of the current financial condition of the guarantor of a security.

The SEC notes in SAB Topic 5M that the FASB ASC 320-10-35 paragraph 33 does not define the phrase "other than temporary" for available for sale equity securities. The SAB notes that the SEC believes that the FASB chose the term "other than temporary" because it did not intend that the test be "permanent impairment." The SAB continues to note that the value of investments in equity securities classified as available-for-sale may decline for various reasons. The market price may be affected by general market conditions which reflect prospects for the economy as a whole or by specific information pertaining to an industry or an individual company. Such declines require further investigation by management.

Management should consider all available evidence, which could include but not be limited to the length of time and the extent to which the market value has been less than cost, the financial condition and near-term prospects of the issuer (including items like changes in technology and discontinuance of a segment), and the intent and ability to retain the investment for a period of time sufficient to allow for any anticipated recovery in market value. Unless evidence exist to support a realizable value equal to or greater than the carrying value of the investment in equity securities classified as available-for-sale, a write down to fair value accounted for as a realized loss should be recorded in the period it occurs. The written-down value becomes the new cost basis.

ASC 320-10-35, paragraphs 34A through 35A, includes the next information related to debt securities:

> If other-than-temporary impairment has occurred, the other-than-temporary impairment recognized in earnings depends on whether an entity intends to sell the security or more likely than not will be required to sell the security before recovery of its amortized cost basis less any current-period credit loss.

> If an entity intends to sell the security or more likely than not will be required to sell the security as described above, the other-than-temporary impairment shall be recognized in earnings equal to the entire difference between the investments amortized cost basis and its fair value at the balance sheet date

> If an entity does not intend to sell the security and it is not more likely than not that the entity will be required to sell the security before recovery of its amortized cost basis less any current-period credit loss, the other-than-temporary impairment shall be separated into the amount representing credit loss and the amount related to all other factors. The amount related to credit loss is recognized in earnings. The amount related to other factors is recognized in other comprehensive income, net of taxes.

> The previous amortized cost basis less the other-than-temporary impairment recognized in earnings becomes the new amortized cost basis. The new amortized cost basis is not adjusted for subsequent recoveries in fair value.

(e) DISCLOSURES. The applicable disclosure requirements are included at ASC 320-10-50, *Investments—Debt and Equity Securities, Disclosure.*

11.5 EQUITY SECURITIES

(a) INTRODUCTION. Equity securities are often purchased to generate dividend income, to realize gains from their sale to other parties, and/or to achieve control over another enterprise. The FASB Codification Master Glossary defines and equity security as

Any security representing an ownership interest in an entity (for example, common, preferred, or other capital stock) or the right to acquire (for example, warrants, rights, and call options) or dispose of (for example, put options) an ownership interest in an entity at fixed or determinable prices. The term equity security does not include any of the following:

a. Written equity options (because they represent obligations of the writer, not investments)
b. Cash-settled options on equity securities or options on equity-based indexes (because those instruments do not represent ownership interests in an entity)
c. Convertible debt or preferred stock that by its terms either must be redeemed by the issuing entity or is redeemable at the option of the investor.

(b) INITIAL RECOGNITION AND MEASUREMENT. Upon acquisition, equity securities are generally recorded at cost, presumably fair value at acquisition, and classified into one of two categories: (1) available for sale or (2) trading. ASC 320-10-30, *Investments—Debt and Equity Securities, Overall, Initial Measurement,* paragraph 4, provides that the initial value of a marketable equity security that should no longer be accounted for under the equity method would be the previous carrying amount of the investment and states that the earnings or losses that relate to the stock retained should remain as a part of the carrying amount of the investment and that the investment account should not be adjusted retroactively.

(c) ACCOUNTING AFTER ACQUISITION. Gains and losses realized on the sale of equity securities are included in earnings and dividend income is recognized upon declaration. Equity securities are carried at fair value. As with debt securities, the accounting for the resulting unrealized gain or loss depends on the equity security's classification. Changes in the fair value of equity securities classified as trading are reflected in earnings while changes in the fair value of equity securities classified as available for sale are reflected in other comprehensive income, net of deferred taxes.

(d) IMPAIRMENT. ASC 320-10-35, paragraph 34, provides that if it is determined in Step 2 that the impairment is other than temporary, an impairment loss should be recognized in earnings equal to the entire difference between the investment's cost and its fair value at the balance sheet date. The measurement of the impairment should not include partial recoveries after the balance sheet date. The fair value of the investment becomes the new cost basis. Impairment is discussed in Section 11.4(d).

Cost method investments impairment guidance differs from investments that are valued at fair value. ASC 325-20 *Investments Other, Cost Method Investments* provides the guidance for cost method investments. For investments in equity securities that are carried on the cost method, FSP FAS 115-1 and FAS 124-1 refers to Paragraph 6 of Accounting Principles Board ("APB") 18 for determining whether an impairment is other than temporary: Under the cost method, an investor records an investment in the stock of an investee at cost, and recognizes as income dividends received that are distributed from net accumulated earnings of the investee since the date of acquisition by the investor. The net accumulated earnings of an investee subsequent to the date of investment are recognized by the investor only to the extent distributed by the investee as dividends. Dividends received in excess of earnings subsequent to the date of investment are considered a return of investment and are recorded as reductions of cost of the investment. A series of operating losses of an investee or other factors may indicate that a decrease in value of the investment has occurred which is other-than-temporary and shall be recognized.

(e) TRANSFERS BETWEEN CATEGORIES.   The transfer of equity securities between categories is accounted for in the same manner as the transfer of debt securities, discussed in Subsection 11.4(c)(iv). Of course, transfers to or from the held-to-maturity category do not apply.

(f) DISCLOSURES.   The applicable disclosure requirements are included at ASC 320-10-50.

11.6 SOURCES AND SUGGESTED REFERENCES

Bort, R., *Corporate Cash Management Handbook*. Boston: Warren, Gorham & Lamont, 1989.

Financial Accounting Standards Board. Accounting Standards Codification (ASC) 210, *Balance Sheet*. Norwalk, CT: Author. As of 2011.

_____ . ASC 310, *Receivables*. Norwalk, CT: Author.

_____ . ASC 320, *Investments—Debt and Equity Securities*. Norwalk, CT: Author.

_____ . ASC 325, *Investments—Other*. Norwalk, CT: Author.

_____ . ASC 340, *Other Assets and Deferred Costs*. Norwalk, CT: Author.

_____ . ASC 450, *Contingencies*. Norwalk, CT: Author.

_____ . ASC 460, *Guarantees*. Norwalk, CT: Author.

_____ . ASC 470, *Debt*. Norwalk, CT: Author.

_____ . ASC 505, *Equity*. Norwalk, CT: Author.

_____ . ASC 815, *Derivatives and Hedging*. Norwalk, CT: Author.

_____ . ASC 820, *Fair Value Measurement*. Norwalk, CT: Author.

_____ . ASC 825, *Financial Instruments*. Norwalk, CT: Author.

_____ . ASC 835, *Interest*. Norwalk, CT: Author.

_____ . ASC 840, *Leases*. Norwalk, CT: Author.

_____ . ASC 860, *Transfers and Servicing*. Norwalk, CT: Author.

_____ . ASC 948, *Financial Services—Mortgage Banking*. Norwalk, CT: Author.

_____ . ASC 958, *Not-for-Profit Entities*. Norwalk, CT: Author.

_____ . ASC 954, *Healthcare Entities*. Norwalk, CT: Author.

Financial Accounting Standards Board. Accounting Standards Update (ASU) 2010-20, *Receivables (Topic 310), Disclosures About Credit Quality of Financing Receivables and the Allowance for Loan Losses*. Norwalk, CT: Author.

_____ . ASU 2011-0, Receivables (Topic 310), *Deferral of the Effective Date of Disclosure about Troubled Debt Restructurings in Update No. 2100-20*. Norwalk, CT: Author.

_____ . ASU 2011-02, *A Creditor's Determination of Whether a Restructuring Is a Troubled Debt Restructuring*. Norwalk, CT: Author.

_____ . ASU 2011-4, *Amendments to Achieve Common Fair Value Measurement and Disclosure Requirements in U.S. GAAP and IFRS*. Norwalk, CT: Author.

Keiso, D. E., J. D. Weygandt, and T. D. Warfield. *Intermediate Accounting*, 14th ed. Hoboken, NJ: John Wiley & Sons, 2012.

Meigs, W. B., E. J. Larsen, and R. F. Meigs. *Principles of Auditing*, 9th ed. Homewood, IL: Irwin, 1988.

O'Reilly, V. M., P. J. McDonnell, B. N. Winograd, J. S. Gerson, and H. R. Jaenicke. *Montgomery's Auditing*, 12th ed. New York: John Wiley & Sons, 1998.

Securities and Exchange Commission. *"Notice of Adoption of Amendments to Regulation S-X and Related Interpretations and Guidelines Regarding Disclosure of Compensating Balances and Short-Term Borrowing Arrangements,"* Accounting Series Release No. 148. Washington, DC: Author, November 1973.

CHAPTER 12

REVENUES AND RECEIVABLES

Alan S. Glazer, PhD, CPA
Franklin & Marshall College

Cynthia L. Krom, PhD, CPA
Franklin & Marshall College

Henry R. Jaenicke, PhD, CPA
Late of Drexel University

12.1 NATURE AND MEASUREMENT OF REVENUE

(a) DEFINITION AND COMPONENTS OF REVENUE.   Statement of Financial Accounting Concepts (SFAC) No. 6, *Elements of Financial Statements* (pars. 78, 79, and 82), issued in December 1985, defines *revenues* and *gains* in this way:

Revenues are inflows or other enhancements of assets of an entity or settlements of its liabilities (or a combination of both) from delivering or producing goods, rendering services, or other activities that constitute the entity's ongoing major or central operations.

Revenues represent actual or expected cash inflows (or the equivalent) that have occurred or will eventuate as a result of the entity's ongoing major or central operations. The assets increased by revenues may be of various kinds—for example, cash, claims against customers or clients, other goods or services received, or increased value of a product resulting from production. Similarly, the transactions and events from which revenues arise and the revenues themselves are in many forms and are called by various names—for example, output, deliveries, sales, fees, interest, dividends, royalties, and rent—depending on the kinds of operations involved and the way revenues are recognized.

Gains are increases in equity (net assets) from peripheral or incidental transactions of an entity and from all other transactions and other events and circumstances affecting the entity except those that result from revenues or investments by owners.

SFAC No. 6 (pars. 87–89) distinguishes revenues from gains (and expenses from losses) in this way:

> Revenues and gains are similar, and expenses and losses are similar, but some differences are significant in conveying information about an enterprise's performance. Revenues and expenses result from an entity's ongoing major or central operations and activities—that is, from activities such as producing or delivering goods, rendering services, lending, insuring, investing, and financing. In contrast, gains and losses result from incidental or peripheral transactions of an enterprise with other entities and from other events and circumstances affecting it. Some gains and losses may be considered "operating" gains and losses and may be closely related to revenues and expenses. Revenues and expenses are commonly displayed as gross inflows or outflows of net assets, while gains and losses are usually displayed as net inflows or outflows.
>
> The definitions and discussion of revenues, expenses, gains, and losses in this Statement give broad guidance but do not distinguish precisely between revenues and gains or between expenses and losses. Distinctions between revenues and gains and between expenses and losses in a particular entity depend to a significant extent on the nature of the entity, its operations, and its other activities. Items that are revenues for one kind of entity may be gains for another, and items that are expenses for one kind of entity may be losses for another. For example, investments in securities that may be sources of revenues and expenses for insurance or investment companies may be sources of gains and losses in manufacturing or merchandising companies. Technological changes may be sources of gains or losses for most kinds of enterprises but may be characteristic of the operations of high-technology or research-oriented enterprises. Events such as commodity price changes and foreign exchange rate changes that occur while assets are being used or produced or liabilities are owed may directly or indirectly affect the amounts of revenues or expenses for most enterprises, but they are sources of revenues or expenses only for enterprises for which trading in foreign exchange or commodities is a major or central activity.
>
> Since a primary purpose of distinguishing gains and losses from revenues and expenses is to make displays of information about an enterprise's sources of comprehensive income as useful as possible, fine distinctions between revenues and gains and between expenses and losses are principally matters of display or reporting (paragraphs 64, 219–220, and 228).

The Financial Accounting Standards Board (FASB) currently is reconsidering the definition of revenue it provided in SFAC No. 6 in order to clarify whether transactions give rise to revenues or gains (see Section 12.4(d)). This chapter does not distinguish between gains and revenues because the distinction is not important in resolving the major issues of revenue recognition and measurement. The distinction is significant, however, in considering income statement presentation of earnings, particularly whether asset inflows and outflows should be shown gross or net and where gains and losses should be reported.

(b) CLASSIFICATION OF REVENUE.   O'Reilly, Hirsch, Defliese, and Jaenicke note that:

> Most companies have one or more major sources of revenues and several less significant types of miscellaneous revenues, commonly referred to as other income. The term used for a given type of revenue usually depends on whether it is derived from one of the enterprise's principal business activities. For example, sales of transformers by an electrical supply company would be "sales,"

while such transactions would be "other income" to an electric utility. Conversely, interest and dividends from investments would be "other income" to almost all enterprises except investment companies, for which interest and dividends are a primary source of revenues.[1]

(c) MEASUREMENT, EARNING, REALIZATION, AND RECOGNITION OF REVENUE.   There is general agreement on the meaning of the terms *measurement* and *earning* as they apply to revenue. However, there has been disagreement regarding usage of two other terms—realization and recognition—that are significant in establishing the accounting period in which revenue should be reported.

(i) Measurement of Revenue.   Paragraph 83 of SFAC No. 5, *Recognition and Measurement in Financial Statements,* states that revenues "are generally measured by the exchange values of the assets (goods or services) or liabilities involved." That measurement criterion, coupled with the FASB definition of revenues, thus excludes from revenues those items commonly referred to as *revenue adjustments,* such as bad debts, discounts, returns, and allowances. (See the discussion in Section 12.5.) In certain circumstances, the time value of money should be acknowledged, and interest implicit in a revenue transaction should be classified separately.

Revenue can be measured by the prices (i.e., "gross" amounts) of goods or services sold to customers or the differences (i.e., "net" amounts) between those prices and the amounts due to third parties that supply the goods or services. Staff Accounting Bulletin (SAB) No. 101 (Topic 13-A.5, Question 10), *Revenue Recognition,* discusses two major questions to be answered when deciding whether to record revenue at gross or net amounts:

1. Does the entity act as a principal (where its compensation, in substance, is gross profit from the transaction) or as an agent or broker (where its compensation, in substance, is a commission or fee)?
2. Does the entity take title to the goods sold or otherwise bear the risks and rewards of ownership (such as the risk of loss for collection, delivery, or returns)?

The Standards Executive Committee Staff concluded that if the entity functions as a principal and bears the risks and rewards of ownership, revenue should be reported at gross amounts, with separate reporting of cost of sales. If, instead, the entity functions as an agent and does not bear those risks and rewards—for example, Internet companies, travel agents, and retailers that stock little or no inventory, do not take title to goods sold to customers, and use third-party service providers to fill orders and ship products to customers—revenue should be reported at net amounts.

Additional factors to consider are provided in Accounting Standards Codification (ASC) 605-45-45, *Overall Considerations of Reporting Revenue Gross as a Principal versus Net as an Agent.* Although its consensus acknowledges that the decisions often involve judgment, ASC 605-45-45, Sections 3 through 14, provides a list of indicators supporting revenue measurement at gross amounts:

- The entity, rather than the supplier, is primarily responsible for meeting customers' needs and ensuring customer satisfaction (i.e., entity is the "primary obligor").
- The entity has the risk of loss before a customer order is placed or after a customer return (i.e., entity bears "general inventory risk").
- The entity has latitude in setting the selling price.
- The entity adds value, such as by physically changing the product or performing part of the service.
- The entity has discretion in choosing from among the different suppliers for the product or service.

---

[1] V. M. O'Reilly, M. B. Hirsch, P. L. Defliese, and H. R. Jaenicke, *Montgomery's Auditing,* 11th ed. (New York: John Wiley & Sons, 1990), p. 371.

- The entity is involved in determining and communicating product or service specifications to the supplier.
- The entity has the risk of loss after a customer order is placed or during shipping (i.e., entity bears "physical loss inventory risk").
- The entity is responsible for collecting the sales price from the customer and paying the supplier, regardless of whether the customer pays the total price (i.e., entity bears "credit risk").

ASC 605-45-45, Sections 15 through 18, provides three indicators that support recognizing revenue at net amounts:

1. The supplier, rather than the entity, is primarily responsible for meeting the customer's needs and ensuring customer satisfaction (i.e., supplier is the "primary obligor").
2. The entity earns a fixed amount, expressed either in terms of dollars or a percentage of the gross amount billed to the customer, suggesting that the entity is serving as an agent of the supplier.
3. The supplier assumes the credit risk, and the entity has little or no credit risk.

No single indicator determines which method should be used. For example, although an entity's not taking title to products sold to customers generally indicates a lack of "general inventory risk" and, therefore, net revenue reporting, an entity's taking title to products is not sufficient, by itself, to justify gross reporting.

For those entities that record revenue based on the gross amount billed to the customer, shipping and handling fees billed to the customer should also be reported at gross amounts and classified as revenue (ASC 605-45-45-20). The costs of shipping and handling should not be netted against those gross revenues.

Disclosures that may be appropriate for entities reporting revenues at net amounts are addressed in ASC 605-45-50. Voluntary disclosure of gross transaction volume for those revenues reported at net amounts is encouraged. Gross amounts can be reported either parenthetically on the face of the income statement or in the related notes, but they may not be characterized as "revenues" or be included in a column that reports net income or loss, with the exception of disclosure of taxes collected and remitted to governmental authorities. The presentation of such taxes on either a gross or net basis is considered to be an accounting policy decision requiring disclosure (ASC 605-45-50-3).

(ii) Earning of Revenue. There is not clear agreement on the question of what "earning" revenue means. According to paragraph 83b of SFAC No. 5, revenues are not recognized until earned. An entity's revenue-earning activities involve delivering or producing goods, rendering services, or other activities that constitute its ongoing major or central operations. Revenues are considered to have been earned when the entity has substantially accomplished what it must do to be entitled to the benefits represented by the revenues. In complex transactions such as multiple-deliverable revenue arrangements, however, it may not be apparent when revenue has been earned. When there are many activities being performed, it is not immediately clear whether revenue is earned as each action is performed or only upon completion of all the agreed-on deliverables. Understanding when revenue should be recognized may require knowledge of the nature of the specific earning process in certain industries.

(iii) Revenue Realization and Recognition. To "recognize" revenue means to report it in the entity's financial statements or to formally record it in the entity's accounts by crediting a revenue account and simultaneously debiting an asset or a liability. At the time revenue is recognized, closely related expenses (such as cost of goods sold) also are recognized, although the particular accounting system (e.g., a periodic inventory system) may cause the actual bookkeeping entry to be made later in the accounting period. At the point of revenue recognition, the accounting for related assets switches from recording entry values—that is, amounts based on purchase prices (such as the historical cost of an asset)—to recording exit values—that is, amounts based on selling prices (such as the selling price of an asset sold in the ordinary course of business). "In traditional accounting terminology, the accountant is said to 'recognize revenue' when he [or she] switches from one measurement approach to the other."[2]

Some authors have used the term *realization* in a very broad sense to mean that the necessary conditions for recognizing revenue have been met. The 1957 revision of the American Accounting Association (AAA) *Accounting and Reporting Standards for Corporate Financial Statements,* for example, states: "The essential meaning of realization is that a change in an asset or liability has become sufficiently definite and objective to warrant recognition in the accounts."[3] Under this broad view, the point of realization (recognition) is movable, and specific rules must be provided to define when it occurs in different types of revenue transactions and earning processes.

ASC 605-10-25, *Revenue Recognition: Overall,* clarifies the term *realization.* Consistent with paragraph 83a of SFAC No. 5, revenues are *realized* when products, merchandise, or other assets are exchanged for cash or claims to cash. Revenues are *realizable* when any related assets received in such an exchange are readily convertible to known amounts of cash or claims to cash.

Despite the widely held view that realization takes place at a single specific point in time, such as the sale date, and recognition of revenue at all other points in time is a departure from or an exception to the realization principle, some departures or exceptions are necessary. ASC 605-10-25-1 notes that revenue recognition depends on consideration of both whether the revenue is earned and whether it is realized or realizable. The Standard further states that sometimes one of those factors is more important and sometimes the other. (See Section 12.3(c).)

(d) REVENUE RECOGNITION ALTERNATIVES.   Revenue can be recognized at various points in the earning process, depending on the circumstances.

Paragraph 84 of SFAC No. 5 notes that revenue is commonly recognized "at time of sale," although six other points are described:

1. *After production and delivery*—if a sale, cash receipt, or both occur before production and delivery of goods or services.
2. *During production*—if a contract exists for which reliable estimates of revenue, total costs, and progress can be made.
3. *As time passes*—if reliable, contractually based measures established in advance are available for services rendered or rights to use assets are provided continuously over a period of time.
4. *At completion of production*—if a product or service can be sold at a price that can be reliably determined with little effort before delivery.
5. *At the time of exchange for nonmonetary assets*—if the fair value of goods or services sold or of nonmonetary assets received can be reliably measured.
6. *As cash is collected*—if collectibility of assets received from the sale of goods or services is doubtful.

The use of each alternative (or basis) in different circumstances is discussed in the next subsections. The general criteria for recognizing revenue and specific factors to be considered in applying those criteria are considered later in this chapter. (See Section 12.3.)

(i) Delivery.   Recognizing revenue when a product is delivered or service rendered, often referred to as the *sale basis,* is most common and has been most widely supported in the literature.

---

[2] G. J. Staubus, *Making Accounting Decisions* (Houston: Scholars Book Co., , 1977), p. 172.
[3] AAA, Committee on Accounting Concepts and Standards, *Accounting and Reporting Standards for Corporate Financial Statements,* 1957 revision (Sarasota, FL: Author, 1957), p. 3.

Paton and Littleton state:

For the great majority of business enterprises the sale basis of measuring revenue clearly meets the requirements of accounting standards more effectively than any other possible basis. Revenue is the financial expression of the product of business operation and hence should be gauged in terms of the decisive stage or step in the stream of activity. Revenue, moreover, should be evidenced and supported by new and dependable assets, preferably cash or near-cash. These fundamental requirements are well met by adopting the completed sale as the test of the realization of revenue.

For most concerns engaged in making or dealing with tangible goods the sale is the most conclusive, and the most financially significant, of the chain of events making up the business process; the sale is the capstone of activity, the end toward which all efforts are directed . . . .

If product is in the form of service, as in transportation, banking, etc., the act or process of furnishing service may be viewed as the equivalent of sale for the purpose of measuring revenue.[4]

One of the six rules adopted by the membership of the American Institute of Certified Public Accountants (AICPA) in 1934, and reprinted in Accounting Research Bulletin (ARB) No. 43, *Restatement and Revision of Accounting Research Bulletins* (Chapter 1, Section A, par. 1), states: "Profit is deemed to be realized when a sale in the ordinary course of business is effected, unless the circumstances are such that the collection of the sale price is not reasonably assured." The APB reaffirmed that view in 1966 in APB Opinion No. 10, *Omnibus Opinion—1966* (par. 12), stating: "Revenues should ordinarily be accounted for at the time a transaction is completed, with appropriate provision for uncollectible accounts," a viewpoint adopted in ASC 605-10-25-3.

George O. May stated the rationale behind the widespread use of the sale basis as long ago as 1943:

The problem of allocation of income to particular short periods obviously offers great difficulty—indeed, it is the point at which conventional treatment becomes indispensable, and it must be recognized that some conventions are scarcely in harmony with the facts. Manifestly, when a laborious process of manufacture and sale culminates in the delivery of the product at a profit, that profit is not attributable, except conventionally, to the moment when the sale or delivery occurred. The accounting convention which makes such an attribution is justified only by its demonstrated practical utility.

It is instructive to consider how it happens that a rule which is violative of fact produces results that are practically useful and reliable. The explanation is, that in the normal business there are at any one moment transactions at every stage of the production of profit, from beginning to end. If the distribution were exactly uniform, an allocation of income according to the proportion of completion of each unit would produce the same result as the attribution of the entire profit to a single stage.

A number of conclusions immediately suggest themselves: first, that the convention is valid for the greatest variety of purposes where the flow of product is most uniform; second, that it is likely to be more generally valid for a longer than for a shorter period; and, third, that its applicability is seriously open to question for some purposes where the final consummation is irregular in time and in amount. Thus, the rule is almost completely valid in regard to a business which is turning out a standard product in relatively small units at a reasonable stable rate of production. It is less generally valid—or, to put it otherwise, the figure of profit reached is less generally significant—in the case of a company engaged in building large units, such as battleships, or carrying out construction contracts.[5]

---

[4] W. A. Paton and A. C. Littleton, *An Introduction to Corporate Accounting Standards* (Sarasota, FL: AAA, 1940), pp. 53–54.

[5] G. O. May, *Financial Accounting: A Distillation of Experience* (New York: Macmillan, 1943), pp. 30–31.

Objections to Using Delivery.   Using delivery as the point of revenue recognition is not without short-comings. Paton and Paton noted these objections that others have raised to this basis as a measure of revenue:

- Accounts receivable may become uncollectible.
- Collection expenses and other costs may be incurred subsequent to sale.
- Merchandise returns and allowances may be made.
- Accounts receivable are not the equivalent of cash and hence do not represent immediately disposable funds.
- Revenue is earned through the entire process of production. Hence it is unduly conservative to postpone recognition until the time of sale.[6]

The first three objections can be overcome through periodic adjustments for uncollectible accounts, anticipated expenses, and returns and allowances. These are considered later in this chapter. (See Section 12.5.)

The fourth objection reflects confusion between income and cash flows. Under the accrual basis of accounting, revenue is not equated with cash receipts, as is implied by the objection. Moreover, that net income may not be disposable need not invalidate delivery as the point of revenue recognition. The measurement of income (results of operations) and the administration of funds generated by those operations are separate and distinct.

The fifth objection—that is, delivery is unduly conservative because revenue is earned throughout the production process—suggests that there should be no distinction between the earning and the recognition of revenue. Revenue is recognized during the entire earning process, as in the percentage-of-completion method, only when certain conditions, discussed under Construction-Type Contracts, are present. If those conditions are not present, a more conservative approach is appropriate.

(ii) Recognition Before Delivery.   As indicated, in certain situations the recognition of revenue may occur prior to the time of delivery. Revenue may be recognized during production, as in the construction industry, or at completion of production, as in farming.

Construction-Type and Production-Type Contracts.   In the construction industry, as well as in other situations in which contract specifications are provided by the customer or another third party, such as a regulatory agency or financial institution, revenue may be recognized on the completed contract or the percentage-of-completion (including units of delivery) basis. (See the detailed discussion in Chapter 31.) As noted in ASC 605-35-05, *Revenue Recognition: Construction-Type and Production-Type Contracts,* long-term contracts are more likely than short-term contracts to give rise to problems in accounting for revenue, and the point or points at which to recognize revenue as earned and costs as expenses is a major issue in accounting for long-term contractual arrangements.

Recognizing revenue in construction-type contracts on the basis of production often is regarded as a desirable departure from the sale basis if total revenue and cost can be reliably estimated.

Accounting for revenue by the *completed contract method*—that is, when the contract has been fully performed—is appropriate if estimates of revenue, expenses, or progress toward completion are not reliable. This method, which is the equivalent of the point of delivery, is conservative because it eliminates the problems created when a contract is canceled after revenue and profit have been recognized. Also, the amount of profit can be more accurately determined because the need for estimates is greatly reduced. The principal limitation of this basis in connection with long-term contracts is that periodic income statements do not reveal what is happening in the enterprise if revenue is recognized in the period of completion rather than as the work progresses. Despite continuous performance, revenue is recognized only sporadically, when contracts are completed, resulting in recognition of income only at the end of the entire earnings process.

---

[6] W. A. Paton and W. A. Paton Jr., *Corporation Accounts and Statements* (New York: Macmillan, 1955), pp. 278–279.

For long-term contracts, as in the construction of roads, buildings, ships, complex aerospace and electronic equipment, and some software or software systems, the recognition of revenue using the *percentage-of-completion method* generally results in periodic net income that is more nearly related to the earning process. Thus, the entity's financial statements reflect the economic substance of transactions more clearly and more timely, with less distortion of the relationships between gross profit from contracts and the related period costs. The use of that basis is justified, however, only if there is reasonable assurance of the profit margin and its ultimate realization. The term *percentage of completion* ordinarily refers to the relationship between costs incurred and the total estimated cost of the completed project, although a percentage based on time or physical units of production may be used. While the basic presumption is that each contract is an individual profit center, there are occasions when a group of contracts may be so closely related that they may be treated as a single profit center. There may also be times when a single contract should be segmented into two or more profit centers.

The percentage-of-completion method, as developed in the construction industry, has been applied, sometimes improperly, to seemingly analogous situations in other industries. Nevertheless, the method is widely used to recognize revenue from production-type contracts and certain service transactions. Contracts specifically not appropriate for percentage-of-completion treatment include sales of standard items even if produced to buyer specifications, magazine subscriptions, and consumer-oriented service contracts, among others.

Extractive Industries and Agriculture.   Recognizing revenue when production is complete may be acceptable in certain extractive industries and agriculture when interchangeable units of the commodities are immediately salable at quoted market prices and without significant distribution costs. The mining of precious metals and growing of crops such as wheat, cotton, and oats are examples. Revenue is recognized before delivery by valuing inventory of products on hand at net realizable value.[7]

ASC 330-10-35-16, *Inventory: Overall,* sanctions this procedure, as described:

> It is generally recognized that income accrues only at the time of sale, and that gains may not be anticipated by reflecting assets at their current sales prices. However, exceptions for reflecting assets at selling prices are permissible for both of the following:
>
> **a.** Inventories of gold and silver, when there is an effective government-controlled market at a fixed monetary value
> **b.** Inventories representing agricultural, mineral, and other products, with all the following criteria:
>
> > **1.** Units of which are interchangeable
> > **2.** Units of which have an immediate marketability at quoted prices
> > **3.** Units for which appropriate costs may be difficult to obtain
>
> Where such inventories are stated at sales prices, they should of course be reduced by expenditures to be incurred in disposal.

Despite the support for recognition prior to delivery in the authoritative accounting literature, in practice revenue is generally recognized on mineral products at the time of delivery. The authoritative literature is silent on the appropriateness of recognizing revenue on agricultural products still in the growth or production stage, even if they are readily marketable at quoted prices.

Multiple-Element Arrangements.   Many companies, particularly technology firms, offer multiple deliverable arrangements (MDAs) to address their customers' needs. For instance, a cellular telephone company may offer an arrangement that includes equipment, activation, and ongoing service. Because there are multiple revenue-generating activities, questions arise as to how to allocate total revenue among the various products and services and how to allocate revenue to the proper period.

---

[7] D. E. Kieso, J. J. Weygandt, and T. D. Warfield, *Intermediate Accounting,* 14th ed. (Hoboken, NJ: John Wiley & Sons, 2012), p. 1092.

In general, in an arrangement with multiple deliverables, each delivered item is considered to be a separate unit of accounting as long as the delivered item has value on a stand-alone basis, the fair value of the undelivered items may be objectively determined, and the delivery or performance of the undelivered item(s) is considered probable and substantially under the seller's control (ASC 605-25-25-2, *Revenue Recognition: Multiple-Element Arrangements*). After the separate units of accounting are determined and an objective, reliable fair value is established for each unit, revenue should be allocated to the separate accounting units based on their relative fair values. Required disclosures include the description and nature of the arrangements and provisions for performance, cancelation, and the like. It is important to realize that separate contracts with the same entity, if entered into at or near the same time, are presumed to be negotiated as a single arrangement unless there is sufficient evidence to the contrary. Sales transactions with multiple deliverables are discussed further in Subsection 12.4(a)(ix).

Milestone Method.   Contracts for research and development (R&D) transactions often include provisions where all or a substantial portion of the consideration is paid upon achieving a milestone event in the R&D efforts. In such an arrangement, or in other situations in which the seller satisfies its performance obligations over a period of time, one or more payments may be contingent upon achieving an uncertain future milestone. Under ASC 605-28 *Revenue Recognition: Milestone Method,* sellers are permitted, but not required, to recognize milestone revenue in its entirety in the period in which the substantive milestone is achieved. In the event the seller elects to recognize revenue using the milestone method, disclosures of the overall arrangement and the contingent consideration, as well as other information, are required by ASC 605-28-50-2.

Accretion.   Paton and Littleton reject considering accretion (increase in value from natural growth or aging) as revenue:

> Allied to the question of the significance of production in relation to revenue is the problem of increase resulting from growth and other natural processes.... In this situation there is no doubt that assets have increased, and the amount of the physical increase is subject to objective verification. The technical process of production, however, remains to be undertaken, followed by conversion into new liquid assets. Assuming that the final product of the enterprise is lumber, it is clearly incorrect to treat accretion as revenue.[8]

They add, however, that there is no serious objection to disclosing measurable increases from accretion as supplementary information, provided cost is not obscured and the resulting credit is clearly labeled as unrealized income. Because revenue from accretion is not recognized, the costs incurred for the purpose of encouraging accretion should, theoretically at least, be added to inventory and recognized as expenses when revenues are recognized at the time the timber, nursery stock, or other property is delivered.

Hendriksen and van Breda note that, in an economic sense, accretion gives rise to revenue. However, from a practical standpoint, the discounted value required to make the necessary comparative inventory valuations often is difficult to determine "because it depends upon expectations regarding future market prices and expectations regarding future costs of providing for growth and future costs of harvesting and getting the product ready for market."[9] Periodic recognition of accretion as revenue has not been adopted in practice.

Appreciation.   Accounting authorities for many years generally have agreed that appreciation of asset values attributable to market changes does not constitute revenue. Paton and Littleton summarize the proposition in this way:

> Appreciation in its various forms is not income. The case for introducing estimated appreciation (or "declination") into the accounts and reports otherwise than as supplementary data is not strong....

---

[8] Paton and Littleton, *Corporation Accounts and Statements,* p. 52.

[9] E. S. Hendriksen and M. F. van Breda, *Accounting Theory,* 5th ed.(Homewood, IL: Irwin, 1992), p. 365.

Without doubt the movement of prices has an important bearing on the economic significance of existing business assets, but there is little warrant for the view that sheer enhancement of market value, however determined, represents effective income. Appreciation, in general, does not reflect or measure the progress of operating activity; appreciation is not the result of any transaction or any act of conversion; appreciation makes available no additional liquid resources which may be used to meet obligations or make disbursements to investors; appreciation has little or no legal standing as income.[10]

Several authorities have expressed approval, to varying degrees, of certain departures from historical practice and for the adoption of alternative approaches to income recognition. Statement of Financial Accounting Standards (SFAS) No. 33, *Financial Reporting and Changing Prices,* provides a good example. Its requirements, however, were amended by SFAS No. 82, *Financial Reporting and Changing Prices: Elimination of Certain Disclosures,* and No. 89, *Financial Reporting and Changing Prices.* Both of those Statements have been subsumed by ASC 255, *Changing Prices,* which makes the supplementary disclosure of current cost/constant purchasing power information voluntary. Also, some financial assets are measured at fair value, and, in some cases, changes in their fair values are recognized as gains or losses.

Cost Savings versus Revenue.   Savings resulting from efficient operation or fortunate purchases generally are classified as reductions of costs, not as revenue. Edwards and Bell define the term *cost saving* as "an increase in the current cost of assets held."[11] That usage of the term has not been widely accepted and is not adopted in this chapter.

(iii) Recognition After Delivery.   As noted earlier, in certain circumstances, revenue may be recognized after delivery. Methods used include the *deposit method* (which is really a nonrecognition method), the *cost recovery method,* and the *installment method.* Both the cost recovery and installment methods are sometimes referred to as *cash bases of revenue recognition.*

The cash basis of revenue recognition should not be confused with the *cash basis of accounting.* As Paton and Littleton noted almost 60 years ago:

> Placing revenue on a cash basis when such treatment is appropriate, it is hardly necessary to say, does not imply that expense should be measured by expenditure. Revenue is the controlling element; expense is the cost of the amount of revenue acknowledged. If receipts from customers are viewed as revenue the applicable expense is the cost of producing such receipts, not the cash disbursements made during the period.[12]

The cash basis of accounting reports revenues collected, expenses paid, and the excess or deficiency of revenues collected over expenses paid rather than revenues, expenses, and income. Revenues collected are measured by cash receipts from customers; expenses paid are measured by cash disbursements to vendors and suppliers.

It also is important to distinguish between an installment sale and the method used to recognize revenue, expense, and income from that type of sale. In installment sales, the purchaser agrees to pay for the purchase in a series of periodic payments, usually, but not always, preceded by an initial disbursement customarily termed a *down payment.* The vendor may account for installment sales in the same manner as other charge sales (i.e., by recognizing income at the time of delivery), or may recognize income either proportionally as the installments are collected or after all costs have been recovered. The latter methods, known as the *installment method* and *cost recovery method,* respectively, are acceptable if certain conditions are present.

Installment Method and Cost Recovery Method.   As noted in ASC 605-25-3, "Revenue should ordinarily be accounted for at the time a transaction is completed." Because revenues should not be recognized until realized (or realizable) and earned, the installment method of revenue recognition is generally

---

[10] Paton and Littleton, *Corporation Accounts and Statements,* pp. 46, 62.
[11] E. O. Edwards and P. W. Bell, *The Theory and Measurement of Business Income* (Berkelely: University of California Press, 1965), p. 93.
[12] Paton and Littleton, *Corporation Accounts and Statements,* p. 59.

not acceptable. However, ASC 605-25-4 allows for exceptional cases when the seller has no reasonable basis to assume it will collect the sale price.

> When such circumstances exist, and as long as they exist, either the installment method or the cost recovery method of accounting may be used . . . . [T]he installment method apportions collections received between cost recovered and profit . . . . Under the cost recovery method, equal amounts of revenue and expense are recognized as collections are made until all costs have been recovered, postponing any recognition of profit until that time.

Deposit Method. In some circumstances, such as in contracts that do not qualify to be recorded as sales in retail land transactions, the *deposit method* should be used (ASC 360-10-55-17, *Property, Plant, and Equipment: Overall, Implementation Guidance and Instructions*). A liability is recognized when cash is received, and no amounts are recognized as revenue until the period has expired during which the customer may cancel and receive a full refund.

12.2 NATURE AND SIGNIFICANCE OF RECEIVABLES

(a) RECEIVABLES DEFINED. *Receivables* is a broad designation applicable to claims for future receipt of money, goods, and services. *Receivables* include claims against customers and others arising from the sale of goods or provision of services as well as from the advancement of funds and may either be originated by an entity or purchased from another entity (ASC 310-10-05-4, *Receivables: Overall*). This broad designation thus includes deposits for purchases and payments for services to be rendered in the future, such as insurance, advertising, and utilities. This chapter uses the more restrictive, but common, definition of *receivables* as a designation for claims collectible in money. Claims collectible in goods or services are termed *prepayments.*

The general classification of receivables depends on whether they are evidenced by a written statement. Thus, receivables are either:

- *Accounts receivable.* Receivables for which no written statement acknowledging the obligation has been received from the obligor.
- *Notes receivable.* Receivables for which a written statement acknowledging the obligation has been received from the obligor.

In addition, receivables may be due for purchases of goods and services charged on credit cards issued by the entity itself or by a financial institution or other organization. The types of receivables are further classified by the situation in which the receivable arose (origin), whether a security interest was obtained with the receivable, and the time of expected cash receipt.

(b) TYPES OF ACCOUNTS RECEIVABLE. Accounts receivable are first classified by the situation giving rise to the receivable. The most frequent situation is the delivery of goods. In practice, the term *accounts receivable* normally is used to designate the recorded amounts owed by trade customers. Other terms are used to designate accounts receivable arising from revenue recognition in the normal course of business in various industries. Examples of such designations are *revenues receivable* (used by public utilities), *rents receivable* (used by real estate agencies), and *subscriptions receivable* (used by publishers).

(c) TYPES OF NOTES RECEIVABLE. The term *notes,* used broadly, includes two types of instruments: promissory notes and drafts. (Capital leases required to be accounted for as receivables in accordance with ASC 840, *Leases,* are discussed in Chapter 15 of this *Handbook.*) Promissory notes and drafts are defined by Mallor et al. in this way:

- *A promissory note* is a promise made by one person, called the *maker,* to pay to the order of another person, called the *payee* (or to bearer), a certain sum of money on demand or at a definite future time.

- *A draft* is an instrument in which one person, called the *drawer,* orders another person, called the *drawee,* to pay a certain sum of money to another person, called the *payee* (or to bearer), on demand or at a definite future time. The drawer and payee may be the same person.[13]

To be "negotiable" within the meaning of the Uniform Commercial Code (Article 3 Section 104), all such instruments must meet these conditions:

- Be written
- Be signed by the maker or drawer
- Contain an unconditional promise or order to pay a certain fixed sum in money
- Be payable to order or to bearer, or otherwise qualify as a check
- Be payable on demand or at a specific time
- Not include any instructions to take any action other than paying money, except as specified in Article 3

A distinctive feature of the typical commercial draft, as compared with a note, is that the former is initiated by the creditor rather than by the debtor. Bills are "orders" to pay; notes are "promises" to pay. Bills arising in domestic commerce are usually referred to as *commercial drafts;* the term *bills of exchange* is generally restricted to instruments used in foreign commerce.

(d) CREDIT CARD RECEIVABLES.   A retail business that accepts credit card drafts in payment of purchases may accept one of three types: (1) bank credit cards, (2) travel and entertainment credit cards, and (3) company credit cards (also called *in-house* credit cards). Each of these requires separate treatment by the retailer. Issuers of travel and entertainment and bank credit cards treat credit card receivables in the same fashion as a retailer treats company credit card receivables (except, of course, that the receivables are forwarded by a retailer rather than being direct sales).

For the retailer, bank and travel and entertainment credit card drafts are receivables from the issuer of the credit card. Although procedures for individual card issuers vary slightly, they generally require that the credit card drafts be accumulated and deposited with a bank, which acts as the issuer's agent. There usually is a merchant's charge (discount) for the credit card drafts, which may be recorded as cash at the time of depositing the accumulated drafts or when the payment is received from the issuer of the card. Company credit card drafts are receivables under a credit card agreement. These agreements vary, but normally they provide for a minimum payment with interest on the unpaid balance.

12.3 CRITERIA FOR RECOGNIZING REVENUE

(a) GENERAL CRITERIA.   As discussed earlier in this chapter, the general criteria for recognition traditionally have followed the realization principle stated in ASC 605, *Revenue Recognition,* namely, that the revenue has been earned and an exchange has taken place. One of the most difficult tasks the accountant faces is applying those general criteria to specific transactions and events for the purpose of determining the most appropriate time in the earning process to recognize all or part of the revenue. For some transactions and events and for some industries, authoritative or quasi-authoritative literature provides, on an ad hoc basis, more specific criteria—and sometimes conditions—that must be met before revenue is recognized; those instances are described in Sections 12.4(a) and (b). The next sections provide guidance for selecting the appropriate method of revenue recognition in the absence of specific authoritative or quasi-authoritative pronouncements.

---

[13] J. P. Mallor et al., *Business Law and the Regulatory Environment: Concepts and Cases,* 11th ed. (Chicago: Irwin McGraw-Hill, 2001), pp. 654–655.

(b) ATTRIBUTES MEASURED BY ENTRY AND EXIT VALUES.   As noted earlier, recognizing revenue results in a shift from accounting for *entry values* to accounting for *exit values*. In theory, two attributes of assets can be measured using entry values: historical cost and current cost. Similarly, three attributes, according to SFAC No. 5 (par. 67), can be measured using exit values: (1) current market value, (2) net realizable value, and (3) present value of expected cash flows.

In general, the existing accounting model measures assets at historical cost before revenues and related expenses are recognized. When revenue is recognized, the attribute measured becomes (expected) selling price in due course of business (i.e., net realizable value). For example, inventory is usually accounted for at historical cost until it is sold. At that time, the cost of inventory is recognized as an expense, and the inventory disappears from the balance sheet. The inventory is replaced by a new asset, often a receivable, which is accounted for at net realizable value, and an equal amount of revenue is recognized.

Of course, other attributes of elements of financial statements besides historical cost or proceeds and the (expected) selling price in due course of business can be measured. The significant point is that when revenue is recognized, a switch is made from some entry to some exit value. Unless otherwise specified, however, this discussion assumes that the entry value is historical cost or proceeds and the exit value is net realizable value—that is, "the historical cost model."

(c) FINANCIAL ACCOUNTING STANDARDS BOARD CONCEPTUAL FRAMEWORK AND REVENUE RECOGNITION.
SFAC No. 1, *Objectives of Financial Reporting by Business Enterprises* (pars. 34 and 37), states the first two *objectives of financial reporting* by business enterprises:

> Financial reporting should provide information that is useful to present and potential investors and creditors and other users in making rational investment, credit, and similar decisions. The information should be comprehensible to those who have a reasonable understanding of business and economic activities and are willing to study the information with reasonable diligence.

> Financial reporting should provide information to help present and potential investors and creditors and other users in assessing the amounts, timing, and uncertainty of prospective cash receipts from dividends or interest and the proceeds from the sale, redemption, or maturity of securities or loans. The prospects for those cash receipts are affected by an enterprise's ability to generate enough cash to meet its obligations.... Thus, financial reporting should provide information to help investors, creditors, and others assess the amounts, timing, and uncertainty of prospective net cash inflows to the related enterprise.

SFAC No. 5 (par. 6) defines recognition as "the process of formally recording or incorporating an item into the financial statements of an entity as an asset, liability, revenue, expense, or the like." Paragraph 63 specifies "fundamental recognition criteria" for recognizing a financial statement element:

> An item and information about it should meet four fundamental recognition criteria to be recognized and should be recognized when the criteria are met, subject to a cost–benefit constraint and a materiality threshold. Those criteria are:

> Definitions—The item meets the definition of an element of financial statements.
> Measurability—It has a relevant attribute measurable with sufficient reliability.
> Relevance—The information about it is capable of making a difference in user decisions.
> Reliability—The information is representationally faithful, verifiable, and neutral.

> All four criteria are subject to a pervasive cost–benefit constraint: the expected benefits from recognizing a particular item should justify perceived costs of providing and using the information.

> Recognition is also subject to a materiality threshold; an item and information about it need not be recognized in a set of financial statements if the item is not large enough to be material and the aggregate of individually immaterial items is not large enough to be material to those financial statements.

The measurability criterion states that the financial statement element "must have a relevant attribute that can be quantified in monetary units with sufficient reliability. Measurability must be considered together with both relevance and reliability" (par. 65). The qualities of relevance and reliability sometimes conflict with each other and require that trade-offs be made. Generally, the sooner that reliable information about revenue transactions can be conveyed to financial statement users, the more relevant it will be to them. By the same token, the earlier in the earning process revenue is recognized, the greater the likelihood of a divergence between the information and the underlying economic reality. Accordingly, the later in the earning process revenue is recognized, the greater the likelihood that the information presented will be reliable, but the lesser the likelihood that it will be relevant for users' decisions.

Because proper revenue recognition is critical, SFAC No. 5 (pars. 83a and 83b) specifies that two conditions must be satisfied, namely, being realized or realizable and being earned.

- Revenues are *realized* when products, other assets, or services are exchanged for cash or claims to cash, and revenues are *realizable* when assets received or held are readily convertible to known amounts of cash or claims to cash. Assets that are readily convertible have "(i) inter-changeable (fungible) units and (ii) quoted prices available in an active market that can rapidly absorb the quantity held by the entity without significantly affecting the price" (par. 83a).

- Revenues are earned "when the entity has substantially accomplished what it must do to be entitled to the benefits represented by the revenues" (par. 83b).

These provisions form the basis of ASC 605-10-25. The FASB, however, may revise the criteria based on the results of a major project on revenue recognition that it began in mid-2002. (See Section 12.4(c).)

(d) SPECIFIC RECOGNITION CRITERIA. The specific criteria discussed in Exhibit 12.1 have been suggested by various individuals or groups as being significant to the timing of revenue recognition. They address characteristics of the event or transaction that gives rise to the revenue, characteristics of the asset received in the transaction, and characteristics of the revenue recognized (see

---

Characteristics of the Revenue Event or Transaction

1. The economic substance of the transaction that precedes the recognition of revenue should be such that:
   a. Reversal of the transaction is remote—that is, the revenue recognized has permanence.
   b. If ownership of property has changed hands, the risks and rewards of ownership also should be transferred.
2. Either an event that serves as the basis of recognizing revenue should not be within the control of the entity, or it should be verifiable by external evidence.

Characteristics of the Asset Received

The asset recorded in a revenue transaction should be:

1. Liquid
2. Free from significant obligations and restrictions
3. Collectible
4. Reliably measurable

Characteristics of the Revenue Recognized

The revenue should be "earned" to the extent that it has been recognized. If the earning process is not complete or substantially complete, either the critical event in the earning process should have occurred or measurable progress should have been made toward the completion of the earning process before revenue is recognized.

Exhibit 12.1 Specific Criteria for Recognizing Revenue

Exhibit 12.1). Despite some degree of overlap in the criteria, the classification scheme seems useful, particularly in resolving problems that are not addressed by authoritative pronouncements.

(e) CHARACTERISTICS OF THE REVENUE EVENT OR TRANSACTION.   Before revenue is recognized, the event or transaction should be nonreversible and the risks and rewards of ownership should be transferred. Both criteria should be applied to the substance, not merely to the form, of the event or transaction. APB Statement No. 4 *"Basic Concepts and Accounting Principles Underlying Financial Statements of Business Enterprises"* (par. 127) discusses substance over form as one of the basic features of financial accounting:

> **F-12. Substance over form.** Financial accounting emphasizes the economic substance of events even though the legal form may differ from the economic substance and suggest different treatment. Usually the economic substance of events to be accounted for agrees with the legal form. Sometimes, however, substance and form differ. Accountants emphasize the substance of events rather than their form so that the information provided better reflects the economic activities represented.

SAB No. 114 (Topic 1), *Financial Statements,* Section I, suggests that economic substance should take priority over legal form to determine the accounting and reporting of a transaction. Although the literature provides such guidance for determining the economic substance of particular transactions in specific industries, it provides little guidance for applying the substance over form notion in general. That may well be because, as noted in SFAC No. 2, *Qualitative Characteristics of Accounting Information* (par. 160), "[S]ubstance over form is, in any case, a rather vague idea that defies precise definition." (See Jaenicke for further discussion.)[14]

(i) Nonreversibility.   If revenue is recognized on the basis of a particular event or transaction and subsequent events or transactions reverse the effect of the earlier one, the problem is not that revenue has been recognized in the wrong accounting period—it should never have been recognized at all because the definition of revenue or asset (or both) has not been met. Thus, in addition to affecting the timing of revenue recognition, the possibility of reversal of the revenue transaction also affects the determination of whether the revenue exists. Windal states that "for an item to be sufficiently definite [to warrant recognition], it must appear unlikely to be reversed. We might say it must appear to have permanence."[15]

In some cases, as in sales with right of return, the possibility of the transaction being permanent exists, and the likelihood of reversal may be predictable. In those cases, revenue should be recognized and appropriate allowances recorded for the estimated returns. In other cases, as in many product financing arrangements that contain repurchase agreements, the possibility of permanence is zero or extremely remote. If the economic substance of the "sale" rather than its formal designation is judged and the "sale" transaction is found to be fictitious, completion of the transaction and permanence of the revenue are absent and no revenue should be recognized. As another example, the receipt of a small down payment and small periodic payments, with a large final "balloon" payment, often suggests that an option to buy an asset has been sold, not the asset itself; the sale of the asset itself may never take place.

"Bill and hold" sales represent another type of transaction that, depending on the underlying circumstances, could be reversible. According to the Securities and Exchange (SEC) Release No. 17878 (June 22, 1981), in a bill-and-hold transaction, "a customer agrees to purchase the goods but the seller retains physical possession until the customer requests shipment to designated locations." SAB No. 114, Topic 13-A.3.a, *Revenue Recognition,* "Bill and Hold Arrangements" (see Section 12.3(h)), provides examples of criteria that must be met when delivery has not occurred.

---

[14] H. R. Jaenicke, *Survey of Present Practices in Recognizing Revenues, Expenses, Gains, and Losses* (Norwalk, CT: FASB, January 1981).

[15] F. W. Windal, "The Accounting Concept of Realization," *Accounting Review* (April 1961): 252.

(ii) Transfer of the Risks and Rewards of Ownership. The criterion that the risks and rewards of ownership should be transferred before revenue is recognized appears in several places in the accounting literature. For example, ASC 840-10-10, *Leases,* states:

> The objective of the lease classification in this Subtopic derives from the concept that a lease that transfers substantially all of the benefits and risks incident to the ownership of property should be accounted for as the acquisition of an asset and the incurrence of an obligation by the lessee and as a sale or financing by the lessor.

SAB No. 114, Topic 13-A.3.d states that in resolving the issue discussed, "the delivery criterion would generally be satisfied when title and the risks and rewards of ownership transfers." In practice, however, applying the criterion does not always yield a definitive answer because, in many transactions, the risks and rewards are divided between the two parties.[16]

Determining whether the "risks and other incidents of ownership" have been transferred to the buyer requires an examination of the underlying facts and circumstances. Five circumstances may raise questions about whether the risks of ownership have, in substance, been transferred:

1. A continuing involvement by the seller in the transaction or in the assets transferred, such as through the exercise of managerial authority to a degree usually associated with ownership, perhaps in the form of a remarketing agreement or a commitment to operate the property

2. Absence of significant financial investment by the buyer in the asset transferred, as evidenced, for example, by a token down payment or by a concurrent loan to the buyer

3. Repayment of debt that constitutes the principal consideration in the transaction dependent on the generation of sufficient funds from the asset transferred

4. Limitations or restrictions on the buyer's use of the asset transferred or on the profits from it

5. Retention of effective control of the asset by the seller

The first three items on the list are suggested by SAB No. 114; the last two are found in Accounting Series Release (ASR) No. 95, *Accounting for Real Estate Transactions Where Circumstances Indicate That Profits Were Not Earned at the Time the Transactions Were Recorded.*

Some of the circumstances just listed may also be useful in assessing whether other criteria noted in Exhibit 12.1 have been met. For example, a continuing involvement by the seller may affect the criteria that the asset received be free of significant obligations, that the earning process be substantially complete, and that the asset received be measurable.

(iii) Recognition Based on Events. Revenues are sometimes recognized on the basis of events rather than transactions. For example, production that precedes revenue recognized on the percentage-of-completion basis is more properly described as an event than as a transaction because it need not involve a transfer of something of value between two or more entities.

An event occurring within the enterprise that precedes the recognition of revenue, such as production, should be verifiable by evidence external to the enterprise, such as an increase in market price or the existence of a firm contract. If revenue recognition is based on an event external to the enterprise, such as a price increase, the event should not be within the control of the enterprise.

(f) CHARACTERISTICS OF THE ASSET RECEIVED. Reflecting paragraph 83 of SFAC No. 5, *Recognition and Measurement in Financial Statements of Business Enterprises,* ASC 605-10-25 states that, before it can be recognized, revenue must be realized or realizable. This criterion is based on the presumption that, at least to some degree, the asset received is liquid, free from significant obligations or restrictions, collectible, and reliably measurable. ASC 605-10-25 specifically requires that the asset received must be readily convertible to known amounts of cash or claims for cash

---

[16] See Jaenicke, *Survey of Present Practices,* Chapter 2, for further discussion.

in order for the revenue to be considered realizable. Those tests would be relevant in addition to any characteristics of assets included in the FASB's asset definition in SFAC No. 6.

(i) Asset Liquidity.   Asset liquidity has long been suggested as a prerequisite for recognizing revenue. Canning observes that one of the usual conditions for recognizing revenue is that "the future receipt of money within one year has become highly probable."[17] Paton and Littleton note that "revenue is realized, according to the dominant view, when it is evidenced by cash receipts or receivables, or other new liquid assets."[18] The liquidity criterion also is generally interpreted as having been met if the financial flow is in the form of a reduction of liabilities that would obviate the subsequent use of liquid assets.

Contrary to the views just expressed, however, the APB did not consider asset liquidity a significant condition for revenue recognition. ASC 845, *Nonmonetary Transactions,* implements APB Opinion No. 29, *Accounting for Nonmonetary Transactions* (par. 18). ASC 845-10-30-1 states:

> In general, accounting for nonmonetary transactions should be based on the fair values of the assets (or services) involved, which is the same basis as that used in monetary transactions. Thus, the cost of a nonmonetary asset acquired in exchange for another nonmonetary asset is the fair value of the asset surrendered to obtain it, and a gain or loss should be recognized on the exchange.

ASC 845 continues, however, indicating that the recorded amount of the nonmonetary asset(s) relinquished should be used in place of fair value of the exchanged assets if neither the fair value of the asset(s) given up nor the asset(s) received is reasonably determinable (ASC 845-10-30-3). This suggests that illiquidity of a nonmonetary asset may prevent its fair value from being determinable (i.e. measurable) and, consequently, prevent the recognition of gain or loss.

The issue of illiquidity interfering with the fair valuation of a nonmonetary asset is reinforced in ASC 845-10-30-8, which states:

> Fair value should be regarded as not determinable within reasonable limits if major uncertainties exist about the realizability of the value that would be assigned to an asset received in a nonmonetary transaction accounted for at fair value . . . . If neither the fair value of a nonmonetary asset transferred nor the fair value of a nonmonetary asset received in exchange is determinable within reasonable limits, the recorded amount of the nonmonetary asset transferred from the entity may be the only available measure of the transaction.

Horngren contends that the receipt of liquid assets per se should not be a condition for recognizing revenue but should serve as evidence that the measurability criterion has been met.[19]

(ii) Absence of Obligations and Restrictions.   The absence of obligations and restrictions as a criterion is expressed by Vatter in this way: "Revenue differs from other asset-increasing transactions in that the new assets are completely free of equity restrictions other than the residual equity of the fund itself." The obligations and restrictions that Vatter had in mind—repayment obligations, obligations to share income, voting rights, and dividend preferences—characterize debt and equity financing. Under this view, sales and excise taxes collected by an enterprise should be recognized as liabilities, not as revenue, because the amounts collected are earmarked for remittance to a governmental agency.[20]

It is conceivable for a "buyer" to impose conditions on a transferred asset which suggest that the risks and rewards of the asset's ownership are not transferred to the "seller." This would be

---

[17] J. B. Canning, *The Economics of Accounting* (New York: Ronald Press 1929), p. 102.

[18] Paton and Littleton, *Corporation Accounts and Statements,* p. 49.

[19] C. T. Horngren, "How Should We Interpret the Realization Concept?" *Accounting Review* (April 1965): 330.

[20] W. J. Vatter, *The Fund Theory of Accounting and Its Implications for Financial Reports* (Chicago: University of Chicago Press, 1947), p. 25.

analogous to the condition that the seller's risks and rewards of ownership should transfer to the buyer if revenue is to be recognized (See Section 12.1(c)).

(iii) Asset Collectibility. As noted in Section 12.1(d), the earliest authoritative statement of revenue recognition, ARB No. 43 (Chap. 1, par. 1), emphasized the collectibility criterion when the asset received is other than cash: "Profit is deemed to be realized when a sale in the ordinary course of business is effected, unless the circumstances are such that the collection of the sale price is not reasonably assured." As discussed in subsequent authoritative and quasi-authoritative pronouncements about typical revenue recognition issues and specialized industry problems, much of the literature has been concerned with defining and refining the collectibility criterion in specific circumstances, such as for retail land sales. Little discussion of collectibility in general exists in the pronouncements of authoritative bodies; however, the collectibility criterion is rarely questioned.

From the case-by-case approach to collectibility taken by rule-making bodies, these conditions may suggest doubtful collectibility:

- Evidence of financial weakness of the purchaser
- Uncertainty resulting from the form of consideration or method of settlement, for example, nonrecourse notes and purchaser's stock
- Small or no down payment
- Concurrent loans to purchasers, presumably to finance the down payment

This list comes from ASR No. 95. Although that release is titled *Accounting for Real Estate Transactions Where Circumstances Indicate That Profits Were Not Earned at the Time the Transactions Were Recorded,* the circumstances discussed have wider applicability and appear in slightly different versions in AICPA Guides issued in the 1970s and subsequently incorporated into FASB Statements. If the conditions listed are present, an event or transaction also may fail to meet other recognition criteria, particularly the "transfer of risks and rewards of ownership" test.

(iv) Asset Measurability. The asset measurability criterion is suggested by Canning as well as by a committee of the AAA. Canning notes that the measurability criterion has two aspects: that "the amount to be received can be estimated with a high degree of reliability" and that "the expenses incurred or to be incurred in the (income) cycle can be estimated with a high degree of accuracy."[21] The AAA 1964 Concepts and Standards Research Committee on the Realization Concept noted in "The Realization Concept" (pp. 314–315):

> It is difficult to be precise about what is the current prevailing practice, but it appears that presently accepted tests for realization require receipt of a current (or liquid) asset capable of objective measurement in a market transaction for services rendered. . . . The committee would stress measurability, and not liquidity, as the essential attribute required for recognition of realized revenue.

The measurability criterion is related to the verifiability, and hence the objectivity, of evidence supporting the amount of revenue to be recognized. Thus the FASB has stated:

> Verifiability . . . generally means that independent measurers using the same methods obtain essentially the same result. Verifiability is in one sense a measure of the objectivity (freedom from bias) of financial statement measures because the more the measure reflects the characteristics of the object or event measured, the more likely that different measurers will agree.[22]

---

[21] Canning, *Economics of Accounting,* p. 102.
[22] FASB Discussion Memorandum, *An Analysis of Issued Related to the Conceptual Framework for Financial Accounting and Reporting: Elements of Financial Statements and Their Measurement* (Norwalk, CT: FASB, 1976), p. 158.

For revenue to be recognized, the asset received should be measurable with a degree of veri-fiability such that approximately the same amount would be used by all accountants and it would thus be free from measurer bias—that is, it would be objective. As discussed previously, mea-surability is one of the four recognition criteria provided in paragraph 63 of SFAC No. 5 and is defined in terms of a financial statement item having "a relevant attribute measurable with sufficient reliability."

The measurability of the asset received, and thus of the revenue recognized, is enhanced if the asset received is liquid. Measurability also is related to the nonreversibility and collectibility criteria discussed earlier. Those criteria suggest that possible later reductions in recorded revenue should be small; the measurability criterion suggests that any such reductions be capable of reasonable estimation.

Measurability problems may arise when the assets received are a customer's common stock, preferred stock, stock warrants, stock options, or other equity instruments. (Accounting by entities issuing the instruments is addressed in ASC 505-50, *Equity-Based Payments to Non-Employees,* and ASC 718, *Compensation—Stock Compensation,* regarding share-based payment transactions.)

Section 10-30-1 of ASC 845, *Nonmonetary Transactions,* requires revenue in these situations to be measured at the fair value of the assets or services sold or the equity instrument received, whichever is more reliably measurable. This is echoed in ASC 505-50-05-5, which specifies

> for transactions involving the receipt of equity instruments in exchange for providing goods or services . . . the fair value of the equity instruments to be received may be more reliably measurable than the fair value of the goods or services to be given.

According to paragraph 7 of SFAS No. 121, *Accounting for the Impairment of Long-Lived Assets and for Long-Lived Assets to Be Disposed Of,* "[q]uoted market prices in active markets are the best evidence of fair value." ASC 323-10-50, *Investments—Equity Method and Joint Ventures,* ASC 420-10-30-2, *Exit or Disposal Cost Obligations,* ASC 820-10-35, *Fair Value Measurement,* and ASC 940-820-50, *Financial Services—Brokers and Dealers,* are a few of the many Standards that require or encourage the use of a quoted market price as the measurement of fair value. Several methods are available to estimate the value of equity instruments when no public market exists, such as obtaining valuations from independent experts; using valuation models, such as the Black-Scholes model for options and warrants; and using comparable arm's-length transactions with independent third parties.

Some transactions involving the receipt of equity instruments, especially those involving multi-period arrangements or arrangements in which the terms may change after the goods or services are provided, raise more complex issues. ASC 505-50 addresses two revenue-related questions when equity instruments are involved. First, the date at which fair value should be measured (i.e., the measurement date) is the earlier of the dates at which (a) "the parties come to a mutual understanding of the terms of the equity-based compensation arrangement and a commitment for performance by the grantee [i.e., the seller] to earn the equity instruments (a 'performance commitment') is reached" or (b) "the grantee's performance necessary to earn the equity instruments is complete (that is, the vesting date)" (ASC 505-50-30-18).

The second question concerns accounting for transactions in which the terms of the equity instruments may be adjusted after the measurement date based on either market conditions or future performance by the seller. ASC 505-50-30-28 indicates that if, on the measurement date, any of the terms of an equity instrument depend on achieving a market condition—for example, when the number of shares to be issued depends on the market price of the stock at some future point—total revenue should be measured as the sum of the fair value of the equity interest without regard to the market condition and the fair value of the issuer's commitment to change those terms if the market condition is met. In the performance-based conditions—for example, when the life of the options originally granted to the seller will be extended if the total number of hits on a buyer's Web site exceeds a specified number—the potential fair value of the commitment to change the terms if the future performance conditions are met should not be taken into account when initially measuring the fair value of the equity instruments. Instead, a range of aggregate fair values should be calculated based on the different possible performance outcomes, and the issuer should use the lowest aggregate amount within that range, even if the amount is zero (ASC 505-50-30-30).

Agreements involving equity instruments issued as consideration in sales transactions also may include a seller's contingent right to receive an equity instrument after performance is completed. These arrangements are discussed in ASC 505-50.

(g) CHARACTERISTICS OF THE REVENUE RECOGNIZED.   One of the most commonly suggested criteria for recognizing revenue is that it be "earned" before it is recognized. SFAC No. 5 (par. 83) states that "revenues are not recognized until earned." This criterion takes several forms.

The first form requires completion or *substantial completion* of the earning process. As noted earlier, APB Statement No. 4, *Basic Concepts and Accounting Principles Underlying Financial Statements of Business Enterprises,* (par. 150) states: "Revenue is generally recognized when both of the following conditions are met: (1) the earning process is complete or virtually complete and (2) an exchange has taken place." Paragraph 153 notes that the earning requirement

> usually causes no problems because the earning process is usually complete or nearly complete by the time of the required exchange. The requirement that revenue be earned becomes important, however, if money is received or amounts are billed in advance of the delivery of goods or rendering of services.

APB Statement No. 4 then suggests that the substantial completion test is not always followed and that revenue is sometimes recognized, as on long-term construction contracts, on the basis of *recognizable progress* toward completion of the earning process, a second form of the criterion. A third variation of the earning criterion, first suggested by Meyers, is that recognition be related to the *critical event* in the earning process.[23]

Waiting until the earning process is substantially complete may, depending on the nature of the transaction, delay the recognition of revenue more than either the "recognizable progress" or the "critical event" form of the earning criterion, thus minimizing the risk of error from incorrectly identifying the critical event or the extent of progress. Moreover, at the point of "substantial completion," the costs associated with the revenue transaction are known with more certainty than under the other two approaches because those costs have already been incurred.

The critical event, or "milestone," form of the earning criterion permits greater flexibility in the timing of revenue, depending on the nature of the event or transaction. The recognizable progress version emphasizes that revenue is, in fact, not earned at a single point in time. Because these two forms of the earning criterion may result in revenue recognition earlier than would the substantial completion form, their use could provide information that is more relevant to the needs of users than that attainable from the substantial completion form, but at a possible sacrifice of reliability.

Determining either the point of substantial completion or the critical event may be difficult if the seller has continuing obligations after the initial transfer of the asset. Thus the criterion that the principal risks and rewards of ownership be transferred is related to the criterion that the revenue be earned. For example, special warranties by the seller, remarketing agreements, or the seller's commitment to operate the property not only may raise the question of whether the critical event or substantial completion has taken place but also whether the risks and rewards of ownership have been transferred.

When sales of products are involved, the condition that "an exchange has taken place" is met "at the date of sale, usually interpreted to mean the date of delivery to customers" (APB Statement No. 4, par. 151). Date of delivery usually coincides with the transfer of title. The FOB (free on board) terms specify precisely when title passes: FOB destination indicates that title passes at the buyer's location; FOB shipping point indicates that title passes at the seller's location. Revenue should not be recognized when products are shipped if the terms are FOB destination.

---

[23] J. H. Meyers, "The Critical Event and the Recognition of Net Profit," *Accounting Review* (October 1959): 528.

(h) SECURITIES AND EXCHANGE COMMISSION STAFF'S VIEWS ON RECOGNIZING REVENUES.   In its SAB No. 114, Topic 13, *Revenue Recognition,* the SEC Staff summarized certain of its views on applying generally accepted accounting principles (GAAP) to revenue reporting. The Staff issued the Bulletin in part because of revenue reporting issues encountered by registrants that came to the Commission's attention, including issues related to earnings management (see Section 12.1).

Topic 13-A.1 of SAB No. 114, incorporated as ASC 605-10-S99, discusses four criteria, all of which must be met to satisfy the GAAP requirement that revenue has been realized or is realizable and has been earned and therefore should be recognized:

1. There is persuasive evidence that an exchange arrangement exists.
2. The product has been delivered or services have been rendered.
3. The price is fixed or determinable.
4. Collectibility is reasonably assured.

(i) Persuasive Evidence of an Arrangement.   The SEC Staff intends the term *arrangement* here to mean the final understanding between the parties as to the specific nature and terms of the transaction. This criterion may be implied in the APB literature, but it is not made explicit there. The implication is that revenue may not be recognizable even though the product has been delivered or service has been rendered, the price is fixed or determinable, and collectibility is reasonably assured.

The Staff provides three examples (Topic 13-A.2) (incorporated in ASC 605-10-S99) to illustrate how the first criterion can be applied:

1. The seller, whose normal and customary business practice for this class of customer is to have a written sales agreement signed by both parties, delivers the product. The seller has signed the agreement but the buyer has not.

   The Staff concludes that the seller may not recognize revenue on the sale. If the buyer had signed the agreement but its final commitment is subject to subsequent approval or execution of another agreement, the seller may not recognize revenue until the subsequent approval is obtained or the other agreement is complete.

   Other kinds of persuasive evidence of an exchange agreement could exist depending on the business practices and processes of the parties, including various forms of written or electronic evidence, such as binding purchase orders or online authorizations. Care must be taken to ensure that all the terms of the arrangement, including concurrent or subsequently executed side agreements, provide the needed persuasive evidence.

2. A seller delivers products to a customer on a consignment basis. Title to the products pass to the customer as the customer consumes the products in its operations. The Staff concludes that the seller may not recognize revenue on the sale until the products are consumed, because until then the seller retains the risks and rewards of ownership of the products.

   However, the Staff does provide an example when revenue may be recognized even though there is limited retention of the title to the goods.

3. A seller in a country that does not provide for a seller's retention of a security interest in goods following the U.S. Uniform Commercial Code may retain a form of title to those goods delivered to customers until the customer actually makes payment. The Staff concludes that, presuming all other revenue recognition criteria are met, this limited form of retained ownership to enable recovery of goods in the event of nonpayment by the customer does not necessarily preclude revenue recognition at the time of delivery.

The Staff also describes examples of circumstances in which revenue may not be recognized even though title has passed:

1. The buyer has a right to return the product and:[24]
   ○ The buyer does not pay at the time of sale, and that obligation to pay is contractually or implicitly excused until the buyer resells, consumes, or uses the product.

---

[24] See ASC 605-15-25.

○ The buyer's obligation would be changed—for example, the seller would forgive the debt or grant a refund—if the product is stolen, destroyed, or damaged.

○ The seller and the buyer do not have separate economic substance.

○ The seller must subsequently perform significantly in causing the buyer to resell the product.

2. The seller must repurchase the product, a substantially identical product, or processed goods that include the product, at specified prices not subject to change except for those due to changes in finance and holding costs, and the payments by the seller will be adjusted to cover substantially all changes in costs, including interest, the buyer incurs in buying and holding the product.[25] The Staff believes that each of the following examples is an indicator of the latter condition:

○ The seller provides financing to the buyer until the products are resold without interest or at interest significantly below market beyond the seller's customary sales terms.

○ The seller pays interest costs to a third party on behalf of the buyer.

○ The seller customarily refunds or intends to refund part of the sales price equal to interest for the period from when the buyer paid the seller until the buyer resells the product.

3. The transaction neither avoids the prohibition on reporting revenue in ASC 840-10-55-12, *Sales of Equipment with Guaranteed Minimum Resale Amount,* nor qualifies for sales-type lease accounting.

4. The product is delivered for demonstration purposes.[26]

SAB No. 114 Topic 13-A.3.f, Question 1, contains six examples developed by the SEC Staff illustrating when revenue from nonrefundable up-front fees should be deferred. The examples include initiation fees at health clubs, activation fees for cellular phone service, fees for various Web site services, and technology access fees for R&D activities.

(ii) Delivery and Performance. The SEC Staff provides examples (SAB No. 114 Topic 13-A.3, incorporated in ASC 605-10-S99) in which questions arise as to whether delivery and performance have been accomplished:

• A seller has received a purchase order for products but the buyer is not yet ready to take delivery.

• The seller has completed manufacturing the products and has segregated them in its own warehouse or has shipped them to a third party but has retained title, and payment by the buyer depends on delivery to a site specified by the buyer.

The Staff concludes that revenue may not be recognized in either of these cases. It believes that title and the risks and rewards of ownership must pass to the buyer, typically when the product is delivered to the buyer (if the terms of sale are FOB destination) or shipped to the buyer (if the terms of sale are FOB shipping point).

Examples of criteria that must be met for revenue to be recognizable when delivery has not occurred are listed next (although meeting all the criteria does not necessarily guarantee that revenue will be recognized):

• The risks of ownership must have passed to the buyer.

• The buyer must have made a fixed commitment to buy, preferably in writing.

• The buyer must have requested, preferably in writing, that the transaction be on a bill-and-hold basis and must have a substantial business reason for doing so.

• The schedule for delivery must be fixed, reasonable, and consistent with the buyer's business purpose.

---

[25] See ASC 470-40-15
[26] See AICPA Statement of Position 97-2. *Software Revenue Reconition. October, 1997.*

- The seller must not have retained any duty to perform, making the earning process incomplete.
- The products must have been segregated and not available for shipment to other buyers.
- The product must be complete and ready for shipment.

The next circumstances also should be considered before revenue is recognized under bill-and-hold arrangements:

- The date by which payment is expected and whether the seller has modified its normal billing and credit terms
- The seller's experiences with such transactions
- Whether the buyer has the risk of loss in case the market value of the products declines
- Whether the seller's risks as custodian have been insured
- Whether extended procedures are needed to make sure that the buyer's business reasons for the bill-and-hold have not introduced a contingency to the buyer's commitment

Delivery to an intermediate site should not result in revenue reporting if a substantial part of the price is payable only on delivery to a specified final site.

In addition to delivery, revenue recognition requires that the products or services have been accepted by the buyer. If the contract contains provisions concerning acceptance by the buyer, such as the right to test the product after receipt, buyer acceptance must occur or the provisions must have lapsed before revenue can be recognized.

The seller's duties under the contract must be substantially complete for delivery or performance to have occurred. Inconsequential or perfunctory actions, however, may remain incomplete if they would not result in a refund or rejection of the products delivered or services performed to date. The costs of all such actions should be accrued.

The delivery or performance of one of multiple deliverables is considered not to have occurred if undelivered deliverables are essential to the functioning of the delivered element. (See Subsection 12.4(a)(ix).)

Revenue recognition should begin in a licensing or similar arrangement when its term begins. During the term, revenue should be recognized based on the substance of the arrangement.

The Staff provides three examples (SAB No. 114 Topic 13-A.3) illustrating how these guidelines should be applied:

1. A company sells goods on layaway, setting the goods aside and collecting a cash deposit. Although a time period to finalize the sale may be set, the buyer need not enter a fixed payment commitment. The buyer receives the goods only on payment of the balance. If the buyer does not pay the balance, the deposit is forfeited. If the goods are lost, damaged, or destroyed, the deposit is refundable or substitute goods are provided.

   The Staff concludes that revenue may be recognized no earlier than when the goods are delivered to the buyer. Until then, the seller has a liability for the deposit.

2. A provider of goods or services may receive a nonrefundable fee at the inception of an arrangement, such as a lifetime membership in a health club or an activation fee for telecommunications services. The buyer may agree to pay the fee to obtain a continuing right to purchase the goods or services, at or below the usual prices. Goods or services may or may not be provided at the inception of the arrangement, and, if so, they may or may not be useful to the buyer without provision of further goods or services.

   The Staff concludes that revenue should be recognized only to the extent that the nonrefundable fee is for products delivered or services performed that represent the culmination of a separate earnings process, but that the rest of the fee should be deferred. Revenue should be recognized systematically as those fees are earned. Activities of the seller such as selling memberships, signing contracts, enrolling buyers, or activating telecommunications services do not constitute culmination of a separate earnings process. The earnings process is completed by performing under the terms of the arrangement.

3. A seller provides a buyer with activity tracking or similar services, such as tracking property tax payment activity or sending delinquency letters on overdue accounts, for a 10-year period. (The arrangement is not covered by ASC 310-20, *Nonrefundable Fees and Other Costs.*) The buyer is required to prepay for all the services to be provided during the period. The seller provides setup procedures at the outset and ongoing services in accordance with the arrangement. None of the fees is refundable if the buyer terminates the arrangement or does not use all the services to which it is entitled. The seller must refund a portion of the fee if the seller terminates the arrangement early.

The Staff concludes that the seller should report revenue on a straight-line basis over the term of the contract or the expected period of service, whichever is longer, unless there is evidence that revenue is earned in a different pattern, in which case revenue should be reported in the different pattern. Revenue should not be recognized as costs are incurred because the setup costs bear no direct relationship to the performance of the contracted services. Also, not all revenue should be reported at the outset with accrual of the remaining costs because the services have not been performed.

(iii) Fixed or Determinable Sales Price. Cancelation or termination clauses, side agreements, and significant transactions with unusual terms and conditions may suggest the existence of a demonstration period, an incomplete transaction, or that the price is otherwise not fixed or determinable. For example, the sales price is not fixed or determinable if the buyer has a cancelation privilege; it becomes determinable ratably if a cancelation privilege expires ratably. Customary short-term rights of return are not cancelation privileges and should be treated in conformity with ASC 605-15-25, *Revenue Recognition—Sales of Product When Right of Return Exists.* (See Subsection 12.4(a)(iv).)

The SEC Staff provides examples to illustrate when to recognize revenue in situations where the existence of a fixed or determinable sales price is questionable (SAB 114 Topic 13-A.4; ASC 605-10-S99):

1. A seller charges a membership fee at the beginning of a contract term for the buyer to have the privilege to buy goods from the seller at discount prices during the membership period. The buyer may cancel the arrangement at any time during the term and receive a full refund of the fee.

The Staff believes that revenue should not be recognized for the fee at the beginning of the term with estimated costs accrued because the seller has an unfulfilled duty to perform services; the earnings process is not complete. Further, the ability of the buyer to obtain a full refund of the fee during the membership period makes the sales price involved in the fee not fixed or determinable during the membership period. The fee should be reported as a liability, which is extinguished only on refund of the fee or expiration of the refund privilege. This conclusion holds regardless of whether there is a large population of transactions that grant buyers the same cancelation privileges and reasonable estimates can be made of the number of buyers who will cancel; service arrangements are specifically excluded from the scope of ASC 605-15.

Nevertheless, existing practice had developed contrary to those conclusions, and the Staff believes it should not require practice to be changed without formal rule making or standard setting. The Staff will therefore not object to recognizing refundable membership fees as revenue, net of estimated refunds, over the membership period, if all of these criteria have been met:

○ The estimated refunds are for a large pool of homogeneous items.

○ Timely reliable estimates of expected refunds can be made. Such estimates cannot be made if:

  ▪ There are recurring, significant differences between experience and estimated cancelation or termination rates, even if the effect of the differences is not material to the consolidated financial statements.

- There are recurring variances between experience and estimated amounts of refunds that are material to revenue or net income in quarterly or annual financial statements.
- The likelihood of required material adjustments to previously reported revenue is not "remote."
- Buyers' termination or cancelation and refund privileges exceed one year.

○ Sufficient company-specific historical experience predictive of future events exists on which to estimate the refunds.

○ The amount of the fee is fixed other than the right to obtain a refund.

If any of those conditions are not met, revenue should not be recognized until the cancelation privileges and refund rights expire. If all of the conditions are met and revenue is recognized over the membership period:

○ The amount of the fees representing estimated refunds should be credited to a refund liability account and the rest to a nonmonetary liability account for unearned revenue.

○ At each reporting date, a footnote schedule should be provided of the beginning and ending balances of refund obligations and unearned revenue, cash received for fees, revenue recognized, refunds paid, and adjustments explained.

○ Adjustments, if any, should be based on a retrospective approach, remeasuring the refund liability and the unearned revenue at each reporting date with the offset to revenue (consistent with ASC 310-20-35-26).

The costs of vouchers issued with new memberships for discounts or other benefits should be charged to expense when issued. Other advertising costs relating to new membership offers should be reported in conformity with ASC 720-35, *Other Expenses: Advertising Costs.* If revenue is deferred until the cancelation or termination privileges expire, incremental direct costs of enrolling customers, such as agents' commissions, should be (a) charged to expense when incurred if the costs are not refundable to the reporting entity when fees are refunded, or (b) reported as an asset until the earlier of termination, cancelation, or refund, if the costs are refundable to the reporting entity when fees are refunded. If revenue, net of estimated refunds, is recognized over the membership period, a like percentage of incremental direct costs should be included in earnings in the same pattern that revenue is recognized. The remainder of the incremental costs should be charged to expense when incurred if the costs are not refundable to the reporting entity when the fees are refundable. If those costs are refundable to the reporting entity when the fees are refundable, they should be reported as an asset (until the refund occurs). All costs other than incremental direct costs should be reported as expense as incurred.

2. A lessor leases retail space under an operating lease for one year for $1.2 million, payable in equal monthly installments on the first day of each month plus contingent rentals of 1 percent of the lessee's net sales in excess of $25 million during the year.

   The Staff believes that the contingent rentals should be recognized as revenue beginning with the date the lessee's sales first exceed $25 million and continuing in subsequent periods as it becomes accruable. This position is consistent with ASC 840-10-55-11, which notes that lease payments that depend on a factor that is not measurable at the inception of the lease are contingent rentals and should be included in income as they accrue.

3. The Staff believes that the next examples of the "other factors" referred to in ASC 605-15-25 that may preclude making a reasonable estimate of product returns:

   ○ "Channel stuffing"—significant increases in or excess levels of inventory in a distribution channel

   ○ The inability to determine or observe the levels of inventory in a distribution channel and the current level of sales to end users

- ○ Expected introductions of new products that may cause technological obsolescence or larger-than-expected returns of current products
- ○ A particular distributor's significance to the reporting entity's or to its segment's business, sales, and marketing
- ○ The newness of the product
- ○ Introduction of competitor's products with superior technology and the like[27]

(iv) Sales of Leased or Licensed Departments. Retailers customarily recognized revenue for sales made by departments leased or licensed to others. Because of developments since the SEC issued SAB No. 1, which did not object to that treatment because of existing industry practices, the Staff now concludes (SAB No. 114, Topic 8-A, included at ASC 605-15-S99-2) that such sales should no longer be included in the retailer's revenue. Retailers may disclose the amounts of such sales in notes to their financial statements. Rents and fees under such arrangements should be recognized when earned.

(v) Staff Accounting Bulletin No. 114. The SEC issued SAB No. 114 in March 2011, to update the guidance contained in all preceding SABs. SAB No. 114 revises or rescinds portions of the SAB guidance to make such guidance consistent with FASB's Accounting Standards Codification. SAB No. 114 is fully incorporated as ASC 605-10-S99. In SAB No. 114 Topic 13.A.1, the Staff applies ASC 605-25, *Revenue Recognition: Multiple-Element Arrangements,*" to various types of revenue transactions. For example, if the deliverables in a contractual arrangement meet the separability criteria in the ASC 605-25, vendors should determine an appropriate revenue recognition policy for each deliverable and should apply that policy when accounting for each separable unit they have identified. If the deliverables in a contractual arrangement do not meet the separability criteria, an appropriate revenue recognition policy should be applied to the entire arrangement.

SAB No. 114 also clarified the accounting for contractual arrangements that do not meet the separability criteria but for which vendors have remaining obligations, including those that are inconsequential or perfunctory as well as those that are essential to the functioning of the delivered portion of the arrangement. Although judgment must be applied in determining how consequential the remaining obligations are and the functionality of the delivered portion, the next guidance applies:

- Revenue should be recognized at the time of delivery and the cost of providing the remaining goods or services should be accrued if (1) other criteria for revenue recognition are met, (2) the undelivered element is inconsequential or perfunctory, and (3) the undelivered element is not essential for the delivered portion of the arrangement to function.

- Revenue should not be recognized at the time of delivery if (1) the undelivered element is essential to the functioning of the delivered portion of the arrangement or (2) failure to complete the undelivered portion of the arrangement would result in customers receiving refunds or rejecting the goods previously delivered or services previously performed.

Subsection 12.4(a)(ix) discusses ASC 605-25 in more detail.

(vi) Revenue Recognition Criteria Used Outside the United States. Rule-making bodies outside the United States also have developed criteria for revenue recognition. For example, paragraphs 14–19 of International Accounting Standard (IAS) No. 18, *Revenue Recognition,* issued in 1982 and modified in 1993, discuss five criteria for recognizing revenue from sales of products:

1. The seller has transferred to the buyer the significant risks and rewards of ownership.
2. The seller retains neither continuing managerial involvement to the degree usually associated with ownership nor effective control over the goods sold.
3. The amount of revenue can be measured reliably.

---

[27] SAB No. 114 as presented in ASC 605-10-S99, Topic 13.A.4.b, Question 1.

4. It is probable that the economic benefits associated with the transaction will flow to the seller.

5. The costs incurred or to be incurred related to the transaction can be measured reliably.

For service transactions, IAS 18 (par. 20) specifies the last three of these criteria plus one additional criterion—the stage of completion at the balance sheet date can be measured reliably—that must be met in order for revenue to be recognized using a percentage-of-completion method. If those criteria are not met, a cost-recovery approach should be used. Other recognition criteria are provided for interest, royalty, and dividend revenues.

The broad recognition criteria and limited number of examples contained in IAS 18 have not, in many people's minds, provided sufficient guidance to cover the range and complexity of revenue transactions. In addition, GAAP and industry practices in many countries are not always consistent with that guidance. As a result, the International Accounting Standards Board (IASB) began a project in 2002 to replace IAS 18 and, if necessary, to revise its *Framework for the Preparation and Presentation of Financial Statements.* That project, being conducted jointly with the FASB to help ensure the guidance issued by both boards converge, is described in Section 12.4(d).

Because of increasing inconsistencies in practice, the United Kingdom's Accounting Standards Board (ASB) began a project to develop additional guidance on accounting for revenue recognition by U.K. companies. Based on a Discussion Paper, *Revenue Recognition,* published in July 2001, the ASB issued Application Note G to its Financial Reporting Standard No. 5, *Reporting the Substance of Transactions.* That Note indicates that turnover (i.e., revenue) should be recognized only after companies have performed under contractual arrangements with customers. Specific guidance also is provided on recognizing revenue for various types of transactions, including long-term contracts, bill-and-hold arrangements, and sales with rights of return. Other issues addressed in the Note include reporting revenue at gross or net amounts and measuring revenue from sales with deferred payment terms and when significant risks exist about customers' ability to pay. The Application Note was issued as interim guidance because the ASB supports the joint FASB/IASB revenue recognition project. (See Section 12.4(d).) The FASB and IASB issued a revised Exposure Draft, *Revenue from Contracts with Customers,* on November 14, 2011 and noted that the effective date of the Standard would be no earlier than for annual periods beginning on or after February 15, 2015. The ASB intends to issue a new Standard for U.K. companies after the IASB completes that project.

12.4 TYPES OF REVENUE TRANSACTIONS

(a) SPECIAL REVENUE RECOGNITION PROBLEMS.   Special revenue recognition problems are posed by events and transactions in which the source of revenue is something other than the sale of a product or the rendering of service in a transaction that is completed over a relatively short period. In some cases, authoritative or quasi-authoritative pronouncements have addressed the issue of the proper timing of revenue recognition. In other cases, such pronouncements do not exist, and the proper recognition policies can be determined only by reference to the criteria suggested earlier in this chapter. Specialized industry practices are discussed in Section 12.4(b).

(i) Revenue Recognition Problems Discussed in Other Chapters.   To avoid duplication, the special revenue recognition problems that are discussed elsewhere in this *Handbook* are listed next, with the relevant chapter numbers.

- *Contributions.* ASC 958-605, *Not-for-Profit Entities Revenue Recognition,* applies to all entities that receive or make contributions. The Standard is discussed in *Handbook* Chapter 28.
- *Installment sales.* Revenue from installment sales contracts extending over more than one accounting period may be recognized at the time of sale, on the installment basis, or on the cost recovery basis, depending on circumstances.
- *Nonmonetary exchanges of fixed assets.* ASC 845, *Nonmonetary Transactions,* specifies the conditions under which gains and losses should be recognized on the exchange of nonmonetary assets; the required accounting varies according to whether the exchange

has commercial substance. Nonmonetary barter transactions are discussed in Subsections 12.4(a)(vii) and (b)(vii).

- *Sale and leaseback transactions.* Recognition or deferral of gains by the seller-lessee in a sale and leaseback transaction is specified ASC 840-40, *Leases: Sale-Leaseback Transactions.* This issue is further discussed in *Handbook* Chapter 15. Accounting for leases by a lessor is prescribed by ASC 840. Leases that are classified in ASC 840-30-25, *Leases: Capital Leases,* as sales-type leases result in recognition of revenue by the lessor at the inception of the lease. Sales-type leases involving real estate are further addressed in ASC 360-20, *Property, Plant, and Equipment: Real Estate Sales.* Chapter 15 also discusses sales-type leases; ASC 840-10-55-12 through 55-25, *Leases: Sales of Equipment with Guaranteed Minimum Resale Amount;* and ASC 605-15-25-5, *Products Sold and Subsequently Repurchased Subject to an Operating Lease.*

(ii) Transfers of Receivables. ASC 860-20, *Transfers and Servicing: Sales of Financial Assets,* provides accounting and reporting standards for distinguishing transfers of financial assets that are sales (in which the entity derecognizes the assets transferred) from transfers that are secured borrowings (in which the entity continues to recognize the assets transferred and recognizes the liabilities it has incurred).

ASC 860 is based on a "financial components" approach that focuses on control. Under that approach, a transferor accounts for a transfer of financial assets as a sale if the transferor surrenders control over the assets to the transferee, to the extent that the transferor receives consideration other than beneficial interests (i.e., rights to receive all or part of the underlying cash flows) in the transferred assets. ASC 860-10-40-5, *Transfers and Servicing: Overall,* states that the transferor is deemed to have surrendered control over the transferred assets if and only if all of these three conditions are met:

1. The transferred assets have been isolated from the transferor—put presumptively beyond the reach of the transferor and its creditors, even in bankruptcy or other receivership.

2. Each transferee (or, if the transferee is a qualifying special-purpose entity whose sole purpose is to engage in securitization or asset-backed financing activities, each third-party holder of its beneficial interests) has the right to pledge or exchange the assets (or beneficial interests) it received, and no condition both constrains the transferee (or holder) from taking advantage of its right to pledge or exchange and provides more than a trivial benefit to the transferor (par. 860-10-40-15 through 40-21).

3. The transferor does not maintain effective control over the transferred assets through: (a) an agreement that both entitles and obligates the transferor to repurchase or redeem them before their maturity (par. 860-10-40-23 through 40-27); (b) the ability to unilaterally cause the holder to return specific assets, other than through a cleanup call (par. 860-10-40-28 through 40-39); or (c) the agreement permits the transferee to require the transferor to repurchase the assets at a price that makes it probable that the transferee will exercise that requirement (par. 860-10-55-42D).

(iii) Product Financing Arrangements. ASC 470-40, *Debt: Product Financing Arrangements,* establishes accounting and reporting standards for transactions in which an enterprise sells and agrees to repurchase inventory, with the repurchase price equal to the original sale price plus carrying and financing costs or other similar terms. ASC 470-40-25-1 requires that a product financing arrangement be accounted for as a borrowing rather than as a sale.

Under ASC 470-40-25-2, product financing arrangements include agreements in which an enterprise seeking to finance a product (referred to as a *sponsor*):

1. Sells the product to another entity (the enterprise through which the financing flows), and in a related transaction agrees to repurchase the product (or a substantially identical product); *or*

2. Arranges for another entity to purchase the product on the sponsor's behalf and, in a related transaction, agrees to purchase the product from the other entity.

Other characteristics that are found in many, but not all, product financing arrangements are specified in ASC 470-40-05-4:

1. The entity that purchases the product from the sponsor or purchases it directly from a third party on behalf of the sponsor was established expressly for that purpose or is an existing trust, nonbusiness organization, or credit grantor.
2. The product covered by the financing arrangement is to be used or sold by the sponsor, although a portion may be sold by the other entity directly to third parties.
3. The product covered by the financing arrangement is stored on the sponsor's premises.
4. The debt of the entity that purchases the product being financed is guaranteed by the sponsor.

According to ASC 470-40-25-2, product financing arrangements that require the sponsor to repurchase the product or a substantially identical product at specified prices, adjusted to cover all costs incurred by the other entity in purchasing and holding the product, should be accounted for by the sponsor in this way:

1. If a sponsor sells a product to another entity and, in a related transaction, agrees to repurchase the product (or a substantially identical product) or processed goods of which the product is a component, the sponsor must record a liability at the time the proceeds are received from the other entity to the extent that the product is covered by the financing arrangement. The sponsor must not record the transaction as a sale and must not remove the covered product from its balance sheet.
2. If the sponsor is party to an arrangement whereby another entity purchases a product on the sponsor's behalf and, in a related transaction, the sponsor agrees to purchase the product or processed goods of which the product is a component from the entity, the sponsor must record the asset and the related liability when the product is purchased by the other entity.

(iv) Revenue Recognition When Right of Return Exists. ASC 605-15-25-1, *Revenue Recognition: Sales of Product When Right of Return Exists,* establishes accounting and reporting standards for sales of an enterprise's product in which the buyer has a right to return the product. Revenue from those sales transactions should be recognized at the time of sale only if all of these six conditions are met:

1. The seller's price to the buyer is substantially fixed or determinable at the date of sale.
2. The buyer has paid the seller, or the buyer is obligated to pay the seller and the obligation is not contingent on resale of the product.
3. The buyer's obligation to the seller would not be changed in the event of theft or physical destruction or damage of the product.
4. The buyer acquiring the product for resale has economic substance apart from that provided by the seller.
5. The seller does not have significant obligations for future performance to directly bring about resale of the product by the buyer.
6. The amount of future returns can be reasonably estimated (par. 8).

ASC 605-15-25-2 states that if revenue is recognized because the listed conditions are met, provision should be made immediately for any costs or losses that may be expected in connection with any returns. In accordance with ASC 450-20, *Contingencies: Loss Contingencies,* amounts of sales revenue and cost of sales reported in the income statement should exclude the portion for which returns are expected. Transactions for which revenue recognition is postponed should be recognized as revenue when the return privilege has substantially expired.

The ability to reasonably predict the amount of future returns depends on many factors. Although circumstances vary from one case to the next, the existence of the next four factors would appear to impair the ability to make a reasonable prediction, as presented in ASC 605-15-25:

1. The susceptibility of the product to significant external factors, such as technological obsolescence or changes in demand.
2. Relatively long periods in which a particular product may be returned.
3. Absence of historical experience with similar types of sales of similar products, or inability to apply such experience because of changing circumstances (e.g., changes in the selling enterprise's marketing policies or relationships with its customers).
4. Absence of a large volume of relatively homogeneous transactions.

(v) Service Transactions. As of this writing, the FASB has not issued a comprehensive statement on accounting for service transactions, although ASC 605-20, *Revenue Recognition: Services,* and ASC 605-25, *Revenue Recognition: Multiple-Element Arrangements,* are clearly relevant to the accounting for service transactions. That may change as the FASB continues to work on its revenue recognition project. (See Section 12.4(d).)

The guidance in ASC 605-20 applies to listed service activities and arrangements including these five:

1. Separately priced extended warranty and product maintenance contracts
2. Commissions from certain insurance arrangements
3. The income from fees for guaranteeing a loan subsequent to the initial recognition of the liability.
4. Services for in-transit freight at the end of a reporting period
5. Advertising barter transactions, in which entities exchange rights to place advertisements with each other

Each of those five service arrangements is unrelated, and the accounting for each is specific to that particular service arrangement. ASC 605-20 covers each of the five under separate headings. Additional information on accounting for warranties may be found in Section 12.5(f); for fees for loan guarantees, in Section 12.6(h); for freight, in Section 12.6(g); and for barter transactions, in Subsection 12.4(a)(vii).

Specifically excluded from the guidance in ASC 605-20 are:

1. Guarantees accounted for as derivatives (covered by ASC 815, *Derivatives and Hedging*)
2. Product warranties other than separately priced extended warranty and product maintenance contracts (see ASC 460-10-25-5 through 25-7, *Guarantees: Recognition—Product Warranties*)
3. Guarantees required to be accounted for as financial guarantee insurance contracts in accordance with ASC 944, *Financial Services: Insurance.*

If a seller offers both a product and a service in a single transaction, or offers multiple services in a single transaction, or any other arrangement in which the seller performs multiple revenue-generating activities, the accounting should be in accordance with ASC 605-25, *Multiple-Element Arrangements.* ASC 605-25 generally requires that the arrangement should be divided into separate units of accounting, that the consideration for the arrangement is allocated among the separate units of accounting based on their relative fair values, and that appropriate revenue recognition criteria are considered separately for each of the separate units of accounting.

A multiple-element arrangement may be within the scope of another Codification Topic, such as *Leases* (ASC 840), *Franchises* (ASC 952), and *Software* (ASC 985), among others. ASC 605-25-15-3A, *Revenue Recognition: Multiple-Element Arrangements—Interaction with Other Codification Topics,* provides guidance for deciding whether ASC 605-25 or another Topic should be primary in determining the appropriate recognition of revenue for each element. (See also Subsection 12.4(a)(ix).)

Various standard setters have used the general criteria for revenue and expense recognition of service transactions to develop specific guidance for a wide variety of service-related industries, including:

- Airlines (AICPA Industry Audit Guide, *Airlines,* Chap. 3)
- Banking (see *Handbook* Chapter 30)
- Broadcasting (see Subsection 12.4(b)(v))
- Brokers and dealers in securities (AICPA Accounting and Audit Guide, *Brokers and Dealers in Securities,* Chap. 7)
- Cable television (see Subsection 12.4(b)(ii))
- Casinos (AICPA Accounting and Audit Guide, *Gaming,* Chap. 2)
- Computer software (see Subsection 12.4(b)(vi))
- Contractors (AICPA Accounting and Audit Guides, *Construction Contractors,* Chap. 2, and *Government Auditing Standards and Circular A-133 Audits,* Chap. 3)
- Franchising (see Subsection 12.4(b)(iii))
- Freight service (ASC 605-20-25-13, *Revenue Recognition: Services for Freight-in-Transit at the End of a Reporting Period*)
- Internet (see Subsection 12.4(b)(vii))
- Leasing (see Chapter 15 in this *Handbook*)
- Motion picture films (see Subsection 12.4(b)(v))
- Not-for-profit organizations (see Chapter 28 in this *Handbook*)
- Record and music (see Subsection 12.4(b)(iv))
- Regulated entities (ASC 980, *Regulated Operations*)

SAB No. 114 Topic 13 and the related FAQs address several issues related to revenue from services, including:

- *Receipt of nonrefundable up-front fees.* To be recognized as revenue over the expected period of performance (SAB No. 114, Topic 13-A.3.f, Question 1, incorporated in ASC 605-10-S99).
- *Receipt of refundable fees for services.* To be recognized ratably if the refund privileges expire ratably over the term of the contract; to be recognized either at expiration or ratably if they expire at the end of the term (SAB No. 114, Topic 13-A.4.a, Question 1, incorporated at ASC 605-10-S99). Revenue should be recognized ratably in the latter situation only if all of these four criteria are met: (1) "the estimates of termination or cancellations and refunded revenues are being made for a large pool of homogenous items"; (2) "reliable estimates of the expected refunds can be made on a timely basis"; (3) "there is a sufficient company-specific historical basis upon which to estimate the refunds, and the company believes that such historical experience is predictive of future events"; and (4) "the amount of the membership fee specified in the agreement at the outset of the arrangement is fixed, other than the customer's right to request a refund."
- *Initial setup fees.* If all other recognition criteria are met, revenue is to be recognized, generally on a straight-line basis, over the longer of (1) the term of the arrangement or (2) the expected period during which the specific services will be performed (SAB No. 114, Topic 13-A.3.f, Question 3). Different accounting, however, is required in different situations, such as activation fees for basic telephone service and installation fees for additional phone jacks, in which additional services are to be provided, depending on whether they can be separated for recognition purposes from the initial services (see FAQ, Topic 13-A.3, Questions 11–12).
- *Licensing and similar arrangement.* Revenue should not be recognized prior to the beginning of the license term (SAB No. 114, Topic 13-A.3.d).

The SEC Staff also notes that long-term contracts to provide services often are similar to other revenue arrangements. Assuming the general criteria for revenue recognition are satisfied, the timing of recognition should mirror the timing in which customers' obligations are satisfied.[28]

Some service providers incur incidental costs in connection with their ongoing operations that are reimbursed by their customers, either as part of the fee charged for the service or based on the actual amount of costs incurred by the service provider. Those "out-of-pocket" costs include airfare, automobile mileage, food and lodging expenditures, photocopies, and other items. ASC 605-45-45-23, *Revenue Recognition: Reimbursements Received for Out-of-Pocket Expenses Incurred,* concludes that reimbursements received for such costs should be reported as revenue, rather than as reduction of expenses, unless specific guidance for the reimbursement transaction has been provided by other Subtopics of the Codification (ASC 605-45-15-4b), such as the guidance for insurance and reinsurance premiums, lending transactions, sales of financial assets, broker-dealer transactions, and certain other specialized industry transactions.

As of this writing, the ASC has issued several other Topics that address various aspects of service revenue. For example:

- Other transactions involving the right to use assets may also inform the accounting for licenses for the use of intellectual property. For example, ASC 840, *Leases,* may offer insight for licenses of intellectual property and suggests that accounting for these arrangements should be similar to leases of physical assets, where initial fees are recognized over the lease term. ASC 926-605, *Entertainment—Films: Revenue Recognition,* and ASC 928-605, *Entertainment—Music: Revenue Recognition,* may be relevant because the nature of the licensed items may be similar to other intellectual property. ASC 952-605, *Franchisors: Revenue Recognition,* which addresses franchise fee recognition, also may be appropriate, although franchise fees generally involve far more than simply intellectual property.
- ASC 985-605, *Software: Revenue Recognition,* specifically addresses recognition of revenue in arrangements regarding the intellectual property of software, regardless of its delivery via a tangible medium. The guidance provided for software may be considered analogous to other intellectual property and, therefore, useful in determining the accounting for sales of nonsoftware intellectual property.

(vi) Sales of Future Revenues. Sales of future revenues occur when an enterprise receives cash from an investor, often a financial institution, and agrees to pay the investor a specified percentage or amount of revenue or income that the enterprise will receive from a particular product line, business segment, trademark, patent, or contractual right. The payment to the investor and the related future revenue or income may be denominated either in dollars or in a foreign currency.

Those types of transactions raise two fundamental issues, which are addressed in ASC 470-10-25, *Debt: Sales of Future Revenues or Various Other Measures of Income,* and ASC 470-10-35, *Debt: Subsequent Measurement.* These major issues are:

1. Whether the enterprise should classify the proceeds from the investor as debt or as deferred income
2. How that debt or deferred income should be amortized

On the first issue, ASC 470 notes that classification as debt or deferred income depends on the specific facts and circumstances of the transaction. However, the existence of any one of the next six factors independently makes the classification of the proceeds as debt appropriate:

1. The transaction does not purport to be a sale (i.e., the form of the transaction is debt).
2. The entity has significant continuing involvement in the generation of the cash flows due the investor (e.g., active involvement in the generation of the operating revenues of a product line, subsidiary, or business segment).

---

[28] SEC Division of Corporate Finance, "Current Accounting and Disclosure Issues in the Division of Corporate Finance," December 1, 2005, Section II.F.2.

3. The transaction is cancelable by either the entity or the investor through payment of a lump sum or other transfer of assets by the enterprise.

4. The investor's rate of return is implicitly or explicitly limited by the terms of the transaction.

5. Variations in the entity's revenue or income underlying the transaction have only a trifling impact on the investor's rate of return.

6. The investor has any recourse to the entity relating to the payments due the investor.

The second factor appears to indicate that deferred income accounting applies only to sales where the seller has no significant control over the timing and amount of cash flows. However, the circumstances in which immediate income recognition might be appropriate have not been clarified.

Concerning the second issue, ASC 470-10-35-3 states that amounts recorded as debt should be amortized under the interest method and that amounts recorded as deferred income should be amortized under the units-of-revenue method. The latter method requires calculating a ratio of the proceeds received from the investor to the total payments expected to be made to the investor over the term of the agreement and then applying that ratio to the period's cash payment.

If the debt is considered a foreign currency transaction, cash flow hedge accounting specified in ASC 815-30, *Derivatives and Hedging: Cash Flow Hedges,* may apply.

(vii) Barter Transactions Involving Barter Credits.   In a barter transaction involving barter credits, an enterprise enters into a transaction to exchange a nonmonetary asset (e.g., inventory) for barter credits. Those transactions may occur directly between principals to the transaction or include a third party whose business is to facilitate these types of exchanges (e.g., a barter company).

The barter credits can be used to purchase goods or services, such as advertising time, from either the barter company or members of its barter exchange network. The goods and services to be purchased may be specified in a barter contract or limited to items made available by members of the exchange network. Some arrangements may require the payment of cash in addition to the barter credits to purchase goods or services. Barter credits also may have a contractual expiration date, at which time they become worthless.

ASC 845-10-5-9 and 10, *Nonmonetary Transactions: Barter,* clarify that transactions in which nonmonetary assets are exchanged for barter credits should be accounted for in accordance with ASC 845. An impairment of the nonmonetary asset exchanged should be recognized before recording the exchange if the fair value of that asset is less than its carrying amount. Recognition of an impairment loss also would be required in an exchange of assets or contractual rights not reported in the balance sheet (e.g., operating leases) if the transferor is not relieved of primary liability for the related obligation. (As discussed ASC 360-10-35-15 through 49, *Property, Plant, and Equipment: Subsequent Measurement—Impairment or Disposal of Long-Lived Assets,* requires that certain long-lived assets be reviewed for impairment whenever events or changes in circumstances indicate that the carrying amount of an asset may not be recoverable, establishes accounting standards for the recognition and measurement of impairment losses and sets forth an approach to determining an asset's fair value. Also, ASC 360-10-35-43 requires that certain long-lived assets held for sale be reported at the lower of their carrying amounts or fair values less costs to sell.)

If an exchange involves the transfer of an operating lease, ASC 360-10-35 also concludes that the impairment of that lease should be measured as the remaining lease costs (rental payments and unamortized leasehold improvements) in excess of the estimated fair value of probable sublease rentals for the remaining lease term.

In reporting the exchange of a nonmonetary asset for barter credits, the fair value of the nonmonetary asset exchanged is presumed to measure more clearly the fair value of the barter credits received, so that the barter credits should be reported at the fair value of the nonmonetary asset exchanged. This presumption might be overcome if an entity can convert the barter credits into cash, as evidenced by a historical practice of converting barter credits into cash, or if independent quoted market prices exist for items to be received upon exchange of the barter credits. It should also be presumed that the fair value of the nonmonetary asset does not exceed its carrying amount unless there is persuasive evidence supporting a higher value. An impairment loss on the barter credits should be recognized if it subsequently becomes apparent that (1) the fair value of any remaining barter credits is less than the carrying amount or (2) it is probable that the enterprise will not use all of the remaining barter credits.

(viii) Revenue Recognition for Separately Priced Extended Warranty and Product Maintenance Contracts. Accounting for sales of separately-priced extended warranty and/or product maintenance contracts are addressed in ASC 605-20-25, *Revenue Recognition: Separately Priced Extended Warranty and Product Maintenance Contracts.* Those contracts should be treated in a manner similar to short-duration insurance contracts. As such, full recognition of the revenue and the accrual of the related estimated future costs at the time of sale is inappropriate. Revenue from separately priced extended warranty and product maintenance contracts should be deferred and recognized in income on a straight-line basis over the contract period, except in those circumstances in which sufficient historical evidence indicates that the costs of performing services under the contract are incurred on other than a straight-line basis. In those circumstances, revenue should be recognized over the contract period in proportion to the costs expected to be incurred in performing services under the contract. Costs of providing those services should be expensed as incurred. This accounting treatment is formulated on the premise that sellers of extended warranty or product maintenance contracts have an obligation to the buyer to perform services throughout the period of the contract and, therefore, revenue should be recognized over the period in which the seller is obligated to perform.

Recognition and measurement issues related to warranties and guarantees that are not separately priced are discussed in Section 12.5(f).

(ix) Sales with Multiple Deliverables. Sales transactions may include arrangements in which entities deliver to customers multiple products at different points in time, provide multiple services over different periods of time, or do a combination of both. Those arrangements may involve up-front fees as well as continuing payments over a period of time. For example, a cellular phone company may sign a contract with a customer to provide phone service and a "free" phone in exchange for an up-front activation fee and a monthly service fee. As another example, an entity may provide unlimited Internet access to customers for a monthly fee and, for an up-front fee, sell specific equipment necessary to access the Internet. Transactions with multiple deliverables may result in the recognition of revenue prior to the time of completion of the contract, as discussed in Subsection 12.1(d)(ii).

ASC 605-25 contains specific guidance concerning when vendors should identify separate units of an arrangement for revenue recognition purposes, when smaller units should be combined or excluded, how total revenue should be allocated to each unit based on its relative fair value, and how revenue recognition is affected by cancelation privileges and future vendor and customer actions. The guidance applies to all arrangements with multiple deliverables except in the next situations:

- The arrangements involve vendors offering customers future consideration for achieving certain levels of sales or remaining as customers for certain time periods. Those types of arrangements are discussed in ASC 605-50, *Revenue Recognition: Customer Payments and Incentives,* as are arrangements for the sale of award credits by loyalty program operators.
- The arrangement qualifies for treatment under the milestone method of revenue recognition, particularly R&D deliverables, as addressed in ASC 605-28, *Milestone Method.*

Additionally, the general guidelines provided in ASC 605-25 may be affected by other sections of the Codification. If the arrangements are within the scope of another section—such as

ASC 840, *Leases;* ASC 952, *Franchisors;* ASC 97X, *Real Estate;* ASC 460, *Guarantees;* ASC 605-20, *Revenue Recognition: Services,* which addresses separately priced extended warranties and product maintenance contracts; ASC 360, *Property, Plant, and Equipment;* ASC 605-35, *Revenue Recognition: Construction-Type and Production-Type Contracts;* ASC 985, *Software;* and ASC 926, *Entertainment—Films*—then more specific guidance applies. The three types of accounting treatments are as follows:

1. When another section addresses both the determination of separate units of accounting and the allocation of the arrangement consideration, the arrangement is fully within the scope of that section and should be accounted for in accordance with the provisions of that section rather than ASC 605-25.

2. When another section addresses the determination of separate units of accounting but not the allocation of the consideration, the other section should be used to determine which elements are inside and outside the scope of that section; the arrangement consideration should be allocated based on the relative selling price of the deliverable elements within and without that section. The elements that do not fall within that particular section should then be further segregated among other relevant section and accounted for within the provisions of that portion of the Codification. Any remaining elements not addressed by other sections of the Codification should then be accounted for by ASC 605-25.

3. When another section provides neither separation nor allocation guidance and is silent on multiple-element arrangements, ASC 605-25 should be followed.

ASC 605-25-25-5 requires that combinations of goods, services, and rights to use assets sold to customers under single contractual arrangements should be divided by vendors into separate units of accounting at an arrangement's inception and as each item is delivered when *all* of these three criteria exist:

1. Delivered items can be either (1) sold separately by a vendor or (2) resold by customers on a stand-alone basis.

2. Evidence of the undelivered items' fair values is objective and reliable.

3. If customers have general refund rights under the arrangements, future deliveries of the items are probable and controlled by the vendors.

If these three criteria are met, ASC 605-25-30 clarifies that vendors should allocate total consideration to each of the separate accounting units based on each unit's relative fair value. When reliable and objective information about each unit's fair value is available, the allocation of total consideration should be based on those fair values. If reliable and objective information about fair value is available only for undelivered items, revenue should be allocated using the residual method—revenue for delivered items should be determined by subtracting the fair value of the undelivered items from the total consideration. ASC 605-25-30-7 notes that "[t]he best evidence of fair value is the price of a deliverable when it is regularly sold on a standalone basis." Such evidence often is "vendor-specific objective evidence," and the guidance in ASC 985-605-25, *Revenue Recognition: Software,* should be followed. The consensus also requires vendors to use appropriate revenue recognition criteria for each unit of accounting, but it does not include specific guidance on those criteria or on how to allocate direct costs to the units.

In March 2011, the SEC issued SAB No. 114, of which Topic 13, *Revenue Recognition,* provides additional guidance on applying ASC 605-25. That guidance is described in Subsection 12.3(h)(v).

(x) Inventory Purchases and Sales with Same Counterparty.   Some enterprises sell inventory to customers from whom they also purchase inventory. Accounting for these types of transactions—commonly called *buy-sell arrangements* in the oil and gas industry[29]—are addressed in ASC 845-10-05-08, *Nonmonetary Transactions: Purchases and Sales of Inventory with the Same Counterparty.* All purchases and sales of inventory with the same counterparty (except for transactions in the software and real estate industries, which are discussed in other authoritative literature, or those accounted for as derivatives, which are discussed in ASC 815) should be combined and considered as a single arrangement if their substance suggests they were undertaken "in contemplation" of one another. ASC 845-10-25-4 delineates factors indicating the purchase and sale transactions were undertaken in contemplation of one another, including:

- The purchase and sale transactions occur simultaneously.
- The transactions do not include terms typical of market transactions.
- The parties to the transactions have a legal right to offset the receivables and payables.
- The reciprocal transaction is relatively certain to occur.

If the substance of the transactions indicates that a single arrangement exists, the next accounting is appropriate:

- Exchanges of finished goods for raw materials or work in progress should be measured at fair value as long as the exchange has commercial substance.
- Exchanges of finished goods for finished goods, or exchanges of raw materials or work in process for other raw materials or work in process or for finished goods, should be measured based on book values of those items, following the principles discussed in ASC 845.

(b) SPECIALIZED INDUSTRY PROBLEMS. Many problems concerning when to recognize revenue are specific to entire industries. For example, all franchisors face the problem of when to recognize as revenue the initial fees from the sale of franchises. As with many non-industry-specific revenue recognition problems, the source of the difficulty is the relatively long period, often several accounting periods, over which the earning of revenue (in its broadest sense, extending through completed performance and collection) takes place. In many instances, authoritative or quasi-authoritative pronouncements have specified the appropriate timing of revenue in various circumstances. In others, the accountant must rely on judgment, but the general revenue recognition criteria suggested earlier in this chapter may be helpful.

(i) Specialized Industries Discussed in Other Chapters. To avoid duplication, the industries that are discussed elsewhere in this *Handbook* are listed next along with the relevant chapter numbers:

Construction industry. Revenue may be recognized when long-term construction contracts are completed (completed contract method) or as construction progresses (percentage-of-completion method), depending on the circumstances surrounding each contract. Those methods and their applicability in varying circumstances are discussed in Chapter 31. The primary sources for information about accounting issues for the construction industry are ASC 605-35, *Revenue Recognition: Construction-Type and Production-Type Contracts,* and ASC 910, *Contractors—Construction.*

Not-for-profit organizations. Recognition and measurement of contributions received are addressed by ASC 958-605, *Not-for-Profit Entities: Revenue Recognition,* and discussed in Chapter 28 of this book.

---

[29] The SEC Staff discusses accounting for "buy-sell arrangements" in letters (see *www.sec.gov/divisions/corpfin/guidance/oilgas021105.htm*) sent to various registrants in February 2005 describing recognition, measurement, and disclosure requirements for these transactions. See SEC Division of Corporation Finance, "Current Accounting and Disclosure Issues," December 1, 2005, Section II.F.1.

Real estate industry. Revenue recognition from the sale of real estate and from retail land sales depends largely on the buyer's assuming the normal risks and rewards of ownership, often evidenced by the size of the down payment, and on the seller's performance under the terms of the sales agreement. Those conditions and other related criteria for recognizing revenue are discussed in ASC 970-605, *Real Estate—General: Revenue Recognition,* and Chapter 31 of this book.

Banking. Various recognition and measurement issues related to loans, leases, and other revenue generating activities of banks and other financial institutions are discussed in Chapter 30 of this book.

(ii) Cable Television Companies.   ASC 922, *Entertainment—Cable Television,* discusses revenue recognition and related accounting problems. ASC 922-360-25 suggests that costs incurred during construction before the first subscriber hookup and a portion of certain costs after the first subscriber hookup, but before construction of the entire system is complete, usually may be capitalized. During that "prematurity" period, all revenues except those from hookups should be reported as system revenues, and the portion of costs, depreciation, and amortization charged to expense, as well as specified period costs, should be included in appropriate categories of costs of services. According to ASC 922-605-25-3, "Initial hookup revenue shall be recognized as revenue to the extent of direct selling costs incurred." According to ASC 922-430-25-1, the remainder in excess of direct selling costs should be deferred. ASC 922-430-35-1 requires that those deferred revenues should be amortized to income over the estimated average period that subscribers are expected to remain connected to the system.

(iii) Franchising Companies.   The major franchise accounting problem concerns the recognition of revenue from the initial franchise fee. ASC 952-605 establishes accounting and reporting standards for franchisors. ASC 952-605-25 requires that initial franchise fees from individual and area franchise sales be recognized as revenue only when a franchisor has satisfied all material conditions or performed substantially all material services relating to the sale. It also discusses accounting for continuing franchise fees, continuing product sales, agency sales, repossessed franchises, franchising costs, commingled revenue, and relationships between a franchisor and a franchisee.

(iv) Record and Music Industry.   ASC 928-605 requires the licensor of a record master or music copyright to recognize the licensing fee as revenue if collectibility of the full fee is reasonably assured and if the licensor:

- Has signed a noncancelable contract
- Has agreed to a fixed fee
- Has delivered the rights to the licensee, who is free to exercise them
- Has no remaining significant obligations to furnish music or records

(v) Motion Picture Films; Broadcasting Industry.   ASC 926-605 discusses revenue recognition for sales and licensing arrangements of feature films, television specials and series, and similar items. According to ASC 926-605-25-1, a licensor should recognize revenue from a sale or licensing arrangement of a film when all of these five conditions are met:

1. Persuasive evidence of a sale or licensing agreement with a customer exists.
2. The film is complete and, in accordance with the terms of the arrangement, has been delivered or is available for immediate and unconditional delivery.
3. The license period of the arrangement has begun and the customer can begin its exploitation, exhibit, or sale.
4. The arrangement fee is fixed or determinable.
5. Collection of the arrangement fee is reasonably assured.

ASC 920-350-25-2, *Entertainment—Broadcasters: Intangibles—Goodwill and Other,* and ASC 920-405-25-1, *Entertainment—Broadcasters: Liabilities,* conclude that broadcasters' accounting for television film license agreements should parallel accounting by the licensor as prescribed in ASC 926, and, accordingly, assets and liabilities should be recorded for the rights acquired and the obligations incurred under such agreements.

ASC 920-845, *Entertainment—Broadcasters: Nonmonetary Transactions,* establishes standards of reporting by broadcasters for transactions in which unsold advertising time is bartered for products or services. According to ASC 920-845-25-1: "Broadcasters may barter unsold advertising time for products or services. Barter revenue shall be reported when commercials are broadcast, and merchandise or services shall be reported when received or used."

(vi) Software Revenue Recognition.   ASC 985-605, provides guidance for recognizing and measuring revenues associated with licensing, selling, leasing, or otherwise marketing various computer software products, updates, enhancements, and related services, including postcontract customer support, installation, training, and consulting. ASC 985-20, *Software: Costs of Software to Be Sold, Leased, or Marketed,* provides guidance for recognizing and measuring associated expenses. Costs related to computer software for an entity's own use should be accounted for in conformity with ASC 350-40, *Intangibles—Goodwill and Other: Internal-Use Software.*

If an arrangement to deliver software requires significant production, modification, or customization of software, it should be accounted for as a construction-type or production-type contract in conformity with ASC 605-35, and the relevant guidelines in ASC 985-605-25-88 through 107. Otherwise, ASC 985-605 requires that revenue be recognized when all of these four criteria are met:

1. Persuasive evidence of an arrangement exists.
2. Delivery has occurred.
3. The vendor's fee is fixed or determinable.
4. Collectibility is probable.

ASC 985-605-25-6 stipulates that, if an arrangement includes multiple deliverables, the allocation should be based on "vendor-specific objective evidence of fair value," such as a price list reflecting the price charged when the same element is sold separately. The revenue allocated to a specific product or service should be recognized when the preceding criteria are met with respect to the product or service. ASC 985-605-25-7 through 14 offer additional guidance for recognizing revenue when a software arrangement includes multiple deliverables.

Some entities sell software or rights to use software that have elements of film, music, or similar types of materials. Revenues from the sale of these multiple elements should be separated based on ASC 605-25. If those guidelines do not require the revenue on bundled deliverables to be separated, general revenue recognition principles should be applied (see Subsection 12.4(a)(ix)).

Instead of selling copies of software, some vendors provide customers with access to software over the Internet or by other electronic means; the software actually resides on a server maintained by vendors or third parties. In those situations, vendors provide customers with both the right to use software and storage of the software (a service called *hosting*). ASC 985-605-55-121 concludes that a hosting arrangement represents a separate software element only if customers (1) have a contractual right to take physical possession of the software during the hosting period without significant penalty and (2) feasibly can run the software on their own computers or can contract with third parties to do so. If those criteria are met, ASC 985-605-55-124 concludes that:

- Delivery of the software is presumed to occur when the customer has the ability to take immediate possession.
- All of the recognition criteria in ASC 985-605-55 must be satisfied before the vendor can recognize revenue.
- A portion of the total revenue must be allocated to each separate element of the transaction, including the hosting arrangement.

- The portion of total revenue allocated to the hosting element should be recognized as that service is provided.

Some software vendors enter into barter transactions in which they accept, in exchange for software and related services, customers' products or services or shares of customers' stock. Revenue would be recognized based on the guidance in ASC 985-845, *Software: Nonmonetary Transactions.* Implementation guidance for nonmonetary transactions involving software and accounting for exchanges of software between companies is discussed in ASC 985-845-55.

Software manufacturers may offer price protection agreements, under which they refund or credit a portion of the original selling price to customers if they subsequently reduce the price offered to other customers. Software manufacturers should set up appropriate allowances for those price concessions when they are authorized.

(vii) Internet Companies.   Many accounting issues have emerged as a result of e-commerce activities and other ways to provide products and services to customers. Those activities have also led to the formation of new types of entities that offer Internet and other services and hardware and other products. Those entities include:

- Service providers—entities that charge fees for providing Internet access
- Portal companies—entities that provide Web site content, accessible with their own or through other entities' search engines, in exchange for fees from arrangements with advertisers that may involve performance guarantees based on benchmarks, such as the number of hits on a Web site
- E-commerce companies—entities that sell goods or services exclusively through the Internet or that earn fees for facilitating transactions between other parties
- Internet-related companies—entities that provide hardware and software for Internet and other electronic transactions

Because of the unique nature of these companies and the goods and services they offer, specific revenue recognition and measurement rules cover a variety of e-commerce and related activities. Some of those issues—such as sales arrangements with separate deliverables (Subsection 12.4(a)(ix)), various types of sales incentives (Section 12.5(d)), and gross versus net reporting (Subsection 12.1(c)(i))—are discussed elsewhere in this chapter. Some types of revenue-related arrangements are unique to Internet companies; these are discussed next.

Some Internet companies receive fees from customers that include payments for providing access to, posting information on, and maintenance of customers' Web sites. ASC 605 requires those fees to be recognized as revenue over the periods in which the services are performed. ASC 605-25 provides additional guidance on arrangements that include separate deliverables (see Subsection 12.4(a)(ix)).

Internet companies also may host customers' auction sites or run their own auction sites. In those situations, the companies ordinarily do not take title to the products sold on the site. Instead, they charge up-front fees for listing products and services for sale as well as fees for facilitating transactions. The guidance provided in ASC 605-20 requires the initial fees to be recognized over the performance period—the period during which customers' products and services are listed on the auction site. Nonrefundable transaction fees ordinarily should be recognized as revenue when the underlying sales transactions are completed. If those fees are refundable, or if the company hosting the auction site is substantially involved with the products or services sold on the site after the sale is completed, some or all of the refundable fees should be deferred until the earnings process is complete.

ASC 605-20-25-14 through 18 concern "banner-for-banner," "click-through for click-through," and similar types of reciprocal or comarketing arrangements in which two entities exchange advertising on each others' Web sites without, in substance, any cash being exchanged. The ASC requires entities to recognize revenues and related expenses from those transactions at fair value when the fair value of the advertising provided can be determined from an entity's past experience involving similar cash transactions with unrelated parties. ASC 605-20-25-16 through 18 provide detailed guidance on how fair value should be determined. If fair value cannot be determined, barter transactions should be recorded based on the carrying value (which in most cases will be zero) of the advertising provided.

Some advertising arrangements made by Internet companies include guarantees on a minimum number of hits or click-throughs during a period. If that minimum is not achieved, the arrangements may include automatic extensions of the advertising until that number, or a larger number, of hits is achieved. Depending on the specific arrangements and the likelihood of achieving the minimum number guaranteed, revenue may be recognized when the guaranteed minimum is achieved or ratably over the period of the arrangement.

Cloud computing is "a style of computing where massively scalable and elastic IT [information technology]–related capabilities are provided 'as a service' using Internet technologies to multiple external customers."[30] A typical cloud service provider (CSP) offering will have multiple elements delivered at different times over the course of the relationship. Separating the multiple elements will drive the timing of revenue recognition for each element, in accordance with ASC 605-25. (See Subsection 12.4(a)(ix).) CSPs may use a subscription model, a usage-based pricing model, an advertising-supported model that is free to users, or a combination thereof. Because this is a quickly-evolving business, capturing radically different contract terms for ongoing activities may drive complex and varied revenue recognition conclusions. CSPs that provide software and application program interfaces in addition to services may need to comply with the revenue recognition standards at ASC 985-605. (See Subsection 12.4(b)(vi).)

(c) NEED FOR ADDITIONAL GUIDANCE. Despite the conceptual guidance and detailed, industry-specific principles described in various sections of this chapter, numerous questions continue to arise concerning when entities should recognize revenue and how it should be measured. Arriving at sound answers to those questions is critical to ensuring that an entity's financial statements present fairly the entity's operating results and financial position. Revenues typically are the largest financial statement item, and many financial statement users analyze revenue numbers and trends in those numbers when making investment, credit, and similar decisions.

Accounting problems involving revenue continue to arise frequently. In its 1999 report, "Fraudulent Financial Reporting: 1987–1997, An Analysis of U.S. Public Companies," the Treadway Commission's Committee of Sponsoring Organizations (COSO) notes that revenue recognition problems existed in about half of the financial reporting misstatement cases described in the SEC's Accounting and Auditing Enforcement Releases (AAER) issued during that period. Similar issues were identified in a study reported by the Panel on Audit Effectiveness's "Report and Recommendations" (Panel Report). That study of AAER cases shows that 70 percent of the problems concerned premature or fictitious revenue, including recognizing revenue before recognition criteria were met (e.g., on consignment sales and bill-and-hold transactions); in the wrong period (e.g., on products shipped after year end); or for transactions that never took place (pars. 2.126–2.142 and Appendix F).

The SEC has grown increasingly concerned about revenue recognition issues and management's ability to use aggressive recognition policies to manage earnings. (See Chapter 5 in this *Handbook*.) In September 1999, the SEC announced charges against 68 organizations and individuals that were accused of financial reporting abuses, many of which involved revenue recognition problems similar to those cited by COSO and the Panel Report. Later that year, the SEC asked the Emerging Issues Task Force (EITF) to consider 20 major Internet-related revenue problems, including recognizing revenue for services provided to customers free of charge, reporting gross instead of net revenues, and recognizing revenue from barter transactions. Those problems are summarized in EITF Issue No. 99-V, *Remaining Issues from the SEC's October 18, 1999 Letter to the EITF.*

---

[30] P. Iyengar, "Application Development in the Cloud: Strategies and Tactics for a New Generation," Gartner, Inc., November 2009.

As a result of the need for more detailed guidance, the SEC issued SAB No. 101, *Revenue Recognition,* in December 1999. (See Section 12.3(h).) The SEC did not intend to create or change revenue recognition principles but to provide guidelines useful for public companies, especially those involved in buying and selling over the Internet, in deciding how to apply existing GAAP. Applying the four criteria that form the foundation of SAB No. 101, however, has proven to be difficult. Part of the problem is that the criteria are drawn from the SEC's experience with Internet-related transactions but the SAB applies to all types of revenue transactions. In addition, the guidance in the SAB is discussed in a series of questions and answers illustrating what the SEC Staff considered to be sound revenue recognition practices in fact-specific situations. A small change in those facts, however, can have a major effect on how the four criteria would apply. As a result, entities and their auditors found it difficult to apply SAB No. 101 to new and increasingly more complex revenue arrangements.

Several developments improved that situation. For example, in response to numerous requests from public companies and their auditors, the SEC issued an FAQ document in October 2000 providing additional, but still very situation-specific, guidance on applying the SAB No. 101 criteria. In addition, the EITF issued consensuses on several significant revenue-related projects described previously, such as Issues No. 99-19 on gross versus net revenue reporting and No. 01-9 on sales incentives. In March 2011, SAB No. 114 was issued to revise or rescind portions of the interpretive guidance included in the codification of the SAB Series, updating the relevant interpretive guidance consistent with the FASB Accounting Standards Codification. Consequently, the SAB Series is represented in its entirety in SAB No. 114.

Despite that additional guidance, revenue recognition problems have continued to arise. For example, the SEC investigated accounting by Dynergy, Global Crossing, and Qwest Communications for "round-trip" swap transactions involving asset and service transfers whose sole purpose seemed to be inflating the companies' reported revenues. Other entities, including Xerox and ConAgra, have restated prior years' revenues following SEC investigations of their allegedly "aggressive" recognition policies.[31] The SEC also has charged members of senior management at several companies, including Homestore and L90, with inflating online advertising revenues through various barter transactions and misleading auditors about the nature of those transactions.[32] The SEC charged Gemstar-TV Guide International with misstating $250 million of revenue from 1999 to 2002 in a variety of ways, including front-end loading revenue from long-term and multiple-element contracts, inflating revenue from barter transactions, and shifting revenue among accounting periods. Gemstar agreed to pay $10 million to settle the SEC's civil case.[33] The SEC subsequently sanctioned the company's auditing firm, KPMG, and four of the firm's auditors for repeated failures in auditing Gemstar's revenue.[34]

More recently, the SEC:

- Charged various executives at Vitesse Semiconductor Corporation with an elaborate channel-stuffing scheme, materially inflating revenue for at least 14 quarters.[35]
- Accused the former chief financial officer of International Commercial Television, Inc. of prematurely and fraudulently recognizing revenue on sales of products through infomercials and through the Home Shopping Network.[36] In addition, Dohan & Company CPAs and three of its principals were accused of improper professional conduct during their audit of ICTV, particularly with regard to revenue recognition issues.[37]

---

[31] See SEC Accounting and Auditing Enforcement Release No. 1864, September 18, 2003, and No. 1874, September 26, 2003.

[32] See SEC Accounting and Auditing Enforcement Release No. 2045, June 23, 2004.

[33] See SEC Accounting and Auditing Enforcement Release No. 2125, October 20, 2004.

[34] See SEC Accounting and Auditing Enforcement Release No. 3137, June 2, 2010.

[35] See SEC Accounting and Enforcement Release No. 3217, December 10, 2010.

[36] See SEC Accounting and Enforcement Release No. 3311, August 4, 2011.

[37] See SEC Accounting and Enforcement Release No. 3171, August 9, 2010.

- Elicited a $25 million civil penalty from Diebold, Inc., and filed fraud and other charges against several of its top executives. The firm and its executives were accused of improper use of bill-and-hold accounting and fraudulent recognition of revenue on a lease agreement, among other charges.[38]

In addition, many companies—including Green Mountain Coffee Roasters, Inc. (Form 8-K, November 19, 2010), Dell, Inc. (Form 8-K, August 13, 2007), and Overstock.com, Inc. (Form 8-K, February 4, 2010)—have had to restate their financial results as a result of errors in recognizing revenue. Huron Consulting Group found that almost 60 percent of the restatements made by public companies in 2004 resulted from revenue problems.[39]

The continuing problems have highlighted the need for what the Panel Report called "an authoritative statement on the broad principles of revenue recognition: (par. 2.142). The broad conceptual guidance provided by SFAC No. 5 and SAB No. 101 has not resulted in entities reporting consistent and comparable information about revenues. In addition, the more detailed guidance issued by the SEC, the EITF, and the AICPA often (1) is issued without adequate due process, (2) applies to a narrow range of problems, and, (3) at times is inconsistent with other literature.

(d) FINANCIAL ACCOUNTING STANDARDS BOARD PROJECT ON REVENUE RECOGNITION.   In mid-2002, the FASB formally recognized the need to provide additional guidance and to promote international convergence of accounting standards for revenue recognition. It initiated a joint project with the IASB to eliminate inconsistencies in the authoritative literature and provide a conceptual foundation for resolving new and emerging revenue recognition and measurement issues. The project's two components were (1) the reorganization of U.S. GAAP into a more user-friendly single source of authoritative standards and (2) the clarification of the principles for recognizing revenue with the goal of developing a common revenue standard for U.S. GAAP and International Financial Reporting Standards.

The objective of the project's first component included developing a comprehensive, principles-based standard on revenue recognition containing clear, concise implementation guidelines for business entities. The FASB's Staff compiled an inventory of the authoritative literature and other sources of guidance (such as industry-specific practices) dealing with revenue recognition. The inventory included over 180 sources of accounting principles,[36] classified under one of four "conventions":

1. *Mark to market.* Revenue is recognized when the fair values of assets or liabilities change.
2. *Proportionate performance.* Revenue is recognized when performance occurs or with the passage of time.
3. *Sales and delivery.* Revenue is recognized when performance is substantially complete.
4. *Collection.* Revenue is recognized when consideration is collected following an exchange or performance.

As noted in Section 12.4(c), much of the then-existing guidance was narrow, applying only to specific industries or types of transactions, and was issued by many different organizations—including the APB, the FASB, and various groups within the AICPA—over a long period of time. The FASB's goals in this first component of the project were to eliminate the inconsistencies and provide more comprehensive guidance for recognizing revenue.

On July 1, 2009, FASB launched the *FASB Accounting Standards Codification* (ASC) as the single source of authoritative nongovernmental U.S. GAAP. The use of the ASC became effective with interim and annual reporting after September 15, 2009, when it superseded all other

---

[38] C. Graciano, "Revenue Recognition: A Perennial Problem," *Financial Executive Magazine,* July 14, 2005.
[39] As of this writing, the FASB's inventory has not been made available to the public.

accounting standards. The Codification reorganized thousands of GAAP pronouncements into a consistent structure and included relevant SEC guidance. Guidelines for revenue recognition are found primarily in ASC 605 but appear in a number of other sections as well.

The second FASB/IASB project component, the "convergence effort," focuses on the need to:

- Remove from existing revenue recognition standards any weaknesses and inconsistencies
- Develop a more robust authoritative framework for addressing revenue recognition issues
- Improve the comparability of revenue recognition practices across jurisdictional and other boundaries
- Reduce the number of authoritative requirements to which entities must refer when preparing financial statements.

The boards issued joint proposals in June 2010. FASB published an Exposure Draft for public comment of proposed Accounting Standards Update (ASU) No. 1820-100, *Revenue Recognition (Topic 605): Revenue from Contracts with Customers)*. The IASB Exposure Draft was similar except for minor differences in spelling, style, and format. About 1,000 comment letters were received, with the two boards agreeing some redrafting was necessary. FASB and IASB anticipate issuing a revised Exposure Draft in the last quarter of 2011 and note that the effective date of the standard would be no earlier than for annual periods beginning on or after January 1, 2015. As of this writing, the boards are undecided whether to permit early application of the standard.[40]

12.5 REVENUE ADJUSTMENTS AND AFTERCOSTS

(a) NATURE OF REVENUE ADJUSTMENTS AND AFTERCOSTS.   Revenue adjustments include *sales returns* and *allowances, discounts,* and *bad debts; warranties* and *guarantees* may be treated either as future revenue or as "aftercosts," depending on the circumstances; costs related to product defects should be treated as expenses.

Practice does not always clearly distinguish between events and transactions that give rise to expenses and those that are more properly treated as adjustments or valuations of revenue. Alternative definitions of the term *revenue* were presented at the beginning of this chapter; expenses are defined in paragraph 80 of SFAC No. 6 as outflows or expirations of assets sold or liabilities incurred in the process of earning revenue (as "earning" was previously defined). Hendriksen and van Breda state that:

> [S]ales returns and allowances, sales discounts, and bad debt losses are all more appropriately treated as reductions of gross revenues than as expenses. None of them represents the use of goods or services to generate revenues; each represents a reduction of the amount to be received in exchange for the product.[41]

(b) SALES RETURNS.   Merchandise returned by a customer is, in effect, a cancelation of the original sales transaction, in whole or in part, and should be treated as a direct offset to gross sales rather than as a revenue adjustment. To maintain a record of sales returns as well as of the amount of gross sales, however, returns are ordinarily recorded in a contra sales account, "sales returns." A special problem arises if the returned merchandise has been used or has deteriorated to a point substantially below its original value. In those cases, the returned goods should be recorded at their net realizable value based on their present condition and estimated costs of making them ready for resale. Losses attributable to returned goods should be recognized as appropriate.

---

[40] FASB Project Update, *Revenue Recognition—Joint Project of the FASB and IASB,* September 21, 2011, available at *www.fasb.org*.
[41] Hendriksen and van Breda, *Accounting Theory,* p. 370.

(c) SALES ALLOWANCES.   Allowances to customers fall into these two general classes:

1. Specific allowances on certain products, such as those for shortages in shipments, breakage, spoilage, inferior quality, failure to meet specifications, or errors in billing or handling of freight
2. Policy allowances, or allowances that the seller makes only because of the possible loss of future business it might suffer in related lines if it did not offer such allowances

Allowances falling in the first class should be treated as a direct offset to gross sales. Allowances in the second class are generally classified as revenue deductions.

(d) SALES INCENTIVES.   Some vendors provide cash, credits, and other consideration to their customers in the form of discounts, coupons, rebates, and free products or services. For example, deductions from gross invoice prices, order quotations, published price lists, and other forms of discounts may be offered as:

- *Cash discounts.* Credit terms often allow customers a cash discount for payment of invoices within a certain period. In the past, cash discounts sometimes were viewed as interest allowances to customers for prompt payment. Sales discounts taken were thus treated as financial expenses; discounts not taken were implicitly included in gross revenue. This accounting can still be found in the literature. The preferred method, however, is to regard cash discounts as revenue adjustments, either by deducting discounts taken from gross sales revenue on the income statement or by initially recording the sales at net prices and treating forfeited discounts as financing revenue. As a practical matter, the amounts involved are usually not material to the financial statements.
- *Trade discounts.* Trade discounts are deductions from list prices, allowed to customers for quantities purchased or for the purpose of establishing different price levels for different classes of customers, such as wholesalers and retailers. Trade discounts also are employed to enable vendors to change the effective prices of articles included in catalogs or similar sales publications by the relatively simple process of issuing a revised discount sheet. Revenues should be recorded after deduction of such discounts.
- *Employee discounts.* Employees are often allowed special discounts on purchases made through the company. The discount may be limited to the company's ordinary products or merchandise, or it may extend to clothing, food, and other commodities carried in a general company store for the benefit of employees and sold to them at cost. If the sales are not recorded net of discounts initially, the total discounts generally should be treated as a revenue deduction. If a discount is in substance additional compensation, it should be treated as an operating expense.

A variety of more complex sales incentive arrangements also are used by companies in the Internet, hospitality, airline, and other industries. These include:

- Free products or services delivered when customers purchase another specified product or service (e.g., two-for-one offers)
- Shares of vendors' stock, stock options, or stock warrants to purchase vendors' stock
- Points or other credits that can be redeemed for various goods and services after customers have accumulated a specified amount "loyalty programs)
- Fees paid to customers to obtain space in customers' selling areas (slotting fees)
- Reimbursements for a portion of customers' advertising costs relating to vendors' products or services (cooperative advertising)
- Reimbursements up to specified amounts if the customers do not resell the vendors' products at greater than a specified minimum price during a specified time period (e.g., buydowns, shortfalls, factory incentives, dealer holdbacks, price protection, and factory-to-dealer incentives)

The accounting issues raised by sales incentives such as these concern how vendors should measure the costs of these arrangements and how those costs should be reported on vendors' income statements. ASC 605-50 provides guidance for accounting for sales incentives. As discussed in Subsection 12.5 (d)(i), the appropriate accounting depends on the type of consideration offered.

(i) Cash or Equity Consideration.   When cash or equity consideration is offered voluntarily and without charge by a vendor to be used in a single exchange transaction or that becomes exercisable by the customer as a result of a single exchange transaction, and this incentive will not result in a loss on the sale of the product or service, the cost of the incentive should be measured at the later of two dates: when the related revenue is recognized by the vendor or when the incentive is offered. ASC 605-50-45 requires that cash consideration be presumed to be a reduction of the selling price of the product or service and should be recognized as a reduction in revenue. This presumption may be overcome if the seller receives, or will receive, an identifiable benefit in exchange for the consideration, and the seller can reasonably estimate the fair value of the benefit received. If the transaction overcomes the presumption, the excess amount of consideration over the fair value of the benefit should be treated as a reduction in revenue.

(ii) Other Forms of Consideration.   Sales incentives offered to customers may involve consideration other than cash or equity instruments, such as gift certificates and offers of "free" products or services. ASC 605-50-45-3 considers those types of incentives to be separate deliverables and requires their cost to be reported as expenses. Although the consensus does not specify the appropriate expense classification, the SEC Staff believes they should be included in cost of sales if they are delivered at the time of the sale of other goods or services. Accounting for points or loyalty programs that offer customers free or discounted goods or services only after reaching a certain level or after being a customer for a certain period of time is specifically excluded from the scope of ASC 605-25, due to their unique nature. However, companies may elect to treat points as a separate unit of accounting under ASC 605-25; the relevant revenue would be deferred and recognized when the points are redeemed.

(iii) Customers' Accounting for Sales Incentives.   ASC 605-50-45-12 presumes that cash consideration received by customers is a reduction in the price of a vendor's goods or services. Customers should not report such consideration as revenue but as reductions in their cost of sales. This presumption can be overcome if either of two conditions exist: (1) the cash consideration is a payment for goods or services delivered to the vendor, in which case the cash consideration should simply be recognized as income; or (2) the cash consideration is a reimbursement of costs to sell the vendor's product, in which case the cash consideration should be treated as a reduction of that cost.

Two common arrangements involving payments from vendors to customers are specifically addressed by ASC 605-50-45-4, *Slotting Fees.* The first type is payments made by a seller to a retailer so the retailer will stock the seller's product in its stores. These and similar product placement fees are to be treated as a reduction of revenue by the vendor. They should generally be treated by the customer as a reduction in the cost of sales, even when the slotting fee arrangement is written in the form of a lease. The second type of arrangement includes buydowns, such as factory to dealer incentives in the automobile industry. These generally involve a vendor agreeing to reimburse a retailer for a specified amount of shortfall in a sales price on specific products during a specific promotional period. Buydowns are required to be treated as a reduction of revenue by the vendor and should generally be treated as a reduction in cost of sales by the retailer customer.

Rebates and coupons are two means by which manufacturers will offer sales discounts to consumers in order to stimulate demand. Frequently, a manufacturer will sell its product to a reseller/retailer, which then sells the product to consumers. Typically, consumers present coupons to the reseller, who honors the coupons at the point of sale and tenders them to the manufacturer for reimbursement. ASC 605-50-45-16 through 22, *Reseller's Characterization of Sales Incentives*

Offered to Customers by Manufacturers, concludes that resellers should account for those reimbursements as reductions in cost of goods sold if the incentives meet all four of these criteria:

1. The incentives are available to consumers to reduce the price paid at any reseller of the manufacturers' products.

2. They are paid directly to resellers from vendors (or vendor-authorized third parties) based on the face value of the incentives.

3. The incentives are determined solely by the terms offered to consumers by manufacturers (i.e., have no terms affected by other incentive arrangements between the manufacturers and resellers).

4. They arise from express or applied agency relationships between manufacturers and vendors in connection with the sales incentive offered by the manufacturers to consumers.

If a sales incentive does not meet all four of these criteria, resellers should apply the guidance in ASC 605-50-45-2 through 45-3.

(e) UNCOLLECTIBLE RECEIVABLES. According to ASC 310-10-35-16, *Receivables: Subsequent Measurement,* "a loan is impaired when, based on current information and events, it is probable that a creditor will be unable to collect all amounts due according to the contractual terms of the loan agreement." (As defined in ASC 310-10-20, *loans* include accounts receivable with terms exceeding one year and notes receivable.) ASC 310 applies to all creditors; its applicability to financial institutions is discussed in Chapter 30 of this *Handbook.* However, ASC 310, *Receivables,* guidance for the accounting for impairment of a loan specifically excludes these four types:

1. Large groups of smaller-balance homogeneous loans that are collectively evaluated for impairment such as credit card loans, residential mortgages, and consumer installment loans

2. Loans that are measured at fair value or lower of cost or fair value, the treatment of which should be in accordance with specialized industry practice

3. Leases, which are addressed in ASC 840

4. Debt securities as defined in ASC 320, *Investments: Debt and Equity Securities*

Uncollectible receivables are accounts and note receivables that probably will not be collected in the future. Providing an allowance for uncollectible receivables is required under SFAS No. 5, *Accounting for Contingencies,* when a loss is probable and can be reasonably estimated. Under the *allowance method,* an allowance account is used to report the estimated uncollectible amount of receivables. ASC 310-10-45-4 specifies that the allowance account be reflected as a contra to the controlling (i.e., gross) receivables account and the individual subsidiary accounts be left intact. When it is decided that a specific amount is uncollectible, it is charged against the allowance account. Bad debt expense is recorded when the allowance account is increased. Although not acceptable for financial statements prepared in conformity with GAAP, the *direct write-off method* is acceptable for income tax purposes. Under this method, no allowance is required; instead, uncollectible accounts are written off during the period in which they are determined to be uncollectible. The loss is charged directly to bad debt expense.

Bad debts can be classified on the income statement as (1) a financial expense or loss, (2) an operating expense (either selling or administrative), or (3) a sales adjustment. The first view assumes that all customers' claims are initially valid in the amount of their face value and that subsequent lack of collection is a financing cost that must be borne by the business as a whole. Under the second interpretation, bad debts are considered one of the costs of operating the business. The third alternative recognizes at the outset that a certain percentage of customers' claims will become uncollectible, that total credit sales are therefore tentative and subject to subsequent adjustment, and that, consequently, no expense or loss should be recognized because no asset has expired or liability been incurred.

When the allowance account is used, there are three methods for estimating its appropriate balance: percentage-of-sales method, percentage-of-receivables method, and aging-of-receivables method.

(i) Percentage-of-Sales Method. The percentage-of-sales method requires charging bad debt expense and crediting the allowance account for an amount determined by applying an estimate of uncollectibles to sales revenue for the period. It can be used with both accounts and notes receivable, either together or separately. As a practical matter, however, this method can be used advantageously with notes *only* when the notes are numerous and arise as a regular credit term granted at the time of the sale. Although the uncollectible expense percentage usually should be based on recent experience and applied to credit sales, often substantially the same result can be attained by using a smaller percentage applied to total sales (assuming the relationship of cash sales to credit sales remains fairly constant). The balance in the allowance account may become excessive or inadequate unless there are periodic reviews of probable losses and consequent adjustments of the allowance account as necessary.

(ii) Percentage-of-Receivables Method. The percentage-of-receivables method requires a determination of collection experience. The total of estimated uncollectibles is thus ascertained by applying the loss percentage to total receivables. The allowance account is then adjusted by the amount necessary to bring the existing balance to the required amount. This method also can be used with both accounts and notes receivable. When the notes held are relatively few in number and originate in the process of collection of accounts receivable or through loans and advances, the percentage-of-receivables method is an appropriate means of valuing notes receivable.

This method often results in a fairly accurate approximation of expected net realizable value of receivables. In terms of bad debt expense on the income statement, however, the method may be deficient in that bad debts are related to all open receivables irrespective of the period in which the claims originated, with the result that uncollectible receivable losses may not be recognized in the period in which the revenue is recorded.

(iii) Aging-of-Receivables Method. The aging-of-receivables method is a variation of the percentage-of-receivables method. The basis for using this method is that the older the receivable, the less likely it is to be collected. The first step in aging receivables is classifying them as to time since (1) billing, (2) end of regular credit period granted, (3) payment due date, or (4) date of last payment. The amount of expected uncollectibles as determined by the aging process becomes the balance to be reflected in the allowance account. The allowance account is adjusted to bring the current balance into agreement with the required balance; the amount of the adjustment is charged to bad debt expense for the period.

If properly applied, the aging method, including use of appropriate supplemental information, provides the most accurate approximation of the expected net realizable value of receivables. Like the percentage-of-receivables method, however, the aging method may fail to recognize bad debt expenses in the period in which they arise. In the aging process, bad debts are related to impairment-of-asset values irrespective of the time of the sales activity. Receivables resulting from the most recent sales, for example, may be regarded as fully collectible in the aging process, only to prove uncollectible in the subsequent period. The aging method can be costly and time consuming when many accounts are involved, although computerized receivables systems have greatly reduced the costs and time required.

(f) WARRANTIES AND GUARANTEES. According to ASC 460-20, *Revenue Recognition: Services,* a warranty is:

> A guarantee for which the underlying is related to the performance (regarding function, not price) of nonfinancial assets that are owned by the guaranteed party. The obligation may be incurred in connection with the sale of goods or services; if so, it may require further performance by the seller after the sale has taken place.

As a result of the uncertain nature of the claims that may be made under warranties, ASC 460-10-25-5 requires that warranty obligations be treated as a contingency. Therefore, losses from warranty obligations must be accrued when the conditions in ASC 450-20-25-2 are met. Those conditions require accrual when it is (1) probable that an asset has been impaired or liability incurred at the date of the financial statements and (2) the amount of the loss can be reasonably estimated. The first accrual condition is met if it is probable that customers will make claims under warranties related to either goods or services that have been sold. The second may be satisfied based on either the experience of the entity or reference to the experience of other entities in the same business. If an enterprise cannot reasonably estimate the amount of the loss, accrual is precluded.

Accounting for separately priced extended warranty and product maintenance contracts is discussed in Subsection 12.4(a)(viii).

(g) OBLIGATIONS RELATED TO PRODUCT DEFECTS.   Obligations, other than warranty obligations, may arise due to injury or damage caused by products or services that have been sold. Such obligations are likely to meet the definition of a loss contingency provided in ASC 450, *Contingencies:* "An existing condition, situation, or set of circumstances involving uncertainty as to possible loss to an entity that will ultimately be resolved when one or more future events occur or fail to occur." The treatment of such a contingency will depend on the probability of the adverse event occurring and whether the loss can be reasonably estimated. ASC 450-20-25 requires accrual if both those criteria are met and the underlying causal event happened before the balance sheet date. ASC 450-20-30-1 provides additional guidance if only a range of loss can be determined.

12.6 ANCILLARY REVENUE

(a) DIVIDENDS.   Generally, investors in equity securities classified as trading or available for sale report cash dividends and dividends paid in property of the payor corporation as "other income" unless the dividends are a major source of income to the recipient; then they are classified as operating revenue. Dividends received in property of the payor corporation are recorded as revenue in amounts equivalent to the fair market value of the property (ASC 845-10-30). The date an investor becomes entitled to receive a dividend is the accepted time for recognizing it as revenue. In practice, organizations often record the revenue when the cash or property is actually received.

As indicated by ASC 505-20-30-7, *Equity: Stock Dividends and Stock Splits,* stock dividends consisting of shares received on holdings of the same class of stock do not represent income to the recipient because the "shareholder's interest in the corporation remains unchanged . . . except as to the number of share units constituting such interest."

Liquidating dividends do not normally result in income until their cumulative total exceeds the recipient's cost of the investment to which they apply.

(b) INTEREST.   Interest generally is classified as "other income," unless, as in financial institutions, it is a major source of income; then it is classified as operating revenue. Interest on obligations of debtors generally should be recorded as it accrues. If collectibility of interest is doubtful, the recognition of interest should be postponed until the interest is received or its collection becomes reasonably certain.

Interest income on long-term investments purchased at a premium is subject to reduction by the amount of the amortization of the premium from the date of purchase to the earliest call date or maturity. The amount of discount on investments purchased at less than face value should be similarly amortized and included in income. If collection of the principal amount of the investment is uncertain, the discount should not be amortized.

(c) PROFITS ON SALES OF MISCELLANEOUS ASSETS.   Profits on sales of miscellaneous assets—those not regularly and customarily offered for sale in the normal conduct of the business—are usually classified as "other income." Such profits include gains and losses on sales of securities, real estate, machinery and equipment, automobiles and trucks, furniture and fixtures, and sundry salvaged materials. Profits on those sales generally are recorded "net"; that is, the selling price is not recorded as revenue and the carrying value of the asset sold is not shown as expense.

A derivative should be reported as either an asset or a liability at fair value. ASC 815, *Derivatives and Hedging,* specifies that any gains or losses, whether realized or unrealized, on derivative instruments held for trading purposes should be shown net when recognized in the income statement (815-10-45-9). Mark-to-market accounting is precluded for energy trading contracts that are not derivatives (ASC 932-330-35-1, *Extractive Activities—Oil and Gas: Inventory*).

(d) RENTS.   Rents receivable should be recorded as revenue in the accounting period during which they accrue. Rents received in advance should be deferred and included in revenue in the period to which they apply.

(e) ROYALTIES.   *Royalties* may be broadly defined as a compensation or a portion of the proceeds paid to an owner for the right to use the owner's property. The payment may be in the form of a share in kind of the product or the right that is exploited or in the form of monetary compensation at agreed rates based on units produced, used, or sold or the equivalent of their market value. The types of property for which royalties may be paid include forests, mineral and oil lands, copyrights, patents, processes, and equipment.

Royalties should be recognized as revenue as they accrue. Periodic royalty reports from the user of the property customarily form the basis for determining the amount to be accrued. Amounts collected as advance royalties or as minimum periodic royalties should be deferred to the extent that such collections may be applied in settlement of royalties accruing in a period subsequent to the period of receipt.

(f) BY-PRODUCT, JOINT PRODUCT, AND SCRAP SALES.   Horngren, Datar and Rajan state:

> Industries abound in which a production process simultaneously yields two or more products, either at the splitoff point or after further processing . . . . [N]o individual product can be produced without the accompanying products appearing . . . .
>
> When a joint production process yields one product with a high total sales value, compared with total sales values of other products of the process, that product is called a main product. When a joint production process yields two or more products with high total sales values compared with the total sales values of other products, if any, those products are called joint products. The products of a joint production process that have low total sales values compared with the total sales value of the main product or of joint products are called byproducts.
>
> Distinctions among main products, joint products, and byproducts are not so definite in practice . . . . Moreover, the classification of products—main, joint, or byproduct—can change over time . . . . In practice, it is important to understand how a specific company chooses to classify its products.[42]

Joint product sales normally are recorded in the same manner as the seller's principal sources of revenue. The major accounting problem in this connection is determining the proportionate share of total product costs to be assigned to joint products. The value of by-products and scrap may be treated either as a reduction of cost or as revenue (or other income), either at the time of production or at the time of sale.

(g) SHIPPING AND HANDLING FEES.   Fees billed to customers in sales transactions for shipping and handling and related costs should be reported as revenue rather than netted against the costs incurred. According to ASC 605-45-45-21, *Revenue Recognition: Shipping and Handling Fees and Costs,* that is appropriate whether amounts billed to customers equal the actual shipping and

---

[42] C. T. Horngren, S. M. Datar, and M. Rajan, *Cost Accounting: A Managerial Emphasis,* 14th ed. (Englewood Cliffs, NJ: Prentice-Hall, 2012).

handling costs incurred or the amounts billed exceed those costs. Although the SEC Staff prefers shipping and handling costs to be reported as part of cost of sales, they may be included in some other income statement classification as long as the total amount of those costs, if material, and the line item in which they are included are disclosed. ASC 605-45-45-21 does not specify what costs are to be considered "shipping and handling" and notes that the components may differ among entities. ASC 605-45-50-2 instructs that shipping and handling costs may be reported in cost of sales or separately on other lines in the income statement. If they are not included in cost of sales, disclosure is required in accordance with ASC 235, *Notes to Financial Statements.*

(h) LOAN GUARANTEES. Entities may guarantee other entities' loans in order to improve those other entities' ability to borrow, or the terms under which those other entities can borrow, from third parties. ASC 605-20-25-9, *Revenue Recognition: Fees for Guaranteeing a Loan,* requires entities to recognize fee revenue from providing those guarantees, and any direct costs associated with the guarantees, over the period during which the guarantees apply. If, however, a fee is in substance a "lending commitment" as defined in ASC 310-20-20, *Receivables: Nonrefundable Fees and Other Costs,* the guidance in ASC 310-20-25-11 through 25-14 applies.

ASC 460-10-50, *Guarantees: Disclosure,* requires entities to disclose in notes to their financial statements these six points of information about material financial guarantees:

1. The nature of the obligation guaranteed, including the approximate term and how the guarantee arose, among other information
2. Substantial information about the maximum amount at risk
3. The current carrying amount of the liability
4. The nature of any recourse provisions
5. The nature of any assets held as collateral or assets held by third parties that the guarantor can liquidate to recover all or a portion of the guaranteed amount
6. If estimable, the extent to which the proceeds from the liquidation of the assets noted in item 5 would cover the maximum amount at risk.

Financial guarantee contracts are considered derivatives under ASC 815 if the payment under the guarantee is based on changes in an underlying, such as the other party's creditworthiness. In conformity with ASC 815-10-30-1, those contracts would be reported at fair value; accounting for changes in fair value is discussed in ASC 815-10-35. ASC 815 does not apply, however, if the contracts "provide for payments to be made solely to reimburse the guaranteed party for failure of the debtor to satisfy its required payment obligations under a nonderivative contract" (ASC 815-10-15-58).

12.7 STATEMENT PRESENTATION

(a) INCOME STATEMENT AND REVENUE-RELATED DISCLOSURES. The income statement should disclose sales for the period, usually net of discounts, returns, and allowances.

Various authoritative pronouncements contain guidance on disclosures about revenue recognition policies and the impact of events and trends on revenue. In addition to the specific disclosures described in various sections of this chapter, this information should be disclosed:

- In providing information about its accounting policies for the reporting of revenue in conformity with ASC 235, a company should disclose:
  ○ Different policies for different kinds of revenue transactions, including barter sales
  ○ The policies for each element, such as product and service, of transactions with multiple elements
  ○ How each of multiple elements are determined and valued

- ○ Changes in estimated returns if material
- ○ The amount of revenue from sales of merchandise, services, and other products and the related costs for each (reported separately)
- ○ ASC 280-10-50, *Segment Reporting: Disclosure,* provides guidance regarding the disclosure of operating segment information in notes to the financial statements. If the chief operating decision maker reviews information about a portion of an entity, such as its Internet operations, separately from other portions, it may be considered a reportable operating segment. Reportable segment disclosures relating to revenue include types of goods and services from which revenues are derived, total revenues from external customers and from other operating segments of the entity, interest revenue, a reconciliation of total reportable segment revenue to total consolidated revenues, and a number of other items (as listed in ASC 280-10-50-21 through 50-31). For interim periods, revenues from external customers and intersegment revenues for each reportable segment are among the items that should be disclosed (see ASC 280-10-50-32 and 50-33).

- Amounts recovered under business interruption insurance claims typically include (1) gross margin that would have been earned if normal operations had not been suspended; (2) a portion of normal fixed costs incurred during the interruption period; and (3) other out-of-pocket costs incurred as a result of the interruption of business. ASC 225-30-45, *Income Statement: Business Interruption Insurance,* concludes that these recoveries could be shown in any section of the income statement as long as the classification is consistent with GAAP. For example, reporting a recovery as an extraordinary gain is acceptable only if the extraordinary item criteria in ASC 225-20, *Income Statement: Extraordinary and Unusual Items,* are satisfied. ASC 225-30 requires the disclosure of a description of the event causing the loss, the total amount of the recoveries included in the income statement, and the line item or items on the income statement in which the recoveries are reported. Companies should describe the types of multiple deliverable arrangements they have with customers, including provisions related to performance, refunds, terminations, and cancelations. Companies also should disclose the recognition policies they use for such arrangements (ASC 605-25).

The SEC Staff has suggested that this information about revenue be disclosed:

- In its management discussion and analysis (MD&A), a company should discuss unusual or infrequent transactions and known trends or uncertainties that have had or might reasonably be expected to have a favorable or unfavorable material effect on revenue, operating income, or net income and the relationship between revenue and the costs of the revenue. The company should evaluate changes in revenue in terms of volume and price changes and disclose the reasons and factors contributing to the changes. Examples of transactions or events that should be disclosed in the MD&A (SAB No. 114, Topic 10.B.1, incorporated at ASC 605-10-S99) include:
  - ○ Late-period shipments that significantly reduce backlog and might reasonably be expected to result in lower shipments and revenue in the next period
  - ○ Granting of extended payment terms and the effect on liquidity and capital resources (the fair value of trade receivables, if it does not approximate the reported amount, should be disclosed in the notes)
  - ○ Changing trends in shipments to and sales from a sales channel or separate class of buyer that could be expected to significantly affect future sales or sales returns
  - ○ Increasing trends toward different classes of buyer, such as to a revenue distribution channel that has a lower gross profit margin or increasing service revenue with higher profit margins

- ○ Seasonal trends or variations in revenue
- ○ Gains or losses from the sales of assets
- Other disclosures as appropriate,[43] such as:
  - ○ Disaggregated product and service information:
  - ○ Product and service revenues (and costs of revenues) separately on the face of the income statement
  - ○ Separate revenues of each major product or service within segment data
  - ○ Description of major revenue-generating products or services
  - ○ For major contracts or groups of similar contracts, descriptions of essential terms, including payment terms and unusual provisions or conditions
  - ○ Details concerning when revenue is recognized, such as:
    - At delivery (indicate whether terms are customarily FOB shipping point or FOB destination)
    - At completion of service
    - At commencement of service
    - Ratably over service period
    - At satisfaction of a significant condition of sale and a description of that condition
    - After customer acceptance
    - After testing of product sold
    - After completion of all terms of contract
    - Over performance period based on progress toward completion
    - At delivery of separate elements in multi-element arrangement
  - ○ If revenue is recognized over the service period based on progress toward completion, or based on separate contract elements or milestones:
    - How the period's revenue is measured
    - How progress is measured—for example, cost to cost, time and materials, units of delivery, units of work performed
    - Types of contract payment milestones, with an explanation of how they relate to substantive performance and revenue recognition events
  - ○ Description of whether contracts with a single counterparty are combined or bifurcated
  - ○ Identification of contract elements permitting separate revenue recognition and a description of how they are distinguished
  - ○ How contract revenue is allocated among elements
  - ○ Whether the relative fair value or residual method is used to allocate elements
  - ○ Whether fair values are based on vendor specific evidence or by other means
  - ○ Material assumptions, estimates, and uncertainties, including:
  - ○ Existing contingencies such as rights of return, conditions of acceptance, warranties, and price protection
  - ○ How those contingencies are accounted for
  - ○ Significant assumptions, material changes, and reasonably likely uncertainties
  - ○ Disclosures and conditions as specified by SAB No. 114 for companies that recognize refundable revenues by analogy to ASC 605-15, *Revenue Recognition: Products.*

---

[43] SEC Division of Corporate Finance, *Current Accounting and Disclosure Issues,* December 1, 2005, Section II.F.3.

The SEC Staff has emphasized that, in order to ensure fair presentation, income statement disclosures of revenues should be classified based on the nature of the underlying events. For example, reported revenues should be reported net of consideration given to customers or resellers and should not include:

1. Amounts intended to offset costs incurred
2. Equity in investees' income
3. Gains or losses from fixed asset or investment sales
4. Other income

The Staff expects companies to clarify and expand their disclosures in SEC filings regarding the accounting policies used for each material revenue-generating activity the company undertakes.[44]

(b) BALANCE SHEET DISCLOSURES.   The basis for presentation of receivables in the balance sheet is the expected time of collection. Receivables expected to be collected within the next operating cycle or fiscal year, whichever is longer, are ordinarily classified as current assets. Several exceptions allowed by ASC 310 are discussed next. Specialized reporting requirements also are discussed.

Kieso, Weygandt, and Warfield summarize the general rules for statement presentation in the receivables section of the balance sheet:

1. Segregate the different types of receivables that an enterprise possesses, if material.
2. Ensure that the valuation accounts are appropriately offset against the proper receivable accounts.
3. Determine that receivables classified in the current assets section will be converted into cash within the year or the operating cycle, whichever is longer.
4. Disclose any loss contingencies that exist on the receivables.
5. Disclose any receivables designated or pledged as collateral.
6. Disclose all significant concentrations of credit risk arising from receivables.[45]

(i) Presentation of Single-Payment Accounts Receivable.   Ordinarily accounts receivable are classified in the balance sheet as *current assets*. Amounts that will not be collected until the next operating cycle or fiscal year, however, should be shown as noncurrent. In the interest of full disclosure, it is considered desirable to limit the accounts receivable designation to current claims attaching to trade customers and to identify separately other major types of receivables, such as amounts due from officers and employees, prepayments, and stock subscriptions receivable.

(ii) Presentation of Installment Receivables.   ASC 310-10-45, *Receivables: Other Presentation Matters,* specifically provides for the inclusion within *current assets* of "installment or deferred accounts and notes receivable if they conform generally to normal trade practices and terms within the business." Thus, installment receivables may be classified as current regardless of the length of the collection period. Designation of annual maturity dates by separate listing of contracts receivable or by parenthetical or note disclosure is recommended to enable readers to ascertain the current position.

Conflicting opinions exist as to the proper classification of the deferred gross profit account related to installment receivables. The FASB concludes[46] that deferred gross profit conceptually should be treated as an asset valuation account. Because deferred gross profit is part of revenue from installment sales not yet realized, the related receivable will be overstated unless deferred gross profit is deducted. Another alternative is to report deferred gross profit as unearned revenue

---

[44] Ibid.

[45] Kieso, Weygandt, and Warfield, *Intermediate Accounting,* p. 391.

[46] SFAC No. 6, par. 234.

in the liability section. This alternative has been criticized, however, because the credit is not an obligation to an outsider.

In preparing an income statement, installment sales, cost of installment sales, and realized gross profit may be shown in the statement, or only the realized gross profit may be reported, with installment sales and cost of sales reflected in a separate supporting schedule. ASC 976-605-55, *Revenue Recognition: Real Estate—Retail Land,* illustrates the financial statement presentation when the installment method is used for retail land sales. Also see Section 12.4(b) of this chapter.

(iii) Interest on Receivables.   Notes receivable arise in many situations in which the legal form of the note specifies an interest rate (including lack of an interest rate) that varies from prevailing interest rates. ASC 835-30, *Interest: Imputation of Interest,* requires that, in these situations, the note receivable be recorded at its present value and that interest be imputed at an appropriate rate. The resulting discount or premium is amortized over the life of the note. ASC 835-30-55-3 exempts these seven receivables:

1. Receivables arising from transactions with customers in the normal course of business which are due in customary trade terms not exceeding approximately one year
2. Receivables that will be applied to the purchase price of other property, goods, or services rather than being repaid
3. Security deposits, retainages, or other amounts intended to provide security to a party to an agreement
4. Receivables from the customary cash lending activities of financial institutions
5. Receivables where interest rates are affected by the tax attributes or legal restrictions prescribed by a governmental agency
6. Receivables from a parent, subsidiary, or another firm with a common parent
7. Obligations assumed in connection with the sale of property, goods, or services, such as product warranties, to which present value measurement techniques are applied

12.8 SOURCES AND SUGGESTED REFERENCES

American Institute of Certified Public Accountants. APB Opinion No. 10, *Omnibus Opinion—1966*. New York: Author, 1966.

_____. APB Opinion No. 29, *Accounting for Nonmonetary Transactions*. New York: Author, 1973.

_____. APB Statement No. 4, *Basic Concepts and Accounting Principles Underlying Financial Statements of Business Enterprises*. New York: Author, 1970.

_____. Civil Aeronautics Subcommittee. Industry Audit Guide, *Airlines*. New York: Author, 2010.

_____. Committee on Accounting Procedure. Accounting Research Bulletin No. 43, *Restatement and Revision of Accounting Research Bulletins*. New York: Author, 1953.

_____. Construction Contractors Guide Committee. Audit and Accounting Guide, *Construction Contractors and Real Estate Ventures*. New York: Author, 2010.

_____. Gaming Industry Special Committee. Audit and Accounting Guide, *Gaming*. New York: Author, 2010.

_____. Government Contractors Guide Special Committee, Audit and Accounting Guide, *Government Auditing Standards and Circular A-133 Audits*. New York: Author, 2010.

_____. Statement of Position 97-2, *Software Revenue Recognition*. New York: AICPA, 1997.

_____. Stockbrokerage and Investment Banking Committee. Audit and Accounting Guide, *Brokers and Dealers in Securities*. New York: Author, 2010.

_____. Technical Practice Aids, Accounting and Auditing Publications Technical Questions and Answers (TIS Section 5100), *Revenue Recognition*. New York: AICPA, 2002.

Accounting Standards Board (U.K.). Amendment to Financial Reporting Standard No. 5, Application Note G, *Reporting the Substance of Transactions: Revenue Recognition*. London: Author, 2003.

———. Discussion Paper, *Revenue Recognition*. London: Author, July 2001.

American Accounting Association. Committee on Accounting Concepts and Standards, *Accounting and Reporting Standards for Corporate Financial Statements (1957 Revision*. Sarasota, FL: Author, 1957.

———. Concepts and Standards Research Committee on the Realization Concept, "The Realization Concept," *Accounting Review*, April 1965.

Canning, J. B. *The Economics of Accounting*. New York: Ronald Press, 1929.

Committee of Sponsoring Organizations of the Treadway Commission. *Fraudulent Financial Reporting: 1987–1997. An Analysis of U.S. Public Companies*. New York: Author, March 1999.

Dell, Inc. Form 8-K Non-Reliance on Previously Issued Financial Statements for the event date August 13, 2007.

Edwards, E. O., and P. W. Bell. *The Theory and Measurement of Business Income*. Berkeley: University of California Press, 1965.

Financial Accounting Standards Board. *Accounting Standards Codification*. Norwalk, CT: Author, 2009.

———. Discussion Memorandum, *An Analysis of Issues Related to Conceptual Framework for Financial Accounting and Reporting: Elements of Financial Statements and Their Measurement*. Norwalk, CT: Author, 1976.

———. Exposure Draft of Accounting Standards Update No. 1820-100, *Revenue Recognition (Topic 605): Revenue from Contracts with Customers*. Norwalk, CT: Author, June 2010.

———. Invitation to Comment, *Accounting for Certain Service Transactions*. Norwalk, CT: Author, 1978.

———. Emerging Issues Task Force, Issue No. 91-9, *Revenue and Expense Recognition for Freight Services in Process*. Norwalk, CT: Author, 1992.

———. Issue No. 99-V, *Remaining Issues from the SEC's October 18, 1999 Letter to the EITF*. Norwalk, CT: Author, 2002.

———. Issue No. 00-21, *Revenue Arrangements with Multiple Deliverables*. Norwalk, CT: Author, 2002.

———. "Project Updates—Revenue Recognition—Joint Project of the FASB and IASB." Norwalk, CT: Author, September 21, 2011.

———. Statement of Financial Accounting Concepts No. 1, *Objectives of Financial Reporting by Business Enterprises*. Norwalk, CT: Author, 1978.

———. Statement of Financial Accounting Concepts No. 2, *Qualitative Characteristics of Accounting Information*. Norwalk, CT: Author, 1980.

———. Statement of Financial Accounting Concepts No. 5, *Recognition and Measurement in Financial Statements of Business Enterprises*. Norwalk, CT: Author, 1984.

———. Statement of Financial Accounting Concepts No. 6, *Elements of Financial Statements*. Norwalk, CT: Author, 1985.

———. Statement of Financial Accounting Standards No. 13, *Accounting for Leases*. Norwalk, CT: Author, 1977.

———. Statement of Financial Accounting Standards No. 48, *Revenue Recognition When Right of Return Exists*. Norwalk, CT: Author, 1981.

———. Statement of Financial Accounting Standards No. 52, *Foreign Currency Translation*. Norwalk, CT: Author, 1981.

———. Statement of Financial Accounting Standards No. 121, *Accounting for the Impairment of Long-Lived Assets and for Long-Lived Assets to Be Disposed Of*. Norwalk, CT: Author, 995.

———. Statement of Financial Accounting Standards No. 133, *Accounting for Derivative Instruments and Hedging Activities*. Norwalk, CT: Author, 1998.

———. Statement of Financial Accounting Standards No. 138, *Accounting for Certain Derivative Instruments and Certain Hedging Activities; An Amendment of FASB Statement No. 133*. Norwalk, CT: Author, 2000.

Graciano, G. "Revenue Recognition: A Perennial Problem," *Financial Executive Magazine*, July 14, 2005.

Green Mountain Coffee Roasters, Inc. Form 8-K Non-Reliance on Previously Issued Financial Statements for the event date November 15, 2010.

Hendriksen, E. S., and M. F. van Breda. *Accounting Theory*, 5th ed. Homewood, IL: Irwin, 1992.

Horngren, C. T. "How Should We Interpret the Realization Concept?" *Accounting Review* (April 1965).

Horngren, C.T., S. M. Datar, and M. Rajan. *Cost Accounting: A Managerial Emphasis*, 14th ed. Englewood Cliffs, NJ: Prentice-Hall, 2012.

International Accounting Standards Committee. International Accounting Standard No. 18, *Revenue*. London: Author, 1993 (amended 1998 and 2009).

Iyengar, P. "Application Development in the Cloud: Strategies and Tactics for a New Generation," Gartner, Inc. (November 2009).

Jaenicke, H. R. *Survey of Present Practices in Recognizing Revenues, Expenses, Gains, and Losses*. Norwalk, CT: FASB, January 1981.

Kieso, D. E., J. J. Weygandt, and T. D. Warfield. *Intermediate Accounting*, 14th ed. Hoboken, NJ: John Wiley & Sons, 2011.

Mallor, J. P., A. J. Barnes, T. Bowers, M. J. Phillips, and A. W. Langvardt. *Business Law and the Regulatory Environment: Concepts and Cases*, 11th ed. Chicago: Irwin McGraw-Hill, 2001.

May, G. O., *Financial Accounting: A Distillation of Experience*. New York: Macmillan 1943.

Meyers, J. H. "The Critical Event and the Recognition of Net Profit," *Accounting Review* (October 1959).

O'Reilly, V. M., M. B. Hirsch, P. L. Defliese, and H. R. Jaenicke. *Montgomery's Auditing*, 11 ed. New York: John Wiley & Sons, 1990.

Overstock.com, Inc. Form 8-K Non-Reliance on Previously Issued Financial Statements or a Related Audit Report of Completed Interim Review for the event date January 29, 2010.

Paton, W. A., and A. C. Littleton. *An Introduction to Corporate Accounting Standards*. Sarasota, FL: AAA, 1940.

Paton, W. A., and W. A. Paton Jr., *Corporation Accounts and Statements*. New York: Macmillan, 1955.

Pulliam, S., and R. Blumenstein. "SEC Broadens Investigation into Revenue-Boosting Tricks," *Wall Street Journal*, May 16, 2002.

Securities and Exchange Commission. Accounting and Auditing Enforcement Release No. 1864, *SEC and United States Attorney Charge Former Homestore Executives with Scheme to Inflate Advertising Revenue*. Washington, DC: Author, September 18, 2003.

——. Accounting and Auditing Enforcement Release No. 1874, *SEC and Justice Department Bring Civil and Criminal Actions Charging Former CFO of Company that Engaged in Fraudulent Barter Deals with Homestore*. Washington, DC: Author, September 26, 2003.

——. Accounting and Auditing Enforcement Release No. 2045, *Gemstar-TV Guide International Agrees to Settle SEC Enforcement Action Charging the Company with Overstating Its Revenues*. Washington, DC: Author, June 21, 2004.

——. Accounting and Auditing Enforcement Release No. 2125, *Order Instituting Public Administrative Proceedings Pursuant to Rule 102(E) of the Commission's Rules of Practice, Making Findings, and Imposing Remedial Sanctions in the Matter of KPMG LLP, Bryan E. Palbaum, CPA, John M. Wong, CPA, Kenneth B. Janeski, CPA, David A. Hori, CPA*. Washington, DC: Author, October 20, 2004.

——. Accounting and Auditing Enforcement Release No. 3137, *SEC Charges Diebold and Former Financial Executives with Accounting Fraud*. Washington, DC: Author, June 2, 2010.

——. Accounting and Auditing Enforcement Release No. 3171, *Order Instituting Public Administrative Proceedings Pursuant to Section 4C of the Securities Exchange Act of 1934 and Rule 102(e) of the Commission's Rules of Practice, In the Matter of Dohan & Company CPAs, Steven H. Dohan, CPA, Nancy L. Brown, CPA and Erez Bahar*, Chartered Accountant *(CA)*. Washington, DC: Author, August 9, 2010.

——. Accounting Series Release No. 95, *Accounting for Real Estate Transactions Where Circumstances Indicate That Profits Were Not Earned at the Time the Transactions Were Recorded*. Washington, DC: Author, 1972.

——. Accounting and Auditing Enforcement Release No. 3217, *SEC Charges Vitesse Semiconductor Corporation and Four Former Vitesse Executives in Revenue Recognition and Options Backdating Schemes*. Washington, DC: SEC, December 10, 2010.

——. Accounting and Auditing Enforcement Release No. 3311, *Judgement of Permanent Injunction and Other Relief Entered Against Defendant Karlheinz Redekopp and Order Instituting Administrative Proceedings, Making Findings and Imposing Sanctions*. Washington, DC: Author, August 4, 2011.

——. Division of Corporation Finance. *Current Accounting and Disclosure Issues*. Washington, DC: Author, December 1, 2005.

——. Exchange Act Release No. 17878, "Order Instituting Proceedings and Opinion and Order Pursuant to Rule 2(e) of the Commission's Rules of Practice *In the Matter of Arthur Andersen & Co.*" Washington, DC: Author, 1981.

_____. Staff Accounting Bulletin No. 101, *Revenue Recognition in Financial Statements*. Washington, DC: Author, 1999.

_____. Staff Accounting Bulletin No. 101, *Revenue Recognition in Financial Statements—Frequently Asked Questions and Answers*. Washington, DC: Author, October 2000.

Staubus, G. J. *Making Accounting Decisions*. Houston: Scholars Book Co., 1977.

Vatter, W. J. *The Fund Theory of Accounting and Its Implications for Financial Reports*. Chicago: University of Chicago Press, 1947.

Windal, F. W. "The Accounting Concept of Realization," *Accounting Review* (April 1961).

CHAPTER 13

INVENTORY

Richard R. Jones, CPA
Ernst & Young LLP

Anna T. Szurgot, CPA
Ernst & Young LLP

13.1 OVERVIEW

Accounting for inventory has been guided more by practice than by pronouncement. As advances in manufacturing processes have occurred, accounting practices have evolved to identify the applicable costs to be allocated to inventory. Authoritative accounting literature related to inventory accounting and financial reporting is not extensive. The accounting profession has made it clear that examining individual facts and circumstances is important when valuing inventory and applying the established standards.

Historical cost is the normal starting point to record inventory as an asset. In determining inventory cost, a cost flow assumption must be selected. Alternate valuation methods that are exceptions to the historical cost convention are used for certain specialized types of inventory (e.g., sales price less cost of disposal for precious metals if certain criteria are met, and net realizable value for trade-in inventory). The write-down of inventory to amounts below cost may be necessary due to factors such as damage or changing market conditions.

This chapter addresses inventory costing in greater detail by identifying the pertinent guidance in the authoritative accounting literature and by citing examples that illustrate the practical application of the fundamental principles. The chapter also explains the various types of inventory and practical ways to determine inventory quantities. Finally, the chapter explores internal control considerations.

13.2 ESSENTIAL INVENTORY CONCEPTS

(a) INVENTORY AS AN ASSET.   Inventory generally is acquired or produced for subsequent exchange. This utility or service potential justifies the classification of inventory as an asset of the enterprise that controls it. Normally, inventory is converted into cash or other assets during the operating cycle of the business. In fact, this process is what establishes the operating cycle. As a result, inventory typically is classified as a current asset for purposes of preparing a classified balance sheet.

(b) DEFINITION OF INVENTORY.   The primary authoritative guidance addressing financial reporting for inventory is Accounting Standard Codification (ASC) 330, *Inventory*. It defines *inventory* as:

> The aggregate of those items of tangible personal property that have any of the following characteristics: (a) held for sale in the ordinary course of business, (b) in process of production for such sale, or (c) to be currently consumed in the production of goods or services to be available for sale.

The definition elaborates that the trading merchandise of a retailer or wholesaler—and the finished goods, work in process, and raw materials of a manufacturer—constitutes inventory and specifically excludes from inventory long-term assets subject to depreciation accounting. Fixed assets such as buildings and equipment provide benefits that generally extend beyond the operating cycle and, therefore, are classified as noncurrent assets. The definition notes that such assets should not be classified as inventory even if they are retired and held for sale.

(c) OBJECTIVES OF ACCOUNTING FOR INVENTORY. The sale of inventory to customers is often the most significant component of revenue for a business enterprise. Matching inventory costs with the revenues received from the sale of the goods in order to determine periodic income is the major objective of inventory accounting. Incurred inventory costs that have not been charged against operations represent the carrying amount of inventory on the balance sheet. The costs allocated to goods on hand should not, however, exceed the utility of those goods. In other words, the recorded inventory balance should not exceed the total revenues less selling costs that will result when those goods are sold.

The methods used to determine and measure the flow of inventory costs should be consistent from period to period. The methods should be objective so that comparable results are produced by similar transactions, to allow for independent verification and to prevent manipulation of results of operations. Adequate disclosure should be made regarding the nature of the inventory and the basis on which it is stated.

13.3 TYPES OF INVENTORY

(a) RETAIL/WHOLESALE. Wholesalers and retailers typically acquire merchandise that is ready for resale to customers. Acquisition cost becomes the basis for carrying the inventory until it is sold.

(b) MANUFACTURING. In a manufacturing operation, a production process creates goods for sale to customers or for use in other operations. Manufacturing inventories often are categorized by stage of completion.

(i) Raw Materials. Goods to be incorporated into a product or used in the production process that have not yet entered the process are referred to as *raw materials inventory*. The output from one process can become the raw material for another process (e.g., subassemblies).

(ii) Work in Process. Goods typically are classified as work in process inventory as soon as they are drawn from raw materials stock and enter the manufacturing process.

(iii) Finished Goods. Products that are complete and ready for sale are considered finished goods inventory.

(iv) Supplies. Materials necessary for the manufacturing operation but not a significant component of the final product are known as *supplies inventory*. For example, small incidental screws may be considered supplies inventory, or oil used to lubricate a grinding machine may be considered supplies inventory. ASC 330 specifically mentions manufacturing supplies as a type of inventory and notes that the fact that a small portion of the supplies may be used for purposes other than production does not require separate classification.

(c) CONSIGNMENT. Arrangements for marketing, storage, distribution, and finishing of a company's products can result in goods being held by a party other than the owner. The consignee (party holding the goods) generally is precluded from recording the inventory because legal title is retained by the consignor and no exchange has taken place. The consignment inventory balance frequently is combined with the work in process or finished goods inventory shown on the consignor's financial statements. Examples include inventories held for sale in a retail store that have been consigned by the manufacturer, and components held by an outside machine shop to be used in a larger product by the consignor.

(d) TRADE-IN. Some companies obtain goods accepted from customers in connection with sales of other products. These goods may or may not be similar to the items sold or other products of the seller. An example is a cell phone accepted in trade by a wireless company when upgrading customer equipment. Trade-in inventory should be valued at net realizable value, defined as estimated selling price less costs of disposal. The discount or allowance deducted from the list price of the goods sold is not an appropriate value to assign to the trade-in inventory, because the discount often pertains to marketing strategy and other factors not related to the trade-in items.

(e) REPOSSESSED.   In connection with its collection efforts, a company may repossess its product from a customer. Companies that provide consumer financing often deal with repossessed inventory. The physical condition of the property may vary widely and will affect the company's decision regarding disposition (e.g., rework, offer for sale at a discount, scrap). Repossessed inventory should be recorded at the lower of the outstanding balance of the note receivable (i.e., cost) or the asset's replacement cost (i.e., cost to purchase or reproduce). Solely considering the outstanding balance of the receivable from the customer is not appropriate, because this approach does not consider the condition and utility of the repossessed item. If replacement cost cannot realistically be determined, net realizable value should be used.

(f) CONTRACT PRODUCTION.   A company may enter into a contract under which the customer provides specifications for producing goods, constructing facilities, or providing services.

(g) PRODUCTS MATURING IN MORE THAN ONE YEAR.   Certain products—such as tobacco, spirits, livestock, and forest products—are held for an extended period of time until they are mature for sale or inclusion in a finished product. Recognized trade practice is to classify such inventory items as current assets despite the required aging process.

(h) SPARE PARTS.   To service their customers, many companies (particularly equipment dealers and manufacturers) maintain a supply of spare parts for their products. Also, transportation companies hold spare parts to allow their fleets to operate continuously. If spare parts are not more appropriately classified as property, plant and equipment, typically they will be classified as inventory as they are either held for sale or will be consumed in the production of a good or service for sale.

(i) Miscellaneous.   Many other types of products may be classified as inventory for financial reporting purposes. Examples include by-products (secondary products that result from the manufacturing process, particularly in the chemicals and the oil and gas industries), reusable items (such as beverage containers), and extractive products.

13.4   DETERMINING PHYSICAL QUANTITIES

(a) INTRODUCTION.   An important aspect of inventory accounting is to establish quantities. This section discusses the two basic methods used to determine the quantities of goods on hand, the periodic system and the perpetual system. In practice, hybrid methods often are used. Also, a company may use a periodic system for certain types of inventories and a perpetual system for others. For example, a steel company may use a perpetual system for work in process and for finished steel products but a periodic system for raw, bulk commodities such as iron ore.

A periodic system employs physical counts to determine physical quantities on hand. A perpetual system maintains detailed records to track quantities based on additions and usage. A perpetual system provides greater internal accounting control because it allows the user to identify and investigate differences between actual quantities on hand and the amounts the records indicate. The additional recordkeeping requirements of a perpetual system generally are justified by the additional control given over high-value and off-site inventories. Further, perpetual systems provide improved management information for individual products that can enhance sales, marketing, and operation decisions. The greater availability and variety of automated systems have led to a proliferation of perpetual inventory systems in recent years.

As discussed at Section 13.5(g), companies may use less sophisticated methods to determine inventory quantities at interim dates, compared to those used in connection with the year-end inventory valuation.

(b) PERIODIC SYSTEM.   The most direct means of determining the physical quantity of inventory on hand is to count it. An inventory system that establishes quantities on the basis of recurring counts is known as a *periodic system*. After establishing quantities on hand, each unit is multiplied by its unit cost to determine its inventory value. Cost of sales is a residual amount obtained by subtracting the ending inventory amount from the cost of goods available for sale:

$$
\begin{array}{l}
\text{Beginning Inventory} \\
+\,\text{Purchases and Costs of Production} \\
\hline
\text{Goods Available for Sale} \\
-\,\text{Ending Inventory} \\
\hline
\text{Cost of Sales} \\
\hline
\end{array}
$$

A periodic system is most likely to be used by a small company or for a department with low-value items that do not warrant more elaborate control procedures. A periodic system also is used for inventories for which reliable usage data cannot practicably be generated (e.g., certain supplies and extractive materials).

(i) Physical Count Procedures.   Written instructions that describe the procedures to be performed by the individuals participating in the count are an important part of the effort and should be prepared and distributed well in advance of the physical inventory date.

The instructions should cover each phase of the procedures and address:

1. Names of persons drafting and approving the instructions
2. Dates and times of inventory taking
3. Names of persons responsible for supervising inventory taking
4. Plans for arranging and segregating inventory, including precautions taken to clear work in process to cutoff points
5. Provisions for control of receiving and shipping during the inventory-taking period and, if production is not shut down, the plans for handling inventory movements
6. Instructions for recording the description of inventory items and how quantities are to be determined (e.g., count, weight, or other measurement)
7. Instructions for identifying obsolete, damaged, and slow-moving items
8. Instructions for the use of inventory tags or count sheets (including their distribution, collection, and control)
9. Plans for determining quantities at outside locations
10. Instructions for review and approval of inventory by department heads or other supervisory personnel
11. Method for transcribing original counts to the final inventory sheets or summaries

Physical inventory count teams should be familiar with the inventory items. The counts should be checked, or recounts should be performed, by persons other than those making the original counts.

(ii) Cutoff.   The process to ensure that transactions are recorded in the proper accounting period is known as *cutoff*. For inventory, the general rule is that all items owned by the entity as of the inventory date should be included, regardless of location. For goods in transit, if they are shipped free on board (FOB) destination, ownership does not pass from the seller to the purchaser until the purchaser receives the goods from the common carrier. For goods shipped FOB shipping point, title passes from the seller to the purchaser once the seller turns the goods over to the common carrier.

In practice, purchases are recorded upon receipt, based on the date indicated on the receiving report. Inventory generally is relieved for items sold as of the date of shipment. In this manner, the accounting entries to record the purchase and sale of inventory correspond to the physical movement of the goods at the company. Assuming an accurate physical count of goods on hand is achieved, companies effectively eliminate cutoff errors by verifying that purchases have been recorded in the period of receipt and sales have been recorded in the period of shipment. This usually is accomplished by matching accounts payable invoices to receiving reports, and matching sales invoices to shipping documents. The procedure just described guarantees that both sides of the accounting entry are recorded in the same period. The inventory amount is recorded through the physical count and valuation, whereas the accounts payable/cost of sales amount is recorded through the matching procedure. This method implies all purchases are FOB destination and all sales are FOB shipping point. Although this is unlikely to be the case, the approach works in practice because goods in transit are typically not significant, and the procedure is applied consistently. Companies that have a significant volume of goods in transit and varying terms regarding transfer of ownership should scrutinize the inventory cutoff calculations. For example, a FOB destination sale that was in transit at period end would be recorded prematurely using the method described above. As a result, pretax income would be overstated by the gross margin on the sale, accounts receivable would be overstated, and inventory would be understated. Such a situation normally is considered more of a revenue recognition issue (discussed in Chapter 12) than an inventory issue. The effect of a similar situation for a purchase would merely affect the balance sheet, because there is no margin involved for the buyer. In situations where a strict legal determination of ownership is impractical or other cutoff questions arise, the terms of the sales agreement, the intent of the parties involved, industry practices, and other factors should be considered.

Achieving an accurate cutoff is enhanced by controlling the shipping, receiving, and transfer activity during the physical count. Also, source documents (e.g., receiving reports, shipping reports, bills of lading) pertaining to goods shipped and received around the inventory date must be reviewed closely to verify that transactions have been recorded in the proper period.

(c) PERPETUAL SYSTEM.   Many businesses require frequent information regarding the quantity of goods on hand or the value of their inventory. A perpetual inventory system meets this need by maintaining records that detail the physical quantity and dollar amount of current inventory items. Technological advances such as scanners and low-cost computer applications have made automated perpetual inventory systems more practical and more popular. Their ease of use and their control over inventory quantities have enhanced the productivity of users. The records are updated constantly to reflect inventory additions and usage. Physical inventory counts are performed periodically to check the accuracy of the perpetual records. Discrepancies between the physical count and the quantities shown on the perpetual records should be investigated to determine the causes. Assuming an accurate physical count was achieved, the accounting records should be adjusted to reflect the results of the count. This entry is commonly referred to as the *book to physical adjustment*. The ability to isolate the book to physical adjustment is a perpetual system control feature not present in a periodic system.

(i) Recordkeeping Procedures.   In a perpetual inventory system, detailed records are maintained on an ongoing basis for each inventory item. The inventory balance is increased as items are purchased or inventoriable costs are incurred, and the balance is reduced as items are sold or transferred. Cost of sales reflects actual costs relieved from inventory. The level of sophistication of the records can vary dramatically, from manual entries posted directly to the general ledger to refined automated systems that use standard costs and detailed subsidiary records.

Cycle counting may be used with a perpetual inventory system to supplement other control procedures and to spread the physical counting effort throughout a period. A cycle count involves physically counting a portion of the inventory and comparing the quantity to that indicated by the perpetual records. Cycle counts test the reliability of the perpetual records. In connection with the ABC method of inventory control, in which higher-cost items receive a greater degree of continuous control than other items, cycle counts are performed more frequently for high-cost items. Successful results from interim-cycle counts can justify reliance on the perpetual records, and thereby eliminate the need to perform a companywide physical inventory at the fiscal year-end date. This approach generally is recommended in situations where unusual book to physical adjustments have not been identified during the interim-cycle counts.

(ii) Cutoff.   The points just made about periodic inventory system cutoff are equally applicable to a perpetual system. In fact, the detailed recordkeeping procedures regularly performed in a perpetual system generally make the period-end cutoff process less burdensome.

(d) PROCEDURES TO CONTROL INVENTORY QUANTITIES.   Implementation of effective accounting procedures and internal accounting controls over inventory quantities can protect the company's investment and reduce costs. A key objective is that goods or services are purchased only with proper authorization. To achieve this objective, some or all of these control procedures may be helpful:

- Approval by designated personnel within specified dollar limits is required for requisitions and purchase orders.
- Receiving, accounts payable, and stores personnel are denied access to purchasing records (e.g., blank purchase orders).
- Purchasing personnel are denied access to blank receiving reports and accounts payable vouchers.
- Purchase orders are compared to a control list or a file of approved vendors.
- Purchase orders are issued in prenumbered order; sequence is independently checked.
- Records of returned goods are matched to vendor credit memos.
- Goods are compared to purchase orders or other purchase authorization before acceptance.
- Unmatched receivers are investigated; unauthorized items are identified for return to the vendor.
- Receipts under blanket purchase orders are monitored; quantities exceeding the authorized total are returned to the vendor.
- Management approves overhead expense budget; variances from budgeted expenditures are analyzed and explained.

Another control objective is to prevent or detect promptly the physical loss of inventory. The next controls may help to achieve this objective:

- Responsibility for inventories is assigned to designated storekeepers; written store requisition or shipping order is required for all inventory issues.
- Perpetual records are regularly checked by cycle count or complete physical count.
- Where no perpetual records are maintained, quantities are determined regularly by physical count, costing, and comparison to the inventory accounts.
- Inventory counts and recordkeeping are independent of storekeepers.
- Written instructions are distributed for inventory counts; compliance is checked.
- Formal policies exist for scrap gathering, measuring, recording, storing, and disposal/recycling; compliance is reviewed periodically.
- Cost of scrap, waste, and defective products is regularly reviewed and standards are adjusted.
- Inventory adjustments are documented and require management approval.
- Complete production is reconciled to finished goods additions.
- Guards and/or alarm system are used.

- Employees are identified by badge, card, and so on.
- Employees are bonded.
- Storage areas are secured against unauthorized admission and protected against deterioration.
- Off-site inventories are stored in bonded warehouses.
- Materials leaving premises are checked for appropriate shipping documents.

13.5 VALUATION METHODS

(a) COST.   The cost principle that underlies today's financial accounting model holds that historical cost is the appropriate basis for recording and valuing assets. ASC 330 states:

> The primary basis of accounting for inventories is cost, which has been defined generally as the price paid or consideration given to acquire an asset. As applied to inventories, cost means in principle the sum of the applicable expenditures and charges directly or indirectly incurred in bringing an article to its existing condition and location.

Section 13.5(b) of this chapter deals with the write-down of inventory to amounts below cost by applying the lower-of-cost-or-market concept. In such circumstances, the reduced amount is considered cost for subsequent accounting periods.

Determining what costs are inventoriable is a matter of professional judgment based on the broad guidance in the authoritative literature referred to above. ASC 330 contains these additional comments pertaining to the determination of inventory costs:

- Selling expenses constitute no part of inventory costs.
- The exclusion of all overheads from inventory costs does not constitute an accepted accounting procedure.
- Items such as idle facility expense, excessive spoilage, double freight, and rehandling costs may be so abnormal as to require treatment as current-period charges rather than as a portion of the inventory cost.
- General and administrative expenses should be included as period charges, except for the portion of such expenses that may be clearly related to production and thus constitute a part of inventory costs (product charges).

(i) Job-Order Costing.   Products produced in individual units or batches, and requiring varying amounts of materials and labor (often to customer specifications) compared to other products, normally are costed using the job-order method. This technique is common in the furniture, printing, and robotics industries.

Costs of direct material and direct labor are assigned to specific jobs, based on actual usage. Usage information frequently is obtained from material requisition forms and labor time cards. Overhead typically is applied using a predetermined annual rate adjusted periodically to approximate actual costs.

(ii) Process Costing.   Products produced in large quantities normally are costed using an averaging method called *process costing*. Production runs are costed based on standard costs, which are the costs expected under efficient operating conditions. The total of all standard costs reported during each period is compared to actual costs incurred, based on general ledger account totals used to capture each cost category. Variances between standard costs and actual costs are analyzed and may be included in inventories or charged to expense, depending on the cause of the variance. No attempt is made to match costs of specific materials and labor to inventory units, because doing so would be highly impractical. A standard cost system can be effective in a process costing environment because of the relative predictability of unit costs. Standard costs can be developed based on each product's bill of materials and engineering specifications.

(iii) Direct Material Component. Materials contained in and traceable to a finished product are designated as direct materials. Because direct materials are a physical component of inventory items, and their cost is based on invoices from vendors, accounting for direct material costs is not difficult as long as quantities are tracked accurately. Freight and other costs of receiving materials also are inventoriable. Generally, freight-in is included as a portion of direct material, whereas receiving costs are included in the overhead pool. The cost of materials should be recorded net of related purchase discounts.

For operational purposes, material price variances and usage variances are identified to highlight deviations from standard amounts. Variances between standard costs and actual costs are analyzed and may be included in inventories or charged to expense, depending on the cause of the variance.

(iv) Direct Labor Component. Payroll and employee benefits costs of employees incurred in the technical operations of converting raw materials to finished product are considered direct labor. It is more difficult to associate labor costs directly with inventory than to associate material costs in that way. Labor reporting systems are often the most cumbersome part of collecting inventory costs. Labor price variances and labor efficiency variances are identified to highlight the reasons for deviations from standard costs. Variances between standard costs and actual costs are analyzed and may be included in inventories or charged to expense, depending on the cause of the variance.

(v) Overhead Component. Overhead, often referred to as *factory overhead* or *indirect manufacturing costs,* consists of all costs—other than direct material and direct labor—directly related to and adding value to the manufacturing process.

ASC 330 states that general and administrative costs can be included in inventories only if they are clearly related to production and that selling expenses should never be included in the inventory. In addition, amounts of wasted materials (spoilage) regardless of whether it is normal or abnormal should be treated as a current period charge. For many companies, determining which costs are appropriate inventoryable costs under these criteria may be difficult. Costs typically included in the overhead pool are:

- Indirect labor and employee benefits (e.g., factory supervision and maintenance).
- Financial statement depreciation related specifically to assets utilized in the manufacturing process is an appropriate inventory cost. (Excess tax depreciation should not be included in inventory cost for financial reporting purposes.)
- Receiving department.
- Insurance costs, such as production workers' compensation and the cost of insuring the manufacturing facilities, are inventoriable. Costs related to product liability coverage and claims should not be included in inventory costs because they are related to goods that have already been sold, not those currently being produced or in inventory.
- Factory utilities.
- Other plant maintenance and repairs.

Other less obvious costs appropriate to charge to the overhead pool include those listed next.

- Net periodic pension costs and other postretirement costs are elements of employee compensation. Therefore, when it is appropriate to capitalize employee compensation in connection with inventory production, the corresponding net periodic pension and other postretirement costs should also be capitalized. Amounts capitalized should be a function of all aspects of pension and/or other postemployment benefits (OPEB) accounting and should include interest cost and any gains or losses from pension and OPEB accounting. In this regard, gains and losses are based on the company's accounting policy (e.g., immediate recognition versus recognition of gains and losses outside the corridor, etc.). The volatility that sometimes results from pension and OPEB accounting would not be considered an "abnormal" variance and should not be excluded from inventory costing. However, a significant variance may trigger lower-of-cost-or-market adjustments.

- Costs of warehousing and handling finished goods may be inventoriable for financial reporting purposes if the warehousing and handling is an integral aspect of bringing the goods to a salable condition (e.g., goods received in bulk at a warehouse that must be repackaged for final sale). In some situations, warehousing and handling costs are considered costs of disposal and are not inventoriable for financial reporting purposes.

- Personnel department costs to the extent they relate to such activities as hiring and administering benefits of production personnel.

- Purchasing department costs are inventoriable to the extent they relate to the acquisition of raw materials or production supplies by manufacturers or the acquisition of goods for resale by wholesalers or retailers.

- Information systems processing costs that are specifically related to a manufacturing or cost accounting system may be included in inventory costs for financial reporting purposes. Data processing costs related to a general ledger or other financial accounting system should not be included in inventory costs.

- Legal costs incurred for labor relations or workers' compensation issues are allocable to inventory for financial reporting purposes. Costs incurred in product liability matters should not be included in inventory costs.

- Officers' salaries are inventoriable to the extent the officers' responsibilities are directly related to the production process (e.g., vice president of production or purchasing). The salary of a general officer, such as the chief operating officer, normally would not be inventoriable even though he or she has certain indirect responsibilities related to manufacturing operations.

ASC 330 specifies that fixed overhead should be allocated to inventories based on the normal capacity of the productive facility.

Evaluating and documenting costs that may be capitalized as part of overhead cost requires judgment based on consideration of a number of factors, including a company's organizational structure and the nature of its accounting records. For example, a company that is highly decentralized may have all of its direct production costs segregated at its manufacturing facilities. The personnel, purchasing, and accounting functions related to manufacturing may all be located at the facility and their costs clearly identified. In contrast, a highly centralized company may have all its personnel, purchasing, and accounting functions in a central location supporting sales and corporate functions as well as manufacturing. In this case, it is more difficult to establish and document a direct relationship to the production process. However, documenting a direct relationship is necessary to support including those costs in inventory under generally accepted accounting principles.

As described, certain costs, such as selling expenses, abnormal costs, and a defined portion of general and administrative costs, are to be excluded from inventory and charged to operations as incurred. ASC 720, *Research and Development,* requires that all research and development costs encompassed by that guidance be charged to expense when incurred. ASC 985-20, *Software—Costs of Software to Be Sold, Leased, or Marketed,* requires that all costs incurred to establish the technological feasibility of a computer software product be charged to expense as research and development. Once technological feasibility is established, software production costs are capitalized and amortized on a product-by-product basis. Capitalization of computer software costs ends when the product is available for general release to customers. Costs related to maintenance and customer support are expensed as incurred or when the related revenue is recognized, whichever occurs first. Costs incurred to duplicate the software, documentation, and training materials and to physically package the product for distribution are capitalized as inventory.

Selling costs are appropriately charged to expense as incurred, because such costs typically cannot be identified with individual sales and relate to goods previously sold rather than to inventory on hand. The question of deferring certain selling and marketing costs that relate to transactions not yet recognized for accounting purposes (i.e., in order to record the expense in the same period as the related revenue) is controversial and beyond the scope of this chapter. Nevertheless, if such costs are deferred, they should not be included with or classified as inventory.

Numerous other types of costs raise questions about whether they should be included in the overhead pool or treated as a period cost. These costs include purchasing and other costs of ordering, quality control, warehousing, cost accounting, and carrying costs such as interest and insurance (on the inventory items and on the warehouse). The decision to include a cost in the overhead pool requires considerable judgment. Challenging whether the cost adds value to the product is often useful. Observation of current practice indicates all of the items just discussed except interest are included in the overhead pool by some companies and excluded by others. ASC 835-20, *Interest—Capitalization of Interest,* states: "Interest cost shall not be capitalized for inventories that are routinely manufactured or otherwise produced in large quantities on a repetitive basis." The FASB decided this based on a cost-benefit rationale.

Including judgmental-type costs in inventory increases current assets and shareholders' equity. The effect on income of a particular period can be in either direction, depending on the relative inventory balances at the beginning and end of the period. However, for a growing company, a broadly defined overhead pool generally serves to increase income reported each period.

(vi) Overhead Allocation.   Because indirect production costs cannot be directly associated with a particular inventory unit, the costs generally are assigned to various units by using allocation methods. There are several means of allocating overhead costs to inventory and cost of sales. The traditional method has been to develop an overhead rate based on overhead cost per direct labor hour or direct labor dollar. This method allocates overhead to inventory and cost of sales in proportion to the amount of labor used. Other allocation bases may be more logical in certain circumstances. For instance, use of machine-hours may be a preferable method of overhead allocation for highly automated processes. Recording overhead costs by function and department can significantly improve the cost allocation process. Logical statistical methods can be established to allocate indirect costs. Such refinements can produce more meaningful results than use of a single plant-wide overhead rate. Increased accuracy and control results from using more specific and relevant overhead allocation methods.

Possible methods of allocating indirect costs include:

Indirect Cost	Allocation Basis
Materials handling	Quantity or weight of materials
Occupancy (depreciation, rent, property taxes, etc.)	Square-footage occupied
Employment related	Number of employees, labor hours, or labor dollars

The level of sophistication in allocating indirect costs and determining overhead absorption rates can profoundly affect the inventory valuation and such other important matters as product margins and pricing.

ASC 330 indicates a change in composition of the elements of cost included in inventory is an accounting change. Reporting of such changes should conform with ASC 250, *Accounting Changes and Error Corrections.* Preference should be based on an improvement in financial reporting, not on the basis of the income tax effect alone.

(b) LOWER OF COST OR MARKET.   Generally accepted accounting principles (GAAP) require the carrying amount of inventory to be reduced below cost whenever the utility of the goods is less than their cost. This is referred to as valuing inventory at the lower of cost or market. Impairment of inventory can occur through damage, obsolescence (technological changes or new fashions have reduced or eliminated customer interest in the product), deterioration, changes in price levels, excess quantities, and other causes. ASC 330 also states that "the offer of a sales incentive that will result in a loss on the sale of a product may indicate an impairment of existing inventory." The lower-of-cost-or-market valuation method is designed to eliminate the deferral of unrecoverable costs and to recognize the reduction in the value of inventory when it occurs.

When valuing inventory at the lower of cost or market, the term *market* means current replacement cost (by purchase or by reproduction, as the case may be) except that:

1. Market should not exceed the net realizable value (i.e., estimated selling price in the ordinary course of business less reasonably predictable costs of completion and disposal); and

2. Market should not be less than net realizable value reduced by an allowance for an approximately normal profit margin.

Use of replacement cost as the starting point for the lower-of-cost -or-market valuation is intended to reflect the utility of the goods based on the cost required to produce equivalent goods currently. Replacement cost also is more practical than net realizable value for establishing a market value for raw materials and component parts because these items may not be sold separately or in their existing condition.

The ceiling of the market valuation just described is net realizable value to ensure that replacement cost valuation does not defer costs that will not be recovered by the ultimate selling price. For example, an inventory item with a net realizable value of $10 would not be carried above that amount even if its replacement cost exceeded $10. The floor of the market valuation is intended to eliminate any write-off of costs that will be recovered from the customer at a normal profit margin even though the replacement cost of the inventory is lower. For example, an item with a normal profit margin of 20 percent to be sold to a customer for $10 would not be carried at less than $8 even if its replacement cost was less than $8.

The lower-of-cost-or-market adjustment may be recorded for each inventory item or may be aggregated for the total inventory or for major inventory categories. The choice depends on the nature of the inventory and should be the one that most clearly reflects periodic income. Once selected, the same method should be applied consistently. Any comparisons of aggregate cost and market offset unrealized gains on certain inventory items against expected losses on other items (if such loss items exist) and, therefore, reduce the amount of the inventory write-down compared to the amount calculated on an item-by-item basis. Notwithstanding the principle of conservatism, the aggregate approach may be preferable when there is only one type of inventory or when no loss is expected on the sale of all goods because price declines of certain components are offset by adequate margins on other components. Similarly, the lower-of-cost-or-market procedure should be applied on an individual item basis for unrelated items and for inventories that cannot practically be classified into categories. Profitable margins on one product line should not be used to eliminate a lower-of-cost-or-market write-down for other unrelated products. ASC 330 specifically requires use of the item-by-item method of applying the lower-of-cost-or-market principle to excess inventory stock (quantity of goods on hand exceeds customer demand).

ASC 330 also states that "if a business is expected to lose money for a sustained period, the inventory should not be written down to offset a loss inherent in the subsequent operations."

Controls that can provide reasonable assurance that obsolete, slow-moving, or overstock inventory is prevented or promptly detected and provided for include:

- Perpetual records show date of last usage; stock levels and usability are regularly reviewed.
- Physical storage methods are regularly reviewed for sources of inventory deterioration.
- Purchase requisitions are compared to preestablished reorder points and economic order quantities.
- Potential overstock is identified by regularly comparing quantities on hand with historical usage.
- Production and existing stock levels are related to forecasts of market and technological changes.
- Bill of materials and part number systems provide for identification of common parts and subassemblies; discontinued products are reviewed for reusable components.
- Work in process is reviewed periodically for old items.

Regular preparation and review of product line income statements can identify products that are losing money and may warrant a lower of cost or market write-down. Another procedure to highlight potential lower-of-cost-or-market concerns is to compare product carrying amounts to selling prices. Inventory should be written down to the lower of cost or market at an interim date unless:

- Substantial evidence exists that market prices will recover before the inventory is sold.
- In the case of last-in, first-out (LIFO) inventories, inventory levels will be restored by year-end.
- The decline is due to seasonal price fluctuations.

In Staff Accounting Bulletin (SAB) Topic No. 100, *Restructuring and Impairment Charges* (Topic 5-BB), the Securities and Exchange Commission (SEC) Staff expressed its view that a write-down of inventory to the lower-of-cost-or-market at the close of a fiscal period creates a new cost basis that subsequently cannot be marked up based on changes in underlying facts and circumstances.

A SEC Staff Observer comment (codified in ASC 420-10-S99-3)[1] on the income statement classification of inventory markdowns associated with a restructuring indicated that the SEC Staff recognizes that there may be circumstances in which it can be asserted that inventory markdowns are costs directly attributable to a decision to exit or restructure an activity. However, the Staff believes that it is difficult to distinguish inventory markdowns attributable to a decision to exit or restructure an activity from inventory markdowns attributable to external factors that are independent of a decision to exit or restructure an activity. Further, the Staff believes that decisions about the timing, method, and pricing of dispositions of inventory generally are considered to be normal, recurring activities integral to the management of the ongoing business. Accordingly, the SEC Staff believes that inventory markdowns should be classified in the income statement as a component of cost of goods sold.

(i) LIFO Considerations.   In 1984, the Accounting Standards Executive Committee (AcSEC) of the American Institute of Certified Public Accountants (AICPA), in Section 6 of an issues paper, *Identification and Discussion of Certain Financial Accounting and Reporting Issues Concerning LIFO Inventories* (the AICPA Issues Paper), indicated that companies may apply the lower-of-cost-or-market provisions of ASC 330 to LIFO inventories on the basis of "reasonable groupings of inventory items." Further, it stated that in general a pool constitutes a reasonable grouping. Section 6 of the AICPA Issues Paper also indicates companies with more than one pool may aggregate pools for purposes of lower-of-cost-or-market determinations if the compositions of the pools are similar. The AICPA Issues Paper emphasizes the importance of "the character and composition" of the inventory in making lower-of-cost-or-market determinations. The AICPA task force responsible for preparing the AICPA Issues Paper (Task Force) also added this caution: If the compositions of the pool are significantly dissimilar, they should not be aggregated.

The AICPA Issues Paper includes a discussion of the treatment of obsolete or discontinued products within the lower-of-cost-or-market review. The Task Force and AcSEC did not agree on this issue. AcSEC believes the item-by-item approach should be used for identified product obsolescence and product discontinuance, while the Task Force believes either the item-by-item approach or the aggregate-by-pool approach is appropriate. Because there was disagreement between the Task Force and AcSEC, companies can use either the item-by-item approach or the aggregate-by-pool approach for identified product obsolescence and product discontinuance. However, whatever approach used should be applied consistently.

(c) RETAIL METHOD.   The retail method offers a simplified, cost-effective alternative of inventory valuation for department stores and other retailers selling many and varied goods. By using estimates of inventory cost based on the ratio of cost to selling price, it generally eliminates the procedure of referring to invoice cost to value each item. This ratio is often referred to as the *cost ratio* or *cost complement*. To avoid distortions arising from differing product mix and margins, a separate calculation generally is performed for each department. This step produces more accurate departmental costs and operating results. Also, because the types of products that constitute the inventory on hand at the balance sheet date may differ significantly from the proportion in which goods were purchased during the period, use of departmental cost ratios reduces the likelihood that these differences will improperly affect the inventory valuation.

---

[1] ASC section 420 is titled *Exit or Disposal Cost Obligations.*

Definitions of certain key terms used in the retail industry and important to the retail inventory method are listed next.

- *Original retail.* The price at which merchandise is first offered for sale
- *Markon.* The difference between the retail price and the cost of merchandise sold or in inventory
- *Markup.* An addition to the original retail price
- *Markdown.* A reduction of original retail price
- *Markup cancelation.* A reduction in marked-up merchandise that does not reduce retail price below the original retail price
- *Markdown cancellation.* An addition to marked-down merchandise that does not raise retail price above the original retail price

Physical inventory counts (e.g., for year-end inventory taking) are initially priced at retail value (i.e., selling prices) and converted to cost using the cost ratio. The retail method also allows for periodic determination of inventory and cost of sales without the need for a physical count by means of a calculation similar to that shown in Exhibit 13.1. Retailers regularly use this type of calculation to value inventory at interim periods.

	Department A Traditional Sleepwear		Department E Cosmetics	
	Cost	Retail	Cost	Retail
Beginning inventory—1/31/X2	$200,000	$ 400,000	$170,000	$ 285,000
Purchases[a]	450,000	865,000	575,000	950,000
Markups	—	5,500	—	3,500
Markup cancellations	—	(500)	—	(1,000)
Total available	650,000	1,270,000	745,000	1,237,500
Cost complement		51.18%		60.20%
Markon		48.82%		39.80%
Sales		(720,000)		(918,000)
Employee discounts		(7,500)		(5,500)
Shrinkage		(11,500)		(14,900)
Markdowns		(78,000)		(1,100)
Markdown cancelations		1,000		—
Promotional markdowns		(10,000)		—
		(826,000)		(939,500)
Ending inventory—1/31/X3				
at retail		$ 444,000		$ 298,000
at lower of cost or market	$227,239	51.18%	$179,396	60.20%

[a]The *National Retail Merchants Association Accounting Manual* states that, for department stores, markon is based on the delivered cost of merchandise and original selling price, adjusted for errors in pricing and additional markups. Markdowns and markdown cancelations do not enter into the calculation of the cost complement. Most accounting references suggest that cash purchase discounts should not be credited to purchases but should be separately accounted for, and a pro rata share of discounts should be netted against the closing inventory. As a practical matter, many retailers either run cash purchase discounts through the purchase journal or record purchases net of discount.

Exhibit 13.1   Example of Retail Inventory Calculation
Source: P. W. Wilson and K. E. Christensen, *LIFO for Retailers* (New York: John Wiley & Sons, New York, 1985).

To perform the retail inventory calculations in a manner similar to that shown in Exhibit 13.1, a record of the cost and the retail value of the beginning inventory and of the current period purchases is kept (often referred to as the *stock ledger*). Net markups (markups less markup cancelations) are added to these amounts to determine the total goods available for sale on both the cost and retail bases. The cost ratio or cost complement calculated by dividing total cost of purchases by total selling price is used to reduce inventory at retail to cost. The markon percentage can be obtained by subtracting the cost ratio from 100 percent. The ending inventory at retail is obtained by subtracting current period sales, net markdowns (markdowns less markdown cancelations), and other reductions from the total goods available for sale on the retail basis. Finally, the ending inventory at retail is multiplied by the cost ratio to obtain the ending inventory at cost.

Note that the calculation in the exhibit excludes net markdowns from the computation of the cost ratio. Markdowns are deducted from the retail amount after the cost ratio is computed. This method values the ending inventory at an estimate of the lower of cost or market. ASC 330 acknowledges that this method is acceptable provided adequate markdowns are currently taken.

In contrast, the retail method is considered to approximate average costs if the calculation includes net markdowns in the computation of the cost ratio. This inclusion reduces the cost ratio denominator and thereby increases the ending inventory figure compared to the lower-of-cost-or-market methodology. To illustrate, the next calculations use the figures for Department A in the exhibit to compute the retail method variation that approximates average costs:

	Cost	Retail
Beginning inventory	$200,000	$ 400,000
Purchases	450,000	865,000
Markups		5,500
Markup cancelations		(500)
Markdowns		(78,000)
Markdown cancelations		1,000
Total available	650,000	1,193,000
Cost complement		54.48%
Sales		(720,000)
Employee discounts		(7,500)
Shrinkage		(11,500)
Promotional markdowns		(10,000)
		(749,000)
Ending inventory		
at retail		$ 444,000
at average cost	$241,891	54.48%

The retail LIFO valuation method is discussed in Section 13.6(c).

(d) ABOVE COST. In certain cases, inventory items possess such widely accepted value and immediate marketability that an exception is made to the normal requirement that an exchange (e.g., sale) must occur for income to be recognized. Examples of inventories often valued above cost (i.e., at sales price less costs of disposal) include precious metals, farm products, minerals, and certain other commodities. This is a practical solution to the difficulty of determining product cost for goods that are obtained from the ground rather than from manufacture but may be used only if specific criteria are met.

ASC 330 indicates that to be valued above cost, inventory items must meet three criteria:

1. Inability to determine appropriate approximate costs
2. Immediate marketability at quoted market price
3. Unit interchangeability

Note that when inventory valuations are based on selling price, holding gains are recognized when the selling price increases and holding losses are recorded when the selling price decreases. When inventories are stated above cost, disclosure of this policy should be made in the financial statements.

Companies often hedge their exposure to commodity price fluctuations by entering into futures contracts or forward contracts. Theoretically, any gain or loss in the market value of the hedged item is directly offset by a change in the market value of the futures or forward contract. ASC 330 states:

> If inventory has been the hedged item in a fair value hedge, the inventory's "cost" basis used in the lower of cost-or-market accounting shall reflect the effect of the adjustments of its carrying amount made pursuant to paragraph 815-25-35-1(b).

ASC 815, *Derivatives and Hedging,* requires all derivative financial instruments to be carried at fair value. If the derivative qualifies for accounting as a hedge of the fair value of inventory, then the changes in the fair value of the derivative are recorded in current earnings. In addition, changes in the fair value of the inventory that occur during the period it is hedged are also recognized in income by adjusting the inventory's carrying amount. If the derivative does not qualify as a hedge of the fair value of the inventory, changes in the fair value of the derivative would be recorded in current earnings, while the carrying amount of the inventory would not be adjusted to reflect the change in its fair value.

(e) REPLACEMENT COST. As described, replacement cost is the starting point for determining market value under the lower-of-cost-or-market valuation method. Replacement cost also is the primary method of valuing repossessed goods.

(f) NET REALIZABLE VALUE. Certain inventory items (scrap, by-products and trade-in inventory) for which cost or replacement cost is not determinable or is inappropriate for valuation purposes are valued at net realizable value, defined as estimated selling price in the ordinary course of business less reasonably predictable costs of completion and disposal.

(g) GROSS MARGIN METHOD. A frequently used technique to estimate the inventory balance without performing a physical count is the gross margin method. Although the gross margin method generally is not acceptable as the inventory valuation method for financial reporting purposes because of its reliance on estimated rather than actual cost information, it is useful for a variety of purposes, including:

- *Estimating the inventory balance at regular interim periods.* This might be required to calculate operating results and to calculate borrowing limits on loans collateralized by inventory. Companies with complicated manufacturing operations may not be able to take a complete physical inventory every quarter and, therefore, might require an estimating technique such as the gross margin method.
- *Preparing budget information.* Budgets usually are centered on sales forecasts. The gross margin method is useful to estimate the cost of goods sold and inventory amounts based on the sales forecast.
- *Estimating the value of inventory destroyed by a casualty, such as a fire.* Such calculations may be required to support insurance claims related to the loss.
- *Checking the reasonableness of an inventory balance determined using a more sophisticated valuation method.*

The gross margin method assumes that the gross margin percentage can be predicted with reasonable accuracy, based on results of prior periods or other calculations. The next example demonstrates the estimation of an inventory balance using the gross margin method:

Cost of Goods Sold

Sales	$100,000
× Gross margin percentage	× 25%
Gross margin	$ 25,000
Sales	$100,000
Less: Gross margin	(25,000)
Cost of goods sold	$ 75,000

Ending inventory

Beginning inventory	$300,000
Purchases	80,000
Cost of goods available for sale	380,000
Less: Cost of goods sold	(75,000)
Ending inventory	$305,000

ASC 270, *Interim Reporting,* recognizes that some companies use the gross margin method to estimate inventory and cost of goods sold for interim reporting purposes (e.g., quarterly reporting to the SEC). Such companies must disclose that this method is used and disclose any significant adjustments that result from reconciliations with the annual physical inventory.

(h) IN CONNECTION WITH A PURCHASE BUSINESS COMBINATION. The next three general guidelines for assigning amounts to inventories acquired in a purchase business combination are contained in ASC 805, *Business Combinations.*

1. Acquired finished goods inventories should be recognized at their fair value, which we believe in many cases approximates a market participant's estimated selling price adjusted for (a) costs of the selling effort and (b) a reasonable profit allowance for the selling effort of the acquiring entity, both estimated from the viewpoint of a market participant. The acquiring entity's results of operations after the acquisition should reflect the costs and outcome of the selling activities that occur after the date of acquisition.

2. Work-in-process inventories are recognized at fair value, which we believe in most cases will approximate a market participant's estimated selling price of the eventual finished inventories adjusted for a market participants expected (a) costs to complete the manufacturing process, (b) costs of the selling effort, and (c) a reasonable profit allowance for the remaining manufacturing and selling effort. Estimated costs to complete the manufacture of work-in-process inventories should consider all inventoriable costs, as discussed in ASC 330, and should be reconcilable with manufacturing cost estimates that would be incurred by a market participant. A market participant's reasonable profit allowance for acquired work-in-process inventories should be greater than the profit allowance associated with comparable acquired finished inventories since the profit allowance for work-in-process inventories includes the value-added portion of manufacturing profit related to the effort to complete the inventory production, in addition to the selling profit allowance associated with acquired finished inventories.

3. Acquired raw material inventories should be recognized at fair value, which we believe generally would be the price a market participant could achieve in a current sale, without regard to whether that sale price is greater or less than a target's historical carrying cost.

Some business combinations accounted for as purchases are nontaxable. In those circumstances, if the acquired company accounted for inventories using the LIFO method and the acquiring company continues that LIFO election, the amounts reported as LIFO inventories for financial statement and for tax purposes will likely differ in the year of combination and in subsequent years.

(i) CONTROL PROCEDURES TO HELP ACHIEVE A PROPER INVENTORY VALUATION.   To record inventory amounts accurately and ensure that costs are assigned to inventory in accordance with the stated valuation method, controls should be implemented. These control procedures can be effective:

- Cost accounting subsidiary records are balanced regularly to the general ledger control accounts.
- Standard unit costs are compared to actual material prices, quantities used, labor rates and hours, overhead expenses, and proper absorption rate.
- Variances, including overhead, are analyzed periodically and allocated to inventory and cost of sales; results are submitted to management for review.
- Written policies exist for inventory pricing; changes are appropriately documented, quantified as to effect, and approved prior to change.

To provide assurance that goods and services are recorded correctly as to account, amount, and period, a company may select control procedures such as these:

- Goods are counted, inspected, and compared to packing slips before acceptance.
- Receiving reports are issued by the receiving/inspection department in prenumbered order; sequence is checked independently or unused receivers are otherwise controlled.
- Services received are acknowledged in writing by a responsible employee.
- Receiving documentation, purchase order, and invoice are matched before the liability is recorded.
- Invoice additions, extensions, and pricing are checked.
- Unmatched receiving reports and invoices are investigated for inclusion in the estimated liability at the close of the period.
- Account distribution is reviewed when recording the liability or when signing the check.
- Vendor statements are regularly reconciled.

In addition to valuing inventory properly at periodic reporting dates, an important objective is that the usage and movement of inventory be recorded correctly by account, amount (quantities and dollars), and period. To achieve this objective, these controls should be considered:

- Periodic comparisons of actual quantities to perpetual records are made for raw materials, purchased parts, work in process, subassemblies, and finished goods.
- Documentation is issued in prenumbered order for receiving, stores requisitions, production orders, and shipping (including partial shipments); sequence is checked independently.
- Shipments of finished goods are checked for appropriate shipping documents.
- Shipping, billing, and inventory records are reconciled on a regular basis.
- Records are maintained for inventory on consignment (in and out), held by vendors, or in outside warehouses; these records are reconciled to reports received from outsiders.
- Inventory accounts are adjusted for results of periodic physical counts.
- Inventory adjustments are documented and require approval.

13.6 FLOW OF COSTS

(a) INTRODUCTION.   For cost-based inventory valuation methods, it is necessary to select an assumption of the flow of costs to value the inventory and cost of sales systematically. The reason is that the unit cost of items typically varies over time, and a consistent method must be adopted for allocating costs to inventory and cost of sales. As items are accumulated in inventory at different costs, a basis must be established to determine the cost of each item sold. The cost flow does not always match the physical movement of the inventory goods. ASC 330 recognizes that several cost flow assumptions are acceptable and that the major objective in selecting a method is to reflect periodic income most clearly. It also states that in some cases, it may be "desirable to apply one of the acceptable methods of determining cost to one portion of the inventory or components thereof and another of the acceptable methods to other portions of the inventory."

(b) FIRST-IN, FIRST-OUT. The first-in, first-out (FIFO) method assumes that costs flow through operations chronologically. Cost of sales reflects older unit costs whereas inventory is valued at most recent costs. In periods of rising prices, FIFO can result in holding gains (also known as *inventory profits*) because older costs are matched against current sales. Proponents of FIFO believe that FIFO is the most logical assumed flow of costs based on the pattern of the physical flow of goods and the valuation of inventory as close to current cost as is reasonably possible under the historical cost basis of accounting. The FIFO method is also relatively simple to apply.

In practice, the FIFO method is applied by valuing inventory items at the most recent costs of acquisition or production. For example, assume a dealer made these purchases of Item A during the year:

Date	Quantity	Unit Cost
Jan. 6	1,000	$4.00
Aug. 12	3,000	5.00
Dec. 18	2,000	6.00

If 4,000 units of Item A were held in inventory at December 31, under the FIFO method they would be valued this way:

2,000 units @ $6.00 each = $12,000
2,000 units @ $5.00 each =   10,000
                           $22,000

Note that, unlike the LIFO method, the FIFO method produces the same results whether the periodic or the perpetual inventory system is used.

(c) LAST-IN, FIRST-OUT. Last-in, first-out (LIFO) is identified in ASC 330 as one of the accepted methods of costing inventory and is widely used in practice. The LIFO method assumes the most recent unit costs are charged to operations. This values inventory at older costs. In periods of increasing prices, LIFO produces a higher cost of sales figure than FIFO or the average cost method and, accordingly, a lower income amount. Advocates of the LIFO method point out that in periods of continuous inflation, LIFO provides a better matching of costs and revenues than other cost flow assumptions because it matches current costs with current revenues in the income statement. Because proponents of LIFO believe that the income statement is more important to users of financial statements than the balance sheet, they give less weight to the counterargument that the LIFO method "understates" the inventory balances (in periods of rising costs) in relation to current costs. In addition, LIFO often improves the company's cash flow because it results in lower income taxes. This situation is attractive to companies seeking to reduce their income tax liability, and, as a result, many companies use the LIFO method for income tax purposes. The IRS regulations contain a "conformity requirement" that companies using LIFO for tax purposes must use LIFO for external financial reporting purposes, but it is acceptable for LIFO calculations to differ for book and tax purposes. Historically, IRS regulations have had a significant effect on LIFO techniques used for financial reporting purposes.

As mentioned previously, LIFO causes the inventory amount on the balance sheet to be carried at older costs. The theory supporting this method is that because a company needs certain levels of inventory to operate its business, carrying inventories at their initial cost is consistent with the historical cost principle. Under the LIFO concept, inventory levels are carried on the balance sheet at their original LIFO cost until they are decreased. Any increases (i.e., new layers) are added to the inventory balance at the current cost in the year of acquisition and are carried forward at that amount to subsequent periods. A liquidation (or decrement) of a LIFO layer occurs when the quantity of an inventory item or pool decreases. The liquidation causes older costs to be charged to operations, failing to achieve the LIFO objective of matching current costs and revenues. To summarize, as long as inventory quantities are maintained (i.e., not decreased), the older, generally low-cost layers are preserved. If inventory quantities decrease, older layers are liquidated and charged to operations, generally increasing earnings.

Principally because of the involved calculations related to inventory pools and layers, LIFO is more complex than other inventory valuation methods. As a result, LIFO may result in higher record-keeping costs and require more management attention and planning. Certain companies, particularly publicly held companies, may be concerned with investor reaction to the lower earnings reported under LIFO when prices are rising. The Internal Revenue Service (IRS) rules that permit companies to make supplemental disclosures of FIFO earnings may help alleviate this concern.

There are two basic methods of determining LIFO cost: specific identification and dollar value. (The latter method includes the double extension technique, the link-chain technique, the retail method, and other techniques to be discussed.)

(i) Specific Goods Method.   The specific goods (or specific identification) method is normally the simplest LIFO approach to apply and understand. Inventory quantities and costs are measured in terms of individual units. Each item or group of similar items is treated as a separate inventory pool (e.g., a specific grade of tobacco).

The advantage of the specific goods method is that it is easy to conceptualize because LIFO costs are associated with specific items in inventory. This method has been used most frequently by companies that have basic inventory items, such as steel or commodities, and deal with a relatively low volume of transactions.

There are disadvantages, however, in using the specific goods method, especially if the inventory has a wide variety of items or if items change frequently (e.g., for technological reasons). In such circumstances, the specific goods method might become complicated, may prove costly to administer, and may produce unwanted LIFO liquidations.

(ii) Dollar-Value Method.   The dollar-value method overcomes most of the disadvantages of the specific identification method. The distinguishing feature of the dollar-value LIFO method is that it measures inventory quantities in terms of fixed dollar equivalents (base-year costs) rather than quantities and prices of individual goods. Similar items of inventory are aggregated to form inventory pools. Changes in quantities and changes in product mix within a pool are ignored. Increases or decreases in each pool are identified and measured in terms of the total base-year cost of the inventory in the pool rather than of the physical quantities of items.

One of the most important aspects of dollar-value LIFO is selecting the pools to be used in the computations. A careful assignment of inventory items to pools will avoid most of the limitations of the specific identification method just noted. Generally, the fewer the pools, the lower the likelihood of a liquidation and the lower the resulting taxable income. Fewer pools also minimize the administrative burden associated with accounting for LIFO inventories. The AICPA Issues Paper concludes that it is not feasible to formulate detailed guidance for selecting pools that could apply to all enterprises. It advises that the objective of LIFO inventory pooling is to group inventory items to match most recently incurred costs to current revenues, after considering the manner in which the company operates its business; establishing separate pools with the principal objective of facilitating inventory liquidations would not be considered acceptable. Items that comprise a similar or identical product sold by the enterprise should be included in the same pool. The existence of separate legal entities (e.g., subsidiaries), by itself, does not justify establishing separate LIFO pools for consolidated financial reporting purposes.

The selection of LIFO pools may be different for tax and financial reporting purposes. For example, for tax purposes, LIFO is applied by legal entity, not by consolidated groups. However, referring to U.S. tax guidelines may be useful in determining a pooling method as long as the objectives of the AICPA Issues Paper are met.

The broadest definition of a pool is the natural business unit pool. This includes, in a single pool, all inventories, including raw materials, work in process, and finished goods. This method is available only to companies—generally manufacturers and processors—whose operations consist of a single product line (or more than one if they are related). The natural business unit pool is attractive to many companies because the use of a single pool simplifies LIFO calculations and reduces the number of layer liquidations.

Companies that do not qualify for natural business unit pooling or that wish to elect LIFO for only a portion of their inventory may elect the multiple pool method. Each of the multiple pools should consist of "substantially similar" inventory items.

Various computational techniques are used to apply the dollar-value method—the double-extension link-chain, internal indexes, the retail LIFO method (a variation of the link-chain technique) and other simplified external index techniques. These techniques have the objective of determining the base-year cost of the current-year inventory. The double-extension technique converts current-year amounts directly to base-year costs. The link-chain technique achieves the objective indirectly by developing an index based on the current-year cost increases and multiplying that index by the prior-year cumulative index. The internal index technique uses a representative sample of the entire population (e.g., 70 percent of all items in the pool or a statistical sample) that are double-extended to convert current-year amounts to base-year costs. The retail LIFO method is a dollar-value method that uses base-year retail value instead of base-year cost to compute inventory changes. The simplified external index technique applies 100 percent of the external index (e.g., price indexes published by the Bureau of Labor Statistics (BLS) to the current-year cost).

(iii) Double-Extension Technique. The double-extension technique extends ending inventory quantities twice—once at current-year costs (unit costs for the current period, determined using another method, typically FIFO) and once at base-year costs. This double extension procedure provides the current-year index (total current-year cost divided by total base-year cost).

To determine the net inventory change for the year, the ending inventory expressed in terms of base-year costs is compared to the beginning-of-the-year inventory expressed in terms of base-year costs. If the ending inventory at base-year costs exceeds the beginning inventory at base-year costs, a new LIFO layer has been created. The new layer is valued by applying the ratio of the ending inventory at current costs (using one of the approaches described at Subsection 13.6(c)(vi)) to the ending inventory at base-year costs. This ratio is generally referred to as *LIFO index*. If the ending inventory at base-year costs is less than beginning inventory at base-year costs, a LIFO liquidation has occurred. When a liquidation has occurred, decrements in base-year costs are deducted from the layers of earlier years beginning with the most recent prior year.

When an item enters the inventory for the first time, a company must either use its current cost or determine its base-year cost. Under IRS regulations, current cost must be used unless the company is able to reconstruct a base-year cost. The use of manufacturing specifications or other methods may allow a company to determine what the cost of a new item would have been in the base year. This effort may be worthwhile, because it may calculate a base-year cost that is lower than the current-year cost, most likely due to inflation in the cost of materials and labor. Use of a lower base-year cost in the LIFO calculations increases the current-year index and, thereby, lowers the inventory balance and pretax income. In other words, by reconstructing a base-year cost for new items, the impact of LIFO is normally maximized.

Companies that use the double-extension technique must retain indefinitely a record of base-year unit costs of all items in inventory at the beginning of the year in which LIFO was adopted as well as any base-year unit costs developed for new items added in subsequent years. Exhibit 13.2 is an example of the LIFO double-extension technique.

The double-extension technique can prove cumbersome, particularly when the base year extends back a number of years. Changes in product specifications and manufacturing methods are common in many industrial companies. The link-chain method eliminates the burden of reconstructing base-year costs and so is a more efficient means of computing LIFO cost. In determining a LIFO index,

This example illustrates the application of the double-extension technique of dollar-value LIFO for one pool. Assume that the company's opening inventory on January 1, 20X1 (the date LIFO is adopted) totaled $150,000. Ending inventory for the next three years is shown.

Item	Quantities in Ending Inventor	Base-Year Cost Unit Cost	Amount	Current-Year Cost Unit Cost	Amount	Index
Year Ended December 31, 20X1						
A	8,000	$ 1.00	$ 8,000	$ 1.15	$ 9,200	
B	7,000	4.00	28,000	4.30	30,100	
C	10,000	7.00	70,000	7.60	76,000	
D	12,000	6.00	72,000	6.35	76,200	
			$178,000		$191,500	107.58
Year Ended December 31, 20X2						
A	12,000	$ 1.00	$ 12,000	$ 1.30	$ 15,600	
B	6,000	4.00	24,000	4.75	28,500	
C	7,000	7.00	49,000	8.15	57,050	
D	15,000	6.00	90,000	6.80	102,000	
E	7,000	9.00	63,000	10.30	72,100	
			$238,000		$275,250	115.65
Year Ended December 31, 20X3						
A	18,000	$ 1.00	$ 18,000	$ 1.50	$ 27,000	
D	17,000	6.00	102,000	7.50	127,500	
E	10,000	9.00	90,000	11.20	112,000	
F	5,000	8.00	40,000	9.75	48,750	
G	3,000	10.00	30,000	12.35	37,050	
			$280,000		$352,300	125.82

Computation of LIFO Cost

	Base-Year Cost	Index	LIFO Cost
December 31, 20X1			
January 1, 20X1, base	$150,000	100.00	$150,000
December 31, 20X1, increment	28,000	107.58	30,122
	$178,000		$180,122
December 31, 20X2			
January 1, 20X1, base	$150,000	100.00	$150,000
December 31, 20X1, increment	28,000	107.58	30,122
December 31, 20X2, increment	60,000	115.65	69,390
	$238,000		$249,512
December 31, 20X3			
January 1, 20X1, base	$150,000	100.00	$150,000
December 31, 20X1, increment	28,000	107.58	30,122
December 31, 20X2, increment	60,000	115.65	69,390
December 31, 20X3, increment	42,000	125.82	52,844
	$280,000		$302,356

Exhibit 13.2   Example of LIFO Double-Extension Technique

an IRS rule of thumb holds that at least 70 percent of the total value of the pool should be matched to the prior-year costs to achieve a representative sample. If a statistical, random sampling technique is used, fewer items may be matched to obtain acceptable results.

(iv) Link-Chain Technique.   Under the link-chain technique, the ending inventory is double- extended at both current-year unit costs and prior-year unit costs. The respective extensions are then totaled, and the totals are used to compute a current-year index. This current-year index is multiplied by the prior-year cumulative LIFO index to obtain a current-year cumulative index. Total current-year costs are divided by the current-year cumulative index to determine base-year costs. If ending inventory stated at base-year cost exceeds beginning inventory stated at base-year cost, a new LIFO layer has been created. The new layer is valued by applying the applicable cumulative index (using one of the approaches described later in this chapter) to the increments stated at base-year cost. If ending inventory stated at base-year cost is less than beginning inventory stated at base-year cost, a LIFO liquidation has occurred. The double-extension and link-chain techniques produce identical results in the year LIFO is adopted. In subsequent years, however, changes in inventory mix and differences in the way new inventory items are handled usually create at least minor differences.

When a liquidation has occurred, decrements in base-year costs are deducted from the layers of earlier years, beginning with the most recent prior year.

If new items are included in the calculation of an index under the link-chain method, a unit cost would be reconstructed using prior-year, rather than base-year, costs. The reason is that the link-chain current-year index attempts to measure inflation for the most recent year. Exhibit 13.3 is an example of the LIFO link-chain technique and compares the results obtained to those calculated using the double-extension technique in Exhibit 13.2.

(v) Retail LIFO Method.   Like the retail inventory method described earlier, the retail LIFO method is used most frequently by department stores and other retailers that sell many and varied goods. In determining the ratio of cost to retail value for the year, the retail LIFO method differs from the conventional retail inventory method (which approximates the lower of average cost or market) in two basic respects: (1) the ratio is based on transactions during the year (beginning inventories are excluded, except in the year of adoption) and (2) net markdowns during the year (exclusive of promotional markdowns) are reflected in determining the sales value of inventory for purposes of calculating the ratio of cost to retail. Use of retail LIFO permits these companies to match most recent costs against current revenues and, as a result, values inventory at older costs. The retail method of LIFO is an adaption of the dollar-value LIFO method. However, the retail method differs from other applications of dollar-value LIFO because in recording inventory input and output, retail sales values are used rather than cost. Items in the closing inventory are initially priced at retail value (i.e., intended sales value), and the retail value of the closing inventory in each department is converted to cost by applying a factor reflecting the relationship of those values to cost.

Most retailers that adopt LIFO continue to maintain their books for internal merchandise management and accounting purposes at the lower of non-LIFO cost or market, following the retail method described earlier in this chapter. The internal records are converted to LIFO only for external financial reporting and tax purposes.

The retail LIFO method requires that retail selling prices be adjusted for markdowns to state inventories at approximate cost rather that at the lower-of-cost-or-market, as frequently followed under the non-LIFO retail method. To state the inventory at cost, the cost complement under the retail LIFO method includes the effects of markdowns. However, temporary or promotional markdowns are not included in the cost complement calculation, because the physical inventory would never reflect such markdowns (i.e., they are applied separately at the time of sale).

Department stores using the retail LIFO method are allowed to use price indexes published by the IRS based on information furnished by the BLS to convert the current-year retail value of the closing inventory to base-year retail value. In addition, other retailers that maintain a reasonably full line of inventory that comprises a representative cross-section of the inventory included in the BLS departmental groupings may use the BLS retail price indexes. Retailers that do not meet

This example, which uses the same inventory items and unit costs as in Exhibit 13.2, illustrates the link-chain technique and compares the results with those achieved using the double-extension technique. Because this example involves only a few items, the entire inventory has been double-extended. A representative sample also may be used with the link-chain technique. As in the double-extension example, assume that the company's opening inventory on January 1, 20X1 (the date LIFO is adopted), totals $150,000.

Item	Quantities in Ending Inventory	Prior-Year Cost		Current-Year Cost		Index	
		Cost	Unit Amount	Cost	Amount	Current Year	Cumulative
Year Ended December 31, 20X1							
A	8,000	$ 1.00	$ 8,000	$ 1.15	$ 9,200		
B	7,000	4.00	28,000	4.30	30,100		
C	10,000	7.00	70,000	7.60	76,000		
D	12,000	6.00	72,000	6.35	76,200		
			$178,000		$191,500	107.58	107.58
					÷107.58		
			Base-Year Cost		$178,000		
Year Ended December 31, 20X2							
A	12,000	$ 1.15	$ 13,800	$ 1.30	$15,600		
B	6,000	4.30	25,800	4.75	28,500		
C	7,000	7.60	53,200	8.15	57,050		
D	15,000	6.35	95,250	6.80	102,000		
E	7,000	9.60	67,200	10.30	72,100		
			$255,250		$275,250	107.84	116.01
					÷116.01		
			Base-Year Cost		$237,264		
Year Ended December 31, 20X3							
A	18,000	$ 1.30	$ 23,400	$ 1.50	$27,000		
D	17,000	6.80	115,600	7.50	127,500		
E	10,000	10.30	103,000	11.20	112,000		
F	5,000	9.15	45,750	9.75	48,750		
G	3,000	11.60	34,800	12.35	37,050		
			$322,550		$352,300	109.22	126.71
					÷126.71		
			Base-Year Cost		$278,036		

(*continues*)

Exhibit 13.3   Example of LIFO Link-Chain Technique

these criteria must develop their own indexes from internally generated figures, unless they make an election to use "simplified" LIFO (under which indexes are based on government-published indexes). Because price indexes are a significant element of the LIFO retail computations, internally generated indexes must be constructed on a sound basis and appropriate records must be maintained for examination by the IRS.

In a retail LIFO calculation, the current year's inventory at base-year retail value is compared with the prior year's inventory at base-year retail value to determine if there is a current-year increment or decrement. A current-year increment at base-year retail value is converted to current-year retail value by use of the BLS or other computed price index and then reduced to LIFO cost by using a factor reflecting the ratio of current-year cost to retail value for the year. The LIFO cost of the increment is added to the beginning-of-year LIFO inventory cost to arrive at the end-of-year LIFO inventory.

Computation of LIFO Cost

	Base-Year Cost	Index	LIFO Cost Using Link-Chain	LIFO Cost Using Double-Extension (From Exhibit 13.2)
December 31, 20X1				
January 1, 20X1, base	$150,000	100.00	$150,000	$150,000
December 31, 20X1, increment	28,000	107.58	30,122	30,122
	$178,000		$180,122	$180,122
December 31, 20X2				
January 1, 20X1, base	$150,000	100.00	$150,000	$150,000
December 31, 20X1, increment	28,000	107.58	30,122	30,122
December 31, 20X2, increment	59,264	116.01	68,752	69,390
	$237,264		$248,874	$249,512
December 31, 20X3				
January 1, 20X1, base	$150,000	100.00	$150,000	$150,000
December 31, 20X1, increment	28,000	107.58	30,122	30,122
December 31, 20X2, increment	59,264	116.01	68,752	69,390
December 31, 20X3, increment	40,772	126.71	51,662	52,844
	$278,036		$300,536	$302,356

Exhibit 13.3   Continued

A current-year decrement is applied against the most recent LIFO layer(s) at base-year retail value. The decrement is converted to retail value applicable to those layers by use of the index associated with such layers. The retail value so determined is reduced to LIFO cost by the factor(s) reflecting the ratio of cost to retail associated with the particular layers being liquidated. The LIFO cost of the decrement is then subtracted from the beginning-of-year LIFO inventory to arrive at the end-of-year LIFO inventory. Exhibit 13.4 is an example of the retail LIFO computation.

(vi) Valuing the Current-Year Layer.   Regardless of the technique used to compute LIFO values, an approach to price any newly created current-year LIFO layer must be selected and used consistently. Three methods are common.

1. *Latest acquisition cost.* This approach is attractive because often it is the easiest to apply. Many companies on LIFO maintain their internal inventory records on FIFO because of its simplicity and because it is a logical starting point for calculating LIFO. If the latest acquisition-cost approach is used, current-year unit costs are available from FIFO inventory valuation. A disadvantage of this approach is that it results in the highest value for the new layer (and, therefore, the highest taxable income) if costs have been consistently rising throughout the year. Another disadvantage is that the company must wait until after year-end to compute current-year cost.

2. *Earliest acquisition costs.* In periods of steadily increasing prices, this approach prices new layers at lower costs than the other approaches do. The result is the lowest tax liability. Another advantage is that current-year unit costs may be computed in the early part of the year. The major disadvantage of this approach is that it may require additional effort, because it generally involves a separate calculation. The separate calculation usually requires double-extending a sample of inventory items at earliest current-year costs to obtain the earliest acquisition-cost index.

This example illustrates the calculation of LIFO using the retail method. (Calculation of the indexes is not shown because those principles have been discussed previously.) The example illustrates the calculation for one department for the first three years the company is on LIFO.

Step No.	Item or Computation	First Year	Second Year	Third Year
1	Purchases at cost	$1,400,000	$1,600,000	$1,800,000
2	Purchases at retail, including markups	$2,900,000	$3,400,000	$3,700,000
3	Less permanent markdowns applicable to purchases	(100,000)	(150,000)	(200,000)
4	Net purchases at retail	$2,800,000	$3,250,000	$3,500,000
5	Cost complement percentage (1 ÷ 4)	50%	49.23%	51.43%
6	Ending inventory at retail	$ 800,000	$ 900,000	$ 950,000
7	Index (computed or BLS)	104.5	109.1	112.3
8	Inventory at base-year retail (6 ÷ 7)	765,550	824,931	845,948
9	Base-year retail, previous year	(700,000)	(765,550)	(824,931)
10	Current-year increment at base-year retail (8 − 9)	65,550	59,381	21,017
11	Valuation of current-year increment (7 × 10)	68,500	64,785	23,602
12	Current-year increment at cost (11 × 5)	34,250	31,894	12,138
13	Prior LIFO basis inventory	$ 350,000*	$ 384,250	$ 416,144
14	LIFO cost of inventory (12 + 13)	$ 384,250	$ 416,144	$ 428,282

*For purposes of this example, assume the cost complement percentage for the beginning inventory also was 50% (assumed opening inventory of $700,000 × 50% = $350, 000).

   If there had been a decrement or liquidation in any of the years, it would have been handled in the same manner as other LIFO methods (i.e., applied to most recent layer).

LIFO Reserve

In order to disclose the LIFO reserve (i.e., the difference between the inventory amount calculated using the retail method and the inventory amount calculated using the retail LIFO method), it is necessary to calculate the cost complement percentage as if the retailer used the retail method. As mentioned, however, this usually is easily derived from the internal records, because most retailers on LIFO maintain their records on the retail method. The calculation for the previous example follows.

	Cost	Retail	Retail Cost Complement
First Year			
Opening inventory	$ 350,000	$ 700,000	
Purchases including markups	1,400,000	2,900,000	
Goods available	$1,750,000	$3,600,000	48.61%
Second Year			
Opening inventory	$388,800	$800,000	
Purchases including markups	1,600,000	3,400,000	
Goods available	$1,988,000	$4,200,000	47.35%
Third Year			
Opening inventory	$426,150	$900,000	
Purchases including markups	1,800,000	3,700,000	
Goods available	$2,226,150	$4,600,000	48.39%

(*continues*)

Exhibit 13.4   Retail LIFO Method

The retail cost method complement percentage (e.g., 48.61% in the first year) is lower than the LIFO cost complement percentage (50% in the first year) because the retail method is a lower-of-cost-or-market method. Conversely, the LIFO method is a cost method. The LIFO reserve disclosure should represent the difference between LIFO cost and the lower of current cost or market.

	First Year	**Second Year**	**Third Year**
Summary of LIFO Reserve			
Inventory at retail	$800,000	$900,000	$950,000
Cost complement percentage	48.61%	47.35%	48.39%
Inventory at retail method	388,880	426,150	459,705
Inventory at LIFO cost above	(384,250)	(416,144)	(428,282)
LIFO reserve	$ 4,630	$ 10,006	$ 31,423

Exhibit 13.4   Continued

3. *Average acquisition cost.* The results obtained from this approach represent a middle ground between the other two approaches. However, this approach may require even more involved calculations than the earliest acquisition approach.

In addition, any other method that in the opinion of the IRS clearly reflects income may be used to price current-year LIFO layers.

(vii) New Items.   The treatment of new items is one of the more controversial aspects involved in using LIFO. Important considerations in this area include what constitutes a new item and how the LIFO cost of new items should be determined.

Improper designation of items as new can significantly affect reported income if base-year costs are not reconstructed. The SEC expresses its concern in this area in Financial Reporting Release (FRR) 1 (Section 205) and again in SAB No. 58, *Last-In, First-Out (LIFO) Inventory Accounting Practices for Financial Reporting Purposes* (SAB Topic 5.L), by stating that "insignificant and sometimes arbitrary" differences are not sufficient justification for new product designation, particularly when it results in a significant increase in reported income.

Section 4-21 of the AICPA Issues Paper provides this guidance for determining if an item should be classified as a new item for financial reporting purposes:

A *new item* is a raw material, product, or cost component not previously present in significant quantities in the inventory. To be considered a new item, the material or product should not be commingled physically with other materials or products so that its identity is lost, and it should be accounted for separately. In addition, the material should have qualities (physical, chemical, or both) significantly different from those previously inventoried items. Items treated as fungible with items already in the pool ordinarily should not be considered *new items.* Changes in the market value of an item or merely purchasing a virtually identical item from a different supplier does not make the item a new item. [Emphasis added.]

The AICPA Issues Paper concludes (Section 4-27) that for financial reporting purposes, if the double-extension or an index technique is used, the base-year cost of the new item should be reconstructed and the base-year cost should be estimated if it is not otherwise objectively determinable. However, if the link-chain technique is used, the AICPA Issues Paper concludes that "reconstruction of prior years' costs is unnecessary because that technique produces approximately the same results as reconstruction." To avoid the problems generally encountered in reconstructing base-year costs, companies may consider using the link-chain method if they meet IRS requirements. Some companies that frequently add new items are not able to satisfy the IRS's stringent qualifications for the use of the link-chain method. In addition, reconstructing base-year costs using vendor quotes or price lists is not always practical. Consequently, these companies would have added new items at current-year costs for tax purposes. Although allowable for tax purposes, adding new items to inventory using current-year costs for financial reporting would conflict with the recommendation in the AICPA Issues Paper.

(viii) Other LIFO Matters.   In SAB Topic 5.L, the SEC Staff endorsed the AICPA Issues Paper, saying it represents an accumulation of existing acceptable LIFO accounting practices, and companies and their auditors should refer to it for guidance.

Deferred taxes should be recognized under ASC 740, *Income Taxes,* for LIFO inventory temporary differences (e.g., an excess of LIFO inventory for financial reporting over its tax basis requires recognition of a deferred tax liability).

(d) AVERAGE COST.   Another fairly common cost flow assumption uses an average cost per unit to determine cost of sales and the inventory value. A weighted average cost (including the cost of the beginning inventory and current period purchases and production) is used in connection with a periodic inventory system. A moving average cost typically is used with a perpetual inventory system. The average cost method is used by companies in many industries and is often viewed as producing results similar to those obtained from the FIFO method. The reason is that the inventory balance is directly influenced by current costs.

(e) SPECIFIC IDENTIFICATION.   Companies in a limited number of industries track the cost of individual items and retain costs in inventory until the related physical goods are sold using the specific identification method. This method is commonly used for large or expensive items such as automobiles or precious gems. Theoretically, this approach is preferable because it matches costs and revenues based on the actual physical flow of specific goods. However, implementing it is often difficult or impossible, because the cost of individual inventory items cannot be determined or the expense of tracking cost by item is not justified by increased accuracy. Also, when the approach is used in situations where inventory items are not unique, manipulation of recorded amounts is possible. For example, a company having similar inventory items with different costs can record in inventory and cost of sales the item that yields the most favorable current results.

(f) OTHER ASSUMPTIONS.   Other cost flow assumptions not commonly used for external reporting but possibly useful for internal purposes include:

- Next-in, first-out
- Cost-of-last-purchase
- Base stock method (similar to LIFO in that it assumes a certain minimum level of inventory is required to operate a business. The base stock is carried at initial cost.)

These methods are not considered to be within GAAP. However, they may assist companies in identifying current product-profit margins, because they match current costs against current sales.

13.7 CONTROL OBJECTIVES AND PROCEDURES

(a) GENERAL CONTROL PROCEDURES.   For most manufacturing and merchandising companies, inventory represents a significant asset, valuable to others as well as to the company. As a result, it is important that proper internal controls are in place to protect this investment. General controls provide an environment that enhances safeguarding the inventory in a planned and systematic manner.

(i) Physical Safeguards.   The use of locks, guards, restricted access, and other physical means to secure valuable inventory items improves control and discourages theft. In addition, proper shelter and storage facilities reduce deterioration and spoilage. As with most control measures, a cost/benefit evaluation should be performed to determine the extent to implement physical safeguards.

(ii) Written Policies. Documentation of the procedures and policies authorized by management for inventory control should exist and be updated regularly for changes. The documentation should be readily available to and understood by employees who perform these procedures. Systems documentation is particularly useful for training new employees and minimizing disruption from other changes in personnel.

(iii) Reconciliations. Regular comparisons of physical goods to the accounting records and reconciliations of various source documents can improve control by identifying losses, problems, or other matters warranting management's timely attention. A perpetual inventory system is required to make effective use of reconciliations as a control. Reconciliations should be reviewed by the individual who supervises the person who prepares them. Many specific inventory reconciliation procedures are included in the lists of specific control procedures presented in Section 13.4(d).

(iv) Budgets. In the inventory area, the use of budgets is most effective for fixed and semifixed costs. Comparison of actual costs to the budgeted amounts can identify matters for further investigation. Explanations of budget variances can assist management in determining whether to record actual costs or standard costs as the inventory amount.

(v) Use of Standard Costs and Analysis of Variances. For variable costs, the use of regularly updated standard costs and the related variance analysis can identify differences between actual costs and standard costs, regardless of the level of volume. These differences should be examined to ascertain what caused them and what corrective action may be required.

(b) SPECIFIED CONTROL PROCEDURES. To support the general control procedures in achieving an effective system of internal control over inventory, specific control procedures must be implemented. Several lists of potential specific control procedures related to inventory are in Sections 13.4(d) and 13.5(i).

13.8 FINANCIAL STATEMENT DISCLOSURE REQUIREMENTS

GAAP requires specific inventory disclosures, including the basis of stating inventory, methods used to recognize and measure costs (e.g., FIFO, LIFO), and LIFO-related information for companies applying the LIFO method. SEC rules require additional qualitative and quantitative disclosures for public companies.

13.9 INTERNATIONAL STANDARDS ON INVENTORY ACCOUNTING

In general, International Financial Reporting Standards (IFRS) are less detailed than GAAP in the area of inventory accounting. IFRS addresses inventory accounting issues in three standards: International Accounting Standard (IAS) 2, *Inventories;* IAS 18, *Revenue;* and IAS 41, *Agriculture.* There are a number of differences between U.S. GAAP and these standards, the most notable being that LIFO is not permitted under IFRS.

IFRS also calls for the valuation of inventories at the lower of cost or net realizable value. (The concept of a ceiling and floor value to determine market value is limited to U.S. GAAP.) IFRS permits write-ups of previously written-down inventory items back to their original cost amounts under certain conditions, whereas U.S. GAAP does not allow write-ups in a subsequent annual period.

IFRS requires write-downs in interim periods. However, under U.S. GAAP, inventory write-downs in interim periods do not have to be made if there are reasonable expectations that the declines will be reversed before year-end.

U.S. GAAP does not have specific inventory guidance for livestock and agricultural products.

13.10 SOURCES AND SUGGESTED REFERENCES

Accounting Standards Executive Committee. *Identification and Discussion of Certain Financial Accounting and Reporting Issues Concerning LIFO Inventories.* New York: AICPA, 1984.

———. Practice Bulletin No. 2. *Elimination of Profits Resulting from Intercompany Transfers of LIFO Inventories.* New York: AICPA, 1987.

Financial Accounting Standards Board. FASB Accounting Standards Codification Topic, 250, *Accounting Changes and Error Corrections as of 2011.*

———. FASB Accounting Standards Codification Topic 270, *Interim Reporting.*

———. FASB Accounting Standards Codification Topic 330, *Inventory.*

———. FASB Accounting Standards Codification Topic 420, *Exit or Disposal Cost Obligations.*

———. FASB Accounting Standards Codification Topic 720, *Research and Development.*

———. FASB Accounting Standards Codification Topic 740, *Income Taxes.*

———. FASB Accounting Standards Codification Topic 805, *Business Combinations.*

———. FASB Accounting Standards Codification Topic 810, *Consolidation.*

———. FASB Accounting Standards Codification Topic 815, *Derivatives and Hedging.*

———. FASB Accounting Standards Codification Subtopic 835-20, *Interest—Capitalization of Interest.*

———. FASB Accounting Standards Codification Subtopic 985, *Software—Costs of Software to Be Sold, Leased, or Marketed*

Securities and Exchange Commission. *LIFO Method of Accounting for Inventories,* Financial Reporting Releases, § 205 (ASR No. 141). Washington, DC: Author, 1973.

———. Financial Reporting Releases, § 205 (ASR No. 293), *LIFO Method of Accounting for Inventories.* Washington, DC: Author, 1981.

———. Staff Accounting Bulletin No. 40, *Codification of SAB Nos. 1–38.* Washington, DC: Author, 1981.

———. Staff Accounting Bulletin No. 100, *Restructuring and Impairment Charges.* Washington, DC: Author, 1999.

———. Staff Accounting Bulletin No. 58, *LIFO Inventory Practice.* Washington, DC: Author, 1985.

Wilson, P. W., and K. E. Christensen. *LIFO for Retailers.* New York: John Wiley & Sons, 1985.

CHAPTER 14

GOODWILL AND OTHER INTANGIBLE ASSETS

James Mraz, CPA, MBA

University of Maryland, University College

14.1 CHARACTERIZATION OF INTANGIBLE ASSETS

Intangible assets are assets—other than financial assets—that lack physical substance yet do have utility and value in the hands of the reporting entity. Examples include patents, copyrights, trade names, customer lists, royalty agreements, databases, and computer software. They also include assets, called leasehold improvements, which are frequently but mistakenly viewed as being tangible assets.

The range of intangibles is quite broad, and this fact is perhaps more clearly understood now than during earlier years, since changing business and economic conditions have brought intellectual property (IP) and certain other intangible assets to much greater prominence than had formerly been the case. While the value of intangibles may still be underappreciated for many, mostly traditional (e.g., manufacturing), businesses, for high-technology and other so-called knowledge-based companies, the primary assets may be intangible ones such as patents and copyrights. Even for professional service firms, the key assets may be "soft" resources, such as knowledge bases and client relationships.

There are several possible taxonomies of intangible assets. First, intangible assets can be classified either as *identifiable*—for example, trademarks and most other intangibles—or as *unidentifiable*—which generally implies goodwill. A second way to classify intangible assets is based on how they are acquired. They can be internally developed or acquired from external sources, which include both simple purchases of one or more intangibles (e.g., groups of related patents) or those that are part of business combinations. Intangible assets acquired in a business combination may be recognized as assets separate from goodwill or as part of goodwill, depending on whether the intangible assets satisfy certain criteria. As discussed in this chapter, the applicable accounting pronouncements and accounting requirements differ significantly, depending on whether the intangible asset is identifiable, whether it is internally developed or acquired externally, and, if acquired externally, whether it was acquired in a business combination.

Yet other classification schemes for intangible assets were first offered by the now-superseded Accounting Principles Board (APB) Opinion No. 17, *Intangible Assets,* which indicated that intangible assets could also be categorized based on either:

1. Expected period of benefit—whether limited by law or contract, related to human or economic factors, or indefinite or indeterminate duration; or
2. Separability from an entire enterprise—rights transferable without title, salable, or inseparable from the enterprise or a substantial part of it.

While the foregoing taxonomies assist one in thinking about intangibles and are to greater or lesser extent incorporated into current generally accepted accounting principles (GAAP; primarily Statement of Financial Accounting Standards (SFAS) No. 142 [Accounting Standards Codification (ASC) 350], perhaps the most important distinctions are between intangibles acquired in business combinations accounted for under SFAS No. 141(R) (ASC 805) or otherwise; between those having finite lives and those having indefinite lives; and between those that are severable from the reporting entity and those that are not. All of these matters are addressed in this chapter.

14.2 ACCOUNTING AND FINANCIAL MANAGEMENT OVERVIEW

Numerous pronouncements provide guidance on the accounting for intangibles. This section provides an overview of those pronouncements.

(a) INTANGIBLE ASSETS INCLUDING GOODWILL ACQUIRED IN A BUSINESS COMBINATION. Under SFAS No. 141(R) (ASC 805), *Business Combinations,* all business combinations must now be accounted for as acquisitions; pooling accounting is no longer permitted. This necessitates purchase price allocation. It provides initial measurement and recognition guidance for intangible assets and goodwill acquired in a business combination, including mandates as to the recognition of intangible assets apart from goodwill.

Subsequent accounting for intangible assets, including goodwill, is provided in SFAS No. 142 (ASC 350), *Goodwill and Other Intangible Assets,* which provides that goodwill should not be amortized; it mandates that impairment tests of goodwill be conducted annually or, in some circumstances, more frequently; and it provides guidance on recognizing impairments. In contrast with earlier GAAP, which required amortization of all intangibles, SFAS No. 142 (ASC 350) addresses whether intangible assets other than goodwill have *indefinite* useful lives, and therefore should not be amortized but instead tested at least annually for impairment, or *finite* useful lives, and therefore should be amortized over their estimated useful life.

Intangible assets with finite useful lives are tested for impairment under SFAS No. 144 (ASC 360), *Accounting for the Impairment or Disposal of Long-Lived Assets.* Intangibles having finite lives and thus are amortized must also be reviewed for recoverability of carrying amounts in a process similar to that under SFAS No. 144 (ASC 360), and useful lives must be reassessed and altered when warranted by circumstances (e.g., technological obsolescence making the useful life of a patent much shorter than the legal term).

(b) INTANGIBLE ASSETS ACQUIRED SEPARATELY OR WITH OTHER ASSETS.   SFAS No. 142 (ASC 350) provides initial recognition and measurement guidance for intangible assets acquired other than in a business combination (i.e., intangible assets acquired individually or together with a group of other assets that do not constitute a business). It also provides guidance to the subsequent accounting for intangible assets, including determining whether they have finite or indeterminate useful lives and therefore whether they should be amortized or not. Finally, it addresses accounting for impairments of intangible assets with indeterminate lives. A separate standard, SFAS No. 144 (ASC 360), provides guidance on impairment of intangible assets with finite useful lives.

(c) INTERNALLY DEVELOPED INTANGIBLE ASSETS.   SFAS No. 142 (ASC 350) addresses the initial and subsequent accounting for internally developed intangible assets. It carries forward the requirement set forth by the predecessor standard, APB No. 17, that the costs of internally developing, maintaining, or restoring intangibles that cannot be identified specifically, have indeterminate lives, or are inherent in an ongoing business and pertain to the entity as a whole cannot be capitalized. Such costs must be expensed currently as incurred.

(d) INTANGIBLE ASSETS RECOGNIZED ON ACQUISITION OF A NONCONTROLLING INTEREST IN A SUBSIDIARY.   SFAS No. 142 (ASC 350) provides guidance on the initial and subsequent accounting for goodwill and other intangible assets recognized on acquisition of noncontrolling interests in a subsidiary. Under current GAAP, goodwill associated with minority (i.e., noncontrolling) interests is not recognized. Note, however, that the Financial Accounting Standards Board (FASB) is currently considering a major change in purchase business combination accounting that will, if adopted, result in the recognition of goodwill associated with minority interests.

(e) GOODWILL RECOGNIZED WHEN APPLYING THE EQUITY METHOD.   SFAS No. 142 (ASC 350) provides that amounts recognized as corresponding to goodwill in applying equity method accounting to investments should not be amortized. Equity method goodwill is tested for impairment under APB Opinion No. 18, *The Equity Method of Accounting for Investments in Common Stock.*

(f) SPECIFIC GUIDANCE ON CERTAIN INTANGIBLES.   Accounting pronouncements, such as Statements of Position issued by the Accounting Standards Executive Committee of the American Institute of Certified Public Accountants (AICPA), provide guidance on the accounting for specific intangible assets, such as start-up costs, internally developed software, and advertising. These matters are addressed later in this chapter in paragraphs 14.5(m), 14.6(f) and 14.5(p) respectively.

(g) INTANGIBLE ASSETS IN SPECIALIZED INDUSTRIES.   Certain FASB Statements and Interpretations provide guidance on accounting for certain intangibles of specialized industries, such as airlines and computer software development. Impairment testing for intangible assets in many specialized industries is performed under the general requirements (SFAS No. 144 (ASC 360)), but for certain industries or assets, such as broadcasters' program rights, guidance under particular AICPA Industry Audit and Accounting Guides must be followed instead.

(h) NEW EMPHASIS ON MANAGEMENT OF INTANGIBLE ASSETS

(i) Sarbanes-Oxley Act of 2002—Implications for the Financial Reporting of Intangible Assets.   Sound financial and operating management of reporting entities has always been a critical concern, of course, but developments in the early 2000s have caused there to be renewed emphasis on managements' and directors' fiduciary duties, including the duty to maximize the value of all assets under management. The widely reported corporate management and financial reporting scandals of the late 1990s, in particular, created a groundswell of demand for reforms in corporate governance practices. Among other things, this led to the hurried passage of the Sarbanes-Oxley Act of 2002 (Sarbanes or the Act), the ramifications of which are still being comprehended.

Sarbanes has generated a considerable amount of interest in, and focus on, the quality of financial reporting and the reliability of internal control systems. The widely publicized and sometimes controversial Section 404 requirements for reporting on the effectiveness of internal controls, certified by both management and the entity's independent accountants, has been a costly and demanding undertaking for many companies, including some whose quality of controls and financial management were previously unquestioned by investors.

Sarbanes has also highlighted the historically troublesome disparity between corporate managers and shareholders regarding many entities' true financial condition, which is sometimes referred to as the "transparency" issue. GAAP-basis financial reporting is based on a "mixed-attribute" model that combines historical costs and current fair values, with some costs subject to amortization and others only sporadically tested for impairment, making financial statements often unsuited for directly assessing the reporting entity's value. Because intangible assets now account for the majority of the stock values of many publicly traded companies (by some estimates, as much as two-thirds), and because accounting for intangibles has been largely overlooked in the accounting pronouncements and literature, this area is now overdue for much greater attention. The demand for greater transparency has increased the pressure on accountants to develop the means to more fully report the value of intangible assets of the companies they manage, report, and/or opine on.

When the 2002 Sarbanes requirements are evaluated in conjunction with the 2001 FASB pronouncements regarding goodwill, intangibles, and business combinations (SFAS Nos. 141(R) (ASC 805) and 142 (ASC 350)), it is clear that today's accountants (both internal staff and outside auditors) must increase their awareness of the intangible assets a company possesses and the value those assets bring to the company. That value, which may in part be driven by the potential value those assets hold for other entities. Even the SEC now recognizes that the way in which intangible assets are accounted for, as well as which valuation method is employed, can have a material effect on investors' decisions. (See discussion by SEC Staff on "market participation" valuation requirements in Subsection 14.3(a)(ii).)

For example, when the accountant considers how off-balance-sheet transactions may impact (either negatively or positively) the financial condition of a company, intangible assets will be, in many instances, a likely asset class to inspect and analyze. Section 401(a) of the Act directed the SEC to enact rules so that:

> each annual and quarterly report required to be filed with the Commission shall disclose all material off-balance-sheet transactions, arrangements, obligations (including contingent obligations), and other relationships of the issuer with unconsolidated entities or other persons, that may have a material current or future effect on financial condition, changes in financial condition, results of operations, liquidity, capital expenditures, capital resources, or significant components of revenues or expenses.

In its rules (Final Rule: Disclosure in Management's Discussion and Analysis about Off-Balance-Sheet Arrangements and Aggregate Contractual Obligations, effective April 7, 2003), the SEC mandated that registrants provide explanations of off-balance-sheet arrangements in separately captioned subsections of the so-called management discussion and analysis (MD&A) section of their periodic filings with the Commission. While certain of these disclosures were already required under MD&A rules, the new requirements are somewhat more comprehensive. These rules do not, however, alter underlying accounting for, or disclosures about, owned intangible assets, nor do they alter the accounting, under GAAP, for transfers or sales of such assets.

The SEC rule does require that executory contracts, such as purchase obligations for goods or services, be included in a new tabular presentation of off-balance-sheet obligations, which is at variance with GAAP requirements but deemed to be important because of liquidity implications. In the case of a license arrangement (e.g., for patent rights previously sold), disclosure in the MD&A under this rule would be appropriate, even though the obligation is not a liability under GAAP definitions.

(ii) Improved Internal Controls Over Intangible Assets Under Sarbanes.   In Section 404(a), the Act addresses a new requirement for management to prepare an internal control report that shall:

1. state the responsibility of management for establishing and maintaining an adequate internal control structure and procedures for financial reporting, and
2. contain an assessment, as of the end of the most recent fiscal year of the issuer, of the effectiveness of the internal control structure and procedures of the issuer for financial reporting.

As discussed earlier, SFAS Nos. 141(R) (ASC 805) and 142 (ASC 350) require revised accounting for intangibles and goodwill arising from business combinations. Similarly, as a company generates new IP through innovation, invention, or operational insights, it may be necessary to establish new accounting procedures to measure the carrying value and fair value of an acquired reporting unit (and perhaps existing reporting units), including the value of intangibles.

Both the cost to create and the cost to protect intangibles are measured and reported in the financial statements, either as an expense (if properly considered research and development costs under GAAP) or as capital assets. In general, due to the strict requirements of SFAS No. 2 (ASC 730), *Accounting for Research and Development Costs,* most of the cost of patent or other IP development, if internally accomplished, will be expensed—one reason that GAAP-compliant financial reporting sometimes underserves entities that rely on IP for their operations and valuation.

An important concern, then, is that if these assets are largely missing from the financial statements, how can these entities ensure that fiduciary responsibilities relative to these hidden assets are properly discharged? There are at least two aspects to this concern: (1) developing and implementing internal controls over these assets such that the requirements of Sarbanes will be met; and (2) that the value of these assets is recognized for the benefit of the shareholders.

An axiom in management is that what is not measured is not managed; a corollary to that is that what is not in plain sight is also likely to not be well managed. The relatively trivial carrying values of IP often can result in undermanagement, meaning a failure to manage these assets for the benefit of shareholders, whether by using them more effectively internally or by seeking external sources of income from these intangible assets.

As part of a comprehensive effort to establish meaningful controls over its intangible assets, entities should consider developing metrics that would raise the profile of both the holdings of intangibles and of the productivity derived therefrom. Productivity measures would address (as appropriate) both internal usage and external revenue generation. By devising and monitoring such internal control procedures, compliance with this section of Sarbanes would seem to have been accomplished.

(iii) Practical Approaches to Internal Control Structures for Intangible Assets.   The development of an internal control structure used to capture, measure, and report the presence and value of intangible assets can be accomplished by assisting personnel in the legal, research, and/or technology transfer departments to establish the appropriate recordkeeping and asset control procedures. Those procedures would relate to documenting the creation, acquisition, and disposal of intellectual assets. Such documentation could include data about the specific identity of the asset, correspondence with appropriate patent, trademark, or copyright offices, ownership and/or assignments, estimated useful lives, associated costs to acquire or create, and, when appropriate, market values.

It is potentially the case that in-house and/or outside counsel may be aware of existing third-party claims that could be asserted against the company as well as claims the company may be able to assert against third parties. Such analyses may already be in process by the tech-transfer and/or legal staff as part of their normal process of selecting what technologies to outlicense or protect through an infringement action. They may also be in possession of demand letters from other entities that are asserting claims based on their intellectual assets.

Accounting for such claims may also suggest that a review of the company's various insurance policies, vendor and customer contracts, and licensing agreements might be warranted. Because the accountant is typically required under SFAS No. 5 (ASC 450), *Accounting for Contingencies,* to assess the likelihood that a loss event will occur, and whether the estimated loss amounts can be reasonably determined, this should be a routine procedure. Under SFAS No. 5 (ASC 450), however, indemnification and insurance provisions may give rise to a recovery claim, but this cannot be offset.

SFAS No. 112 (ASC 712), *Employers' Accounting for Postemployment Benefits—an amendment of FASB Statements No. 5 and 43,* amended SFAS No. 5 (ASC 450) in this way:

> The Board decided not to apply the additional Statement 5 disclosures to postemployment benefit obligations because it believes that the additional cost of compliance is not warranted. Thus, this Statement requires disclosure only if an obligation for postemployment benefits is not accrued accordance with Statements 5 or 43 solely because the amount cannot be reasonably estimated.

SFAS No. 114 (ASC 310), *Accounting by Creditors for Impairment of a Loan—an amendment of FASB Statements No. 5 and 15,* amended SFAS No. 5 (ASC 450) to clarify that a creditor should evaluate the collectability of both contractual interest and contractual principal of all receivables when assessing the need for a loss accrual.

As part of an assessment of the company's disclosure controls, it may be helpful to prepare documentation procedures throughout the life cycle of the intangible asset. If the company is International Organization for Standardization (ISO) compliant, much of the key information regarding intangibles may already be documented relating to:

- Creation and acquisition identification of the intangible asset
- Applicable filings and prosecution of applications to obtain a formal or registered IP right for the intangible asset
- Encumbrances to ownership rights, including licensing and assignments that may narrow or eliminate rights for the intangible asset
- Maintenance of the asset, such as repair and upkeep or the payment of appropriate registration fees
- Outlicensing and/or cross-licensing agreements
- Infringement claims against and/or by third parties regarding the intangible asset
- Disposal, retirement, or expiration of the asset

An additional reference to assist accountants to structure internal control procedures is the guidance presented in the AICPA toolkit, *The Fair Value Measurement Valuation Toolkit for Financial Accounting Standards Board Statements of Financial Accounting Standards No. 141, Business Combinations, and No. 142 (ASC 350), Goodwill and Other Intangible Assets.*

Much of the foregoing is directed toward maintaining a current record of the existence of intangible assets and various agreements, such as licensing arrangements. Another aspect, and one vital to the goal of maximizing shareholder wealth, is to address those actions that are not currently being taken but that could be valuable for the enterprise and its various stakeholders. Doing this requires that external data sources be incorporated into the entity's information system. Without external references, poor performance may be misread as good simply because of an improvement over prior periods.

One cited statistic, for example, is that each patent in existence (circa 2000) was producing an average of $60,000 in licensing revenues per year, or about $1 million over its economic life. Information about the average licensing revenue per patent is an external metric that can be used to evaluate the entity's own licensing portfolio. Over time, such analyses can be used to gauge portfolio trends, to show whether the licensing revenue of the patent portfolio is acceptable versus expected licensing revenues, based on statistical averages. If not, an investigation can be focused to determine why not. This control mechanism is fully consistent with the explicit requirements and implicit objectives of Sarbanes.

This type of information also sets out a framework for an internal metric. The licensing revenue per patent can be determined for a company patent portfolio. An average licensing revenue can be determined and tracked over time. Patents that are underperforming can be reviewed to ascertain whether these should be preserved for commercial purposes other than licensing, or whether they should be sold or abandoned. Trend data can be accumulated over time to report on whether the portfolio is underperforming based on internally set expectations.

Some examples of metrics that can be used to evaluate an IP program include the number of patents or patent applications owned, by type (utility or design), country, the royalty income received from each patent, and an average royalty for each type of patent or type of technology. Patents owned should include all patents to which the company has unimpaired title. (Title would be deemed impaired if the reporting entity is not the sole assignee.) The dollar value of sales for products covered by the patents is another metric that permits such evaluations of a patent portfolio or IP program.

14.3 INITIAL RECOGNITION AND MEASUREMENT OF INTANGIBLE ASSETS

(a) ACQUIRED INTANGIBLE ASSETS.   SFAS No. 142 (ASC 350), issued in June 2001, superseded the former standard, APB Opinion No. 17. It uses the term *intangible assets* to refer to intangible assets other than goodwill. While amortization is no longer universally required, as it had been for over 30 years under APB No. 17, SFAS No. 142 (ASC 350) did carry forward certain of the requirements of that former standard.

(i) Cost Allocation and Other Valuation Issues.   An intangible asset acquired either individually or with a group of other assets—other than as part of a business combination—is initially recognized and measured based on its fair value. The cost of a group of assets acquired in a transaction other than a business combination is allocated to the individual assets acquired based on their relative fair values, and cannot result in the recognition of goodwill.

Intangible assets acquired in a business combination are initially recognized and measured in conformity with SFAS No. 141(R) (ASC 805). SFAS No. 141(R) (ASC 805) requires an acquirer to recognize the assets acquired, the liabilities assumed, and any noncontrolling interest in the acquiree at the acquisition date, measured at their fair values as of that date. This replaces SFAS No. 141's cost allocation price method. SFAS No. 141(R) (ASC 805) requires the acquirer to recognize goodwill as of the acquisition date, measured as a residual, which in most types of business combinations will result in measuring goodwill as the excess of the consideration transferred plus the fair value of any noncontrolling interest in the acquire at the acquisition date over the fair values of the identifiable net assets acquired.

(ii) SEC/PCAOB Valuation Issues for Intangible Assets—More Changes, Greater Confusion on the Horizon.   In unofficial remarks before the December 2004 AICPA National Conference on Current SEC and PCAOB Developments, a staff member of the SEC's Office of the Chief Accountant explained why fair value, determined by using the actual amounts negotiated by the buyer and seller (referred to later as "entity specific") would be superseded by an "estimated" fair value based on an analysis from a "marketplace participant" perspective. In these remarks, it was stated that:

> An underpinning to the determination of fair value of an acquired intangible asset under SFAS No. 141 is that it is determined from the perspective of a marketplace participant.

> This is clear in SFAS No. 141, paragraph B174, which indicates that the fair value estimate,

> should incorporate assumptions that marketplace participants would use in making estimates of fair value, such as assumptions about future contract renewals and other benefits such as those that might result from acquisition-related synergies.

> In contrast, the useful life concept in SFAS No. 142 (ASC 350) is not necessarily viewed from that of a marketplace participant. Rather the useful life of an intangible asset is inherently related to the expectations of the particular entity and therefore would incorporate entity specific assumptions.

In this context, the entity may believe that the fair value determination should therefore be entirely consistent with the useful life then assigned to the intangible asset as in this case, both were developed based on entity specific assumptions.

I would point out, however, that the utilization of entity specific assumptions to determine fair value in this case is just a proxy for those assumptions that may be developed by a marketplace participant.

Subsequent to these remarks the FASB issued an Exposure Draft of SFAS No. 141(R) (June 2005), which in many particulars is based on an analysis of international accounting standards. SFAS No. 141(R) (ASC 805) was issued in December 2007. Paragraph 3(i) of SFAS No. 141(R) (ASC 805) defines fair value as the price that would be received to sell an asset or paid to transfer a liability in an orderly transaction between market participants at the measurement date.

Paragraph 20 of SFAS No. 141(R) states:

The acquirer shall measure the identifiable assets acquired, the liabilities assumed, and any non-controlling interest in the acquiree at their acquisition date fair values.

Paragraphs A57 through A61 provide guidance on measuring the fair values of particular identifiable assets and a noncontrolling interest in an acquiree.

The SEC remarks and the FASB exposure draft provisions are indicative of a changing landscape of the acceptable valuation methodologies and technical experts to whom the accountant can turn for support when computing an intangible's fair value.

FASB Concept Statement No. 7 (ASC 915), *Accounting and Reporting by Development Stage Enterprises,* was identified in SFAS No. 142 (ASC 350), issued in 2002, as guidance for valuation methodologies, principally citing the comparables and income method approaches. However, often intangible asset values measured in actual business transactions are based more on expected and potential benefits rather than on historical and/or actual revenues. Therefore, the application of the income approach requires a stacking or layering of assumptions. As the number of those assumptions increases, compliance with Rule 201 of the AICPA Code of Professional Conduct (specifically concerning the reliance on sufficient relevant data in support of any professional opinion) becomes more and more difficult.

There are real-world situations where technical experts from other disciplines have addressed the situation of determining the fair value of intangibles where historical cash flows do not exist. One of those situations arises during the dispute resolution process, and a second is seen in the technology-transfer industry.

(iii) Valuation Approaches Supported by Court Opinions. In the federal courts, a jury is frequently asked to estimate the damages attributable to a violation of intellectual property rights. Several cases, including *Georgia-Pacific v. United States Plywood Corp.* and *Panduit Corp. v. Stahlin Bros. Fibre Works, Inc.,* have compiled a technical body of knowledge regarding methodologies to determine the fair value of intangible assets. For example, *Panduit* sets forth these four tests:

1. Is there demand for the patented product?
2. Are there acceptable noninfringing alternatives to the infringing product?
3. Does the patent holder have the manufacturing and marketing capacity to make and sell more of the product?
4. Can the damages consultant quantify the lost profits to a reasonable degree of certainty?

In the earlier *Georgia-Pacific* case, the court considered 15 factors as a means to compute damages arising from a dispute over intangible assets:

1. The royalties received by Georgia-Pacific for licensing the patent, proving or tending to prove an established royalty
2. The rates paid by the licensee for the use of other similar patents

3. The nature and scope of the license, such as whether it is exclusive or nonexclusive, restricted or nonrestricted in terms of territory or customers

4. Georgia-Pacific's policy of maintaining its patent monopoly by licensing the use of the invention only under special conditions designed to preserve the monopoly

5. The commercial relationship between Georgia-Pacific and licensees, such as whether they are competitors in the same territory in the same line of business or whether they are inventor and promoter

6. The effect of selling the patented specialty in promoting sales of other Georgia-Pacific products; the existing value of the invention to Georgia-Pacific as a generator of sales of nonpatented items; and the extent of such derivative or "convoyed" sales

7. The duration of the patent and the term of the license

8. The established profitability of the patented product, its commercial success, and its current popularity

9. The utility and advantages of the patent property over any old modes or devices that had been used

10. The nature of the patented invention, its character in the commercial embodiment owned and produced by the licensor, and the benefits to those who used it

11. The extent to which the infringer used the invention and any evidence probative of the value of that use

12. The portion of the profit or selling price that is customary in the particular business or in comparable businesses

13. The portion of the realizable profit that should be credited to the invention as distinguished from any nonpatented elements, manufacturing process, business risks, or significant features or improvements added by the infringer

14. The opinion testimony of qualified experts

15. The amount that Georgia-Pacific and a licensee would have agreed on at the time the infringement began if they had reasonably and voluntarily tried to reach an agreement

In a subsequent case based in part on the *Panduit* findings, the courts have held that damages based on a loss of market share can be used to compute damages (*State Industries, Inc. v. Mor-Flo Industries, Inc.*). In *State Industries,* the Federal Circuit accepted evidence of the patentee's market share to prove that the patentee would have made at least a percentage of the infringer's sales had there been no infringement. Quantifying market share allows the patentee to measure lost profits in the ratio of their original market share to their diluted market share after the infringement.

In these cases and several others, the courts have held that intellectual property owners may be entitled to lost profits that can never be realized (hence the claim for "lost" profits), but were nonetheless measured to "a reasonable degree of accounting certainty."

(iv) Valuation Approaches Used by Tech-Transfer Practitioners.   Taking a page from the dispute resolution practitioners, several technology transfer specialists (also referred to as licensing professionals) have adopted market-based measures of value. Here, however, rather than measure the amount of damages, the computation is made for the purpose of measuring the amount of benefits that would be recognized by the adoption of the licensor's technology by the licensee. In 2002 Ted Hagelin analyzed different concepts and methods of valuation, including the cost, market, and income methods.[1] Other valuation methods developed especially for intellectual property law were also examined, including the "25 percent" rule, industry standards, ranking, surrogate measures, disaggregation, Monte Carlo, and option methods. In his article, Hagelin presented a newly devised

---

[1] Ted Hagelin, "A New Method to Value Intellectual Property," *American Intellectual Property Law Association Quarterly Journal* 30 (2000): 33.

tech-transfer valuation model labeled "Competitive Advantage Valuation (CAV)" and suggested that:

> The major premise of the CAV method is that intellectual property assets have no inherent value: the value of intellectual property assets resides entirely in the value of the tangible assets which incorporate them.

> The minor premise of the CAV method is that the value of a given intellectual property asset can best be measured by the competitive advantage which that asset contributes.

When one incorporates this tech-transfer CAV approach with the previously cited assertion by SEC Staff that "market-participant" value drivers must be considered under SFAS Nos. 141 and 142 (ASC 350), it becomes obvious that there are multiple, well-established, fully vetted intangible asset valuation approaches that accounting practitioners can employ when answering the question "What are the values of these intangible assets?"

(v) Valuation Approaches Seen in Wall Street Transactions.   An additional market validation of the alignment of these various intangible asset valuation approaches is found in the emergence of numerous intellectual asset-based transactions on Wall Street. One of the most familiar transactions seen in the entertainment and garment industries is the securitization of anticipated intangible asset-based revenues, as reflected in the Bowie Bond (David Bowie) and Bill Blass securitizations.

Another example is the adaptation of the traditional lending structure known as a sale/ leaseback (used for tangible assets) that has been deployed using intangible assets and has been referred to as a sale/license-back. In a presentation to the National Knowledge and Intellectual Property Management Taskforce's annual executive briefing in September 2002, Mitchell Fillet, of Riderwood Group, Incorporated, stated:

> We are in the midst of a paradigm shift that is so economically powerful that it ranks with the other two that have defined our economic history . . . .

> I am suggesting that intellectual property, primarily patents and derivative products from those patents, as well as licenses to use that intellectual property is emerging as an important asset class both on corporate balance sheets and off them, as collateral for loans and legally separate securitizations.

As a result of the sale/license-back structure, intangible assets are now being acquired by large investment banking firms, much like mortgage portfolios were acquired starting in the 1970s, thus giving birth to a highly liquid market for what had previously been difficult-to-trade assets. As such, the value drivers associated with intangible assets now reflect several of the financial modeling aspects found in commercial paper and various asset-backed securitizations.

As evidence of the importance such intangible assets have, and the market-based impact they can make, we can review the Federal Reserve chairman's October 2005 comments on this market built on intangibles, citing the significant economic benefits to the U.S. economy of the secondary market launched in the mid-1970s:

> These increasingly complex financial instruments have contributed to the development of a far more flexible, efficient, and hence resilient financial system than the one that existed just a quarter-century ago. After the bursting of the stock market bubble in 2000, unlike previous periods following large financial shocks, no major financial institution defaulted, and the economy held up far better than many had anticipated.[2]

---

[2] Alan Greenspan, speech on economic flexibility, presented before the National Italian American Foundation, Washington, DC, October 12, 2005. See: *www.federalreserve.gov/boarddocs/speeches/2005/20051012/default.htm*.

To gain an understanding about how intangible assets account for such significant market values, the accounting of a sale/license-back transaction can be reviewed; both the buyer and the seller in this transaction recognize distinct benefits.

From the seller's position, the closing would generate significant pretax earnings, as the only significant offset to sales price paid for internally generated intangibles would be the transaction fees (attorneys, financial consultants, valuation experts) and any unamortized capitalized cost of the underlying assets. In the sale/license-back structure, the attributes of the intangible assets permit the transaction to unleash earnings (unlike the sale/leaseback that was treated as a financing), principally because title to the intangible asset is transferred to the buyer.

Additionally, any license-back provision would qualify as a fully deductible expense for tax purposes. Unlike the sale/leaseback of a tangible asset, which is governed by SFAS No. 13 (ASC 840), *Accounting for Leases,* the "license" in a sale/license-back is a period expense and not debt; the license is consumed in the period in which the expense is incurred. Such accounting treatment suggests that the seller's cost of capital would be reduced to the extent that the proceeds from the sale are used to reduce bank or other outstanding debt, thereby deleveraging the balance sheet.

From the buyer's perspective, intangible assets with measurable, market-based value (presumably from outlicensing potential) can be selectively acquired, without incurring all of the fixed and sunk costs attributed to a research and development facility. Generally speaking, the licensing activity of a large corporation enjoys a greater contribution margin than the company taken as a whole. Additionally, the operating costs would be partially offset by the license granted to the seller, and the intangible assets acquired would be treated as an amortizable asset.

(vi) Identifiable Intangibles Distinguishable from Goodwill. Paragraphs 12 through 14 of SFAS No. 141(R) (ASC 805) provide that intangible assets acquired in a business combination are to be recognized as an asset *apart from goodwill,* but only if they meet the definitions of assets and liabilities in FASB's Statement of Financial Accounting Concept No. 6, *Elements of Financial Statements.* In addition, to qualify for recognition as part of applying the acquisition method, the identifiable assets acquired and liabilities assumed must be part of what the acquirer and the acquire (or its former owners) exchanged in the business combination transaction rather than the result of separate transactions.

Paragraph A39 of SFAS No. 141(R) (ASC 805) stipulates that if an entity establishes relationships with its customers through contracts, those customer relationships arise from contractual rights. Therefore, customer contracts and the related customer relationships acquired in a business combination meet the contractual-legal criterion, even if confidentiality or other contractual terms prohibit the sale or transfer of a contract separately from the acquire.

Paragraph A41 of SFAS No. 141(R) (ASC 805) states that a customer relationship exists between an entity and its customer if (a) the entity has information about the customer and has regular contact with the customer and (b) the customer has the ability to make direct contact with the entity. Customer relationships meet the contractual-legal criterion if an entity has a practice of establishing contracts with its customers, regardless of whether a contract exists at the acquisition date.

Examples of intangible assets that meet the "legal/contractual" criterion include trademarks, newspaper mastheads, Internet domain names, order backlog, books, magazines, musical works, license agreements, construction permits, broadcast rights, mortgage servicing contracts, patented technology, and computer software. Examples of assets that meet the separability criterion include customer lists, noncontractual customer relationships, unpatented technology, and databases such as title plants. Note that it is not necessary for the acquiring entity actually to intend to dispose of, sell, or rent the separable intangible in order to satisfy this criterion.

SFAS No. 141(R) (ASC 805) presents a lengthy listing of intangibles that are to be separately recognized, along with the useful lives relevant for amortization purposes. Certain exceptions are identified, such as for those intangibles having indefinite lives, as is the case for perpetually renewable broadcast licenses, which are maintained at cost (subject to potential impairment writedowns) until a finite life can be ascertained, if ever. These intangibles generally can be categorized as being:

1. Customer- or market-based assets (e.g., customer lists, newspaper mastheads, and trade-marked brand names)
2. Contract-based assets (e.g., covenants not to compete, broadcast rights)
3. Artistic-based assets (e.g., plays, other literary works, musical compositions)
4. Technology-based assets (e.g., title plant, databases, computer software)

With the exception of indefinite-life intangibles, all identifiable intangibles are to be amortized over their estimated useful lives, defined as the period over which the intangible asset is expected to directly or indirectly generate cash flows for the entity.

Paragraph A30 of Appendix A to SFAS No. 141(R) (ASC 805) identifies intangible assets that have characteristics that meet one of the two criteria (legal/contractual or separability). However, depending on the facts and circumstances, a specific acquired intangible asset might not meet the criteria. A good approach would be to first consider whether the acquired intangibles are among those specifically described by FASB and then to consider whether other intangibles also meeting the two criteria for separate capitalization might also be present.

Identified intangibles can be aggregated into permits, intellectual property, technology tools, procurement rights, competitor arrangements, and customer arrangements. *Permits* include:

- *Broadcast rights.* A license to transmit over certain bandwidths in the radio frequency spectrum, granted by the operation of communication laws
- *Certification marks.* The right to be able to assert that a product or service meets certain standards of quality or origin, such as "ISO 14000 Certified"
- *Collective marks.* Rights to signify membership in an association
- *Construction permits.* Rights to build a specified structure at a specified location
- *Franchise rights.* Permits to engage in a trade-named business, to sell a trademarked good, or to sell a service-marked service in a particular geographic area
- *Internet domain names.*
- *Operating rights.* Permits to operate in a certain manner, such as that granted to a carrier to transport specified commodities
- *Use rights.* Permits to use specified land, property, or air space in a particular manner, such as the right to cut timber, expel emissions, or land airplanes

Intellectual property includes, inter alia:

- *Copyrights.* The rights to reproduce, distribute, and so on, an original work of literature, music, art, photography, or film
- *Newspaper mastheads.* The rights to use the information that is displayed on the top of the first pages of newspapers
- *Patents.* Rights to make, use, or sell an invention for a specified period
- *Service marks.* Rights to use the name or symbol that distinguishes a service. Service marks include:
  - *Trade dress.* Access to the overall appearance and image (unique color, shape, or package design) of a product
  - *Trademarks.* Rights to use the word, logo, or symbol that distinguishes a product
  - *Trade names.* The right to use the name or symbol that distinguishes a business
  - *Trade secrets.* Information, such as a formula, process, or recipe, that is kept confidential
  - *Unpatented technology.* Access to the knowledge about the manner of accomplishing a task

Technology tools may consist of computer software, including programs, procedures, and documentation associated with computer hardware as well as databases, which are collections of a particular type of information, such as scientific data or credit information.

Procurement rights include:

- *Construction contracts.* Rights to acquire the subject of the contract in exchange for taking over the remaining obligations (including any payments)
- *Employment contracts.* Rights to take the seller's place as the employer under the contract and thus obtain the employee's services in exchange for fulfilling the employer's remaining duties, such as payment of salaries and benefits, under the contract
- *Lease agreements.* If assignable, rights to step into the shoes of the lessee and thus obtain the rights to use assets that are the subject of the agreement, in exchange for making the remaining lease payments
- *License agreements.* Rights to access or use properties that are the subjects of licenses in exchange for making any remaining license payments and adhering to other responsibilities as licensee
- *Royalty agreements.* Rights to take the place of payors and thus assume the payors' remaining rights and duties under the agreements
- *Service or supply contracts.* Rights to become the customer of particular contracts and thus purchase the specified products or services for the prices specified in those contracts

Competitor arrangements may include:

- *Noncompete agreements.* Rights to assurances that companies or individuals will refrain from conducting similar businesses or selling to specific customers for an agreed-on period
- *Standstill agreements.* Convey rights to assurances that companies or individuals will refrain from engaging in certain activities for specified periods

Customer arrangements are items such as:

- *Customer lists.* Information about companies' customers, including names, contact information, and order histories that a third party, such as a competitor or a telemarketing firm, would want to use in its own business
- *Customer relationships.* The relationships between entities and their customers for which:
  - The entities have information about the customers and have regular contacts with the customers, and
  - The customers have the ability to make direct contact with the entity
- *Contracts and related customer relationships.* Arise through contracts and are of value to buyers who can step into the shoes of the sellers and assume their remaining rights and duties under the contracts, and which hold the promise that the customers will place future orders with the entity
- *Noncontractual customer relationships.* Arise through means such as regular contacts by sales or service representatives, the value of which are derived from the prospect of the customers placing future orders with the entities
- *Order or production backlogs.* Provide buyers rights to step into the shoes of sellers on unfilled sales orders for services and for goods in amounts that exceed the quantity of finished goods and work in process on hand for filling the orders

(b) INTERNALLY DEVELOPED INTANGIBLE ASSETS.   Costs of internally developing, maintaining, or restoring intangible assets including goodwill that are not specifically identifiable, that have indeterminate lives, or that are inherent in a continuing business and related to a reporting entity as a whole are recognized as an expense when incurred. This rule was grounded, in part, on the traditional aversion to recognition of self-developed goodwill, which is a prohibition nominally still in effect (although the prescribed procedures for the impairment testing of goodwill under SFAS No. 142 implicitly allow for recognition of self-created goodwill, to the extent that it replaces acquired goodwill).

As a practical matter, capitalization of internally developed intangibles is generally obviated by the requirements of SFAS No. 2 (ASC 730), which requires that all research and development (R&D) costs be expensed as incurred. This rule, which is controversial (e.g., the corresponding international financial reporting standard requires expensing of research costs but capitalization of development expenditures) and likely to become more so (as general awareness of the importance of intangibles increases and as the move toward the "knowledge-based economy" continues and even accelerates), probably would preclude most costs incurred in connection with internal generation of intangibles from being recognized as assets in any event.

14.4 ACCOUNTING FOR INTANGIBLE ASSETS

(a) DETERMINING THE USEFUL LIFE OF AN INTANGIBLE ASSET.   The accounting for recognized intangible assets is based on their useful lives *to the reporting entity*. Note that these may well differ from the legal or contractual lives and could also easily diverge from the useful lives in the hands of *other* reporting entities holding similar or even identical assets. The amounts of intangible assets with finite useful lives are amortized while the amounts assigned to intangible assets with indefinite useful lives are not amortized. The useful lives of intangible assets to a reporting entity are the respective periods over which the assets are expected to contribute directly or indirectly to the future cash flows of the reporting entity. The estimates of the useful lives of intangible assets to the reporting entity are based on analyses of all pertinent factors. Particular attention is to be given to:

- Expected use of the assets by the entity
- Expected useful lives of another asset or groups of assets to which the useful life of the intangible asset may relate, such as mineral rights to depleting assets
- Any legal, regulatory, or contractual provisions that may limit the useful lives
- Any legal, regulatory, or contractual provisions that enable renewal or extension of the asset's legal or contractual life without substantial cost, provided there is evidence to support renewal or extension, and renewal or extension can be accomplished without material modifications of the respective existing terms and conditions
- The effects of obsolescence, demand, competition, and other economic factors, such as the stability of the industry, known technological advances, legislative action that results in an uncertain or changing regulatory environment, and expected changes in distribution channels
- The levels of maintenance expenditures required to obtain the expected future cash flows from the asset; for example, a material level of required maintenance in relation to the carrying amount of the asset may suggest a very limited useful life

If no legal, regulatory, contractual, competitive, economic, or other factors limit the useful life of an intangible assets to the reporting entity, the useful life of the asset shall be considered to be indefinite, which does not mean *infinite*.

(b) INTANGIBLE ASSETS SUBJECT TO AMORTIZATION.   The amounts of recognized intangible assets recognized are to be amortized over the useful lives of the respective assets to the reporting entity, unless those lives are determined to be indefinite. Paragraph 12 of SFAS No. 142 (ASC 350) requires that the recorded amount of an intangible asset with an finite life, but without precisely a known life, be amortized over the best estimate of its useful life. The methods of amortization should reflect the pattern by which the economic benefits of the intangible asset are consumed or otherwise used up. If the pattern cannot be reliably determined, the straight-line amortization method is to be used. Intangible assets are not written down or off in the period of acquisition unless impairments occur during that initial period, which is unlikely but not impossible.

According to paragraph 13 of SFAS No. 142 (ASC 350), the amount of an intangible asset subject to amortization is the value initially assigned to the asset less any residual value. However, the residual value of an intangible asset shall be assumed to be zero unless at the end of the useful life to the reporting entity the asset is expected to continue to have a useful life to another entity *and* (a) the reporting entity has a commitment from a third party to purchase the asset at the end of its useful life to the reporting entity, or (b) the residual value can be determined by reference to an exchange transaction in an existing market for that asset and that market is expected to exist at the end of the asset's useful life. In practice, residual values are rarely justified for intangibles subject to amortization.

Paragraph 14 of SFAS No. 142 (ASC 350) requires reporting entities to evaluate the remaining useful life of an intangible asset that is being amortized each reporting period to determine whether events and circumstances warrant a revision to the remaining periods of amortization. If the estimate of the intangible asset's useful life is changed, the remaining carrying amount of the intangible asset shall be amortized prospectively over that revised remaining useful life.

If an intangible asset that is being amortized is subsequently determined to have indefinite useful life, the asset shall be tested for impairment, as discussed in paragraph 17 of SFAS No. 142 (ASC 350). These intangible assets are then no longer amortized and are instead accounted for the same way as other intangible assets not subject to amortization.

Intangible assets subject to amortization are to be reviewed for impairments in conformity with SFAS No. 144 (ASC 360). After an impairment loss is recognized, the adjusted carrying amount of that intangible asset is its new accounting basis. A previously recognized impairment loss is not subsequently reversed, despite evidence of value recovery.

(c) INTANGIBLE ASSETS NOT SUBJECT TO AMORTIZATION.   Intangible assets that were determined to have indefinite useful lives are not amortized until their respective useful lives are determined to no longer be indefinite. The reporting entity is required to evaluate the remaining useful lives of intangible assets not being amortized each reporting period, in order to determine whether events and circumstances continue to support indefinite useful lives. Intangible assets not being amortized, but subsequently determined to have finite useful lives, are tested for impairment, as discussed next. The assets are then amortized prospectively over their estimated remaining useful lives and accounted for the same way as other intangible assets subject to amortization.

Intangible assets not subject to amortization are to be tested for impairments annually or more frequently if events or changes in circumstances indicate that the assets might have become impaired. Paragraph 5 of SFAS No. 121, *Accounting for the Impairment of Long-Lived Assets and for Long-Lived Assets to Be Disposed Of,* includes examples of impairment indicators.[3] The impairment tests shall consist of a comparison of the fair value of an intangible asset with its carrying amount. If the carrying amount for a given intangible asset exceeds its fair value, an impairment loss is recognized in an amount equal to the excess. After an impairment loss is recognized, the asset's adjusted carrying amount is the intangible asset's new accounting basis. A previously recognized impairment loss cannot be reversed.

In Emerging Issues Task Force (EITF) Issue No. 02-7, *Unit of Accounting for Testing Impairment of Indefinite-Lived Intangible Assets,* there was a consensus that separately recorded indefinite-lived intangible assets should be combined into a single unit of accounting for impairment testing purposes if they are operated as a single asset and are therefore essentially inseparable. EITF Issue No. 02-7 includes indicators and illustrations of when intangible assets should be, and when they should not be, combined.

Indicators that suggest that indefinite-lived intangibles should be combined as a single unit of accounting include:

1. The intangibles will be used together to construct or enhance a single asset.
2. If the intangibles had been part of the same acquisition, they would have been recorded as a single asset.

---

[3] Superseded by SFAS No. 144 (ASC 360).

3. The intangibles, as a group, represent "the highest and best use of the assets" (e.g., they could probably realize a higher sales price if sold together than if they were sold separately). Indicators pointing to this situation are:

   a. The degree to which it is unlikely that a substantial portion of the assets would be sold separately, *or*

   b. The fact that, should a substantial portion of the intangibles be sold individually, there would be a significant reduction in the fair value of the remaining assets in the group.

4. The marketing or branding strategy of the entity treats the assets as being complementary (e.g., a trademark and its related trade name, formulas, recipes, and patented or unpatented technology can all be complementary to an entity's brand name).

Indicators that imply that indefinite-lived intangibles should not be combined as a single unit of accounting include:

1. Each separate intangible generates independent cash flows.

2. In a sale, it would be likely that the intangibles would be sold separately. If the entity had previously sold similar assets separately, this would constitute evidence that combining the assets would not be appropriate.

3. The entity is either considering or has already adopted a plan to dispose of one or more of the intangibles separately.

4. The intangibles are used exclusively by different asset groups (as defined in SFAS No. 144 (ASC 360)).

5. The assets have different useful economic lives.

EITF Issue No. 02-7 provided additional guidance regarding the "unit of accounting" determination that must be made for impairment testing purposes.

1. Goodwill and finite-lived intangibles may not be combined in the "unit of accounting" since they are subject to different impairment testing rules (set forth by SFAS No. 142 (ASC 350) and No. 144 (ASC 360), respectively).

2. If the indefinite-lived intangible assets collectively constitute a business, they may not be combined into a unit of accounting.

3. If the unit of accounting includes intangibles recorded in the separate financial statements of consolidated subsidiaries, it is possible that the sum of impairment losses recognized in the separate financial statements of the subsidiaries will not equal the consolidated impairment loss.

4. If the unit of accounting used to test impairment of indefinite-lived intangible assets is contained in a single reporting unit, the same unit of accounting and associated fair value should be used for purposes of measuring a goodwill impairment loss in accordance with paragraph 20 of SFAS No. 142 (ASC 350).

Identifiable intangible assets, such as franchise rights, customer lists, trademarks, patents and copyrights, and licenses, are to be amortized over their expected useful economic lives, even if they exceed the former 40-year ceiling. However, if longer amortization periods (useful lives) are elected, impairment reviews of the assets' recoverability are required when necessitated by changes in facts and circumstances in the same manner as set forth in SFAS No. 144 (ASC 360) for tangible long-lived assets. SFAS No. 144 (ASC 360) also requires consideration of the residual values of intangible assets (which are analogous to salvage values for tangible assets) in determining the amounts of the intangibles to amortize. *Residual value* is defined as the value of the intangible to the entity at the end of its (entity-specific) useful life reduced by any estimated disposition costs. The residual value of an amortizable intangible is assumed to be zero unless the intangible will continue to have a useful life to another party after the end of its useful life to its current holder, and one or both of the these two criteria are met:

1. The current holder has received a third-party commitment to purchase the intangible at the end of its useful life, *or*
2. A market for the intangible exists and is expected to continue to exist at the end of the asset's useful life as a means of determining the residual value of the intangible by reference to marketplace transactions.

A broadcast license is nominally subject to expiration in five years, but might be indefinitely renewable at little additional cost to the broadcaster. If cash flows can be projected indefinitely, and assuming a market exists for the license, no amortization is to be recorded until such time as a finite life is predicted. However, it is required that the asset be tested for impairment at least annually, to ensure that it is carried at no greater than its fair value.

14.5 CERTAIN IDENTIFIABLE INTANGIBLE ASSETS

(a) PATENTS.   Accounting for patents is affected by the laws governing the legal rights of a patent holder. A U.S. patent is a nonrenewable right granted by the United States Patent and Trademark Office, an agency of the United States Department of Commerce, that enables the recipient to exclude others from the manufacture, sale, or other use of an invention for a period of 20 years from the date of grant. Enforceability of a patent begins only on its grant, and the exclusive right of use is not retroactive. However, the filing of a patent application provides protection from the claims of a later inventor for the same item so that the period of partial protection may be considered to extend from the date of the original application. While the legal term of the patent is 20 years, the effective period of competitive advantage may extend beyond the original 20-year patent term if additional patents are obtained as improvements are made. Many patent holders do endeavor to create various modifications and improvements that can be patented in their own right, to accomplish this de facto extension of protection for many years. The rights to a patent may be assigned in whole or in part, as can the right to use the patent (i.e., licenses under the patent) on a royalty or other basis.

(i) Capitalizable Amounts for Patents.   Patents may be purchased from others or developed internally as a result of R&D activities. The cost of a purchased patent includes the purchase price and any related expenditures, such as attorneys' fees. If a patent is developed internally, its cost includes legal fees in connection with patent applications, patent fees, litigation fees, litigation costs, costs of sale or licensing, and filing fees. Any related research, experimental and developmental expenditures, including the cost of models and drawings not specifically required for a patent application, are R&D costs and should be expensed as incurred in accordance with paragraph 12 of SFAS No. 2 (ASC 730).

   The grant of a patent through the U.S. Patent and Trademark Office is no guarantee of protection. Often it is necessary to defend the patent's validity in court tests and also to refute allegations of infringement of other patents and to prosecute infringement of the patent by others. The costs of successful court tests may be capitalized as additional costs of the patent and then amortized over the remaining useful life of the underlying patent. However, if the litigation is unsuccessful, the costs of the litigation should be written off immediately, as should any carrying value of the patent that has been stripped of its economic value.

(ii) Amortization of Patents.   A U.S. patent has a specified legal life. It provides protection for 20 years, and that is the maximum amortization period. The period used in practice is often less because of technological or market obsolescence factors, such as the issuance of new patents to competitors, improved models, substitutes, or general technological progress. These factors must be taken into account in determining the original useful life and during the subsequent reviews of remaining economic life. The amortization period should not extend beyond the market life of the product with which the patent is associated, unless it is demonstrable that the patent can also be used in other applications. However, if it is possible to extend a patent's economic life by obtaining additional patents, it is permissible to amortize the remaining balance of the costs of the old patent over the estimated economic lives of the new ones. (For example, if a patent is half amortized when a successor patent is issued and the estimated life of the successor is 10 years, the unamortized carrying value of the original patent should be added to the cost of the new one, with the entire sum then amortized over 10 years.)

The impairment accounting guidance in SFAS No. 144 (ASC 360) is applicable to patents. Once it is determined that the monopolistic advantage offered by use and ownership of the patent no longer exists, the remaining unamortized balance should be written off. Also, any increases in separately identified deferred costs, due to such factors as an additional lawsuit establishing the validity of the patent, should be written off over the remaining estimated economic life of the patent.

(b) COPYRIGHTS. A copyright is the exclusive right to reproduce, publish, and sell a literary product or artistic work. Title 17 of the United States Code, Chapter 3, "Duration of Copyright §302 Duration of Copyright: Works Created on or After January 1, 1978"[4] states:

(a) In General—Copyright in a work created on or after January 1, 1978, endures for a term consisting of the life of the author and 70 years after the author's death.

(b) Joint Works—In the case of a joint work prepared by two or more authors who did not work for hire, the copyright endures for a term consisting of the life of the last surviving author and 70 years after such last surviving author's death.

As in the case of a patent, the rights to a copyright may be assigned, licensed, or sold.

(i) Capitalizable Amounts for Copyrights. The costs of developing copyrights and the costs of purchased copyrights may be substantial and should be deferred. For a copyright developed internally, costs include expenditures for government filing fees and attorneys' fees and expenses as well as outlays for wages and materials in the preparation of the material to be copyrighted and expenditures incurred to establish the right. If a copyright is purchased, the initial valuation includes the acquisition price plus any costs incurred in establishing the right and costs associated with defending a copyright.

(ii) Amortization of Copyrights. Copyrighted materials, for various reasons, often do not have an active market past the first few years after the issuance of the copyright. It is rare that copyrighted materials will have lengthy economic lives, although there are exceptions. The capitalized amounts are to be amortized over the number of years in which sales or royalties related to the copyright can be expected to occur.

SFAS No. 144 (ASC 360) provides guidance on the impairment of intangible assets with finite lives, such as copyrights. Continuing review of the status of copyrights is essential to determine whether they have continuing value. If the copyrighted material will no longer be used, it should be written off.

(c) CUSTOMER AND SUPPLIER LISTS. Customer and supplier lists can be particularly valuable to a business, as they represent groups of customers or suppliers with whom business relations have been established. The value of such lists is based on the assumption of continuing business relationships, as well as possibly reducing the marketing costs that would otherwise be necessary (e.g., to develop customer lists).

(i) Capitalizable Amounts for Customer and Supplier Lists. Customer or supplier lists often are developed internally, and the cost specifically identified with development generally is impossible to determine. These costs are often analogous to R&D expenditures and accordingly such costs are not

---

[4] *www.copyright.gov/title17/92chap3.html*

deferred. However, when lists are purchased from others, the acquisition cost should be deferred. While generally these are identifiable assets and thus separately recognizable, a customer or supplier list acquired in a business combination would not meet the criteria for recognition apart from goodwill if there are terms of confidentiality or other agreements that prohibit the selling, leasing, or otherwise exchanging of the acquired customer or supplier information.

(ii) Amortization of Customer and Supplier Lists.   The value of customer or supplier lists decreases as customers or suppliers are lost or cease to exist. Ideally, the cost of a list should be written off based on these factors—that is, on a units-lost basis. However, since it often is difficult to track lost customers or suppliers precisely, straight-line amortization over a reasonable average customer or supplier retention period is commonly used. The estimate of the useful life should consider all available information and be reevaluated each reporting period. Rapid turnover of customers or suppliers suggests that little or even no value should have been attributed to the acquired lists.

(d) FRANCHISES.   Franchises may be granted by governmental units, individuals, or corporate entities. Public utilities are granted franchises by the communities they serve. These franchises establish the right to operate and specify the conditions under which utilities must function. Such franchises may place certain restrictions on the enterprise concerning rates and operating conditions, but they also confer certain privileges, ranging from minor ones to the granting of a full monopoly.

Private franchises are contracts for the exclusive right to perform certain functions or to sell certain (usually branded) products or services. Such agreements involve the use by the franchisee of a trademark, trade name, patent, process, or know-how of the franchisor for the term of the franchise. For example, a manufacturer may grant a dealer a franchise to market a product within a given territory and agree not to allow other dealers to market the same product in that area.

Costs of obtaining a franchise include any fees paid to the franchisor as well as legal and other expenditures incurred in obtaining the franchise. If a franchise agreement covers a specified period of time, the cost of the franchise should be written off over that period unless the economic life is anticipated to be less. If the franchise is perpetual, the franchisee should evaluate the expected useful life of the franchise, considering the effect of obsolescence, demand, competition, and other relevant economic factors. Additional periodic payments based on revenues or other factors may be required in addition to initial fees. These period costs should be expensed as incurred, because they pertain only to the current period and represent no future benefit. The franchise agreement may also require certain property improvements that should be capitalized and included in property, plant, and equipment.

(e) LEASES AND LEASEHOLD RIGHTS.   A favorable lease is one in which the property rights obtained under the lease could be obtained currently only at a higher rental. This concept is not to be mistaken for the issue of capitalized leases or capital additions classified as leasehold improvements. Favorable leases may be recognized when a business is purchased or when a payment is made to an existing lessee for the right to sublease, if indeed there is sufficient evidence to demonstrate a below-market rate of rental payments.

(i) Capitalizable Amounts for Favorable Leases and Leasehold Rights.   The favorable lease usually is measured by the present value of the cost differential between the terms of the lease and the amount that could be obtained currently in an arm's-length transaction. This corresponds to the economic or fair value of the favorable terms.

(ii) Amortization of Favorable Leases.   The cost assigned to a favorable lease is amortized over the lease term. A lump-sum payment at the inception of the lease should be amortized to rent expense over the life of the lease.

(f) ORGANIZATION COSTS.   Organization costs are expenditures made to promote and organize a concern, including costs (i.e., legal and state filing fees) of establishing the entity's existence. Under Statement of Position (SOP) 98-5, *Reporting on the Costs of Start-Up Activities,* start-up activities include organization costs (ASC 720). This SOP defines start-up activities as one-time activities an entity undertakes when it opens a new facility, introduces a new product or service, conducts business in a new territory or with a new class of customer or beneficiary, initiates a new process in an existing facility or commences some new operation. This SOP also concludes that costs of start-up activities, including organization costs, should be expensed as incurred.

(g) REGISTRATION COSTS.   The Securities and Exchange Commission Staff in Standards Advisory Board Topic 5A, *Expenses of Offering,* stated that specific incremental costs directly attributable to a proposed or actual offering of securities may properly be deferred and charged against the gross proceeds of the offering. However, management salaries or other general and administrative expenses may not be allocated as costs of the offering. Costs of an aborted offering may not be deferred and charged against a subsequent offering. According to SEC Staff, a short postponement of up to 90 days does not represent an aborted offering.

(h) RESEARCH AND DEVELOPMENT COSTS.   So-called R&D expenses have long been a controversial accounting topic. Prior to the imposition of current GAAP, it had been common to defer such costs, and investors often were dismayed at sporadic "big baths" when the hoped-for developments failed to be consummated or proved to have less economic value than expected. In reaction to the formerly liberal practices of deferring R&D costs, therefore, one of FASB's first acts was to impose SFAS No. 2 (ASC 730), which requires that all R&D costs be charged to expense as incurred.

SFAS No. 142 (ASC 350) did not change the stringent accounting requirements of SFAS No. 2 (ASC 730). It includes these definitions of R&D:

> Research is planned search or critical investigation aimed at discovery of new knowledge with the hope that such knowledge will be useful in developing a new product or service . . . or a new process or technique . . . or in bringing about a significant improvement to an existing product or process.

> Development is the translation of research findings or other knowledge into a plan or design for a new product or process or for a significant improvement to an existing product or process whether intended for sale or use. It includes the conceptual formulation, design, and testing of product alternatives, construction of prototypes, and operation of pilot plants. It does not include routine or periodic alterations to existing products, production lines, manufacturing processes, and other on-going operations even though those alterations may represent improvements and it does not include market research or market testing activities. [SFAS No. 2, para. 8]

The distinction between *research* and *development* is more than semantic. For example, under International Financial Reporting Standards (IFRS), while research costs must be expensed at once, as under U.S. GAAP, development costs are to be deferred and amortized over the economic lives of the resultant products or processes. Even under U.S. GAAP, the distinction between *research* and *development* is germane, albeit not as a general principle. However, for certain categories of software development costs, costs incurred before technological feasibility has been demonstrated (i.e., what are analogous to research costs) are expensed while those incurred after feasibility is demonstrated (which are, arguably, more suggestive of development costs) are capitalized and amortized.

Given the huge economic significance of R&D expenditures and the growing recognition that substantial amounts of assets are being omitted from many reporting entities' balance sheets (with an equivalent understatement of net stockholders' equity), this is likely to receive renewed attention. Particularly given the FASB commitment to "converge" U.S. GAAP and IFRS, there would appear to be some possibility that future GAAP will permit or require deferral of development-type expenses, subject to amortization and, perhaps, impairment assessments.

R&D costs, according to SFAS No. 2 (ASC 730), include these elements:

> *Materials, Equipment and Facilities.* The cost of materials . . . and equipment or facilities that are acquired or constructed for research and development activities and that have alternative future uses . . . shall be capitalized as tangible assets when acquired or constructed. The cost of such materials consumed in research and development activities and the depreciation of such equipment

or facilities used in those activities are research and development costs. However, the costs of materials, equipment, or facilities that are acquired or constructed for a particular research and development project and that have no alternative future uses … are research and development costs at the time the costs are incurred.

Personnel. Salaries, wages, and other related costs of personnel engaged in research and development activities shall be included in research and development costs.

Intangibles Purchased from Others. The costs of intangibles that are purchased from others for use in research and development activities and that have alternative future uses … shall be accounted for in accordance with FASB Statement No. 142 (ASC 350), "Goodwill and Other Intangible Assets." … The amortization of those intangible assets used in research and development activities is a research and development cost. However, the costs of intangibles that are purchased from others for a particular research and development project and that have no alternative future uses … are research and development costs at the time the costs are incurred.

Contract Services. The costs of services performed by others in connection with the research and development activities of an enterprise, including research and development conducted by others in behalf of the enterprise, shall be included in research and development costs.

Indirect Costs. Research and development costs shall include a reasonable allocation of indirect costs. However, general and administrative costs that are not clearly related to research and development activities shall not be included as research and development costs. SFAS No. 2 (ASC 730) requires that all costs of activities identified as R&D be charged to expense as incurred. The only exception is that government-regulated enterprises may be required to defer certain costs for rate-making purposes. This occurs when the rate regulator reasonably assures the recovery of R&D costs by permitting the inclusion of the costs in allowable costs for rate-making purposes. SFAS No. 2 also requires disclosure of total R&D costs charged to expense in each period. [SFAS No. 2 (ASC 730), paras. 11–13]

There are three ways in which R&D costs may be incurred by a reporting entity:

1. Conducting R&D activities for the benefit of the reporting entity itself
2. Conducting R&D for others under a contractual arrangement
3. Purchasing R&D from other entities

As noted, under SFAS No. 2 (ASC 730), all R&D expenditures must be expensed as incurred. Examples of such R&D costs include:

- Laboratory research to discover new knowledge
- Searching for applications of new research findings or other knowledge
- Conceptual formulation and design of possible product or process alternatives
- Testing in search for or evaluation of product or process alternatives
- Modification of the formulation or design of a product or process
- Design construction, and testing of pre-production prototypes and models
- Design of tools, jigs, molds, and dies involving new technology
- Design, construction, and operation of a pilot plant that is not of a scale economically feasible to the enterprise for commercial production
- Engineering activity required to advance the design of a product to the point that it meets specific functional and economic requirements and is ready for manufacture

Not all costs that appear related to R&D are to be accounted for as such, however. Examples of costs that are *not* considered R&D include:

- Engineering during an early phase of commercial production
- Quality control for commercial production
- Troubleshooting during a commercial production breakdown

- Routine, ongoing efforts to improve products
- Adaptation of existing capacity for a specific customer or other requirements
- Seasonal design changes to products
- Routine design of tools, dies, and so on.
- Design, construction, start-up, and so on, of equipment except that used solely for R&D

In many cases, entities will pay other parties to perform R&D activities on their behalf. In some instances, these are simply rational business decisions and are not undertaken with any financial reporting motive ("earnings management") in mind. In some instances, however, the intent of "outsourcing" certain R&D activities is to try to avoid the immediate expensing requirement of SFAS No. 2 (ASC 730) and to instead disguise these expenditures as capital asset purchases.

In applying substance over form in evaluating these arrangements, a financial reporting result cannot be obtained indirectly if it would not have been permitted if accomplished directly. Thus, if costs are incurred to engage others to perform R&D activities that, in substance, could have been performed by the reporting entity itself, those costs must be expensed as incurred. However, if the payment is to acquire intangibles for use in R&D activities, and these assets have other uses, then the expenditure is capitalized and accounted for in accordance with SFAS No. 142 (ASC 350).

When R&D costs are incurred as a result of contractual arrangements, the nature of the agreement dictates the accounting treatment of the costs involved. The key determinant is the transfer of the risk associated with the R&D expenditures. If the business receives funds from another party to perform R&D and is obligated to repay those funds regardless of the outcome, a liability must be recorded and the R&D costs expensed as incurred. In order to conclude that a liability does not exist, the transfer of the financial risk must be substantive and genuine.

The SEC Staff has stated that, if a significant portion of the purchase price in a business combination is expensed as purchased R&D, the Staff may raise issues such as these:

- Purchased R&D must be valued based on appropriate assumptions and valuation techniques; it may not be determined as a residual amount similar to goodwill.
- Allocation of purchase price to purchased R&D will be questioned if differing significantly from the estimated replacement cost for the acquiring enterprise.
- Policies used for internally developed products should be used to determine if R&D is in process or complete and whether alternative future uses exist.
- If substantially all of the purchase price is allocated to purchased R&D, the staff will challenge whether some should be allocated to other identifiable intangible assets and goodwill and would object to useful lives of those intangible assets and goodwill exceeding five to seven years.

The AICPA has issued the following Practice Aid on accounting for R&D projects acquired in a business combination: *Assets Acquired in a Business Combination to Be Used in Research and Development Activities: A Focus in Software, Electronic Devices, and Pharmaceutical Industries.*

(i) RESEARCH AND DEVELOPMENT ARRANGEMENTS.   R&D arrangements may take a variety of forms, but a central feature of each of these is to conduct R&D that is to be financed by another entity. According to SFAS No. 68 (ASC 730), *Research and Development Arrangements,* certain of these arrangements are actually financing transactions, and funds to be repaid, irrespective of the outcome of the research, must be reported as liabilities, with actual research or development costs expensed as incurred by the reporting entity. Only if there is a substantive risk transfer to the entity providing financing will it be appropriate not to record such a liability.

The actual obligation can take various forms, including an outright unconditional commitment to repay the funds advanced, an option giving the other entity the right to require that the reporting entity purchase the other party's interest in the outcome of the R&D efforts, and a firm obligation to issue debt or equity instruments to the funding party at completion. In all such instances, the payment for R&D is actually a loan, not a purchase of R&D services. Accordingly, the reporting entity (the party conducting R&D) must currently expense all R&D expenditures.

To the extent that the financial risk associated with the R&D has been transferred because repayment of any of the funds provided is conditioned on the results of the R&D having future economic benefit, however, the reporting entity is to account for its obligation as a contract to perform R&D for others, not as debt.

(j) ACQUIRED IN-PROCESS RESEARCH AND DEVELOPMENT.   So-called in-process research and development (IPRD) has long been a difficult financial reporting issue. On one hand, purchase business combination accounting suggests that the purchase cost be allocated to the fair value of all assets acquired; on the other hand, to allow capitalization of IPRD would result in deferral of costs that would have to be immediately expensed under SFAS No. 2 (ASC 730) if incurred directly by the reporting entity.

In many business combinations, a part of the premium (i.e., the amounts in excess of the fair value of tangible net assets) paid is in recognition of the value of the acquiree's previously expensed R&D efforts. Since what is banned under GAAP (e.g., capitalization of R&D costs) if accomplished directly cannot be attained indirectly (e.g., via a business combination), it was logical to prohibit the creation of an intangible asset in purchase business combinations to reflect the value of R&D already completed by the acquiree entity.

IPRD is virtually the only asset acquired in a purchase business combination transaction that is expensed rather than being capitalized. This includes not only the amount paid for actual in-process work (which was, per SFAS No. 2 (ASC 730), already expensed as incurred by the acquiree entity) but also certain tangible assets used in R&D. As stated in FASB Interpretation No. 4, *Applicability of FASB Statement No. 2 to Business Combinations Accounted for by the Purchase Method,* any identifiable assets of the acquiree to be used in R&D projects that do not also have an alternative future use should be first valued as part of the purchase price allocation and then charged to expense of the combined companies simultaneous with consummation of acquisition. This matter was considered by the EITF in Issue 86-14, *Purchased Research and Development Projects in a Business Combination,* but no changes to the requirement were made. SFAS No. 141(R) (ASC 805) nullified FASB Interpretation No. 4 and EITF Issue 86-14.

In the mid- to late 1990s, overly aggressive use of the mandate that IPRD costs be immediately expensed upon consummation of a purchase business combination became something of a concern. In many acquisitions, a disproportionately large part of the premium paid was assigned to IPRD, on the assumption that immediate charge-offs as part of purchase accounting were less of a concern to stockholders and other stakeholding parties than would be regular periodic charges against earnings lasting many years. There were even some instances, in fact, where more than 99 percent of the entire purchase cost was allocated to IPRD cost and then immediately written off. This phenomenon drew the attention of the SEC as well as of accounting standard setters. The elimination of goodwill amortization by SFAS No. 142 (ASC 350) reduced the motivation for exaggerated allocations to IPRD, but this remains a concern.

In response to this perceived problem, the FASB at first indicated an intent to develop a new requirement that would have, it was widely presumed, imposed a requirement that purchased IPRD costs be capitalized and amortized. However, upon further reflection, it became clear that to have a diametrically opposite rule for IPRD costs, versus internally generated R&D, would be neither logical nor defensible. Consequently, no action was taken by FASB, and the requirement that purchased IPRD be immediately expensed, after purchase cost is first allocated to it, remained.

Clearly, the last chapter has not yet been written regarding proper accounting for research and/or development costs, in general, or IPRD acquired in purchase transactions, in particular.

(k) ROYALTY AND LICENSE AGREEMENTS.   Royalty and license agreements are contracts allowing the use of patented, copyrighted, or proprietary (trade secrets) material in return for royalty payments. An example is the licensing of a patented chemical process for use in a customer's operating system.

The costs to be assigned to royalty and license agreements include any initial payments required plus legal costs incurred in establishing the agreements. Royalty or usage fees are expensed as incurred, because they relate to services of products and not to future benefits.

The capitalized costs of royalty and license agreements should be amortized over the lesser of the life of the agreement or the expected economic life, with the useful life reassessed each reporting period. Unamortized costs of royalty and license agreements should be written off when it is determined that they have become worthless.

(l) SECRET FORMULAS AND PROCESSES.   A formula or process known only to a particular producer may be a valuable asset, even if not patented. As in the case of a patent, the value of a trade secret is derived from the exclusive control that it gives. Trade secrets, like patents and copyrights, are recognized legal property and are transferable. Costs that can be directly identified with secret formulas and processes are properly capitalized, except that costs of activities constituting R&D as defined by SFAS No. 2 (ASC 730) must be expensed. Costs are normally assigned only to acquired secret formulas and processes. Because secret formulas and secret processes have unlimited lives in a legal sense, costs capitalized are amortized over the useful life of the secret formula or are not amortized if the secret formula is determined to have an indefinite useful life. Whether the value of the formula or process is impaired because of lack of demand for the related product, development of a substitute product or process, loss of exclusivity, or other factors should be determined as discussed in Section 14.4(b) or (c), as appropriate.

(m) START-UP ACTIVITIES.   Under SOP 98-5, costs of start-up activities, including organization costs, should be expensed as incurred. For purposes of the SOP, *start-up activities* are defined broadly as those one-time activities related to opening a new facility, introducing a new product or service, conducting business in a new territory, conducting business with a new class of customer or beneficiary, initiating a new process in an existing facility, or commencing some new operation. Start-up activities include activities related to organizing a new entity (commonly referred to as organization costs). The SOP applies to all nongovernmental entities and would apply to development-stage entities as well as established operating entities.

(n) TOOLING COSTS.   Initial tooling costs are sometimes treated as an intangible asset, but they are more often considered an element of property, plant, and equipment or, in the case of certain long-term contracts, inventory. SFAS No. 2 (ASC 730) states that the design of tools, jigs, molds, and dies involving new technology is an R&D cost, which must be expensed as incurred. However, routine design of those items is not R&D, and the cost may be deferred and amortized over the periods expected to benefit. Deferred tooling may be written off over a period of time (generally less than five years, with shorter periods used when tooling relates to products with frequent style or design obsolescence) or anticipated production (using the unit-of-production method). Replacements of parts of tooling for reasons other than changes in the product are usually expensed.

If deferred initial tooling costs are material, the accounting policy regarding those costs should be disclosed. SEC registrants are required to state, if practicable, the amount of unamortized deferred tooling costs applicable to long-term contracts or programs (Regulation S-X, Rule 5.02-6(d)(i)).

EITF Issue No. 99-5, *Accounting for Pre-Production Costs Related to Long-Term Supply Arrangements,* provides guidance on design and development and tooling costs related to new long-term supply arrangements. The Task Force concluded that:

- Design and development costs for products to be sold under long-term supply arrangements should be expensed as incurred.
- Design and development costs for molds, dies, and other tools that a supplier will own and that will be used in producing the products under the long-term supply arrangements should, in general, be capitalized as part of the cost of the molds, dies, and other tools. However, if the molds, dies, and tools involve new technology, their costs should be expensed as incurred.
- If the supplier will not own the molds, dies, and other tools, the design and development costs should be capitalized only if the supply arrangement provides the supplier the noncancelable right to use them during the supply arrangement. Otherwise, the design and development

costs should be expensed as incurred, including costs incurred before the supplier receives a noncancelable right to use the molds, dies, and other tools during the supply arrangement.

- Design and development costs that would otherwise be expensed should be capitalized if the supplier has a contractual guarantee for reimbursement of those costs. A contractual guarantee means a legally enforceable agreement under which the amount of the reimbursement can be objectively measured and verified.

SEC registrants are expected to disclose their accounting policy for preproduction design and development costs and the aggregate amount of:

- Assets recognized pursuant to agreements that provide for contractual reimbursement of preproduction design and development costs
- Assets recognized for molds, dies, and other tools that the supplier owns
- Assets recognized for molds, dies, and other tools that the supplier does not own

Design and development costs for molds, dies, and other tools that are capitalized are subject to impairment assessment under SFAS No. 144 (ASC 360).

(o) TRADEMARKS AND TRADE NAMES. Broadly defined, a *trademark* is any distinguishing label, symbol, or design used by a concern in connection with a product or service. A trade name identifies the entity.

Trademarks can be registered with the U.S. Patent and Trademark Office to provide access to the federal courts for litigation and to serve as notice of ownership. Proof of prior and continuing use of the trademark is required to obtain and retain the right to use the registered item. Protection of trademarks and trade names that cannot be registered or are not registered can also be sought through common law. These assets have an unlimited life as long as they are used continuously. A "Declaration of Use Section 8 of the Trademark Act, 15 U.S.C. §1058" must be filed between the fifth and sixth year following registration. In addition, a combined "Declaration of Use and Application for Renewal under Sections 8 and 9" must be filed between the ninth and tenth year after registration, and every 10 years thereafter. If these documents are not timely filed, the registration will be cancelled and cannot be revived or reinstated.

Trademarks and trade names may also be registered under the laws of most states. It is customary to consider trademarks and trade names as being of value only as long as they are used. The value of a trademark or trade name consists of the product differentiation and identification that it provides, which theoretically contributes to revenue by enabling a business to sell such products at a higher price than unbranded products. Although closely related to goodwill, trademarks and trade names are property rights that are separately identifiable and, as such, can be assigned or sold.

(i) Capitalizable Amounts for Trademarks and Trade Names Costs. The cost of a trademark or trade name developed internally consists of legal fees associated with successful litigation involving the trademark or trade name, registration fees, and all developmental expenditures that can be reasonably associated with trademarks, such as payments to design firms. The cost of a purchased trademark or trade name is its purchase price and any other costs required to maintain exclusive use of the mark or name. Obviously, much of the value of a trademark or trade name is established by continuing operations that create a reputation with customers. Some of that reputation, however, may have been gained through the use of advertising and other marketing techniques.

The costs should be amortized over the trademark's or trade name's useful life to the entity, unless the trademark or trade name is determined to have an indefinite useful life, in which case it is not amortized, as discussed in Section 14.4(c). The expected useful life should be reassessed each reporting period. These expenditures should be accounted for under SOP 93-7, which is discussed next.

(ii) Amortization of Trademarks and Trade Names.   Because of the legal status of trademarks and trade names, established trademarks and trade names have unlimited legal lives as long as they are used. There is no specified statutory life that restricts the amortization period.

(p) ADVERTISING.   While many, if not most, businesses engage in some forms of advertising, it has long been held that demonstrating the actual effectiveness of such efforts is too speculative to warrant deferral of costs to future periods. Put another way, advertising has been held to be a sunk cost and thus must be expensed as incurred. However, SOP 93-7, *Reporting on Advertising Costs,* did provide a limited exception to this general principle.

Under this SOP, the costs of advertising should be expensed either as incurred or the first time the advertising takes place, unless the advertising is direct-response advertising that meets specific, rather rigorous criteria, in which case deferral and amortization is prescribed. Examples of first-time advertising include the first public showing of a television commercial for its intended purpose, or the first appearance of a magazine advertisement for its intended purpose. The cost of direct-response advertising is deferred and reported as an asset, subject to amortization, if the primary purpose of the advertising is to elicit sales to customers who can be shown to have responded specifically to the advertising *and* if the advertising results in *probable* future benefits. Showing that a customer responded to specifically identifiable direct-response advertising requires documentation, including a record that can identify the name of the customer and the advertising that elicited the direct response. Such documentation could include, for example, files listing the customer names and the related direct-response advertisement; a coded order form, coupon, or response card included with the advertisement that would indicate the customer's name; or a log of customers who made phone calls responding to a number appearing in an advertisement.

Probable future benefits are highly likely future primary revenues resulting from the direct-response advertising, net of future costs to realize the revenues. Probable future primary revenues are limited to revenues from sales to customers receiving and responding to the direct-response advertising. To demonstrate that direct-response advertising will result in probable future benefits, an entity is required to provide persuasive evidence that the results of the advertising will be similar to the results of its past direct-response advertising activities that had future benefits. The evidence should include verifiable historical patterns of results specific to the entity. To determine if results will be similar, attributes to consider include the demographics of the audience, the method of advertising, the product, and economic conditions. Industry statistics would not provide objective evidence of probable future benefits in the absence of the entity's own operating history.

Other requirements of the SOP include:

- Costs of direct-response advertising should include only incremental direct costs incurred in transactions with independent third parties plus payroll and payroll-related costs for the activities of employees that are directly associated with the direct-response advertising project. Allocated administrative costs, rent, depreciation, and other occupancy costs are not costs of direct-response advertising activities.

- The costs of the direct-response advertising directed to all prospective customers, not just the cost related to the portion of the potential customers that is expected to respond to the advertising, should be deferred.

- Deferred direct-response advertising costs should be amortized using a cost-pool method over the period during which the future benefits are expected to be received. The amortization should be the ratio that current-period revenues for a cost pool bear to the total current and estimated future-period revenues for that cost pool. The amount of estimated future revenues should not be discounted, but it may be adjusted in subsequent periods. The ratio should be recalculated at each reporting date.

- The realizability of the deferred advertising should be evaluated, at each balance sheet date, by comparing, on a cost pool-by-cost pool basis, the carrying amount of the deferred advertising with the probable remaining future net revenues expected to result directly from such advertising. Only probable future primary revenues should be used to determine the probable remaining future net revenues.

- Certain disclosures are required, such as:
  - The accounting policy selected for advertising
  - The total amount charged to advertising
  - A description of the direct-response advertising reported as assets (if any)
  - The accounting policy and amortization period of direct-response advertising, the total amount of advertising reported as assets
  - The amounts, if any, written down to net realizable income

The SEC Staff considers the requirements for deferral of direct-response advertising costs to be met only if the advertising results in a direct revenue-generating response; for example, if the respondent orders the product when placing the call to the advertised number. The Staff believes capitalization is not appropriate for advertising that results not in sales but only in sales opportunities, even if these are likely to produce results. For example, an advertisement for aluminum siding that includes a phone number to call to schedule a visit from a sales representative would not qualify for capitalization as direct-response advertising because the advertisement leads only indirectly to the revenue-generating transaction. The SEC Staff also would object to the classification of deferred advertising costs as current assets, because such costs do not meet the definition of a current asset in Accounting Research Bulletin No. 43, *Restatement and Revision of Accounting Research Bulletins.*

(q) WEB SITE DEVELOPMENT COSTS.   With the rapid growth in so-called e-commerce in the late 1990s, many reporting entities incurred costs to develop and maintain Web sites.

EITF Issue No. 00-2, *Accounting for Web Site Development Costs,* provided this guidance for accounting for Web site development costs:

- During the planning phase, an entity develops a project plan, determines the desired functionalities of the Web site, identifies the needed hardware and software applications, and determines whether suitable technology exists. All costs incurred in the planning stage should be expensed as incurred.
- During the Web site development phase, the entity acquires or develops hardware and software to operate its Web site and develops appropriate graphics. Costs related to software and graphics should be accounted for under SOP 98-1, *Accounting for the Costs of Computer Software Developed or Obtained for Internal Use,* as software for internal use unless the entity has or is developing a plan to market the software. Software, including graphics, to be marketed should be accounted for under SFAS No. 86 (ASC 985), *Computer Software to Be Sold, Leased, or Otherwise Marketed.* See Section 14.6(f) for a discussion of SOP 98-1 and SFAS No. 86 (ASC 985). Costs incurred for Web site hosting should generally be expensed over the period of benefit.

14.6 INTANGIBLE ASSETS IN SPECIALIZED INDUSTRIES

Intangible assets are particularly significant or receive unique accounting treatment in certain industries. These requirements are generally to be found in AICPA Industry Audit and Accounting Guides or in SOPs.

(a) AIRLINES.   Under the AICPA Industry Audit Guide, *Audits of Airlines,* as amended by SOP 88-1, *Accounting for Developmental and Pre-operating Costs, Purchases and Exchanges of Take-off and Landing Slots, and Airframe Modifications,* and SOP 98-5, *Reporting on the Costs of Start-Up Activities,* the capitalization of preoperating costs related only to the integration of new types of aircraft. The costs of acquiring take-off and landing slots, whether by exchange of stock or through purchase, are identifiable intangible assets. Developmental costs related to preparation of new routes should not be capitalized.

(b) BANKING AND THRIFTS.   During the thrift and banking crises of the late 1980s and early 1990s, precipitated in part by the high interest rate environment and negative interest rate spreads of those years, many insured financial institutions, when evaluated on a fair value basis, were threatened with insolvency or already were insolvent. The federal insurers (Federal Deposit Insurance Corporation; Federal Savings and Loan Insurance Corporation) were themselves facing insolvency and would likely have been unable to repay all depositors of closed institutions from available reserves. It was hoped that, with an anticipated return to a normal interest rate environment, many of these banks and thrifts would regain solvency and survive, sparring the insurers (and ultimately the taxpayers) these losses.

Given this situation, there was a concerted political effort to postpone bank and thrift closings, and one perhaps ill-conceived solution was to encourage the takeovers of failing banks and thrifts by offering the acquirers the ability to treat the net liabilities acquired (measured at fair value) as so-called supervisory goodwill. Although this did not comport with the traditional GAAP concept of goodwill, the profession accommodated this regulatory mandate. Under SFAS No. 72, *Accounting for Certain Acquisitions of Banking or Thrift Institutions,* this goodwill was to be amortized over the terms set forth in the assisted, supervisory mergers (often 20 or more years), even though the so-called core deposit intangible (related to the expected holding term of deposits acquired) would have a much shorter expected life.

The elimination of goodwill amortization by SFAS No. 142 (ASC 350) necessitated a change to many of the SFAS No. 72 provisions. SFAS No. 147, *Acquisitions of Certain Financial Institutions,* eliminated the special accounting imposed by SFAS No. 72, with the exception that mergers between mutual enterprises continue to be governed by that standard. Thus, as amended, SFAS No. 72 applied only to acquisitions of financial institutions that were mutual enterprises by other financial institutions that were also mutual enterprises. For those acquisitions, goodwill that was created by an excess of the fair value of liabilities assumed over the fair value of tangible and identified intangible assets acquired was to be amortized by the interest method over a period no greater than the estimated remaining life of the long-term, interest-bearing assets acquired. If the assets acquired did not include a significant amount of long-term, interest-bearing assets, such goodwill was to be amortized over a period not exceeding the estimated average life of the existing customer (deposit) base acquired.

At the effective date of SFAS No. 147, any remaining unidentified intangible other than that arising from a business combination continued to be amortized, while that arising from business combinations (e.g., the assisted supervisory mergers) was to be reclassified as goodwill and thereafter tested for impairment per SFAS No. 142 (ASC 350). Transitional impairment testing procedures were also specified.

(c) MORTGAGE BANKING.   Under paragraph 13 of SFAS No. 140 (ASC 860), *Accounting for Transfers and Servicing of Financial Assets and Extinguishments of Liabilities,* servicing of mortgage loans becomes a distinct asset or liability only when contractually separated from the underlying amounts by sale or securitization of the assets with servicing retained, or through the separate purchase or assumption of the servicing rights. SFAS No. 156 (ASC 860), *Accounting for Certain Hybrid Financial Instruments—an amendment of FASB Statements No. 133 and 140,* deleted paragraph 13 of SFAS No. 140; replacing it with this wording:

> An entity shall recognize and initially measure at fair value, if practicable, a servicing asset or servicing liability each time it undertakes an obligation to service a financial asset by entering into a servicing contract in any of the following situations:
>
> **a.** A transfer of the servicer's financial assets that meets the requirements for sale accounting
>
> **b.** A transfer of the servicer's financial assets to a qualifying SPE [special-purpose entity] in a guaranteed mortgage securitization in which the transferor retains all of the resulting securities

and classifies them as either available-for-sale securities or trading securities in accordance with FASB Statement No. 115, *Accounting for Certain Investments in Debt and Equity Securities*

c. An acquisition or assumption of a servicing obligation that does not relate to financial assets of the servicer or its consolidated affiliates

An entity that transfers its financial assets to a qualifying SPE in a guaranteed mortgage securitization in which the transferor retains all of the resulting securities and classifies them as debt securities held-to-maturity in accordance with Statement 115 may either separately recognize its servicing assets or servicing liabilities or report those servicing assets or servicing liabilities together with the asset being serviced.

An entity that undertakes a contract to service financial assets shall recognize either a servicing asset or a servicing liability, unless the transferor transfers the assets in a guaranteed mortgage securitization, retains all of the resulting securities, and classifies them as debt securities held-to-maturity in accordance with SFAS No. 115 "Accounting for Certain Investments in Debt and Equity Securities" (ASC 320), in which case the servicing asset or liability may be reported together with the asset being serviced. SFAS No. 159 (ASC 825), *The Fair Value Option for Financial Assets and Financial Liabilities,* amendments to SFAS No. 115 (ASC 320) do not affect a contract to service financial assets. Each sale or securitization with servicing retained or separate purchase or assumption of servicing results in a servicing contract. Each servicing contract results in a servicing asset (when the benefits of servicing are expected to be more than adequate compensation to the servicer for performing the servicing) or a servicing liability (when the benefits of servicing are not expected to compensate the servicer adequately for performing the servicing). If the servicer is more than adequately compensated and if the servicing was retained in a sale or securitization, the servicer shall account for the contracts to service the mortgage loans separately from the loans by initially measuring the servicing assets at their allocated previous carrying amounts based on relative fair value at the date of sale or securitization. If the servicing asset is purchased or servicing liability assumed, it is measured at fair value. If the servicer is not adequately compensated, a servicing liability undertaken in a sale or securitization is measured at fair value.

Servicing assets are amortized in proportion to and over the period of estimated net servicing income—the excess of service revenues over servicing costs. Servicing liabilities are amortized in proportion to and over the period of estimated net servicing loss—the excess of servicing costs over servicing revenues, if practicable.

Paragraph 63(f) of SFAS No. 156 stipulates that the impairment of servicing assets should be measured in this way:

1. Stratify servicing assets based on one or more of the predominant risk characteristics of the underlying assets.
2. Recognize impairment through a valuation allowance for an individual stratum for the amount by which the carrying amount of the servicing assets for the stratum exceeds their fair value.
3. Adjust the valuation allowance to reflect changes in the measurement of impairment subsequent to the initial measurement of impairment.

Rights for future income from the serviced assets that exceed contractually specified servicing fees should be accounted for separately. Those rights are not servicing assets; they are financial assets, effectively interest-only strips to be accounted for in accordance with paragraph 14 of SFAS No. 140 (ASC 860).

In EITF No. 95-5, *Determination of What Risks and Rewards, If Any, Can Be Retained and Whether Any Unresolved Contingencies May Exist in a Sale of Mortgage Loan Servicing Rights,* the issue addressed was whether the inclusion of any provision that results in the seller's retention of specified risk (1) precludes recognition of a sale at the date title passes or (2) allows recognition of the sale at that date if (a) the seller can reasonably estimate, and record a liability for, the costs related to protection provisions, or (b) the sale agreement provides for substantially all risks and rewards to irrevocably pass to the buyer, and the seller can reasonably estimate, and record a liability for, the minor protection provisions.

The EITF consensus was that sales of rights to service mortgage loans should be recognized when these conditions are met: (1) title has passed, (2) substantially all risks and rewards of ownership have irrevocably passed to the buyer, and (3) any protection provisions retained by the seller are minor and can be reasonably estimated. If a sale is recognized and minor protection provisions exist, a liability should be accrued for the estimated obligation associated with those provisions. The seller retains only minor protection provisions if (a) the obligation associated with those provisions is estimated to be no more than 10 percent of the sales price and (b) risk of prepayment is retained for no longer than 120 days. Mortgage banking is covered in more detail in Chapter 30.

(d) BROADCASTING INDUSTRY. The principal intangible assets in the broadcasting industry are Federal Communications Commission (FCC) licenses, broadcast rights (license agreement to program material), and network affiliation agreements. Television and radio stations may not operate without a FCC license, which specifies, for example, the frequency to be used. A broadcasting license is granted for a 10-year period and is renewable for additional 10-year periods if the entity provides at least an average level of service to its customers and complies with applicable FCC rules and policies. Licenses thus may be renewed indefinitely at little cost.

If the entity intends to renew the license indefinitely and has the ability to do so, a broadcast license would be deemed to have an indefinite useful life. It would not be amortized until its useful life was no longer deemed to be indefinite. Impairment would be tested as provided in Section 14.4(c). If the entity does not intend to renew a broadcast license indefinitely, however, it would amortize the license over its remaining useful life and follow the impairment guidance in SFAS No. 144 (ASC 360).

(i) Broadcast Rights. SFAS No. 63 (ASC 920), *Financial Reporting by Broadcasters,* contains industry-specific GAAP. Its primary mandate is that broadcasters must account for license agreements for program materials as purchases of rights, thus necessitating the presentation of assets and liabilities on the entities' balance sheets. Broadcast rights result from a contract or license to exhibit films, programs, or other works and permit one or more exhibitions during a specified license period. Compensation is ordinarily payable in installments over a period shorter than the period of the licensing contract, but it may also take the form of a lump-sum payment at the beginning of the period. The license expires at the end of the contract period. SFAS No. 139 amends SFAS No. 63 (ASC 920) to clarify that the requirements of SOP 00-2, *Accounting by Producers or Distributors of Films* apply to a film owned by broadcaster. Previously, SFAS No. 63 (ASC 920) addressed licensing agreements only.

Amounts recorded for broadcasting rights are to be segregated on the balance sheet as current and noncurrent assets based on estimated usage within one year. Rights should be amortized based on the estimated number of future showings. Items that may be used on an unlimited basis, rather than a limited number of showings, may be amortized over the period covered by the agreement. An accelerated method of amortization is required when the first showing is more valuable than reruns, as is usually the case. Straight-line amortization is allowable only when each telecast or broadcast is expected to generate approximately the same revenue.

Feature programs are to be amortized on a program-by-program basis; however, amortization as a package may be appropriate if it approximates the amortization that would have been provided on a program-by-program basis. The capitalized costs of rights to program material should be reported in the balance sheet at the lower of unamortized cost or estimated net realizable value on a program-by-program, series, package, or "daypart" basis, as appropriate. If management's expectations of the programming usefulness of a program, series, package, or daypart are revised downward, it may be necessary to write down unamortized cost to estimated net realizable value. *Daypart* is defined in SFAS No. 63 (ASC 920) as an aggregation of programs broadcast during a particular time of day (e.g., daytime, evening, late night) or programs of a similar type (e.g., sports, news, children's shows). A write-down from unamortized cost to a lower estimated net realizable value establishes a new cost basis.

(ii) Revoked or Nonrenewed Broadcast Licenses.   When broadcasting licenses are not renewed or are revoked, unamortized balances should be written off. If a network affiliation is terminated and is not immediately replaced or under agreement to be replaced, the unamortized balance of the amount originally allocated to the network affiliation agreement should be charged to expense. If a network affiliation is terminated and immediately replaced or under agreement to be replaced, a loss is recognized to the extent that the unamortized cost of the terminated affiliation exceeds the fair value of the new affiliation. Gain is not to be recognized if the fair value of the new network affiliation exceeds the unamortized cost of the terminated affiliation.

(e) CABLE TELEVISION.   Cable television companies experience a long preoperating and development period. SFAS No. 51 (ASC 922), *Financial Reporting by Cable Television Companies,* defines the "pre-maturity period" as that during which a cable television system is partially under construction and partially in service. Costs incurred during this period that relate to both current and future operations are partially expensed and partially capitalized. In a cable system, portions or segments that are in the pre-maturity period and can be clearly distinguished from the remainder of the system should be accounted for separately. Costs incurred to obtain and retain subscribers and general and administrative expenses incurred during the pre-maturity period are to be expensed as period costs. Programming costs and other system costs that will not vary significantly regardless of the number of subscribers are allocated between current and future operations. The amount currently expensed is based on a relationship of subscribers during the current month (as prescribed in the SFAS) and the total number of subscribers expected at the end of the pre-maturity period. The capitalized portions decrease each month as the cable company progresses toward the end of the pre-maturity period. Prior to the pre-maturity period, system-related costs are capitalized; subsequent thereto, none of these costs is deferred. Capitalized costs should be amortized over the same period used to depreciate the main cable television plant. Costs of successful franchise applications are capitalized and amortized in accordance with SFAS No. 142 (ASC 350). Costs of unsuccessful applications and abandoned franchises are charged to expense.

(f) COMPUTER SOFTWARE.   SFAS No. 86 (ASC 985), *Computer Software to Be Sold, Leased, or Otherwise Marketed,* prescribes the accounting for the costs of computer software purchased or internally developed as a marketable product by itself. Costs incurred to establish the technological feasibility are charged to expense when incurred as required by SFAS No. 2 (ASC 730). Technological feasibility is established on completion of all planning, designing, coding, and testing activities necessary to establish that the product can be produced. The completion of a detailed program design or completion of a working model provides evidence of the establishment of technological feasibility.

Costs incurred subsequent to the establishment of technological feasibility are capitalized. Software used as an integral part of product or process is not capitalized until both technological feasibility has been established for the software and all R&D activities for the other components have been completed. When the product is available for release to customers, capitalization ceases. Costs of maintenance and customer support are expensed when the related revenue is recognized or when the costs are incurred, whichever occurs first. Purchased software that has alternative future uses should be capitalized but subsequently accounted for according to its use.

Paragraph 8 of SFAS No. 86 (ASC 985) stipulates that:

> ...capitalized software costs shall be amortized on a product-by-product basis. The annual amortization shall be the greater of the amount computed using (a) the ratio that current gross revenues for a product bear to the total of current and anticipated future gross revenues for that product or

(b) the straight-line method over the remaining estimated economic life of the product including the period being reported on. Amortization shall state when the product is available for general release to customers.

Paragraph 10 of SFAS No. 86 (ASC 985) stipulates that:

> ...at each balance sheet date, the unamortized capitalized costs of a computer software product shallbe compared to the net realizable value of that product. The amount by which the unamortized capitalized costs of a computer software product exceed the net realizable value of that asset shall be written off. The amount of the write down shall not be subsequently restored.

The unamortized computer costs included in the balance sheet, the total amortization charged to expense in each income statement presented, and amounts written down to net realizable value should be disclosed.

FASB Interpretation (FIN) No. 6, *Applicability of FASB Statement No. 2 to Computer Software— an interpretation of FASB Statement No. 2,* par. 4, states that, to the extent the acquisition, development, or improvement of a process for use in selling and administrative activities includes costs for computer software, these costs are not R&D costs. Examples given of excluded costs are the development by an airline of a computerized reservation system or the development of a general management information system. SFAS No. 86 (ASC 985) does not cover accounting for costs of software used internally. For that subject, see the discussion of SOP 98-1 in this subsection.

In EITF Issue No. 96-6, *Accounting for the Film and Software Cost Associated with Developing Entertainment and Educational Software Products,* the EITF considered the issue of how companies should account for the film and software costs associated with developing entertainment and educational software (EE) products such as computer games, interactive videos, and other multimedia products. The SEC Staff announced that EE products that are sold, leased, or otherwise marketed are subject to the accounting requirements of SFAS No. 86 (ASC 985). The SEC Staff believes that the film costs incurred in development of an EE product should be accounted for under the provisions of SFAS No. 86 (ASC 985). In addition, exploitation costs should be expensed as incurred unless those costs include advertising costs that qualify for capitalization in accordance with SOP 93-7. Because of the SEC Staff's position, the EITF was not asked to reach a consensus on this issue.

In EITF Issue No. 97-13, *Accounting for Costs Incurred in Connection with a Consulting Contract or an Internal Project That Combines Business Process Reengineering and Information Technology Transformation,* the EITF addressed the accounting for business process reengineering costs. These costs may be included in a contract that combines business process reengineering and a project to acquire, develop, or implement internal-use software. The issue does not address the accounting for internal-use software development costs (which was, however, dealt with subsequently by SOP 98-1, *Accounting for the Costs of Computer Software for Internal Use*). The EITF reached a consensus that costs of business process reengineering, whether done internally or by third parties, should be expensed as incurred. If the project is carried out by a third party and some of the costs are capitalizable, such as fixed asset costs, the EITF concluded that the total contract cost should be allocated to various activities based on the relative fair value of the separate activities. The allocation should be based on the objective evidence of the fair value of the elements in the contract, not separate prices stated within the contract. The consensus opinion identified the following as third-party or internally generated costs typically associated with business process reengineering activities that should be expensed as incurred:

- Preparation of request for proposal
- Current state assessment
- Process reengineering
- Restructuring the workforce

The cost of software used internally is accounted for under SOP 98-1. The SOP divides the process of computer software development into three stages:

1. *Preliminary project stage.* Conceptual formulation and evaluation of alternatives, determination of existence of needed technology, and final selection of alternatives
2. *Application development stage.* Design of chosen path, coding, installation to hardware, and testing
3. *Postimplementation/operation stage.* Training and application maintenance

Computer software costs that are incurred in the preliminary project stage should be expensed as incurred.

Once the capitalization criteria of the SOP have been met, external direct costs of materials and services consumed in developing or obtaining internal-use computer software, payroll costs for employees who are directly associated with and who devote time to the project, and interest costs incurred in developing the software should be capitalized. Capitalization should cease no later than the point at which a computer software project is substantially complete and ready for its intended use.

Internal and external training costs and maintenance costs incurred in the postimplementation/operation stage should be expensed as incurred. General and administrative costs and overhead costs should not be capitalized as costs of internal-use software.

(g) EXTRACTIVE INDUSTRIES.   Intangible assets in the extractive industries include leased or purchased rights to exploit mineral and other natural resources based on lump-sum, periodic, or production-based payments. The rights are usually included in the property section of the balance sheet.

(h) PRODUCERS OR DISTRIBUTORS OF FILMS.   SOP 00-2 provides guidance on the accounting for costs related to all types of films and is applicable to both producers and distributors of films. The costs of producing a film include film costs, participation costs, exploitation costs, and manufacturing costs. Marketing and other exploitation costs, other than advertising, should be expensed as incurred. Advertising costs should be accounted for under SOP 93-7. Paragraph 34 of SOP 00-2 requires entities to amortize film costs using the individual-film-forecast-computation method. That method provides for amortization of costs in the same ratio that current-period actual revenue (numerator) bears to estimated remaining unrecognized ultimate revenue as of the beginning of the current fiscal year. Amortization begins when a film is released and the entity begins to recognize revenue from the film.

Certain events or changes in circumstances, such as an adverse change in the expected performance of a film or a substantial delay in completion of the film, indicate that the fair value of the film may be less than the related unamortized film costs. If such an event occurs, an entity should assess whether the fair value of the film is less than its unamortized film costs. If the unamortized capitalized film costs exceed the film's fair value, the excess should be written off and may not be subsequently restored. See Chapter 37 for more on this topic.

(i) PUBLIC UTILITIES.   The general provisions of accounting for intangible assets of various types apply to public utilities. However, since public utilities are required by regulatory agencies to maintain their accounts in accordance with accounting practices that may vary from GAAP, certain differences in treatment may result. An example is R&D costs, which certain regulatory agencies allow to be deferred.

The rate regulator may reasonably assure the existence of an asset by permitting the inclusion of a cost in allowable costs for rate-making purposes. Paragraph 9 of SFAS No. 71 (ASC 980), *Accounting for the Effects of Certain Types of Regulation,* sets forth two criteria that must both be met in order for a utility to capitalize a cost that would otherwise be required, under GAAP, to be expensed currently:

1. It is probable that future revenue in an amount at least equal to the capitalized cost will result from inclusion of that cost in allowable costs for rate-making purposes.

2. Based on available evidence, the future revenue will be provided to permit recovery of the previously incurred cost rather than to provide for expected levels of similar future costs. If the revenue will be provided through an automatic rate-adjustment clause, this criterion requires that the regulator's intent clearly be to permit recovery of the previously incurred cost.

SFAS No. 90 amended SFAS No. 71 (ASC 980) in this way:

- Footnote 6 to paragraph 9 is superseded by the following:
  - "The term *probable* is used in SFAS No. 90 consistent with its use in SFAS No. 5 (ASC 450), *Accounting for Contingencies.* Statement No. 5 defines *probable* as an area within a range of the likelihood that a future event or events will occur. That range is from probable to remote:
    - *Probable.* The future event or events are likely to occur.
    - *Reasonably possible.* The chance of the future event or events occurring is more than remote but less than likely.
    - *Remote.* The chance of the future event or events occurring is slight.
  - The next footnote is added at the end of the first sentence of paragraph 9:
  - Costs of abandoned plants shall be accounted for in accordance with paragraphs 3-6 of SFAS No. 90, *Regulated Enterprises—Accounting for Abandonments and Disallowances of Plant Costs."*

SFAS No. 92 amends SFAS No. 71 (ASC 980) and SFAS No. 90 in this way:

- The next sentence is added to the end of the footnote, added by paragraph 9(b) of SFAS No. 90, at the end of the first sentence of paragraph 9 of SFAS No. 71:

Phase-in plans shall be accounted for in accordance with SFAS No. 92, *Regulated Enterprises—Accounting for Phase-in Plans.*

- Paragraph 14 of SFAS No. 71 (ASC 980) is superseded by this text:

The following specific standards and the standards in SFAS No. 90 and 92 are derived from the general standards in paragraphs 9–12. The specific standards in paragraphs 15–17 and the standards in SFAS No. 90 and 92 shall not be used as guidance for other applications of the general standards in paragraphs 9–12.

- Paragraph 9(d) of SFAS No. 90 is deleted.

If at any time the capitalized cost no longer meets those two criteria above, as shown in paragraph 14.6(i), it is to be expensed. The value of an asset may be impaired by a regulator's rate actions. If a rate regulator excludes all or part of a capitalized cost from allowable costs and the cost was capitalized based on the above criteria, the asset should be reduced to the extent of the excluded cost. Whether other assets have been impaired is determined under the general rules for impairment, which are described in Section 14.4(b) and (c).

If an enterprise discontinues application of SFAS No. 71 (ASC 980) because, for example, its operations have been deregulated, it would eliminate from its GAAP balance sheet assets consisting of costs capitalized that would not have been capitalized by unregulated entities. Numerous state legislatures and/or regulatory commissions have approved or are considering deregulating utilities' generation (production) cost of electricity, although the portion of the kilowatt charge attributable to transmission of the electricity to the local area and the distribution cost to the customer are not being deregulated. If some, but not all, of a utility's operations are regulated, SFAS No. 71 (ASC 980) should be applied to the portion of the operations that continue to meet the requirements of SFAS No. 71 (ASC 980) for regulatory accounting. SFAS No. 101 (ASC 980), *Regulated Enterprises—Accounting for the Discontinuation of Application of FASB Statement No. 71,* addresses how an entity that ceases to meet the criteria for application of SFAS No. 71 (ASC 980) to all or part of its operations should report that event in its financial statements.

An issue related to the current deregulation environment is when an entity should cease to apply the regulated enterprise accounting model prescribed by SFAS No. 71 (ASC 980) to the generation portion of its operations if deregulation is under consideration. In EITF Issue No. 97-4, *Deregulation of the Price of Electricity—Issues Related to the Application of FASB Statements No. 71 and 101,* the EITF reached a consensus that when deregulatory legislation or a rate order is issued that contains sufficient detail to determine how the deregulatory plan will affect the portion of the business being deregulated, the entity should stop applying SFAS No. 71 (ASC 980) to that separable portion of its business. The Task Force considered this fact situation: If legislation is passed requiring deregulation of generation charges at the end of five years, the date the legislation is passed is the latest date that the entity can discontinue application of the SFAS No. 71 (ASC 980) accounting model to the generation portion of its operations. The consensus does not address whether an entity should stop applying SFAS No. 71 (ASC 980) at an earlier time. The Task Force also observed that the financial statements should segregate, either on their face or in the notes, the amounts that pertain to the separable portion.

With regard to goodwill, a regulator may permit a utility to amortize purchased goodwill over a specified period, may direct a utility not to amortize goodwill, or may direct the utility to write off goodwill. SFAS No. 71 (ASC 980) requires the goodwill to be amortized for financial reporting purposes over the period during which it will be allowed for rate-making purposes. If the regulator either excludes amortization from allowable costs for rate-making purposes or directs the utility to write off goodwill, goodwill should not be amortized, and it should be accounted for under SFAS No. 142 (ASC 350).

(j) RECORD AND MUSIC INDUSTRY.   Significant intangible assets in the record and music industry include record masters, recording artist contracts, and copyrights. Accounting for copyrights generally follows that used in other industries, but the accounting for record masters and recording artist contracts is unique.

SFAS No. 50 (ASC 928), *Financial Reporting in the Record and Music Industry,* is the primary source of accounting principles in this area. Paragraph 5 of AICPA SOP 76-1 "Accounting Practices in the Record and Music Industry" provides that the costs of producing a record master include the costs of musical talent; technical talent for engineering, directing, and mixing; equipment to record and produce the master; and studio facility charges. Paragraph 40 of SOP 76-1 also provides:

> When past performance of an artist provides a reasonable basis for estimating that the cost of a record master borne by the record company will be recovered from future sales, that cost should be recorded as an asset and, when material, should be separately disclosed. The cost of record masters should be amortized by a method that reasonably relates the cost to the net revenue expected to be realized. Ordinarily, amortization occurs over a very short period. Unamortized amounts should be written off when it becomes apparent that they will not be recovered through future sales. The cost of the record master recoverable from the artist's royalties is to be accounted for as an advance royalty.

A recording artist contract is an agreement for personal services. A major portion of the artist's compensation consists of participation in earnings (measured by sales and license fee income, commonly referred to as a "royalty") or of a nonrefundable advance against royalties. Advances should be recorded as an asset (as a prepaid royalty, classified as current or noncurrent depending on when amounts are expected to be realized) if it is anticipated that they will be recovered against royalties otherwise payable to the artist. When it is determined that a prepayment will not be recovered, the balance should be written off.

(k) TIMBER INDUSTRY. Companies in the forest products industry may make lump-sum payments for timber-cutting rights, which allow them to remove trees for a specified period or in specified quantities. Lump-sum payments made at the inception of an agreement are properly deferred and amortized over the period of the agreement or on the basis of estimates of recoverable timber. Periodic or production-based payments are expensed as they do not represent future benefits. Cutting rights are ordinarily included in the property section of the balance sheet and are stated at cost less amortization. The amortization policy should be disclosed.

14.7 ACCOUNTING FOR GOODWILL

(a) INITIAL VALUATION. SFAS Nos. 141, *Business Combinations,* and 142 were both issued in June 2001. Those Statements replaced APB Opinions No. 16, *Business Combinations,* and No. 17, *Intangible Assets,* and respectively SFAS No. 141(R) (ASC 805), issued in December 2007, replaces SFAS No. 141. SFAS No. 141 and SFAS No. 142 (ASC 350) define goodwill in this way:

> The excess of the cost of an acquired entity over the net of the amounts assigned to assets acquired and liabilities assumed. The amount recognized as goodwill includes acquired intangible assets that do not meet the criteria in paragraph 39 of SFAS No. 141, *Business Combinations,* for recognition as an asset apart from goodwill.

SFAS No. 141(R) (ASC 805) defines goodwill in this way:

> Goodwill is an asset representing the future economic benefits arising from other assets acquired in a business combination that are not individually identified and separately recognized.

The above-referenced criteria for separate recognition of intangibles are discussed in Section 14.3(a). For accounting purposes, the cost of purchased goodwill is the residual cost remaining after all other identifiable assets and liabilities have been valued.

(b) SUBSEQUENT ACCOUNTING. Goodwill is not amortized. It is tested for impairment at a level of reporting referred to as a reporting unit (see Subsection 14.7(b)(iv) for a definition of a reporting unit). Impairment is the condition that exists when the carrying amount of goodwill is greater than its implied fair value. A two-step impairment test, discussed next, is used to identify potential goodwill impairment and measure the amount of a goodwill impairment loss to be recognized, if any.

(i) Recognition and Measurement of an Impairment Loss. The first step of a goodwill impairment test compares the fair value of a reporting unit with its carrying amount, including goodwill, applying the guidance in Subsection 14.7(b)(ii). If the fair value of the reporting unit is more than its carrying amount, goodwill of the reporting unit is considered not impaired, and the second step of the impairment test is not performed. If the carrying amount of the reporting unit is more than its fair value, the second step of the goodwill impairment test, discussed next, is performed to measure the amount of impairment loss, if any.

The second step of the goodwill impairment test compares the implied fair value of reporting unit goodwill (explained in the next paragraph) with the carrying amount of the goodwill. If the carrying amount of reporting unit goodwill is more than the implied fair value of the goodwill, an impairment loss is recognized in an amount equal to the excess. The loss recognized cannot exceed the carrying amount of goodwill. When a goodwill impairment loss is recognized, the adjusted carrying amount of goodwill is its new accounting basis. Subsequent to the measurement and recognition of the goodwill impairment loss, a later recovery in value cannot be recognized. Thus, goodwill impairments cannot be reversed.

The implied fair value of goodwill is determined in the same way as is the amount of goodwill to be recognized in a business combination. The reporting entity allocates the fair value of the reporting unit to all of the assets and liabilities of the unit, including any unrecognized intangible assets, the same way it would be allocated had the reporting unit been acquired in a business combination and had the fair value of the reporting unit been the price paid to acquire the reporting unit. The excess of the fair value of the reporting unit over the amounts assigned to its assets and liabilities is the *implied fair value of goodwill.*

The above-described allocation process is performed only for the purpose of testing goodwill for impairment. A reporting entity does not write up or down a recognized asset or liability, and it does not recognize a previously unrecognized intangible asset as a result of the allocation process.

If the second step of the goodwill impairment test is not complete before the financial statements are issued and a goodwill impairment loss is probable and can be reasonably estimated, the best estimate of the loss is recognized in those financial statements. Paragraph 47(c) of SFAS No. 142 (ASC 350) requires disclosure of the fact that the measurement of the impairment loss is an estimate. Any adjustment to the estimated loss based on completion of the measurement of the impairment loss is recognized in the next reporting period.

(ii) Fair Value Measurements.   SFAS No. 142 defines *fair value* the same way FASB Statement of Concepts No. 7, *Using Cash Flow Information and Present Value in Accounting Measurements,* does:

> The amount at which that asset (or liability) could be bought (or incurred) or sold (settled) in a current transaction between willing parties, that is, other than in a forced or liquidation sale.

According to that definition, the fair value of a reporting unit is the amount at which the unit as a whole could be bought or sold in a current transaction between willing parties. Quoted market prices in active markets are the best evidence of fair value and shall be used as the basis for measurement, if available. However, the market price of an individual equity security and thus the market capitalization of a reporting unit with publicly traded equity securities may not be representative of the fair value of the reporting unit as a whole, because of a control premium. The quoted market price of an individual equity security, therefore, need not be the sole measurement basis of the fair value of a reporting unit. SEC registrants should be aware that the SEC Staff has sometimes questioned valuations not based on the market price of the equity security.

If quoted market prices are not available, the estimate of fair value is based on the best information available, including prices for similar assets and liabilities and the results of using other valuation techniques. A present value technique is often the best available technique with which to estimate the fair value of a group of net assets (i.e., a reporting unit). If a present value technique is used to measure fair value, estimates of future cash flows used in the technique are to be consistent with the objective of measuring fair value. The cash flow estimates should incorporate assumptions that marketplace participants would use in their estimates of fair value. If that information is not available without undue cost and effort, a reporting entity may use its own assumptions.

An entity should base the cash flow estimates on reasonable and supportable assumptions after consideration of all available evidence. The weight given to the evidence should be commensurate with the extent to which the evidence can be verified objectively. If the entity estimates a range for the amount or timing of possible cash flows, it should consider the likelihood of possible outcomes. Paragraphs 39-54 and 75-88 of FASB Concepts Statement No. 7 discusses the use of present value techniques in measuring the fair value an asset or a liability. It states that an "expected cash flow approach" which uses the sum of probability-weighted present values in a range of estimated cash flows adjusted for risk, all discounted using the same interest rate convention, is the preferred—but not required—approach. FASB has indicated that such a technique is a more effective measurement tool than was the traditional present value approach, especially in situations in which the timing or the amount of estimated cash flows is uncertain, as is the case in measuring nonfinancial assets and liabilities.

In estimating the fair value of a reporting unit, a valuation technique based on multiples of earnings or revenue or a similar performance measure may be used if that technique is consistent with the objective of measuring fair value. Use of such multiples may be appropriate, for example, when the fair value of an entity that has comparable operations and economic characteristics is observable and the relevant multiples of the comparable entity are known. Conversely, such multiples are not appropriate in situations in which the operations or activities of an entity whose multiples are known are not of a comparable nature, scope, or size as the reporting unit for which fair value is being estimated.

(iii) When to Test Goodwill for Impairment. Goodwill of a reporting unit is tested for impairment annually and between annual tests in certain circumstances, as discussed below in this same paragraph. The annual goodwill impairment test may be performed any time during the fiscal year, provided the timing of the test is consistent from year to year. Different reporting units may be tested for impairment at different times.

A detailed determination of the fair value of a reporting unit may be carried forward from one year to the next if all of the next criteria have been met:

- The assets and liabilities that make up the reporting unit have not changed significantly since the most recent fair value determination.
- The most recent fair value determination resulted in an amount that exceeded the carrying amount of the reporting unit by a substantial margin.
- Based on an analysis of events that have occurred and circumstances that have changed since the most recent fair value determination, the likelihood that a current fair value determination would be less than the current carrying amount of the reporting unit is remote.

Goodwill of a reporting unit is tested for impairment between annual tests if an event occurs or circumstances change that would more likely than not reduce the fair value of a reporting unit below its carrying amount.

Examples of such events or circumstances include:

- A significant adverse change in legal factors or in the business climate
- An adverse action or assessment by a regulator
- Unanticipated competition
- A loss of key personnel
- A more-likely-than-not expectation that a reporting unit or a significant portion of a reporting unit will be sold or otherwise disposed of
- Testing for recoverability under paragraph 8 of SFAS No. 144 (ASC 360) of a significant asset group within a reporting unit
- Recognition of a goodwill impairment loss in the financial statements of a subsidiary that is a component of a reporting unit

Also see Subsection 14.7(b)(vi) for the need to test goodwill for impairment after a portion of goodwill has been allocated to a business to be disposed of.

If goodwill and another asset or asset group of a reporting unit are tested for impairment at the same time, the other asset or asset group is tested before goodwill. If the asset or asset group is found to be impaired, the impairment loss is recognized before goodwill is tested for impairment.

(iv) Reporting Unit. A reporting unit is an operating segment or one level below an operating segment, referred to as a component. An operating segment is defined by paragraph 10 of SFAS No. 131 (ASC 280), *Disclosures about Segments of an Enterprise and Related Information.* A component of an operating segment is a reporting unit if the component constitutes a business, as discussed in EITF Issue No. 98-3 *Determining Whether a Nonmonetary Transaction Involves Receipt of Productive Assets or of a Business,* for which discrete financial information is available and segment management, as defined by SFAS No. 131, regularly reviews the operating results of that component.

Segment management may consist of one or more segment managers. Two or more components of an operating segment are aggregated and deemed a single reporting unit if the components have similar economic characteristics, as discussed in SFAS No. 131. An operating segment is deemed a reporting unit if all of its components are similar, if none of its components is a reporting unit, or if it comprises only a single component.

Because considerable judgment is required for entities to determine their reporting units and the guidance in SFAS No. 142 is quite limited, the FASB Staff provided further clarification of that guidance in EITF Topic No. D-101, *Clarification of Reporting Unit Guidance in Paragraph 30 of FASB Statement No. 142*. The basic guidance is that a component of an operating segment is a reporting unit if (1) it constitutes a business, (2) discrete financial information on the component is available, and (3) segment management regularly reviews the operating results of the reporting unit. A fourth requirement provides that components with similar economic characteristics should be combined into one reporting unit. EITF Topic No. D-101 provides that the first three factors are required for a component to be a reporting unit, but no one factor is individually determinative.

The determinative factors are how an entity manages its operations and how an acquired entity is integrated with the acquiring entity. EITF Topic No. D-101 provides this clarification of each factor:

- *Component constitutes a business.* Judgment is required to determine whether a component constitutes a business, and entities are required to consider the guidance in EITF Issue No. 98-3 in determining that. To be a business under the guidance in EITF Issue No. 98-3, the activities and assets should include "all the inputs and processes necessary" to conduct normal operations. The fact that operating information may be available does not mean the operations constitute a business. They may be just a part of a business, such as one product line. The guidance in Section 805-10-55 should be considered in determining whether a group of assets constitutes a business.

- *Discrete financial information.* For purposes of both SFAS No. 131 and SFAS No. 142 (ASC 350), discrete financial information can consist of just operating information, with no balance sheet information prepared for the component. However, if the component is a reporting unit, the entity would be required to identify and allocate assets and liabilities applicable to the component to test goodwill for impairment.

- *Reviewed by segment management.* Under SFAS No. 131 (ASC 280-10-50-7 through 50-8), segment management may be one level below the chief operating decision maker, and there may be one or more segment managers. According to ASC 280-10-50-7 a segment manager is directly accountable to and maintains regular contact with the chief operating decision maker to discuss operating activities, financial results, forecasts or plans for the segment. The focus of SFAS No. 142 (ASC 350) is on how operating segments are managed rather than on how the entity as a whole is managed.

- *Similar economic characteristics.* The evaluation of whether two components have similar economic characteristics requires consideration of the factors in paragraph 17 of SFAS No. 131 (ASC 280):

  - Similar economic characteristics, such as similar long-term average gross margins

  - The nature of the products and/or services; the nature of production processes

  - The type or class of customers

  - The methods used to distribute products and provide services

  - The nature of any regulatory environment

  EITF Topic No. D-101 provides that not all factors have to be met for economic similarity to exist and the evaluation should be more qualitative than quantitative.

EITF Topic No. D-101 also provides additional factors to consider when evaluating whether components should be combined in a reporting unit because they are economically similar:

- How an entity operates its business and the nature of the operations
- Whether goodwill is recoverable from the separate operations of each component business or from the components working together because, for example, the components are economically interdependent
- The extent to which the component businesses share assets and other resources
- Whether the components provide support and receive benefits from the same R&D projects

Components of different operating segments, as explained in Part 1 of EITF Topic No. D-101, cannot be combined into the same reporting unit, even if they have similar economic characteristics. This might occur, for example, if the entity organized its operating segments on a geographic basis.

Questions have arisen about whether one or more components of operating units aggregated into one reporting unit under SFAS No. 131 (ASC 280) could be economically dissimilar and therefore be in separate reporting units under SFAS No. 142 (ASC 350). EITF Topic No. D-101 provides two explanations of why that could happen:

1. The determination of reportable segments under SFAS No. 131 (ASC 280) requires identification of operating segments and then determination of whether economically similar operating segments should be aggregated. However, the determination of reporting units under SFAS No. 142 (ASC 350) begins with operating segments and then requires an analysis of whether economically dissimilar components of an operating segment should be disaggregated for the purpose of testing goodwill for impairment.
2. For a component of an operating segment to be an operating segment under SFAS No. 131 (ASC 280), its operating performance must be regularly reviewed by the chief operating decision maker. That same component, however, could be a reporting unit if a segment manager regularly reviews its operating performance.

For the purpose of testing goodwill for impairment, acquired assets and assumed liabilities are assigned to a reporting unit as of the acquisition date if both of the next criteria are met:

1. The asset will be employed in or the liability relates to the operations of a reporting unit.
2. The asset or liability will be considered in determining the fair value of the reporting unit.

Assets or liabilities that an entity considers part of its corporate assets or liabilities are also assigned to a reporting unit if both of the preceding criteria are met. Examples are environmental liabilities that relate to an existing operating facility of the reporting unit and a pension obligation that would be included in the determination of the fair value of the reporting unit. Some assets or liabilities may be employed in or relate to the operations of multiple reporting units. The methodology used to determine the amount of those assets or liabilities to assign to a reporting unit is on a reasonable and supportable basis and applied in a consistent manner. For example, assets and liabilities not directly related to a specific reporting unit but from which the reporting unit benefits could be allocated according to the benefit received by the different reporting units or based on the relative fair values of the different reporting units. A pro rata allocation based on payroll expense might be used for pension items.

For the purpose of testing goodwill for impairment, paragraph 34 of SFAS No. 142 (ASC 350) requires all goodwill acquired in a business combination is assigned to one or more reporting units as of the acquisition date. Goodwill must be assigned to reporting units of the acquiring entity expected to benefit from the synergies of the combination even though other assets or liabilities of the acquired entity may not be assigned to that reporting unit. The total amount of acquired goodwill may be divided among a number of reporting units. The methodology used to determine the amount of goodwill to assign to a reporting unit should be reasonable and supportable and applied in a consistent manner. Also, the methodology should be consistent with the objectives of the process of assigning goodwill to reporting units described next. In concept, the amount of goodwill assigned to a reporting unit would be determined in a manner similar to how the amount of goodwill recognized in a business combination is determined.

The fair value of the acquired business or portion of the acquired business that will be included in a particular reporting unit is, in essence, the purchase price of that business. The entity allocates that purchase price to the assets acquired and liabilities incurred related to (the portion of) the acquired business assigned to the reporting unit. Any excess purchase price is the amount of goodwill assigned to that reporting unit. However, if the goodwill is to be assigned to a reporting unit that has not been assigned any of the assets acquired or liabilities assumed in that acquisition, the amount of goodwill to be assigned to that unit might be determined by applying a "with and without" computation. That is, the difference between the fair value of that reporting unit before the acquisition and its fair value after the acquisition represents the amount of goodwill to be assigned to that reporting unit.

When an entity reorganizes its reporting structure in a manner that changes the composition of one or more of its reporting units, the guidance given earlier in this section (also paragraphs 32 and 33 of SFAS No. 142 (ASC 350) for assigning acquired assets and assumed liabilities to reporting units must be used to reassign assets and liabilities to the reporting units affected. However, goodwill is reassigned to the reporting units affected using a relative fair value allocation approach similar to that used when a portion of a reporting unit is to be disposed of, which is discussed in Subsection 14.7(b)(vii). For example, if existing reporting unit A is to be integrated with reporting units B, C, and D, goodwill of reporting unit A would be assigned to units B, C, and D based on the relative fair values of the three portions of reporting unit A before those portions are integrated with reporting units B, C, and D.

(v) Goodwill Impairment Testing by a Subsidiary.   All goodwill recognized by a public or nonpublic subsidiary in its separate financial statements prepared in conformity with GAAP, known as subsidiary goodwill, is accounted for in conformity with SFAS No. 142 (ASC 350). It is tested for impairment at the subsidiary level using the subsidiary's reporting units. If a goodwill impairment loss is recognized at the subsidiary level, goodwill of the reporting unit or units at the consolidated level in which the subsidiary's reporting unit with impaired goodwill resides is tested for impairment if the event that gave rise to the loss at the subsidiary level more likely than not would reduce the fair value of the reporting unit at the consolidated level below its carrying amount. A goodwill impairment loss is recognized at the consolidated level only if goodwill at the consolidated level is impaired.

(vi) Goodwill Impairment Testing When a Noncontrolling Interest Exists.   Goodwill from a business combination with a continuing noncontrolling (minority) interest is tested for impairment using an approach consistent with the approach used to measure the noncontrolling interest at the acquisition date. For example, if goodwill is first recognized based on only the controlling interest of the parent, the fair value of the reporting unit used in the impairment test is based on the controlling interest and does not reflect the portion of fair value attributable to the noncontrolling interest. Similarly, the implied fair value of goodwill determined in the second step of the impairment test used to measure the impairment loss reflects only the parent's interest in the goodwill.

(vii) Disposal of All or a Portion of a Reporting Unit.   When a reporting unit is to be disposed of in its entirety, the carrying amount of goodwill of the reporting unit is included in the carrying amount of the reporting unit in determining the gain or loss on disposal. When a portion of a reporting unit that constitutes a business is to be disposed of, the carrying amount of goodwill associated with the business is included in the carrying amount of the business in determining the gain or loss on disposal. The portion of the carrying amount of goodwill to be included in that carrying amount is based on the relative fair values of the business to be disposed of and the portion of the reporting unit to be retained. However, if the business to be disposed of was never integrated into the reporting unit after its acquisition and thus the benefits of the acquired goodwill were never realized by the rest of the reporting unit, the current carrying amount of the acquired goodwill should be included in the carrying amount of business to be disposed of. When only a portion of goodwill is be allocated to a business to be disposed of, the goodwill remaining in the portion of the reporting unit to be retained is tested for impairment in accordance with paragraphs 19 to 22 of SFAS No. 142 (ASC 350).

(viii) Equity Method Investments. The portion of the difference between the cost of an investment and the amount of underlying equity in net assets of an equity method investee recognized as goodwill in conformity with paragraph 19(b) of APB Opinion No. 18, *The Equity Method of Accounting for Investments in Common Stock,* known as equity method goodwill, should not be amortized. However, equity method goodwill is not tested for impairment in conformity with SFAS No. 142 (ASC 350).

Equity method investments continue to be reviewed for impairment in conformity with paragraph 19(h) of APB Opinion No. 18.

(ix) Entities Emerging from Bankruptcy. SOP 90-7, *Financial Reporting by Entities in Reorganization Under the Bankruptcy Code,* provides that when an entity applies fresh-start accounting on emerging from bankruptcy, the reorganization value should be allocated to all tangible and intangible assets following the procedures in APB Opinion No. 16. SFAS No. 142 (ASC 350) stipulates that entities should report the excess reorganization value as goodwill and account for it in the same manner as other elements of goodwill.

14.8 DEFERRED INCOME TAXES

SFAS No. 142 (ASC 350) did not change the requirements in SFAS No. 109, *Accounting for Income Taxes,* paragraphs 30, 261, and 262, for recognition of deferred income taxes related to goodwill and intangible assets.

14.9 FINANCIAL STATEMENT PRESENTATION

(a) INTANGIBLE ASSETS. At a minimum, all intangible assets are aggregated and presented as a separate (one) line item in the statement of financial position. In addition, individual intangible assets or classes of intangible assets may be presented as separate line items. Amortization expense and impairment losses for intangible assets are presented in income statement line items within continuing operations as deemed appropriate for each entity. An impairment loss resulting from such an impairment test should not be recognized as a change in accounting principle.

(b) GOODWILL. The aggregate amount of goodwill is presented as a separate line item in the statement of financial position. The aggregate amount of goodwill impairment losses are presented as a separate line item in the income statement before the subtotal *income from continuing operations,* or a similar caption, unless a goodwill impairment loss is associated with a discontinued operation. A goodwill impairment loss associated with a discontinued operation is included net of tax within the results of discontinued operations.

14.10 DISCLOSURES

The next information is disclosed in the notes to the financial statements in the period of acquisition of intangible assets acquired either individually or with a group of assets.

  A. For intangible assets subject to amortization:
    1. The total amount assigned and the amount assigned to any major intangible asset class
    2. The amount of any significant residual value, in total and by major intangible asset class
    3. The weighted-average amortization period, in total and by major intangible asset class
  B. For intangible assets not subject to amortization, the total amount assigned and the amount assigned to any major intangible asset class
  C. The amount of R&D assets acquired and written off in the period and the line item in the income statement in which the amounts written off are aggregated

The next information is disclosed in the financial statements or the notes to the financial statements for each period for which a statement of financial position is presented:

  A. For intangible assets subject to amortization:
    1. The gross carrying amount and accumulated amortization, in total and by major intangible asset class
    2. The aggregate amortization expense for the period
    3. The estimated aggregate amortization expense for each of the five succeeding fiscal years
  B. For intangible assets not subject to amortization, the total carrying amount and the carrying amount for each major intangible asset class
  C. The changes in the carrying amount of goodwill during the period, including:
    1. The aggregate amount of goodwill acquired
    2. The aggregate amount of impairment losses recognized on goodwill
    3. The amount of goodwill included in the gain or loss on disposal of all or a portion of a reporting unit

Reporting entities that report segment information in conformity with SFAS No. 131 (ASC 280) must provide the preceding information about goodwill in total and for each reportable segment and must disclose any significant changes in the allocation of goodwill by reportable segment. If any portion of goodwill has not yet been allocated to a reporting unit at the date the financial statements are issued, that unallocated amount and the reasons for not allocating the amount are disclosed. For each impairment loss recognized related to an intangible asset, the next information should be disclosed in the notes to the financial statements that include the period in which the impairment loss is recognized.

  • Description of the impaired intangible asset and the facts and circumstances leading to the impairment
  • Amount of the impairment loss and the method for determining fair value
  • Caption in the income statement or the statement of activities in which the impairment loss is aggregated
  • If applicable, the segment in which the impaired intangible asset is reported under SFAS No. 131 (ASC 280)

For each goodwill impairment loss recognized, the next information should be disclosed in the notes to the financial statements that include the period in which the impairment loss is recognized.

  • A description of the facts and circumstances leading to the impairment
  • The amount of the impairment loss and the method of determining the fair value of the associated reporting unit

- If a recognized impairment loss is an estimate that has not yet been finalized, that fact and the reasons for it and, in subsequent periods, the nature and amount of any significant adjustments made to the initial estimate of the impairment loss

14.11 EFFECTIVE DATE AND TRANSITION PROVISIONS OF SFAS NO. 142 (ASC 350)

The provisions of SFAS No. 142 (ASC 350) were initially applied in fiscal years beginning after December 15, 2001, to all goodwill and other intangible assets recognized in a reporting entity's statement of financial position at the beginning of that fiscal year, regardless of when those previously recognized assets were first recognized. Early application was permitted for entities with fiscal years beginning after March 15, 2001, provided that the first interim financial statements had not been issued previously. The provisions of the statement were to be first applied at the beginning of a fiscal year. They were not being applied retroactively.

Provisions of SFAS No. 142 (ASC 350) are not to be applied to previously recognized goodwill and intangible assets acquired in a combination between two or more mutual enterprises, acquired in a combination between not-for-profit organizations, or from the acquisition of a for-profit business entity by a not-for-profit organization until interpretive guidance related to the application of the purchase method to those transactions is issued. As of late 2005, this guidance has yet to be promulgated, although this is anticipated to occur in the near future. SFAS 164 (ASC 958-805) amends paragraph 48C of SFAS 142 (350) to now include guidance for goodwill acquired by a not-for-profit entity.

Paragraph 61 of SFAS No. 141 transition provisions related to goodwill and intangible assets acquired in business combination for which the acquisition date was before July 1, 2001, that were accounted for by the purchase method. Paragraphs A131 to A134 of SFAS No. 141(R) (ASC 805) provides transition provisions for mutual entities that had purchase business combinations accounted for in accordance with Opinion 16 of Statement 72. These provisions are similar to that in SFAS No. 141.

(a) GOODWILL AND INTANGIBLE ASSETS ACQUIRED AFTER JUNE 30, 2001. Goodwill acquired in a business combination for which the acquisition date is after June 30, 2001, should not be amortized. Intangible assets other than goodwill acquired in a business combination or other transaction for which the date of acquisition is after June 30, 2001, are amortized or not amortized in conformity with the discussion in Sections 14.4(b) and (c). Goodwill and intangible assets acquired in a transaction for which the acquisition date is after June 30, 2001, but before the date that SFAS No. 142 (ASC 350) was first applied in its entirety were to be reviewed for impairment in conformity with APB Opinion No. 17 or SFAS No. 121 (as appropriate) until the date SFAS No. 142 (ASC 350) was applied in its entirety. The financial statement presentation and disclosure provisions of SFAS No. 142 (ASC 350) were not to be applied to those assets until SFAS No. 142 (ASC 350) was applied in its entirety.

Goodwill and intangible assets acquired in a combination between two or more mutual enterprises, acquired in a combination between not-for-profit organizations, or from the acquisition of a sec for-profit business entity by a not-for-profit organization for which the acquisition date is after June 30, 2001, continue to be accounted for in conformity with APB Opinion No. 17 until the FASB issues guidance on issues related to the application of the purchase method to such transactions. APB Opinion No. 17 was superseded by paragraph D1(a) of SFAS No. 142 (ASC 350), which was issued in June 2001. SFAS No. 164 (ASC 958) amended SFAS 142 (ASC 350.)

(b) PREVIOUSLY RECOGNIZED INTANGIBLE ASSETS. To apply SFAS No. 142 (ASC 350) to previously recognized intangible assets (those acquired in a transaction for which the acquisition date is on or before June 30, 2001), the useful lives of those assets are reassessed using the guidance in Section 14.4(a), and the remaining amortization periods are adjusted accordingly. For example, the amortization period for a previously recognized intangible asset might be increased if its original useful life was estimated to be longer than the 40-year maximum amortization period allowed by APB Opinion No. 17. The reassessment was to be completed before the end of the first interim period of the fiscal year in which SFAS No. 142 (ASC 350) was first applied.

Previously recognized intangible assets deemed to have indefinite useful lives should be tested for impairment as of the beginning of the fiscal year in which SFAS No. 142 (ASC 350) was first applied. The transitional intangible asset impairment test was to be completed in the first interim period in which SFAS No. 142 (ASC 350) was first applied, and any resulting impairment loss was to be recognized as the effect of a change in accounting principle. The effect of the accounting change and related income tax effects were to be presented in the income statement between the captions "extraordinary items" and "net income." The per share information presented in the income statement included the per share effect of the accounting change.

(c) PREVIOUSLY RECOGNIZED GOODWILL. At the date SFAS No. 142 (ASC 350) was first applied, the reporting entity was required to establish its reporting units based on its reporting structure at that date and the guidance described in Subsection 14.7(b)(iv). Recognized net assets, excluding goodwill, should be assigned to those reporting units using the guidance in paragraphs 32 and 33 of SFAS No. 142 (ASC 350). Recognized net assets and liabilities that did not relate to a reporting unit, such as an environmental liability for an operation previously disposed of, did not need to be assigned to a reporting unit. All goodwill recognized in a reporting entity's statement of financial position at the date that SFAS No. 142 (ASC 350) was first applied was to be assigned to one or more reporting units. Goodwill was to be assigned in a reasonable and supportable manner. The sources of previously recognized goodwill were to be considered in making that initial assignment as well as the reporting units to which the related acquired net assets were assigned. Subsection 14.7(b)(iv) provides guidance on assigning goodwill to reporting units on initial application of SFAS No. 142 (ASC 350).

Goodwill in each reporting unit should be tested for impairment as of the beginning of the fiscal year in which SFAS No. 142 (ASC 350) was first applied in its entirety. The first step of the goodwill impairment test is to be completed within six months from the date the reporting entity first applied SFAS No. 142 (ASC 350). The amounts used in the transitional goodwill impairment test should be measured as of the beginning of the year of first application. If the carrying amount of the net assets of a reporting unit (including goodwill) exceeded the fair value of the reporting unit, the second step of the transitional goodwill impairment test was completed as soon as possible, but no later than the end of the year of first application.

An impairment loss as a result of a transitional goodwill impairment test was recognized as the effect of a change in accounting principle. The effect of the accounting change and related income tax effects should be presented in the income statement between the captions extraordinary items and net income. The per share information presented in the income statement included the per share effect of the accounting change. Although a transitional impairment loss for goodwill could be measured in other than the first interim reporting period, it was to be recognized in the first interim period regardless of the period in which it was measured, consistent with paragraph 10 of SFAS No. 3, *Reporting Accounting Changes in Interim Financial Statements.* SFAS No. 154 (ASC 320), *Accounting Changes and Error Corrections—a replacement of APB Opinion No. 20 and FASB Statement No. 3,* issued May 2005, replaced SFAS No. 3. Paragraph 15 of SFAS No. 154 (ASC 250) provides guidance for reporting a change in an accounting principle.

The financial information for the interim periods of the fiscal year that preceded the period in which the transitional goodwill impairment loss was measured was to be restated to reflect the accounting change in those periods. The aggregate amount of the accounting change is included in restated net income of the first interim period of the year of first application (and in any year-to-date or last-12-months-to-date financial reports that included the first interim period). Whenever financial information is presented that includes the periods that precede the period in which the transitional goodwill impairment loss was measured, that financial information should be presented on the restated basis.

A reporting entity was required to perform the required annual goodwill impairment test in the year that SFAS No. 142 (ASC 350) was first applied in its entirety, in addition to the transitional goodwill impairment test, unless the reporting entity designated the beginning of its fiscal year as the date for its annual goodwill impairment test.

(d) EQUITY METHOD GOODWILL. When SFAS No. 142 (ASC 350) was first applied, the portion of the excess of cost over the underlying equity in net assets of an investee accounted for using the equity method that has been recognized as goodwill was no longer to be amortized. However, equity method goodwill is not to be tested for impairment under paragraph 40 of SFAS No. 142 (ASC 350). Rather, the guidance under APB No. 18 continues to be applicable in assessing impairment of equity method investments.

(e) TRANSITIONAL DISCLOSURES. Expanded disclosures were mandated during the initial implementation period for SFAS No. 142 (ASC 350). Since all entities have now fully adopted this standard, and since comparative disclosures including preimplementation periods are now unlikely to be encountered in practice, this will not be described in detail.

14.12 SOURCES AND SUGGESTED REFERENCES

Accounting Principles Board. Accounting Research Bulletin No. 43, *Restatement of Revision of Accounting Research Bulletins*. New York: AICPA, 1968.

――――. APB Opinion No. 22, *Disclosure of Accounting Policies*. New York: AICPA, 1973.

――――. APB Opinion No. 30, *Reporting the Results of Operations*. New York: AICPA, 1973.

American Accounting Association Financial Accounting Standards Committee. "Equity Valuation Models and Measuring Goodwill Impairment," *Accounting Horizons* (June 2001).

American Institute of Certified Public Accountants. Issues Paper, *Push Down Accounting*. New York: Author, 1979.

――――. Statement of Position 88-1, *Accounting for Developmental and Preoperating Costs, Purchases and Exchanges of Take-off and Landing Slots, and Airframe Modifications*. New York: Author, 1988.

――――. Statement of Position 90-7, *Financial Reporting by Entities in Reorganization Under the Bankruptcy Code*. New York: Author, November 19, 1990.

――――. Statement of Position 93-7, *Reporting on Advertising Costs*. New York: Author, December 29, 1993.

――――. Statement of Position 98-1, *Accounting for the Costs of Computer Software Developed or Obtained for Internal Use*. New York: Author, 1998.

――――. Statement of Position 98-5, *Reporting on the Cost of Start-Up Activities*. New York: Author, 1998.

――――. Statement of Position 00-2, *Accounting by Producers or Distributors of Films*. New York: AICPA, 2000.

――――. AICPA Practice Aid Series, *Assets Acquired in a Business Combination to Be Used in R&D Activities: A Focus on Software, Electronic Devices, and Pharmaceutical Industries*. New York: Author, 2001.

Anwar, D., F. Jamil, S. Sidju, S. Thota, and S. Bai. "Intangible Assets." April 28, 2010. *http://intangible assetscois20077.wikidot.com/start*.

Day, J. W. "Theme: Intangible Assets." *www.reallifeaccounting.com/pubs/Article_Theme_Intangible_Assets.pdf*, 2008.

"Financial Accounting: AICPA Issues New Rules for Film Industry," *Journal of Accountancy* (August 2000).

Financial Accounting Standards Board. EITF Issue No. 95-3, *Recognition of Liabilities in Connection with a Purchase Business Combination*. Norwalk, CT: Author, 1995.

――――. EITF Issue No. 95-5. *Determination of What Risks and Rewards, If Any, Can Be Retained and Whether Any Unresolved Contingencies May Exist in a Sale of Mortgage Loan Servicing Rights*. Norwalk, CT: Author, 1995.

――――. EITF Issue No. 95-8, *Accounting for Contingent Consideration Paid to the Shareholders of an Acquired Enterprise in a Purchase Business Combination*. Norwalk, CT: Author, 1995.

――――. EITF Issue No. 96-6, *Accounting for the Film and Software Costs Associated with Developing Entertainment and Educational Software Products*. Norwalk, CT: Author, 1996.

――――. EITF Issue No. 97-4, *Deregulation of the Price of Electricity—Issues Related to the Application of FASB Statements 71 and 101*. Norwalk, CT: Author, 1997.

_____ . EITF Issue No. 97-8, *Accounting for Contingent Consideration Issued in a Purchase Business Combination*. Norwalk, CT: Author, 1997.

_____ . EITF Issue No. 97-13, *Accounting for Costs Incurred in Connection with a Consulting Contract or an Internal Project That Combines Business Process Reengineering and Information Technology Transformation*. Norwalk, CT: Author, 1997.

_____ . EITF Issue No. 02-7, *Unit of Accounting for Testing Impairment of Indefinite-Lived Assets*. Norwalk, CT: Author, 2002.

_____ . EITF Issue No. 02-13, *Deferred Income Tax Considerations in Applying the Goodwill Impairment Test in FASB Statement No. 142*. Norwalk, CT: Author, 2002.

_____ . EITF Issue No. 02-17, *Recognition of Customer Relationship Intangible Assets Acquired in a Business Combination*. Norwalk, CT: Author, 2002.

_____ . EITF Issue No. 03-9, *Interaction of Paragraphs 11 and 12 of FASB Statement No. 142 Regarding Determination of the Useful Life and Amortization of Intangible Assets*. Norwalk, CT: Author, 2003.

_____ . EITF Issue No. 04-1, *Accounting for Pre-Existing Contractual Relationships Between the Parties to a Business Combination*. Norwalk, CT: Author, 2004.

_____ . EITF Issue No. 04-2, *Whether Mineral Rights Are Tangible or Intangible Assets and Related Issues*. Norwalk, CT: Author, 2004.

_____ . Exposure Draft, *Fair Value Measurements*. Norwalk, CT: Author, June 2004.

_____ . Exposure Draft, *SFAS No. 141(R) Business Combinations (a Replacement of FASB Statement No. 141)*. Norwalk, CT: Author, June 2005.

_____ . Interpretation No. 6, *Applicability of FASB Statement No. 2 to Computer Software (An Interpretation of FASB Statement No. 2)*. Norwalk, CT: Author, 1975.

_____ . Invitation to Comment, Selected Issues Relating to Assets and Liabilities with Uncertainties. Norwalk, CT: Author, September 2005.

_____ . Staff Position 141-1 and 142-1, *Interaction of FASB Statements No. 141, Business Combinations, and No. 142, Goodwill and Other Intangible Assets, and EITF Issue No. 04-2, Whether Mineral Rights Are Tangible or Intangible Assets*. Norwalk, CT: Author, 2003.

_____ . Statement of Financial Accounting Standards No. 2, *Accounting for Research and Development Costs*. Norwalk, CT: Author, 1974.

_____ . Statement of Financial Accounting Standards No. 45, *Accounting for Franchise Fee Revenue*. Norwalk, CT: Author, 1981.

_____ . Statement of Financial Accounting Standards No. 50, *Financial Reporting in the Record and Music Industry*. Norwalk, CT: FASB, 1981.

_____ . Statement of Financial Accounting Standards No. 51, *Financial Reporting by Cable Television Companies*. Norwalk, CT: Author, 1981.

_____ . Statement of Financial Accounting Standards No. 63, *Financial Reporting by Broadcasters*. Norwalk, CT: Author, 1982.

_____ . Statement of Financial Accounting Standards No. 71, *Accounting for the Effects of Certain Types of Regulation*. Norwalk, CT: Author, 1982.

_____ . Statement of Financial Accounting Standards No. 86, *Accounting for the Costs of Computer Software to Be Sold, Leased, or Otherwise Marketed*. Norwalk, CT: FASB, 1985.

_____ . Statement of Financial Accounting Standards No. 90, *Regulated Enterprises—Accounting for Abandonments and Disallowances of Plant Costs—An Amendment of FASB Statement No. 71*. Norwalk, CT: Author, December 1986

_____ . Statement of Financial Accounting Standards No. 92, *Regulated Enterprises—Accounting for Phase-in Plans—An Amendment of FASB Statement No. 71*. Norwalk, CT: Author, August 1987

_____ . Statement of Financial Accounting Standards No. 95, *Statement of Cash Flows*. Norwalk, CT: Author, 1987.

_____ . Statement of Financial Accounting Standards No. 102, *Statement of Cash Flows—Exemption of Certain Enterprises and Classification of Cash Flows from Certain Securities Acquired for Resale—An Amendment of FASB Statement No. 95*. Norwalk, CT: Author, February 1989.

_____ . Statement of Financial Accounting Standards No. 104, *Statement of Cash Flows—Net Reporting of Certain Cash Receipts and Cash Payments and Classification of Cash Flows from Hedging Transactions—An Amendment of FASB Statement No. 95*. Norwalk, CT: Author, December 1989.

_____. Statement of Financial Accounting Standards No. 109, *Accounting for Income Taxes*. Norwalk, CT: Author, February 1992.

_____. Statement of Financial Accounting Standards No. 112, *Employers' Accounting for Postemployment Benefits—An Amendment of FASB Statements No. 5 and 43*. Norwalk, CT: Author, November 1992.

_____. Statement of Financial Accounting Standards No. 131, *Disclosures about Segments of an Enterprise and Related Information*. Norwalk, CT: Author, 1997.

_____. Statement of Financial Accounting Standards No. 139, *Rescission of FASB Statement No. 53 and Amendments to FASB Statements No. 63, 89 and 121*. Norwalk, CT: Author, June 2000.

_____. Statement of Financial Accounting Standards No. 140, *Accounting for Transfers and Servicing of Financial Assets and Extinguishments of Liabilities—A Replacement of FASB Statement No. 125*. Norwalk, CT: Author, 2000.

_____. Statement of Financial Accounting Standards No. 141 (Revised 2007), *Business Combinations*. Norwalk, CT: Author, December 2007.

_____. Statement of Financial Accounting Standards No. 142, *Goodwill and Other Intangible Assets*. Norwalk, CT: Author, June 2001.

_____. Statement of Financial Accounting Standards No. 144, *Accounting for the Impairment or Disposal of Long-Lived Assets*. Norwalk, CT: Author, June 2001.

_____. Statement of Financial Accounting Standards No. 146, *Accounting for Costs Associated with Exit or Disposal Activities*. Norwalk, CT: Author, June 2002.

_____. Technical Bulletin No. 88-1, *Issues Relating to Accounting for Leases*. Norwalk, CT: FASB, 1988.

Garland, P. J. "Fresh-Start Reporting For Entities Emerging from Chapter 11 Reorganization: Financial Accounting Valuation Insights," *Insights* (Winter 2004). *www.willametteinsights.com/04/Winter04article1.pdf*.

Gore, R., and D. Zimmerman. "Is Goodwill an Asset?" *CPA Journal* (June 2010).

Lamoreaux, M. G. "Double Accounting for Goodwill: A Problem Redefined," *Journal of Accountancy* (April 2009).

Levine, M. H., and J. G. Siegel. "Accounting Changes for the Film Industry," *CPA Journal* (October 2001).

Maples, L., and M. Earles. "When Should Advertising Be Capitalized?: The IRS and FASB Have Specific Guidelines Companies Should Follow," *Journal of Accountancy* (May 1999).

Miller, R. I., and P. H. Pashkoff. "Regulations Under the Sarbanes-Oxley Act: What Auditors/Audit Committees Need to Know and Do to Comply," *Journal of Accountancy* (October 2002).

Mueller, J. "Judgment Replaces Amortization For Many Intangibles" Abstracted from "Amortization of Certain Intangible Assets," *Journal of Accountancy* (December 2004).

Noll, D. "Resolved: Start-up Costs Are Not Assets." AllBusiness.com. *www.allbusiness.com/accounting-reporting/corporate-taxes/691087-1.html#ixzz1YpRAh6Fj*.

Securities and Exchange Commission. Staff Accounting Bulletin Topic 5A, *Expenses of Offering*. Washington, DC: Author: 1975.

_____. Staff Accounting Bulletin Topic 2-A3, *Acquisitions Involving Financial Institutions*. Washington, DC: Author: 1981.

_____. Staff Accounting Bulletin Topic 5J, *Push Down Basic of Accounting Required in Certain Limited Circumstances*. Washington, DC: Author: 1983.

Siegal, P., and C. Borgia. "The Measurement and Recognition of Intangible Assets," *Journal of Business and Public Affairs* 1, no. 1 (2007). *www.scientificjournals.org/journals2007/articles/1006.htm*.

United States Code, Title 17. Chapter 3, Duration of Copyright § 302. "Duration of Copyright: Works Created on or after January 1, 1978." *www.law.cornell.edu/uscode/17/usc_sec_17_00000302—-000-.html*.

Waxman, R. N. "Goodwill Convergence," *CPA Journal* (October 2001).

CHAPTER 15

LEASES

Francis E. Scheuerell Jr., CPA
Navigant Consulting

15.1 INTRODUCTION AND BACKGROUND INFORMATION

A *lease* is an agreement conveying the right to use property, plant, or equipment, usually for a stated period of time. Since World War II, the leasing industry has become a major economic force, and leasing has become a method by which to finance acquisitions of property.

The rapid growth created by the demand to lease everything from equipment to automobiles, furniture, and even people has caused a highly price-competitive environment. Lessors earn their profits by buying equipment at lower prices than ordinary buyers, charging brokerage fees, and getting tax deductions for equipment write-offs. However, the 1986 Tax Reform Act eliminated tax credits, removing some of the traditional cash flow advantages that lessors could gain upon initiating a leasing transaction.

Traditionally, lessees prefer to have operating leases rather than capital leases so that the future lease payment obligations do not appear on the balance sheet as a liability.

(a) FINANCING ADVANTAGES OF LEASING.   The financing advantages associated with leasing include, but are not limited to, the following:

- Leasing permits 100 percent financing, whereas a normal equipment loan may require a 20 to 40 percent initial down payment. Leasing can thereby conserve cash and working capital.
- Longer terms than are normally available with loans can be arranged for leasing many types of capital equipment.
- Financing of initial acquisition costs is possible because these costs can be included in a lease. Such costs—for example, delivery charges, interest on advance payments, sales or use taxes, and installation costs—are not normally financed under other methods of equipment financing.
- Leasing offers greater convenience than either debt or equity financing because of the reduced documentation.
- The risk of obsolescence can be avoided by the lessee as compared with the risk he or she would assume on the purchase of such equipment.

(b) FINANCING DISADVANTAGES OF LEASING.   Some of the financing disadvantages associated with leasing include, but are not limited to, the following:

- The effective interest rate is generally greater than if the lessee obtained a bank loan for the same term. This may not be true, however, for leveraged leases.

- The lessee suffers the loss of residual rights to the property at the termination of the lease.
- The lessee does not enjoy the tax benefits of accelerated depreciation and interest expense.

15.2 ACCOUNTING ISSUES AND PRONOUNCEMENTS

Prior to 2009, there were over 60 separate pronouncements providing guidance for leases and that is an indication of the complexity and controversy surrounding the accounting for leases. The manufacturer or dealer is concerned with the issue of when a lease becomes a sale with the respective profit and loss recognition. Other lessors are perceived as either renting out their asset or providing financing for the acquisition of this asset by a lessee, depending on the circumstances. Likewise, the lessee either has an asset and a liability or is committed to an obligation to rent an asset. The accounting issues can then be summarized according to four questions:

1. On whose balance sheet should the leased asset appear?
2. What is the timing of financial statement recognition of lease events?
3. How are measurements made for both balance sheet and income statement effects of leases?
4. What disclosures should be made in the financial statements?

The Financial Accounting Standards Board (FASB) issued Statement of Financial Accounting Standards No. 13, *Accounting for Leases,* in November 1976 to address the accounting for leases. At that time, FASB Statement No. 13 superseded all preceding technical literature and established the primary current standard in accounting for leases. Under this pronouncement, when substantially all of the risks and rewards of ownership have passed from the lessor to the lessee, the leased property transfers from the lessor to the lessee. The questions of whose asset it is and the related income statement effect are answered by establishing where the substantial risks and rewards of ownership lie. Timing is at the inception of the lease, and measurement is usually at the fair value of the leased property to the lessor at that date.

Effective for interim and annual periods ending after September 15, 2009, the FASB *Accounting Standards Codification*® (Codification) became the source of authoritative generally accepted accounting principles (GAAP) recognized by the FASB for all nongovernmental entities. The Codification supersedes all previous issued accounting pronouncements. As a result, Codification Topic 840, *Leases* ([ASC] 840 or Topic 840), is now the primary authoritative source for the accounting and reporting for leases by both lessees and lessors.

This chapter provides an overview of lease accounting from the viewpoint of both lessee and lessor as well as sale-leaseback transactions and other leasing issues.

(a) DETERMINING IF AN ARRANGEMENT IS A LEASE.   Topic 840 applies to all nongovernmental entities and defines a *lease* as "an agreement conveying the right to use property, plant, or equipment (land and (or) depreciable assets) usually for a stated period of time."

At the inception of an arrangement, a purchaser (lessee) should analyze the terms of the arrangement to determine if the substance of the arrangement is a lease or contains a lease using all facts and circumstances. For an arrangement to contain a lease, the arrangement must identify either explicitly or implicitly the property, plant, and equipment (i.e., land or depreciable assets) that the lessee has the right to use.

Arrangements that are contracts for services that do not transfer the right to use property, plant, or equipment from one contracting party to the other do not meet the definition of a lease. In addition, if fulfillment of an arrangement is not dependent on the use of the property, plant, or equipment, even if explicitly identified in the arrangement, it is not a lease under Topic 840. Furthermore, assets that are not depreciable, such as, but not limited to, inventory (including equipment parts inventory), minerals, and precious metals or other natural resources do not meet the definition of a lease under Topic 840. In addition, intangible assets such as, but not limited to, an employee workforce and licensing arrangements for items such as motion picture films, plays, manuscripts, patents, and copyrights are excluded from the scope of Topic 840 even though those assets may be amortized.

After the purchaser (lessee) has identified the arrangement is dependent on the explicit or implicit use of property, plant, or equipment (the identified assets), the lessee then will need to determine if the arrangement conveys the right to control the use of the identified assets. The right to control the use of the identified assets is present if any of these conditions exist:

1. The purchaser (lessee) has the ability or right to operate the identified assets or direct others to operate the identified assets in a manner it determines while obtaining or controlling more than a minor amount of the output or other utility of the identified assets. The lessee's ability to operate the identified assets may be evidenced by (but is not limited to) the lessee's ability to hire, fire, or replace the property's operator or the lessee's ability to specify significant operating policies and procedures in the arrangement with the owner-seller (lessor) having no ability to change such policies and procedures. A requirement to follow prudent operating practices (or other similar requirements) generally does not convey the right to control the identified assets. Similarly, a contractual requirement designed to enable the lessee to monitor or ensure the lessor's compliance with performance, safety, pollution control, or other general standards generally does not establish control over the identified asset.

2. The purchaser (lessee) has the ability or right to control physical access to the identified assets while obtaining or controlling more than a minor amount of the output or other utility of the identified assets.

3. It is remote, based on the facts and circumstances, that one or more parties other than the lessee will take more than a minor amount of the output or other utility that will be produced or generated by the identified assets during the term of the arrangement, and the price that the lessee will pay for the output is neither contractually fixed per unit of output nor equal to the current market price per unit of output as of the time of delivery of the output.

Arrangements that transfer the right to use identified assets meets the definition of a lease for purposes of Topic 840 even though the arrangement may require the lessor to provide substantial services in connection with the operation or maintenance of such assets. Topic 840 includes arrangements that, although not nominally identified as leases, meet the definition of lease, such as a heat supply contract for nuclear fuel.

If facts or circumstances change, the parties to the arrangement may need to reassess their original conclusions.

Subsequent to the initial assessment to determine whether the arrangement is, or contains, a lease, the following changes in facts and circumstance require a reassessment of the initial conclusions:

1. Formal or informal changes or modifications to the terms to the contractual arrangement
2. Change in the determination as to whether or not fulfillment is dependent on specified identified assets
3. Substantial physical change to the identified assets

Both the owner-seller (lessor) and the purchaser (lessee) are required to reassess whether the arrangement contains, or is, a lease, if the owner-seller (lessor) modified the identified asset to increase its capacity.

If the only modification is to renew or extend the original arrangement before the end of the term of the original arrangement, then the arrangement is evaluated only with respect to the renewal or extension period. The accounting for the remaining term of the original arrangement does not change. The exercise of a renewal option that was included in the lease term at the inception of the arrangement is not considered a renewal for the purpose of reevaluating the arrangement. Accordingly, the exercise of the renewal option, absent any modification, does not trigger a reassessment.

(b) LEASE ACCOUNTING CLASSIFICATION—LESSEE. From the standpoint of the lessee, a lease may be classified as either a capital lease or an operating lease. At the inception date of the lease, if the lease meets any one of the following four criteria, then the lessee should classify and account for the arrangement as a capital lease:

1. *Ownership transfer.* The lease transfers ownership of the property to the lessee at the end of the lease term (ASC 840-10-25-1(a)).
2. *Bargain purchase option.* The lease contains a bargain purchase option (ASC 840-10-25-1(b)).
3. *Lease term.* The lease term is equal to at least 75 percent of the estimated economic life of the property. (If the beginning of the lease term falls within the last 25 percent of the total estimated life including earlier use, this criterion should not be used; ASC 840-10-25-1(c)).
4. *Minimum lease payments.* The present value of the minimum lease payments at the beginning of the lease term, excluding that portion of the payments representing executory costs, is 90 percent or more of the fair value of the leased property to the lessor at the inception date, less any related investment tax credit retained by and expected to be realized by the lessor. The discount rate that the lessee used in computing the present value of the lease payments is the lessee's incremental borrowing rate, defined in Topic 840 as "the rate that, at the inception of the lease, the lessee would have incurred to borrow the funds necessary to buy the leased asset on a secured loan with repayment terms similar to the payment schedule called for in the lease." However, if the lessee knows the implicit rate used by the lessor and that rate is less than the lessee's borrowing rate, Topic 840 requires use of the implicit rate. (If the beginning of the lease term falls within the last 25 percent of the total estimated life including earlier use, this criterion should not be used; ASC 840-10-25-1(d)).

Leases that do not meet any of these criteria are classified as operating leases by the lessee.

(c) LEASE ACCOUNTING CLASSIFICATION—LESSOR. Topic 840 specifies these classifications of leases for lessors:

- Direct financing
- Sales type
- Operating
- Leveraged

A lease is classified as a direct financing lease if it meets any one of the four lease classification criteria and, in addition, meets both of the following criteria:

1. Collectibility of the minimum lease payments is reasonably predictable.
2. No important uncertainties surround the amount of unreimbursable costs yet to be incurred by the lessor under the lease.

A lease is classified as a sales-type lease if it qualifies as a direct financing lease and, in addition, has a fair market value in excess of the property's carrying value. Sales-type leases are generally associated with dealers and manufacturing lessors. Leases that do not meet these criteria are classified as operating leases.

(d) DEFINITIONS OF LEASE TERMS. The following technical terms have been defined in the Codification:

- *Bargain purchase option.* A provision allowing the lessee, at the lessee's option, to purchase the leased property for a price that is sufficiently lower than the expected fair value of the property at the date the option becomes exercisable so that exercise of the option appears, at the inception of the lease, to be reasonably assured.
- *Bargain renewal option.* A provision allowing the lessee, at the lessee's option, to renew the lease for a rental sufficiently lower than the fair rental of the property at the date the option becomes exercisable so that exercise of the option appears, at the inception of the lease, to be reasonably assured. In this context, fair rental of a property is the expected rental for equivalent property under similar terms and conditions.
- *Capital lease.* A lease that must be capitalized by a lessee because it meets one of the four lease classification criteria discussed in Topic 840.
- *Contingent rentals.* The increases or decreases in lease payments that result from changes occurring subsequent to the inception of the lease in the factors (other than the passage of time) on which lease payments are based, except as provided in the following sentence. Any escalation of minimum lease payments relating to increases in construction or acquisition cost of the leased property or for increases in some measure of cost or value during the construction or preconstruction period shall be excluded from contingent rentals. The term contemplates an uncertainty about future changes in the factors on which lease payments are based. Lease payments that depend on a factor directly related to the future use of the leased property, such as machine hours of use or sales volume during the lease term, are contingent rentals and, accordingly, are excluded from minimum lease payments in their entirety. However, if it is probable that the lessee will reach the specified target, the lessee should recognize contingent rental expense, in both annual and interim periods, before reaching the specified target that triggers the contingent rental expense. Subsequently, if the lessee determines that it is no longer probable that it will reach the specified target, at that time previously recognized contingent rental expense is reversed into income.

  For a sales-type or direct financing lease, a lessor should include in contingent rentals in the determination of income as accruable.

  In addition, lease payments that depend on an existing index or rate, such as the consumer price index or the prime interest rate, should be included in minimum lease payments based on the index or rate existing at the inception of the lease; any increases or decreases in lease payments that result from subsequent changes in the index or rate are contingent rentals and thus affect the determination of income as accruable.
- *Direct financing lease.* A lease that meets any one of the four Topic 840 lease classification criteria for a lessor plus two additional criteria:

  a. Collectability of minimum lease payments must be reasonably predictable. However, simply because the receivable is subject to an estimate of uncollectability based on experience with groups of similar receivables does not prohibit a lessor from classifying a lease a direct financing lease.

  b. No important uncertainties may surround the amount of unreimbursable costs to be incurred by the lessor under the lease. For example, important uncertainties are, but are not limited to, commitments by the lessor to guarantee performance of the leased property in a manner more extensive than the typical product warranty or to effectively protect the lessee from obsolescence of the leased property. However, the necessity of estimating executory costs such as insurance, maintenance, and taxes to be paid by the lessor, as discussed in paragraph 30-30-6(a) of Topic 840, does not by itself constitute an important uncertainty. If the property covered by the lease is yet to be constructed or has not been acquired by the lessor at lease inception, the lessor should determine the lease classification at the date that construction of the property is completed or the property is acquired by the lessor.

And the lease does not give raise to manufacturer's or dealer's profit (loss) to the lessor and does not meet the criteria for a leveraged lease in Topic 840.

- *Estimated economic life of leased property.* The estimated remaining period during which the property is expected to be economically usable by one or more users, with normal repairs and maintenance, for the purpose for which it was intended at the inception of the lease, without limitation by the lease term.

- *Estimated residual value of leased property.* The estimated fair value of the leased property at the end of the lease term.

- *Executory costs.* Those costs such as insurance, maintenance, and taxes incurred for leased property, whether paid by the lessor or lessee. Amounts paid by a lessee in consideration for a guarantee from an unrelated third party of the residual value are also executory costs. If executory costs are paid by a lessor, any lessor's profit on those costs is considered the same as executory costs.

- *Fair value of the leased property.* The price for which the property could be sold in an arm's-length transaction between unrelated parties. Examples of the determination of fair value follow.

  a. When the lessor is a manufacturer or dealer, the fair value of the property at the inception of the lease will ordinarily be its normal selling price, reflecting any volume or trade discounts that may be applicable. However, the determination of fair value should be made in light of market conditions prevailing at the time, which may indicate that the fair value of the property is less than the normal selling price and, in some instances, less than the cost of the property.

  b. When the lessor is not a manufacturer or dealer, the fair value of the property at the inception of the lease will ordinarily be its cost, reflecting any volume or trade discounts that may be applicable. However, when there has been a significant lapse of time between the acquisition of the property by the lessor and the inception of the lease, the determination of fair value should be made in light of market conditions prevailing at the inception of the lease, which may indicate that the fair value of the property is greater or less than its cost or carrying amount, if different.

- *Finance lease.* A financing device by which a user can acquire use of an asset for most of its useful life. Rentals are net to the lessor, and the user is responsible for maintenance, taxes, and insurance. Rent payments over the life of the lease are sufficient to enable the lessor to recover the cost of the equipment plus interest on its investment.

- *Inception of the lease.* The date of the lease agreement or commitment, if earlier. For purposes of this definition, a commitment should be in writing, signed by the parties in interest to the transaction, and should specifically set forth the principal provisions of the transaction. If any of the principal provisions are yet to be negotiated, such a preliminary agreement or commitment does not qualify for purposes of this definition.

- *Initial direct costs.* Only those costs incurred by the lessor that are (a) costs to originate a lease incurred in transactions with independent third parties resulting directly from and essential to acquiring that lease and which would not have been incurred had that leasing transaction not occurred, and (b) certain costs directly related to specified activities performed by the lessor for that lease. Those activities include evaluating the prospective lessee's financial condition; evaluating and recording guarantees, collateral, and other security arrangements; negotiating lease terms; preparing and processing lease documents; and closing the transaction. The costs directly related to those activities include only that portion of the employees' total compensation and payroll-related fringe benefits directly related to time spent performing those activities for that lease and other costs related to those activities that would not have been incurred but for that lease. Initial direct costs do not include costs related to activities performed by the lessor for advertising, soliciting potential lessees, servicing existing leases, and other ancillary activities related to establishing and monitoring credit policies, supervision, and administration. They also do not include administrative costs, rent, depreciation, any other occupancy and equipment costs and employees' compensation and fringe benefits related to ancillary activities, unsuccessful origination efforts, and idle time.

- *Interest rate implicit in the lease.* The discount rate that, when applied to (a) the minimum lease payments, excluding that portion of the payments representing executory costs to be paid by the lessor, together with any profit thereon, and (b) the unguaranteed residual value accruing to the benefit of the lessor causes the aggregate present value at the beginning of the lease term to be equal to the fair value of the leased property to the lessor at the inception of the lease, minus any investment tax credit retained by the lessor at the inception of the lease and minus any investment tax credit retained by the lessor and expected to be realized by the lessor. (This definition does not necessarily purport to include all factors that a lessor might recognize in determining his rate of return.)

- *Lease.* An agreement conveying the right to use property, plant, or equipment (land or depreciable assets or both) usually for a stated period of time.

- *Lease term.* The fixed noncancelable term of the lease plus each of the following items, except where noted:

  a. All periods, if any, covered by bargain renewal options.

  b. All periods, if any, for which failure to renew the lease imposes a penalty on the lessee in such amount that a renewal appears, at the inception of the lease, to be reasonably assured.

  c. All periods, if any, covered by ordinary renewal options during which a guarantee by the lessee of the lessor's debt directly or indirectly related to the leased property is expected to be in effect or a loan from the lessee to the lessor directly or indirectly related to the leased property is expected to be outstanding.

  d. All periods, if any, covered by ordinary renewal options preceding the date as of which a bargain purchase option is exercisable.

  e. All periods, if any, representing renewals or extensions of the lease at the lessor's option. However, in no case shall the lease term be assumed to extend beyond the date a bargain purchase option becomes exercisable. A lease that is cancelable only upon the occurrence of some remote contingency, only with the permission of the lessor, only if the lessee enters into a new lease with the same lessor, or only if the lessee incurs a penalty in such amount that continuation of the lease appears, at inception, reasonably assured shall be considered "noncancelable" for purposes of this definition.

The existence of a fiscal funding clause in a lease agreement requires an assessment of the likelihood of lease cancelation through exercise of the fiscal funding clause. If the likelihood of exercise of the fiscal funding clause is assessed as being remote, a lease agreement containing such a clause should be considered a noncancelable lease; otherwise, the lease should be considered cancelable and thus classified as an operating lease.

- *Lessee's incremental borrowing rate.* The rate that, at the inception of the lease, the lessee would have incurred to borrow over a similar term the funds necessary to purchase the leased asset. This definition does not proscribe the lessee's use of a secured borrowing rate as its incremental borrowing rate if that rate is determinable, reasonable, and consistent with the financing that would have been used in the particular circumstances.

- *Leveraged lease.* A lease that meets the definition as a direct financing lease for a lessor and, in addition, has all the following characteristics:

  a. At least three partners are involved: a lessee, a lessor (the equity participant), and a long-term creditor.

  b. The amount of creditor financing provided is sufficient to provide substantial leverage to the transaction and is without recourse to the general credit lessor, although the creditor may have recourse to the specific property leased and the unremitted rentals relating to it.

c. The lessor's net investment declines during the early years of the lease and rises during the latter years of the lease. Such decreases and increases in the net investment balance may occur more than once.

• *Minimum lease payments*

a. From the standpoint of the lessee: The payments that the lessee is obligated to make or can be required to make in connection with the leased property. However, contingent rentals, any guarantee by the lessee of the lessor's debt, and the lessee's obligation to pay (apart from the rental payments) executory costs, such as insurance, maintenance, and taxes, in connection with the leased property are excluded from minimum lease payments. If the lease contains a bargain purchase option, only the minimum rental payments over the lease term and the payment called for by the bargain purchase option should be included in the minimum lease payments. Otherwise, minimum lease payments include:

   i. The minimum rental payments called for in the lease over the lease term.

   ii. Any guarantee by the lessee or any party related to the lessee of the residual value at the expiration of the lease term, whether or not payment of the guarantee constitutes a purchase of the leased property. If the lessor has the right to require the lessee to purchase the property at termination of the lease for a certain or determinable amount, that amount is considered a lessee guarantee of the residual value. If the lessee agrees to make up any deficiency below a stated amount in the lessor's realization of the residual value, the residual value guarantee to be included in the minimum lease payments is the stated amount rather than an estimate of the deficiency to be made up.

   iii. Any payment that the lessee must make or can be required to make upon failure to renew or extend the lease at the expiration of the lease term, whether or not the payment would constitute a purchase of the lease property. In this connection, it should be noted that the definition of lease term includes "all periods, if any, for which failure to renew the lease imposes a penalty on the lessee in an amount such that renewal appears, at the inception of the lease, to be reasonably assured." If the lease term has been extended because of that provision, the related penalty is not included in minimum lease payments.

   iv. Payments made before the beginning of the lease term are considered as part of minimum lease payments and included in the 90 percent test, as specified in paragraph 10-25-1(d) of Topic 840, at their future value at the beginning of the lease term—that is, to give effect to the time value of money, the future value at the beginning of the lease term of the lease payments are calculated just as payments during the lease term are discounted back to the beginning of the lease term for purposes of applying the 90 percent test in that paragraph. The lessee should use the same interest rate to accrete payments to be made before the beginning of the lease term that it uses to discount lease payments to be made during the lease term.

   v. Fees that are paid by the lessee to the owners of the special-purpose entity for structuring the lease transaction are included as part of minimum lease payments (but are not included in the fair value of the leased property) for purposes of applying the 90 percent test in paragraph 10-25-1(d) of Topic 840.

b. From the standpoint of the lessor: The payments described immediately above for a lessee plus any guarantee of the residual value or of rental payments beyond the lease term by a third party unrelated to either the lessee or the lessor, provided the third party is financially capable of discharging the obligations that may arise from the guarantee.

• *Net lease.* In a net lease, executory costs in connection with the use of the asset are to be paid by the lessee and are not a part of the rental. For example, taxes, insurance, and maintenance are paid directly by the lessee. Most finance leases are net leases.

• *Nonrecourse financing.* Lending or borrowing activities in which the creditor does not have general recourse to the debtor but rather has recourse only to the property used for collateral in the transaction or other specific property.

- *Operating lease.* A lease that does not meet any of the lease classification criteria of a capital lease (lessee) or direct financing lease (lessor). Also describes a short-term rental agreement by which a user can acquire use of an asset for a fraction of the useful life of that asset.

- *Penalty.* Any requirement that is imposed or can be imposed on the lessee by the lease agreement or by factors outside the lease agreement to disburse cash, incur or assume a liability, perform services, surrender or transfer an asset or rights to an asset or otherwise forgo an economic benefit, or suffer an economic detriment. Factors to consider when determining if an economic detriment may be incurred include, but are not limited to, the uniqueness of purpose or location of the property, the availability of a comparable replacement property, the relative importance or significance of the property to the continuation of the lessee's line of business or service to its customers, the existence of leasehold improvements or other assets whose value would be impaired by the lessee vacating or discontinuing use of the leased property, adverse tax consequences, and the ability or willingness of the lessee to bear the cost associated with relocation or replacement of the leased property at market rental rates or to tolerate other parties using the leased property.

- *Related parties.* A parent company and its subsidiaries, an owner enterprise and its joint ventures (corporate or otherwise) and partnerships, and an investor (including a natural person) and its investees, provided that the parent company, owner enterprise, or investor has the ability to exercise significant influence over operating and financial policies of the related party. In addition to the foregoing examples of significant influence, significant influence may be exercised through guarantees of indebtedness, extensions of credit, or through ownership of warrants, debt obligations, or other securities. If two or more enterprises are subject to the significant influence of a parent company, owner enterprise, investor (including a natural person), or common officers or directors, those enterprises should be considered related parties with respect to each other.

- *Renewal or extension of a lease.* The continuation of a lease agreement beyond the original lease term including a new lease under which the lessee continues to use the same property.

- *Sale-leaseback accounting.* A method of accounting for a sale-leaseback transaction, in which the seller-lessee records the sale, removes all property and related liabilities from its balance sheet, recognizes gain or loss from the sale, and classifies the leaseback as a financing or operating lease as appropriate.

- *Sales recognition.* Any method to record a transaction involving real estate, other than the deposit method, or the methods to record transactions accounted for as financing, leasing, or profit-sharing arrangements. Profit recognition methods commonly used to record transactions involving real estate include, but are not limited to, the full accrual method, the installment method, the cost recovery method, and the reduced profit method.

- *Sales-type lease.* A direct financing lease that also contains a dealer or manufacturer's profit; the fair market value of the property at lease inception exceeds the related carrying value.

- *Sublease.* A transaction in which a leased property is released by the original lessee to a third party, and the lease agreement between the two original parties remains in effect.

- *Unguaranteed residual value.* The estimated residual value of the leased property exclusive of any portion guaranteed by the lessee or by a third party unrelated to the lessor.

15.3 OPERATING LEASES

(a) LESSEE ACCOUNTING FOR OPERATING LEASES. An operating lease does not result in a lessee recognizing an asset or liability on the balance sheet. Normally, rental payments on an operating lease are charged to expense over the lease term as the payments become due. If rental payments are not made on a straight-line basis, rental expense nevertheless is recognized on a straight-line basis unless another systematic and rational basis is more representative of the time pattern in which use benefit is derived from the leased property, in which case that basis would be used.

(b) LESSEE DISCLOSURES FOR OPERATING LEASES.   A lessee should make the following disclosures related to an operating lease either on the face of the financial statements or in the notes thereto:

1. The nature and extent of leasing transactions with related parties been disclosed (ASC 840-10-50-1).

2. A general description of leasing arrangements including, but not limited to (ASC 840-10-50-2):

    a. The basis on which contingent rental payments are determined.

    b. The existence and terms of renewal or purchase options and escalation clauses.

    c. Restrictions imposed by lease agreements such as those concerning dividends, additional debt, and further leasing.

3. For operating leases:

    a. For each period for which an income statement is presented, disclose (ASC 840-20-50-1) (*note:* Rental payments under leases with terms of a month or less that were not renewed need not be included):

        i. Rental expense.

        ii. Separate amounts for minimum rentals, contingent rentals, and sublease rentals.

    b. For operating leases having initial or remaining noncancelable lease terms in excess of one year, disclose (ASC 840-20-50-2):

        i. Future minimum rental payments required as of the date of the latest balance sheet presented, in the aggregate and for each of the five succeeding fiscal years.

        ii. The total amount of minimum rentals to be received in the future under noncancelable subleases as of the date of the latest balance sheet presented.

    c. Include rental costs in the lessee's income from continuing operations (ASC 840-20-45-1).

In addition to the above disclosure requirements, Topic 460, *Guarantees,* requires that a lessee disclose:

1. The nature of the guarantee (including residual value guarantees on operating leases), how the guarantee arose, and the events or circumstances that would require the guarantor to perform under the guarantee

2. The maximum potential amount of future payments the guarantor could be required to make under the lease contract

3. The current carrying amount of the liability for the guarantor's obligations under the guarantee

4. The nature of (a) any recourse provisions that would enable the guarantor to recover from third parties any of the amount paid under the guarantee and (b) assets held either as collateral or by third parties that, upon the occurrence of any triggering event or condition under the guarantee, the guarantor can obtain and liquidate to recover all or a portion of the amounts paid under the guarantee.

(c) LESSOR ACCOUNTING FOR OPERATING LEASES.   Operating leases are accounted for by the lessor as follows:

- Leased property is included with or displayed near other property, plant, and equipment in the balance sheet.

- Depreciation is recorded following the lessor's normal depreciation policy for like assets, and accumulated depreciation is displayed as a reduction of the leased property.

- Rent is recorded as income over the lease terms as it becomes receivable under the provisions of the lease. However, if the rentals vary from the straight-line basis, the income is recognized on a straight-line basis unless another systematic and rational basis is more representative of the time pattern in which the benefit from the leased property is diminished, in which case that basis is used.

- Initial direct costs are deferred and allocated over the lease term in proportion to revenue recognition under the lease. However, these costs may be expensed when incurred if the effect is not materially different from that which would have resulted from the use of the straight-line method prescribed above.

- A lessor should also disclose, in addition to the items just described, the following items related to an operating lease:

  a. The nature and extent of leasing transactions with related parties (ASC 840-10-50-1).

  b. A general description of the lessor's leasing arrangements, if leasing (exclusive of leveraged leasing) is a significant part of the lessor's business activities in terms of revenue, net income, or assets (ASC 840-10-50-4).

  c. Lessors that recognize contingent rental income disclose (ASC 840-10-50-5):

   i. The accounting policy for recognizing contingent rental income.

   ii. If contingent rental income is recognized (accrued) prior to the lessee's achievement of the specified target that triggers the contingent rents, the impact on rental income as if the lessor's accounting policy was to defer contingent rental income until the specified target is met.

  d. The cost and carrying amount, if different, of property on lease or held for leasing, by major classes of property according to nature or function, and the amount of accumulated depreciation in total as of the date of the latest balance sheet presented.

  e. Minimum future rentals on noncancelable leases as of the date of the latest balance sheet presented, in the aggregate and for each of the five succeeding fiscal years.

  f. Total contingent rentals included in income for each period for which an income statement is presented.

(d) EXAMPLE OF OPERATING LEASES.   The AMS Realty Group leases property with a cost and fair value of $5,000 and a life of 10 years to the GCS Generator Corporation for 4 years with a rental of $2,000 per year for years 1 and 2 and $1,000 per year for years 3 and 4.

AMS Realty Group		
Years 1 and 2		
Cash	$2,000	
Rent Income		$1,500
Deferred Rent Income		500
To recognize rental income on a straight-line basis		
Depreciation Expense	500	
Accumulated Depreciation		500
To recognize depreciation expense ($5,000/10 years = $500)		
Years 3 and 4		
Deferred Rent Income	500	
Cash	1,000	
Rent Income		1,500
To recognize rental income on a straight-line basis		
Depreciation Expense	500	
Accumulated Depreciation		500
To recognize depreciation expense ($5,000/10 years = $500)		

GCS Generator Corporation
Years 1 and 2

Rent Expenses	$1,500	
Prepaid Rent	500	
Cash		$2,000
To recognize rental expense on a straight-line basis		

Years 3 and 4

Rent Expenses	1,500	
Prepaid Rent		500
Cash		1,000
To recognize rental expense on a straight-line basis		

This example assumes that some other time pattern other than straight line is not of benefit to the lessee and diminution of benefit to the lessor does not exist. For simplicity, the straight-line depreciation method was used although other methods could be selected by the lessor.

15.4 CAPITAL LEASES

(a) ACCOUNTING FOR CAPITAL LEASES. For capital leases, the lease transaction is viewed as a form of financing in which an asset is acquired and a liability is incurred. The lessee records a capital lease as an asset and a liability on the balance sheet. The amount recorded on the balance sheet is the present value of the minimum lease payments. Executory costs such as insurance, maintenance, and taxes to be paid by the lessor are excluded from the minimum payments. However, the amount recorded as an asset and liability must not exceed the fair value of the leased property.

The lessee will record amortization expense and interest expense on capitalized leases. A lessee should amortize a capitalized asset in a manner consistent with the lessee's normal amortization policy. The amortization period to be used is the lease term (including the renewal period(s) if used in determining the lease term), unless there is a bargain purchase or transfer of ownership at the end of the lease term, in which case the amortization is over the life of the assets, as if owned.

Interest expense is recognized by the lessee in proportion to the remaining balance of the capitalized lease obligation. This is accomplished by allocating each minimum lease payment between interest expense and reduction of the lease obligation so as to produce a constant periodic rate of interest on the remaining lease obligation. This method is called the *effective interest method.*

(b) DISCLOSURES FOR CAPITAL LEASES. For capital leases, in addition to the first three disclosure items under operating leases, a lessee should make the following disclosures (ASC 840-30-45-1 through 45-3; 840-30-50-1):

1. Assets recognized as capital leases and the accumulated amortization thereon as of the date of each balance sheet presented.
2. The gross amount of assets recorded under capital leases as of the date of each balance sheet presented by major classes according to nature or function. (*Note:* This information may be combined with the comparable information for owned assets.)
3. Separately identify obligations under capitalized leases in the balance sheet and appropriately classify as current and noncurrent liabilities.
4. Future minimum lease payments as of the date of the latest balance sheet presented, in the aggregate and for each of the five succeeding fiscal years, with separate deductions from the total for the amount representing executory costs (including any profit thereon) that are included in the minimum lease payments and for the amount of the imputed interest necessary to reduce the net minimum lease payments to present value.

5. The total of minimum sublease rentals to be received in the future under noncancelable subleases as of the date of the latest balance sheet presented.

6. Total contingent rentals actually incurred for each period for which an income statement is presented.

7. Amortization of capitalized leases separately reported on the income statement or presented in a note to the financial statements. (The amortization may be combined with depreciation expense, but that fact must be disclosed.)

(c) EXAMPLE OF CAPITAL LEASE—LESSEE.   Topic 840 offers an example illustrating classification and accounting for leases. Assume that lessee and lessor sign a lease with these provisions:

- The lease has a noncancelable term of 30 months, and payments of $135 are due at the beginning of each month.
- The equipment costs $5,000, has a 5-year economic life, and has a residual value guaranteed by lessee of $2,000.
- Lessee receives any excess of the sales price over the guaranteed amount.
- Lessee pays executory costs.
- Lessee's incremental borrowing rate is 10.5 percent.
- The interest rate implicit in the lease is unknown to the lessee because the lessor's unguaranteed residual value assumption is unknown to the lessee.
- Lessee depreciates similar equipment on a straight-line basis.
- No investment tax credit is available.

(i) Minimum Lease Payments.   Minimum lease payments for both lessee and lessor are calculated as follows:

Payments $135 × 30 months	$4,050
Residual value guarantee	2,000
Total minimum lease payments	$6,050

(ii) Lease Classification.   The lease is classified by reviewing the four lease capitalization criteria presented in Section 15.2(a).

1. *Not met.* The lease does not transfer ownership (ASC 840-25-1(a)).

2. *Not met.* The lease does not contain a bargain purchase option (ASC 840-25-1(b)).

3. *Not met.* The lease is not for a term equal to or greater than 75 percent of the economic life of the property (ASC 840-25-1(c)).

4. *Met.* For the lessee, the present value of the minimum lease payments using the lessee's incremental borrowing rate exceeds 90 percent of the fair value of the property at the inception of the lease (calculations follow). Even if the lessee knows the implicit rate, he or she uses the incremental borrowing rate because it is lower. Therefore, lessee classifies the lease as a capital lease (ASC 840-25-1(d)).

Present values using lessee's incremental borrowing rate of 10.5 percent are:

Present value:	
Rental payments (present value of $135 at 0.875% per month for 29 months)	$3,580
Residual guarantee (present value of $2,000 in 30 months at 0.875% per month)	1,540
Total	$5,120

Although the lessee's incremental borrowing rate produces a present value of $5,120 for lease classification criteria, Topic 840 stipulates that the lease is not to be capitalized in excess of fair value, or $5,000 in this example. When the present value is adjusted to total $5,000, the interest rate rises to 12.036 percent, or 1.003 percent per month, as shown:

Present value:

Rental payments (present value of $135 at 1.003% per month for 29 months)	$3,517
Residual guarantee (present value of $2,000 in 30 months at 1.003% per month)	$1,483
Total	$5,000

(iii) Lessee Accounting at Inception.   At the beginning of the lease, the lessee's journal entries are:

Equipment under capital lease	$5,000	
Capital lease obligation		$5,000
To record capital lease at the fair value of the property.		

(Because the present value of the minimum lease payments using the lessee's incremental borrowing rate as the discount rate [see ASC 840-10-25-31 for selection of rate to be used] is greater than the fair value of the property, the lessee capitalizes only the fair value of the property. See ASC 840-30-30-1 through 30-4.)

The first month's payment is recorded as:

Capital lease obligation	135	
Cash		135
To record first month's rental payment.		
Interest expense	49	
Accrued interest		49
To recognize interest expense for the first month of the lease.		

Obligation balance outstanding during the month is $4,865 ($5,000 − $135) × 1.003% (rate implicit in the liquidation of the $5,000 obligation through (a) 30 monthly payments of $135 made at the beginning of each month and (b) a $2,000 guarantee of the residual value at the end of 30 months) = $49. (See ASC 840-30-35-6 through 35-8.)

Then at the beginning of the second month:

Capital lease obligation	86	
Accrued interest	49	
Cash		135
To record rental payment on capital lease obligation.		

(iv) Lessee Amortization.   Amortization would be taken on a straight-line basis over 30 months.

Total amortization to be taken equals the capitalized lease value of $5,000, less its estimated residual value of $2,000. Each month's depreciation would be recorded as follows:

Amortization expense	$100	
Accumulated amortization—		
Equipment under capital lease		$100
To record first month's amortization on a straight-line basis over 30 months to a salvage value of $2,000, which is the estimated residual value to the lessee. (See ASC 840-30-35-1(b).)		

(v) Lease Payments. Each lease payment contains both interest and principal, and Topic 840 requires that interest be calculated on the effective interest method, as follows:

Payment Number	Lease Payment	Interest (1.003%) on Principal	Reduction of Principal	Net Lease Obligation
1	$135	0	0	$4,865
2	135	$49	$86	4,779
3	135	48	87	4,692
4	135	47	88	4,604
5	135	46	89	4,515

15.5 DIRECT FINANCING LEASES

(a) ACCOUNTING FOR DIRECT FINANCING LEASES.   In a direct financing lease, a lessor accounts for the investment in the lease as a receivable. A direct financing lease is accounted for by recording the following:

- *Gross investment.* The minimum lease payments (excluding executory costs paid by the lessor including any profit thereon) and any unguaranteed residual value accruing to the lessor are recorded as the gross investment in finance leases. The estimated residual value used to calculate this amount should not exceed the amount estimated at lease inception. However, the lessor should consider the effect of a provision to escalate minimum lease payments for certain activities during the construction or preacquisition period in the determination of the estimated residual value of the leased property at lease inception.

- *Unearned income.* The difference between the gross investment and the cost or carrying amount, if different, of the leased property is recorded as unearned income. This unearned income, reduced by an amount equal to initial direct costs, is amortized to income over the lease term, applying the effective interest method to produce a constant rate of return on the net investment in the lease.

- *Net investment.* The net investment consists of the gross investment less the unearned income.

- *Initial direct costs.* These costs are expensed as incurred.

- *Earned income.* Earned income consist of two elements: (1) An amount equal to initial direct costs, which is recorded at the inception of the lease; and (2) the remaining unearned income, which is amortized to income over the lease term using the effective interest method.

(b) EXAMPLE OF DIRECT FINANCING LEASES.   Assume that a lessor executes the same lease described earlier. In addition, for simplicity, assume that there were no initial direct costs. This lease does not meet the first three criteria for a direct finance lease, but it does meet the 90 percent of fair value test. Having met this test and assuming that the collectibility and uncertainty tests are also met, the lessor will classify this lease as a direct financing lease. The interest rate implicit in this lease is the internal rate of return that discounts the minimum lease payments ($135 × 30 plus $2,000 residual value) to the fair value of the property at the inception of the lease ($5,000). That rate is 12.036 percent, or 1.003 percent per month.

In this case, the rate is shown by adding the present values of the components of return:

Present value of 29 payments of $135 at 1.003% per month	$3,382
Plus $135 for first payment	135
Equals present value of rental payments	3,517
Plus present value of $2,000 in 30 months at 1.003% per month	1,483
	$5,000

The lessor uses this rate to calculate the present value of the minimum lease payments in the 90 percent of fair value test, as shown:

Present value	
Rental payments	$3,517
Residual guarantee	1,483
Total	$5,000
Fair value of property at inception of lease	$5,000
Present value of minimum lease payments as percentage of fair value	100 percent

In all direct financing leases where an unguaranteed residual value is recorded, the fair value of property will exceed the present value of minimum lease payments. This is because the unguaranteed residual value is excluded from the lessor's present value calculation. The lessor must produce the following information to record the lease:

- Gross investment is $6,050. Payments of $135 × 30 plus $2,000 guaranteed residual value.
- Unearned income is $1,050. Gross investment less $5,000 cost of equipment.
- Net investment is $5,000. The gross investment less the unearned income.

The entries for the lessor at the inception of the lease are:

Minimum lease payments receivable	$6,050	
Equipment		$5,000
Unearned income		1,050
To recognize lessor's investment in direct financing lease (see ASC 840-30-30-6 and 840-30-30-11 through 30-13).		
Monthly lease payments would be recorded as:		
Cash	135	
Minimum lease payments receivable		135
To recognize receipt of first month's rental payment under the lease.		

Earned income (excluding any applicable income to cover initial direct costs) for the first month would be recorded as:

Unearned income	$49	
Earned income		$49
To recognize the portion of unearned income that is earned during the first month of the lease.		

Net investment outstanding for month is computed to be $4,865 (gross investment $5,915 ($6,050 − $135) less unearned income ($1,050) × 1.003% (monthly implicit rate in the lease) = $49 (see ASC 840-30-30-11 through 30-13).

A similar pattern is followed for the remainder of the lease term.

The following table summarizes the income recognition and net investment of the lessor over the term of the lease.

Payment Number	Payment	Interest Income on Net Investment	Principal Reduction	Net Investment Beginning of Month
1	$ 135	$ 0	$ 35	$4,865
2	135	49	86	4,779
3	135	48	87	4,692
4	135	47	88	4,604
—	—	—	—	—
—	—	—	—	—
—	—	—	—	—
30	135	21	114	1,980
	0	20	(20)	$2,000
	$4,050	$1,050	$3,000	

15.6 SALES-TYPE LEASES

The major difference between a direct financing lease and a sales-type lease is the presence of a manufacturer's profit in a sales-type lease; for example, the fair market value of the property is greater than the carrying value of such property.

(a) ACCOUNTING FOR SALES-TYPE LEASES. A sales-type lease is accounted for by recording the following four items:

1. *Gross investment.* Gross investment combines the minimum lease payments (excluding executory costs paid by the lessor including any profit thereon) and any unguaranteed residual value accruing to the lessor are recorded as the gross investment in finance leases. The estimated residual value used to calculate this amount should not exceed the amount estimated at lease inception. However, the lessor should consider the effect of a provision to escalate minimum lease payments for certain activities during the construction or preacquisition period in the determination of the estimated residual value of the leased property at lease inception.

2. *Unearned income.* Unearned income is initially measured as the difference between: (a) the gross investment in the sales-type lease and (b) the sum of the present values of the two components of the gross investment. This unearned income is amortized to income over the lease term, applying the effective interest method to produce a constant rate of return on the net investment in the lease.

3. *Net investment.* The net investment consists of the minimum lease gross investment less the unearned income.

4. *Sales price.* The sales price equals the present value of the minimum lease payments (net of executory costs, including any profit thereon), computed at the interest rate implicit in the lease.

5. *Cost of goods sold or cost of sales.* This cost equals the cost or carrying amount of the lease property less the present value of any unguaranteed residual value accruing to the benefit of the lessor.

(b) DISCLOSURE REQUIREMENTS FOR DIRECT FINANCING AND SALES-TYPE LEASES. For direct financing and sales-type leases, in addition to the first three disclosure items under operating leases, a lessor should make the following disclosures (ASC 840-30-50-4):

1. The four components of the net investment in sales-type and direct financing leases as of the date of each balance sheet presented:
    a. Future minimum lease payments to be received with separate deductions for: (i) amounts representing executory costs, including any profit thereon, included in the minimum lease payments; and (ii) the accumulated allowance for uncollectible minimum lease payments receivable
    b. The unguaranteed residual values accruing to the benefit of the lessor
    c. Initial direct costs (for direct financing leases only)
    d. Unearned income
2. Future minimum lease payments to be received for each of the five succeeding fiscal years as of the date of the latest balance sheet presented.
3. Total contingent rentals included in income for each period for which an income statement is presented.

(c) EXAMPLE OF SALES-TYPE LEASES. In the case presented in Section 15.5, assume that the lessor produces the equipment for a cost of $4,000. The information needed to record the sales-type lease consists of these four items:

1. Gross investment is $6,050 ($4,050 of lease payments plus $2,000 of guaranteed residual value).
2. Unearned interest income is $1,050 (gross investment of $6,050 less $5,000).
3. Sales price is $5,000 (present value of minimum lease payments).
4. Cost of goods sold is $4,000 less the present value of any unguaranteed residual value accruing to the benefit of the lessor. Because there is no unguaranteed residual value, the cost of goods sold equals the lessor's cost to produce the equipment under lease.

The transaction is recorded by the lessor as:

Lease payments receivable	$6,050	
Cost of goods	4,000	
Sales revenue		$5,000
Equipment		4,000
Unearned income		1,050

Thereafter, the accounting for lessors would follow the example of the direct financing lease.

Balance Sheet Presentation—Capital Lease—Lessee

Long-lived assets:	
Leased property under capital leases less accumulated amortization	$XXX
Current liabilities:	
Obligations under capital leases	$XXX
Long-term liabilities:	
Obligations under capital leases	$XXX

Balance Sheet Presentation—Capital Lease—Lessor

Current assets:	
Net investment in direct financing and sales-type leases—current portion	$XXX
Noncurrent assets:	
Net investment in direct financing and sales-type leases	$XXX
Long-lived assets:	
Property on operating leases and property held for leases net of accumulated depreciation	$XXX

15.7 SALE OR ASSIGNMENT OF A LEASE OR OF PROPERTY SUBJECT TO A LEASE ACCOUNTED FOR AS A SALES-TYPE OR DIRECT FINANCING LEASE

According to Paragraph 30-40-8 of Topic 840, the sale or assignment of a lease or of property subject to a lease that was accounted for as a sales-type lease or a direct financing lease should not negate the original accounting treatment for the lease. A transfer of minimum lease payments or guaranteed residual values subject to a sales-type lease or direct financing lease must be accounted in conformity with Topic 860, *Transfers and Servicing*. Transfers of unguaranteed residual values are not subject to Topic 860.

15.8 LEVERAGED LEASES

(a) LEVERAGED LEASE ACCOUNTING.   Leveraged leases derive their name from a characteristic of the transaction, namely that the lessor tends to have a small equity in the leased property and borrows or otherwise finances a large part of the cost of owning the asset. Frequently the lessor's equity is reduced by an immediate return from investment tax credits related to the leased property, which offsets income taxes otherwise payable by the lessor. The lessor (equity participant) often is a financial institution able to finance the leverage at a relatively low cost. This combination, together with the security of a high-quality lessee (or lease), tends to produce a comparatively low usage cost of the asset to the lessee.

The lessor's investment in a finance lease may be zero or even negative at certain times during the lease period. The concept of recognizing a profit during a period of negative investment caused some theoretical problems in determining the proper accounting for leveraged leases.

(i) Characteristics of a Leveraged Lease.   Topic 840 defines a *leveraged lease* as one having all of these four characteristics:

1. It meets the definition of a direct financing lease.
2. It involves at least three parties: a lessee, a long-term creditor, and a lessor (commonly called the *equity participant*).
3. The financing provided by the long-term creditor is nonrecourse as to the general credit of the lessor (although the creditor may have recourse to the specific property leased and the unremitted rentals relating to it), and the amount of the financing is sufficient to provide the lessor with substantial "leverage" in the transaction.
4. The lessor's net investment declines during the early years once the investment has been completed and rises during the later years of the lease before its final elimination. Such decreases and increases in the net investment balance may occur more than once.

Provided the lease meets these requirements and the investment tax credit, if any, is not accounted for using the flow-through method, the lease is treated as a leveraged lease.

In addition, as discussed in Topic 840, a lease involving real estate that does not give rise to manufacturer's or dealer's profit should be classified as a leveraged lease if the lease qualifies as a direct financing lease (i.e., meets any of the criteria of ASC 840-10-25-1 and both of the criteria of ASC 840-10-25-42) and the lease qualifies as a leveraged lease under ASC 840-10-25-43(c).

(ii) Lessee Accounting.   From the viewpoint of the lessee, leveraged leases are classified and accounted for in the same manner as nonleveraged leases.

(iii) Lessor Accounting for Investment.   The lessor records the investment in a leveraged lease net of the nonrecourse debt. The net balance of the following four accounts represents the initial and continuing investment in leveraged leases:

1. Rentals receivable, net of that portion of the rental applicable to principal and interest on the nonrecourse debt
2. A receivable for the amount of the investment tax credit to be realized on the transaction
3. The estimated residual value of the leased asset
4. Unearned and deferred income (the remaining amount of estimated pretax lease income or loss and investment tax credit to be allocated to income over the lease term, after deducting initial direct costs)

(iv) Lessor Recognition of Income.   The lessor in a leveraged lease transaction recognizes income by use of the investment with the separate phases method. Under this method, lease income is recognized at a level after-tax rate of return on net investment in those years in which the net investment at the beginning of the period is positive. Deferred taxes should be used to calculate the net investment for use in computing income from the lease. However, deferred taxes should not be offset against the investment in the lease for balance sheet presentation. Usually the lessor's net investment in a leveraged lease is as follows:

- *Early period.* Positive, due to the initial investment in leased property.
- *Middle period.* Negative, due to income tax reductions provided by accelerated depreciation, interest on nonrecourse debt, and investment tax credits, the cash flows are shielded from payment of taxes. In this period, the lessor has not only recovered the initial investment but has received additional funds, which are temporarily invested in other operations.
- *Later period.* Positive, due to a transfer from a tax shelter position to a tax-paying position arising primarily from reduced depreciation and interest charges.
- *Final period.* Zero, when the residual value is realized on sale of the property.

The investment with the separate phases method identifies two separate and distinct types of earnings: primary earnings and earnings from reinvestment. Primary earnings consist of three elements: pretax lease income, tax effect of pretax lease income, and investment tax credit. The income that is recognized at a level rate of return in the years in which the net investment is positive consists only of the primary earnings from the lease.

In the middle years of a leveraged lease, the net investment is typically negative. The lessor has recovered the initial investment and has the further use of cash that is shielded from tax by high depreciation and interest expense charges. The earnings from the reinvestment of excess funds are taken into income during the years when the net investment is negative and are independent of the reporting of the leveraged lease income. The result is that lease income is recognized at a level rate of return on the net investment (cost of property less nonrecourse debt and less the investment tax credit) in the years in which the net investment is positive at the beginning of the year. During the years when the net investment is negative, only the earnings from the reinvested funds are realized.

(b) LEVERAGED LEASE DISCLOSURES.   For leveraged leases, a lessor should make the following additional disclosures:

1. Present the amount of related deferred taxes separately from the remainder of the net investment in leveraged leases in the balance sheet (ASC 840-30-45-5).
2. Present separately (in the income statement or in related notes) pretax income from the leveraged lease, the tax effect of pretax income, and the amount of investment tax credit recognized as income during the period (ASC 840-30-45-5).
3. If leveraged leasing is a significant part of the lessor's business activities in terms of revenue, net income, or assets, disclose the following components of the net investment balance in leveraged leases (ASC 840-30-25-8, ASC 840-30-50-5):
   a. Rentals receivable

   b. Investment tax credit receivable

   c. Estimated residual value of the leased assets

   d. Unearned and deferred income

  4. If accounting for the effect on leveraged leases of the change in tax rates results in a significant variation from the customary relationship between income tax expense and pretax accounting income and the reason for that variation is not otherwise apparent, disclose the reason for that variation (ASC 840-30-50-6).

15.9 REAL ESTATE LEASES

(a) DETERMINING WHAT IS REAL ESTATE.   In Subtopic 360-20, *Real Estate Sales,* definition of *real estate* includes property with improvements or integral equipment. Property improvements and integral equipment are any physical structure or equipment attached to the real estate that cannot be removed and used separately without incurring significant cost.

The concepts and determination of whether equipment is integral equipment is based on the significance of the cost to remove the equipment from its existing location (which would include the cost of repairing damage done to the existing location as a result of the removal), combined with the decrease in the value of the equipment as a result of that removal. The decrease in the value of the equipment as a result of its removal, at a minimum, is the estimated cost to ship and reinstall the equipment at a new site.

However, when there are multiple potential users of the leased equipment, the estimate of the fair value of the equipment as well as the costs to ship and install the equipment should assume that the equipment will be sold to the potential user that would result in the greatest net cash proceeds to the seller (current lessor). In addition, the nature of the equipment, and the likely use of the equipment by other potential users, should be considered in determining whether any additional diminution in fair value exists beyond that associated with costs to ship and install the equipment.

When the combined total of both the cost to remove and the decrease in value (for leasing transactions, the information used to estimate those costs and the decrease in value is as of lease inception) exceeds 10 percent of the fair value of the equipment (installed) (for leasing transactions, at lease inception), the equipment is integral equipment. For example, buried fiber optics cable is considered integral equipment whereas copying machines or desktop computers are not considered integral equipment.

As a result, careful analysis and judgment should be given to arrangements that involve property improvements or equipment but not the underlying land because of the guidance in Topic 840.

Paragraph 10-25-46 of Topic 840 indicates that a lessor must evaluate an arrangement with integral equipment as a real estate lease. Paragraphs 10-25-48 through 10-25-50 of Topic 840 provide additional guidance for the transfer-of-ownership criterion for a lease involving integral equipment for which no statutory title registration system exists. The transfer-of ownership criteria is met if either of the following events occur:

- Upon the lessee's performance in accordance with the terms of the lease, the lessor will execute and deliver to the lessee such documents (including, if applicable, a bill of sale for the equipment) as may be required to release the equipment from the lease and to transfer ownership thereto to the lessee.

- The lease agreement requires the payment by the lessee of a nominal amount (e.g., the minimum fee required by statutory regulation to transfer ownership) in connection with the transfer of ownership.

However, it is a purchase option, if the lease provides that ownership of the leased property is not transferred to the lessee if the lessee elects not to pay the specified fee (whether nominal or not) and, as a result, would not satisfy the transfer-of-ownership criterion.

For purposes of performing the minimum-lease payments test for leases involving both land and building (as discussed in greater detail in the section on real estate leases below), if the lessee provides a residual value guarantee in a lease of both land and building(s), and the fair value of the land is 25 percent or more of the total fair value of the leased property at lease inception the annual minimum lease payments applicable to the land are determined for both the lessee and lessor by multiplying the fair value of the land by the lessee's incremental borrowing rate. As a result, the remaining minimum lease payments, including the full amount of the residual value guarantee, are attributed to the building.

(b) REAL ESTATE LEASES. Leases involving real estate can be categorized in one of five ways:

1. Land-only leases
2. Land and building leases
3. Real estate and equipment leases
4. Leases involving part of a building
5. Leases involving facilities owned by a government unit or authority

(i) Leases Involving Land Only. *Lessee's Accounting.* If land is the only item of property leased and the lease transfers ownership of the property (ASC 840-10-25-1(a)) or contains a bargain purchase option (ASC 840-10-25-1(b)), the lessee should account for the lease as a capital lease; because ownership of the land is expected to pass to the lessee, the asset recorded under the lease is not normally amortizable. However, the lease-term criterion (ASC 840-10-25-1(c)) and the minimum-lease-payments criterion (ASC 840-10-25-1(d) do not apply to classifying a land lease; as a result, the lessee should account for the lease as an operating lease.

Lessor's Accounting. The lessor accounts for a lease involving only land as follows:

1. If the lease meets the transfer of ownership criterion (ASC 840-10-25-1(a)) and gives rise to manufacturer's or dealer's profit (or loss), the lessor should classify the lease as a sales-type lease and account for the transaction using the guidance in Subtopic 360-20, *Real Estate Sales,* in the same manner as a seller of the same property.
2. If the lease meets the transfer of ownership criterion (ASC 840-10-25-1(a)) and both the additional collectibility and uncertainty criteria in ASC 840-10-25-42, but the lease does not give rise to manufacturer's or dealer's profit, the lessor should account for the lease as either a direct financing or leveraged lease, as appropriate.
3. If the lease meets the bargain-purchase-option criterion (ASC 840-10-25-1(b)) and both the additional collectibility and uncertainty criteria in ASC 840-10-25-42, the lessor should account for the lease as a direct financing, leveraged, or operating lease, as appropriate.
4. If the lease does meet both the additional collectibility and uncertainty criteria in ASC 840-10-25-42, the lessor should account for the lease as an operating lease.

However, the lease-term criterion (ASC 840-10-25-1(c)) and the minimum-lease-payments criterion (ASC 840-10-25-1(d)) do not apply to classifying a land lease. As a result, the lessor should account for the lease as an operating lease.

(ii) Leases Involving Land and Buildings. When the lease either transfers ownership or contains a bargain purchase option, there are two forms of accounting:

1. *Lessee's accounting.* If the lease transfers ownership or contains a bargain purchase option, the land and the buildings are capitalized separately by the lessee. The present value of the minimum lease payments (after deducting executory costs, including any profit thereon) is apportioned between land and buildings in relation to their fair values at the inception of the lease. However, if the lease agreement or commitment, if earlier, includes a provision

to escalate minimum lease payments for increases in construction or acquisition cost of the leased property or for increases in some other measure of cost or value, such as general price levels, during the construction or preacquisition period, lessee should consider the effect of any increases that have occurred in the determination of fair value of the leased property at lease inception. The building should be amortized under the normal accounting policies of the lessee.

2. *Lessor's accounting.* If the lease transfers ownership and meets both the collectibility and uncertainty criteria in ASC 840-10-25-42, the lessor accounts for the lease as a single unit. If there is a manufacturer or dealer profit, the lease is a sales-type lease and the lessor accounts for the transaction using the guidance in Subtopic 360-20 in the same manner as a seller of the same property. Without such profit, the lessor would account for the lease as a direct financing lease or leveraged lease, as appropriate. If the lease meets the bargain-purchase option criterion and there is a manufacturer or dealer profit, the lessor classifies and accounts for the lease as an operating lease. Without such profit, the lessor would account for the lease as a direct financing or leveraged lease if the lease meets both the additional collectibility and uncertainty criteria in ASC 840-10-25-42. If the lease does not meet these tests, the lessor accounts for the lease as an operating lease.

When the lease neither transfers ownership nor contains a bargain purchase option, whether the land and the building are considered together or separately depends on the relation of the fair value of the land to the total fair value of the leased property.

If the fair value of the land is less than 25 percent of the total fair value of the leased property, both the lessee and the lessor must consider the land and the building as a single unit, the economic life of the building.

If the lease term is at least 75 percent of the property's estimated economic life or if the present value of the minimum lease payments is 90 percent or more of the fair value of the property, the lessee capitalizes the land and buildings as a single unit and amortizes it. If the lease does not meet those requirements, it is accounted for as a single unit as an operating lease.

If the lease term is at least 75 percent of the property's economic life or if the present value of minimum lease payments is 90 percent or more of the fair value of the property and both the collectibility and uncertainty tests are met, the lessor accounts for the lease as a single unit, a direct financing lease, a leveraged lease, or an operating lease as appropriate based on the guidance in ASC 840-10-25-43. If the lease does not meet those requirements, it is accounted for as an operating lease.

If the building in the lease meets the economic life or 90 percent fair value tests, the building is accounted for as a capital lease by the lessee. The land element of the lease is separately accounted for as an operating lease. However, if the building element in the lease meets neither the economic life nor the fair value test, both the building and the land are accounted for as a single operating lease by the lessee.

If the building in the lease meets the economic life or fair value test as well as the criteria for uncertainty and collectibility, the lessor accounts for the building elements as a direct financing lease, leveraged lease, or operating lease, as appropriate. The land is accounted for as an operating lease. If the building does not meet the economic life or fair value tests and does not meet the tests for collectibility, both the building and the land are accounted for collectively as a single operating lease.

(iii) Leases Involving Land and Equipment.   If a lease involves land and equipment, the portion of the minimum lease payments applicable to the equipment is estimated by whatever means is appropriate and reasonable. The equipment is then to be treated separately for purposes of applying the criteria and accounted for separately according to its classification by both lessee and lessor.

(iv) Leases Involving Only Part of a Building.   When the leased property is part of a larger entity, its cost and fair value may not be objectively determinable as, for example, if a floor in an office building was leased. If the cost and fair value of the leased property are objectively determinable, both the lessee and the lessor should classify and account for the lease as described above for a lease involving land and a building..

Unless both the cost and the fair value are objectively determinable, the lease is classified and accounted for in two ways:

1. *Lessee.* If the fair value of the leased property is not objectively determinable, the lessee should classify the lease pursuant to whether it meets the 75 percent of economic life test.

2. *Lessor.* If either the cost or the fair value of the property is not objectively determinable, the lessor should account for the lease as an operating lease.

(c) LEASES INVOLVING FACILITIES OWNED BY A GOVERNMENT UNIT OR AUTHORITY. Because of special provisions normally present in leases involving various types of facilities owned by a governmental unit or authority, the economic life of such facilities for purposes of classifying the lease is essentially indeterminate. In addition, the concept of fair value is not applicable to such leases. Because such leases also do not provide for a transfer of ownership or a bargain purchase option, they are classified as operating leases. Leases of other facilities owned by a governmental unit or authority wherein the rights of the parties are essentially the same as in a lease of airport facilities are also classified as operating leases. Examples of such leases may be those involving facilities at ports and bus terminals. The guidance is intended to apply to leases only if all of the following conditions are met;

1. The leased property is owned by a governmental unit or authority.

2. The leased property is part of a larger facility, such as an airport, operated by or on behalf of the lessor.

3. The leased property is a permanent structure or a part of a permanent structure, such as a building, that normally could not be moved to a new location.

4. The lessor, or in some circumstances a higher governmental authority, has the explicit right under the lease agreement or existing statutes or regulations applicable to the leased property to terminate the lease at any time during the lease term, such as by closing the facility containing the leased property or by taking possession of the facility.

5. The leased property or equivalent property in the same service area cannot be purchased nor can such property be leased from a nongovernmental unit or authority. Equivalent property in the same service area is property that would allow continuation of essentially the same service or activity as afforded by the leased property without any appreciable difference in economic results to the lessee.

Leases of property not meeting all of the conditions in the guidance from ASC 840-10-25-25 are subject to the same criteria for classifying leases that are applicable to the various types of real estate leases that do not involve government-owned property.

15.10 SELECTED ISSUES IN LEASE ACCOUNTING

(a) PARTICIPATION BY THIRD PARTIES. The sale or assignment of a lease or property subject to a lease to a third party does not change the original accounting for the lease. Any profit or loss on the sale should be recognized at the time of the transaction, unless the transaction is between related parties or is sold with recourse (see Topic 860, *Transfer and Servicing*).

(b) RELATED PARTY LEASES. In general, related party leases are classified in accordance with the same criteria as all other leases, unless it is clear that the terms of the transaction have been significantly affected by the relationship of the lessees and lessor. The economic substance of such a transaction may cause the accounting for such leases to be modified from that which would be suggested by the strict terms of the lease.

(c) SUBLEASES. The accounting by the original lessee and lessor in a sublease situation depends on the terms of the sublease arrangement and the extent to which the original lessee's is relieved of its obligation after the sublease occurs. In all sublease situations, the new lessee treats the sublease as if it is a new lease and, as a result, should classify the lease in accordance with the lease classification criteria and account for it as an operating or capital lease. In addition, an original lessee may not offset sublease payments received against obligations paid unless the transaction qualifies for right of offset under Subtopic 210-20, *Offsetting.*

(i) Original Lessee's Accounting—Relieved of Obligation. In a sublease situation where the original lessee is no longer the primary obligor under the original lease, the transaction is considered a termination of the original lease agreement. The lessee's accounting for a capital lease termination is discussed in the following section. However, if the original lessee under an operating lease is no longer the primary obligor but now is secondarily liable under the sublease agreement, the lessee should recognize a guarantee obligation in accordance with Subtopic 405-20, *Extinguishment of Liabilities.*

If the original lease was a capital lease of property other than real estate (including integral equipment) the lessee should (1) remove the asset and obligation representing the original lease from its accounts; (2) recognize a gain or loss for the difference between the asset and obligation; and (3) recognize a guarantee obligation if the original lessee is secondarily liable. The lessee should include any consideration paid or received in determining the amount of gain or loss to recognize.

If the original lease was a capital lease of real estate (including integral equipment), the original lessee should follow the guidance in Subtopic 360-20 to determine whether it should remove the asset held under the capital lease and the related obligation from its balance sheet. If the criteria for sale recognition are met, the original lessee should (1) remove the asset and obligation representing the original lease from its accounts and (2) recognize any consideration paid or received upon termination or any guarantee obligation in accordance with the preceding guidance for property other than real estate. The original lessee may recognize a gain if the transaction meets the requirements for recognition of profit by the full accrual method; otherwise, the lessee should recognize the gain using one of the other appropriate profit recognition methods discussed in Subtopic 360-20. However, an original lessee should immediately recognize any loss on the transaction.

Although not lease contract, a contingent obligation arising out of a terminated lease or a guarantee of a third-party lease obligation is subject to the disclosure requirements of Subtopic 825-10-50, *Financial Instruments—Disclosures.*

(ii) Original Lessee's Accounting—Not Relieved of Obligation. If the original lessee is not relieved of its primary obligation under the original lease, the original lessee (as sublessor) accounts for both the original lease and the new lease as operating leases. If costs expected to be incurred under an operating sublease (i.e., executory costs and either amortization of the leased asset or rental payments on an operating lease, whichever is applicable) exceed anticipated revenue on the operating sublease, the original lessee should immediately recognize a loss.

If the original lessee is not relieved of its primary obligation under the original capital lease, original lessee (as sublessor) should account for the sublease as follows:

1. Continue to account for the obligation related as a capital lease.
2. If the original capital lease met either the transfer-of-ownership criterion or the bargain-purchase-option criterion, the original lessee (as sublessor) appropriately determines the classification of the new lease and does one of the following:
   a. Determines that the new lease is a capital lease (either a sale-type or direct financing lease) and treats the unamortized balance of the asset under the original capital lease as the cost basis of the leased asset under the sublease arrangement
   b. Otherwise accounts for the new lease as an operating lease
3. If the original capital lease met either the lease-term criterion or the minimum-lease-payments criterion but did not meet the transfer-of-ownership criterion or the bargain-purchase option

criterion, the original lessee (as sublessor) should classify the new lease with lease-term criterion and the additional incremental criteria applicable to lessors as follows:

a. The original lessee (as sublessor) accounts for the new lease as a direct financing lease and treats the unamortized balance of the asset under the original lease as the cost basis of the leased asset. Otherwise, the original lessee (as sublessor) classifies and accounts for the new lease as an operating lease.

b. However, there is an exception if the timing and other circumstances suggest that the intent of the sublease was an integral part of an overall transaction in which the original lessee serves only as an intermediary. In that situation, the original lessee (as sublessor) should classify the sublease according to the lease-term criterion and the minimum-lease payments criterion and both the additional incremental criteria.

In some situations, the original lessee (sublessor) will need to recognize a loss on a direct financing sublease.

The original lessee, if sublease transactions are material, should disclose the gross amount of its guarantees or obligations under the original lease, along with the expected rentals to be received under an enforceable legal assignment or sublease for the asset.

(iii) Original Lessor's Accounting.   The original lessor continues to account for the lease without change, if the original lessee enters into a sublease or sells or otherwise transfers the original lease arrangement to a third party.

However, if the original agreement is substituted with a new arrangement, the lessor accounts for the termination of the original lease and classification and accounting for the new lease as separate transactions. The lessor should account for the termination of the original lease by: removing the net investment from its accounts; recognizing the leased asset at the lower of its original cost, present fair value, or present carrying amount; and recognizing an adjustment to income of the period.

(d) CHANGES IN THE PROVISIONS OF LEASES.   From the standpoint of the lessor, three changes can take place:

1. The change does not give rise to a new agreement. A new agreement is defined as a change that, if in effect at the inception of the lease, would have resulted in a different classification.

2. The change does give rise to a new agreement that would be classified as a direct financing lease.

3. The change gives rise to a new agreement classified as an operating lease.

If either (1) or (2) occur, the balance of the minimum lease payment receivable and the estimated residual value are adjusted to reflect the effect of the change. The net adjustment is to be charged (or credited) to the unearned income account, and the accounting for the lease adjusted to reflect the change.

If the new agreement is an operating lease, then the transaction should be accounted for under the sale-leaseback requirements.

(e) RENEWAL, EXTENSION, OR TERMINATION OF LEASES.   A renewal or extension involves one of two circumstances that affect the accounting for an existing lease:

1. A guarantee or penalty is rendered inoperative.

2. A new agreement exists.

In both circumstances, the lessee in a capital lease adjusts the current balance of the leased asset and obligation to the present value of the future minimum lease payments based on the implicit interest rate in the original lease. If a new agreement exists and it is classified as an operating lease, then the lessee continues to account for the existing capital lease until the end of the term. The renewal or extension is an operating lease and is accounted for as such. In both circumstances, the lessor in a direct financing lease would adjust the lease receivable and estimated residual value charging or crediting unearned income for the difference. An upward revision to estimated residual value is prohibited, however. If a renewal or extension constitutes a new agreement and is an operating lease, then the lessor continues to account for the existing lease until the end of the term and accounts for the renewal/extension as an operating lease. If the new agreement is a sales-type lease, the renewal or extension is accounted for as a sales-type lease providing the renewal/extension occurred at or near the end of the existing lease term.

In a termination, the lessor eliminates the remaining net investment and records the leased asset at its lower of present fair value, current book value, or historical cost. The net difference is reflected in the income statement of the current period. The lessor in a capital lease will eliminate the asset and obligation from the financial statements recording a gain or loss on termination. In an operating lease, no adjustment is required.

(f) LEASES AND BUSINESS COMBINATIONS.   If, in connection with a business combination, the provisions of a lease are modified such that the revised lease is essentially a new agreement, this new lease should be classified as any new lease would be.

In a purchase, unless the terms of the lease have been changed, the previous classification would remain in effect. However, the amounts assigned to the assets and liabilities arising from the accounting for leases should be determined in accordance with the guidelines under Topic 805, *Business Combinations*.

(g) CHANGE IN RESIDUAL VALUE.   A lessor should at a minimum annually review the estimated residual values in any leasing transactions. If the review results in a lower estimate than had been previously established, the lessor should determine whether the decline in the estimated residual value is other than temporary. If the decline in estimated residual value is judged to be other than temporary, the lessor should revise the accounting for the transaction using the changed estimate and should recognize the resulting reduction in the net investment as a loss in the period in which the estimate is changed. An upward adjustment of the leased property's estimated residual value (including any guaranteed portion) is prohibited.

(h) SALE AND LEASEBACK.   A sale and leaseback transaction is one involving the sale of property by the owner (seller-lessee), who simultaneously leases it back from the new owner. Sale and leaseback transactions are frequently entered into as a means of raising additional cash from assets that are owned and used by a company. For example, a company may sell a building it owns and simultaneously lease it back. The facilities of the building are still available to the company. The cash received can be invested in the company's productive process or business at a relatively high rate of return. Since real estate investors, who purchase and lease the building, frequently accept lower rates of return than are available to the company from its normal operations, overall rate of return is improved. In effect, the company transfers funds invested in real estate (or similar) assets to higher-yielding, more active investments. The lease in a sale and leaseback transaction is frequently a net lease, which provides that the lessee remains liable for all executory costs, taxes, maintenance, and so on.

(i) Lessee Involvement with Construction.   In addition, a sale-leaseback transaction may arise in situations in which the lessee never owned the leased property. To illustrate, an entity (lessee) may be involved on behalf of an owner-lessor with the construction of a building that will be leased to the lessee when the owner-lessor has completed construction of the building. In this situation, the lessee is considered the owner of an asset during the construction period and thus is subject to the sale-leaseback requirements, if the lessee has substantially all of the construction period risks. Various forms of the lessee's involvement during the construction period raise questions about whether the lessee is acting as an agent for the owner-lessor or is, in substance, the owner of the asset during the construction period. The lessee's involvement during the construction period may include any of the following:

- Being obligated to begin making lease payments regardless of whether the project is complete (a date-certain lease)
- Guaranteeing the construction debt or providing construction financing either directly or indirectly
- Being primarily or secondarily obligated on construction contracts
- Serving as an agent for the construction, financing, or ultimate sale of the asset for the owner-lessor
- Acting as a developer or being the general contractor
- Being obligated to purchase the asset if the construction is not successfully completed by an agreed-upon date
- Being obligated to fund cost overruns and so forth

(ii) Build-to-Suit Leases. As a result of the above guidance, lessee involvement in build-to-suit leases will require careful consideration of the guidance at ASC 840-40-55-2 through 55-16; otherwise the lessee may find itself in a situation where it will have to capitalize the construction in progress and the related debt. Furthermore, a lessee is considered the owner for accounting purposes of the construction in progress if the lessee incurred any hard costs in connection with a construction project or otherwise commences construction activities prior to entering into a lease arrangement with the developer-owner.

(iii) Other Sale-Leaseback Issues. It is not uncommon for a special-purpose entity to be used in leasing transactions. For the construction of government-owned properties, the lessee will need to determine if it is considered the owner of the property (i.e., has substantially all of the construction period risk) and account for the arrangement using the sale-leaseback guidance.

Also, if the terms of an arrangement require the lessee to indemnify the lessor or its lenders for preexisting environmental contamination, the lessee should assess at the lease inception date the likelihood of loss based on existing laws and regulations. If the loss is reasonably possible, the lessee is considered to have purchased, sold, and then leased the property and the transaction is subject to the sale-leaseback guidance.

Furthermore, except in the circumstance involving the refunding of tax-exempt debt (ASC 840-30-35-10), if a change in the provisions of a capital lease gives rise to a new agreement classified as an operating lease, the lessee should account for the transaction as sale-leaseback transaction.

However, ASC 840-40-25-9 through 25-18 may require that an entity account for a sale-leaseback transaction involving real estate (including integral equipment) as a borrowing or as a deposit (see Subsection 15.10(h)(vi) on sale-leaseback for real estate). Sale-leasebacks of personal property are not within the scope of the sale-leaseback guidance, unless the sale-leaseback includes integral equipment.

(iv) Lessee Accounting. If a sale of property is accompanied by a leaseback of all or any part of its remaining economic life and the lease meets one of the criteria for classification as a capital lease, the seller-lessee accounts for it as a capital lease. If the lease does not meet one of the criteria, then it is an operating lease.

In general, any profit or loss on the sale is deferred and recognized in proportion to the amortization of the leased asset in a capital lease or to the gross rental expense in an operating lease. The three exceptions to the general rule are:

1. The seller-lessee relinquishes rights to substantially all of the property sold, retaining only a minor portion of such use. The seller-lessee leased back a minor portion if the present value of a reasonable amount of rentals for the leaseback period is not more than 10 percent of the value of the asset sold. Both the sale and leaseback are accounted for as separate transactions unless they require an adjustment due to the unreasonable amount of rentals called for by the leaseback compared to market conditions at the inception of the lease.

2. The seller-lessee retains more than a minor part of the property but less than substantially all of the leaseback property and realizes profit on the sale in excess as follows:

   ○ If classified as an operating lease, the present value of the minimum lease payments over the lease term.

   ○ If classified as a capital lease, the recorded amount of the leased asset.

   ○ Only the profit on the sale in excess of the present value of the minimum lease payments or recorded value of the leased asset is recognized at the date of sale.

3. At the date of the transaction the fair value of the property is less than its net book value, in which case a loss should be immediately recognized. The amount of the loss is the difference between the undepreciated cost and fair value.

However, it is a financing transaction if the seller-lessee retains, through a leaseback, substantially all of the benefits and risks incident to the ownership of the property sold. If sale-leaseback transaction is a financing transaction the seller-lessee does not recognize any profit on the sale of an asset. As a result, the sale-leaseback guidance does not permit the lessee to recognize any profit on a sale if a related leaseback of the entire property sold meets one of the criteria in paragraph 840-10-25-1 for classification as a capital lease. A lessee is also required to defer any profit realized by the lessee during the construction period (for example, rental income paid to the lessee during the construction period under a ground lease or fees paid for construction or development services) in those transactions. In addition, an entity that may become the lessee as a result of the exercise of an option following construction completion is required to defer any profit realized during the construction period.

Any deferred profit where the leased asset is land only is amortized over the term of the lease. Otherwise, any deferred profit related to a capital lease is amortized in relationship to the amortization of the leased asset or for an operating lease in relationship to the related gross rental recognized as expense over the lease term.

Executory costs of the leaseback are excluded from the amount of profit to be deferred on a sale-leaseback transaction irrespective of who pays the executory costs or the classification of the leaseback.

However, if the fair value of the asset sold is more than its carrying amount, any indicated loss on the sale is probably in substance a prepayment of rent, and thus, the entity should defer that indicated loss as prepaid rent and amortize it over the lease term.

(v) Lessor Accounting.   If the lease meets any one of the lease classification criteria and both criteria for collectibility and uncertainty, the purchaser-lessor must record the transaction as a purchase and a direct financing lease. If the lease does not meet these criteria, the lessor records the transaction as a purchase and an operating lease.

(vi) Sale-Leaseback for Real Estate.   The Codification's Real Estate subsection guidance applies to sale-leaseback transactions:

1. That qualify for sales recognition under ASC 360-20-40-57 through 40-59
2. In which the seller-lessee sells property improvements or integral equipment to a buyer-lessor and leases them back while retaining the underlying land
3. That involve:
   ○ Only real estate
   ○ Real estate with equipment or equipment integral to the real estate
   ○ Real estate with equipment in which the equipment and the real estate are sold and leased back as a package, irrespective of the relative value of the equipment and the real estate
   ○ Real estate with equipment that include separate sale and leaseback agreements that are with (a) the same entity or related parties and (b) consummated at or near the same time, suggesting they were negotiated as a package.

The Codification's Real Estate subsection guidance does not apply to sale-leaseback transactions that do not qualify for sales recognition under the guidance in ASC 360-20-40-56.

A seller-lessor may use sale-leaseback accounting only if the sale-leaseback transaction meets all of the following criteria:

- Meets the definition of a normal leaseback (a lessee-lessor relationship that involves the active use of the property by the seller-lessee in consideration for payment of rent, including contingent rentals that are based on the future operations of the seller-lessee, and excludes other continuing involvement provisions or conditions).
- Payment terms and provisions adequately demonstrating the buyer-lessor's initial and continuing investment in the property as described in paragraphs 40-9 through 40-24 of Subtopic 360-20.
- Payment terms and provisions transferring all of the other risks and rewards of ownership as demonstrated by the absence of any other continuing involvement by the seller-lessee.

Terms and provisions such as, but not limited to, the sale price, interest rates, or loan terms substantially different from those that an independent lessor or lessee would normally accept are considered an exchange of unstated rights or privileges that should be considered in evaluating continuing involvement by the seller-lessee.

A sale-leaseback that does not qualify for a normal leaseback because of the continuing involvement by the seller-lessee should be accounted for by the deposit method or as a financing.

The various types of continuing involvement that do not transfer the risks or rewards of ownership are described in ASC 360-20-40-37 through 40-64. It is not uncommon for a sale-leaseback transaction to include the following types or forms of continuing involvement:

- Seller-lessee is obligated or has an option to repurchase the property or the buyer-lessor can compel the seller-lessee to repurchase the property.
- Seller-lessee provides a default remedy that allows the buyer-lessor to put the leased property to the seller-lessee. This is essentially a purchase option by the seller-lessee because it would be within the control of the seller-lessee to economically compel the buyer-lessor to put the leased property to the seller-lessee.
- Seller-lessee guarantees the buyer-lessor's investment or a return on that investment for a limited or extended period of time.
- Seller-lessee is obligated to pay the buyer-lessor at the lease termination date for a decrease in the fair value of the property below the estimated residual value on some basis other than excess wear and tear of the property levied on inspection of the property at the end of the lease.
- Seller-lessee provides nonrecourse financing to the buyer-lessor for any portion of the sales proceeds or provides recourse financing in which the only recourse is to the leased asset.
- Seller-lessee is not relieved of the obligation under any existing debt related to the property.
- Seller-lessee provides collateral on behalf of the buyer-lessor other than the property directly involved in the sale-leaseback transaction, the seller-lessee or a related party to the seller-lessee guarantees the buyer-lessor's debt, or a related party to the seller-lessee guarantees a return of or on the buyer-lessor's investment.
- Seller-lessee's rental payment is contingent on some predetermined or determinable level of future operations of the buyer-lessor.
- Seller-lessee enters into a sale-leaseback transaction involving property improvements or integral equipment without leasing the underlying land to the buyer-lessor.
- Buyer-lessor is obligated to share with the seller-lessee any portion of the appreciation of the property.
- Seller-lessee participates in any future profits of the buyer-lessor or the appreciation of the leased property.

In addition, a partial sale transaction precludes the use of sale-leaseback accounting due to the continuing involvement of the seller-lessee.

An uncollateralized, irrevocable letter of credit is not a form of continuing involvement that would prevent sale-leaseback accounting. Also, a lessee is not precluded from providing an independent third-party guarantee of the lease payments in a sale-leaseback transaction. However, all written contracts that exist between the seller-lessee in a sale-leaseback transaction and the issuer of a letter of credit should be considered. For example, a financial institution's right of setoff of any amounts on deposit with that institution against any payments made under the letter of credit constitutes collateral and, therefore, is a form of continuing involvement that would prevent sale-leaseback accounting.

In addition, an entity's unsecured guarantee of its own lease payments is not a form of continuing involvement because such a guarantee does not provide the buyer-lessor with additional collateral that reduces the buyer-lessor's risk of loss, except in the event of the seller-lessee's bankruptcy.

Furthermore, an unsecured guarantee of the lease payments of one member of a consolidated group by another member of the consolidated group is not a form of continuing involvement that would prevent sale-leaseback accounting in the consolidated financial statements. However, an unsecured guarantee of the lease payments of one member of a consolidated group by another member of the consolidated group is a form of continuing involvement that precludes sale-leaseback accounting in the separate financial statements of the seller-lessee because such a guarantee provides the buyer-lessor with additional collateral that reduces the buyer-lessor's risk of loss.

The financial statements of a seller-lessee should include a description of the terms of the sale-leaseback transaction, including future commitments, obligations, provisions, or circumstances that require or result in the seller-lessee's continuing involvement.

The financial statements of a seller-lessee that has accounted for a sale-leaseback transaction by the deposit method or as a financing should disclose the obligation for future minimum lease payments in the aggregate and for each of the five succeeding fiscal years, and the total of minimum sublease rentals in the aggregate and for each of the five succeeding fiscal years.

(i) ASSET RETIREMENT OBLIGATIONS.   According to paragraph 15-3(e) of Subtopic 410-20, *Asset Retirement Obligations,* if obligations of a lessee in connection with leased property, whether imposed by a lease agreement or by a party other than the lessor, meet the provisions of an asset retirement obligation discussed in ASC 410-20-15-2 but do not meet the definition of either minimum lease payments or contingent rentals, the lessee should account for those obligations in accordance with the requirements of Subtopic 410-20.

In addition, a lessor should consider its asset retirement obligations that are within the scope of Subtopic 410-20 when determining lease classification. For example, the results of the minimum-lease payments could be affected if the recorded cost of an asset leased by a lessor is affected by the requirements of Subtopic 40-20.

15.11 EXAMPLES OF LEASE DISCLOSURE

Exhibits 15.1 and 15.2 provide comprehensive illustrations of lease disclosure. Exhibit 15.1 presents a lessee's disclosure of capital and operating leases. Exhibit 15.2 presents a lessor's disclosure.

15.12 FASB ADDS LEASE ACCOUNTING BACK ON ITS AGENDA

In 2006, the FASB decided to reconsider the existing guidance on lease accounting as identified in this chapter. The Board announced that it would do so with the International Accounting Standards Board (IASB) as part of the convergence of GAAP project.

In August 2010, the FASB issued an Exposure Draft, *Leases,* which would significantly change the lease accounting requirements in Topic 840 for both lessees and lessors. The comment period

NOTES TO CONSOLIDATED FINANCIAL STATEMENTS
Note L—Lease Obligations

Certain airport and other retail facilities, a cruise ship, buses and bus terminals (primarily subleased), plants, offices, and equipment are leased. The leases expire in periods ranging from 1 to 46 years, and some provide for renewal options ranging from 1 to 25 years. Also, certain leases contain purchase options. Leases that expire are generally renewed or replaced by similar leases.

Capital leases included in the cost of property and equipment aggregate $40,992,000 and $79,395,000 at December 31, 20X8 and 20X7, respectively, with related accumulated depreciation of $28,704,000 and $45,656,000, respectively.

At December 31, 20×8, future minimum payments and related sublease rentals receivable with respect to capital leases and noncancelable operating leases with terms in excess of one year, are as shown:

(000 omitted)	Capital Leases	Operating Leases				
		Airport Terminal Concessions	Buses	Cruise Ship	Other	Total
20X9	$ 4,621	$ 42,942	$20,138	$12,949	$ 37,144	$113,173
20X0	4,570	42,116	19,479	12,949	33,763	108,307
20X1	4,973	46,125	19,466	12,949	30,720	109,260
20X2	4,858	47,174	17,996	12,949	25,188	103,307
20X3	4,641	49,354	7,048	12,949	22,078	91,429
Thereafter	41,002	93,239		23,742	133,183	250,164
Total future minimum lease payments	64,665	$320,950	$84,127	$88,487	$282,076	$775,640
Less imputed interest	$27,795					
Present value of future minimum capital lease payments	$36,870					

Rentals Receivable under Subleases
(000 omitted)

	Subleased Buses	Other (Principally Airport Concessions)	Total
20X9	$21,727	$ 16,628	$ 38,355
20X0	21,043	16,546	37,589
20X1	21,043	16,628	38,467
20X2	19,576	17,290	36,866
20X3	7,325	15,632	22,957
Thereafter		39,622	39,622
	$90,714	$123,142	$213,856

Information regarding net operating lease rentals for the three years ended December 31, 20×8, is as shown:

(000 omitted)	20X8	20X7	20X6
Minimum rentals	$130,795	$88,120	$50,617
Contingent rentals	$ 38,925	$18,676	$12,179
Sublease rentals	(55,753)	(32,285)	(1,112)
Total net rentals	$113,967	$74,511	$61,684

Contingent rentals on operating leases are based primarily on sales and revenues for buildings and leasehold improvements and usage for other equipment.

Exhibit 15.1   Lessee Disclosure

SUN COMPANY, INC.
NOTES TO CONSOLIDATED FINANCIAL STATEMENTS
8 (in part): Long-Term Receivables and Investments

	December 31	
	20X7	**20X6**
Investment in:	(millions of dollars)	
Leveraged leases	$ 85	$ 79
Direct financing and sales-type leases	276*	271
	361	350
Accounts and notes receivable	114	68
Investments in and advances to affiliated companies	27	34
Other investments, at cost	19	12
	$521	$464

*Include $129 million used with $26 million of other assets as collateral for $87 million recourse long-term debt-leasing notes associated with sales-type leases (Note 12).

Sun, as lessor, has entered into leveraged, direct financing, and sales-type leases of a wide variety of equipment including oceangoing vessels, aircraft, mining equipment, railroad rolling stock, and various other transportation and manufacturing equipment. The components of Sun's investment in these leases at December 31, 20X7 and 20X6, are set forth next (in millions of dollars):

	Leveraged Leases December 31		Direct Financing and Sales-Type Leases December 31	
	20X7	20X6	20X7	20X6
Minimum rentals receivable	$63*	$50*	$401	$417
Estimated unguaranteed residual value of leased assets	61	61	60	55
Unearned and deferred income	(39)	(32)	(185)	(201)
Investment in leases	85	79	$276	$271
Deferred taxes arising from leveraged leases	(60)	(54)		
Net investment in leveraged leases	$25	$25		

*Net of principal of and interest on related nonrecourse financing aggregating $234 and $247 million in 20X7 and 20X6, respectively.

The following is a schedule of minimum rentals receivable by years at December 31, 20X7 (in millions of dollars):

	Leveraged Leases	Direct Financing and Sales-Type Leases
Year ending December 31:		
20X8	$ 4	$ 51
20X9	5	49
20X0	5	48
20X1	4	46
20X2	6	37
Later years	39	170
	$63	$401

Exhibit 15.2   Lessor Disclosure

ended December 15, 2010. Since that time, the FASB and IASB have been redeliberating the conclusions reached in the Exposure Draft.

In July 2011, the FASB and IASB decided to "re-expose their revised proposals for a common leasing standard." Although the Boards have reaffirmed the major change to lease accounting, which is to report lease obligations and the related right to use on the balance sheet, other decisions taken to date were sufficiently different from those published in the Exposure Draft to warrant re-exposure of the revised proposals. The new Exposure Draft is expected to be issued by the end of 2011, with final guidance issued by June 2012. Some of the tentative decisions that the Boards have reached though their August 2011 meetings are as follows.

As mentioned previously, the Boards reaffirmed that a lessee will account for a lease under a right-of-use model. Under a right-of-use model, a lessee in an arrangement that is, or contains, a lease would recognize an asset representing its right to use an underlying asset during the lease term and a liability representing its obligation to make lease payments during the lease term. However, the Boards have not concluded their discussion on the application of the right-of-use model by a lessor.

Under the proposed guidance, lessees would apply a single accounting approach for all leases. This accounting approach would require a lessee to:

- Initially recognize a liability to make lease payments and a right-of-use asset, both measured at the present value of the lease payments
- Subsequently measure the liability to make lease payments using the effective interest method
- Amortize the right-of-use asset on a systematic basis that reflects the pattern of consumption of the expected future economic benefits

However, the Boards tentatively decided that for short-term leases, a lessee need not recognize lease assets or lease liabilities. For those leases, the lessee should recognize lease payments in profit or loss on a straight-line basis over the lease term, unless another systematic and rational basis is more representative of the time pattern in which use is derived from the underlying asset. The Boards have tentatively defined a *short-term lease* as:

A lease that, at the date of commencement of the lease, has a *maximum* possible term, including any options to renew, of 12 months or less. [emphasis added]

In addition, the Boards tentatively decided that a lessor should apply a "receivable and residual" accounting approach as follows:

- The lessor would recognize a right to receive lease payments and a residual asset at the date of the commencement of the lease.
- The lessor would initially measure the right to receive lease payments as the sum of the present value of the lease payments, discounted using the rate the lessor charges the lessee.
- The lessor would initially measure the residual asset as an allocation of the carrying amount of the underlying asset and would subsequently measure the residual asset by accreting it over the lease term using the rate the lessor charges the lessee.
- If profit on the right-of-use asset transferred to the lessee is reasonably assured, the lessor would recognize that profit at the date of the commencement of the lease. The profit would be measured as the difference between (a) the carrying amount of the underlying asset and (b) the sum of the initial measurement of the right to receive lease payments and the residual asset.
- If profit on the right-of-use asset transferred to the lessee is not reasonably assured, the lessor would recognize that profit over the lease term. In that case, the lessor would initially measure the residual asset as the difference between the carrying amount of the underlying asset and the right to receive lease payments. The lessor would subsequently accrete the residual asset,

using a constant rate of return, to an amount equivalent to the underlying asset's carrying amount at the end of the lease term as if the underlying asset had been subject to depreciation.

• If the right to receive lease payments is greater than the carrying amount of the underlying asset at the date of the commencement of the lease, the lessor would recognize, as a minimum, the difference between those two amounts as profit at that date.

These are just some of the decisions reached to date, and the Boards still have more decisions to reach before they can expose the guidance for more comments, including the effective date of the new guidance.

Although it is not likely the new guidance would be effective before 2014, an organization that has a significant amount of leases currently classified as operating leases under Topic 840 should begin to put a plan place to transition to the new guidance. At a minimum, the organization should review its existing debt covenants and evaluate whether its existing accounting systems are adequate to implement the significant changes.

15.13 SOURCES AND SUGGESTED REFERENCES

Bisgay, L. "FASB Issues Statement 98," *Management Accounting* 70 (August 1988): 63.

Byington, J. R., C. T. Moores, and P. H. Munter. "How Initial Direct Costs Affect Lessors," *CPA Journal* 58 (February 1988): 67–69.

Financial Accounting Standards Board. Statement of Financial Accounting Standards No. 66, *Accounting for Sales of Real Estate*. Stamford, CT: Author, 1982.

————. Statement of Financial Accounting Standards No. 140, *Accounting for Transfers and Servicing of Financial Assets and Extinguishments of Liabilities*. Norwalk, CT: Author, 2000.

"Firms Now Lease Everything But Time," *U.S. News & World Report*, August 14, 1989, p. 45.

Johnson, J. M. *Fundamentals of Finance for Equipment Lessors: A Transaction Orientation*. Arlington, VA: American Association of Equipment Lessors, 1986.

McMeen, A. R. *Treasurer's and Controller's New Equipment Leasing Guide*. Englewood Cliffs, NJ: Prentice-Hall, 1984.

Nailor, H., and A. Lennard. *Leases: Implementation of a New Approach*. Norwalk, CT: Financial Accounting Standards Board, February 2000.

Vernor, J. D. "Comparative Lease Analysis Using a Discounted Cash Flow Approach," *Appraisal Journal* 56 (July 1988): 391–398.

CHAPTER 16

PROPERTY, PLANT, EQUIPMENT, AND DEPRECIATION

George I. Victor, CPA
Giambalvo, Stalzer & Company, CPAs, P.C.

16.1 NATURE OF PROPERTY, PLANT, AND EQUIPMENT

(a) DEFINITION.   Property, plant, and equipment (PP&E) are presented as noncurrent assets in a classified balance sheet. The category includes such items as land, buildings, equipment, furniture, fixtures, tools, machinery, and leasehold improvements. It excludes intangibles and investments in affiliated companies.

(b) CHARACTERISTICS.   PP&E have several important characteristics:

- A relatively long life
- The production of income or services over their life
- Tangibility—having physical substance

(c) AUTHORITATIVE LITERATURE.   Generally accepted accounting principles (GAAP) for PP&E have evolved without the promulgation of any Level A or B GAAP rule making on a comprehensive basis. Because of this lack of authoritative literature, many believe that diversity in practice has developed with respect to both the type of costs capitalized and the amounts.

In 2001, the Accounting Standards Executive Committee (AcSEC) of the American Institute of Certified Public Accountants (AICPA) issued an Exposure Draft (ED) of a Statement of Position (SOP) titled *Accounting for Certain Costs and Activities Related to Property, Plant and Equipment.* The proposal was not adopted, since the Financial Accounting Standards Board (FASB) indicated that it addressed significant issues that should be addressed by the FASB. Nevertheless, in the absence of subsequent action by the FASB, this document reflects the "best thinking" of the AcSEC at the time.

The proposal addresses accounting for costs related to initial acquisition, construction, improvements, betterments, additions, repairs and maintenance, planned major maintenance, turnaround, overhauls, and other similar costs related to PP&E, outlined as follows:

1. Preliminary Stage

   This stage occurs before the acquisition of any specific PP&E asset and before it is probable that a specific PP&E asset will be acquired or constructed. All costs, with the exception of costs related for payment of an option to acquire PP&E, should be charged to expense during the preliminary stage.

2. Preacquisition Stage

   This stage is similar to the preliminary stage as no PP&E asset has yet been acquired. However, acquisition or construction of a specific PP&E asset is considered probable. All costs related to PP&E incurred during this stage should be charged to expense unless the costs are directly identifiable with the specific PP&E. Directly identifiable costs include only (a) incremental direct costs incurred in transactions with independent third parties and (b) payroll and payroll-benefit-related costs for employees who devote time to the PP&E activity. All general and administrative and overhead costs should be charged to expense and should not be capitalized as a cost of PP&E.

3. Acquisition-or-Construction Stage

   This stage begins when the entity obtains ownership of the PP&E. Only directly identifiable costs from the pre-acquision stage are capitalizable along with depreciation of machinery and equipment used directly in the construction of PP&E and inventory used directly in the construction or installation of PP&E. All general and administrative and overhead costs should also be charged to expense and should not be capitalized as a cost of PP&E.

4. In-Service Stage

   This stage begins when a PP&E asset is substantially complete and ready for its intended use. All costs incurred in this stage are charged to expense except for costs relating to replacement of existing components of a PP&E asset or acquisition of additional components. The principles outlined under the acquisition-or-construction stage are used to determine what costs of the replacements or additional components are capitalizable. Accordingly, all costs of repairs and maintenance are charged to expense, because they cannot be considered replacements or additional components. In conjunction with the replacement of a component of PP&E, an estimate of the remaining net book value of that replaced component should be charged to expense in the period of replacement.

5. Planned Major Maintenance Activities

   The ED prohibited these accounting methods for planned major maintenance activities:

   ○ Accrual of a liability before incurring the costs for a planned major maintenance activity

   ○ Deferral and amortization of the cost of a planned major maintenance activity

   ○ Current recognition of additional depreciation to cover future costs of a planned major maintenance activity

6. Component Accounting

   A component of a PP&E asset is defined as a tangible part or portion that can be separately identified as an asset, and it is expected to provide economic benefit for more than one year. The ED provided that if a component has an expected useful life that differs from the expected useful life of the PP&E asset to which it relates, the cost of the component should be accounted for separately and depreciated over its separate expected useful life.

7. Current Practice

Over 400 comment letters were received by AcSEC in response to this proposed SOP. The ED would have made these major changes in existing practice:

○ The capitalization criteria would have prohibited capitalization of indirect costs, overhead, and general and administrative costs, which many entities currently capitalize as a part of their PP&E cost.

○ Many entities currently use the methods prohibited under the section titled "Planned Major Maintenance Activities" to account for plant turnarounds and other major maintenance activities.

○ Requirements to use component accounting would have effectively prohibited entities from using group and composite methods of accounting for depreciation.

Since the withdrawal of this ED, the FASB has not taken action in providing guidance on these issues.

16.2 COST

PP&E usually are recorded at cost, defined as the amount of consideration paid or incurred to acquire or construct an asset. Cost consists of several elements. Welsch and Zlatkovich explain:

The capitalizable costs include the invoice price (less discounts), plus other costs such as sales tax, insurance during transit, freight, duties, ownership searching, ownership registration, installation, and break-in costs.[1]

(a) DETERMINING COST.   Generally, three principles are followed for determining the cost of an asset:

1. An asset acquired by exchanging cash or other assets is recorded at cost—that is, the amount of cash disbursed or the fair value of the other assets distributed

2. An asset acquired by incurring liabilities is recorded at cost—that is, at the present value of the future amounts to be paid.

3. An asset acquired by issuing shares of stock of the acquiring corporation is recorded at the fair value of the asset—that is, shares of stock issued are recorded at the fair value of the consideration received for the stock. That fair value is considered cost.

(i) Acquisition by Exchange.   PP&E may be acquired by exchange as well as by purchase. In that case, the applicable accounting requirements are set forth in paragraph 3c of Accounting Principles Board (APB) Opinion No. 29, *Accounting for Nonmonetary Transactions,* (FASB Accounting Standard Codification [ASC] 845-10) which defines an exchange as "a reciprocal transfer between an enterprise and another entity that results in the enterprise's acquiring assets or services or satisfying liabilities by surrendering other assets or services or incurring other obligations."

After defining nonmonetary assets (par. 3b) to include PP&E, Opinion No. 29 (par. 18) (FASB Accounting Standard Codification [ASC] 845-10)[2] further provides the general rule:

Accounting for nonmonetary transactions should be based on the fair values of the assets (or services) involved . . . . Thus, the cost of a nonmonetary asset acquired in exchange for another nonmonetary asset is the fair value of the asset surrendered to obtain it, and a gain or loss should

---

[1] Glenn A. Welsch and Charles T. Zlatkovich, *Intermediate Accounting,* 8th ed. (Homewood, IL: Irwin, 1989).

[2] References "FASB ASC XX" refer to sections of the recent Codification of FASB literature.

be recognized on the exchange. The fair value of the asset received should be used to measure the cost if it is more clearly evident than the fair value of the asset surrendered.

However, paragraph 21 of Opinion No. 29 (FASB ASC 845-10) recognizes an exception to its general rule if an exchange of nonmonetary assets "is not essentially the culmination of an earning process." In that case, the accounting "should be based on the recorded amount (after reduction, if appropriate, for an indicated impairment of value) of the nonmonetary asset relinquished."

Among the exchanges of nonmonetary assets that do not culminate the earning process, paragraph 21b of Opinion No. 29 (FASB ASC 845-10) includes "an exchange of a productive asset [defined to include property, plant, and equipment] not held for sale in the ordinary course of business for a similar productive asset or an equivalent interest in the same or similar productive asset."

However, the rule about basing exchanges of productive (nonmonetary) assets on recorded amounts has its own exception if the exchange includes monetary consideration. In that case, paragraph 22 of Opinion No. 29 (FASB ASC 845-10) states:

> The Board believes that the recipient of the monetary consideration has realized gain on the exchange to the extent that the amount of the monetary receipt exceeds a proportionate share of the recorded amount of the asset surrendered. The portion of the cost applicable to the realized amount should be based on the ratio of the monetary consideration to the total consideration received (monetary consideration plus the estimated fair value of the nonmonetary asset received) or, if more clearly evident, the fair value of the nonmonetary asset transferred. The Board further believes that the entity paying the monetary consideration should not recognize any gain on [an exchange not culminating the earning process] but should record the asset received at the amount of the monetary consideration paid plus the recorded amount of the nonmonetary asset surrendered. If a loss is indicated by the terms of [an exchange not culminating the earning process], the entire indicated loss on the exchange should be recognized.

FASB's Emerging Issues Task Force (EITF) later reached a consensus (EITF Issue No. 86-29; FASB ASC 845-10) that an exchange of nonmonetary assets should be considered a monetary (rather than nonmonetary) transaction if monetary consideration is significant, and agreed that "significant" should be defined as at least 25 percent of the fair value of the exchange.

(ii) Acquisition by Issuing Debt. If PP&E are acquired in exchange for payables or other contractual obligations to pay money (referred to collectively as *notes*), paragraph 12 of Accounting Principles Board (APB) Opinion No. 21, *Interest on Receivables and Payables* (FASB ASC 310-10) states:

> There should be a general presumption that the rate of interest stipulated by the parties to the transaction represents fair and adequate compensation to the supplier for the use of the related funds.

However, the Opinion continues:

> That presumption ... must not permit the form of the transaction to prevail over its economic substance and thus would not apply if (1) interest is not stated, or (2) the stated interest rate is unreasonable ... or (3) the stated face amount of the note is materially different from the current cash sales price for the same or similar items or from the market value of the note at the date of the transaction.

In any of these circumstances, both the assets acquired and the note should be recorded at the fair value of the assets or at the market value of the note, whichever can be more clearly determined. If the amount recorded is not the same as the face value of the note, the difference is a discount or premium, which should be accounted for as interest over the life of the note. If there is no established price for the assets acquired and no evidence of the market value of the note, the amount recorded should be determined by discounting all future payments on the note using an imputed rate of interest.

In selecting the imputed rate of interest to be used, paragraph 14 of APB Opinion No. 21 (FASB ASC 835-30) states that consideration should be given to:

(a) An approximation of the prevailing market rates for the source of credit that would provide a market for sale or assignment of the note; (b) the prime or higher rate for notes which are discounted with banks, giving due weight to the credit standing of the maker; (c) published market rates for similar quality bonds; (d) current rates for debentures with substantially identical terms and risks that are traded in open markets; and (e) the current rate charged by investors for first or second mortgage loans on similar property.

(iii) Acquisition by Issuing Stock.   Assets acquired by issuing shares of stock should be recorded at either the fair value of the shares issued or the fair value of the property acquired, whichever is more clearly evident.

Smith and Skousen further explain:

When securities do not have an established market value, appraisal of the acquired assets by an independent authority may be required to arrive at an objective determination of their fair market value. If satisfactory market values cannot be obtained for either securities issued or the assets acquired, values may have to be established by the board of directors for accounting purposes. The source of the valuation should be disclosed on the balance sheet.[3]

(iv) Mixed Acquisition for Lump Sum.   Several assets may be acquired for a lump-sum payment. This type of acquisition is often called a *basket purchase*. It is essential to allocate the joint cost carefully, because the assets may include both depreciable and nondepreciable assets, or the depreciable assets may be depreciated at different rates.

Welsch and Zlatkovich discuss the methods of allocating joint costs:

The allocation of the purchase price should be based on some realistic indicator of the relative values of the several assets involved, such as current appraised values, tax assessment, cost savings, or the present value of estimated future earnings.[4]

(v) Donated Assets.   PP&E may be donated to an entity. The accounting for such donations is addressed by Statement of Financial Accounting Standards (SFAS) No. 116, *Accounting for Contributions Received and Contributions Made.* Paragraph 8 (FASB ASC 958-605) concludes that donated PP&Eshould be measured at fair value.

Paragraph 19 (FASB ASC 958-605) provides guidance for determining the fair value of donated assets and indicates that quoted market prices, if available, are the best evidence of the fair value. It further indicates that if quoted market prices are not available, fair value may be estimated based on quoted market prices for similar assets, independent appraisals, or valuation techniques, such as the present value of estimated cash flows.

(b) OVERHEAD ON SELF-CONSTRUCTED ASSETS.   Companies often construct their own buildings and equipment. Materials and labor directly identifiable with the construction are part of its cost.

As to whether overhead should be included in the cost of construction, Lamden, Gerboth, and McRae suggest:

In the absence of compelling evidence to the contrary, overhead costs considered to have "discernible future benefits" for the purpose of determining the cost of inventory should be presumed

---

[3] Jay M. Smith and K. Fred Skousen, *Intermediate Accounting, Comprehensive Volume,* 9th ed. (Cincinnati: Southwestern Publishing, 1987).
[4] Welsch and Zlatkovich, *Intermediate Accounting.*

to have "discernible future benefits" for the purpose of determining the cost of a self-constructed depreciable asset.[5]

Mosich and Larsen agree and go on to discuss two alternative views as to what overhead should be included:

Allocate Only Incremental Overhead Costs to the Self-Constructed Asset. This approach may be defended on the grounds that incremental overhead costs represent the relevant cost that management considered in making the decision to construct the asset. Fixed overhead costs, it is argued, are period costs. Because they would have been incurred in any case, there is no relationship between the fixed overhead costs and the self-constructed project. This approach has been widely used in practice because it does not distort the cost of normal operations.

Allocate a Portion of All Overhead Costs to the Self-Constructed Asset. The argument for this approach is that the proper function of cost allocation is to relate all costs incurred in an accounting period to the output of that period. If an enterprise is able to construct an asset and still carry on its regular activities, it has benefited by putting to use some of its idle capacity, and this fact should be reflected in larger income. To charge the entire overhead to only a portion of the productive activity is to disregard facts and to understate the cost of the self-constructed asset. This line of reasoning has considerable merit.[6]

(c) INTEREST CAPITALIZATION.   Paragraph 6 of SFAS No. 34, *Capitalization of Interest Cost* (FASB ASC 835-20) states:

The historical cost of acquiring an asset includes the costs necessarily incurred to bring it to the condition and location necessary for its intended use. If an asset requires a period of time in which to carry out the activities necessary to bring it to that condition and location, the interest cost incurred during that period as a result of expenditures for the asset is a part of the historical cost of acquiring the asset.

Paragraph 9 (FASB ASC 835-20) describes the assets that qualify for interest capitalization:

- Assets that are constructed or otherwise produced for an enterprise's own use (including assets constructed or produced for the enterprise by others for which deposits or progress payments have been made)
- Assets intended for sale or lease that are constructed or otherwise produced as discrete projects (e.g., ships or real estate developments)

The amount of interest capitalized is computed by applying an interest rate to the average amount of accumulated expenditures for the asset during the period. To the extent that specific borrowings are associated with the asset, the interest rate on those borrowings may be used. Otherwise, the interest rate should be the weighted average rate applicable to other borrowings outstanding during the period. In no event should the total interest capitalized exceed total interest costs incurred for the period. Imputing interest costs on equity is not permitted.

Descriptions of capitalized interest are often seen in footnotes, such as the next example from 1989 financial statements:

Delta Air Lines, Inc.

Notes to Consolidated Financial Statements

Note 1. Summary of Significant Accounting Policies

---

[5] Charles Lamden, Dale L. Gerboth, and Thomas McRae, *Accounting for Depreciable Assets,* Accounting Research Monograph No. 1 (New York: AICPA, 1975).
[6] A. N. Mosich and John E. Larsen, *Intermediate Accounting,* 6th ed. (New York: McGraw-Hill, 1986).

Interest Capitalized—Interest attributable to funds used to finance the acquisition of new aircraft and construction of major ground facilities is capitalized as an additional cost of the related asset. Interest is capitalized at the Company's average interest rate on long-term debt or, where applicable, the interest rate related to specific borrowings. Capitalization of interest ceases when the property or equipment is placed in service.

(d) COST OF LAND.   Determining the cost of land presents particular problems, as described by Pyle and Larson:

> When land is purchased for a building site, its cost includes the amount paid for the land plus real estate commissions. It also includes escrow and legal fees, fees for examining and insuring the title, and any accrued property taxes paid by the purchaser, as well as expenditures for surveying, clearing, grading, draining, and landscaping. All are part of the cost of the land. Furthermore, any assessments incurred at the time of purchase or later for such things as the installation of streets, sewers, and sidewalks should be debited to the Land account because they add a more or less permanent value to the land.[7]

Excavation of land for building purposes, however, is chargeable to buildings rather than to land.

See Chapter 31 for a discussion of the accounting for land acquired as part of a real estate operation.

(i) Purchase Options.   If a company acquires an option to purchase land and later exercises that option, the cost of the option generally becomes part of the cost of the land. Even if an option lapses without being exercised, its cost can be capitalized if the option is one of a series of options acquired as part of an integrated plan to acquire a site. In that case, if any one of the options is exercised, the cost of all may be capitalized as part of the cost of the site.

(ii) Interest.   Paragraph 11 of SFAS No. 34 (FASB ASC 835-20) describes the proper accounting for interest cost related to land:

> Land that is not undergoing activities necessary to get it ready for its intended use is not [an asset qualifying for interest capitalization]. If activities are undertaken for the purpose of developing land for a particular use, the expenditures to acquire the land qualify for interest capitalization while those activities are in progress. The interest cost capitalized on those expenditures is a cost of acquiring the asset that results from those activities. If the resulting asset is a structure, such as a plant or a shopping center, interest capitalized on the land expenditures is part of the acquisition cost of the structure. If the resulting asset is developed land, such as land that is to be sold as developed lots, interest capitalized on the land expenditures is part of the acquisition cost of the developed land.

(iii) Other Carrying Charges.   Paragraph 6 of SFAS No. 67, *Accounting for Costs and Initial Rental Operations of Real Estate Projects* (FASB ASC 970-340) states:

> Costs incurred on real estate for property taxes and insurance shall be capitalized as property cost only during periods in which activities necessary to get the property ready for its intended use are in progress. Costs incurred for such items after the property is substantially complete and ready for its intended use shall be charged to expense as incurred.

Even though the scope of the Statement excludes "real estate developed by an enterprise for use in its own operations, other than for sale or rental," this guidance is followed in capitalizing carrying charges generally.

---

[7] William W. Pyle and Kermit D. Larson, *Fundamental Accounting Principles,* 10th ed. (Homewood, IL: Irwin, 1984).

(e) COST OF ASSETS HELD FOR RESEARCH AND DEVELOPMENT ACTIVITIES. Although paragraph 12 of SFAS No. 2, *Accounting for Research and Development Costs* (FASB ASC 730-10) generally requires that research and development costs be charged to expense when incurred, it makes an exception (par. 11a; FASB ASC 730-10) for "the costs of materials (whether from the enterprise's normal inventory or acquired specially for research and development activities) and equipment or facilities that are acquired or constructed for research and development activities and that have alternate future uses (in research and development projects or otherwise)." These costs, the Statement says, "shall be capitalized as tangible assets when acquired or constructed."

16.3 IMPAIRMENT OF VALUE

(a) AUTHORITATIVE PRONOUNCEMENTS. SFAS No. 144, *Accounting for the Impairment or Disposal of Long-Lived Assets* (FASB ASC 360-10), prescribes the accounting for the impairment of long-lived assets, including PP&E. The SFAS applies to PP&E that is "held and used" and to PP&E that is held for disposal (referred to in the Statement as *assets to be disposed of*).

(b) ASSETS TO BE HELD AND USED. SFAS No. 144 (FASB ASC 360-10) requires this three-step approach for recognizing and measuring the impairment of assets to be held and used:

1. Consider whether indicators of impairment of PP&E are present.
2. If indicators of impairment are present, determine whether the sum of the estimated undiscounted future cash flows attributable to the assets in question is less than their carrying amounts.
3. If less, recognize an impairment loss based on the excess of the carrying amount of the assets over their fair values.

(i) Recognition. SFAS No. 144 (FASB ASC 360-10) requires that PP&E that are used in operations be reviewed for impairment whenever events or changes in circumstances indicate that the carrying amount of the assets might not be recoverable—that is, information indicates that an impairment might exist. Accordingly, companies do not need to perform a periodic assessment of assets for impairment in the absence of such information. Instead, companies would assess the need for an impairment write-down only if an indicator of impairment is present. The SFAS lists these examples of events or changes in circumstances that may indicate to management that an impairment exists:

- A significant decrease in the market price of a long-lived asset (asset group)
- A significant adverse change in the extent or manner in which an asset (asset group) is used or in its physical condition

A significant adverse change in legal factors or in the business climate that could affect the value of a long-lived asset (asset group), including an adverse action or assessment by a regulator An accumulation of costs significantly in excess of the amount originally expected for the acquisition or construction of a long-lived asset (asset group) A current-period operating or cash flow loss combined with a history of operating or cash flow losses or a projection or forecast that demonstrates continuing losses associated with the use of a long-lived asset (asset group) A current expectation that, more likely than not, a long-lived asset (asset group) will be sold or otherwise disposed of significantly before the end of its previously estimated useful life. The term *more likely than not* refers to a level of likelihood that is more than 50 percent. The preceding list is not all-inclusive, and there may be other events or changes in circumstances, including circumstances that are peculiar to a company's business or industry, indicating that the carrying amount of a group of assets might not be recoverable and thus impaired. If indicators of impairment are present, companies must then disaggregate the assets by grouping them at the lowest level for which there are identifiable cash flows that are largely independent of the cash flows of other groups of assets. Then future cash flows expected to be generated from the use of those assets and their eventual disposal must be estimated. That estimate is comprised of the future cash inflows expected to be generated by the assets less the future cash outflows expected to be necessary to obtain those inflows. If the estimated undiscounted cash flows are less than the carrying amount of the assets, an impairment exists, and an impairment loss must be calculated and recognized.

The FASB recognized that certain long-lived assets could not be readily identified with specific cash flows (e.g., a corporate headquarters building and certain property and equipment of not-for-profit organizations). In those situations, the assets should be evaluated for impairment at an entity-wide level. If management estimates that the entity as a whole will generate cash flows sufficient to recover the carrying amount of all assets used in its operations, including its corporate headquarters building, no impairment loss would be recognized.

SFAS No. 144 (FASB ASC 360-10) provides little guidance for estimating future cash flows, even though the accounting consequences of small changes in those estimates could be significant. Accordingly, estimating future undiscounted cash flows requires a great deal of judgment. Companies must make their best estimate based on reasonable and supportable assumptions and projections that are applied on a consistent basis. The Statement indicates that all available evidence should be considered in developing the cash flow estimates, and the weight given that evidence should be commensurate with the extent to which the evidence can be verified objectively.

(ii) Measurement.   Once it is determined that an impairment exists, an impairment loss is calculated based on the excess of the carrying amount of the asset over the asset's *fair value*.

In September 2006, the FASB issued SFAS Statement No. 157, *Fair Value Measurements* (FASB ASC 820-10). It defines fair value, establishes a framework for measuring fair value in GAAP, and expands disclosure about fair value measurements. The effective date of SFAS No. 157 is for financial statements of fiscal years beginning after November 15, 2007. SFAS No. 157 (FASB ASC 820-10) defines *fair value* as "the price that would be received to sell an asset or paid to transfer a liability in an orderly transaction between market participants at the measurement date." FAS 157 (FASB ASC 820-10) discusses changes to current practice related to the definition of fair value and the methods used to measure fair value and expands disclosures about fair value measurements.

FAS 157 (FASB ASC 820-10) clarifies that the exchange price is the price in an orderly transaction between market participants to sell the asset or transfer the liability in the market in which the reporting entity would transact for the asset or liability (i.e., the principal or most advantageous market for the asset or liability). The transaction to sell the asset or transfer the liability is a hypothetical transaction at the measurement date, considered from the perspective of a market participant that holds the asset or owes the liability. Therefore, the definition focuses on the price that would be received to sell the asset or paid to transfer the liability (an exit price), not the price that would be paid to acquire the asset or received to assume the liability (an entry price).

Once management determines that an asset (or a group of assets) is impaired and the asset is written down to fair value, the reduced carrying amount represents the new cost basis of the asset. As a result, subsequent depreciation of the asset is based on the revised carrying amount, and companies are prohibited from reversing the impairment loss should facts and circumstances change or conditions improve in the future.

(c) ASSETS TO BE DISPOSED OF.   SFAS No. 144 (FASB ASC 360-10) indicates that assets to be disposed of other than by sale (e.g., abandonment, exchange for another long-lived asset) should continue to be classified as held and used until they are disposed of. An asset or asset group to be disposed of by sale should be classified as held for sale during the period in which all of these criteria are met:

- Management commits to a plan of disposal.
- The asset is available for immediate sale.
- An active program to locate a buyer has been initiated.
- Sale of the asset within one year is probable.

- The asset is being actively marketed for sale at a reasonable price.
- Actions required to complete the plan indicate that it is unlikely the plan will be significantly modified or withdrawn.

If at any time while an asset is classified as held for sale any of these criteria are no longer met or the entity's plans change, the asset should be reclassified to the held and used category. The asset should be reclassified at the lower of the original carrying amount immediately before it is transferred to held for sale (adjusted for any depreciation expense that would have been recognized had the asset been continuously classified as held and used) or fair value at the date of the change in status. An asset classified as held for sale should be measured at the lower of its carrying amount or fair value less incremental direct costs of sale. An asset classified as held for sale should not be depreciated. SFAS No. 144 (FASB ASC 360-10) requires subsequent revisions to the carrying amount of assets classified as held for sale if the estimate of fair value less cost to sale changes during the holding period. After an initial write-down of an asset to fair value less cost to sell, the carrying amount can be increased or decreased depending on changes in the fair value less cost to sell of the asset. However, an increase in carrying value cannot exceed the carrying amount of the asset immediately before its classification into the held for sale category.

SFAS No. 144 (FASB ASC 360-10) also supersedes APB Opinion No. 30 (FASB ASC 225-20) with respect to discontinued operations. The Statement indicates that the results of operations relating to assets to be disposed of comprising a component of an entity should be classified as discontinued operations if both of the next conditions are met:

1. The operations and cash flows of the component have been eliminated or will be eliminated from the ongoing operations of the entity as a result of the disposal.
2. The entity will not have any continuing involvement in the operations of the component after the disposal.

A *component of an entity* is defined as operations and cash flows that can be clearly distinguished from the rest of the entity both operationally and for financial reporting purposes. The definition of *component of an entity* under SFAS No. 144 (FASB ASC 360-10) is much broader than the APB Opinion No. 30 (FASB ASC 225-20) definition of a *segment of a business.* Accordingly, many more discontinued operations will be reported under SFAS No. 144 (FASB ASC 360-10) than previously. For example, if a real estate entity disposes of an individual property, that property would likely qualify as a component of an entity under SFAS No. 144 (FASB ASC 360-10) but generally would not have qualified as a disposal of a segment of a business under APB Opinion No. 30 (FASB ASC 225-20).

16.4 EXPENDITURES DURING OWNERSHIP

(a) DISTINGUISHING CAPITAL EXPENDITURES FROM OPERATING EXPENDITURES.   After PP&E have been acquired, additional expenditures are incurred to keep the assets in satisfactory operating condition. Certain of these expenditures—capital expenditures—are added to the asset's cost. The remainder—operating expenditures (sometimes called *revenue expenditures*)—are charged to expense.

Kohler defines a capital expenditure in two ways:

1. An expenditure intended to benefit future periods, in contrast to a revenue expenditure, which benefits a current period; an addition to a capital asset. The term is generally restricted to expenditures that add fixed-asset units or that have the effect of increasing the capacity, efficiency, life span, or economy of operation of an existing fixed asset.
2. Hence, any expenditure benefiting a future period.[8]

---

[8] Eric Louis Kohler, *Kohler's Dictionary for Accountants,* 6th ed. (Englewood Cliffs, NJ: Prentice-Hall, 1983).

Although the distinction is important, immaterial capital expenditures can be charged to expense. Expenditures during ownership fall into four categories:

1. Maintenance and repairs
2. Replacements, improvements, and additions
3. Rehabilitation
4. Rearrangement and reinstallation

(b) MAINTENANCE AND REPAIRS.   The terms *maintenance* and *repairs* generally are used interchangeably. However, Kohler defines them separately, and his definitions are useful in identifying expenditures that should be accounted for as maintenance and repairs. He defines *maintenance* as:

> The keeping of property in operable condition; also, the expense involved. Maintenance costs include outlays for (a) labor and supplies; (b) the replacement of any part that constitutes less than a retirement unit; and (c) major overhauls the items of which may involve elements of the first two classes. Items falling under (a) and (b) are always regarded as operating costs, chargeable to current expense directly or through the medium of a maintenance reserve.... Costs under (c) are similarly treated unless they include the replacement of a retirement unit the outlay for which is normally capitalized. [p. 315]

He defines *repairs* as:

> The restoration of a capital asset to its full productive capacity, or a contribution thereto, after damage, accident, or prolonged use, without increase in the asset's previously estimated service life or productive capacity. The term includes maintenance primarily "preventive" in character, and capitalizable extraordinary repairs. [p. 428]

(i) Accounting Alternatives.   As Kohler states, except for extraordinary repairs (or major overhauls), discussed in the next subsection, maintenance and repairs expenditures are accounted for in two ways:

1. Charge to expense when the cost is incurred
2. Charge to a maintenance allowance account

Charge to Expense When the Cost Is Incurred. Since ordinary maintenance and repairs expenditures are regarded as operating costs, they are usually charged directly to expense when incurred.

Charge to a Maintenance Allowance Account. The charge to expense may be accomplished through an allowance account. In some cases, the purpose of an allowance account is to equalize monthly repair costs within a year. Total repair costs are estimated at the beginning of the year, and the total is spread evenly throughout the year. The difference between the estimated and actual amounts at the end of the year is usually spread retroactively over all months of the year rather than being absorbed entirely by the last month. In the balance sheet, this allowance account may be treated as a reduction of the related asset account.[9]

This latter approach is supported by paragraph 16a of APB Opinion No. 28, *Interim Financial Reporting* (FASB ASC 270-10):

> When a cost that is expensed for annual reporting purposes clearly benefits two or more interim periods (e.g., annual major repairs), each interim period should be charged for an appropriate portion of the annual cost by the use of accruals or deferrals.

In other cases, the purpose of a maintenance allowance account is to charge the costs of major repairs over the entire period benefited, which may be longer than one year. When airlines acquire

---

[9] Ibid., p. 428.

new aircraft, for example, they begin immediately to accrue the cost of the first engine overhaul, which usually is scheduled for more than one year hence. As illustrated by the next example from 1987 financial statements, the accrual charges are credited to a maintenance allowance account, which is then charged for cost of the overhaul.

Stateswest Airlines, Inc. and Subsidiaries

Notes to Consolidated Financial Statements

Summary of Significant Accounting Policies

Engine Overhaul Reserve. For all the leased aircraft, the Company accrues maintenance expense, on the basis of hours flown, for the estimated cost of engine overhauls.

(ii) Extraordinary Repairs. Welsch, Anthony, and Short define *extraordinary repairs* as repairs that

> . . . occur infrequently, involve relatively large amounts of money, and tend to increase the economic usefulness of the asset in the future because of either greater efficiency or longer life, or both. They are represented by major overhauls, complete reconditioning, and major replacements and betterments.[10]

Because expenditures for extraordinary repairs increase the future economic usefulness of an asset, they benefit future periods and are therefore capital expenditures. Ordinarily, they are added to the related asset account, as illustrated in the next example from 1987 financial statements.

Air Midwest, Inc. and Subsidiaries

Notes to Consolidated Financial Statements

Note 1. Summary of Significant Accounting Policies

d. Maintenance and Repairs

Major renewals and betterments are capitalized and depreciated over the remaining useful life of the asset.

Some authorities recommend that the expenditures for extraordinary repairs be charged against the accumulated depreciation account. The rationale for charging accumulated depreciation is provided by Smith and Skousen:

> Often it is not possible to identify the cost related to a specific part of an asset. In these instances, by debiting accumulated depreciation, the undepreciated book value is increased without creating a build-up of the gross asset values.[11]

Other authorities argue against debiting accumulated depreciation for extraordinary repairs because the accumulated depreciation on the asset may be less than the cost of the repairs and because the practice allows the original cost of any parts replaced to remain in the asset account.

(c) REPLACEMENTS, IMPROVEMENTS, AND ADDITIONS. Replacements, improvements, and additions are related concepts. Kohler defines a *replacement* as "the substitution of one fixed asset for another, particularly of a new asset for an old, or of a new part for old part." He defines an *improvement* (which he calls a "betterment") as "an expenditure having the effect of extending the useful life of an existing fixed asset, increasing its normal rate of output, lowering its operating cost, increasing rather than merely maintaining efficiency or otherwise adding to the worth of benefits it

---

[10] Glenn A. Welsch, Robert N. Anthony, and Daniel G. Short, *Fundamentals of Financial Accounting* (Homewood, IL: Irwin, 1984).

[11] Smith and Skousen, *Intermediate Accounting, Comprehensive Volume.*

can yield."[12] Improvements ordinarily do not increase the physical size of the productive facility. Such an increase is an addition.

The distinctions among replacement, improvement, and addition notwithstanding, the accounting for all three is substantially the same. Expenditures for them are capital expenditures, that is, additions to PP&E. (In practice, immaterial amounts are often charged to expense.) The cost of existing assets that are replaced, together with their related accumulated depreciation accounts, is eliminated from the accounts.

(d) REHABILITATION.   Expenditures to rehabilitate buildings or equipment purchased in a rundown condition with the intention of rehabilitating them should be capitalized. Normally the acquisition price of a rundown asset is less than that of a comparable new asset, and the rehabilitation expenditures benefit future periods. Capitalization of the expenditures is therefore appropriate. However, the total capitalized cost of the asset should not exceed the amount recoverable through operations.

When rehabilitation takes place over an extended period, care should be taken to distinguish between the cost of rehabilitation and the cost of maintenance.

(e) REARRANGEMENT AND REINSTALLATION.   Kieso and Weygandt describe rearrangement and reinstallation costs and the accounting for them:

> Rearrangement and reinstallation costs, which are expenditures intended to benefit future periods, are different from additions, replacements and improvements. An example is the rearrangement and reinstallation of a group of machines to facilitate future production. If the original installation cost and the accumulated depreciation taken to date can be determined or estimated, the rearrangement and reinstallation cost can be handled as a replacement. If not, which is generally the case, the new costs if material in amount should be capitalized as an asset to be amortized over those future periods expected to benefit. If these costs are not material, if they cannot be separated from other operating expenses, or if their future benefit is questionable, they instead should be expensed in the period in which they are incurred.[13]

(f) ASBESTOS REMOVAL OR CONTAINMENT.   Removal or containment of asbestos is regulated and required by various federal, state, and local laws. The diversity of practice in capitalizing or expensing the cost of asbestos removal or containment resulted in asbestos removal being considered by the EITF. Issue No. 89-13 (FASB ASC 410-20) asked "whether the costs incurred to treat asbestos when a property with a known asbestos problem is acquired should be capitalized or charged to expense" and "whether the costs incurred to treat asbestos in an existing property should be capitalized or charged to expense."

The EITF concluded that the costs incurred to treat asbestos within a reasonable time period after a property with a known asbestos problem is acquired should be capitalized as part of the cost of the acquired property subject to an impairment test for that property. The consensus on existing property was not as conclusive and stated that the costs "may be capitalized as a betterment subject to an impairment test for that property."

The EITF also reached a consensus that when costs are incurred in anticipation of a sale of property, they should be deferred and recognized in the period of the sale to the extent that those costs can be recovered from the estimated sales price.

The SEC observer at the EITF meeting noted that regardless of whether asbestos treatment costs are capitalized or charged to expense, Securities and Exchange Commission (SEC) registrants should disclose significant exposure for asbestos treatment costs in "Management's Discussion and Analysis."

---

[12] Kohler, *Kohler's Dictionary for Accountants.*
[13] Donald E. Kieso and Jerry J. Weygandt, *Intermediate Accounting,* 5th ed. (New York: John Wiley & Sons, 1986).

The EITF in Issue No. 90-8 (FASB ASC 410-30) affirmed the Issue No. 89-13 (FASB ASC 410-30) consensus but did not provide further guidance on capitalizing or charging to expense the costs incurred on existing properties. In practice, there continues to be wide diversity of the types of costs capitalized, if any, and the accrual of costs to remove or contain asbestos in existing properties.

(g) COSTS TO TREAT ENVIRONMENTAL CONTAMINATION. Costs to remove, contain, neutralize, or prevent existing or future environmental contamination may be incurred voluntarily or as required by federal, state, and local laws. In Issue No. 90-8 (FASB ASC 410-30), the EITF considered whether environmental contamination treatment costs should be capitalized or charged to expense.

The EITF reached a consensus that, in general, environmental contamination treatment costs should be charged to expense unless the costs are recoverable and meet one of three criteria:

1. The costs extend the life, increase the capacity, or improve the safety or efficiency of property owned by the company. For purposes of this criterion, the condition of that property after the costs are incurred must be improved as compared with the condition of that property when originally constructed or acquired, if later.

2. The costs mitigate or prevent environmental contamination that has yet to occur and that otherwise may result from future operations or activities. In addition, the costs improve the property compared with its condition when constructed or acquired, if later.

3. The costs are incurred in preparing for sale property currently held for sale.

Costs to remediate environmental contamination that do not meet one of these criteria should be expensed under the provisions of the AICPA's SOP No. 96-1, *Environmental Remediation Liabilities* (FASB ASC 410-30), which provides authoritative guidance on the recognition, measurement, display, and disclosure of environmental remediation liabilities. The AICPA issued SOP No. 96-1 (FASB ASC 410-30) to improve and narrow the manner in which existing authoritative accounting literature, principally SFAS No. 5, *Accounting for Contingencies* (FASB ASC 450-10), is applied in recognizing, measuring, and disclosing environmental liabilities.

SFAS No. 5 (FASB ASC 450-10) generally requires loss contingencies to be accrued when they are both probable and estimable. According to SOP No. 96-1 (FASB ASC 410-30), the probability criterion of SFAS No. 5 is met for environmental liabilities if both of the next conditions have occurred on or before the date the financial statements are issued:

- Litigation, a claim, or an assessment has been asserted, or is probable of being asserted.
- It is probable that the outcome of such litigation, claim, or assessment will be unfavorable.

The AICPA concluded that there is a presumption that the outcome will be unfavorable if litigation, a claim, or an assessment has been asserted, or is probable of assertion and if the entity is associated with the site. Assuming that both of the preceding conditions are met, a company would need to accrue at least the minimum amount that can reasonably be estimated as an environmental remediation liability.

Once a company has determined that it is probable that a liability has been incurred, the entity should estimate the remediation liability based on available information. In estimating its allocable share of costs, a company should include incremental direct costs of the remediation effort and postremediation monitoring costs that are expected to be incurred after the remediation is complete. An entity also should include in its estimate costs of compensation and related benefit costs for employees who are expected to devote a significant amount of their time directly to the remediation effort. The accrual of expected legal defense costs related to remediation is not required.

In cases in which joint and several liability exists and the company is one of several parties responsible for remediation, which often is the case, the entity is required to estimate the percentage of the liability that it will be allocated. The entity also must assess the likelihood that each of the other parties will pay its allocable share of the remediation liability. An entity would accrue its estimated share of amounts related to the site that will not be paid by other parties or the government.

SOP No. 96-1 (FASB ASC 410-30) provides that discounting environmental liabilities is permitted, but not required, only if the aggregate amount of the obligation and the amount and timing of the cash payments are fixed or reliably determinable. Because of the nature of the remediation process and the inherent subjectivity involved in estimating remediation liabilities, most companies will find it difficult to meet the criteria for discounting.

An asset relating to recoveries can be recognized only when realization of the claim for recovery is deemed probable. If a claim for recovery is the subject of litigation, a rebuttable presumption exists that realization of the claim is not probable. An environmental liability should be evaluated independently from any potential claim for recovery. SOP No. 96-1(FASB ASC 410-30) requires that probable recoveries be recorded at fair value. However, discounting a recovery claim is not required in determining the value of the recovery when the related liability is not discounted and the timing of the recovery is dependent on the timing of the payment of the liability.

The EITF provided examples of applying the consensus in Issue No. 90-8 (FASB ASC 410-30).

16.5 DISPOSALS

Asset disposals may be voluntary, through retirement, sale, or trade-in, or involuntary, from fire, storm, flood, or other casualty. In general, these terms have the same meaning for accounting purposes as they do in ordinary discourse. The one exception is retirement, which for accounting purposes means the removal of an asset from service, whether the asset is removed physically or not. This is clear from Kohler's definition of retirement as "the removal of a fixed asset from service, following its sale or the end of its productive life, accompanied by the necessary adjustment of fixed asset and depreciation-reserve accounts."

(a) RETIREMENTS, SALES, AND TRADE-INS.   Davidson, Stickney, and Weil describe the accounting for retirements, which applies also to assets that are sold or traded in:

> When an asset is retired from service, the cost of the asset and the related amount of accumulated depreciation must be removed from the books. As part of this entry, the amount received from the sale or trade-in and any difference between that amount and book value must be recorded. The difference between the proceeds received on retirement and book value is a gain (if positive) or a loss (if negative).[14]

As discussed next, when composite or group rate depreciation is used, no gain or loss on disposal is recognized.

When an asset is traded in, the amount that should in theory be recorded as received from the trade-in is the asset's fair market value (which is not necessarily the amount by which the cash purchase price of the replacement asset is reduced). However, in practice, a reliable market value for the old asset may not be available. In that case, the usual practice is to recognize no gain or loss on the exchange but to record as the acquisition cost of the replacement asset the net book value of the old asset plus the cash or other consideration paid.

(b) CASUALTIES.   Casualties, the accidental loss or destruction of assets, can give rise to gain or loss, even when the assets are replaced. Paragraph 2 of FASB Interpretation No. (FIN) No. 30, *Accounting for Involuntary Conversions of Nonmonetary Assets to Monetary Assets* (FASB ASC 605-40) makes this clear:

> Involuntary conversions of nonmonetary assets to monetary assets are monetary transactions for which gain or loss shall be recognized even though an enterprise reinvests or is obligated to reinvest the monetary assets in replacement nonmonetary assets.

---

[14] Sidney Davidson, Clyde P. Stickney, and Roman L. Weil, *Financial Accounting: An Introduction to Concepts, Methods and Uses,* 5th ed. (Hinsdale, IL: Dryden Press, 1988).

16.6 ASSET RETIREMENT OBLIGATIONS

SFAS No. 143, *Accounting for Asset Retirement Obligations* (FASB ASC 410-20) was issued in June 2001. This project was undertaken by the FASB because diversity in practice had developed in accounting for the obligations associated with the retirement of long-lived assets. Some entities were accruing the obligations over the life of the related asset either as a liability or a reduction of the carrying amount of the asset while others did not recognize the liability until the asset was retired. The Statement requires that a liability be recorded for legal obligations resulting from the acquisition, construction, or development and normal operations of a long-lived asset.

(a) INITIAL RECOGNITION AND MEASUREMENT.   If a reasonable estimate of an asset retirement obligation can be made, an entity should recognize the fair value of the liability in the period in which it is incurred. In accordance with FAS 143 par 8 (FASB ASC 410-20):

> An expected present value technique will usually be the only appropriate technique with which to estimate the fair value of a liability for an asset retirement obligation. An entity, when using that technique, shall discount the expected cash flows using a credit-adjusted risk-free rate. Thus, the effect of an entity's credit standing is reflected in the discount rate rather than in the expected cash flows. Proper application of a discount rate adjustment technique entails analysis of at least two liabilities—the liability that exists in the marketplace and has an observable interest rate and the liability being measured. The appropriate rate of interest for the cash flows being measured shall be inferred from the observable rate of interest of some other liability, and to draw that inference the characteristics of the cash flows shall be similar to those of the liability being measured.

When an asset retirement obligation is initially recognized, the entity should capitalize an asset retirement cost by increasing the carrying amount of the related long-lived asset by the same amount. This cost should be charged to expense over the estimated useful life of the asset. When the asset is tested for impairment under SFAS No. 144 (FASB ASC 360-10), the asset retirement cost should be included in the carrying value tested for impairment.

(b) SUBSEQUENT RECOGNITION AND MEASUREMENT.   Subsequent to initial recognition, an entity should recognize period-to-period changes in the asset retirement liability for the passage of time and revisions to either the timing or amount of the original estimate of undiscounted cash flows. Adjustments for the passage of time should use an interest method based on the credit-adjusted risk-free rate at the time of initial recognition of the liability. The adjustment should increase the amount of the liability and be charged to accretion expense. Adjustments relating to revisions in the timing or amounts of cash flows will increase or decrease the asset retirement liability and the related asset.

16.7 DEPRECIATION

PP&E used by a business in the production of goods and services is a depreciable asset. That is, its cost is systematically amortized by charges to goods produced or to operations over the asset's estimated useful service life. That meaning is captured by International Accounting Standards (IAS) Statement No. 4, *Depreciation Accounting,* which defines *depreciable assets* as

> assets that (a) are expected to be used during more than one accounting period, and (b) have a limited useful life, and (c) are held by an enterprise for use in the production or supply of goods and services, for rental to others, or for administrative purposes.

(a) *DEPRECIATION* DEFINED.   Despite its widespread use, *depreciation* has no single, universal definition. Economists, engineers, the courts, accountants, and others have definitions that meet their particular needs. Seldom are the definitions identical.

The generally accepted accounting definition is set forth in Accounting Terminology Bulletin No. 1 (AICPA, 1961):

Depreciation accounting is a system of accounting which aims to distribute the cost or other basic value of tangible capital assets, less salvage (if any), over the estimated useful life of the unit (which may be a group of assets) in a systematic and rational manner. It is a process of allocation, not of valuation. Depreciation for the year is the portion of the total charge under such a system that is allocated to the year.

As the definition says, depreciation accounting is "a process of allocation, not of valuation." That is, its purpose is to allocate the net cost (cost less salvage) of an asset over time, not to state the asset at its current or long-term value.

Depreciation, as accountants use the term, applies only to buildings, machinery, and equipment. It is thus distinguished first from depletion, which is a process of allocating the cost of wasting resources, such as mineral deposits, and second from amortization, which is a process of allocating the cost of intangible assets.

(b) BASIC FACTORS IN THE COMPUTATION OF DEPRECIATION.   Three basic factors enter in the computation of depreciation:

1. The estimate of the service life (sometimes called the *useful life*) of the asset
2. The determination of the depreciation base
3. The choice of a depreciation method

16.8 SERVICE LIFE

(a) SERVICE LIFE AS DISTINGUISHED FROM PHYSICAL LIFE.   Depreciation allocates the net cost of an asset over its service life, not its physical life. The service life of an asset represents the period of usefulness to its present owner. The physical life of an asset represents its total period of usefulness, perhaps to more than one owner. For any given asset, and any given owner, physical and service life may be identical, or service life may be shorter. For example, a company that supplies automobiles to its sales force may replace its automobiles every 50,000 miles. An automobile's physical life is usually longer than 50,000 miles. But to this particular company, the service life of an automobile in its fleet is 50,000 miles, and the company's depreciation policies would allocate the net cost of its automobiles over 50,000 miles.

(b) FACTORS AFFECTING SERVICE LIFE.   Service life may be affected by two factors physical or functional as follows:

1. Physical factors:
   a. Wear and tear
   b. Deterioration and decay
   c. Damage or destruction
2. Functional factors:
   a. Inadequacy
   b. Obsolescence

(i) Physical Factors.   Mosich and Larsen discuss physical factors:

Physical deterioration results largely from wear and tear from use and the forces of nature. These physical forces terminate the usefulness of plant assets by rendering them incapable of performing the services for which they were intended and thus set the maximum limit on economic life.[15]

Wear and tear and deterioration and decay act gradually and are reasonably predictable. They are ordinarily taken into consideration in estimating service life. Damage or destruction, however, usually occurs suddenly, irregularly, infrequently, and unpredictably. Either one is ordinarily not taken into consideration in estimating service life. Its effects are therefore usually not recognized in the depreciation charge but as a charge to expense when the damage or destruction occurs.

(ii) Functional Factors.   Asset inadequacy may result from business growth, requiring the company to replace existing assets with larger or more efficient assets. Or assets may become inadequate because of changes in the market, in plant location, in the nature or variety of products manufactured, or in the ownership of the business. For example, a warehouse may be in good structural condition, but if more space is needed and cannot be economically provided by adding a wing or a separate building, the warehouse has become inadequate, and its remaining service life to its present owner is ended.

Obsolescence usually arises from events that are more clearly external, such as progress, invention, technological advances, and improvements. For example, the Boeing 707 and the Douglas DC-8 jet aircraft made many propeller-driven airplanes obsolete, at least as to major airlines, because propeller-driven planes were no longer economical in long-range service, compared to more modern and efficient jets.

A distinction should be made between ordinary obsolescence and extraordinary obsolescence. Ordinary obsolescence is due to normal, reasonably predictable technical progress; extraordinary obsolescence arises from unforeseen events that result in an asset being abandoned earlier than expected. For example, computers and related software generally have a short service life span in anticipation of more advanced computers and software releases in the market within a few years.

According to the American Accounting Association (AAA) publication, *A Statement of Basic Accounting Theory:* "Obsolescence, to the extent it can be quantified by equipment replacement studies or similar means, should be recognized explicitly and regularly." Thus ordinary obsolescence, like wear and tear, should be considered in estimating useful life so that it can be recognized in the annual depreciation charge. But extraordinary obsolescence, like damage or destruction, is recognized outside depreciation accounting as a charge when it occurs.

(c) EFFECT OF MAINTENANCE.   As Welsch and Zlatkovich note, "The useful life of operational assets also is influenced by the repair and maintenance policies of the company."[16] The expected effect of a company's maintenance policy is therefore considered in estimating service lives.

(d) STATISTICAL METHODS OF ESTIMATING SERVICE LIVES.   In several industries, notably utilities, estimates of service lives have been based on historical analyses of retirement rates for specific groups of assets, such as telephone or electric wire poles. These analyses have resulted in the development of statistical techniques for predicting retirement rates and service lives. Utilities have used such techniques in defending depreciation practices, replacement needs and policies, and investment valuations for rate-making purposes. Statistical techniques are appropriate for any group of homogeneous assets where estimating individual service lives is not possible or practical (e.g., mattresses and linens in a hotel, overhead and underground cables of telephone companies, and rails and ties for railroads).

Grant and Norton mention two other statistical approaches to determining service lives:

1. *Actuarial methods,* which aim at determining survivor curves and frequency curves for annual retirements, as well as giving estimates of average life. These methods are generally similar to the methods developed by life insurance actuaries for the study of human mortality. They require plant records in sufficient detail so that the age of each unit of plant is known at all times.

---

[15] Mosich and Larsen, *Intermediate Accounting.*
[16] Welsch and Zlatkovich, *Intermediate Accounting.*

2. *Turnover methods,* which aim only at estimating average life. Since turnover methods require only information about additions and retirements, they require less detail in the plant records than do actuarial methods.[17]

(e) SERVICE LIVES OF LEASEHOLD IMPROVEMENTS.   Leasehold improvements are depreciated over the shorter of the remaining term of the lease or the expected life of the asset. Lease renewal terms are usually not considered unless renewal is probable.

In February 2005, almost concurrent with the filing of the first wave of Sarbanes-Oxley Section 404 filings, the SEC clarified that certain accounting principles for leasehold improvements, rent holidays and landlord/tenant incentives should be followed, despite "industry practice" that had arisen where these principles were not always being adhered to. This clarification forced a spate of restatements and material weakness determinations by some larger retail establishments. The timing of this announcement made it difficult for some companies to remediate the control deficiency in time to avoid reporting a material weakness in internal controls. The letter from the SEC Chief Accountant Don Nicolaison can be found at: *www.sec.gov/info/accountants/staffletters/cpcaf020705.htm.*

(f) REVISIONS OF ESTIMATED SERVICE LIVES.   Service life estimates should be reviewed periodically and revised as appropriate. The National Association of Accountants (NAA) Statement on Management Accounting Practices No. 7, *Fixed Asset Accounting: The Allocation of Costs,* suggests that reviews of estimates involve operations, management, engineering, and accounting personnel.

A change in the estimated useful lives of depreciable assets should be accounted for as a change in an accounting estimate. As prescribed by SFAS No. 154, *Accounting Changes and Error Corrections* (FASB ASC 250-10), a change in accounting estimate should be accounted for in the period of change if the change affects that period only or in the period of change and future periods if the change affects both. A change in accounting estimate should not be accounted for by restating or retrospectively adjusting amounts reported in financial statements of prior periods or by reporting pro forma amounts for prior periods.

If future periods are affected, the Opinion also requires disclosure of the effect on income from continuing operations, net income (or other appropriate captions of changes in the applicable net assets or performance indicator), and any related per-share amounts of the current period. An example of this disclosure from 2007 financial statements follows.

Tanger Properties Ltd. Partnership/Form 10-K (Period-End 12/31/07)

Change in Accounting Estimate

During the first quarter of 2007, the general partner's Board of Trustees formally approved a plan to reconfigure our center in Foley, Alabama. As a part of this plan, approximately 42,000 square feet was relocated within the property by September 2007. The depreciable useful lives of the buildings demolished were shortened to coincide with their demolition dates throughout the first three quarters of 2007 and the change in estimated useful life was accounted for as a change in accounting estimate. Approximately 28,000 relocated square feet had opened as of December 31, 2007, with the remaining 14,000 square feet expected to open in the next two quarters. Accelerated depreciation recognized related to the reconfiguration reduced income from continuing operations and net income by approximately $6.0 million for the year ended December 31, 2007. The effect on income from continuing operations per diluted unit and net income per diluted unit was a decrease of $.32 per unit for the year ended December 31, 2007.

---

[17] E. Grant and P. Norton, *Depreciation* (New York: Ronald Press, 1955).

16.9 DEPRECIATION BASE

The cost to be depreciated, otherwise known as the *depreciation base,* is the total cost of an asset less its estimated net salvage value. When immaterial, net salvage value is commonly ignored.

(a) NET SALVAGE VALUE.   *Kohler's Dictionary for Accountants* defines *salvage* as: "Value remaining from a fire, wreck, or other accident or from the retirement or scrapping of an asset."[18] Salvage value may be determined by reference to quoted market prices for similar items or to estimated reproduction costs, reduced by an allowance for usage. Salvage value reduced by the cost to remove the asset is net salvage value.

Net salvage value can be taken into account in either of two ways: directly, by reducing the depreciation base, or, indirectly, by adjusting the depreciation rate.

To illustrate the latter, assume an asset with a total cost of $1,000, a service life of 10 years, and an estimated net salvage value of $250. A 7.5 percent rate applied to the cost will yield the same annual depreciation charge as a 10 percent rate applied to cost less estimated net salvage value. This point should be borne in mind in interpreting stated rates of depreciation; the rates may be applied to the asset cost or to cost less net salvage value.

(b) PROPERTY UNDER CONSTRUCTION.   Assets are generally not depreciated during construction, which includes any necessary pilot testing or breaking in. Such assets are not yet placed in service, and the purpose of depreciation accounting is to allocate the cost of an asset over its service life.

An exception to the general rule arises when an asset under construction is partially used in an income-producing activity. In that case, the part in use should be depreciated. An example is a building that is partially rented while still under construction.

(c) IDLE AND AUXILIARY EQUIPMENT.   NAA Statement on Management Accounting Practices No. 7 recommends that depreciation be continued on idle, reserve, or standby assets. When the period of idleness is expected to be long, the assets should be separately disclosed in the balance sheet; however, depreciation should continue.

(d) ASSETS TO BE DISPOSED OF.   SFAS No. 144 (FASB ASC 360-10) prohibits depreciation from being recorded during the period in which the asset is being held for disposal, even if the asset is still generating revenue.

(e) USED ASSETS.   The depreciation base of a used asset is the same as for a new asset, that is, cost less net salvage value. The carrying value of a used asset in the accounts of the previous owner should not be carried over to the accounts of the new owner. See, however, Chapter 8 for the accounting for assets acquired in a business combination.

16.10 DEPRECIATION METHODS

Assets are depreciated by a variety of methods, including these five:

1. Straight-line method
2. Usage methods:
   a. Service-hours method
   b. Productive-output method
3. Decreasing-charge methods:
   a. Sum-of-digits method

---

[18] Kohler, *Kohler's Dictionary for Accountants*

    b. Fixed-percentage-of-declining-balance method

    c. Double-declining-balance method

  4. Interest methods:

    a. Annuity method

    b. Sinking-fund method

  5. Other methods:

    a. Appraisal method

    b. Retirement method

    c. Replacement method

    d. Arbitrary assignment

(a) STRAIGHT-LINE METHOD.   This method recognizes equal periodic depreciation charges over the service life of an asset, thereby making depreciation a function solely of time without regard to asset productivity, efficiency, or usage. The periodic depreciation charge is computed by dividing the cost of the asset, less net salvage value, by the service life expressed in months or years:

$$\frac{\text{Cost} - \text{Net salvage value}}{\text{Service life}} = \text{Depreciation charge per period}$$

Assuming an asset cost \$15,000 and has an estimated net salvage value of \$750 (5 percent of cost) and a service life of 10 years, the annual depreciation charge would be \$1,425, calculated as:

$$\frac{\$15,000 - \$750}{10 \text{ years}} = \$1,425$$

When the use or productivity of an asset differs significantly over its life, the straight-line method produces what some believe is a distorted allocation of costs. For example, if an asset is more productive during its early life than later, some view an equal amount of depreciation in each year as distorted. Nevertheless, the method is widely used because of its simplicity.

A survey reported by Lamden, Gerboth, and McRae showed that the straight-line method is most frequently used for financial statement purposes by companies with these five characteristics:

  1. Relatively large investments in depreciable assets

  2. Relatively high depreciation charges

  3. Stock traded on one of the major stock exchanges or in the over-the-counter market

  4. Managements with a high level of concern for (a) matching costs with revenues and (b) maintaining comparability with other firms in the industry

  5. Managements with a low level of concern for conforming depreciation for financial statement to depreciation for tax purposes[19]

(b) USAGE METHODS.   Two other methods, the service-hours method and the productive-output method, vary the periodic depreciation charge to recognize differences in asset use or productivity.

(i) Service-Hours Method.   This method assumes that if an asset is used twice as much in period 1 as in period 2, the depreciation charge should differ accordingly. The depreciation rate is calculated as it is for the straight-line method, except that service life is expressed in terms of hours of use:

$$\frac{\text{Cost} - \text{Net salvage value}}{\text{Service life}} = \text{Rate per hour of use}$$

---

[19] Lamden, Gerboth, and McRae, *Accounting for Depreciable Assets.*

If an asset cost $15,000 and had an estimated net salvage value of $750 and an estimated service life of 38,000 hours, the calculation would be:

$$\frac{\$15,000 - \$750}{38,00 \text{ hours}} = \$0.375 \text{ per hour of use}$$

If the asset is used 4,000 hours in the first year, the annual depreciation charge would be $1,500 (4,000 hours × $0.375 per hour).

Welsch and Zlatkovich state, "The service hours method usually is appropriate when obsolescence is not a primary factor in depreciation and the economic service potential of the asset is used up primarily by running time."[20]

(ii) Productive-Output Method. This method is essentially the same as the service-hours method, except that service life is expressed in terms of units of production rather than hours of use. If the asset just described had a service life of 95,000 units of production rather than 38,000 hours of use, the depreciation rate would be calculated as:

$$\frac{\$15,000 - \$750}{95,00 \text{ units}} = \$0.15 \text{ per unit of product}$$

Depreciation by the productive-output method is illustrated by the next example from 1987 financial statements:

McDermott International, Inc.

Notes to Consolidated Financial Statements

Note 3. Change in Depreciation Method

Effective April 1, 1986, McDermott International changed the method of depreciation for major marine vessels from the straight-line method to a units-of-production method based on the utilization of each vessel. Depreciation expense calculated under the units-of-production method may be less than, equal to, or greater than depreciation expense calculated under the straight-line method in any period. McDermott International employs utilization factors as a key element in the management of marine construction operations and believes the units-of-production method, which recognizes both time and utilization factors, accomplishes a better matching of costs and revenues than the straight-line method. The cumulative effect of the change on prior years at March 31, 1986, of $25,711,000, net of income taxes of $17,362,000 ($0.70 per share), is included in the accompanying Consolidated Statement of Income (Loss) and Retained Earnings for the fiscal year ended March 31, 1987. The effect of the change on the fiscal year ended March 31, 1987, was to increase Income from Continuing Operations before Extraordinary Items and Cumulative Effect of Accounting Change and decrease Net Loss $6,556,000 ($0.18 per share). Pro forma amounts showing the effect of applying the units-of-production method of depreciation retroactively, net of related income taxes, are presented in the Consolidated Statement of Income (Loss) and Retained Earnings.

The productive-output method is sometimes used to adjust depreciation calculated by the straight-line method, when asset usage varies from normal. The adjustment may be limited to a specified range, as illustrated in this example drawn from 1986 financial statements:

Wheeling-Pittsburgh Steel Corporation

Notes to Financial Statements

---

[20] Welsch and Zlatkovich, *Intermediate Accounting.*

Note G. Property, Plant, and Equipment

The Corporation utilizes the modified units-of-production method of depreciation which recognizes that the depreciation of steelmaking machinery is related to the physical wear of the equipment as well as a time factor. The modified units-of-production method provides for straight-line depreciation charges modified (adjusted) by the level of production activity. On an annual basis, adjustments may not exceed a range of 60% (minimum) to 110% (maximum) of related straight-line depreciation. The adjustments are based on the ratio of actual production to a predetermined norm. Eighty-five percent of capacity is considered the norm for the Corporation's primary steelmaking facilities; 80% of capacity is considered the norm for finishing facilities. No adjustment is made when the production level is equal to norm. In 1986 depreciation under the modified units of production method exceeded straight-line depreciation by $1.5 million or 3.2%. For 1985 and 1984 aggregate straight-line depreciation exceeded that recorded under the modified units-of-production method by $10.1 million or 18.3%, $7.0 million or 12.6%, respectively.

The productive-output method recognizes that not all hours of use are equally productive. Therefore, the theory underlying the preference for a usage method would point to the productive-output method as the better of the two.

(c) DECREASING-CHARGE METHODS.   Decreasing-charge methods allocate a higher depreciation charge to the early years of an asset's service life. These methods are justified on the next grounds:

- Most equipment is more efficient (hence more productive) in its early life. Therefore, the early years of service life should bear more of the asset's cost.
- Repairs and maintenance charges generally increase as an asset gets older. Therefore, depreciation charges should decrease as the asset gets older so as to produce a more stable total charge (repairs and maintenance plus depreciation) for the use of the asset during its service life.

(i) Sum-of-Digits Method.   This method applies a decreasing rate to a constant depreciation base (cost less net salvage value). The rate is a fraction. The denominator is the sum of the digits representing periods (years or months) of asset life. The numerator, which changes each period, is the digit assigned to the particular period. Digits are assigned in reverse order. For example, if an asset has an estimated service life of five years, the denominator would be 15, calculated as:

$$1 + 2 + 3 + 4 + 5 = 15$$

In the first year the rate fraction would be 5/15, in the second year 4/15, in the third year 3/15, and so on. The denominator may be calculated by means of the next formula, where n is the service life in years or months:

$$\frac{n+1}{2} \times n = \text{Denominator}$$

For example, if the service life is estimated to be 25 years:

$$\frac{25+1}{2} \times 25 = 325$$

(ii) Fixed-Percentage-of-Declining-Balance Method.   This method produces results similar to the sum-of-digits method. However, whereas the sum-of-digits method multiplies a declining rate times a fixed balance, the fixed-percentage-of-declining-balance method multiplies a fixed rate times a declining balance. The rate is calculated by means of the next formula, where n equals the service life in years:

$$\text{Depreciation rate} = 1 - \sqrt[n]{\frac{\text{Net salvage value}}{\text{Cost}}}$$

The rate thus determined is then applied to the cost of the asset, without regard to salvage value, reduced by depreciation previously recognized. The result is to reduce the cost of the asset to its estimated net salvage value at the end of the asset's service life. (Some salvage value must be assigned to the asset, since it is not possible to reduce an amount to zero by applying a constant rate to a successively smaller remainder. In the absence of an expected salvage value, a nominal value of $1 can be assumed.)

To illustrate, assume an asset with a cost of $10,000, an estimated salvage value of $1,296, and an estimated service life of four years:

$$\text{Depreciation rate} = 1 - \sqrt[4]{\frac{\$1,296}{\$10,000}} = 1 - \frac{6}{10} = 40\%$$

The first year's depreciation will be $4,000 ($10,000 × 40%), the second year's $2,400 [($10,000 − $4,000) × 40%], and so on, leaving at the end of the fourth year a net asset of $1,296.

(iii) Double-Declining-Balance Method. The double-declining-balance method was introduced into the income tax laws in 1954. Since then, it has gained increased acceptability for financial reporting as well. This method differs from the fixed-percentage-of-declining-balance method by specifying that the fixed rate should be twice the straight-line rate. Otherwise the two methods are identical: The fixed rate is applied to the undepreciated book value of the asset—a declining balance.

To illustrate, assume an asset with a cost of $15,000, an estimated net salvage value of $750, and an estimated service life of 10 years. Twice the straight-line rate would be 20 percent. Exhibit 16.1 shows the calculation for the first four years.

Note that, as with the fixed-percentage-of-declining-balance method, the rate is applied to the cost of the asset without regard to net salvage value. This means that by the end of the asset's estimated service life, some amount of undepreciated book value will be left in the asset account. But since the depreciation rate is determined without regard to estimated net salvage value, the undepreciated amount left in the account will likely differ from net salvage value. For example, at the end of the 10-year service life of the asset illustrated in Exhibit 16.1, the asset's book value would be $1,611, which is $861 greater than estimated net salvage value. To avoid such differences, companies usually switch from the double-declining-balance method to the straight-line method sometime during an asset's service life.

To calculate the straight-line depreciation charge at the time of the switch, the net book value (cost less accumulated depreciation), less estimated net salvage value, is divided by the estimated

Year	Book Value Beginning of Period	Rate (%)	Annual Depreciation Charge	Book Value End of Period
1	$15,000	20	$3,000	$12,000
2	12,000	20	2,400	9,600
3	9,600	20	1,920	7,680
4	7,680	20	1,536	6,144

Exhibit 16.1   Depreciation Using the Double-Declining-Balance Method

Year	Straight-Line	Sum-of-Digits	Double-Declining-Balance, Switch to Straight-Line
1	$ 14,250	$ 2,591	$ 3,000
2	1,425	2,322	2,400
3	1,425	2,073	1,920
4	1,425	1,814	1,536
5	1,425	1,555	1,229
6	1,425	1,295	983
7	1,425	1,036	796
8	1,425	777	796
9	1,425	518	795
10	1,425	259	795
	$ 14,250	$ 14,250	$ 14,250

Exhibit 16.2   Comparison of Annual Depreciation Charges: Straight-Line, Sum-of-Digits, and Declining-Balance with Switch to Straight Line

remaining service life. For example, if an asset has a remaining depreciation base (cost less estimated net salvage value) of $4,620 and seven years of remaining service life, a straight-line charge of $660 for the next seven years will depreciate the asset to its net salvage value.

The optimal time to make a switch is when the year's depreciation computed using the straight-line method exceeds depreciation computed using the double-declining-balance method. That is usually sometime after the midpoint of the asset's life.

Exhibit 16.2 compares the annual depreciation charges computed by the straight-line method, the sum-of-digits method, and the double-declining-balance method with switch to straight-line.

Note that although all three methods charge the same total amount to expense over the same service life, the amounts charged at the midpoint of the asset's service life differ:

1. Straight-line has charged 50 percent of the total.
2. Sum-of-digits has charged nearly 73 percent.
3. Double-declining-balance with switch to straight-line has charged about 71 percent.

(d) INTEREST METHODS. Two methods, the annuity method and the sinking-fund method, compute depreciation using compound interest factors. Both methods produce an increasing annual depreciation charge. Neither method is used much in practice.

(i) Annuity Method. The annuity method equalizes each year's sum of depreciation and an imputed interest charge calculated at a constant rate on the asset's undepreciated book value. Each year's sum of depreciation and imputed interest is calculated by the next formula, where n is the estimated service life of the asset in years and i is the imputed rate of interest:

$$\frac{\text{Cost of asset less present value of net salvage value}}{\text{Present value of an ordinary of annuity of } n \text{ payments of 1 at } i}$$

Assume, for example, that an asset with an economic life of five years and a net salvage value of $67,388 is acquired at a cost of $800,000. Using an imputed rate of interest of 10 percent, each year's sum of depreciation and imputed interest would be computed as:

$$\frac{\$800,000 - (\$67,388 \times 0.620921^*)}{3.790787}$$

$$\frac{\$800,000 - \$41,843}{3.790787}$$

$$= \$200,000$$

*Present Value of $1 for five periods at 10%.

The result is presented in Exhibit 16.3.

Imputed interest is computed only for purposes of computing depreciation; it is not charged to expense.

(ii) Sinking-Fund Method. The sinking-fund method produces a depreciation pattern that is identical to that of the annuity method but by means of a different rationale and a different formula. Under the sinking-fund method, the amount of annual depreciation is equal to the increase in a hypothetical interest-earning asset replacement fund. The increase in the fund consists of assumed equal periodic deposits to the fund plus interest at the assumed rate on the fund balance.

Each year's depreciation charge is calculated by the next formula, where n is the remaining service life of the asset in years and i is the assumed rate of interest:

$$\text{Depreciation} = \frac{\text{Cost of asset less net residual value}}{\text{Ordinary annuity of } n \text{ payments of 1 at } i}$$

Using the same facts as in Exhibit 16.3 (an asset cost of $800,000, a 5-year life, a net salvage value of $67,388, and a 10 percent interest rate), the first year's depreciation would be computed as:

$$\text{Depreciation} = \frac{\text{Cost of asset less net residual value}}{\text{Ordinary annuity of 5 payments of 1 at 10\%}}$$

$$\frac{\$800,000 - \$67,388}{6.1051}$$

$$= \$120,000$$

Year	Combined Depreciation and Imputed Interest	Imputed Interest (10% of Carrying Amount)	Depreciation	Accumulated Depreciation	Carrying Amount of Asset
0					$800,000
1	$ 200,000	$ 80,000	$120,000	$120,000	680,000
2	200,000	68,000	132,000	252,000	548,000
3	200,000	54,800	145,200	397,200	402,800
4	200,000	40,280	159,720	556,920	243,080
5	200,000	24,308	175,692	732,612	67,388
	$1,100,000	$267,388	$732,612		

Exhibit 16.3 Depreciation Using the Annuity Method
Source: Adapted from A. N. Mosich and E. John Larsen, *Intermediate Accounting,* 6th ed. (New York: McGraw-Hill, 1986), p. 627.

(e) DEPRECIATION FOR PARTIAL PERIODS.   Since assets are often acquired and disposed of throughout the year, companies must compute depreciation for partial periods. Five computation alternatives are found in practice:

1. Depreciation is recognized to the nearest whole month. Assets acquired on or before the fifteenth of the month or sold after the fifteenth are reduced by a full month's depreciation; assets acquired after the fifteenth or sold on or before the fifteenth are excluded from the month's depreciation computation.

2. Depreciation is recognized to the nearest whole year. Assets acquired during the first six months or sold during the last six months are reduced by a full year's depreciation; assets acquired during the last six months or sold during the first six months are excluded from the year's depreciation computation.

3. One-half year's depreciation only is recognized on all assets purchased or sold during the year.

4. No depreciation is recognized on all assets purchased or sold during the year.

5. A full year's depreciation is recognized on assets acquired during the year; none is recognized on assets retired during the year.

(f) CHANGE IN DEPRECIATION METHOD.   A change in depreciation method is a change in an accounting principle. In accordance with SFAS No. 154 (FASB ASC 250-10), the cumulative effect of the change is recognized in net income of the period of change.

16.11 DEPRECIATION RATES

(a) SOURCES OF DEPRECIATION RATES.   Information concerning depreciation rates for various classes of business property is available from several sources. Depreciation rates have been given attention by authors of manuals on accounting, engineering, management, rate making, and other aspects of the business process. They have been the subject of special investigation by industry through individual studies and studies conducted under the auspices of manufacturing and other trade associations.

The choice of depreciation rates has also been influenced by the requirements of tax law and regulation, discussed later in Section 16.12 of this chapter.

(b) GROUP AND COMPOSITE RATES.   A group of assets may be depreciated at a single rate. Assets of electrical utilities and hotels are sometimes depreciated in this manner. The two most common methods of depreciating asset groups are the group depreciation method and the collective depreciation method.

(i) Group Depreciation.   Mosich and Larsen define *group depreciation* as the "process of averaging the economic lives of a number of plant assets and computing depreciation on the entire class of assets as if it were an operating unit."[21] Smith and Skousen elaborate:

> Because the accumulated depreciation account under the group procedure applies to the entire group of assets, it is not related to any specific asset. Thus, no book value can be calculated for any specific asset and there are no fully depreciated assets. To arrive at the periodic depreciation charge, the depreciation rate is applied to the recorded cost of all assets remaining in service, regardless of age.[22]

To illustrate, assume that a company purchased a group of 100 similar machines having an average expected service life of five years at a total cost of $200,000. Of this group, 30 machines

---

[21] Mosich and Larsen, *Intermediate Accounting.*

[22] Smith and Skousen, *Intermediate Accounting, Comprehensive Volume.*

End of Year	Depreciation (20% of cost)	Asset			Accumulated Depreciation			Asset Book Value
		Debit	Credit	Balance	Debit	Credit	Balance	
		$200		$200				$200
1	$40			200		$40	$40	160
2	40			200		40	80	120
3	40			200		40	120	80
4	40		$ 60	140	$ 60	40	100	40
5	28		80	60	80	28	48	12
6	12		60	—	60	12	—	—
	$200	$200	$200	$200	$200	$200		

Exhibit 16.4   Group Depreciation (All Amounts in Thousands)

are expected to be retired at the end of four years, 40 at the end of five years, and the remaining 30 at the end of six years. Under the group depreciation method, depreciation is based on the average expected service life of five years, which converts to an annual depreciation rate of 20 percent. This rate is applied to those assets in service each year. Assuming the machines are retired as expected, the charges for depreciation and the changes in the group asset and accumulated depreciation accounts are summarized in Exhibit 16.4.

It should be noted that the depreciation charge per machine-year is $400—one-fifth of the unit price of $2,000. In each of the first four years, 100 machines are in use, and the annual depreciation charge is $40,000. In the fifth year, when the number of machines in use drops to 70, the charge is $28,000. In the sixth year, when only 30 units are in use, the charge is $12,000.

When an asset in the group is disposed of, no gain or loss is recognized. The asset's cost is removed from the group asset account, and the difference between the cost and the asset's actual net salvage value is removed from the accumulated depreciation account.

The advantage of group depreciation, according to Smith and Skousen, is "an annual charge that is more closely related to the quantity of productive facilities being used. Gains and losses due solely to normal variations in asset lives are not recognized, and operating results are more meaningfully stated."[23]

But what Smith and Skousen see as an advantage, Geiger sees as a weakness:

> Since, for all practical purposes, the actual depreciation rate of an item is unknown and is not used, the true gain or loss at time of its sale or disposal cannot be computed. Accordingly, gain or loss on disposal of fixed assets is not recognized in the income accounts.[24]

Smith and Skousen counter: "With normal variations in asset lives, the losses not recognized on early retirements are offset by the continued depreciation charges on those assets still in service after the average life has elapsed."[25]

(ii) Composite Depreciation.   Composite depreciation applies group depreciation procedures to groups of dissimilar assets with varying service lives.

Exhibit 16.5 illustrates the calculation of composite rates. The composite life of the assets is 9.96 years; the resulting composite depreciation rate is 9.2 percent. To determine the annual depreciation, the composite rate of 9.2 percent is applied to the asset account balance at the beginning of the

---

[23] Smith and Skousen, *Intermediate Accounting, Comprehensive Volume.*
[24] H. Dwight Geiger, "Composite Depreciation under Depreciation Guidelines," *AAA Bulletin* 44, no. 11 (July 1963).
[25] Smith and Skousen, *Intermediate Accounting, Comprehensive Volume.*

Asset Item	Cost	New Salvage Value	Depreciation Base	Annual Rate	Depreciation
A	$ 2,000	$ —	$ 2,000	20.0%	$ 400
B	5,000	500	4,500	12.0	540
C	8,000	1,000	7,000	10.0	700
D	15,000	1,000	14,000	8.0	1,120
Group	$30,000	$2,500	$27,500		$2,760

Composite life: $27,500 ÷ $2,760 = 9.96 years.
Composite rate: $2,760 ÷ $30,000 = 9.2%.

Exhibit 16.5   Composite Depreciation

year. The total acquisition cost of $30,000 is thus reduced to the estimated salvage value of $2,500 in 9.96 years.

As in group depreciation, when an asset is disposed of, no gain or loss is recognized. The asset's cost is removed from the group asset account, and the difference between cost and actual net salvage value is removed from the accumulated depreciation account.

Once a composite rate has been established, it is usually continued until a significant event indicates the need for a new rate. Such an event may be a material change in the service lives of the assets included in the group, a major asset addition, or a major asset retirement. Composite depreciation is based on the assumptions that assets are regularly retired near the end of their service lives and that the retired assets are replaced with similar assets. If replacements do not take place according to the assumptions, if the service lives of replacement assets differ substantially from the service lives of the assets replaced, or if the cost of replacement assets differs materially from the cost of the assets replaced, continued use of the same composite rate is inappropriate.

Mosich and Larsen discuss the advantages and disadvantages of composite depreciation:

The primary disadvantage ... is that the averaging procedure may obscure significant variations from average. The accuracy of the ... composite depreciation rate may be verified by recomputing depreciation on the straight-line basis for individual plant assets. Any significant discrepancies between the two results require a change in the composite depreciation rate.

The advantages ... are simplicity, convenience, and a reduction in the amount of detail involved in plant asset records and depreciation computations. The availability of computers has reduced the force of this argument.[26]

(c) EFFECTS OF REPLACEMENTS, IMPROVEMENTS, AND ADDITIONS.

As stated in Section 16.4(c), major expenditures that extend the service lives of assets or otherwise benefit future years are capitalized. Such expenditures require new depreciation computations. The new periodic depreciation charge is determined by dividing the asset's new book value by the new remaining service life, illustrated for straight-line depreciation, as shown:

Original asset cost (original estimated life, 10 years)	$8,000
Six years' depreciation	−4,800
Net book value before capital expenditure	3,200
Net increase in book value resulting from capital expenditure	2,400
New book value (new estimated life, eight years)	$5,600
New annual depreciation charge ($5,600 ÷ 8)	$ 700

[26] Mosich and Larsen, *Intermediate Accounting*.

Retroactive adjustment of previous years' depreciation is not appropriate, since the expenditures benefit future years only.

(d) TOOLS AND RELATED ASSETS.   Tools are sometimes divided into two classes: semidurable (lives of five years or more) and perishable. The cost of semidurable tools is capitalized and depreciated, usually at a group or composite rate. The rate is usually high because tools are hard to control.

Perishable tools may be handled in a variety of ways. Their cost may be charged directly to the appropriate expense or production cost account. Or the cost may be capitalized, often at some arbitrarily reduced amount, and written down when periodic inventories reveal shrinkage and deterioration. A third method is to capitalize the original cost and charge all subsequent expenditures for replacements to expense.

16.12 DEPRECIATION FOR TAX PURPOSES

Tax regulations contain their own depreciation requirements. Before 1954, the Internal Revenue Service generally allowed only the straight-line method of depreciation. Subsequently, the tax laws and regulations have been amended several times to permit accelerated depreciation methods and arbitrarily short asset lives. As a result, depreciation for financial reporting purposes and depreciation for tax purposes commonly differ. The difference between an asset's tax and accounting basis is a temporary difference that requires interperiod tax allocation under SFAS No. 109, *Accounting for Income Taxes* (FASB ASC 740-10) (see Chapter 17).

(a) CURRENT REQUIREMENTS.   Depreciation for tax purposes is currently determined under the modified accelerated cost recovery system (MACRS), enacted in the Tax Reform Act of 1986 (TRA). The TRA made significant changes to the previous Accelerated Cost Recovery System (ACRS) and created the modified ACRS (MACRS). MACRS provides for accelerated write-offs. In many cases, the asset service lives allowable for tax purposes under MACRS are shorter than the realistic economic service lives used for financial reporting purposes.

(b) MODIFIED ACCELERATED COST RECOVERY SYSTEM.   MACRS is mandatory for most tangible depreciable property placed in service after December 31, 1986.

Under MACRS, property other than real estate is depreciated over 3, 5, 7, 10, 15, or 20 years, depending on its classification. Real estate is classified as residential rental property, which is depreciated over 27.5 years, or nonresidential real property, which is depreciated over 39 years, for purchases made after May 13, 1993..

Most property can be depreciated using an alternate method, which computes depreciation using the straight-line method with no salvage value over the applicable MACRS class life.

(c) ADDITIONAL FIRST-YEAR DEPRECIATION.   The Internal Revenue Code also allows, with certain limitations, qualified tangible personal property to be deducted as an expense in the year acquired. The additional expense must be deducted from cost to determine the asset's depreciable base for tax purposes.

16.13 FINANCIAL STATEMENT PRESENTATION AND DISCLOSURE

(a) GENERAL REQUIREMENTS.   Paragraph 5 of APB Opinion No. 12, *Omnibus Opinion—1967* (FASB ASC 360-10) requires these four disclosures in the financial statements or notes:

1. Depreciation expense for the period
2. Balances of major classes of depreciable assets, by nature or function, at the balance sheet date

3. Accumulated depreciation, either by major asset classes or in total, at the balance sheet date
4. A general description of the method or methods used in computing depreciation for major classes of depreciable assets

Special disclosures may include the method of accounting for fully depreciated assets and liens against property. Ordinarily, the basis of valuation is also disclosed. Chapter 5 discusses the SEC's requirements.

(b) CONSTRUCTION IN PROGRESS.   Payments to contractors for construction in progress are usually recorded as advances, since the payor does not acquire ownership until completion of the construction. Self-constructed assets are normally classified separately as construction in progress until construction is complete.

(c) GAIN OR LOSS ON RETIREMENT.   Under paragraph 23 of APB Opinion No. 30, *Reporting the Results of Operations* (FASB ASC 225-20), gains or losses from the sale or abandonment of PP&E used in the business are usually not reported as extraordinary items. They are expected to recur as a consequence of customary and continuing business activities. Exceptions are recognized for gains and losses that are "a direct result of a major casualty (such as an earthquake), an expropriation, or a prohibition under a newly enacted law or regulation" and that clearly meet both criteria of unusual nature and infrequency of occurrence.

(d) FULLY DEPRECIATED AND IDLE ASSETS.   Many authorities recommend that the cost and accumulated depreciation of fully depreciated assets still in use be kept in the accounts until the assets are sold or retired. Stettler recommends disclosure not only of fully depreciated assets in use but also of idle assets:

> Disclosure should also be made if there are material amounts of fully depreciated assets still in use or material amounts of assets still subject to depreciation that are not currently in productive use.[27]

(e) IMPAIRMENT OF ASSETS

(i) Presentation.   SFAS No. 144 (FASB ASC 360-10) requires that impairment losses related to assets to be held and used in operations and that impairment losses from initial adjustments (and gains and losses from subsequent adjustments) of the carrying amount of assets to be disposed of be reported as a component of income from continuing operations, before income taxes. However, it provides these options as to how such losses may be presented within the financial statements:

- As a separate line item in the income statement
- Aggregated in an appropriate line item in the income statement (e.g., as part of "other expenses") with the amount of the loss noted parenthetically on the face of the income statement
- Aggregated in an appropriate line item in the income statement supplemented by disclosure in the notes to be financial statements of the amount of impairment loss and the income statement caption in which the loss is included

If a company presents a subtotal in its income statement (e.g., income from operations, or operating income), the impairment loss must be included in such subtotal.

---

[27] Howard F. Stettler, *Auditing Principles,* 5th ed. (Englewood Cliffs, NJ: Prentice-Hall, 1982).

(ii) Disclosures for Assets to Be Held and Used. SFAS No. 144 (FASB ASC 360-10) requires these disclosures in the notes to the financial statements when an impairment loss is reported:

- A description of the assets that are impaired and the facts and circumstances leading to the impairment
- If not separately presented on the face of the statement, the amount of the impairment loss and the caption in the income statement or the statement of activities that includes that loss
- The method or methods for determining fair value (whether based on a quoted market price, prices for similar assets, or another valuation technique)
- If applicable, the business segment(s) affected

(iii) Disclosures for Assets to Be Disposed Of

SFAS No. 144 (FASB ASC 205-20) states that the following information shall be disclosed in the notes to the financial statements that cover the period in which a long-lived asset (disposal group) either has been sold or is classified as held for sale:

- A description of the facts and circumstances leading to the expected disposal, the expected manner and timing of that disposal, and, if not separately presented on the face of the statement, the carrying amount(s) of the major classes of assets and liabilities included as part of a disposal group
- The gain or loss recognized and if not separately presented on the face of the income statement, the caption in the income statement or the statement of activities that includes that gain or loss
- If applicable, amounts of revenue and pretax profit or loss reported in discontinued operations
- If applicable, the segment in which the long-lived asset (disposal group) is reported

(f) SEGMENT INFORMATION. SFAS No. 131, *Disclosures about Segments of an Enterprise and Related Information* (FASB ASC 280-10), requires disclosure of two items of information about PP&E for each reportable segment:

1. Total assets, for each reportable segment
2. The aggregate amount of depreciation, depletion, and amortization expense and the amount of capital expenditures for each reportable segment

16.14 SOURCES AND SUGGESTED REFERENCES

American Accounting Association. *A Statement of Basic Accounting Theory* by the Committee to Prepare a Statement of Basic Accounting Theory. Sarasota, FL: Author, 1966.

Accounting Principles Board. APB Opinion No. 12, *Omnibus Opinion—1967*. New York: AICPA, 1967. (FASB ASC topics 310, 360, 505,710, and 835)

———. APB Opinion No. 20, *Accounting Changes* (FASB ASC 250). New York: AICPA, 1971.

———. APB Opinion No. 21, *Interest on Receivables and Payables* (FASB ASC 835). New York: AICPA, 1971.

———. APB Opinion No. 28, *Interim Financial Reporting* (FASB ASC 270). New York: AICPA, 1973.

———. APB Opinion No. 29, *Accounting for Nonmonetary Transactions* (FASB ASC 845). New York: AICPA, 1973.

———. APB Opinion No. 30, *Reporting the Results of Operations* (FASB ASC 225). New York: AICPA, 1973.

American Accounting Association. *A Statement of Basic Accounting Theory.* Sarasota, FL: Author, 1966.

American Institute of Certified Public Accountants. *Accounting Research and Terminology Bulletins—Final Edition.* New York: Author, 1961.

———. Accounting for the Inability to Fully Recover the Carrying Amount of Long-Lived Assets, Issues Paper. New York: Author, July 15, 1980.

———. *Illustrations of Accounting for the Inability to Fully Recover the Carrying Amounts of Long-Lived Assets.* New York: Author, April 1987.

———. Proposed Statement of Position, *Accounting for Certain Costs and Activities Related to Property, Plant, and Equipment.* New York: Author, 2001.

———. Statement of Position No. 96-1, *Environmental Remediation Liabilities.* New York: Author, October 1996.

Bendel, C. W. "Streamlining the Property Accounting Procedures," *NACA Bulletin* 31, no. 11 (1950).

Davidson, S., C. P. Stickney, and Roman L. Weil. *Financial Accounting: An Introduction to Concepts, Methods and Uses,* 5th ed. Hinsdale, IL: Dryden Press, 1988.

Financial Accounting Standards Board. EITF Issue No. 86-29, *Nonmonetary Transactions: Magnitude of Boot and the Exceptions to the Use of Fair Value* (FASB ASC 845). Stamford, CT: Author, December 3–4, 1986, January 15, 1987, and February 26, 1987.

———. EITF Issue No. 89-13, *Accounting for the Cost of Asbestos Removal* (FASB ASC 410). Norwalk, CT: Author, October 26, 1989.

———. EITF Issue No. 90-8, *Capitalization of Costs to Treat Environmental Contamination* (FASB ASC 410). Norwalk, CT: Author, May 31, 1990, and July 12, 1990.

———. FASB Interpretation No. 4, *Applicability of FASB Statement No. 2 to Business Combinations Accounted for by the Purchase Method* (FASB ASC 350). Stamford, CT: Author, 1975.

———. FASB Interpretation No. 30, *Accounting for Involuntary Conversions of Nonmonetary Assets to Monetary Assets* (FASB ASC 605). Stamford, CT: Author, 1979.

———. Statement of Financial Accounting Concepts No. 7, *Using Cash Flow Information and Present Value in Accounting Measurements.* Norwalk, CT: Author, 2000.

———. Statement of Financial Accounting Standards No. 2, *Accounting for Research and Development Costs* (FASB ASC 730). Stamford, CT: Author, 1974.

———. Statement of Financial Accounting Standards No. 34, *Capitalization of Interest Cost* (FASB ASC 835). Stamford, CT: Author, 1979.

———. Statement of Financial Accounting Standards No. 67, *Accounting for Costs and Initial Rental Operations of Real Estate Projects* (FASB ASC 970). Stamford, CT: Author, 1982.

———. Statement of Financial Accounting Standards No. 109, *Accounting for Income Taxes* (FASB ASC 740). Norwalk, CT: Author, 1992.

———. Statement of Financial Accounting Standards No. 131, *Disclosures about Segments of an Enterprise and Related Information* (FASB ASC 310). Norwalk, CT: Author, 1997.

———. Statement of Financial Accounting Standards No. 143, *Accounting for Asset Retirement Obligations* (FASB ASC 410). Norwalk, CT: Author, 2001.

———. Statement of Financial Accounting Standards No. 144, *Accounting for the Impairment or Disposal of Long-Lived Assets* (FASB ASC 360). Norwalk, CT: Author, 2001.

———. Statement of Financial Accounting Standards No. 157, *Fair Value Measurements* (FASB ASC 820). Norwalk, CT: Author, 2006.

Financial Executives Institute. *Survey of Unusual Charges.* Morristown, NJ: Author, September 26, 1986.

Geiger, H. D. "Composite Depreciation under Depreciation Guidelines," *NAA Bulletin* 44, no. 11 (July 1963).

Grant, E., and P. Norton. *Depreciation.* New York: Ronald Press, 1955.

International Accounting Standards Committee. International Accounting Standards No. 4, *Depreciation Accounting.* London: Author, 1977.

Kieso, D. E., and J. J. Weygandt. *Intermediate Accounting,* 5th ed. New York: John Wiley & Sons, 1986.

Kohler, E. L. *Kohler's Dictionary for Accountants,* 6th ed. Englewood Cliffs, NJ: Prentice-Hall, 1983.

Lambert, S. J. III, and J. C. Lambert. "Concepts and Applications in APB Opinion No. 29," *Journal of Accountancy* (March 1977): 60–68.

Lamden, C., D. L. Gerboth, and T. McRae. *Accounting for Depreciable Assets*, Accounting Research Monograph No. 1. New York: AICPA, 1975.

Mosich, A. N., and E. J. Larsen., *Intermediate Accounting*, 6th ed. New York: McGraw-Hill, 1986.

National Association of Accountants, Management Accounting Practices Committee, Statement on Management Accounting Practices No. 4, *Fixed Asset Accounting: The Capitalization of Costs*. New York: Author, 1973.

————. Statement on Management Accounting Practices No. 7, *Fixed Asset Accounting: The Allocation of Costs*. New York: Author, 1974.

Pyle, W. W., and K. D. Larson. *Fundamental Accounting Principles*, 10th ed. Homewood, IL: Irwin, 1984.

Smith, J. M., and K. F. Skousen. *Intermediate Accounting, Comprehensive Volume*, 9th ed. Cincinnati: South-Western Publishing, 1987.

Stettler, H. F. *Auditing Principles*, 5th ed. Englewood Cliffs, NJ: Prentice-Hall, 1982.

Welsch, G. A., R. N. Anthony, and D. G. Short. *Fundamentals of Financial Accounting*. Homewood, IL: Irwin 1984.

Welsch, G. A., and C. T. Zlatkovich. *Intermediate Accounting*, 8th ed. Homewood, IL: Irwin, 1989.

CHAPTER 17

ACCOUNTING FOR INCOME TAXES

Lynne Glennon, CPA, MST

17.1 ACCOUNTING RECOGNITION OF INCOME TAXES

(a) BASIC PROBLEM. Accounting for income taxes is one of the most complex and controversial accounting subjects in this country. The basic problem is that transactions and events may be reported in different years for financial reporting and for income tax purposes. This may be because different accounting methods are used for each purpose—for example, accrual accounting versus cash basis accounting, straight-line depreciation versus an accelerated depreciation method, the percentage-of-completion versus the completed contract methods on long-term contracts, or revenue recognition at time of sale versus the installment method. It may also be because a different estimated useful life is elected for depreciation or amortization. These differences may occur because the income tax reporting requirements and generally accepted accounting principles (GAAP) are different for a particular event or transaction or because a taxpayer is able to elect to report differently.

The accounting procedure employed to recognize the tax effects of amounts that are reported in different years for financial reporting and for income tax reporting has been known as *interperiod income tax allocation* or *tax effect accounting*. The more neutral description of "recognition" of income taxes is used in this chapter, and the other terms are not generally used.

Several different approaches to the recognition of income taxes have been used at various times in the United States. An income statement approach known as the *deferred method* of interperiod income tax allocation was adopted in 1967 in Accounting Principles Board (APB) Opinion No. 11, *Accounting for Income Taxes.* Under that method, amounts reported in different years for financial reporting and for income tax reporting are known as *timing differences.* Using accelerated depreciation on the income tax return and straight-line depreciation in the income statement, for example, causes a timing difference to originate each year during the early life of an asset; the timing difference reverses, or "turns around," during the later life of the asset. Other items, known as *permanent differences,* are not considered taxable income, are not tax deductible, or are special deductions for income tax reporting purposes. Because they always differ for financial and income tax reporting purposes, there is a permanent, nonrecurring difference. For example, interest income from state and local government bonds is financial revenue that is not taxable under the federal income tax.

The *liability method* is a balance sheet approach to accounting for income taxes. That method was first adopted in the United States in Statement of Financial Accounting Standards (SFAS) No. 96, *Accounting for Income Taxes,* and was continued in the replacement for that Statement in Financial Accounting Standards Board (FASB) Accounting Standard Codification (ASC) 740 (formerly SFAS No. 109), *Accounting for Income Taxes.* Under that method, differences between the amounts reported in the balance sheet for assets and liabilities and the income tax bases of those assets and liabilities are known as *temporary differences.* Thus, whereas the difference between the amount of depreciation on the tax return and in the income statement in a single year is a timing difference under APB Opinion No. 11, the cumulative difference at the balance sheet date between the tax basis of the asset and its cost (or other amount) reported in the balance sheet is a temporary difference under FASB ASC 740. Temporary differences may also result from causes other than cumulative timing differences (see Subsection 17.2(c)(i)). Because the concepts underlying timing differences and temporary differences are so different, the term *timing difference* will be used in this chapter only in the explanation of APB Opinion No. 11 and earlier accounting requirements; elsewhere the more current term *temporary difference* in FASB ASC 740 will be used.

(b) TAX RECOGNITION CONCEPTS.   Income taxes are seldom, if ever, paid completely in the period to which they relate. Thus, the cash basis is not acceptable under GAAP. Income taxes, like other expenses, should be recognized on an accrual basis of accounting. Although there is agreement that, at a minimum, income tax expense should include income taxes paid and payable for a period as determined on the income tax return for the period, the taxes payable method ignores timing and temporary differences and is not acceptable under GAAP.

(i) Development in the United States.   There has long been general agreement in this country on the need for, at a minimum, recognition of deferred taxes for nonrecurring material differences that will reverse in a relatively short period. That partial recognition position was taken in 1944 in Accounting Research Bulletins (ARB) No. 23, *Accounting for Income Taxes,* carried forward in 1953 in ARB No. 43, *Restatement and Revision of Accounting Research Bulletins,* and reaffirmed in 1954 in ARB No. 44, *Declining-Balance Depreciation.* In 1958 ARB No. 44 (Revised), *Declining-Balance Depreciation,* further called for tax allocation even though depreciation differences were of a recurring nature, or a plant was expanding, so there would be long-term deferral of an increasing tax balance. That comprehensive recognition approach extended the applicability of the interperiod income tax allocation procedure to depreciation differences to which it had not previously been broadly applied. In 1962, APB Opinion No. 1, *New Depreciation Guidelines and Rules,* further extended the applicability of that procedure to differences arising from adoption of shorter lives for income tax depreciation in relation to those used for financial reporting.

Whether the concepts in those pronouncements applied for timing differences other than depreciation was uncertain, however, and interperiod income tax allocation was not literally required for most timing differences until APB Opinion No. 11 became effective in 1968. That Opinion also generally resolved the question of which method should be applied in favor of the deferred method with comprehensive allocation. Although the deferred method was preferred in earlier pronouncements, the liability and net-of-tax methods were also acceptable. In the research study published by the American Institute of Certified Public Accountants (AICPA) before APB Opinion No. 11 was issued, Black discussed those methods in detail.[1] They are summarized next.

Deferred Method.   The deferred method is an income statement approach to interperiod income tax allocation that seeks to match the tax effects of revenues and expenses with those items in the period for which they are recognized for financial reporting purposes. Deferred taxes are determined on the basis of tax rates in effect when timing differences originate and are not adjusted for changes in tax rates or for new taxes. The tax effect of a timing difference that reduces income tax currently payable is reported as an increase in income tax expense in the income statement and as a deferred tax credit in the balance sheet; conversely, the tax effect of a timing difference that increases income tax currently payable is reported as a reduction in income tax expense in the income statement and as a deferred tax charge (or reduction of deferred tax credits) in the balance

---

[1] Homer A. Black, *Interperiod Allocation of Corporate Income Taxes,* Accounting Research Study No. 9 (New York: AICPA, 1966).

sheet. Because the beginning amount of income tax expense in the income statement is based on taxes currently payable, in concept the deferred method adjusts tax expense as if originating timing differences for the period were included in taxable income. The tax effects of reversing timing differences likewise adjust tax expense, but in concept at the tax rates in effect when those timing differences originated. Paragraph 57 of APB Opinion No. 11 states that "deferred charges and deferred credits relating to timing differences represent the cumulative recognition given to their tax effects and as such do not represent payables or receivables in the usual sense."

Liability Method.   The liability method is a balance sheet approach to accounting for income taxes. The method seeks to determine the liability for income taxes payable in the future or the asset for prepaid income taxes and, accordingly, measures the tax effect of a temporary difference at the tax rate or rates in effect when the difference will reverse. If tax rates change or new taxes are imposed, the balance sheet accounts are adjusted with a corresponding adjustment to income tax expense.

Net-of-Tax Method.   The net-of-tax method is a method of valuing an asset or liability and the related revenue or expense by recognizing that those amounts are worth more or less because of their tax status. Under this method, if straight-line depreciation is used for financial reporting and accelerated depreciation is used for income tax, the tax effect of the difference is an adjustment to depreciation expense and to the allowance for depreciation. Accordingly, in the early years of an asset's life, the net book value of the asset is less (in relation to what it would be under other methods) because of the increased allowance. In later years, depreciation expense and the addition to the allowance are less each year than straight-line depreciation. The theory is that an asset's *tax* depreciability is used up, it is worth less and its book value should reflect that fact. Tax effects under the net-of-tax method may be determined using either a deferred or a liability approach.

Comprehensive Recognition.   Under comprehensive recognition of deferred taxes, the tax effects of all timing and temporary differences are recognized. Thus, recurring transactions will have both originating and reversing timing or temporary differences that may offset in the tax return but nevertheless leave temporary differences in the balance sheet. In this case the deferred taxes in the balance sheet roll over in a revolving account, as do accounts receivable or accounts payable. Recurring timing or temporary differences of continually increasing amounts cause deferred income taxes in the balance sheet to likewise continually increase. An expanding company using various elections to defer income taxes currently payable on recurring transactions will have an increasing balance of deferred income taxes under comprehensive recognition.

Partial Recognition.   Partial recognition of deferred taxes ignores recurring timing or temporary differences and timing or temporary differences that will not reverse for long periods. Income tax expense is based on income taxes currently payable, adjusted for the tax effects of nonrecurring timing or temporary differences that will materially increase or decrease income taxes payable in a relatively short period, such as five years. Accordingly, balance sheet amounts for deferred income taxes would be considerably less for most companies under partial recognition than under comprehensive recognition of deferred taxes.

Although APB Opinion No. 11 was generally a comprehensive approach to accounting for income taxes, exceptions were made for several special areas. Although some of these exceptions continue, FASB ASC 740 (formerly SFAS No. 109) eliminates some significant exceptions, and the exceptions discussed later in this section are the only items for which it allows partial recognition. Because APB Opinion No. 11 only considered the tax effects of timing differences in any single year, other tax effects of basis differences were ignored, such as an increase in the tax basis of assets in a taxable business combination accounted for as a pooling of interests when the former book values of the assets are carried forward for financial reporting. In FASB ASC 740 (formerly SFAS No. 109), such differences are considered temporary differences for which deferred taxes must be recognized and eliminates those exceptions to tax allocation that existed under APB Opinion No. 11.

(ii) Move to the Liability Method. The FASB issued SFAS No. 96 adopting the liability method in December 1987 as the culmination of a six-year project to reconsider the accounting for income taxes. For various reasons, preparers, auditors, users, and educators had strongly supported moving from the deferred method to the liability method when the FASB undertook the project and while it was in process. Some objected to the increasing amounts of deferred taxes reported in balance sheets under APB Opinion No. 11 even though corporate income tax rates had been declining. Others believed income tax allocation under APB Opinion No. 11 had become too complex and viewed the liability method as a simpler approach. Still others thought the results obtained from applying the deferred method could only be explained procedurally and believed the liability method would be conceptually superior.

The amounts reported as liabilities under the liability method do not conform with the FASB's definition of *liabilities,* which is:

> probable future sacrifices of economic benefits arising from present obligations of a particular entity to transfer assets or provide service to other entities in the future as a result of past transactions or events.

It therefore is an unsound method.[2] The FASB states three tests, *all* of which must be passed for an amount to conform with the definition. The third test is: "Has the transaction or other event obligating the entity already happened?" The FASB states that the test is passed because "[d]eferred tax liabilities result from the same past events that create taxable temporary differences."[3] The FASB does not identify the past events it alludes to in that Statement, so the reader has to infer them. They are (1) preparing a tax return one way and (2) preparing financial statements another way. The second of those events is bookkeeping. Because a reporting entity's own bookkeeping cannot be one of the events necessary to cause the reporting entity to incur a liability, a real-world detrimental relationship it has with another entity, the test is failed. Were it a liability, it could be paid off by restating the financial statements. Liabilities cannot be paid off by restating financial statements.

(iii) Delay and Reconsideration. Some companies adopted SFAS No. 96 in their 1987 financial statements before they were required to do so, but others complained that the Statement was too complex and difficult to apply and disagreed with some of the results of applying it. In December 1988, the FASB issued SFAS No. 100, *Accounting for Income Taxes—Deferral of the Effective Date of FASB Statement No. 96,* to delay the required application of SFAS No. 96 by one year to 1990. In large part, the delay was to permit the FASB to provide implementation guidance. At the same time, the FASB began considering requests to simplify the application of SFAS No. 96, to relax its requirements for recognizing a deferred tax asset, and to modify several other specific requirements. In December 1989, the FASB issued SFAS No. 103, *Accounting for Income Taxes—Deferral of the Effective Date of FASB Statement No. 96,* further delaying the required application of SFAS No. 96 until 1992 to continue consideration of those requests. In June 1991, the FASB issued an Exposure Draft, *Accounting for Income Taxes,* of a replacement for SFAS No. 96, and in February 1992, it issued FASB ASC 740 (formerly SFAS No. 109) to supersede SFAS No. 96. SFAS No. 108, *Accounting for Income Taxes—Deferral of the Effective Date of FASB Statement No. 96,* further delayed the required application of SFAS No. 96 so that it never became mandatory. FASB ASC 740 is required for financial statements for fiscal years beginning after December 15, 1992. The APB Opinion No. 11, *Accounting for Income Taxes,* or SFAS No. 96 are permitted to be applied for financial statements for earlier periods.

Criticisms and concerns with SFAS No. 96 focused on (1) the restrictive criteria for recognition and measurement of deferred tax assets and (2) the complexity of scheduling the future reversals of temporary differences and of considering hypothetical tax-planning strategies that were, to a large

---

[2] Paul Rosenfield and William C. Dent, "No More Deferred Taxes," *Journal of Accountancy* (February 1983).

[3] FASB, Statement of Financial Accounting Standards No. 109, *Accounting for Income Taxes,* par. 79.

degree, a consequence of those criteria for deferred tax assets. FASB ASC 740 resulted from a comprehensive reconsideration of both APB Opinion No. 11 and SFAS No. 96. It permits, in more instances than SFAS No. 96, recognition of deferred tax assets that are expected to be realized and reduces the complexity of scheduling and consideration of tax-planning strategies. Other changes from SFAS No. 96 in FASB ASC 740 that should reduce the cost and complexity of deferred tax accounting are the revised requirements for transfers of assets (see Subsection 17.1(c)(v)), foreign nonmonetary assets (see Subsection 17.1(c)(vi)), measurement of deferred tax liabilities and assets when graduated tax rates or the alternative minimum tax are a significant factor (see Subsection 17.2(d)(iv)), and balance sheet classification (see Section 17.4(b)).

(iv) FASB Accounting Standards Codification.   SFAS No. 109 was superseded by FASB ASC 740, for interim and annual periods ending after September 15, 2009. The FASB ASC effectively combines SFAS No. 109 with all other authoritative literature that affects accounting for income taxes and organizes that literature within a single ASC Topic—FASB ASC 740, *Income Taxes*. This chapter reflects the Codification.

(c) GENERAL APPROACH TO RECOGNITION OF INCOME TAXES AND EXCEPTIONS.   The GAAP for recognition of income taxes are specified by FASB ASC 740. It also includes a limited number of long-standing exceptions to its recognition principles and provides some specific exceptions. For example, some basis differences are not temporary differences because their reversals are not expected to result in future taxable or deductible amounts. In other situations, FASB ASC 740 provides certain exceptions to the basic principles of the Statement. A more recent noteworthy change to the recognition principles is the addition to GAAP for uncertain tax positions in FASB ASC 740-10 (formerly FASB Interpretation (FIN) 48, *Accounting for Uncertainty in Income Taxes;* see Section 17.3 for full discussion.)

(i) General Approach to Recognition.   FASB ASC 740 requires comprehensive recognition of the effects of income taxes for temporary differences by the liability method. Under that method, the tax effect of a temporary difference is computed by multiplying the difference by the enacted tax rate(s) scheduled to be in effect for the year(s) the difference is expected to be reported in an income tax return(s). The tax effect may be either a deferred tax asset or a deferred tax liability. The Statement, however, provides certain exceptions.

(ii) Accounting for Uncertainty in Income Taxes.   FASB ASC 740-10 (formerly FIN 48) requires a specific threshold that an individual tax position must meet before such position can be recognized in the financial statements. A tax position may not be recognized unless it is more likely than not to pass a tax audit based solely on the technical merits of the position and the reported amount in the financial statements. The term *more likely than not* means a level of likelihood that is more than 50 percent.

Discussions and examples in this chapter assume that tax positions satisfy the more-likely-than-not requirement unless specifically stated otherwise. Accounting for uncertainty in income taxes is discussed thoroughly in Section 17.3.

(iii) Valuation Allowance.   A valuation allowance is recognized to reduce a deferred tax asset if it is more likely than not that some portion or all of the deferred tax asset will not be realized. The term *more likely than not* has the same meaning as described earlier with respect to uncertain tax positions.

(iv) Goodwill and Leveraged Lease Exceptions.   FASB ASC 805-740-25-3 prohibits the recognition of a deferred tax liability for the reported amount of goodwill (or portion thereof) that is not deductible for tax purposes. This was a practical decision because recognizing a deferred tax liability would increase goodwill by a like amount since goodwill is merely the amount of the purchase price that cannot be allocated to identifiable assets in a business combination accounted for as a purchase. Because of FASB ASC 805-740-25-3, an excess of book goodwill over tax-deductible goodwill will not result in the recording of deferred taxes at the date of a business combination. However, if there is an excess of tax-deductible goodwill over book goodwill at the acquisition date, a deferred tax asset should be provided in accordance with FASB ASC 805-740-25-8 through 25-9. (See Subsection 17.2(e)(iii) for a more detailed discussion.) Not changing the accounting specified by FASB ASC 840-30, *Leases—Capital Leases,* formerly SFAS No. 13, *Accounting for Leases,* for income taxes related to leveraged leases also represented a practical decision. Although that accounting is not consistent with FASB ASC 740, the FASB concluded that changing it would require reconsidering the accounting for leveraged leases.

(v) Transfers of Assets.   Ordinarily, there are tax effects when an asset is sold or transferred at a profit between affiliated companies that are consolidated for financial statement purposes but file separate tax returns. FASB ASC 740-10-25-3(e) (formerly SFAS No. 109, paragraph 9), however, prohibits recognition of a deferred tax asset for the difference between the tax basis of assets to the buyer and their cost in consolidated financial statements. Thus, FASB ASC 740 is consistent with FASB ASC 810-10-45-8 (formerly paragraph 17 of ARB No. 51, *Consolidated Financial Statements*) which states, "If income taxes have been paid on intra-entity profits on assets remaining within the consolidated group, those taxes shall be deferred or the intra-entity profits to be eliminated in consolidation shall be appropriately reduced."

(vi) Foreign Nonmonetary Assets.   Under FASB ASC 830, *Foreign Currency Matters* (formerly SFAS No. 52, *Foreign Currency Translation*), the U.S. dollar is the functional currency for certain foreign operations, and nonmonetary assets are remeasured using historical exchange rates. Changes in exchange rates and indexing for tax purposes will create differences between the foreign currency equivalent of the U.S. dollar cost of those assets and their foreign currency tax basis. However, FASB ASC 740-10-25-3(f) prohibits recognition of a deferred tax liability or asset for those differences. Otherwise, deferred taxes would be recognized for the effect of changes in exchange rates on nonmonetary assets that are measured at historical U.S. dollar cost.

(vii) Other Special Areas.   APB Opinion No. 11 provided exceptions to recognition of deferred taxes in the areas addressed by APB Opinion No. 23, *Accounting for Income Taxes—Special Areas.* It did not address deposits in statutory reserve funds by U.S. steamship companies. SFAS No. 109 expands the APB Opinion No. 23 exception for foreign undistributed earnings to include the total the book basis exceeds the tax basis of an investment in a foreign subsidiary or corporate joint venture. The SFAS No. 109 requirements for the other APB Opinion No. 23 exceptions grandfather temporary differences that arose prior to certain dates and require recognition of a deferred tax liability for temporary differences that arise after those dates. The grandfathered temporary differences are undistributed earnings of a domestic subsidiary or corporate joint venture and "policyholders' surplus" of a stock life insurance company that arose in fiscal years beginning on or before December 15, 1992, and "bad-debt reserves" of savings and loan associations that arose in tax years beginning before December 31, 1987. A deferred tax liability for APB Opinion No. 23 exceptions that continue under SFAS No. 109 (as described) is not recognized unless it becomes apparent that those temporary differences will reverse in the foreseeable future.

In summary, under FASB ASC 740 (formerly SFAS No. 109), deferred taxes should not be recognized for the next types of temporary differences unless it becomes apparent that they will reverse in the foreseeable future:

1. The temporary difference related to an investment in a foreign subsidiary or foreign corporate joint venture that is essentially permanent in duration

2. Undistributed earnings of a domestic subsidiary or a domestic corporate joint venture that is essentially permanent in duration that arose in fiscal years beginning on or before December 15, 1992

3. Bad debt reserves for tax purposes of U.S. savings and loan associations (and other qualified thrift lenders) that arose in tax years beginning before December 31, 1987

4. Policyholders' surplus of stock life insurance companies that arose in fiscal years beginning on or before December 15, 1992

In addition, FASB ASC 740 requires U.S. steamship companies to record deferred taxes related to deposits in statutory reserve funds on a prospective basis.

17.2 APPLYING FASB ASC 740

(a) SCOPE OF FASB ASC 740. FASB ASC 740 applies to all business entities subject to income taxes. It includes a company's domestic and foreign operations that are consolidated, combined, or accounted for by the equity method and to foreign companies that prepare financial statements in accordance with U.S. GAAP. FASB ASC 740-10-20 defines income taxes as all federal, foreign, state, and local taxes, including franchise taxes based on income. However, FASB ASC 740-10-15-4 specifically excludes a franchise tax to the extent that it is based on capital and there is no additional tax based on income or a withholding tax for the benefits of the recipients of a dividend.

(b) AUTHORITATIVE LITERATURE. FASB ASC 740 covers this primary guidance with respect to accounting for income taxes:

- Computing deferred tax assets or liabilities
- Presenting income tax expense in the income statement
- Disclosing information about income taxes
- Recognizing the effects of operating loss carrybacks and carryforwards
- Accounting for changes in tax rates
- Accounting for changes in a company's tax status

(i) Pre-Codification Authoritative Literature for Income Taxes. The next tax-related topics were addressed by other pre-Codification pronouncements:

- Income taxes in interim periods
- Investment tax credits
- Income taxes related to leveraged leases
- Tax benefits of tax deductions for stock compensation plans
- Discounting deferred tax assets and liabilities

Some of the other tax-related pronouncements were combined with the guidance in SFAS No. 109 to become Topic 740 within the FASB ASC; some were codified within other FASB ASC Topics; and others were not codified and are no longer authoritative as a result of the Codification.

(ii) FASB Special Report. The FASB issued a special report entitled *A Guide to Implementation of Statement 109 on Accounting for Income Taxes* to provide additional guidance after SFAS No. 109 was issued. The Special Report was primarily codified into FASB ASC 740. The key topics addressed in the Special Report are:

- Scheduling
- Disclosure
- Recognition and measurement
- Allocation of tax expense
- Change in tax status
- Tax-planning strategies

(iii) FASB Emerging Issues Task Force Discussions on Income Taxes. The Emerging Issues Task Force (EITF) has addressed several issues related to GAAP for income taxes. Some of these issues, as included in the FASB Accounting Standards Codification, remain relevant and are listed for reference in Subsection 17.2(e) (vi) of this chapter.

(c) BASIC OBJECTIVES AND PRINCIPLES. The basic objective of accounting for income taxes under FASB ASC 740-10-10-1 (formerly SFAS No. 109) is to recognize the tax consequences of all events recognized in the financial statements or income tax returns. The goal is to match tax expense with the economic income earned by the entity. Thus, when an "event" is recognized in the financial statements, the eventual tax consequences of the "event" should also be recognized (i.e., "match" tax to the same financial statement period that includes the gain or loss).

Most transactions and events are reported at the same time and in the same manner in the financial statements and in the tax return, and income taxes currently payable or refundable are determined from the tax return. Some items reported in the financial statements, however, are never reported in the tax return. These book-to-tax differences are known as *permanent items,* and although the term is not specifically defined in FASB ASC 740, the concept is described through examples. Interest income from municipal bonds is not taxable on a U.S. federal income tax return, for example, and certain fines paid are not deductible. Unlike temporary differences, which eventually reverse and equal out between the financial statements and the income tax return, permanent differences never reverse.

Items that are reported partially or completely in different periods or in different amounts in the financial statements and in the tax return create temporary differences. For example, a temporary difference between the reported amount of depreciable assets and their tax basis is created when depreciation is deducted sooner in the tax return than the expense is reported in the income statement. A deferred tax liability or asset is recognized for the estimated tax effects in future years as a result of temporary differences between the reported amount of an enterprise's assets and liabilities and their tax basis. The deferred tax liability or asset is measured applying enacted tax law for the future years in which temporary differences will result in taxable or deductible amounts. Tax planning strategies are considered when determining the need for and amount of a valuation allowance for a deferred tax asset. The only exceptions to comprehensive recognition of deferred taxes are described in Section 17.1(c).

Based on the described objectives and principles under FASB ASC 740, the basic calculation of the yearly tax provision consists of the steps in Exhibit 17.1.

(i) Temporary Differences. Tax laws and financial accounting standards differ as to when or how some items are recognized or measured. Consequently, items may be reported sooner or later or in different amounts on the tax return than in the financial statements, as noted in FASB ASC 740-10-25-20.

Following are seven examples.

1. *Revenue or gain that is recognized in income before it is taxable.* The receivable for an installment sale is a temporary difference that becomes taxable when collected.
2. *Expense or loss that is recognized in income before it is deductible for taxes.* A liability for product warranty cost is a temporary difference that becomes deductible when settled.
3. *Revenue or gain that is taxable before it is recognized in income.* Prepaid rental income is taxable when cash is received. The liability for financial reporting is a temporary difference that becomes deductible (or results in nontaxable income) when the liability is settled.
4. *Expense or loss that is deductible before it is recognized in income.* An asset may be expensed or depreciated by an accelerated method on the tax return but depreciated straight-line for financial reporting. The amount by which the undepreciated cost exceeds the tax basis is a temporary difference that becomes taxable when the undepreciated cost is recovered.
5. *Differences caused by tax credits.* Investment tax credit or other tax credits may reduce the tax basis of an asset, and deferred ITC reduces the cost of the related asset for financial

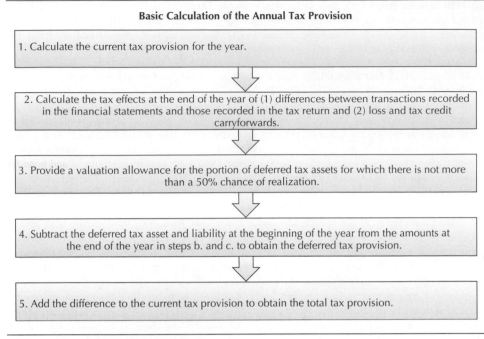

Basic Calculation of the Annual Tax Provision

1. Calculate the current tax provision for the year.

2. Calculate the tax effects at the end of the year of (1) differences between transactions recorded in the financial statements and those recorded in the tax return and (2) loss and tax credit carryforwards.

3. Provide a valuation allowance for the portion of deferred tax assets for which there is not more than a 50% chance of realization.

4. Subtract the deferred tax asset and liability at the beginning of the year from the amounts at the end of the year in steps b. and c. to obtain the deferred tax provision.

5. Add the difference to the current tax provision to obtain the total tax provision.

Exhibit 17.1   Basic Calculation of the Annual Tax Provision

reporting. In either case, the difference between the accounting cost and tax basis is a temporary difference.

6. *Purchase business combinations.* The amounts assigned to assets and liabilities in a business combination accounted for by the purchase method may differ from their tax bases. Those differences are temporary differences. In general, business combinations will create temporary differences when there is no step-up to fair value in tax basis of the assets and liabilities of acquired company, or even if there is a step-up, the purchase price allocations of assets differ between book and tax.

7. *An increase in the tax basis of assets because of indexing whenever the local currency is the functional currency.* Certain tax jurisdictions may require a tax basis adjustment for depreciable (or other) assets for the effects of inflation. For tax purposes, the inflation-adjusted basis would be used to determine future depreciation deductions or to calculate gain or loss upon disposition of the asset. The amount received upon future recovery of the local currency historical cost of the asset will be less than the remaining tax basis of the asset and is a temporary difference.

A difference between the tax basis of an asset or liability computed pursuant to the requirements in FASB ASC 740-10 for tax positions and the amount at which it is reported in the balance sheet is a temporary difference. In other words, temporary differences are differences between the tax bases of assets and liabilities that are *more likely than not* to be sustained in a tax audit and the financial reporting bases reported in the financial statements. (*Note:* The remainder of this discussion assumes that the tax information discussed and illustrated—taxable income, tax basis, temporary difference, and so on—represents the amount acknowledged for financial reporting purposes [i.e., after considering any uncertainty following the guidance in former FIN 48] unless specifically stated otherwise.)

The temporary difference will be deductible or taxable in some future year when the related asset is recovered or the related liability is settled. An assumption inherent in financial statements prepared in accordance with GAAP is that amounts reported for assets will be recovered and for liabilities will be settled. A tax liability or asset is recognized for the deferred tax consequences of temporary differences. A valuation allowance is recognized for the portion (or all) of a deferred tax asset for which it is more likely than not a tax benefit will not be realized.

A few temporary differences do not relate to a particular asset or liability on the balance sheet. FASB ASC 740-10-25-25 cites two examples of temporary differences that cannot easily be identified with a particular asset or liability for financial reporting. The first example discusses organization costs that are immediately expensed for financial reporting purposes but are capitalized for tax purposes. The other is a contract accounted for by the percentage-of-completion method for which amounts billed have been collected but reported by the completed-contract method for tax purposes. Both examples are temporary differences for which no identifiable amount appears in the balance sheet. In those situations, there is an asset or liability for tax purposes and none for financial reporting.

Two types of differences between the tax basis of an asset and the amount at which it is reported in the balance sheet might or might not be temporary differences depending on the manner in which the asset will be recovered. One type is cash surrender value of life insurance in excess of premiums paid. It is a temporary difference if that asset will be recovered by cashing in the policy. Recovery of the asset in that manner will result in taxable amounts in future years. There is no temporary difference if that asset will be recovered from the proceeds of the policy upon the death of the insured. Under current U.S. tax law, those proceeds are not taxable.

The other type of difference is the amount the book basis of an investment in a domestic subsidiary (more than 50 percent owned) exceeds its tax basis. It is a temporary difference if that asset will be recovered by sale of the subsidiary because recovery of the investment in that manner will result in taxable amounts in future years. There is no temporary difference if the investment will be recovered by a tax-free liquidation or merger that is structured in accordance with certain requirements specified under current U.S. tax law.

(ii) Annual Computation.   Income taxes generally should be separately computed for each tax jurisdiction and for each tax-paying component in each tax jurisdiction with certain exceptions. (See the blended rate discussion in Subsection 17.2(d)(iv).) One reason, for example, is that a loss carryforward for a subsidiary in tax jurisdiction A does not offset taxable income for another subsidiary in tax jurisdiction B. Another reason is that different tax jurisdictions have different enacted tax laws and tax rates.

The first step is to determine the type and amount of all temporary differences at the date of the financial statements. Temporary differences that will result in taxable amounts in future years are referred to as *taxable temporary differences*. Temporary differences that will result in deductible amount in future years are referred to as *deductible temporary differences*. In addition, the nature and amount of each type of loss and tax credit carryforward (collectively referred to as *carryforwards*) and the remaining length of the carryforward period for each must be determined.

The next step is to measure and recognize the total deferred tax liability for all taxable temporary differences and the total deferred tax asset for all deductible temporary differences and carryforwards.

The final step is to assess whether a valuation allowance is needed for the deferred tax asset. All available evidence, both positive and negative, should be assessed. A valuation allowance is needed if the weight of that evidence indicates that some portion or the entire deferred tax asset will not be realized. The criterion for making that assessment is more likely than not. The amount of valuation allowance recognized equals the amount of deferred tax asset for which it is more likely than not that a tax benefit will not be realized.

(d) RECOGNITION AND MEASUREMENT.   Deferred tax liabilities and assets are recognized and measured under FASB ASC 740 by applying enacted tax laws and rates to determine the estimated tax effects in future years as a result of temporary differences and carryforwards that exist at the date of the financial statements. Discounting is not permitted.

(i) Recognition of Deferred Tax Liabilities and Assets.   Deferred tax liabilities and deferred tax assets are recognized separately. Thus, a deferred tax liability is recognized for all taxable temporary differences, and a deferred tax asset is recognized for all deductible temporary differences and carryforwards. Likewise, a valuation allowance for the deferred tax asset, if needed, is recognized separately. Some netting is permitted for balance sheet presentation, but disclosure of the total of all deferred tax liabilities, deferred tax assets, and valuation allowances is required. To illustrate, assume that at the end of the current year, an enterprise has $600 of taxable temporary differences and $500 of deductible temporary differences. The enacted tax rate for the last several years and all future years is 34 percent. The enterprise would recognize a deferred tax liability in the amount of $204 ($600 at 34 percent) and a deferred tax asset in the amount of $170 ($500 at 34 percent). All available evidence would be considered to determine whether a valuation allowance is needed for some portion or all of the $170 deferred tax asset.

The next chart summarizes how deferred tax assets and deferred tax liabilities arise:

Deferred Tax Asset	Deferred Tax Liability
1. Expenses currently recognized for book purposes, but not for tax purposes	1. Expenses currently recognized for tax purposes but not book purposes.
2. Revenues currently recognized for tax purposed but not for book purposes FUTURE: Book Income > Taxable Income (As item reverses)	2. Revenues currently recognized for book purposes but not tax purposes FUTURE: Taxable Income > Book Income (As item reverses)

The next example provides a detailed analysis and computation of the previously described recognition and measurement principles regarding a book-to-tax depreciation temporary difference.

MACRS Depreciation Example

- XYZ Corp. purchased office equipment for $100,000 on January 1, 2005.
- The equipment had an estimated useful life of 7 years and estimated salvage value of $0. XYZ uses the straight-line method to compute depreciation expenses under GAAP.
- Under the *Modified Accelerated Cost Recovery System* (*MACRS*), the equipment has a tax life of 5 years and is depreciated using the 200% declining balance depreciation method.
- Results in higher depreciation expense early in life of the asset for tax purposes compared to book.

Analysis

In year of deduction:

Tax Depreciation	>	Book Depreciation
Taxable Income	<	Pretax Book Income
Taxes Actually Paid	<	Provision for Taxes

In subsequent years:

Tax Depreciation	<	Book Depreciation
Taxable Income	>	Pretax Book Income
Taxes Actually Paid	>	Provision for Taxes

- A deferred tax liability is booked to account for the temporary difference, equal in amount to the difference between the book and tax basis of the asset times the expected tax rate.
- The temporary difference reverses as accumulated book depreciation catches up to the accumulated depreciation over the life of the asset.

Computation of Deferred Taxes Over the Life of the Asset

		2005	2006	2007	2008	2009	2010	2011
Depreciation Expense	**Book**							
	Depreciation Expense	14,286	14,286	14,286	14,286	14,286	14,286	14,286
	Tax							
	Depreciation Expense	20,000	32,000	19,200	11,520	11,520	5,760	
	MACRS %	20.0%	32.0%	19.2%	11.52%	11.52%	5.76%	
Balance Sheet	**Book**							
	Asset	100,000	100,000	100,000	100,000	100,000	100,000	100,000
	Less: Accum Dep.	14,286	28,571	42,857	57,143	71,429	85,714	100,000
	(b) Carrying Value	85,714	71,429	57,143	42,857	28,571	14,286	-
	Tax							
	Asset	100,000	100,000	100,000	100,000	100,000	100,000	
	Less: Accum Dep.	20,000	52,000	71,200	82,720	94,240	100,000	
	(t) Carrying Value	80,000	48,000	28,800	17,280	5,760	-	-
	Temporary Differences (t-b)	(5,714)	(23,429)	(28,343)	(25,577)	(22,811)	(14,286)	-
	Deferred Tax Liability (balance)	2,000	8,200	9,920	8,952	7,984	5,000	-
Income Statement	Pre-Tax Book Income	50,000	50,000	50,000	50,000	50,000	50,000	50,000
	Δ Temporary Differences	(5,714)	(17,714)	(4,914)	2,766	2,766	8,526	14,286
	Taxable Income	44,286	32,286	45,086	52,766	52,766	58,526	64,286
	Current Tax Expense (35%)	15,500	11,300	15,780	18,468	18,468	20,484	22,500
	Deferred Tax Expense	2,000	6,200	1,720	(968)	(968)	(2,984)	(5,000)
	Total Tax Expense	17,500	17,500	17,500	17,500	17,500	17,500	17,500
	Effective Tax Rate	35%	35%	35%	35%	35%	35%	35%

(ii) Recognition of a Valuation Allowance.   Under FASB ASC 740, the objective is to produce accounting results that come closest to the expected outcome (i.e., recognition of deferred tax assets that are expected to be realized and nonrecognition of deferred tax assets that are not expected to be realized). To accomplish that objective, a deferred tax asset is recognized for all deductible temporary differences and carryforwards, and a valuation allowance is recognized if it is more likely than not that the asset will not be realized. *More likely than not* means a level of likelihood that is more than 50 percent. Thus, companies must reduce deferred tax assets by a valuation allowance if, based on available evidence, it is more likely than not some or all of the deferred tax assets will not be realized.

Recognizing deferred tax assets is a complex and subjective area of FASB ASC 740. Judgment is needed, and assessing the need for a valuation allowance generally includes assumptions and estimates involving forecasts of future operating results. There are no bright-line tests to apply. In fact, the FASB stopped short of imposing a mandatory valuation allowance when an entity reported cumulative pretax losses for financial reporting in the current and two preceding years due to the uncertainty of continued losses into the future. Therefore, application of this provision will be affected by each company's circumstances and by management's evaluation of those circumstances.

For companies that have a history of being profitable and expect that trend to continue, the judgment required to conclude the future realization of deferred tax assets is more likely than not to occur is generally straightforward. The evaluation of whether a valuation allowance needs to be provided is more complex when there is negative evidence, which generally applies to loss companies, marginally profitable or break-even companies, or companies experiencing a high degree of volatility in profits.

A deferred tax asset is realized by reducing the amount of tax paid on taxable income. A deferred tax asset might not be realized, and a valuation allowance might be needed, for any of three reasons. One obvious reason is that there might not be enough taxable income to realize the deferred tax asset. Equally important, the taxable income must occur within the right time period (i.e., sometime during the carryback or carryforward years specified by the tax law). Finally, the nature or type of taxable income sometimes is important (e.g., if future capital gains are the only way to realize a deferred tax asset for a capital loss carryforward).

Thus, the critical factor in determining whether a valuation allowance is needed for a deferred tax asset is taxable income—a sufficient amount of the appropriate type of taxable income that occurs during the required time period. FASB ASC 740-10-30-18 identifies four potential sources of taxable income:

1. Future reversals of taxable temporary differences
2. Future taxable income exclusive of those reversals
3. Taxable income in the current or prior years for which loss carryback is permitted by the tax law
4. Tax-planning strategies

In the example given earlier, the enterprise recognized a deferred tax liability in the amount of $204 for $600 of taxable temporary differences and a deferred tax asset in the amount of $170 for $500 of deductible temporary differences. Future realization of the deferred tax asset must be assessed to determine whether a valuation allowance should be recognized. Future realization could occur as a result of any one or combination of the four potential sources of taxable income. To illustrate, a tax benefit might be realized for the $500 of deductible temporary differences by offsetting one of four sources:

1. $500 of taxable income that results from reversing taxable temporary differences in future years
2. $500 of taxable income (exclusive of reversals) that results from operations in future years
3. $500 of taxable income in the current or prior years by loss carryback to those years
4. $500 of taxable income in any of the three circumstances above *and* as a result of a tax-planning strategy

The four sources of taxable income may be considered in any sequence. If one source is sufficient to eliminate the need for a valuation allowance, the other three sources do not need to be considered. Or if two sources are sufficient, the other two do not need to be considered, and so forth. Thus, it may make sense to first consider the source(s) that, potentially, is the most fertile source of taxable income. Alternatively, some may prefer to first consider the source(s) that is easiest to evaluate.

Recognition of a valuation allowance when none is needed, however, is prohibited. When a valuation allowance is recognized, each of the four sources of taxable income must be considered to determine the amount of the valuation allowance. For example, recognition of a valuation allowance that is measured based on a consideration of two of the sources and without regard to taxable income from the other two sources is not permitted. The valuation allowance should reduce the deferred tax asset to the amount that is expected to be realized, and it should not reduce the deferred tax asset below that amount.

Future Reversals of Taxable Temporary Differences. The future reversal of taxable temporary differences is a ready source of taxable income for future realization of a deferred tax asset for deductible temporary differences and carryforwards. This future taxable income is already "on hand," so to speak, at the balance sheet date.

One note of caution is appropriate. The taxable temporary differences must reverse sometime within the window of opportunity for realizing a tax benefit for deductible temporary differences and carryforwards. Thus, in the case of tax attributes such as net operating and capital loss and credit carryforwards, it is important to know when the attributes are expiring and to consider any law changes that impact the analysis, such as expanded carryback or carryforward periods. In the case of net operating losses, the U.S. federal tax jurisdiction has a very large window. The window of opportunity generally is 23 years (the reversal year, two carryback years, and 20 carryforward years). One exception is that there is no time limit for alternative maximum tax (AMT) credit carryforwards. The window of opportunity, however, is in many cases much smaller for state, local, and foreign tax jurisdictions and thus requires a close review of each taxing jurisdiction's statute.

In the case of capital losses and foreign tax credit carryforwards, it is also important to consider the character of any potential future income. For example, current federal income tax law allows corporations to deduct capital losses only if they offset capital gains. Foreign tax credit (FTC) carryforwards can be used only to reduce taxes on foreign source income such as dividends from foreign subsidiaries.

A general understanding of the timing of future reversals of temporary differences is, in many cases, relevant in assessing the need for a valuation allowance. Most temporary differences reverse when the related asset is recovered or the related liability is settled. Since most enterprises know, at least approximately, when their assets and liabilities will be recovered and settled, those enterprises already have a general understanding of the timing of the future reversals of their temporary differences. However, in the case where a more complex analysis is required, a company may use scheduling to determine the timing of future reversals of taxable temporary items, and it may find it useful to categorize future reversal patterns by these specific time periods:

1. The reversal pattern is recovered over a certain time frame and is easy to determine (e.g., depreciating an asset with a tax life of 5 years using the 200 percent declining balance under MACRS, but for GAAP, the asset had an estimated useful life of 7 years and uses the straight-line method to compute depreciation expense).

2. The reversal pattern is not clear-cut, and estimates may be required in such cases (e.g., reserves for litigation where settlement date may not be certain).

3. The reversal pattern is indefinite, and the temporary item is not expected to reverse in the foreseeable future (e.g., nondepreciable assets such as land that the company does not intend to sell).

FASB ASC 740 does not require scheduling but does require an informed decision about the need for a valuation allowance. The FASB stated in SFAS No. 109, *Special Report:* "Because of cost-benefit considerations, the Board has chosen not to specify in detail how the reversal patterns for each class of temporary differences should be treated. In many cases there is more than one logical approach." Based on such rationale, the amount of scheduling, if any, that will be required will depend on the facts and circumstances of each situation. In some cases, the amount of scheduling can be reduced by using estimates or aggregate FASB ASC 740 (former SFAS No. 109, *Special Report,* Q1) offers this guidance when selecting a scheduling method:

1. A method may be used that minimizes the complexity of determining reversal patterns.
2. The method used should be systematic and logical.
3. The same method should be used for all temporary differences within a particular category.
4. Different methods may be used for different categories of temporary differences.

Future Taxable Income Exclusive of Reversals. Unlike the first source, taxable temporary differences, this source of future taxable income is not already on hand at the balance sheet date. This source results from earning taxable income (exclusive of reversals) in future years. Thus, assessments of this source of taxable income are more subjective, and more judgment is required. The subjective nature of the assessments and the need for judgment, however, do not provide reasons either to ignore this source of potential taxable income or to arbitrarily assume, in the name of conservatism or anything else, that future taxable income will be zero.

Sometimes this source of future taxable income may be the easiest and most fruitful starting point. For example, assume that an enterprise has $500 of deductible temporary differences and that it has earned taxable income of at least $100 in each of the last three years. This enterprise is relatively free of negative evidence, and future operations are reasonably expected to be equally profitable. That level of future taxable income is more than sufficient to realize a tax benefit for $500 of deductible temporary differences during the window of opportunity in the U.S. federal tax jurisdiction. In other circumstances, however, there may be a considerable amount of negative evidence, or the relationship between the amount of deductible temporary differences and the expected level of future taxable income may be less favorable. In those circumstances, determining the need for a valuation allowance based on an assessment of future taxable income (exclusive of reversals) is more difficult.

In practice, a company's management forecast of future pretax income or loss may be a helpful tool to support valuation allowance assessments so that a company with a history of operating losses may be able to recognize deferred tax assets if it can overcome such negative evidence with positive evidence. However, it should also be noted that in some cases, management maybe overly optimistic about the future, and the company may want to take a more conservative approach for this purpose. In cases where management either has not prepared a forecast or has limited experience, a company may need to rely on other factors to determine valuation allowances, such as revenue or industry trends as well as current economic conditions.

FASB ASC 740-10-30-17 (paragraph 20 of former Statement No. 109) states:

> All available evidence, both positive and negative, shall be considered to determine whether, based on the weight of that evidence, a valuation allowance for deferred tax assets is needed. Information about an entity's current financial position and its results of operations for the current and preceding years ordinarily is readily available. That historical information is supplemented by all currently available information about future years. Sometimes, however, historical information may not be available (for example, start-up operations) or it may not be as relevant (for example, if there has been a significant, recent change in circumstances) and special attention is required.

FASB ASC 740 10-30-21 and FASB ASC 740-10-30-22 provide examples of negative and positive evidence respectively. The next chart highlights the examples provided.

Negative Evidence	Positive Evidence
Cumulative losses	Cumulative profits
History of expiring losses	No history of losing attributes
Unsettled circumstances that would negatively impact profits	Existing backlogs of sales or firm contracts
Brief carryback or carryforward period	Long or indefinite carryback or carryforward period
Unrealized tax loses (depreciated assets)	Unrealized tax gains (appreciated assets)
Losses occurred in recent past or are expected to occur in near future	Losses are an isolated event

The examples of negative and positive evidence in FASB ASC 740 are truly intended to be no more than examples. They are not intended to be used as a checklist for determining when a valuation allowance is or is not required. Furthermore, the examples provided are not all-inclusive lists. All available evidence should be considered—regardless of whether a particular type of evidence is one of the examples cited in FASB ASC 740. However, usually objective evidence (historical data) is weighted more heavily than subjective evidence (forecasted earnings). The objective is to determine whether the weight of the available evidence indicates a valuation allowance is needed.

Judgment is required in considering the relative impact of negative and positive evidence. An accounting standard obviously cannot set forth requirements for how to apply judgment, but it can provide guidelines. FASB ASC 740 740-10-30-21 states that "forming a conclusion that a valuation allowance is not needed is difficult when there is negative evidence such as cumulative losses in recent years." FASB ASC 740-10-30-23 further acknowledges that "a cumulative loss in recent years is a significant piece of negative evidence that is difficult to overcome" and requires that the weight given to the potential effect of negative and positive evidence "be commensurate with the extent to which it can be objectively verified." Thus, a forecast of future taxable income is inherently subjective and may not be sufficient to overcome negative evidence that includes cumulative losses in recent years, particularly if the projected future taxable income is dependent on an anticipated turnaround to operating profitability that has not yet been demonstrated.

It should be noted that the Securities and Exchange Commission (SEC) has questioned registrants with three-year cumulative losses and no valuation allowance and has requested documentation to support such determination. Thus, in practice, for those companies incurring cumulative losses, it may be difficult to avoid a valuation allowance.

Taxable Income in the Current or Prior Years. Taxable income in the current or prior years for which loss carryback is permitted by the tax law is another ready source of taxable income for future realization of a deferred tax asset for deductible temporary differences. Like taxable temporary differences, this taxable income is already on hand, so to speak, at the balance sheet date.

Referring again to the previous example, the enterprise needs to determine whether a valuation allowance is needed for the $170 deferred tax asset for $500 of deductible temporary differences. Assume that the tax jurisdiction is the U.S. federal tax jurisdiction and that taxable income and the tax paid for the current year exceed $500 and $170, respectively. If the deductible temporary differences will reverse within the next three years, nothing needs to be known about future taxable income exclusive of reversals. Regardless of whatever else occurs in the future, the deferred tax asset is realizable by loss carryback to the current year.

Tax-Planning Strategies. Tax planning strategies are another potential source of taxable income to be considered in determining the need for a valuation allowance. For example, a strategy to switch from tax-exempt to taxable investments would result in additional future taxable income that could reduce or eliminate the need for a valuation allowance at the end of the current year.

FASB ASC 740-10-30-19 defines *tax-planning strategies* as actions that (1) are prudent and feasible, (2) an entity ordinarily might not take but would take to prevent an operating loss or tax credit carryforward from expiring unused, and (3) would result in realization of deferred tax assets. All three criteria must be met in order to be considered a tax planning strategy under FASB ASC 740. Thus, an action that is prudent and feasible but does not result in the realization of deferred tax assets would not be considered a qualifying tax-planning strategy.

A strategy is prudent and feasible if management has the *ability to implement* the strategy and *expects* to do so if necessary in future years. For example, the sale of equipment that is critical to operations would not be prudent because the equipment would need to be replaced. However, a strategy to sell the equipment and lease it back may be considered prudent. However, the strategy would only feasible only if the company is expected to find a purchaser that would be willing to enter into the sale-leaseback transaction. The dominant consideration is that management is *able* to apply and *intends* to apply the strategy to realize the tax benefits of operating loss or tax credit carryforwards unless circumstances change.

The term does *not* refer to all of the various actions, assumptions, strategies, and so forth that are implicit either in the normal course of conducting a business or in estimates of expected future taxable income. For example, a company's practice of deferring taxable income whenever possible by structuring sales to qualify as installment sales for tax purposes is not considered a tax-planning strategy as the term is used in FASB ASC 740.

Most tax-planning strategies involve actions or elections that accelerate or delay taxable or deductible items, change the character of taxable or deductible amounts (e.g., from ordinary income or loss to capital gain or loss), or change the nature of the income (e.g., from tax-exempt income to taxable income). Some examples of these strategies include:

1. A company modifies transfer pricing or other intercompany fee arrangements to shift income from one jurisdiction to another.

2. A company that uses accelerated depreciation methods elects straight-line method for future acquisitions if the additional income from reduced depreciation would enable it to utilize a loss carryforward.

3. A company elects out of the installment basis to the accrual basis for measuring taxable income on future sales for federal income tax purposes, so that gains may be recognized immediately.

4. A company sells investments in securities to generate capital gains so capital loss carryforwards may be used.

Some tax-planning strategies may involve actions that would result in incurring significant expenses (e.g., lawyers' and other fees) or recognizing significant losses (e.g., from the sale of investments carried at cost if market value is less). In those cases, the expenses or losses, net of any related and realizable tax benefits, are recognized by including them as a component of the valuation allowance.

Tax-planning strategies pertain only to the determination of a valuation allowance for deferred tax assets, and tax-planning strategies may not be considered for purposes of nonrecognition of a deferred tax liability. A deferred tax liability is recognized for all taxable temporary differences except the particular types of taxable temporary differences for which exceptions are specified in FASB ASC 740 (see Section 17.1(c)).

Furthermore, ASC 740-10-30-20 states:

> When a tax-planning strategy is contemplated as a source of future taxable income to support the realizability of a deferred tax asset, the recognition and measurement requirements for tax positions in paragraphs 740-10-25-6 through 25-7; 740-10-25-13; and 740-10-30-7 shall be applied in determining the amount of available future taxable income.

Thus, if a tax-planning strategy fails the more-likely-than-not recognition criterion of GAAP for uncertainty in income taxes-FASB ASC 740-10 (formerly FASB Interpretation No. 48), that tax-planning strategy should not be considered a source of future taxable income for determining the amount of a deferred tax asset valuation allowance.

FASB ASC 740-10-55-41 addresses the question as to what extent must management actively search for valid tax planning strategies since the use of such strategies is not elective. The FASB provides guidance by stating:

> [M]anagement should make a reasonable effort to identify those qualifying tax planning strategies that are significant. Management's obligation to apply qualifying tax-planning strategies in determining the amount of valuation allowance required is the same as its obligation to apply the requirements of other Topics for financial accounting and reporting. However, if there is sufficient evidence that taxable income from one of the other sources of taxable income listed in paragraph 740-10-30-18 will be adequate to eliminate the need for any valuation allowance, a search for tax-planning strategies is not necessary.

Documentation.   A company may find that its external auditors may challenge the valuation allowance amount it provided (or has not provided), or it may receive a SEC comment letter inquiring as to how the company made its assessment, since the analysis can be quite subjective. Such challenges apply especially in the case when a company is transitioning from incurring losses to becoming profitable, or vice versa. Therefore, a company will find it helpful to document its analysis in support of its conclusion for the amount of valuation allowance it is providing.

(iii) Recognition of a Change in the Valuation Allowance. The gross amount of a deferred tax asset will change because of deductible temporary differences and carryforwards that originate or are realized during the year or that expire unused at the end of the year. The need for and, if so, the amount of a valuation allowance for a gross deferred tax asset is redetermined at least annually. A change in the net amount of a deferred tax asset (i.e., the gross asset less the valuation allowance) results in deferred tax expense or benefit. The general requirements for the allocation of tax expense or benefit among continuing operations and other items are discussed in Section 17.4(a).

Sometimes there will be a change in the amount of valuation allowance for particular deductible temporary differences and carryforwards that exist at both the beginning and the end of the year. That ordinarily will occur because a significant change in the enterprise's facts and circumstances causes a change in judgment about the amount of taxable income (exclusive of reversals) expected in future years. In those circumstances, deferred tax expense from an increase in the valuation allowance always is allocated to continuing operations, and deferred tax benefit from a decrease in the valuation allowance also is allocated to continuing operations unless the tax benefit is one of those that are never recognized in comprehensive income (see Section 17.4(a)).

(iv) Measurement of Deferred Tax Liabilities and Assets. Measurements of deferred tax liabilities for taxable temporary differences and deferred tax assets for deductible temporary differences and carryforwards are based on enacted tax laws and rates. The objective is to measure the estimated future tax effects of temporary differences and carryforwards that exist at the date of the financial statements.

In the U.S. federal tax jurisdiction, if taxable income exceeds a certain amount, all taxable income is taxed at a single tax rate. Lower levels of taxable income are taxed at graduated tax rates. Deferred tax liabilities and assets are measured using (1) the single tax rate for enterprises that ordinarily are not subject to graduated tax rates and (2) an estimated average graduated tax rate for enterprises that ordinarily are subject to graduated tax rates. The estimated average graduated tax rate is based on the estimated average annual taxable income in the future years that deferred tax liabilities and assets are estimated to be settled and realized.

Sometimes there may be a different enacted tax rate for certain types of income, such as capital gains. If, for example, the enacted tax rate for capital gains is different, that enacted tax rate is used to measure a deferred tax liability for taxable temporary differences that, when they reverse, will result in capital gains.

A zero tax rate cannot be used to measure deferred tax liabilities and assets even if losses are expected in future years. A zero tax rate is not used to measure deferred tax liabilities because the FASB decided, for practical reasons, that anticipation of the tax consequences of future losses or expenses to eliminate a deferred tax liability should not be permitted. A zero tax rate is not used to measure deferred tax assets because future losses (more precisely, the absence of future taxable income) are a factor that is considered in determining the need for a valuation allowance. Thus, in circumstances when the tax rate otherwise might be zero, deferred tax liabilities and assets are measured using the single tax rate or the lowest graduated tax rate depending on the type of enterprise.

Blended-Rate Approach. FASB ASC 740-10-55-25 allows tax computations for two or more jurisdictions to be combined when (1) the same operations are taxed in two or more jurisdictions and (2) either there are no significant differences between the tax laws of the or any difference in computation would have no significant effect, given the company's facts and circumstance. Based on these criteria, many companies use a "blended rate" approach at the legal-entity level to simplify the income tax calculation for entities operating in multiple U.S. states.

When companies are subject to income taxes in only one state, the calculation of deferred taxes is straightforward. The enacted federal tax rate is adjusted to reflect the interaction of federal and state income taxes. That is, state taxes are deductible for federal purposes, and the federal rate is adjusted for the benefit of the state tax deduction.

Blended Rate Example

State tax rate		6%
Federal tax rate		34%
Deduction for state income taxes:	(34% × 6%)	(2%)
Federal rate net of state benefit		32%
Combined federal and state tax rate		38%

When companies are subject to income taxes in more than one state, they apportion their federal taxable income between all of the states according to state laws. Therefore, different rates may apply to different portions of federal taxable income. In such instances, one approach to calculating deferred income taxes is to use a weighted average rate.

Weighted Average Tax Rate Example

Assume that a company operates in two states.

- State A imposes a 9 percent income tax.
- State B imposes a 4 percent income tax

Approximately 75 percent of the company's taxable income is allocated to State A. The weighted average tax rate would be determined as:

- State A: 75% × 9%
- State B: 25% × 4%

For many companies, the effects of the different rates on the calculation of deferred tax assets and liabilities are not likely to be significant, and a single rate may be appropriate to use in such cases. Whatever approach is applied, management should be able to support its decision based on the criteria set forth in FASB ASC 740-10-55-25, after considering materiality thresholds.

Tax Credits.   Since tax credits provide a dollar-for-dollar reduction of income taxes, the deferred tax asset is simply the amount of tax credit carryforwards available. Thus, in the case of credits, one should *not* tax effect the credits by the applicable rate.

Alternative Minimum Tax.   Under FASB ASC 740-10-30-11, the AMT tax rate is never used to measure deferred tax liabilities and assets. Instead, the regular tax rate is used, and a deferred tax asset is recognized for any AMT credit carryforward and then assessed to determine whether a valuation allowance is needed. The window of opportunity for realization of a deferred tax asset for an AMT credit carryforward encompasses the entire life of the enterprise. That positive factor distinguishes this type of deferred tax asset from virtually every other type of deferred tax asset.

What if, however, the enterprise will always be an AMT taxpayer? A valuation allowance is needed if the AMT credit carryforward is expected to expire unused at the end of the life of the enterprise. But that future scenario might not occur as often as some people might intuitively expect. AMT credit carryforwards arise primarily because of either "timing" differences (such as depreciation) or preference items (such as certain special deductions). If an enterprise is an AMT taxpayer because of timing differences, those differences ultimately will unwind (toward the end of the life of the enterprise) and thereby provide an opportunity to realize the AMT credit carryforward. Alternatively, if an enterprise is an AMT taxpayer because of preference or other items, income earned from the investment of funds available at the end of the life of the enterprise (i.e., prior to the final distribution of those funds to shareholders) might provide an opportunity to realize an AMT credit carryforward.

Enacted Change in Tax Laws or Rates.   Deferred tax liabilities and assets are adjusted for the effects of changes in tax laws or rates. A change in tax laws or rates is accounted for as a discrete event that is recognized in the period that includes the enactment date. In the U.S. federal tax jurisdiction, the enactment date is the date that the change is signed into law by the president. If an enterprise prepares its annual financial statements on a calendar-year basis, a change that is enacted any time in year 2 through December 31 is recognized in the financial statements for year 2, and a change that is enacted any time in year 3 starting on January 1 is recognized in the financial statements for year 3. Disclosure of the effect of a change that is enacted after the end of the year and before issuing the financial statements for that year usually is necessary.

An understanding of the timing of future reversals of temporary differences is needed when there is a phased-in change in tax rates. For example, assume that the new enacted tax rates for future years are X percent for years 2 to 4, Y percent for years 5 to 7, and Z percent for year 8 and thereafter. Deferred tax liabilities and assets for the estimated future tax effects of temporary differences are measured in this way: (1) at X percent for temporary differences that will reverse in years 2 to 4, (2) at Y percent for temporary differences that will reverse in years 5 to 7, and (3) at Z percent for temporary differences that will reverse in year 8 and thereafter.

Different enacted tax rates for different years create another, related issue that occasionally might be encountered in practice. Sometimes an enterprise may know or expect that the deferred tax liability for taxable temporary differences reversing in a particular future year will not be settled in that year or that the deferred tax asset for deductible temporary differences reversing in a particular future year will not be realized in that year. That would occur, for example, if there is a loss in the future reversal year, and if the reversing taxable and deductible temporary differences only serve to decrease or increase that loss. If the loss is carried back, it will decrease taxes for an earlier year, or if it is carried forward, it will decrease taxes for a later year. When there are different enacted tax rates for the reversal (loss) year and the carryback or carryforward year, the deferred tax liability and asset for temporary differences reversing in the loss year should be measured using the enacted tax rate for the carryback or carryforward year.

Change in Tax Status.   A change in the tax status of an enterprise also is accounted for as a discrete event. A deferred tax liability or asset is recognized or eliminated in the period that the change in tax status occurs. The date of change is the approval date if the change is voluntary, and it is the enactment date of a change in tax law that changes the tax status of an enterprise. If approval of a voluntary change is not necessary, the date of change is the filing date (e.g., changes to or from the taxable C corporation status or nontaxable S corporation status in the U.S. federal tax jurisdiction). FASB ASC 740-10-50-4 (formerly Questions 11 and 12 in the FASB Special Report on implementation of SFAS No. 109 provide additional guidance.)

(e) SPECIAL APPLICATIONS.   FASB ASC 740 provides for a number of special applications.

(i) Regulated Companies.   FASB ASC 980, *Regulated Operations,* provides special accounting rules for companies that are rate regulated, such as utilities. A company subject to FASB ASC 980, for example, may be required to capitalize a cost that other companies would charge to expense. If capitalization of that cost creates a temporary difference, a deferred tax liability is recognized. If it is probable that future revenue will be provided for the payment of that deferred tax liability, a new asset is recognized for that probable future revenue. That asset and the deferred tax liability are shown as an asset and liability and are not offset. Similar accounting also may result from other special accounting rules for rate-regulated companies, such as those for (1) the equity component of the allowance for funds used during construction, (2) tax benefits that are flowed through to customers when temporary differences originate, and (3) adjustments of a deferred tax liability or asset for an enacted change in tax law or rates. (See Chapter 36 on regulated utilities in this *Handbook*).

(ii) Leveraged Leases.   FASB ASC 840-30, *Leases—Capital Leases,* specify special accounting for the tax benefits associated with a leveraged lease. However, FASB ASC 740-10-25-3(c) does not change the basic model for accounting for leveraged leases. Taxable temporary differences arising from leveraged leases do not enter into the computation of a deferred tax liability. Instead, a deferred tax credit is calculated in accordance with the FASB ASC 840-30 model. (See Chapter 15 in this *Handbook*).

(iii) Business Combinations.[4]   FASB ASC 805-10-05-4 requires business combinations to be accounted for using the acquisition method by measuring each asset acquired, liability assumed, and any noncontrolling interest in an acquired entity at its fair value at the acquisition date. Generally, under the acquisition method differences between the carrying amounts of the assets and liabilities recorded under GAAP and the amounts recorded for income tax reporting should be accounted for following the requirements of FASB ASC 740.

FASB ASC 805-740-25-2 and ASC 805-740-30-1 provide that the acquirer must determine the potential tax effects of temporary differences, carryforwards, and income tax uncertainties of an acquiree that exist at the acquisition date, or that arise as a result of the acquisition. The next discussion considers the key considerations that need to be examined when dealing with a business combination in order to determine such amounts.

Tax Structure (Asset versus Stock Purchase).   The tax basis of the assets acquired and liabilities assumed is determined differently depending on whether the business combination is *taxable* or *nontaxable*. Thus, it is important to understand the tax structure even though the basis amount for financial reporting purposes will be the same, regardless of the form of the business combination.

If an enterprise's assets are acquired and its liabilities are assumed (asset acquisition), the purchase is treated as a *taxable* transaction. In a *taxable* transaction, the tax bases of the assets acquired and liabilities assumed are adjusted (*stepped up*) to fair value. A step-up in tax basis generally requires allocating the consideration for the acquisition to identifiable assets acquired and liabilities assumed based on their fair values, with the difference between the consideration and the amounts allocated accounted for as goodwill. The acquisition of a business through the purchase of its shares (stock acquisition) generally is treated as a *nontaxable* transaction. This can be effected either through a taxable sale of stock or tax-free reorganization if the exchange qualifies under the Internal Revenue Code. In a nontaxable transaction, the historical tax bases (*carryover basis*) of the assets and liabilities, net operating losses, and other tax attributes of the target generally carryover to the acquirer. For federal income tax purposes, if the appropriate tax election is made under the Internal Revenue Code (section 338(h)(10) election), a stock acquisition can be treated as an asset acquisition for tax purposes.

---

[4]SFAS No. 141(R), *Business Combinations,* which is codified in FASB ASC 805, replaced the guidance on business combinations in SFAS No. 141 with new guidance effective for combinations occurring in years beginning on or after December 15, 2008.

Tax Status. The tax status of an enterprise impacts the determination of temporary differences. Therefore, the determination as to how the entity or entities acquired will be treated for tax purposes (e.g., corporate entities [taxable], partnerships [nontaxable], limited liability corporations [taxable or nontaxable]) must also be considered. For example, while the assets and liabilities of a limited liability corporation (LLC) that is taxed as a partnership (i.e., a nontaxable enterprise) might give rise to taxable or deductible temporary differences, no deferred taxes are recorded in the LLC's financial statements. This is due to the fact that the tax consequences of the LLC will be reported by its members under the tax law. However, if the LLC members are taxable enterprises, those members must provide deferred taxes on any temporary difference associated with the LLC interest. It should be noted that the tax status of the enterprise does not affect whether a business combination is considered taxable or nontaxable; instead, these commonly used terms refer to whether the acquirer records the tax bases of assets and liabilities of the acquired entity on the basis of their historical tax basis or at fair market value or another remeasurement technique required by the tax law.

Temporary Differences. Entities must identify, on the basis of enacted tax law as of the date of acquisition, the tax bases of identifiable assets acquired and liabilities assumed. The next step is to compare the recognized tax bases of the assets and liabilities with the financial reporting fair values of the acquired assets and assumed liabilities to determine the temporary differences. Nontaxable business combinations generally result in significantly more temporary differences than do taxable business combinations because the tax basis of the assets acquired and liabilities assumed is carryover basis.

The process for recording deferred taxes for the acquired entity's temporary differences is essentially the same for taxable and nontaxable business combinations. That is, determine if the temporary differences are deductible temporary differences or taxable temporary differences, and record the appropriate deferred tax assets (DTAs) or deferred tax liabilities (DTLs). In nontaxable business combinations, two approaches are commonly used for recording deferred taxes. The *de novo approach* is where all existing deferred taxes are removed from the acquired entity's books and new temporary differences are calculated on the basis of the differences between book and tax bases in acquired assets and assumed liabilities. The acquirer sometimes shortcuts the de novo approach by limiting its analysis to the change in book bases from historically reported amounts. This *layering-on approach* is labeled as such because the new book bases are recorded as an incremental adjustment to the historical book bases. The change from old to new book bases is added to (or subtracted from) the historical temporary differences. It should be noted that this method may not be as reliable as the de novo approach in cases where it may be difficult to substantiate the historical deferred tax balances. The next example illustrates these two different approaches that can be used to record deferred taxes in a business combination.

Example

- Company A pays $5,000 to acquire Target Company (TC) stock in a nontaxable business combination.
- The fair value of the identifiable assets is $3,500 ($2,500 tangible, $1,000 intangible).
- TC has no liabilities except for its DTLs.
- TC had some historical goodwill from a prior taxable business combination.
- The historical book and tax bases of the acquired assets, along with the historical DTL, are presented in the next table.
- Assume that 40 percent is the applicable tax rate for calculating tax deferred taxes.

Processes for Recording Deferred Taxes in a Business Combination

	Fair Value A	Historical Book Bases B	Historical Tax Bases C	Existing Deferred Tax Layer D	Existing Deferred Tax Layer (A–B) × 40%	De NovoMethod (A–C) × 40%
Assets	2500	1500	375	−450	−400	− 850
Intangibles	1000	750	125	−250	−100	− 350
Goodwill		250	0	−100	100*	0
DTL				−800		
Total DTL recorded					−500	−1200

Note: D + E (tax layer) = layering-on approach.
*Historical DTL related to tax-deductible goodwill must be removed.

Journal Entry to Record the Business Combination

	Debit	Credit
Assets	2500	
Intangibles	1000	
Goodwill§	2700	
DTL		1200
Cash		5000

§Represents $1,500 of goodwill ($5,000 purchase price less the $3,500 assigned to the fair value of tangible and intangible assets) plus the $1,200 of DTL. No DTL is recognized for the excess of financial reporting goodwill over tax-deductible goodwill because such recognition is precluded by ASC 740, *Acquired Tax Attributes.*

FASB ASC 805-740-25-2 addresses acquired tax benefits such as net operating losses (NOLs), credit carryforwards, or other relevant tax attributes. It requires that that deferred tax assets be recorded as part of the business combination, unless they are not considered to be realizable. In that case, a valuation allowance is required, and the next considerations need to be made:

1. *Acquiring company's valuation allowance adjustment.* Tax laws may allow an acquiring company's deductible temporary differences and operating loss or tax credit carryforwards to reduce future taxable income attributable to the acquired company if consolidated tax returns are filed after the acquisition. In that case, the acquiring company should assess its existing deferred tax asset valuation allowances based on realization by the combined company when accounting for the business combination. If a valuation allowance is provided for a deferred tax asset for an acquiring company's deductible differences or carryforwards at the acquisition date, FASB ASC 805-740-30-3 states that reduction of a valuation allowance relating to deductible temporary differences or carryforwards is recognized as an income tax benefit (or credited directly to contributed capital). In other words, the tax benefits of those items that are later realized (i.e., through elimination of the valuation allowance) should reduce income tax expense since the tax benefit does not result from using the acquired company's deductible temporary differences or carryforwards.

2. *Acquired entity's adjustments.* Adjustments, within the measurement period, to an acquired entity's valuation allowance established for DTAs at the date of acquisition that are the

result of new information about facts and circumstances that existed at the acquisition date are reflected as adjustments to goodwill. All other adjustments inside or outside the measurement period are recorded as a component of income tax expense.

3. *Decreases in valuation allowances due to subsequent changes in tax laws.* If a valuation allowance is reduced or eliminated due to subsequent changes in tax laws, FASB ASC 805-740-45-2 requires the effect of an adjustment related to an acquired company's operating loss carryforwards (or deductible temporary differences or other carryforwards) to be recognized as an income tax benefit (or credited directly to contributed capital).

Tax Uncertainties. FASB ASC 805-740-45-4 generally requires changes in an acquired tax position, or new tax positions that arise as a result of the acquisition, to be accounted for following GAAP for uncertainties in income taxes (formerly FIN 48). Therefore, as of the acquisition date, uncertain tax positions are recognized if they meet the more-likely-than-not recognition threshold and are measured at the largest amount of benefit that is greater than 50 percent likely to be realized upon settlement with a taxing authority that has full knowledge of all relevant information. In general, after the acquisition date, adjustments to an acquired entity's uncertain tax positions are recorded in income tax expense, not goodwill. A required adjustment that is based on new information about facts and circumstances that existed as of the acquisition date may be recorded to goodwill if the company is in the process of finalizing its accounting during the measurement period.

Acquisition-Related Costs

Professional Fees.   Attorney, accountant, investment banker fees, and other professional fees incurred as a result of the acquisition must be expensed as incurred under U.S. GAAP. For U.S. federal tax purposes, such costs may or may not be deductible. However, a temporary difference exists if acquisition-related costs are deductible for tax purposes and if that deduction occurs in a period different from that in which they are expensed for US GAAP purposes. In that case, any related deferred taxes will be recorded as a component of income tax expense (i.e., outside the business combination).

Debt Issuance Costs. Generally, debt issuance costs are capitalized and amortized using the effective interest method over the term of the related debt for U.S. GAAP purposes. Tax may or may not follow book treatment. Deferred taxes should be provided if there is a difference between the book and tax approaches to recognizing debt issue costs.

Registration and Issuing Equity Costs. For U.S. GAAP purposes, registration and issuance costs for equity securities are generally treated as a reduction in additional paid-in capital. Such costs are generally neither deductible nor amortizable for tax purposes, and therefore no temporary differences should exist.

Deferred Taxes Related to Goodwill.   It is not unusual for the recorded amounts of book and tax goodwill to be different. This is a result of differences in tax laws and financial reporting rules and whether the business combination is taxable or nontaxable. For example, book and tax have may have different valuation methods and allocation rules. In addition, there are book and tax accounting differences for determining the amount of consideration transferred due to different treatment of contingencies or for expenses incurred for the transaction. In a taxable acquisition, the taxpayer must allocate the consideration paid among the various assets acquired according to a residual method prescribed by Internal Revenue Code 1060. Section 197 of the Code identifies the allocated purchase price amounts that should be classified as intangibles and that are eligible for 180-month (15-year) amortization. In certain cases, value assigned as a separate Section 197 intangible for tax purposes, such as customer-based intangibles, are included as part of goodwill for book purposes. Therefore, it is important to review valuations to confirm that tax allocations between Section 197 intangibles and goodwill are correct in order to ensure that the goodwill components and deferred taxes are calculated accurately.

Goodwill Components.   In a taxable acquisition, goodwill is either tax deductible or nondeductible. If goodwill is deductible for tax, goodwill for financial reporting purposes and tax-deductible goodwill

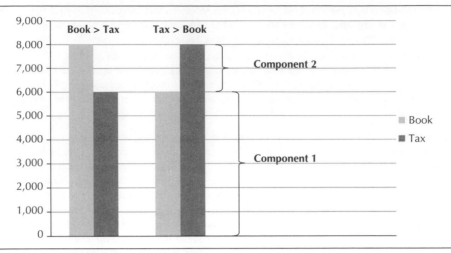

Exhibit 17.2   Goodwill Separated into Two Components

must be separated into two components as of the acquisition date. This allocation is necessary to calculate the appropriate amount of deferred taxes.

The first component of goodwill (*component 1* goodwill) equals the lesser of (1) goodwill for financial reporting purposes or (2) tax-deductible goodwill. The second component of goodwill (*component 2* goodwill) equals (1) the greater of financial reporting goodwill or tax-deductible goodwill less (2) the amount calculated as component 1 goodwill.

FASB ASC 805 prescribes the recognition of a deferred tax benefit resulting from tax-deductible goodwill that is in excess of book goodwill. The tax benefit of the excess tax goodwill is recognized as a deferred tax asset at the acquisition date, which increases the values assigned to the acquired net assets and correspondingly decreases book goodwill. This further increases (1) the difference between book goodwill and tax-deductible goodwill and (2) the corresponding deferred tax balance. To deal with this recursive process, the computation of the deferred tax asset can be reduced to the next equation:

$$(\text{Tax rate}/(1 - \text{Tax rate})) \times \text{Preliminary temporary difference} = \text{DTA}$$

The resulting amount of deferred tax asset reduces book goodwill. If book goodwill is reduced to zero, any additional amounts recognized result in a bargain purchase gain.

For example, at the date of a business combination, goodwill should be separated into the two components shown in Exhibit 17.2 at the acquisition date.

The first components of the financial basis and tax basis of goodwill are the same, so there is no temporary difference. Any difference that arises between the financial and tax basis of the first component due to tax basis amortization and financial basis impairment in future years is a temporary difference for which a deferred tax asset or liability is recognized. A deferred tax asset is recognized for the second component of goodwill only if it represents an excess of tax-deductible goodwill over financial reporting goodwill. The deferred tax asset is recognized with a corresponding reduction in the carrying amount of goodwill. However, if the second component represents an excess of the financial basis of goodwill over tax-deductible goodwill, the excess is, in effect, a permanent difference, and deferred taxes are not recognized because of ASC 805-740-25-3, which provides that an excess of book goodwill over tax-deductible goodwill will not result

Step 1: Compute the excess of the second component for tax reporting over the second component of the carrying amount of goodwill. The excess is referred to as the *preliminary temporary difference,* which is $2,000.

	Financial Basis	Tax Basis
Component 1	$6,000	$6,000
Component 2	0	2,000
Total Goodwill	$6,000	$8,000

Preliminary Temp. Difference

Step 2: Compute the deferred tax asset (DTA) that is recorded through an offsetting credit to goodwill.

The asset is computed by multiplying the preliminary temporary difference by a percentage equal to the ratio of the tax rate to the residual of the tax rate. The equation can be expressed as follows:

DTA = preliminary temporary difference × [tax rate ÷ 1 – tax rate].

Assuming the tax rate is 40%:
(1) The percentage would be 66.7%, which is 40% ÷(1 – 40% = 60%).
(2) The DTA would be $1,333, which is 66.7% of the $2,000 preliminary temporary difference. The asset would be recorded through a *debit* to DTA and a *credit* to goodwill.

The adjusted carrying amount of goodwill would be $4,667, which is $6,000 –the $1,333 deferred tax asset.

Exhibit 17.3   Deferred Tax Effects

in the recording of deferred taxes at the date of a business combination. Therefore, enterprises are prohibited from establishing a deferred tax liability when goodwill recorded for financial reporting is not tax deductible or in excess of tax-deductible goodwill.

For example, if the financial basis and tax basis of deductible goodwill are $6,000 and $8,000, respectively, at the date of a business combination, goodwill should be separated into two components (financial and tax) at the acquisition date, and the deferred tax effects are recorded as shown in Exhibit 17.3.

(iv) Quasi Reorganizations. In a quasi reorganization, charges or credits go directly to contributed capital, and any deficit in retained earnings is eliminated by a charge to contributed capital. Because a quasi reorganization is considered an accounting "fresh start," any unrecognized tax benefits of deductible temporary differences and carryforwards existing at the time of the quasi reorganization are credited directly to contributed capital if subsequently recognized. The only exception is for enterprises that have previously both adopted SFAS No. 96 and effected a reorganization that involved only a deficit reclassification from retained earnings; the tax benefit of carryforwards for that limited exception are reported in income normally and then are reclassified to contributed capital.

(v) Separate Financial Statements of a Subsidiary. If separate financial statements are issued for companies that are included in a consolidated tax return, total tax expense for the group should be allocated to the individual members using a method that is systematic, rational, and consistent with the broad principles of FASB ASC 740. One example of a method that meets those criteria is the "separate return" method. Examples of unacceptable methods are methods that (1) allocate only current tax expense to a member that has taxable temporary differences, (2) are fundamentally different from the asset and liability method, and (3) allocate no current or deferred tax expense because the group has no current or deferred tax expense.

(vi) Issues Addressed by the Emerging Issues Task Force. The FASB's EITF has addressed a number of implementation issues on the accounting for income taxes. They are listed next in chronological order by EITF Issue number with FASB ASC cross references.

- Issue 91-8 (ASC 740-10-55-140 through 55-144) addresses the combination of a state franchise tax and an income tax and concludes that the income tax portion is only the portion that will exceed the franchise tax.
- Issue 92-8 (ASC 830-740-25-2 and 25-3; 830-740-45-2) addresses the accounting for income tax when there is a change in the functional currency of a foreign operation because the foreign economy ceases to be highly inflationary.
- Issue 93-9 (ASC 830-740) addresses the accounting for income taxes in foreign financial statements restated for general price-level changes.
- Issue 93-13 (ASC 740-10) specifies that retroactive changes in enacted tax rates should be determined as of the date of enactment.
- Issue 93-16 (ASC 830-740-25-6 through 25-8) addresses the recognition of deferred income taxes related to "inside" basis differences of foreign subsidiaries that meet the indefinite reversal criterion of APB Opinion No. 23, *Accounting for Income Taxes—Special Areas.*[5]
- Issue 93-17 (ASC 740-30-25-10) addresses the recognition of deferred tax assets for a parent company's excess tax basis in the stock of a subsidiary that is accounted for as a discontinued operation.
- Issue 94-1 (ASC 323-740) addresses the accounting for investments subject to the affordable housing income tax credit. It specifies that investments that meet specified conditions may be accounted for by the effective yield method; other investments should be consolidated if appropriate or accounted for by the equity method unless a limited partner's investment is so minor as to have virtually no influence, in which case the cost method should be used with amortization of the investment.
- Issue 94-10 (ASC 740-10-45-21; 740-20-45-11) addresses the accounting for income tax effects of transactions among shareholders or between the company and its shareholders and specifies those tax effects that should be recognized in income and those that should be recognized in stockholders' equity.
- Issues 95-9 and 95-10 (ASC 740-10) address the tax effects of distributions to shareholders by companies in France and Germany where different tax rates (or tax credits) apply to income distributed as dividends and income retained.

---

[5] Accounting Principles Board, APB Opinion No. 23, *Accounting for Income Taxes—Special Areas* (New York: AICPA, 1972).

- Issue 95-20 (ASC 740-10-25-41) addresses measurement of deferred taxes in the consolidated financial statements of a parent company related to the operations of a foreign subsidiary that receives tax credits related to dividend payments.
- Issue 98-11(ASC 740-10) addresses the treatment of acquired temporary differences in purchase transactions that are not accounted for as business combinations.
- Issue 02-13 (ASC 350-20) addresses deferred income tax considerations in applying the goodwill impairment test in FASB Statement No. 142.
- Issue 05-8 (ASC 740-10-55-51) addresses income tax consequences of issuing convertible debt with a beneficial conversion feature.
- Issue 06-11(ASC 740-10-45-8 through 45-12) addresses accounting for income tax benefits of dividends on share-based payment awards.

17.3 FASB ASC 740-10: *ACCOUNTING FOR UNCERTAINTY IN INCOME TAXES*

(a) BACKGROUND. In June 2006, the FASB released FASB Interpretation No. 48, *Accounting for Uncertainty in Income Taxes* (FIN 48 or the Interpretation), which under the codification of accounting standards is included in FASB Accounting Standards Codification subtopic 740-10, *Income Taxes* (ASC 740-10). Under FASB ASC 740-10, enterprises are required to assess an income tax position to determine whether the benefit of the position can be recognized in U.S. GAAP financial statements. Additionally, it requires significant disclosures related to uncertain tax positions (UTPs) and resulting liabilities.

Prior to the adoption of FASB ASC 740-10, any uncertainty concerning the tax positions reported in a tax return were reported as tax reserves and recognized, measured, and disclosed following the guidance in SFAS No. 5, *Accounting for Contingencies*. In practice, there was considerable diversity in how tax positions were recognized, with different approaches being applied for establishing and applying the SFAS No. 5 "probable" threshold of recording contingent liabilities. These inconsistencies, as well as a lack of guidance, resulted in the need to establish an objective and systematic approach. The FASB believed that the result from adoption should be "increased relevance and comparability in financial reporting of income taxes because all tax positions will be evaluated for recognition, derecognition, and measurement using consistent criteria." The FASB concluded that this along with the additional disclosure provisions will provide greater transparency concerning the reporting of the uncertainty in income tax assets and liabilities.

In summary, the most significant changes from prior practice include these:

- There is a much greater focus on identification of uncertain tax positions.
- Each exposure is assessed individually and cannot be commingled or offset with other items in any manner
- A more likely than not threshold (MLTN) requirement must be met in order to recognize any tax benefit.
- A "cumulative probability" approach is applied to measure the amount of recognized benefit that may be reported.
- Consideration of detection risk is explicitly prohibited when analyzing the degree of uncertainty of a tax position.
- Reserves for timing items require balance sheet classification.
- Each taxing jurisdiction is presented separately (i.e., no netting is allowed).
- A set framework for adjusting reserves is provided.

- Improved processes and increased documentation are necessary in order to properly identify, analyze, and support management's conclusions concerning uncertain tax positions.
- A significant increase in required disclosures.

(b) SCOPE. FASB ASC 740-10 applies to all individual tax positions for all open tax years with respect to any federal, state, local, and international taxes based on income. The FASB determined that by including all positions, the creation of a more complex rules-based standard and the potential for inconsistent application would be avoided. Thus, highly certain positions—that is, those positions based on clear and unambiguous tax law—are subject to FASB ASC 740-10.

All public and private business enterprises that are *potentially* subject to income taxes are subject to FASB ASC 740-10. This means that even tax-exempt nonprofit and pass-through entities must also consider its application. For example, such entities may need to consider some of the next issues:

- Have any events occurred that would jeopardize the entity's tax exempt status?
- Is the tax-exempt nonprofit subject to unrelated business income taxes and was the proper amount reported?
- Does the entity qualify for pass through status in all jurisdictions in which if files a return?
- In the case of state and local taxes, is the income tax paid by the entity attributable to the entity or its owners?
- Has the entity made an election to be an association taxable as a corporation (check-the-box election)?
- In the case of a Subchapter S election, was the election made in a timely manner, and is it still valid?
- Are there built in gains resulting from a recent conversion from a C corporation to an S corporation that would subject the entity to tax?

(i) Consolidated or Combined Financial Statements. Consolidated or combined financial statements should include all tax positions for each entity within the consolidated or combined group that is subject to income tax or has taxable income, regardless of the reporting entity's tax status. Therefore, a nontaxable reporting entity has to apply FASB ASC 740-10 to all taxable entities included in the consolidated or combined financial statements even though the reporting entity may be a pass-through entity. For example, assume that a partnership owns a 100 percent interest in a taxable entity and that the partnership is required to issue consolidated financial statements. In that case, the partnership is required to consider the tax positions of the taxable subsidiary regardless of the partnership's tax status.

(c) TAX POSITION. A tax position is generally any rationale used to support the amounts included (or not included) on an entity's tax return. The term *tax position* as used in this Interpretation refers to a position taken in a previously filed tax return or expected to be taken in a future tax return that is used to measure current or deferred income tax assets or liabilities for interim or annual periods. A tax position can result in a permanent reduction of income taxes payable, a deferral of income taxes otherwise currently payable to future years, or a change in the expected realizability of deferred tax assets.

These items are examples of tax positions:

- A decision not to file a return
- An allocation (or shift) of income between jurisdictions
- The characterization of income

- A decision to not report a portion of taxable income in a tax return
- A decision to classify a transaction, entity, or other tax position as tax exempt
- An entity's status, including its status as a pass-through entity or a tax-exempt nonprofit entity

(d) DETERMINING "UNIT OF ACCOUNT." Individual tax positions should be determined at the appropriate unit of account. FASB ASC 740-10-25-13 states that the "appropriate unit of account for determining what constitutes an individual tax position, is a matter of judgment based on the individual facts and circumstances of that position evaluated in light of all available evidence." Furthermore, the unit of account should be consistently applied to similar positions from period to period unless a change in facts and circumstances indicates that a different unit of account is more appropriate.

Although FASB ASC 740-10 does not define *unit of account,* it requires that the determination of a unit of account consider two factors:

1. The manner in which the enterprise prepares and supports its income tax return.
2. The approach the enterprise anticipates the taxing authority will take during an examination. For example, if a particular tax return amount is supported and will be examined at a project level, the appropriate unit of account for recognizing and measuring the financial statement effects of the tax position is the project level.

The process of identifying the appropriate unit of account for all tax positions can be applied by using a top-down, risk-based assessment of uncertain tax positions. Whatever the approach, the process used should be documented to identify all potentially significant uncertain tax positions. Documentation may be reduced for low-risk tax positions or for amounts that are immaterial. The next items should be considered during the identification process:

- Consider all sources of information to identify positions.
- Review and/or perform nexus and permanent establishment studies in the various taxing jurisdictions for all operations.
- Consider all open years in significant jurisdictions.

(e) RECOGNITION AND MEASUREMENT REQUIREMENTS. FASB ASC 740-10 proposes a two-step structured approach to accounting for uncertainty in income taxes. These steps are recognition and measurement. Tax positions that meet the MLTN recognition criterion are recognized in the financial statement computations of current and deferred income tax assets and liabilities, subject to the measurement guidelines of FASB ASC 740. Conversely, tax positions that do not meet the MLTN recognition criterion should not be recognized in the current and deferred income tax computations.

(i) Step 1: Recognition. The first step is to determine whether any amount of a tax benefit may be recognized with respect to a tax position. This will be the case only when such position is MLTN to be sustained based on the technical merits of the position.

The MLTN recognition threshold is a likelihood of more than 50 percent. The conclusion assumes that a tax position will be examined by a taxing authority. Additionally, this means that no settlements or trading off of tax issues with the taxing authority may be taken into account in the recognition process. Each position must stand on its own merits, that is, without consideration of the possibility of offset or aggregation with other positions.

Because tax law is complex and subject to diverse interpretation, the analysis as to whether a tax position will satisfy the MLTN recognition threshold is a matter of judgment based on facts and circumstances and evaluated in light of all available evidence. Legal authority including favorable statutes, legislative history, regulations, case law, and rulings are considered when making this determination. However, the lack of specific authoritative guidance or case law does not automatically deny a MLTN determination. Instead, other sources of authoritative tax law, although they may not specifically address the position, may be considered relevant in concluding whether a position meets the MLTN criteria. Not all positions, however, are controversial and thus may need minimal analysis. Thus, in cases where the tax law is unambiguous and favorable, supporting legal authority will clearly satisfy the MLTN standard.

The FASB provided these examples in the proposed Interpretation when evaluating a tax position as support that the position meets the recognition threshold:

1. Whether there is an unambiguous tax law that supports the tax position
2. Whether a "should" tax opinion has been issued by a qualified expert (note that the "should" threshold was revised to a MLTN standard in the final Interpretation)
3. Whether similar positions were clearly presented in prior years' returns that have been accepted or not challenged by the tax authority
4. Whether similar positions were taken by other taxpayers where analogy is proper and favorable results were produced through litigation with tax authorities

FASB ASC 740-10-25 further notes that widely understood "past administrative practices and precedents of a taxing authority in its dealings with the enterprise or similar enterprises" may be considered. Administrative practices and precedents typically deal with limited technical violations of the tax law or include a well-understood policy by a particular taxing jurisdiction. For example, state, local, or foreign taxing jurisdictions may have developed in practice a policy not to review returns more than a certain number of years old where it was asserted that there was no nexus or no permanent establishment, and so on, to support a position not to charge a tax liability for prior years (more than X years).

Documentation.   In gathering evidence to support a MLTN determination, an enterprise should think about all of the sources of evidence available and then document its analysis of such evidence for benefit recognition and measurement of all uncertain tax positions. When documenting each UTP:

- Consider the level of materiality and complexity of the UTP.
- Apply reasonable judgment and common sense as a basis for determining the amount of documentation needed.
- Review formal as well as informal guidance from the taxing authority and other sources, and then weigh in on the different pieces of evidence based on their persuasiveness.
- Support management's conclusions with the appropriate level of evidential matter.
- In cases where complex tax planning strategies have been implemented:
  ○ Obtain an opinion from a qualified outside tax consultant.
  ○ Update tax opinions for significant older unsettled UTPs.

A company's process for documenting UTPs should be an area of continuing focus. The process should include a yearly evaluation that ensures that any new uncertain tax positions have been identified and documented. In addition, a company should make sure that it has documentation about any new information for both recognition and measurement of tax positions. Additionally, a company will want to document its process to avoid the need to reassess recognition, even when a tax position meets the MLTN recognition threshold.

(ii) Step 2: Measurement—Cumulative Probability Approach.   Once it has been established that a tax position meets the requisite MLTN threshold, the next step is to determine the amount of tax benefit that can be recognized applying a cumulative probability approach. FASB ASC 740-10-30-7-states:

> [A] tax position that meets the more-likely-than-not recognition threshold shall initially and subsequently be measured as the largest amount of tax benefit that is greater than 50 percent likely of being realized upon ultimate settlement with a taxing authority that has full knowledge of all relevant information.

There is no prescribed formula for assigning probabilities, and therefore the task is a highly judgmental process. Instead, FASB ASC 740-10-30-7 further states that "facts, circumstances, and information available at the reporting date (i.e., date of the enterprise's most recent statement of financial position), are to be used" when considering the amounts and probabilities of the outcomes that could be realized upon ultimate settlement. However, detection risk may not be considered as the basis for probabilities but the probabilities may include these issues:

- Materiality of amount reported in tax return
- Weight of favorable tax law
- Company audit experience with similar positions
- Issues previously settled with tax authority
- Expert advice rendered (opinion letter)
- Willingness to litigate position

Measurement Example

This example illustrates the cumulative probability approach to measurement.

Facts

Company takes a tax credit on the tax return that creates an "as filed" tax benefit of $1,000.

- The position is greater than 50 percent likely of being sustained on technical merit (Step 1).
- The company estimates the distribution of outcomes (Step 2) shown next.

Cumulative Probability Assessment

Management Expectation— Tax Credit	% Likelihood Tax Position Will Be Sustained at This Level	Cumulative Probability
$1000	5%	5%
800	25%	30%
600	25%	55%
500	20%	75%
400	20%	95%
200	5%	100%

Conclusion:

Because $600 is the largest amount of benefit that is greater than 50 percent likely of being realized upon ultimate settlement, the enterprise would recognize a tax benefit of $600 in the financial statements.

Recognition and Measurement Example

This example illustrates how to apply the two-step model for recognition and measurement.

Permanent Item Example

Assume

Co A enters into a transaction that results in a $100 benefit from a permanent difference. Co A concludes:

The transaction is MLTN of being sustained. The largest amount of the tax benefit from taking the deduction that is MLTN to be sustained upon settlement is $80.

○ Book basis $0

○ UTP basis $80

○ Tax basis $100

Determine Amount of Benefit Recognized

Compare book basis to UTP basis to determine the amount of benefit to be recognized	Book basis $0	UTP basis $80
	$80 benefit recognized	

Record UTP Liability

Compare tax basis to UTP basis to determine the amount of liability to be recognized	UTP basis $0	Tax basis $100
	$20 UTP liability	

Current Tax Expense

The journal entry to record the UTP liability:

(Dr) Refundable taxes $100

   (Cr) UTP liability $20

   (Cr) Tax benefit $80

Thus, in the case of a permanent item, an increase in the liability for unrecognized tax benefits will increase the current tax provision and effectively eliminate the tax benefits of uncertain tax positions from the income statement.

Temporary Difference Example

Facts

In year 1, Company A acquired a separately identifiable intangible asset for $60 million that has an indefinite life for financial reporting purposes and is, thus, cannot be amortized. Based on some uncertainty in the tax code, the company decides for tax purposes to deduct the entire cost of the asset in year 1. While the company is certain that the full amount of the intangible is ultimately deductible for tax purposes, the timing of deductibility is uncertain under the tax code.

Analysis

In applying the recognition criterion of FASB ASC 740-10, the company has determined that the tax position qualifies for recognition and should be measured. The company believes it is 45 percent likely it would be able to realize immediate deduction upon ultimate settlement, and it is certain that it could sustain a 15-year amortization for tax purposes.

Conclusion

The largest year 1 benefit that is greater than 50 percent likely of being realized upon ultimate settlement is the tax effect of $4 million or $1.6 million assuming a 40% tax rate (the year 1 deduction from straight-line amortization of the asset over 15 years). The determination of this amount and it effects on the financial statements follows:

Assume

Co A enters into a transaction that results in a $24 million benefit from a temporary difference ($60 million @ 40% tax rate)

Co A concludes:

The transaction is MLTN of being sustained over 15 years. In year 1, the largest amount of the tax benefit from taking the deduction that is MLTN to be sustained upon settlement is $1.6 million ($60 million/15 years @ 40% tax rate).

- Book basis $24
- UTP basis $22.4
- Tax basis $0

Determine Amount of Recognized Benefit

Compare book basis to UTP basis to determine the amount of benefit to be recognized	Book basis $24 million	UTP basis $22.4 million
	$1.6 million recognized benefit	

Record UTP Liability

Compare tax basis to UTP basis to determine the amount of liability to be recognized	UTP basis $22.4 million	Tax basis $0
	$22.4 million UTP liability	

Deferred Tax Expense

The journal entry to record the deferred tax liability recognized in year 1 assuming a 40 percent tax rate:

(Dr) Deferred tax expense $ 1.6 million

(Cr) Noncurrent deferred tax liability $ 1.6 million

- $4 million taxable temporary difference created
- $60 million financial statement basis versus $56 million UTP adjusted tax basis
- $1,600,000 noncurrent deferred tax liability created at 40 percent effective tax rate

Current Tax Expense

The journal entry to record the UTP liability in year 1 assuming a 40 percent tax rate:

> (Dr) Refundable taxes $ 24 million
> > (Cr) Noncurrent UTP liability $ 22.4 million
> > (Cr) Current benefit $ 1.6 million
>
> ○ $56 million IRS adjustment anticipated
> ○ $60 million tax deduction versus.$4 million MLNT amortization
> ○ $22.4 million noncurrent liability created at 40 percent effective tax rate
> ○ Cash payment not anticipated within one year or the operating cycle, if longer

Net Impact to Balance Sheet

> (Dr) Refundable taxes $ 24 million
> > (Cr) UTP liability $ 22.4 million
> > (Cr) DTL $ 1.6 million

Net Impact to P&L

> (Dr) Deferred tax expense $ 1.6
> > (Cr) Current Tax Benefit $ 1.6

Other than potential interest and penalties, there is has no net P&L impact (e.g., the journal entry decreases the current tax benefit by $22,400,000 and decreases the deferred tax expense by $22,400,000, leaving the P&L with a current tax benefit of $1,600,000 and a deferred tax expense of $1,600,000).

(f) SUBSEQUENT RECOGNITION, DERECOGNITION, AND MEASUREMENT.   The recognition and measurement of UTPs is a continuous process and should be reassessed (using the two-step model) at each reporting date. Any reassessment can potentially change not only the measurement of the benefit recorded but also the determination as to whether the recognition threshold has been or continues to be met.

A tax position that fails the MLTN recognition criterion should not be recognized until the first reporting period that one of the next three conditions is met:

1. The MLTN recognition criterion is satisfied.
2. The tax position is effectively settled through examination, negotiation, or litigation.
3. The statute of limitations has expired for the relevant taxing authority to examine and challenge the tax position.

Conversely, a previously recognized tax position should be derecognized in the first reporting period that it fails the MLTN recognition criterion (i.e., the position is no longer more likely than not to be sustained upon examination). Note that providing a valuation allowance is not a substitute for derecognizing the tax benefit of a previously recognized tax position.

Definitive triggering events are not needed to cause a change in assessment. However, a change in assessment must be based upon new information, as opposed to a reevaluation of preexisting information.

Some potential sources of "new information" to consider include:

- Developments in a tax audit
  - Audit plans
  - Oral statements by tax authority
  - Prefiling agreements
- Experience in prior audits
- Taxing authority program changes
- Advanced pricing agreement, competent authority
- Notice of proposed adjustment
- Revenue agent's report
- Changes in the tax law
- Public statements made by tax authority
  - Audit guidelines
  - Designation for litigation
  - Listing of transactions

(g) INTEREST AND PENALTIES. A taxpayer is required to accrue interest and penalties that would be incurred if the uncertain tax position is not ultimately sustained based on the relevant law of the taxing jurisdiction. Thus, such amount is not necessarily the amount that a taxpayer ultimately expects to pay.

The reporting of such amounts is determined in this way:

- *Recognition.* Interest and penalties are recorded based on the provisions of the tax law for the periods for which the taxing authority would assess interest and penalties should the position not be sustained.
- *Measurement.* Interest expense is computed by applying the applicable statutory interest rate based on the difference between the benefit recognized in the financial statement and the amount previously taken (or expected to be taken) on a tax return that would give rise to the penalty.

Interest may be classified in the financial statements as either income taxes or interest expense. Penalties may be classified in the financial statements as either income taxes or another expense classification. In practice, it is common for companies to elect to treat interest and penalties as a component of income tax expense. Classification of interest and penalties in the income statement is an accounting policy election and must be consistently applied. Additionally, a company is required to disclose its accounting policy for classifying interest and penalties, the amount of interest and penalties charged to expense for each period, and the cumulative amounts recorded in the balance sheet.

(h) BALANCE SHEET PRESENTATION. UTP liabilities will be classified and presented in the balance sheet as either:

- A reduction of deferred tax assets resulting from a deductible temporary difference or net operating loss or tax credit carryforward, OR
- A current or noncurrent liability, based on the expected timing of cash payments.

The only liabilities that should be classified as a deferred tax liabilities are ones that arise from a taxable temporary difference that meets the MLTN recognition threshold.

A rolling 12-month analysis is used to reclassify long-term UTP liability amounts as current if such amounts are expected to be paid within the next 12 months or the operating cycle, if longer. Expected decreases in the UTP liability that do not require actual cash payments (e.g., pending changes in judgment, lapsing of statute of limitations) should not be reclassified as a current liability. From a practical standpoint, the progression from filing a tax return to examination and final resolution often spans several years, and thus many of the UTP liabilities will be classified as long term.

(i) DISCLOSURES FOR EXTERNAL REPORTING

(i) Tabular Reconciliation of Aggregate Beginning and Ending Unrecognized Tax Benefits.   ASC 740-10-50 requires financial statement filers to provide various annual disclosures. While the particular line items will depend on a company and its circumstances, the next items must be presented separately in the table at the end of each annual period:

- The gross amounts of the increases and decreases in unrecognized tax benefits as a result of tax positions taken during a prior period
- The gross amounts of the increases and decreases in unrecognized tax benefits as a result of tax positions taken during the current period
- The amount of decreases in unrecognized tax benefits relating to settlements with taxing authorities
- Reductions to unrecognized tax benefits as a result of lapse of the applicable statute of limitations

Sample Tabular Reconciliation

Balance, January 1, 2010	$141
Additions for current-year tax positions	22
Additions for prior-year tax positions	99
Reductions for tax positions of prior years for:	
Changes in judgment	(2)
Settlements	(10)
Statute of Limitation lapses	(3)
Balance, December 31, 2010	$247

Additional Disclosures: These additional items must be disclosed by a company if relevant:

- The amount of unrecognized tax benefits that, if recognized, would change the effective tax rate
- The classification of interest and penalties, the amount of interest and penalties included in the income statement each period, and the total amount of interest and penalties accrued in the statement of financial position
- If it is reasonably possible that estimate of the tax benefit will change significantly within 12 months (sometimes known as the early warning disclosure):
  - The nature of the uncertainty
  - The nature of the event that would cause the change
  - An estimate of the range of the reasonably possible change, or state that an estimate cannot be made
- Description of open tax years by major jurisdiction

Nonpublic entities. Nonpublic entities are not required to disclose a tabular reconciliation of unrecognized tax benefits and the effects the unrecognized tax benefits would have on the effective tax rate if they were recognized. However, according to Accounting Standards Update No. 2009-06, such entities are required to comply with all other disclosure requirements, including the requirement to disclose information about tax positions for which it is reasonably possible that the unrecognized tax benefits will significantly change in the next 12 months.

Level of Disclosure. There is no specific guidance on the proper level of aggregation of information, so companies must use judgment when determining how much detail should be disclosed. If very little detail is disclosed or some information is omitted, the SEC typically issues comment letters and will request that a company revise its disclosure and provide additional information. The early warning disclosure has been the most discussed and controversial of the just- described disclosure requirements. Many companies believe that it may provide a roadmap for taxing authorities. The FASB considered this concern and concluded that the disclosures provided aggregate totals of all uncertain tax positions, so taxing authorities should not be able to identify specific tax positions for audit. However, in January 2010, the IRS issued Announcement 2010-9 (I.R.B. 2010-7, 408) to inform taxpayers that it was developing a schedule that would require the reporting of uncertain tax positions with the filing of tax returns "in order to improve tax compliance and administration" due to the lack of detail provided in financial statements. The new requirement to file a schedule for uncertain tax positions (Schedule UTP) is the latest in a series of steps taken by the IRS designed to improve transparency and to further assist the IRS auditors with examinations.

(ii) Uncertain Tax Position Statement (Schedule UTP). According to the IRS, preparation of Schedule UTP[6] is expected to flow from the preparation of financial statements and requires a company to report:

1. U.S. income tax positions for which a reserve has been established in audited financial statements, OR
2. Those positions for which a decision not to reserve was made because of an expectation to litigate.

For tax years beginning in 2010, a public or privately held corporation must file Schedule UTP if all of these four points apply:

1. The corporation files IRS Form 1120, Form 1120-F, Form 1120-L, or Form 1120-PC.
2. The corporation or a related party issued audited financial statements prepared using GAAP, International Financial Reporting Standards (IFRS), or a country-specific accounting standard that reports all or a portion of the corporation's operations for all or a portion of the corporation's tax year.
3. The corporation has at least one tax position that must be reported on Schedule UTP.
4. The corporation's total assets equal or exceed Schedule UTP's phase-in amount of $100 million. (For 2012 tax years, the total asset phase-in amount is lowered to $50 million and further lowered to $10 million for 2014 tax years.)

After a five-year phase-in period, all corporations that satisfy the first three criteria will be required to file Schedule UTP.

(iii) Pass-Through Entities and Tax-Exempt Entities. The IRS has announced that it will consider whether to extend all or a portion of the requirements to 2011 or later tax years for pass-through entities and tax-exempt entities. However, the Employer Identification Number (EIN) of a pass-through is included on a company's Schedule UTP if the tax position taken by the company relates to a tax position of a pass-through entity.

(j) IRS ACCESS TO TAX ACCRUAL WORKPAPERS. Schedule UTP inevitably raises the topic regarding the IRS' ability to access highly sensitive tax accrual workpapers, since such workpapers can provide the IRS with a roadmap of issues to review on audit. This topic has a long history of being litigated in a number of cases, starting with the landmark Supreme Court case decided

---

[6] Instructions for Schedule UTP, *www.irs.gov/pub/newsroom/2010_instructions_for_sch_utp.pdf*

more than 25 years ago. In United States vs. *Arthur Young,* 465 U.S. 805, 53 AFTR 2d 84-866 (1984), the Supreme Court affirmed the IRS's right to obtain tax accrual workpapers prepared by a taxpayer's independent auditors and held that tax accrual workpapers were not privileged. Despite the IRS win, in Announcement 84-46 (1984-18 I.R.B. 18) the IRS informed taxpayers that it would restrain itself and request tax accrual workpapers only in unusual circumstances. According I.R.M. 4.10.20.3.1 (July 12, 2004), an "unusual circumstance" is when the IRS cannot obtain the factual data it needs to support the information provided on the tax return from the taxpayer's records or from third parties. The IRS has continued to apply this policy of restraint except in cases where a taxpayer has participated in certain "listed transactions" as identified by the IRS. These types of transactions have been determined by the IRS to contain abusive tax-avoidance properties.

Independent auditors typically request copies of legal opinions and other workpapers to assess the adequacy of reserves for uncertain tax liabilities in reviewing financial statements. This information may be considered "privileged" under attorney-client privilege, tax advice privilege (Code section 7525), or the work product doctrine. In the recently decided *Textron* and *Deloitte* court cases, the IRS asserted that, by supplying information related to tax reserves to the independent auditor, the company had waived privilege. In *U.S. v. Textron,*[7] the U.S. Court of Appeals for the First Circuit held that tax accrual workpapers prepared by the client for purposes of preparing financial statements did not qualify as privileged under the work product doctrine. On May 24, 2010, the Supreme Court denied the taxpayer's request to hear the case. On June 29, 2010, the U.S. Court of Appeals for the DC Circuit issued an opinion in *U.S. v. Deloitte LLP*[8] that questioned the First Circuit's analysis in the *Textron* opinion.

Based on these cases, the IRS's policy with respect to access to tax accrual workpapers was raised as a concern once again by many companies when the draft Schedule UTP was issued since some of the required information to be disclosed on the Schedule UTP is based on legal or tax advice when determining the company's ability to sustain a tax deduction.

At the same time that it issued the final Schedule UTP, the IRS released Announcement 2010-76[9] in order to address such concerns. In the announcement, the IRS stated:

> [I]f a document is otherwise privileged under attorney-client privilege, tax advice privilege (Code section 7525), or work product doctrine and the document was provided to an independent auditor as part of an audit of the taxpayer's financial statements, the Service will not assert during an examination that privilege has been waived by such disclosure.

Additionally, the IRS acknowledged that

> other than requiring the disclosure of the information on the schedule, the requirement to file Schedule UTP does not affect the policy of restraint.

However, this policy will not apply if the taxpayer has engaged in any activity or taken any action, that would waive the attorney-client privilege, the tax advice privilege, or the work product doctrine, or a request for tax accrual workpapers is made because unusual circumstances exist or the taxpayer has claimed benefits of one or more listed transactions. One additional observation is that the policy of restraint seems to apply only to the IRS examination function. Thus, there is a question as to whether the policy would be applicable in other situations, such as the IRS appeals process or tax litigation.

Finally, Announcement 2010-76 states that taxpayers are allowed to redact:

- Working drafts, revisions, or comments concerning the concise description of tax positions reported on Schedule UTP
- The amount of any reserve related to a tax position reported on Schedule UTP

---

[7] *United States v. Textron Inc.,* 577 F.3d 21 (1st Cir.), *cert. denied,* 130 S. Ct. 3320 (2010).

[8] *U.S. v Deloitte LLP,* 610 F.3d 129 (D.C. Cir. 2010).

[9] Announcement 2010-76, Requests for Documents Provided to Independent Auditors, *Policy of Restraint and Uncertain Tax Positions, www.irs.gov/pub/irs-drop/a-10-76.pdf*

- Computations determining the ranking of tax positions to be reported on Schedule UTP or the designation of a tax position as a major tax position (defined as at least 10 percent of the year's total reserve activity)

17.4 FINANCIAL REPORTING

(a) TAX ALLOCATION WITHIN A PERIOD. The process of allocating income taxes among income from continuing operations and other items within a period is known as *intraperiod tax allocation.* (This should not be confused with tax allocation among interim periods of a year, which is discussed later in this section.) Intraperiod income tax allocation is the apportionment of total income tax for the period among income from continuing operations, discontinued operations, extraordinary items, other comprehensive income, and direct entries to stockholders' equity.

FASB ASC 740-20-45-1 through 45-14 describes the basic model for intraperiod allocation, which is sometimes referred to as the with-and-without or incremental approach. The three key steps to apply when using the basic model are shown in Exhibit 17.4.

In general, the first step in intraperiod income tax allocation under FASB ASC 740 is to compute the total tax expense or benefit (both current and deferred) for the period. The next step is to determine the tax expense or benefit related to income from continuing operations. The difference between that amount and total tax expense or benefit is the tax effect to be allocated to all of the other items listed. If there is only one other item (e.g., an extraordinary item), the remaining tax effect is allocated to it. If there is more than one item, the remaining tax effect is allocated between (or among) them in this way:

- Determine the tax benefit of all items with a loss.
- Allocate the tax benefit for all loss items pro rata among those items.
- Allocate the difference between (a) the tax expense or benefit determined earlier for income or loss from all items other than continuing operations and (b) the tax benefit determined in (1) above for all items with a loss (c) pro rata among all items with a gain.

Summary of Steps

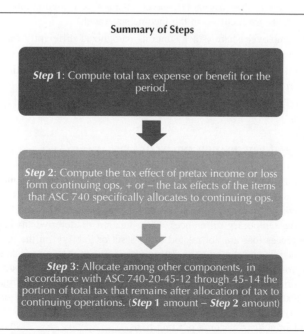

Step 1: Compute total tax expense or benefit for the period.

Step 2: Compute the tax effect of pretax income or loss form continuing ops, + or − the tax effects of the items that ASC 740 specifically allocates to continuing ops.

Step 3: Allocate among other components, in accordance with ASC 740-20-45-12 through 45-14 the portion of total tax that remains after allocation of tax to continuing operations. (*Step* 1 amount − *Step* 2 amount)

Exhibit 17.4   Summary of Steps

The general approach is supplemented by specific requirements for allocation of the tax expense or benefit attributed to certain types of items. These specified requirements override the general approach whenever the general approach would produce a different result.

Specifically, FASB ASC 740-20-45-8 (formerly Paragraph 35 of SFAS No. 109) provides that the amount allocated to continuing operations is the tax effect of the pretax income or loss from continuing operations that occurred during the year, plus or minus income tax effects of:

a. Changes in circumstances that cause a change in judgment about the realization of deferred tax assets in future years

b. Changes in tax laws or rates

c. Changes in tax status

d. Tax-deductible dividends paid to shareholders (except for dividends paid on unallocated shares held by an employee stock ownership plan or any other stock compensation arrangement)

Any remaining amount is than allocated to items other than continuing operations.

FASB ASC 740-20-45-11 (formerly Paragraph 36 of SFAS No. 109) addresses allocation involving certain items charged directly to other comprehensive income (OCI) or stockholders' equity, and provides that the tax effects of such items are also generally charged or credited directly to other comprehensive income or the related components of stockholders' equity. Some examples of items that impact OCI include unrealized holding gains and losses on marketable securities classified as available for sale, foreign currency translation adjustments, and gains and losses from certain foreign currency transactions. The list of items charged or credited to shareholders equity as provided in FASB ASC 740 are:

1. Adjustments of the opening balance of retained earnings for certain changes in accounting principles or for an error correction.

2. An increase or decrease in contributed capital.

3. Changes in the tax bases of assets and liabilities caused by transactions among or with shareholders, including the effect of valuation allowances initially required upon recognition of any related deferred tax assets. (However, changes in valuation allowances occurring in subsequent periods are included in the income statement.)

4. Expenses for employee share (stock) options recognized differently for financial reporting and tax purposes.

5. Dividends paid on unallocated shares held by an employee stock option plan and charged to retained earnings.

6. Certain deductible temporary differences and carryforwards that existed at the date of a quasi reorganization.

(b) FINANCIAL STATEMENT PRESENTATION AND DISCLOSURE.   FASB ASC 740 requires deferred tax liabilities or assets to be classified as current and noncurrent in a classified balance sheet. The classification is determined for each tax jurisdiction, and offset of liabilities and assets attributable to different tax jurisdictions is not permitted. Deferred tax liabilities and assets are classified as current or noncurrent based on the classification of the nontax assets and liabilities that give rise to the underlying temporary differences. Classification of deferred tax liabilities and assets for temporary differences that are not related to an asset or liability on the balance sheet and for carryforwards are classified as current or noncurrent according to the reversal dates of the temporary differences or carryforwards. In other words, the portion of those deferred tax assets and liabilities that will reverse during the next year should be classified as current, and the portion that will reverse after the next year should be classified as noncurrent. As a result of that requirement, some scheduling may be necessary. The valuation allowance for a particular deferred tax asset is classified as current or noncurrent on a pro rata basis.

Disclosure of the total of all (1) deferred tax liabilities, (2) deferred tax assets, and (3) valuation allowances is required. The net change in the total of all valuation allowances is also disclosed. Public companies disclose the approximate tax effect of each type of temporary difference or carryforward that constitutes a significant portion of deferred tax liabilities and deferred tax assets. In practice, a particular type of temporary difference may be considered significant if its deferred tax effects equal 5 percent or more of either total deferred tax assets (i.e., before valuation allowance) or total deferred tax liabilities, whichever is greater. Nonpublic companies also disclose the types of temporary differences and carryforwards but need not disclose the tax effects of each.

The income statement or notes must disclose these eight components of income tax expense for continuing operations for each income statement presented as provided in FASB ASC 740-10-50-9:

1. Current tax expense or benefit
2. Deferred tax expense or benefit, not including the effects of other components below
3. Investment tax credits
4. Government grants that reduce income tax expense
5. Benefits of operating loss carryforwards
6. Adjustments of deferred tax assets or liabilities for changes in tax laws, tax rates, or tax status (i.e., the company becomes taxable or tax exempt)
7. Adjustments of a valuation allowance because of a change in judgment about realization in future years
8. Tax expense that results from allocating certain tax benefits directly to contributed capital

Note that although the current and deferred components of income tax expense include taxes from all applicable tax jurisdictions (i.e., federal, foreign, state, and local taxes), taxes from each jurisdiction typically are not shown separately on the income statement.

Disclosure is also required for the amount of tax expense or benefit allocated to continuing operations and the amounts separately allocated to other items for each year whenever those items are reported. FASB ASC 740-10-55-79 further states:

> The sum of the amounts disclosed for the components of tax expense should equal the amount of tax expense that is reported in the statement of earnings for continuing operations. Insignificant components that are not separately disclosed should be combined and disclosed as a single amount so that the sum of the amounts disclosed will equal total income tax expense attributable to continuing operations.

An amount or percentage reconciliation of the income tax expense for continuing operations to the comparable tax that would result from applying domestic federal statutory tax rates is required (regular tax rates if there are alternative tax systems). Public companies must disclose the nature and estimated amount of each significant reconciling item; nonpublic companies may omit the amount. A public company not subject to income tax because its income is taxed directly to its owners (such as a publicly held limited partnership) must disclose that fact and the net difference between its reported assets and liabilities and their tax bases.

Companies that have not recognized a deferred tax liability for any of the exceptions listed in Subsection 17.1(c)(vii) must disclose:

- The type of temporary difference involved and what would cause it to become taxable
- The cumulative amount of the temporary difference
- The amount of the unrecognized tax liability (If determination of the amount related to foreign investees is not practicable, that fact may be disclosed instead.)

FASB ASC 740-10-55-80 (formerly Question 18 of the FASB Special Report) states that the amount to be disclosed as the tax benefit of operating loss carryforwards is the amount by which total income tax expense from continuing operations has been reduced by the operating loss. The tax benefits of the loss carryforward may be disclosed using the gross or net methods.

Disclosure is required of the amounts and expiration dates of operating loss and tax credit carryforwards for tax purposes for any portion of the valuation allowance for deferred tax assets for which subsequently recognized tax benefits will be credited directly to contributed capital.

In separately issued financial statements, a company that is included in a consolidated tax return must disclose these two items:

1. The current and deferred tax expense for each income statement presented and any tax-related amounts due to or from affiliates for each balance sheet presented
2. How the consolidated tax expense is allocated to members of the group and the nature and effect of any change in the method of allocation or determining amounts to or from affiliates for the periods included in item 1

The SEC's disclosure requirements in Rule 4-08(h) of Regulation S-X related to the accounting for income taxes reflect the issuance of FASB ASC 740 and require these two disclosures that are not required by FASB ASC 740:

1. Domestic and foreign pretax accounting income if income (loss) from operations located outside the registrant's home country is 5 percent or more of total pretax accounting income
2. The tax related to the amounts disclosed under item 1 above is 5 percent or more of total tax expense

As does FASB ASC 740, the SEC requires a reconciliation of tax expense to what tax expense would be at federal domestic statutory tax rates. If the statutory rate used is not the U.S. federal corporate income tax rate, the rate used and the basis for using that rate must be disclosed.

(c) OTHER DISCLOSURES. The following additional disclosures are required when they are applicable:

Significant accounting policy. FASB ASC 235-10-50-1 requires that a company disclose in its financial statements all significant accounting policies that it follows. The authoritative literature does not specifically require disclosure of the method of accounting for income taxes. However, many companies disclose their income tax accounting policies at least in a general way.

Other comprehensive income (OCI). FASB ASC 220-10 requires disclosure of the amount of income tax expense allocated to each component of OCI.

Uncertain tax positions (UTPs). See Subsection 17.3 for separate discussion concerning required disclosures for UTPs.

Investment tax credit (ITC). FASB ASC 740-10-50-20, *Income Taxes—Overall—Disclosure,* calls for disclosure of the method used to account for the ITC and any material amounts involved.

Interim income tax provision. The interim income tax provision requires disclosure of the reasons for any significant variations from the expected relationship between income tax expense and pretax GAAP income, if they are not otherwise apparent from the financial statements or from the nature of the company's business. The financial statements need not disclose the current and deferred components of the interim provision. Tax law and tax rate changes enacted subsequent to reporting period but prior to issuance of financials should be disclosed, if significant.

Management discussion and analysis (MD&A). SEC registrants, in their MD&A, should disclose the reasons for significant changes in the effective income tax rate from year to year and the effect income tax payments would have on liquidity and capital resources. In addition, they are required to disclose one-time items that impact the effective rate.

Other SEC requirements. A company that was granted a tax holiday must disclose in the notes the per share tax effects of such a holiday.

17.5 ACCOUNTING FOR INCOME TAXES IN INTERIM PERIODS

(a) OVERVIEW. FASB ASC 740-270 specifies the general concepts for accounting for income taxes in interim periods. FASB ASC 740-270-25-1 states:

> This guidance addresses the issue of how and when income tax expense (or benefit) is recognized in interim periods and distinguishes between elements that are recognized through the use of an estimated annual effective tax rate applied to measures of year-to-date operating results, referred to as ordinary income (or loss), and specific events that are discretely recognized as they occur.

Thus, FASB ASC 740-270 prescribes an estimated annual effective tax rate (ETR) approach for calculating a tax provision for interim periods. However, in the case of "discrete" items, income taxes associated with significant unusual or extraordinary items are reported in the interim period in which they occur; thus, they are not be prorated over the balance of the fiscal year.

It is important to note that this chapter discusses only some of the key considerations and general rules of this very complex topic. For example, there are limited exceptions to the use of the estimated annual effective tax rate approach and on the amount of benefits that can be recognized for losses, credits, and rate differentials in loss periods. A number of additional scenarios that present unique challenges when accounting for income taxes in interim periods are beyond the scope of this chapter.

(b) ESTIMATED ANNUAL EFFECTIVE TAX RATE. FASB ASC 740-270-20 defines certain terms that are used in special ways for interim period income taxes

> *"Ordinary" income (or loss).* This term refers to "income (or loss) from continuing operations before income taxes (or benefits) excluding significant unusual or infrequently occurring items." Extraordinary items, discontinued operations, and cumulative effects of changes in accounting principles are also excluded from this term. The term is *not* used in the income tax context of ordinary income versus capital gain.
>
> *Tax (or benefit)* is the total income tax expense (or benefit), including the provision (or benefit) for income taxes both currently payable and deferred.[10]
>
> *Extraordinary item.* The definition of "ordinary income (or loss)" in FASB ASC 740-270-20 refers to the definition of the term "extraordinary item" in ASC 225-20-20, which provides these definitions:
>
> - *Unusual nature.* The underlying event or transaction should possess a high degree of abnormality and be of a type clearly unrelated to, or only incidentally related to, the ordinary and typical activities of the entity, taking into account the environment in which the entity operates (see ASC 225-20-60-3).
> - *Infrequency of occurrence.* The underlying event or transaction should be of a type that would not reasonably be expected to recur in the foreseeable future, taking into account the environment in which the entity operates (see ASC 225-20-60-3).

The estimated annual effective tax rate is the estimated income tax for the year allocated to ordinary income divided by the estimated ordinary income for the year. The estimated income tax for the year includes federal, foreign, and state and local income taxes, including the effects of:

1. Credits
2. Special deductions (e.g., Internal Revenue Code Section 199 deduction under the American Jobs Creation Act or percentage depletion)
3. Capital gains taxed at different rates
4. Valuation allowances for current-year changes in temporary differences and losses or income arising during the year

---

[10] Words in parentheses here are deleted in the following discussions.

In theory, the estimated income tax for the year is determined by forecasting what the balances of income taxes payable and deferred income taxes will be at year-end and adjusting for beginning-of-the-year balances. In practice, estimates of tax for the year may suffice. Having estimated income tax for the year, the procedures described in this section for intraperiod income tax allocation are used to allocate the estimated income tax for the year between ordinary income and the items that are treated separately (e.g., unusual, infrequently occurring, and extraordinary items and discontinued operations). A new estimate of the annual effective tax rate should be made whenever assumptions change significantly.

(c) INTERIM PERIOD TAX.   The income tax for the current interim period is determined in several steps.

1. The year-to-date ordinary income is multiplied by the current estimated annual effective tax rate to determine the applicable year-to-date tax.
2. The total tax applicable to ordinary income for prior interim periods of that fiscal year is subtracted to determine tax applicable to ordinary income for the current interim period.
3. Income tax allocated to unusual or infrequently occurring items and similar items included in income from continuing operations but handled on a discrete basis is added.

The result is the income tax applicable to income from continuing operations for the current interim period.

Procedures such as the recognition of the tax benefit of a loss or tax credit carryforward must be properly applied in computing the estimated annual effective tax rate to correctly determine the interim-period income tax rate.

The ETR approach is modified by FASB ASC 740-270-30-30 through 30-34. The effect of this modified approach is to limit the tax benefit recognized for a loss in interim periods to the amount that is expected to be (1) realized during the year or (2) recognizable as a deferred tax asset at the end of the year. The limitations should be applied in determining the estimated annual effective tax rate and the year-to-date benefit for a loss.

FASB ASC 740-270-4 addresses the intraperiod allocation rules and notes that its provisions should be used to allocate the interim provision throughout the interim financial statements using basically the same with-and-without model used for annual periods.

(d) SPECIAL INTERIM-PERIOD PROBLEMS.   FASB ASC 740-270 addresses several special interim-period problems. The next four issues are some of the special issues that are addressed.

1. *It may not be possible to make a reliable estimate of the annual effective tax rate.* In those situations, the actual effective tax rate for the year to date may be the best estimate of the annual effective tax rate. Also, if components of ordinary income or the related tax cannot be reliably estimated, those components may be excluded from the overall estimated annual effective tax rate and handled on an actual effective tax rate for the year to date.
2. *Several estimated annual effective tax rates may have to be computed for one company.* For example, a company that is subject to income tax in several jurisdictions may have losses in some jurisdictions for which no tax benefit can be recognized. Separate annual effective tax rates must be estimated for those loss jurisdictions. Another example is a U.S. company that has foreign operations and is unable to make a reliable estimate *in dollars* of the ordinary income or of the related tax for the foreign operations. Those amounts must be reported on a discrete basis.
3. *New tax legislation poses special problems for reporting income taxes in interim periods.* In the past, some companies have anticipated the effect of proposed tax legislation, but FASB ASC 740-270-25-5 makes it clear that the tax effects of new legislation, such as a change in tax rates, are not recognized prior to enactment.

4. *The tax effect of a change in a valuation allowance because of a change in judgment about realization in future years is recognized in the period that the change in judgment occurs.* It is not allocated to subsequent interim periods by an adjustment of the estimated annual effective tax rate for the remainder of the year.

17.6 INTERNATIONAL FINANCIAL REPORTING STANDARDS

(a) BACKGROUND. IFRS is a set of established accounting standards that is quickly gaining worldwide recognition. The standards are promulgated by the International Accounting Standards Board (IASB; *www.iasb.org*), which includes representatives from major countries, including the United States. In general, IFRS applies a principles-based approach and is therefore less reliant on detailed rules and interpretation than U.S. GAAP.

IAS 12, *Income Taxes,* provides the guidance for income tax accounting under IFRS. The overall approach is the same as FASB ASC 740, as both pronouncements focus on the matching principle, the balance sheet approach, and providing deferred taxes on temporary differences. However, there are also significant differences between the two accounting standards.

(i) IFRS Convergence. In 2002, FASB and IASB affirmed their commitment to the convergence of IFRS and U.S. GAAP in the Norwalk Agreement (*www.fasb.org/news/memorandum.pdf*). The SEC also generally agreed that timely completion of the convergence efforts would best position IFRS to serve as the single set of global accounting standards. Most recently, on May 26, 2011, the SEC issued a staff paper, *Exploring a Possible Method of Incorporation,* that presents a proposed framework for incorporating IFRS into the U.S. financial reporting system.[11] The framework has been referred to as "condorsement" by SEC Staff since it proposes a combination of the convergence and endorsement approaches to incorporation. It is not certain how differences between FASB ASC 740 and IAS 12 may be addressed under this framework since no recent advancement has been made in arriving at a converged standard.

(ii) Accounting for Income Taxes Convergence Project. From a practical standpoint, it appears that many companies find IAS 12 challenging to implement, as indicated by the frequent inquiries received by the IFRS Interpretation Committee and IASB staff. The concepts underlying deferred tax are not intuitive and require significant judgment in some areas. Income tax is also consistently mentioned as a source of significant reconciling items for U.S.-listed foreign registrants applying IFRS. Due to these challenges, accounting for income taxes was included as a short-term convergence project of the IASB and the FASB as part of the 2006 Memorandum of Understanding (MOU).[12] The project goal is to resolve problems in practice under IAS 12, *Income Taxes,* without changing the fundamental approach under IAS 12 and to avoid increasing divergence with U.S. GAAP.

In September 2008, the IASB and the FASB issued an updated MOU. At that time, the FASB decided to postpone its income tax project until it had an opportunity to evaluate its strategy on the ongoing short-term convergence projects, bringing up the possibility that U.S. financial issuers may be transitioning to IFRS in the near term.

In March 2009, the IASB issued an Exposure Draft, *Income Tax* (ED 2009/2)[13] proposing amendments to IAS 12. The Board received many unfavorable comments that the proposed changes were too complex. As a result, both Boards postponed undertaking a fundamental review of the accounting for income taxes.

In its March 2010 IASB Boardmeeting, Board members noted that a full reassessment of income tax accounting would take years and was something that would need to be considered and

---

[11] *www.sec.gov/spotlight/globalaccountingstandards/ifrs-work-plan-paper-052611.pdf*
[12] *www.iasb.org/NR/rdonlyres/874B63FB-56DB-4B78-B7AF-49BBA18C98D9/0/MoU.pdf*
[13] *www.iasb.org/NR/rdonlyres/8A6D0AC9-B6BE-4B87-BD02-B058B5F12148/0/ EDIncomeTaxesStandard.pdf*

prioritized after June 2011. Therefore, the IASB decided to limit the scope of the project to these specific, less divisive practice issues:

- Uncertain tax positions
- Deferred tax on property remeasurement at fair value (amended December 20, 2010)

The Board also decided to consider the next proposals that were on the whole favorably received by respondents to the Exposure Draft issued in 2009 :

- The introduction of an initial step to consider whether the recovery of an asset or settlement of liability will affect taxable profit
- The recognition of a deferred tax asset in full and an offsetting valuation allowance to the extent necessary
- Guidance on assessing the need for a valuation allowance
- Guidance on substantive enactment
- The allocation of current and deferred taxes within a group that files a consolidated tax return

The Board acknowledged that it also intends to examine the treatment of the tax effect of dividends paid by real estate investment trusts and cooperatives.

(iii) Deferred Tax on Property Remeasurement at Fair Value.   On December 20, 2010, the IASB made amendments to IAS 12 and issued *Deferred Tax: Recovery of Underlying Assets.* IAS 12 requires an entity to measure deferred tax relating to an asset by assessing whether the entity expects to recover the carrying amount of the asset through use or sale, as prescribed by the fair value model of IAS 40, *Investment Property.* The amendments were implemented to provide a practical solution to a standard that had proven to be difficult and subjective to apply. The effect of the amendments to IAS 12 can be summarized in this way:

- There is a rebuttable presumption that deferred tax on investment property measured using the fair value model of IAS 40 should be based on the premise that the carrying amount of the underlying asset will be recovered through sale. The presumption is rebutted if investment property is depreciable and the enterprise's business plan is to hold the asset and consume all the economic benefits over time rather than through sale.
- Deferred tax on nondepreciable property using the IAS 16 (*Property, Plant and Equipment*) revaluation model must always be measured on a sale basis.
- IASC Standing Interpretations Committee (SIC) 21, *Income Taxes—Recovery of Revalued Non-Depreciable Assets,* would no longer apply to investment properties carried at fair value.
- The amendments also incorporate into IAS 12 the remaining guidance previously contained in SIC-21, which has been withdrawn.

(b) IAS 12, *CALCULATION OF DEFERRED TAX.*   The flowchart in Exhibit 17.5 shows the steps necessary to calculate a deferred tax provision in accordance with IAS 12.

(c) IAS 12 VERSUS U.S. GAAP.   This section highlights some of the key similarities and significant differences between U.S. GAAP and IAS 12. *Note:* It is not a comprehensive list of the principal differences and similarities between income tax accounting under U.S. GAAP and IFRS.

(i) Key Similarities
- The scope is limited to income taxes (IAS 12.2; ASC 740-10-15-3).
- In general, the current tax effects and the expected future tax consequences of events are recognized using an asset and liability approach (IAS 12.IN2 and .15-.18 ; ASC 740-10-10-1).

IAS 12 Calculation of Deferred Tax

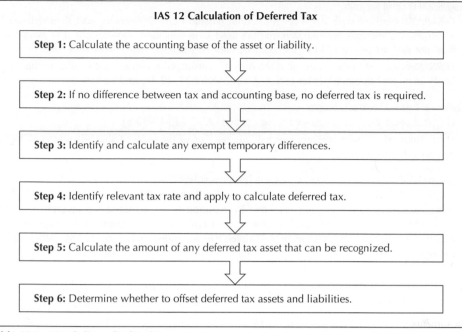

Step 1: Calculate the accounting base of the asset or liability.

Step 2: If no difference between tax and accounting base, no deferred tax is required.

Step 3: Identify and calculate any exempt temporary differences.

Step 4: Identify relevant tax rate and apply to calculate deferred tax.

Step 5: Calculate the amount of any deferred tax asset that can be recognized.

Step 6: Determine whether to offset deferred tax assets and liabilities.

Exhibit 17.5   IAS Calculation of Deferred Tax

- Deferred taxes for temporary differences arising from nondeductible goodwill are not recorded (ASC 740-10-25-3(d): IAS 12.15).
- The tax effects of items accounted for directly in equity during the current year are also allocated directly to equity (IAS 12.61A; ASC 740-20-45-11).
- The discounting of deferred taxes is not allowed (IAS 12.53; ASC 740-10-30-8).

(ii) Significant Differences

Tax Basis
GAAP. Tax basis is determined under the tax law, and when uncertainty exists, it is determined in accordance with ASC 740-10-25.

IFRS. Tax basis is generally the amount deductible or taxable for tax purposes. The manner in which management intends to settle or recover the carrying amount affects the determination of tax basis (IAS 12.51).

Uncertain Tax Positions
GAAP. Prescribes a methodology based on the probability of a tax position being sustained. Detection risk is precluded from being considered in the analysis (ASC 740-10-25-6).

IFRS. Does not include specific guidance. Accounting for tax consequences reflects management's expectations and indicates that tax assets and liabilities should be measured at the amount expected to be paid. Practice varies regarding the consideration of detection risk in the analysis.

Initial Recognition Exemption
GAAP. Does not include an exemption.

IFRS. Deferred tax effects arising from the initial recognition of an asset or liability are not recognized when (1) the amounts did not arise from a business combination and (2) upon occurrence the transaction affects neither accounting nor taxable profit (e.g., acquisition of nondeductible assets; IAS 12.15 and 12.24).

Recognition of Deferred Tax Assets

GAAP. Recognized in full (except for certain outside basis differences) and then reduced by a valuation allowance. Reduce deferred tax asset by a valuation allowance if it is more likely than not that all or a portion of the asset will not be realized (ASC 740-10-30-5(e)).

IFRS. Recognized to the extent that recovery is considered probable and similar to the "more likely than not" threshold under U.S. GAAP (IAS 12.24, 12.34, and 12.56).

Calculation of Deferred Tax Asset or Liability

GAAP. Enacted tax rates required to be applied (ASC 740-10-30-8).

IFRS. Enacted or "substantively enacted" tax rates as of the balance sheet date are required to be applied (IAS 12.47).

Recognition of Deferred Tax Liabilities from Investments in Subsidiaries or Joint Ventures

GAAP. Deferred tax is recognized on all undistributed earnings, occurring after 1992, of domestic subsidiaries and joint ventures. Recognition is not required for investment in foreign subsidiary or corporate joint venture that is effectively permanent in duration, unless it becomes evident that the difference will reverse in the foreseeable future (ASC 740-30-25-18 through 25-19).

IFRS. Recognition is required unless the reporting entity has control over the timing of the reversal of the temporary difference and it is probable ("more likely than not") that the difference will not reverse in the foreseeable future (IAS 12.39).

Taxes on Intercompany Transfers of Assets that Remain Within a Consolidated Group

GAAP. Taxes paid on intercompany profits are deferred. Prohibits the recognition of deferred taxes on the differences between the tax bases of assets transferred between entities/tax jurisdictions that remain within the consolidated group (ASC 740-10-25-3(e)).

IFRS. Requires taxes paid on intercompany profits to be recognized as incurred. Allows recognition of deferred taxes on differences between the tax bases of assets transferred between entities and tax jurisdictions that remain within the consolidated group.

Share-Based Payments

GAAP. Deferred tax is computed on the GAAP expense recognized and trued up or down at realization of the tax benefit or expense. Deferred tax adjustment for current share price is be recorded on settlement (ASC 718-740-25-2 through 25-3).

IFRS. Deferred tax is computed on the basis of the tax deduction for the share-based payment under the applicable tax law. Deferred tax assets is adjusted each period to the amount of tax deduction that the entity would receive if the award was tax deductible as of the reporting date based on the current market price of the shares (IAS 12.68B).

Deferred Taxes on Nonmonetary Foreign Asset/Liabilities Remeasured from Local to Functional Currency

GAAP. Prohibits recognition of deferred taxes for differences related to assets and liabilities that are remeasured from the local currency into the functional currency using historical exchange rates and that result from changes in exchange rates or indexing for tax purposes (ASC 740-10-25-3(f)).

IFRS. Deferred taxes must be recognized for temporary differences that arise when nonmonetary assets and liabilities are measured in their functional currency but have a tax base determined in a different currency (IAS 12.41).

Classification of Deferred Tax Assets and Liabilities

GAAP. Classified between current and noncurrent components based on the classification of the underlying asset or liability or on the expected reversal of items not related to an asset or liability (ASC 740-10-45-4 through 45-10).

IFRS. Always classified as noncurrent (IAS 12.IN11).

Reconciliation of Actual and Expected Tax Expense

GAAP. Required for public entities. Expected tax expense is calculated by applying the domestic federal statutory rate to pretax income from continuing operations using percentages or dollar amounts. Nonpublic entities must disclose the nature of the reconciling items but not the amounts and may omit a numerical reconciliation (ASC 740-10-50-12 through 50-14).

IFRS. Required for all entities. Expected tax expense is computed by applying the applicable tax rate(s) to accounting profit, disclosing the basis on which any applicable tax rate is computed using a numerical reconciliation (IAS 12.81c).

17.7 SOURCES AND SUGGESTED REFERENCES

Accounting Principles Board. APB Opinion No. 2, *Accounting for the Investment Credit*. New York: AICPA, 1962.

————. APB Opinion No. 4, *Accounting for the "Investment Credit"* (Amending No. 2). New York: AICPA, 1964.

————. APB Opinion No. 11, *Accounting for Income Taxes*. New York: AICPA, 1967.

————. APB Opinion No. 16, *Business Combinations*. New York: AICPA, 1970.

————. APB Opinion No. 23, *Accounting for Income Taxes—Special Areas*. New York: AICPA, 1972.

————. APB Opinion No. 25, *Accounting for Stock Issued to Employees*. New York: AICPA, 1992.

————. APB Opinion No. 28, *Interim Financial Reporting*. New York: AICPA, 1973.

Accounting Standards Board. Discussion Paper, *Accounting for Tax*. London: Author, 1995.

————. "Deferred Tax," Financial Reporting Standard 19. London: Author, 2000.

Accounting Standards Committee. Statement of Standard Accounting Practice No. 15, *Accounting for Deferred Taxation*. London: Institute of Chartered Accountants in England and Wales, 1978, revised 1985.

American Institute of Accountants. Accounting Research Bulletin No. 23, *Accounting for Income Taxes*. New York: AIA (now AICPA), 1944.

————. Accounting Research Bulletin No. 43, *Restatement and Revision of Accounting Research Bulletins*. New York: AIA (now AICPA), 1953.

————. Accounting Research Bulletin No. 44, *Declining-Balance Depreciation*. New York: AIA (now AICPA), 1954.

————. Accounting Research Bulletin No. 44, *Declining-Balance Depreciation* (Revised). New York: AIA (now AICPA), 1958.

American Institute of Certified Public Accountants. APB Opinion No. 1 , *New Depreciation Guidelines and Rules*. New York: Author, 1962.

American Institute of CPAs, *Survey of International Accounting Practices*. New York: AICPA, 1991.

————. Internal Revenue Bulletin. Announcement 2010-9, I.R.B.2010-7, 408. (2010)

————. Announcement 84-46, 1984-18 I.R.B. 18. (1984)

Black, H. A. *Interperiod Allocation of Corporate Income Taxes*, Accounting Research Study No. 9. New York: AICPA, 1966.

FASB Emerging Issues Task Force. *EITF Abstracts—A Summary of Proceedings of the FASB Emerging Issues Task Force*. Norwalk, CT: 2001 (published annually by FASB).

Financial Accounting Standards Board. Accounting Standards Update No. 2009-06, *Income Taxes (Topic 740)—Implementation Guidance on Accounting for Uncertainty in Income Taxes and Disclosure Amendments for Nonpublic Entities*. Stamford, CT: Author, September 2009

————. FASB Interpretation No. 18, *Accounting for Income Taxes in Interim Periods—An Interpretation of APB Opinion No. 28*. Stamford, CT: Author, 1977.

————. FASB Interpretation No. 21, *Accounting for Leases in a Business Combination*. Stamford, CT: Author, 1978.

————. Proposed Statement of Financial Accounting Standards, *Accounting for Income Taxes*. Norwalk, CT: Author, June 5, 1991.

_____. Statement of Financial Accounting Standards No. 2, *Accounting for Research and Development Costs*. Stamford, CT: Author, 1974.

_____. Statement of Financial Accounting Standards No. 13, *Accounting for Leases*. Stamford, CT: Author, 1977.

_____. Statement of Financial Accounting Standards No. 16, *Prior Period Adjustments*. Stamford, CT: Author, 1977.

_____. Statement of Financial Accounting Standards No. 37, *Balance Sheet Classification of Deferred Taxes*. Stamford, CT: Author, 1980.

_____. Statement of Financial Accounting Standards No. 52, *Foreign Currency Translation*. Stamford, CT: Author, 1981.

_____. Statement of Financial Accounting Standards No. 71, *Accounting for the Effects of Certain Types of Regulation*. Stamford, CT: Author, 1982.

_____. Statement of Financial Accounting Standards No. 96, *Accounting for Income Taxes*. Stamford, CT: Author, 1987.

_____. Statement of Financial Accounting Standards No. 100, *Accounting for Income Taxes—Deferral of the Effective Date of FASB Statement No. 96*. Norwalk, CT: Author, 1988.

_____. Statement of Financial Accounting Standards No. 103, *Accounting for Income Taxes—Deferral of the Effective Date of FASB Statement No. 96*. Norwalk, CT: Author, 1989.

_____. Statement of Financial Accounting Standards No. 108, *Accounting for Income Taxes—Deferral of the Effective Date of FASB Statement No. 96*. Norwalk, CT: Author 1991.

_____. Statement of Financial Accounting Standards No. 109, *Accounting for Income Taxes*. Norwalk, CT: Author, 1992.

_____. Statement of Financial Accounting Standards No. 123, *Accounting for Stock-Based Compensation*. Norwalk, CT: Author, 1995.

_____. Statement of Financial Accounting Standards No. 142, *Goodwill and Other Intangible Assets*. Norwalk, CT: Author, June 2001.

Fitzgerald, R. D., A. D. Stickler, and T. R. Watts, eds. *International Survey of Accounting Principles and Reporting Practices*. Scarborough, Ontario: Butterworth & Co., 1979.

Grant Thornton International Ltd. "Deferred Tax—A Chief Financial Officer's Guide to Avoiding the Pitfalls: Understanding Deferred Tax Under IAS 12 Income Taxes," November 2009.

International Accounting Standards Committee. IAS 12 (Revised), *Income Taxes*. London: Author, 1996.

I.R.M. 4.10.20.3.1, July 12, 2004.

Perry, R. E., and E. R. Simpson. *A Guide to Implementation of Statement No. 109 on Accounting for Income Taxes—Questions and Answers*. Norwalk, CT: FASB, 1992.

Securities and Exchange Commission. Accounting Series Release No. 96, *Accounting for the "Investment Credit."* Washington, DC: Author, 1963.

_____. Regulation S-X, Part 210 of Title 17 of the Code of Federal Regulations, *Form and Content of and Requirements for Financial Statements*. Washington, DC: Author, as amended through July 1995.

Simpson, E. Raymond, J. M. Cassel, J. Peperone Giles, and G. J. Jones. *Special Report: A Guide to Implementation of Statement 96 on Accounting for Income Taxes—Questions and Answers*. Norwalk, CT: FASB, 1989.

United States vs. Arthur Young, 465 U.S. 805, 53 AFTR 2d 84-866 (1984).

United States v. Textron Inc., 577 F.3d 21 (1st Cir.), *cert. denied,* 130 S. Ct. 3320 (2010).

U.S. v. Deloitte LLP, 610 F.3d 129 (D.C. Cir. 2010).

17.8 VALUABLE WEB SITES

Announcement 2010-75, *Reporting of Uncertain Tax Positions: www.irs.gov/pub/irs-drop/a-10-75.pdf*

Announcement 2010-76, *Requests for Documents Provided to Independent Auditors, Policy of Restraint and Uncertain Tax Positions: www.irs.gov/pub/irs-drop/a-10-76.pdf*

Financial Accounting Standards Board: *www.fasb.org*

Frequently Asked Questions on Schedule UTP: *www.irs.gov/businesses/article/0,,id=237538,00.html*

Internal Revenue Manual, Part 4, Chapter 10, Section 20: "Requesting Audit, Tax Accrual, or Tax Reconciliation Workpapers": *www.irs.gov/irm/part4/irm_04-010-020.html*

International Accounting Standards Board (IASB): *www.iasb.org/home.htm*

International Financial Reporting Standards (IFRS): *www.ifrs.org*

Schedule UTP: *www.irs.gov/pub/irs-pdf/f1120utp.pdf*

Schedule UTP Instructions: *www.irs.gov/pub/newsroom/2010_instructions_for_sch_utp.pdf*

CHAPTER 18

LIABILITIES

Frederick Gill, CPA
American Institute of Certified Public Accountants, Accounting Standards Team

This chapter was updated for the 12th edition by the editor. The views of Mr. Gill, as expressed in this publication, do not necessarily reflect the views of the AICPA. Official AICPA positions are determined through certain specific committee procedures, due process, and deliberation.

18.1 NATURE OF LIABILITIES

(a) DEFINITION OF *LIABILITIES*.   Financial Accounting Standards Board (FASB) Statement of Financial Accounting Concepts No. 6, *Elements of Financial Statements,* defined *liabilities* as:

> [P]robable future sacrifices of economic benefits arising from present obligations of a particular entity to transfer assets or provide services to other entities in the future as a result of past transactions or events.

Probable is used with its usual general meaning and refers to that which can reasonably be expected on the basis of available evidence but is not certain. *Obligation* is broader than "legal obligation," referring to duties imposed legally or socially and to that which one is bound to do by contract, promise, or moral responsibility. Paragraph 36 of Concepts Statement No. 6 elaborates that a liability has three essential characteristics:

1. [I]t embodies a present duty or responsibility to one or more other entities that entails settlement by probable future transfer or use of assets at a specified or determinable date, on occurrence of a specified event, or on demand,
2. the duty or responsibility obligates a particular entity, leaving it little or no discretion to avoid the future sacrifice, and
3. the transaction or other event obligating the entity has already happened.

(i) Executory Contracts as Liabilities.   The furnishing of goods, services, or money to another party is usually a prerequisite for the recording of a liability. Agreements for the exchange of resources in the future that are at present unfulfilled commitments on both sides are not recorded until one of the parties at least partially fulfills its commitment. The effects of some executory contracts, however, are recorded, for example, losses under purchase commitments. In Concepts Statement No. 5, paragraph 107, the FASB stated:

> Several respondents urged the Board to address in this Statement certain specific recognition and measurement issues including definitive guidance for recognition of contracts that are fully executory (i.e., contracts as to which neither party has as yet carried out any part of its obligations, which are generally not recognized in present practice) and selection of measurement attributes for particular assets and liabilities. Those issues have long been, and remain, unresolved on a general basis.

(ii) Credit Balances That Are Not Liabilities.   Items such as minority interest and deferred gross profit on installment sales are sometimes found on the right side of balance sheets. On occasion, such items are confused with liabilities. Neither minority interest nor deferred gross profit on installment sales is a liability, and the presentation of those items in financial statements should be such as to clearly segregate them from any long-term liabilities.

(b) OFFSETTING OF LIABILITIES AGAINST ASSETS. Accounting Principles Board (APB) Opinion No. 10, *Omnibus Opinion—1966,* originally stated in paragraph 7 that "[i]t is a general principle of accounting that the offsetting of assets and liabilities in the balance sheet is improper except where a right of setoff exists." FASB Interpretation No. 39, *Offsetting of Amounts Related to Certain Contracts,* clarifies that a *right of setoff* is a debtor's legal right, by contract or otherwise, to discharge all or a portion of the debt owed to another party by applying against the debt an amount that the other party owes to the debtor. The Interpretation states in paragraph 5 that a right of setoff exists when all of these conditions are met:

- Each of *two* parties owes the other determinable amounts.
- The reporting party has the right to set off the amount owed by the other party.
- The reporting party intends to set off the amount owed by the other party.
- The right of setoff is enforceable at law.

A debtor having a valid right of setoff may offset the related asset and liability and report the net amount (see Accounting Standard Codification [ASC] 210–20).

For purposes of the Interpretation, cash on deposit at a financial institution is to be considered by the depositor as cash rather than as an amount owed to the depositor. Thus, for example, an overdraft in a bank account at a particular bank may not be offset against a cash balance at the same institution because the cash balance is not considered an amount owed to the depositor.

The Interpretation addresses offsetting of amounts recognized for forward, interest-rate swap, currency swap, option, and other conditional or exchange contracts (ASC 815). The fair value of those contracts or an accrued receivable or payable arising from those contracts, rather than the notional amounts or the amounts to be exchanged, is recognized in the statement of financial position. The fair value of contracts in a loss position should not be offset against the fair value of contracts in a gain position unless a right of setoff exists. Similarly, amounts recognized as accrued receivables should not be offset against amounts recognized as accrued payables unless a right of setoff exists. An exception is made to permit offsetting of fair value amounts recognized for forward, swap, and other conditional or exchange contracts executed with the same counterparty under a master netting arrangement, without regard to whether the reporting party intends to set them off. A master netting arrangement exists if the reporting entity has multiple contracts, whether for the same type of conditional or exchange contract or for different types of contracts, with a single counterparty that are subject to a contractual agreement that provides for net settlement of all contracts through a single payment in a single currency in the event of default on or termination of any one contract. Offsetting the fair values recognized for forward, interest rate swap, currency swap, option, and other conditional or exchange contracts outstanding with a single counterparty results in the net fair value of the position between the two counterparties being reported as an asset or a liability in the statement of financial position.

Various accounting pronouncements specify accounting treatments in circumstances that result in offsetting or in a presentation in a statement of financial position that is similar to the effect of offsetting, for example, the accounting for pension plan assets and liabilities under FASB Statement No. 87, *Employers' Accounting for Pensions* (ASC 715) and the accounting for advances received on construction contracts under the American Institute of Certified Public Accountants (AICPA) Audit and Accounting Guides *Construction Contractors* and *Audits of Federal Government Contractors.* Interpretation No. 39 does not modify the accounting treatment prescribed by other pronouncements.

FASB Interpretation No. 41, *Offsetting of Amounts Related to Certain Repurchase and Reverse Repurchase Agreements,* modified Interpretation No. 39 (ASC 210) to permit offsetting in the statement of financial position of payables and receivables that represent repurchase agreements, without regard to whether the reporting party intends to set them off, if conditions specified in the Interpretation are met.

(c) MEASUREMENT OF LIABILITIES.   Paragraph 67 of FASB Concepts Statement No. 5 recognized that items currently reported in financial statements are measured by different attributes, depending on the nature of the item. Liabilities that involve obligations to provide goods or services to customers are generally reported as historical proceeds, which is the amount of cash, or its equivalent, received when the obligations were incurred and may be adjusted after acquisition for amortization or other allocations. Liabilities that involve known or estimated amounts of money payable at unknown future dates—for example, trade payable or warranty obligations—generally are reported at their net settlement value, which is an undiscounted amount. Long-term payables are reported at their present value, discounted at the implicit or historical rate, which is the present value of future outflows required to settle the liability. Many liabilities result from financial instruments, for example, bonds and notes payable. (See "Disclosures about Fair Value of Financial Instruments" at 18.1(d) for the definition of a financial instrument.) The FASB concluded in Statement No. 133, *Accounting for Derivative Instruments and Hedging Activities,* issued in June 1998 (ASC 815), that fair value is the most relevant measure for financial instruments and that fair value measurement is practical for most financial assets and liabilities. Paragraph 334 of Statement No. 133 stated:

> The Board is committed to work diligently toward resolving, in a timely manner, the conceptual and practical issues related to determining the fair values of financial instruments and portfolios of financial instruments. Techniques for refining the measurement of the fair values of financial instruments continue to develop at a rapid pace, and the Board believes that all financial instruments should be carried in the statement of financial position at fair value when the conceptual and measurement issues are resolved.

Only certain liabilities resulting from financial instruments, such as liabilities resulting from derivative financial instruments and guarantees, are currently reported at fair value.

The fair value of a liability is commonly said to be the amount at which that liability could be settled in a current transaction between willing parties, that is, other than in a forced or liquidation transaction. Quoted market prices in active markets are the best evidence of fair value. Thus, if a quoted market price is available for an instrument, its fair value is the product of the number of trading units of the instrument times that market price. If an instrument trades in more than one market, the price in the most active market for that instrument should be used. If quoted market prices are not available, the estimate of fair value may be based on the best information available in the circumstances, including prices for similar liabilities and the results of using other valuation techniques such as the present value technique. (Fair value is further defined and discussed in ASC 820 and in Chapter 24 of this *Handbook.*)

In February 2000, the FASB issued Concepts Statement No. 7, *Using Cash Flow Information and Present Value in Accounting Measurements.* The Board introduced in that Concepts Statement the expected cash flow approach, which focuses on explicit assumptions about the range of possible estimated cash flows and their respective probabilities. That approach differs from the traditional approach to present value applications, which have typically used a single set of estimated cash flows and treated uncertainties implicitly in the selection of a single interest rate.

The Board also concluded in that Concepts Statement that, when using present value techniques to estimate the fair value of a liability, the objective is to estimate the value of the assets required currently to (1) settle the liability with the holder or (2) transfer the liability to an entity of comparable credit standing. In either case, the measurement should reflect the credit standing of the entity obligated to pay. Thus, an improvement in a debtor's credit standing would result in the debtor's reporting a greater liability in its statement of financial position; deterioration in the debtor's credit standing would result in the debtor reporting a smaller liability. The income statement results of that treatment have been challenged.

FASB Concepts Statements do not establish standards prescribing accounting procedures or disclosure practices for particular items or events. They do, however, guide the Board in developing accounting and reporting standards and may provide some guidance in analyzing new or emerging problems of financial accounting and reporting in the absence of applicable authoritative pronouncements.

Recently, the Board proposed that essentially all financial assets and liabilities could be stated at their fair values, as expressed in FASB Statement No. 159, *The Fair Value Option for Financial Assets and Liabilities* (ASC 825-10-25).

(d) DISCLOSURES ABOUT FAIR VALUES OF FINANCIAL INSTRUMENTS.   Paragraph 3 of FASB Statement No. 107, *Disclosures about Fair Values of Financial Instruments* (ASC 825) defines a *financial instrument* as

Cash, evidence of an ownership interest in an entity, or a contract that both:

(a) Imposes on one entity a contractual obligation (1) to deliver cash or another financial instrument to a second entity or (2) to exchange other financial instruments on potentially unfavorable terms with the second entity.

(b) Conveys to that second entity a contractual right (1) to receive cash or another financial instrument from the first entity or (2) to exchange other financial instruments on potentially favorable terms with the first entity.

Contractual obligations encompasses both those that are conditioned on the occurrence of a specified event and those that are not. All contractual obligations that are financial instruments meet the definition of a liability set forth in FASB Concepts Statement No. 6, *Elements of Financial Statements,* although some may not be recognized as liabilities in financial statements; that is, they may be "off-balance sheet," because they fail to meet some other criterion for recognition. For some financial instruments, the obligation is owed to or by a group of entities rather than a single entity.

Examples of contractual obligations that are financial instruments include:

- Loans
- Bonds
- Notes payable
- Trade payables
- Deposit liabilities of banks
- Interest rate swaps
- Foreign currency contracts
- Put and call options on stock, foreign currency, or interest rate contracts
- Commitments to extend credit
- Guarantees of the indebtedness of others, regardless of whether explicit consideration was received for the guarantees

FASB Statement No. 107 requires disclosure, either in the body of the financial statements or in the accompanying notes, of: (1) the fair value of financial instruments, regardless of whether recognized in the statement of financial position, for which it is practicable to estimate that value; and (2) the method(s) and significant assumptions used to estimate the fair value of financial instruments.

Practicable, in this context, means that an estimate of fair value can be made without incurring excessive costs.[1]

If it is not practicable to estimate the fair value of a financial instrument or a class of financial instrument, Statement No. 107 requires disclosure of:

- Information pertinent to estimating the fair value of that financial instrument or class of financial instruments, such as the carrying amount, effective interest rate, and maturity
- The reasons why it is not practicable to estimate fair value

---

[1] Until recently, companies relied on the practicability provison to avoid disclosure of the fair value of guarantees of the indebtedness of others. FASB Interpretation No. 45, *Guarantor's Accounting and Disclosure Requirements for Guarantees, Including Indirect Guarantees of Indebtedness of Others,* however, contains no such provison.

Quoted market prices, if available, should be used to measure fair value. If quoted market prices are not available, management's best estimate of fair value may be based on the quoted market price of a financial instrument with similar characteristics or on valuation techniques (e.g., the present value of estimated cash flows using a discount rate commensurate with the risks involved, option pricing models, or matrix pricing models). In estimating the fair value of deposit liabilities, a financial entity should not take into account the value of core deposit intangibles. For deposit liabilities without defined maturities, the fair value to be disclosed is the amount payable on demand at the date of the financial statements.

The disclosures about fair value are not required for:

- Employers' and plans' obligations for pension benefits, other post retirement benefits including healthcare and life insurance benefits, employee stock option and stock purchase plans, and other forms of deferred compensation arrangements
- Substantively extinguished debt
- Insurance contracts other than financial guarantees and investment contracts
- Lease contracts
- Warranty obligations
- Unconditional purchase obligations

In addition, no disclosure is required for trade payables when their carrying amount approximates fair value.

18.2 INTEREST

There is a general presumption that, if a contractual obligation to pay money on a fixed or determinable date (referred to herein for convenience as a *note*) was exchanged for property, goods, or services in a bargained transaction entered into at arm's length, the rate of interest stipulated by the parties to the transaction represents fair and adequate compensation to the supplier for the use of the money. That presumption does not apply, however, if:

- Interest is not stated.
- The stated interest rate is unreasonable.
- The stated face amount of the note is materially different from the current cash sales price for the same or similar items or from the market value of the note at the date of the transaction.

In those circumstances, APB Opinion No. 21, *Interest on Receivables and Payables* (ASC 835) requires that the note, the sales price, and the cost of the property, goods, or services exchanged for the note be recorded at the fair value of the property, goods, or services or at an amount that reasonably approximates the market value of the note, whichever is more clearly determinable. Established exchange prices may be used to determine the fair value of the property, goods, or services exchanged for the note; when notes are traded in an open market, the market rate of interest and market value of the notes are evidence of fair value. In other circumstances, the present value of the note should be determined by discounting all future payments on the note using an imputed interest rate.

The interest rate should be selected by reference to interest rates on similar instruments of the same or comparable issuers, with similar maturities, security, and so on. APB Opinion No. 21 notes that the objective is

> to approximate the rate that would have resulted if an independent lender had negotiated a similar transaction under comparable terms and conditions with the option to pay the cash price upon purchase or to give a note for the amount of purchase which bears the prevailing rate of interest to maturity.

The difference between the amount at which the note is recorded and the face amount of the note is referred to as a *premium* or *discount*.

The premium or discount is amortized[2] as interest expense or income over the life of the note using the interest method, or capitalized in accordance with FASB Statement No. 34, *Capitalization of Interest Cost* (ASC 835). The interest method allocates the premium or discount over the life of the note in such as way as to result in a constant rate of interest when applied to the amount outstanding at the beginning of any given period.[3] The interest method is discussed further in Section 18.5.

APB Opinion No. 21 does not apply to:

- Receivables and payables arising from transactions with customers or suppliers in the normal course of business that are due in customary trade terms not exceeding approximately one year

- Amounts that will be applied to the purchase price of the property, goods, or services involved, for example, deposits or progress payments on construction contracts, advance payments for acquisition of resources and raw materials, advances to encourage exploration in the extractive industries

- Amounts intended to provide security for one party to an agreement, for example, security deposits, retainages on contracts

- The customary cash lending activities and demand or savings deposit activities of financial institutions whose primary business is lending money

- Transactions where interest rates are affected by the tax attributes or legal restrictions prescribed by a governmental agency (e.g., industrial revenue bonds, tax exempt obligations, government guaranteed obligations, or income tax settlements)

- Transactions between a parent and its subsidiary or between subsidiaries of a common parent

18.3 CURRENT LIABILITIES

(a) NATURE OF CURRENT LIABILITIES.   Accounting Research Bulletin (ARB) No. 43, *Restatement and Revision of Accounting Research Bulletins,* Chapter 3, paragraph 7, as amended by FASB Statement No. 78, *Classification of Obligations That Are Callable by the Creditor* (ASC 470), states, in part:

> The term current liabilities is used principally to designate obligations whose liquidation is reasonably expected to require the use of existing resources properly classifiable as current assets, or the creation of other current liabilities. As a balance-sheet category, the classification is intended to include obligations for items which have entered into the operating cycle, such as payables incurred in the acquisition of materials and supplies to be used in the production of goods or in providing services to be offered for sale; collections received in advance of the delivery of goods or performance of services; and debts which arise from operations directly related to the operating cycle, such as accruals for wages, salaries, commissions, rentals, royalties, and income and

---

[2] Amortization of a discount is sometimes referred to as "accumulation" or "accretion" of the discount. Those usages are incorrect, because the balance of the discount is systematically being reduced, not increased. It is correct, however, to refer to "accretion" of the carrying amount of a loan.

[3] The interest method came over time to be widely accepted as the conceptually superior method of amortizing premiums or discounts. The superiority of the interest method was challenged by Leonard Lorenson in AICPA Accounting Research Monograph No. 4, *Accounting for Liabilities,* published in 1992. The FASB acknowledged in Concepts Statement No. 7, *Using Cash Flow Information and Present Value in Accounting Measurements,* that "no allocation method can be demonstrated to be superior to all others in all circumstances." The Board nevertheless maintains that the interest method is generally considered more relevant than other methods when applied to assets and liabilities that exhibit one or more of the next characteristics:

   a. The transaction giving rise to the asset or liability is commonly viewed as a borrowing and lending.

   b. Period-to-period allocation of similar assets or liabilities employs an interest method.

   c. A particular set of estimated future cash flows is closely associated with the asset or liability.

   d. The measurement at initial recognition was based on present value.

other taxes. Other liabilities whose regular and ordinary liquidation is expected to occur within a relatively short period of time, usually twelve months, are also intended for inclusion.... The current liability classification is also intended to include obligations that, by their terms, are due on demand or will be due on demand within one year (or operating cycle, if longer) from the balance sheet date, even though liquidation may not be expected within that period. It is also intended to include long-term obligations that are or will be callable by the creditor either because the debtor's violation of a provision of the debt agreement at the balance sheet date makes the obligation callable or because the violation, if not cured within a specified grace period, will make the obligation callable.

Under FASB Statement No. 109, *Accounting for Income Taxes* (ASC 740), deferred tax liabilities (i.e., the deferred tax consequences attributable to taxable temporary differences) are classified as current or noncurrent based on the classification of the related asset or liability for financial reporting. A deferred tax liability that is not related to an asset or liability, including deferred tax assets related to carryforwards, is classified according to the expected reversal date of the temporary difference.

A suggestion has been made to eliminate the classification of current liabilities (and current assets).[4]

(i) Long-Term Obligations Approaching Maturity.   If part of a long-term liability matures or otherwise becomes payable within one year after the balance sheet date, for example, serial maturities of long-term obligations and amounts required to be expended within one year under sinking fund provisions, that part of the liability should be classified as current.

(ii) Short-Term Obligations to Be Refinanced.   Under FASB Statement No. 6, *Classification of Short-Term Obligations Expected to Be Refinanced,* short-term obligations other than obligations arising from transactions in the normal course of business that are due in customary terms are classified as noncurrent if:

- The enterprise intends to refinance the obligations on a long-term basis.
- The intent to refinance on a long-term basis is evidenced either by (a) an actual post–balance-sheet-date issuance of long-term debt or equity securities or (b) the enterprise having entered into a firm agreement, before the balance sheet is issued, to make an appropriate refinancing.

If short-term obligations are excluded from current liabilities pursuant to Statement No. 6, the financial statements should disclose:

- A general description of the financing arrangement
- Terms of any new obligation incurred or expected to be incurred, or equity securities issued or expected to be issued, as a result of the refinancing

Obligations that do not qualify for exclusion from current liabilities based on expected refinancing include:

- Obligations for items that have entered into the operating cycle, such as payables incurred in the acquisition of materials and supplies to be used in the production of goods or in providing services to be offered for sale
- Collections received in advance of the delivery of goods or performance of services
- Debts that arise from operations directly related to the operating cycle, such as accruals for wages, salaries, commissions, rentals, royalties, and income and other taxes

---

[4] See L. Heath, Accounting Research Monograph No. 3, *Financial Reporting and the Evaluation of Solvency* (New York: AICPA, 1978).

FASB Interpretation No. 8, *Classification of a Short-Term Obligation Repaid Prior to Being Replaced by a Long-Term Security* (ASC 470) clarified that, if a short-term obligation is repaid after the balance sheet date and subsequently a long-term obligation or equity securities are issued whose proceeds are used to replenish current assets before the balance sheet is issued, the short-term obligation may not be excluded from current liabilities at the balance sheet date.

(iii) Classification of Obligations Callable by the Creditor.   FASB Statement No. 78, *Classification of Obligations That Are Callable by the Creditor* (ASC 470) stated that current liability classification includes obligations that are due on demand or that will be due on demand within one year (or operating cycle, if longer) from the balance sheet date, even though liquidation may not be expected within that period.

Current classification also applies to long-term obligations that are or could become callable by the creditor either because the debtor's violation of a provision of the debt agreement at the balance sheet date makes the obligation callable or because the violation, if not cured within a grace period, will make the obligation callable. However, long-term classification is appropriate if the creditor has waived or subsequently lost the right to demand repayment for more than a year, or if it is probable that the violation will be cured within a grace period. In the latter case disclosure is required of the circumstances.

(iv) Demand Notes.   Loan agreements may specify the debtor's repayment terms but may also enable the creditor, at his discretion, to demand payment at any time. The loan arrangement may have wording such as "the term *note* shall mature in monthly installments as set forth therein or on demand, whichever is earlier," or "principal and interest shall be due on demand, or if no demand is made, in quarterly installments beginning on . . . ." The Emerging Issues Task Force (EITF) in Issue No. 86-5 concluded that such an obligation should be considered a current liability in accordance with FASB Statement No. 78. Further, under FASB Technical Bulletin No. 79-3, *Subjective Acceleration Clauses in Long-Term Debt Agreements,* the demand provision is not a subjective acceleration clause as discussed below. (See ASC 470.)

(v) Subjective Acceleration Clause in Long-Term Debt Agreements.   FASB Statement No. 6 defines a subjective acceleration clause contained in a financing agreement as one that would allow the cancellation of an agreement for the violation of a provision that can be evaluated differently by the parties. The inclusion of such a clause in an agreement that would otherwise permit a short-term obligation to be refinanced on a long-term basis would preclude that short-term obligation from being classified as long term. However, Statement No. 6 does not address financing agreements related to long-term obligations. Under FASB Technical Bulletin No. 79-3, the treatment of long-term debt with a subjective acceleration clause would vary depending on the circumstances. In some situations, only disclosure of the existing clause would be required. Neither reclassification nor disclosure would be required if the likelihood of the acceleration of the due date was remote, such as when the lender historically has not accelerated due dates in similar cases, and the borrower's financial condition is strong and its prospects are good (ASC 470).

(b) KINDS OF CURRENT LIABILITY.   Common kinds of current liability include:

- Accounts payable and accrued expenses
- Short-term notes payable
- Dividends payable
- Deferred income or revenue
- Advances and deposits
- Withheld amounts
- Estimated liabilities

Accounts payable includes all trade payable arising from purchases of merchandise or services. In published balance sheets, this classification normally also includes the liability related to nonfinancial expenses that are incurred continuously (i.e., estimated amounts payable for wages and salaries, rent, and royalties). Accrued interest and taxes are also normally included under this caption. Federal income taxes payable are frequently shown separately. The traditional distinction between accounts payable and accrued expenses has tended to disappear, and the common practice today is to include the two items in one heading.

In most cases, notes payable, if shown as a separate category, refers to a definite borrowing of funds, as distinguished from goods purchased through the use of trade acceptances. In this latter case, relatively rare today, notes payable may be presented as part of accounts payable. Dividends payable, the liability to shareholders representing dividend declarations, has traditionally been viewed as a distinct kind of obligation. Deferred revenues appear when collection is made in whole or part prior to the actual furnishing of goods or services. A common example is found in the insurance industry, where premiums are regularly collected in advance. Tickets, service contracts, and subscriptions are other deferred revenue items.

Advances and deposits required to guarantee performance and returnable to the depositor are current liabilities. The returnable containers used in many industries are sometimes included in this category. Withheld amounts, also referred to as *agency obligations,* result from the collection or acceptance of cash or other assets for the account of a third party. By far the most common items today are federal, state, and local income taxes and payroll taxes withheld from wages.

Estimated liabilities refer to obligations whose amount may be uncertain but the existence of which is unquestioned. Examples include product and service guarantees and warranties.

(c) ACCOUNTS PAYABLE: TRADE. In some cases, the term *accounts payable* is restricted to trade creditors' accounts, represented by unpaid invoices for the purchase of merchandise or supplies. In other cases, *accounts payable* includes all unpaid invoices, regardless of their nature. In the accounting system, of course, accounts payable will normally be limited to those transactions for which the company has received an invoice. As stated previously, for financial statement presentation purposes, it is common to include "accrued expenses" in the same balance sheet caption.

Accounts payable may be recorded at gross invoice price (i.e., without deducting discounts offered for prompt payment), or they may be shown net. Although it has been argued that the latter treatment is conceptually superior regardless of the circumstances, in practice receivables tend to be recorded gross. Accounts payable should be recorded net, however, if it is customary in an industry to permit customers to take the discount regardless of when the invoice is paid. If the discount is always allowed, it amounts to a purchase price reduction and should be accounted for as such. If it is allowed only within the discount period, it appears to be more in the nature of a financial item.

The practical difficulties of apportioning small discounts to a series of items on one invoice lead most companies to account for discounts separately from the purchase price of merchandise. Inventory is recorded at the gross price, and the credit balances resulting from the discount are normally netted against the total year's purchases. In principle, year-end adjustments should be made for that portion of the purchases that remains in inventory, but in practice that is rarely done.

Some companies consider that the rate of interest implicit in the usual trade discount is so large that substantial efforts should be devoted to assuring that it is not lost. If conditions preclude the taking of the discount, the difference between the gross price actually paid and the net price that would have been paid may be accounted for as "discount lost." The balance of this account may be interpreted as a financial expense or as evidence of inefficiency in the accounts payable operation.

(d) NOTES PAYABLE: BANK. Bank loans evidenced by secured or unsecured notes payable to commercial banks are a common method of short-term financing. Ordinarily the notes are interest bearing, and in such cases the amount borrowed and the liability to be recorded is the face amount of the note.

In some instances, however, non-interest-bearing or "discount" paper is issued. In such transactions, the bank deducts the interest in advance from the amount given to the borrower, who subsequently repays the full amount of the note.

Assume, for example, that the X Company gives the bank a $1,000 non-interest-bearing two-month note on a 12 percent basis. The customary entry to record the borrowing is:

Cash	$980	
Prepaid interest	20	
Notes payable—bank		$1,000

Reporting of the discount as "prepaid interest" has been objected to on the ground that the company has borrowed only $980 and that, therefore, the $20 asset is in no way a prepaid item. Essentially the same problem arises on a long-term basis when bonds are issued at a discount. This matter is discussed in Subsection 18.4(f).

In some cases bank loans or notes are taken for short periods but with the intent on the part of both borrower and lender that the note will be continuously refinanced.

(e) NOTES PAYABLE: TRADE AND OTHERS.   Short-term notes payable often arise directly or indirectly from purchases of merchandise, materials, or equipment. If such notes arise directly from purchases, they may be classified in the financial statements with accounts payable. If, however, the notes arise indirectly, or have substantially different payment dates from the usual trade payables, they should be shown separately.

(f) ACCRUED EXPENSES.   An accounts payable figure can be determined at the balance sheet date from the control account, even though normally it is necessary to review all invoices paid for a reasonable period subsequent to the balance sheet date (search for unrecorded liabilities) to assure that all amounts actually payable at the balance sheet date are properly recorded. In contrast, although some part of the balance of accrued expenses may be determined from recurring expense accruals, in general it is necessary to make a thorough review of all the company's relevant expense accounts—rent, salaries, and so on—to determine the appropriate amount at year-end. Thus accrued liabilities (expenses) arise principally only when financial statements are prepared. When preparing the accruals for the different expenses, it is well to keep in mind a sense of balance between the possibility of producing financial statements with every conceivable accrual determined precisely and the added economic value of that precision. In many cases the amount of extra work necessary to estimate certain accruals with extreme accuracy may not be justified by their value to a user of the financial statements. For such immaterial items, relatively rough estimates may suffice.

(i) Interest Payable.   Outside of financial institutions, it is usually not deemed necessary to accrue interest liabilities from day to day, but it is essential that such liabilities be fully recognized at the close of each period. Accrued interest must be calculated in terms of the various outstanding obligations that bear interest such as accounts, notes, bonds, and capitalized leases.

(ii) Accrued Payrolls.   Full recognition of the liability for wages and salaries earned, but not paid, should be made at the close of each accounting period. Accruals should include not only hourly wages and salaries up to the close of business on the last day of the period but also estimates of bonuses accrued, commissions earned, employer share of Social Security, and so on.

The liability for unclaimed wages is a related item usually of minimal size but of some legal significance. Payroll checks that have been outstanding for a period should be restored to the bank account and credited to unclaimed wages. In many states the amount of unclaimed wages escheats to the state after a number of years and therefore should be carefully accounted for until such payment is made. In other states the balance of unclaimed wages should be credited to income after a reasonable period.

(iii) Vacation Pay. Prior to FASB Statement No. 43, *Accounting for Compensated Absences* (ASC 710-10-25), practice related to accruing for vacation pay varied. Most companies did not make such accruals, but a minority did. The prevalent practice was to record compensation for vacation pay as paid. Statement No. 43 requires an employer to accrue a liability for employees' right to receive compensation for future absences if all of these four conditions are met:

1. The employer's obligation relating to employees' rights to receive compensation for future absences is attributable to services already rendered.
2. The obligation relates to rights that vest or accumulate. *Accumulate* means that earned but unused rights to compensated absences may be carried forward to one or more periods subsequent to that in which they are earned, even though there may be a limit to the amount that may be carried forward.
3. Payment of the compensation is probable.
4. The amount can be reasonably estimated.

If the first three conditions are met but the employer does not accrue the cost because of an inability to reasonably estimate the amount, that fact must be disclosed.

(iv) Commissions and Fees. All liabilities for commissions, fees, and similar items should be accrued whenever financial statements are prepared. The principal problem is the determination of the precise amount to be accrued as of a given date. In the case of sales people's commissions, which are in no sense contingent or conditional, if all sales have been recorded, the precise amount usually is readily determinable. However, commissions are subject to reduction in the event of cancellation of sales, uncollectability, or other contingencies, it is not possible to make an exact determination of the liability. In such circumstances, a reasonable estimate should be made, taking into consideration the maximum liability based on performance to date, reduced by the expected amount of adjustments due to cancellations and similar contingencies.

In the case of professional services, such as those furnished by accountants and lawyers, the client often finds it difficult to determine the amount due or earned as of a given date. If billing from accountants or lawyers is based on hourly or per diem rates, a statement to date can be obtained and no difficulty is involved in setting up the proper liability. If, however, the engagement has been undertaken for a lump sum, or if the fee will not be determined until the outcome is known, as is common in legal services, the accrual may be very difficult to estimate. If no reasonable estimate can be made, and the amount may be material, the matter should be disclosed in the notes to the financial statements.

(v) Federal Income Taxes. The determination of the precise liability for federal corporate income taxes is a complex process. In the rush accompanying preparation of year-end financial statements and annual reports, it is not uncommon to obtain an automatic extension for the filing of a tax return (Form 4868) and to delay the preparation of the return, hence determination of the precise tax liability, until after the financial statements have been prepared. It is necessary, under such circumstances, to make an estimate of the income taxes payable and to record that estimate as a liability in the financial statements.

In some instances, there may be income tax items for which the appropriate tax treatment is unclear. Attitudes toward the treatment of such items vary, but many companies will tend to resolve them in their own favor and await possible disallowance by Internal Revenue Service (IRS) examining agents. The calculation of current and deferred taxes for financial reporting purposes should be based on the probable tax treatment.[5] In addition, interest may need to be accrued for expected adjustments by the taxing authorities.

---

[5] The FASB issued *Accounting for Uncertain Tax Positions—An Interpretation of FASB Statement No. 109* (Fin 48). This topic is more fully discussed in Chapter 17 of this *Handbook.*

If the estimate of the tax liability proves to be reasonably accurate, small corrections are usually adjusted to the expense account in the following period.

The determination of the federal income tax liability in interim statements is a more difficult problem, as it requires an estimate of the year's tax burden.

(vi) Property Taxes.   Tax laws, income tax regulations, and court decisions have mentioned various dates on which property taxes may be said to accrue legally. Such dates include assessment date, date on which tax becomes a lien on the property, and date or dates tax is payable, among others. The IRS holds that property taxes accrue on the assessment date, even if the amount of tax is not determined until later (ASC 720-30).

The legal liability for property taxes must be considered when title to property is transferred at some point during the taxable year in order to determine whether buyer or seller is liable for the taxes and to adjust the purchase price accordingly. For normal accounting purposes, however, the legal liability concept is held to be secondary to the general consideration that property taxes arise ratably over time.

(vii) Rent Liabilities.   If property is held under a lease agreement with cash rents payable currently to the lessor and the lease is classified as an operating lease under FASB Statement No. 13 (ASC 840), rent should be accrued ratably with occupancy as an expense and any unpaid portions shown as current lease liabilities. (See Chapter 15 of this *Handbook*.)

Rent advanced by a tenant represents deferred revenue on the books of the lessor and should also be classed as a liability. Generally, tenants' deposits and sureties should be recorded as separate items. In some jurisdictions, interest must be paid on tenants' deposits and should be accrued.

(g) ADVANCES FROM OFFICERS AND EMPLOYEES.   Advances from officers and employees are related party transactions that may require disclosure in accordance with FASB Statement No. 57, *Related Party Disclosures* (ASC 850), and, for Securities and Exchange Commission (SEC) registrants, Regulations S-X and S-K. Related party disclosures are not required, however, for compensation arrangements, expense allowances, and other similar items in the ordinary course of business. The requirements for disclosure of related party transactions are discussed in Subsection 18.8(a)(i).

(h) DIVIDENDS PAYABLE.   The amount of cash dividends declared, but unpaid, is commonly treated as a current liability in balance sheets.

Stock dividends declared, constituting only a rearrangement of the equity accounts, are not recorded as a liability.

(i) Deferred Revenue.   Advances by customers or clients that are to be satisfied by the future delivery of goods or performance of services are liabilities and should be shown as such. These items are often labeled "deferred revenue" or "deferred credits." It is better disclosure to provide a title that clearly describes the nature of the item, such as "advances from customers." Commonly such accounts are payable in goods or services rather than in cash, and as a rule a margin of profit will emerge in making such payment. For a discussion of timing of the recognition of income associated with this type of transaction, see Chapter 12 of this *Handbook*.

(i) CONTINGENCIES.   In paragraph 1 of Statement No. 5, *Accounting for Contingencies* (ASC 450), the FASB defines a contingency as:

> [A]n existing condition, situation, or set of circumstances involving uncertainty as to possible gain or loss to an enterprise that will ultimately be resolved when one or more future events occur or fail to occur. Resolution of the uncertainty may confirm the acquisition of an asset or the reduction of a liability or the loss or impairment of an asset or the incurrence of a liability.

Not all the uncertainties inherent in the accounting process result in the type of contingencies foreseen by Statement No. 5 (ASC 450). Estimates, such as those required in the determination of useful lives, do not make depreciation a contingency. Similarly, a requirement that the amount of a liability be estimated does not produce a contingency as long as there is no uncertainty that the obligation has been incurred. Thus, amounts owed for services received, such as advertising and utilities, are not contingencies, although the amounts actually owed may have to be estimated at the time financial statements must be prepared.

(i) Likelihood of Contingencies. In Statement No. 5, the FASB indicated that the likelihood of contingencies occurring may vary and stipulates different accounting depending on that likelihood. The standard suggests three possibilities:

1. *Probable.* The future event or events are likely to occur.
2. *Reasonably possible.* The chance of the future event or events occurring is more than remote but less than likely.
3. *Remote.* The chance of the event or future events occurring is slight.

Unfortunately, these word distinctions are of little help in relating the concepts to real-world issues and problems. Some accountants might operationalize the word *remote* to mean a 5 percent chance or less of occurrence. The term *probable* may be operationalized in the range of 75 to 80 percent or more in the probability of occurrence, clearly more than just "likely" (which might imply a 51% or greater chance).

(ii) Examples of Loss Contingencies. Among the kinds of loss contingencies are:

- Collectability of receivables
- Obligations related to product warranties and product defects
- Risk of loss or damage of enterprise property by fire, explosion, or other hazards
- Threat of expropriation
- Pending or threatened litigation
- Actual or possible claims or assessments
- Risk of loss from catastrophes assumed by property and casualty insurance companies
- Guarantees of indebtedness of others
- Obligations of commercial banks under "standby letters of credit"
- Agreements to repurchase receivables (or to repurchase the related property) that have been sold

Some of these contingencies involve impairment of an asset rather than the incurrence of a liability.

Contingencies may involve either short-term obligations or long-term obligations, or both. Contingent liabilities are addressed in this section without regard to when they are expected to be settled.

(iii) Accrual of Loss Contingencies. The FASB requires that an estimated loss from a loss contingency be accrued by a charge to income if both of the next two conditions are met:

1. Information available prior to the issuance of the financial statements indicates that it is probable that an asset had been impaired or a liability had been incurred at the date of the financial statements. This condition implies that it must be probable that one or more future events will occur confirming the fact of the loss.
2. The amount of loss can be reasonably estimated.

Items become liabilities of an entity only as a result of transactions or other events or circumstances that have already occurred.

(iv) Estimating Amounts to Be Accrued. As noted, an estimated loss be accrued when it appears that a liability has been incurred and the amount of the loss can be reasonably estimated.

The term *reasonably estimated* is susceptible to interpretation. In many cases, particularly with litigation and claims, estimates of the amount of the loss may be difficult. Although Statement No. 5 does not define *reasonably estimated* specifically, FASB Interpretation No. 14, *Reasonable Estimation of the Amount of a Loss* (ASC 450) attempts to define the term more clearly.

If a reasonable estimate of the loss is a range, Interpretation No. 14 indicates that the "reasonably estimated" criterion is satisfied. If no value in the range is more likely than any other, the minimum amount should be accrued. Thus, if the loss from a contingency is probable and will be within a range of $4 million to $6 million, and there is no better estimate within that range, $4 million should be accrued. If within the $4 million to $6 million range, $5.5 million is the most likely outcome, that latter amount should be accrued.

(v) Disclosure of Loss Contingencies.   The disclosure of the nature of an accrual should made pursuant to its provisions. In some circumstances, the amount accrued may be necessary for the financial statements to be not misleading.

In many circumstances, a loss contingency exists but does not satisfy the two conditions calling for accrual, or exposure to loss exists in excess of the amount accrued. In such cases, Statement No. 5 requires disclosure of the loss contingency. Disclosure is required when there is at least a reasonable possibility that a loss or additional loss may have occurred. The disclosure should indicate the nature of the contingency and should give an estimate of the possible loss or range of loss or state that such an estimate cannot be made.

FASB Statement No. 5 also requires disclosure of guarantees such as (1) guarantees of the indebtedness of others, (2) obligations of commercial banks under "standby letters of credit," and (3) guarantees to repurchase receivables (or, in some cases, to repurchase the related property) that have been sold or otherwise assigned, even though the possibility of loss may be remote. The requirement also applies to other contingencies that in substance have the characteristic of a guarantee. The disclosure must include the nature and amount of the guarantee. Consideration should also be given to disclosing, if estimable, the value of any recovery that could be expected to result, for example, from the guarantor's right to proceed against an outside party.

FASB Interpretation No. 45, *Guarantor's Accounting and Disclosure Requirements for Guarantees, Including Indirect Guarantees of Indebtedness of Others* (ASC 460-10-50-8), provides further guidance on accounting for and disclosure of guarantee obligations.

SEC Codification of Financial Reporting Policies Section 104 points out that oral guarantees, even if legally unenforceable, may have the same financial reporting significance as written guarantees.

In accordance with APB Opinion No. 28 (ASC 270 and ASC 450), contingencies and other uncertainties that could be expected to affect the fairness of presentation of financial data at an interim date should be disclosed in interim reports in the same manner required for annual reports. Such disclosures should be repeated in interim and annual reports until the contingencies have been removed, resolved, or become immaterial.

Financial statements sometimes contain a contingency conclusion that addresses the estimated total unrecognized exposure to one or more loss contingencies. It may state, for example, that "management believes that the outcome of these uncertainties should not have (or 'may have') a material adverse effect on the financial condition, cash flows, or operating results of the enterprise." Alternatively, the disclosure may indicate that the adverse effect could be material to a particular financial statement or to results and cash flows of a quarterly or annual reporting period. AICPA Statement of Position (SOP) No. 96-1, *Environmental Remediation Liabilities* (ASC 410), states this about contingency conclusions:

> Although potentially useful information, these conclusions are not a substitute for the required disclosures of . . . FASB Statement No. 5, such as [its] requirement to disclose the amounts of material reasonably possible additional losses or to state that such an estimate cannot be made. Also, the assertion that the outcome should not have a material adverse effect must be supportable. If an entity is unable to estimate the maximum end of the range of possible outcomes, it may be difficult to support an assertion that the outcome should not have a material adverse effect.

AICPA SOP No. 94-6, *Disclosure of Certain Significant Risks and Uncertainties* (ASC 275 and ASC 410), requires disclosure about significant estimates used to determine the carrying amounts of assets or liabilities and the disclosure of gain or loss contingencies if (1) it is at least reasonably possible that the estimate of the effect on the financial statements of a set of circumstances that existed at the financial statement date will change in the near term due to one or more future confirming events and (2) the effect of the change would be material. *Near term* is a period not to exceed one year from the date of the financial statements. Disclosure requirements include the nature of the uncertainty and an indication that it is at least reasonably possible that a material change will occur in the near term. Disclosure of factors causing the uncertainty is encouraged but not required. If an uncertainty is a loss contingency, disclosure must also provide an estimate of the possible loss or range of loss. If the SOP's disclosure criteria are not met as a result of the use of risk-reduction techniques, the disclosures that would otherwise be required by the SOP and disclosure of the risk-reduction techniques are encouraged but not required.

Examples of estimates subject to change in the near term include litigation-related obligations, contingent liabilities for guarantees of other entities, and amounts reported for pensions and other benefits.

(vi) Uninsured Risks.   Enterprises may decide to insure against certain risks by specifically obtaining coverage. In other cases risks may be borne by the company either through use of deductible clauses in insurance contracts or by not purchasing insurance at all. Insurance policies purchased from a subsidiary or investee, to the extent that policies have not been reinsured with an independent insurer, are considered not to constitute insurance. Some risks, such as a decline in business, may not be insurable.

The absence of insurance does not mean that an asset has been impaired or that a liability has been incurred at the date of the enterprise's financial statements. Therefore, exposure to uninsured risks does not constitute a contingency requiring either disclosure or accrual. However, GAAP does not discourage disclosure of noninsurance or underinsurance in appropriate circumstances, and may require disclosure. For example, when the noninsurance or underinsurance violates a debt covenant, disclosure may be warranted.

If an event has occurred, such as an accident, for which the enterprise is not insured and for which some liability is suggested, the proper accounting or disclosure of that event must be considered within the framework of the standard.

(vii) Litigation, Claims, and Assessments.   Accounting for and disclosure of litigation, claims, and assessments, either actual or possible, often presents problems. Those problems may involve the probability of payment, estimates of amounts, and, in a particularly sensitive area, the reluctance of companies to disclose information that may be actually or potentially adverse. Full disclosure or the accrual of a loss contingency, when litigation is threatening or pending, may well be seized on by the opposing party as evidence to support its case.

Accounting for contingencies (ASC 450) does not exempt from its accounting or disclosure provisions entities that believe complying with those provisions could damage their position in litigation. If the underlying cause of the litigation, claim, or assessment is an event occurring before the date of the financial statements, the probability of an unfavorable outcome must be assessed to determine whether it is probable that a liability has been incurred. Among the factors that should be considered are:

- The nature of the litigation, claim, or assessment, the progress of the case (including progress after the date of the financial statements but before those statements are issued)
- The opinions or views of legal counsel and other advisers
- The company's experience in similar cases
- The experience of other companies in similar cases
- Any decision of the company's management as to how the company intends to respond to the lawsuit, claim, or assessment (e.g., a decision to contest the case vigorously or a decision to seek an out-of-court settlement)

The fact that legal counsel is unable to express an opinion that the outcome will be favorable should not necessarily be interpreted to mean that a loss is probable.

Among the most difficult issues to resolve is that of unasserted claims. An unasserted claim exists, for example, when the company knows that an event such as a product failure has occurred, but no actions have yet been brought against the company. It is conceivable that disclosure of the event, along with a discussion indicating the possibility of claims being asserted, could trigger litigation adverse to the company that might not have been brought in the absence of the company's own disclosure. A judgment must first be made as to whether the assertion of a claim is probable. If the judgment is that assertion is not probable, no accrual or disclosure would be required. If, however, the judgment is that assertion is probable, a second judgment must be made as to the degree of probability of an unfavorable outcome.

For both asserted and unasserted litigation, claims, and assessments, if an unfavorable outcome is determined to be probable and the amount of loss is reasonably estimable, the loss should be accrued. If an unfavorable outcome is determined to be reasonably possible but not probable, or if the amount of loss cannot be reasonably estimated, a loss should not be accrued, but the disclosures required for other contingencies would be required.

Caution should be used in disclosing "contingency conclusions." In at least one case, a disclosure to the effect that the outcome of litigation should not have a material adverse effect on the financial condition, cash flows, or operating results of the enterprise was the basis for the awarding by a jury of punitive damages well in excess of those originally sought in a lawsuit.

(viii) General Reserves for Contingencies Not Permitted.   In the past, some companies have provided, sometimes through income, reserves for general contingencies. In other cases, such reserves have been established as appropriations of retained earnings. GAAP does not permit such general contingency reserves to be charged to income. Appropriation of retained earnings is not prohibited provided that it is shown within the stockholders' equity section of the balance sheet and is clearly identified as an appropriation of retained earnings.

(ix) Warranty Obligations.   The obligation to satisfy a product warranty, incurred in connection with the sale of goods or services, is a loss contingency of the kind that requires accrual. That is, future obligations under warranties should be estimated and provided for. Such estimates may be difficult, particularly if new products or changed warranty terms are involved. Still, an effort should be made to determine the liability. If necessary, reference may be made to the experiences of other companies.

If there is inadequate information to permit a reasonable estimate of the obligation for warranties, the propriety of recording a sale of the goods until the warranty period has expired should be questioned.

(x) Accounting for Environmental Liabilities.   SOP No. 96-1, *Environmental Remediation Liabilities* (ASC 410) provides accounting guidance on environmental remediation liabilities that relate to pollution arising from some past act. Such liabilities should be accrued when the criteria of FASB Statement No. 5 (ASC 460) are met, and it includes benchmarks to aid in determining when environmental liabilities should be recognized.

The SOP establishes a presumption that, given the legal framework within which most environmental remediation liabilities arise, (1) if litigation has commenced or a claim or assessment has been asserted or if commencement of litigation or assertion of a claim or assessment is probable and (2) if the company is associated with the site—that is, if it in fact arranged for the disposal of hazardous substances found at a site or transported hazardous substances to the site or is the current or previous owner or operator of the site—the outcome of such litigation, claim, or assessment will be unfavorable.

The estimate of the liability should include (1) the entity's allocable share of the liability for a specific site and (2) the entity's share of amounts related to the site that will not be paid by other potentially responsible parties or the government.

Costs to be included in the measurement of the liability are both incremental direct costs of the remediation effort and costs of compensation and benefits for those employees who are expected to devote a significant amount of time directly to the remediation effort.

The measurement of the liability should be based on enacted laws and existing regulations and policies—no changes in regulations or policies should be anticipated. The measurement of the liability should be based on the reporting entity's estimate of what it will cost to perform all elements of the remediation effort when they are expected to be performed, using remediation technology that is expected to be approved to complete the remediation effort. The measurement of the liability, or of a component of the liability, may be discounted to reflect the time value of money if the aggregate amount of the liability or component of the liability and the amount and timing of cash payments for the liability or component are fixed or reliably determinable.

The SOP provides financial statement display guidance and encourages, but does not require, a number of disclosures that are incremental to the FASB Statement No. 5 and SOP No. 94-6 requirements.

For SEC registrants, SEC Staff Accounting Bulletin (SAB) No. 92, *Accounting and Disclosures Relating to Loss Contingencies,* provides additional accounting, display, and disclosure guidance concerning environmental liabilities. SAB No. 92 also states that the Staff would not object to a registrant accruing site restoration, postclosure and monitoring, or other environmental exit costs that are expected to be incurred if that is established accounting practice in the registrant's industry. In other industries, the Staff would raise no objection provided that the liability is probable and reasonably estimable. If the use of an asset in operations gives rise to growing exit costs that represent a probable liability, the accrual of the liability should be recognized as an expense in accordance with the consensus in EITF Issue No. 90-8, *Capitalization of Costs to Treat Environmental Contamination* (ASC 410).

(xi) Vulnerability from Concentrations. Vulnerability due to concentrations arises because of exposure to risk of loss greater than an enterprise would have had if it mitigated its risk through diversification. Although an exposure to risk from a concentration is not the same as a liability, the subject is included in this chapter because it tends to be associated with the subject of liabilities.

GAAP requires disclosure of these kinds of concentrations:

- Concentrations in volume of business with a particular customer, supplier, lender, grantor, or contributor
- Concentrations in revenue from particular products, services, or fundraising events
- Concentrations in available sources of supply of materials, labor or services, or licenses or other rights used in operations
- Concentrations in the market or geographic area in which the entity operates

Disclosure is required if all of the next conditions are met:

- The concentration exists at the balance sheet date.
- The enterprise is vulnerable to a near-term severe impact as a result of the concentration.
- It is at least reasonably possible that the events that could cause the severe impact will occur in the near term.

Severe impact, which is defined as a significant financially disruptive effect on the normal functioning of the entity, is a higher threshold than material, but the concept includes matters that are less than catastrophic, such as those that would result in bankruptcy.

The disclosure requirements also apply to group concentrations, which may arise if a number of counterparties or items have similar economic characteristics.

Although other kinds of concentrations may create equal, or even greater, vulnerability, they were not covered by SOP No. 94-6 for practical reasons. For example, a business's dependence on key management personnel might make it vulnerable to a severe impact in the event of the loss of services of those persons. However, a requirement to disclose that the occurrence of an adverse effect of that vulnerability is reasonably possible in the near term might violate accepted rights to privacy (e.g., by causing information about an individual's health or marital problems to be revealed) and place an unreasonable burden on the accountant to know that information.

Disclosure should include information that is adequate to inform users of the general nature of the risk associated with the concentration. For labor subject to collective bargaining agreements meeting the disclosure requirements, the notes should include the percentage of the labor force covered by collective bargaining agreements and the percentage of the labor force covered by agreements that will expire within one year. For operations outside the home country, the disclosures should include the carrying amount of net assets and geographical areas in which the assets are located. (See ASC 275 and ASC 280.)

(j) EXIT OR DISPOSAL ACTIVITY OBLIGATIONS.   An entity's commitment to a plan to exit an activity, by itself, does not create a present obligation to others that meets the definition of a liability. FASB Statement No. 146, *Accounting for Exit or Disposal Activities* (ASC 420), requires recognition of a liability for costs associated with an exit or disposal activity when a liability has been incurred and points out that a liability is not incurred until a transaction or event occurs that leaves an entity with little or no discretion to avoid the future transfer or use of assets to settle the liability.

(i) One-Time Termination Benefits.   Under FASB Statement No. 146 (ASC 420), a one-time benefit arrangement exists at the date the plan of termination meets all of the next criteria and has been communicated to employees:

- Management, having the relevant authority to approve the action, commits to a plan of termination.
- The plan identifies the number of employees to be terminated, their job classifications or functions and their locations, and the expected completion date.
- The plan establishes the terms of the benefit arrangement, including the benefits that employees will receive upon termination, in sufficient detail to enable employees to determine the kind and amount of benefits they will receive if they are involuntarily terminated.
- Actions required to complete the plan indicate that it is unlikely that significant changes to the plan will be made or that the plan will be withdrawn.

The timing of recognition of and measurement of a liability for one-time termination benefits depends on whether employees are required to render service until they are terminated in order to receive the termination benefits and, if so, whether they will be retained beyond the minimum retention period. If employees are not required to render service until they are terminated (i.e., if employees are entitled to receive the termination benefits regardless of when they leave) or if they will not be retained to render service beyond the minimum retention period, a liability is recognized and measured at fair value at the date the plan of termination has been communicated to the employees (referred to as the *communication date*).

If employees are required to render service until they are terminated in order to receive termination benefits and will be retained to render service beyond the minimum retention period, a liability for termination benefits is measured initially at the communication date based on the fair value of the liability as of the termination date. The liability should be recognized ratably over the future service period. Any change resulting from a revision to either the timing or the amount of estimated cash flows over the future service period should be measured using the credit-adjusted risk-free rate that was used to measure the liability initially, and the cumulative effect of the change should be recognized as an adjustment to the liability in the period of the change.

If a plan of termination changes and employees who were expected to be terminated within the minimum retention period are retained beyond that period, a liability previously recognized at the communication date should be adjusted to the amount that would have been recognized had the employees originally been expected to render service beyond the minimum retention period. The cumulative effect of the change should be recognized as an adjustment of the liability in the period of the change.

If a plan of termination includes both involuntary termination benefits and termination benefits offered for a short period in exchange for employees' voluntary termination of service, a liability for the involuntary termination benefits should be recognized in accordance with Statement No. 146 and a liability for the excess of the voluntary termination benefit amount over the involuntary termination benefit amount should be recognized in accordance with FASB Statement No. 88, *Employers' Accounting for Settlements and Curtailments of Defined Benefit Pension Plans and for Termination Benefits* (ASC 715).

(ii) Contract Termination Costs.   A liability for costs to terminate, in connection with an exit activity, an operating lease or other contract before the end of its term should be recognized and measured at its fair value when the entity terminates the contract in accordance with the contract terms (e.g., by giving written notice or otherwise negotiating a termination with the lessor). No liability for contract termination costs may be recognized solely because of an entity's commitment to an exit or disposal plan. The termination of a capital lease should be accounted for in accordance with FASB Statement No. 13, *Accounting for Leases* (ASC 840).

A liability for costs that will continue to be incurred under a contract for its remaining term without economic benefit should be recognized and measured at its fair value when the entity ceases using the right conveyed by the contract (referred to as the *cease-use date*). If the contract is an operating lease, the fair value of the liability at the cease-use date is determined based on the remaining lease rentals, reduced by estimated sublease rentals that could reasonably be obtained for the property, even if the entity does not intend to sublease. Remaining rentals may not be an amount less than zero.

(iii) Other Associated Costs.   A liability for other costs associated with an exit or disposal activity, such as costs to consolidate or close facilities and relocate employees, should be recognized and measured at its fair value in the period in which the liability is incurred, which is generally when goods or services associated with the activity are received. No liability should be recognized before it is incurred, even if the costs are incremental to other operating costs and will be incurred as a direct result of a plan.

(iv) Financial Statement Presentation.   Costs associated with an exit or disposal activity should be included either in income from continuing operations before income taxes or in results of discontinued operations, depending on whether the exit or disposal activity involves a discontinued operation. If an exit or disposal activity does not involve a discontinued operation, the costs may not be presented in the income statement net of taxes or in any manner that implies they are similar to an extraordinary item.

If an entity's responsibility to settle a liability for a cost associated with an exit or disposal activity recognized in a prior period is discharged or removed, the liability should be reversed and the costs should be reversed through the same income statement line items used when the costs were recognized initially.

(v) Disclosure.   GAAP requires disclosure of the next information in the period in which an exit or disposal activity is initiated and any subsequent period until the activity is completed:

1. A description of the exit or disposal activity, including the facts and circumstances leading to the expected activity and the expected completion date
2. For each major kind of cost associated with the activity (e.g., one-time termination benefits, contract termination costs, and other associated costs)
   ○ The total amount expected to be incurred in connection with the activity, the amount incurred in the period, and the cumulative amount incurred to date
   ○ A reconciliation of the beginning and ending liability balances showing separately the changes during the period attributable to costs incurred and charged to expense, costs paid or otherwise settled, and any adjustments to the liability with an explanation of the reasons therefore

3. The line item(s) in the income statement or the statement of activities in which the cost in number 2 are aggregated

4. For each reportable segment, the total amount of costs expected to be incurred in connection with the activity, the amount incurred in the period, and the cumulative amount incurred to date, net of any adjustments to the liability with an explanation of the reasons therefore

5. If a liability for a cost associated with an activity is not recognized because fair value cannot be reasonably estimated, that fact and the reasons therefore

(k) TRANSLATION OF LIABILITIES IN FOREIGN CURRENCIES.   When a domestic corporation consolidates a foreign branch or subsidiary or when an importer purchases goods or incurs liabilities expressed in foreign currencies, the problem arises of translating the liabilities into U.S. dollar amounts. Accounting principles in this area have undergone considerable change in recent years.

(l) STATEMENT PRESENTATION OF CURRENT LIABILITIES.   As indicated previously, obligations expected to be liquidated within the next operating cycle by the use of current assets or the creation of other current obligations should be classified as current liabilities.

(i) Balance Sheet Classification.   The SEC, in Regulation S-X, Rule 5.02(19), requires this classification in balance sheets:

Accounts and notes payable. State separately amounts payable to:

1. Banks for borrowings
2. Factors or other financial institutions for borrowings
3. Holders of commercial paper
4. Trade creditors
5. Related parties
6. Underwriters promoters, and employees (other than related parties)
7. Others

Rule 5.02(19) also requires disclosure of the amount and terms of unused lines of credit for short-term financing.

(ii) Other Current Liabilities.   Regulation S-X, Rule 5.02(20), requires the separate statement in the balance sheet or in a note thereto of any item in excess of 5 percent of total current liabilities. Such items may include, but are not limited to, accrued payrolls, accrued interest, taxes, indicating the current portion of deferred income taxes, and the current portion of long-term debt. Remaining items may be shown in one amount.

Many companies disclose arrangements for compensating balances in the note covering short-term debt, although these are covered in Regulation S-X under requirements related to cash.

An example of a note that presents the required SEC information is given in Exhibit 18.1.

NOTE 7. SHORT-TERM DEBT

The Company borrows on a short-term basis, as necessary, by the issuance of commercial paper and by obtaining short-term bank loans. The maximum and average amount of short-term borrowings during 1988 were $112 million and $56 million, respectively, at a weighted average interest rate of 7.77 percent. The Company has an agreement for a line of credit for up to $200 million through December 1991. No short-term debt was outstanding at December 31, 1988. The line of credit is on a fee basis.

Exhibit 18.1   Sample Presentation of Short-Term Liabilities as Required by the SEC
Source: Oklahoma Gas & Electric Co., 1988 Annual 10-K Report.

In the less detailed form used in published reports to shareholders, it is common to present current liabilities in this way:

- Payable to banks
- Accounts payable and accrued expenses
- Federal income taxes payable
- Current portion of long-term debt

As a general rule, current liabilities should not be offset against related assets. For example, an overdraft at one bank should not be canceled against a debit balance at another bank; such offsetting distorts the current ratio. An exception to the general rule is indicated by APB Opinion No. 10, *Omnibus Opinion—1966,* in the instance of short-term government securities "when it is clear that a purchase of securities (acceptable for the payment of taxes) is in substance an advance payment of taxes that will be payable in the relatively near future" (ASC 740).

Supplemental disclosure should be used to indicate partially and fully secured current claims, overdue payments, and special conditions of future payment.

18.4 NATURE AND ISSUE OF BONDS PAYABLE

(a) BONDS DEFINED.   Bonds are essentially long-term notes issued under a formal legal procedure and secured either by the pledge of specific properties or revenues or by the general credit of the issuer. In the last case, the bonds are considered "unsecured." The most common bonds are those issued by corporations, governments, and governmental agencies. A significant difference, from the viewpoint of the holder although not the issuer, is that most obligations of state and local governmental units are free of federal income taxes on interest and sometimes of state taxes as well. Both state and local government bonds are usually called *municipals.* Agency bonds are obligations of government agencies and frequently carry a form of guarantee from the government unit. The typical bond contract, known as an *indenture,* calls for a series of "interest" payments semiannually and payment of principal or face amount at maturity. Bonds differ from individual notes in that they represent fractional shares of participation in a group contract, under which a trustee acts as intermediary between the corporation and holders of the bonds. The terms are set forth in the trust indenture covering the entire issue. Indentures are frequently long and complex documents and normally contain various conditions and restrictions related to the operations of the borrower.

The conditions and restrictions referred to as *covenants* may include restrictions on dividend payments and an agreement to maintain a minimum amount of working capital. Failure to comply with covenants would lead to default and acceleration of the due date of the debt. This event may trigger default on other obligations of the corporation under cross-covenant provisions.

Bonds, like stocks, are a means of providing the funds required for the long-run operation of the corporation and have been used for this purpose on a large scale, particularly in the utility field. The primary difference between the two broad classes of securities is that bonds represent a contractual liability whereas stocks represent a residual equity. Failure to pay interest and principal as agreed under the bond indenture usually results in definite legal action to protect the rights of the bondholder. As long as the corporation meets all obligations as prescribed, the bondholder has little or no influence on the administration of the company. However, if the issuer violates one or more of the restrictive covenants in the indenture, the power of the holders may increase substantially.

Bonds are normally long-term securities and are often issued for periods of ten years or longer. Maturities vary with industry and with general conditions at the time of issue. Intermediate-term securities, with maturities of one to five years, like bonds in every other respect, are normally called *notes.* Whereas bonds are usually issued in units of $1,000, prices are quoted in multiples of $100. Thus a bond quoted at $85 would actually be priced at $850. Alternatively, bond prices may be quoted in terms of their interest yield.

(b) BONDS CLASSIFIED. Bonds may be classified in a number of different ways. The security given in connection with the bond may range from a first or senior lien on specific physical property, such as a first mortgage bond or an equipment obligation, to securities that are a general lien, such as debentures, and finally to conditional promises with no lien, such as income bonds. The traditional distinction between bonds and stocks became blurred through the increasing use of hybrid types such as convertible bonds, bonds with stock-purchase warrants attached, and redeemable preferred stocks. Similarly, the popularity of serial bonds, in which a portion of the issue matures each year, has blurred distinctions based on maturities.

For financial statement purposes, clear identification of bonds that are "secured" and similarly clear labeling of the assets involved are absolute requirements.

(i) Convertible Bonds. Bonds may have characteristics of both the typical senior security and the typical common stock. The most common form of privileged *issue* is the convertible bond, which includes a provision giving the right to the holder to exchange the bond for common stock on certain stipulated terms. Another method of introducing an equity element into a bond is the bond with warrants attached, under which holders of the bond may purchase common shares in amounts, at prices and during periods that are stipulated in advance.

These privileged issues have created several other problems in accounting. Aside from the accounting required upon conversion, the existence of warrants or a conversion feature provides difficulties in the determination of the amount of discount.

(ii) Serial Bonds and Sinking Funds. Sinking funds may be established for the retirement of bonds, either as a requirement of the bond indenture or voluntarily. A disadvantage of bond sinking funds is that as a result of transferring cash to the sinking fund, a portion of the money borrowed for use in the business is not available for that purpose.

Generally, the same type of protection sought by a sinking fund can be obtained by the use of serial bonds, issues that mature in installments. For most serial bonds, coupon interest rates differ with each maturity, and the issue price is relatively similar for all maturities. In principle, a default of any issue in a serial maturity or a failure to make a sinking fund payment causes the entire issue to become due and payable. In practice, as long as the issuer continues to meet interest payments, some remedy short of total default is normally arranged.

(c) AUTHORITY TO ISSUE BONDS. The general right of a corporation to create a bonded indebtedness is found in the power to borrow funds granted by statute, and specific authorization of such action is usually included in the charter or bylaws. However, the authority of the directors to place a mortgage on corporate assets may be subject to shareholder approval. Securing such approval is often advisable, even if not required, in the event of a heavy borrowing program, in view of the effect of such a program on the shareholders' position. Under some statutes, corporate borrowing is subject to general restrictions (e.g., limitation to a certain percentage of total capital stock).

(d) OUTLINE OF ISSUING PROCEDURE. An outline of 14 procedural steps when bonds are issued through investment bankers follows.

1. Directors authorize management to proceed with negotiations.
2. Investment bankers are interviewed by corporation's representatives.
3. Propositions of investment bankers are submitted to board of directors, and board approves a particular proposal.
4. Plan is submitted to corporation's attorneys.
5. Meeting of shareholders is called, and resolution is passed approving the bond issue.
6. Appraisers and certified public accountants, acceptable to bankers, are instructed to make an investigation and submit reports.
7. Attorneys examine titles and arrange legal details.
8. An underwriting agreement with investment bankers is drawn up.

9. Trust indenture is prepared and trustee is appointed.

10. Application for registration is made to the SEC if bonds are to be marketed outside the state of origin.

11. Application is made to state commissions of states in which bonds are to be sold.

12. Certificates are printed and prepared for delivery.

13. Bonds are signed by corporate officers and trustee.

14. Bonds are delivered to underwriter and money is received by corporation.

(e) RECORDING ISSUE OF BONDS.   If the entire issue is "sold" to the underwriters, which is the most frequent procedure, and the corporation has no responsibility with respect to the process of distribution, the entries covering the issue boil down to a charge to the underwriters—or directly to "cash," if payment is made upon delivery—and a credit to "bonds payable." If the corporation disposes of the bonds through the efforts of its own organization, the accounting will be more extended and may include the recording of subscriptions.

Assume, for example, that a company authorizes debenture bonds in the par amount of $1 million and undertakes to dispose of the bonds at par through its own office. Assume, further, that subscriptions are taken at par for 700 bonds of $1,000 each. The next general entries are required:

Subscriptions to bonds	$700,000	
Debenture bonds subscribed		$700,000

Assuming cash is received in full for 500 bonds, the entries are:

Cash	$500,000	
Subscriptions to bonds		$500,000

When the bonds are issued, the account with bonds subscribed is charged and the regular liability account, "bonds payable," is credited.

When bond subscriptions are collected on the installment plan, it may be advisable to set up separate accounts for each installment receivable as a means of controlling collections and segregating balances past due. In any event, detailed records of each subscription must be maintained.

On the balance sheet, bond subscriptions are preferably shown as a receivable, with bonds subscribed reported as a form of liability.

(i) Origin of Bond Discount and Premium.   *Bond discount* is defined as the excess of face or maturity value over the amount of cash or equivalent paid in by the original bondholder. Conversely, *premium* is defined as the excess of cash paid in over maturity value. The explanation of this excess is the fact that in the discount case, the nominal or "coupon" rate of interest stated on the bond, is less than the market rate. In this case the investor is unwilling to pay maturity value for the bond, since this price would yield only the coupon rate. Instead, the price of the bond is set at some lower point at which the yield to the buyer is the same as the market rate of interest on comparable securities. In the case of a premium, the coupon interest rate exceeds the market rate, and the price of the bond is set at a point above maturity value that will yield to the investor only the market rate of interest.

Until the 1950s, it was common for companies to issue bonds with low, even-percentage coupons (such as 4 percent) to demonstrate the solidity of the company. The result, frequently, was large amounts of discount, accompanied by major accounting disputes over proper treatment. It has since become common to state the nominal rate of interest on bonds in rather precise fractions. An attempt is usually made to align the nominal rate as closely as possible with the market or effective rate, and the absolute magnitude of the discount or premium tends to be small. This condition does not simplify the accounting for discount and premium, but it does suggest that in many cases theoretical arguments will be disposed of on grounds of materiality.

(ii) Issue of Bonds at Discount and Premium. Bonds are recorded in the main liability account at par or maturity value. If issued for less than par, the difference is charged to a discount account, illustrated as shown:

Cash	$ 97,550	
Discount on bonds payable	2,450	
Bonds payable		$100,000
Or, if subscriptions are involved,		

(1)

Bond subscriptions	97,550	
Discount on bonds payable	2,450	
Bonds subscribed		100,000
To record taking of subscriptions.		

(2)

Cash	97,550	
Bond subscriptions		97,500
To record collection of subscriptions.		

(3)

Bonds subscribed	100,000	
Bonds payable		100,000
To record issue of certificates to bondholders.		

An account "discount on bond subscriptions" may be used to reflect the discount until the bond subscriptions are collected in full, at which time the account will be transferred to "discount on bonds payable."

If bonds are issued for cash in excess of the face amount of the bonds, the excess is credited to a premium account as shown:

Cash	$102,700	
Bonds payable		$100,000
Premium on bonds payable		2,700

The entries for bond subscriptions at a premium would correspond with the discount illustration just shown.

The practice of recording the face amount of the bonds and discount (or premium) in separate accounts is thoroughly established, in spite of the fact that on the investors' books, it is good practice to record the purchase of the bond at cost without regard to face or maturity value. It is theoretically correct to credit "bonds payable" with the proceeds of the bond issue, but the practice illustrated above is not objectionable, provided it is properly interpreted and reported.

(iii) Segregation of Bond Issue Costs. Charges connected with the issue of new bonds—such as legal expenses in preparing the bond contract and mortgage, cost of printing certificates, registration costs, and commission to underwriters—are costs of the use of capital obtained for the whole life of the issue and should be capitalized and written off over that period.

It is common practice to lump these costs with actual discount (or net them against premium, as the case may be). Good accounting requires careful distinction between these costs and bond discount, which is properly an offset to the maturity value of the bonds. Issue costs should likewise not be offset against the premium liability.

Occasionally the amount of bond issue costs is difficult to determine. That is particularly true where bonds are sold through underwriters who share expenses. As a general rule, the difference between the amount paid in by the first bona fide bondholders and maturity value represents premium or discount. The difference between this amount paid in and net proceeds to the issuer represents bond issue cost.

For example, if bonds with a face value of $1 million are issued through underwriters to original holders at a price of 100 1/2, and if the net proceeds to the issuer are 98 1/4, out of which bond issue costs amounting to $15,000 are paid, the entries are:

(1)

Cash	$982,500	
Bond issue costs	22,500	
Bonds payable		$1,000,000
Premium on bonds payable		5,000
To record receipt of bond proceeds from underwriters.		

(2)

Bond issue costs	15,000	
Cash		15,000

Bond issue costs of $37,500 are classified on the balance sheet as an intangible asset and amortized over the life of the bond issue on a straight-line basis.

(iv) Allocation of Debt Issue Costs in a Business Combination.   In SAB No. 77, *Allocation of Debt Issue Costs in a Business Combination,* the SEC's staff took the position that fees paid to an investment banker for advisory services, including financing services, must be allocated between direct costs of the acquisition and debt issue costs.. The allocation would apply whether the services were billed as a single amount or separately. Tests of reasonableness should consider such factors as fees charged by investment bankers in connection with other recent bridge financings and fees charged for advisory services when obtained separately. The allocation should result in an effective debt service cost and interest and amortization of debt issue costs that are comparable to the effective cost of other recent debt issues of similar investment risk and maturity.

The bridge financing costs should be amortized over the estimated interim period preceding the placement of the permanent financing; any unamortized amounts should be charged to expense if the bridge loan is repaid prior to the expiration of the estimated interim period.

(v) Bonds Issued between Interest Dates.   When a bond is sold after the stated issue date, the price paid by the purchaser will include interest accrued at the coupon rate from the issue date on the bond. At the outset this accrued interest represents a liability to the issuer covering the amount of interest advanced by the investor, in view of the date of purchase, and payable at the next interest date.

For example, 10 percent bonds in maturity amount of $100,000 and dated January 1 are marketed at par and accrued interest one month after the stated date. The entries to record the sale and the initial payment of interest are:

February 1

Cash	$100,833.34	
Bonds payable		$100,000.00
Bond interest payable		833.34

July 1

Bond interest payable	833.34	
Bond interest charges	4,066.66	
Cash		5,000.00

When a bond is finally sold after one or more interest coupons have matured, the matured coupons are detached by the issuing company and the buyer is charged only with interest accrued since the last interest payment date.

(f) DETERMINATION OF BOND ISSUE PRICE.   When investors buy a bond, they acquire two rights: (1) the right to receive periodic interest payments from the date of purchase to maturity and (2) the right to receive face value at maturity date. It follows that the current price of the bond is the sum of (1) the present value of the interest payments, plus (2) the present value of the face amount.

For example, a corporation plans to issue $1 million face value, 20-year bonds. The bonds bear interest (coupon rate) of 9 percent, payable semiannually. If the market yield (rate of interest) on securities of this quality is 10 percent at the date of issue, the sale price of the bond is the sum of:

1. The present value of 40 semiannual payments of $45,000 each
2. The present value 40 periods hence of $1,000,000

Here both present values are calculated to yield 10 percent per annum (or, more precisely, 5 percent each six months, since interest is compounded semiannually).

The present value of item 1, an annuity of $45,000 for 40 periods at 5 percent, is $772,158.89. The present value of the maturity payment of $1,000,000, payable in 20 years at 10 percent, is $142,045.68. Thus we can compute the value of the bond and the discount as:

Present value of interest payments	$ 772,158.89
Present value of principal	+ 142,045.68
Value of the bond	914,204.57
Less face value of bond	− (1,000,000.00)
Discount on issue	$ 85,795.43

The effect of various yield rates on the issue price of this bond issue can be shown by calculating the bond issue price at various yields, as shown in the next table:

(1) Assumed Semiannual Yield Rate	(2) Present Value of Interest Payments	(3) Present Value of Payment at Maturity	(4) Present Value Price (col. 2 + col. 3)
7%	$599,926.90	$66,780.38	$666,707.28
6%	677,083.36	97,222.19	774,305.55
5%	772,158.89	142,045.68	914,204.57
4.5%	828,071.30	171,928.70	1,000,000.00
4%	890,674.82	171,928.70	1,098,963.86

As shown in the 4.5 percent line of the table, when the yield rate is the same as the coupon rate, the investor pays face value for the bonds.

In some cases, the issue price of the bonds is determined first; then the problem arises of estimating the effective rate established by that price. More sophisticated financial calculators are capable of determining the yield under such conditions.

(g) BOND DISCOUNT AND PREMIUM IN THE BALANCE SHEET.   It was standard practice for many years to show bond discount on the balance sheet as a deferred charge and bond premium as a deferred credit, with the bond liability account remaining at face value throughout the life of the bonds.

A debate over this accounting practice raged for decades. However, it was ended by APB Opinion No. 21 (ASC 835), which stated: "[D]iscount or premium resulting from the determination of present value in cash or non-cash transactions is not an asset or liability separable from the note which gives rise to it."

Also, GAAP call for the presentation in the balance sheet of discount or premium as direct deduction or addition to the face amount of the note. Such an amount should not be classified as a deferred charge or credit.

Examples from APB Opinion No. 21 show discount presented either in parenthetical form in the caption for a note or as a separate statement amount deducted from the outstanding balance of the note. The Opinion notwithstanding, some companies apparently classify discount or premium in some other account when the amount is inconsequential. As noted earlier, this is frequently the case when coupon values are almost identical to market interest rates.

18.5 BOND INTEREST PAYMENTS, PREMIUM, AND DISCOUNT AMORTIZATION

(a) ACCRUAL OF BOND INTEREST.   Interest payment dates may not coincide with accounting period dates. In such circumstances, it is necessary to accrue interest on outstanding bonds. And even when the stated date of payment and the end of the accounting period are the same, systematic accrual of interest expense and liability is good procedure, especially since interest money may be deposited prior to the interest date and payment of all coupons may not be effected on that date. A regular monthly accrual is usually desirable.

For example, if 12 percent bonds in the par amount of $1,000,000 are issued at par on June 1, the issuing company may well make entries at the end of each month throughout the life of the bonds as shown:

Bond interest charges	$10,000.00	
Bond interest payables		$10,000.00

(b) PAYMENT OF INTEREST.   Bond interest is ordinarily paid semiannually. Thus the regular cash requirement for interest on an issue of $1,000,000 of 12 percent bonds is 6 percent, or $60,000 every six months. Interest may be paid directly by the issuer or through the trustee. In the former case, the issuer mails checks to all registered holders and makes a deposit in some specified bank sufficient to cover all outstanding coupons (or, in some instances, makes payments by check or in actual cash to parties presenting coupons). In the latter case, the issuer deposits the required interest money with the trustee and depends on the trustee to carry out the actual process of paying the individual bondholders. Assuming that deposit with the trustee is tantamount to payment, the entries covering such deposit are, for example:

Bond interest payable	$60,000	
Cash		$60,000

However, a more complete and satisfactory treatment is to charge the trustee with the money deposit and cancel the liability when payment of coupons has been reported (or coupons have been returned). Thus:

	(1)	
Interest fund—Blank Trust Co.	$60,000	
Cash		$60,000
	(2)	
Bond interest payable	60,000	
Interest fund—Blank Trust Co.		60,000

The amount of unredeemed coupons due at any time is represented by the balance of "bond interest payable," and the amount available for payment is the balance of the interest fund. If desired, the amount of past-due coupons may be transferred to a distinct account.

Paid or canceled coupons should be filed systematically either by the issuing company or by the trustee.

(I) Interest on Treasury Bonds.   Any matured coupons attached to treasurybonds (either unissued or reacquired) should be removed, canceled, and filed. The interest entries should be confined to bonds actually outstanding. When payment is made by the trustee, coupons on bonds in the treasury may be forwarded with the check for interest on outstanding bonds, or they may be filed by the company with notice to the trustee that the bonds are in the treasury.

(ii) Interest on Bonds Held by Trustee.   Bonds of the company's own issue in the hands of the trustee are not truly outstanding, and any "interest" payments on such bonds required by the trust agreement should not be permitted to affect the interest accounts of the issuer. A requirement that "interest" be deposited on bonds already held by the trustee is simply a means of accelerating the accumulation of the sinking fund.

Assume, for example, that 10 percent of an issue on which the total semiannual interest is $20,000 is in the hands of the trustee and that the agreement calls for deposit of the entire amount. The appropriate entries are:

(1)

Bond interest charges	$18,000	
Bond interest payable		$18,000
To record accrual of interest on outstanding bonds.		

(2)

Interest and sinking fund—Blank Trust Co.	20,000	
Cash		20,000
To record periodic payment to trustee.		

(3)

Bond interest payable	18,000	
Interest and sinking fund—Blank Trust Co.		18,000
To record payment of coupons by trustee.		

(c) PREMIUM AND DISCOUNT AMORTIZATION. GAAP requires that bond discount or premium be charged systematically to income as interest expense or income over the life of the bond issue using the interest method. The effect on the income statement of systematic amortization of premium or discount is to show interest expense at the effective amount.

As an illustration of the interest method, assume a $1,000,000 issue of five-year bonds with 8 percent annual interest (payable semiannually), priced to yield 10 percent to investors, for a market price of $922,782.65.

The interest method is a procedure for absorbing the discount or premium in accord with the ordinary mathematical interpretation of the composition of the issue price; it provides for spreading of the total interest charge in terms of the effective or market rate of interest. Under the interest method, the periodic amortization is the difference between the interest due and effective rates of interest applied to the carrying amount of bonds outstanding at the interest date. For the illustrative issue, the entry to record interest and the amortization of discount for the first period is:

Bond interest expense (5% × $922,782.65)	$46,139.13	
Discount on bonds payable		$ 6,139.13
Bond interest payable (4% × $1,000,000)		40,000.00

In each subsequent period, bond interest expense will be charged with the effective rate of interest times the carrying amount of the bonds, and the periodic amortization will be the difference between that amount and the bond interest liability. The amortization of premium is given similar treatment.

An accumulation table for the bonds above for the first three years under the interest method is:

Half-Year Period	Carrying Amount of Bonds	Interest Expense	Interest Payments	Amortization of Discount
1	$922,782.65	$46,139.13	$40,000.00	$6,139.13
2	928,921.78	46,446.09	40,000.00	6,446.09
3	935,367.87	46,768.39	40,000.00	6,768.39
4	942,136.26	47,106.81	40,000.00	7,106.81
5	949,243.07	47,462.15	40,000.00	7,462.15
6	956,705.22	47,835.26	40,000.00	7,835.26

In practice, it is common to develop such tables when bonds are first issued, to provide a basis for subsequent accounting. As interest dates are not likely to coincide with financial reporting dates, tables are frequently developed on a monthly or daily basis to permit correct entries whenever financial statements are prepared. Similar entries and tables result for the amortization of bond premium.

(d) DISCOUNT ON CONVERTIBLE BONDS AND BONDS WITH WARRANTS. Bonds that may eventually be converted into a certain number of shares of common stock and bonds that have warrants attached, permitting the purchase of common stock at a fixed price, have achieved considerable popularity. The attraction to the buyer of such issues is obvious—they provide the fixed income of bonds along with the opportunity to participate in an equity increase. An attraction of such issues to the issuing corporation is that they are typically sold at interest rates below those that would be required for similar securities in the absence of the equity privileges. In some cases, the corporation's credit may be such that debt could not be issued at all without the conversion privilege or warrants.

APB Opinion No. 14, *Accounting for Convertible Debt and Debt Issued with Stock Purchase Warrants* (ASC 470) stated that no portion of the proceeds from the issuance of convertible debt or debt with nondetachable stock purchase warrants should be accounted for as attributable to the conversion feature. Such securities include debt securities that are convertible into common stock of the issuer or an affiliated company at a specified price at the option of the holder and that are sold at a price or have a value at issuance not significantly in excess of face amount. The terms of such securities generally include:

- An interest rate that is lower than the issuer could obtain for nonconvertible debt
- An initial conversion price that is greater than the market value of the common stock at the time of issuance
- A conversion price that does not decrease except pursuant to antidilution provisions

If convertible debt is issued at a substantial premium, there is a presumption that the premium represents paid-in capital.

GAAP requires that the proceeds of debt securities with detachable stock purchase warrants be allocated between the debt and paid-in capital, based on the relative fair values of the two securities at the time of issuance. Any resulting discount or premium on the debt securities should be accounted for as such. The same accounting treatment applies to issues of debt securities (issued with detachable warrants) that may be surrendered in settlement of the exercise price of the warrant.

EITF Issue No. 98-5, *Accounting for Convertible Securities with Beneficial Conversion Features or Contingently Adjustable Conversion Ratios* (ASC 470), addressed the accounting for a convertible security with a nondetachable conversion feature that is in-the-money at the commitment date. That issue also addressed certain convertible securities that have a conversion price that is variable based on future events. A number of practical issues regarding the application of the guidance in Issue No. 98-5 were raised subsequent to the final consensus. The EITF addressed those issues in Issue No. 00-27, *Application of Issue No. 98-5 to Certain Convertible Instruments* (ASC 470).

(e) BLOCKS ISSUED AT DIFFERENT RATES. In some cases bonds of a particular class and series are marketed at different times and at different prices. Assume, for example, that of an issue with a maturity amount of $1 million, the first $600,000 is sold at 102 and the second $400,000 at 105. Under such conditions two alternative procedures are available. The two blocks of the issue may be accounted for separately, and the premium on each block may be amortized at the effective rate involved. The alternative is to combine both blocks in the accounts and to apply an overall approximate rate, determined in the light of the conditions under which the two blocks were issued. Separate computations are generally advisable where considerable time elapses between issue dates and there is a substantial difference between the effective rates involved.

(f) TREATMENT OF SERIAL BONDS. In the rare case of various maturities of serial bonds being issued at the same yield rate, that rate can be applied to the net book value of the entire issue to determine amortization as in the interest method illustrations above.

In the much more common case of serial bonds that are issued with different yields on each maturity, the interest method of amortization of discount or premium should be applied to each maturity, treating it as if it were a separate issue. Formerly, such treatment was considered "too complex," but the development of sophisticated financial calculators obviates that argument.

18.6　BOND REDEMPTION, REFUNDING, AND CONVERSION

(a) PAYMENT AT MATURITY.　No special accounting problems arise when bonds are paid as agreed at maturity, assuming that items of bond issue cost and of discount or premium have been disposed of systematically.

The amount of any matured bonds not presented for redemption by the holder at maturity date should be segregated in a special account. That balance should be carried as a current liability except where a special fund—not reported in current assets—is maintained to redeem the bonds when they are presented. No interest accrues on matured bonds not in default.

(b) SETTLEMENT AFTER MATURITY.　If default occurs at maturity, no special entries are required prior to the settlement made through reorganization procedure, although the fact that the liability has matured but remains unpaid should be indicated in the balance sheet. Occasionally, creditors consent to a postponement of payment provided the corporation continues to pay interest at a specified rate. Where a special settlement following default at maturity provides for issue of new securities to replace the defaulted bonds, the book value assigned to such securities presumably will equal the maturity amount of the bonds (plus any unpaid interest accruing since maturity), except as conditions clearly warrant some other treatment.

(c) DEFAULTED BONDS.　Default of bonds prior to maturity creates a situation similar to that of default at maturity. Generally, no entries are called for, but the condition of default should be clearly described in the statements. Interest continues to accrue on defaulted bonds under conditions prescribed in the contract and should be recorded.

(d) CLASSIFICATION OF OBLIGATIONS BY THE CREDITOR.　In EITF Issue No. 86-30 (ASC 470), the EITF considered whether the waiver of a lender's rights resulting from the violation of a covenant with retention of the periodic covenant test represents, in substance, a grace period. If viewed as a grace period, the borrower must classify the debt as current, unless it is probable that the borrower can cure the violation (comply with the covenant) within the grace period. The Task Force's consensus was that unless the facts and circumstances would indicate otherwise, the borrower should classify the obligation as noncurrent unless (1) a covenant violation has occurred at the balance sheet date or would have occurred absent a loan modification and (2) it is probable that the borrower will not be able to cure the default at measurement dates that are within the next 12 months.

(e) COMPOSITIONS WITH CREDITORS.　Compositions with creditors in the event of financial weakness often involve a scaling down of acknowledged liabilities, either through actual cancellation of the claims or through issue of stock to cover some element of the total debt. Chapter 11 of the Bankruptcy Act is designed to facilitate such agreements, to eliminate losses due to forced sale of property, and to prevent cash payments to dissenting minorities when a revision in the debt structure is agreed to by a substantial majority of claimants of the same class. These procedures tend to encourage continued operations under the same management when this seems desirable (see Chapter 39 of this *Handbook*).

(f) REDEMPTION BEFORE MATURITY.　Many bond contracts provide for the calling of any portion, usually selected by random draw, or all of the issue at the option of the company at a stated price, usually above par, to allow the corporation to reduce its debt before maturity as the occasion arises. When interest rates decline, debtors may consider transactions that would use the leverage of an existing call provision to reduce the higher interest rate on an older debt issue. For example, the debtor may exchange new noncallable debt with a lower interest rate for old callable debt or have the creditor pay a fee in return for an agreement not to exercise the call provision for the life of the debt or for a shorter period. In periods of high interest rates, buyers of new bonds prefer indentures that restrict the call privilege. Also, bonds are often retired piecemeal through sinking fund operations, or acquired by the issuer on the open market.

FASB Statement No. 140, *Accounting for Transfers and Servicing of Financial Assets and Extinguishment of Liabilities* (ASC 860), provides guidance as to when debt should be considered to be extinguished for financial reporting. See Section 18.9(b) for further discussion. As interest rates rose in the 1970s, some corporations retired older, low-interest bonds (and, in some cases, low-yielding convertible bonds) to increase earnings by passing the gain on retirement through income. In many cases, these retirements appeared to be uneconomic, suggesting that earnings creation was the principal reason. See Subsection 18.6(f)(i) for a more complete discussion.

Outstanding bonds acquired by the issuer may be permanently retired or—if the conditions of acquisition permit—they may be held in the corporate treasury for reissue at some later date. If the bonds were issued at par and are redeemed at par, the only special problem is the absorption of any bond issue costs remaining on the books. Additional problems arise when there is unabsorbed discount or premium on the books at the time of redemption, or where the redemption price differs from the maturity value.

Assuming outright redemption, all balances relating to the bonds redeemed should be eliminated.

The M Co., for example, has outstanding a bond issue of $100,000 maturity amount. On the books related to this issue are unamortized bond issue costs of $2,000 and unamortized discount of $3,000. At this point the entire issue is called at 105, and costs are incurred in the carrying out of this transaction of $1,500. The summarized entries are:

Bonds payable	$100,000	
Loss on redemption of bonds	11,500	
Bond issue costs		$ 2,000
Discount on bonds payable		3,000
Cash		106,500

When bonds are redeemed by purchase on the market, a book profit may result.

Assume conditions as in the preceding example except that instead of calling the entire issue, the M Co. bought bonds in par amount of $20,000 on the market at a total expenditure, including all charges, of $15,000. The summarized entries are:

Bonds payable	$20,000	
Bond issue costs		$ 400
Discount on bonds payable		600
Cash		15,000
Gain on redemption of bonds		4,000

In this case, with 20 percent of the issue retired, the write-off of issue costs and discount is restricted to 20 percent.

(i) Gains and Losses from Extinguishment of Debt.   Losses resulting from unamortized bond issue costs, unamortized discount, call premium, or a combination of these factors and gains or losses resulting from market conditions, upon retirement, should be recognized currently as income of the period in which the debt extinguishment takes place.

Previously, all gains and losses on extinguishment of debt were classified as extraordinary. Currently, only gains and losses that meet both the *unusual nature* and *infrequency of occurrence* criteria of ASC 225-20 are classified as extraordinary.

The SEC in SAB No. 94 stated that disclosures as to a planned extinguishment and its likely effects would be required in notes to financial statements and in the management discussion and analysis. The Staff also indicated that announcement of a plan to extinguish debt in the future does not in itself result in a requirement to recognize a loss, nor does an irrevocable offer to repurchase a debt obligation. A debt holder's acceptance of that offer prior to the balance sheet date by tendering the security and surrendering all rights is considered an extinguishment. When debt is called, extinguishment does not occur until interest ceases to accrue or accrete under the obligation as a result of the call.

(ii) Noncash Extinguishments. FASB Technical Bulletin No. 80-1, *Early Extinguishment of Debt through Exchange for Common or Preferred Stock* (ASC 470), indicates that the rules from APB Opinion No. 26 apply to all extinguishments of debt effected by issuance of common or preferred stock, including redeemable and fixed maturity preferred stock, unless the extinguishment is a troubled debt restructuring or a conversion (a) pursuant to conversion privileges provided in the terms of the debt at issuance or (b) when conversion privileges provided in the terms of the debt at issuance are changed to induce conversion. The reacquisition price is determined by the value of the common or preferred stock issued or the value of the debt, whichever is more clearly evident.

In EITF Issue No. 96-19, *Debtor's Accounting for Modification or Exchange of Debt Instruments* (ASC 470), the Task Force reached a consensus that an exchange of debt instruments with substantially different terms is a debt extinguishment and should be accounted for in accordance with FASB Statement No. 125. (Statement No. 125 has since been superseded by FASB Statement No. 140 [ASC 860], which revises the standards for accounting for securitizations and other transfers of financial assets and collateral and requires certain disclosures but carries over most of Statement No. 125's provisions without reconsideration.)

(g) TREATMENT AND REISSUE OF TREASURY BONDS. Bonds acquired by the corporation as a result of call or purchase may be canceled by formal action, or they may be held in substantially the same category as authorized bonds that have never been issued. The most common modern form of presentation is to show only the net amount of bonds outstanding on the balance sheet and to indicate the existence of treasury bonds in a note to the statements.

It follows from this that the acquisition by a corporation of its own bonds amounts to redemption of those bonds, and disposition of any balances of unamortized premium or discount, or bond issue costs, should follow the recommendations presented earlier in Subsection 18.6(f)(i), permitting recognition of book gain or loss.

Where the earlier recommendations for accounting for acquisition of treasury bonds have been followed, accounting for reissue is essentially the same as for bonds that have never before been outstanding. If the par amount of the treasury bonds is carried in a special account, that account is credited at par when the bonds are issued.

(h) USE OF SINKING FUNDS. Retirement of bonds through the operation of a special fund is familiar financial practice. The fund procedure may be a plan adopted by the issuing corporation and entirely within its control, or it may be an arrangement provided by contract, involving a trustee.

Most commonly, the sinking fund is an arrangement rather than an actual fund. That is, the bond indenture requires the borrowing corporation to make specific, periodic payments to the trustee, who then acquires the necessary bonds. Whether the sinking fund actually holds the bonds or arranges for their retirement is actually a moot question, since when held by the sinking fund, the bonds are effectively retired. In the past, sinking funds might actually consist of a fund, holding assets other than the debt in question. Because the purpose of the sinking fund arrangement is to provide gradual retirement of the debt, there is no reason for the fund to undertake the risk of holding securities of another issuer. In another common arrangement, the company may acquire bonds in the open market or through calls, hold them as treasury bonds, then deposit them in satisfaction of sinking fund requirements at appropriate dates. In the case of some convertible debt, the conversion of enough bonds may satisfy the sinking fund requirements.

When the trustee has used the funds to acquire the corporation's bonds, either at or before maturity, the bonds so acquired are in effect retired and should be reported as such on the balance sheet of the corporation. Accounting for corporation bonds acquired by a sinking fund trustee should follow the same procedures described in Section 18.6(f). This treatment is proper even when the bonds are kept "alive" by the trustee for the purpose of accumulating "interest" from the corporation issuer. "Interest" payments by the corporation to the trustee on the corporation's own bonds held in the fund should be treated simply as additional deposits.

(i) Payment by Refunding. In the utility field, in particular, the funded debt is often viewed as a permanent part of the capital structure. This means that corporate policy is not always directed toward the permanent retirement of long-term liabilities; instead, the usual procedure is to secure the funds to meet maturing obligations by floating new loans.

A distinction should be drawn between retirement of bonds through an exchange and payment by refunding or refinancing. In the typical refunding operation a new bond issue, with new terms, is floated through investment channels, and the funds so provided are specifically employed to retire the preceding bond issue. However, in some cases the holders of the old issue are given the opportunity to exchange their bonds directly for bonds of the new issue. To the extent that direct exchange can be arranged by the issuing corporation, the cost of refinancing is minimized.

No additional accounting problems are encountered when bonds are refunded at maturity. The retirement of the old bonds and the issue of the new bonds are separate transactions.

(i) DETERMINING WHEN TO REFUND. Ignoring effect on taxes and other special factors, there is no object in refunding prior to maturity except when more favorable terms can be secured, particularly with respect to interest rate. However, the bare fact that the market rate has fallen does not justify refunding. To retire a complete issue of outstanding bonds prior to maturity ordinarily necessitates exercise of right of call, and this means payment of a redemption premium, usually substantial. Moreover, the costs of refunding must be considered. When the old issue is called before maturity, the trustee will require a fee for additional services. There will be legal and accounting fees, taxes, and printing costs. More serious are the added costs of registration and marketing the issue. Another factor that may be important is the additional interest charge required by the overlapping of the two issues.

There has been considerable discussion in financial circles as to the proper method of computing the savings—if any—to be realized by refunding under a specified set of conditions. Probably the most significant approach is that which compares the present values at the prevailing effective rate of the cash requirements of the two programs, considering the new issue to run for only the remaining life of the old. (It is pure speculation to make the comparison for a longer term.)

For example, the M Co. has outstanding $1,000,000, maturity amount, of six percent bonds, with 10 years yet to run. These bonds are callable at any interest date at 105. Assume that the effective market rate of interest for this class of security is currently only four percent, for loans of 10 years or longer. The service costs of various kinds required to call the old bonds and float the new loan are estimated at $30,000. The present cash value of the obligations under the old contract is found as shown:

Present value of amount due in 20 periods (10 years) at 2% per period	$ 672,971.33
Present value of annuity of $30,000 per period for 20 periods at 2%	490,543.00
	$1,163,514.33

The amount of cash required to meet these claims through the medium of a new loan is $1,080,000 (including redemption premium of $50,000 and costs of $30,000). By comparison, it appears that an advantage is realized by refunding.

It is important to note that the question of book loss realized on redemption has no bearing on the determination of the financial advantage of a refunding program over continuation of the existing contract.

However, as noted in connection with early retirement of bonds and notes, some companies have undertaken early retirement to produce reported earnings, even though the transactions are inherently uneconomical.

The desire to realize a book loss for tax purposes in the form of unamortized discount and expense may be an important or even a decisive factor in bringing about a decision to refund. It is even possible for a situation to develop in which a refunding might seem to be advantageous, in view of the tax angle, although no saving in interest charges results.

(j) BOND CONVERSION. When convertible bonds issued at par are converted into stock at par, dollar for dollar, the conversion is ordinarily assumed to be the equivalent of the payment of the liability and the issue of additional stock at par. The entries necessary to recognize conversion under these conditions, accordingly, consist essentially of a charge to bonds outstanding and a corresponding credit to capital stock. In the case of the conversion of bonds issued at a premium into stock on a par-for-par basis, the unamortized premium on the date of conversion is preferably treated as a form of stock premium. Similarly, an unaccumulated discount attaching to bonds converted into stock on a par-for-par basis should be set up as a type of stock discount, although that discount would presumably not represent an amount that might be collected from shareholders by assessment. The schedule of accumulation of discount or amortization of premium set up for convertible bonds should disregard the possibility of conversion and should be adhered to until conversion takes place.

When bonds are convertible into stock at some specified price other than par or stated value, the book value of the bonds converted is generally made the basis of the credit to capital stock.

Assume, for example, that a company has outstanding an issue of debenture bonds in the par amount of $1 million, with applicable unamortized discount of $50,000, and that those bonds are convertible into the common stock of the company on any interest date at a price of $25 per share or on the basis of 40 shares of stock for each bond in the maturity amount of $1,000. The shares of this class of stock have a stated value of $10 each. At this point 10 percent of the bond issue is presented for conversion, and shares are issued in accordance with the exchange ratio. The summarized entries are:

Debenture bonds—Maturity amount	$100,000	
Discount on debenture bonds		$ 5,000
Capital stock—Stated value		40,000
Capital stock—Contributions in excess of stated value		55,000

In some cases the specified conversion price of the stock increases in terms of stated periods. The contract may also provide for termination of the conversion privilege at a specified date. A minor complication arises when the exchange ratio is such that conversion calls for issue of fractional shares. In that situation the converting bondholder may pay an additional contribution—in sufficient cash to entitle him or her to a whole number of shares. Alternatively, the corporation may make an appropriate cash payment in lieu of the fractional share, or the corporation may actually issue the fractional shares.

The treatment of unamortized bond issue cost on conversion date is something of a problem. As a matter of convenience, such cost may be absorbed in the conversion entries in the same manner as bond discount. However, a better treatment would be to retain the balance of issue cost as in effect a cost of stock financing. A convertible bond is potential capital stock and may become actual stock at any time the bondholder elects. As long as the bonds are outstanding, the schedule of amortization of issue costs based on the total life of the bonds should be maintained, as conversion is not assured and is beyond the control of the issuer. Upon conversion, nevertheless, the contingency becomes controlling, and the balance of bond issue cost becomes a cost of issuing stock.

(k) INDUCED CONVERSION. FASB Statement No. 84, *Induced Conversions of Convertible Debt* (ASC 470), specifies that when a convertible debt is converted to equity securities of the debtor pursuant to an inducement offer, the debtor should recognize an expense (not extraordinary) equal to the fair value of all securities and other consideration transferred in excess of the fair value of securities issuable pursuant to the original conversion terms.

Measurement of the fair value of the securities should be as of the date the inducement is accepted. Usually that is when conversion takes place or a binding agreement is signed.

Inducement includes changes made by the debtor to the conversion privileges for purposes of inducing conversion. The Statement applies only to conversions occurring pursuant to changed conversion privileges that are exercisable for a limited period and include the issuance of all of the equity securities issuable pursuant to conversion privileges included in the terms of the debt at issuance for each debt instrument that is converted. Inducements include reducing the original conversion price, issuing warrants or other securities not included in the original terms, or payment of cash.

(l) ACCRUED INTEREST UPON CONVERSION OF CONVERTIBLE DEBT. In Issue No. 85-17 (ASC 470), the EITF concluded that when accrued but unpaid interest is forfeited at the date of conversion of convertible debt, either because the conversion date falls between interest payment dates or because there are no interest payment dates (a zero coupon convertible instrument), interest should be accrued or imputed to the date of conversion of the debt instrument. Accrued interest from the last interest payment date, if applicable, to the date of conversion, net of unrelated income tax effects, if any, should be charged to expense and credited to capital as part of the cost of the securities issued. Thus, accrued interest is accounted for in the same way as the principal amount of the debt and any unamortized issue or premium discount.

(m) SUBSCRIPTION RIGHTS AND WARRANTS SOLD WITH BONDS. Bonds are sometimes sold with warrants or subscription rights attached. The rights or warrants permit their holder to purchase other securities, normally common shares, at some fixed or determinable price in a future period or at a certain future date. The warrants are essentially calls or options on the common stock. The theory, of course, is that the combination of the warrant and the bond enables the company to market the bond at a lower interest rate.

As mentioned previously, Opinion No. 14 (ASC 260) requires that the proceeds of debt securities with detachable stock purchase warrants be allocated between the debt and paid-in capital, based on the relative fair values of the two securities at the time of issuance. Any resulting discount or premium on the debt securities should be accounted for as such. The same accounting treatment applies to issues of debt securities (issued with detachable warrants) that may be surrendered in settlement of the exercise price of the warrant.

As an illustration of the accounting for a bond with warrants, consider this example. A company issues a bond at par with an 8.75 percent yield. Each bond has a warrant attached that permits the holder of the warrant to purchase a share of the company's stock for $20 within five years. The common shares are currently selling for $50. It is determined that the company's bond, without the warrant attached (a straight bond), could have been sold for 95 (i.e., $950 per bond).

The underwriter handling the issue estimates that the warrant will be worth about $75 when issued. Note that APB Opinion No. 14 calls for this valuation (and that of the comparable straight bond) to be made "at the time of issuance," which it defines as "the date when agreement as to terms has been reached and announced." That is not the actual date of issue of the securities, when relative market values for the two securities could be determined. The date given in APB Opinion No. 14 is earlier. Thus the fair value will be approximated or estimated by someone, probably the underwriter.

The allocation required under APB Opinion No. 14 is:

$$\frac{\text{Value of bonds}}{\text{Value of bonds without warrants} + \text{Value of warrants}} \times \text{Purchase price} = \text{Value assigned to bonds}$$

$$\frac{\$950}{\$950 + \$75} \times \$1,000 = \$927.00$$

$$\frac{\text{Value of warrants}}{\text{Value of bonds without warrants} + \text{Value of warrants}} \times \text{Purchase price} = \text{Value assigned to warrants}$$

$$\frac{\$75}{\$950 + \$75} \times \$1,000 = \$73.00$$

The entries, for the issuance assuming one bond, would be:

Cash	$927	
Discount on bonds	73	
Bonds payable		$1,000
Cash	73	
Paid-in capital		73

This accounting applies to warrants that are "separable" from the bonds, which is the most common situation. If the warrants were required to trade with the bond, the issue would be almost identical to a convertible bond and should be accounted for as a convertible.

18.7 STATEMENT PRESENTATION OF LONG-TERM DEBT

There is general agreement about the nature of information that should be presented on the balance sheet or in the notes to the financial statements concerning long-term debt. That information includes:

- The major categories of debt (e.g., notes payable to banks, mortgages notes payable, notes to related parties)
- Maturity dates
- Interest rates
- Methods of liquidation
- Conversion features
- Assets pledged as collateral
- Covenants to reduce debt, maintain working capital, or restrict dividends
- Other significant matters (e.g., subordinated features)

Paragraph 18 of FASB Statement No. 5, *Accounting for Contingencies,* requires disclosure of unused letters of credit, assets pledged as security for loans, and commitments such as those for plant acquisition or an obligation to reduce debts, maintain working capital, restrict dividends.

FASB Statement No. 47, *Disclosure of Long-Term Obligations* (ASC 440), requires disclosure of the maturities and sinking fund requirements, if any, for all long-term borrowings for each of the five years following the balance sheet date.

FASB Statement No. 129, *Disclosure of Information about Capital Structure* (ASC 505), requires disclosure of this information concerning debt that is a security:

An entity shall explain, in summary form within its financial statements, the pertinent rights and privileges of the various securities outstanding. Examples of information that shall be disclosed are . . . liquidation preferences . . . call prices and dates, conversion or exercise prices or rates and pertinent dates, sinking fund requirements, and significant terms of contracts to issue additional shares.

FASB Statement No. 107, *Disclosures about Fair Value of Financial Instruments,* as amended by FASB Statement No. 126, *Exemption from Certain Required Disclosure about Financial Instruments for Certain Nonpublic Entities,* and FASB Statement No. 133 *Accounting for Derivative Instruments and Hedging* (ASC 815), require public entities with total assets equal to at least $100 million to disclose both the fair value and the bases for estimating the fair value of long-term debt unless it is not practicable to estimate that value.

SOP No. 94-6 (ASC 275) requires disclosure of current vulnerability due to a concentration in the volume of business transacted with a particular lender if the concentration makes the borrower vulnerable to the risk of a near-term severe impact and it is at least reasonably possible that the events that could cause the severe impact will occur in the near term.

General requirements of the SEC for disclosure of long-term debt are stated in Regulation S-X, Rule 5-02(22):

> Bonds, mortgages and other long-term debt . . . (a) State separately in the balance sheet or in a note thereto, each issue or type of obligation and such information as will indicate (1) the general character of each type of debt including the interest rate; (2) the date of maturity, or if maturing serially, a brief indication of the serial maturities . . . ; (3) if the payment or principal or interest is contingent, an appropriate indication of such contingency; (4) a brief indication of priority; (5) if convertible, the basis.

Other disclosures called for by the SEC in Regulation S-X include:

- Rule 4.08(b). Security
- Rule 4.08(c). Defaults
- Rule 4.08(f). Significant changes in bonds, mortgages, and similar debt
- Rule 5.02(23). Indebtedness to related parties
- Rule 12.29. Scheduled mortgage loans on real estate

Exhibit 18.2 provides a sample presentation on long-term debt.

18.8 OTHER LONG-TERM LIABILITIES

(a) MORTGAGES AND LONG-TERM NOTES. A mortgage is essentially a pledge of title to physical property as security for repayment of a loan. The term mortgage refers to the security for a debt, not the debt itself. A promissory note usually accompanies the granting of a mortgage. On the balance sheet, the liability should appear as "Mortgage Notes Payable" or "Notes Payable—Secured" with a brief reference to the property pledged. The term *mortgage payable* as a liability caption is, nevertheless, occasionally found in financial statements.

If mortgages are payable on the installment plan, the liability account is charged each payment date with the amount of principal paid. When the periodic installments are fixed amounts covering both payment on principal and accrued interest, the payments must be apportioned between principal and interest (see Section 18.8(b)).

With respect to individual mortgages and accompanying notes, the borrower usually receives cash in the face amount of the note; in this case, the face amount is the true liability and discount or premium is not involved. However, when the consideration for the note is in the form of property, as is the case when a mortgage is given on the property purchased or when points are given, the liability may be more or less than the face of the note. Points are the analogue, in mortgage financing, of original issue discount for bonds. They raise the effective interest rate above that specified in the note. A point is 1 percent of the face of the note. For example, if a 20-year mortgage note for $100,000 face were signed, but the banker demanded 4 points, the borrower would receive 4 percent less than $100,000, or $96,000. If the note carried an interest rate of 10.75 percent, for example, the borrower would still be obligated to make the monthly payments on $100,000 (i.e., $1,015 per month). Since the borrower received only $96,000, his or her effective interest rate is increased to about 12.3 percent on the money received.

In some mortgage loan arrangements, the lender is entitled to participate in appreciation in the market value of the mortgaged real estate project or the results of operations of the mortgaged real estate project, or in both.

(i) Related Party Transactions. Companies sometimes borrow from related parties, such as principal owners, management, or members of their immediate family, or from other subsidiaries of a common parent. FASB Statement No. 57 (ASC 850) requires disclosure of material transactions

R. Debt	2001	2000
Short-term debt (1)		
Commercial paper		$ 56
U.S. dollar bank loans/overdrafts	$ 416	55
Other currency bank loans/overdrafts	48	121
Total short-term debt	$ 464	$ 232
Long-term debt		
U.S. dollars:		
Credit facility borrowings (2)	$1,402	$1,962
Private placements		
7.54% due 2005	105	105
Senior notes and debentures:		
7.13% due 2002	350	350
6.75% due 2003 (3)	400	400
6.75% due 2003	200	200
8.38% due 2005	300	300
7.00% due 2006 (3)	300	300
8.00% due 2023	200	200
7.38% due 2026	350	350
7.50% due 2096	150	150
Other indebtedness:		
Rates in 2001 ranging from 2.00% to 10.77%, due 2002 through 2015	60	106
	3,817	4,423
Other currencies:		
Credit facility borrowings (2)	741	353
6.00% Euro bond due 2004	266	281
Other indebtedness in various currencies		
(average rates in 2001 ranging from 3.54% to		
14.3%), due 2003 through 2010	13	35
Capital lease obligations in		
various currencies	19	25
Total long-term debt (3)	4,856	5,117
Less: current maturities	(381)	(68)
Long-term debt, less current maturities	$4,475	$5,049

(1) The weighted average interest rates for commercial paper outstanding during 2000 and 1999 were 5.9% and 4.9% respectively. The weighted average interest rates for bank loans and overdrafts outstanding during 2001, 2000, and 1999 were 5.7%, 7.0% and 5.5% respectively.

(2) A committed $2,500 multicurrency revolving credit facility was in place at both December 31, 2001, and December 31, 2000. At December 31, 2001, $257 was available under the credit facility.

(3) On December 12, 1996, two wholly owned finance subsidiaries located in the United Kingdom and France sold public debt securities that were fully guaranteed by the Company. The face value of the notes bear interest ranging from 6.75% to 7.0%. The offerings by the subsidiaries, amounting to $700, were simultaneously converted into fixed rate, 8.28% Sterling and 5.75% Euro obligations through cross-currency swaps with various counterparties. In May 2000, the cross-currency swap on the Euro obligation was converted to a floating rate instrument with a coupon rate of EURIBOR less .89%. At December 31, 2001, the equivalent rate was 2.46%.

Exhibit 18.2   Sample Presentation of Long-Term Debt
Source: Crown Cork & Seal, 2001 Annual Report.

Aggregate maturities of long-term debt for the five years subsequent to December 31, 2001, are $381, $2,777, $272, $407, and $305, respectively. Cash payments for interest during 2001, 2000 and 1999 were $469, $385, and $377, respectively (including amounts capitalized of $1 in each of the three years).

The estimated fair value of the Company's long-term borrowings, based on quoted market prices for the same or similar issues, was $3,612 at December 31, 2001.

On March 2, 2001, the Company amended and restated its $2,500 multicurrency revolving credit facility and obtained a new $400 term loan. The amended and restated credit facility bears interest at LIBOR plus 2.5%, and the maturity date was extended from February 4, 2002 to December 8, 2003. The term loan bears interest at LIBOR plus 3.5%, with a maturity date of February 4, 2002. In connection with the new facility and the term loan, the Company pledged as collateral the stock of certain of the Company's subsidiaries and substantially all of the assets of the borrowing companies and the Company's domestic subsidiaries, except for those assets which are already pledged, are precluded from being pledged under existing or anticipated agreements, or are impractical to pledge under local law. The credit facility and term loan contain covenants which include (i) interest coverage and leverage ratios, (ii) restrictions on the repayment of notes, debentures, and private placements, (iii) restrictions on the assumption of indebtedness and payment of dividends, and (iv) restrictions on the use of proceeds from asset sales. Any credit facility or term loan repayments made using proceeds from the sale of assets will permanently reduce the funds available under the agreement. At December 31, 2001, there were outstanding letters of credit of $115 including $100 which reduced the borrowings available under the credit facility.

On January 30, 2002, the maturity date for $225 of the term loan was extended to August 4, 2002, and the remaining $175 was subsequently repaid on its original due date using net proceeds of $100 from asset sales and $75 of availability under the credit facility. The term loan balance was further reduced to $201 during the first quarter of 2002 using additional asset sale proceeds. The amended term loan bears an interest rate of LIBOR plus 4.5%.

Exhibit 18.2 *Continued*

with related parties unless those transactions are eliminated in the preparation of consolidated or combined financial statements. The disclosures must include:

- The nature of the relationship(s) involved
- A description of the transactions, including transactions to which no amounts or nominal amounts were ascribed, for each of the periods for which income statements are presented, and such other information deemed necessary to an understanding of the effects of the transactions on the financial statements
- The dollar amounts of transactions for each of the period for which income statements are presented and the effects of any change in the method of establishing the terms from that used in the preceding period
- Amounts due from or to related parties as of the date of each balance sheet presented and, if not otherwise apparent, the terms and manner of settlement

If necessary to the understanding of the relationship, the name of the related party should be disclosed.

Transactions involving related parties cannot be presumed to be carried out on an arm's-length basis, as the requisite conditions of competitive, free-market dealings may not exist. Representations about transactions with related parties, if made, may not imply that the related party transactions were consummated on terms equivalent to those that prevail in arm's-length transactions unless those representations can be substantiated.

For SEC registrants, SEC Regulation S-X, Rules 4-08(k)(1) and (2), set forth these additional requirements:

(k) Related party transactions which affect the financial statements. (1) Related party transactions should be identified and the amounts stated on the face of the balance sheet, income statement, or statement of cash flows.

(2) In cases where separate financial statements are presented for the registrant, certain investees, or subsidiaries, separate disclosure shall be made in such statements of the amounts in the related consolidated financial statements which are (i) eliminated and (ii) not eliminated. Also, any intercompany profits or losses resulting from transactions with related parties and not eliminated and the effects thereof shall be disclosed.

In addition, SEC Regulation S-K (Regulation Section 229.404) sets forth nonfinancial statement disclosure requirements concerning certain relationships and related transactions.

(ii) Debtor's Accounting for Forfeiture of Real Estate Subject to a Nonrecourse Mortgage. EITF Issue No. 91-2 dealt with a situation where a borrower under a nonrecourse loan purchases real property. The only security for the loan is the real property, and the lender accepts that limitation. After repaying a portion of the loan, the borrower transfers the property, which by then has a reduced fair value, in satisfaction of the loan balance, which exceeds the value of the property. For example, assume the purchased property cost of $1000, which was totally financed. After repaying $200, the borrower transfers the property, which now has a fair value of $600, to the lender in full satisfaction of the balance due. The issue is whether FASB Statement No. 15 (ASC 320) applies in this case.

If Statement No. 15 on troubled debt restructuring applies, the borrower would record a loss on the asset of $400, and a gain of $200 on the extinguishment of the debt. The FASB Staff and the SEC Observer agree that Statement No. 15 applies in this case and calls for the two-step approach illustrated earlier.

An alternative one-step approach would be for the borrower to record a loss of $200, the difference between the asset carrying amount of $1000 and the $800 balance of the loan.

The Task Force did not reach a consensus on this issue.

(b) INSTALLMENT PURCHASE CONTRACTS. Installment purchase contracts are a popular means of financing asset acquisitions. In the typical case, the buyer secures possession upon making a down payment and agrees to pay the balance in a series of installments, usually with interest, over an extended period. In some cases, buyers with excellent credit ratings are not required to provide down payments. Transfer of title is often deferred until payment of the final installment. Proper accounting requires showing the asset at full cost and the balance of the contract payable as a liability.

Purchase contracts are commonly payable in equal periodic installments. The regular installment may include both interest on the contract balance and a payment on the principal, or it may apply entirely to principal, with interest paid separately.

To illustrate the first plan, assume a contract covering the purchase of equipment for $5,000, with interest at 12 percent, which provides for semiannual payments of $500 each until the entire obligation has been discharged. The division of these payments between interest and retirement of principal, at an interest rate of 12 percent, compounded semiannually, is shown in the next table. The entries in this case for the first semiannual payment (assuming no interim accrual of interest) are:

Purchase contract payable	$200	
Interest on purchase contract	300	
Cash		$500

Half-Year Period	Balance of Debt	Interest 6% per Period	Payment	Amortization of Debt
1	$5,000.00	$ 300.00	$ 500.00	$ 200.00
2	4,800.00	288.00	500.00	212.00
3	4,588.00	275.28	500.00	224.72
4	4,363.28	261.80	500.00	238.20
5	4,125.08	247.50	500.00	252.50
6	3,872.58	232.36	500.00	267.64
7	3,604.94	216.30	500.00	283.70
8	3,324.24	199.27	500.00	300.73
9	3,020.51	181.23	500.00	318.77
10	2,701.74	162.10	500.00	337.90
11	2,363.84	141.83	500.00	358.17
12	2,005.67	120.34	500.00	379.66
13	1,626.01	97.56	500.00	402.44
14	1,223.57	73.41	500.00	426.59
15	796.98	47.82	500.00	452.18
16	$ 344.80	$ 20.69	$ 365.49	$ 344.80
		$ 2,865.49	$7,865.49	$5,000.00

In this example, the fair value of the property is assumed to be the full contract price of $5,000, because interest is provided at a presumably adequate rate. If no interest rate were provided, the imputed interest provisions would apply.

(c) LONG-TERM LEASES.   Leasing, as a means of financing the acquisition of long-term assets, has seen a rapid expansion in the United States and other countries since World War II. It was not until the 1960s, however, that authoritative accounting pronouncements began to significantly affect lease accounting. There now exist several major pronouncements and many interpretations. The related accounting is complex. Chapter 15 in this *Handbook* is devoted entirely to lease accounting, from both the lessee and lessor points of view.

(d) DEFERRED REVENUE OBLIGATIONS.   *Deferred revenue* is the term often applied to liabilities that arise from the receipt of payment in advance of furnishing the service for which the funds are received. Usually deferred revenues are current, in that the service will be rendered in the next accounting period and the obligation discharged. A more complete discussion of accounting for deferred revenue has already been given in connection with current liabilities. In some cases, however, payments are received covering a period of years, and here it is necessary to reduce the obligation each period by an appropriate amount, with a concurrent credit to revenue. Such long-term collections in advance should be shown as long-term liabilities in the balance sheet, under an appropriate title. The amount to be discharged in the following accounting period should be classed as current, with only the balance shown as a long-term liability.

Casualty insurance premiums are frequently collected three to five years in advance, and the long-term portions of such premiums represent long-term liabilities on the books of the insurer.

(e) LONG-TERM EXPENSE ACCRUALS.   Although most accruals of expenses are properly classified as current liabilities, some commitments, such as three- to five-year product and service warranties, self-insurance programs, and pension plans, deserve classification as long-term obligations. The amount of the obligation is estimated in light of a company's past experience and is established by an expense charge. The facts that the amount is estimated and the identity of the specific obligee may be unknown at the time the obligation is recognized do not affect the propriety of the entry. Subsequently, when payment or service is made, the long-term liability account is eliminated.

The extent to which inflation should be recognized in long-term expense accruals is unclear. If, for example, a company gives a five-year repair warranty on a product, it is reasonable to assume that the labor cost of repair work performed in five years will be considerably higher than it is today. It is not clear whether the accrual of the liability for the warranty work should be made at current prices or at estimated future prices.

Paragraph 6.12 of SOP No. 96-1 states:

> The measurement of environmental remediation liabilities should be based on the reporting entity's estimate of what it will cost to perform each of the elements of the remediation effort . . . when those elements are expected to be performed. Although this approach is sometimes referred to as "considering inflation," it does not simply rely on an index and should take into account factors such as productivity improvements due to learning from experience with similar sites and similar remedial action plans. In situations in which it is not practicable to estimate inflation and such other factors because of uncertainty about the timing of expenditures, a current-cost estimate would be the minimum in the range of the liability to be recorded until such time as these cost effects can be reasonably estimated.

That guidance may be applicable to other kinds of liabilities by analogy (ASC 410-30).

In the past, it was common to refer to such long-term expense accruals as operating or liability reserves, which, on occasion, were located ambiguously between the liability and equity sections of the balance sheets. These amounts are clearly liabilities and should be presented as such. The use of the term *reserve* in this context is not good practice.

(f) BORROWINGS ON OPEN ACCOUNT.   Long-term borrowings on open account from affiliated corporations or other parties are a kind of long-term liability and should normally be shown separately.

Long-term advances received for future use of property or merchandise, or for service to be rendered, represent a liability on the books of the party obligated to furnish property or render the service. Classification of this type of item as a "deferred credit" is not recommended.

(g) ASSET RETIREMENT OBLIGATIONS.   FASB Statement No. 143, *Accounting for Assets Retirement Obligations* (ASC 410-20), sets forth accounting and disclosure requirements for legal obligations associated with the retirement of a tangible long-lived asset that result from the acquisition, construction, or development and (or) the normal operation of a long-lived asset. Accounting for assets is discussed in Chapter 16 of this *Handbook*.

(h) PENSION PLANS AND DEFERRED COMPENSATION CONTRACTS.   Plans for payment of employee pensions and other retirement allowances involve assumption of obligations that are deferred until employee retirement dates. Accounting for retirement plans is the subject of Chapter 27 of this *Handbook*.

(i) FUTURE INCOME TAXES.   The objectives of accounting for income taxes, as set forth in FASB Statement No. 109 (ASC 740) are:

> to recognize (a) the amount of taxes payable or refundable for the current year and (b) deferred tax liabilities and assets for the future tax consequences of events that have been recognized in an enterprise's financial statements or tax returns.

Four basic principles are applied in accounting for income taxes at the date of the financial statements:

1. A current tax liability or asset is recognized for the estimated taxes payable or refundable on tax returns for the current year.
2. A deferred tax liability or asset is recognized for the estimated future tax effects attributable to temporary differences and carryforwards.
3. The measurement of current and deferred tax liabilities and assets is based on provisions of the enacted tax law; the effects of future changes in tax laws or rates are not anticipated.
4. The measurement of deferred tax assets is reduced, if necessary, by the amount of any tax benefits that, based on available evidence, are not expected to be realized.

A complete discussion of this subject is in Chapter 17 of this *Handbook*.

(j) DISCLOSURE OF UNCONDITIONAL PURCHASE AND OTHER LONG-TERM OBLIGATIONS.   FASB Statement No. 47 (ASC 440) requires that an enterprise disclose its commitments under unconditional purchase obligations, such as take-or-pay contracts or through-put contracts that are associated with suppliers' financing arrangements. Such arrangements result in obligations to transfer funds in the future for fixed or minimum amounts or quantities of goods or services at fixed or minimum prices. Disclosure is required of an unconditional purchase obligation that (par. 6):

a. Is noncancelable, or cancelable only
   1. Upon the occurrence of some remote contingency or
   2. With the permission of the other party or
   3. If a replacement agreement is signed between the same parties or
   4. Upon payment of a penalty in an amount such that continuation of the agreement appears reasonably assured
b. Was negotiated as part of arranging financing for the facilities that will provide the contracted goods or services or for costs related to those goods or services
c. Has a remaining term in excess of one year

If the obligation is not recognized on the purchaser's balance sheet, the required disclosures, which may be combined for similar or related obligations, include (par. 7):

a. The nature and the term of the obligation(s)

b. The amount of the fixed and determinable portion of the obligation(s) as of the date of the latest balance sheet presented in the aggregate and, if determinable, for each of the five succeeding fiscal years

c. The nature of any variable components of the obligation(s)

d. The amounts purchased under the obligation(s) for each period for which an income statement is presented

Disclosure of the amount of imputed interest necessary to reduce the unconditional purchase obligation(s) to present value is encouraged but not required. The discount rate to determine the present value of the obligation(s) should be the interest rate of the borrowings that financed the facilities that will provide the goods or services, if known by the purchaser. If not, the rate should be the purchasers' incremental borrowing rate at the date the obligation is entered into.

For obligations that are recognized on the balance sheet, Statement No. 47 requires these disclosures for each of the five years following the latest balance sheet date (par. 10):

1. The aggregate amount of payments for unconditional purchase obligations

2. The combined aggregate amount of maturities and sinking fund requirements for all long-term borrowings

(k) GUARANTEE OBLIGATIONS. FASB Interpretation No. 45 (ASC 460), issued in November 2002, changed dramatically the accounting for guarantees within its scope by creating the concept of a noncontingent obligation to "stand ready" to perform over the term of the guarantee in the event that specified triggering events or conditions occur.

Guarantors are now required to recognize, at the inception of a guarantee, a liability for the fair value of the obligations they have undertaken in issuing the guarantee. The liability consists of two elements:

1. Any contingent liability that meets the recognition criteria of FASB Statement No. 5.

2. A liability for the guarantor's ongoing obligation to stand ready to perform over the term of the guarantee in the event that the specified triggering events or conditions occur. This element is considered to be noncontingent; thus, the liability is recognized even if it is not probable that the specified triggering events or conditions will occur. Furthermore, the liability is recognized regardless of whether any explicit premium or other compensation was received for the guarantee.

(i) Scope of Interpretation No. 45. Interpretation No. 45 applies only to direct and indirect guarantees with any of these contract characteristics:

- Contracts and indemnification agreements that contingently require the guarantor to make payments (in cash, financial instruments, other assets, shares of its stock, or provision of services) to the guaranteed party based on changes in an underlying that is related to an asset, a liability, or an equity security of the guaranteed party. An "underlying" is a variable such as a specified interest rate or commodity price. An underlying also includes the occurrence or nonoccurrence of a specified event, such as a scheduled payment under a contract or an adverse judgment in a lawsuit.

- Indirect guarantees of the indebtedness of others (meaning the creditor's claim against the guarantor is based solely on the right to enforce the debtor's claim against the guarantor), even though the payment to the guaranteed party may not be based on changes in an underlying that is related to an asset, a liability, or an equity security of the guaranteed party.

- Contracts that contingently require the guarantor to make payments (in cash, financial instruments, other assets, shares of its stock, or provision of services) to the guaranteed party based on another entity's failure to perform under an obligating agreement (performance guarantees).

Examples of guarantees that meet the characteristic-based scope provisions of the Interpretation are presented next.

- A financial standby letter of credit, which is an irrevocable undertaking (typically by a financial institution) to guarantee payment of a specified financial obligation
- A guarantee to repurchase receivables that have been sold or otherwise assigned
- A market value guarantee on either a financial asset (such as a security) or a nonfinancial asset owned by the guaranteed party
- A guarantee of the market price of the common stock of the guaranteed party
- A guarantee of the collection of the scheduled contractual cash flows from individual financial assets held by a special-purpose entity (SPE)
- An indemnification against an adverse judgment in a lawsuit
- An indemnification against the imposition of additional taxes due to either a change in the tax law or an adverse interpretation of the tax law
- A performance standby letter of credit, which is an irrevocable undertaking by a guarantor to make payments in the event a specified third party fails to perform under a nonfinancial contractual obligation

Examples of arrangements that do not meet the characteristic-based scope provisions of the Interpretation are presented next.

- Guarantees of an entity's *own* performance
- Guarantees of funding, such as commercial letters of credit and other loan commitments
- Subordination agreements, wherein one class of investors agrees not to receive any cash until investors in a priority class are paid

Interpretation No. 45 also provides numerous specific scope exclusions—some from the entire Interpretation, others solely from the initial recognition and measurement provisions. Those exclusions are summarized next.

Excluded from the Entire Interpretation	**Excluded from the Initial Recognition Requirements (Disclosure Only)**
Guarantees that are excluded from the scope of FASB Statement No. 5 under paragraph 7 of that Statement (e.g., pensions and stock options)	Contracts that guarantee the functionality of nonfinancial assets that are owned by the guaranteed party (e.g., product warranties)
Residual value guarantees issued by a lessee that accounted for a lease as a capital lease	Guarantees that are accounted for under FASB Statement No. 133 as a derivative instrument at fair value
Guarantees that require payments due to changes in an underlying that belongs to the guaranteed party but that are accounted for as contingent rents	Guarantees issued in a business combination that represent contingent consideration
Guarantees issued by either an insurance or a reinsurance company and accounted for under specified FASB Statements	Guarantees for which the guarantor's obligation would be reported as an equity item (rather than a liability) under GAAP
Guarantees that require payments due to changes in an underlying that belongs to the guaranteed party but provide vendor rebates by the guarantor based	Guarantees issued by an original lessee that has become secondarily liable under a new lease that relieved the original lessee of the primary obligation under the original lease

on either the sales revenues of or the number of units sold by, the guaranteed party

Guarantees issued either between parents and their subsidiaries or corporations under common control

Guarantees that prevent the guarantor from accounting for a transaction as a sale or recognizing the profit from that sale transaction in earnings

Guarantees by a parent of its subsidiary's debts to third parties

Guarantees by a subsidiary of debts owed to third parties by either its parent or other subsidiaries of that parent

(ii) Initial Recognition. If a guarantee is issued in a stand-alone arm's-length transaction with an unrelated party, the liability should be recognized initially at the amount of the premium received or receivable by the guarantor. If a guarantee is issued as part of a transaction with multiple elements with an unrelated party, the liability should be recognized initially at its estimated fair value. If a guarantee is issued as a contribution to an unrelated party, the liability should be recognized initially at its fair value.

If, at the inception of the guarantee, the guarantor is required to recognize a liability under FASB Statement No. 5 (ASC 450) for a contingent loss, the liability to be initially recognized for that liability is the greater of (1) the amount that satisfies the fair value objective described in the preceding paragraph or (2) the contingent liability amount required to be recognized by Statement No. 5. It would be unusual, however, for the contingent liability amount required to be recognized by Statement No. 5 to be greater than the amount that satisfies the fair value objective.

The Interpretation does not prescribe a specific account for the guarantor's offsetting entry when it recognizes the liability at the inception of the guarantee. The offsetting entry depends on the circumstances in which the guarantee was issued. For example,

- If a guarantee is issued in connection with the sale of assets or a business, the overall proceeds received from the transaction would be allocated between consideration for the guarantee and proceeds from the sale.
- If a guarantee is issued in connection with the formation of a joint venture, the offsetting entry would probably be to the investment in the joint venture.
- If a guarantee is issued by a lessee when entering into an operating lease, the offsetting entry would be to prepaid rent.

(iii) Subsequent Accounting. Subsequent to initial recognition, the noncontingent liability typically would be reduced by a credit to income as the guarantor is released from risk under the guarantee. Depending on the nature of the guarantee, the release from risk is typically recognized over the term of the guarantee (1) only upon either expiration or settlement of the guarantee, (2) by a systematic and rational amortization method, or (3) as the fair value of the guarantee changes. Some view the selection of methods for subsequent reduction of the noncontingent liability as an accounting policy election. Any contingent liability required to be recognized under Statement No. 5 should be adjusted accordingly.

(iv) Disclosure. Interpretation No. 45 requires disclosures about guarantees within its scope in addition to those required by FASB Statement Nos. 5, 57, and 107:

- The nature and approximate term of the guarantee, the circumstances that gave rise to the guarantee, and the conditions that require the guarantor to make payments under the guarantee.
- Except for product warranties, the maximum potential amount of future payments (undiscounted and not reduced for possible recoveries) under the guarantee. If the guarantor cannot estimate the amount, the reason should be disclosed.
- The carrying amount of the guarantor's contingent and noncontingent obligation under the guarantee.

- The nature and extent of recourse provisions and collateral related to the guarantee and, if estimable, the extent to which the maximum potential loss under the guarantee would be covered.

- The fair value of financial guarantees.

- For product warranties, (1) the accounting policy and methodology used in determining the guarantor's liability (including any liability associated with extended warranties) and (2) a tabular reconciliation of the changes in the guarantor's aggregate product warranty liability for the period. The reconciliation should present the beginning balance of the aggregate product warranty liability, aggregate reductions in the liability for payments made (in cash or in kind), aggregate changes in the liability for accruals related to warranties issued during the period, aggregate changes in the liability for accruals related to preexisting warranties (including changes in estimates), and the ending balance of the aggregate product warranty liability.

18.9 FINANCIAL INSTRUMENTS WITH CHARACTERISTICS OF BOTH LIABILITIES AND EQUITY

(a) FINANCIAL INSTRUMENTS CLASSIFIED AS LIABILITIES.   The dividing line between equity and liabilities seems clear in concept. FASB Concepts Statement No. 6 defines equity as net assets, that is, the residual interest that remains in the assets of an entity after deducting its liabilities. In practice, however, the difference may be obscured. Certain securities issued by business enterprises seem to have characteristics of both liabilities and equity in varying degrees, or the name given to some securities may not accurately describe their essential characteristics.

FASB Statement No. 150, *Accounting for Certain Financial Instruments with Characteristics of Both Liabilities and Equity* (ASC 480), provides guidance on accounting for *freestanding* financial instruments that have both liability and residual-interest characteristics, including those that comprise more than one option or forward contract. Financial instruments are freestanding if they are entered into separately from other interests or transactions or are legally detachable and separately exercisable. At the time of this writing, the FASB has on its agenda a project to develop a comprehensive standard on financial instruments with characteristics of equity, liabilities, or both. That project is also expected to produce amendments to the definition of a liability in Concepts Statement No. 6, aspects of which are already reflected in Statement No. 150.

Three classes of freestanding financial instruments are required to be classified as a liability (or an asset in some cases):

1. Mandatorily redeemable financial instruments
2. Obligations to repurchase the issuer's equity shares by transferring assets
3. Certain obligations to issue a variable number of shares

(i) Mandatorily Redeemable Financial Instruments.   A mandatorily redeemable financial instrument is one that embodies an unconditional obligation requiring the issuer to redeem it by transferring its assets at a specified or determinable date (or dates) or upon an event that is certain to occur. Mandatorily redeemable financial instruments must be classified as liabilities unless redemption is required to occur only upon the liquidation or termination of the reporting entity. An example of a common mandatorily redeemable financial instrument is mandatorily redeemable preferred stock, which, prior to the effective date of Statement No. 150, typically was classified in the "mezzanine" between liabilities and equity. Another example is stock of a privately held company that must be sold back to the company upon the holder's termination of employment by the company or upon the holder's death.[6]

---

[6] An insurance contract covering the cost of redemption does not affect the classification of the stock as a liability.

Contingently redeemable financial instruments become mandatorily redeemable—and, therefore, liabilities—when the contingency is satisfied.

(ii) Obligations to Repurchase the Issuer's Equity Shares.   A financial instrument that, at inception, embodies or is indexed to an obligation to repurchase the issuer's equity shares, may require the issuer to settle the obligation by transferring assets. Common examples are a forward purchase contract that is to be physically settled or net cash settled and a written put option on the issuer's equity shares that is to be physically settled or net cash settled.

(iii) Certain Obligations to Issue a Variable Number of Shares.   Some financial instruments may contain an unconditional obligation, or a conditional obligation, that the issuer must or could settle by issuing a variable number of its equity shares. This would be the case if, at inception, the monetary value of the obligation is based solely or predominantly on any of these points:

1. A fixed monetary amount known at inception (e.g., a payable settleable with a variable number of the issuer's equity shares)
2. Variations in something other than the fair value of the issuer's equity shares (e.g., a financial instrument whose value is based on a stock market index and that is can be settled with a variable number of the issuer's equity shares)
3. Variations inversely related to changes in the fair value of the issuer's equity shares (e.g., a written put option that could be settled by one party delivering stock equal to the fair value of the counterparty's gain; net share settled)

(b) MEASUREMENT.   With one exception, all instruments within the scope of Statement No. 150 (ASC 480) are measured initially at their fair value. The exception is that, for freestanding "physically settled" forward purchase contracts that obligate the issuer to purchase a fixed number of its own shares for cash, fair value is adjusted for any consideration or unstated rights or privileges that may have affected the terms of the transaction. For example, if the underlying shares are expected to pay dividends before the repurchase date, the dividends should be reflected in the implicit interest rate used in determining the fair value of the instrument. For another example, if a physically settled forward purchase contract on the issuer's own shares is issued to a customer to whom the issuer simultaneously sold a product at a discount, that discount would be taken into account in arriving at an appropriate implied discount rate.

With two exceptions, all instruments within the scope of Statement No. 150 are subsequently measured at fair value, with changes in fair value recognized in earnings. The two exceptions are the physically settled forward purchase contracts discussed earlier and mandatorily redeemable instruments. If both the amount to be paid under a physically settled forward purchase contract or a mandatorily redeemable instrument and the settlement date are fixed, the liability is measured subsequently at the present value of the amount to be paid at settlement, accruing interest cost at the rate implicit at inception. If either the amount to be paid or the settlement date varies based on specified conditions, the liability is measured subsequently at the amount of cash that would be paid under the conditions specified in the contract if settlement occurred at the reporting date, and the difference between the amount so determined and the amount reported for the liability at the previous reporting date would be reflected in interest cost.

(c) PRESENTATION AND DISCLOSURE.   Entities that have only one class of "equity" instruments, all of which are mandatorily redeemable financial instruments required to be classified as liabilities, must describe those instruments in the balance sheet as "shares subject to mandatory redemption" to distinguish them from other liabilities. Similarly, payments to holders of such instruments and related accruals must be presented separately from payments to and interest due to other creditors in the statement of cash flows and in the income statement. In addition, such entities must disclose the related par value and paid-in capital amounts separately from retained earnings or accumulated deficit.

FASB Statement No. 150 requires disclosure of detailed information about each financial instrument within its scope. In addition, FASB Statement No. 129 (ASC 505) requires entities that issue redeemable stock to disclose the amount of redemption requirements, separately by issue or combined, for all issues of capital stock that are redeemable at fixed or determinable prices on fixed or determinable dates in each of the five years following the date of the latest statement of financial position presented.

18.10 RESTRUCTURING AND EXTINGUISHMENT OF LIABILITIES

(a) TROUBLED DEBT RESTRUCTURINGS.
If a debtor has difficulty making scheduled payments on a debt, a restructuring of the debt may be arranged. That is, the creditor may agree to alter the payments of principal, interest, or both in such a manner as to make it more likely that the debtor can make the payments. For example, the creditor may agree to a reduction in the original interest rate, deferral of interest payments, extension of the time for payment of principal, a reduction in the absolute value of the principal amount, or some combination thereof. Creditors may also accept cash, other assets, or an equity interest in the debtor in satisfaction of the debt even though the value received is less than the amount of the debt.

FASB Statement No. 15, *Accounting by Debtors and Creditors for Troubled Debt Restructurings* (see ASC 310 and ASC 470), governs the accounting for the restructuring of a

> contractual . . . obligation to pay money on demand or on fixed or determinable dates that is already included as . . . [a] liability in the . . . debtor's balance sheet at the time of the restructuring.

Examples of such obligations are accounts payable, debentures and bonds, and related accrued interest. Statement No. 15 does not apply, however, to lease agreements; employment-related agreements; or debtors' failure to pay trade payables according to their terms, or creditors' delays in taking legal action to collect overdue amounts of interest and principal, unless they involve an agreement between the debtor and creditor to restructure.

Under FASB Statement No. 15, if the debtor transfers its receivables from third parties, real estate, or other assets to a creditor to settle fully a debt, the debtor should recognize a gain on "restructuring" of the debt equal to the excess of (1) the carrying amount of the debt settled (including accrued interest and unamortized premium or discount, finance charges, and issue costs, as applicable) over (2) the fair value of the assets transferred. Fair value of assets is measured by (in order of preference): (1) their market value in an active market, (2) the selling prices of similar assets for which there is an active market, or (3) a forecast of expected cash flows, discounted at a rate commensurate with the risk involved.

If only the terms of the debt are modified (i.e., no assets or equity interest are transferred), the carrying amount of the payable at the time of the restructuring is not changed unless it exceeds the total future cash payments (undiscounted) specified by the new terms. If the total future cash payments specified by the new terms are less than the carrying amount of the payable:

- The carrying amount of the payable is reduced to the amount of the total future cash payments specified by the new terms.
- Unless indeterminate future cash payments are involved , a gain is recognized on restructuring equal to the amount of the reduction.

If the debtor may be required to pay additional amounts based on a contingency such as its financial condition improving, the debtor must assume that the contingent future payments will have to be paid and include them in the "total future cash payments specified by the new terms" to the extent necessary to prevent recognition of a gain on restructuring that may be offset in future periods. The same principle applies if the amount of future payments is uncertain (e.g., if the number of future interest payments is uncertain because the principal and accrued interest are payable on demand).

If a troubled debt restructuring involves a partial settlement by transferring assets or granting an equity interest and a modification of terms of the remaining payable, the carrying amount of the payable should first be reduced by the fair value of the assets transferred or equity interest granted. The difference between the carrying amount and the fair value of the assets transferred is recognized as a gain or loss. The reduced carrying amount of the debt is then compared with the total future cash payments specified by the new terms in accounting for the portion of the restructuring that is a modification of terms of the remaining debt.

Interest expense is recorded by the debtor subsequent to the restructuring so that a constant effective interest rate is applied to the carrying amount of the payable at the beginning of the period between the restructuring and the maturity. That is, in substance, the interest method prescribed by APB Opinion No. 21 and described in Sections 18.2 and 18.5. If a gain is recognized on a troubled debt restructuring, no interest expense is recognized on the debt going forward, other than for any contingent interest payments.

Also, Statement No. 15 requires disclosure of the principal features of a restructuring, of any gain or loss, and of the per share effects.

FASB Technical Bulletin No. 81-6, *Applicability of FASB Statement 15 to Debtors in Bankruptcy Situations* (ASC 470), indicates that the principles of troubled debt restructuring of Statement No. 15 do not apply if a company is involved in a chapter 3 bankruptcy proceeding that will result in a restatement of all of its indebtedness, say at 50 cents on the dollar. However, Statement No. 15 would apply to an isolated troubled debt restructuring by a debtor involved in a bankruptcy proceeding as long as it did not result in a general restatement of the debtor's liabilities.

The next conditions would indicate that a debt restructuring may not be a troubled debt restructuring for purposes of Statement No. 15:

- The fair value of cash, other assets, or an equity interest accepted by a creditor from a debtor in full satisfaction of its receivable at least equals the creditor's recorded investment in the receivable.

- The fair value of cash, other assets, or an equity interest transferred by a debtor to a creditor in full settlement of its payable at least equals the debtor's carrying amount of the payable.

- The creditor reduces the effective interest rate on debt primarily to reflect a decrease in market interest rates in general or a decrease in the risk so as to maintain a relationship with the debtor that can readily obtain funds from other sources at the current market interest rate.

- The debtor issues in exchange for its debt new marketable debt having an effective interest rate based on its market price that is at or near the current market interest rates of debt with similar maturity dates and stated interest rates issued by nontroubled debtors.

Statement No. 15 notes that, in general, a debtor that can obtain funds from sources other than the existing creditor at market interest rates at or near those for nontroubled debt is not involved in a troubled debt restructuring.

EITF Issue No. 02-4, *Determining Whether a Debtor's Modification or Exchange of Debt Instruments Is within the Scope of FASB Statement No. 15* (ASC 470), provides further guidance for determining whether an event is a troubled debt restructuring for purposes of Statement No. 15. If a modification or exchange of debt instruments is not within the scope of Statement No. 15, the provisions of EITF No. 96-19, *Debtor's Accounting for a Modification or Exchange of Debt Instruments* (also ASC 470), should be applied.

(b) EXTINGUISHMENT OF LIABILITIES.   FASB Statement No. 140 (ASC 860) provides guidance to debtors as to when debt should be considered to be extinguished for financial reporting purposes:

- The debtor pays the creditor and is relieved of its obligations with respect to the debt. This includes the debtor's reacquisition of its outstanding debt securities in the public securities markets, regardless of whether the securities are canceled or held as so-called treasury bonds.

- The debtor is legally released from being the primary obligor under the debt either judicially or by the creditor.

Previously under FASB Statement No. 76, *Extinguishment of Debt,* a debtor considered debt to be extinguished if it irrevocably placed cash or other assets in a trust to be used solely for satisfying scheduled payments of both interest and principal of a specific obligation and the possibility that the debtor would be required to make future payments with respect to the debt was remote. An in-substance defeasance transaction does not meet Statement No. 140's criteria for derecognizing a liability. For debt that was considered defeased under the provisions of FASB Statement No. 76, there should continue to be a general description of the defeasance transaction and the amount of the debt that is considered extinguished at the end of the period so long as that debt remains outstanding.

If a creditor releases a debtor from primary obligation on the condition that a third party assumes the obligation and the original debtor becomes secondarily liable as guarantor, the original debtor treats the release as an extinguishment. However, as a guarantor, the original debtor must recognize a guarantee obligation in the same manner as if he or she had never been primarily liable to that creditor, with due regard for the likelihood that the third party will perform on its obligation. The guarantee obligation is initially measured at its fair value, and that amount reduces the gain or increases the loss recognized on extinguishment.

In EITF Issue No. 96-19, the Task Force reached a consensus that an exchange of debt instruments with substantially different terms is debt extinguishment and should be accounted for in accordance with paragraph 16 of Statement No. 125 (paragraph 16 of that statement is now included in FASB Statement No. 140). Thus, a substantial modification of terms should be accounted for like, and reported in the same manner as, an extinguishment.

EITF No. 96-19 (ASC 470) concluded that, from the debtor's perspective, an exchange of debt instruments between or a modification of a debt instrument by a debtor and a creditor in a nontroubled debt situation is deemed to have been accomplished with debt instruments that are *substantially different* if present value of the cash flows under the terms of the new debt instrument is at least *10 percent* different from the present value of the remaining cash flows under the terms of the original instrument.

Cash flows can be affected by changes in principal amounts, interest rates, or maturity. They can also affected by fees exchanged between the debtor and creditor to change:

- Recourse or nonrecourse features
- Priority of the obligation
- Collateralized (including changes in collateral) or noncollateralized features
- Debt covenants, waivers, or both
- The guarantor (or elimination of the guarantor)
- Option features

If the terms of a debt instrument are changed or modified in any of the ways just described and the cash flow effect on a present value basis is less than 10 percent, the debt instruments are not considered to be substantially different.

The next guidelines are to be used to calculate the present value of the cash flows for purposes of applying the 10 percent test:

1. The cash flows of the new debt instrument include all cash flows specified by the terms of the new debt instrument plus any amounts paid by the debtor to the creditor less any amounts received by the debtor from the creditor as part of the exchange or modification.

2. If the original debt instrument, the new debt instrument, or both have a floating interest rate, the variable rate in effect at the date of the exchange or modification is to be used to calculate the cash flows of the variable-rate instrument.

3. If either the new debt instrument or the original debt instrument is callable or puttable, separate cash flow analyses are to be performed assuming exercise and nonexercise of the call or put. The cash flow assumptions that generate the smaller change would be the basis for determining whether the 10 percent threshold is met.

4. If the debt instruments contain contingent payment terms or unusual interest rate terms, judgment should used to determine the appropriate cash flows.

5. The discount rate to be used to calculate the present value of the cash flows is the effective interest rate, for accounting purposes. of the original debt instrument.

6. If within a year of the current transaction the debt has been exchanged or modified without being deemed to be substantially different, the debt terms that existed a year ago should be used to determine whether the current exchange or modification is substantially different.

If it is determined that the original and new debt instruments are substantially different, the calculation of the cash flows related to the new debt instrument at the effective interest rate of the original debt instrument is *not* used to determine the initial amount recorded for the new debt instrument or to determine the debt extinguishment gain or loss to be recognized. The new debt instrument should be initially recorded at fair value, and that amount should be used to determine the debt extinguishment gain or loss to be recognized and the effective rate of the new instrument.

If it is determined that the original and new debt instruments are not substantially different, a new effective rate must be determined based on the carrying amount of the original debt instrument and the revised cash flows.

Fees paid by the debtor to the creditor or received by the debtor from the creditor (fees may be received by the debtor from the creditor to cancel a call option held by the debtor or to extend a no-call period) as part of the exchange or modification are to be accounted for in this way:

- If the exchange or modification is to be accounted for in the same manner as a debt extinguishment and the new debt instrument is initially recorded at fair value, the fees paid or received are to be associated with the extinguishment of the old debt instrument and included in determining the debt extinguishment gain or loss to be recognized.
- If the exchange or modification is not to be accounted for in the same manner as a debt extinguishment, the fees are to be associated with the replacement or modified debt instrument and, along with any existing unamortized premium or discount, amortized as an adjustment of interest expense over the remaining term of the replacement or modified debt instrument using the interest method.

Costs incurred with third parties directly related to the exchange or modification (such as legal fees) are to be accounted for in this way:

- If the exchange or modification is to be accounted for in the same manner as a debt extinguishment and the new debt instrument is initially recorded at fair value, the costs are to be associated with the new debt instrument and amortized over the term of the new debt instrument using the interest method in a manner similar to debt issue costs.
- If the exchange or modification is not to be accounted for in the same manner as a debt extinguishment, the costs should be expensed as incurred.

EITF Issue No. 96-19 also carried over the consensus from EITF Issue No. 86-18, which it superseded, that a borrower should not account for the original debt securities as extinguished and that those securities should not be offset against the receivable from the third party in the borrower's financial statements in the next situation:

- A borrower, instead of acquiring debt securities directly, loans funds to a third party, who in turn acquires the borrower's original debt securities.
- The borrower and third party agree that they may settle their respective receivables and obligation by right of setoff as payments become due, contingent on the third party's continued retention of the borrower's original debt.

18.11 ACCOUNTING FOR SELECTED FINANCING INSTRUMENTS

(a) INTRODUCTION. In recent years numerous modifications to traditional debt instruments have required the EITF to address the accompanying accounting issues. In one instance, a traditional convertible debt instrument was modified by giving the buyer the option to put (sell) the issue back to the issuer at a premium. Other modifications to traditional debt have included debt issuances that have altered the traditional way in which interest rates are set. There have been issuances of debt with increasing interest rates and deferral of the setting of interest rates as well as issuances of debt instruments that provide not only for principal repayment, but also contingent payments. Companies have also sold their marketable securities granting the buyer the right to sell those assets back to the issuer. Those modifications have led to such fundamental questions as whether the transaction is a sale or a borrowing, the amount of liability to be accrued, the amount of interest expense and pattern of interest recognition, and the method of accounting for possible impairments. The next section summarizes both the accounting issues that have arisen from these financial instrument modifications and the EITF consensus agreements on acceptable accounting.

(i) Convertible Bonds with a Premium Put. The EITF considered convertible bonds issued at par value with a put allowing the bondholder to require that the corporation redeem the bonds at a future date for cash at a premium to the bond's par value. At the date of issue, the carrying amount of the bonds exceeds the market value of the common stock into which they are convertible.

The questions addressed in Issue No. 85-29 are:

- Should a liability be accrued for the put premium and, if so, over what period?
- Should the liability continue to be accrued if the value of debt or equity changes, making exercise of the put unlikely?
- If the put expires unexercised, should the put be recognized as income or paid-in capital, amortized as a yield adjustment, or continue to be carried as part of debt?

The EITF reached this consensus:

- The issuer should accrue the put premium over the period from the date of issuance to the first put date. The accrual should continue even if changes in market value of the bond or underlying common stock indicate the put will not be exercised.
- If the put expires unexercised, the amount accrued should be credited to additional paid-in capital if the market value of the common stock exceeds the put price. Otherwise, if the put price exceeds the market value of the common stock, the put premium should be amortized as a yield adjustment over the remaining life of the bonds.

FASB Statement No. 133 (ASC 815) partially nullified this consensus. Under Statement No. 133, the embedded feature warrants separate accounting as a derivative. However, because Statement No. 133 permits entities not to account separately for certain derivatives embedded in pre-1998 or pre-1999 hybrid instruments, the consensus on this issue continues to apply to those convertible bonds for which the embedded derivative is not accounted for separately.

(ii) Increasing-Rate Debt. The EITF dealt with debt that matures three months from date of issuance but may be extended at the discretion of the issuer for an additional period at each maturity date until final maturity. The rate of interest increases each time the note's maturity is extended.

Issue No. 86-15 (ASC 470) addressed these issues:

- How should the borrower's interest expense be determined and what maturity date should be used in establishing the interest rate?
- How should the debt be classified?
- What period is to be used for amortization?
- If debt is paid at an earlier date than that assumed in arriving at the interest rate, how should the excess accrual be accounted for?

The EITF reached this consensus:

- The borrower's periodic interest cost should be based on the estimated outstanding term of the borrowing. Plans, intent, and ability to service debt should be considered in estimating the term of the debt.
- Classification of debt as current or noncurrent should reflect the borrower's anticipated source of repayment and is not necessarily identical to the time period used to establish periodic interest rate. That is, if short-term debt is expected to be used to refinance the debt, then the original debt is current. If FASB Statement No. 6 requirements are met, the debt is noncurrent.
- Debt issuance costs should be amortized over the same period used in interest cost determination.
- If debt is redeemed at par value before estimated maturity, the excess interest expense accrual is an adjustment to interest expense and is not an extraordinary item.

The first point just mentioned was affected, however, by FASB Statement No. 133, as amended. Under Statement No. 133, the term-extending provisions of the debt instrument should be analyzed to determine whether those provisions constitute an embedded derivative that warrants separate accounting as a derivative.

(iii) Accounting Implications of Indexed Debt Instruments. The EITF Task Force (in EITF Issue No. 86-28) considered debt instruments with both contingent and guaranteed payments. The contingent payments were linked to the price of specific commodities or a specific index. In some instances, the right to the contingent payment is separable from the debt instrument.
The issues are:

- Should the proceeds be allocated between the debt liability and the investor's right to receive the contingent payment?
- How should the issuer account for changes in the underlying commodity or index values?

The EITF reached this consensus:
If the investor's right to a contingent payment is separable, the issuer should allocate the proceeds between the debt instrument and the right. The premium or discount on the debt instrument should be accounted for in accordance with APB Opinion No. 21. No consensus was reached on situations where the contingent payments are not separable.

Whether there is any initial allocation of proceeds to the contingent payment or not, if the index changes so that the issuer would have to pay the investor a contingent payment at maturity, the issuer must recognize a liability. The amount recognized is measured by the extent to which the contingent payment exceeds the amount, if any, originally allocated to that feature. When no proceeds are originally allocated to the contingent payment, the additional liability is an adjustment to the carrying amount of the debt.

This EITF Issue was effectively nullified prospectively by FASB Statement No. 133 (ASC 815). The consensus would not apply to debt instruments that contain an embedded derivative that is accounted for under Statement No. 133. However, Statement No. 133 permits entities not to account separately for certain derivatives embedded in pre-1998 or pre-1999 hybrid instruments, including indexed debt instruments.

(iv) Accounting for Derivative Financial Instruments Indexed to, and Potentially Settled in, a Company's Own Stock. EITF Issue No. 00-19 (ASC 815) codified a consensus reached in earlier EITF Issues concerning a situation in which notes are issued with detachable warrants that include a put. The notes mature in about seven years. The detachable warrants give the holder the right to purchase 6,250 shares of stock for $75 per share and also the right to sell back (put) these warrants to the firm for $2,010 per share at a date several months after the notes mature.
The issues are:

- Should the proceeds received at date of issuance be allocated between the debt and warrant?
- Should the carrying amount of the warrants be accrued to the put price?

- If there is an accrual, should the charge be to interest expense or immediately to retained earnings associated with the equity instrument?

The EITF's consensus is:

The proceeds should be allocated between warrants and debt based on their relative fair values, and the discount should be amortized using the effective interest rate approach in APB Opinion No. 21.

(v) Convertible Bonds with Issuer Option to Settle for Cash Upon Conversion.   EITF Issue No. 90-19 considered a situation in which a company issues a debt instrument convertible into a fixed number of shares of stock. Upon conversion, the issuer is either required or has the option to satisfy part or all of the obligation in cash. If the instrument is not converted, cash is paid by the issuer at maturity. Three variants of this transaction are:

1. Upon conversion, the issuer is required to satisfy the entire obligation in cash.
2. Upon conversion, the issuer may satisfy the entire obligation in either cash or stock.
3. Upon conversion, the issuer must satisfy the accreted value in cash and may satisfy the conversion spread in either cash or stock.

The Task Force addressed whether under these three variants the issuer should separately account for the debt obligation and the conversion feature. It also addressed the accounting for the conversion spread (excess of conversion value over accreted amount).

This Issue was subsequently affected by FASB Statement No. 133 (ASC 815), which would require the embedded derivative in transaction 1 to be separated from the debt host contract and accounted for separately as a derivative instrument. Transactions 2 and 3 should continue to be accounted for in accordance with the consensus, which was that:

- Combined accounting for the conversion feature and debt obligation is appropriate.
- Transaction 2 should be accounted for as conventional convertible debt.
- Transaction 3 should be accounted for similar to indexed debt obligations. The issuer should adjust the carrying amount of the instrument in each reporting period to reflect the current stock price, but not below the accreted value of the instrument. Adjustments to the carrying amount are included currently in income and not spread over future periods.

(b) ASSET-SECURITIZATION TRANSACTIONS.   Under FASB Statement No. 140 (ASC 860), a transfer of financial assets (or all or a portion of a financial asset) in which the transferor surrenders control over those financial assets is accounted for as a sale to the extent that consideration other than beneficial interests in the transferred assets is received in exchange. The transferor has surrendered control over transferred assets if and only if all of the next conditions are met:

- The transferred assets have been isolated from the transferor—put presumptively beyond the reach of the transferor and its creditors, even in bankruptcy or other receivership.
- Each transferee (or, if the transferee is a qualifying special-purpose entity, each holder of its beneficial interests) has the right to pledge or exchange the assets (or beneficial interests) it received, and no condition both constrains the transferee (or holder) from taking advantage of its right to pledge or exchange and provides more than a trivial benefit to the transferor.
- The transferor does not maintain effective control over the transferred assets through (1) an agreement that both entitles and obligates the transferor to repurchase or redeem them before their maturity or (2) the ability to unilaterally cause the holder to return specific assets, other than through a "clean-up call."

If a transfer of financial assets does not meet criteria for sales recognition, the transferor accounts for the transaction as a secured borrowing with a pledge of collateral.

18.12 FAIR VALUE OPTION

In an important move toward fair value accounting, the FASB in Statement No. 159 (ASC 825-10-25) permits companies to select fair value accounting for any monetary asset or liability account. The implication is that for such optioned items, changes in the market value of these items (gains and losses) will be reflected in earnings in each period. This election is a one-time initial election by security or by issue; therefore, once the election is made, it cannot be changed for that specific instrument. However, since the election is made by individual instrument, the financial statements might reflect an aggregation of financial assets or liabilities using different accounting principles. The permission to use this principle includes investments carried under the equity method of accounting.

18.13 INTERNATIONAL PERSPECTIVE

There are some important differences between International Accounting Standards (IAS)[7] and (U. S.) GAAP in the area of current and long-term liabilities. Over time, convergence is planned; however, these differences can result in significantly different presentations and amounts in the financial statements. A joint project to address instruments with attributes of both liabilities and equity is ongoing.

Issues of differing presentation include:

- Many IAS statements present long-term liabilities before current liabilities in the statements.
- Some entities, such as financial institutions, may present liabilities in the order of their liquidity.
- IAS uses the term *provisions* to describe estimated liabilities.
- If there is an agreement in place by the date of the financial statements to refinance the current portion of long-term debt, then that debt would be classified as long term. Under GAAP, the date by which the agreement needs to be in place is the issue date of the financial statements.
- Bonds are presented *net* of any premium or discount. The accounts premium and discount are not used.
- Under IAS, convertible debt is apportioned to the liability and equity sections of the balance sheet based on its relative fair value.

Issues of differing accounting and measurement include:

- IFRS does not allow for applying the fair value option principle to equity investments.
- Estimated liabilities under IAS are based on the best estimate (generally the middle point of a range) whereas GAAP uses the lower end of the range,
- Contingent liabilities are recognized under IAS if they are "more likely than not" (e.g., more than 50 percent likely) to be realized. GAAP suggests the threshold of "probable" for recognition.
- IAS is considered more permissive than GAAP in recognizing contingent gains.
- Bond issue costs under IAS reduce the carrying amount of the bonds. Under GAAP they are treated as an asset. This treatment difference will impact the effective interest rate of the securities.
- IAS does not have specialized accounting guidance, such as that available under GAAP for environmental liabilities.

---

[7] See IAS 1, *Presentation of Financial Statements*, and IAS 37, *Provisions, Contingent Liabilities and Contingent Assets.*

18.14 PREDECESSOR LITERATURE AND OTHER REFERENCE MATERIALS

Accounting Principles Board. APB Opinion No. 10, *Omnibus Opinion—1966.* New York: AICPA, 1966.

_____. APB Opinion No. 14, *Accounting for Convertible Debt and Debt Issued with Stock Purchase Warrants.* New York: AICPA, 1969.

_____. APB Opinion No. 21, *Interest on Receivables and Payables.* New York: AICPA, 1971.

_____. APB Opinion No. 26, *Early Extinguishment of Debt.* New York: AICPA, 1972.

Accounting Standards Executive Committee. Statement of Position No. 94-6, *Disclosure of Certain Significant Risks and Uncertainties.* New York: AICPA, 1994.

_____. Statement of Position 96-1, *Environmental Remediation Liabilities.* New York: AICPA, 1996.

_____. Statement of Position 97-1, *Accounting by Participating Mortgage Loan Borrowers.* New York: AICPA, 1997.

Bragg, S. M. *Wiley GAAP 2012: Interpretation and Application of Generally Accepted Accounting Principles.* Hoboken, NJ: John Wiley & Sons, 2011.

AICPA. Committee on Accounting Procedure. Accounting Research Bulletin No. 43, Chapter 24, "Working Capital." New York: AICPA, 1953.

Financial Accounting Standards Board. Author Interpretation No. 8, *Classification of a Short-Term Obligation Repaid Prior to Being Replaced by a Long-Term Security.* Stamford, CT: Author, 1976.

_____. Author Interpretation No. 14, *Reasonable Estimation of the Amount of a Loss.* Stamford, CT: Author, 1976.

_____. Author Interpretation No. 39, *Offsetting of Amounts Related to Certain Contracts (an Interpretation of APB Opinion No. 10 and Author Statement No. 105).* Norwalk, CT: Author, 1993.

_____. Author Interpretation No. 41, *Offsetting of Amounts Related to Certain Repurchase and Reverse Repurchase Agreements (an Interpretation of APB Opinion No. 10 and a Modification of Author Interpretation No. 39).* Norwalk, CT: Author, 1994.

_____. Author Interpretation No. 45, *Guarantor's Accounting and Disclosure Requirements for Guarantees, Including Indirect Guarantees of Indebtedness of Others—an Interpretation of Author Statements No. 5, 57, and 107 and Rescission of Author Interpretation No. 34.* Norwalk, CT: Author, 2002.

_____. Author Interpretation No. 47, *Accounting for Conditional Asset Retirement Obligations.* Norwalk, CT: Author, 2005.

_____. Author Staff Position No. EITF 00-19-1, *Application of EITF Issue No. 00-19 to Freestanding Financial Instruments Originally Issued as Employee Compensation.* Norwalk, CT: Author, 2005.

_____. Author Staff Position No. FAS 129-1, *Disclosure Requirements under Author Statement No. 129, Disclosure of Information about Capital Structure, Relating to Contingently Convertible Securities.* Norwalk, CT: Author, 2004.

_____. Author Staff Position No. FAS 146-1, *Determining Whether a One-Time Termination Benefit Offered in Connection with an Exit or Disposal Activity Is, in Substance, an Enhancement to an Ongoing Benefit Arrangement.* Norwalk, CT: Author, 2003.

_____. Author Staff Position No. FAS 150-2, *Accounting for Mandatorily Redeemable Shares Requiring Redemption by Payment of an Amount that Differs from the Book Value of Those Shares, under Author Statement No. 150, Accounting for Certain Financial Instruments with Characteristics of both Liabilities and Equity.* Norwalk, CT: Author, 2003.

_____. Author Staff Position No. FAS 150-3, *Effective Date, Disclosures, and Transition for Mandatorily Redeemable Financial Instruments of Certain Nonpublic Entities and Certain Mandatorily Redeemable Non-controlling Interests under Author Statement No. 150, Accounting for Certain Financial Instruments with Characteristics of Both Liabilities and Equity.* Norwalk, CT: Author, 2003.

_____. Author Staff Position No. FAS 150-4, Issuers' *Accounting for Employee Stock Ownership Plans under Author Statement No. 150, Accounting for Certain Financial Instruments with Characteristics of both Liabilities and Equity.* Norwalk, CT: Author, 2003.

_____. Author Staff Position No. FAS 150-5, *Issuers' Accounting under Statement 150 for Freestanding Warrants and Other Similar Instruments on Shares That Are Redeemable.* Norwalk, CT: Author, 2005.

_____. Author Staff Position No. FIN 45-1, *Accounting for Intellectual Property Infringement Indemnifications under Author Interpretation No. 45, Guarantor's Accounting and Disclosure Requirements for Guarantees, Including Indirect Guarantees of Indebtedness of Others.* Norwalk, CT: Author, 2003.

_____. Author Staff Position No. FIN 45-2, *Whether Author Interpretation No. 45, Guarantor's Accounting and Disclosure Requirements for Guarantees, Including Indirect Guarantees of Indebtedness of Others, Provides Support for Subsequently Accounting for a Guarantor's Liability at Fair Value*. Norwalk, CT: Author, 2003.

_____. Author Staff Position No. FIN 45-3, *Application of Author Interpretation No. 45 to Minimum Revenue Guarantees Granted to a Business or Its Owners*. Norwalk, CT: Author, 2005.

_____. Discussion Memorandum, *Distinguishing between Liability and Equity Instruments and Accounting for Instruments with Characteristics of Both*. Norwalk, CT: Author, 1990.

_____. EITF Issue No. 84-5, *Sale of Marketable Securities with a Put Option*. Stamford, CT: Author, 1984.

_____. EITF Issue No. 85-29, *Convertible Bonds with a Premium Put*. Stamford, CT: Author, 1985.

_____. EITF Issue No. 85-30, *Sale of Marketable Securities at a Gain with a Put Option*. Stamford, CT: Author, 1985.

_____. EITF Issue No. 85-40, *Comprehensive Review of Sales of Marketable Securities with Put Arrangements*. Stamford, CT: Author, 1985.

_____. EITF Issue No. 86-15, *Increasing-Rate Debt*. Stamford, CT: Author, 1986.

_____. EITF Issue No. 86-28, *Accounting Implications of Indexed Debt Instruments* Stamford, CT: Author, 1986.

_____. EITF Issue No. 86-30, *Classification of Obligations When a Violation Is Waived by the Creditor*. Stamford, CT: Author, 1986.

_____. EITF Issue No. 88-11, *Allocation of Recorded Investment When a Loan or Part of a Loan Is Sold*. Norwalk, CT: FASB, 1988.

_____. EITF Issue No. 89-2, *Maximum Guarantees on Transfers of Receivables with Recourse*. Norwalk, CT: Author, 1989.

_____. EITF Issue No. 90-19, *Convertible Bonds with Issuer Option to Settle for Cash Upon Conversion*. Norwalk, CT: Author, 1991.

_____. EITF Issue No. 91-2, *Debtors Accounting for Forfeiture of Real Estate Subject to a Nonrecourse Mortgage*. Norwalk, CT: Author, 1991.

_____. EITF Issue No. 92-2, *Measuring Loss Accruals by Transferors for Transfers of Receivables With Recourse*. Norwalk, CT: Author, 1992.

_____. EITF Issue No. 94-3, *Liability Recognition for Certain Employee Termination Benefits and Other Costs to Exit an Activity (including Certain Costs Incurred in a Restructuring)*. Norwalk, CT: Author, 1994.

_____. EITF Issue No. 96-19, *Debtor's Accounting for a Modification or Exchange of Debt Instruments*. Norwalk, CT: Author, 1997.

_____. EITF Issue No. 98-5, *Accounting for Convertible Securities with Beneficial Conversion Features or Contingently Adjustable Conversion Ratios*. Norwalk, CT: Author, 1998.

_____. EITF Issue No. 00-19, *Accounting for Derivative Financial Instruments Indexed to, and Potentially Settled in, a Company's Own Stock*. Norwalk, CT: Author, 2000.

_____. EITF Issue 00-27, *Application of Issue No. 98-5 to Certain Convertible Instruments*. Norwalk, CT: Author, 2000.

_____. EITF Issue No. 02-4, *Determining Whether a Debtor's Modification or Exchange of Debt Instruments is within the Scope of Author Statement No. 15*. Norwalk, CT: Author, 2002.

_____. Statement of Financial Accounting Concepts No. 6, *Elements of Financial Statements*. Stamford, CT: Author, 1985.

_____. Statement of Financial Accounting Concepts No. 7, *Using Cash Flow Information and Present Value in Accounting Measurements*. Norwalk, CT: Author, 2000.

_____. Statement of Financial Accounting Standards No. 5, *Accounting for Contingencies, Stamford*. CT: Author, 1975.

_____. Statement of Financial Accounting Standards No. 6, *Classification of Short-Term Obligations Expected to Be Refinanced*. Stamford, CT: Author, 1975.

_____. Statement of Financial Accounting Standards No. 13, *Accounting for Leases*. Stamford, CT: Author, 1976.

_____. Statement of Financial Accounting Standards No. 15, *Accounting by Debtors and Creditors for Troubled Debt Restructurings*. Stamford, CT: Author, 1977.

_____ . Statement of Financial Accounting Standards No. 37, *Balance Sheet Classification of Deferred Income Taxes*. Stamford, CT: Author, 1980.

_____ . Statement of Financial Accounting Standards No. 43, *Accounting for Compensated Absences*. Stamford, CT: Author, 1980.

_____ . Statement of Financial Accounting Standards No. 47, *Disclosure of Long-Term Obligations*. Stamford, CT: Author, 1981.

_____ . Statement of Financial Accounting Standards No. 49, *Accounting for Product Financing Arrangements.* Stamford, CT: Author, 1981.

_____ . Statement of Financial Accounting Standards No. 78, *Classification of Obligations That Are Callable by the Creditor*. Stamford, CT: Author, 1983.

_____ . Statement of Financial Accounting Standards No. 107, *Disclosures about Fair Value of Financial Instruments*. Norwalk, CT: Author, 1991.

_____ . Statement of Financial Accounting Standards No. 109, *Accounting for Income Taxes*. Stamford, CT: Author, 1991.

_____ . Statement of Financial Accounting Standards No. 126, *Exemption from Certain Required Disclosures about Financial Instruments for Certain Nonpublic Entities*. Norwalk, CT: Author, 1996.

_____ . Statement of Financial Accounting Standards No. 129, *Disclosure of Information about Capital Structure*. Norwalk, CT: Author, 1997.

_____ . Statement of Financial Accounting Standards No. 140, *Accounting for Transfers and Servicing of Financial Assets and Extinguishments of Liabilities*. Norwalk, CT: Author, 2000.

_____ . Statement of Financial Accounting Standards No. 145, *Rescission of Author Statements No. 4, 44, and 64, Amendment of Author Statement No. 13, and Technical Corrections*. Norwalk, CT: Author, 2002.

_____ . Statement of Financial Accounting Standards No. 146, *Accounting for Costs Associated with Exit or Disposal Activities*. Norwalk, CT: Author, 2002.

_____ . Statement of Financial Accounting Standards No. 150, *Accounting for Certain Financial Instruments with Characteristics of both Liabilities and Equity*. Norwalk, CT: Author, 2003.

_____ . Technical Bulletin No. 80-1, *Early Extinguishment of Debt through Exchange for Common or Preferred Stock*. Stamford, CT: Author, 1980.

_____ . Technical Bulletin No. 80-2, *Classification of Debt Restructurings by Debtors and Creditors*. Stamford, CT: Author, 1980.

_____ . Technical Bulletin No. 81-6, *Applicability of Author Statement 15 to Debtors in Bankruptcy Situations*. Stamford, CT: Author, 1981.

Heath, L. *Financial Reporting and the Evaluation of Solvency*, Accounting Research Monograph No. 3. New York: AICPA, 1978.

International Accounting Standards Committee. *Framework for the Preparation and Presentation of Financial Statements*. London: Author, 1989.

Lorenson, L. *Accounting for Liabilities*, Accounting Research Monograph No. 4 New York: AICPA, 1992.

Schroeder, A. D., and W. S. Upton. A *Fresh Look at Statement 5, Author Status Report No. 244*. Norwalk, CT: FASB.

Securities and Exchange Commission. *Codification of Financial Reporting Policies*. Washington, DC: Author, Current.

_____ . Regulation S-X, *Form and Content of and Requirements for Financial Statements*. Washington, DC: Author, Current.

_____ . Staff Accounting Bulletin No. 77, *Allocation of Debt Issue Costs in a Business Combination*. Washington, DC: Author, 1988.

_____ . Staff Accounting Bulletin No. 92, *Accounting and Disclosures Relating to Loss Contingencies*. Washington, DC: Author, 1993.

_____ . Staff Accounting Bulletin No. 94, *Recognition of a Gain or Loss on Early Extinguishment of Debt*. Washington, DC: Author, 1995.

Storey, R., and S. Storey. *The Framework of Financial Accounting Concepts and Standards*, Special Report. Norwalk, CT: FASB, 1998.

CHAPTER 19

SHAREHOLDERS' EQUITY

George I. Victor, CPA
Giambalvo, Stalzer & Company, CPAs, P.C.

19.1 THE CORPORATION

(a) DEFINITION.   A *corporation* is a statutory form of organization created under rules promulgated by the legislature of the state in which it is incorporated. It is "an artificial being, invisible, intangible, and existing only in contemplation of law. Being the mere creature of law, it possesses only those properties which the charter of its creation confers upon it."[1] Thus, a corporation is a distinct and unique entity, separate from the personal affairs and other interests of its owners.

(b) ADVANTAGES OF CORPORATE FORM. The important advantages of doing business as a corporation are:

- Continuity of life
- Limited liability for owners
- Ease of transferability of ownership

The combination of these advantages provides the corporation with the ability to raise large sums of capital. It is the sources of this capital and the claims on it that are of concern to the accountant.

(c) OWNERS' INTERESTS. Since the corporation is separate and distinct from its owners, owners merely have claims against its net assets. These claims and their nature and origin are presented in the shareholders' equity section of the corporate balance sheet. Shareholders' equity generally comprises three broad categories:

1. Capital stock or legal capital
2. Additional paid-in capital
3. Retained earnings (deficit)

The reporting of transactions affecting these classifications is influenced by legal as well as by accounting principles.

(d) CERTIFICATE OF INCORPORATION. In order to form a corporation, incorporators—usually at least three—file articles of incorporation with the secretary of state in the state of incorporation. The Model Business Corporation Act (MBCA), prepared by the American Bar Association and adopted in a majority of states, lists in Section 54 the required provisions of the articles. Those provisions of relevance to this section are listed next:

- The aggregate number of shares which the corporation shall have authority to issue; if such shares are to consist of one class only, the par value of each of such shares, or a statement that all of such shares are without par value; or, if such shares are to be divided into classes, the number of shares of each class, and a statement of the par value of the shares of each such class or that such shares are to be without par value.
- If the shares are to be divided into classes, the designation of each class and a statement of the preferences, limitations and relative rights in respect of the shares of each class.

When the secretary of state determines that the articles of incorporation conform to law, he or she issues a certificate of incorporation, after which corporate life commences.

19.2 SHARES OF STOCK

(a) CERTIFICATES REPRESENTING SHARES. Shares of a corporation are represented by stock certificates that include these 10 items:

1. State in which the corporation was organized
2. Date of issuance of the stock
3. Name of the person to whom issued

---

[1] *The Trustees of Dartmouth College v. Woodward,* 4 Wheaton 518; 4 L. Ed. 629 (1819).

4. Certificate number

5. Class of shares, and the designation of the series, if any, which the certificate represents

6. Par value of each share represented by the certificate, or a statement that the shares are without par value

7. Name of the issuing corporation

8. Number of shares represented by the certificate

9. Number and classes of shares authorized

10. Rights of each class of stock

Certificates for shares may not be issued until the full amount of consideration has been received; however, New York and other states provide an exception to this rule for shares purchased under employee stock option plans.[2] Neither promissory notes nor future services constitute payment or part payment for shares of a corporation.

Shares of stock are classified as either preferred or common with subclassifications within each of these two major classifications.

(b) COMMON STOCK.   A corporation has the power to create and issue the number of shares for the various classes of stock stated in its certificate of incorporation. Holders of shares have the right to vote, the right to share in profits through dividend distributions, and the right to share in assets distributed in full or partial liquidation. Traditionally, common shareholders had *preemptive* rights, such as the right to maintain their proportionate interest when more shares are issued. More recently, however, the cost of satisfying this requirement has led many corporations to eliminate it. The certificate of incorporation may limit these rights; however, limitation of the rights of any class is precluded unless one class has no such limitations.

Preferred stock generally contains limitations of all of these rights. Because of these limitations, the holders are given various preferences as to dividends and in liquidation. Common stock contains no limitations as to voting, dividend distributions, or liquidation distributions. However, the shares represent residual interests; preferred shares must receive dividends first, and in liquidation all obligations, including those to preferred shareholders, must be satisfied before the common shareholders receive anything.

Generally, a corporation has only one class of common stock. However, some corporations, such as Ford Motor Co., have two or more classes of common stock with each class reflecting different voting or dividend rights.

(c) PREFERRED STOCK.   Preferred stock is given preference over common stock as to distributions of corporate earnings and distributions of assets in the event of corporate liquidations. Sometimes, in involuntary liquidations, the preference is in excess of the par or stated value of the shares. Financial Accounting Standard (FAS) No. 129, *Disclosure of Information About Capital Structure* (Financial Accounting Standards Board [FASB] Accounting Standard Codification [ASC] 505-10), states:

> An entity that issues preferred stock (or other senior stock) that has a preference in involuntary liquidation considerably in excess of the par or stated value of the shares shall disclose the liquidation preference of the stock (the relationship between the preference in liquidation and the par or stated value of the shares). That disclosure shall be made in the equity section of the statement of financial position in the aggregate, either parenthetically or "in short," rather than on a per-share basis or through disclosure in the notes. In exchange for these preferences, preferred shareholders usually relinquish certain rights, such as the right to vote.

Preferred stock generally has a fixed dividend rate and usually has a par value of $100. In some aspects it is similar to a bond; however, dividends on preferred stock are not deductible for income

---

[2] New York Business Corporation Law, § 505(e).

tax purposes, whereas interest on bonds is tax deductible. Therefore, capital obtained through the issuance of preferred stock is expensive. Nevertheless, corporations may use this method at times because of these three circumstances:

1. A high debt-to-equity ratio may adversely affect bond ratings.
2. Investors, such as pension funds, prefer this type of investment.
3. Banks and insurance companies that desire to minimize the risks inherent in equity securities favor preferred stock. Although an investment in bonds minimizes risks even further, interest is fully taxable to most corporate investors, whereas 70 percent of preferred dividends are excluded from corporate taxable income.

In recent years, preferred stock has acquired even more of the characteristics of bonds because of mandatory redemption provisions.

(i) Preferred Stock Subject to Mandatory Redemption. A corporation, at its option, may redeem its stock at the market price or at a price stated in the stock certificate. However, recently corporations have issued preferred stock with mandatory redemption provisions. The FASB has not provided guidance as to how the issuing corporation should classify this type of stock. It has, however, in Statement of Financial Accounting Standards (SFAS) No. 129, *Disclosure of Information About Capital Structure* (FASB ASC 505-10), states that for each of the five years following the date of the balance sheet presented, "an entity that issues redeemable stock shall disclose the amount of redemption requirements, separately by issue or combined, for all issues of capital stock that are redeemable at fixed or determinable prices on fixed or determinable dates."

(ii) Classification Requirements for Mandatory Redeemable Preferred Stock. The FASB has been silent about classification requirements of the issues of mandatory redeemable preferred stock. It did state, however, in SFAS No. 115, *Accounting for Certain Investments in Debt and Equity Securities* (FASB ASC 310-20), that an equity security "does not include . . . preferred stock that by its terms either must be redeemed by the issuing enterprise or is redeemable at the option of the investor."

The Securities and Exchange Commission (SEC), however, has been rigorous in its requirements for issuers of mandatory redeemable preferred stock. In 1979, the SEC amended Regulation S-X to modify the financial statement presentation of preferred stocks subject to mandatory redemption requirements or whose redemption is outside the control of the issuers. Companies having these types of securities outstanding are required to present separately in their balance sheets amounts applicable to these three general classes of securities:

1. Preferred stocks subject to mandatory redemption requirements or whose redemption is outside the control of the issuer
2. Preferred stocks that are not redeemable or are redeemable solely at the option of the issuer
3. Common stocks

A general heading, "Stockholders' Equity," is prohibited as is presentation of a combined total for equity securities, inclusive of mandatorily redeemable preferred stock.

Companies have been reporting mandatory redeemable preferred stock on their balance sheets between the last liability account and the equity section. The SEC suggests that in these circumstances, the equity section be captioned "Non-Redeemable Preferred Stocks, Common Stocks, and Other Stockholders' Equity."

In addition, the SEC requires disclosure in the notes to financial statements. The note should be captioned "Redeemable Preferred Stocks" and should include (1) terms of redemption, (2) five-year maturity date, and (3) changes in these securities. Aggregate redemption amounts are required to be presented on the face of the balance sheet.

(iii) Dividends on Mandatory Redeemable Preferred Stock.   The SEC has not established whether this type of preferred stock is, in fact, debt; therefore, there is no change in the calculation of debt equity ratios. In addition, dividends paid on these securities are accounted for in the same manner as dividends paid on other equity securities—a reduction of retained earnings.

(iv) Carrying Amount of Mandatory Redeemable Preferred Stock.   When mandatory redeemable preferred stock is issued, it should be recorded at its fair value at date of issue. If the fair value of the security at date of issue is less than the mandatory redemption amount, its carrying amount should be increased by periodic accretions, using the interest method, so that the carrying amount will equal the redemption amount at the mandatory redemption date. The corresponding entry for the periodic accretion is a reduction of retained earnings.

(v) Callable Preferred Stock.   Since preferred stock is a burden of which corporations want to be relieved, many preferred issues contain a callable feature. This feature gives the corporation the right to call in the preferred stock at a stated redemption price, generally in excess of the par value or issue price of the stock. This excess is to compensate the owner for his involuntary loss. When preferred stock is called, all dividend arrearages must be satisfied.

SFAS No. 129 (FASB ASC 505-10) requires these disclosures: either on the face of the balance sheet or in the notes to financial statements the aggregate or per share amounts at which preferred shares may be called or are subject to redemption through sinking fund operations or otherwise

(vi) Cumulative Preferred Stock.   Generally, preferred stock contains a cumulative provision whereby dividends omitted in previous years must be paid before dividends on other outstanding shares may be paid. Inasmuch as dividends do not become a corporate liability until declared, dividend arrearages should be disclosed.

(vii) Fully Participating Preferred Stock.   Participating preferred stock is entitled to dividends in excess of its specified rate after the common stock has received the same rate. Preferred stock may be fully or partially participating. If it is fully participating with a 5 percent dividend rate, then, after the common stockholders receive 5 percent dividends, both the common and the preferred shareholders receive additional dividends on a pro rata basis. The dividend rate is based on the par values of the stocks, and the allocation of excess dividends between common and preferred stockholders is based on the total par values of the classes of stock involved.

(viii) Partially Participating Preferred Stock.   If preferred stock is partially participating, it shares with common stock dividends in excess of its specified rate, limited by its participation percentage. If 5 percent preferred stock is partially participating up to a maximum of an additional 10 percent, it and the common stock may receive up to 15 percent on par value; thereafter the common shareholders receive all additional dividends.

Participating preferred stock is not common today; the overwhelming majority of preferred stock currently issued is nonparticipating.

(ix) Convertible Preferred Stock.   Convertible preferred stock may be converted into common shares at a specified ratio at the option of the shareholder. This type of stock is issued in order to make the preferred stock more attractive to investors while at the same time reducing the dividend rate. Under certain conditions, convertible preferred is considered to be a common stock equivalent for the computation of earnings per share.

When conversion occurs, a realignment of the components of stockholders' equity takes place. This realignment may result in an increase in additional paid-in capital or a decrease in retained earnings; it may not result in an increase in retained earnings.

At the time of conversion, the company must reduce its preferred stock and additional paid-in capital-preferred stock accounts for the amount originally received for the stock. This amount is then credited to the common stock and additional paid-in capital-common stock accounts. For example, if a $100 par value preferred share, convertible into six shares of $1 par value common, was issued at $103, the journal entry to record the conversion is:

Preferred stock—$100 par value	$100	
Capital in excess of par value—preferred stock	3	
Common stock—$1 par value		$ 6
Capital in excess of par value—common stock		97

If, however, the par value of the common stock was $20, the journal entry to record the conversion would be:

Preferred stock—$100 par value	$ 100	
Capital in excess of par value—preferred stock	3	
Retained earnings	17	
Common stock—$20 par value		$120

(x) Increasing-Rate Preferred Stock—Staff Accounting Bulletin Topic 5.Q. Staff Accounting Bulletin (SAB) Topic 5.Q (FASB ASC 22510) expresses the staff's views regarding accounting for increasing-rate preferred stock. Essentially, increasing-rate preferred stock is cumulative preferred and carries either a zero dividend rate in the early years after issuance or a low dividend rate, which increases over time to a higher "permanent" rate. The higher dividend rate is usually a market rate for dividend yield given the characteristics of the preferred stock, other than scheduled cash dividend entitlements (voting rights, liquidation preference, etc.), as well as the registrant's financial condition and future prospects. Therefore, the issue price is well below the amount that could be expected, based on the future permanent dividend.

Balance Sheet Treatment. The SEC Staff's view is that the increasing-rate preferred stock should be recorded initially at its fair value at the date of issuance. Thereafter, the carrying amount should be increased periodically.

Amortization of Discount. It is unacceptable to recognize the dividend costs according to their stated schedules. Any discount due to the absence of dividends, or gradually increasing dividends, for an initial period represents prepaid, unstated dividend cost. The discount is based on the price the stock would have sold for had the permanent dividend been in effect from the date of issuance. The discount should be amortized over the periods preceding commencement of the perpetual dividend by charging imputed dividend cost against retained earnings and increasing the carrying amount of the preferred stock by a corresponding amount.

Computation of Discount and Amortization. The discount at the time of issuance should be computed as the present value of the difference between (1) any dividends that will be payable in the periods preceding commencement of the perpetual dividend and (2) the perpetual dividend amount for a corresponding number of periods, discounted at a market rate for dividend yield on preferred stocks that are comparable (other than with respect to dividend payment schedules) from an investment standpoint.

The amortization in each period should be the amount that, together with any stated dividend for the period, results in a constant rate of effective cost relative to the carrying amount of the preferred stock (the market rate that was used to compute the discount). The SEC Staff believes that this approach is consistent with APB Opinion No. 21, *Interest on Receivables and Payables* (FASB ASC 835-30).

The imputed dividends would be considered an adjustment of net income in the computation of earnings per common share during the amortization period.

If stated dividends on an increasing-rate preferred stock are variable, computations of the initial discount and subsequent amortization should be based on the value of the applicable index at the date of issuance and should not be affected by subsequent changes in the index.

(xi) Voting Rights of Preferred Stock. Each share of stock, regardless of classification, is entitled to one vote. The corporation may, however, in its articles of incorporation, deny voting rights to any class of stock. This usually is done with preferred stock.

The denial of voting rights to preferred stock is generally contingent on the maintenance of dividends. The New York Stock Exchange (NYSE) will deny listing to any preferred issue that does not give holders the right to elect at least two members of the board of directors if six quarterly dividends are passed. Some companies will make the next disclosure in the financial statements:

Holders of the series of preferred stock will not have voting rights, except that if six quarterly dividends shall be in arrears in part or in full,... holders of preferred stock voting separately as a class... will be entitled to elect two directors of the Company until such time as all such dividends... in arrears on all outstanding shares of preferred stock have been satisfied.

(d) PAR AND NO PAR VALUE STOCK. Prior to 1912, all shares of corporate stock contained a par value—an arbitrarily assigned amount below which the stock could not be issued. The function of the par value was to provide an upper limit to the shareholder's liability, while at the same time indicating to creditors the minimum amount of permanent capital of the corporation.

In the late 1800s and early 1900s, corporations generally issued stock with high par values. However, as corporations split their stock, par values declined. In addition, many states assess corporate taxes based on the par value of a company's stock, thereby providing an incentive for low par value stock.

In 1912, New York State enacted a law permitting corporations to issue no par value stock. Most states quickly followed New York and enacted similar laws. When no par value stock is issued, the board of directors may give it a stated value after which, for accounting purposes, it is reported in a manner similar to par value stock.

(e) RECORDING THE ISSUANCE OF STOCK. When par value stock is issued at par value, the stock account is increased by the amount of the proceeds. When par value stock is issued at a price in excess of par value, the excess is included in the additional paid-in capital of that class of stock. Section 18 of the MBCA states that shares may be issued for not less than their par values; however, in states where this is not mandated, shares may be issued for a price below par value and the difference, the *discount,* is reported as a deduction in the stockholders' equity section of the balance sheet. The discount is the amount the stockholders who paid less than par value for the stock may be forced to ultimately pay to the corporation.

When no par value stock with a stated value is issued, the consideration in excess of the stated value increases the additional paid-in capital for that class of stock. When no par value stock without a stated value is issued, the entire proceeds are included in the account of that class of stock.

(f) STATED CAPITAL. Section 2(j) of the MBCA defines *stated capital* as the sum of these three items:

1. The par value of all shares of the corporation having a par value that have been issued
2. The amount of the consideration received by the corporation for all shares of the corporation without par value that have been issued, except such part of the consideration therefrom as may have been allocated to capital surplus in a manner permitted by law
3. Such amounts not included in items 1 and 2 as have been transferred to stated capital of the corporation, whether upon the issue of shares as a share dividend or otherwise, minus all reductions from such sum as have been effected in a manner permitted by law.

Thus, the stated or legal capital of the corporation represents the permanent investment of the shareholders; it is that portion of the net assets that cannot be distributed legally to stockholders prior to partial or total liquidation.

(g) BALANCE SHEET PRESENTATION. Next is the shareowners' equity section of Eastman Kodak Company, a company with one class of par value stock outstanding, as presented in its December 27, 1987, balance sheet.

(dollars in thousands)

	1987	1986
Shareowners' equity:		
Common stock, par value $2.50 per share	$ 933	$ 622
500,000,000 shares authorized; issued		
at December 27, 1987—373,379,570		
at December 28, 1986—248,705,111		
Additional capital paid or transferred from retained earnings	—	314
Retained earnings	7,139	6,533
	8,072	7,469
Less Treasury stock at cost	2,059	1,081
at December 27, 1987—49,008,666 shares		
at December 28, 1986—34,007,309 shares		
Total shareowners' equity	$6,013	$6,388

The stockholders' equity section of a company with no par value common stock and authorized but unissued preferred stock is presented in the balance sheet as follows:

	20X1	20X0
Stockholders' equity:		
Preferred stock, no par value authorized		
1,000,000 shares, none issued	$ —	$ —
Common stock, no par value, authorized		
8,000,000 shares, shares issued and outstanding of		
2,688,198 in 19X1 and 2,347,074 in 19X0	10,320,000	5,673,000
Retained earnings	19,726,000	17,014,000
Total stockholders' equity	$30,046,000	$22,687,000

Although no preferred stock has been issued, it is reported on the balance sheet. Rule 5-02 of Regulation S-X (FASB ASC 210-10) requires the disclosure of all classes of stock and the number of shares authorized and issued or outstanding, as appropriate. The stockholders' equity section also indicates that the no par value stock does not have a stated value since there is no additional paid-in capital.

The stockholders' equity section of a company with both preferred stock and common stock outstanding is presented in the balance sheet as shown next.

	20X1	20X0
Stockholders' equity:		
Senior preferred stock, without par or stated value		
Authorized 3,000,000 shares, issued and outstanding		
1,600,000 shares, preference in liquidation—$40,000	$ 40,000	
Preferred stock, without par or stated value		
Authorized 1,000,000 shares, issued and outstanding		
204,000 shares, preference in liquidation—$10,200	7,132	$ 7,132
Common stock, par value $1 per share		
Authorized 20,000,000 shares, issued and outstanding		
9,908,000 and 6,024,000 shares respectively	9,908	6,024
Additional paid-in capital	71,370	53,438
Retained earnings	38,925	7,966
Total stockholders' equity	$167,335	$74,560

As required by paragraph 5 of SFAS No. 129 (FASB ASC 505-10):

An entity shall disclose within its financial statements the number of shares issued upon conversion, exercise, or satisfaction of required conditions during at least the most recent annual fiscal period and any subsequent interim period presented.

19.3 ISSUANCE OF STOCK

(a) AUTHORIZED CAPITAL STOCK.   The maximum number of shares of stock a corporation is authorized to issue is specified in its articles of incorporation. However, a corporation may, with stockholder approval, amend its articles to increase the number of its authorized shares.

Rule 5-02 of Regulation S-X of the SEC (FASB ASC 210-10) requires the corporate balance sheet to state, for each class of stock, these four items:

1. Title of the issue
2. Number of shares authorized
3. Number of shares issued or outstanding, as appropriate
4. Dollar amount of the shares issued or outstanding

A company may issue its shares immediately for full consideration, or it may receive payments in installments and not issue its shares until all installments have been collected.

(b) COST OF ISSUING STOCK.   When a corporation issues stock, it incurs certain costs, such as printing of certificates; security registration and listing fees; legal and accounting fees; and commissions, fees, and expenses of its investment bankers and underwriters. SAB Topic 5A (FASB ASC 340–10) states that specific incremental costs directly attributable to a proposed or actual offering of securities may properly be deferred and charged against the gross proceeds of the offering.

Section 507 of the New York Business Corporation Law states:

The reasonable charges and expenses of formation or reorganization of a corporation, and the reasonable expenses of and compensation for the sale of underwriting of its shares may be paid or allowed by the corporation out of consideration received by it in payment for the shares without thereby impairing the fully paid and nonassessable status of such shares.

If a corporation withdraws shares it intended to issue, the costs incurred for the contemplated sale are charged to income in the year of withdrawal. The charge is *not* an extraordinary item.

(c) ISSUANCE OF SHARES FOR CASH.   From an accounting perspective, the par value or stated value of capital serves one purpose only: That amount, and only that amount, appears in the stock account of the corporate records. The excess is included in an appropriate additional paid-in capital account. Thus, if common stock with a par value of $10 is issued for $12 and the consideration is cash, the entry is:

Cash	$12	
Common stock		$10
Capital in excess of par value—common stock		2

The consideration for the issuance of shares may be paid, in whole or in part, in other than cash.

(d) ISSUANCE OF SHARES FOR PROPERTY OR SERVICES.   Under the MBCA, in the absence of fraud, the judgment of the board of directors or the shareholders as to the value of consideration received for shares shall be conclusive. Paragraph 182 of Accounting Principles Board Statement No. 4,

Basic Concepts and Accounting Principles Underlying Financial Statements of Business Enterprises (FASB ASC 740-10), states:

> Measurements of owners' investments are generally based on the fair value of the assets or the discounted present value of liabilities that are transferred. The market value of stock issued may be used to establish an amount at which to record owners' investments but this amount is only an approximation when the fair value of the assets transferred cannot be measured directly.

Thus, when a publicly held corporation issues its stock for property or services, the market value of the stock issued may be used to approximate the fair value of the consideration received. However, a closely held corporation will have to rely on its board of directors to determine the fair value of consideration other than cash received for its stock.

(e) SUBSCRIPTION FOR SHARES. Sale of stock on a subscription basis generally occurs when a closely held corporation sells stock either to outsiders or to employees or when a publicly held corporation offers stock to its employees. When stock is sold on a subscription basis, the full price of the stock is not received and the stock generally is not issued until full payment is made.

(i) Recording Subscription. When stock is sold on a subscription basis, two accounts are set up: subscriptions receivable and capital stock subscribed. For example, if common stock with a par value of $10 is subscribed to for $12, the entry would be:

Subscriptions receivable	$12	
Common stock subscribed		$10
Additional paid-in capital		2

The common stock subscribed account is similar to the common stock account in that only the par value or stated value of the stock is entered in this account. As cash is collected on the subscription, the receivable is reduced, and when the final payment is made, the common stock subscribed account is reduced and the common stock account is increased by a similar amount.

(ii) Balance Sheet Presentation. If common stock subscribed has not been issued, it is still reported on the balance sheet as part of stockholders' equity, either as a separate caption or as part of the common stock with appropriate disclosure.

Subscriptions receivable may be presented in the balance sheet as an asset or as a deduction from stockholders' equity. However, Rule 5-02 of Regulation S-X (FASB ASC 210-10) requires a company to show the total dollar amount of capital shares subscribed but unissued, reduced by subscriptions receivable in the capital shares section of stockholders' equity. The shareholders' equity section of the balance sheet of a company that has stock subscriptions receivable is presented next.

Shareholders' equity:	
Common stock, $.10 per value, authorized	
5,000,000 shares; outstanding 1,769,500 shares subscribed 57,000 shares	$ 182,650
Capital surplus	4,612,598
	4,795,248
Less—Common stock subscriptions receivable	(114,000)
	$4,681,248

The total shares of 1,769,500 outstanding plus 57,000 subscribed equal 1,826,500 shares. This number multiplied by the par value of 10 cents equals the common stock amount of $182,650.

(iii) Defaulted Subscriptions. The disposition of the cash received before default is determined by state law. Under the New York Business Corporation Law, if the subscriber paid at least 50 percent of the subscription price, the shares subscribed for must be offered for sale for cash. The offering price must be sufficient to pay the full balance owed by the subscriber plus all expenses incidental to the sale. Excess proceeds realized must be remitted to the delinquent subscriber.

If less than 50 percent of the subscription price has been paid, or if there is no cash offer sufficient to pay expenses plus the full balance owed by a delinquent subscriber who paid at least 50 percent of the subscription price, the shares subscribed for must be canceled. Under these conditions, payments previously made by the subscriber are forfeited to the corporation and credited to an additional paid-in capital account.

(f) STOCK PREMIUM AND STOCK DISCOUNT.   The accounting treatment for stock issued at a premium is covered in Accounting Terminology Bulletins (ATB) No. 1, *Review and Resume.* Paragraph 66 states:

> These [stockholder] interests include the entire proprietary capital of the enterprise, frequently divided further, largely on the basis of source, as follows:
>
> 1. Capital stock, representing the par or stated value of the shares.
> 2. Capital surplus, representing (a) capital contributed for shares in excess of their par or stated value or (b) capital contributed other than for shares.

In a subsequent paragraph, however, the Bulletin states that the use of the term *surplus* should be discontinued and in its place should be the term *capital contributed for,* or *assigned to, shares in excess of such par on stated value.*

Rule 5-02 of Regulation S-X (FASB ASC 210-10) requires separate captions in the stockholders' equity section for paid-in additional capital and other additional capital.

If stock is issued at a discount, the discount is reported in the balance sheet as a deduction from capital contributed. The discount is a liability of the shareholder to the creditors of the corporation, not to the corporation. The stockholders' equity section of the balance sheet of a company that has issued stock in excess of par value and below par value is shown next.

	20X1	20X0
Stockholders' equity		
Capital stock:		
Preferred—$100 par value, authorized		
260,000 shares, issued 99,817 shares, less discount		
of $1,500,000	$ 8,482,000	$ 8,482,000
Common—$.625 par value, authorized		
7,500,000 shares, issued 5,795,061 shares	3,622,000	3,622,000
Capital in excess of par value	6,246,000	6,246,000
Retained earnings	40,892,000	33,812,000
Less—common stock in treasury,		
311,503 and 328,753 shares respectively	(2,090,000)	(2,206,000)
Total stockholders' equity	$57,152,000	$49,956,000

19.4 COMMON STOCK ADJUSTMENTS

(a) STOCK SPLITS.   Corporations can achieve wider distribution of shares or maintain the market price of shares within a specified range by means of stock splits. Chapter 7B of Accounting Research Bulletins (ARB) No. 43, *Restatement and Revision of Accounting Research Bulletins* (FASB ASC 505–20), defines a split as the issuance

> by a corporation of its own common shares to its common shareholders without consideration and under conditions indicating that such action is prompted mainly by a desire to increase the number of outstanding shares for the purpose of effecting a reduction in their unit market price and thereby, of obtaining wider distribution and improved marketability of the shares.

(i) Split with Change in Par Value. Generally, a stock split is executed by changing the par value of the stock. In the early part of 1979, the stock of IBM was selling for approximately $300 a share. The stockholders approved a 4-for-1 split of its stock when the par value of the shares was $5. After the split, the shares traded at approximately $75 and the par value was reduced to $1.25 a share. This type of stock split requires no monetary entry on the corporation's books; however, a memorandum entry should be made to note the change in the number of shares outstanding and the change in the par value.

(ii) Split with No Change in Par Value. A corporation may execute a stock split without changing the par value of its stock; it may transfer from additional paid-in capital to common stock an amount equal to the additional shares issued multiplied by the par value. For example, if 1 million shares of common stock with a par value of $10 are split 2 for 1 without adjusting the par value, $10 million will be transferred from additional paid-in capital to common stock. A corporation may also increase the number of its shares outstanding by means of a stock dividend. This adjustment is explained in the discussion of dividends.

(iii) Reverse Splits. At times, a corporation may wish to raise the market price of its shares and reduce the number of shares outstanding. This may be accomplished by means of a reverse split, in which the number of shares outstanding is reduced and the par value is increased proportionately. For example, if a company with 1 million shares of its $5 par value stock outstanding desires to reduce the number of outstanding shares, it may execute a 1-for-2 reverse split. The outstanding shares would be reduced to 500,000 and the par value would be increased to $10.

19.5 REACQUISITION AND RETIREMENT OF CAPITAL STOCK

(a) TREASURY STOCK. Treasury shares are shares that were issued by a corporation and subsequently reacquired that have not been canceled or restored to the status of authorized but unissued shares. Treasury shares are issued but not outstanding and may be resold below par value without liability attaching to their purchase.

A corporation may purchase its own shares unless restricted by its certificate of incorporation or the corporation law of its state of incorporation. Section 513 of the New York Business Corporation Law applies to the purchase or redemption by a corporation of its own shares. It states::

1. A corporation may purchase its own shares or redeem its redeemable shares out of surplus except when the corporation is insolvent or would be made insolvent by the purchase.
2. A corporation may redeem or purchase its redeemable shares out of stated capital except when the corporation is insolvent or would be made insolvent by the transaction.

A reporting entity never actually purchases its own shares. A purchase is an exchange, a reciprocal transfer as defined by APB Statement No. 4 (FASB ASC 740-10), a two-way transaction in which the reporting entity obtains something of value to it and sacrifices something of value to it. In a reacquisition of its own shares, the reporting entity gives up something of value to it, money, but does not receive anything of value to it (its own shares are not an asset to it). To the reporting entity, a reacquisition of shares is simply a partial nonproportional liquidating dividend.

(i) Restrictions on Retained Earnings. The corporation laws of most states provide that distributions from retained earnings—in some states, retained earnings plus additional paid-in capital—are restricted to the extent of the cost of treasury shares until the shares are either disposed of or canceled. Rule 4-08 of Regulation S-X (FASB ASC 235-10) states: "Disclosure shall be made of any restriction upon retained earnings that arises from the fact that upon involuntary liquidation the aggregate preferences of the preferred shares exceeds the par or stated value of such shares."

(ii) Agreements to Purchase. Several states allow a corporation to contract to purchase its own shares, even though at the time of the agreement it is unable to pay for them because of the insolvency provisions of the law. Section 514 of the New York Business Corporation Law permits such an agreement if, at the time of partial or full payment, the corporation is solvent and the payment will not render it insolvent.

(b) BALANCE SHEET PRESENTATION OF TREASURY STOCK. Under ARB No. 43, Chapter 1B, paragraph 7 (FASB ASC 505–30), a corporation may report its treasury stock in three ways:

1. The cost of acquired stock may be shown separately as a deduction from the total capital stock, additional paid-in capital, and retained earnings.
2. The stock may be accorded the treatment appropriate for retired stock.
3. In rare circumstances, treasury shares may be shown as an asset.

Generally, treasury shares are reported as described in (1) and (2) above. Treasury stock is rarely reported as an asset because it is difficult to justify classifying what is essentially equivalent to unissued stock as an asset. However, occasionally corporations acquire their own stock to satisfy a specific obligation and classify these reacquired shares as assets. The SEC Staff has indicated that asset classification of treasury stock is appropriate only if the shares repurchased are expected to be reissued promptly (within one year) under existing stock plans.

In FAS No. 135 (FASB ASC 235-10), the FASB indicated that it is no longer acceptable to show stock of a corporation held in its own treasury as an asset.

Reporting the cost of reacquired shares as a deduction from the total stockholders' equity is commonly known as the *cost method* or the *single-transaction* and *unallocated deduction method.* Treating reacquired shares as retired stock is commonly known as the *par value method* or the *two-transaction* and *contraction of capital method.*

(c) REPORTING TREASURY STOCK TRANSACTIONS—COST METHOD. The cost method is more frequently used than the par value method in reporting treasury stock transactions. Seiden and Rikert noted that in 1994, of the 600 annual reports reviewed, 373 disclosed treasury stock. Of these, 342 reported treasury shares under the cost method, 23 under the par value method, and 8 under other methods.[3]

Under the cost method, the acquisition of treasury shares is treated as the initial step of a financing operation that will culminate in the resale of these shares (i.e., the purchase and sale are viewed as one continuous transaction). As a result, treasury stock assumes the status of a capital element in suspense, and the ultimate disposition of the shares marks the time for recognizing any adjustment among the various capital elements. A treasury stock account is debited for the cost of the shares purchased, and on resale the account is credited for the cost. If possible, the cost of each acquisition should be accounted for separately. When the treasury stock is resold, it should be reissued on the basis of specific identification. If specific identification is not possible, the stock may be assigned a cost on the basis of first-in, first-out (FIFO) or, as a last resort, average cost.

(i) Disposition of Treasury Stock. When treasury stock is sold for less than its cost, the charge for the loss depends on the laws of the state of incorporation and the status of shareholders' equity accounts in excess of legal or stated capital. It is customary to assign losses on treasury stock transactions to these accounts in the order given: capital in excess of par value from previous treasury stock transactions of the same class of shares, capital in excess of par value from original sale of the same class of shares, pro rata, and retained earnings.

When treasury stock is sold for more than its cost, the gain is credited to additional paid-in capital, treasury stock transactions for that class of stock.

(ii) Treasury Stock Retired. When reacquired stock is retired, the stock account is debited for the amount credited when the stock was issued originally, the treasury stock account is credited at cost, and if the difference is a gain, it is credited to capital in excess of par value—retired stock. If the retirement results in a loss, it is debited to the next three accounts in the order given:

---

[3] N. Seiden and R. Rikert, eds., *Accounting Trends and Techniques,* 49th ed. (New York: AICPA, 1995).

1. Capital in excess of par value to the extent of the credit when the stock was issued
2. Capital in excess of par value from previous treasury stock transactions of the same class of stock
3. Retained earnings

Paragraph 28 of APB Opinion No. 9, *Reporting the Results of Operations* (FASB ASC 505-10), reaffirmed the provisions of Chapter 1B of ARB No. 43 and stated:

> [T]he following should be excluded from the determination of net income or the results of operations under all circumstances: (a) adjustments or charges or credits resulting from transactions in the company's own stock.

Under both generally accepted accounting principles (GAAP) and provisions of the Internal Revenue Code (IRC), gains and losses on treasury stock transactions are not included in determining income and, therefore, do not affect provisions for income taxes.

(d) REPORTING TREASURY STOCK TRANSACTIONS—PAR VALUE METHOD.

Under the par value method for treasury stock, the reacquisition is viewed as the termination of the contract between the corporation and the shareholder, requiring the elimination of all capital elements identified with these shares. As a result, any adjustment between the retiring and remaining equity holders is made at the time of acquisition. The subsequent disposition of the treasury shares is regarded as a completely independent transaction. The purchase and resale of stock constitutes two transactions. Although accounting practitioners have turned increasingly to the cost method, the par value method has received more theoretical support.

Under the par value method, the acquisition of treasury shares has essentially the same effect on paid-in capital as the purchase and retirement of the stock. The treasury stock account is debited for the par (or stated) value of the stock acquired. The related capital in excess of par (or stated) value accounts is debited for the same amount as was identified with the stock when originally sold. If the reacquisition cost exceeds the original sales proceeds, the excess is charged to retained earnings. When the original sales proceeds exceed the reacquisition price, the difference is credited to capital in excess of par (or stated) value—treasury stock. If the company cancels the reacquired stock, proper accounting requires that the balance in the treasury stock account be transferred to the account credited when the stock was originally sold.

The subsequent resale of acquired stock is accounted for in a manner similar to that for the sale of unissued stock. The treasury stock account is credited for par (or stated) value. Any proceeds from the sale in excess of the par (or stated) value should be credited to capital in excess of par (or stated) value—treasury stock. Should the proceeds be less than par (or stated) value, the difference is debited to retained earnings because no discount liability attaches to the sale of treasury stock.

(e) DONATED TREASURY STOCK.

In situations not so common today, shareholders may donate shares of company stock to the company. Whatever the reasons for the donation, it does not affect either total assets or total stockholders' equity. Kieso and Weygandt discuss three methods of accounting for donated stock when it is received:

1. Treasury stock is debited and donated capital is credited for the current market value of the donated shares. When the donated treasury shares are received, they are accounted for in the same manner as other treasury stock applying the cost method.
2. Treasury stock is debited for the par or stated value (or if it is true no-par stock, the average price paid in may be used), paid-in capital in excess of par or stated value is debited for the original premium paid in at the time of issuance, and donated capital is credited for the sum of the two debits. When the donated shares are reissued, they are accounted for in the same manner as other treasury stock applying the par value method (i.e., as newly issued shares).

3. The donated shares are assumed to have no cost. Only a memorandum record is made indicating the number of shares received. The entire proceeds from reissuance of the donated treasury shares would be credited for donated capital.[4]

(f) CONTRAST IN ACCOUNTING FOR TREASURY STOCK TRANSACTIONS UNDER THE COST AND PAR VALUE METHODS.
The cost and par value methods of accounting for treasury stock transactions are illustrated next. Assume these facts:

Common stock, $10 par value; issued and outstanding 1,000 shares	$10,000
Capital contributed in excess of par value	1,000
Retained earnings	9,000
Total stockholders' equity	$20,000

Furthermore, assume:

1. Company acquired 200 shares of its stock, 100 at $12 and 100 at $9.
2. **a.** Sold the 200 shares for $13.
   b. Sold the 200 shares for $7.

The journal entries are:

	Cost Method		Par Value Method	
1. To record purchase of shares at $12 and $9				
Treasury stock	$1,200		$1,000	
Capital contributed in excess of par value			100	
Retained earnings			100	
Cash		$1,200		$1,200
Treasury stock	$ 900		$1,000	
Capital contributed in excess of par value				
Treasury stock transactions				$ 100
Cash		$ 900		900
2(a). To record sales of shares at $13				
Cash	$2,600		$2,600	
Contributed capital, Treasury stock transactions		$ 500		$ 600
Treasury stock		2,100		2,000
2(b). To record sale of shares at $7				
Cash	$1,400		$1,400	
Capital contributed in excess of par value	200		100	
Capital in excess of par value, Treasury stock transactions			100	
Retained earnings	500		400	
Treasury stock		$2,100		$2,000

---

[4] Donald E. Kieso and Jerry J. Weygandt, *Intermediate Accounting,* 6th ed. (New York: John Wiley & Sons, 1989).

(g) PRESENTATION OF TREASURY STOCK IN SHAREHOLDERS' EQUITY. Presented next are the shareholders' equity sections of the balance sheets of two companies showing the usual manner of reporting treasury stock under both methods.

COST METHOD

Shareholders' equity (dollars in thousands):

Preference stock	$ 248
Common stock, par value $2.50 per share; authorized 100,000,000 shares;	
issued 28,988,757 shares	72,472
Additional paid-in capital	206,316
Retained earnings	734,020
	1,013,056
Less common stock in treasury, at cost; 1,249,110 shares	68,440
Total shareholders' equity	$ 944,616

PAR VALUE METHOD

Shareholders' equity:

Capital stock	
Common stock; authorized 10,000,000 shares of $2.50 par value each;	
issued 4,316,045 shares	$ 10,790,000
Less: treasury stock—157,611 shares	394,000
Outstanding—4,158,434 shares	$ 10,396,000
Capital in excess of par value	35,487,000
Retained earnings	108,297,000
Total shareholders' equity	$154,180,000

In its notes to the consolidated financial statements, this company indicated that its capital in excess of par value is increased for the proceeds of the sale of treasury stock in excess of par value and decreased by the cost in excess of par value of treasury stock purchased.

Other companies using the par value method for reporting treasury stock merely report the number of shares outstanding and parenthetically state the number of shares held in the treasury.

(h) PURCHASE OF TREASURY SHARES AT A PRICE SIGNIFICANTLY IN EXCESS OF CURRENT MARKET PRICE. Companies that have been targets of unfriendly takeover attempts have paid prices in excess of market for their stock to persons holding the stock in an attempt to prevent the takeover. These payments have been called *greenmail*. FASB Technical Bulletin (FTB) No. 85–6 (FASB ASC 505–30) requires companies to allocate the cost of the reacquired stock to treasury stock for the market price of the stock and to other elements of the transaction for the balance. The other elements should be accounted for according to their substance.

FTB No. 85-6 (FASB ASC 505-30) also requires disclosure of the allocation of the cost of the reacquired stock and the accounting treatment of the allocated costs.

19.6 SHARE-BASED PAYMENTS

(a) USE OF SHARE-BASED PAYMENTS. Corporations attempt to make debt more appealing but less costly, stock more desirable, and employees more committed. Stock equivalents are used to achieve these goals. Tax incentives also have served to enhance the use of stock equivalents. For purposes of this section, *stock equivalents* are comprised of:

- Stock warrants and stock rights
- Employee stock options
- Employee stock ownership plans (ESOPs)

(b) STOCK WARRANTS AND STOCK RIGHTS.   Stock warrants can be issued in conjunction with and attached to debt securities, can be sold separately, or can be given to investment bankers, stockbrokers, and attorneys as compensation for services rendered in the issuance of the company's stock. Stock warrants entitle the holder to purchase a specific amount of company shares, generally its common stock, at a specified price, either within a given period or for an indefinite period.

(i) Issued with Debt.   When stock warrants are issued with debt or any other security, they may be either detachable from the other security or nondetachable.

Paragraph 16 of APB Opinion No. 14, *Accounting for Convertible Debt and Debt Issued with Stock Purchase Warrants* (FASB ASC 470-20), states that "the portion of the proceeds of debt securities issued with detachable stock purchase warrants which is allocable to the warrants should be accounted for as paid-in capital." The allocation is based on the relative fair values of the two securities at time of issuance, and the amount allocated to the warrant either increases the bond discount or reduces the bond premium. If, however, the warrant is not detachable, no allocation is made and the proceeds are attributed entirely to the debt.

Fair values may not be readily determinable when the company's securities are not publicly traded. In these circumstances, the company should estimate what the interest rate on the debt would be without the accompanying warrant. This rate would naturally be higher than the rate on the debt and warrant. The future cash flows from the payment of the debt and the interest payments should be discounted to the present. The difference between this amount and the amount received for the debt and the warrant is attributable to the warrant.

(ii) Sale of Warrants.   When stock warrants are sold, the transaction is reported in a manner similar to the sale of stock; that is, the proceeds are credited to a paid-in capital account, generally stock warrants outstanding.

(iii) Issued for Services.   When stock warrants are issued for services, the fair market value of the services or the warrants, whichever is more clearly determinable, should be credited to paid-in capital.

(iv) Exercise of Warrants.   When the stock warrant is exercised, part of the cost of the stock is considered to be the value allocated to the warrant. Therefore, this amount is removed from the stock warrants outstanding account and, together with the cash received, credited to the stock account for the par or stated value. Any excess is credited to the capital in excess of par value account.

(v) Stock Rights.   Stock rights and stock warrants are, for all practical purposes, the same. The differences are essentially mechanical. Stock warrants may be sold alone, whereas stock rights are usually sold in conjunction with a debt or equity security. Generally, one warrant, but more than one right, is required to acquire one share of stock. Whatever the esoteric differences may be between stock rights and stock warrants, they are reported in a similar manner for accounting purposes.

(vi) Lapsed Warrants and Rights.   When stock warrants and stock rights lapse, the accounts should be closed and a paid-in capital account should be credited. The next stockholders' investment section of a company's comparative balance sheets shows the results of a lapse of warrants.

	2009	2008
Stockholders' Investment:		
Common stock—$.10 per value,		
5,000,000 shares authorized, 1,816,318		
shares issued and outstanding	$ 181,632	$181,632
Warrants outstanding	—	15,000
Paid-in capital	982,833	967,833
Retained earnings (deficit)	693,834	(676,867)
	$1,858,299	$487,598

In 2008, the warrants expired and the $15,000 was added to paid-in capital.

(vii) Tax Consequence of Lapsed Warrants. A company may have taxable income when its warrants lapse. In these circumstances, the company could avoid adverse tax consequences by extending the expiration date of the warrants. Before any action is taken, however, the company should consult with its tax adviser.

(viii) Reacquisition of Warrants. When stock warrants are reacquired, the amount paid in excess of the amount assigned to the warrants at issuance is charged to retained earnings. If the warrants are reacquired at a price less than the amount originally assigned to them, the difference is credited to additional paid-in capital.

(c) EMPLOYEE STOCK OPTIONS. Stock options are nontransferable rights granted by a corporation to its employees to purchase shares of the corporation at a stated price, either at a specified date or during a specified period. FAS No. 123R, *Share-Based Payment* (SFAS No. 123R; FASB ASC 718-10), provides guidance related to accounting for employee stock options.

(i) Accounting for Share-Based Payments Transactions. The cost of employee services received in exchange for awards of equity instruments is based on the fair value of the equity instrument at the grant date, less any amount paid or to be paid by the employee.

Compensation is the difference between the fair value of the equity share options at the measurement date and the amount, if any, that the employee is required to pay. The amount allocated to compensation costs is credited to a paid-in capital account. Kieso and Weygandt illustrate the accounting and reporting of a compensatory stock option plan with the next example.

On January 1, 1989, a company grants options to its officers for 10,000 shares of its $1 par value common stock. The options may be exercised at any time within the next 10 years, commencing two years after the date of the grant. At the time of the grant, the fair value of the stock option is $70 a share and the option price for the stock is $60; therefore, there is an element of compensation in this option to the extent of $100,000 ($10 × 10,000). The company will record these entries in 1989:

January 1, 1989		
Deferred compensation expense	$100,000	
Paid-in capital-stock options		$100,000
December 31, 1989		
Compensation expense	$ 50,000	
Deferred compensation expense		$ 50,000

At December 31, 1989, the stockholders' equity section of the company's balance sheet is:

Stockholders' equity:		
Common stock, $50 par, 20,000 shares		
issued and outstanding		$1,000,000
Paid-in capital-stock options	$100,000	
Less deferred compensation	50,000	50,000
Total stockholders' equity		$1,050,000

At December 31, 1990, the remaining $50,000 to the deferred compensation account is written off and charged to income. If 20 percent or 2000 of the 10,000 options were exercised on June 1, 1992, this entry would be recorded:

Cash (2000 × $60)	$120,000	
Paid-in capital-stock option		
(20% × $100,000)	20,000	
Common stock (2,000 × $1)		$ 2,000
Paid-in capital in excess of par		138,000

If the remaining stock options lapse, the balance in the paid-in capital—stock option account is transferred to a new account, paid-in capital—expired stock options."[5]

(ii) Disclosure Requirements.   Paragraph A240 of FAS No. 123R (FASB ASC 718–10) states the disclosure requirements for stock options. For further discussion on developing the underlying amounts for accounting and disclosure for share-based payments, refer to Chapter 23 in this *Handbook*.

(d) EMPLOYEE STOCK OWNERSHIP PLANS; REPORTING THE ESOP.   An employee stock ownership plan (ESOP) is a plan under which employees acquire stock of their employer. It is also a means by which the corporation can obtain additional capital. Generally, the ESOP borrows from the bank and uses the proceeds to buy the company's shares, either from the corporation or from shareholders with significant holdings. The corporation guarantees the loan made to the ESOP, and the ESOP repays the loans from tax-deductible contributions made to it by the corporation.

Therefore, under the ESOP and variations of it, such as a Tax Reduction Act stock ownership plan (TRASOP), the stockholders' equity section of the company reports a deduction to the extent of the ESOP outstanding debt that it guaranteed.

Financial reporting by the corporation of its ESOP is determined by the provisions of SOP 93-6, *Employers' Accounting for Employee Stock Ownership Plans* (FASB ASC 718-40). The financial reporting requirements of Statement of Position No. 93-6 (FASB ASC 718-40) are described in the next paragraphs.

(i) Reporting the Purchase of Shares by Employee Stock Ownership Plans.   Employers should do the following:

- For a leveraged ESOP, report the issuance of shares or the sale of shares when they occur. The corresponding charge should be to unearned ESOP shares, a contra account to be reported separately in the stockholders' equity section.
- If a leveraged ESOP buys outstanding employers' shares in the market, the employer should charge unearned ESOP shares and credit either cash or debt, depending on whether the ESOP is internally or externally leveraged.

(ii) Reporting the Release of Employee Stock Ownership Plan Shares.   When ESOP shares are committed to be released by a leveraged ESOP, unearned ESOP shares should be credited and compensation cost, dividends payable, or compensation liabilities should be charged, depending on the purpose for which the shares are released.

The difference between the fair value of the shares committed to be released and the cost of those shares to the ESOP should be charged or credited to additional paid-in capital.

(iii) Reporting Dividends on Employee Stock Ownership Plan Shares.   Dividends should be reported in two ways:

1. For a leveraged ESOP:
   a. Dividends on unallocated shares used to pay debt service should be reported as reduction of either debt on accrued interest payable.
   b. Dividends on unallocated shares paid to participants or added to participant accounts should be reported as compensation expense.
   c. Dividends on allocated shares should be charged to retained earnings.
2. For a nonleveraged ESOP, dividends on shares held by the ESOP should be charged to retained earnings.

(iv) Reporting Redemptions of Employee Stock Ownership Plan Shares.   Employers should report their purchase of shares held by ESOP participants as the purchase of treasury stock.

---

[5] Ibid.

19.7 RETAINED EARNINGS

(a) DEFINITION.   According to the MBCA, *retained earnings* of a corporation are

> equal to its net profits, income, gains and losses from the date of incorporation or from the latest date when a deficit was eliminated by an application of its capital surplus or stated capital or otherwise, after deducting subsequent distributions to shareholders and transfers to stated capital and capital surplus.

A corporation is an entity separate and distinct from its shareholders, and legally it cannot make a distribution to shareholders from permanent capital. Therefore, a credit balance in the retained earnings account represents the maximum potential claim that the shareholders have against the net assets of the corporation. The claim is no longer potential when, and to the extent that, the company's board of directors declares a dividend.

The board of directors may declare a dividend except when the corporation is insolvent or when the dividend payment would render the corporation insolvent. Dividends may be declared only out of the unreserved and unrestricted retained earnings of the corporation; however, in some states, dividends may also be declared out of additional paid-in capital.

(b) EVENTS AFFECTING RETAINED EARNINGS.   The balance in the retained earnings account is increased by net income and reduced by net loss. In addition, the balance is affected by these five things:

1. Prior-period adjustments
2. Dividends
3. Recapitalizations and reorganizations
4. Treasury stock transactions
5. Stock redemptions

Treasury stock transactions and stock redemptions were discussed earlier in this section. The first three items are discussed next.

(c) PRIOR-PERIOD ADJUSTMENTS.   The theoretical undesirability of prior-period adjustments has been acknowledged for many years:

> [I]t is plainly desirable that all costs, expenses, and losses, and all profits of a business, . . . be included in the determination of income. If this principle could in practice be carried out perfectly, there would be no charges or credits to earned surplus [retained earnings] except those relating to distributions and appropriations of final net income. This is an ideal upon which all may agree, but because of conditions impossible to foresee it often fails of attainment. [ARB No. 43, Chapter 2B, paragraph 3]

Although Chapter 2B has been superseded, the undesirability of prior-period adjustments is still recognized. Conditions under which prior-period adjustments may be recorded have been narrowed so that except for items specifically noted in authoritative pronouncements, only one item may be accounted for as a prior-period adjustment and recorded directly in the retained earnings account.

(i) Correction of an Error in Previously Issued Financial Statements.   Paragraph 25 of SOP No. 154, *Accounting Changes and Error Corrections* (SFAS No. 154; FASB ASC 250), states:

> Any error in the financial statements of a prior period discovered subsequent to their issuance shall be reported as a prior-period adjustment by restating the prior period financial statements. Restatement requires that:
>
> **(a)** The aggregate effect of the error is applied to the carrying amount the accounts affected in the statements of the first period presented.

(b) If there is an impact on retained earnings or equity, then that should also be reflected in the earliest period presented financials.

(c) Financial statements for each individual prior period presented shall be adjusted to reflect correction of the period-specific effects of the error.

Paragraph 2h of SFAS No. 154 (FASB ASC 250), defines an error in previously issued financial statements as

an error in recognition, measurement, presentation, or disclosure in financial statements resulting from mathematical mistakes, mistakes in the application of GAAP, or oversight or misuse of facts that existed at the time the financial statements were prepared.

When an accounting principle is changed and the change is to conform with GAAP, then that is treated like a correction of an error.

(ii) Reporting Prior-Period Adjustments.   SFAS No. 154 (FASB ASC 250-10) states:

Those items that are reported as error corrections shall, in single period statements, be reflected as adjustments of the opening balance of retained earnings. When comparative statements are presented, corresponding adjustments should be made of the amounts of net income (and the components thereof) and retained earnings balances (as well as of other affected balances) for all of the periods reported therein, to reflect the retroactive application of the error corrections.

(d) OTHER PRIOR-PERIOD ADJUSTMENTS.   In addition to the adjustment of retained earnings required by SFAS No. 154 (FASB ASC 250-10), other events require an adjustment of retained earnings.

The FASB has made many of its pronouncements effective on a retroactive basis. This requires restatements of all prior years' statements presented and, if applicable, an adjustment of the opening retained earnings of the earliest year presented.

In addition to FASB requirements for retained earnings adjustments, paragraph 25 of SFAS No. 154 (FASB ASC 250-10) requires an entity to report a change in accounting principle through retrospective application of the new accounting principle to all prior periods, unless it is impracticable to do so.

(e) DIVIDENDS.   Dividends are pro rata distributions of a company's assets to its shareholders, limited by business considerations, availability of resources, and, in most states, the amount of retained earnings. They represent the portion of the accumulated earnings that the board decides it can distribute without adversely affecting the operations of the company.

Although shareholders have the right to share in the earnings of the company, they are not entitled to receive the earnings or any part thereof without action by the board of directors. The declaration by the board and the distribution by the corporation of dividends involve three dates:

1. Declaration date
2. Record date
3. Payment date

Dividends are of five types:

1. Cash
2. Stock
3. Property

4. Scrip or liability

5. Liquidating

(f) DIVIDEND DATES. For dividends other than stock dividends, the corporation incurs a liability at the time of declaration. This is the date when the board of directors meets and votes the dividend. At this meeting, the board also establishes the record date and the payment date for the dividend. When a stock dividend is declared, the board may rescind it prior to distribution.

At declaration date for other than a stock dividend, the company reduces its retained earnings by the amount of the dividend and records a liability. The record date does not affect the corporation. It must pay dividends on the number of shares outstanding; the record date merely establishes who will receive the dividend. For stocks that are publicly traded, generally the stock is traded ex-dividend—without the dividend—four or five days prior to the record date.

On the record date, the person responsible for distributing the dividend determines the individuals who will receive the dividend, and on the payment date, the dividend is remitted to the stockholder. On the record date, no entry is required on the corporate books; on the payment date, the corporation eliminates its liability by distributing the assets necessary to satisfy the liability.

(g) CASH DIVIDENDS. Declaration of a cash dividend is the usual manner in which the board initiates a distribution to the shareholders. The declaration is usually quarterly and may be stated as either a percentage of the par value of the shares or a dollar amount per share. However stated, at the date of declaration the corporation has assumed a liability and must therefore record it with a corresponding reduction of retained earnings.

As noted earlier, the company makes no entry in recognition of the record date of the dividend. On the payment date, the corporation satisfies its liability by distributing the cash.

(h) STOCK DIVIDENDS. Chapter 7B, paragraph 1 of ARB No. 43 (FASB ASC 260-10) defines a stock dividend in this way:

> An issuance by a corporation of its own common shares to its common shareholders without consideration and under conditions indicating that such action is prompted mainly by a desire to give the recipient shareholders some ostensibly separate evidence of a part of their respective interests in accumulated corporate earnings without distribution of cash or other property which the board of directors deems necessary or desirable to retain in the business.

A stock dividend is the second most common type of dividend, and it is the only one that, when declared, does not create a legally enforceable corporate liability. The declaration of a stock dividend is not a commitment to distribute corporate assets; it merely indicates an intent to realign the accounts constituting stockholders' equity by issuing additional stock to current shareholders.

(i) Small Stock Dividend. According to Chapter 7B of ARB No. 43 (FASB ASC 505-20), a distribution less than 20 to 25 percent of the shares previously outstanding would be considered a small stock dividend. Recipients of small stock dividends view them as distributions of corporate earnings, usually in an amount equal to the fair value of the shares received. Paragraph 10 states:

> [I]t is to be presumed that such views of recipients are materially strengthened in those instances, which are by far the most numerous, when the issuances are so small in comparison with the shares previously outstanding that they do not have any apparent effect upon the share market prices and, consequently, the market value of the shares previously held remains substantially unchanged. The committee therefore believes that when these circumstances exist the corporation should in the public interest account for the transaction by transferring from earned surplus to the category of permanent capitalization (represented by the capital stock and capital surplus accounts) an amount equal to the fair value of the additional shares issued.

Therefore, when a small stock dividend is declared or distributed (see below for time of recording), the corporation must:

- Reduce retained earnings by the fair value of the shares
- Increase the common stock account by the par or stated value of the shares
- Increase capital paid in excess of par or stated value by the difference between such value and the amount determined in the first bullet point

If no par value stock is distributed, its total market value should be credited to the common stock account.

(ii) Large Stock Dividend.   A distribution of 20 to 25 percent or more of the shares previously outstanding is considered a large stock dividend; therefore, it is reasonable to assume a reduction in the market value of outstanding shares. Under these circumstances, the retained earnings account is reduced and the stock account increased by the par or stated value of the shares. If no par value stock is distributed, the amount is computed by multiplying the number of shares distributed by the average amount per share paid in.

(iii) Closely Held Corporation.   For closely held corporations, market value is not a factor in determining the amount of the stock dividend. Under these circumstances, Chapter 7B, paragraph 12 of ARB No. 43 (FASB ASC 505-20) states that "there is no need to capitalize earned surplus other than to meet legal requirements." Therefore, the par or stated value of the shares distributed determines the amount of the reduction of retained earnings.

(iv) Record Date.   Since there is no legally enforceable obligation at the declaration date to issue the stock, the dividend should be recorded at the market value on the date the stock is distributed. However, many accountants prefer to record the dividend at the date of declaration. When this is done, the corporation establishes a new account, stock dividend distributable, which, at the date of declaration, is credited for the par or stated value of the shares to be distributed.

(v) Reasons for Stock Dividends.   Stock dividends usually are declared for four reasons:

1. To permanently retain earnings in the business by capitalizing a portion of accumulated earnings
2. To maintain a record of paying dividends without affecting corporate assets
3. To increase the number of shares outstanding without affecting the market price significantly
4. To take advantage of the nontaxability of stock dividends

The last reason is significant since not only are stock dividends not taxable on receipt, but the stock is assumed to have the same holding period as the shares on which the dividend was declared.

(i) PROPERTY DIVIDENDS.   Occasionally, a corporation will pay a dividend in kind, that is, it will pay the dividend in property, inventory, real estate, marketable securities of other corporations. Prior to the adoption of APB Opinion No. 29, *Accounting for Nonmonetary Transactions* (FASB ASC 845-10), dividends of this nature were accounted for at book value.

Paragraph 18 of APB Opinion No. 29 states:

> A transfer of a nonmonetary asset to a stockholder or to another entity in a nonreciprocal transfer should be recorded at the fair value of the asset transferred, and a gain or loss should be recognized on the disposition of the asset.

However, if the transfer is a spinoff or other form of reorganization or liquidation, it should be recorded at book value, not market value.

The recording of a property dividend is explained in the next example. Assume that a corporation owns 1,000 shares of X Corp. stock, which it acquired at $10 a share and which now has a market value of $25. If it declares a property dividend of 600 shares, it must record a gain on the disposal of the 600 shares. Therefore, at the declaration date, it increases its investment by $9,000 (600 shares × $15) and credits an account, gain on disposal of investment. It then reduces retained earnings by $15,000 (600 shares × $25) and records its liability. The $9,000 gain is reported in the income statement; however, for income tax purposes, this gain is not taxable. Since this item does not have tax consequences, it is not considered when computing income taxes under the provisions of SFAS No. 109, *Accounting for Income Taxes.* (FASB ASC 740)

(j) SCRIP OR LIABILITY DIVIDENDS. Although it is rarely done, a corporation may pay a dividend in scrip—a note. The accounting and reporting is the same as for a cash dividend, except that the corporation records notes payable rather than dividends payable as the liability. Notes payable for dividends bear interest that, when accrued, is charged to the interest expense account.

One reason for scrip dividends is that the shareholders may want a cash dividend; however, at the time of declaration, the corporation wishes to conserve its cash. After the shareholders receive the notes for the dividend, they can discount them and thereby obtain the desired cash.

(k) LIQUIDATING DIVIDENDS. A liquidating dividend is any dividend not based on profits; therefore, it must be recorded as a reduction of paid-in capital. Dividends of this nature are common in industries involved in natural resources. Section 45(b) of the MBCA recognizes the possibility of this kind of dividend. It states:

> If the articles of incorporation of a corporation engaged in the business of exploiting natural resources so provide, dividends may be declared and paid in cash out of the depletion reserves, but each such dividend shall be identified as a distribution of such reserves and the amount per share paid from such reserves shall be disclosed to the shareholders receiving the same concurrently with the distribution thereof.

Liquidating dividends also may be declared as a result of contraction of a corporation's operations. For example, a corporation may dispose of a division or a subsidiary and decide not to reinvest the proceeds.

When a liquidating dividend is declared and stock is not redeemed, accounts other than the retained earnings and capital stock accounts must be reduced. These accounts are capital in excess of par value, donated capital, capital arising from treasury stock transactions, or some similar capital account.

(l) QUASI REORGANIZATION. In the early years of a corporation's existence, it is not unusual for the corporation to be unprofitable and build up an accumulated deficit. When the corporation becomes profitable, it will not be able to pay dividends until this deficit is eliminated. One way of eliminating the deficit is a reorganization—an adjustment of the financial structure of the company.

Reorganizations may be formal and be subject to the provisions of the Federal Bankruptcy Law and the jurisdiction of the bankruptcy courts, or they may be informal. Informal reorganizations, generally called *quasi reorganizations,* adjust the corporate capital structure without recourse to the courts. In addition to speeding up the reorganization process, a quasi reorganization is less costly than the more formal court-supervised reorganization.

GAAP states that "capital surplus, however created, should not be used to relieve the income account of the current or future years of charges which would otherwise . . . be made" according to Chapter 1A, paragraph 2 of ARB No. 43 (FASB ASC 505–10). However, exceptions to this rule are provided for in the case of a quasi reorganization.

(i) Procedures in a Quasi Reorganization. Chapter 7A of ARB No. 43 (FASB ASC 852-20) explains the procedures used in a quasi reorganization. Assets are revalued downward to fair value at the date of adjustment; however, upward adjustments of items within the same asset classification are permitted so long as the net effect of the adjustments does not result in a write-up of the net assets (see SAB No. 115, Topic 5 S, *Quasi-Reorganization*). The net reduction in assets is a charge to the accumulated deficit of the corporation. After all asset adjustments are completed, the accumulated deficit is written off against any additional paid-in capital accounts. If the total in these accounts is not sufficient to absorb the accumulated deficit, additional paid-in capital should be created by means of a reduction in the par or stated value of the stock.

(ii) Retained Earnings After Readjustment. In Chapter 7, section A, paragraph 9, ARB No. 43 (FASB ASC 852-20) states: "When the readjustment has been completed, the company's accounting should be substantially similar to that appropriate for a new company." Therefore, retained earnings must be zero, and thereafter, whenever a balance sheet is prepared, the retained earnings should be dated to indicate from which date these earnings have been accumulated.

Dating of retained earnings may be done either on the face of the balance sheet or in the notes to financial statements. In its 1988 balance sheet, Genentech, Inc., reported:

	1988	1987
Shareholders' Equity:		
Preferred stock, $.02 par value; authorized		
100,000,000 shares; none issued	$ —	$ —
Common stock, $.02 par value; authorized		
297,00,000 shares;		
outstanding: 1988—82,924,439; 1987—78,739,896	1,658	1,575
Earnings convertible restricted stock $.02 par		
value; authorized 3,000,000 shares;		
outstanding: 1988—none; 1987—2,927,260	—	59
Additional paid-in capital	366,518	336,267
Notes receivable from sale of stock	—	(320)
Retained earnings (since October 1, 1987, quasi reor-		
ganization in which a deficit of $329,457 was eliminated)	31,119	17,831
Total stockholders' equity	399,295	355,412
Total liabilities and stockholders' equity	$668,755	$618,973

In its notes to financial statements explaining its reorganization, the company stated:

On February 18, 1988 the Company's Board of Directors approved the elimination of the Company's accumulated deficit through an accounting reorganization of its stockholders' equity accounts (quasi-reorganization) effective October 1, 1987. The quasi-reorganization did not involve any revaluation of assets or liabilities. The effective date of the quasi-reorganization (October 1, 1987) reflects the beginning of the quarter in which the Company received approval for and commenced marketing of its second major product, and as such, marks a turning point in the Company's operations. The accumulated deficit was eliminated by a transfer from additional paid-in capital in an amount equal to the accumulated deficit. The Company's stockholders' equity accounts at October 1, 1987 before and after the quasi-reorganization, are reflected in the consolidated statements of stockholders' equity. The tax benefits recognized subsequent to the quasi-reorganization that relate to items occurring prior to the quasi-reorganization have been reclassified from retained earnings to additional paid-in capital.

(iii) Tax Loss Carryforwards. A corporation that undertakes a quasi reorganization probably has operating loss or tax credit carryforwards that have not been recognized as assets. When the benefits of these carryforwards are realized subsequent to the quasi reorganization, they should be reported as a direct addition to contributed capital. If, however, the quasi reorganization involved only the elimination of the accumulated deficit by a reduction in contributed capital, subsequent recognition of prior operating loss or tax credit carryforwards should be accounted for as if the quasi reorganization had not occurred. That is, it should be recognized in the income statement. However, after this recognition, the tax benefit should be reclassified from retained earnings to contributed capital.

(m) RESTRICTIONS OF RETAINED EARNINGS. Although the retained earnings category indicates the maximum that may be distributed to shareholders, this amount may be subject to certain constraints and restrictions. Paragraph 199 of APB Statement No. 4, *Reporting Gains and Losses from Extinguishment of Debt—An Amendment of APB Opinion No. 30,* states that information about restrictions on assets and of owners' equity should be disclosed.

Restrictions of retained earnings are classified as legal, contractual, or voluntary.

(i) Legal Restrictions. A legal restriction on retained earnings was noted in Section 19.5(a) which discussed treasury stock. Under Section 6 of the MBCA, a corporation has the right to acquire its stock but only to the extent of unreserved or unrestricted retained earnings. The section further states:

> To the extent that earned surplus or capital surplus is used as the measure of the Corporation's right to purchase its own shares, such surplus shall be restricted so long as such shares are held as treasury shares.

(ii) Contractual Restrictions. Bond indentures and loan agreements with banks usually contain restrictions on retained earnings. Typical of these restrictions and the related disclosure is the note in the 1987 financial statements of Occidental Petroleum Corporation:

> At December 31, 1987, under the most restrictive covenants of certain financing agreements, the capacity for the payment of all cash dividends and other distributions on, and for acquisitions of, capital stock was approximately $2.2 billion, assuming that such dividends, distributions or acquisitions were made without incurring additional borrowing. The net assets of certain subsidiaries of Occidental are restricted from being advanced, loaned, or dividended to Occidental and its affiliates by certain financing agreements. At December 31, 1987, net assets of consolidated subsidiaries so restricted were approximately $1.1 billion.

(iii) Voluntary Restrictions. Occasionally, a corporation will voluntarily restrict the distribution of dividends because of some loss contingency that does not qualify for deduction on the income statement or because of future plans for major construction or renovation. In these situations, the corporation is merely informing the user of its financial statements that it has voluntarily restricted the payment of dividends.

(iv) Liquidating Value of Preferred Stock. The question of whether the excess of the liquidating value of preferred stock over its par value is a restriction on retained earnings is a legal determination. When state law is unclear, the uncertainty should be disclosed.

(n) APPROPRIATIONS OF RETAINED EARNINGS. Usually, restrictions of retained earnings are disclosed in the notes to financial statements and recorded on the books by means of a memorandum entry. Sometimes, by action of the board of directors, retained earnings may be appropriated (i.e., total retained earnings is reduced and a new account, appropriated retained earnings, is established). However, the total retained earnings remains the same. Rarely is appropriated retained earnings reported on the balance sheet.

(o) LOSS CONTINGENCIES.   Appropriated retained earnings may not relieve the income statement of an expense. SFAS No. 5 (par. 15) (FASB ASC 505–10) states:

> Some enterprises have classified a portion of retained earnings as "appropriated" for loss contingencies.... Appropriation of retained earnings is not prohibited by this Statement provided that it is shown within the stockholders' equity section of the balance sheet and is clearly identified as an appropriation of retained earnings. Costs or losses shall not be charged to an appropriation of retained earnings, and no part of the appropriation shall be transferred to income.

When the event for which the appropriation was established has passed, the appropriated retained earnings account is reduced by the amount originally established and the retained earnings account increased by a similar amount.

19.8 OTHER ITEMS AFFECTING STOCKHOLDERS' EQUITY

(a) NONCONTROLLING INTEREST.   In December 2007, the FASB issued SFAS No. 160, *Noncontrolling Interests in Consolidated Financial Statements* (FASB ASC 810-10), which amended ARB No. 51, *Consolidated Financial Statements*. FAS No. 160 (FASB ASC 810-10) changed the terminology traditionally known as *minority interest* to *noncontrolling interest*. Another change is that noncontrolling interests in the subsidiary is to be reported in the consolidated statement of financial position within equity, separately from the parent's equity. A company that has noncontrolling interest in more than one subsidiary can present all the noncontrolling interests in the aggregate.

Presented next is an example of a company with noncontrolling interests.

The Boeing Company and Subsidiaries
Consolidated Statements of Financial Position

(Dollars in millions, except per share data)

December 31

Shareholders' equity:		
Common stock, par value $5.00 – 1,012,261,159 shares issued	**5,061**	5,061
Additional paid-in capital	**3,866**	3,724
Treasury stock, at cost	**(17,187)**	(15,911)
Retained earnings	**24,784**	22,746
Accumulated other comprehensive loss	**(13,758)**	(11,877)
ShareValue Trust		(1,615)
Total shareholders' equity	**2,766**	2,128
Noncontrolling interest	**96**	97
Total equity	**2,862**	2,225
Total liabilities and equity	**$ 68,565**	$ 62,053

(b) COMBINED FINANCIAL STATEMENTS.   Consolidated financial statements are required when one company owns more than 50 percent of the outstanding voting shares of another company. However, a group of independent companies may have common controlling shareholders. For example, an individual may have controlling interest in two or more corporations or a parent company may have more than one subsidiary. When these commonly controlled companies present financial information, "combined financial statements ... are more meaningful than ... separate statements," according to ARB No. 51 (FASB ASC 810-10).

When combined financial statements are presented, intercompany transactions and profits or losses must be eliminated. When combining balance sheets, all components are combined except for the outstanding stock of the separate entities, which is presented separately. The shareholders' equity section of the 1983 combined balance sheet of AMP Incorporated and Pamcor, Inc. and their subsidiaries was presented as shown next.

	1983	1982
Shareholders' equity:		
AMP Incorporated		
Common stock, without par value—		
Authorized 50,000,000 shares, issued 37,440,000 shares	$ 12,480	$ 12,480
Pamcor, Inc.		
Common stock, par value $1.00 per share—		
Authorized and issued, 20,000 shares	20	20
Other capital	27,235	26,262
Cumulative translation adjustments	(39,439)	(24,665)
Retained earnings	853,845	748,085
	854,141	762,182
Less—Treasury stock, at cost	53,288	47,685
Total shareholders' equity	$800,853	$714,497

In the notes to combined financial statements, the principles of combination were explained in this way:

The financial statements of AMP and Pamcor and their subsidiaries (all wholly owned with one exception) are combined, as each company is owned beneficially by identical shareholders. Intercompany and affiliated company accounts are eliminated in the combination.

(c) INVESTOR AND INVESTEE TRANSACTIONS.

There are situations where a parent–subsidiary relationship exists and the subsidiary issues additional shares to someone other than its parent. In these circumstances, the parent's percentage interest in the subsidiary decreases, and the book balance of its investment may change, depending on the price at which the new stock is sold.

Assume that on January 2, 1989, Company P owns a 90 percent interest in Company S whose balance sheet on that date is:

Assets	$10,000
Liabilities	$ 1,000
Stockholders' equity	9,000
Total	$10,000

Company S has outstanding 1,000 shares of which Company P owns 900 shares; each share has a book value of $9. Further assume that, when Company P acquired its shares, there was no goodwill; therefore, at January 2, 1989, its investment account has a balance of $8,100 (90% × $9,000).

(i) Investee Sale at Book Value. Assume Company S sells 500 shares to the public on January 2, 1989, at its book value of $9 a share or $4,500. The outstanding shares therefore increase to 1,500 and the balance sheet of Company S is:

Assets	$14,500
Liabilities	$ 1,000
Stockholders' equity	$13,500
Total	$14,500

Company P's ownership dropped to 60 percent (900 shares of 1,500 outstanding), but 60 percent of $13,500 still equals $8,100, and the transaction does not affect the carrying value of the investor's investment.

(ii) Investee Sale in Excess of Book Value.   If Company S sells the 500 shares for $10 a share ($1 over book value) or $5,000, the result is different. After the sale, the balance sheet of Company S is:

Assets	$15,000
Liabilities	$ 1,000
Stockholders' equity	14,000
Total	$15,000

Under these circumstances, Company P's investment account should reflect a balance of 60 percent of $14,000, or $8,400. The increase represents 60 percent of $500 (the amount paid in excess of book value). This increase is not an item of income nor is it an item to be credited to retained earnings. It is a capital transaction; the investment account must be increased by $300, and the corresponding credit is to an additional paid-in capital account.

(iii) Investee Sale Below Book Value.   If Company S sells the 500 shares below book value—$7 a share, or $3,500—a different situation exists. After the sale, the balance sheet of Company S is:

Assets	$13,500
Liabilities	$ 1,000
Stockholders' equity	12,500
Total	$13,500

Under these circumstances, Company P's investment account should reflect a balance of 60 percent of $12,500, or $7,500. The decrease represents 60 percent of $1,000 (the amount paid below book value). Company P therefore must reduce its investment account by $600 and reduce additional paid-in capital by a similar amount. If there is not a sufficient balance in the additional paid-in capital account of Company P, the excess must be applied to a reduction of retained earnings.

(iv) Staff Accounting Bulletin No. 51.   The SEC, in this SAB No. 51, stated that where the investee sales are not part of a planned reorganization, it would permit the investor to recognize the gain or loss in its income statement as a separate line item.

(v) No Parent–Subsidiary Relationship.   If the investor company owns more than 20 percent but 50 percent or less of the outstanding voting stock of the investee, the same treatment must be accorded investee transactions in its own stock. However, if the investor's interest falls below 20 percent, no adjustment is made to the investment account, as stated in APB Opinion No. 18, *The Equity Method of Accounting for Investments in Common Stock* (FASB ASC 323-10).

If an investor company initially owns less than 20 percent of the voting stock of the investee and in a subsequent period increases its percentage ownership to 20 percent or more, either by its actions or by the actions of the investee, "the investment, results of operations (current and prior periods presented), and retained earnings of the investor should be adjusted retroactively in a manner consistent with the accounting for a step-by-step acquisition of a subsidiary," as explained in APB Opinion No. 18. The mechanics of a step-by-step acquisition of a subsidiary are explained in ARB No. 51 (par. 10)

(d) REPORTING COMPREHENSIVE INCOME.   Paragraph 8 of SFAS No. 130, *Reporting Comprehensive Income,* refers to FASB Concepts Statement No. 6 (FASB ASC 220-10), which defines *comprehensive income* as "the change in equity of a business enterprise during a period from transactions and other events and circumstances from nonowner sources." Paragraph 10 (FASB ASC 220-10) states:

> This Statement uses the term comprehensive income to describe the total of all components of comprehensive income, including net income. This Statement uses the term other comprehensive income to refer to revenues, expenses, gains, and losses that under generally accepted accounting principles are included in comprehensive income but excluded from net income.

Paragraph 26 of SFAS No. 130 (FASB ASC 505-10) states:

> The total of other comprehensive income for a period shall be transferred to a component of equity that is disclosed separately from retained earnings and additional paid-in capital in a statement of financial position at the end of an accounting period. . . . An enterprise shall disclose accumulated balances for each classification in that separate component of equity on the face of a statement of financial position, in a statement of changes in equity, or in notes to the financial statements.

The provisions of SFAS No. 130 (FASB ASC 220-10) are effective for fiscal years beginning after December 15, 1997. I

In June 2011, the FASB released Accounting Standards Update 2011-05, *Comprehensive Income* (ASU 2011-05) (FASB ASC 220), which revised the options for presentation of comprehensive income. Upon the effective date of ASU 2011-05, Other Comprehensive Income ("OCI") can no longer be included in the statement of owners' equity. OCI can be presented in *either*

- A **single continuous statement** of comprehensive income, or
- **Two separate but consecutive statements**.

In both choices, the entity is required to present:

- each component of net income along with total net income,
- each component of other comprehensive income along with a total for other comprehensive income, and
- a total amount for comprehensive income.

In the two-statement approach, the income statement must be immediately followed by the statement of OCI, which will present the amount for total comprehensive income.

ASU 2011-05 should be applied retrospectively, and is effective as follow:

- For public entities, the amendments are effective for fiscal years, and interim periods within those years, beginning after December 15, 2011. For nonpublic entities, the amendments are effective for fiscal years ending after December 15, 2012, and interim and annual periods thereafter. Early adoption is permitted.

19.9 DISCLOSURE OF INFORMATION ABOUT CAPITAL STRUCTURE

SFAS No. 129 (FASB ASC 505-10) essentially consolidated disclosure requirements found in other authoritative pronouncements. Disclosures concerning a company's stock include:

- Dividend and liquidation preferences
- Participation rights
- Call prices and dates
- Conversion or exercise prices or rates and pertinent rates

- Sinking fund requirements
- Unusual voting rights
- Significant terms of contracts to issue additional shares
- Number of shares issued upon conversion, exercise, or satisfaction of required conditions during at least the most recent annual fiscal period and any subsequent interim period presented

(a) PREFERRED STOCK.   A company that issues preferred stock or other senior stock with a preference in involuntary liquidation considerably in excess of par or stated value should disclose the relationship between the liquidation preference and the par or stated value. This disclosure should be made in the equity section of the balance sheet in the aggregate.

The company should also disclose (1) the aggregate or per share amounts at which preferred stock may be called or is subject to redemption and (2) the aggregate and per share amounts of arrearages in cumulative preferred stock.

19.10 SOURCES AND SUGGESTED REFERENCES

Accounting Principles Board. APB Opinion No. 9, *Reporting the Results of Operations* (FASB ASC 250–10). New York: AICPA, 1966.

_____ . APB Opinion No. 14, *Accounting for Convertible Debt and Debt Issued with Stock Purchase Warrants* (FASB ASC 470–20). New York: AICPA, 1969.

_____ . APB Opinion No. 18, *The Equity Method of Accounting for Investments in Common Stock* (FASB ASC 323–10). New York: AICPA, 1971.

_____ . APB Opinion No. 21, *Interest on Receivables and Payables* (FASB ASC 470–10). New York: AICPA, 1971.

_____ . APB Opinion No. 29, *Accounting for Nonmonetary Transactions* (FASB ASC 845-10). New York: AICPA, 1973.

_____ . APB Statement No. 4, *Basic Concepts and Accounting Principles Underlying Financial Statements of Business Enterprises* (FASB ASC 740–10). New York: AICPA, 1970.

American Bar Association, Committee on Corporate Laws of Section of Corporation, Banking and Business Law: Model Business Corporation Act. Philadelphia: American Law Institute—American Bar Association Committee on Continuing Professional Education, 1975.

American Institute of Certified Public Accountants. Accounting Research Bulletin No. 43, *Restatement and Revision of Accounting Research Bulletins* (FASB ASC 605–10). New York: Author, 1953.

_____ . Accounting Terminology Bulletin No. 1, *Review and Resume*. New York: Author, 1953.

_____ . Accounting Research Bulletin No. 51, *Consolidated Financial Statements* (FASB ASC 810–10). New York: Author, 1959.

_____ . Statement of Position No. 93–6, *Employers' Accounting for Employee Stock Ownership Plans* (FASB ASC 718–10). New York: Author, 1993.

Financial Accounting Standards Board. Statement of Financial Accounting Concepts No. 1, *Objectives of Financial Reporting by Business Enterprises*. Stamford, CT: Author, 1978.

_____ . Statement of Financial Accounting Concepts No. 2, *Qualitative Characteristics of Accounting Information*. Stamford, CT: Author, 1980.

_____ . Statement of Financial Accounting Concepts No. 5, *Recognition and Measurement in Financial Statements of Business Enterprises*. Stamford, CT: Author, 1984.

_____ . Statement of Financial Accounting Concepts No. 6, *Elements of Financial Statements* Stamford, CT: Author, 1985.

_____ . Statement of Financial Accounting Standards No. 5, *Accounting for Contingencies*. Stamford, CT: Author, 1975.

_____ . Statement of Financial Accounting Standards No. 109, *Accounting for Income Taxes* (FASB ASC 740–10). Stamford, CT: Author, 1992.

_____ . Statement of Financial Accounting Standards No. 123R, *Share Based Payments* (FASB ASC 505–10). Stamford, CT: Author, 2004.

_____ . Statement of Financial Accounting Standards No. 129, *Disclosure of Information about Capital Structure* (FASB ASC 505–10). Stamford, CT: Author, 1997.

_____ . Statement of Financial Accounting Standards No. 130, *Reporting Comprehensive Income* (FASB ASC 220–10). Stamford, CT: Author, 1997.

_____ . FASB Technical Bulletin No. 85–6, *Accounting for a Purchase of Treasury Shares at a Price Significantly in Excess of the Current Market Price of the Shares and the Income Statement Classification of Costs Incurred in Defending against a Takeover Attempt* (FASB ASC 505–30). Stamford, CT: Author, 1985.

Griffin, C. H., T. H. Williams, and K. D. Larson. *Advanced Accounting*, 4th ed. Homewood, IL: Irwin, 1980.

Kieso, D. E., and J. J. Weygandt. *Intermediate Accounting*, 6th ed. New York: John Wiley & Sons, 1989.

Melcher, B. Accounting Research Study No. 15, *Stockholders' Equity.* New York: AICPA, 1973.

Securities and Exchange Commission. Regulation S-X, *Accounting Rules.* Washington, DC: Author.

_____ . Staff Accounting Bulletin No. 51, *Accounting for Sales of Stock by Subsidiary.* Washington, DC: Author, 1983.

_____ . Staff Accounting Bulletin No. 57, *Views Concerning Accounting for Contingent Warrants in Connection with Sales Agreements with Certain Major Customers.* Washington, DC: Author, 1984.

_____ . Staff Accounting Bulletin No. 68, *Increasing Role of Preferred Stock.* Washington, DC: Author, 1987.

_____ . Staff Accounting Bulletin No. 78, *Views Regarding Certain Matters Relating to Quasi Reorganizations, Including Deficit Eliminations.* Washington, DC: Author, 1988.

Seiden, N., and R. Rikert, eds. *Accounting Trends and Techniques*, 49th ed. New York: AICPA, 1995.

CHAPTER 20

PARTNERSHIPS AND JOINT VENTURES

Francis E. Scheuerell Jr., CPA
Navigant Consulting

The editors wish to acknowledge the previous contribution to this chapter by George N. Dietz, CPA, American Institute of Certified Public Accountants; Gerard L. Yarnall, CPA, Deloitte & Touche; and Ronald J. Patten, PhD, CPA, DePaul University.

20.1 NATURE AND ORGANIZATION OF THE PARTNERSHIP ENTITY

(a) DEFINITION OF *PARTNERSHIP*. The Uniform Partnership Act (UPA), which has been adopted by most of the U.S. states, defines a partnership as an association of two or more persons who contribute money, property, or services to carry on as co-owners a business for profit.

A partnership may be general or limited. In the general partnership, each partner may be held personally responsible for all the firm's debts, whereas in the limited partnership, the liability of certain partners is limited to their respective contributions to the capital of the firm. The limited partnership is composed of a general partner and limited partners with the latter playing no role in the management of the business. Limited partnerships are discussed in Section 20.6.

While partnerships remain popular as a form of business organization, they are not as common as they once were. The Tax Reform Act of 1986 has served to dampen the attractiveness of limited partnerships as tax shelters. Similarly, new accounting standards that require consolidation of investees have made the use of partnerships and joint venture for purposes such as research and development less advantageous. At the same time, many law firms and public accounting firms that were organized as general partnerships are tending to organize themselves as professional corporations as a result of the favorable tax status that can flow from that structure as well as the easing of state laws forbidding professional firms to incorporate.

(b) ADVANTAGES AND DISADVANTAGES OF A PARTNERSHIP. Jules I. Bogen states:

> The partnership form of organization is superior to the proprietorship because it permits several persons to combine their resources and abilities to conduct a business. It is easier to form than a corporation, and retains a personal character making it more suitable in professional fields.[1]

A distinct advantage of a partnership over a corporation is the close relationship between ownership and management. This provides more flexible administration as well as more management talent with a personal interest in the problems and success of the business.

Historically, the three outstanding disadvantages of the partnership form of organization, as compared with corporate form, were recognized as (1) unlimited liability of the partners for business debts, (2) mutual agency power of each partner as it pertains to business actions, and (3) limited life of the partnerships. However, the existence of a number of large partnerships, particularly in the fields of law, accountancy, and investment banking, indicates that to a great degree many

---

[1] J. I. Bogen, "Advantages and Disadvantages of Partnership," in J. I. Bogen, ed., *Financial Handbook,* 4th ed., p. 5 (New York: Ronald Press, 1968).

of these disadvantages may be more apparent than real. In addition, partnerships have devised a number of ways to overcome some of the drawbacks. For example, since the partnership is subject to dissolution upon the death, bankruptcy, insanity, or retirement of a partner—events that do not affect the continuity of a corporation—long-term commitments for the business unit are difficult to obtain. Many partnership agreements overcome this drawback by providing for automatic continuation by the remaining partners subject to liquidation of the former partner's interest. In a sense, these partnerships have an unlimited life.

Still, the unlimited liability condition, which creates the possibility of loss of personal assets on the part of each partner, is a retardant to many. This risk of loss is especially important when one considers that each party is assumed to be an agent for all partnership activities, with the power to bind other partners as a result of his or her actions. Again, however, some partnerships have managed to overcome these difficulties, at least partially, by adopting variations of the partnership form of organizations. Such variants include:

- *Limited liability companies.* Limited liability companies (LLCs) are a relatively new form of business entity in the United States and have characteristics of both corporations and partnerships. LLCs shield their owners (or members) from personal liability for certain of the entity's debts and obligations, in much the same manner as a corporation. At the same time, a properly organized LLC can be treated as a partnership for federal income tax purposes, enabling it to enjoy the tax item pass-through and other benefits of the standard partnership form.

- *Registered limited liability partnerships.* Registered limited liability partnerships (LLPs), a distant relative of the LLC, are a type of general partnership that protects the partners' personal assets if another of their partners is sued for malpractice. However, the assets of the partnership itself remain at risk, as do the personal assets of the accused partner, and all partners still retain the standard joint-and-several liabilities of the partnership (e.g., lease obligations and bank loans).

- *Limited partnerships.* The limited partnership form has proliferated in recent years as a vehicle for raising capital for a particular project or undertaking. Limited partnerships are particularly common in the leasing and oil and gas industries. Prior to the Tax Reform Act of 1986, the limited partnership form also served as the organizational structure for a number of tax shelters. Limited partners risk losing their limited liability the more they participate in the management or control of the partnership's activities, thus reducing the attractiveness of the limited partnership structure for some potential partners. See Section 20.6 for further discussion of limited partnerships.

- *Joint ventures.* The formation and operation of joint ventures often includes partnerships. In a typical corporate joint venture, two or more entities form a partnership to undertake a specific business project, often for a specific, agreed-upon period. Each party's contributions to the venture may vary widely from case to case. For example, one corporation may provide technology, personnel, or facilities while the other contributes only the cash or other operating capital required for the undertaking. Alternatively, the venturers may jointly provide some or all of these elements. In any event, the entities form an enterprise that will function as a partnership, even if that partnership has the legal status of a corporation. See Section 20.8 for further discussion of joint ventures.

(c) TAX CONSIDERATIONS.   Even though a partnership is not considered a separate taxable entity for purposes of paying and determining federal income taxes, it is treated as such for purposes of making various elections and for selecting its accounting methods, taxable year, and method of depreciation.

Under Section 761(a) of Subchapter K of the Internal Revenue Code (IRC) of 1954, certain unincorporated organizations may be excluded, completely or partially, from treatment as partnerships for federal income tax purposes. This exclusion applies only to those organizations used (1) for investment purposes rather than as the active conduct of a business, or (2) for the joint extraction, production, or use of property, but not for the purpose of selling the products or services extracted or produced.

The use of limited partnerships because of favorable tax considerations has been significantly reduced as a result of the Tax Reform Act of 1986. Prior to passage of that Act, limited partnerships as a form of tax-sheltered investment had been used in real estate, motion picture production, oil drilling, cable television, cattle feeding, and research and development. The limited partnership gave investors the tax advantages of the partnership such as the pass-through of losses while at the same time limiting their liability to the original investment. The Tax Reform Act of 1986 changed the situation considerably, however.

IRC Section 465 generally limits a partner's loss to the amount that the partner has "at risk" and could actually lose from an activity. These rules, which apply to individuals and certain closely held corporations, are designed to prevent taxpayers from offsetting trade, business, or professional income with losses from investments in activities that are, for the most part, financed by nonrecourse loans for which they are not personally liable. If it is determined that the loss is deductible under these "at-risk" rules, the taxpayer is subjected to "passive activity" loss rules. Generally, losses from passive trade or business activities, such as in a partnership where the partner is not active, may not be deducted from other types of income such as wages, interest, or dividends according to IRC Section 469.

Some substantial tax benefits can still be enjoyed by investing in a triple net lease limited partnership. These partnerships buy buildings that are used by fast-food, auto parts, and other chains and franchises that do not want mortgage debt on their balance sheet. The partnerships collect rent and pass it along to the partners net of three costs—insurance, upkeep, and property taxes—paid by the tenants.

(d) IMPORTANCE OF THE PARTNERSHIP. In the United States, the single proprietorship is the most common form of business organization in terms of number of establishments, and the corporate form does by far the greatest volume of business. Nevertheless, the partnership form of organization holds an important place in both respects and fills a significant need. It is widely employed among the smaller business units and in professional fields such as medicine, law, dentistry, and accountancy, activities in which the partners are closely identified with the operation of the business or profession. Partnerships are also found in financial lines, such as investment banks. Occasionally a substantial trading or other business is conducted as a partnership.

(e) FORMATION OF A PARTNERSHIP. The agreement among the copartners that brings the partnership into existence may be oral or written. The latter is much to be preferred. According to Bedford, Perry, and Wyatt:

> Since a partnership is based on a contract between two or more persons, it is important, although not necessarily a legal requirement, that special attention be given to the drawing up of the partnership agreement. This agreement is generally referred to as the "Articles of Copartnership." In order to avoid unnecessary and perhaps costly litigation at some later date, the Articles should contain all of the terms of the agreement relating to the formation, operation, and dissolution of the partnership.[2]

Each partner should sign the articles and retain a copy of the agreement. It is desirable that a copy of the agreement be filed with the recorder, clerk, or other official designated to receive such documents in the county in which the partnership has its principal place of business. In the case of a limited partnership, such filing is imperative. There may also be a requirement that the agreement be published in newspapers.

---

[2] N. M. Bedford, K. W. Perry, and A. H. Wyatt, *Advanced Accounting—An Organization Approach* (New York: John Wiley & Sons, 1979).

According to Bogen, the articles of copartnership should cover these 12 matters:

1. Names of partners and the firm name
2. Kind of business to be conducted
3. Capital contribution of each partner
4. Duration of the partnership contract
5. The time to be devoted to the business by each, and any limitation upon outside business interests
6. Method of dividing profits and losses
7. Restrictions upon the agency powers of the partners
8. Salaries to be paid partners, or limitations upon the withdrawal of profits
9. Method of admitting new partners
10. Provision for insurance on lives of partners for benefit of firm
11. Procedure to be followed in voluntary dissolution
12. Procedure upon death or withdrawal of partner, including method of valuation of tangible assets and goodwill, and provision for continuation of the business by the remaining partners[3]

In the event that contributions of assets other than cash are being made to the new firm, the articles should also cover the matter of income tax treatment upon the subsequent disposal of such assets. In general, such assets retain the tax basis of the previous owner so that the taxable gain or loss when ultimately disposed of may be greater or less than the gain or loss to the partnership.

Many partnerships have been plagued, if not entirely destroyed, by disagreements that could have been avoided, or greatly minimized, by the exercising of more care and skill in the drafting of the original agreement.

(f) INITIAL BALANCE SHEET. Section 8 of the UPA states that:

- All property originally brought into the partnership or subsequently acquired, by purchase or otherwise, on account of the partnership is partnership property.
- Unless the contrary intention appears, property acquired with partnership funds is partnership property.

It follows that the initial balance sheet should explicitly identify the assets contributed by partners as belonging to the partnership and assign values to these assets that are agreeable to all partners. Debts assumed by the partnership will receive comparable treatment. The initial balance sheet should also show the total initial proprietorship and the partners' shares therein. According to Moonitz and Jordan:

> The most direct manner of accomplishing this result is to include the initial balance sheet in the partnership agreement itself. If it is not expedient to include it as an integral part of the agreement, reference to the initial balance sheet should be made in the agreement, and the balance sheet, as a separate document, should be signed by each partner.[4]

Unambiguous identification of assets and obligations at the inception of the partnership is important for at least two reasons:

1. Partnership creditors have no claim against the assets of individual partners until the partnership assets have been exhausted. (Special cases are discussed in Parts III and VI of the UPA.)

---

[3] Bogen, "Advantages and Disadvantages of Partnership."
[4] M. Moonitz and L. H. Jordan, *Accounting—An Analysis of Its Problems,* 2 vols., rev. ed. (New York: Holt, Rinehart and Winston, 1963).

2. Unless specifically provided for in the partnership agreement, partnership assets may be used only for partnership purposes; partners' personal assets are, of course, subject to no such limitations.

20.2 ACCOUNTING FOR PARTNERSHIP OPERATIONS

(a) PECULIARITIES OF PARTNERSHIP ACCOUNTING. In many respects, the accounting problems of the partnership are the same as those of other forms of business organization. The underlying pattern of the accounting for the various assets and current goods and service costs, including departmental classification and assignment, is not modified by the type of ownership and method of raising capital employed. The same is true of the recording of revenues and the treatment of liabilities. The special features of partnership accounting relate primarily to the recording and tracing of capital, the treatment of personal services furnished by the partners, the division of profits, and the adjustments of equities required upon the occasion of reorganization or liquidation of the firm.

(b) METHODS OF DIVIDING PROFITS AND LOSSES. As stated in Section 18 of the UPA, partnership income is shared equally unless otherwise provided for in the partnership agreement. In some cases, the agreement may specify division of profits in an arbitrary ratio (which of course includes the equal ratio already mentioned), referred to elsewhere in this discussion as the *income ratio.* Such a specified ratio (e.g., 60–40, $\frac{2}{3}-\frac{1}{3}$) may or may not be related to the original capital contributions of the respective partners. It is reiterated that the essential point is agreement among the partners as to how they wish profits to be divided.

Another example of profit division by a single set of relationships is afforded by division in proportion to capital balances. Since this phrase is ambiguous, the agreement should specify which of these bases are intended:

1. Original capital
2. Capital at the beginning of the year
3. Capital at the end of the year
4. Average capital (if this is specified, the method of computation should be outlined)

(c) EXAMPLE USING AVERAGE CAPITAL RATIO. The next example shows the division of profits and losses on the basis of average capital ratios.

The Articles of Co-partnership of Bracey and Maloney provide for the division of profits on the basis of the average capital balances as shown for the year by the books of the partnership. Effect is to be given to all contributions and withdrawals during the year. The capital accounts for the year appear as follows:

	Bracey		Maloney	
	Debit	*Credit*	*Debit*	*Credit*
January 1		$60,000		$48,000
March 1	$6,000			
April 1			$3,000	
June 1		12,000		
July 1			6,000	
September 1		3,000		21,000
October 1	9,000		9,000	
December 1				6,000

Computation of average capital is as follows:

	Debits	Credits	Balance	Time Maintained	Dollar-Months
			Bracey		
January 1		$60,000	$60,000	2 mos.	$120,000
March 1	$ 6,000		54,000	3	162,000
June 1		12,000	66,000	3	198,000
September 1		3,000	69,000	1	69,000
October 1	9,000		60,000	3	180,000
	$15,000	$75,000	$60,000	12 mos.	$729,000
					$ 60,750

Average capital ($729,000 ÷ 12)

	Debits	Credits	Balance	Time Maintained	Dollar-Months
			Maloney		
January 1		$48,000	$48,000	3 mos.	$144,000
April 1	$ 3,000		45,000	3	135,000
July 1	6,000		39,000	2	78,000
September 1		21,000	60,000	1	60,000
October 1	9,000		51,000	2	102,000
December 1	—	6,000	57,000	1	57,000
	$18,000	$75,000	$57,000	12 mos.	$576,000
					$ 48,000

Average capital ($576,000 ÷ 12)

If net profit for the year is $36,000, it is distributed as follows:

Bracey	$ 60,750	6,075 ÷ 10,875 × $36,000	$20,110.35
Maloney	48,000	4,800 ÷ 10,875 × 36,000	15,889.65
	$108,750		$36,000.00

This method assumes each month to be of equal significance. If the contributions and withdrawals are dated irregularly, it might be desirable to use days rather than months as the time unit.

(d) TREATMENT OF TRANSACTIONS BETWEEN PARTNER AND FIRM. It has often been pointed out that no single profit-sharing ratio can yield equitable results under all circumstances in view of the various contributions of the partners to the firm activities. Accordingly, the articles may well include provisions regarding allowances for (1) interest on invested capital, (2) salaries for services rendered, and (3) bonuses. The ratio for dividing the profit or loss remaining after applying such provisions must, of course, also be specified.

(i) Interest on Invested Capital. The partnership agreement should cover at least four points in the matter of allowing interest on invested capital:

1. Specific rate or directions for determining the rate
2. Procedure to be followed if the net income before interest is less than the interest requirement
3. Procedure to be followed if the partnership experiences a loss
4. Capital balance (beginning, closing, or average) on which interest is to be allowed (and, if an average balance, method by which the average is to be determined)

The rate of interest may be stated specifically or it may be determined by reference to the call money market, the yield of certain governmental obligations, the charge made by local banks for commercial loans, or some other available measure.

If the articles provide for a regular interest allowance, there should be included a statement of how to deal with the cases in which the firm operates at a loss or has a net profit of less than the interest. Two ways of dealing with these contingencies are: (1) the interest allowance may be dropped or reduced (when there is some profit) for the period in question; (2) the full interest may be allowed and the resulting net debit in the income account apportioned in the income (profit-sharing) ratio. The second procedure is customary for cases in which the articles do not cover the point precisely.

(ii) Partners' Salaries. Each working partner should be entitled to a stated salary as compensation for his or her services, just as each investing partner should receive interest on his or her capital investment. (The general rule, from a legal standpoint, is that a partner is not entitled to compensation for services in carrying on the business, other than his or her share in the profits, unless such compensation is specifically authorized in the partnership agreement.) It is always desirable that the articles of partnership specify the amounts of salaries or wages to be paid to partners or indicate clearly how the amounts are to be determined. The agreement regarding salaries should also cover the contingencies of inadequate income and net losses in particular periods.

Charges for salaries designed to represent reasonable allowances for personal services rendered by the partners are often viewed as operating expenses, and this interpretation may be included in the agreement. Under this interpretation, there would seem to be good reason for concluding that regular salaries should be allowed, whether or not the business is operated at a profit. As is the case with interest allowances on capital investments, there is strong presumption that if salaries are authorized in the agreement, they must be allowed, regardless of the level of earnings, in all cases in which a contrary treatment is not prescribed.

Treatment of salary allowances as business expenses is convenient from the standpoint of accounting procedure, particularly in that this treatment facilitates appropriate departmentalization of such charges. However, it must not be forgotten that partners' salaries, like interest allowances, are essentially devices intended to provide equitable treatment of partners who are supplying unlike amounts of capital and services to the firm; the purpose, in other words, is to secure an equitable apportionment of earnings.

According to Bedford, a distinct rule, "derived from custom and from law," that applies in accounting for partnership owners' equities is that "the income of a partnership is the income before deducting partners' salaries; partners' salaries are treated as a means of dividing partnership income."[5]

Dixon, Hepworth, and Paton, however, indicate that the interpretation of partners' salaries should vary with the circumstances:

> Where there are a substantial number of partners, and salaries are allowed to only one or two members who are active in administration, there is practical justification for treating such salaries as operating charges closely akin to the cost of services furnished by outsiders. This is especially defensible where the salaries are subject to negotiation from period to period and are in no way dependent upon the presence of net earnings. Where there are only two partners, and both capital investments and contributions of services are substantially equal, there is less need for salary adjustments; if "salaries" are allowed in such a situation it would seem to be reasonable to interpret them as preliminary distributions of net income—an income derived from a coordination of capital and personal efforts in a business venture. Between these two extremes there lies a range of less clear-cut cases.[6]

---

[5] N. M. Bedford, *Introduction to Modern Accounting* (New York: Ronald Press, 1962).

[6] R. L. Dixon, S. R. Hepworth, and W. A. Paton, Jr., *Essentials of Accounting* (New York: Macmillan, 1966).

(iii) Bonuses. Where a particular partner furnishes especially important services, the device of a bonus—usually expressed as a percentage of net income—may be employed as a means of providing additional compensation. The principal question that arises in such cases is the interpretation of the bonus in relation to the final net amount to be distributed according to the regular income ratio, as illustrated in the next example.

Stark and Bruch share profits equally. Per the partnership agreement, Bruch is to receive a bonus of 20 percent of the net income of the firm, before allowing the bonus, for special services to the firm. If in a particular year the credit balance of the expense and revenue account is $27,000 before allowing the bonus, profits are divided as follows:

	Stark	Bruch	Total
Bonus, 20% of $27,000		$ 5,400	$ 5,400
Balance equally	$10,800	10,800	21,600
	$10,800	$16,200	$27,000

If the bonus is to be treated as an expense item in the computation of the final net income, the $27,000 credit balance of the expense and revenue account represents both the bonus and the final net income. Hence the $27,000 is 120 percent of the net income, and the net income is 100 percent, or $22,500. Under this method, the profits are divided as follows:

	Stark	Bruch	Total
Bonus, 20% of $22,500		$ 4,500	$ 4,500
Balance equally	$11,250	11,250	22,500
	$11,250	$15,750	$27,000

(iv) Debtor–Creditor Relationship. At times, when a partnership is formed, a partner may not be interested in investing more than a certain amount of assets on a permanent basis. That partner, therefore, may make an advance to the partnership that is viewed as a loan rather than an increase in his or her capital account. The firm may thus obtain the initial financing it needs without having to negotiate with an outside source on less favorable terms. The loan may be interest bearing and may be repayable in installments. Interest charges on such loans should be treated as an expense of the partnership, and the loan itself should be disclosed clearly as a liability of the firm.

Occasionally, a partner may withdraw a sum from the partnership. This type of transaction should be treated in the manner dictated by the circumstances. If the loan is material relative to the partner's net personal assets, if no repayment terms are stipulated, and if the loan has been long outstanding, the loan is, in effect, a withdrawal and should be viewed as a contraction of the firm's capital. If, however, the partner has every intention of repaying the sum, the loan may be regarded as a valid receivable.

(v) Landlord–Tenant Relationship. In some cases, a partner may rent property from or to the partnership. Transactions of this type should be handled exactly as rental agreements with others are handled. The only possible difference in recording this type of event would find the rent receivable from a partner being debited to his or her drawing or capital account instead of to a "rent receivable" account. If the rent was owed to the partner, the payable could be recorded as a credit to either the partner's drawing or capital account. To minimize the possibility of confusion, it is preferable to record rental transactions with partners in the same manner as other rental agreements.

(vi) Statement Presentation. Receivables and payables arising out of transactions between a partner and the firm of which he or she is a partner should be classified in the balance sheet in the same manner as are receivables and payables arising out of transactions with nonpartners. However, any such receivables and payables included in the balance sheet should be set forth separately; they should not be combined with other receivables and payables. Accounting Standards Codification (ASC) Statement of Financial Accounting Standards (SFAS) No. 57 indicates that receivables or payables involving partners stem from a related party transaction and, as such, if material, should be disclosed in such a way as to include these four items:

1. The nature of the relationship(s) involved
2. A description of the transactions including transactions to which no amounts or nominal amounts were ascribed, for each of the periods for which income statements are presented, and such other information deemed necessary to an understanding of the effects of the transaction on the financial statements
3. The dollar amounts of transactions for each of the periods for which income statements are presented and the effects of any change in the method of establishing the terms from that used in the preceding period
4. Amounts due from or to related parties as of the date of each balance sheet presented and, if not otherwise apparent, the terms and manner of settlement

(e) CLOSING OPERATING ACCOUNTS.   The operating accounts are closed to the expense and revenue account in the usual manner. That account is then closed by crediting each partner's capital account with his or her share of the net income or debiting it with his or her share of the net loss. The drawing account of each partner is then closed to the respective capital account.

(i) Division of Profits Illustrated.   The articles of co-partnership of the fictitious firm of Ahern and Ciecka include these provisions as to distribution of profits:

Partners' loans. Loans made by partners to the firm shall draw interest at the rate of 6% per annum. Such interest shall be computed only on December 31 of each year regardless of the period in which the loan was in effect.

Partners' salaries. On December 31 of each year, salaries shall be allowed by a charge to the expense and revenue account and credits to the respective drawing accounts of the partners at the following amounts per annum: Ahern $14,400; Ciecka, $12,000. Partners' salaries are to be allowed whether or not earned.

Interest on partners' invested capital. Each partner is to receive interest at the rate of 6% per annum on the balance of his capital account at the beginning of the year. Such interest is to be allowed whether or not earned.

Remainder of profit or loss. The balance of net income after provision for salaries, interest on loans, and interest on invested capital is to be divided equally. Any loss resulting after provision for the above items is to be divided equally.

On December 31, the books of the partnership show these balances before recognition of interest and salary adjustments:

Sundry assets	$309,000	
Sundry liabilities		$ 66,000
Ahern, capital		120,000
Ahern, drawings	15,000	
Ciecka, capital		60,000
Ciecka, drawings	9,000	
Ciecka, loan		30,000
Expense and revenue	–	57,000
	$333,000	$333,000

AHERN AND CIECKA, PARTNERSHIP
Schedule of Division of Net Income
For the year Ended December 31, 20XX

	Total	Ahern	Ciecka
Interest on loan	$ 1,350		$ 1,350
Interest on capital	9,180	$ 6,300	2,880
Salaries allowed	26,400	14,400	12,000
Remainder—equally	20,070	10,035	10,035
Profit earned	$57,000	$30,735	$26,265

Exhibit 20.1   Division of Profits

Balances of the capital accounts on January 1 were: Ahern $105,000; Ciecka $48,000. The loan from Ciecka was made on April 1. Division of profits is as shown in Exhibit 20.1.

(ii) Statement of Partners' Capitals Illustrated.   Formal presentation of the activity of the partners' capital accounts is often made through the statement of partners' capitals (Exhibit 20.2).

(f) INCOME TAXES.   According to William H. Hoffman, Jr.:

Unlike corporations, estates, and trusts, partnerships are not considered separate taxable entities. Instead, each member of a partnership is subject to income tax on their distributive share of the partnership's income, even if an actual distribution is not made. (Section 701 of Subchapter K of the 1954 Code contains the statutory rule that the partners are liable for income tax in their separate or individual capacities. The partnership itself cannot be subject to the income tax on its earnings.) Thus, the tax return (Form 1065) required of a partnership serves only to provide information necessary in determining the character and amount of each partner's distributive share of the partnership's income and expense.[7]

Some states, however, impose an unincorporated business tax on a partnership that for all practical purposes is an income tax.

AHERN AND CIECKA, PARTNERSHIP
Statement of Partners' Capitals
For the year Ended December 31, 20XX

	Total	Ahern	Ciecka
Balances: January 1	$153,000	$105,000	$48,000
Add: additional investments	27,000	15,000	12,000
net income for year — per schedule	57,000	30,735	26,265
Total	237,000	150,735	86,265
Less: withdrawals	24,000	15,000	9,000
Investment, December 31	$213,000	$135,735	$77,265

Exhibit 20.2   Sample Statement of Partners' Capitals

---

[7] W. H. Hoffman, Jr., ed., *West's Federal Taxation: Corporations, Partnerships, Estates and Trusts* (St. Paul, MN: West, 1978).

20.3 ACCOUNTING FOR CHANGES IN FIRM MEMBERSHIP

(a) EFFECT OF CHANGE IN PARTNERS. From a legal point of view, the withdrawal of one or more partners or the admission of one or more new members has the effect of dissolving the original partnership and bringing into being a new firm. This means that the terms of the original agreement as such are not binding on the successor partnership. As far as the continuity of the business enterprise is concerned, however, a change in firm membership may be of only nominal importance; with respect to character of the business, operating policies, relations with customers, and so on, there may be no substantial difference between the new firm and its predecessor.

To determine the value of the equity of a retiring partner or the amount to be paid for a specified share by an incoming partner, a complete inventory and valuation of firm resources may be required. Estimation of interim profits and unrealized profits on long-term contracts may be involved. In any event, there should be a careful adjustment of partners' equities in accordance with the new relationships established.

A withdrawing partner may continue to be liable for the firm's obligation incurred prior to his or her withdrawal unless the settlement includes specific release therefrom by the continuing partners and by the creditors.

A person admitted as a partner into an existing partnership is liable for all the obligations of the partnership arising before his or her admission as if he or she had been a partner when such obligations were incurred, except that this liability shall be satisfied only out of partnership property.

(b) NEW PARTNER PURCHASING AN INTEREST. It is possible for a party to acquire the interest of a partner without becoming a partner. A member of a partnership may sell or assign his or her interest, but unless this has received the unanimous approval of the other partners, the purchaser does not become a partner; one partner cannot force copartners into partnership with an outsider. Under the UPA, the buyer in such a case acquires only the seller's interest in the profits and losses of the firm and, upon dissolution, the interest to which the original partner would have been entitled. The buyer has no voice in management, nor may he or she obtain an accounting except in case of dissolution of the business; ordinarily the buyer can make no withdrawal of capital without the consent of the partners.

To illustrate some of the possibilities in connection with purchase of an interest, assume that the firm of Hirt, Thompson, and Pitts negotiates with Davis for the purchase of a capital interest. Data are as follows:

	Capital Accounts	*Income Ratio*
Hirt	$20,000	50%
Thompson	12,000	40
Pitts	8,000	10
	$40,000	100%

(i) Purchase at Book Value. If Davis purchases a one-fourth interest for $10,000, it is clear that she is paying exactly book value, and the entry would be:

Hirt, capital	$5,000	
Thompson, capital	3,000	
Pitts, capital	2,000	
Davis, capital		$10,000

The cash payment would be divided in the same manner (i.e., Hirt $5,000, Thompson $3,000, and Pitts $2,000) and would pass directly from Davis to them without going through the firm's cash account.

(ii) Purchase at More than Book Value. Assume now that Davis agrees to pay $12,000 for a one-fourth interest; this is more than book value. In general, two solutions are possible.

Bonus Method. Under this method, the extra $2,000 paid by Davis is considered to be a bonus to Hirt, Thompson, and Pitts and is shared by them in the income ratio. The entry is:

Hirt, capital	$5,000	
Thompson, capital	3,000	
Pitts, capital	2,000	
Davis, capital		$10,000

The cash payment of $12,000 is divided as shown:

	Hirt	Thompson	Pitts	Total
Capital transferred	$5,000	$3,000	$ 2,000	$10,000
Premium—in income ratio	1,000	800	200	2,000
Cash received	$6,000	$3,800	$2,200	$12,000

Goodwill Method. That Davis is willing to pay $12,000 for a one-fourth interest indicates that the business is worth $48,000. Existing assets are therefore undervalued by $8,000. Under the goodwill or revaluation of assets method, if specific assets can be revalued, this should be done. If not, or if the agreed revaluation is less than $8,000, the difference may be assumed to be goodwill. Dividing the gain in the income ratio results in this entry:

Sundry, assets and/or goodwill	$8,000	
Hirt, capital		$4,000
Thompson, capital		3,200
Pitts, capital		4,800

The entry to record Davis's admission would then be:

Hirt, capital	$6,000	
Thompson, capital		$ 3,800
Pitts, capital		2,200
Davis, capital		12,000

The cash payment will be received in amounts equal to the transfer from the capital accounts.

(iii) Purchase at Less than Book Value. Assume next that Davis agrees to pay only $9,000 for a one-fourth interest—that is, less than book value. Again two solutions are possible.

Bonus Method. Under this method, the same transfers are made from the three partners to Davis's capital account as if she had paid book value, but the difference of $1,000 is apportioned to determine the cash settlement, as follows:

	Hirt	Thompson	Pitts	Total
Capital transferred	$5,000	$3,000	$2,000	$10,000
Loss—in income ratio	500	400	100	1,000
Cash received	$4,500	$2,600	$1,900	$ 9,000

Revaluation of Assets Method. This approach reasons that a price of $9,000 for a one-fourth interest indicates that the business is worth $36,000 and that assets should be revalued downward by $4,000. Where a portion of the write-down can be identified with specific tangible assets, the appropriate accounts should be adjusted. Otherwise, existing goodwill should be included in the write-down. The entries would be:

	(1)	
Hirt, capital	$2,000	
Thompson, capital	1,600	
Pitts, capital	2,400	
Sundry, assets and/or goodwill		$4,000
	(2)	
Hirt, capital	$4,500	
Thompson, capital	2,600	
Pitts, capital	1,900	
Davis, capital		$9,000

(c) NEW PARTNER'S INVESTMENT TO ACQUIRE AN INTEREST.   The admission of a new partner when he or she makes an investment in the firm to acquire a capital interest is illustrated by the following cases.

Assume that the capital account balances of the partnership of Andrews and Bell prior to the admission of Cohen are:

	Capital Accounts	*Income Ratio*
Andrews	$18,000	60%
Bell	12,000	40
	$30,000	100%

(i) Investment at Book Value.   If Cohen invests $10,000 in the firm for a one-fourth interest, the entry is:

Cash (or other assets)	$10,000	
Cohen, capital		$10,000

(ii) Investment at More than Book Value.   If Cohen is willing to invest $14,000 for a one-fourth interest, the total capital will be $44,000.

Bonus Method.   Under this method, Cohen's share is one-fourth or $11,000, and the $3,000 premium is treated as a bonus to the old partners by the entry:

Cash (or other assets)	$14,000	
Andrews, capital		$ 1,800
Bell, capital		1,200
Cohen, capital		11,000

Goodwill Method.   If Cohen invests $14,000 for a one-fourth interest, it would seem that the total worth of the firm should be $56,000. Since total capital is $44,000, under the goodwill or revaluation of assets method, there is justification in assuming that existing assets are undervalued to the extent of $12,000. Circumstances may indicate that the $12,000 undervaluation is in the form of goodwill. If it is to be recognized, the entries are:

	(1)	
Goodwill	$12,000	
Andrews, capital		$ 7,200
Bell, capital		4,800
	(2)	
Cash	$14,000	
Cohen, capital		$14,000

If the understatement of the capital of the old partners was attributable to excessive depreciation allowances, land appreciation, an increase in inventory value, or some combination of such factors, an appropriate adjustment of the asset or assets involved would be substituted for the charge to "goodwill."

(iii) Investment at Less Than Book Value.

Bonus Method.   If Cohen invests $8,000 for a one-fourth interest, it may indicate the willingness of the old partners to give Cohen a bonus to enter the firm.

Since the total capital is now $38,000, a one-fourth interest is $9,500 and the entry is:

Cash	$8,000	
Andrews, capital	900	
Bell, capital	600	
Cohen, capital		$9,500

Revaluation of Assets Method.   Under this method, the investment by Cohen of only $8,000 for a one-fourth interest may be taken to mean that the existing net assets are worth only $24,000. The overvaluation of $6,000 could be corrected by crediting the overvalued assets and charging Andrews and Bell in the income ratio. The entries would be:

	(1)	
Andrews, capital	$3,600	
Bell, capital	2,400	
Sundry assets		$6,000
	(2)	
Cash	$8,000	
Cohen, capital		$8,000

(iv) Goodwill Method.

A third method sometimes offered to handle this situation is the goodwill method, which assumes that the new partner contributes goodwill (of $2,000 in this case) in addition to the cash and is credited for the amount of his interest at book value ($10,000 in this case). This seems illogical, however, since it contradicts the original fact that Cohen's investment was to be $8,000.

(d) SETTLING WITH WITHDRAWING PARTNER THROUGH OUTSIDE FUNDS.

The withdrawal of a partner where settlement is effected by payments made from personal funds of the remaining partners directly to the retiring partner is illustrated by the firm of Adams, Bates, & Caldwell:

	Capital Balances	*Income Ratio*
Adams	$30,000	50%
Bates	24,000	30%
Caldwell	16,000	20%
	$70,000	100%

(i) Sale at Book Value.

If Caldwell retires, selling her interest at book value to the other partners in their income ratio and receiving payment from outside funds of Adams and Bates, the entry is:

Caldwell, capital	$16,000	
Andrews, capital		$10,000
Bates, capital		6,000

The total payment to Caldwell is $16,000, and payments by Adams and Bates are $10,000 and $6,000, respectively.

(ii) Sale at More Than Book Value.   If payment to Caldwell exceeds book value, either the bonus or the goodwill method may be used.

Bonus Method.   If total payment to Caldwell is $18,000, the premium of $2,000 may be treated as a bonus to Caldwell. The entry to record the withdrawal of Caldwell is the same as above, and payment would be:

	Adams	Bates	Total
Capital per books	$10,000	$6,000	$16,000
Premium paid	1,250	750	2,000
Cash required	$11,250	$6,750	$18,000

Goodwill Method.   In the following situation, Adams and Bates are willing to pay a total of $2,000 more than book value for Caldwell's interest. Since the latter receives 20 percent of the profits, this implies that assets are undervalued by $10,000. Under the goodwill or revaluation of assets method, all or part of this amount may be goodwill. The entries to record this situation are:

	(1)	
Goodwill or sundry assets	$10,000	
Adams, capital		$5,000
Bates, capital		3,000
Caldwell, capital		2,000
	(2)	
Caldwell, capital	$18,000	
Adams, capital		$11,250
Bates, capital		6,750

(iii) Sale at Less Than Book Value.   If Caldwell should agree to accept $15,000 for her interest, this is $1,000 less than book value.

Bonus Method.   The $1,000 may be considered to be a bonus to Adams and Bates. The entry would be the same as in the first example, but the cash payments would be calculated as follows:

	Adams	Bates	Total
Capital, per books	$10,000	$6,000	$16,000
Less discount allowed	625	375	1,000
Cash required	$ 9,375	$ 5,625	$15,000

Revaluation of Assets Method.   In this example, it can be argued under the revaluation of assets approach that the discount of $1,000 for a 20 percent share in firm profits implies an overstatement of book values of assets by $5,000. If this correction is to be made, the entries to adjust the books and record the subsequent withdrawal of Caldwell are:

	(1)	
Adams, capital	$ 2,500	
Bates, capital	1,500	
Caldwell, capital	1,000	
Sundry assets		$5,000
	(2)	
Caldwell, capital	$15,000	
Adams, capital		$9,375
Bates, capital		5,625

In preceding examples, the so-called bonus method and revaluation of assets method have been presented as alternatives. Although each method results in different capital account balances in the new firm that comes into being, it should be observed that the partners in the new firm are treated relatively the same under either method. This is subject to the basic qualification that the old partners who remain in the new firm must continue to share profits and losses as between themselves in the same ratio as before.

(e) SETTLEMENT THROUGH FIRM FUNDS.   The withdrawal of a partner where settlement is to be made from funds of the business is illustrated by the firm of Arnold, Brown & Cline.

	Capital Balances	Income Ratio
Arnold	$ 40,000	30%
Brown	50,000	30
Cline	60,000	40
	$150,000	100%

(i) Premium Paid to Retiring Partner.   Payment is to be made to Cline from the assets of the partnership. Payment is $64,000, to be made one-half in cash and the balance in notes payable. Under one treatment, the premium of $4,000 is viewed as chargeable to the remaining partners in their income ratio. The entry is:

Arnold, capital	$ 2,000	
Brown, capital	2,000	
Cline, capital	60,000	
Cash		$32,000
Notes payable		32,000

A second method treats the $4,000 premium as payment for Cline's share of the unrecognized goodwill of the firm. The following entry would be made:

Goodwill	$ 4,000	
Cline, capital	60,000	
Cash		$32,000
Notes payable		32,000

A third possibility for recording the retirement of Cline is to recognize a total goodwill or asset revaluation implied by the premium paid for the retiring partner's share. Since a $4,000 premium was paid for a 40 percent share, total implied goodwill or asset revaluation is $10,000, and the entries are:

	(1)	
Goodwill or sundry assets	$10,000	
Arnold, capital		$3,000
Brown, capital		3,000
Cline, capital		4,000
	(2)	
Cline, capital	$64,000	
Cash		$32,000
Notes payable		32,000

Many accountants are inclined to approve of the first treatment on the grounds that it is "conservative." Meigs, Johnson, and Keller state that it is "consistent with the current trend toward viewing a partnership as a continuing business entity, with asset valuations and accounting policies remaining undisturbed by the retirement of a partner."[8] The second treatment is supported by reference to the rule that it is proper to set up goodwill only when it has been purchased. The third interpretation relies on the idea that it is inconsistent to recognize the existence of an intangible asset and then to record it at only a fraction of the proper amount.

The accountant may distinguish between a payment for goodwill and one that represents a partner's share of the increase in value of one or more of the firm's assets. In the latter case, it is generally not reasonable to record only the increase attaching to the retiring partner's equity. Suppose, for example, that an inventory of merchandise has a market value on the date of settlement substantially above book value. Clearly, the most appropriate treatment here is that under which the inventory is adjusted to market value—the value at which it is in effect acquired by the new firm; to add to book value only the withdrawing partner's share of the increase would result in figures unsatisfactory from the standpoint both of financial accounting and operating procedure.

(ii) Discount Given by Retiring Partner.   Assuming that Cline receives $57,000 for his interest in the firm and payment is made by equal amounts of cash and notes payable, two possible accounting treatments are available.

First, the discount of $3,000 may be credited to the remaining partners in their income ratio:

Cline, capital	$60,000	
Cash		$28,500
Notes payable		28,500
Arnold, capital		21,500
Brown, capital		21,500

In the second method, the implied overvaluation of assets is recognized. Since Cline's share (40 percent) was purchased at a discount of $3,000, the total overvaluation of firm assets may be considered as $7,500. The following entries are made:

	(1)	
Arnold, capital	$ 2,250	
Brown, capital	2,250	
Cline, capital	3,000	
Sundry assets		$7,500
	(2)	
Cline, capital	$57,000	
Cash		$28,500
Notes payable		28,500

(f) ADJUSTMENT OF CAPITAL RATIOS.   Circumstances may arise in partnership affairs when it becomes desirable to adjust partners' capital account balances to certain ratios—most often the income ratio. This may happen in connection with the admission of a new partner, the withdrawal of a partner, or at some time when no change in personnel has occurred. Only a simple case involving a continuing firm is illustrated here.

---

[8] W. B. Meigs, C. E. Johnson, and T. F. Keller, *Advanced Accounting I* (New York: McGraw-Hill, 1966).

Assume the following data for the firm of Emmett, Frye, and Gable:

	Capital Balances	Income Ratio
Emmett	$50,000	50%
Frye	25,000	30
Gable	15,000	20
	$90,000	100%

If the partners wish to adjust their capital balances to the income ratio without changing total capital, it is obvious that Frye should pay $2,000 and Gable $3,000 directly to Emmett and that the entry should be:

Emmet, capital	$5,000	
Frye, capital		$2,000
Gable, capital		3,000

Adjustment of the capital balances to the income ratio by the minimum additional investment into the firm (as distinguished from the preceding personal settlement) could, of course, be effected by the additional investment of $5,000 each by Frye and Gable.

20.4 INCORPORATION OF A PARTNERSHIP

According to Meigs, Johnson, and Keller:

> Most successful partnerships give consideration at times to the possible advantages to be gained by incorporating. Among the advantages are limited liability, ease of attracting outside capital without loss of control, and possible tax savings.

> A new corporation formed to take over the assets and liabilities of a partnership will usually sell stock to outsiders for cash either at the time of incorporation or at a later date. To assure that the former partners receive an equitable portion of the total capital stock, the assets of the partnership will need to be adjusted to fair market value before being transferred to the corporation. Any goodwill developed by the partnership should be recognized as part of the assets transferred.

> The accounting records of a partnership may be modified and continued in use when the firm changes to the corporate form. As an alternative, the partnership books may be closed and a new set of accounting records established for the corporation.[9]

20.5 PARTNERSHIP REALIZATION AND LIQUIDATION

(a) BASIC CONSIDERATIONS.   A partnership may be disposed of either by selling the business as a unit or by the sale (realization) of the specific assets followed by the liquidation of the liabilities and final distribution of the remaining assets (usually cash) to the partners. A basic principle to be observed carefully in all such cases is that losses (or gains) in realization or sale must first be apportioned among the partners in the income ratio, following which, if outside creditors have been paid in full or cash reserved for that purpose, payments may be made according to the remaining capital balances of the partners.

---

[9] Ibid.

Discussions of partnership liquidations usually point out that the proper order of cash distribution is: (1) payment of creditors in full, (2) payment of partners' loan accounts, and (3) payment of partners' capital accounts. Actually, the stated priority of the partners' loans appears to be a legal fiction. An established legal doctrine called the right of offset requires that any credit balance standing in a partner's name be set off against an actual or potential debit balance in his capital account. Application of this right of offset always produces the same final result as if the loan or undrawn salary account were a part of the capital balance at the beginning of the process. For this reason, no separate examples are given that include loan accounts. If they are encountered, they may be added to the capital account balance at the top of the liquidation statement. (The existence of partners' loan accounts might have an effect on profit sharing, however, in the sense that interest on partners' loans is usually provided for and profits might be shared in the average capital ratio; loans presumably would be excluded from the computation.)

Realization of all assets and liquidation of liabilities may be completed before any cash is distributed to partners. Or, if the realization process stretches over a considerable period of time, so-called installment liquidation may be employed.

(b) LIQUIDATION BY SINGLE CASH DISTRIBUTION.   The next illustration demonstrates the realization of assets, payment of creditors, and final single cash distribution to the partners. Losses are first allocated to the partners in the income ratio, followed by cash payment to creditors and then to partners.

Rogers, Stevens, and Troy are partners with capital balances of $20,000, $15,000, and $10,000, respectively. Profits and losses are shared equally. On a particular date they find that the firm has assets of $80,000, liabilities of $47,000, and undistributed losses of $12,000. At this point the assets are sold for $59,000 cash. The proper distribution of the cash is as follows:

		Total	Rogers	Stevens	Troy
Capital balances		$45,000	$20,000	$15,000	$10,000
Less undistributed losses		12,000	4,000	4,000	4,000
Adjusted balances		33,000	16,000	11,000	6,000
Less loss on sale of assets		21,000	7,000	7,000	7,000
Adjusted balances		12,000	9,000	4,000	(1,000)
Payment by Troy for deficiency		1,000			1,000
Balances before distribution		$13,000	$ 9,000	$ 4,000	$ 0
Cash available	$60,000				
Paid to creditors	47,000				
Cash paid to partners		$13,000	$ 9,000	$ 4,000	$ 0

In this example, it was assumed that Troy was financially able to make up the $1,000 deficiency that appeared in his capital account. Only by making this payment does he bear his agreed share of the losses. If Troy had been personally insolvent and therefore unable to make the $1,000 payment, the statement from that point on would have taken this form:

		Total	Rogers	Stevens	Troy
Adjusted balances		$12,000	$9,000	$4,000	$(1,000)
Apportion deficiency in income ratio			(500)	(500)	1,000
Balances before distribution		$12,000	$8,500	$3,500	$ 0
Cash available	$59,000				
Paid to creditors	47,000				
Cash paid to partners		$12,000	$8,500	$3,500	$ 0

Troy is now personally indebted to Rogers and Stevens in the amount of $500 each. Just how this debt would rank in the settlement of Troy's personal affairs depends on the state having jurisdiction. Under the UPA, his personal creditors (not including Rogers and Stevens) have prior claim to his personal assets; because he was said to have been personally insolvent, the presumption is that Rogers and Stevens would collect nothing. In a common-law state, a deficiency of this sort is considered to be a personal debt and would generally rank along with the other personal creditors. In this event, Rogers and Stevens would presumably make a partial recovery of the $500 due each of them.

(c) LIQUIDATION BY INSTALLMENTS. It is sometimes necessary to liquidate on an installment basis. Two of the many possible cases are illustrated—in the first there is no capital deficiency to any partner when the first cash distribution is made; in the second there is a possible deficiency of one partner at the time of the first cash distribution. The situation involving a final deficiency of a partner was discussed earlier in the partnership of Rogers, Stevens, and Troy. If this situation should appear in the winding up of an installment liquidation, its treatment would be the same as described there.

The role of the liquidator is especially important in the case of installment liquidation. In addition to the liquidator's obvious responsibility to see that outside creditors are paid and to convert the various assets into cash with a maximum gain or a minimum loss, he or she must protect the interests of the partners in their relationship to each other. Other than for reimbursement of liquidation expenses, no cash payment can be made to a partner, even on loan accounts or undrawn profits, except as the total standing to his or her credit exceeds his or her share of total possible losses on assets not yet realized. Improper payment by the liquidator might result in personal liability. Therefore, recovery could not be made from the partner who was overpaid.

(d) CAPITAL CREDITS ONLY—NO CAPITAL DEFICIENCY. The balance sheet of Burns & Mantle as of April 30, when installment liquidation of the firm began, is presented next. The partners share profits and losses equally.

Assets		Liabilities and Capital	
Cash	$ 6,200	Liabilities	$ 56,000
Other assets	350,000	Burns, capital	220,200
		Mantle, capital	80,000
	$356,200		$356,200

During May, assets having a book value of $220,000 are sold for cash of $198,000, and $39,000 is paid to creditors. During June, the remaining assets are sold for $90,000, the balance due creditors is paid, and liquidation expenses of $8,000 are paid. Distribution of cash to the partners should be made as follows:

	Total	Burns	Mantle
Capital, per balance sheet	$300,200	$220,200	$ 80,000
Less realization loss in May	22,000	11,000	11,000
Balance after loss	278,200	209,200	69,000
Cash available to partners	148,200		
Possible loss divided	130,000	65,000	65,000
Balances paid in cash		144,200	4,000
Balances, June 1		65,000	65,000
Less realization loss in June	40,000	20,000	20,000
Balances after loss	90,000	45,000	45,000
Less liquidation expense	8,000	4,000	4,000
Final cash payment	$ 82,000	$ 41,000	$ 41,000

Cash available to partners at May 31 is calculated as follows

Cash, per balance sheet	$ 6,200	
Received from sale of assets—May	198,000	$204,200
Paid to creditors—May	39,000	
Reserved for creditors	17,000	56,000
Available for distribution to partners		$148,200

In this example, the first payment of $148,200 reduces the capital claims to the profit and loss ratios, and all subsequent charges or credits to the partners' capital accounts are made accordingly.

(i) Capital Credits Only—Capital Deficiency of One Partner.   This situation is illustrated in Exhibit 20.3 using the previous balance sheet but assuming the next liquidation data:

BURNS & MANTLE
Statement of Liquidation
May 1 to July 31

	Total	Burns	Mantle
Capital balances, May 1	$300,200	$220,200	$80,000
Less realization loss in May	30,000	15,000	15,000
Balances after loss, May 31[a]	270,200	205,200	65,000
Less realization loss in June	40,000	20,000	20,000
Balances after loss, June 30	230,200	185,200	45,000
Cash available to partners[b]	60,200		
Possible loss apportioned	170,000	85,000	85,000
Balances after apportionment		100,200	(40,000)
Further possible loss to Burns		(40,000)	40,000
Cash payment to Burns		60,200	
Balances, July 1		125,000	45,000
Less realization loss in July	25,000	12,500	12,500
Balances after loss, July 31	145,000	112,500	(32,500)
Less liquidation expense	8,000	4,000	4,000
Final cash payment	$137,000	$108,500	$28,500

Calculation:

Cash, per balance sheet	$ 6,200	
Received from sale of assets — May	50,000	$ 56,200
Paid to creditors — May	39,000	
Reserved for creditors	17,000	56,000
Available to partners — not distributed, May 31		$ 200

	Assets Sold	Cash Received	Creditors Paid	Expenses Paid
May	$ 80,000	$ 50,000	$39,000	
June	100,000	60,000	17,000	
July	170,000	145,000		$8,000

[a]No cash was distributed to partners at May 31 because only $200 was available at that time.
[b]This amount is the $200 not distributed at May 31 plus the $60,000 received in June from sale of assets.

Exhibit 20.3   Sample Statement of Liquidation

In Exhibit 20.3, each partner received in total the balance of his or her capital account per the balance sheet minus his or her share (50 percent) of realization losses and expenses, the same as if one final cash payment had been made on July 31. Note that if Mantle had had a loan account of, say, $20,000 and a capital balance of $60,000, the first cash distribution of $60,200 would still have gone entirely to Burns. At this point, after exercising the right of offset, Mantle would still have had a future possible deficiency of $40,000.

(ii) Installment Distribution Plan. A somewhat different approach to the problem of installment liquidation is illustrated below.

Fox, Green, and Harris are partners sharing profits equally. Shown next is the partnership balance sheet as of December 31, at which time it is decided to liquidate the firm by installments.

Assets		Liabilities and Capital	
Cash	$ 3,000	Liabilities	$ 24,000
Other assets	186,000	Fox, capital	79,000
		Green, capital	52,000
		Harris, capital	34,000
	$189,000		$189,000

Using this balance sheet, computation of correct cash distribution is as follows:

	Total	Fox	Green	Harris
Partners' capital balances	$165,000	$79,000	$52,000	$34,000
Loss that would eliminate				
Harris, who is least able to absorb	102,000	34,000	34,000	34,000
Balances	$63,000	$45,000	$18,000	
Loss that would eliminate				
Green	36,000	18,000	18,000	
Balances	$ 27,000	$27,000		

The amount of the loss that will extinguish each partner's capital account is determined by dividing his or her capital account by his or her percentage of income and loss sharing. Hence, for Harris, this amount is $34,000 ÷ 33 1/3 percent, or $102,000.

From the computations, it is possible to prepare a schedule for the distribution of cash as follows:

	Cash	Liabilities	Fox	Green	Harris
First	$21,000	$21,000			
Next	27,000		All		
Next	36,000		1/2	1/2	
All in excess of	84,000		1/3	1/3	1/3

It is assumed that the $3,000 cash on hand on December 31 is used in payment of liabilities. The following liquidation data are given:

	Assets Sold	Cash Received	Creditors Paid
January	$64,000	$41,000	$24,000
February	60,000	37,000	
March	62,000	54,000	
Totals	$186,000	$132,000	$24,000

Based on these data, the application of the computations already made results in the following payments to creditors and partners:

	Amount	Liabilities	Fox	Green	Harris
January	$ 41,000	$21,000	$20,000		
February	37,000		7,000		
			15,000	$15,000	
March	54,000		3,000	3,000	
			16,000	16,000	$16,000
Totals	$132,000	$21,000	$61,000	$34,000	$16,000

20.6 LIMITED PARTNERSHIPS

(a) DEFINITION. *Limited partnerships* are business partnership structures that permit partners to invest capital with the proviso that there will be limited control over business operations and, accordingly, assumption of liability limited to the extent of capital contributions.

In general partnerships, the potential liability that can accrue to individual partners is unlimited. That unlimited liability has always been a major drawback of the partnership structure. Limited partnerships evolved to a great extent in order to overcome that disadvantage.

The legal provisions governing limited partnerships are provided by the Uniform Limited Partnership Act and the Revised Uniform Limited Partnership Act, which have been adopted in some form by each state government.

(b) DIFFERENCES BETWEEN LIMITED PARTNERSHIPS AND GENERAL PARTNERSHIPS. In addition to limitations on the liability of partners, limited partnerships differ from general partnerships in these ways:

- Limited partners have no participation in the management of the limited partnership.
- Limited partners may invest only cash or other assets in a limited partnership; they may not provide services as their investment.
- The surname of a limited partner may not appear in the name of the partnership.

(c) FORMATION OF LIMITED PARTNERSHIPS. The formation of limited partnerships is generally evidenced by a certificate filed with the county recorder of the principal place of business of the limited partnership rather than a partnership agreement such as that described in Section 20.1(e). Such certificates include many of the items present in the typical partnership contract of a general partnership. In addition, certificates must include:

- Name and residence of each general partner and limited partner
- Amount of cash and other assets invested by each limited partner
- Provision for return of a limited partner's investment
- Any priority of one or more limited partners over other limited partners
- Any right of limited partners to vote for election or removal of general partners, termination of the partnership, amendment of the certificate, or disposal of all partnership assets

Interests in limited partnerships are offered to prospective limited partners in units subject to the Securities Act of 1933. Thus, unless provisions of that act exempt a limited partnership, it must file a registration statement for the offered units with the Securities and Exchange Commission (SEC) and undertake to file periodic reports with the SEC. Large limited partnerships that engage in ventures such as oil and gas exploration and real estate development and issue units registered with the SEC are called *master limited partnerships*. The SEC has provided guidance for such registration and reporting in Industry Guide 5, *Preparation of Registration Statements Relating to Interests in Real Estate Limited Partnerships.*

(d) ACCOUNTING AND FINANCIAL CONSIDERATIONS. As a general rule, the accounting records of limited partnerships are kept on a cash basis. However, the SEC requires that limited partnerships registrants prepare and file basic financial statements in conformity with generally accepted accounting principles (GAAP). For example, paragraph 10-S99-5 of ASC Topic 505-10, *Equity,* requires, for a public reporting company, the equity section of the limited partnership's balance sheet to distinguish between general partner and limited partner equity, with a separate statement of changes in partnership equity for each type of participation provided for each period for which a limited partnership income statement is presented.

The SEC staff also believes it is appropriate for a limited partnership registrant to include financial data on a tax basis of accounting, with an appropriate reconciliation of differences in major disclosure areas between tax and financial accounting. Whether GAAP-basis financial statements (along with the data necessary for income tax return preparation) should be distributed to the participants of SEC-reporting limited partnerships is a matter covered by the proxy rules.

ASC Topic 272, *Limited Liability Entities,* provides reporting guidance along with guidance on certain accounting issues regarding the application of existing authoritative literature for limited liability companies and limited liability partnerships (jointly referred to herein as LLCs).

(i) Financial Statement Reporting Issues. According to ASC Topic 272, a complete set of LLC financial statements should include:

- Statement of financial position as of the end of the reporting period
- Statement of operations for the period
- Statement of cash flows for the period
- Accompanying notes to financial statements

LLCs should also present information related to changes in members' equity for the period, either in a separate statement combined with the statement of operations or in the notes to the financial statements. The headings of an LLC's financial statements should identify clearly the financial statements as those of a limited liability company.

ASC Topic 272 stipulates that the financial statements of an LLC should be similar in presentation to those of a partnership. Since the owners of an LLC are referred to as *members,* the equity section in the statement of financial position should be titled *members' equity.* If more than one class of members exists, each having varying rights, preferences, and privileges, the LLC is encouraged to report the equity of each class separately within the equity section. If the LLC does not report the amount of each class separately within the equity section, it should disclose those amounts in the notes to the financial statements.

Even though a member's liability may be limited, if the total balance of the member's equity account or accounts described in the preceding paragraph is less than zero, a deficit should be reported in the statement of financial position.

If the LLC maintains separate accounts for components of members' equity (e.g., undistributed earnings, earnings available for withdrawal, or unallocated capital), ASC Topic 272 permits disclosure of those components, either on the face of the statement of financial position or in the notes to the financial statements.

If the LLC records amounts due from members for capital contributions, such amounts should be presented as deductions from members' equity. ASC Topic 272 notes that presenting such amounts as assets is inappropriate except in very limited circumstances when there is substantial evidence of ability and intent to pay within a reasonably short period of time.

Presentation of comparative financial statements is encouraged, but not required, by ASC Subtopic 205-10-45, *Other Presentation Matters.* If comparative financial statements are presented, amounts shown for comparative purposes must in fact be comparable with those shown for the most recent period, or any exceptions to comparability must be disclosed in the notes to the financial statements. Situations may exist in which financial statements of the same reporting entity for periods prior to the period of conversion are not comparable with those for the most recent period presented—for example, if transactions such as spin-offs or other distributions of assets occurred prior to or as part of the LLC's formation. In such situations, sufficient disclosure should be made so the comparative financial statements are not misleading. If the formation of the LLC results in a new reporting entity, a company should follow the guidance in paragraph 45-21 of ASC Topic 250, *Accounting Changes and Error Corrections,* and apply the change retrospectively to the financial statements of all prior periods presented to show financial information for the new reporting entity for those periods.

(ii) Financial Statement Disclosure Issues. ASC Topic 272 requires that these disclosures be made in the financial statements of a limited liability company:

- Any limitation of its members' liability should be described.
- The different classes of members' interests and the respective rights, preferences, and privileges of each class. If the LLC does not report separately the amount of each class in the equity section of the statement of financial position, those amounts should be disclosed.
- LLCs subject to income tax should make the disclosures required by ASC Topic 740, *Income Taxes.*
- If the LLC has a finite life, the date the LLC will cease to exist should be disclosed.
- For LLCs formed by combining entities under common control or by conversion from another type of entity, the notes to the financial statements for the year of formation should disclose that the assets and liabilities previously were held by a predecessor entity or entities. LLCs formed by combining entities under common control are encouraged to make the relevant disclosures in paragraphs 50-50-1 through 50-50-4 of ASC Topic 805, *Business Combinations.*

(iii) Accounting Issues. ASC Topic 272 requires that an LLC formed by combining entities under common control or by conversion from another type of entity initially should state its assets and liabilities at amounts at which they were stated in the financial statements of the predecessor entity or entities in a manner similar to a pooling of interests.

LLCs generally are classified as partnerships for federal income tax purposes. An LLC that is subject to federal (U.S.), foreign, state, or local (including franchise) taxes based on income should account for such taxes in accordance with ASC Topic 740.

ASC Topic 272 points out that in accordance with ASC Topic 740, an entity whose tax status in a jurisdiction changes from taxable to nontaxable should eliminate any deferred tax assets or liabilities related to that jurisdiction as of the date the entity ceases to be a taxable entity. ASC Topic 740 requires disclosure of significant components of income tax expense attributable to continuing operations including "adjustments of a deferred tax liability or asset for . . . a change in the tax status of the enterprise."

20.7 NONPUBLIC INVESTMENT PARTNERSHIPS

ASC Topic 946, *Financial Services—Investment Companies,* provides financial reporting guidance for investment partnerships that are exempt from SEC registration pursuant to the Investment Company Act of 1940 and defined as an investment company, except for:

- Investment partnerships that are brokers and dealers in securities subject to regulation under the Securities Exchange Act of 1934 (registered broker-dealers) and that manage funds only for those who are officers, directors, or employees of the general partner
- Investment partnerships that are commodity pools subject to regulation under the Commodity Exchange Act of 1974

ASC Topic 946 provides that the financial statements of an investment partnership, when prepared in conformity with GAAP, should, at a minimum, include a condensed schedule of investments in securities owned by the partnership at the close of the most recent period. Such a schedule should categorize investments by:

- Type (such as common stocks, preferred stocks, convertible securities, fixed-income securities, government securities, options purchased, options written, warrants, futures, loan participations, short sales, other investment companies, etc.)
- Country or geographic region
- Industry

The schedule should report the percentage of net assets that each such category represents and the total value and cost for each type of investment and country or geographic region. The schedule should also disclose the name, shares or principal amount, value, and type of:

- Each investment (including short sales) constituting more than 5 percent of net assets
- All investments in any one issuer aggregating more than 5 percent of net assets

In applying the 5 percent test, total long and total short positions in any one issuer should be considered separately.

Other investments (those that are individually 5 percent or less of net assets) should be aggregated without specifically identifying the issuers of such investments and be categorized by type, country or region, and industry. Also note that the foregoing information is required when the partnership's proportional share of any security owned by an individual investee exceeds 5 percent of the reporting partnership's net assets. Disclosure of the required information for such securities may be made either on the schedule itself or in a note thereto.

ASC Topic 946 also requires that investment partnerships present, among other things, separate disclosure of dividend income and interest income and realized and unrealized gains (losses) on securities for the period.

Investment companies organized as limited partnerships typically receive advisory services from the general partner. For such services, a number of partnerships pay fees chargeable as expenses to the partnership, whereas others allocate net income from the limited partners' capital accounts to the general partner's capital account, and still others employ a combination of the two methods. ASC Topic 946 states that the amounts of any such payments or allocations should be presented in either the statement of operations or the statement of changes in partners' capital, and the method of computing such payments or allocations should be described in the notes to the financial statements.

20.8 JOINT VENTURES

Forming a joint venture is a common way to create alliances and gain entry to or expand business operations in various domestic and foreign markets. As an alternative to a complete sale of a business, a company may form a joint venture if it is the company's desire to exit a business only partially while still maintaining an interest the rest of the business.

A company needs to use significant judgment and careful analysis regarding the accounting for joint ventures. Generally, the investors' accounting for the formation of a joint venture, including the receipt of noncash assets by the venture, provide for complex issues to sort through. Also adding to the complexities, a joint venture investor must evaluate its joint venture interests under the Variable Interest Entities Subtopics of ASC Topic 810, *Consolidations,* first to determine if the joint venture is a variable interest entity and whether one investor, or another enterprise with a variable interest in the entity, is the primary beneficiary and may be required to consolidate the joint venture.

Chapter 9 of this *Handbook* discusses the requirements to consolidate a variable interest entity.

(a) DEFINITION.   *Joint ventures* are partnerships formed when two or more parties pool resources for the purpose of undertaking a specific project, such as the development or marketing of a product. Joint ventures are owned, operated, and jointly controlled by a small group of owners or investors as separate business projects operated for the mutual benefit of the ownership group. Joint ventures may take the legal form of partnerships or they may be separately incorporated entities.

The owners or investors (venturers) in a joint venture may or may not have equal ownership interests in the venture. A venturer's share may range from as low as 5 percent or 10 percent to over 50 percent, but no less. All venturers usually participate in the overall management of the venture. Significant decisions generally require the consent of all venturers regardless of the percentage of ownership so that no individual venturer has unilateral control. It should be noted that an entity that is controlled by another entity is by definition not a joint venture. In addition, joint control, by itself, is not necessarily sufficient to use joint venture accounting.

ASC Topic 323, *Investments—Equity Method and Joint Ventures,* defines a corporate joint venture as follows:

> A corporation owned and operated by a small group of entities (the joint venturers) as a separate and specific business or project for the mutual benefit of the members of the group. A government may also be a member of the group. The purpose of a corporate joint venture frequently is to share risks and rewards in developing a new market, product or technology; to combine complementary technological knowledge; or to pool resources in developing production or other facilities. A corporate joint venture also usually provides an arrangement under which each joint venturer may participate, directly or indirectly, in the overall management of the joint venture. Joint venturers thus have an interest or relationship other than as passive investors. An entity that is a subsidiary of one of the joint venturers is not a corporate joint venture. The ownership of a corporate joint venture seldom changes, and its stock is usually not traded publicly. A noncontrolling interest held by public ownership, however, does not preclude a corporation from being a corporate joint venture.

(b) ACCOUNTING BY JOINT VENTURES.   Regardless of their legal form of organization, joint ventures must maintain accounting records and prepare financial statements just like any other enterprise. The primary users of the joint ventures financial statements are the venturers, who need to record their share of the profit or loss of the venture and to value their investment in it. Most of the accounting principles and procedures used by joint ventures are the same as those used by other business enterprises.

The most significant accounting issue for most joint ventures is the recording of initial capital contributions, particularly noncash contributions. Such contributions should be recorded on the books of the venture at the fair value of the assets contributed on the date of contribution, unless the fair value of the assets is not readily or reliably determinable or the recoverability of that value is in doubt. This general rule does not apply, however, to assets contributed by a venturer who controls a venture. In those circumstances, the assets should be recorded on the books of the venture at the same amount at which they were carried on the venturer's books because there has been no effective change in control over the assets.

(c) ACCOUNTING FOR INVESTMENTS IN JOINT VENTURES.   Since joint venturers have rights and obligations that may differ from their ownership percentages assuring them of significant influence even at ownership percentages of less than 20 percent, the application of customary equity or consolidation accounting is not always appropriate. Interests in incorporated joint ventures are accounted for in accordance with ASC Topic 323, which mandates use of the equity method. Accounting for interests in joint ventures that are organized as partnerships or undivided interests is discussed in ASC Subtopic 323-30, *Partnerships, Joint Ventures, and Limited Liability Entities.*

Chapter 9 in this *Handbook* discusses the requirements of the equity method of accounting.

20.9 SOURCES AND SUGGESTED REFERENCES

American Institute of Certified Public Accountants. Statement of Auditing Standards No. 45, *Related Party Transactions*. New York: Author, 1983.

Anderson, R. J. *External Audit*. Toronto: Pitman Publishing, 1977.

Bedford, N. M. *Introduction to Modern Accounting*. New York: Ronald Press, 1962.

Bedford, N. M., K. W. Perry, and A. H. Wyatt. *Advanced Accounting—An Organization Approach*. New York: John Wiley & Sons, 1979.

Blein, D. M., M. L. Fischer, and T. D. Skekel. *Advanced Accounting*. Hoboken, NJ: John Wiley & Sons, 2004.

Bogen, J. I. "Advantages and Disadvantages of Partnership." In Jules I. Bogen, ed., *Financial Handbook*, 4th ed. New York: Ronald Press, 1968.

Defliese, P. L., K. P. Johnson, and R. K. Macleod. *Montgomery's Auditing*, 9th ed. New York: Ronald Press, 1975.

Dixon, R. L., S. R. Hepworth, and W. A. Paton, Jr. *Essentials of Accounting*. New York: Macmillan, 1966.

Financial Accounting Standards Board. Statement of Financial Accounting Standards No. 57, *Related Party Disclosures*. Stamford, CT: Author, 1982.

Hoffman, W. H., Jr., ed. *West's Federal Taxation: Corporations, Partnerships, Estates and Trusts*. St. Paul, MN: West, 1978.

Jeter, D. C., and P. K. Chaney. *Advanced Accounting*. Hoboken, NJ: John Wiley & Sons, 2010.

Meigs, W. B., C. E. Johnson, and T. F. Keller. *Advanced Accounting*. New York: McGraw-Hill, 1966.

Moonitz, M., and L. H. Jordan. *Accounting—An Analysis of Its Problems*, 2 vols., rev. ed. New York: Holt, Rinehart and Winston, 1963.

CHAPTER 21

PROSPECTIVE FINANCIAL STATEMENTS

Don M. Pallais, CPA

21.1 TYPES OF PROSPECTIVE FINANCIAL STATEMENTS

(a) DEFINITIONS. *Prospective financial information* is future oriented; that is, it is financial information about the future. *Prospective financial statements* are future-oriented presentations that present, at a minimum, certain specific financial information.

The American Institute of Certified Public Accountants (AICPA) *Guide for Prospective Financial Information* (2009) defines prospective financial statements as presentations of an entity's financial position, results of operations, and cash flows for the future. In addition to the AICPA *Guide,* Statements on Standards for Attestation Engagements (SSAEs) (AT[1] 301) establish enforceable standards for accountants' services on prospective financial reporting. As the AICPA *Guide* incorporates all of the AT 301 requirements as well as establishing the presentation guidelines and definitions, for efficiency, this chapter quotes and provides references to the *Guide* only.

Entity means an individual, organization, enterprise, or other unit for which financial statements could be prepared in conformity with generally accepted accounting practices (GAAP). It is not necessary for the entity to have been formed at the time the prospective financial statements are prepared—prospective financial statements may be prepared for entities that may be formed in the future. In fact, before committing capital to proposed entities, prospective investors or lenders often insist on seeing prospective financial statements covering the early years of proposed operations.

Although the AICPA *Guide* defines prospective financial statements as presentations of future financial position, results of operations, and cash flows, three full financial statements are not always required. Prospective financial statements may be presented in summarized or condensed form. A presentation of future financial data is considered to be a prospective financial statement if it discloses at least these nine items, to the extent that they apply to the entity and would be presented in the entity's historical financial statements for the period covered:

1. Sales or gross revenue
2. Gross profit or cost of sales
3. Unusual or infrequently occurring items
4. Provision for income taxes
5. Discontinued operations or extraordinary items
6. Income from continuing operations
7. Net income
8. Basic and diluted earnings per share (required only when disclosure is also required for the entity's historical financial statements)
9. Significant changes in financial position (i.e., significant balance sheet changes not otherwise disclosed in the presentation)

---

[1] AT is the abbreviation for the codification of the AICPA attestation standards.

The definition of prospective financial statements does not specify the *length* of the future period. For a presentation to be prospective, however, *some* of the period covered must be in the future even though a part of the period may have expired. Thus, a calendar 20X1 presentation done on December 30, 20X1, would still, in theory, be a prospective presentation since there would still be an unexpired day in the period. Determining the period to be covered by prospective financial statements is discussed in more detail in Section 21.3(c)(ii).

There are two kinds of prospective financial statements: financial forecasts and financial projections. In practice, though, prospective financial statements are often given other names, such as budgets, business plans, and studies.

Although the terms *forecast* and *projections* sometimes are used interchangeably in popular usage, in the technical accounting literature, forecasts and projections differ in what they purport to represent. Forecasts represent expectations whereas projections are hypothetical analyses.

(i) Financial Forecasts. *Financial forecasts* are defined as prospective financial statements that present, to the best of management's knowledge and belief, an entity's expected financial position, results of operations, and cash flows based on management's assumptions reflecting conditions it expects to exist and the course of action it expects to take. In some cases forecasts can be prepared by persons other than current management, such as a potential acquirer of the entity, but usually the person (or persons) who take responsibility for the assumptions is someone who expects to be in a position to influence the entity's operations during the forecast period. The AICPA *Guide* refers to the person who takes responsibility for the assumptions as the *responsible party*.

Despite the inherent uncertainty of future events and the softness of prospective data, a forecast cannot be prepared without a *reasonably objective basis*. That is, sufficiently objective assumptions must be capable of being developed to present a forecast. Without a reasonably objective basis, management has no grounds for any expectations; all it would have is guesses.

The determination of whether a reasonably objective basis for a forecast exists is primarily an exercise in judgment. The key question is whether assumptions, based on the entity's plans, made by persons who are informed about the industry in which the entity operates, would generally fall within a relatively narrow range. If so, there may be a reasonably objective basis for the forecast. If, however, there is so much uncertainty regarding significant assumptions that consensus would be unlikely to be reached, there may not be a reasonably objective basis, precluding preparation of a forecast (although a projection could be developed). For example, there would be no reasonably objective basis to forecast the winnings of a thoroughbred being reared to race.

If prospective financial data are necessary but no reasonably objective basis exists to present a forecast, management might hypothesize the assumption that is not subject to reasonable estimation and call the presentation a *projection* or, alternatively, quantify only those assumptions that have a reasonably objective basis and prepare a *partial presentation*. However, both of these alternatives are limited in their usefulness. (See Sections 21.2(a)–(d) for a further discussion.)

Exhibit 21.1 presents factors to consider in determining whether there is a reasonably objective basis to present a forecast.

Occasionally an entity may need to present a forecast but cannot do so because of an uncertainty about the actions the *users* of the forecast may take. For example, an assumption may relate to passage of a referendum when the forecast is to be used by voters deciding on the referendum. In those cases, despite the high level of uncertainty, management can select one of the alternative outcomes as its assumption and then call the presentation a forecast if:

- The assumption is subject to only two possible outcomes (an either/or situation).
- The outcome of that assumption is dependent on the actions of the users of the presentation.
- The alternative selected is not unreasonable on its face.
- The presentation discloses that the forecast represents management's expectations only if the prospective action of users takes place.

Regardless of the need for a reasonably objective basis and management's efforts to present its expectations, a forecast is not a prediction. A forecast is not judged on whether, in hindsight,

SUFFICIENTLY OBJECTIVE ASSUMPTIONS—MATTERS TO CONSIDER

Basis	Less Objective	More Objective
Economy	Subject to uncertainty	Relatively stable
Industry	Emerging or unstable— high rate of business failure	Mature or relatively stable
Entity		
Operating history	Little or no operating history	Seasoned company; relatively stable operating history
Customer base	Diverse, changing customer group	Relatively stable customer group
Financial condition	Weak financial position; poor operating results	Strong financial position; good operating results
Management's Experience with:		
Industry	Inexperienced management	Experienced management
The business and its products	Inexperienced management; high turnover of key personnel	Experienced management
Products or Services		
Market	New or uncertain market	Existing or relatively stable market
Technology	Rapidly changing technology	Relatively stable technology
Experience	New products or expanding product line	Relatively stable products
Competing Assumptions	Wide range of possible outcomes	Relatively narrow range of possible outcomes
Dependency of Assumptions on Outcome of Forecasted Results	More dependency	Less dependency

Exhibit 21.1   Determining a Reasonably Objective Basis
Source: AICPA, *Guide for Prospective Financial Information,* Exhibit 7-1 (New York: Author, 2009).

it came true. A forecast is a presentation intended to provide financial information regarding management's plans and expectations for the future. It augments information in historical financial statements and other sources of data to help prospective investors, lenders, or others make better financial decisions.

(ii) Financial Projections.   Financial projections present, to the best of management's knowledge and belief, an entity's future financial position, results of operations, and cash flows given the occurrence of one or more *hypothetical assumptions.* Financial projections are sometimes prepared to analyze alternative courses of action, as in response to a question such as "What would happen if . . . ?"

The hypothetical assumptions in a projection are those that are not necessarily expected to occur but are consistent with the reason the projection was prepared. There is no explicit limit on the number of hypothetical assumptions used in a projection. However, since a projection is a presentation of expectations based on the occurrence of the hypothetical assumptions, a presentation in which all significant assumptions have been hypothesized would not be a projection because it depicts no dependent expectations. Thus, at some point the number of hypothetical assumptions may grow so large that the presentation is not a projection.

Hypothetical assumptions need not be reasonable or plausible; in fact, they may even be improbable if their use is consistent with the reason the projection is prepared. For example, it is generally improbable that a hotel would experience 100 percent occupancy. But use of that occupancy rate as a hypothetical assumption would be appropriate if the projection were prepared to demonstrate the maximum return on investment of a hotel. However, there are special disclosure rules when hypothetical assumptions are improbable. (See Section 21.4(c)(ii).)

All the non-hypothetical assumptions in a projection are expected to occur if the hypothetical assumption occurred, which may be different from expecting the non-hypothetical assumptions actually to occur. For example, a company may hypothesize adding a new product line and intend to use the resulting projection in deciding whether to do so. As a result of the assumption about a new product line, the projection might include assumptions about hiring new sales personnel. Management may not actually expect to hire new sales personnel, but it would hire them if it started a new product line; thus, the assumption is not actually expected, but it is expected given the occurrence of the hypothetical assumption.

(b) OTHER PRESENTATIONS THAT LOOK LIKE PROSPECTIVE FINANCIAL STATEMENTS.   A number of presentations look like prospective financial statements but are not. These include presentations for wholly expired periods, partial presentations, pro forma financial statements, and financial analyses.

(i) Presentations for Wholly Expired Periods.   Prospective financial statements are presentations for a future period. If the period covered by a presentation is wholly expired, such as a prior-year budget, it is not a prospective financial statement.

(ii) Partial Presentations.   Partial presentations are presentations of prospective financial information that omit one or more minimum items required of prospective financial statements. (See Section 21.1(a).) They are not subject to the same rules as prospective financial statements.

(iii) Pro Formas.   Pro forma financial statements are historical financial statements adjusted for a prospective transaction. Although one transaction has not occurred at the time of presentation, the statements are essentially historical ones. In essence, such statements answer the question "What would have happened if . . . ?" Guidance for compilations of pro formas is established by Statements on Standards for Accounting and Review Services (SSARS) No. 14, *Compilation of Pro Forma Financial Information* (AR[2] 120); guidance for examinations and reviews can be found in AT 401.

(iv) Financial Analyses.   *Financial analyses* are defined in the AICPA *Guide* as presentations in which the independent accountant rather than management develops and takes responsibility for the assumptions. Such presentations are normally a by-product of a consulting engagement in which management asks the accountant to analyze a condition and make recommendations about possible or prudent courses of action.

These analyses are not prospective financial statements because the party who takes responsibility for the assumptions (the accountant) is not, and does not expect to be, in a position to influence the entity's operations in the future period. If, however, management adopts the assumptions used, it may present the statements as a forecast or projection.

21.2 LIMITATIONS ON THE USE OF PROSPECTIVE FINANCIAL STATEMENTS

(a) HOW PROSPECTIVE FINANCIAL STATEMENTS ARE USED.   The use of prospective financial statements is neither required nor recommended by AICPA literature. Nonetheless, they are used for many purposes in practice. For example, they are used by management in internal planning, by potential suppliers of capital in making investment decisions, and by government agencies for monitoring or approving an entity's operations.

The AICPA *Guide* (Chapter 4) categorizes all the potential uses of prospective financial statements into two broad classes: *general use,* which refers to passive users, and *limited use,* which refers to use by management only or use by persons who are negotiating directly with management.

The AICPA *Guide* states that forecasts are appropriate for either general or limited use; projections are generally appropriate only for limited use.

---

[2] AR (accounting and review) is the abbreviation for the relevant section of the AICPA Professional Standards in Volume 2.

Unlike Securities and Exchange Commission (SEC) registration rules, the type of use is not dependent on the *number* of users of the prospective financial statements. A user is considered a limited user if it is negotiating directly with the entity; if it is not, it is a general user. Thus, even one passive user would constitute general use; whereas an entity may negotiate directly with numerous users, each of whom can change the terms of the transaction, and each would be considered a limited user.

(b) GENERAL USE.   *General use* means use of the prospective financial statements by persons who are not negotiating directly with management. General users are passive users; that is, they can use the prospective financial statements to determine their own course of action, but they cannot affect the company's actions or the terms of their investment. For example, after considering an entity's prospective financial statements, a potential investor in a limited partnership can decide whether to invest in it and, if so, how much to invest but cannot change the terms of the investment. Thus, the user would be considered a general user. A user who can change the terms of the investment would be considered a limited user.

Because general users cannot negotiate the terms of their involvement with the entity, their information needs are much like those of shareholders in a public company. To make informed decisions, general users would ordinarily be served best by a presentation of management's estimate of future financial results—a forecast.

A presentation of results based on a hypothetical assumption that does not reflect management's expectations (i.e., a projection) would not serve general users because such a presentation would tell them only what is *not* necessarily expected to happen, not what is. This would be analogous to providing shareholders with pro forma financial statements including transactions that did not occur instead of with historical financial statements.

Accordingly, financial projections are not ordinarily issued to general users unless the projections supplement a forecast *for the period covered by the forecast.* Thus, general users may benefit from an analysis of a hypothetical course of action when it supplements a presentation of management's expectations for that period but not when it stands alone as the only presentation of prospective results for a period.

That forecasts are appropriate for general use, of course, does not suggest that they will meet all the users' information needs. Potential investors or lenders often need to consider other information as well before making economic decisions, just as they do when presented with historical financial statements.

(c) LIMITED USE.   *Limited use* of prospective financial statements means use by the entity itself or use by persons with whom the entity is negotiating directly. Negotiating is an active concept. It includes more than the user's ability to ask questions of the entity; it refers to the user's ability to affect the terms of its business with the entity beyond merely deciding whether to participate and the amount of its participation.

There is no limit on the potential number of limited users in a particular circumstance except for the limit of the number of parties that management can practically negotiate with at any one time. It is also unnecessary to specifically identify the limited users at the time the prospective financial statements are prepared.

Because limited users can negotiate the terms of their involvement and challenge or propose changes to the hypothetical assumptions, they can use presentations that do not present management's best estimates. Accordingly, projections are often useful for limited users.

Similarly, because limited users can demand additional information as a condition of their participation (or, when there is a lack of needed information, increase the cost of capital in response to a perceived increase in risk), partial presentations or financial analyses may be appropriate for them.

Of course, financial forecasts are appropriate for limited users as well as general users.

(d) INTERNAL USE.   *Internal use* means use of the prospective financial statements only by the entity itself. It is a type of limited use. Limitation of the prospective financial statements to internal use does not affect the type of statements that are appropriate in the circumstances, but it affects the type of services that an independent accountant can perform on them. This is discussed in more detail in Section 21.9(a).

21.3 DEVELOPING PROSPECTIVE FINANCIAL STATEMENTS

(a) GENERAL GUIDELINES.   Chapter 6 of the AICPA *Guide* presents 11 guidelines for preparation of prospective financial statements. Although forecasts and projections can be developed without adhering to those guidelines, using them often results in more reliable prospective data.

The AICPA guidelines are listed in Exhibit 21.2. They apply to projections as well as forecasts, although in many cases they do not apply to the hypothetical assumptions in projections.

A general approach to developing prospective financial statements involves three steps:

1. Identifying key factors
2. Developing assumptions for each key factor
3. Assembling the prospective financial statements

(b) IDENTIFYING KEY FACTORS.   The AICPA *Guide* (Section 6.28) states: "Key factors are those significant matters upon which an entity's future results are expected to depend. Those factors are basic to the entity's operations and serve as a foundation for the prospective financial statements."

Key factors vary by entity and industry. They are general matters such as manufacturing labor, sales, or capital asset needs. Knowledge of the entity's industry and proposed operations is necessary to identify all the key factors that will form the basis for the prospective financial statements.

(c) DEVELOPING ASSUMPTIONS.   Assumptions are developed for each key factor. In a forecast, the assumptions represent management's best estimate of future conditions and courses of action. In a projection, the hypothetical assumptions are consistent with the purpose of the projection, and all the other assumptions represent management's best estimate of future conditions and courses of action given the occurrence of the hypothetical assumptions.

Approaches to developing assumptions range from highly sophisticated mathematical models to estimates based on personal opinion. Regardless of the approach taken to quantify the assumptions, to determine whether the assumptions are appropriate, management considers whether:

- There appears to be a rational relationship between the assumptions and the underlying facts and circumstances.
- Assumptions have been developed for each key factor.

Financial forecasts are prepared in good faith.

Financial forecasts are prepared with appropriate care by qualified personnel.

Financial forecasts are prepared using appropriate accounting principles.

The process used to develop financial forecasts provides for seeking out the best information that is reasonably available at the time.

The information used in preparing financial forecasts is consistent with the plans of the entity.

Key factors are identified as a basis for assumptions.

Assumptions used in preparing financial forecasts are appropriate.

The process used to develop financial forecasts provides the means to determine the relative effect of variations in the major underlying assumptions.

The process used to develop financial forecasts provides adequate documentation of both the financial forecasts and the process used to develop them.

The process used to develop financial forecasts includes, where appropriate, the regular comparison of the financial forecasts with attained results.

The process used to prepare financial forecasts includes adequate review and approval by the responsible party at the appropriate levels of authority.

Exhibit 21.2   Guidelines for Preparation of Prospective Financial Statements
Source: AICPA, *Guide for Prospective Financial Information,* Section 6.08 (New York: Author, 2009).

- Assumptions have been developed without undue optimism or pessimism.
- Assumptions are consistent with the entity's plans and expectations.
- Assumptions are consistent with each other.
- Individual assumptions make sense in the context of the prospective financial statements taken as a whole.

It is not always necessary to obtain support for each significant assumption, but developing support often results in more reliable prospective financial information. In any case, the significant considerations in developing a forecast are (1) whether management has a reasonably objective basis (see Section 21.1(a)(i)) for its expectations and (2) whether the assumptions are consistent with its expectations.

(i) Mathematical Models.   Forecasts may be based on sophisticated mathematical techniques such as regression analysis. However, merely extrapolating historical results into the future does not result in a forecast. To forecast, management satisfies itself that it has identified the conditions and course of action it intends to take in the future period. If, based on consideration of key factors, management believes that historical conditions are indicative of future results, it then might use an estimation technique based on historical results.

(ii) Length of the Prospective Period.   The AICPA *Guide* states that the length of time to be covered by prospective financial statements should be based on the needs of the user and management's ability to estimate future financial results.

In establishing a minimum length, the AICPA *Guide* (Section 8.33) states that to be meaningful to users, a forecast or projection should include at least one full year of normal operations. For example, an entity forecasting a major acquisition would present at least the first full year following the acquisition; a newly formed entity would show at least the first full year of normal operations in addition to its start-up period.

When the entity has a long operating cycle or when long-term results are necessary to evaluate the investment consequences involved, it may be necessary to forecast farther into the future to meet the needs of users.

Uncertainty increases as the horizon stretches farther in the future. At some point, the underlying assumptions become so subjective that no reasonably objective basis exists to present a forecast.

The AICPA *Guide* (Section 8.33) limits the maximum length of the forecast period to three to five years. It states that ordinarily it would be difficult to establish that a reasonably objective basis for a forecast exists for a longer period. However, the *Guide* recognizes that, in some cases, forecasts can be presented for longer periods, such as when long-term contracts exist that specify the timing and the amount of revenue and costs can be controlled within reasonable limits (as in the case of real estate projects with long-term leases). It also recognizes that in some cases, it may be hard to justify even a three-year forecast, such as for certain start-up or high-technology companies.

The SEC rules are generally more restrictive than the AICPA's. For prospective financial statements included in SEC filings, the SEC has stated that "for certain companies in certain industries a [forecast] covering a two or three year period may be entirely reasonable. Other companies may not have a reasonable basis for [forecasts] beyond the current year" (Reg. 229.10(b)(2)).

In determining how far into the future it can forecast, management considers the key factors and resulting assumptions for each future period presented. Considering them in detail for, say, one year and merely extrapolating the results for an additional two years beyond that does not result in a three-year forecast, but in a one-year forecast and a two-year projection.

(d) ASSEMBLING THE PROSPECTIVE FINANCIAL STATEMENTS.   Assembling the prospective financial statements involves converting the assumptions into prospective amounts and presenting the amounts and assumptions in conformity with AICPA presentation guidelines. Those guidelines are discussed in more detail in the next sections.

21.4 PRESENTATION AND DISCLOSURE OF PROSPECTIVE FINANCIAL STATEMENTS

(a) AUTHORITATIVE GUIDANCE. The primary source of guidance for presentation and disclosure of financial forecasts and projections is Chapter 8 of the AICPA *Guide*. In the absence of pronouncements by formally established accounting standard setters, such as the Financial Accounting Standards Board, the *Guide* establishes the equivalent of GAAP for prospective financial statements.

Although the *Guide* establishes guidelines for presentation and disclosure, it does not require or recommend the presentation of prospective financial statements in any circumstance. The decision to present prospective financial statements is generally management's, based on its needs and desires and those of potential financial statement users.

Other bodies have also established rules concerning presentation and disclosure of forecasts and projections. For example, the SEC, the North American Security Administrators Association, and individual state securities commissions have established rules that are applicable in certain situations. Issuers of prospective financial statements used in offering statements should be aware of those rules as well, but it is beyond the scope of this chapter to discuss all of them.

Occasionally, potential users of prospective financial statements also require a specific form or content for the statements. For example, users may specify the level of detail presented or the period covered, or they may require the completion of prescribed forms. Issuers of prospective financial statements should consider how those requirements compare with those in the AICPA *Guide* and whether compliance with the user's requirements may cause difficulties in obtaining an independent accountant's services on the statements.

(b) FORM OF PROSPECTIVE FINANCIAL STATEMENTS. Unlike historical financial statements, the form of prospective financial statements is flexible. Flexibility is permitted in order to present the most useful information in the circumstances.

Presenting prospective financial statements in the same form as the historical financial statements expected to be issued at the end of the prospective period facilitates later comparison. Accordingly, if later comparison is expected, an entity may issue a prospective balance sheet, income statement, and statement of cash flows.

If no later comparison is intended, or if more aggregated data are desired, the prospective financial statements may be presented in a summarized or condensed format. The amount of condensation or summarization is flexible as long as the next nine minimum items, to the extent that they are applicable and would be presented in the historical financial statements, are either presented or otherwise derivable from the presentation:

1. Sales or gross revenue
2. Gross profit or cost of sales
3. Unusual or infrequently occurring items
4. Provision for income taxes
5. Discontinued operations or extraordinary items
6. Income from continuing operations
7. Net income
8. Basic and diluted earnings per share
9. Significant changes in financial position

A summarized presentation should disclose significant cash flows and other significant changes in balance sheet accounts for the prospective period. The specific items to be presented depend on the circumstances but often include cash flows from operations.

Exhibit 21.3 illustrates a condensed format for a financial forecast.

(i) Amounts Presented. The prospective financial statements may be presented in terms of single-point estimates or ranges.

XYZ Company, Inc.
Summarized Financial Forecast
Year Ending December 31, 20X3
(in thousands except per-share amounts)

	Forecasted	Comparative Historical Information*	
	20X3	20X2	20X1
Sales	$101,200	$91,449	$79,871
Gross profit	23,700	21,309	19,408
Income tax expense	3,400	3,267	2,929
Net income	4,500	3,949	3,214
Earnings per share	4.73	4.14	3.37
Significant anticipated changes in financial position: Cash provided by operations	4,100	3,103	4,426
Net increase (decrease) in long-term borrowings	3,400	300	(300)
Dividend (per share 20X3: $1.50; 20X2: $1.35; 20X1: $1.00)	1,400	1,288	954
Additions to plant and equipment	4,400	2,907	2,114
Increase (decrease) in cash	1,400	(334)	1,017

See accompanying Summary of Significant Forecast Assumptions and Accounting Policies

*Comparative historical information is not part of the minimum presentation.

Exhibit 21.3   Illustration of Condensed Format for Prospective Financial Statements
Source: AICPA, *Guide for Prospective Financial Statements,* Exhibit 9-2 (New York: Author: 2009).

Ranges are sometimes presented when management wants to present a forecast but cannot refine its estimate of expected results sharply enough to present a single point as its best estimate. If the prospective financial statements are presented in terms of ranges, the range is not selected in a biased manner. That is, one end of the range is not significantly more likely than the other. In addition, the range is not characterized as representing the best and worst cases, since actual results might fall outside of the range.

Any of these formats for a forecast might be acceptable:

Single-point estimate:

Sales	$XXX
Cost of Sales	XXX

Range (from X to Z) showing an intermediate point (Y):

	X	Y	Z
Sales	$XXX	$YYY	$ZZZ
Cost of sales	XXX	YYY	ZZZ

Range showing a one line item only; example assumes the range is based on a forecasted range of sales prices and demand is inelastic:

Sales	$XXX—$YYY
Cost of Sales	$XXX

(ii) Titles.   Titles of financial forecasts should include the word *forecast* or *forecasted.* Titles of financial projections should refer to the hypothetical assumptions. Titles such as "budget" are avoided since they offer no indication whether the presentation is a forecast or a projection.

(c) DISCLOSURES.   In addition to the items listed at the beginning of Section 21.4(b), the AICPA *Guide* requires that these three matters be disclosed in prospective financial statements:

1. Description of what the presentation intends to depict
2. Summary of significant assumptions
3. Summary of significant accounting policies

Each page of the prospective financial statements should direct the readers' attention to the summaries of significant assumptions and accounting policies. A legend such as "The accompanying summaries of significant assumptions and accounting policies are an integral part of the financial forecast" or "See accompanying summaries of significant assumptions and accounting policies" is generally used.

(i) Description of the Presentation.   The prospective financial statements should include a description of what management intends the statements to present, a statement that the assumptions are based on management's judgment at the time the prospective information was prepared, and a caveat that the prospective results may not be achieved.

The description is usually presented as the introduction to the summary of significant assumptions.

The introduction to the assumptions for a financial forecast would disclose the necessary information, as shown next.

> This financial forecast presents, to the best of management's knowledge and belief, the Company's expected financial position, results of operations, and cash flows* for the forecast period. Accordingly, the forecast reflects its judgment, as of [date], the date of this forecast, of the expected conditions and its expected course of action. The assumptions disclosed herein are those that management believes are significant to the forecast. There will usually be differences between the forecasted and actual results, because events and circumstances frequently do not occur as expected, and those differences may be material.

---

*If the presentation is summarized or condensed, this might read "summary of the Company's expected results of operations and changes in financial position."

The introduction to the summary of significant assumptions for a financial projection would be similar to that for a forecast except that it would clearly explain the special purpose and limitations on the usefulness of the presentation. Such an introduction might read:

> This financial projection is based on sales volume at maximum productive capacity and presents, to the best of management's knowledge and belief, the Company's expected financial position, results of operations, and cash flows* for the projection period if such volume were attained. Accordingly, the projection reflects its judgment, as of [date], the date of this projection, of the expected conditions and its expected course of action if such sales volume were experienced. The presentation is designed to provide information to the Company's board of directors concerning the maximum profitability that might be achieved if current production were expanded through the addition of a third production shift and should not be considered to be a presentation of expected future results. Accordingly, this projection may not be useful for other purposes. The assumptions disclosed herein are those that management believes are significant to the projection. Management considers it highly unlikely that the stated sales volume will be experienced during the projection period. Further, even if the stated sales volume were attained, there will usually be differences between the projected and actual results, because events and circumstances frequently do not occur as expected, and those differences may be material.

---

*If the presentation is summarized or condensed, this might read "summary of the Company's expected results of operations and changes in financial position."

If the presentation is shown as a range, the introduction also makes it clear that presentation is shown as a range, that the range represents managements' expectations, and that there is no assurance that actual results will fall within the range. A sample introduction follows.

> This financial forecast presents, to the best of management's knowledge and belief, the Company's expected financial position, results of operations, and cash flows for the forecast period at occupancy rates of 75 percent and 95 percent of available apartments. Accordingly, the forecast reflects its judgment, as of [date], the date of this forecast, of the expected conditions and its expected course of action at each occupancy rate. The assumptions disclosed herein are those that management believes are significant to the forecast. Management reasonably expects, to the best of its knowledge and belief, that the actual occupancy rates achieved will be within the range shown; however, there can be no assurance that it will. Further, even if the actual occupancy rate is within the range shown, there will usually be differences between the forecasted and actual results, because events and circumstances frequently do not occur as expected, and those differences may be material, and the actual results may be outside the range presented by the forecast.

(ii) Significant Assumptions.   The assumptions form the basis for the prospective financial statements; for the statements to be meaningful to users, the assumptions should be disclosed.

Numerous assumptions are made in developing prospective financial statements. Only *significant* assumptions are required to be disclosed. Significance is generally considered to be measured in terms of the magnitude of an assumption's effect on the prospective financial statements.

Assumptions, however, may be considered significant even though they may not have a direct and large dollar effect on the statements. Four other types of assumptions also need to be disclosed; they are:

1. Sensitive assumptions (i.e., assumptions about which there is a reasonable possibility of the occurrence of a variation that may significantly affect the prospective results)
2. Significantly changed conditions (i.e., assumptions about anticipated conditions that are expected to be significantly different from current conditions)
3. Hypothetical assumptions used in a projection
4. Other matters deemed important to the statements or their interpretation

The form and placement of assumptions is flexible and can be based on management's judgment in the circumstances. The guiding principle is that the disclosure is understandable by the persons expected to use the statements.

Disclosure of the basis or rationale underlying the assumptions assists users in understanding and making decisions based on prospective financial statements. Such disclosure is recommended, but not required, by the AICPA *Guide.*

The next examples show the form of disclosure of significant assumptions that might be appropriate in various circumstances.

As a footnote in a formal presentation:

2. *Sales.* Sales of the Company's product in 20X2 are expected to increase 20 percent over those experienced in 20X1 ($1,000,000).

As a footnote in a formal presentation, including basis and rationale:

2. *Sales.* Based on commitments received and its current expansion into the Midwest market, management expects unit sales to increase by 15 percent over the number of units sold in 20X1. In addition, the Company expects to increase sales prices by an average of five percent over the year to cover expected increases in raw material costs. Increasing sales prices is not expected to adversely affect units sold since raw material cost increases will affect the entire industry and management anticipates industry-wide price increases. (Disclosure might also include discussion of other product lines, marketing plans, and other related information.)

Informal, shown on the face of the statements:

Sales (units up 15 percent over 20X1, price up 5 percent) $1,200,000

Informal, shown as output of factors used in an electronic spreadsheet:

Sales = 1.2* 20X1Sal

The appropriateness of each approach depends on the expected use of the prospective financial statements. The formal presentation that includes the basis and rationale would be most useful for general users; the informal printout of factors from a spreadsheet might be appropriate, and least costly to prepare, for internal use.

The disclosure of significant assumptions should also indicate which assumptions are *hypothetical* and which are *particularly sensitive.*

The *hypothetical* assumptions used in a projection should be identified specifically. In addition, if any of the hypothetical assumptions are considered *improbable,* the disclosure should indicate it.

Particularly sensitive assumptions are those for which there is a relatively high probability of variation that would significantly affect the prospective financial statements. The presentation should indicate which assumptions appeared to be particularly sensitive at the time of preparation of the statements (even though hindsight might indicate that others actually were particularly sensitive).

The disclosure of sensitivity is flexible. Examples of disclosures that might be appropriate in the circumstances are presented next.

With sensitivity quantified:

9. *Interest Expense.* The forecast assumes that the debt to be placed will carry an interest rate of 10 percent; however, the rate will not be determined until closing. For each $\frac{1}{4}$ of 1 percent that the actual interest rate differs from the rate assumed, forecasted income before income taxes would be raised or lowered by $25,000 and after-tax cash flow would change by approximately $16,000. If the rate exceeds $11\frac{1}{4}$ percent, the forecast would not indicate sufficient cash flow from the new project to service the debt.

Without sensitivity quantification:

9. *Interest Expense.* The forecast assumes the debt to be placed will carry an interest rate of 10 percent. The actual rate will not be determined until closing and may be higher or lower. To the extent that the actual rate exceeds 10 percent, forecasted income would be adversely affected.

Informal, printout of factors in an electronic spreadsheet:

Int exp = 0.1*debt! part. sensitive

(iii) Significant Accounting Principles.   The prospective financial statements should include disclosure of the *significant accounting principles* used in the statements. The basis of accounting and the accounting principles used in the prospective statements are generally those that are expected to be used during the prospective period. Thus, if the prospective statements accompany historical financial statements, this disclosure may be accomplished by referring the reader to the appropriate note in the historical statements.

If the basis of accounting used in the prospective statements is a non-GAAP basis, the basis used should be disclosed as well as that it is different from GAAP.

If the basis of accounting used is different from that expected to be used in the historical financial statements for the prospective period (such as presenting cash-flow forecast for an entity that uses GAAP for its historical financial statements), the use of a different basis of accounting in the prospective statements should be disclosed. The differences in prospective results that are caused by the use of the different basis usually would be reconciled in the statements unless the reconciliation would not be useful.

If the accounting principles used differ from those expected to be used (such as in a projection that analyzes the effect of a possible change in accounting principles), the use of a different principle in the projection should be disclosed. The results in the projection may also be reconciled to those that would result from using the principle used in the historical financial statements.

If management expects to change an accounting principle during the prospective period, the change in principle should be reflected in the prospective financial statements the same way it would be in the historical financial statements covering the prospective period. Other specific disclosures required for historical financial statements, such as those regarding pensions and income taxes, are not required for prospective financial statements.

(iv) Other Matters.   The *date* of preparation of the prospective financial statements should be disclosed. This disclosure provides information to users about how current the information underlying the statements is likely to be. The date generally is disclosed in the introduction to the summary of significant assumptions.

Occasionally management recognizes that users need information for periods beyond its ability to forecast. For example, management may plan a refinancing of debt or the introduction of new products after the end of the forecast period. Or management may expect expiration of a significant contract or future adverse tax consequences to investors.

If users are considered limited users, management may present projections or partial presentations for the more distant periods.

If, however, the users are general users, presentation of a projection outside of the forecast period would be considered inappropriate. The AICPA *Guide* (Section 8.42) provides guidance for disclosure of significant post forecast-period matters.

Such a disclosure should include:

- A title indicating that it presents information about periods beyond the financial forecast period.

- An introduction indicating that the information presented does not constitute a financial forecast and indicating its purpose.

- Use of significant assumptions and identification of those that are hypothetical, as well as the specific plans, events, or circumstances that are expected to have a material effect on results beyond the forecast period.

- A statement that (1) the information is presented for analysis purposes only, (2) there is no assurance that the events and circumstances described will occur, and, if applicable, (3) the information is less reliable than the forecast.

The disclosures are part of the forecast presentation; they are generally in the summary of significant assumptions. The *Guide* prohibits presenting them comparative to the forecasted results on the face of the forecast, in related summaries of benefits (such as in a summary of investor benefits), or as a financial projection.

21.5 TYPES OF ACCOUNTANTS' SERVICES

(a) OBJECTIVE OF ACCOUNTANTS' SERVICES.   Companies generally retain independent accountants to provide services on prospective financial statements for either of two reasons: to add credibility to prospective statements expected to be used by third parties or to provide consultation or assistance in developing statements expected to be used primarily by the client. The AICPA performance and reporting standards recognize that the type of service that is appropriate in the circumstances may vary depending on the expected use.

The AICPA standards provide three standard accountants' services for prospective financial statements expected to be used by third parties: *compilation, examination,* and application of *agreed-upon procedures.* (No review or moderate-level assurance service is permitted.) When third-party use is not reasonably expected, the accountant may provide the three standard services or other types of services and reports that more closely reflect the purpose of the engagement.

(b) STANDARD ACCOUNTANTS' SERVICES.   The accountant is required to compile, examine, or apply agreed-upon procedures whenever:

- The presentation includes prospective financial statements.
- The statements are, or reasonably might be, expected to be used by a third party.
- The accountant either (1) submits to the client or others statements that he or she has assembled or assisted in assembling or (2) reports on the statements.

There are three exceptions to this rule:

1. The accountant need not report on *drafts* of prospective financial statements submitted if they are clearly marked as such.
2. The accountant need not provide one of the standard services when the prospective financial statements are used solely in connection with engagements involving potential or pending litigation before a trier of fact in connection with the resolution of a dispute between two or more parties (often called *litigation support services*). In such circumstances, the accountant's work is ordinarily subjected to detailed analysis and challenge by each party to the dispute. However, the exception does not apply when the prospective financial statements are used by third parties that do not have the opportunity for such analysis and challenge. For example, creditors may not have that opportunity when a financial forecast is submitted to them to secure their agreement to a plan of reorganization.
3. The accountant who submits interim historical financial statements in a document that also contains prospective financial statements need not provide one of the standard services on the prospective statements if the prospective statements are labeled "budget," they do not extend beyond the end of the current fiscal year, the accountant's report states that the accountant did not apply any of the standard services to them, and the accountant's report disclaims an opinion or any other form of assurance on the statements.

(i) Prospective Financial Statements.   If the presentation does not meet the minimum disclosure requirement of prospective financial statements (see Section 21.1(a)), it is a *partial presentation* rather than prospective financial statements. In that case, the accountant is not required to provide a standard service on the prospective data. Chapter 23 of the AICPA *Guide* contains guidelines for compilations, examinations, and application of agreed-upon procedures to partial presentations. It does not *require* those services on partial presentations but provides guidance for the accountant who is engaged to provide them.

(ii) Third-Party Use.   Third parties generally are any persons outside the entity presenting the prospective financial statements. Some outsiders, however, are not considered third parties for the purpose of determining whether the guidance on accountants' services applies.

The AICPA *Guide* (Section 10.2) provides these guidelines for determining whether outsiders are considered third parties:

In deciding whether a party that is or reasonably might be expected to use an accountant's report is considered to be a third party, the accountant may consider the degree of consistency of interest between [management] and the user regarding the forecast. If their interests are substantially consistent (e.g., both the [preparer] and the user are employees of the entity about which the forecast is made), the user would not be deemed to be a third party. On the other hand, where the interests of the [preparer] and user are potentially inconsistent (e.g., the [preparer] is a nonowner manager and the user is an absentee owner), the user would be deemed a third party. In some cases, this determination will require the exercise of considerable professional judgment.

In considering whether the statements will be restricted to internal use, the accountant may generally rely on management's oral or written representations, unless something leads the accountant to believe that, despite management's representations, the statements are likely to be distributed to a third party.

(iii) Assemble and Submit.   *Assembly* means the "manual or computer processing of mathematical or other clerical functions related to the presentation of the prospective financial statements" (AICPA *Guide,* Section 3.16). The term refers to converting the assumptions into prospective amounts or putting the amounts into the form of statements. Assembly does not mean merely copying or collating statements prepared by someone else.

(c) INTERNAL USE.   The accountant may provide compilation, examination, or agreed-upon procedures engagements for internal use if engaged to do so. However, for internal use, the accountant has more flexibility to accommodate the varying circumstances of the engagement. Normally, these engagements involve consulting or planning (such as in management consulting or tax planning services) rather than third-party reliance. Common reporting options for internal use include *assembly reports* and *plain-paper* prospective financial statements. Internal-use services are discussed in more detail in Section 21.9.

(d) PROHIBITED ENGAGEMENTS.   The AICPA *Guide* prohibits the accountant from submitting or reporting on prospective financial statements intended for third-party use if those statements omit the disclosure of significant assumptions. Similarly, the accountant is prohibited from submitting or reporting on a projection for third-party use if it does not identify the hypothetical assumption or describe the limitations on the usefulness of the presentation.

The accountant also should not submit or report on a financial projection that is intended for general use (unless it supplements a forecast for the same period) because such use is considered inappropriate. (See Section 21.2(b).) This prohibition means that the accountant could not assemble and submit such a presentation even if management agreed not to present the accountant's report or refer to the accountant in the document containing the projection that would be presented to general users.

(e) MATERIALITY.   Accountants consider *materiality* in conducting engagements on prospective financial statements much as they do for historical financial statements. The AICPA *Guide* (Section 10.32) states, however, "Materiality is a concept that is judged in light of the expected range of reasonableness of the information; therefore, users should not expect prospective information (information about events that have not yet occurred) to be as precise as historical information."

It follows, then, that materiality criteria would be higher for prospective statements than for the same company's historical statements. That is, an amount that would be material to the historical statements might not be material to the prospective financials. There is no consensus in practice, however, as to just how much higher materiality should be for prospective financial statements.

(f) SECURITIES AND EXCHANGE COMMISSION PERSPECTIVE.   Relevant SEC rules regarding accountants' services on prospective financial statements in filings subject to the SEC's authority include the Safe Harbor Rule for Projections and as policies stated in equation S-K Section 229.10. These rules, however, add relatively little to the requirements for accountants' procedures and reports established by the AICPA *Guide.* The more significant SEC policies in this area are less formal ones. Two particularly significant positions taken by the SEC involve *compilation services* and *independence rules.*

(i) Compilations in Securities and Exchange Commission Filings. Although not stated in formal SEC rules, the Commission's Staff has been reluctant to accept compilations of prospective financial statements. Thus, although that service is allowed under the AICPA literature for both public and nonpublic entities (unlike compilations of historical statements, which are appropriate only for nonpublic companies), they generally are not an option for filings subject to SEC authority.

(ii) Independence. The SEC independence rules differ from those established by the AICPA. As a general rule, AICPA literature considers independence impaired when the accountant either has a financial interest in the client or when the accountant is acting in the capacity of management or an employee. Thus, providing a service on prospective financial statements would not, in and of itself, affect the auditor's independence for the audit of its historical financial statements or any other service.

The SEC rules, however, are based on a different concept, which the SEC refers to as "mutuality of interest." The SEC considers that the accountant's assistance in preparing prospective financial statements creates a mutuality of interest in the prospective results. Thus, it has stated that, generally, an accountant who actively participates in the preparation of the prospective data loses the independence necessary to examine and report on that prospective data.

In a letter to an accountant, the SEC Staff pursued this reasoning even further, stating that active assistance in the preparation of a company's prospective financial statements would also affect the accountant's independence in regard to its *historical financial statements* for the length of the prospective period. This independence impairment would occur regardless of whether the prospective statements were forecasts or projections or whether they were issued to the public or restricted to internal use.[3]

(g) INTERNAL REVENUE SERVICE PERSPECTIVE. Internal Revenue Service (IRS) Circular 230 applies to prospective financial statements included in tax shelter offerings. It states that an accountant who reports on prospective financial statements in such offerings must either provide a *tax shelter opinion* or rely on one issued by another professional, such as another accountant or a lawyer.

A tax shelter opinion under Circular 230 states whether, in the professional's opinion, it is more likely than not that an investor will prevail on the merits of each material tax issue that involves a reasonable possibility of challenge by the IRS and an overall evaluation of the extent to which the material tax benefits are likely to be realized in the aggregate.

21.6 COMPILATION SERVICES

(a) SCOPE OF THE COMPILATION SERVICE. A *compilation* of prospective financial statements is similar to a compilation of historical financial statements performed subject to SSARS. It relies primarily on an informed reading of the statements with an eye for obvious problems, but it does not provide any assurance on the statements.

The AICPA *Guide* states that a compilation of prospective financial statements involves:

- Assembling, to the extent necessary, the prospective financial statements based on management's assumptions
- Performing the required compilation procedures, including reading the prospective financial statements with their summaries of significant assumptions and accounting policies and considering whether they appear to be presented in conformity with AICPA presentation guidelines and are not obviously inappropriate
- Issuing a compilation report

---

[3] Letter from Chief Accountant to Amper, Politzner, and Mattia, April 14, 1987; CCH, 1990, par. 7986.

(b) ASSEMBLY.   Assembly, which is defined in Section 21.5(b)(iii), refers to performing the necessary mathematics to turn assumptions into prospective financial data and drafting prospective financial statements in the appropriate form. In some cases, such as when the client has a sophisticated financial reporting function and prepares its own statements, assembly may not be required in a compilation. Often, however, assembly assistance is one of the primary benefits the client receives from the accountant.

Assembly does not include identifying key factors or developing assumptions, although accountants often help clients in these areas in a compilation.

(c) COMPILATION PROCEDURES.   The compilation procedures required by AICPA standards are listed in Exhibit 21.4.

There are two principal differences between the procedures done in a compilation of prospective statements and a compilation of historical statements: the requirement to consider the *actual results* for any expired portion of the prospective period and the requirement to obtain *signed representations* from the client.

In performing a compilation of prospective financial statements the practitioner should, where applicable—

a. Establish an understanding with the client regarding the services to be performed. The understanding should include the objectives of the engagement, the client's responsibilities, the practitioner's responsibilities, and limitations of the engagement. The practitioner should document the understanding in the attest documentation, preferably through a written communication with the client. If the practitioner believes an understanding with the client has not been established, he or she should decline to accept or perform the engagement.

b. Inquire about the accounting principles used in the preparation of the prospective financial statements.

    ○ For existing entities, compare the accounting principles used to those used in the preparation of previous historical financial statements and inquire whether such principles are the same as those expected to be used in the historical financial statements covering the prospective period.

    ○ For entities to be formed or entities formed that have not commenced operations, compare specialized industry accounting principles used, if any, to those typically used in the industry. Inquire about whether the accounting principles used for the prospective financial statements are those that are expected to be used when or if the entity commences operations.

c. Ask how the responsible party identifies the key factors and develops its assumptions.

d. List, or obtain a list of, the responsible party's significant assumptions providing the basis for the prospective financial statements and consider whether there are any obvious omissions in light of the key factors upon which the prospective results of the entity appear to depend.

e. Consider whether there appear to be any obvious internal inconsistencies in the assumptions.

f. Perform, or test the mathematical accuracy of, the computations that translate the assumptions into prospective financial statements.

g. Read the prospective financial statements, including the summary of significant assumptions, and consider whether—

    ○ The statements, including the disclosures of assumptions and accounting policies, appear to be not presented in conformity with the AICPA presentation guidelines for prospective financial statements.[1]

    ○ The statements, including the summary of significant assumptions, appear to be not obviously inappropriate in relation to the practitioner's knowledge of the entity and its industry and, (1) for a financial forecast, the expected conditions and course of action in the prospective period or (2) for a financial projection, the purpose of the presentation.

h. If a significant part of the prospective period has expired, inquire about the results of operations or significant portions of the operations (such as sales volume), and significant changes in financial position, and consider their effect in relation to the prospective financial statements. If historical financial statements have been prepared for the expired portion of the period, the practitioner should read such statements and consider those results in relation to the prospective financial statements.

i. Confirm his or her understanding of the statements (including assumptions) by obtaining written representations from the responsible party. Because the amounts reflected in the statements are not supported by historical books and records but rather by assumptions, the practitioner should obtain representations in which the responsible party indicates its responsibility for the assumptions. The representations should be signed by the responsible party at the highest level of authority who the practitioner believes is responsible for and knowledgeable, directly or through others, about matters covered by the representations.

Exhibit 21.4   Standard Compilation Procedures
Source: Adapted from AICPA, *Guide for Prospective Financial Information,* Section 12.11 (New York: Author, 2009).

○ *For a financial forecast,* the representations should include the responsible party's assertion that the financial forecast presents, to the best of the responsible party's knowledge and belief, the expected financial position, results of operations, and cash flows for the forecast period and that the forecast reflects the responsible party's judgment, based on present circumstances, of the expected conditions and its expected course of action. The representations should also include a statement that the forecast is presented in conformity with guidelines for presentation of a forecast established by the AICPA. The representations should also include a statement that the assumptions on which the forecast is based are reasonable. If the forecast contains a range, the representation should also include a statement that, to the best of the responsible party's knowledge and belief, the item or items subject to the assumption are expected to actually fall within the range and that the range was not selected in a biased or misleading manner.

○ *For a financial projection,* the representations should include the responsible party's assertion that the financial projection presents, to the best of the responsible party's knowledge and belief, the expected financial position, results of operations, and cash flows for the projection period given the hypothetical assumptions, and that the projection reflects its judgment, based on present circumstances, of expected conditions and its expected course of action given the occurrence of the hypothetical events. The representations should also (1) identify the hypothetical assumptions and describe the limitations on the usefulness of the presentation, (2) state that the assumptions are appropriate, (3) indicate if the hypothetical assumptions are improbable, and (4) if the projection contains a range, include a statement that, to the best of the responsible party's knowledge and belief, given the hypothetical assumptions, the item or items subject to the assumption are expected to actually fall within the range and that the range was not selected in a biased or misleading manner. The representations should also include a statement that the projection is presented in conformity with guidelines for presentation of a projection established by the AICPA.

j. Consider, after applying the above procedures, whether he or she has received representations or other information that appears to be obviously inappropriate, incomplete, or otherwise misleading and, if so, attempt to obtain additional or revised information. If such information is not received, the practitioner should ordinarily withdraw from the compilation engagement.[2] (The omission of disclosures, other than those relating to significant assumptions, would not require the practitioner to withdraw.)

---

[1] Presentation guidelines for entities that issue prospective financial statements are set forth and illustrated in the AICPA *Guide for Prospective Financial Information.*
[2] The practitioner need not withdraw from the engagement if the effect of such information on the prospective financial statements does not appear to be material.

Exhibit 21.4 *Continued*

In a compilation of prospective financial statements, the *working papers* (i.e., documentation) ordinarily should indicate that:

- The work was adequately planned and supervised.
- The required compilation procedures were performed as a basis for the compilation report.

(d) REPORTING ON A COMPILATION. The *standard report* on a compilation of prospective financial statements includes seven things:

1. An identification of the prospective financial statements presented by the responsible party
2. A statement that the accountant has compiled the prospective financial statements in accordance with attestation standards established by the AICPA
3. A statement that a compilation is limited in scope and does not enable the accountant to express an opinion or any other form of assurance on the prospective financial statements or the assumptions
4. A caveat that the prospective results may not be achieved
5. A statement that the accountant assumes no responsibility to update the report for events and circumstances occurring after the date of the report
6. The manual or printed signature of the accountant's firm
7. The date of the compilation report

The standard form of compilation report for a financial forecast is presented next.

We have compiled the accompanying forecasted balance sheet, statements of income, retained earnings, and cash flows of XYZ Company as of December 31, 20XX,* and for the year then ending, in accordance with attestation standards established by the American Institute of Certified Public Accountants.

A compilation is limited to presenting in the form of a forecast information that is the representation of management and does not include evaluation of the support for the assumptions underlying the forecast. We have not examined the forecast and, accordingly, do not express an opinion or any other form of assurance on the accompanying statements or assumptions. Furthermore, there will usually be differences between the forecasted and actual results, because events and circumstances frequently do not occur as expected, and those differences may be material. We have no responsibility to update this report for events and circumstances occurring after the date of this report.

[Signature]

[Date]

---

*If the presentation is summarized, the opening sentence of the report would begin: "We have compiled the accompanying summarized forecast of XYZ Company as of December 31, 20XX."

The standard form of report for the compilation of a financial projection is presented next.

We have compiled the accompanying projected balance sheet, statements of income, retained earnings, and cash flows of XYZ Company as of December 31, 20XX,* and for the year then ending, in accordance with attestation standards established by the American Institute of Certified Public Accountants. The accompanying projection was prepared for [state special purpose, e.g., "the purpose of negotiating a loan to expand XYZ Company's plant"].

A compilation is limited to presenting information in the form of a projection that is the representation of management and does not include evaluation of the support for the assumptions underlying the projection. We have not examined the projection and, accordingly do not express an opinion or any other form of assurance on the accompanying statements or assumptions. Furthermore, even if [describe hypothetical assumption, for example, "the loan is granted and the plant is expanded"], there will usually be differences between the projected and the actual results, because events and circumstances frequently do not occur as expected, and those differences may be material. We have no responsibility to update this report for events and circumstances occurring after the date of this report.

The accompanying projection and this report are intended solely for the information and use of [identify specified parties, for example, "XYZ Company and DEF Bank"] and are not intended to be and should not be used by anyone other than these specified parties.

[Signature]

[Date]

---

*If the presentation is summarized, the opening sentence of the report would begin: "We have compiled the accompanying summarized projection of XYZ Company as of December 31, 20XX."

If the presentation is shown as a range, the accountant's report also includes a paragraph that states that management has shown the results of one or more assumptions as a range. An example of such a paragraph is presented next.

As described in the summary of significant assumptions, management of XYZ Company has elected to portray forecasted [description of the financial statement element or elements for which the expected results of one or more assumptions fall within a range, and identification of the assumptions expected to fall within a range, e.g., "revenue at the amounts of $XX and $YY, which is predicated upon occupancy rates of XX% and YY% of available apartments"] rather than as a single-point estimate. Accordingly, the accompanying forecast presents forecasted financial position, results of operations, and cash flows [description of the assumptions expected to fall within a range, e.g., "at such occupancy rates"]. However, there can be no assurance that the actual results will fall within the range of [description of the assumptions expected to fall within a range, e.g., "occupancy rates"] presented.

(e) PROBLEM SITUATIONS.   Potential problems in a compilation engagement include scope limitations, deficiencies in the prospective financial statements, and lack of independence.

(i) Scope Limitations.   Scope limitations might include a client's inadequate responses to the limited inquiries required in a compilation or its refusal to supply signed representations. The AICPA *Guide* does not allow a scope-limitation compilation report. An accountant who cannot apply all the necessary procedures cannot complete the engagement and ordinarily should withdraw.

(ii) Presentation Deficiencies.   Possible deficiencies in the prospective financial statements might affect either the assumptions or the other required disclosures. If the deficiency affects disclosures *other than assumptions,* the accountant mentions it in the compilation report. For example, if management chose to omit the disclosure of significant accounting policies, the accountant might add this paragraph to the compilation report:

> Management has elected to omit the summary of significant accounting policies required by the guidelines for presentation of a financial forecast established by the American Institute of Certified Public Accountants. If the omitted disclosures were included in the forecast, they might influence the user's conclusions about the Company's financial position, results of operations, and cash flows for the forecast period. Accordingly, this report is not intended for those who are not informed about such matters.

If the deficiency affects the disclosure of *assumptions* and the accountant is unable to have it corrected, the accountant is not permitted merely to mention it in the report. In that case, the accountant ordinarily would withdraw from the engagement.

(iii) Independence.   Since a compilation provides no assurance, an accountant may compile prospective financial statements when not independent. In that case, the report would indicate the lack of independence. The next sentence would be added to the compilation report to indicate the lack of independence:

> We are not independent with respect to XYZ Company.

The accountant may choose to also disclose the reason for the independence impairment, using this form:

> We are not independent with respect to XYZ Company because [identify reason].

21.7 EXAMINATION SERVICES

(a) SCOPE OF AN EXAMINATION.   An examination of prospective financial statements is similar to an audit of historical financial statements. It is based on evidence-gathering procedures and results in positive assurance about the statements. The main difference between the two services involves the evidence-gathering procedures. Because completed transactions generally do not constitute the bulk of the data underlying prospective financial statements, the accountant's procedures generally consist primarily of inquiry and analysis rather than document inspection and confirmation.

An examination of prospective financial statements involves:

- Evaluating the preparation of the statements
- Evaluating the support underlying the statements
- Evaluating the presentation of the statements for conformity with AICPA presentation guidelines

- Issuing a report as to whether, in the accountant's opinion,
    - **a.** The prospective financial statements are presented in conformity with AICPA presentation guidelines and
    - **b.** The assumptions provide a reasonable basis for the forecast or, for a projection, whether the assumptions provide a reasonable basis given the hypothetical assumptions

(i) Evaluating Preparation.   The accountant considers the process that management uses to develop its prospective financial statements to determine how much support will need to be accumulated. This consideration is analogous to, but less detailed than, the consideration an auditor gives to a company's internal control in planning and performing an audit of historical financial statements. The better controlled the process of developing the financial statements, the less work the accountant generally needs to do in obtaining support for them.

In judging the process the entity uses in developing its prospective financial statements, the accountant generally compares the process to the guidelines discussed in Section 21.3(a).

(ii) Evaluating Assumptions.   The accountant performs procedures to determine whether the assumptions provide a reasonable basis for the prospective financial statements. The accountant can decide that they provide such a basis if he or she can conclude that:

- Management has identified all key factors expected to affect the entity during the prospective period.
- Management has developed assumptions for each key factor.
- The assumptions are suitably supported.

To determine whether management has identified all *key factors* and developed assumptions for each one, the accountant needs to possess, or obtain during the engagement, an appropriate knowledge of the industry in which the entity will operate and the accounting principles and practices of that industry.

The accountant can conclude that the assumptions are *suitably supported* if the preponderance of information supports each significant assumption. *Preponderance* here does not imply a statistical majority of information. A preponderance exists if the weight of available information tends to support the assumption. The AICPA *Guide* states, however, "Because of the judgments involved in developing assumptions, different people may arrive at somewhat different but equally reasonable assumptions based on the same information."

The accountant need not obtain support for the *hypothetical* assumptions in a projection, since they are not necessarily expected to occur. For a projection, the accountant considers whether the hypothetical assumptions are consistent with the purpose of the projection and whether the other assumptions are suitably supported, given the hypothetical assumption.

In evaluating the support for the assumptions, the accountant considers whether:

- Sufficient pertinent sources of information, both internal and external to the entity, have been considered.
- The assumptions are consistent with the sources from which they are derived.
- The assumptions are consistent with each other.
- The historical financial information and other data used in developing the assumptions are sufficiently reliable for that purpose.
- The historical information and other data used in developing the assumptions are comparable over the periods specified or whether the effects of any lack of comparability were considered in developing the assumptions.
- The logical arguments or theory, considered with the data supporting the assumptions, are reasonable.

Support for assumptions may include market surveys, engineering studies, general economic indicators, industry statistics, trends and patterns developed from an entity's operating history, and internal data and analysis, accompanied by their supporting logical argument or theory.

The accountant determines whether the assumptions provide a reasonable basis for the statements but cannot conclude that any outcome is expected because:

- Realization of prospective results may depend on management's intentions, which cannot be examined.
- There is substantial uncertainty in the assumptions.
- Some of the information accumulated about an assumption may appear contradictory.
- Different but similarly reasonable assumptions concerning a particular matter might be derived from common information.

(iii) Evaluating Presentation.   The accountant compares the presentation of the prospective financial statements to the AICPA presentation guidelines. (See Sections 21.4(b) and (c).)

(b) STANDARD EXAMINATION REPORT.   The accountant's *standard report* on an examination of prospective financial statements includes:

- A title that includes the word *independent*
- An identification of the prospective financial statements presented
- An identification of the responsible party and a statement that the prospective financial statements are the responsibility of the responsible party
- A statement that the accountant's responsibility is to express an opinion on the prospective financial statements based on the examination
- A statement that the examination of the prospective financial statements was conducted in accordance with attestation standards established by the AICPA and, accordingly, included such procedures as the accountant considered necessary in the circumstances
- A statement that the accountant believes that the examination provides a reasonable basis for the opinion
- The accountant's opinion that the prospective financial statements are presented in conformity with AICPA presentation guidelines and that the underlying assumptions provide a reasonable basis for the forecast or for the projection, given the hypothetical assumptions
- A caveat that the prospective results may not be achieved
- A statement that the accountant assumes no responsibility to update the report for events and circumstances occurring after the date of the report
- The manual or printed signature of the accountant's firm
- The date of the examination report

The standard report on the examination of a financial forecast is shown next.

Independent Accountant's Report

We have examined the accompanying forecasted balance sheet, statements of income, retained earnings, and cash flows of XYZ Company as of December 31, 20XX, and for the year then ending.* XYZ Company's management is responsible for the forecast. Our responsibility is to express an opinion on the forecast based on our examination.

Our examination was conducted in accordance with attestation standards established by the AICPA and, accordingly, included such procedures as we considered necessary to evaluate both the assumptions used by management and the preparation and presentation of the forecast. We believe that our examination provides a reasonable basis for our opinion.

In our opinion, the accompanying forecast is presented in conformity with guidelines for presentation of a forecast established by the American Institute of Certified Public Accountants, and the underlying assumptions provide a reasonable basis for management's forecast. However, there will usually be differences between the forecasted and actual results, because events and circumstances frequently do not occur as expected, and those differences may be material. We have no responsibility to update this report for events and circumstances occurring after the date of this report.

[Signature]

[Date]

---

*If the presentation is summarized, the opening sentence of the report would begin: "We have examined the accompanying summarized projection of XYZ Company as of December 31, 20XX."

The standard report on the examination of a financial projection is shown next.

Independent Accountant's Report

We have examined the accompanying projected balance sheet, statements of income, retained earnings, and cash flows of XYZ Company as of December 31, 20XX, and for the year then ending. XYZ Company's management is responsible for the projection, which was prepared for [state special purpose, e.g., "the purpose of negotiating a loan to expand XYZ Company's plant"]. Our responsibility is to express an opinion on the projection based on our examination.

Our examination was conducted in accordance with attestation standards established by the American Institute of Certified Public Accountants and, accordingly, included such procedures as we considered necessary to evaluate both the assumptions used by management and the preparation and presentation of the projection. We believe our examination provides a reasonable basis for our opinion.

In our opinion, the accompanying projection is presented in conformity with guidelines for presentation of a projection established by the American Institute of Certified Public Accountants, and the underlying assumptions provide a reasonable basis for management's projection [describe the hypothetical assumption, e.g., "assuming the granting of the requested loan for the purpose of expanding XYZ Company's plant as described in the summary of significant assumptions"]. However, even if [describe hypothetical assumption, for example, "the loan is granted and the plant is expanded"], there will usually be differences between the projected and actual results, because events and circumstances frequently do not occur as expected, and those differences may be material. We have no responsibility to update this report for events and circumstances occurring after the date of this report.

The accompanying projection and this report are intended solely for the information and use of [identify specified parties, e.g., "XYZ Company and DEF National Bank"] and are not intended to be and should not be used by anyone other than these specified parties.

[Signature]

[Date]

When the prospective financial statements are presented as a range, the report also includes a separate paragraph describing the range. (See Section 21.4(c)(i) for an example.)

(c) MODIFIED EXAMINATION REPORTS.   There are four types of modified examination reports:

1. A *qualified* report, used when the statements depart from the AICPA presentation guidelines but the deficiency does not affect the assumptions (If the matter is highly material, the accountant may, however, issue an adverse report.)
2. An *adverse* report, used when the statements fail to disclose significant assumptions or when the assumptions do not provide a reasonable basis for the presentation

3. A *disclaimer* used when the accountant is precluded from applying procedures considered necessary in the circumstances

4. A *reference* to another accountant, used when another accountant examines the prospective financial statements of a significant portion of the entity, such as a major subsidiary

(i) Qualified Opinion. The accountant issues a qualified opinion if there is a material presentation deficiency that does not affect the assumptions. The next examination report is qualified because of a presentation deficiency.

Independent Accountant's Report

We have examined the accompanying forecasted balance sheet, statements of income, retained earnings, and cash flows of XYZ Company as of December 31, 20XX, and for the year then ending. XYZ Company's management is responsible for the forecast. Our responsibility is to express an opinion on the forecast based on our examination.

Our examination was conducted in accordance with attestation standards established by the American Institute of Certified Public Accountants and, accordingly, included such procedures as we considered necessary to evaluate both the assumptions used by management and the preparation and presentation of the forecast. We believe our examination provides a reasonable basis for our opinion.

The forecast does not disclose significant accounting policies. Disclosure of such policies is required by guidelines for presentation of a forecast established by the American Institute of Certified Public Accountants.

In our opinion, except for the omission of the disclosure of the significant accounting policies as discussed in the preceding paragraph, the accompanying forecast is presented in conformity with guidelines for presentation of a forecast established by the American Institute of Certified Public Accountants, and the underlying assumptions provide a reasonable basis for management's forecast. However, there will usually be differences between the forecasted and actual results, because events and circumstances frequently do not occur as expected, and those differences may be material. We have no responsibility to update this report for events and circumstances occurring after the date of this report.

[Signature]

[Date]

(ii) Adverse Report. The accountant issues an adverse opinion when a significant assumption is unsupported or is not disclosed. An adverse opinion is also issued when the accountant believes that a departure from the presentation guidelines not involving the assumptions is serious enough to warrant it. Next is an example of an adverse report issued by the accountant because an assumption was unreasonable.

Independent Accountant's Report

We have examined the accompanying forecasted balance sheet, statements of income, retained earnings, and cash flows of XYZ Company as of December 31, 20XX, and for the year then ending. XYZ Company's management is responsible for the forecast. Our responsibility is to express an opinion on the forecast based on our examination.

Our examination was conducted in accordance with attestation standards established by the American Institute of Certified Public Accountants and, accordingly, included such procedures as we considered necessary to evaluate both the assumptions used by management and the preparation and presentation of the forecast. We believe our examination provides a reasonable basis for our opinion.

As discussed under the caption "Sales" in the summary of significant forecast assumptions, the forecasted sales include, among other things, revenue from the Company's federal defense contracts continuing at the current level. The Company's present federal defense contracts will expire in March 20XX. No new contracts have been signed and no negotiations are under way for new federal defense contracts. Furthermore, the federal government has entered into contracts with another company to supply the items being manufactured under the Company's present contracts.

In our opinion, the accompanying forecast is not presented in conformity with guidelines for presentation of a financial forecast established by the American Institute of Certified Public Accountants because management's assumptions, as discussed in the preceding paragraph, do not provide a reasonable basis for management's forecast. We have no responsibility to update this report for events and circumstances occurring after the date of this report.

[Signature]

[Date]

There is no caveat about actual results differing from those forecasted since the accountant believes the forecast assumptions to be unreasonable.

(iii) Disclaimer.   The accountant who cannot apply all the procedures deemed necessary to support an opinion on the statements issues a disclaimer. An example of a disclaimer is presented next.

Independent Accountant's Report

We were engaged to examine the accompanying forecasted balance sheet, statements of income, retained earnings, and cash flows of XYZ Company as of December 31, 20XX, and for the year then ending. XYZ Company's management is responsible for the forecast.

As discussed under the caption "Income from Investee" in the summary of significant forecast assumptions, the forecast includes income from an equity investee constituting 23 percent of forecasted net income, which is management's estimate of the Company's share of the investee's income to be accrued for 20XX. The investee has not prepared a forecast for the year ending December 31, 20XX, and we were therefore unable to obtain suitable support for this assumption.

Because, as described in the preceding paragraph, we are unable to evaluate management's assumption regarding income from an equity investee and other assumptions that depend thereon, the scope of our work was not sufficient to express, and we do not express, an opinion with respect to the presentation of, or the assumptions underlying, the accompanying forecast. We have no responsibility to update this report for events and circumstances occurring after the date of this report.

[Signature]

[Date]

In a disclaimer there is no caveat about differences between actual and forecasted assumptions since the accountant is not satisfied about the reasonableness of the assumptions.

Notwithstanding his or her scope limitation, if the accountant is aware of material deficiencies in the forecast, those deficiencies should be discussed in the disclaimer.

(iv) Divided Responsibility.   When another accountant is involved in the examination, the principal accountant may refer to the work of the other accountant as a basis, in part, for the principal accountant's own report. The reference is done in essentially the same way divided-responsibility reports are done for audits of historical financial statements.

(d) INDEPENDENCE.   The accountant who examines prospective financial statements is required to be independent. If not, the accountant generally issues a compilation report rather than disclaim an opinion after the examination.

21.8 AGREED-UPON PROCEDURES

(a) SCOPE OF SERVICE. An engagement to apply agreed-upon procedures to prospective financial statements involves applying the procedures specified by the users of the statements and reporting the results of their application. The level of service is flexible, but the accountant's report may be distributed only to the users who specified the procedures. Thus, it is a limited-distribution service.

(b) PROCEDURES. The procedures applied in an engagement may be limited or extensive, depending on the users' needs. For example, the service may consist of procedures below the level done in a compilation (such as mere assembly) or may be similar to those done in an examination. Alternatively, the service may consist of different levels of procedures applied to different amounts in the statements, such as a high level of work done on forecasted sales and very limited procedures on forecasted expenses.

An accountant may perform an agreed-upon procedures attest engagement on prospective financial statements provided that the next 10 conditions are met:

1. The accountant is independent.
2. The accountant and the specified parties agree -upon the procedures performed or to be performed by the accountant. Generally, the accountant's procedures may be as limited or as extensive as the specified parties desire, as long as the specified parties take responsibility for their sufficiency. However, mere reading of a financial forecast does not constitute a procedure sufficient to permit an accountant to report on the results of applying agreed-upon procedures.
3. The specified parties take responsibility for the sufficiency of the agreed-upon procedures for their purposes.
4. The prospective financial statements include a summary of significant assumptions.
5. The prospective financial statements to which the procedures are to be applied are subject to reasonably consistent evaluation against criteria that are suitable and available to the specified parties.
6. Criteria to be used in the determination of findings are agreed-upon between the accountant and the specified parties.
7. The procedures to be applied to the prospective financial statements are expected to result in reasonably consistent findings using the criteria.
8. Evidential matter related to the prospective financial statements to which the procedures are applied is expected to exist to provide a reasonable basis for expressing the findings in the accountant's report.
9. Where applicable, the accountant and the specified users agree on any agreed-upon materiality limits for reporting purposes.
10. Use of the report is to be restricted to the specified parties.

(c) REPORTS. The accountant's report on the results of applying agreed-upon procedures should contain these elements:

- A title that includes the word *independent*
- Identification of the specified parties
- Reference to the prospective financial statements covered by the accountant's report and the character of the engagement
- A statement that the procedures performed were those agreed to by the specified parties identified in the report

- Identification of the responsible party and a statement that the prospective financial statements are the responsibility of the responsible party

- A statement that the agreed-upon procedures engagement was conducted in accordance with attestation standards established by the AICPA

- A statement that the sufficiency of the procedures is solely the responsibility of the specified parties and a disclaimer of responsibility for the sufficiency of those procedures

- A list of the procedures performed (or reference to them) and related findings

- Where applicable, a description of any agreed-upon materiality limits

- A statement that the accountant was not engaged to and did not conduct an examination of prospective financial statements; a disclaimer of opinion on whether the presentation of the prospective financial statements is in conformity with AICPA presentation guidelines and on whether the underlying assumptions provide a reasonable basis for the forecast, or a reasonable basis for the projection given the hypothetical assumptions; and a statement that if the accountant had performed additional procedures, other matters might have come to the accountant's attention that would have been reported

- A statement of restrictions on the use of the report because it is intended to be used solely by the specified parties

- Where applicable, reservations or restrictions concerning procedures or findings

- A caveat that the prospective results may not be achieved

- A statement that the accountant assumes no responsibility to update the report for events and circumstances occurring after the date of the report

- Where applicable, a description of the nature of the assistance provided by a specialist

- The manual or printed signature of the accountant's firm

- The date of the report

An example of a report on the application of agreed-upon procedures is presented next.

Independent Accountant's Report on Applying Agreed-Upon Procedures

Board of Directors—XYZ Corporation

Board of Directors—ABC Company

At your request, we have performed certain agreed-upon procedures, as enumerated below, with respect to the forecasted balance sheet, statements of income, retained earnings, and cash flows of DEF Company, a subsidiary of ABC Company, as of December 31, 20XX, and for the year then ending. These procedures, which were agreed to by the Boards of Directors of XYZ Corporation and ABC Company, were performed solely to assist you in evaluating the forecast in connection with the proposed sale of DEF Company to XYZ Corporation. DEF Company's management is responsible for the forecast.

This agreed-upon procedures engagement was conducted in accordance with attestation standards established by the American Institute of Certified Public Accountants. The sufficiency of these procedures is solely the responsibility of the specified parties. Consequently, we make no representation regarding the sufficiency of the procedures described below either for the purpose for which this report has been requested or for any other purpose.

a. With respect to forecasted rental income, we compared the occupancy statistics about expected demand for rental of housing units used in the forecast to occupancy statistics for the following comparable properties. Comparable properties for this purpose are defined as [describe characteristics of comparability, e.g., those located in Sample City with between xxx and yyy rental units, rental prices within z percent of those used in the forecast.]

b. [List comparable properties]

As a result of performing this procedure, we found occupancy statistics used in the forecast were [describe findings].

    a. We traced each amount in the forecast to underlying schedules prepared by management and tested the arithmetical accuracy of management's calculations of rental income, operating income, and income tax expense contained thereon.

We found no differences as a result of these procedures.

We were not engaged to, and did not, conduct an examination, the objective of which would be the expression of an opinion on the accompanying prospective financial statements. Accordingly, we do not express an opinion on whether the prospective financial statements are presented in conformity with American Institute of Certified Public Accountants presentation guidelines or on whether the underlying assumptions provide a reasonable basis for the presentation. Had we performed additional procedures, other matters might have come to our attention that would have been reported to you. Furthermore, there will usually be differences between the forecasted and actual results, because events and circumstances frequently do not occur as expected, and those differences may be material. We have no responsibility to update this report for events and circumstances occurring after the date of this report.

This report is intended solely for the information and use of the Boards of Directors of ABC Company and XYZ Corporation and is not intended to be and should not be used by anyone other than these specified parties.

[Signature]

[Date]

21.9 INTERNAL USE SERVICES

(a) SCOPE OF SERVICES. The accountant who assembles and submits or reports on prospective financial statements for *third-party use* must compile, examine, or apply agreed-upon procedures to them. However, for *internal use,* the accountant's services and reports can be more flexible.

Internal use services generally are provided in the form of consulting, tax planning, or so-called controllership services. In these types of service, the objective of the service is not to lend credibility to the statements and there is no third-party reliance on them, so AICPA guidelines allow the accountant to structure the engagement and report to fit the circumstances.

The accountant may provide compilation, examination, or agreed-upon procedures for internal use prospective financial statements but is not required to do so.

(b) DETERMINING WHETHER USE IS INTERNAL. The accountant may provide internal use services if the accountant believes that third-party use is not reasonably expected. In arriving at this belief, the accountant may rely on the oral or written representation of management, unless something comes to his or her attention to contradict management's representation.

The AICPA *Guide* (Section 10.2) provides these guidelines for determining whether outsiders are considered third parties:

In deciding whether a party that is or reasonably might be expected to use an accountant's report is considered to be a third party, the accountant may consider the degree of consistency of interest between [management] and the user regarding the forecast. If their interests are substantially consistent (e.g., both the [preparer] and the user are employees of the entity about which the forecast is made), the user would not be deemed to be a third party. On the other hand, where the interests of the [preparer] and user are potentially inconsistent (e.g., the [preparer] is a nonowner manager and the user is an absentee owner), the user would be deemed a third party. In some cases, this determination will require the exercise of considerable professional judgment.

(c) PROCEDURES.   The procedures applied in an internal use engagement are usually based on the nature of the engagement. They may focus on developing prospective data, or they may focus on improving operations or financial planning with prospective data being only a by-product of the engagement.

(d) REPORTS.   The accountant's report for internal use services is flexible. Such reports sometimes speak solely to the prospective financial statements, but often they focus on alternative or recommended courses of action.

The standard compilation, examination, or agreed-upon procedures reports may be issued for internal use but often they are not.

Reports on prospective financial statements for internal use generally take three broad forms: *plain paper, legend,* and *formal.* Where there is a report on the statements, it may stand alone or may be incorporated into another report, such as a consultant's report.

(i) Plain Paper.   *Plain paper* means that the accountant provides neither a report on the statements nor any other written communication that accompanies them. In a plain-paper situation, there would be nothing apparent to the reader to associate the accountant with the statements.

(ii) Legend.   When an accountant's written communication (such as a transmittal letter) accompanies the prospective financial statements, the AICPA *Guide* (Section 22.9) requires that the accountant include (1) a caveat that prospective results may not be achieved and (2) a statement that the prospective financial statements are for internal use only. Many accountants choose to present this as a *legend* on the statement itself.

(iii) Formal Report.   The accountant may decide to issue a report on a service. However, the accountant is not permitted to report on a forecast or projection, even for internal use, if it does not disclose the significant assumptions.

According to the AICPA *Guide* (Section 22.6), a report for internal use preferably:

- Is addressed to management
- Identifies the statements being reported on
- Describes the character of work performed and the degree of responsibility taken with respect to the statements
- Includes a caveat that the prospective results may not be achieved
- Indicates the restrictions as to the distribution of the statements and report
- Is dated as of the date of the completion of the accountant's procedures
- For a projection, describes the limitations on the usefulness of the presentation

An example of a report on an internal use service consisting of assembly of a forecast is presented next.

To Mr. John Doe, President

XYZ Company

We have assembled, from information provided by management, the accompanying forecasted balance sheet, statements of income, retained earnings, and cash flows of XYZ Company* as of December 31, 20XX, and for the year then ending. We have not compiled or examined the financial forecast and express no assurance of any kind on it. Further, there will usually be differences between the forecasted and actual results, because events and circumstances frequently do not occur as expected, and those differences may be material. In accordance with the terms of our engagement, this report and the accompanying forecast are restricted to internal use and may not be shown to any third party for any purpose.

---

*If the presentation is summarized as discussed in Section 21.4(b), the first sentence would read, in part: "We have assembled...he accompanying summarized forecast of XYZ Company as of..."

An example of a report on the assembly of a projection is presented next.

To Mr. John Doe, President

XYZ Company

We have assembled, from information provided by management, the accompanying projected balance sheet, statements of income, retained earnings, and cash flows, and summaries of significant assumptions and accounting policies of XYZ Company as of December 31, 20XX, and for the year then ending. The accompanying projection and this report were prepared for [description of the special purpose, e.g., "presentation to the Board of Directors of XYZ Company for its consideration as to whether to add a third operating shift"]. We have not compiled or examined the financial projection and express no assurance of any kind on it. Further, even if [description of the hypothetical assumption, e.g., "the third operating shift is added"], there will usually be differences between the projected and actual results, because events and circumstances frequently do not occur as expected, and those differences may be material. In accordance with the terms of our engagement, this report and the accompanying projection are restricted to internal use and may not be shown to any third party for any purpose.

---

*If the presentation is summarized as discussed in Section 21.4(b), the first sentence would read, in part: "We have assembled...the accompanying summarized forecast of XYZ Company as of...."

In addition, the accountant's report on prospective financial statements for internal use would:

- Indicate if the accountant is not independent with respect to the client (The report would not express any assurance on the statements if there is a lack of independence.)
- Note any disclosures required under the presentation guidelines (see Section 21.4(a)) whose omission comes to the accountant's attention (other than omitted assumptions)

The report might either describe the omitted disclosures or merely note the omission of disclosures in a manner such as:

This financial forecast was prepared to help you develop your personal financial plan. Accordingly, it does not include all disclosures required by the guidelines established by the AICPA for presentation of a financial forecast.

21.10 SOURCES AND SUGGESTED REFERENCES

American Institute of Certified Public Accountants. Accounting and Review Services Committee, Statements on Standards for Accounting and Review Services. *AICPA Professional Standards*, vol. 2. June 1, 2011. New York: Author.

―――. Auditing Standards Board. Statements on Standards for Attestation Engagements, *AICPA Professional Standards*, vol. 1. New York: AICPA, June 1, 2011.

―――. *Guide for Prospective Financial Information*. New York: AICPA, 2009.

Pallais, D., and S. D. Holton. *Guide to Forecasts and Projections*, 26th ed. Fort Worth, TX: Practitioners Publishing, 2011.

INDEX